THE BLACKWELL COMPANION TO SOCIAL MOVEMENTS

BLACKWELL COMPANIONS TO SOCIOLOGY

The *Blackwell Companions to Sociology* provide introductions to emerging topics and theoretical orientations in sociology as well as presenting the scope and quality of the discipline as it is currently configured. Essays in the Companions tackle broad themes or central puzzles within the field and are authored by key scholars who have spent considerable time in research and reflection on the questions and controversies that have activated interest in their area. This authoritative series will interest those studying sociology at advanced undergraduate or graduate level as well as scholars in the social sciences and informed readers in applied disciplines.

The Blackwell Companion to Social Movements

Edited by

David A. Snow, Sarah A. Soule, and Hanspeter Kriesi

Blackwell
Publishing

BLACKWELL PUBLISHING
350 Main Street, Malden, MA 02148-5020, USA
9600 Garsington Road, Oxford OX4 2DQ, UK
550 Swanston Street, Carlton, Victoria 3053, Australia

First published 2004 by Blackwell Publishing Ltd
First published in paperback 2007 by Blackwell Publishing Ltd

4   2010

Library of Congress Cataloging-in-Publication Data

The Blackwell companion to social movements / edited by David A. Snow,
Sarah A. Soule, and Hanspeter Kriesi.
     p. cm. – (Blackwell companions to sociology)
Includes bibliographical references and index.
  ISBN 978-0-631-22669-7 (alk. paper) – ISBN 978-1-4051-7561-6 (paperback : alk. paper)
  1. Social movements. I. Snow, David A. II. Soule, Sarah Anne, 1967–
III. Kriesi, Hanspeter. IV. Series.

HM881.B53 2004
303.48′4—dc22

                                                              2003020377

A catalogue record for this title is available from the British Library.

Set in 10/12 pt Sabon
by SPi Publisher Services, Pondicherry, India
Printed in Singapore
by Ho Printing Singapore Pte Ltd

For further information on
Blackwell Publishing, visit our website:
www.blackwellpublishing.com

Contents

Contributors

Edwin Amenta is Professor of Sociology at New York University. His research is in political sociology, comparative and historical sociology, social movements, and social policy. He has published articles on these subjects in, among other places, the *American Sociological Review*, the *American Journal of Sociology*, *Social Forces*, *Social Problems*, and the *Annual Review of Sociology*. He is completing a book on the consequences of social movements, *When Movements Matter: The Impact of the Townsend Plan and U.S. Social Spending Challengers*, to be published by Princeton University Press.

Robert D. Benford is Professor and Chair of Sociology at Southern Illinois University, Carbondale. He has published on framing processes, narratives, collective identity, and other social constructionist issues associated with social movements in various journals, including the *American Sociological Review*, the *Annual Review of Sociology*, *Social Forces*, *Sociological Quarterly*, and the *Journal of Contemporary Ethnography*.

Steven M. Buechler is Professor of Sociology at Minnesota State University, Mankato. His areas of interest include social movements, political economy, and social theory. He has written on women's movements and social movement theory. His most recent book is *Social Movements in Advanced Capitalism: The Political Economy and Cultural Construction of Social Activism* (2000).

Gene Burns is Associate Professor of Social Relations at James Madison College, Michigan State University. His areas of interest include moral conflict, reproductive politics, and the politics of religion. A new project examines religious mobilization in American politics. Publications include *The Frontiers of Catholicism: The Politics of Ideology in a Liberal World* (1992) and *The Moral Veto: Stalemate and Change in American Debates over Contraception and Abortion* (forthcoming). His articles have appeared in the *American Journal of Sociology, Theory and Society,* and *Sociology of Religion.*

Neal Caren is a PhD candidate in Sociology at New York University. His areas of interest include social movements and political sociology, and his dissertation explores variation in the levels and forms of political participation across American cities since the 1970s. His co-authored articles have appeared in the *Annual Review of Sociology, Qualitative Sociology,* and *Research in Political Sociology.*

Elisabeth S. Clemens is Associate Professor of Sociology at the University of Chicago. She works at the intersection of political, organizational, and historical sociology. *The People's Lobby* (1997) addressed the role of social movements and voluntary organizations in processes of institutional change. In 2003 her research addresses how formal political institutions structure organizational fields in the context of both state expansion and contemporary policies of privatization.

Donatella della Porta is Professor of Sociology at the Department of Political and Social Sciences of the European University Institute in Florence. Her areas of research include social movements, with particular attention to protest policing, political violence, and urban protest. In 2003 she is conducting comparative research on the global movement, the Europeanization of the public sphere, and mobilizations regarding unemployment and migrant issues. Among her recent volumes on social movements are (with M. Andretta, L. Mosca, and H. Reiter) *Global, noglobal, new global: Le proteste contro il G8 a Genova* (2002); (co-edited with H. Kriesi, and D. Rucht) *Social Movement in a Globalizing World* (1999); and (with M. Diani) *Social Movements: An Introduction* (1999).

Mario Diani is Professor of Sociology at the University of Trento and the European editor of *Mobilization.* His work has focused on ethnonationalism, environmental politics, social capital, and social network approaches to the study of social movements. Publications include (with Doug McAdam) *Social Movements and Networks* (2003), (with Bob Edwards and Michael Foley) *Beyond Tocqueville* (2001), and (with Donatella della Porta) *Social Movements: An Introduction* (1999).

Jennifer Earl is an Assistant Professor of Sociology at the University of California, Santa Barbara. Her research focuses on social movements and the sociology of law, with research emphases on social movement outcomes, social movement repression, Internet contention, and legal change. Her published work has appeared in the *American Sociological Review, Sociological Theory, Sociological Perspectives,* the *Journal of Historical Sociology, Research in Political Sociology,* and *Research in Social Movements, Conflicts and Change.*

Bob Edwards is Associate Professor of Sociology and Coastal Resources Management at East Carolina University in Greenville, NC. He is co-editor of *Beyond Tocqueville: Civil Society and the Social Capital Debate in Comparative Perspective* (2001) and author of articles and chapters on social movement organizations, environmental justice, civil society, and social capital. In 2003 he is collaborating with Kenneth Andrews on a systematic analysis of the structure, activities, and impact of local and state-level environmental organizations in North Carolina.

Rick Fantasia is Professor of Sociology at Smith College. He studies labor and culture and their interpenetration in the US and in France. He is the author of *Cultures of Solidarity: Consciousness, Action, and Contemporary American Workers* (1988). More recently he has been a frequent contributor to *Le Monde Diplomatique* in addition to various other French and US publications, and his book (with Kim Voss) *Des Syndicats Domestiques Répression patronale et résistance syndicale aux États-Unis* is forthcoming (2003) in English from the University of California Press.

Myra Marx Ferree is Professor of Sociology at the University of Wisconsin-Madison where she is also on the executive committees of the women's studies and European studies programs. Her work focuses on women's movements in the US and Germany, and includes such co-authored and co-edited books as *Controversy and Coalition: The New Feminist Movement in the US*; *Feminist Organizations*; and *Shaping Abortion Discourse*.

Olivier Fillieule is Professor of Political Sociology at the University of Lausanne (Switzerland). His areas of research include studies of public protests in various cultural areas, anti-AIDS movements and the sociology of AIDS, environmental movements, unemployment protests, and antiglobalization organizations. Publications include *Le désengagement militant* (2003), (with M. Bennani Chraïbi) *Résistances et protestations dans les sociétés musulmanes* (2003), (with C: Broqua) *Trajectoires d'engagement: AIDES et Act Up* (2001), *Stratégies de la rue: Les manifestations en France* (1997), *Sociologie de la protestation: Les formes contemporaines de l'action collective en France* (1993), *Lutter ensemble: Les théories de l'action collective* (1993).

William A. Gamson is Professor of Sociology and co-directs, with Charlotte Ryan, the Media Research and Action Project (MRAP) at Boston College. He has most recently co-authored *Shaping Abortion Discourse: Democracy and the Public Sphere in Germany and the United States* (2002), and is the author of *Talking Politics* (1992) and *The Strategy of Social Protest* (2nd ed., 1990) among other books and articles on political discourse, the mass media, and social movements. He is a past president of the American Sociological Association and a Fellow of the American Academy of Arts and Sciences.

Marco G. Giugni is a researcher and teacher in the Department of Political Science at the University of Geneva. His work addresses social movements and political opportunity structures, with a focus on the consequences of protest activities. Publications include several co-authored and co-edited books on social movements, including *New Social Movements in Western Europe* (1995), *Histoires de mobilisation politique en Suisse* (1997), *From Contention to Democracy* (1998), *How Social Movements Matter* (1999), and *Political Altruism?* (2001), as well as articles in major French-, English-, and Italian-speaking journals. In 2003 his research focuses on political claims-making in the fields of immigration, unemployment, and social exclusion.

Jeff Goodwin is Professor of Sociology at New York University. He is the author of *No Other Way Out: States and Revolutionary Movements* (2001) and coeditor (with James M. Jasper and Francesca Polletta) of *Passionate Politics: Emotions and Social Movements* (2001). He has published articles on movements and revolutions in the *American Sociological Review,* the *American Journal of Sociology, Theory and Society, Mobilization,* and other journals.

Scott A. Hunt is Associate Professor of Sociology at the University of Kentucky. His research focuses on deviance, identity, and social movements. In the area of social movements, he has published on issues pertaining to collective identity construction and framing. He is co-author (with Pamela Wilcox and Kenneth C. Land) of *Criminal Circumstance: A Dynamic Multicontexual Criminal Opportunity Theory* (2003). He has published in the *Journal of Contemporary Ethnography, Sociological Inquiry, Symbolic Interaction,* and *Sociological Quarterly.*

James M. Jasper has written and edited a number of books and articles on social movements, including *The Social Movement Reader* (2003) and *Rethinking Social Movements* (2003), both edited with Jeff Goodwin. His main work in this field is *The Art of Moral Protest* (1997).

Bert Klandermans is Professor of Applied Social Psychology and Dean of the Faculty of Social Sciences of Free University Amsterdam, the Netherlands. He studies social movement participation and mobilization. His recent work concerns the politicization of collective identity and political participation among migrants. He is author of *The Social Psychology of Protest* (1997), has co-authored a number of edited collections on social movement studies, the most recent being *Methods of Social Movement Research* (with Suzanne Staggenborg, 2002), and has published in various journals, including the *American Sociological Review* and *the European Journal of Social Psychology.* He is editor of the series Social Movements, Protest, and Contention published by the University of Minnesota Press.

Fred Kniss is Associate Professor of Sociology at Loyola University Chicago, and Director of its McNamara Center for the Social Study of Religion. His previous research has examined religious conflict, faith-based social change organizations, and the so-called "culture wars." His 2003 research studies the impact of religion on new immigrants' engagement with civil society. He is the author of *Disquiet in the Land: Cultural Conflict in American Mennonite Communities* (1997), and has published articles in the *Journal for the Scientific Study of Religion, Sociology of Religion,* and *Review of Religious Research.*

Ruud Koopmans is Professor of Sociology at the Free University Amsterdam. Before, he was senior researcher and co-director of the Research Group Political Communication and Mobilization at the Wissenschaftszentrum Berlin für Sozialforschung (WZB). He does research on immigration politics, European integration, and social movements. In the latter field, he has particularly worked on political and discursive opportunity structures, as well as on protest waves, with an empirical focus on cross-national comparative analyses. His publications include (with Paul Statham) *Challenging Immigration and Ethnic Relations Politics* (2000), and articles in journals such as the *American Journal of Sociology*, the *American Sociological Review*, the *European Journal of Political Science*, and *Revue Européenne des Migrations Internationales*.

Hanspeter Kriesi is Professor of Political Science at the University of Zurich. His areas of research include political sociology, comparative politics, and social movements. He has published widely on topics such as new social movements and the radical right in Western Europe, opinion formation and change, electoral behavior, direct-democratic voting, political elites, and business interest associations. Publications include (with Ruud Koopmans, Jan Willem Duyvendak, and Marco G. Giugni) *New Social Movements in Western Europe: A Comparative Analysis* (1995); Movements of the Left, Movements of the Right: Putting the Mobilization of Two New Types of Social Movements into Political Context, in *Continuity and Change in Contemporary Capitalism* (1999); (with Donatella della Porta and Dieter Rucht) *Social Movements in a Globalizing World* (1999); as well as articles published in the *American Journal of Sociology*, *European Journal of Political Research*, the *British Journal of Political Science*, and the *American Political Science Review*.

Sam Marullo is Associate Professor and Chair of the Department of Sociology and Anthropology at Georgetown University. He is the Director of Research at the Center for Social Justice at Georgetown University and the Director and founder of the Washington DC Community Research and Learning Network. His research on social movements has focused on the peace movement and more recently on community organizing. He co-edited (with John Lofland) *Peace Action in the 1980s* (1990) and has authored *Ending the Cold War at Home: From Militarism to a More Peaceful World Order* (1993) and *Community-Based Research and Higher Education* (2003). His recent articles have appeared in the *Michigan Journal of Community Service Learning*, *American Behavioral Scientist*, and *Teaching Sociology*.

John D. McCarthy is Professor of Sociology and Graduate Director at Pennsylvania State University. In addition to his widely published work (with Mayer N. Zald) *Social Movements in an Organizational Society* (1987), which articulated a resource mobilization approach to studying social movements, his more recent work includes studies of both selection and description bias in media coverage of protests, the policing of protest events, campus/community disruptions of public order (all with Clark McPhail), and studies of social movement organizations. In 2003 he is a Co-Principal Investigator of two ongoing projects, one that traces the entire range of US protest events through the later part of the twentieth century and the other that traces, with Clark McPhail, the simultaneous evolution of the US social movement organizational sector.

David S. Meyer is Associate Professor of Sociology and Political Science at the University of California, Irvine. He is author or editor of four books, most recently, *Social Movements: Identity, Culture, and the State*, co-edited with Nancy Whittier and Belinda Robnett (2002). He is also author of numerous articles on social movements in a range of sociology and political science journals, and is most interested in the connections among institutional politics, public policy, and social movements.

Debra C. Minkoff is Associate Professor of Sociology at the University of Washington. Her areas of interest include social movements, political sociology, and organizational theory and research. She is the author of *Organizing for Equality: The Evolution of Women's and Racial-Ethnic Organizations in America* (1995). She has also published articles on the organizational dynamics of contemporary social movements in the *American Journal of Sociology, American Sociological Review*, and *Social Forces*.

Aldon D. Morris is Professor of Sociology and Associate Dean of Faculty Affairs at Northwestern University. His areas of research include social movements, civil rights movement, and race. He has published books and articles on the civil rights movement, social movement theory, and racial inequality. His publications have appeared in the *American Sociological Review, Contemporary Sociology, Ethnicities*, and the *Annual Review of Sociology*.

Carol McClurg Mueller is Professor of Sociology at Arizona State University West in the Department of Social and Behavioral Sciences. Her research has long been on social movements with primary emphasis in 2003 on the multiple layering and linkages of the international women's movement. Among her books are (with Aldon Morris) *Frontiers in Social Movement Theory* (1992), (with Mary Fainsod Katzenstein) *The Women's Movements of the U.S. and Western Europe* (1987), and (with Christian Davenport and Hank Johnston, forthcoming) *Repression and Mobilization*. Her articles have appeared in the *American Sociological Review*, the *American Journal of Sociology, Mobilization, Social Problems*, and *Social Forces*, among others.

Susan Olzak is Professor of Sociology at Stanford University. Her areas of research include studies of ethnic conflict, protest movements, and tactics using event-history and event-count methods of analysis. She has authored two books on race and ethnic competition and conflict, and has published articles on these topics in the *American Journal of Sociology*, the *American Sociological Review, Social Forces, Annual Review of Sociology*, and *Mobilization*.

Francesca Polletta is Associate Professor of Sociology at Columbia University. She has published on the cultural dimensions of protest and politics, on legal mobilization, and on institutional experiments in democracy. She is the author of *Freedom Is an Endless Meeting: Democracy in American Social Movements* (2002), and co-editor, with Jeff Goodwin and James Jasper, of *Passionate Politics: Emotions and Social Movements* (2001).

Christopher Rootes is Reader in Political Sociology and Environmental Politics, and Director of the Centre for the Study of Social and Political Movements, at the University of Kent at Canterbury. He is joint editor of the journal *Environmental Politics*, and Chair of the Green Politics Standing Group of the European Consortium for Political Research. He has published on student movements, green parties and environmental protest as well as on resource mobilization, class politics, and political opportunity structures. Most recently, he has authored *Environmental Protest in Western Europe* (2003).

Dieter Rucht is Professor of Sociology at the Social Science Research Center Berlin. His research interests include political participation, social movements and political protest. Among his recent books are (co-edited with Donatella della Porta and Hanspeter Kriesi) *Social Movements in a Globalizing World* (1999); (with Myra Marx Ferree, William Gamson, and Jürgen Gerhards) *Shaping Abortion Discourse: Democracy and the Public Sphere in Germany and the United States* (2002); (co-edited with Lee Ann Banaszak and Karen Beckwith) *Women's Movements Facing the Reconfigured State* (2003). He has published articles in the *American Journal of Sociology*, *West European Politics*, and other journals.

Jackie Smith is Associate Professor of Sociology at the State University of New York at Stony Brook. Her main research focus is on how global integration influences social movement mobilization, and vica versa. She has co-edited three volumes on various aspects of this topic, and the most recent one (co-edited with Joe Bandy) is *Coalitions Across Borders: Negotiating Difference and Unity in Transnational Alliances Against Neoliberalism*. Her work has appeared in *Research in Social Movements Conflict and Change*, *International Sociology*, *Mobilization*, *Social Forces*, and in various edited collections.

David A. Snow is Professor of Sociology at the University of California, Irvine. Within the study of collective action and social movements, he has conducted research on crowd dynamics; recruitment and conversion to religious movements; the emergence, operation and consequences of movements among the homeless in the US; framing processes and outcomes; and on identity. He has published extensively on these topics in a variety of edited volumes and professional journals, including the *American Journal of Sociology*, the *American Sociological Review*, the *Annual Review of Sociology*, and *Social Problems*. He has also authored *Shakubuku: A Study of the Nichiren Shoshu Buddhist Movement in America, 1960–1975* (1993) and co-authored with Doug McAdam *Social Movements: Readings on their Emergence, Mobilization, and Dynamics* (1997).

Sarah A. Soule is an Associate Professor of Sociology at the University of Arizona. Her areas of research include social movements and political sociology. She has published articles on diffusion in the *American Journal of Sociology*, *Social Forces*, the *Annual Review of Sociology*, *Sociological Perspectives*, and *The Annals of the American Academy of Political and Social Sciences*.

Suzanne Staggenborg is Professor of Sociology at McGill University. She is co-editor, with Bert Klandermans, of *Methods of Social Movement Research* (2002). Her articles on the women's movement and abortion politics, movement / counter-movement dynamics, social movement communities, and movement survival and transformation have appeared in the *American Sociological Review*, the *American Journal of Sociology*, *Social Problems*, and *Gender & Society*.

Judith Stepan-Norris is Professor of Sociology at the University of California, Irvine. She has published books and articles concerning the American Labor Movement, with an emphasis on the role of political relations and democracy within CIO unions. Publications include (with Maurice Zeitlin) *Left Out: Reds and America's Industrial Unions* (2003), (with Maurice Zeitlin) *Talking Union* (1996), and articles on these topics in the *American Sociological Review*, the *American Journal of Sociology*, *Social Forces*, *Social Problems*, and the *Annual Review of Sociology*.

Verta Taylor is Professor of Sociology at the University of California, Santa Barbara, and Associate Editor of the Series on Social Movements, Protest, and Societies in Contention of the University of Minnesota Press. Her work focuses on social movement abeyance, gender and social movements, collective identity, emotions, and other cultural processes associated with social movements. She has published several books on women's and gay and lesbian movements including (with Leila J. Rupp) *Drag Queens at the 801 Cabaret* (2003) and *Survival in the Doldrums: The American Women's Rights Movement, 1945 to the 1960s* (1987), and *Rock-a-by Baby: Feminism, Self-Help and Postpartum Depression* (1996). Her articles have appeared in a variety of journals, such as the *American Sociological Review*, *Signs*, and the *Journal of Homosexuality*.

Nella Van Dyke is Assistant Professor of Sociology at Washington State University. Her research focuses on the dynamics of student protest, social movement coalitions, protest tactics, and the factors influencing right-wing mobilization. Recent publications include articles in *Social Problems* and *Mobilization*.

Nancy Whittier is Associate Professor of Sociology at Smith College. She is the author of *Feminist Generations: The Persistence of the Radical Women's Movement*, and co-editor of *Social Movements: Identity, Culture, and the State*. Her work on the women's movement, social movement, culture and collective identity, activist generations, and activism against child sexual abuse has appeared in numerous scholarly collections and journals, including *Social Problems* and *Mobilization*.

Rhys H. Williams is Professor and Department Head of Sociology at the University of Cincinnati. His research interests focus on the intersection of American politics, religion, culture, and social movements. He is author or editor of four books and numerous articles in journals such as the *American Sociological Review*, *Sociological Theory*, *Social Problems*, and *Theory and Society*. In 2003 he edits the *Journal for the Scientific Study of Religion*.

Acknowledgments

The prospect of editing a compilation of original essays on some substantive field of inquiry almost always seems to be a reasonably appealing undertaking when considered a number of years in advance of the recommended date of completion. After all, the editor only has to identify a set of topics for discussion, enlist one or more authorities on the topics to write original essays, provide some substantive feedback on each of the original drafts, and then assemble the finals drafts and ship them off to the publisher. Not a particularly onerous set of tasks, right? Perhaps not when viewed temporally from a distance. But as anyone who has ever taken on such a task knows, the reality of doing it typically turns out to be much more challenging than originally anticipated. Not only is there usually insufficient space to cover all of the topics relevant to the broader area of research, but it is rarely possible to include as authors all of the accomplished scholars in the area. Thus, decisions have to be made about coverage and authorship. Moreover, once these matters have been settled, there is the challenge of coaxing the targeted authors to write the first drafts of the designated chapters within a limited span of time. And finally, there is the seemingly endless task of badgering the authors to revise their chapters in accordance with the reviewers' substantive suggestions, which may be quite extensive, and to submit their revised drafts in a timely manner.

Not surprisingly to those who have traveled this road before, we experienced all of these challenges in editing this volume, with some being much more time-consuming than initially anticipated. A case in point was the review process. At least two of us, and sometimes all three, reviewed each of the contributions, and there was no hesitancy in calling for extensive changes, both in coverage and organization. As a consequence, our reviews ranged from a minimum of two pages to as many as eight pages, with a few insisting on an almost completely new draft as a condition of continued inclusion.

Such editorial challenges notwithstanding, we prevailed. And we did so not only because of our belief in the utility of the volume for scholars and students of social movements, but also because of the commitment and assistance of a number of individuals and institutions, to whom we owe a measure of gratitude. Foremost among the individuals are the chapter authors themselves, most of whom found the idea of the volume to be as important as we did. Obviously, if they had not stuck with us, tolerating our frequent badgering and coming through in the end, this volume would not have seen the light of day.

We also acknowledge Blackwell's former sociology editor, Susan Rabinowitz, who initially proposed that the lead editor (Snow) pursue this project, and a number of other editors associated with Blackwell, namely Assistant Editor Ken Provencher, on-screen copy editor Eldo Barkhuizen, and desk editor Mary Dortch. Fergus Breck, Catherine Corrigall-Brown and Sharon Oselin, sociology graduate students, and Jeannine Jacobs, a sociology staff member, at the University of California, Irvine, also warrant thanks for their assistance in assembling the volume.

We also express our gratitude to three institutions that provided varying degrees of support: the Center for Advanced Study in the Behavioral Sciences (CASBS) at Stanford, California, the Department of Sociology at the University of Arizona, and the Center for the Study of Democracy and the Department of Sociology at the University of California, Irvine. The volume was conceived and outlined while the lead editor was a Fellow at CASBS in 1999–2000, and developed, massaged, and completed in the subsequent years with the assistance provided by the above-mentioned units associated with the Universities of Arizona and California, Irvine. Our thanks to each of these institutional contexts for the temporal, staff, and financial support provided.

David A. Snow, Sarah A. Soule, and Hanspeter Kriesi

Part I

Introduction

1

Mapping the Terrain

DAVID A. SNOW, SARAH A. SOULE, AND HANSPETER KRIESI

Social movements are one of the principal social forms through which collectivities give voice to their grievances and concerns about the rights, welfare, and well-being of themselves and others by engaging in various types of collective action, such as protesting in the streets, that dramatize those grievances and concerns and demand that something be done about them. Although there are other more institutionalized and publicly less conspicuous venues in which collectivities can express their grievances and concerns, particularly in democratic societies, social movements have long functioned as an important vehicle for articulating and pressing a collectivity's interests and claims. Indeed, it is arguable that an understanding of many of the most significant developments and changes throughout human history – such as the ascendance of Christianity, the Reformation, and the French, American, and Russian revolutions – are partly contingent on an understanding of the workings and influence of social movements, and this is especially so during the past several centuries. In this regard, it is interesting to note that *Time* magazine's December 31, 1999, centennial issue (McGeary 1999) included Mohandas Gandhi, the inspirational leader of one the more consequential movements of the past century, among its three major candidates for the person of the century. Why Gandhi? Because "(h)e stamped his ideas on history, igniting three of the century's great revolutions – against colonialism, racism, violence. His concept of nonviolent resistance liberated one nation and sped the end of colonial empires around the world. His marches and fasts fired the imagination of oppressed people everywhere" (1999: 123). And "his strategy of nonviolence has spawned generations of spiritual heirs around the world" (1999: 127), including Martin Luther King Jr., Cesar Chavez, Lech Walesa, Benigno Aquino Jr., and Nelson Mandela – all erstwhile, internationally prominent leaders of a major, consequential social movement in their respective homelands.

While one might quibble with *Time's* estimation of Gandhi's influence, the more important point is that some of the major events and figures of the past century, as well as earlier, are bound up with social movements. And that is particularly true today, as social movements and the activities with which they are associated have become an increasingly conspicuous feature of the social landscape. Indeed, rarely does a day go by in which a major daily newspaper does not refer to social movement activity in relation to one or more of the hotly contested issues of our time: abortion, animal rights, civil rights, human rights, democratization, environmental protection, family values, gay/lesbian rights, gender equality, governmental intrusion and overreach, gun control, immigration, labor and management conflict, nuclear weapons, religious freedom, terrorism, war, world poverty, and so on. In fact, it is difficult to think of major national or international social issues in which social movements and related collective action events are not involved on one or both sides of the issues. Of course, not all social movements speak directly to or play a significant role in relation to major national or international issues, as some are primarily local in terms of the scope and target of their actions. Examples include ordinary worshipers demonstrating against the Church hierarchy in scattered parishes around Italy; a public gathering of placard-carrying citizens protesting the removal of scenic *Benjamin ficus* trees in a California beach community; a series of neighborhood, "not in my backyard" (NIMBY) mobilizations protesting the proposed relocation of the Salvation Army shelter in Austin, Texas; squatters occupying apartment buildings in Amsterdam and Berlin; local youth mobilizing for a "free" cultural space in Zurich; and a Christmas Eve march of the homeless, carrying banners proclaiming "Still No Room at the Inn," through the streets of Tucson, Arizona, and their subsequent two-week encampment on the front lawn of the county building. In addition to being local in terms of their constituents and targets, such movements typically go unnoticed beyond the local context because they operate beneath the radar of the national and international media. Nonetheless, such local movement activity probably occurs much more frequently than the large-scale protest events that are more likely to capture the media's attention.

Because of such observations and considerations, it might be argued that we live in a "movement society" (Meyer and Tarrow 1998), and perhaps even in a movement world. In the preface to the reissue of his highly regarded historical account of the people, ideas, and events that shaped the New Left in the 1960s, titled *Democracy Is in the Streets*, James Miller (1994) ponders the legacy of that period, and concludes that perhaps its most enduring contributions were cultural. Maybe so, but only insofar as the cultural includes models for political participation and action. Why? Because whatever the significant consequences of the 1960s, certainly one of the most important was that the movements of that period pushed open the doors to the streets wider than ever before as a major venue for aggrieved citizens to press their claims. And large numbers of citizens have been "takin' it to the streets" ever since in the US and elsewhere to express their collective views on all kinds of issues.[1] Citing World Values Survey Data, Norris (2002: 200) shows that in 17 out of 22 countries, the percentage of respondents reporting participation in demonstrations increased rather dramatically between 1980 and 1990. In the Netherlands, for example, the percent reportedly participating in demonstrations increased from 12 percent in 1980 to 25 percent in 1990. In West Germany, the increase was somewhat less but still significant, from nearly 14 to 19.5 percent over the same period. The difference in the corresponding figures in the United States was even less – from 12 percent in 1980 to 15 percent in 1990, but the trend was still upwards. It is arguable, then, that social movements and the activities they sponsor have become a kind of fifth estate in the world today. If so, then understanding our own societies, as well as the larger social world in which they are embedded, clearly requires some knowledge and understanding of social movements and the activities with which they are associated.

Just as social movement activity appears to have become a more ubiquitous social form in the world today, even to the point of becoming a routinized avenue for expressing publicly collective grievances, so there has been a corresponding proliferation of scholarly research on social movements and related activity throughout much of the world, and particularly within Europe and the US. Taking what are generally regarded as the top four journals in American sociology (*American Sociological Review*, *American Journal of Sociology*, *Social Forces*, and *Social Problems*), for example, there has been a steady increase in the proportion of collective action and social movement articles published in these journals since the middle of the past century: from 2.23 percent for the 1950s, to 4.13 percent for the 1970s, to 9.45 percent for the 1990s.[2] Also suggestive of growing scholarly interest in the study of social movements is the relatively large number of edited volumes, based principally on social movement conference proceedings, published since the early 1990s (e.g., Morris and Mueller 1992; Laraña et al. 1994; Jenkins and Klandermans 1995; Johnston and Klandermans 1995; McAdam et al. 1996; Smith et al. 1997; Costain and McFarland 1998; Meyer and Tarrow 1998; della Porta et al. 1999; Stryker et al. 2000; Goodwin et al. 2001; Mansbridge and Morris 2001; Meyer et al. 2002; Diani and McAdam 2003). As well, there have been a number of social movement texts (Garner 1996; Tarrow 1998; della Porta and Diani 1999; Buechler 2000) and edited, textlike readers (Darnovsky et al. 1995; Lyman 1995; Buechler and Cylke 1997; McAdam and Snow 1997; Goodwin and Jasper 2003) published within the past decade. The publication of two international journals of research and theory about social movements and related collective actions – *Mobilization* (published in the US) and *Social Movement Studies* (published in the UK) – also points to increasing scholarship in this area. And finally, McAdam et al. (2001) recent synthetic project, and the debate it has generated provide further indication of a vibrant area of study.[3]

Clearly there has been a proliferation of research and writing on social movements during the past several decades, and particularly during the 1990s. Yet, there is no single volume that provides in-depth, synthetic examinations of a comprehensive set of movement-related topics and issues in a fashion that reflects and embodies the growing internationalization of social movement scholarship. That is what this volume seeks to do. In contrast to most of the conference-based edited volumes that are narrowly focused on particular dimensions, processes, or contexts relevant to social movements – such as culture, emotion, identity, networks, and globalization – this volume covers the major processes and issues generally regarded as relevant to understanding the course and character, indeed the dynamics, of social movements. And, in doing so, it provides broader coverage, and thus is more comprehensive, than other existing edited volumes and texts on social movements. But this topical breadth is afforded without sacrificing focus and detail, as each of the contributions to the volume provides an in-depth, state-of-the-art overview of the topics addressed, whether it be a facilitative context or condition, a particular set of outcomes, or a major social movement. And finally, in recognition of the growing internationalization of social movement scholarship, the volume was compiled with the additional objective of reflecting this internationalization in terms of both empirical substance and chapter authorship. Our objective with this volume, then, is to provide in-depth, synthetic examinations of a comprehensive set of movement-related topics and issues by a significant cross-section of internationally recognized scholars.

Before outlining how we have organized the contributions that comprise this volume, we seek to establish a conceptualization of social movements that is sufficiently broad so as not to exclude the various and sundry types of social movements while sufficiently bounded to allow us to distinguish movements from other social phenomena that may bear a resemblance to social movements but yet are quite different.

Conceptualizing Social Movements

Definitions of social movements are not hard to come by. They are readily provided in most textlike treatments of the topic (e.g., Turner and Killian 1987; Tarrow 1998; della Porta and Diani 1999), in edited volumes of conference proceedings and previously published articles and scholarly papers (e.g., McAdam and Snow 1997; Meyer and Tarrow 1998; Goodwin and Jasper 2003), and in summary, encyclopedia-like essays (e.g., McAdam et al. 1988; Benford et al. 2000). Although the various definitions of movements may differ in terms of what is emphasized or accented, most are based on three or more of the following axes: collective or joint action; change-oriented goals or claims; some extra- or non-institutional collective action; some degree of organization; and some degree of temporal continuity. Thus, rather than begin with a straightforward conceptualization, we consider first these conceptual axes.[4]

Social Movements as a Form of Collective Action outside of Institutional Channels

Social movements are only one of numerous forms of collective action. Other types include much crowd behavior, as when sports and rock fans roar and applaud in unison; some riot behavior, as when looting rioters focus on some stores or products rather than others; some interest-group behavior, as when the National Rifle Association mobilizes large numbers of its adherents to write or phone their respective congressional representatives; some "gang" behavior, as when gang members work the streets together; and large-scale revolutions. Since these are only a few examples of the array of behaviors that fall under the collective action umbrella, it is useful to clarify the character of social movements as a type of collective action.

At its most elementary level, collective action consists of any goal-directed activity engaged in jointly by two or more individuals. It entails the pursuit of a common objective through joint action – that is, people working together in some fashion for a variety of reasons, often including the belief that doing so enhances the prospect of achieving the objective. Since collective action so defined obviously includes a large number of human behaviors, it is useful to differentiate those collective actions that are institutionalized or normatively sanctioned from those that are not and that fall outside of institutional channels. Since social movements are defined *in part* by their use of noninstitutionalized means of action, such as appropriating and using public and quasipublic places for purposes other than those for which they were designed or intended, introducing this distinction clearly reduces the number of joint actions that bear a family resemblance to movements. As Sidney Tarrow notes in this regard: collective action not only "takes many forms – brief or sustained, institutionalized or disruptive, humdrum or dramatic," but "most of it occurs within institutions on the part of constituted groups acting in the name of goals that would hardly raise an eyebrow" (1998: 3).

Social Movements and Collective Behavior

Parsing collective action via the institutional/noninstitutional distinction still leaves numerous collective actions within the latter category. Traditionally, most of these noninstitutional collective actions, including those associated with social movements, have been treated as varieties of collective behavior. Broadly conceived, collective behavior refers to "extrainstitutional, group-problem solving behavior that encompasses an array of collective actions, ranging from protest demonstrations, to behavior in disasters, to mass or diffuse phenomena, such as fads and crazes, to social movements and even revolution" (Snow and Oliver 1995: 571). Thus, just as social movements are a form of collective action, so it has been argued that they also constitute a species of collective behavior. But they also differ significantly from most other variants of collective behavior – such as crowds, panics, fads, and crazes – in terms of their other central defining characteristics discussed below.[5]

Social Movements and Interest Groups

Just as social movements overlap to some degree with some forms of collective behavior, so they also overlap with interests groups, which also comprise another set of collective actors that are often equated with social movements. Clearly interest groups, such as Planned Parenthood and the Christian Coalition, and some social movements, such as the pro-choice and pro-life movements, are quite similar in terms of the interests and objectives they share with respect to some aspect of social life. Yet there are also noteworthy differences. First, interest groups are generally defined in relation to the government or polity (Walker 1991), whereas the relevance and interests of social movements extend well beyond the polity to other institutional spheres and authorities. Second, even when social movements are directly oriented to the polity or state, their standing is different. Interest groups are generally embedded within the political arena, as most are regarded as legitimate actors within it. Social movements, on the other hand, are typically outside of the polity, or overlap with it in a precarious fashion, because they seldom have the same standing or degree of access to or recognition among political authorities.

A third difference follows: interest groups pursue their collective objectives mainly through institutionalized means, such as lobbying and soliciting campaign contributions, whereas social movements pursue their collective ends mainly via the use of noninstitutional means, such as conducting marches, boycotts, and sit-ins. Social movements may sometimes operate squarely within the political arena as well, as when they focus on influencing and even controlling party platforms at national political conventions in the US (Bunis 1993). But their action repertoires are generally skewed in the direction of extrainstitutional lines of action. Thus, to paraphrase William Gamson (1990), interests groups and politically oriented social movements are not so much different species as members of the same species positioned differently in relation to the polity or state. But that differential positioning is sufficiently important to produce different sets of strategic and tactical behaviors, and thus different kinds of collectivities.[6]

Connections and Overlaps

To note the distinction among social movements, other varieties of collective behavior, and interest groups is not to assert that they do not overlap at times. The relationship between nonconventional crowd activity and social movements is illustrative. Although some crowds arise spontaneously and dissipate just as quickly, others are the result of prior planning, organization, and negotiation. In such cases, they often are sponsored and organized by a social movement, and constitute part of its tactical repertoire for dramatizing its grievances and pressing its claims (see chapter 12 in this volume). When this occurs, which is probably the dominant pattern for most protest crowds or demonstrations, neither the crowd phenomena nor the movement can be thoroughly understood without understanding the relationship between them. Thus, while social movements can be distinguished conceptually from other forms of collective action and collective behavior, social movements and some crowd phenomena often are intimately linked. Social movements and interest groups can be closely connected too, as when they form an alliance to press their joint interests together. Moreover, as social movements develop over time, they often become more and more institutionalized, with some of them evolving (at least partially) into interest groups or even political parties.

Social Movements as Challengers to or Defenders of Existing Authority

There is generalized acknowledgment that social movements are in the business of seeking or halting change, but there is a lack of consensus as to the locus and level of changes sought. Must it be at the political institutional level? That is, must the changes or objectives sought be in terms of seeking concessions from or altering political institutions? What about changes at the individual or personal level? Do other kinds of changes count, such as those associated with so-called self-help groups, or animal rights, or lifestyles? And to what extent should the amount or degree of change be considered in conceptualizing movements?

Whatever the components of various definitions of social moments, all emphasize that movements are in the business of promoting or resisting change with respect to some aspect of the world in which we live. Indeed, fostering or halting change is the *raison d'être* for all social movements. But scholars are not of one mind when it comes to specifying the character of the change sought. Some leave the question open-ended, stating simply that social movements are "collective attempts to promote or resist change in a society or group" (Turner and Killian 1987: 223; Benford et al. 2000: 2717); others narrow the range of targets of change primarily to those within the political arena, as reflected in the recent conceptualization of movements as a variant of "contentious politics" (McAdam et al. 2001). Contentious politics is a cover term encompassing "collective political struggle" that is "episodic" in the sense of not being regularly scheduled on the political docket, "public" in the sense of excluding claim-making "that occurs entirely within-well bounded organizations," and "manifestly political" in the sense that a government is involved as a claimant, target, or mediator (McAdam et al. 2001: 5).

Neither the open-ended nor the manifestly political conceptual strategy is entirely satisfactory. The open-ended one is too ambiguous; the emphasis on "collective political struggle" is too institutionally narrow, excluding challenges rooted in other institutional and sociocultural contexts.[7] Thus, in order to have an understanding of social movements that is both more inclusive in terms of what gets counted as social movement activity, and yet more tightly anchored institutionally and culturally, we argue that movements be considered as challengers to or defenders of existing *institutional authority* – whether it is located in the political, corporate, religious, or educational realm – or patterns of *cultural authority*, such as systems of beliefs or practices reflective of those beliefs.[8]

Movements as Organized Activity

Earlier it was noted that social movements, as a form of collective action, involve joint action in pursuit of a common objective. Joint action of any kind implies some degree of coordination, and thus organization. Scholars of social movements have long understood the relevance of organization to understanding the course and character of movement activity, but they have rarely agreed about the forms, functions, and consequences of organization with respect to social movements. The seeds of this debate were sown in the early twentieth century – with the juxtaposition of the revolutionary Lenin's (1929) call for organization as the key to stimulating working class consciousness to Luxemburg's (Waters 1970) and Michels's ([1911] 1962) critique of formal party organization as retarding rather than promoting progressive politics and democracy – and flowered full bloom in the latter quarter of the century. Carrying Luxemburg's banner, for example, Piven and Cloward (1977) argued that too much emphasis on organization was antithetical to effective mobilization, particularly among the poor. In contrast, McCarthy and Zald (1977), among others (Gamson 1990; Lofland 1996), argued that social movement organizations (SMOs) were fundamental not only for assembling and deploying resources necessary for effectively mounting movement campaigns, but they were also key to the realization of a movement's objectives. Thus SMOs were proffered as the orienting, focal unit of analysis for understanding the operation of social movements (McCarthy and Zald 1977; Lofland 1996). But again not all scholars agreed. This time it was not because of fear of the constraining effects of formal organization, but because movements, according to della Porta and Diani (1999: 16) "are not organizations, not even of a peculiar kind," but "networks of interaction between different actors which may either include formal organizations or not, depending on shifting circumstances."

Given these contrasting arguments regarding the relationship between organization and social movements, it seems reasonable to ask whether one is more accurate than another, or if we must choose one over another? The answer to both questions is "no!" There is absolutely no question about the fact that social movement activity is organized in some fashion or another. Clearly there are different forms of organization (e.g., single SMO vs. multiple, networked SMOs) and degrees of organization (e.g., tightly coupled vs. loosely coupled), and clearly there are differences in the consequences of different forms and degrees of organization. But to note such differences is not grounds for dismissing the significance of organization to social movements.

Tarrow (1998: 123–4) helps clarify these issues when he distinguishes between social movements as formal organizations, the organization of collective action, and social movements as connective structures or networks. Conceptually, the issue concerns neither the form nor consequences of organizations, but the fact that the existence of social movement activity implies some degree of organization. To illustrate, consider the civil rights movement of the 1960s, and some of its leaders, such as Martin Luther King and Stokely Carmichael, as well as various organizational representatives, such as the Southern Christian Leadership Conference (SCLC) and the Student Nonviolent Coordinating Committee (SNCC). Indeed, it is difficult to comprehend the civil rights movement in the absence of the leaders and organizations associated with it. The same can be said as well about many other social movements. Take, for example, the student-led pro-democracy movement in Beijing. Not only were the actions of demonstrators coordinated, but there were various organizing groups.

Thus in many movements we see the interests and objectives of a particular constituency being represented and promoted by one or more individuals associated with one or more organizations now routinely referred to in the literature as "SMOs." While the organizations associated with these movements may vary in a variety of ways, the point still remains that much of the activity, including the relations between participating organizations, was itself organized. It is because of such observations that a semblance of organization needs to be included as a component of the conceptualization of social movements, but without specifying the character and degree of organization for any specific movement.

Movements as Existing with Some Temporal Continuity

The final axis of conceptualization concerns the extent to which social movements operate with some degree of temporal continuity. Some scholars have suggested that social movements are "episodic" in the sense of not being regularly scheduled events (McAdam et al. 2001: 5), which is certainly true inasmuch as social movements are not routinely on the community or national calendar. To be sure, social movement events and activities get placed on the community calendar from time to time, but such is the result of application and/or negotiation processes with officials rather than routine calendarization of a movement's activities.

Yet, to note that movements are temporally episodic is not to suggest that they are generally fly-by-night fads that are literally here today and gone tomorrow. Clearly there is considerable variability in their careers or life course, as some movements do indeed last for a very short time, as with most neighborhood, NIMBY oppositions; while others endure for decades, as with the Heaven's Gate "cult" that was first observed in the US in the 1970s (Balch 1995) and the Sokagakkai/Nichiren Shoshu Buddhist movement that was first introduced into the US in the early 1960s (Snow

1993); and still others persist across generations, alternating between periods of heightened activism and dormancy, as with the women's movement (Rupp and Taylor 1987). And for many, and perhaps most movements, they are clustered temporally within "cycles of protest" that wax and wane historically (Tarrow 1998; see also chapter 2 in this volume). So clearly, there is striking temporal variability in the life span of social movements.

However, the kinds of changes movements pursue, whatever their degree or level, typically require some measure of sustained, organized activity. Continuity, like organization, is a matter of degree, of course. But, it is difficult to imagine any movement making much progress in pursuing its objectives without fairly persistent, almost nagging, collective action. Accordingly, some degree of sustained collective action, and thus temporal continuity, is an essential characteristic of social movements.

A Conceptualization

Having explored the various conceptual axes pertaining to social movements, we are now in position to suggest a working conceptualization of social movements based on the various elements highlighted. Accordingly, social movements can be thought of as *collectivities acting with some degree of organization and continuity outside of institutional or organizational channels for the purpose of challenging or defending extant authority, whether it is institutionally or culturally based, in the group, organization, society, culture, or world order of which they are a part.*

The major advantage of this conceptualization over other definitions, and particularly those that link social movements to the polity or government, is that it is more inclusive, thus broadening what gets counted and analyzed as social movements. So, from this vantage point, not only do the spring 1989 pro-democracy student protests in China, the broader pro-democracy stirrings in Eastern Europe that contributed to fall of Communist regimes throughout the region in the late 1980s, and the wave of worldwide antiwar protests associated with the US/UK–Iraq war (variously framed as an "invasion" and a "liberation") of 2003 constitute social movements, but so do local, NIMBY movements, the spread of culturally imported religious movements like Hare Krishna and Sokagakkai/Nichiren Shoshu, the rebellion among parishioners to the sexual abuse scandal in the Catholic Church, and even erstwhile cultish, escapist movements such as Heaven's Gate and the followers of Jim Jones.[9] In some fashion or another, each of these movements constituted challenges to institutional, organizational, or cultural authority or systems of authority.

Organization of Volume

Social movements, so conceptualized, can be examined in terms of various contextual factors, dimensions, and processes from a variety of overlapping perspectives via a number of methods. Most edited volumes on movements are typically organized in terms of a few focal contextual factors, dimensions and/or processes. This volume is arranged in terms of these considerations as well, but, consistent with our previously mentioned objective of compiling a comprehensive set of detailed, synthetic discussions of the range of factors associated with the dynamics of social movements, we organize the volume in terms of a broader array of contextual factors, dimensions, and processes than is customary.

Contextual factors reference the broader structural and cultural conditions that facilitate and constrain the emergence and operation of social movements. Metaphorically, contextual conditions constitute the soil in which movements grow or languish. Part II of the volume consists of five chapters that focus on and elaborate the relevance of a variety of contextual factors to the course and character of social movements. These include historical contexts and associated cycles of protest, contexts of strain and conflict, and political, cultural, and resource contexts.

Dimensions encompass characteristic aspects of social movements, such as organizational forms, organizational fields, leadership, tactical repertoires, collective action frames, emotion, collective identity, and consequences; whereas *processes* encompass the ways in which dimensions evolve and change temporally over the course of a movement's operation, such as participant mobilization, tactical innovation, diffusion, and framing. Parts III, IV, and V of the volume examine a broad range of movement-relevant dimensions and processes. Part III consists of eight chapters that dissect and elaborate various meso- or organizational-level dimensions and processes that together constitute the dynamic field of action in which movements operate. Included here are chapters on social movement organizations, leadership, allies and adversaries, bystanders and the media, tactics, and diffusion and transnational processes. Part IV includes five chapters that illuminate key microstructural and social-psychological dimensions and processes relevant to participant mobilization and related issues. It should be understood that the dimensions and processes examined in this section – such as social networks, framing, emotions, and collective identity – operate in conjunction with the meso-organizational level factors considered in the previous section, but are separated for analytical purposes because they are partly either microstructural or social-psychological phenomena.

In Part V, attention is turned to the outcome dimension or aspect of social movements. Here there are two guiding questions: What are the consequences of social movements? And in what ways or domains do they make a difference? The four chapters in this section provide different answers to these questions by focusing on four different sets or domains of consequences: legislative and beneficiary, personal or biographic, cultural, and movement-related.

The final section of the volume, Part VI, presents a variety of general social movements that are operative throughout most of the world in one fashion or another. Social movements are known publicly primarily through the framing of their grievances and their tactical collective actions, and the domains or categories of social life with which those public framings and actions are associated, such as the workplace, the environment, and the treatment and rights of labor, women, ethnic minorities, and other categories, including animals. This section includes focused, synthetic discussions of six different general social movements that are known publicly in these ways throughout much of the world, although their particular manifestations or forms have been and will probably continue to be quite variable temporally and culturally. The six major movements examined include labor, women's, environmental, antiwar and peace, ethnic and national, and religious movements.

Rarely is a volume that seeks comprehensive coverage of a field of study completely successful in covering all relevant phenomena or issues variously referenced in discussions of the field. This volume is no different. Clearly there are very significant general movements other than those covered in the final section, such as the human rights movements and what some scholars call revolutionary movements. We had planned to have a chapter on human rights movements, but the prospective author of the chapter failed to deliver, so we had to set sail without it. But what about revolutionary movements? Here we decided not to include a chapter on revolutionary movements, certainly not because we thought such movements are any less important than those covered. Rather, we thought it might be difficult to do justice to the study of revolution because of a number of intersecting considerations. First, there is the difficulty of compressing the vast literature on the topic into a single chapter. Second, it is arguable that the study of revolutions constitutes its own separate field. And third, in spite of the efforts of McAdam et al. (2001) to integrate the study of social movements and revolutions by identifying and examining common, underlying mechanisms and processes, the overlap among scholars of revolution and movements is neither clear nor tidy. For example, many of the most prominent scholars of revolution (e.g., Crane Brinton, Chalmers Johnson, Samuel Huntington, Barrington Moore, Jeffery Paige, Theda Skopol) have shown comparatively little interest in the study of social movements per se, and relatively few scholars of social movements have given equal attention to the study of revolution – Charles Tilly (1978), Jack Goldstone (1991), and Jeff Goodwin (2001) being three prominent exceptions. For these reasons, then, we chose not to include a chapter on revolution in the volume. Finally, we offer no synthetic or integrative chapter at the end – partly because doing so seemed overly daunting in light of the array of movement-related contexts, processes, and dimensions covered, and partly because of McAdam et al.'s (2001) recent synthetic treatise. Better at this point, we thought, to provide a comprehensive discussion of the array of factors relevant to the operation of social movements that may, in turn, provide a basis for evaluating aspects of current synthetic efforts and perhaps contribute to the development of further synthesis.

These omissions notwithstanding, it is our hope that, by providing a compilation of original, state-of-the-art essays on a comprehensive set of movement-related contexts, dimensions, and processes, as well as on a variety of the world's most significant general social movements, this volume will prove to be a useful companion to those interested in social movements in general and, more particularly, in the array of factors relevant to understanding their emergence, dynamics, and consequences.

Notes

1   We use "the streets" both literally and metaphorically: literally as the site or social space in which much social protest occurs, and metaphorically as a cover-term for the array of movement-related tactical actions, many of which now extend beyond the streets (see chapter 12 in this volume). The doors to the street as a literal site for protest had been partially opened well before the 1960s, at least a century or so earlier, as Charles Tilly has emphasized in his numerous works elaborating his seminal and historically grounded

concept of "repertoires of contention" (e.g., Tilly 1986, 1995. Also, see Tarrow 1998, especially chs. 2 and 6). Thus our point is not that the streets constituted a new space for protest, but that the 1960s appear to have provided a template or model for collective action that would be adopted by citizens from all walks of life associated with all kinds of causes, as our foregoing examples suggest.

2   We wish to acknowledge the assistance of Catherine Corrigall-Brown, who conducted the analysis from which these data are derived.

3   For illustration of this debate, see the critiques of Diani, Koopmans, Oliver, Rucht, and Taylor, and the responses of McAdam and Tarrow, in the symposium in *Mobilization* (Vol. 8, 2003: 109–41). Also, see Snow 2002.

4   Portions of this discussion are drawn from Snow and McAdam's introduction to their edited volume consisting of previously published work on social movements (McAdam and Snow 1997: xviii–xxvi). This discussion is also influenced by the conceptual efforts of McAdam et al. (2001), Tarrow (1998), and Turner and Killian (1972, 1987). The reader familiar with these works will note that the way in which our conceptualization differs from the conceptualizations provided by these works is more nuanced than discordant

5   For an examination of collective behavior broadly construed, see Turner and Killian 1972, 1987. For an incisive critical examination of the literature on crowds, as well as of the utility of the crowd concept, see McPhail 1991.

6   Burstein (1998, 1999) has questioned the analytic utility of distinguishing between interest groups and social movements, arguing that both concepts should be abandoned in favor of "interest organizations." In chapter 11 in this volume, Gamson suggests (in note 2) in response to Burstein that the distinction between interest groups and social movements is of sufficient theoretical value to justify their retention, even though both can be construed as "advocacy groups," albeit different types. Clearly our position is aligned with Gamson's for the reasons noted.

7   It is both interesting and important to note that McAdam et al. would appear to agree with this charge, as they soften their initial conceptualization by suggesting that "contention involving non-state actors" is not beyond the scope of their approach so long as "at least one member and one challenger [are] actively engaged in contestation over the shape of a given organizational or institutional field" (2001: 342–3).

8   The rationale for expanding the conceptualization of social movements in this fashion is elaborated in Snow 2002.

9   Some students of social movements do not consider escapist or other-worldly cults or sects and communes as social movements per se, but a strong case can be made that they constitute significant challenges, albeit often indirect, to their encompassing cultural and/ or political systems. Indeed, we would argue, in the language of Hirschman (1970), that "exit" may sometimes not only constitute a form of "voice," but may even speak louder and be more threatening than the voices associated with more conventional challenges (see Snow 2002, for an elaboration of this argument).

References

Balch, Robert W. (1995) Waiting for the Ships: Disillusionment and the Revitalization of Faith in Bo and Peep's UFO Cult. In James R. Lewis (ed.), *The Gods Have Landed: New Religions from Other Worlds*. Albany: State University of New York Press, 137–66.

Benford, Robert D., Timothy B. Gongaware, and Danny L. Valadez (2000) Social Movements. In Edgar F. Borgatta and Rhonda J. V. Montgomery (eds.), *Encyclopedia of Sociology*. 2nd ed. Vol. 4. New York: Macmillan, 2717–27.

Buechler, Steven M. (2000) *Social Movements and Advanced Capitalism: The Political Economy and Cultural Construction of Social Activism*. New York: Oxford University Press.

Buechler, Steven M., and F. Kurt Cylke Jr. (1997) *Social Movements: Perspectives and Issues.* Mountain View, CA: Mayfield.

Bunis, William K. (1993) Social Movement Activity and Institutionalized Politics: A Study of the Relationship Between Political Party Strength and Social Movement Activity. PhD dissertation, University of Arizona.

Burstein, Paul (1998) Interest Organizations, Political Parties, and the Study of Democratic Politics. In Anne N. Costain and Andrew S. McFarland (eds.), *Social Movements and American Political Institutions: People, Passions, and Power.* Lanham, MD: Rowman & Littlefield, 39–56.

——(1999) Social Movements and Public Policy. In Marco Giugni, Doug McAdam, and Charles Tilly (eds.), *How Social Movements Matter.* Minneapolis: University of Minnesota Press, 3–21.

Costain, Anne N., and Andrew S. McFarland (eds.) (1998) *Social Movements and American Political Institutions: People, Passions, and Power.* Lanham, MD: Rowman & Littlefield.

Darnovsky, Marcy, Barbarta Epstein, and Richard Flacks (eds.) (1995) *Cultural Politics and Social Movements.* Philadelphia, PA: Temple University Press.

della Porta, Donatella, and Mario Diani (1999) *Social Movements: An Introduction.* Oxford: Blackwell.

della Porta, Donatella, Hanspeter Kriesi, and Dieter Rucht (eds.) (1999) *Social Movements in a Globalizing World.* London: Macmillan.

Diani, Mario, and Doug McAdam (eds.) (2003) *Social Movements and Networks.* New York: Oxford University Press.

Gamson, William A. (1990) *The Strategy of Social Protest.* 2nd ed. Belmont, CA: Wadsworth.

Garner, Roberta (1996) *Contemporary Movements and Ideologies.* New York: McGraw-Hill.

Goldstone, Jack (1991) *Revolution and Rebellion in the Early Modern World.* Berkeley: University of California Press.

Goodwin, Jeff (2001) *No Other Way Out: States and Revolutionary Movements, 1945–1991.* Cambridge: Cambridge University Press.

Goodwin, Jeff, and James M. Jasper (2003) *The Social Movements Reader: Cases and Concepts.* Oxford: Blackwell.

Goodwin, Jeff, James M. Jasper, and Francesca Polletta (eds.) (2001) *Passionate Politics: Emotions and Social Movements.* Chicago: University of Chicago Press.

Hirschman, Albert O. (1970) *Exit, Voice, and Loyalty: Responses to Declines in Firms, Organizations, and States.* Cambridge, MA: Harvard University Press.

Jenkins, J. Craig, and Bert Klandermans (eds.) (1995) *The Politics of Social Protest: Comparative Perspectives on States and Social Movements.* Minneapolis: University of Minnesota Press.

Johnston, Hank, and Bert Klandermans (eds.) (1995) *Social Movements and Culture.* Minneapolis: University of Minnesota Press.

Laraña, Enrique, Hank Johnson, and Joseph. R. Gusfield (eds.) (1994) *New Social Movements: From Ideology to Identity.* Philadelphia, PA: Temple University Press.

Lenin, V. I. (1929) *What Is to Be Done? Burning Questions of our Movements.* New York: International.

Lofland, John (1996) *Social Movement Organizations: Guide to Research on Insurgent Realities.* New York: Aldine de Gruyter.

Lyman, Stanford M. (ed.) (1995) *Social Movements: Critiques, Concepts, Case-Studies.* New York: New York University Press.

McAdam, Doug, and David A. Snow (eds.) (1997) *Social Movements: Readings on their Emergence, Mobilization, and Dynamics.* Los Angeles: Roxbury.

McAdam, Doug, John D. McCarthy, and Mayer N. Zald (1988) Social Movements. In Neil Smelser (ed.), *Handbook of Sociology.* Beverly Hills, CA: Sage, 695–737.

——(eds.) (1996) *Comparative Perspectives on Social Movements: Political Opportunities, Mobilizing Structures, and Cultural Framings*. New York: Cambridge University Press.

McAdam, Doug, Sidney Tarrow, and Charles Tilly (2001) *Dynamics of Contention*. New York: Cambridge University Press.

McCarthy, John D., and Mayer N. Zald (1977) Resource Mobilization and Social Movements: A Partial Theory. *American Journal of Sociology*, 82, 1212–41.

McGeary, Johanna (1999) Mohandas Gandhi. *Time*, 154, December 31, 118–23.

McPhail, Clark (1991) *The Myth of the Maddening Crowd*. New York: Aldine de Gruyter.

Mansbridge, Jane, and Aldon D. Morris (eds.) (2001) *Oppositional Consciousness: The Subjective Roots of Social Protest*. Chicago: University of Chicago Press.

Meyer, David S., and Sidney Tarrow (eds.) (1998) *The Social Movement Society: Contentious Politics for a New Century*. Boulder, CO: Rowman & Littlefield.

Meyer, David S., Nancy Whittier, and Belinda Robnett. (eds.) (2002) *Social Movements: Identity, Culture, and the State*. New York: Oxford University Press.

Michels, Robert ([1911] 1962) *Political Parties: A Sociological Study of the Oligarchical Tendencies of Modern Democracy*. New York: Free Press.

Miller, James (1994) *Democracy Is in the Streets: From Port Huron to the Siege of Chicago*. Cambridge, MA: Harvard University Press.

Morris, Aldon D., and Carol McClurg Mueller (eds.) (1992) *Frontiers in Social Movement Theory*. New Haven: Yale University Press.

Norris, Pippa (2002) *Democratic Phoenix: Reinventing Political Activism*. Cambridge: Cambridge University Press.

Piven, Francis Fox, and Richard A. Cloward (1977) *Poor People's Movements*. New York: Vintage.

Rupp, Leila, and Verta Taylor (1987) *Survival in the Doldrums: The American Women's Rights Movement, 1945 to the 1960s*. Columbus: Ohio State University Press.

Smith, Jackie, Charles Chatfield, and Ron Pagnucco (eds.) (1997) *Transnational Social Movements and Global Politics: Solidarity beyond the State*. Syracuse, NY: Syracuse University Press.

Snow, David A. (1993) *Shakubuku: A Study of the Nichiren Shoshu Buddhist Movement in America, 1960–1975*. New York: Garland.

——(2002) Social Movements as Challenges to Authority: Resistance to an Emerging Conceptual Hegemony. Paper presented at Authority in Contention Conference, Notre Dame University.

Snow, David A. and Pamela Oliver (1995) Social Movements and Collective Behavior: Social Psychological Dimensions and Considerations. In K. Cook, G. Fine, and J. House (eds.), *Sociological Perspectives on Social Psychology*. Boston: Allyn and Bacon, 571–99.

Stryker, Sheldon, Timothy J. Owens, and Robert W. White (eds.) (2000) *Self, Identity, and Social Movements*. Minneapolis: University of Minnesota Press.

Tarrow, Sidney (1998) *Power in Movement: Social Movements, Collective Action and Politics*. 2nd ed. New York: Cambridge University Press.

Tilly, Charles (1978) *From Mobilization to Revolution*. Reading, MA: Addison-Wesley.

——(1986) *The Contentions French*. Cambridge, MA: Harvard University Press.

——(1995) *Popular Contention in Great Britain, 1758–1834*. Cambridge, MA: Harvard University Press.

Turner, Ralph H., and Lewis M. Killian (1972) *Collective Behavior*. 2nd ed. Englewood Cliffs, NJ: Prentice-Hall.

——(1987) *Collective Behavior*. 3rd ed. Englewood Cliffs, NJ: Prentice-Hall.

Walker, Jack L. (1991) *Mobilizing Interest Groups in America: Patrons, Professions, and Social Movements*. Ann Arbor: University of Michigan Press.

Waters, Mary-Alice (1970) *Rosa Luxemburg Speaks*. New York: Pathfinder.

Part II

Facilitative Contexts and Conditions

2

Protest in Time and Space: The Evolution of Waves of Contention

Ruud Koopmans

Introduction

Instances of collective action are often treated as independent events that can be understood outside of their spatial and historical contexts, and irrespective of other instances of political action. For instance, a whole subfield of analysis asks whether repression increases or decreases collective action. Some studies investigate large numbers of (usually country-by-year) measures of repression and mobilization and correlate them as if collective action-repression sequences were interchangeable and equivalent and their properties analyzable irrespective of their insertion in time and space. Other studies analyze single events or movements in a case-study approach, which is only seemingly more sensitive to spatial and temporal insertion. For all their descriptive detail, they, too, often treat instances of collective action as independent events, and for the quantitative analysts' assumption of interchangeability they substitute an equally ahistorical uniqueness. The perspective presented in this chapter holds that instances of collective action are not independent (see also chapters 13 and 23 in this volume). They are neither understandable in their own, unique terms, nor are they merely interchangeable instances of general classes of events. The most fundamental fact about collective action is its connectedness, both historically and spatially, and both with other instances of collective action of a similar kind, and with the actions of different claim-makers such as authorities and countermovements.

Consider this well-known example: On Monday October 9, 1989, 70,000 people gathered outside the Nikolai Church in Leipzig to demonstrate for democratic reforms of the East German communist regime and the freedom to travel abroad.[1] Their major slogan on that day, however, was "No Violence!" When one observed the scene in and around the city, the reason was obvious. There was a heavy police presence in the city, and around it army troops had been placed in position. In anticipation of things to come, shops and schools had been closed early, and local hospitals had followed the authorities' instructions to increase their blood plasma stocks. As was widely feared then and confirmed afterwards, Party Chairman Erich Honecker had instructed the police and the army to prevent the demonstrators – if necessary by shooting to kill – from marching through the city. As it turned out, Honecker's orders were not followed and a last-minute call by local Party officials and community leaders for "peaceful dialogue" miraculously prevailed. The 70,000 then marched unhindered through the city, along the way inventing the rallying cry "We Are the People!" for which the East German revolution became famous.

This critical event in the East European revolutions of 1989–1991 is perhaps best known for its wide-ranging consequences. Although it has still not become clear what exactly caused the sudden withdrawal of security forces, the failure of the regime hardliners to impose their will proved to be a breaking point that ultimately sealed the fate of the GDR. Protests surged, and within days, Erich Honecker had been ousted as state leader, within weeks the Wall had come down, and within months the Socialist Unity Party was no more. While the East German regime crumbled, citizens' movements sprang up or were reinvigorated in the other Eastern Bloc countries, including the Soviet Union itself. When this tidal wave of events subsided, the world was a different place.

But the origins of October 9 were equally wide-ranging. Monday gatherings had been held weekly in the Nikolai Church since way back in 1982, their content slowly and then in an accelerating pace radicalizing from the regime-conformist call for peace to demands for free travel and democratic reforms, and ultimately, after October 9, to reunification with West Germany. This radicalization and expansion of "voice" (Hirschman 1970) was made possible by the pressure exerted on the regime by the massive exodus of East German citizens – mostly young and well-educated – who at the end of the summer holidays chose the "exit" option of seeking a better life in West Germany, after the reform-communist government of Hungary had torn down the Iron Curtain along the border with Austria. Needless to say, this decision of the Hungarian government – and its reform course more generally – was contingent on the loosening of Soviet control over Eastern Europe under Gorbachev's politics of *perestroika / glasnost*. But the events on October 9 were not just influenced by the current of reform in parts of the communist world. Erich Honecker's decision to have the army and police crush the rising citizens' movement was directly inspired by the events in Beijing in June of the same year. That, in spite of Honecker's orders for October 9, a "Chinese solution" was prevented is certainly to no small degree due to Mikhail Gorbachev's stance during his official visit to the GDR just a few days before the Leipzig events. On the occasion of the celebration of the GDR's fortieth anniversary, Gorbachev made it clear to his hosts that the Soviet Union was not going to come to the regime's assistance, adding his famous prophecy that "those who come too late, will be punished by life" – Honecker sure was, but so was his successor Egon Krenz, as well as, ultimately, Gorbachev himself along with the Soviet Union he tried to reform.

Thus a tightly knit web of linkages connected October 9 to previous and subsequent events, both in East Germany itself, and across its borders, from Hungary to China, from West Germany to the Soviet Union. The massive surge of protest of which the events in Leipzig were a part, and that swept across the communist world, is just one example of the highly unequal distribution of political contention across time and space. Periods of relative quiet alternate with waves of intense mobilization that encompass large sections of societies, and quite often affect many societies simultaneously. "Revolution years" such as 1848, 1917, or 1989 are but the most punctuated examples of this phenomenon. More temporally drawn-out examples are the postwar decolonization movements, the conglomerate of movements of "the sixties," or the "new social movements" of the 1970s and 1980s in Western Europe.

This interdependence of contention across space and time poses formidable challenges to the predominant theoretical paradigms in the study of contentious politics. Most studies in the field focus on individual movements in particular temporal and spatial settings (or static comparisons among such settings) and explain them in terms of the value and nature of explanatory variables (be they grievances, resources, opportunities or cultural frames) for that particular setting and that particular movement. But how far does an analysis of grievances among the GDR population prior to the autumn of 1989, or of the political opportunity structure of the East German regime get us, if events (and perceptions of grievances and opportunities) were to such an important extent influenced by what happened elsewhere? And what does an analysis of the resources and cultural frames available to East German dissident movements tell us, when we know that these were almost nonexistent prior to 1989, and subsequently were produced *within* the wave of contention? And how can these theories come to terms with the counterfactual that a slightly different course of events (not more than the wrong rumor at the wrong time might have been sufficient to tip the balance) on October 9 could have led to a completely different outcome: not only a "Chinese solution" for the GDR, but perhaps a wholly different future for Eastern Europe?

To confront these challenges we must move beyond single movements, and consider dynamic interactions among a multitude of contenders, including not only challenging protestors, but also their allies and adversaries – elite and nonelite, as well as the whole range of forms of claims-making from the most conventional and institutionalized, to the most provocative and disruptive. In addition, we must dynamize our explanatory variables, which during intense waves of protest may be as much in flux as the movements they are supposed to explain. Important theoretical advances in this direction have been made since the early 1990s or so, and it is on these that this chapter builds. Many concepts and topics that are important for understanding the dynamics of protest waves can be touched upon only briefly here, but will be treated in more detail in subsequent chapters (e.g., political opportunities, diffusion, allies and adversaries, tactical innovation, movements' consequences for each other; see chapters 4, 9, 12, 13, and 23 in this volume). The task I set myself in this chapter is to demonstrate that during periods of protracted contention the workings of these variables and mechanisms can be understood only in conjunction and in their effects on many contenders simultaneously.

I follow Sidney Tarrow's definition of a protest cycle as "a phase of heightened conflict and contention across the social system" (1994: 153). However, I prefer to use the terminology *wave* instead of *cycle*. The notion of a cycle suggests a periodically recurring sequence of phenomena,[2] an assumption that, as we will discuss below, is untenable (see also McAdam et al. 2001: 66). The wave metaphor does not imply such assumptions of regularity, and simply refers to the strong increase and subsequent decrease in the level of contention. I will use the terms "protest wave" and "wave of contention" interchangeably. While the former is often used in daily speech to refer to periods of intense protest, the latter is analytically more precise in that it acknowledges the fact that social movements as collective actors, and protest as a type of action, cannot be understood in isolation but only in relation to other contenders for power and to other types of political action (Koopmans and Statham 1999a).

Three fundamental features seem universal to waves of contention. Trivial truths though they may seem, to explain them is a challenging task. First, protest waves are characterized by a strong *expansion* of contention across social groups and sectors, superseding the narrow boundaries of policy fields, and often transcending national borders. Second, protest waves are invariably characterized by a *transformation* of contention, that is, changes in strategies, alliance structures, identities, and so forth, which inevitably arise in processes of dynamic interaction and ensure that no protest wave ends up where it began. That protest waves come to an end is the third seemingly trivial truth, but the reasons for that *contraction* of contention have commanded little attention in the literature so far. This chapter will be structured along the lines of these three fundamental processes that drive the development of waves of contention. This is not meant to suggest that protest waves pass through distinct phases of expansion, transformation, and contraction. Expansionist forces work throughout a wave, though they will obviously be less powerful – at least relative to contractive forces – towards its end. Transformative and contractive mechanisms and processes are likewise not confined to the later stages of a protest wave, but are present right from the beginning and may, in fact, prevent a wave from taking off altogether.

EXPANSIVE MECHANISMS

Protest waves often seemingly emerge out of nowhere, but then rapidly engulf broad geographical areas and sectors of society. This observation of protest waves as emergent and apparently spontaneous phenomena has led many mass psychologists and collective behavioralists to compare protest waves to epidemics (evidenced by the use of the term "contagion"), panics or fads. The explanation for such sudden eruptions of protest given by classical theories of collective behavior emphasized social-structural strains and their psychological consequences in the form of relative deprivation (Gurr 1970), anomie (Kornhauser 1959), and the spread of "generalized beliefs" (Smelser 1962). However, as has been demonstrated especially by the work of Charles Tilly and his collaborators (e.g., Shorter and Tilly 1974; Tilly et al. 1975), the historical record does not reveal a direct connection between profound social-structural changes and the rhythm of contention, but rather an indirect one, mediated by changes in political alignments and relations of power. Moreover, studies within the resource mobilization tradition have convincingly criticized the classical model's emphasis on irrationality and the loss of individuality under the spell of "the crowd." They showed that those who protest are often better integrated and less deprived than those who do not, and that different sites of protest are often connected by way of tight social networks rather than by random contagion (e.g., Oberschall 1973; Useem 1980).

From these criticisms of the collective behavior approach follows that the parameters of contention are first and foremost relational and defined by conflict lines, network links, and power relations among actors, both elite and extra-institutional. Usually, this web of relations that makes up a polity is in a state of relative equilibrium. For instance, in relation to nationalist movements, Beissinger (1996: 104) has aptly remarked that

> in times of "normalized" politics, a given crystallization of state boundaries is backed by the effective authority of the state and is not subject to open challenge from within. In such conditions, there is a strong tendency for individuals to adjust their beliefs to the boundaries of the possible, accepting a given institutional arrangement as unalterable and even natural.

Such equilibria should not be confused with stasis, because even in the most frozen, authoritarian regimes, there will always be small dissident groups testing the limits of the possible, as well as regime fluctuations between relative closure and "thaw." In democratic regimes, there is a much broader latitude for gradual change. But although the limits of the possible are comparatively wide and regime flexibility to respond with gradual reform is relatively great, even in democracies existing institutional arrangements, power relations, and cultural idioms set boundaries that are not easily transcended.

Protest waves, however, are characterized by the transcendence of such boundaries and a radical destabilization of social relations within the polity. Ari Zolberg (1972) has used the phrase "moments of madness" to capture the widespread feeling during intense waves of contention that "everything is possible." Usually, this "everything" includes both euphoric hopes for revolutionary change, and fears of repressive reaction – as in Leipzig on October 9 when many demonstrators sensed a historic moment without knowing whether it would be one of revolutionary breakthrough or an East German version of the Tiananmen massacre. Contrary to the collective behavior tradition, these "moments of madness" do not have their origins in psychological changes in the states of mind of protesters, but in the radicalized unpredictability of interactions across the social system. Still, in 1988, the few lone dissidents in the GDR "knew" the regime they opposed, and the regime and its security apparatus knew "their" dissidents. In the autumn of 1989, the regime's reactions had become unpredictable (even for Erich Honecker!), and its opponents were no longer just a few easily recognizable and controllable dissidents with well-known aims and strategies.

Expanding Political Opportunities

What causes, then, the destabilization of the web of social relations within a polity? One way in which social-structural changes may influence sociopolitical relations is through their impact on the relative amounts of resources controlled by different actors. Social change may make certain social groups more numerous or more economically powerful, and thereby – at least potentially – more politically relevant. McAdam (1982) has for instance shown this with regard to the origins of the US civil rights movement. The emergence of a black middle class, as well as black migration to the North improved both the resource basis for black activism and its potential political leverage.

While such social-structural changes may point towards potentials for change and may help identify the groups most likely to contribute to such changes, they are insufficient to account for the emergence of protest waves. A widely held view in the literature nowadays is that changes in the structure of political opportunities, which reduce the power disparity between authorities and challengers, are of decisive importance (e.g., Koopmans 1993; Tarrow 1994; McAdam 1995; see also chapter 4 in this volume). The reasoning behind this idea is that normally the power disparity between power-holders and challengers is so large that even a substantial increase in the amount of resources controlled by a challenging group will be far from sufficient to shift the balance of power. Only when the regime is weakened or divided will challengers stand a chance to make a difference.

However, the availability of political opportunities does not automatically and immediately translate into increased protest. Latent conflicts among the political elite and other regime weaknesses have to be perceived and made manifest before they can affect contention (Gamson and Meyer 1996). Two ideal-typical paths toward such a manifestation of political opportunities can be discerned, one top-down, the other bottom-up (reality of course often containing a mixture of both). The top-down variant most unequivocally demonstrates the relevance of political opportunities. When elites are divided among themselves, factions among them may choose to mobilize popular support in order to strengthen their position *vis-à-vis* rival elites, either by directly sponsoring or even initiating protest campaigns, or by encouraging dissent in more subtle ways. An example is Mikhail Gorbachev's politics of glasnost and his occasional direct encouraging of public criticism and protest against his opponents within the Soviet leadership. Opposition to Gorbachev was likewise often encouraged or even orchestrated from within the Soviet elite, be it by people like Boris Yeltsin for whom Gorbachev's reforms were not radical enough, or by anti-reformist elites in the Soviet periphery who put themselves at the head of nationalist movements (Beissinger 1996). Very similar patterns of active involvement of the communist elite in ethno-nationalist agitation could be observed in the former Yugoslavia (Oberschall 2000).

This is a common pattern for shifts in political opportunity structures to become manifest, particularly in authoritarian regimes where power disparities are so great that sustained protest is hardly imaginable without active elite support. Often, however, pressure from below is necessary to expose latent regime weaknesses and conflicts of interest within the elite. Political contention is an iterative process, and, as indicated, even in the most authoritarian contexts, there will always be dissident groups who occasionally test the regime's steadfastness. While these attempts usually fail because they meet with the resistance of a unified elite, the dissidents' fate may suddenly reverse when their actions reveal a split within the elite and are not, as usual, repressed or ignored.

Contentious Innovations and their Diffusion

A simple repetition of past patterns of protest by dissidents is however unlikely to lead to such an exposure of political opportunities. Regimes have established ways of dealing with known types of protest and elite controversies are unlikely to emerge over how to respond to them. The possibilities for exposing political opportunities are therefore greatly enhanced if there is a novel quality to protest. Such novelty can consist of new actors involved in protest or a redefinition of their collective identities, new tactics or organizational forms, or demands and interpretive frames that challenge the regime's legitimacy in novel ways. It is significant in this respect that Eastern European communist regimes were not brought down by traditional dissident movements, but by a much more diffuse challenge that included ordinary workers (posing a particular ideological problem in these alleged "workers' paradises") and ethnic and linguistic minorities – whose leverage was greatest where a quasi-federal state structure made it difficult to deny such groups public legitimacy (Beissinger 1996; Bunce 1999). In the GDR, the linkage of traditional dissidents to the refugee crisis and advocates of free travel was of decisive importance (Joppke 1995).

Such successful innovations in patterns of contention are, however, very rare. Much like their regime opponents, challenging groups have established patterns of action, with clearly circumscribed constituencies and collective identities, limited and relatively inert tactical repertoires (Tilly 1978), and predictable demands and interpretive frames. Occasionally, often helped by particular precipitating circumstances, dissident groups are able to invent new combinations of identities, tactics, and demands. These creative moments are extremely important, for they may provide the initial sparks that expose regime weaknesses. However, if the history of contention would depend on such *de novo* inventions alone, protest waves would be extremely rare and limited in scope.[3] Most movements, in fact, borrow inventions from other movements, either within the same polity or from abroad. By incorporating such innovations in their established repertoires, they not only introduce an element of novelty in their interactions with the regimes they oppose, but may also, if successful, establish a new recombination of identities, tactics, and demands that can in turn inspire other movements.

Here we arrive at the crucial importance of diffusion processes in the expansion of contention. In the words of McAdam (1995: 231), "initiator movements are nothing more than clusters of new cultural items – new cognitive frames, behavioral routines, organizational forms, tactical repertoires, etc. – subject to the same diffusion dynamics as other innovations." Such diffusion processes have commanded considerable attention in the recent social movement literature and there is much we can learn here from more established diffusion theories in other fields. Since chapter 13 in this volume is entirely devoted to this important problematic, I will here only highlight some of the most important characteristics of diffusion processes.

Diffusion is responsible for the emergent and eruptive character of protest waves that puzzled collective behaviorists and mass psychologists, and was subsequently neglected by the resource mobilization school, probably because this aspect of protest waves stood in uneasy tension with the idea of social movements as carefully planned, organized, rational actors. What epidemics, fads, contentious innovations, or any other diffusion process have in common is that they are socially embedded: they can only spread by way of communication from a source to an adopter, along established network links (Strang and Soule 1998; Myers 2000). Granovetter (1973) has argued that "weak ties" are particularly important in the diffusion of innovations because they link constituencies which have relatively few social relations in common, whereas communication along strong network ties is less likely to contain information that is novel to the recipient.[4] In modern open societies, the mass media are the weak tie *par excellence*, and may communicate innovations between groups who share no social links at all – apart of course from their watching or reading the same news media. Therefore, the mass media play a crucial (but understudied) role in the diffusion of protest in modern democracies (Myers 2000).

A second important characteristic of social diffusion (and here the parallel with contagion and epidemics ends) is that adopters are generally not passive recipients, but choose whether or not to adopt a particular innovation.[5] Innovations may be helpful for one group, but be seen as useless or inapplicable by another. The process by which groups make such decisions about the applicability of innovations to their context is sometimes denoted as "attribution of similarity" (Strang and Meyer 1993). Apart from internal characteristics of the adopting group, the perceived similarity of the political context will play an important role in such considerations. It is certainly no coincidence that the diffusion of contention that started in the autumn of 1989 respected clearly circumscribed geopolitical boundaries. All Eastern European countries whose regimes were directly existentially linked to the Soviet Union were affected by it, as were communist countries in immediate geographical and cultural proximity such as Yugoslavia and Albania. But the wave neither spread to the non-European communist world, nor to noncommunist countries within Europe.

Linkages Between Political Opportunities and Diffusion

Such limits to the scope of diffusion depend strongly on the actual linkages of opportunity structures in different contexts. Protests could spread across Eastern Europe not just because these were structurally and culturally similar communist countries, but also because a weakening of one regime had immediate consequences for the strength of another. Earlier revolts in the Eastern Bloc had always been smothered in the threat or actual use of military force by the "brother countries," first and foremost the Soviet Union. Starting with Gorbachev's explicit indication that the Soviet Union would this time not intervene, every subsequent failure of a regime to contain or repress opposition made the position of remaining hardliners more precarious until even those who did choose the road of repression, such as Ceausescu in Romania, were no longer able to scare regime opponents from the streets. Such "opportunity cascades" may be an important mechanism for protest diffusion. They may, it should be noted, themselves be partly the result of diffusion processes. Innovations also spread within elite networks, subject to similar constraints as protest diffusion. Thus glasnost and perestroika, Yeltsinite radical reformism, as well as the strategy of mobilizing ethno-nationalism as a means of elite survival, all diffused throughout Eastern Europe's communist elites, and differential adoption of such strategic models often introduced conflicts within formerly consensual regimes.

The linkage between diffusion and political opportunities is reinforced by a third and final central characteristic of diffusion processes. Contrary to the assumption of irrational contagion that is prevalent in the collective behavior approach, numerous studies have shown that adoption depends on the perceived success of innovations. For instance, in his study of the early history of airplane hijackings, Holden (1986) showed that only successful hijackings increased the subsequent rate of hijacking, whereas unsuccessful hijackings had no discernable impact. This is the main reason why protest innovations can spread more easily if opportunities are conducive. Innovations that fail to help those who employ them to achieve their aims are unlikely to be adopted by others. However, success or failure may not always be so easy to determine, certainly if more long-term strategic aims are concerned. Especially in authoritarian contexts, the mere fact that mobilization is not repressed may be a sufficient indicator of success for that type of mobilization to spread. In democratic contexts the media again play an important role. It is sometimes more important that a protest practice is portrayed in the media as successful than whether it really is so – particularly if activists are not themselves directly affected by a tactic's success or failure (Soule 1999).

Reactive Mobilization

An expansive process different from diffusion (although sometimes wrongly subsumed under it) is that successful mobilization by one group may affect, or threaten to affect the interests of another group in such a way that it provokes countermobilization or competitive mobilization among the members of that group. Countermobilization refers to the mobilization of a different constituency, which is (threatened to be) adversely affected by the mobilization of initial contenders (see Meyer and Staggenborg 1996). For instance, the mobilization of a nationalist movement among the members of one ethnic group tends to provoke counternationalisms among those groups with whom it shares disputed territories or who live as minorities among them. Thus the attempt to impose Serbian hegemony in Yugoslavia reinforced or even gave birth to ethno-nationalist movements among Croats, Bosnians, and Kosovars. Competitive mobilization, by contrast, refers to attempts to mobilize the same constituency by groups or organizations whose control over that constituency is (threatened to be) affected by the initial movement, or who seek to capture the mobilization potential revealed by it. Ethno-nationalist mobilization in Eastern Europe again provides many examples, for instance in the form of the competitive bidding among different Serbian nationalist leaders and warlords that contributed importantly to the escalation of ethnic conflict.

It is important to note that countermovements and competitive mobilization are as dependent on the availability of political opportunities as their adversaries. The mere presence of a movement that threatens another group's interests is as insufficient to explain the latter's mobilization as is the presence of grievances among the constituency of the initial movement. However, political opportunities for countermovements in the form of direct or indirect elite support are almost by definition given if the initial movement poses a credible threat to established interests. Countermovements often receive strong support or are even initiated from within the political elite. The situation is a bit different for competitive groups. Since they mobilize a similar constituency with similar demands as the initial movement, their opportunity structures overlap to a large extent. They may, however, tap different sources of elite support. Political elite groups may also directly initiate competitive mobilization if the challenger group threatens to make inroads into their popular constituency. This form of competitive mobilization is most likely in democratic contexts where established political parties often support or initiate moderate competitors to more radical groups, in order to prevent the radicals from eroding their constituency. This increased institutional support for moderate groups in order to undermine more radical ones is often referred to as the "radical-flank effect" (Haines 1984). For instance, faced with growing competition from Green parties from the end of the 1970s onwards, many social-democratic parties in Europe became active supporters of the moderate wings of the peace and environmental movements (Koopmans 1995a).

Together, expanding political opportunities, diffusion of contentious innovations, and reactive mobilization are the three major mechanisms behind the rapid expansion of waves of contention. Diffusion and reactive mobilization are chiefly responsible for the rapidity of this process, and political opportunities may or may not act as a brake on this expansion. If fault lines within a regime's ruling elite remain shallow and the resulting opportunities localized, the limits of expansion may be quickly reached. If changes in political opportunities take the form of what has been called a "generalized regime crisis" (McAdam 1995: 222–3), conflict may expand to such a level that the regime collapses in revolution or civil war. However, it is usually only possible to tell after the fact which of these two scenarios we are dealing with. The more initial mobilization has destabilized the web of social relations in a polity, the more contention has spread to different social groups, and the more initial challenger successes set in motion a spiral of opportunities and threats (McAdam et al. 2001) that activate imitators, countermovements, and competitive mobilization, the more unpredictable the course of events becomes. It is to these transformations over the course of protest waves that we now turn.

TRANSFORMATIVE MECHANISMS

Over their course, waves of contention often display shifts between conflictive and accommodating interactions, radical alterations in the balance of power between groups, and profound realignments of patterns of coalition and opposition among actors. These often striking changes have long inspired a quest for recurrent patterns in such transformations. Several stage models of social movements (e.g., Rammstedt 1978), and revolutions (Brinton 1959; Edwards 1965) have been proposed. This "natural history" tradition assumes that social movements or revolutions pass through a recurrent sequence of phases, and often draw on biological or medical analogies to explain their course. Crane Brinton, for instance, compares revolutions to fevers, and posits that revolutions "work up, not regularly but with advances and retreats, to a crisis, frequently accompanied by delirium, the rule of the most violent revolutionaries, the reign of terror... Finally the fever is over, and the patient is himself again" (1959: 18).

Because of their deterministic character, these theories did not have a lasting influence (for a critique see Rule and Tilly 1972). After a longer period in which questions of movement development past their emergence were strongly neglected, Sidney Tarrow's innovative work on protest cycles (1989) put the question of protest transformations firmly back on the agenda. While he departed from the rigid stage models of the past, his formulation of the dynamics of protest cycles stuck to the idea that recurrent patterns, which explained their parabolic rise and fall, could be distinguished. In early formulations of the theory, Tarrow emphasized increased competition between movement groups and organizations as the main mechanism of change, leading to institutionalization and a turn towards conventional politics of some organizations, and a radicalization and increasing sectarianism of others.

Both processes, institutionalization and radicalization, in tandem contribute to the decline of the cycle, as people are either satisfied by reforms, or scared from the streets by violence. A similar explanation had earlier been proposed by Sabine Karstedt-Henke (1980) in her theory on the origins of terrorist movements. However, while Tarrow emphasized mechanisms internal to the social movement sector, she stressed the counterstrategies of state authorities, who in a classical "carrot and stick" strategy react to some movement groups with concessions and co-optation, while marginalizing and repressing groups with more radical demands. Such divide-and-rule strategies of authorities thus amplify strategic differences within movements to the extent that the latter disintegrate into pacified and institu-tionalized moderates, and marginalized and increasingly sectarian radicals. The link between both perspectives is, of course, that the success of differential external strategies of facilitation and repression both depends on, and reinforces internal processes of movement institutionalization and radicalization (Koopmans 1993).

In later reformulations, Tarrow has gradually backed away from the idea of recurrent patterns within protest cycles. In *Power in Movement* (1994) he continues to emphasize opportunities and diffusion as crucial to the expansion of protest, but stresses that the endings of protest cycles can be very diverse. In my own restatement of protest wave dynamics among the new social movements of Western Europe (Koopmans 1995b), I likewise emphasized variance between protest waves, and explained such variation as a consequence of different patterns of state–movement interaction. In contexts where the political system offers multiple channels of insti-tutionalized access to challengers and where authorities react by accommodation and concessions, institutionalization will predominate, and radicalization may remain very limited. If, however, the regime offers few channels of access, responds by repression and is unwilling to reform, radicalization will be the dominant outcome.

But even such amended versions of cyclical theory cannot do justice to the variety of paths that waves of contention may follow (see also the critique in McAdam et al. 2001: 66–8). Access and concessions may lead to demobilization through institu-tionalization, but they may just as well increase protesters' appetite. Short-lived Party leader Egon Krenz soon found this out after he had ousted Erich Honecker, initiated a dialogue with the citizens' movement, and opened the Wall: these were yesterday's demands; the East Germans now wanted nothing short of the end of Party rule and reunification with the West. In a similar vein, regime steadfastness and repression may contribute to the marginalization of protest through submission or sectarian radicalization, but just as often such a strategy backfires and serves only to reinforce the challenge to the regime. Where the Chinese succeeded, Nicolae Ceausescu met his end.

These strong variations among waves of contention, and the apparent absence in them of fixed causal linkages, between, say, repression and demobilization, or concessions and pacification, reflects the radical unpredictability of contentious interactions during intense protest waves, the contingency of their outcomes, and the path dependence of the interactive sequences they consist of. To appreciate this, it is instructive to reflect on the mechanisms that structure contentious interactions in times of "normal politics," when social relations in the polity are relatively stable.

Three Mechanisms of Strategic Change

Three basic mechanisms underlying strategic change in contentious politics can be discerned. The first, which I call "strategic anticipation," denotes the type of forward-looking rational decision-making that is central to rational choice theory. In trying to achieve their aims, contenders consider several alternatives for action, anticipate the reactions of other actors to them, and choose the option that provides the optimal balance of costs and benefits. The adequacy of forward-looking problem-solving by any particular actor depends of course on the accuracy of her predictions of the range of relevant contenders to a set of strategic interactions, as well as of her anticipation of the identities, aims, and discursive and tactical reper-toires of these other contenders. These preconditions may sometimes be approxi-mated – though obviously never quite fulfilled – in times of normal politics. When the web of social relations in the polity is relatively stable, the range of competitors, opponents, and allies and the balance of power among them are reasonably well known, and their reactions are fairly predictable. Since such knowledge is not just held by the one contender which we take as our point of departure, but by all relevant contenders, change as a result of strategic anticipation is subject to strong equilibrating pressures: if A can anticipate pretty well what B will do, the reverse is usually true as well, and A and B's interactions will be highly routinized, save for limited oscillations and perhaps some very gradual change. As late as 1988, the GDR was probably a fairly good approximation of a polity where such conditions prevailed. This balance of forces, which had been established after the construction of the Wall in 1961 and had undergone only minor changes since then, condemned the small dissident movement to an existence at the margins of the polity, easily held in check by the powerful state security apparatus.

However, even in times of high political stability, explanations of the course of contentious interactions based only on this model of rationality have a limited reach. While they have achieved much in their dealings with the physical (and to some extent biological) environment (which have the advantage of not reacting strategic-ally in response to attempts to manipulate them: atoms do not change their "strat-egies" if we attempt to split them), humans are quite poor social problem-solvers. The reason is the sheer complexity of social life and the fact that even in times of normal politics, anticipations of other actors' behavior are always imperfect and subject to counteranticipations. The more relevant parties there are to a conflict and the more actors' calculations extend over several interactive sequences, the less effective forward-looking rationality becomes, both from a strategic and an explana-tory point of view (Luhmann 1999: 430).[6]

But strategic decision-making is not a one-off process without history. Much strategic change results from a less demanding form of rationality, which we may call "strategic adaptation." It is based on the iterative, trial-and-error character of interactions and consists of the simple decision rule: shift towards strategies that were successful in past interactive sequences and away from strategies that failed. Attempts at problem-solving that do not achieve the anticipated outcomes, will thus ultimately disappear from a contender's strategic repertoire, and those that do will be retained. Strategic adaptation as a form of learning by doing is a more realistic explanation for changes in patterns of contention than strategic anticipation, because it neither assumes that contenders have a crystal-clear overview of the field of contention, nor that they are able to adequately predict the behavior of all other relevant actors – it merely requires that they learn from their mistakes. But strategic adaptation, too, depends on the relatively stable conditions of normal politics. Iterative adaptation works only if there is time for convergence, that is, if different solutions to the strategic problem can subsequently be put to a test in similar circumstances. In analytic terms, strategic adaptation requires relatively stable opportunity structures, and under these conditions, like problem-solving, it tends to reproduce a state of relative equilibrium in that it routinizes strategic interactions among contenders.

Both anticipation and adaptation are situated at the level of individual contenders. However, as we have seen, instances of collective action are connected to one another through processes of diffusion and reactive mobilization. Knowledge of other instances of collective action influences anticipation and adaptation by signaling new opportunities and threats and by providing examples of successful and failed strategies. This allows contenders to learn from others' mistakes instead of making their own, and to adopt successful solutions to collective action problems rather than independently inventing them. However, of all the (attempted) collective action that occurs in a polity, only a relatively small portion reaches the attention of a wider audience and can thereby spur imitation and reaction. This is so because diffusion and reaction depend on the communicative channels of the public sphere, which tend to have a limited carrying capacity relative to the multitude of events that vie for inclusion (Hilgartner and Bosk 1988). This is the basis for the third and final mechanism of strategic change that I call "environmental selection."[7]

In authoritarian societies such as the former GDR, selective pressures are extremely severe. A free circulation of information in such polities is prevented through media censorship, strong limitations to the freedom of association and the expression of dissident opinions, as well as a strict surveillance of dissidents and restrictions of their movements. As a result, dissident groups have to operate in isolation with hardly any possibilities to spread their messages to a wider audience. The opening of political opportunities at the end of the 1980s in the GDR was to no small extent due to the regime's loss of control over the flow of information. Mikhail Gorbachev's politics of glasnost led to a liberalization of opinions expressed in the Soviet press, which was also widely read in the GDR. In an act of unprecedented defiance, the GDR regime at one time even banned several Soviet publications, but quickly pulled back following protests by the Soviet leadership. Among the Eastern European countries, the GDR was also in the unique position that it was strongly exposed to counterinformation from the West in the form of West German television, which could be received in large parts of the country. This, too, contributed to the GDR regime's gradual loss of its information monopoly over the course of the 1980s. Only in the valley of the Elbe around Dresden could West German television not be received, and it is no coincidence that this "valley of the ignorant" (*Tal der Ahnungslosen*), as the East Germans used to call it, played a conspicuously marginal role in the revolution of 1989.

In democratic societies, too, selective pressures operate, albeit less severely. The mass media play a preponderant role in this respect. As recent research on media selection processes of contentious events has shown, mass media coverage is highly selective but in relatively systematic ways (e.g., McCarthy et al. 1996; Hocke 1999). The media privilege events that satisfy certain "news values," for example the

prominence of the actor, the relevance of the issue or the degree of conflict. Moreover, media coverage is seldom neutral and ascribes legitimacy to certain actors,
demands, and strategies, while denying it to others (for a more extensive treatment,
see Koopmans 2001). Thus, the news media prestructure the information that
people receive about contentious events and thereby affect which of them become
available as templates for imitation and reaction. Paraphrasing the famous one-liner
about the role of agency in history, one might say that people make their own
history, but on the basis of an information input not of their own making. Besides
the media, the political system itself acts as a powerful instrument of selection. For
instance, the design of the electoral system (e.g., majoritarian or proportional, the
size and boundaries of constituencies, electoral hurdles) determines how easily new
parties may gain access to the parliamentary arena and to the public visibility,
legitimacy, and resources that such access entails. More generally, differential state
facilitation and repression affect the chances of different forms of contention to
diffuse to a wider audience, and like the news media, the state ascribes or denies
legitimacy to such contention.

Like anticipation and adaptation, selection processes tend to reproduce a state of
relative equilibrium in times of normal politics. A relatively stable "discursive
opportunity structure" (Koopmans and Statham 1999b: 228–9) in such periods
leads to recurrent and self-reproducing patterns of access to the news media and
to political resources, and settled notions of which ideas are considered "sensible,"
which constructions of reality are seen as "realistic," and which claims and contenders are held as "legitimate."

Punctuated Equilibrium, Contingency, and Path Dependence

The powerful centripetal tendencies, which we have just discussed, give some idea of
the odds against the kind of radical change within a polity that we see during waves
of contention. However, I want to argue that beyond a certain threshold of deviation
from habitual patterns of interaction, centripetal forces rapidly erode and make
place for a much more disorderly, unpredictable, and innovative course of events.
For this, I adopt the notion of "punctuated equilibrium" proposed by the biologists
Niles Eldredge and Stephen Jay Gould (1972).[8] This idea is based on the observation
of alternations of long periods of great stability in the fossil record with (geologically
speaking) short periods of radical change in which large numbers of ancient species
become extinct and many new ones make their first appearance. This idea is
contested in evolutionary biology because it challenges the classical Darwinian
idea of glacial change, expressed in Darwin's ([1859] 1985: 222–3) dictum that
natura non facit saltum (nature does not make leaps). Whatever its value in biology,
the historical record of waves of contention and revolution suggests that human
politics does make leaps and that political change is indeed often concentrated in
relatively short periods of radical transformation.[9]

To understand what drives the pace of change during waves of contention, we
return to the three mechanisms of strategic change and ask how they operate under
conditions of uncertainty. As I have argued above, expanding political opportunities
stand at the basis of the processes that drive the expansion of protest waves.
Translated into the terms of our mechanisms, such shifts in political opportunities
imply a significant reduction in selective pressures – generally or for some specific

groups – and allow new contenders, tactics, and demands to enter the scene. Diffusion of contentious innovations and reactive mobilization may then quickly expand the scope of contention to other groups, societal sectors, and geographical areas. As a result, all contenders, not just those who have newly sprung up or taken up innovations from elsewhere, but including the established elite, face an unknown situation for which previous experience provides little guidance. In the relatively stable environment of normal politics, contenders may solve this problem by trial and error. However, during waves of contention, the strategic problem of contenders is a moving target. Because many groups adapt their strategies at the same time, interactions lose the recurrent character they have in times of normal politics and which allow the gradual emergence of a stable strategic response. During waves of contention most contenders will have the impression that they are constantly running behind the facts. Past experience does not provide much guidance since today's situation is too different, and forward-looking problem-solvers will often find out tomorrow that they have solved the problems of yesterday.

With selection significantly relaxed, its rules in flux, and adaptation on the basis of recurrent trials no longer a viable option, the main burden of guiding strategic change comes to rest on strategic anticipation. But as indicated above, humans are not nearly as good at solving new strategic problems as they like to think (not because of a lack of intelligence, but because their interactive counterparts are equally intelligent), and events usually follow a course that is different from anything anybody had anticipated. Just consider the strategic failure of a man of vision, courage, and intelligence like Mikhail Gorbachev, whose attempt to reform the Soviet Union ended up destroying it.

The nonrecurrent character of strategic interactions during waves of contention greatly enhances the effects of contingent events. In times of relative political stability, an unexpected event such as the death of a demonstrator (e.g., at the G7 summit in Genoa in 2001 or at the EU summit in Göteborg in 2000) may cause temporary indignation and protest, but does not usually alter the course of history. In Prague in the autumn of 1989, the rumor of the death of a demonstrator at the hands of the police (which later turned out to be false) brought people massively into the streets and played an important role in bringing down the regime. The opening of the Berlin Wall on November 9, 1989, provides another example. The move had been decided by the Politburo as a concession to the opposition and proof of its willingness to reform. As it was, the regime never even got the chance to reap the strategic advantages it must have hoped to gain from its move. At a press conference in the early evening, the government's press speaker, Günther Schabowski, mistakenly announced that the government had decided to open the border to West Berlin "if I am correctly informed, immediately." Instead of the orderly granting of travel visas on an individual basis to be started as of November 10 (which was what the government had really decided) tens of thousands of East Berliners swelled to the border crossings to West Berlin and simply overran the few, unprepared, and confused border guards. Instead of an orderly regime concession, the fall of the Wall had become a triumph of the people.

Errors, false rumors, misunderstandings, and inconsistent behaviors not only have a much larger potential impact during intense waves of contention; they are also more likely to occur under these circumstances. Schabowski's mistake, for instance, can only be understood in the context of the enormous strategic pressure under which the regime operated at that point, which meant that decisions were taken hastily without enough time to adequately consider and communicate them. The mistake also reflects the uncertainty of the situation, both from the point of view of the regime and from that of the population. Given the dramatic twists and turns of events in the preceding weeks, Schabowski (and the population) could well imagine that the regime had decided to open the Wall immediately and without preconditions. Only a month before, Schabowski would never have thought the government capable of such a decision, and even if he had announced such a thing, most people would have assumed he had erred and would have waited for confirmation from higher authorities.

Nonrecurrence and contingency together imply that intense waves of contention become radically path dependent. Depending on the choices made by actors at critical junctures, interactions are led into certain paths while other possible paths may be permanently closed off.[10] Returning to the events with which we started this chapter, let us try to imagine what would have happened if Erich Honecker would have had his way and the police and army had crushed the demonstration in Leipzig on October 9, 1989? Of course, we can only speculate, but we can be pretty sure that things would have taken a very different course from the one we know (a crushed rebellion like in China, a *coup d'état* against Honecker, a violent revolution?), with attendant effects on what subsequently happened in other Eastern European countries, and on the ultimate geopolitical outcome. At the same time, the consequences of the choice *not* to crush the Leipzig demonstration, made it almost impossible for the East German leadership to revert to the option of massive repression later on. After the success of the Leipzig demonstration, mobilization surged across East Germany, the leadership itself no longer stood united, and the police and army could no longer be counted on to follow orders to repress a movement that now so clearly had majority support among the population.

To be theoretically meaningful, path dependence must mean more than just that subsequent events depend on what came before (Pierson 2000: 252). This, one may argue, is always true in historical processes. For example, if a strategic failure of an actor leads him to change his tactic, we may well say that prior events affect subsequent events, but we are not dealing here with path dependence in any meaningful sense. Path dependence is a particular way in which subsequent developments depend on prior events, namely when prior events increase the likelihood of subsequent events *of the same type*. For example, when not repressing a movement at t1 makes it more difficult to repress that movement at t2, and if again not repressing it at t2 makes it even more difficult to repress it at t3, etc., then we are dealing with a path-dependent process. The radicalness of path dependence simply depends on how important single, critical choices are. That is, if not repressing at t1 makes repressing at t2 only slightly more difficult, we are dealing with moderate path dependence. If, as in the Leipzig case, not repressing at t1 makes repressing at t2 almost impossible, then we may call such path dependence radical.[11]

Scope Conditions for Further Generalizations

Does all this mean that it is futile to search for generalizable patterns of transformation over the course of protest waves? Given the role of unpredictability, contingency, and radical path dependence in waves of contention, the answer must on a general level be yes. If the argument advanced in this chapter holds, a general theory of waves of contention can only consist of an account of the basic mechanisms that drive transformations, but will (precisely because of the inherent unpredictability resulting from these mechanisms) have to refrain from generalizations regarding the nature of the transformations that result from their interplay (see McAdam et al. 2001).

At the same time, however, it is important to realize that while much of the polity may be in flux during intense waves of contention, there are also elements that remain fairly stable. The degree to which this is the case is of course itself variable among waves of contention and is small in the case of revolutions, intermediate in the case of politywide but nonrevolutionary waves of protest, and large in the case of protest waves that are limited to a circumscribed set of contenders. In the case of revolutions such as those in Eastern Europe in 1989, it is probably indeed futile to look for generalizations that would contribute to a general theory of revolutions. Such generalizations require that there are relevant parts of the political environment of a wave of contention that remain relatively stable (and allow comparison with and generalizations to other cases, with similar stable structures) and which exert selective pressures on the development of contention that provide consistent positive feedback to some patterns of interaction and consistent negative feedback to others, and thereby make some outcomes more likely than others. When, however, contention escalates into an *Umwertung aller Werte* (full-scale revolution), there are too few such external constants on which a generalizing account of transformations might build.

However, in the case of more limited waves of contention, such generalizations are in principle possible, albeit within clearly circumscribed conditions.[12] For instance, the development of protest waves in democracies under the rule of law is affected by several limiting and facilitating features that are absent in nondemocratic regimes. Repression in such regimes is constrained by legal norms, while many forms of nonviolent contention are guaranteed and protected by law. At the same time, the availability of such legal protection for nonviolent protest make the use of violence much less legitimate in the eyes of the wider population than in regimes that do not offer such legal opportunities (consider for instance the failed attempts to import the "urban guerilla" tactic from the authoritarian context of Latin America to Western Europe and the USA in the 1960s and 1970s). Next to legal opportunities for protest and constraints on repression, democratic regimes of course offer the important channel of access of the electoral process, which radically alters the conditions for interaction between political elites and challengers compared to nondemocratic regimes. In democracies, political elites are dependent on the citizenry for reelection, and protest movements derive power from the electoral leverage of their adherents that movements in authoritarian regimes lack. This forces democratic elites to be much more responsive than their counterparts in authoritarian regimes, and institutionalizes and routinizes the alteration of political incumbency, which in authoritarian regimes is only possible by way of intra-elite coup d'état or revolution from below. In democracies, the very existence of institutionalized access and routinized change of incumbency exerts very strong selective pressures against a revolutionary overthrow of the regime from below.

Among regimes of the same type, there are also structural differences that are fairly stable and that make some developmental trajectories more likely than others. For instance, in the case of new social movements in Western Europe, it was no coincidence that radicalization tendencies were relatively strong in Germany and France, and weak in the Netherlands and Switzerland, because of the differential responsiveness and institutional openness of these regimes to social movements generally, and the new social movements in particular (Kriesi et al. 1995). Likewise, the highly centralized nature of the French polity and the comparative lack of institutional channels of interest mediation and conflict resolution produces typically eruptive patterns of protest with strong upsurges and declines versus much smoother trajectories in the Swiss case with its multiple channels of access and consensual elite strategies (Duyvendak 1995; Giugni 1995). Here is not the place to dwell on these differences between political regimes. They will be discussed at length in the chapter on political opportunity structures. Here it suffices to conclude that generalizations on trajectories of waves of contention beyond the general mechanisms of change discussed in this chapter can only be made for specified regime types. The boundaries set by relatively stable features of a regime's political opportunity structure act as powerful constraints on the transformation of protest waves, which gives them a much different (and more "contained") dynamics in democratic than in nondemocratic regimes, and probably also implies differences between protest now, with democratic norms geopolitically firmly in place and exerting normative pressure also on nondemocratic regimes, than in the past, when democracy was still the exotic exception. The implication of this view is that while they do not have general applicability, hypotheses about protest trajectories such as those developed by Tarrow (1989) or Koopmans (1993) may well have a more limited validity for the case of contemporary (Western?) democratic regimes.

Contractive Mechanisms

The fact that the trajectories of waves of contention can be highly varied and contingent implies that there is no typical way in which protest waves end. The range of possible endings is principally unlimited and includes regime replacement through revolution, civil war or foreign intervention, repression, elite closure, reform, institutionalization, co-optation, altered conflict and alliance structures, a new balance of electoral power and changes in government incumbency, or any combination of these. Moreover, the endings of waves of contention may be sudden and dramatic, or take the form of an unspectacular "petering out" of protest. The outcomes in terms of a comparison between the level of contention before and after a wave also span a range of possibilities from a radical reduction of the level of contention (e.g., the stabilization of the Russian Revolution under Stalin) to a permanent residue of strongly increased levels of contention (e.g., in Eastern Europe after 1989). Because time's arrow points in just one direction, the only outcome that can be principally excluded is that a wave ends up where it began. Even if at the end the same actors would hold power as at the beginning, and no concessions had been granted or permanent defeats had been suffered by any of the contenders, the situation would still be very different from the status-quo-ante. Actors would have gained additional experiential knowledge about their opponents' and allies' intentions, tactics, strengths, and weaknesses, as well as those of themselves. As a result, each of them would enter a new round of interaction wiser and with adapted strategies aiming to improve upon previous experiences.

One more thing is certain: one way or another, sooner or later, each wave of contention comes to an end. To date, the explanation of protest decline is perhaps the weakest chain in social movement theory and research (Oegema and Klandermans 1994). Often, simple exhaustion, disappointment or a loss of interest in political life are offered as an explanation, which raises rather than answers the question (e.g., Hirschman 1982). As indicated in the above section on transformative mechanisms, others have argued in terms of a combination of radicalization and institutionalization. Since, however, the combination of these processes is not a generalizable feature of protest waves, it can not function as a general explanation of why and how they end. Another explanation is that protest declines because tactical innovations lose their novelty, and thereby their ability to attract media attention and to take adversaries by surprise (e.g., Freeman 1979; Rochon 1988; Koopmans 1993). This explanation is problematic, too. As has often been emphasized, protest waves are "the crucibles out of which new weapons of protest are fashioned" (Tarrow 1994: 156). That is, waves of contention provide a particularly fertile ground for tactical innovation and therefore there is no reason why once the strategic and media effects of initial tactical innovations wane, others cannot take their place. A decrease in the level of tactical innovation over the course of a protest wave is a symptom, not a cause of protest decline.

The most popular argument for why protest waves decline (one that is virtually universally found in studies of protest waves) is a "closure" of political opportunities. This argument is wrong when "closure" refers to a reduced responsiveness of political elites or the closure of channels of access, because this may lead to demobilization or mobilization, depending on the circumstances. Moreover, demobilization may also result from the opposite, *increased* regime responsiveness or access. The "closure" argument is tautological when it is simply derived from the effect on mobilization, for example when reform and other favorable changes are subsumed under "closure" because both may have the effect of decreasing the level of mobilization.

Restabilization through Interactive Convergence

For a more satisfactory explanation of the contraction of contention, we must return to what makes it expand, namely the destabilization of the web of social relations in the polity resulting from expanding opportunities, diffusion and reactive mobilization. In a similar vein, the contraction of protest waves is best conceptualized as a process of *restabilization* and reroutinization of patterns of interaction within the polity. It is worth emphasizing that this is a very different approach to contraction than traditional accounts in terms of "decline" or "closure." The latter perspective leads one to search for worsening opportunities, declining resources or a loss of discursive resonance for a movement's demands and frames. Or, in the "reform" and "institutionalization" variant, the explanation is sought in newly gained power and resources and discursive breakthroughs. But neither defeat nor victory is a satisfactory explanation for demobilization. History is full of examples of movements that kept on fighting in the face of defeat, and of victories that served only to open up new horizons.

The fundamental error of this type of explanation for contraction is that it argues from the point of view of one particular actor in a wave of contention, usually the social movement under study. The crux of an adequate account of contraction is not that the situation becomes more or less favorable for any one actor, but that relations *between actors* become more stable. To explain contentious contraction we must account for why *all* (or at least the large majority of) actors decrease their levels of mobilization. Any account that explains only why one contender demobilizes is incomplete. Because if those in a favorable position demobilize, why wouldn't the less fortunate try to make up for their losses? And conversely, if the disfavored give up the struggle, why wouldn't those on top try to increase their piece of the cake a bit more still?

What matters, then, is not whether any conflict party has lost or gained, or has been weakened or strengthened, but whether relations between actors converge on a new equilibrium in which neither party can hope to make substantial gains by continuing to raise the stakes of contention. Like the expansion of contention, this is an iterative process. Conflict parties gradually learn, both that they themselves have reached the limits of their possibilities, and that others, too, do not command sufficient power to further alter the balance of power in their favor. Importantly, such a stabilization of social relations does not usually imply complete mutual demobilization. The new equilibrium may well consist of a stabilization of mobilization on a level that clearly exceeds the status quo before the start of the wave. For instance, the residue of the movements of the 1960s seems to have been a permanently increased legitimacy and broad usage of (formerly "unconventional" but now routinized) extraparliamentary forms of protest such as demonstrations, consumer boycotts, and different forms of civil disobedience, coupled with the establishment of new ways of containing these forms of protest on the side of the forces of law and order (della Porta and Reiter 1998).

Especially when antagonisms between conflict parties are deep (or have become so over the course of interactions) and few extracontentious social network links between them exist, a restabilization of patterns of interaction may be difficult to achieve. The problem here is not so much the depth of differences of interests and ideology between parties (after all, relations between sworn enemies may be very stable – such as those between the USA and the USSR during much of the Cold War), but the distrust that results from it.[13] Restabilization depends on increased predictability of other parties' intentions and behavior. Conflict parties in deeply conflictive situations, however, tend to distrust their adversaries to such an extent that even if the other party consistently responds in an accommodating way, the adversaries' fear is often that this is only to lure them into sleep in order to hit back harder later on. The conflicts between Catholics and Protestants in Northern Ireland, between different ethno-religious groups in the former Yugoslavia, or between Israelis and Palestinians are examples of such conflicts that have proved very hard to stabilize.

Conflict Mediation and Resolution

This difficulty for parties engaged in intense conflicts to arrive at the kind of mutual predictability and reliability necessary for a routinization of their interactions can be overcome by way of forms of conflict mediation and resolution, often involving more or less neutral and mutually respected third parties. This type of conflict resolution is an integral and defining characteristic of democratic systems under the rule of law. Such polities offer many institutionalized forms of conflict resolution and mediation that can help to stabilize contentious interactions and prevent their escalation to revolutionary or civil war proportions. These forms of conflict resolution and mediation include third parties, such as the electorate, parliament, or the courts, whose legitimacy is accepted by all conflict parties, and which may settle conflicts authoritatively. Second, democratic systems offer routinized forums for negotiations, such as the systems of collective bargaining, often with the state as a mediator, which have contributed importantly to reducing strike levels in many West European countries. Third, but certainly not least important, routinized forms of mediation offer possibilities for information exchange between conflict parties. Insecurity about other parties' intentions and capacities stands in the way of a stabilization of relations between conflict parties as it breeds misunderstandings, overreactions, and unpleasant surprises that keep parties permanently on red alert.

The fundamental weakness of authoritarian systems is that they lack such routinized forms of conflict resolution and mediation. Used to repressing contention altogether, the elites of such polities are at a loss once challengers succeed in achieving public visibility, and they then lack the means to contain or channel protest short of full-scale repression. This is why seemingly innocent forms of protest and initially limited demands may ultimately have huge repercussions in such regimes, as the history of Solidarnosc in Poland or of the East German citizens' movement illustrate. Another consequence is that in authoritarian contexts a stabilization of contention can often be achieved only by way of the complete elimination or surrender of one side to the conflict: either the regime collapses, or those who challenge it are repressed.

The Role of External Effects

The importance of third parties in stabilizing or resolving conflicts points to a parallel with the process of contentious expansion. There, the mobilization or success of initial contenders provokes reactive mobilization by other actors who see their interests threatened or see new opportunities opened up. But contention may also have external effects on other actors in such a way that these develop an interest not in joining contention, but in ending it. For instance, the breakdown of the Eastern Bloc at the end of the 1980s led to a huge immigration wave to Western Europe,[14] and the surging ethnic conflicts in the Soviet Union and Yugoslavia were perceived as a threat to political stability in Europe more generally. In reaction, Western European countries (with Germany as the most directly affected country in the forefront) set up extensive programs of support for the fledgling East European democracies and offered them the prospect of joining the European Union. In ex-Yugoslavia, third-party intervention from the side of the EU and the USA also included direct brokerage of peace agreements and military and humanitarian intervention to contain the escalation of ethnic conflicts and stem the tide of refugees. In a similar vein, US mediation efforts in the Israeli--Palestinian conflict have often been directly linked to the negative external effects of this conflict on US geopolitical interests, most recently in the context of the US government's efforts to mobilize international support for the war against terror.

Conclusions

Much of the social movement literature either searches for generalizations across movements at different times and places, or focuses on single movements at one particular time and place. Both approaches, I have argued, fail to appreciate that instances of political contention are not independent events, but depend in a most fundamental sense on what came before and on what happens elsewhere. Acts of contentious claims-making are not instances of a general class of events, which can be correlated and regressed with other variables disregarding their ordering in time and space. But neither are they, as strong versions of culturalist accounts would have it, occurrences that are understandable only in the unique terms of their own particular times and places. Instead, what we need is an approach that transcends the isolated view of single movements and inserts them in time and space, but treats the latter not as dimensions on which to sample "cases," but as variables that are an intrinsic and central part of the analysis of contention. Such an approach has been gaining ground in recent years, in different forms such as historical-sociological approaches, population models in the study of organizations, diffusion studies, and event analyses.

The most explicit theoretical attempt to deal with the role of time and space in contentious politics has been the concept of protest cycles or waves. The basic observation from which this perspective flows is that contention is highly unequally distributed across time and space, and that much of it is concentrated in intense waves of contention with a broad scope in geographical and social space. Against the focus on single movements, this approach argues that contention is always a multi-actor process that cannot be adequately understood by focusing attention on one actor and reducing the others to the role of context variables. Instead, inter-actions between actors become the fundamental units of analysis.

The elaboration of this approach presented in this chapter can be summarized in three main points. First, acknowledging the insertion of contention in geographical and social space requires an *ecological* perspective. Any particular form of conten-tion is part of a complex web of social relations linking particular contenders to supporters, opponents, competitors, and neutral third parties, and stretching across societal sectors, social groups, and often across national boundaries. Political op-portunities for a specific group, in this view, are not structural variables somehow external to contention, but consist of nothing else than the actions of other contend-ers. Because contenders are ecologically interdependent on one another (either directly or indirectly via third parties) the mobilization of one contender has impli-cations for many other contenders. Even slight openings of opportunities for one particular group can therefore set in motion an expansion of contention when its strategies diffuse to other social sectors, groups, and geographical areas, and pro-voke the mobilization of countermovements and competitors. These in turn, feed back into the mobilization of the original movement, and may have many new side effects, which draw still other groups into contention. The reverse process of the contraction of contention depends on ecological factors, too. Demobilization, like mobilization, is an iterative and interactive process, which depends on feedback processes involving several contenders simultaneously. Often the termination or stabilization of conflicts depends on the mediating involvement of initially uninvolved third actors, who are drawn into this role by the negative external effects of continued contention on their interests.

Second, to acknowledge the insertion of contention in time, I have taken an *evolutionary* perspective. Political change, in this view, is driven by the constant attempts of various contenders to improve their relative positions of power and control over material and ideological resources. There are always actors (especially those who find themselves in a disadvantaged position in the current state of affairs) who are trying to devise new strategies of contention, be they innovative forms of action or organization, novel alliances, or reformulated demands and ideological frames. While most of these innovations fail and are abandoned, some are successful and retained and may diffuse across the polity and be adopted by other groups. Which innovations are able to diffuse and which are not is not a random process, but is determined in a coevolutionary process by the reactions of other contenders to them. Partly, this selection of contentious innovations takes the form of strategic decision-making by individual contenders, either in the form of anticipation of others' reactions, or by way of a process of adaptation in which previously unsuccessful strategic models are abandoned, and successful ones are retained. In addition, environmental selection plays an important role in that many attempts at claims-making never reach the public visibility, resonance, and legitimacy that would allow them to be perceived and considered as a model by potential adopters. Political processes consist of chains of many such sequences of innovation, selection (or not), and diffusion (or not), the end of one being at the same time the beginning of another. Time's arrow relentlessly pushes this process forward so that no sequence is ever repeated in the same way under the same circumstances. As a result, contentious politics is fundamentally path dependent, both because avenues that might have been taken but were not are permanently closed off, and because opportunities are opened up that could only become available by way of the particular path by which they were reached.

Third and finally, I have distinguished protest waves as periods of intense and widespread contention from times of normal politics – essentially an empirical observation rather than a theoretical assumption. The explanation for this unequal distribution of contention over time and space hinges on the self-reinforcing dynamics of both political stability and instability, giving contentious interactions the features of "tipping games," as Mark Beissinger (1996: 129) has aptly remarked. In times of political stability, contenders can often anticipate each other's actions, the recurrent pattern of interactions allows gradual co-adaptation, and the selective pressures of the environment are relatively stable. As a result, interactions tend to reproduce relations of power, control over resources, and notions of what is true, possible, and legitimate rather than fundamentally altering them, thereby reconstituting the preconditions for relative stability. By contrast, during intense waves of contention, uncertainty and contingency are the defining characteristics, and they, too, tend to be self-reproducing. The history of the GDR illustrates this contrast between times of almost frozen stability and times of radical instability in an exemplary way. Still in 1988, nothing was as boring and predictable as East German politics. One year later, it was difficult to imagine anything more amazing and unpredictable than the course of events that brought down the Wall.

Seen from this perspective, what needs to be explained in analyses of waves of contention is not adequately conceptualized in terms of the ascent and decline of protest, or the opening and closure of political opportunities. Rather, the problem should be formulated in terms of what accounts for the destabilization of social relations within the polity, and what explains their ultimate restabilization around a particular new equilibrium of forces. This chapter does not present more than the tentative beginnings of an answer, but at least, I would maintain, it has clarified the questions to be asked.

Notes

1 For accounts of the East German revolution of 1989 see, e.g., Joppke (1995) and Mueller (1999).

2 E.g., the *Wordsworth Concise English Dictionary* (edited by G. W. Davidson et al. 1994; Ware, UK: Wordsworth Editions, 1994) defines a cycle as "a period of time in which events happen in a certain order, and which constantly repeats itself; a recurring series of changes..." A wave, by contrast, is defined less demandingly as "a swelling up or increase, normally followed by a subsidence or decline".

3 This is so not only because of the rarity of innovations, but also because such innovations will be effective only if they occur in a situation of at least latently available political opportunities. It is never the innovation as such that sparks a protest wave, but the coincidence of particular innovations with political conditions that allow them to have a destabilizing effect on power relations within the polity. In this sense, the history of protest innovations parallels the history of technology, which is also rife with inventions – sometimes technically superior to later successful ones – that never made it because they occurred in a context that did not fulfil the conditions for their adoption.

4 Granovetter's distinction between strong and weak ties is roughly similar to Soule's distinction in chapter 13 of this volume between direct and indirect channels of diffusion.

5 Snow and Benford (1999) make a useful distinction between types of diffusion processes, depending on whether or not the transmitter and adopter are involved in promoting the diffusion of a certain practice from one context to another.

6 Consider the difficulty and unpredictability of chess, a game with only two players, each of whom moves (always one at a time and in strict alternation between the players) 16 pieces (each with limited capabilities) around a board with 64 fields. Compared to contentious politics, this game is laughably simple. Even if a "game" of contention starts with only two players, any number of players may join over its course, players may split in two or join forces, new pieces and playing fields may be introduced, and perhaps, most importantly, the rules of the game are themselves are subject to contestation and therefore subject to change along the way.

7 A related theory of change based on selective pressures can be found in the literature on the ecology of organizational populations (e.g., Hannan and Carroll 1992), which has sometimes also been applied to social movement organizations (Minkoff 1999). The main differences with the argument advanced here are twofold. First, organizational ecologists take organizations as the unit of analysis and investigate their birth rates and death rates under conditions of competition. In the present argument, the units of selection are neither collective actors, nor collective action events, but (clusters of) characteristics of collective action. These may consist of certain demands, tactics, self-identifications, collective action frames, organizational forms, or any specific combination of these. The second difference is that selection processes in organizational ecology rest on the problematic assumption of "structural inertia" of organizations, i.e. the idea that individual organizations do not

fundamentally change over their careers and that organizational change on the population level can be reduced to the disbanding of unsuccessful and the founding of new and better adapted organizations. The present argument does not assume structural inertia among collective actors and does not posit a contradiction between change through adaptation or anticipation and by way of selection. Adaptation and anticipation are assumed to occur, however, on the basis of a range of alternatives and information about those alternatives that is strongly structured by selection processes.

8   The concept of punctuated equilibrium has also been picked up by Baumgartner and Jones (1993) for explaining policy change. The idea of longer periods of "normal politics" alternated by short periods of intense contention also has interesting parallels with Thomas Kuhn's (1962) theory of scientific development in which he differentiates between periods of "normal science," and revolutionary paradigmatic shifts, followed by a renewed normalization of scientific practice around a new paradigm.

9   See, e.g., Goldstone's (1980) re-analysis of Gamson's data, in which he shows regarding the success of social movement organizations, long periods in which few groups were successful alternated with short periods of broad regime crisis in which many groups were able to make substantive gains or obtain policy access.

10 For a related discussion of the effects of contingency and path dependence in the development of organizational populations, see Carroll and Harrison 1994.

11 Note that this example is a bit different from those given by Pierson (2000), who emphasizes "increasing returns" as the mechanism behind path dependence. The returns of the regime's nonrepressive approach were negative rather than positive, and they became worse rather than better along the way. However, as Pierson (2000: 252) notes, the *relative* returns of current strategies are decisive. Even though the regime's strategies of accommodation failed most of the time, they were after Leipzig always and increasingly preferable to the alternative of repression.

12 Here my approach deviates from that of McAdam et al. (2001), whose most different systems design leads them to search for generalizations across a range that includes democratic and nondemocratic regimes, Western and non-Western cultures, contemporary and historical periods, and limited protest movements as well as full-scale revolutions. As I have argued along similar lines as these authors, the only generalizations possible at this level of abstraction from time and place are mechanisms, not patterns of transformation. However, while these authors claim that the search for recurrent patterns of transformation is misleading and futile, my argument is that such generalizations are possible within specified scope conditions. I.e., the search for mechanisms across forms of contention and regime types is legitimate and important, but it does not take away the need, nor preclude the possibility of specific theoretical generalizations for, say, nationalist contention, contention in democratic regimes, or transitions to democracy.

13 Thus the importance for stability of routinizing the Cold War and making it more predictable by way of telephone hotlines, disarmament treaties, or (proof that the kind of trust required need go no further than predictability) the expectation of mutually assured destruction in the case of nuclear war.

14 Germany alone witnessed a yearly influx of more than half a million East European immigrants (mostly asylum seekers and ethnic Germans) at the beginning of the 1990s.

References

Baumgartner, Frank R., and Bryan D. Jones (1993) *Agendas and Instability in American Politics*. Chicago: University of Chicago Press.

Beissinger, Mark R. (1996) How Nationalisms Spread: Eastern Europe Adrift the Tides and Cycles of Nationalist Contention. *Social Research*, 63 (1), 97–146.

Brinton, Crane (1959) *The Anatomy of Revolution*. New York: Vintage.

Bunce, Valerie (1999) *Subversive Institutions: The Design and the Destruction of Socialism and the State*. Cambridge: Cambridge University Press.

Carroll, Glenn R., and J. Richard Harrison (1994) On the Historical Efficiency of Competition between Organizational Populations. *American Journal of Sociology*, 100 (3), 720–49.

Darwin, Charles ([1859] 1985) *The Origin of Species by Means of Natural Selection*. London: Penguin.

della Porta, Donatella, and Herbert Reiter (eds.) (1998) *Policing Protest: The Control of Mass Demonstrations in Western Democracies*. Minneapolis: University of Minnesota Press.

Duyvendak, Jan Willem (1995) *The Power of Politics*. Boulder, CO: Westview.

Edwards, Lyford P. (1965) *The Natural History of Revolution*. New York: Russell & Russell.

Eldredge, Niles, and Stephen Jay Gould (1972) Punctuated Equilibria: An Alternative to Phyletic Gradualism. In T. J. M. Schopf (ed.), *Models of Paleobiology*. San Francisco: Freeman, Cooper, 81–115.

Freeman, Jo (1979) Resource Mobilization and Strategy: A Model for Analyzing Social Movement Organization Actions. In Mayer N. Zald and John D. McCarthy (eds.), *The Dynamics of Social Movements: Resource Mobilization, Social Control, and Tactics*. Cambridge, MA: Winthrop, 167–89.

Gamson, William, and David A. Meyer (1996) Framing Political Opportunity. In Doug McAdam, John D. McCarthy, and Mayer N. Zald (eds.), *Comparative Perspectives on Social Movements: Political Opportunities, Mobilizing Structures, and Cultural Framings*. Cambridge: Cambridge University Press.

Giugni, Marco (1995) *Entre stratégie et opportunité: Les nouveaux mouvements sociaux en Suisse*. Zurich: Seismo.

Goldstone, Jack A. (1980) The Weakness of Organization: A New Look at Gamson's *The Strategy of Social Protest*. *American Journal of Sociology*, 85, 1017–42.

Granovetter, Mark (1973) The Strength of Weak Ties. *American Journal of Sociology*, 78, 1360–80.

Gurr, Ted Robert (1970) *Why Men Rebel*. Princeton, NJ: Princeton University Press.

Haines, Herbert (1984) Black Radicalization and the Funding of Civil Rights: 1957–1970. *Social Problems*, 32, 31–43.

Hannan, Michael T., and Glenn R. Carroll. (1992) *Dynamics of Organizational Populations: Density, Legitimation, and Competition*. Oxford: Oxford University Press.

Hilgartner, Stephen, and Charles L. Bosk (1988) The Rise and Fall of Social Problems. *American Journal of Sociology*, 94, 53–78.

Hirschman, Albert O. (1970) *Exit, Voice and Loyalty: Responses to Decline in Firms, Organizations and States*. Cambridge, MA: Harvard University Press.

——(1982) *Shifting Involvements: Private Interest and Public Action*. Princeton, NJ: Princeton University Press.

Hocke, Peter (1999) Determining the Selection Bias in Local and National Newspaper Reports on Protest Events. In Dieter Rucht, Ruud Koopmans, and Friedhelm Neidhardt (eds.), *Acts of Dissent: New Developments in the Study of Protest*. Lanham, MD: Rowman & Littlefield, 131–63.

Holden, Robert T. (1986) The Contagiousness of Aircraft Hijacking. *American Journal of Sociology*, 91 (4), 874–904.

Joppke, Christian (1995) *East German Dissidents and the Revolution of 1989: Social Movement in a Leninist Regime*. New York: New York University Press.

Karstedt-Henke, Sabine (1980) Theorien zur Erklärung terroristischer Bewegungen. In E. Blankenberg (ed.), *Politik der inneren Sicherheit*. Frankfurt am Main: Suhrkamp, 198–234.

Koopmans, Ruud (1993) The Dynamics of Protest Waves: West Germany, 1965 to 1989. *American Sociological Review*, 58, 637–58.

——(1995a) *Democracy from Below: New Social Movements and the Political System in West Germany.* Boulder, CO: Westview.

——(1995b) The Dynamics of Protest Waves. In Hanspeter Kriesi, Ruud Koopmans, Jan Willem Duyvendak, and Marco G. Giugni (eds.), *New Social Movements in Western Europe: A Comparative Analysis.* Minneapolis: University of Minnesota Press, 111–42.

——(2001) Repression and the Public Sphere: Discursive Opportunities for Repression Against the Extreme Right in Germany in the 1990s. Paper presented at the conference Mobilization and Repression: What We Know and Where We Should Go from Here, University of Maryland.

Koopmans, Ruud, and Paul Statham (1999a) Political Claims Analysis: Integrating Protest Event and Political Discourse Approaches. *Mobilization*, 4 (1), 40–51.

——(1999b) Ethnic and Civic Conceptions of Nationhood and the Differential Success of the Extreme Right in Germany and Italy. In Marco Giugni, Doug McAdam, and Charles Tilly (eds.), *How Social Movements Matter.* Minneapolis: University of Minnesota Press, 225–52.

Kornhauser, William (1959) *The Politics of Mass Society.* Glencoe, IL: Free Press.

Kriesi, Hanspeter, Ruud Koopmans, Jan Willem Duyvendak, and Marco G. Giugni (eds.) (1995) *New Social Movements in Western Europe: A Comparative Analysis.* Minneapolis: University of Minnesota Press.

Kuhn, Thomas S. (1962) *The Structure of Scientific Revolutions.* Chicago: University of Chicago Press.

Luhmann, Niklas (1999) *Die Gesellschaft der Gesellschaft, Band 1.* Frankfurt am Main: Suhrkamp.

McAdam, Doug (1982) *Political Process and the Development of Black Insurgency, 1930–1970.* Chicago: University of Chicago Press.

——(1995) "Initiator" and "Spin-off" Movements: Diffusion Processes in Protest Cycles. In Mark Traugott (ed.), *Repertoires and Cycles of Collective Action.* Durham, NC: Duke University Press, 217–39.

McAdam, Doug, Sidney Tarrow, and Charles Tilly (2001) *Dynamics of Contention.* Cambridge: Cambridge University Press.

McCarthy, John D., Clark McPhail, and Jackie Smith (1996) Images of Protest: Estimating Selection Bias in Media Coverage of Washington Demonstrations, 1982, 1991. *American Sociological Review*, 61 (3), 478–99.

Meyer, David S., and Suzanne Staggenborg (1996) Movements, Countermovements, and the Structure of Political Opportunity. *American Journal of Sociology*, 101, 1628–60.

Minkoff, Debra C. (1999) Bending with the Wind: Strategic Change and Adaptation by Women's and Racial Minority Organizations. *American Journal of Sociology*, 104 (6), 1666–1703

Mueller, Carol (1999) Claim "Radicalization?" The 1989 Protest Cycle in the GDR. *Social Problems*, 46 (4), 528–47.

Myers, Daniel J. (2000) The Diffusion of Collective Violence: Infectiousness, Susceptibility, and Mass Media Networks. *American Journal of Sociology*, 106 (1), 173–208.

Oberschall, Anthony (1973) *Social Movements and Social Conflicts.* Englewood-Cliffs, NJ: Prentice-Hall.

——(2000) Social Movements and the Transition to Democracy. *Democratization*, 7 (3), 25–45.

Oegema, Dirk, and Bert Klandermans (1994) Why Social Movement Sympathizers Don't Participate: Erosion and Nonconversion of Support. *American Sociological Review*, 59, 703–22.

Pierson, Paul (2000) Increasing Returns, Path Dependence, and the Study of Politics. *American Political Science Review*, 94, 251–67.

Rammstedt, Otthein (1978) *Soziale Bewegung*. Frankfurt am Main: Suhrkamp.

Rochon, Thomas R. (1988) *Mobilizing for Peace: The Antinuclear Movements in Western Europe*. Princeton, NJ: Princeton University Press.

Rule, James, and Charles Tilly (1972) 1830 and the Unnatural History of Revolution. *Journal of Social Issues*, 28, 49–76.

Shorter, Edward, and Charles Tilly (1974) *Strikes in France, 1830–1968*. Cambridge: Cambridge University Press.

Smelser, Neil J. (1962) *Theory of Collective Behavior*. New York: Free Press.

Snow, David A., and Robert D. Benford (1999) Alternative Types of Cross-National Diffusion in the Social Movement Arena. In Donatella della Porta, Hanspeter Kriesi, and Dieter Rucht (eds.), *Social Movements in a Globalizing World*. Houndmills: Macmillan, 23–39.

Soule, Sarah (1999) The Diffusion of an Unsuccessful Innovation. *Annals of the American Academy of Political and Social Science*, 566, 120–31.

Strang, David, and John W. Meyer (1993) Institutional Conditions for Diffusion. *Theory and Society*, 22, 487–511.

Strang, David, and Sarah Soule (1998) Diffusion in Organizations and Social Movements: From Hybrid Corn to Poison Spills. *Annual Review of Sociology*, 24, 265–90.

Tarrow, Sidney (1989) *Democracy and Disorder: Protest and Politics in Italy 1965–1975*. Oxford: Clarendon.

——(1994) *Power in Movement: Social Movements, Collective Action and Politics*. Cambridge: Cambridge University Press.

Tilly, Charles (1978) *From Mobilization to Revolution*. Reading, MA: Addison-Wesley.

Tilly, Charles, Louise Tilly, and Robert Tilly (1975) *The Rebellious Century, 1830–1930*. Cambridge, MA: Harvard University Press.

Useem, Bert (1980) Solidarity Model, Breakdown Model, and the Boston Anti-Busing Movement. *American Sociological Review*, 45, 357–69.

Zolberg, Aristide R. (1972) Moments of Madness. *Politics and Society*, 2, 183–207.

3

The Strange Career of Strain and Breakdown Theories of Collective Action

Steven M. Buechler

Since the 1970s, social movement theory has changed dramatically. One reason is that "the study of social movements is volatile because the phenomena under consideration change so rapidly" (Garner 1997: 1). In this imagery, theory changes to reflect changes in its subject matter. However, theoretical change often has less to do with faithful reflections of a changing subject matter than with rapid shifts in assumptions, perspectives, and questions (Kuhn 1962). A broader sociology of knowledge suggests that theories also change in response to altered sociohistorical contexts and new generations of theorists who bring different experiences to their theoretical work and to the very definition of their subject matter.

Within sociology as a whole, all these factors prompted the paradigm shifts of the post-World War II period. The functionalist orthodoxy of the 1950s gave way to several alternatives in the 1960s because social phenomena changed, social and political currents also changed, and new generations of sociologists brought different experiences to their work. The theoretical disputes between functionalism, conflict theory, critical theory, phenomenology, feminist theory, and other alternatives defined the broader context in which paradigm shifts occurred in subfields like collective behavior and social movements. The story of social movement theory is not just a function of movements themselves, but also of the social and intellectual histories of the countries and disciplines in which the theories evolve.

The major paradigm shift in social movement theory is indexed by the inelegant but revealing nomenclature of "collective behavior/social movements"; the forward slash testifies to the conceptual confusion and disagreement that characterizes this area. It was not always so. For much of the twentieth century, there was a consensually designated subfield called "collective behavior," and social movements were seen as one subtype of collective behavior along with panics, crazes, crowds, rumors, and riots. During this time, a major explanation for the emergence of all kinds of collective behavior was that periods of strain and breakdown generate collective behavior because the social controls and moral imperatives that normally constrain such behavior are weakened or absent. Strain and breakdown theories were thus tied to a whole series of assumptions about the nature of collective behavior and the subsumption of social movements under that rubric. When those assumptions were challenged and that rubric was undermined, theorists began to emphasize the differences between collective behavior and social movements, and to focus more exclusively on the latter as requiring a separate analysis. In so doing, strain and breakdown theories were both actively challenged and passively marginalized as part of a broader paradigm shift.

As often happens, the role of strain and breakdown in precipitating collective behavior was probably overstated by the collective behavior paradigm and under-stated by its critics. Tracing the strange career of strain and breakdown theories promises to restore some balance to our understanding of the role of such factors in collective action while also shedding light on how paradigms shift. This chapter is organized into four parts. First, I summarize the role of strain and breakdown theories in the earlier collective behavior paradigm. Second, I trace the demise of these theories with the decline of the collective behavior paradigm and the emergence of the resource mobilization approach. Third, I document how such theories nonetheless persisted throughout the predominance of resource mobilization theory. Finally, I identify how they have returned, in a new guise and nomenclature, to a central role in the analysis of collective action.

THE CLASSICAL ERA OF STRAIN AND BREAKDOWN THEORIES

The concepts of strain and breakdown imply a social order whose normal condition is one of integration. If the social order remains sufficiently integrated, strain and breakdown may be avoided altogether and collective behavior may be precluded. In this logic, all roads lead to Durkheim's overriding concern with social integration and the problematic consequences of insufficient integration in modern societies (Durkheim [1893] 1964). Premodern societies were less problematic as the *conscience collective* and mechanical solidarity underwrote social integration and minimized strain and breakdown. With the decline of the *conscience collective* and increases in dynamic density and social differentiation, modern societies became more prone to such problems. In theory, the emergent division of labor would provide the functional integration and organic solidarity to bind modern societies together. In reality, Durkheim was well aware that modern societies did not conform to the theoretical expectation. His classic analyses of anomie and egoism identified breaches in the social order that could lead to chronic strains or acute breakdowns. One indication of such problems was elevated suicide rates, but suicide was merely one example of a range of antisocial, dysfunctional behaviors that could result from strain and breakdown (Durkheim [1897] 1951). The remedy was increased social integration through more explicit normative regulation to guide conduct and strengthened social bonds to contain excessive individualism. While Durkheim said relatively little about collective behavior as the term came to be understood in the twentieth century, his analysis provided a major foundation for subsequent theories of strain and breakdown as explanations of such behavior.

A more direct link between social breakdown and collective behavior was forged by European theorists of crowd behavior who were Durkheim's contemporaries. In their view, "The cause of civil violence...was the breakdown of rational control over human behavior through the spread of what one might call 'crowd mentality'" (Rule 1988: 83). Crowds were theorized to act under the sway of intense emotional states generated by physical proximity; such behavior was in marked contrast to the rational and orderly behavior that prevailed in conventional social settings. It was Robert Park (Park and Burgess 1921; Park 1972) who introduced this tradition into US sociology by positing a fundamental distinction between social integration and control on the one hand and innovative forms of collective behavior that emerge with the breakdown of social control on the other hand. Park broadened the theory beyond crowds to include other forms of collective behavior, and – unlike the European crowd theorists – he recognized that collective behavior could be a positive, healthy element in social life (Rule 1988: 97). Park's work laid the foundation for what would become the classical collective behavior tradition in US sociology.

Herbert Blumer built on this foundation to definitively establish collective behavior as a recognizable subfield in sociology. For Blumer (1951), collective behavior involves group activity that is largely spontaneous, unregulated, and unstructured. It is triggered by some disruption in standard routines of everyday life that promotes circular reaction or interstimulation with the qualities of contagion, randomness, excitability, and suggestibility. It is this social unrest that provides the crucible out of which all forms of collective behavior emerge, including crowds, masses, publics, and social movements. Turner and Killian (1987) codified Blumer's approach to collective behavior, while emphasizing how initially unstructured collective behavior may promote emergent norms and incipient forms of order through symbolic communication and interaction. Despite the modifications introduced by subsequent theorists, several assumptions define this tradition. First, collective behavior is triggered by some breakdown, strain, or disruption in normal social routines. Second, as such, collective behavior is sharply set off from conventional behavior, with elements of contagion, excitability, spontaneity, and emotionality as prevalent themes. In some versions of the theory, these assumptions frame collective behavior as irrational, disruptive, dangerous, and excessive. This image has persisted despite Park's recognition of the positive consequences of collective behavior, Turner and Killian's emphasis on the rational processes of communication in many crowd settings, and the emergence of a "second Chicago school" more concerned with processual dynamics than with structural strain (Snow and Davis 1995). Rightly or wrongly, the negative image of collective behavior that has been attributed to collective behavior theorists played a major role in the subsequent decline of strain and breakdown theories of collective action.

Another variation in the collective behavior tradition involves theories of relative deprivation (Davies 1962; Geschwender 1968; Gurr 1970). In this case, the strain is most evident on the social-psychological level of how people assess their current situation against various reference groups or past or anticipated future situations. Whenever they find a benchmark that implies they could or should be better off than they are, a condition of relative deprivation exists and this psychological strain triggers participation in collective behavior. In Geschwender's (1968) synthesis around the concept of cognitive dissonance and Gurr's (1970) invoking of frustration–aggression mechanisms, the concept of strain becomes a psychological mechanism invoked to explain people's propensity to engage in collective behavior.

The collective behavior tradition also includes a structural version of strain and breakdown theories of collective behavior. Structural-functionalism provides the link between Durkheim's ([1893] 1964) concerns with social integration, Parsons' (1951) theory of functionally integrated social systems, and Smelser's (1962) theory of collective behavior. Smelser proposed a value-added scheme of six factors that are individually necessary and collectively sufficient to cause an episode of collective behavior. The forms of collective behavior range from panics, crazes, and fads to riots and reform and revolutionary movements. In all cases, the behavior emerges from a sequence of structural conduciveness, structural strain, generalized beliefs, precipitating factors, mobilization for action, and the breakdown of social control. Structural strain is loosely defined as ambiguities, deprivations, conflicts, and discrepancies in social structure. When strain does provoke collective behavior in the context of the other determinants, such behavior involves a short-circuiting of levels of social action that gives it a crude, excessive, eccentric, or impatient quality. This quality is amplified by the generalized beliefs that accompany the behavior and are inherently irrational cognitive responses. If effective social controls are in place, any one of these stages can be prevented and the sequential development of collective behavior can be aborted; hence the breakdown of such controls is a crucial determinant. Smelser thus manages to combine the concepts of strain and breakdown into a macrostructural theory of collective behavior.

Mass society theory is an important variant on functionalist approaches to collective behavior that evokes Durkheim's classical concerns with the dangers of anomie and egoism in modern society. For this perspective, modernity is distinguished by the emergence of large-scale social structures but the disappearance of mid-level groups that provide social anchors for individuals (Kornhauser 1959). With the demise of small social groups, modern society becomes a mass society in which isolation, depersonalization, and alienation prevail. Mass society theory predicted that the most isolated and alienated individuals would gravitate toward participation in collective behavior because it offered one of the few available social anchors. Although this prediction proved spectacularly unsuccessful (because isolated actors are no more likely to join collective behavior than any other collective undertaking), the assumptions reiterated structural-functionalism's premise: that social order normally precludes collective behavior which must be explained in terms of social strain or breakdown that leads to psychological discontent, irrational ideation, and deviant behavior.

The concepts of strain and breakdown are the threads that connect an otherwise diverse group of social thinkers. From Durkheim and the European crowd theorists through the early Chicago School to the structural-functionalists, sociologists have regularly invoked strain and breakdown as explanations for collective behavior. One crude measure of this approach's predominance is an overview of the field published by Marx and Wood (1975) in the first *Annual Review of Sociology*. They offer a lengthy discussion of the strains underlying collective behavior and a detailed review of the theorists discussed above. While criticizing specific versions of the theory, they nonetheless argue for retaining the concept of strain as a generalized and central explanation for collective behavior. Moreover, the section of their article devoted to social strain is the only discussion of causal factors underlying collective behavior.

To judge from this history and summary, strain and breakdown theories enjoyed a preeminent position and a bright future. Less than ten years later, J. Craig Jenkins (1983) published a similar overview in the ninth *Annual Review of Sociology*. There is a brief discussion of movement formation that assesses the relative causal weight of various factors, but there is no mention of strain or breakdown in precipitating social movements. The contrast between these two assessments hints at the paradigm shift that occurred from the mid-1970s to the mid-1980s in the study of collective action. Like all such shifts, this one raised new questions and marginalized old ones; in the process, the role of strain and breakdown theories were effectively driven underground.

The Demise of Strain and Breakdown Theories

Strain and breakdown theories virtually disappeared because they were seen – rightly or wrongly – as inextricably linked to a collective behavior paradigm that came under relentless criticism from resource mobilization theorists. Like most paradigm shifts, this one involved a blend of scientific and extra-scientific elements. There were serious problems with the collective behavior tradition. But this shift also followed larger disciplinary trends as approaches stressing values, integration, and consensus gave way to those emphasizing conflict, domination, and resistance. And these larger trends were themselves linked to social changes and political challenges beginning with the civil rights movement and expanding into the myriad social movements and legitimation challenges of the 1960s. Hence this paradigm shift had something to do with inherent weaknesses of the collective behavior tradition and everything to do with a rapidly changing sociohistorical context and the ways in which a new generation of sociologists imported those changes into the discipline (Buechler 2000).

McAdam's (1982) critique of the collective behavior tradition highlights several problems. For example, the claim that social movements are a response to social strain is deeply problematic. It ignores the larger political context in which movements arise, and it assumes a mechanistic and linear relationship between macrolevel strain and microlevel behavior. The identification of individual discontent as the proximate cause of social movements constitutes a second problem. In at least some versions of the theory, this presumes an abnormal psychological profile that sharply distinguishes participants from nonparticipants in collective behavior. But aside from this difficulty, the individual level of analysis invoked here ignores how individual mental states are translated into genuinely collective phenomena. Finally, the individualistic emphasis denies the political dimension of collective behavior by implying that it is nothing more than a "convenient justification for what is at root a psychological phenomenon" (McAdam 1982: 17). When such assumptions guide the analysis, collective behavior is more likely to be perceived as deviant behavior than political action.

The resource mobilization alternative challenged the accepted wisdom about collective behavior in at least four ways. First, it rejected the subsumption of social movements under collective behavior and suggested that the former were different enough from the latter to warrant their own mode of analysis. Second, social movements were seen as exhibiting enduring, patterned, institutionalized elements, thereby challenging the traditional classification of them as noninstitutional behavior. Third, newer approaches explicitly argued that participants in social movements were "at least as rational as those who study them" (Schwartz 1976: 135), and this premise of the rational actor became a cornerstone of social movement analysis. Finally, newer approaches accentuated the political dimension of movement challenges by conceptualizing them as rooted in collective understandings of group interests; this political interpretation largely displaced the earlier psychological interpretation of collective behavior. Having disentangled social movements from other forms of collective behavior (and assumptions about that behavior), resource mobilization theory proceeded to analyze movements as political struggles over conflicting interests that share many organizational dynamics with more institutionalized forms of action (McCarthy and Zald 1973, 1977; Oberschall 1973; Tilly 1978). In sharp contrast to the collective behavior tradition, resource mobilization theory thus viewed social movements as normal, rational, political challenges by aggrieved groups. Resource mobilization theory thereby redefined the study of collective action from an example of deviance and social disorganization to a case study in political and organizational sociology.

In addition to broad critiques of the collective behavior tradition, there were several direct challenges to the role of strain and breakdown in explaining collective behavior. One predated the emergence of the resource mobilization perspective, but it anticipated that perspective's critique of the collective behavior tradition and its alternative conceptualization of collective behavior. The topic was the urban race riots of the 1960s, and the challenge came in Skolnick's (1969) report to a national commission on violence. Skolnick identified the two prevailing explanations of collective behavior as focusing on either the social strain and tension that produce frustration and hostility, or the breakdown of normal systems of social control that otherwise preclude collective behavior. In both cases, the resulting collective behavior is conceived as nonconforming or even deviant behavior that is unstable, disorderly, and irrational. Moreover, participants are portrayed as destructive and irrational while authorities are seen as normal and reasonable. Having reviewed the available evidence, Skolnick concluded that such explanations are deeply flawed. First, the concepts of frustration and tension are too vague and psychologistic to adequately explain the urban riots of the 1960s. Moreover, such explanations obscure the political nature of those riots and the fact that otherwise normal and presumably rational people participated in them. Finally, Skolnick concluded that the violence was less a quality of the rioters than an emergent product of the interactions between protesters and authorities. Skolnick's critique thus challenged many assumptions of the collective behavior paradigm, including strain and breakdown explanations.

The second challenge came from Tilly (Tilly et al. 1975), and it was part of the rise of the resource mobilization alternative. Tilly traced the development of strain and breakdown theories from Durkheim through Smelser, but questioned whether strain and breakdown consistently produce anomie and whether anomie consistently produces either individual or collective disorder. Tilly's alternative explanation argued that group solidarity is the key factor in explaining collective action. Tilly sought to undermine any sharp distinction between routine political struggle and violence by arguing that the same political dynamics and solidarity processes underlay both. Like Skolnick, when violence occurs it is best seen as an interactive product that emerges between protesters and authorities rather than a quality of protesters themselves. Moreover, Tilly claims that when collective violence does occur, participants do not act impulsively or unreflectively but rather with a clear grasp of their actions. Finally, protesters rarely choose between violence or nonviolence directly; they rather choose different tactics and strategies that, in conjunction with the response of authorities, have differential chances of leading to violence. While Tilly's specific target here was stereotypical views of violent and irrational mass behavior, his broader ambition was to shift explanations of such incidents from strain and breakdown (and all their related assumptions about collective behavior) to solidarity and organization (and an alternative set of related assumptions). Tilly's conclusion heralded a major paradigm shift:

> Breakdown theories of collective action . . . suffer from irreparable logical and empirical difficulties. Some sort of solidarity theory should work better everywhere. No matter where we look, we should rarely find uprooted, marginal, disorganized people heavily involved in collective violence. All over the world we should expect collective violence to flow out of routine collective action and continuing struggles for power. (Tilly et al. 1975: 290)

Within a short time, the major debates were within the resource mobilization paradigm rather than between rival paradigms. As these debates unfolded, it became clear that this paradigm implicitly marginalized strain and breakdown while pursuing other questions. The broadest example was the shift from a deterministic collective behavior paradigm (with strain and breakdown as major determinants) to an agency-oriented resource mobilization paradigm in which actors' purposes, interests, and goals displace deterministic factors. The insistence that collective action was political and not psychological foreclosed questions about the subjective states of movement actors and the possible role of strain. The promotion of the rational actor model dismissed issues of emotion, frustration, and strain. The emphasis on resources downplayed grievances and their relationship to social strains. The focus on internal movement dynamics displaced questions of external causal mechanisms. The narrowing of the boundary between routine and nonroutine forms of collective action eclipsed the role of strain and breakdown explanations. The privileging of formal organization obscured spontaneous forms of protest more amenable to analysis via strain and breakdown theories. In every case, the salience of strain and breakdown was marginalized by the new concerns associated with the resource mobilization framework.

These were the circumstances that allowed an authoritative review article published during the height of resource mobilization's predominance (Jenkins 1983) to avoid any reference to strain and breakdown theories as explanations of collective action. Such explanations were driven underground in three ways. First, direct critiques of strain and breakdown theories challenged them on their own terms. Second, the rise of the resource mobilization paradigm undermined the collective behavior tradition within which strain and breakdown theories had been embedded. And third, the research program launched by resource mobilization theory pursued questions and sought answers that rendered strain and breakdown marginal to social movement theory. By the mid-1980s, it appeared that strain and breakdown theories were completely moribund. Nonetheless, such theories persisted despite these challenges.

The Persistence of Strain and Breakdown Theories

Although resource mobilization theory successfully wrested social movements from the grab bag of collective behavior, they were quickly conceptualized in an insular way that privileged reform movements and formal organization. One irony of this development is that until very recently (e.g., McAdam et al. 2001) theory and research into revolutionary movements has remained largely divorced from much of the work done in the resource mobilization paradigm despite Tilly's (1978) claim that revolutionary movements involve the same dynamics as more limited social protest. In any case, the study of revolution became one place where strain and breakdown theories retained a foothold in the explanation of collective action. Not surprisingly, some breakdown theories of revolution were derived from the same functionalist tradition that spawned Smelser's (1962) theory of collective behavior. Johnson's (1966) theory of revolutionary change echoed Smelser's emphasis on system disequilibrium as a trigger of rapid change. In classic functionalist style, such disruption could be avoided if various social subsystems grew in tandem. If and when some subsystems develop more rapidly or independently of others, the resulting strain and imbalance will foster anomie and predispose people to look for alternative social arrangements. Huntington (1968) built on this tradition to argue that it is when educational and economic growth outstrip political development that such institutional imbalances foster revolutionary change. Like Smelser's classic approach, these theories point to a combination of structural strain and social breakdown to explain collective action.

In the more recent work of Goldstone (1986, 1991a, 1991b), the concept of state breakdown looms large in the explanation of revolution. Goldstone (1991a) argues that revolutions follow similar causal processes involving state breakdown, revolutionary contention, and state rebuilding. The origin of state breakdown involves a conjunction of state fiscal distress, elite alienation and conflict, and high mobilization potential among the general populace. In this interactive model, all three elements must be present if a full revolutionary challenge is to unfold. The background causes of this conjunctural model of state breakdown are historically specific, though they often involve demographic growth and population shifts that put new pressure on state resources (Goldstone 1991b). Ideological and cultural factors enter into the revolutionary process, but more as supporting actors than lead performers. Ideologies are not created *de novo* as much as preexisting ideologies are reinterpreted in revolutionary circumstances. Thus cultural factors do not account for the collapse of existing social structures, but they do shape the political order that follows (Goldstone 1991b). In his most definitive statement, Goldstone concludes that state breakdowns from 1500 to 1850 resulted from a single basic process of population growth that overwhelmed agrarian bureaucratic states and prompted fiscal instability, intra-elite conflicts, popular unrest, and revolutionary ideology. This pattern triggered state breakdown in the sixteenth and early seventeenth centuries as well as the late eighteenth and early nineteenth centuries, when the population grew significantly in the early modern world (Goldstone 1991b).

Goldstone's work developed in relative isolation from the resource mobilization approach to social movements and vice versa. This isolation has reinforced the split between the resource mobilization paradigm and any serious consideration of strain and breakdown variables in the emergence of collective action. The lack of resonance between these approaches is perhaps overdetermined. Where resource mobilization theory tends to favor actor-centered, purposive, and goal-oriented efforts at social change, Goldstone's model emphasizes deterministic background factors like demographic changes. Where resource mobilization theory tends to favor internal variables like resource control and micromobilization efforts, Goldstone's model cites external variables like fiscal instability and elite divisions. And where resource mobilization approaches credit the strength of challenging groups as the determining factor in movement success, Goldstone's approach underscores regime weakness and state breakdown as determining factors. In all these ways, the causal imagery of Goldstone's theory is more reminiscent of the classical collective behavior tradition than of the newer approaches to social movements, and hence it is not surprising that there has been little cross-fertilization of these perspectives.

One notable exception involves Goldstone's (1980) critique of Gamson's (1975) *The Strategy of Social Protest*. In that work, Gamson analyzed a historical sample of challenging groups to identify factors that contributed to movement success or failure. Gamson outlined two types of success in the form of acceptance or new advantages, yielding a fourfold set of possibilities ranging from complete success to co-optation to preemption to failure. Gamson concluded that a movement's choice of goals, tactics, and organization all significantly affected the probability of success. Goldstone challenged these findings by claiming that Gamson overstated the role of organization and other movement variables on movement success. The specific critique concerns Gamson's operationalization of success versus failure and his decision to lump together groups that won partial advantages and no advantages as failures for the sake of analysis. Goldstone claims that if groups that won partial advantages are redefined as successes, then the only variable that is important is whether groups seek to displace powerholders. All of the nondisplacing groups were successful by Goldstone's more generous definition of success, while fully 75 percent of the displacing groups failed in this reinterpretation. Goldstone offered an alternative explanation in which the timing of movement success is correlated with larger systemic shocks like wars or political and economic crises when elites are more willing to make concessions. Having undermined the role of internal factors like movement organization and tactics, Goldstone's critique thus sought to underscore the importance of external factors like societal strain and breakdown as accounting for movement success.

Gamson's response focused on how success is defined. He pointed out that Goldstone oversimplified the issue of success by dealing only with new advantages and not acceptance, and he defended his exclusion of groups that won only peripheral or equivocal advantages from the success category. Indeed, where Goldstone claimed the original analysis was too stringent in its operationalization of success and excluded groups that should have been seen as successes, Gamson argued that the original analysis was too lax in using a definition of success that included "shadow successes" and "tag-a-long" successes that would be better coded as nonsuccesses (Gamson 1980). Gamson's defense stressed more complex combinations of movement successes and failures that in turn required analysis of variables like organization, goals, and tactics to differentially explain movement outcomes. Gamson also noted that his original argument acknowledged the importance of crisis periods in influencing movement success or failure, but did not assign it the overwhelming importance it assumed in Goldstone's critical revision. While this debate is complex and the positions may be incommensurable, the most telling comment was from Gamson's conclusion which stated his "personal preference . . . to pursue arguments that rely on manipulable variables" such as mobilization and organization "because these are things that challenging groups can control. Hence, the argument has immediate relevance for practice" (Gamson 1980: 1058). Gamson acknowledged that Goldstone had a different perspective on the issues and that the data are subject to multiple interpretations. Thus one of the few direct exchanges between a breakdown theorist and a resource mobilization theorist ends with a metatheoretical reflection acknowledging foundational differences between agency-centered resource mobilization approaches and deterministic breakdown theories.

The persistence of breakdown theories may also be seen in Piven and Cloward's (1977) work on poor people's movements. It is telling that, like Goldstone, they defend the importance of breakdown processes while criticizing the role of organization in protest. While Goldstone questioned the explanatory relevance of organization to differential outcomes, Piven and Cloward challenged it on strategic grounds. For them, it is not possible for formal organizations to compel concessions from elites that can sustain those organizations over time; organizations rather endure by abandoning their oppositional politics. In an argument reminiscent of Michels (1961), they see formal organization as unwittingly providing elites with a mechanism for containing and channeling protest. Moreover, the emphasis on formal organization has obscured the efficacy of unorganized protest and mass defiance, which they claim has been responsible for the limited but important gains of poor people's movements. In this view, resource mobilization's emphasis on formal organization amounts to conceptual blinders that preclude analysts from considering other forms of protest.

Piven and Cloward emphasize the extent to which social structures limit opportunities for protest and diminish its force when it does occur. If social institutions typically preclude opportunities for protest, then it is only under rare and exceptional circumstances that deprived groups will be in a position to pursue their grievances. Thus major social dislocations are necessary before longstanding grievances can find expression in collective defiance. It is here that they point to social breakdowns in society's regulatory capacity and everyday routines as providing rare but potent opportunities for mass defiance. But breakdown is not enough; people must also see their deprivations and problems as unjust, mutable, and subject to their action. Such insights are likely only when the scale of distress is high or when the dominant institutions are obviously malfunctioning. Societal breakdown thus not only disrupts regulatory capacity and everyday routines; it also opens a cognitive space in which people can begin to consider and pursue alternative social arrangements.

When protest happens, it is shaped by the institutional structures in which it occurs as people choose targets, strategies, and tactics. Mass defiance will be effective to the extent that it disrupts institutions that are important to elites. Defiance is thus best seen as a negative sanction imposed by protesters to extract concessions. Whereas the logic of strikes or boycotts involves withholding valuable resources like labor or purchasing power, the only thing deprived groups may be able to withhold is their acquiescence to the social order. Mass defiance thus provides the only true leverage they have, and it is precisely such defiance that is likely to be tamed by formal protest organizations. In an interesting twist, breakdown is not just a background causal factor in protest but is also a deliberate strategy as protesters seek to exacerbate institutional disruption to the point where they win concessions they would not otherwise realize. While mass defiance may be able to win only limited victories that are subsequently overturned, Piven and Cloward argue that these may be the only meaningful victories that are possible for poor people's movements.

This argument achieved considerable notoriety and sparked sharp debate over the role of formal organization in protest. One issue concerns the generalizability of the argument. Piven and Cloward's experience in the welfare rights movement of the 1960s may have colored their interpretations of the civil rights movement and the poor people's movements of the 1930s; if so, their argument may not fully apply to all the cases in their book. Others have challenged the applicability of the argument to other poor people's movements (Cress and Snow 1996), as well as to movements with different constituencies. For groups with a resource base, formal organization may not necessarily spell the death of effective protest. In any event, their advocacy of breakdown theories of protest fits a larger pattern that includes a critical stance toward the efficacy of formal organization in protest and toward the resource mobilization paradigm that has championed the role of organization in movement success. There is one other element that fits the pattern. Even though Piven and Cloward write as advocates of the movements they analyze (unlike classical theorists of strain and breakdown), there is a decidedly deterministic and pessimistic cast to their conclusions about the probabilities that such movements will achieve significant and lasting results.

In a subsequent programmatic statement, Piven and Cloward (1992) offer an explicit defense of breakdown theories – what they call the malintegration (MI) approach – and a sharp critique of the resource mobilization perspective. They argue that resource mobilization advocates sought to normalize protest by emphasizing the similarities between conventional action and protest behavior. In so doing, the distinction between normative and non-normative forms of protest was seriously blurred, and the role of organization in protest was exaggerated. Piven and Cloward note that non-normative protest is a more basic challenge to power since it not only pursues a specific agenda but does so in a way that challenges elite power and rule-making. The distinction is critical to the debate: "MI analysts do not claim that breakdown is a necessary precondition of normative forms of group action. What they emphasize instead is that breakdown is a precondition of collective protest and violence, of riot and rebellion . . . In effect, the MI tradition is being dismissed for an argument it never made" (Piven and Cloward 1992: 306).

They proceed to challenge the role of organization – what they call lateral integration – in facilitating protest by arguing that such organization is often present over long periods of time and in circumstances that don't generate protest. If true, the "variable" of protest cannot be explained by the "constant" of organization. For Piven and Cloward, it is vertical integration that is crucial. Hierarchical social structures normally constrain opportunities for protest, but it is when those linkages are weakened through social breakdown and when grievances intensify that defiance is likely to emerge. In all these ways, they chastise the resource mobilization approach for marginalizing lower-stratum protest. The normalization of protest by the resource mobilization paradigm has its own history; it was part of an effort to disentangle the equation of protest with deviant, spontaneous, contagious, irrational, and dangerous action in the classical collective behavior tradition. In winning that battle, however, the distinction between normative and non-normative protest was indeed blurred, and the wholesale rejection of breakdown theories – recall Tilly's sweeping statement quoted above – was an ill-considered and premature conclusion. In support of their position, Piven and Cloward note that malintegration ideas are returning to some resource mobilization arguments as analysts try to square theoretical assumptions with empirical realities. Even so, they do so with a different conceptual language that obscures similarities to breakdown arguments. Along with Goldstone's work on revolution, the contributions of Piven and Cloward illustrate the persistence of strain and breakdown theories during the predominance of the resource mobilization paradigm.

Another example of the persistence of breakdown theories is provided by a well-known study of the Boston antibusing movement. Useem (1980) distinguished between two versions of breakdown theory. The mass society version predicted that socially isolated individuals are more likely to become involved in collective action, while the discontent version said that discontent increases along with disorganization and that increasing discontent motivates protest. Both versions have been criticized by solidarity theorists. In the Boston antibusing movement, Useem found that high community attachment and secondary group participation were correlated with movement participation. He concluded that these findings validate the solidarity model and refuted the mass society variant of breakdown theory. However, he also found that high levels of discontent were correlated with movement participation. With further analysis, Useem argued that while disorganization did not increase discontent, an increase in discontent nonetheless occurred and it contributed to movement participation. Useem concludes that "solidarity increases discontent by multiplying the effects of grievance-producing events" (Useem 1980: 366). The partial validity of one version of the breakdown model is taken to reveal a flaw in the solidarity model's assumption that grievances and discontent are constant factors for aggrieved groups. In the antibusing movement, the discontent identified by breakdown theory made an independent contribution alongside solidarity processes in motivating participation. Useem's conclusion that "both the breakdown and solidarity theories help to explain protest" (1980: 368) is a rare example of a more nuanced and interactive understanding of how breakdown and solidarity may be related.

A more recent reformulation of breakdown theories extends this effort to overcome what may be a false dichotomy between breakdown and solidarity approaches. Snow et al. (1998) suggest that although the terms "strain" and "breakdown" are often used interchangeably, breakdown is a specific form of the broader concept of strain. Traditional breakdown theories viewed collective action as rooted in rapid social change and disintegration, which weakens social cohesion and exacerbates tensions and frustrations. Snow et al. (1998) acknowledge that breakdown theories fell out of favor in the last third of the twentieth century because of conceptual vagueness, empirical weakness, and theoretical fads. However, they argue that the rejection of breakdown approaches was premature, and that a revised version of breakdown theory can be formulated that is compatible with the role of solidarity in generating collective action and that empirically fits with a wide range of collective action.

The core of their argument is that the link between social breakdown and collective action is the disruption of the quotidian nature of social life. The latter refers to all the taken-for-granted aspects of everyday life; more specifically, the quotidian consists of daily practices and routines that comprise habitual social action, alongside the natural attitude of routinized expectations and the suspension of doubt about the organization of the social world and one's role within it. "When the quotidian is disrupted, then, routinized patterns of action are rendered problematic and the natural attitude is fractured" (Snow et al. 1998: 5). In this way, a specific type of breakdown is seen as the impetus to collective action. As with all forms of breakdown theory, there are many ways in which people might respond to disruptions of the quotidian, so it remains to specify which disruptions are most likely to provoke collective action rather than social withdrawal, individual coping, or anti-social behavior. At a minimum, the disruption must be experienced collectively and it must not have a normal, institutional resolution if it is to provoke collective action (Snow et al. 1998: 6).

Four categories of events fit these guidelines. First, accidents that disrupt a community's routines or threaten its existence through "suddenly imposed grievances" are likely to spark collective action; Walsh's (1981) study of the community response to the nuclear accident at Three Mile Island is the classic example. Second, intrusions into or violations of community space by strangers or outsiders can provoke such responses: the cases of anti-drunk driving movements, antibusing movements, or neighborhood movements that resist halfway houses, group homes, or toxic waste dumps provide examples here. Third, changes in taken-for-granted subsistence routines can provoke collective action: the response of homeless people to disruptions in habituated survival routines provides examples of this type. Finally, and perhaps most evidently, dramatic changes in structures of social control can disrupt quotidian routines and provoke collective action: research on prison riots provide examples here.

Several implications of this reformulated version of breakdown theory are worth emphasis. First, this formulation resonates with both theory and intuition suggesting that people respond more rapidly to threats to existing resources and routines than to opportunities for changing them. Second, quotidian disruption may thereby substitute – within limits – for factors like framing, resources, and organization because actors motivated by threatened losses will have higher levels of motivation that may reduce the need for other resources. Finally, and perhaps most importantly, Snow and his associates challenge the presumed dichotomy between breakdown and solidarity by specifying that breakdown involves patterns and expectancies of everyday life rather than associational ties between individuals. Thus the breakdown of everyday routines can occur alongside strong ties within groups, and it is this combination that may be most likely to promote collective action. This more sophisticated treatment of the classic breakdown hypothesis thereby rescues a prematurely abandoned concept, removes the taint of irrationality, undermines the dichotomy between breakdown and solidarity, and fits a wide range of collective phenomena. As such, it suggests the utility of a more carefully specified breakdown theory.

Earlier I cited review articles to illustrate the prevalence of strain and breakdown theories until 1975 and their decline by the mid-1980s. Despite the decline, their persistence is documented in Useem's (1998) recent review of breakdown theories.

Useem reiterates that while breakdown theories were the classical explanation for riots, rebellion and civil violence, their popularity eroded in the 1970s with the rise of resource mobilization approaches and the corresponding argument that solidarity rather than breakdown is crucial to explaining collective action. Useem's review makes several helpful observations about this paradigm shift. First, he argues that breakdown theories and resource mobilization theories analyze different phenomena, and the field needs to be open to both types of explanation. While this seems almost self-evident, it is remarkable how rarely the debate has paused to make distinctions between different types of collective action that may indeed require different explanations. Second, one such distinction is between routine and non-routine collective action. Whereas Tilly (1978) and others sought to erode this distinction and thereby reject breakdown theories, the distinction should be preserved and the role of breakdown in explaining nonroutine collective action should be examined more closely. Third, the same distinction would specify the role of organization, which is admittedly crucial to routine forms of collective action but may be less important to nonroutine collective action. Fourth, Useem cites a range of evidence that provides at least partial support for breakdown theories, including reassessments of the urban riots of the 1960s, factors promoting criminal activity among youth, the dynamics of poor people's movements, spirals of ethnic conflict, and disruptions of the quotidian.

Perhaps Useem's most interesting observations concern the implicit value biases of these paradigms. At some risk of oversimplification, he suggests that resource mobilization theorists interpret all government response as repression that raises costs for protesters, whereas breakdown theorists recognize that this can be a moral response expressing widely held societal views. This is really a subterranean debate about the legitimacy of dissent versus social order that appears inextricably intertwined with the concepts of the two paradigms. In a similar vein, Useem argues that resource mobilization theorists emphasize the positive aspects of aggression, whereas breakdown theorists are more likely to see its negative aspects. As noted earlier, this is a longstanding tension that originated in the classical collective behavior paradigm's negative view of collective behavior and was self-consciously challenged by resource mobilization's valorization of collective action. It would appear that such valuations remain deeply embedded in the theoretical concepts used to analyze collective action. In any event, Useem concludes that the breakdown perspective warrants further investigation with particular emphasis on the emergence of nonroutine forms of collective action that result from faltering social control or disrupted cultural routines.

The contributions of Goldstone, Piven and Cloward, Snow et al., and Useem illustrate how strain and breakdown have persisted as explanations of at least some forms of collective action despite the predominance of a paradigm that has been relentlessly hostile to such ideas. More broadly, this history illustrates how classical concepts and theories never completely disappear from the discipline, though they may undergo significant revision. Indeed, if there is any cumulative progression in the development of sociological explanation, it may arise from a dialectic whereby classical notions are thoroughly challenged but persist in revised and more carefully specified forms. This process seems evident in the persistence and perhaps even the return of strain and breakdown approaches in social movement theory.

THE RETURN OF STRAIN AND BREAKDOWN THEORIES

The thesis of this brief section is that strain and breakdown theories have already returned to mainstream social movement theory. Indeed, it can be argued that they never really left, even during the ascendancy of the resource mobilization approach. My contention is that there is considerable conceptual overlap between what classical theorists mean by strain or breakdown and what resource mobilization theorists mean by opportunity. What separates the approaches and obscures this equation is the valuational bias of each set of concepts. The very terms "strain" and "breakdown" inherently connote negative, problematic conditions to be prevented, avoided, or repaired. As these terms functioned in the classical collective behavior paradigm, there can be little argument that they conveyed deeply embedded negative value judgments about the appropriateness of collective behavior. And as Useem (1998) has recently reminded us, breakdown theorists to this day are more likely to see social control in a positive light and protester aggression in a negative light. My further contention is that it was not just the notion of breakdown as a neutral causal mechanism that provoked the ire of resource mobilization theorists; it was also the halo of negative value judgments surrounding the concept that drew their fire.

The concept of opportunity was tailor-made for this debate. On the one hand, it provided the transvaluation sought by resource mobilization proponents that allowed them to paint collective action in a positive light. Particularly in the US context, the concept of "opportunity" inherently signifies something to be sought, desired, seized, enjoyed, valued, and maximized. On the other hand, it preserved a way of talking about changes in structural conditions and cultural contexts that facilitate collective action. By substituting the concept of opportunity for that of breakdown, resource mobilization theorists retained a powerful explanation for collective action while reversing the valuations placed on that action. There are as many different versions of opportunity in recent approaches as there are variations on breakdown in the classical tradition, and this is not the place for an exhaustive review. However, a brief overview will illustrate some ways in which "opportunity" has become a substitute for "breakdown."

The concept of opportunity has been there from the beginning as an element in Tilly's (1978) mobilization model of collective action. Most basically, it was defined as the increased vulnerability of other groups and governments to the actions of a contender pursuing its interests. The flip side of opportunity is threat: the extent to which other groups are able to make claims that would damage a contender's interests. Closely related are repression or facilitation; these are usually the province of governments whose actions may raise or lower the costs of collective action. Opportunities emerge when the established order becomes vulnerable to the actions of contenders and when their costs of acting are reduced. While not the same thing, it seems evident that strains and breakdowns in existing social and cultural structures would precisely increase their vulnerability to contender's claims and reduce the latter's costs of acting. Conversely, a strongly integrated social order with minimal strain or tendencies toward breakdown would be one in which contenders are more vulnerable than authorities and the costs of acting collectively are considerably higher. Increases or decreases in strain or breakdown thus mirror increases or decreases in movement opportunity, including the costs of acting. Both sets of concepts refer to external factors typically beyond the control of claimants, and both function as variables suited to explaining the episodic nature of collective action.

McAdam's (1982) well-established political process model recognizes a central role for opportunity in the emergence of collective action. Alongside organizational readiness and insurgent consciousness, political opportunities constitute the third essential ingredient in this recipe for insurgency. Alterations in political opportunity structures reduce power discrepancies between authorities and challengers and increase the cost of repressing protest. While phrased somewhat differently, this is Tilly's logic reiterated; once again, increasing strain or breakdown is mirrored in increased power for challengers relative to authorities and increased costs of social control for authorities. In a more recent synthetic statement by Tarrow (1994), opportunity is also recognized as a crucial variable in the emergence of social protest. While some types of opportunity are relatively consistent features of the political environment that correspond to a notion of social strain, others are more variable (unstable alignments, divided elites) and correspond to a notion of breakdown. Tarrow also underscores the ways in which movements not only seize preexisting opportunities but strategize to create opportunities in which to act. A parallel in breakdown theory may be found in Piven and Cloward's argument that social disorganization is not just a cause of defiance but also a goal of that defiance because heightened disorganization is a means of extracting concessions from authorities. In all these ways, where a classical theorist sees strain or breakdown, a resource mobilization theorist sees opportunity. While the valuations placed on these concepts are diametrically opposed, they do essentially the same work in each theory as external, variable conditions that alter the balance of power between authorities and contenders, and hence the likelihood of collective action itself.

European new social movement theory provides another example where the concept of opportunity looms large as an understudy for what might otherwise be considered strain and breakdown. The work of Kriesi et al. (1995) provides an impressive example in which different types of political opportunity structures are defined and explored cross-nationally. In addition to this recognition of opportunity as a stand-in for breakdown, new social movement theory has always been more comfortable with notions of strain or breakdown as explanations for collective action. This may well be because recent European social movement theory is more politicized and resistant to the negative image of protest that plagued US versions of breakdown theory; hence the European versions were less likely to toss the baby out with the bath water. As a result, notions of strain and breakdown feature prominently in several new social movement theories (Buechler 1995). The most global version may be found in Habermas's arguments that political instability and anomic situations constitute legitimation and motivation crises (1975) or the colonization of the lifeworld by systemic imperatives (1987) that in turn spur collective action. This image of a social system under strain that provokes collective action is very similar to classical strain and breakdown theories. What obscures the similarity is the political subtext of the theory. Classical breakdown theory valued social order and integration over collective behavior, whereas new social movement theorists typically write as critics of social systems who champion efforts to transform them.

The concept of political opportunity has become a well-established element in a theoretical synthesis in social movement theory built around the concepts of political opportunities, mobilizing structures, and framing processes (McAdam et al. 1996).

While I have not claimed that opportunity and breakdown are the same thing, I have suggested that they do the same work in each respective theoretical tradition. Both concepts refer to external, variable processes that increase the likelihood of collective behavior. Put more polemically, a political process theorist might argue that to whatever extent strain and breakdown are causally relevant, that relevance is captured in the notion of opportunity structures. What is jettisoned are the negative connotations of traditional strain and breakdown theories. To the extent that opportunity has become a stand-in for strain and breakdown, it can be concluded that the latter never really disappeared from social movement theory.

Conclusion

Strain and breakdown theories have indeed had a strange career in the sociological explanation of collective action. From the classical era of sociology until well into the twentieth century, they were the central mechanisms for analyzing collective behavior. Then, in the 1970s, such theories were unceremoniously displaced by a ferocious barrage of criticism that ushered in the resource mobilization perspective. Such criticism was directed at the logical and empirical flaws of those approaches as well as the negative imagery of collective behavior implicit in them. Alongside this antagonism to breakdown explanations, resource mobilization theory's assumptions about agency, rationality, politics, and organization led it to ask different questions and pursue different answers than the classical collective behavior tradition. Nevertheless, strain and breakdown approaches persisted at the margins of the resource mobilization perspective and in the work of critics of that tradition who still saw a role for them. Finally, it can be argued that the concepts of strain and breakdown never really disappeared from social movement theory as much as they went underground and reappeared in the guise of a new conceptual language about opportunity. Given recent pronouncements about new syntheses emerging in social movement theory, perhaps it is time for a reconsideration of the role of strain and breakdown in any such synthesis.

Any successful effort in this direction will require three levels of specification. Most obviously, we need greater specificity about what it is that undergoes strain or breakdown. The candidates include formal authority structures, informal normative understandings, institutional patterns and processes, and quotidian life. The only obviously nonviable candidate is social ties among potential participants in collective action; this is the one instance in which breakdown (of such ties) will reduce rather than increase the chances of collective action.

Second, we need greater specificity about the mechanisms by which any type of strain or breakdown is translated into collective action. Even when specified more carefully, strain and breakdown remain broad background factors that could promote an equally wide range of responses. We need to tease out the conditions under which strain and breakdown will lead to collective action rather than social isolation, criminal activity, or antisocial behavior. There is a start in the suggestion that the breakdown must be experienced collectively and that there must not be a ready-made institutional response (Snow et al. 1998), but we still need to understand more clearly under what circumstances breakdown leads to collective action rather than to something else.

Third, we need greater specificity about what types of collective action are most likely to emerge from specific types of breakdown and strain. The classical collective behavior approach presumed an extremely broad spectrum, from panics, crazes, and fads to riots, movements, and revolutions. Recent social movement theory has fractured the spectrum and claimed movements as its domain while paying less attention to other forms of collective action. This is precisely where a revised breakdown theory may have its greatest relevance. Hence, the distinction between routine forms of collective action that are more amenable to resource mobilization explanations and nonroutine forms that may derive from strain and breakdown needs to be further explored if we are to specify which types of collective action are most likely to be associated with social strain and breakdown.

Finally, while we introduce greater specificity to notions of strain and breakdown, we must do the same with the concept of opportunity (McAdam 1996) so we can then explore the relationships between strain, breakdown, and opportunity more carefully. To do so promises to advance social movement theory while also providing a fascinating test of the extent to which concepts embedded in antithetical theoretical traditions are capable of genuine synthesis.

References

Blumer, Herbert (1951) The Field of Collective Behavior. In A. M. Lee (ed.), *Principles of Sociology*. New York: Barnes & Noble, 167–222.

Buechler, Steven M. (1995) New Social Movement Theories. *Sociological Quarterly*, 36, 441–64.

—— (2000) *Social Movements in Advanced Capitalism*. New York: Oxford University Press.

Cress, Daniel M., and David A. Snow (1996) Resources, Benefactors and the Viability of Homeless SMOs. *American Sociological Review*, 61, 1089–1109.

Davies, James (1962) Toward a Theory of Revolution. *American Sociological Review*, 27, 5–19.

Durkheim, Emile ([1893] 1964) *The Division of Labor in Society*. New York: Free Press.

—— ([1897] 1951) *Suicide*. New York: Free Press.

Gamson, William (1975) *The Strategy of Social Protest*. Homewood, IL: Dorsey.

—— (1980) Understanding the Careers of Challenging Groups: A Commentary on Gladstone. *American Journal of Sociology*, 85, 1043–60.

Garner, Roberta (1997) *Social Movement Theory and Research: An Annotated Bibliographical Guide*. Salem: Scarecrow.

Geschwender, James (1968) Explorations in the Theory of Social Movements and Revolutions. *Social Forces*, 47, 127–35.

Goldstone, Jack (1980) The Weakness of Organization: A New Look at Gamson's *The Strategy of Social Protest*. *American Journal of Sociology*, 85, 1017–42.

—— (1986) Introduction: The Comparative and Historical Study of Revolutions. In Jack Goldstone (ed.), *Revolutions: Theoretical, Comparative, and Historical Studies*. San Diego: Harcourt Brace Jovanovich, 1-17.

—— (1991a) An Analytical Framework. In Jack Goldstone, Ted Robert Gurr, and Farrokh Moshiri (eds.), *Revolutions of the Late Twentieth Century*. Boulder, CO: Westview, 37-51.

—— (1991b) *Revolution and Rebellion in the Early Modern World*. Berkeley: University of California Press.

Gurr, Ted (1970) *Why Men Rebel*. Princeton, NJ: Princeton University Press.

Habermas, Jürgen (1975) *Legitimation Crisis*. Boston: Beacon.

——(1987) *The Theory of Communicative Action*. Vol. 2. Boston: Beacon.

Huntington, Samuel (1968) *Political Order in Changing Societies*. New Haven: Yale University Press.

Jenkins, J. Craig (1983) Resource Mobilization Theory and the Study of Social Movements. *Annual Review of Sociology*, 9, 527–53.

Johnson, Chalmers (1966) *Revolutionary Change*. Boston: Little, Brown.

Kornhauser, William (1959) *The Politics of Mass Society*. New York: Free Press.

Kriesi, Hanspeter, Ruud Koopmans, Jan Willem Duyvendak, and Mario G. Giugni (1995) *New Social Movements in Western Europe*. Minneapolis: University of Minneapolis Press.

Kuhn, Thomas (1962) *The Structure of Scientific Revolutions*. Chicago: University of Chicago Press.

McAdam, Doug(1982) *The Political Process and the Development of Black Insurgency*. Chicago: University of Chicago Press.

——(1996) Conceptual Origins, Current Problems, Future Directions. In Doug McAdam, John D. McCarthy, and Mayer N. Zald (eds.), *Comparative Perspectives on Social Movements*. New York: Cambridge University Press, 23–40.

McAdam, Doug, John McCarthy, and Mayer N. Zald (1996) Introduction: Opportunities, Mobilizing Structures and Framing Processes – Toward a Synthetic, Comparative Perspective on Social Movements. In Doug McAdam, John D. McCarthy, and Mayer N. Zald (eds.), *Comparative Perspectives on Social Movements*. New York: Cambridge University Press, 1–20.

McAdam, Doug, Sidney Tarrow, and Charles Tilly (2001) *Dynamics of Contention*. New York: Cambridge University Press.

McCarthy, John D., and Mayer N. Zald (1973) *The Trend of Social Movements in America: Professionalization and Resource Mobilization*. Morristown, NJ: General Learning.

——(1977) Resource Mobilization and Social Movements: A Partial Theory. *American Journal of Sociology*, 82, 1212–41.

Marx, Gary, and James L. Wood (1975) Strands of Theory and Research in Collective Behavior. *Annual Review of Sociology*, 1, 363–428.

Michels, Robert (1961) *Political Parties*. New York: Free Press.

Oberschall, Anthony (1973) *Social Conflict and Social Movements*. Englewood Cliffs, NJ: Prentice-Hall.

Park, Robert E. (1972) *The Crowd and the Public, and Other Essays*. Chicago: University of Chicago Press.

Park, Robert E., and Ernest W. Burgess (1921) *Introduction to the Science of Sociology*. Chicago: University of Chicago Press.

Parsons, Talcott (1951) *The Social System*. Glencoe, IL: Free Press.

Piven, Frances Fox, and Richard A. Cloward (1977) *Poor People's Movements*. New York: Vintage.

——(1992) Normalizing Collective Protest. In Aldon Morris and Carol Mueller (eds.), *Frontiers in Social Movement Theory*. New Haven: Yale University Press, 301–25.

Rule, James (1988) *Theories of Civil Violence*. Berkeley: University of California Press.

Schwartz, Michael (1976) *Radical Protest and Social Structure*. New York: Academic.

Skolnick, Jerome (1969) *The Politics of Protest*. New York: Ballantine.

Smelser, Neil (1962) *Theory of Collective Behavior*. New York: Free Press.

Snow, David A., and Phillip W. Davis (1995) The Chicago Approach to Collective Behavior. In Gary Alan Fine (ed.), *A Second Chicago School?* Chicago: University of Chicago Press, 188–220.

Snow, David, Daniel M. Cress, Liam Downey, and Andrew W. Jones (1998) Disrupting the "Quotidian": Reconceptualizing the Relationship between Breakdown and the Emergence of Collective Action. *Mobilization*, 3, 1–22.

Tarrow, Sidney (1994) *Power in Movement*. Cambridge: Cambridge University Press.

Tilly, Charles (1978) *From Mobilization to Revolution*. Reading, MA: Addison-Wesley.

Tilly, Charles, Louise Tilly, and Richard Tilly (1975) *The Rebellious Century, 1830–1930*. Cambridge: Harvard University Press.

Turner, Ralph, and Lewis Killian (1987) *Collective Behavior*. 3rd ed. Upper Saddle River, NJ: Prentice-Hall.

Useem, Bert (1980) Solidarity Model, Breakdown Model, and the Boston Anti-Busing Movement. *American Sociological Review*, 45, 357–69.

——(1998) Breakdown Theories of Collective Action. *Annual Review of Sociology*, 24, 215–38.

Walsh, Edward J. (1981) Resource Mobilization and Citizen Protest in Communities around Three Mile Island. *Social Problems*, 29, 1–21.

4

Political Context and Opportunity

Hanspeter Kriesi

Introduction

In his study of popular contention in Great Britain during the late eighteenth and early nineteenth century, Charles Tilly (1995) observed a basic shift in the means of popular protest or claims-making – a shift away from short-term, local, and highly variable forms of contention towards a new repertoire of long-term, national, and generally applicable forms. These massive changes in contention involved a parliamentarization and nationalization of claims-making. Thus the timing of claims-making came to depend more closely on the rhythms of parliamentary discussion and governmental action. Britain was the first, but by no means the only country, where such a large-scale shift took place. As Tilly (1995: 364–77) explains, these shifts occurred because the "entire structure of political opportunity changed." More specifically, they were the result of four related processes which converged to profoundly change the opportunities of popular protest: state-making, economic and demographic change, and contention's cumulative history interwove to create the preconditions for a new repertoire of popular protest that was large in scale and national in scope. In addition, they enhanced the strategic advantage and maneuvering room of formally constituted associations, especially those with national constituencies, as a basis for popular contention. First, war-driven expansion, strengthening, and centralization of the British state gave increasing political advantage to groups that could convey their demands directly to Parliament, whose fiscal and regulative powers were augmented from decade to decade. Second, capitalization, commercialization, and proletarianization of economic life created the basis for the class-cleavage and gave workers and employers increasing incentives and opportunities to band together on a regional or national scale. Third, population growth, migration, urbanization, and the creation of larger producing organizations gave additional advantage to organizations and political entrepreneurs capable of connecting and coordinating the actions by dispersed clusters of people. Finally, the shared beliefs, memories, models, and precedents of previous episodes of popular contention contributed to the shaping of episodes to come.

This account of the momentous change in popular contention in the British past provides an excellent illustration of the political process approach to social movements and its key concept – political opportunity structure. Typically, authors working within this approach explain a specific aspect of popular contention (here the change in the action repertoire of contention) by a change in the political opportunity structure. Tilly's notion of "political opportunity" may be broader than that applied by other authors sharing the same approach and it may, in the present example, be more "structural" than some other examples in his own work. But it very well illustrates the general strategy adopted by the practitioners of the political process approach.

Jon Elster (1989: 13) reduces this general strategy to its basic elements – his most elementary "nuts and bolts." He argues that we can see individual human action (such as individual participation in popular protest) as the result of two successive filtering operations. The first filter is made up of all the constraints that an individual faces. The actions consistent with these constraints form an actor's "opportunity set." The second filter is a mechanism that determines which action within the opportunity set will actually be carried out. The choice among the options that have passed the first filter will be determined by the actor's "desires" – his interests, preferences, values, action intentions, or goals.

Elster adds (1989: 20) that even if opportunities are objective, external to the actor, what explains the action is the actor's desire together with "his *beliefs* about the opportunities." This emphasis (in the original) is crucial, because an actor may not be aware of certain opportunities, or he may overestimate some aspects of the available opportunities. Thus movement activists typically tend to overestimate the degree of political opportunity, and, as Gamson and Meyer (1996: 285) observe, "if they did not, they would not be doing their job wisely." However, information about the beliefs of the actors involved in episodes of contentious politics tend to be difficult to come by, which induces the practitioners of the political process approach to make some simplifying heuristic assumptions about the behavior of the actors involved. Thus they often assume the rationality principle – that political actors do what they think will allow them to attain their goals under the given opportunity set. Making this assumption and having a good idea of the actors' goals and their opportunity set, the scientific observers proceed to predict what the actors will do by "vicarious problem-solving," that is, by putting themselves "vicariously" in the same situation and figuring out what they would do if they were there (Schelling 1984; Aya 1990: 9).[1]

The political process approach has become very popular in social movement research. Some observers even believe it has become "the hegemonic paradigm among social movement analysts" (Goodwin and Jasper 1999: 28). It certainly provides a very powerful tool for the study of popular contention. The popularity of the political process approach has, however, had its drawbacks, too: it has given rise to all sorts of interpretations of its key terms, they have been used in many different ways and "consensus regarding the term 'political opportunity' has proven elusive" (McAdam 1996: 24). Indeed, as so many other popular concepts, the term "political opportunity" suffers from definitional sloppiness and "conceptual stretching" (see Sartori 1968, 1991), which tends to reduce its heuristic and theoretical value. Gamson and Meyer (1996: 275) even maintain that the concept of "political opportunity structure" is "in danger of becoming a sponge that soaks up virtually every aspect of the social movement environment – political institutions and culture, crises of various sorts, political alliances, and policy shifts. . . . It threatens to become an all-encompassing fudge factor for all the conditions and circumstances that form the context for collective action." In this chapter, I shall try to put some order into the conceptualization of political context and opportunity and to underline the continued usefulness of this approach by providing some illustrations of its explanatory power.

The General Framework of the Political Process Approach

It is useful to start out by distinguishing different modes of analysis: frameworks, theories, and models (Ostrom 1999: 39 ff.). The political process approach first of all provides a framework for the study of social movements, that is, a general conceptual toolkit that helps analysts to generate the questions that need to be addressed in studying social movements and to delimit the field of research. Frameworks have a heuristic function, but they do not yet provide explanations or predictions (Schlager 1999: 234). The development of theories enables the analyst to specify which elements of the framework are particularly relevant for certain kinds of questions and to formulate specific hypotheses about the relationship between these elements. The political process approach has been elaborated into specific theories for specific questions. Models, in turn, make precise assumptions about a limited set of parameters and variables. Models allow for the testing of specific parts of the theory.

Figure 4.1 provides a framework for the study of the political context. This framework is an updated version of an earlier attempt to come to terms with the conceptual complexity characteristic of the field (Kriesi and Giugni 1995: xvi). Political context is a more general concept than that of political opportunity. Depending on the specific questions asked by different authors, different elements of the political context have been selected and combined to study the relevant "political opportunity set" of the actors concerned. The present framework distinguishes between three sets of variables – structures, configurations of power, and interaction contexts (see also della Porta 1996: 80). Let us look at the different elements of each set.

Structures

The "political opportunity structure" constitutes what we could call the hard core of the political process framework. The basic idea of the framwork is that "political opportunity structures influence the choice of protest strategies and the impact of social movements on their environment" (Kitschelt 1986: 58). Since Eisinger (1973) first introduced the notion of "political opportunity structures," students of social movements have distinguished between "open" and "closed" structures, that is, structures which allow for easy access to the political system or which make access

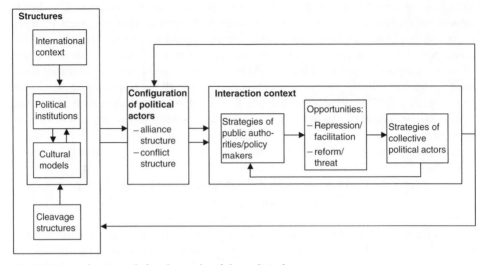

Figure 4.1   A framework for the study of the political context.

more difficult. Kitschelt (1986) introduced the additional distinction between "input" and "output" structures, that is, structures referring specifically either to the openness of the political system in the input phase of the policy cycle or to its capacity to impose itself in the output phase. In practice, it proved to be difficult to separate these two types of structures clearly from one another: Open systems tend to have only a limited capacity to act, whereas closed systems tend to have a somewhat greater capacity to act.

The core of the structures, in turn, is made up of the formal political institutions. The degree of openness of the political system is a function of its (territorial) central-ization and the degree of its (functional) separation of power. The greater the degree of decentralization, the wider is the formal access and the smaller the capacity of any one part of the system to act. Decentralization implies a multiplication of state actors, and, therefore, of points of access and decision-making. In federal states, such as those of Germany, Switzerland, or the United States, there are multiple points of relevant access on the national, regional, and local level. In centralized states, such as those of France, the Netherlands, or Sweden, regional and local access points are rather insignificant. In addition, the system's openness is closely related to the (functional) separation of power. The greater the separation of power between the legislature (parliamentary arena), the executive (government and public administration), and the judiciary, as well as within each one of these powers, the greater the degree of formal access and the more limited the capacity of the state to act.

Parameters characterizing the parliamentary arena more specifically concern the electoral system and the party system. Electoral systems provide more or less access depending on their degree of proportionality: proportional systems are more easily accessible for emerging political actors than majoritarian or plurality systems. The more proportional an electoral system, the greater usually the number of parties, which again increases the possibilities of access. The number of parties, in turn, determines, together with the internal makeup of the parties – that is, the number of factions and groups that exist within parties – the process of coalition formation.

Very roughly, we can distinguish party systems with disciplined parties that can be considered as unitary actors from party systems with heterogenous, undisciplined parties. Highly disciplined, single-party government such as the British Cabinet provides limited access and has a strong capacity to act, whereas multiparty coalitions made up of undisciplined parties, such as the grand coalitions we find in Switzerland, are likely to provide multiple access points and to have a limited capacity to act. With regard to the public administration, parameters specifying the degree of openness refer to the amount of resources, internal coordination, professionalization, and availability of movement allies in the public service. The greater the amount of resources at its disposal, and the greater its internal coordination and professionalization, the stronger and the less accessible the public service is likely to be. By contrast, the larger the number and power of movement allies within the public service, the more accessible it will be and the more likely movement actors will have the possibility to influence public policy.

There are two useful conceptual distinctions to summarize the degree of institutional accessibility of political systems. First, we can distinguish between strong and weak states (see Krasner 1978; Badie and Birnbaum 1979; Birnbaum 1985; Koopmans and Kriesi 1995: 27): strong states are characterized by institutional structures that limit their accessibility with respect to their environment and make them capable of getting things done, whereas weak states have institutions that open them up, but also limit their capacity to act. France constitutes the paradigmatic case of a strong state, the US the typical example of a weak state. Another way to summarize the degree of institutional accessibility of the political system is to adopt Lijphart's (1999) distinction between majoritarian and consensus democracies: majoritarian democracies concentrate political power within and between institutions, which limits their accessibility and enhances their capacity to act, while consensus democracies divide political power and thus increase the institutional accessibility and constrain the capacity to act. Britain is the paradigmatic case of a majoritarian democracy and France is also rather majoritarian, while the small Western European states are typical examples of a consensus democracy. The United States share the majoritarian, Anglo-Saxon heritage, but contrary to the British unitary state, they have a federalist state characterized by a far-reaching separation of power, which contributes to its high accessibility.

In our comparative study of new social movements in Western Europe, in addition to institutional structures we introduced the notion of "prevailing strategies," which refers to the procedures typically employed by members of the political system when they are dealing with challengers (Koopmans and Kriesi 1995: 34 ff.). We distinguished between exclusive (repressive, confrontational, polarizing) and integrative (facilitative, cooperative, assimilative) strategies. These prevailing strategies have a long tradition in a given country and they are related to its institutional structure. Thus political authorities in consensus democracies are rather more likely to rely on integrative strategies than their colleagues in majoritarian democracies. In these countries, the tendency to rely on integrative strategies is the result of a collective learning experience that reaches back to the resolution of the religious conflicts, which have torn these countries apart for centuries. The resolution of these conflicts provided the models for dealing with political challenges for centuries to come (Lehmbruch 1996, 1998; Christin 1997). Similarly, the tendency to rely on repressive strategies is a result of historical experiences, such as is argued by Gallie (1983), who traces the repressive reactions of the French ruling elites to the challenge by labor movement protest after World War I back to the earlier experience of repressing the Parisian Commune in 1871.

The prevailing strategies of how to deal with challengers constitute a first example of cultural models which have a generally facilitative or constraining effect on the mobilization of social movements and their possible success. A second major category of cultural models concerns the political-cultural or symbolic opportunities that determine what kind of ideas become visible for the public, resonate with public opinion and are held to be "legitimate" by the audience. Koopmans and Statham (1999: 228) proposed the term "discursive opportunity structure" to denote this second type of cultural models. They apply the concept to the mobilization by the extreme right – a social movement that mobilizes an ethnic-cultural framing of national identity against the idea of the nation as a political or civic community. They test and confirm the following hypothesis: "the resonance of the extreme-right frame, and consequently its chances of mobilization and success, will be greater (1) the more the dominant discourse on national identity and citizenship corresponds to and legitimates the ethnic-cultural ideal-type of national identity, and (2) the less the dominant conception of the nation is grounded in and legitimized by civic-political elements" (229).

The cultural models can be combined with the political institutional structures in order to arrive at more complex and more focused opportunity sets. Kriesi (1995b: 177) combines institutional structures and prevailing strategies to arrive at four general settings for the approach of polity members toward challengers. Koopmans and Statham (1999: 247–8) combine discursive and institutional opportunities to arrive at a fourfold typology of predicted movement outcomes: where neither discursive nor institutional opportunities are available, the challenger will find no support for his ideas and demands, nor will he be able to gain access to the polity. Where discursive opportunities are available but the political system is closed, the challenger is likely to be preempted by the political elite: it will take up those demands and frames of the challengers that do not conflict with dominant ideas, while simultaneously excluding or even repressing them as a collective actor. In the opposite situation – open access, but unfavorable discursive opportunities – the challenger is likely to be co-opted without obtaining real substantive concessions. Full response finally is the outcome, where the challenger obtains both, access and substantive success, an outcome expected only when opportunities are available in both the institutional and the discursive realms.

The concept of "cultural models" that I have introduced here is narrower than the more general distinction between cultural and institutional dimensions of opportunity by Gamson and Meyer (1996: 279 ff.). It only refers to the stable elements of the cultural repertoire in a given political system that influence the elite's and the public's reaction to challengers.

Both institutional structures and cultural models are influenced by even more fundamental structures, which we should include in our conceptualization of the structural political context in the broad sense of the term. Political institutions and cultural models are influenced by the country-specific political cleavage structures and by the country's international context. The specific political cleavage structure of a country, in turn, is rooted in the social and cultural conflict structure of its society. Social and cultural conflicts do not automatically become political cleavages, of course, but only if they are organized as such (Bartolini and Mair 1990: 216). While the social-structural basis of a political conflict emerges from social change, the conflict itself results from the coupling of the processes of social change – urbanization, population growth, industrialization, globalization and the like – with the processes of democratization, politicization, and mobilization. Social change determines structural and cultural potentials for political mobilization that remain latent as long as they are not politicized by a collective political actor such as a social movement.

Traditional social and cultural cleavages constitute the basis of the political cleavage structure even today. In the case of Western European societies, the impact of such traditional cleavages on the political cleavage structure has proven to be very resistant to change (Lipset and Rokkan 1967; Bartolini and Mair 1990; Bartolini 2000). Thus, still today, the Western European party systems reflect the structure of religious and class conflicts of past centuries. The mobilization capacity of new challengers, such as the new social movements that have mobilized in Western Europe since the late sixties, crucially depends on the remaining mobilization potential of traditional political conflicts (Brand 1985: 322–3). To the extent that traditional conflicts are still salient and segment the population into mutually conscious adversarial groups, there is little maneuvering space for new types of challengers who attempt to articulate a new kind of social or cultural conflict. Comparing the mobilization of new social movements in four Western European countries in the seventies and eighties, Kriesi and Duyvendak (1995) have found evidence for the existence of such a "zero-sum" relationship between traditional and new political cleavages.

So far, my discussion of structures has focused on the national political context. In contemporary multilevel systems of governance, the nation-state constitutes, however, only one level among several. Although I believe that the national level is still the most significant one as far as the political context for the mobilization of social movements is concerned (see della Porta and Kriesi 1999), it is important that we do not lose sight of the other levels involved. On the one hand, nation-states are subdivided in regional and local levels of governance. The variance of the opportunity structure between regions or member-states is of great importance above all in federal states, but the significance of the variations in local contexts for the mobilization of social movement are highly relevant everywhere. On the other hand, nation-states are increasingly inserted into supra- or international systems of governance that impose constraints and open opportunities for social movement actors. Thus, Imig and Tarrow (2001: 7–8) hypothesize that, if Europe is becoming a polity, "sooner or later ordinary citizens will turn their claims and their forms of contentious politics beyond their borders and toward this new level of governance." They think that "contentious politics is one way they will do this – with profound consequences for the Europe of elites." Second, they also suggest that "Europe's authorities not only tolerate but encourage the expression of claims through lobbying and other routine forms and that this has a containing effect on more contentious forms of collective action."

Configurations of Actors

The next set of variables refers to the configurations of actors. From the point of view of a mobilizing social movement, this configuration has three major components

(Hunt et al. 1994): the protagonists, antagonists, and bystanders – that is, the configuration of allies (policymakers, public authorities, political parties, interest groups, the media, related movements), the adversaries (public authorities, repressive agents, countermovements) and the not directly involved, but nevertheless attentive audience (see chapter 11 in this volume) respectively. The analytical distinction between the configuration of political actors and the third level of analysis, the interaction context, implicitly assumes an ordering of contentious episodes in time. Actor configurations represent what we know of the set of actors at a given point in time – their capabilities, perceptions and evaluations of the outcomes obtainable (their "payoffs" in terms of game theory), and the degree to which their interests are compatible or incompatible with each other. The configuration describes the level of potential conflict, the "logic of the situation" at that point in time, but it does not specify how the situation is going to evolve, nor does it say how it has been created (see also Scharpf 1997: 72). On the one hand, any given configuration of political actors is the result of processes of actor and coalition formation – the formation/destruction of groups (identities and categories), alliances, and their infrastructures (organizations and networks), in short, CATNETs (Tilly 1978) that have taken place previously. On the other hand, the configuration of political actors in a given context constitutes the starting point for the analysis of a given episode of strategic interaction between a social movement, its allies and its adversaries – the interaction context.

The configuration of political actors at any given point in time is partly determined by the structures of the political context. Thus the new social movements we have analyzed in Western Europe faced a very different alliance structure depending on the configuration of the left, their "natural ally," which was, in turn, decisively shaped by the heritage of the prevailing strategies to deal with challengers in a given country. Thus the heritage of exclusive strategies in a country like France had caused the radicalization and eventual split of the labor movement into a moderate, social-democratic left and a radical communist left. This split in the labor movement, in turn, contributed to the continued salience of the class conflict, which, at the time of the emergence of the French new social movements in the latter part of the seventies, limited the availability of the left for the mobilization of the new social movements. In the French situation, where the left was dominated by the Communist Party up to the late 1970s, the Socialists could not become unconditional allies of the new social movements. They had to continue to appeal to the working class in traditional class terms to ward off Communist competition, and both the Socialists and the Communists tended to instrumentalize the new social movements – especially the peace movement and the solidarity movement – for their own electoral purposes (Kriesi 1995a).

However, the configuration of political actors is less stable than the structural component of the political context. Thus the alliance structure of a given movement may change decisively at any election, depending on whether the political party which constitutes a "natural ally" for the social movement in question is elected into the government or loses its government position. Thus, the social-democrats tended to support the Western European new social movements when they were in opposition, whereas they were much less reliable allies when in government (Kriesi 1989, 1995a). Moreover, it is also much easier for social movements to modify the configuration of political actors than to modify the structural context. As Tarrow

(1994: 98) points out, social movements can create political opportunities for elites: "Both in a negative sense, when their actions provide grounds for repression; and, in a positive one, when opportunistic politicians seize the opportunity created by challengers to proclaim themselves tribunes of the people." Protesters on their own, he explains, seldom have the power to affect the policy priorities of elites. The goal of challengers is, as Wolfsfeld (1997: 29) points out, "to generate dissensus among the powerful. Challengers attempt to make inroads among elites, who represent more legitimate sources for providing alternative frames." According to Tarrow (1994: 98), reform is most likely "when challenges from outside the polity provide a political incentive for elites within it to advance their own policies and careers."

While authors who analyze the mobilization of social movements in a comparative (cross-national, cross-regional, or cross-local) perspective heavily rely on explanations involving structural elements, authors who do case studies within national contexts tend to put the accent more on configurations of political actors. Most importantly, they tend to adopt a longitudinal perspective involving comparisons across time and important shifts in the configurations of political actors. In their view, it is the shifts in the configurations of political actors – the instability of political alignments, which create the opportunity for successful mobilization (Tarrow 1994: 87–8). Such instability may relate to the changing electoral fortunes of major parties. According to the "social cleavage model" of political realignments (Flanagan and Dalton 1984),[2] the increasing gap between the functioning of the political system and the people's aspirations contributes to an increasingly intense sense of frustration or dissatisfaction on the part of the citizens. This increasing dissatisfaction, in turn, leads to a dealignment in the party system: it weakens existing party identifications among the electorate, makes for greater voter volatility, creates tensions and conflicts in the party system, undermines established leaders, and contributes to internal splits in the major parties. Eventually, as parties and their electorates adjust their positions to the new cleavage, a realignment will occur in the party system, a durable change in the electoral alignments that is produced at the occasion of one or several "critical elections." As Martin (2000) points out, we should distinguish between a "breaking election," which marks the breakdown of the old alignments, and an "election of realignment," which marks the beginning of a durable new electoral era. While the two critical elections may coincide, they need not necessarily do so. The period of transition between the two may last for many years and include several additional elections. The uncertainty created by such a realignment process may induce elites to compete for support from outside the polity. The civil rights movement in the United States provides a well-known example for the leverage created by electoral realignments: both the decline of the Southern white vote and the movement of African-American voters to the Northern cities increased the incentive for the Democrats to seek black support. With its "razor-thin electoral margin, the Kennedy administration was forced to move from cautious footdragging to seizing the initiative for civil rights, a strategy that was extended by the Johnson administration to the landmark Voting Rights Act of 1965" (Tarrow 1994: 87).

The instability of political alignments may also refer to a policy-specific situation. In other words, shifting opportunities for mobilization and success may be policy-domain specific (Gamson and Meyer 1996: 280, 285; Rucht 1998: 119). Following

Sabatier and Jenkins-Smith (1999), we can assume that the actor configuration in a given policy domain is structured into a number of advocacy coalitions. These coalitions do not all have the same amount of influence in the policy domain in question, but policymaking in a given domain is typically dominated by one of the coalitions that exerts what Baumgartner and Jones (1993) have termed a "policy monopoly." A "policy monopoly" has two important characteristics that closely parallel the two basic characteristics of an advocacy coalition: a definable institutional structure responsible for policymaking that limits access to the policy process; and a powerful supporting idea connected to core political values associated with the structure in question. The institutional structure in question may be simply the structure of cooperative interactions between the members of the advocacy coalition, all of whom share the same supporting ideas. Now, some exogenous shock, such as changes in socioeconomic conditions, catastrophes, system-wide governing coalitions, or policy outputs from other subsystems may destabilize the domain-specific equilibrium. Social and cultural shifts and unpredictable catastrophic events may cause policy failures in the domain in question, system-wide power shifts may cause corresponding domain-specific shifts, and policy outputs of other subsystems may cause disarray in the traditional problem-solving routines in the domain in question. Following the model of Baumgartner and Jones, the policy process in a given policy-domain can be conceptualized as a "punctuated equilibrium": long periods of stability and incremental policymaking under the auspices of a dominant coalition are interrupted by shorter intervals of major policy change. As the policy monopoly of the dominant coalition destabilizes, established policy paradigms weaken their hold on the policymakers' minds and controversy is introduced. This provides a "window of opportunity" (Kingdon 1984: 173–204) for policy change in general and for the intervention of social movement actors in particular.

American nuclear power is an example of the construction and collapse of a policy monopoly. By the middle 1950s, a tight policy-monopoly had been constructed by technological enthusiasts in the US centering on the civilian uses of nuclear power. By 1974, not only had the domain-specific subsystem collapsed, but the civilian nuclear option was, for all practical purposes, dead. No new nuclear power plants have been ordered in the US since 1977, and more than a hundred previously ordered plants have been abandoned or canceled. The policy monopoly of the supporters of nuclear power was first challenged by insiders, technical staff from the Atomic Energy Commission (AEC) who began to question the agency's safety decisions. The conflict within the policy community began to expand outward as scientists in the agency leaked information to the Union of Concerned Scientists and other antinuclear groups. This connection gave external opponents the credibility they needed to attack the system. An external legitimacy crisis developed by 1972, as the challengers and the allies in the emerging antinuclear movement contested all license hearings. The oil crisis and the rising antinuclear movement (with the latter reinforced by the former) brought nuclear power from the realm of "iron triangles" and closed doors into the glare of media coverage and partisan debates. Baumgartner and Jones (1993: 70) maintain that the opponents won primarily by getting their vision of the issue accepted and by altering the nature of the decision-making process by expanding the range of participants involved. When the industry lost control of the issue, when the venue had been expanded by opponents to include licensing, oversight, and rate making, the future was determined. Whatever the ultimate reason for the breakdown of the nuclear power coalition in the US (see below), the case of US nuclear power illustrates the opportunities that open up for social movements as the hold of dominant coalitions over a policy domain loosens up.

Policy-domain specific shifts may create new opportunities for movements operating in the policy-domain in question. But some policy-domains are also more or less accessible than others for structural reasons. Thus Duyvendak and Giugni (1995: 96–8) distinguish between what they call "high profile" and "low profile" policy-domains. "High profile" domains are characterized by their critical importance for the maintenance of the established power relations in a given polity. Examples of "high profile" domains include national security, energy, or immigration, while cultural policy would be an example of a "low profile" domain. Access for challengers in "high profile" domains is likely to be more difficult than for those in "low profile" domains.

Finally, as critics have pointed out (Goodwin and Jasper 1999: 34), not all social movements are equally focused on the political process and, therefore, dependent to the same degree on political opportunities for their mobilization and success. For some movements, which have been called "identity oriented" (Cohen 1985; Raschke 1985; Rucht 1988), "subcultural," or "countercultural" (Kriesi et al. 1995), the expression of collective identities through collective action or the implementation of social and cultural change are of primary concern. Such movements will have a greater degree of autonomy from the political context and thus be less adequately explained by the present approach. The women's movement, or at least part of it, is an obvious and important example, and it is probably no coincidence that this movement has received less attention from the political process approach than it deserves (see Koopmans 1999: 98), although this situation is changing (see Minkoff 1995, 1997; Banaszak 1996; Soule et al. 1999; McCammon et al. 2002).

Interaction Context

The third level of analysis concerns the interaction context. This is the level of the mechanisms linking structures and configurations to agency and action, and it is at this level that the strategies of the social movements and their opponents come into view. Several authors sympathetic with the general framework of the political process approach have criticized the "structural bias" and the determinism involved in much of the recent work in this area (see Joppke 1993; Midttun and Rucht 1994; Goodwin and Jasper 1999; McAdam et al. 2001). Such critics wish to put the emphasis more on the processual elements. They insist on the specificities of the movement-specific contexts, on the dynamics of the interaction between the actors in one and the same context, and on the subjective interpretations of the actors involved.

In principle, nothing in the general approach prevents such an emphasis. Thus the earliest version of the political process model – McAdam's (1982: 48–51) account of the civil rights movement – was already very much aware of the subjective elements mediating between opportunity and action. He already insisted that "Mediating between opportunity and action are people and the subjective meanings they attach to their situations," and he, at the time, criticized the proponents of both the classic and resource mobilization perspectives for ignoring this crucial attribution process. More recently, McAdam et al. (2001: 46) insist on the same point:

> "Threats" and "opportunities" cannot be automatically read from the kinds of objective changes on which analysts have typically relied. Let us return to Rosa Parks. This was no demure southern lady who automatically took advantage of an objective structure of opportunities. She had a history of civil rights activism which led her and her Montgomery supporters to attribute an opportunity, not only to the injustice of bus segregation but to the potential economic clout of the city's black population.

The general framework is sufficiently open to accommodate such a perspective, even if its proponents do not all agree on where to put the emphasis.

The context-specific opportunities may take very different forms, depending on the structures of the political system, which constitutes the general context, the system-wide and domain-specific configurations of actors, and precipitating events (see below). Nevertheless, we can systematize them in a simple way, assuming strategic behavior on the part of the movement actors (Tilly 1978: 100–15, 133–8; Koopmans and Kriesi 1995: 38 ff.; Koopmans 1999: 102–3): by distinguishing between factors influencing the costs and benefits of collective action itself (the "means" side), and factors related to the goals of such action (the "ends" side). Regarding both, movement actors may anticipate positive and negative reactions from the political environment to a particular strategic option for action, that is, chances and risks of that option. With respect to goals, authorities may be expected to respond favorably – that is, to change their policies in the direction of the movement's goals (we may call this reform); or unfavorably – that is, to change policies in the opposite direction (we may call this threat). There is also the possibility of some mix of reform and threat or of no response at all. With regard to collective action, authorities may be expected either to apply sanctions that increase the costs of collective action (repression) or to reward collective action, for instance by providing resources or moral support (facilitation). Again, the anticipated response may also be a mix of repression and facilitation, or no response at all.

Movement actors will make their strategic choices on the basis of their appreciation of the specific chances of reform and threat, and the specific risks of repression and facilitation they face. As Gamson and Meyer (1996: 283) suggest, the definition of opportunity, that is, the appreciation of the concrete situation, is typically highly contentious within a social movement and they suggest that "we focus on the process of defining opportunity and how it works." The debates within movements typically turn on questions of "relative opportunity" for different courses of action. This debate is missed, Gamson and Meyer (1996: 284) point out, when we speak of opportunity for the movement as a whole. Opportunity may shift in favor of some specific part of the movement, the radicals for example, and may result in a radicalization of the movement as a whole. According to the political process approach, however, the "relative opportunities" are to a large extent determined by the configuration of actors and the structural context. The outcome of the internal debates of the movements in other words is constrained by the larger political context, which the strategically oriented movement actors will not fail to take into account in their deliberations.

Once the interaction between the movement and its antagonists is set in motion, it will contribute to the modification of its larger political context: above all, episodes of contentious interaction are likely to modify the relevant configuration of actors and, thus, to change the specific opportunities for future options for collective action. McAdam et al. (2001) introduce a number of mechanisms that focus on the modification of the configuration of actors in the course of the interaction sequence. Such mechanisms may serve to facilitate further movement action: thus "brokerage" contributes to the linking of different actors or sites, that is, to the strengthening of supportive alliances; "social appropriation" is a process by which movement activists appropriate existing organizations for their own purposes; "object shifts" may unite previously unrelated movement actors around a common adversary; "identity shifts" may bring in new groups into the movement; "certification" by supportive actors may serve to enhance the salience and legitimacy of movement actors. Analogous processes may contribute to the strengthening of the movement's adversaries and, thus, increase the risks for further movement action. In addition, the movement's alliance may be weakened by unfavorable "object" and "identity shifts" among its own ranks, by focused attemps at "decertification," by failed attempts at "brokerage" and, of course, by repressive measures more generally.

SELECTED RESULTS

So far, I have laid out the elements of the general framework of the political process approach. Building theories and models on the basis of these elements implies that we specify the variables to be explained. Which aspects of the political context are theoretically important will depend on the aspect of popular contention we wish to explain (McAdam 1996: 29–31): the emergence, timing, and rhythm of contentious actions, the levels and forms they take, or the levels and forms of their success. Moreover, we should distinguish theories according to the level of analysis they address: theories may focus on the microlevel of single contentious episodes (such as the campaign of the peace movement against cruise missiles), the mesolevel of specific movements or parts of the social movement sector (such as the new social movements), or on the macrolevel of the entire social movement sector or such all-encompassing phenomena as protest cycles or revolutions. Combining the two criteria, we arrive at a straightforward classification of phenomena to be explained in the framework of the political process approach.

There are basically two designs to test the theory: longitudinal case studies and cross-sectional comparisons at different levels (local, regional, national, or international) of the political governance structure (McAdam et al. 1996: 17). Longitudinal designs are particularly suited to the study of the concrete opportunities within an interaction context, while cross-sectional designs are particularly effective for the analysis of the impact of the structural context.

The Emergence of Popular Contention

Aspects of the political context have above all been used to account for the emergence of popular contention. A famous example of the kind of reasoning involved here is Skocpol's (1979) book on states and social revolutions. At the origin of the three social revolutions she studied, Skocpol finds a conjunction of two key factors: a political crisis and agrarian sociopolitical structures (i.e., a given form of national cleavage structures) that gave rise to widespread peasant discontent and facilitated insurrections against landlords. The political crisis is brought about by the intensification of international pressure (shifts in the geopolitical context structure) that leads to a military and fiscal crisis of the state (institutional strain and even breakdown), which in turn gives rise to profound divisions in the ruling elites over how to respond to the state's declining effectiveness and fiscal problems (realignments in the configuration of actors). The peasant revolts become uncontrollable at the moment, where regime defections become widespread, where the elite loses its cohesion and is no longer capable of exercising its social control (by repressive measures). Goldstone (1998) gives an analogous account of the breakdown of the communist regime in the former Soviet Union. According to this account, the Soviet Union in the 1980s revealed all the major trends typical of a society headed for revolution: a weakening state hamstrung by economic and political failures; an elite sharply divided over how to respond to the state's problems and with a vast number of educated and talented but frustrated aspirants to elite positions who had come to reject the legitimacy of the leadership and the system that sustained it; and a population suffering marked declines in living standards and readily mobilized to support elites seeking radical change.

Skocpol (1979: 154) claims to have identified the sufficient causes of social revolutionary situations. But I would insist that the various elements of the political context define only a set of necessary conditions for the emergence of contention – its "opportunity set." The transformation of a potentially explosive situation into the unfolding of the events within the interaction context is historically contingent, and, therefore, quite unpredictable. "Precipitating factors," "contingent" or "catalyzing" events, and "suddenly imposed grievances" play a crucial role in such a transformation (Rucht 1998: 126). In addition to the "opportunity set," the unfolding of the events crucially depends on the second filter mentioned by Elster – the choices made by actors on the basis of their preferences (see also Dunn 1985: 86).

Thus the events leading up to the French Revolution were set in motion by the king's move to invite the population to submit its grievances to the authorities (*cahiers de doléances*) – a "window of opportunity" with quite unanticipated consequences. The death of Franco touched off the transition to democracy in Spain – a somewhat more predictable outcome. The incident with Rosa Parks launched the Montgomery Bus Boycott, which stood at the beginning of the civil rights movement. The declaration of the state of emergency in Kenya in 1952 resulted in the arrest of nationalist leader Jomo Kenyata and 145 other Kenyan political figures, which unleashed the Mau Mau revolt. The assassination of opposition leader Benigno Aquino was the origin of the Philippines "Yellow Revolution." The accidents at Three Mile Island and Chernobyl were crucial for the mobilization of the antinuclear movement. The contingency of the precipitating event may vary from one occasion to the other. As McAdam et al. (2001: 147) observe, "the catalytic event is often neither accidental, nor the primordial starting point of the episode," but the culmination of a longstanding conflict. To the extent that the buildup of a political conflict systematically increases the opportunity for mobilization, we are more likely to be able to account for the unfolding of the subsequent contentious episodes.

The Level and Form of Mobilization

The political opportunity structures are ideally suited to the explanation of the volume and form of popular contention. A number of longitudinal and cross-sectional studies illustrate its usefulness for the explanation of these aspects of collective action. Tilly's (1995) longitudinal study of the change in the action repertoire of British protest, which introduced this chapter, provides an example of how a shift in the institutional opportunity structure can bring about a shift in the repertoire of popular protest. The study of the institutional origins of civic voluntarism in the US by Skocpol et al. (2000) is another example with a longitudinal design. This example shows the strong impact of the widely understood and prestigious model of the US Constitution on cross-local organization building in an era when popular mobilization made sense for all kinds of purposes: the civic organizations that came to dominate American civic life were vast and interlocking membership associations, organized along the lines of the federal political system, with local units loosely linked together in state branches, and these in turn sending representatives to national bodies.

A third example of the longitudinal type is provided by Koopmans' study (1993, 1995) of the dynamics of protest waves in Germany. It shows how the action repertoire of popular contention typically changes across protest waves, as a result of the shifting opportunities facing movement actors in the interaction context. As Koopmans explains, initially, newly mobilizing movements depend on novelty. Confrontational protests, like occupations, sit-ins, and blockades are attracting media attention, although the movement does not yet have a large mobilizing capacity. This initial strategic model is, however, inherently unstable. Tactical innovations lose their ability to surprise and to attract media attention, and authorities learn to deal with such actions more effectively. Social movements must compensate the loss of novelty by increased numbers or increased militancy – the two basic alternative strategic options. The choice of a strategy to increase numbers is favored if strong allies are available. Support from allies, however, has its price: it is likely to induce the movement to moderate its strategies and goals, which may lead to friction with its more radical activists who will resort to greater militancy to make themselves heard. The bifurcated reactions by the authorities – repression of radicals and concessions to moderates – are likely to deepen the split between moderates and radicals. At least partially satisfied by the concessions they obtained, the moderates tend to demobilize, while the increasingly isolated radicals find it difficult to obtain some additional measure of success. With the decline of the overall level of the movement's mobilization, the action repertoire, therefore, tends to radicalize and the internal conflict tends to increase. As long as the prospects for success are favorable, different factions may find a common ground, or at least agree to "peaceful co-existence." Once things go wrong, however, internal conflict substantially weakens a movement. This happened, as Koopmans (1992: 201–6) argues, to the German peace movement after the government decided to deploy cruise and Pershing missiles in 1983.

Eisinger's (1973) original article provides a first example of a comparative design. He compared protest across American cities and was able to show that protest occurs most frequently in cities whose structure of political opportunities reflects a mix of open and closed characteristics. His finding of a curvilinear relationship between opportunities and levels of protest has been replicated by several later studies. Protest is not likely to occur in extremely closed (repressive) or extremely open (facilitative) systems. Eisinger's (1973: 15) explanation of the curvilinear relationship is still couched in the language of the classic theory: "Protest occurs in a mixed system because the pace of change does not keep up with expectations, even though change is occurring." This is the language of "rising expectations" typical of the classic deprivation theory. More in line with the political process approach, I would rather argue with strategic considerations: in an extremely open system, reform is forthcoming anyway – that is, the social movement actors do not need to mobilize; while in an extremely closed system, reform is never forthcoming and repression is so great that movement actors do not have any opportunity to mobilize or to form in the first place.

Amenta and Zylan (1991) analyze the Townsend movement by comparing its level of mobilization across the US states. The Townsend movement was promoting an Old Age Pension Plan for all Americans 60 years of age and older. It started out in the Depression and declined in World War II. The cross-sectional analysis of the two authors confirms that the movement flourished, where it could count on strong movement allies (the labor movement) and on strong partisan allies (the Democrats), who had gained their power in nontraditional, competitive party systems (traditional, patronage-based Democratic parties did not support them). They also show in some detail how state institutions and bureaucratic forces selectively promoted the movement: the extension of voting rights influenced where the movement mounted a challenge, and a state bureaucracy with a strong capacity in the social policy domain contributed to the promotion of the movement.

In a cross-national study of four Western European countries, Koopmans and Kriesi (1995: 46) show that the level and the form of collective action vary quite closely as a function of the openness of the political system of the respective countries. They found that the openness of the Swiss system facilitates the mobilization for collective action. The existence of direct-democratic institutions in particular invites the citizens to mobilize collectively. At the same time, the openness of the system and the availability of conventional channels of protest, such as the direct-democratic channels, has a strong moderating effect on the strategic choice of the Swiss movement actors. They have learnt to use the available direct-democratic instruments, and they continue to use them even if they are not very successful in doing so (Epple 1988). By contrast, the relative closure of the French system provides little facilitation for the mobilization by collective actors, which not only dampens the level of mobilization, but also contributes to the radicalization of the movements' action repertoires.

Outcomes

Outcomes are still less often studied than the emergence and mobilization of social movements. There is, however, one movement whose success has frequently been the object of studies with a political process perspective – the antinuclear movement. It provides an excellent illustration of how the different aspects of the political context have been used to explain a movement's outcomes. Kitschelt's

(1986) influential paper has set the stage. He put the accent on the structural element and compared the movement's impacts in four countries with quite distinct political opportunity structures – Germany, France, Sweden, and the US. Kitschelt (1986: 72) made the general point that "high mobilization does not necessarily lead to profound impacts if the political opportunity structures are not conducive to change. Conversely, lower mobilization may have a disproportionate impact owing to properties of the political opportunity structure." More specifically, he argued that in Germany, Sweden, and the US, where political opportunity structures were conducive to popular participation, greater responsiveness to the antinuclear opposition invariably led to extremely tight and often changing safety regulations (1986: 79). Once formulated, these new safety standards allowed opponents to intervene to insist that they be complied with. Construction delays were the result, especially in the US and Germany – the two countries with fragmented implementation structures. Much shorter delays were typical of France and Sweden, where tight implementation procedures offered few opportunities for outside intervention. In Sweden, he conceded, nuclear policy was ultimately changed, not by disrupting the policy implementation process, but by the shifting electoral fortunes of major parties and changes in government.

Other authors have added to this account and modified it, without, however, fundamentally changing its basic message. Joppke (1993: 199), who compares the German and the US case, closely follows Kitschelt's lead, but takes issue with his "overly rigid and static view of the political opportunity structures" and puts more weight on short-term changes. While accepting, for example, Kitschelt's general assessment of the German state, he insists that the development of the antinuclear conflict in Germany, that is, the polarization between the emergent antinuclear movement and the state, could not be divorced from the fact that the Social-democratic Party was the ruling party at the time.

Rucht (1994) also agrees with Kitschelt's general assessment of the movement's policy impact in France, Germany, and the US. In his attempt to explain these differences, he adds other elements to arrive at a more complex explanatory framework. Thus, with respect to the French movement's lack of substantive success, he relies on the same factors as Kitschelt (unfavorable opportunity structures) but adds the lack of allies and the absence of resonance of major contingent events), which, incidentally, may also be a result of the closed French political opportunity structure (see Duyvendak and Koopmans 1995), as well as the self-reinforcing negative effects of contingent events during mobilization episodes (Rucht 1994: 497–9). With regard to the remaining two cases, he attributes the difference in timing of the respective movement's success – earlier in the US than in Germany – to some extent to the configuration of power: the early support by powerful allies was crucial for the early success in the US. In addition, he introduces a factor more closely linked to a political-economy perspective (see also Midttun and Rucht 1994: 389–96): the stronger market-orientation of the US energy industry rapidly gave cost-benefit considerations greater weight than in Germany, where the energy industry remained heavily linked to state interest, considerations that undermined the nuclear power industry's position. He also adds a number of other political factors: the change in public opinion, the increasing support within the public administration, and last but not least, the increasingly well-organized resistance by the movement (Rucht 1994: 493–7).

Jasper (1990), to mention yet another contributor to this debate, also compares the nuclear policy in three of Kitschelt's four countries – France, Sweden, and the United States. But he clearly disagrees with his general assessment of the movement's impact (269): according to Jasper, none of the movements had a strong effect on nuclear power in its country. He concedes that the movements – together with the oil crisis – put energy policy on the agenda of politicians and the media. But the policy outcomes were, according to his interpretation, primarily influenced by political struggles within the state and within each state organization. On the one hand, he puts great weight on individual discretion, personal skills, individual and collective beliefs and cultural models of politicians and bureaucrats as well as on the flexibility of seemingly stable structures. On the other hand, he insists on the long-term consequences of policy decisions once they have been taken. According to his account, the oil crisis constituted a kind of critical juncture in the domain of energy policy. Politicians and bureaucrats in the three countries all had to make decisive choices in the three years following this crisis. As a function of the political struggles, the choices made differed considerably from one country to the other, with important consequences for the nuclear power industry in the years to come.

Jasper's interpretation is particularly interesting: while he downplays the role of the movement in these political struggles, the details he provides about them actually indicate its importance, and, what is more, they show that the movement's substantive impact was a function of the relative institutional openness and of the actors' configuration in a given context. Consider his presentation of the Swedish case. What made the Swedish situation different from other countries in the mid-seventies was its party system – a result of the particular Swedish cleavage structure and the proportional electoral system. The Swedish Center Party – one of the three major bourgeois parties – provided a home for antinuclear protest in a way unavailable in the other countries. Its composition, ideology, and history predisposed it to moral ecologism and to leaders like Fälldin, who, after the elections of 1976, became the first non-Social Democratic Prime Minister in many years. As Jasper notes, it was the antinuclear, ecological stand that had made the Center Party the largest of the three center-right coalition partners and Fälldin the coalition's prime minister. Jasper also notes (1990: 226) that the Social Democrats – Sweden's hegemonic party – saw nuclear energy as the main reason why they were out of office. Their leader then announced that he supported a national referendum to be held on the question of nuclear energy – another indication of the remarkable openness of the Swedish political system. Jasper sees the way the referendum was constructed as "a small victory for the same bueaucrats who had transformed Fälldin's political and moral attack on nuclear energy into a narrow technical question about rock formations" (229). But he also observes that the pro-nuclear positions in the referendum (held in 1980) did not differ very much in substance from the antinuclear ones: they all foresaw a gradual phase-out of nuclear power plants, although at different speeds. Jasper concludes (228) that "in a system that insists on compromise (as opposed to stalemate, as the United States tolerates) moralists often win." In other words, the antinuclear moralists won, because they were largely supported by the institutional structure, the prevailing cultural models, and the configuration of power in the Swedish system. The fact that the struggle about nuclear energy in Sweden took place mainly within the institutional framework and not out in the streets does, however, not imply, as Jasper seems to suggest, that the movement was contributing little to the eventual phasing out of nuclear energy. Much to the contrary, this is another illustration of the powerful effect the political context can have not only on the substantive policy impact of a popular challenge, but also on the ways the challenge is articulated and processed by the political system in question.

CONCLUSION

Let me conclude with three remarks concerning the future perspectives of the political process approach. First of all, this approach has so far mainly been applied to the national political contexts of Western liberal democracies, and to social revolutions of the past. However, its general framework is by no means restricted to the analysis of these contexts. It holds out much promise for the analysis of claims-making in nondemocratic political contexts, and for the analysis of the increasingly important popular contention at the inter-, supra-, or transnational level (McAdam 1998). The contributions to della Porta et al. (1999) provide a general introduction to an extension of the approach to the global level. The contributions united by Imig and Tarrow (2001) show for Europe in particular that the existence of a supranational opportunity structure is starting to have an impact on European claims-making. Tarrow (2001: 237) summarizes the central finding of these contributions: "Europeans are beginning to recognize more and more that the sources of many of their claims – especially occupational ones – are increasingly found in Europe's integrated market and institutions. And in some cases, they are beginning to organize themselves transnationally." The development of the European Union as a "crossterritorial, intergovernmental, and multilevel" polity "opens opportunities for coalitions of actors and states to formulate common positions and overcome their diversity and dispersion to exploit its political opportunities" (243–4).

Second, the political process approach is of particular interest for the integration of fields of study that have been leading separate academic lives. This is illustrated by the recent joint effort by McAdam et al. (2001) who elaborated the general framework of this approach to apply it to such diverse phenomena as revolution, democratization, nationalism, or social movements. I believe that the approach is especially well suited for the integration of the study of social movements and public policy analysis. Meyer and Tarrow (1998: 23–4) have observed some mechanisms contributing to the institutionalization of contemporary protest politics in liberal democracies: social movement activists have learnt to employ conventional and unconventional collective actions; police practices increasingly encourage the routinization of contention; the tactics used by movement organizations and those used by more institutionalized groups increasingly overlap. Such mechanisms at the same time contribute to the increasing integration of social movement actors into the policymaking process and to the adoption of social movement strategies by routine participants in the policymaking process. Moreover, the attention social movement scholars increasingly pay to the outcomes produced by popular claims-making and contention (Giugni 1998; Giugni et al. 1998, 1999) also brings them closer to the analysis of public policymaking, which in turn, enhances the usefulness of the political process approach.

My final remark concerns the role of the media, public space, and public opinion for the political process approach. As Gamson and Meyer (1996: 287) point out, mass media are another component of political opportunity structure – a component that has both structural and dynamic elements. The structure of the media and the way they operate (their norms and practices) affect the opportunities and constraints under which movements operate. Movement actors typically attempt to attract the attention of the media for their concerns by staging "protest events." The media reports about these events are expected to create public controversy and reinforce the position of sponsors of the movement's concerns within the policymaking domain (Gamson 1988: 228; Gamson et al. 1992: 383; Hamdan 2000: 72). Indirectly, the goal of the movement's action is to split the policymaking community and to reinforce the opposition within the elite. This crucial mechanism linking popular contention and policymaking has not been effectively integrated into the general framework presented in this chapter. Extending this framework in such a way that it accommodates the role of the media and the public space will be crucial for its continued relevance in a society, where politics are increasingly focused on the public space.

Notes

1 Schelling (1984: 206) calls this "cheap theory," because one only makes minimal assumptions about the actor's choice behavior.
2 There is also a "functional model" of realignment, which suggests that socioeconomic trends are diminishing the relevance of parties for the political process and individual citizens, leading to a continuing pattern of partisan de-alignment.

References

Amenta, Edwin, and Yvonne Zylan (1991) It Happened Here: Political Opportunity, the New Institutionalism, and the Townsend Movement. *American Sociological Review*, 56 (4), 250–65.

Aya, Rod (1990) *Rethinking Revolutions and Collective Violence: Studies on Concept, Theory, and Method*. Amsterdam: Het Spinhuis.

Badie, Bertrand, and Pierre Birnbaum (1979) *La sociologie de l'Etat*. Paris: Grasset.

Banaszak, Lee A. (1996) *Why Movements Succeed or Fail: Opportunity, Culture and the Struggle for Women's Suffrage*. Princeton, NJ: Princeton University Press.

Bartolini, Stefano (2000) *The Political Mobilization of the European Left, 1860–1980: The Class Cleavage*. Cambridge: Cambridge University Press.

Bartolini, Stefano, and Peter Mair (1990) *Identity, Competition, and Electoral Availability: The Stability of European Electorates, 1885–1985*. Cambridge: Cambridge University Press.

Baumgartner, Frank R., and Bryan D. Jones (1993) *Agendas and Instability in American Politics*. Chicago: University of Chicago Press.

Birnbaum, Pierre (1985) *States and Collective Action: The European Experience*. Cambridge: Cambridge University Press.

Brand, Karl-Werner (1985) Vergleichendes Resümee. In Karl-Werner Brand (ed.), *Neue soziale Bewegungen in Westeuropa und den USA: Ein internationaler Vergleich*. Frankfurt am Main: Campus, 306–34.

Christin, Olivier (1997) *La paix de religion: l'autonomisation de la raison politique au XVIe siècle*. Paris: Editions du Seuil.

Cohen, Jean L. (1985) Strategy and Identity: New Theoretical Paradigms and Contemporary Social Movements. *Social Research*, 52, 663–716.

della Porta, Donatella (1996) Social Movements and the State: Thoughts on the Policing of Protest. In Doug McAdam, John D. McCarthy, and Mayer N. Zald (eds.), *Comparative Perspectives on Social Movements: Political Opportunities, Mobilizing Structures, and Cultural Framings*. Cambridge: Cambridge University Press, 62–92.

della Porta, Donatella, and Hanspeter Kriesi (1999) Social Movements in a Globalizing World: An Introduction. In Donatella della Porta, Hanspeter Kriesi, and Dieter Rucht (eds.), *Social Movements in a Globalizing World*. London: Macmillan, 2–22.

della Porta, Donatella, Hanspeter Kriesi, and Dieter Rucht (eds.) (1999) *Social Movements in a Globalizing World*. London: Macmillan.

Dunn, John (1985) *Rethinking Modern Political Theory*. Cambridge: Cambridge University Press.

Duyvendak, Jan Willem, and Marco G. Giugni (1995) Social Movement Types and Policy Domain. In Hanspeter Kriesi, Ruud Koopmans, Jan Willem Duyvendak, and Marco G. Giugni (eds.), *New Social Movements in Western Europe: A Comparative Analysis*. Minneapolis: University of Minnesota Press, 82–110.

Duyvendak, Jan Willem, and Ruud Koopmans (1995) The Political Construction of the Nuclear Energy Issue. In Hanspeter Kriesi, Ruud Koopmans, Jan Willem Duyvendak, and Marco G. Giugni (eds.), *New Social Movements in Western Europe: A Comparative Analysis*. Minneapolis: University of Minnesota Press, 145–64.

Eisinger, Peter K. (1973) The Conditions of Protest Behavior in American Cities. *American Political Science Review*, 67, 11–28.

Elster, Jon (1989) *Nuts and Bolts for the Social Sciences*. Cambridge: Cambridge University Press.

Epple, Ruedi (1988) *Friedensbewegung und direkte Demokratie in der Schweiz*. Frankfurt am Main: Haag & Herchen.

Flanagan, Scott C., and Russell J. Dalton (1984) Parties under Stress: Realignment and Dealignment in Advanced Industrial Societies. *West European Politics*, 7 (1), 7–23.

Gallie, Duncan (1983) *Social Inequality and Class Radicalism in France and Britain*. Cambridge: Cambridge University Press.

Gamson, William A. (1988) Political Discourse and Collective Action. In Bert Klandermans, Hanspeter Kriesi, and Sidney Tarrow (eds.), *From Structure to Action: Comparing Social Movement Research across Cultures*. Greenwich, CT: JAI, 219–44.

Gamson, William A., and David S. Meyer (1996) Framing Political Opportunity. In Doug McAdam, John D. McCarthy, and Mayer N. Zald (eds.), *Comparative Perspectives on Social Movements: Political Opportunities, Mobilizing Structures, and Cultural Framings*. Cambridge: Cambridge University Press, 275–90.

Gamson, William A., David Croteau, William Hoynes, and Theodore Sasson (1992) Media Images and the Social Construction of Reality. *Annual Review of Sociology*, 18, 373–93.

Giugni, Marco G. (1998) Was it Worth the Effort? The Outcomes and Consequences of Social Movements. *Annual Review of Sociology*, 98, 171–93.

Giugni, Marco G., Doug McAdam, and Charles Tilly (eds.) (1998) *From Contention to Democracy*. Boulder, CO: Rowman & Littlefield.

——(eds.) (1999) *How Social Movements Matter*. Minneapolis: University of Minnesota Press.

Goldstone, Jack A. (1998) Theories of Revolution, Elite Crisis, and the Transformation of the U.S.S.R.. In Mattei Dogan and John Higley (eds.), *Elites, Crises, and the Origins of Regimes*. Boulder, CO: Rowman and Littlefield.

Goodwin, Jeff, and James M. Jasper (1999) Caught in a Winding, Snarling Vine: The Structural Bias of Political Process Theory. *Sociological Forum*, 14 (1), 27–92.

Hamdan, Fouad (2000) Aufdecken und Konfrontieren: NGO-Kommunikation am Beispiel Greenpeace. *Forschungsjournal NSB*, 13 (3), 69–74.

Hunt, Scott A., Robert D. Benford, and David A. Snow (1994) Identity Fields: Framing Processes and the Social Construction of Movement Identities. In Enrique Laraña, Hank Johnston, and Joseph R. Gusfield (eds.), *New Social Movements: From Ideology to Identity*. Philadelphia, PA: Temple University Press, 185–208.

Imig, Doug, and Sidney Tarrow (eds.) (2001) *Contentious Europeans: Protest and Politics in an Emerging Polity*. Boulder, CO: Rowman & Littlefield.

Jasper, James M. (1990) *Nuclear Politics: Energy and the State in the United States, Sweden, and France*. Princeton, NJ: Princeton University Press.

Joppke, Christian (1993) *Mobilizing against Nuclear Energy: A Comparison of Germany and the United States*. Berkeley: University of California Press.

Kingdon, John W. (1984) *Agendas, Alternatives, and Public Policies*. Boston: Little, Brown.

Kitschelt, Herbert (1986) Political Opportunity Structures and Political Protest: Anti-Nuclear Movements in Four Democracies. *British Journal of Political Science*, 16, 57–85.

Koopmans, Ruud (1992) *Democracy from Below: New Social Movements and the Political System in West Germany*. Boulder, CO: Westview.

——(1993) The Dynamics of Protest Waves: West Germany, 1965 to 1989. *American Sociological Review*, 58 (5), 637–58.

——(1995) The Dynamics of Protest Waves. In Hanspeter Kriesi, Ruud Koopmans, Jan Willem Duyvendak, and Marco G. Giugni (eds.), *New Social Movements in Western Europe: A Comparative Analysis*. Minneapolis: University of Minnesota Press, 111–42.

——(1999) Political. Opportunity. Structure: Some Splitting to Balance the Lumping. *Sociological Forum*, 14 (1), 93–105.

Koopmans, Ruud, and Hanspeter Kriesi (1995) Institutional Structures and Prevailing Strategies. In Hanspeter Kriesi, Ruud Koopmans, Jan Willem Duyvendak, and Marco G. Giugni (eds.), *New Social Movements in Western Europe: A Comparative Analysis*. Minneapolis: University of Minnesota Press, 26–52.

Koopmans, Ruud, and Paul Statham (1999) Ethnic and Civic Conceptions of Nationhood and the Differential Success of the Extreme Right in Germany and Italy. In Marco G. Giugni, Doug McAdam, and Charles Tilly (eds.), *How Social Movements Matter*. Minneapolis: University of Minnesota Press, 225–52.

Krasner, Stephen D. (1978) United States Commercial and Monetary Policy: Unraveling the Paradox of External Strength and Internal Weakness. In Peter J. Katzenstein (ed.), *Between Power and Plenty*. Madison: University of Wisconsin Press, 51–88.

Kriesi, Hanspeter (1989) The Political Opportunity Structure of the Dutch Peace Movement. *West European Politics*, 12, 295–312.

——(1995a) Alliance Structures. In Hanspeter Kriesi, Ruud Koopmans, Jan Willem Duyvendak, and Marco G. Giugni (eds.), *New Social Movements in Western Europe: A Comparative Analysis*. Minneapolis: University of Minnesota Press, 53–81.

——(1995b) The Political Opportunity Structure of New Social Movements: Its Impact on their Mobilization. In J. Craig Jenkins and Bert Klandermans (eds.), *The Politics of Social Protest: Comparative Perspectives on States and Social Movements*. Minneapolis: University of Minnesota Press, 167–98.

——(1996) The Organizational Structure of New Social Movements in a Political Context. In Doug McAdam, John D. McCarthy, and Mayer N. Zald (eds.), *Comparative Perspectives on Social Movements: Political Opportunities, Mobilizing Structures, and Cultural Framings*. Cambridge : Cambridge University Press, 152–84.

Kriesi, Hanspeter, and Jan Willem Duyvendak (1995) National Cleavage Structures. In Hanspeter Kriesi, Ruud Koopmans, Jan Willem Duyvendak, and Marco G. Giugni (eds.),

New Social Movements in Western Europe: A Comparative Analysis. Minneapolis: University of Minnesota Press, 3–25.

Kriesi, Hanspeter, and Marco G. Giugni (1995) Introduction. In Hanspeter Kriesi, Ruud Koopmans, Jan Willem Duyvendak, and Marco G. Giugni (eds.), *New Social Movements in Western Europe: A Comparative Analysis*. Minneapolis: University of Minnesota Press, ix–xxvi.

Kriesi, Hanspeter, Ruud Koopmans, Jan Willem Duyvendak, and Marco G. Giugni (eds.) (1995) *New Social Movements in Western Europe: A Comparative Analysis*. Minneapolis: University of Minnesota Press.

Lehmbruch, Gerhard (1996) Die korporative Verhandlungsdemokratie in Westmitteleuropa. *Revue suisse de science politique*, 2 (4), 19–40.

—— (1998) Negotiated Democracy, Consociationalism and Corporatism in German Politics: The Legacy of the Westphalian Peace. Paper presented at Harvard University, Center for European Studies.

Lijphart, Arend (1999) *Patterns of Democracy*. New Haven: Yale University Press.

Lipset, Seymour M., and Stein Rokkan (1967) Cleavage Structures, Party Systems, and Voter Alignments: An Introduction. In Seymour M. Lipset and Stein Rokkan (eds.), *Party Systems and Voter Alignments: Cross-National Perspectives*. New York: Free Press, 1–64.

McAdam, Doug (1982) *Political Process and the Development of Black Insurgency, 1930–1970*. Chicago: University of Chicago Press.

—— (1996) Conceptual Origins, Current Problems, Future Directions. In Doug McAdam, John D. McCarthy, and Mayer N. Zald (eds.), *Comparative Perspectives on Social Movements: Political Opportunities, Mobilizing Structures, and Cultural Framings*. Cambridge: Cambridge University Press, 23–40.

—— (1998) Conclusion: The Future of Social Movements. In Marco G. Giugni, Doug McAdam, and Charles Tilly (eds.) (1998) *From Contention to Democracy*. Boulder, CO: Rowman & Littlefield, 229–45.

McAdam, Doug, John D. McCarthy, and Mayer N. Zald (1996) Introduction: Opportunities, Mobilizing Structures, and Framing Processes. In *Comparative Perspectives on Social Movements: Political Opportunities, Mobilizing Structures, and Cultural Framings*. Cambridge: Cambridge University Press, 1–20.

McAdam, Doug, Sidney Tarrow, and Charles Tilly (2001) *Dynamics of Contention*. Cambridge: Cambridge University Press.

McCammon, Holly J., Karen E. Campbell, Ellen M. Granberg, and Christine Mowery (2002) How Movements Win: Gendered Opportunity Structures and U.S. Women's Movements, 1866 to 1919. *American Sociological Review*, 66 (1), 49–70.

Martin, Pierre (2000) *Comprendre les évolutions électorales: La théorie des réalignements revisitée*. Paris: Presses de sciences politiques.

Meyer, David S., and Sidney Tarrow (1998) A Movement Society: Contentious Politics for a New Century. In David S. Meyer and Sidney Tarrow (eds.), *The Social Movement Society: Contentious Politics for a New Century*. Boulder, CO: Rowman & Littlefield, 1–28.

Midttun, Atle, and Dieter Rucht (1994) Comparing Policy Outcomes of Conflicts over Nuclear Power: Description and Explanation. In Helena Flam (ed.), *States and Anti-Nuclear Movements*. Edinburgh: Edinburgh University Press, 383-415.

Minkoff, Debra C. (1995) *Organizing for Equality: The Evolution of Women's and Racial-Ethnic Organizations in America, 1955–1985*. New Brunswick, NJ: Rutgers University Press.

—— (1997) The Sequencing of Social Movements. *American Sociological Review*, 62 (5), 779–99.

Ostrom, Elinor (1999) Institutional Rational Choice: An Assessment of the Institutional Analysis and Development Framework. In Paul A. Sabatier (ed.), *Theories of the Policy Process*. Boulder, CO: Westview, 35–72.

Raschke, Joachim (1985) *Soziale Bewegungen: Ein historisch-systematischer Grundriss.* Frankfurt: Campus.

Rucht, Dieter (1988) Themes, Logics, and Arenas of Social Movements: A Structural Approach. In Bert Klandermans, Hanspeter Kriesi, and Sidney Tarrow (eds.), *From Structure to Action: Social Movement Participation across Cultures.* Greenwich, CT: JAI, 305–28.

——(1994) *Modernisierung und neue soziale Bewegungen.* Frankfurt am Main: Campus.

——(1998) Komplexe Phänomene – komplexe Erklärungen: Die politischen Gelegenheitsstrukturen der neuen sozialen Bewegungen in der Bundesrepublik. In Kai-Uwe Hellmann and Ruud Koopmans (eds.), *Paradigmen der Bewegungsforschung.* Opladen: Westdeutscher Verlag, 109–30.

Sabatier, Paul A., and Hank C. Jenkins-Smith (1999) The Advocacy Coalition Framework: An Assessment. In Paul A. Sabatier (ed.), *Theories of the Policy Process.* Boulder, CO: Westview, 117–66.

Sartori, Giovanni (1968) The Sociology of Parties: A Critical Review. In Otto Stammer (ed.), *Party Systems, Party Organizations and the Politics of the New Masses.* Berlin: Institut für Wissenschaft an der Freien Universität, 150–82.

——(1991) Comparing and Miscomparing. *Journal of Theoretical Politics,* 3 (3), 243–57.

Scharpf, Fritz W. (1997) *Games Real Actors Play: Actor-Centered Institutionalism in Policy Research.* Boulder, CO: Westview.

Schelling, Thomas C. (1984) *Choice and Consequence: Perspectives of an Errant Economist.* Cambridge, MA: Harvard University Press.

Schlager, Edella (1999) A Comparison of Frameworks, Theories, and Models of Policy Processes. In Paul A. Sabatier (ed.), *Theories of the Policy Process.* Boulder, CO: Westview, 233–60.

Skocpol, Theda (1979) *States and Social Revolution: A Comparative Analysis of France, Russia and China.* Cambridge: Cambridge University Press.

Skocpol, Theda, Marshall Ganz, and Ziad Munso (2000) A Nation of Organizers: The Institutional Origins of Civic Voluntarism in the United States. *American Political Science Review,* 94 (3), 527–46.

Soule, Sarah A., Doug McAdam, John McCarthy, and Yang Su (1999) Protest Events: Cause or Consequence of State Action? The U.S. Women's Movement and Federal Congressional Activities, 1956–1979. *Mobilization,* 4 (2), 239–55.

Tarrow, Sidney (1994) *Power in Movement: Social Movements, Collective Action and Politics.* Cambridge: Cambridge University Press.

——(2001) Contentious Politics in a Composite Polity. In Doug Imig and Sidney Tarrow (eds.), *Contentious Europeans: Protest and Politics in an Emerging Polity.* Boulder, CO: Rowman & Littlefield, 233–51.

Tilly, Charles (1978) *From Mobilization to Revolution.* Reading, MA: Addison-Wesley.

——(1995) *Popular Contention in Great Britain. 1758–1834.* Cambridge, MA: Harvard University Press.

Wolfsfeld, Gadi (1997) *Media and Political Conflict: News from the Middle East.* Cambridge: Cambridge University Press.

5

The Cultural Contexts of Collective Action: Constraints, Opportunities, and the Symbolic Life of Social Movements

Rhys H. Williams

That the study of social movements and collective action in the US took a "cultural turn" beginning in the 1980s is not news. One can chart culture's popularity in the recent scholarly literature (e.g., Laraña et al. 1994; Darnovsky et al. 1995; Johnston and Klandermans 1995), but in 2003 development is approaching two decades old. Even as the "resource mobilization" approach was establishing itself as the dominant theoretical lens for studying social movements (e.g., Jenkins 1983; Zald and McCarthy 1987), and "political process" models were amending the conception of "structure" in movements (e.g., McAdam 1982; Morris 1984), scholars were developing and refining approaches to understanding culture and social movements. Several chapters in this volume report on the fruits of this engagement – or perhaps "re-engagement" – with culture and collective action. The topics covered include such concepts as "framing," and "collective identity," or the study of the roles of emotions in movement actions and the resulting cultural consequences from activism. This chapter contributes to the consideration of culture by making an argument for increased attention to the "cultural environment" in which movements occur and how that environment shapes collective action. This involves a de-centering of the individual social movement as the level of analysis, and increased attention to how the availability of legitimated cultural resources channels and often constrains movement activity. I begin with a review of the general cultural turn in the study of social movements.

The Recent Cultural Turn in the Study of Social Movements

There is a general consensus that the cultural turn has comprised two relatively distinct approaches.[1] One was the interpretation of "new social movement (NSM) theory" that North American scholars drew from Western European scholars such as Habermas (1981), Melucci (1985, 1989), and Offe (1985); a good overview of this perspective is in Cohen (1985). As a whole, new social movements scholarship emerged as a response to and interpretation of contemporary European social movements, such as the Greens, that were focused on cultural, moral, and identity issues, rather than on economic distribution. Much postwar European sociology was more influenced by Marxist theory than was its American counterpart; as such, it had often assumed that collective action came out of material interests and that collective actors were economic classes. "The social movement," for many European scholars, was the labor-socialist movement. By contrast, NSMs were often thought to be more like "moral crusades" (see Eder 1985; Scott 1990), and as such appeared as a new phenomenon that needed to be theorized distinctly for the historical moment in which they occurred. Thus the cultural component of new social movement theory had to do with the *content* of movement ideology, the *concerns motivating activists*, and the *arena* in which collective action was focused – that is, cultural understandings, norms, and identities rather than material interests and economic distribution. New social movement theory was generally macro in orientation, and retained the traditional Marxian concern with articulating the ways in which societal infrastructures produced and are reflected by culture and action.[2]

New social movement theory garnered attention, support, and critique from scholars. Many North American critics, not surprisingly, questioned whether the social movements themselves, or the social conditions that helped to produce them, were in fact "new." For example, US scholars are used to thinking of social movements as moral crusades (e.g., Gerlach and Hine, 1970; Gusfield 1986) and are familiar with movements organized around cultural concerns rather than direct material interests. Nor did the explicit reliance on "culture" as a mode of understanding the context and causes of the emergence of collective action strike US scholars as new. Segments of the "collective behavior" tradition in the US (e.g., Park and Burgess 1967; Gurr 1970; see the review in Gusfield 1994) had long maintained that cultural and structural sources of distress – such as "strain," "anomie," or "relative deprivation" – could produce the motives for action.[3] Further, approaches to American society and politics that fell under the canard of "American exceptionalism" (e.g., Huntington 1981; Lipset 1996) recognized that particular historical and structural situations produced a distinct "American culture" that was conducive to protest and movement mobilization.

These critiques aside, the study of social movements in the US gained much from new social movement theory. Focusing on "culture" as an *arena* of action, and cultural change as a *consequence* of movement efforts (as well as a *causal* factor in mobilization) provided important addenda to the movements-as-political-reform perspective that was characteristic of structural approaches such as resource mobilization (see, e.g., Hannigan 1991; Buechler 1995). For example, NSM scholars' theorizing "collective identity" and its role in movement emergence, strategy, and impact was an important conceptual step. It provided an avenue away from the rational actor theory of some structuralist approaches and preoccupation with the "free rider" problem that dominated the study of social movement organizations following Olson (1965; see the analysis in Polletta and Jasper 2001). Another important contribution from NSM was the explicit attention to the connections between the forms of collective action and the historical moments and societal formations in which they existed. Much new social movement theory was explicitly oriented to development within Marxian analytic traditions (e.g., Epstein 1991), and did not affect American sociology more widely. However, the conceptual and analytic contributions, without the Marxian problematic, diffused throughout the sociology of social movements.

In contrast, most of the cultural turn in the United States has been geared toward "bringing meaning back in" and has focused on the ways in which movements have used symbols, language, discourse, identity, and other dimensions of culture to recruit, retain, mobilize, and motivate members. This work arose out of various versions of interactionist theory, inspired by the work of Herbert Blumer (1969), Turner and Killian (1987), and Erving Goffman (1974). Scholars in this tradition have been particularly interested in the interpersonal processes through which people understand what they are doing and how they find the ideational, moral, and emotional resources to keep doing it. In that regard, there has been some continuity with the parts of the "collective behavior" tradition that focused on interpersonal relations, emergent norms, and the discontinuities between moments of collective action and everyday social life (e.g., Blumer 1939; Turner and Killian 1987; Piven and Cloward 1992).

The best known of these culturalist approaches is widely called the "framing" perspective and has been presented, elaborated, reviewed, and critiqued in a number of places (e.g., Snow and Benford 1992; Benford 1997; Jasper 1997; Benford and Snow 2000; Oliver and Johnston 2000; Williams and Benford 2000; Westby 2002), including chapters in this collection. Its most important contribution, in my view, is calling attention to and explicitly theorizing the symbolic and meaning work done by movement activists as they articulate grievances, generate consensus on the importance and forms of collective action to be pursued, and present rationales for their actions and proposed solutions to adherents, bystanders, and antagonists. The central metaphor of "framing" came from Erving Goffman's work, so the emphasis on human agency and interpretation is not surprising. The intuitive appeal of the idea, and its important place in supplying missing dimensions to structuralist movement theories, has resulted in a proliferation of framing studies (e.g., Benford 1993; Swart 1995; Williams and Williams 1995; Carroll and Ratner 1996; Mooney and Hunt 1996; Cornfield and Fletcher 1998; Haydu 1999), and has had considerable scholarly impact.

Framing studies, given their American and interactionist heritage, focus primarily on how people "do things" with culture – that is, the deployment of symbols, claims, and even identities in the pursuit of activism. For example, Benford (1993) analyzes the stories activists share about the efficacy of social action and how that is used to produce and bolster participant motivation. Berbrier (2002) looks at how three movements use "transformation frames" to distance themselves from stigmatized statuses and relocate themselves in cultural space. And Bernstein (1997) draws upon examples of gay and lesbian activism to argue that movements can deploy identity strategically in pursuit of various ends.

Framing has not been the only culturalist approach in American sociology, of course, and other scholars drew inspiration from semiotics (e.g., Steinberg 1999), discourse and narrative analysis (e.g., Fine 1995; Polletta 1998; Davis 2002), studies of ideology (e.g., Williams 1996b; Oliver and Johnston 2000; Platt and Williams

2002; Westby 2002), as well as more traditional attention to norms, values, and ideas (e.g., Inglehart 1990; Rochon 1998). However, almost all of these approaches share both a concern with *meaning*, and a more-or-less *agency-oriented* theoretical perspective. In the former, they parted company with the resource mobilization heritage that explicitly eschewed the study of meaning; in the latter, they parted company with the functionalist collective behavior tradition that viewed culture as a static, integrative, and binding force.

Along with an interactionist understanding of culture and cultural production, what most of these culturalist studies have in common is a "movement-centric" approach to their analysis. That is, a social movement, its activists, and the meanings associated with the movement are the units of analysis, the things to be explored. This has resulted in great strides in understanding what I have termed the "internal" dimensions of movement culture (see Williams 1995). (Analytically, internal movement culture is the norms, beliefs, symbols, identities, stories and the like that produce solidarity, motivate participants, and maintain collective action) (e.g., Fantasia 1988; Benford 1993; Fine 1995). In that regard, "movement culture" has mostly been about the roles traditionally assigned to culture in sociology – motivational, expressive, and integrative functions.[4] Whereas much structuralist movement research has studied the ways in which movements have affected change in the wider society, framing-based approaches to movement culture initially were interested in the internal dynamics of starting and maintaining collective action efforts. This focus has expanded over time, and more recent framing work is clearly interested in questions of public efficacy and the like. But the "center of gravity" in the framing literature has rested on issues distinct to the mobilization and maintenance of a movement or group of movements.

Framing studies have increased our sociological understanding of the emergence and articulation of grievances, the dynamics of recruitment and mobilization, and the maintenance of solidarity and collective identity. For example, Snow and Benford (1988) have analyzed the three component functions of collective action frames, the "diagnostic," the "prognostic," and the "motivational." Relatedly, Gamson (1992) argues that for a frame to go from understanding to motivating action it must have three elements, "injustice," "agency," and "identity." These provide a useful understanding of the problems and dilemmas confronting activists and organizers, and the ways in which grievances develop to foster social action. This has been a powerful corrective to a too often overly rationalized and instrumental approach to movement action. Nonetheless, framing scholars have generally asked what might be called traditional "social movements" questions, but direct those questions to issues of culture. That is, how does movement culture, help form, sustain, and give identity to a social movement?

This movement-centric approach to culture is, analogously, much like the "resource mobilization" school of understanding social movements. Focused on structural factors such as membership, money, organization, and other material resources, resource mobilization scholars studied the factors relevant to specific movements, and that were generally thought of as located "within" the movements themselves (see McAdam 1982). The "demand" side of collective action – such as grievances or shared identity – was generally held to be constant if latent, and movement emergence occurred when a class of persons could muster the necessary social resources.[5]

Ideology as a 'resource' to be 'mobilized'?

From a structuralist perspective, the political process model and its related approach, political opportunity structure theory, added important contextualizing understandings to structural approaches to movements. Political process scholars maintain, and rightly so, that the societal environments in which aggrieved groups exist both affect their capacities to gather resources, and affect the efficacy of their use of those resources once gathered. The social context, conceptualized most often as the "political opportunity structure" of elites, state power, oppositional movements, and the like (see Tarrow 1994; McAdam 1996: 27; Meyer and Staggenborg 1996), became an important factor in understanding social movements. This effectively moved some of the analytic attention off the movements themselves, and on to the contours and dynamics of the wider society in which the movements operate.

It is exactly the analytic move from a movement-centric to a contextual focus – from a *culturalist* perspective – that I wish to highlight and develop in this chapter. By reviewing the work of a number of scholars, including examples from some of my own research, I hope to contribute to understanding the *cultural* contexts in which movements grow, flourish, and wither. Just as movements face different challenges, chart different courses, and have different levels of success in different structural environments, so too do movements fare differently in varying cultural environments.

Thus this chapter offers two analytic shifts from what have been the dominant trends in recent social movement research. The first analytic shift is from a unit of analysis that privileges the movement itself to one that privileges a larger cultural array in which the movement is but one set of actors or meaning-systems. Second is a move from analyses that privilege the configurations of law, political access and representation, economic relations, and other systems that are defined through rational-bureaucratic means, to a perspective in which the configuration or structure of formal and informal meanings, symbols, rituals, and language is highlighted. These shifts, of course, require some consideration as to why this might be an advantage. For example, what questions can we ask and answer with this perspective that a movement-centric analysis cannot? Moreover, how do we think about culture conceptually in ways that are useful to understanding collective action?

BROADENING THE CULTURAL PERSPECTIVE

I have so far talked in terms of the "cultural environment." This general idea has been called by a number of different terms by a variety of scholars. Examples include "codes" (Alexander and Smith 1993; Hart 1996; Kane 1997), "scripts" or "tool kits" (Swidler, 1986, 1995), "mentalities" (Tarrow 1992), the "discursive context" (Koopmans and Statham 1999), "cultural structure" (Rambo and Chan 1990), or the "cultural opportunity structure" (Noonan 1995; McAdam 1996; Benford and Snow 2000). Given that many of these terms are used as metaphors, there is not always a clear reason to choose one over another. Yet, the terms can have implications or connotations that push thinking in one direction or another. The phrase "cultural opportunity structure," for example, is used by scholars primarily interested in the cultural conditions that facilitate movement emergence and affect movement success. The notion of a "structure" lends a fixity and static quality to the phenomenon, although it potentially lends itself to quantitative analysis and macrocomparative work (see the work in Kriesi et al. 1995; McAdam et al. 1996). The "tool kit" metaphor, on the other hand, implies a too instrumentalist and agentic approach to culture, wherein cultural elements almost become transparent over more fundamental impulses such as interests. Thinking of cultural elements as "tools" underplays the affective, moral, and even unacknowledged ways in which culture holds and shapes those within it (see Schudson 1989). While Swidler's (1986) initial formulation of the "tool kit" idea entwined that notion with the metaphor of repertoire, as I parse them here the former has a more instrumentalist, and less structured, implication than the latter.

The terms "code" and "discursive context" seem best suited for analysis of written and spoken language, and less suited to actions, and nonverbal symbols such as dress, drawings, or photographs, and indeed, have been used that way in empirical work (e.g., Alexander and Smith 1993; Koopmans and Statham 1999). "Script" may imply actions as well as words ("stage directions," to push the metaphor) and has the advantage of calling attention to the channeling power of culture. But, in turn, the notion of script seems to suggest a linear, almost deterministic, quality to the organization of culture, and provides less theoretical room for innovation and agency.

While others may disagree with my inferences regarding the connotations of these different metaphors, the conceptual issues should not be lost. The appropriate concept should include room for both the structuring power of history and institutional legitimacy, while still providing space for change, development, and innovation. Further, the culture concept must be able to deal with written and spoken language used as rhetoric – that is, instrumentally meant to persuade – as well as capturing the distinctive properties of actions, rituals, and other expressive dimensions of symbols. As Kniss (1996) notes, the interpretive elasticity varies among different types of symbols. While all may be multivocal, some are more so than others – for example, one either wears a yellow star or pink triangle or does not. The meanings implied and inferred from such an act may vary, but the fact of wearing such a symbol is less ambiguous than an attitudinal commitment to "liberty" or "equal rights."

The metaphor of the "repertoire" (in the study of collective action, usually credited to Tilly 1978) seems to combine a sense of choice within structured options, leaving theoretical room for agency and strategic decisions, while still recognizing that cultural and historical circumstances circumscribe the options available, and even privilege some choices over others. The dictionary definition of "repertoire" plays on both the structuring and agentic aspect of the term. It defines repertoire as the plays or operas a company is prepared to perform, as a list of skills an individual or group possesses, and as a complete supply of devices or ingredients used in a particular field or practice. Thus it is both the storehouse of available elements, as well as those that actors have the knowledge and capacity to use. However, whatever the term or metaphor scholars use to describe the cultural environment, the shared analytic concern moves inquiry away from any particular movement itself and its internal movement culture; rather, the analytic core of the approach is the *socially and culturally available* array of symbols and meanings from which movements can draw.

THINKING ABOUT CULTURE

Conceptualizing the "cultural environment" in which social movements move is a multilevel task. A brief review of several recent developments in the sociology of culture may provide some leverage in that regard. Culture is a widely used term, but used in a variety of ways with a number of meanings. That ambiguity is part of the term's appeal, and its ability to evoke multiple interpretations is often analytically useful as well. However, the task is perhaps no more tricky conceptually than defining and operationalizing the notion of "structure." This is not the place for a full exposition on the culture concept, but a brief review of one analytic tool will provide a helpful reference.

Griswold (1987), Wuthnow (1987), and Wuthnow and Witten (1988) have offered analytic templates for the analysis of culture. In another venue (Williams 1996a), I proposed something of a hybrid scheme that offered a five-pointed "star," where each point is a site in which one can study culture (defined as the "symbolic-expressive" dimensions of human life). Those five points included: (1) the cultural object itself; (2) culture producers; (3) culture consumers/receivers; (4) the institutional context in which culture is produced and used; and (5) the cultural field or environment in which cultural objects are produced and received. Most sociology of culture looks at the connections between any two, or sometimes three, of these points.

[margin handwritten note: analytic scheme for studying culture.]

Given its interactionist heritage, it is not surprising that a central thrust of the framing literature is to examine the connections between cultural *producers* (in most cases, movement activists and elites), cultural *receivers* (rank-and-file members, bystander publics, or potential adherents), and the cultural *object* itself (usually a public claim made by a social movement). Important concepts such as "frame alignment" (Snow et al. 1986) ask how activists and movement leaders formulate and articulate claims, both to motivate adherents and influence the public. Other scholars (e.g., Williams and Blackburn 1996; Platt and Williams 2002) focus on how those who compose various audiences interpret what they hear or read, and show the extent to which the "consensus" a movement culture develops is partial and fluid. In these examples, and the ones cited above from the framing literature, one can clearly see the authors' commitments to understanding the agency and meaning-work of those involved with movement action, both those producing messages about a putative social condition and those hearing and interpreting those messages.

Other scholars (e.g., Williams and Williams 1995; Carroll and Ratner 1996) elaborate the focus on the *cultural object* by examining questions about the "internal logic" of movement claims and appeals. That is, they analyze the cultural object in itself, and seek to find some of its meaning-giving properties in the internal grammar and logic of the text/claim/discourse itself. In a sense, this is a "structural" approach to meaning, as the cultural object is treated as stable, and the structured relationships among elements within the object are seen as the key to shaping the meanings available to actors. Scholars using this approach often draw heavily from linguistics-based discourse analysis. Williams and Benford (2000), analyze the framing literature by noting the division between those scholars who pursue a more structural understanding of the composition of *frames*, and those who purse a more interpretive understanding of the interactive processes of *framing*. Both approaches, however, focus on the relations among the cultural object, cultural producers, and cultural receivers.

Understanding the cultural *environment* in which movements exist, for the most part, deemphasizes the first three points of the five-point cultural star: the object, the producers, and the receivers. This leaves the two points, which broadly can be termed "the social world" (Griswold 1987) – the institutional context and the cultural field. The former is conventionally thought of as the world of "social structures," such as polities, organizations, institutions, and the like. In the sociology of culture, focusing on the organizational bases for cultural production has been enormously profitable (Crane 1992). Rather than treating cultural objects as reflections of stable elements of the social world such as social classes or institutional locations – what Griswold (1987) calls "reflection theory" – the "production of culture" perspective has examined how the organization of industry, cultural producers, and institutional constraints have shaped or channeled the symbolic objects. This approach has found profit in the study of social movements as well (e.g., McCarthy et al. 1991; Evans 1997; Cornfield and Fletcher 1998), as research has shown how the directions that social movement culture takes – for example, the frames employed by leaders or the issues that become salient in the political arena – are channeled by the contours of the institutional sites in which movement activity takes place. Things as diverse as the tax laws governing nonprofit organizations (McCarthy et al. 1991) to organizational routines of media organizations (McCarthy 1994) put constraints on some movement activities and open opportunities for other actions. The institutional context is a powerful shaping force.

The "cultural field" is the last of the points on the "culture star" and the focus of the rest of this chapter. Just as the institutional context can constrain, shape, and channel what directions a movement takes – and just as the structure of political opportunities makes some collective action targets feasible and vulnerable and others less so – so too does the cultural context both constrain and enable collective action. We are still left with the challenge of conceptualizing what the cultural field is, as well as best operationalizing it in social research. To that task I turn.

CONCEPTUALIZING THE CULTURAL ENVIRONMENT

While there is no "right" answer to the definition of culture, given its ambiguity and multilevel usefulness, certain approaches work better to illuminate the dynamics of social movements than do others. Traditionally in sociology, of course, culture was usually conceptualized as "norms and values" that were widely shared, and usually deeply held, within a population. Following this lead, the "civic culture" or "political culture" traditions examined the norms, values, and ideas regarding political arrangements, justice, citizenship, and the like (e.g., Almond and Verba 1965; Devine 1972). The cultural environment was this array of values, which were widely and deeply held, and solidly institutionalized. Culture remained integrative and expressive, and served to delimit the boundaries within which legitimate social action could occur; that is, a movement had to work within societally acceptable norms and values in order to effect change. Culture was, in that sense, a matter of constraint, preventing social fragmentation and sanctioning action with social approval or stigma.

The primary critique of this approach has been its static quality and inability to account clearly for cultural change. However, more recent versions of "values-based" theories of culture have produced important emendations to the approach. For example, Huntington (1981) posits that there is an "American Creed" comprising several key values. These values, due both to their centrality and to some ambiguity in their definition, are always available as ideals with which to criticize existing institutional arrangements. Thus there is an impulse toward critique and change built into American culture and its politics; it is, he says the "promise of disharmony." Huntington does not offer an explicit approach to understanding political challenges or social activism.

More significant to movement scholars is Rochon's (1998) understanding of how culture "moves" through examining the relationships among ideas, activism, and the diffusion of changing values within a society. While focused on ideas and values, Rochon offers an explanation for cultural change and movements' roles in that change. He ties this culture work to particular social groupings that he calls "critical communities." These communities first formulate new "value perspectives." Social movements then take these new values to the wider public through activism in the media and political arena, and translate the generalized values into more restricted but clearly articulated policy claims. Through activism, and successes in institutionalizing proposed changes, changing values diffuse through society. Rochon maintains, however, that values are widely and deeply held, which is why he notes that cultural change is a contentious struggle – and often requires the critical community-social movement nexus in order to be accomplished. Thus he attempts to balance the understanding of values, as the deep feature of culture that serve to integrate social life, with the fact and processes of dynamic social change.

Another response to the critiques of "norm and value" culture theories has been adoption of more literary, narrative, and discursive approaches to culture. That is, rather than conceptualizing values or norms as more or less discreet units held by individuals or social groups, culture is seen as the collection of shared symbols, stories, and public performances that a people use to understand themselves and their world. This is sometimes thought of as a "dramaturgical" approach to culture and is often associated with the work of Clifford Geertz (1973). That is, for Geertz, culture exists in its dramatic enactment in public. One studies not norms and values, nor hearts and minds, but the public display of significant events, stories, and rituals such as funeral marches, coronations, and village cockfights.

In particular, Geertz used this approach to understand cultures in transition, under crisis from exogenous forces of social change, and moments of discontinuity in symbolic worlds. Geertz was not concerned with social movements per se, or even much with collective action geared at purposeful change. Rather, he focused on adaptation to changing circumstances and how culture members used stories and performance to embody meanings in social action.

Neither was Geertz particularly concerned with defining the cultural environment in which social change occurred. He understood human action by examining the ways in which people drew upon the stories, symbols, and narratives available to them as culture members, but spent little effort on delimiting the culture storehouse conceptually or empirically. Partly this is an aspect of his inductive and ethnographic approach to research, and his focus on the creative and agentic properties of action – culture became fluid and evolving, with multiple meanings and a variety of uses in interpreting events. Importantly, Geertz's approach led him away from thinking of culture only as constraint on action. Certain actions, expressions, and even thoughts became possible because of the availability of cultural elements for making sense of proximate events. Just as Giddens (1976) notes that "structures" are simultaneously enabling and constraining, so too is culture, and its conceptualization must be adequate to that task.

Thus in two ways – the dramaturgical shift and the move away from constraint – Geertz produced an understanding of culture distinct from the Durkheimian and functionalist approaches from which he began his study. His conception of culture as stories – and the dynamics of storytelling – is a major contribution to understanding culture.[6]

Swidler (1995) notes that Geertz helped move our understanding of the role of culture in social movements and social change out of the heads of actors and into some type of cultural environment – examining culture from the "outside in" (1995: 31). Beyond the deeply held ideas of Weber's (1958/1904) and Walzer's (1965) Protestant saints, or the taken-for-granted generalized values of the civic culture tradition, culture comprises sets of practices and symbols that are external to movements and their members. As such, culture is largely public symbols, often embodied in the practices of institutions, and thus "variations in the ways social contexts bring culture to bear on action may do more to determine culture's power than variations in how deeply culture is held" (Swidler 1995: 31). The interactions among overlapping social and cultural contexts produce sites in which meanings are ambiguous, definitions of the situation contested, and cultural challenge and change is possible. Understanding cultural change becomes less a matter of how individuals change their minds (or hearts) and more a matter of understanding how symbolic practices get combined and recombined.

This review of conceptions of culture, while certainly not exhaustive, points to a number of requirements for thinking about social movements' cultural environment systematically. First, static accounts of culture, and approaches that focus on its integrative features, are *insufficient for understanding processes of challenge, contestation, and change*. Particularly when thinking of the cultural context in which collective action occurs, any unified concept of a culture is sure to miss the ways in which fluid meanings, rival interpretations, and symbolic innovation are the fertile soil of social movements. This is well recognized in the current sociology of social movements.

Second, and less recognized in the theory and practice of social movements research, locating culture only "within" – within individuals or within social movement groups – misses the extent to which it is the *public enactment of culture* that is at stake with many social movement challenges. The publicness of cultural displays aimed at social change produces distinct challenges to understanding the cultural resources used by movements (Williams 1995: 127). Public enactments form much of the cultural context that shapes the substance, form, and trajectory of movement challenges and the meanings of the cultural resources that movements use (Williams 1995: 128).

Third, while a focus on the cultural environment – and its constraining and enabling capacities to shape action – necessarily places some limits on theoretical expressions of actor agency, culture must be understood as interpretive, multivocal, and socially constructed. Culture's structuring properties, and the social power represented in its functioning, must not overwhelm actors and their actions.

BOUNDEDNESS AND RESONANCE

So, how best to think about the cultural environment? Two analytic requirements stand paramount for a systematic conception of the cultural environment. First is "boundedness." If we are to claim that something "external" to a social movement is either (or both) a storehouse of symbolic elements from which a movement can draw, or a source of constraint on possible movement actions and ideas, then we must be able to say what is "in" the culture and what is not. If we are to say that certain historical periods or cultural formations are conducive to social movement activities and others are not, then we must be able to set analytic boundaries on what is culturally relevant when. It is important to avoid overly unified notions of culture, and the attendant assumption that "a culture" is internally consistent or logical. This is particularly necessary as we incorporate theoretical room for power and social conflict. Nonetheless, there must still be a way of discerning the "boundaries of the legitimate" (see Williams and Demerath 1991) within which social actors work.

Second is "resonance." Even if we have identified a set of cultural resources that have a certain boundedness and perhaps even internal coherence, the salience and applicability of the various symbolic elements will vary. Some cultural elements will be more important and held more dearly. Even within the boundaries of the legitimate, cultural effectiveness will vary. The variation will occur across groups within the general population, across issue areas or arenas of social life, and over time, depending on events. In social movement terms, some cultural resources – such as frames, or symbols, or ideologies – will resonate and others will not. When and where this is so involves resonance.

The intersection of boundedness and resonance in effect creates the conditions we can think of as a cultural environment. There is variation in – but some limits on – the opportunities that culture offers to collective actors. This variation may have a fair amount of consistency – hence we can think of it as being "structured" – and variation in salience affects culture's effectiveness in social action. Yet any structuring aspect of culture is malleable based on the uses and constructions of groups in action. Movement activity thus "enacts" culture and provides the precedent and reference that affects future efforts at cultural sense-making.[7] In sum, the interplay between boundedness and resonance, and between the structured existence of cultural elements and their innovative use by agents, provides the theoretical groundwork for the cultural environment. I consider boundedness, resonance, and the relations between them in turn.

Boundedness and Public Power

Any discussion of boundaries and social life immediately calls to mind the important work of sociologists of culture such as Mary Douglas (1966, 1973), Pierre Bourdieu (1984), and Michele Lamont (1999, 2000). These scholars' intellectual projects are not identical, but they share a common theme in their attempt to understand how humans make distinctions and the social consequences of those distinctions. Thus Douglas delineates principles through which members of societies construct solidarity (the famous "group" and "grid" principles), and make distinctions between what is proper, clean, and pure and what is not. Bourdieu, in contrast, saw distinctions as a mechanism for the construction and maintenance of inequality within societies. It is a structuring process that creates social fields and the cultural meanings that differentiate between them. Lamont extends Bourdieu's work, not only examining how symbolic boundaries create and reinforce inequality (Lamont and Fournier 1992), but also investigating the broad intellectual, religious, and political currents that provide individuals with the cultural resources they use in this boundary work (Lamont 2000) – in effect, investigating and comparing cultural repertoires.

While little of this work is geared toward the problems associated with social movements, it highlights the importance of understanding boundaries in any analysis of culture. What is "inside" a culture and what is not, what is valued and what is sanctioned, what counts as "legitimate" and what does not, are fundamental processes of identification and judgment, applied to collective actors as to any social phenomena. Both culturally central and culturally marginal groups, while differently positioned within a society, are faced with certain boundaries governing what can and cannot be expressed publicly, particularly in pursuit of social change. What "can be expressed" has two components: *intelligibility* (can this even be understood by nonmembers of our group?); and *legitimacy* (will this have the moral and ideational authority to be persuasive or even binding?).

We may assume that to some extent social movements have dealt with the issue of intelligibility, at least at a basic level. Movements arise within a cultural milieu, adherents talk with each other, read each others' writings, and attend events where others are present and acting. This has to be done in a shared language, with at least some shared understandings about the meanings of key symbols, to allow even the simplest forms of collective action to happen at all. Movement members write publications, deliver speeches, create websites, and make media statements for various publics. This has to been done in a language that they at least expect some portion of the public to understand. Often, of course, the discourse "backstage" among movement activists and "frontstage" in public forums are different (Kubal 1998). But the general problem of intelligibility seems so generic to any type of social action that one need not resort to the sociology of social movements to gain perspective on it.

Beyond this base level, however, intelligibility becomes more contingent, less reliable, and – when considering public claims calling for social change – more open to ambiguity, multiple interpretations, and indexical disputes. Movements vary, of course, in how much they attempt to control and constrain the interpretations of their discourse and public symbols. Even within movements, the extent to which positions and ideologies are defined and elaborated varies. Further, some communication technologies allow for ideational development while others rely on fleeting images, nonverbal actions, and mediated "sound bites."

But there is an inherent contradiction between the scope of social change envisioned by movements, and the variation in interpretative construction of the movement's visions. That is, attempts at moderate change – so-called "reform" movements – usually do not ask publics for radical revisions of their conceptions of societal arrangements, or their visions of what constitutes the "good society" (Williams 1995, 1999a). They appeal to movement members and nonmembers in a readily accessible, and hence broadly legitimate, language. It is usually a language that accepts and ratifies many dimensions of status quo social arrangements, while focusing change on specified or delimited arenas of life. However, the sheer range of the audiences involved means that a variety of interpretations arise as to what the social movement is "actually" saying. Meanings are only partially shared, and the dispersion of meanings ranges broadly within the available cultural repertoire.

Radical attempts at social change, on the other hand, often require a more "elaborated" rationale, in which proponents explicitly articulate their critiques of the extant, and the dimensions of the desired future society. These elaborated codes are less enmeshed in immediate social structure than "restricted" codes, and thus can take less advantage of taken-for-granted, indexical knowledge; the speaker makes her or his intentions more explicitly articulate (Douglas 1973: 44, 48–52). By definition, they call into question more social arrangements and cultural meanings.[8] But the very expanse of those challenges pushes movement claims closer to the boundaries of the legitimate, falling outside what many people are able to "hear" as acceptable visions of society. This is, of course, not a purely cognitive exercise in articulating positions on social "issues." Many movement challenges are embodied in the person, dress, behavior, or even existence of activists themselves (e.g., African Americans using "whites only" public facilities, or gay couples openly expressing affection). The more articulated and sweeping the challenge, the more publics who will find it beyond their scope of the intelligible and the legitimate.

Because social movements are about effecting change in society, and this naturally entails running up against extant ways of doing things, there is a crucial element of power involved when assessing the cultural environments that form movements and the cultural resources movements use in pursuing their ends. For the most part, movements must work within the boundaries of the legitimate in expressing their claims. This means that every attempt at expressing a public claim contains a degree of accommodation to that publicness, an implicit acknowledgment that symbols must resonate with audiences who are themselves outside the subculture/group/social movement/community of origin. And, in turn, groups who do not control much public space – that is, groups for whom the dominant public symbols are not part of "their" culture – must step outside their "home" languages in order to communicate publicly.

While adjusting one's rhetorical appeals to take account of cultural receptivity can be a strategic action by movements, it also reflects differences in social power. Some groups choose – and some are forced – to use cultural expressions that originated with their rivals in order to achieve a place in public life. For example, consider the "right to life" language of the anti-abortion movement. The phrase "right to life" is evocative and effective, at least in part because it calls upon the deep American commitment to individual rights in the pursuit of "life, liberty and happiness" (Williams and Williams 1995). However, for major portions of the anti-abortion movement, their actual ideological commitments are antithetical to the type of society and political philosophy that originated the notion of "rights" (Williams and Blackburn 1996). Indeed, many activists are concerned with creating a society that emphasizes the duties that individuals have to the collective – a society where collective moral health allows individual discretion and preferences to be curtailed (see Williams 1995). The variance between the logic of anti-abortion rhetoric and the grounding assumptions of their worldview presents problems both for the public presentation of anti-abortion arguments and for the practical political compromises pro-life movements can make (Williams and Blackburn 1996). They are often forced into a "liberalism" with which they fundamentally disagree. Thus all social groups involved with public life must contend with the autonomy – and potential universality – of public symbolism. This is true even for those social groups that provide the substantive content for public culture (Williams 1999b).

While public cultural space for social movement claims may indeed be bounded, it would be wrong to overstate the extent to which individuals and groups identify with the substantive moral message that their discursive symbols evoke. The multivocality of symbols provides for a number of possible readings of any given symbol, and subcultural processes of meaning-creation make many particular readings plausible. Public actors may participate in the discursive structure of public culture without identifying with the substantive content with which other groups imbue their symbols. However, symbols are not totally arbitrary and transparent – they are more than only plastic masks over material interests. And all symbols are not equally elastic. Adjusting the public culture of movement challenges channels a movement's arguments, actions, and claims into particular directions. That direction may be away from the sentiment pools and commitments that helped mobilize activists in the first place. This presents a challenge to both established and challenger groups when they encounter and try to influence a pluralist public.

As noted above, the very process of "publicness" itself contributes to the diffusion of meaning. Cultural expressions entered into the public sphere cannot be completely controlled by those who originate them. Strategic rhetoric may originate in the interests of particular groups, but its trajectory and ultimate destination can be altered. Competing groups may both adopt or adapt rhetorical frames, for example, the way religious groups use rights language to frame abortion politics as either a "right to life" or a "right to choose"; or the way the Fathers' Rights movement has adopted the "gender neutrality" of liberal feminism to argue against women's interests in custody disputes (Williams and Williams 1995). Particular cultural symbols may not resonate with members of other groups in ways intended by the originators, thus limiting the ability to recruit or persuade. In any case, social movement expressions, to the extent that they do become authentically part of the public cultural repertoire, do not stay the sole symbolic property of the groups who first used them. They become open for rival interpretation and potential transcendence in meaning (Williams 1999b). The ability of public actors to wield symbols in pursuit of their ends demonstrates that cultural resources can be used strategically by a variety of agents. But the need for intelligibility and legitimacy with a variety of publics makes it important that any given cultural resource be firmly within a recognized repertoire.

RESONANCE AND CULTURAL POWER

Snow and Benford (1988) entered the idea of "resonance" into the study of social movement culture. It is, in one sense a straightforward and intuitively appealing idea – whatever frames actors use must "resonate" if audiences are to respond. Some frames "work" better than others because they resonate with audiences who are prepared to hear the claim, or have experiences commensurate with the claims being made. In this sense resonance is the "fit" between frames and audiences' previous beliefs, worldviews, and life experiences. As a result, most approaches to "frame resonance" have been concerned with how audiences "consume" movement culture by interpreting the messages being offered, making them meaningful, and using them as a basis for action (Williams and Kubal 1999).

Benford and Snow (2000: 619) elaborated upon their initial formulation by noting that resonance is shaped by the intersection of two factors, credibility and salience. Credibility applies to both the frame content and those who proffer it ("claims-makers"). That is, is the frame internally consistent, does it seem believable, and what is the claims-maker's status in the eyes of potential adherents? Second, one assesses salience by determining the centrality, experiential commensurability, and narrative fidelity of a frame to the lives of those who are the "targets of mobiliza-tion" (2000: 621). The first two dimensions relate to targets' lives and how a frame resonates with their values, beliefs, and experiences. Narrative fidelity is the extent to which a frame fits within existing cultural narratives and meanings. Thus reson-ance for Snow and Benford includes aspects of the frame itself, characteristics of the claims-makers, and dimensions of the audience's lives. In the context of use, and the examples used, frame resonance is primarily a matter of articulation between claims-makers and those who are their targets.

Equally important to consider, however, is the resonance between movement frames and the existing cultural sets within the bounded legitimate culture. This is a "cultural resonance" that complements the "frame resonance" studies inspired by Snow and Benford's work (Williams and Kubal 1999).[9] However, determining what symbol sets have this cultural resonance is a potential trap, both conceptually and empirically. How is one to measure resonance? If it is only determined "post hoc" the entire process risks tautology – we claim a frame works because it resonates, and we know something has resonated because it "worked."

For those studying social movement adherence and mobilization, frame resonance is clearly an important concept. It highlights the extent to which communication exists between framers and audiences; the current crop of framing studies focused on frame interpretations by movement members is part of understanding resonance (see, e.g., Platt and Williams 2002). Resonance also plays a crucial role in the projection of movement power into the public sphere. Movement discourse, ideolo-gies, and actions must be culturally resonant – coherent within some shared cultural repertoire – if they hope to strike bystander publics as legitimate, or neutralize oppositional positions by elites and countermovements. Thus movement culture must resonate with people outside the movement community even as it recruits and mobilizes (Williams 1995). Movements' public claims must have a "cultural power" (Williams and Demerath 1991) that is effective even with people who are not on board in terms of attitudes, beliefs, or issues.

In my view, resonance is conceptually distinct from "salience." A discourse or collective action frame might resonate with a particular cultural repertoire, and yet not have a high salience or stature within the wider culture. For example, a consistent theme in American culture is the purity of untouched natural wilderness. Albanese (1990) and Nash (1989) demonstrate how "nature" or the "wilderness" has often taken on religious significance apart from – or often in contrast to – humans' fallen nature. As Halle (1993) notes, the most common form of art in American households is landscapes – almost universally unpopulated by humans. And yet, this is a "minor chord" in American political culture (Williams 1995), usually overshadowed by approaches to nature that subordinate it to human needs and view progress as the developing control of the natural world (see Gamson 1992). Thus nature as sacred may be culturally resonant, but not salient, particularly if arrayed against economic interests or personal commitments to leisure and comfort.

Resonant cultural discourses are particularly important in getting challenger groups accepted as legitimate players in public debate over political issues. For example, Williams and Demerath (1991) show how a coalition of black clergy were able to use religious symbols – both discursive arguments and the symbols of the black church – to gain a public voice in debating economic development policies in Springfield, Massachusetts. The resonance of religious imagery, and the presumptive legitimacy of religion as a cultural system, meant that City Hall and economic elites responded to the coalition with public respect, compromise offers, and moderate incorporation into decision-making processes. Religious arguments are not the most salient references when constructing the terms of economic debate (as opposed to market logic), but they are culturally resonant ways for understanding and evaluating social arrangements. Resonant movement discourse gave the challengers a cultural power that was distinct from any structural bases of influence or mobilization.

THE INTERSECTION OF BOUNDEDNESS AND RESONANCE

Delineating the boundaries of available cultural repertoires and the cultural resonance of the themes and elements within the repertoires are tricky conceptual problems. Recent research on the cultural environment of movement discourse reveals two methodological approaches to discovering the content of that cultural environment. A first approach proceeds through a form of deduction – it compares the extant discourse actually used by social movements with the universe of framings potentially available if all symbolic constructions were hypothetically available to actors. The "failure" of particular rhetorics or framings – assessed by their absence or their inability to capture the terms of public debate – provides some indication of the boundaries beyond which public claims may not venture. If agenda setting and dictating the terms with which public issues are discussed are a mark of cultural success for social movements, using rhetoric that fails to do so can indicate its lack of cultural resonance.

So, for example, Williams (1995; 1999a; 1999b; Williams and Kubal 1999) examines the "visions of the good society," the rhetoric about what social arrangements constitute the "public good," by analyzing the public claims used by a sample of social movements in the contemporary US. Three rhetorical models are widely

[handwritten margin notes: "Resonance 1."]

[handwritten note at bottom: If internal movement culture rejects larger cultural areas, then adopting those might be harmful to group solidarity]

available and commonly seen in a variety of movement discourses. Most common is a language of *individual rights*, such as that used by the pro-choice movement or the movements seeking to recognize gays and lesbians as full citizens. Second is a language of *individual duties*, where individual liberties are subordinated to the social good; this assumption about the good society undergirds many anti-abortion arguments, or the efforts by the left to constrain the uses and profits of private property. Finally, there is a language of *collective duties*, such as that found in many forms of environmentalism, wherein the collective as a whole is bound to responsibilities to future generations or other societies. The missing cell in this analysis of American public political language is a developed notion of *collective rights*. It is theoretically available as a way to press challenger claims to public power. Further, collective rights is an available discourse in some parts of the world (Ramet 1997; Beaman 2002).

However, articulating a public claim for the rights of a social *group*, rather than on behalf of citizens as individuals, usually results in charges of "discrimination" in American politics. Attempts at justifying affirmative action, or Native American tribal prerogatives, or making an argument for slavery reparations through a language of collective rights has helped lead to the failures of those public claims.[10] Thus one can identify a boundary beyond which "legitimate" cultural discourse cannot venture successfully. Symbols, frames, or rhetorics drawn from that marginalized language – while theoretically available and perhaps appealing as mobilization tools for particular populations – are not culturally legitimate or resonant.

A second approach to cultural resonance is historically grounded and logically inductive. Scholars may examine the sources of symbols, meanings, and ideologies used by a variety of collective actors within a society, and through comparisons with other societies or across historical periods, come to conclusions about the resonant quality of the cultural repertoires in question. For example, given its frequent appearance in contemporary and historical American social movement discourse, it is reasonable to conclude that religion is a particularly useful resource to those trying to mobilize movements for collective action (Williams 1994, 2001; Smith 1996; Young 2002).

Religion's special place in American public culture – its wide resonance – is not about the "sacred" quality of culture in some Durkheimian sense. Nor is it just a matter of the widespread personal beliefs and practices of Americans. Religion is a useful cultural resource for a variety of movement groups due both to several inherent properties of religious discourse, and due to religion's wide dispersion across American social groups (Zald and McCarthy 1998). Religious meaning systems have many elements that make them useful for movement activity (for additional perspective on religious movements, per se, see Kniss and Burns's chapter in this volume). Many religious expressions have an inherent note of challenge in their content, simply because they do not take the world-as-it-is as an ultimate value. There is a transcendence built into a religious worldview that can relativize any societal arrangement. Further, in American culture religious language is democratically available to movements from a wide array of social groups, both the institutionally powerful and the disenfranchised (Williams 2002).

Moreover, moral and religious language is clearly and easily understood by large portions of the American people as a way of conceptualizing public life. Not only are Americans generally religious as a people, but religion has a deep and presumptive public legitimacy even among many who are not personally pious. As a result, religious culture forms the basis for a variety of cultural repertoires at several analytic levels. For example, religious language can be used directly as a way of articulating movement goals and justifying collective action (e.g., Williams and Alexander 1994; Platt and Williams 2002). Alternatively, language and forms of speech that originated in religious sentiments and communities can be "de-sectarianized" – stripped of their specific and particularistic religious content – but remain recognizable to believers, and familiar to those outside the community (e.g., Billings 1990; Williams 1995, 1999a) as religious-like. At another cultural level, religious practices such as public confession can be part of the action repertoire used by movements pursuing both religious and secular ends (e.g., Young 2002). And, of course, religious communities form valuable organizational bases for organizing and mobilizing protest (Morris 1984; Nepstad 1996; Smith 1996; Zald and McCarthy 1998).

And yet, there are boundaries on legitimate public religious language as well. In general, narrow sectarian language has receded as a public language, particularly as a public political language (see Bates 1995). Morality and moral language is vitally important, as well as a type of civil or civic religious language that understands the nation as divinely blessed (Williams and Demerath 1991). But the discourse must be, at least on the surface, nonsectarian, inclusive, and embracing. Indeed, there is some expectation that even a civil religious language of critique – calling the nation to account for its lapses – should be framed in positive and optimistic terms. Even our public religious language has an important debt to the idea of "progress." Thus, even in cases where many people do not agree with a movement's stated position on an issue, they will view favorably the religious language in which it is pitched, so long as it is the "right" type of public religious language (Williams 1999b).

Importantly, both the deductive and inductive approaches to investigating the cultural environment that are outlined here lend themselves to comparative research. In one sense, they demand a certain comparative focus, as they de-center the individual movement as the level of analysis and shift attention to wider cultural patterns. These patterns could be investigated across movements, across time (perhaps as a cultural analogue to the research on cycles of contention; Tarrow 1994; McAdam 1996), or across societies and cultures. Research could examine public frames for the presence or absence of certain content-based themes. Alternatively, after recording the existence of cultural themes in collective action frames, the frequency or distribution with which such themes appear could be charted historically (e.g., Gamson 1992; Haydu 1999). A "trace-back" method can examine the diffusion of a frame and its relative dominance vis-à-vis other rhetorical constructions (e.g., Koopmans and Statham 1999). Or the relative salience of "religious" or "collectivist" frames could be compared between different collective actors in different societal settings. In each case, the research purpose is to understand the intersecting principles of the cultural environment – its boundedness and resonance.

CONCLUSION

Maintaining a culture concept useful to the understanding of social movements is both an important and often elusive task. Culture played a too important role in much functionalist sociology, but cultural change was underserved. Agency-based approaches highlighted innovation and change, but lost sight of the ways in which history, structures, and power shaped what could and could not be used by actors. And culture was too often simply dismissed from materialist perspectives. Maintaining a conceptualization that allows both for culture's facilitative and constraining power – how it shapes and propels – requires attention to agency and structure. I have proposed a theoretical project geared to illuminating empirical study of collective actors. By moving inductively through the cultural resources used by social movements in particular settings, the "boundaries of the legitimate" and the cultural resonance of symbolic repertoires can be revealed. Within these boundaries lie the cultural environments in which movements emerge, grow, change, and die.

Notes

1 Of course, as with any attempt at summarizing and synthesizing the work of large numbers of engaged and skillful scholars, there is some imprecision in my categories. I have no doubt every reader will be able to offer an example that does not fall neatly into the analytic distinction developed here. Nonetheless, I think there is an important difference in the "central tendency" between US and Western European culturalist approaches to social movements, and the "ideal types" created in this section are designed to highlight that difference. The benefit of doing so is that it allows me to show briefly the analytic advances in the study of culture since the 1980s as well as to point to general areas where I see room for conceptual development.

2 Not all the study of the so-called "new social movements" was from a Marxian perspective. For example, Kriesi et al. (1995) draw from "political opportunity structure," "resource mobilization," and other traditions more directly within the sociology of social movements. Nonetheless, I would maintain that the reception of NSM theory in North America – particularly in ways that influenced the cultural turn in the study of social movements – drew from scholars such as Habermas and Melucci, whose formulations were heavily informed by Marxian paradigms (see Epstein 1991; Hannigan 1991; Buechler 1995; Pichardo 1997). The purpose of this review, of course, is less to show all the nuances in the study of the so-called new social movements as it is to show how a particular trend in European NSM theory helped bring culture back in to social movement analyses in the US.

3 There is not, of course, a single "collective behavior" tradition, and different writers within that general rubric had different approaches to culture. Some posited a more-or-less direct connection from social structural developments to social psychological effects, and bypassed any direct engagement with an autonomous cultural level of analysis. Others, however, understood structural changes as disruptive to the integrating function of culture, and thus posited culture as the proximate cause of collective behavior.

4 Dividing the symbolic world into "internal" and "external" culture has a somewhat arbitrary quality, and blurs some of the fluidity of collective action in the empirical world. However, some research demonstrates that framings and discourse within movement groups are distinct from those used for public claims (e.g., Bates 1995; Kubal 1998), while other research shows that frames or collective identities that are effective in mobilizing those already committed have trouble reaching those not yet fully persuaded (Maurer 2002). A key argument in this chapter is that an advantage to studying cultural repertoires, rather than just movement frames, is that it offers an angle into the relations between internal and external movement culture, and the relations between them (see Williams 1995: 138–40).

5 I do note that Zald and McCarthy often listed what might be called a cultural factor, "legitimacy" (e.g., 1987: 22), among the resources they considered important. However, their theoretical development and empirical attention were devoted to "material" resources of money, members, and organization.

6 I note that many social movements scholars have used "dramaturgical" insights profitably (e.g., Gamson 1989; Benford and Hunt 1992), but that these approaches once again speak to the strategic projection of movement influence or the internal construction of collective identity. This perspective in general does not study the ways in which external culture affects a movement and shapes its available culture resources.

7 Obviously, laying out the theoretical problem in this way brings to mind the attempt at understanding the "duality of structure" in Giddens (1976, 1984) and Sewell (1992).

8 Snow and Benford (1992) describe "elaborated" master frames as those which are open and inclusive, flexibly oriented to a wide variety of meanings and audiences. My use of the term here is more influenced by Mary Douglas's (1973) interpretation of Bernstein.

9 Benford and Snow (2000: 622) observe that the idea of "narrative fidelity" describes a relationship between a collective action frame and its cultural environment – that is, the narratives in question are collective stories such as "myths." They note that this is similar to the concept of "cultural resonance." This is an important way in which Snow and Benford link their interest in the meaning work of movement mobilization with concerns about the cultural environment. Nonetheless, the central tendency of the framing literature and its conception of "frame resonance" is to examine the relationship between movement culture producers and target audiences.

10 Some Native American groups have succeeded in enforcing hunting and fishing rights based on collective identity institutionalized in treaties. The legal rationale and procedures, however, are distinct from the public discourse around the issue, which has vociferously contested any Indian claims based on tribal membership and collective identity. To see how these types of claims work differently in other societies, see Beaman (2002).

References

Albanese, Catherine L. (1990) *Nature Religion in America*. Chicago: University of Chicago Press.

Alexander, Jeffrey, and Philip Smith (1993) The Discourse of American Civil Society: A New Proposal for Cultural Studies. *Theory and Society*, 22, 151–208.

Almond, Gabriel, and Sidney Verba (1965) *The Civic Culture*. Boston: Little, Brown.

Bates, Vernon L. (1995) Rhetorical Pluralism and Secularization in the New Christian Right: The Oregon Citizens Alliance. *Review of Religious Research*, 37, 46–64.

Beaman, Lori G. (2002) Aboriginal Spirituality and the Legal Construction of Freedom of Religion. *Journal of Church and State*, 44, 135–49.

Benford, Robert D. (1993) You Could Be the Hundredth Monkey: Collective Action Frames and Vocabularies of Motive within the Nuclear Disarmament Movement. *Sociological Quarterly*, 34, 195–216.

——(1997) An Insider's Critique of the Social Movement Framing Perspective. *Sociological Inquiry*, 67, 409–30.

Benford, Robert D., and Scott A. Hunt (1992) Dramaturgy and Social Movements: The Social Construction and Communication of Power. *Sociological Inquiry*, 62, 36–55.

Benford, Robert D., and David A. Snow (2000) Framing Process and Social Movements: An Overview and Assessment. *Annual Review of Sociology*, 26, 611–39.

Berbrier, Mitch (2002) Making Minorities: Cultural Space, Stigma Transformation Frames, and the Categorical Status Claims of Deaf, Gay, and White Supremacist Activists in Late Twentieth Century America. *Sociological Forum*, 17, 553–91.

Bernstein, Mary (1997) Celebration and Suppression: The Strategic Uses of Identity by the Lesbian and Gay Movement. *American Journal of Sociology*, 103, 531–65.

Billings, Dwight B. (1990) Religion as Opposition: A Gramscian Analysis. *American Journal of Sociology*, 96, 1–31.

Blumer, Herbert (1939) Collective Behavior. In R. E. Park, (ed.), *An Outline of the Principles of Sociology*. New York: Barnes & Noble, 218–80.

——(1969) *Symbolic Interactionism*. Englewood Cliffs, NJ: Transaction.

Bourdieu, Pierre (1984) *Distinction: A Social Critique of the Judgment of Taste*. Cambridge, MA: Harvard University Press.

Buechler, Steven M. (1995) New Social Movement Theories. *Sociological Quarterly*, 36: 441–64.

Carroll, William K., and R. S. Ratner (1996) Master Framing and Cross-Movement Networking in Contemporary Social Movements. *Sociological Quarterly*, 37, 601–25.

Cohen, Jean L. (1985) Strategy or Identity: New Theoretical Paradigms and Contemporary Social Movements. *Social Research*, 54, 663–716.

Cornfield, Daniel B., and B. Fletcher (1998) Institutional Constraints on Social Movement "Frame Extension": Shifts in the Legislative Agenda of the American Federation of Labor, 1881–1955. *Social Forces*, 76, 1305–21.

Crane, Diane (1992) *The Production of Culture*. Newbury Park, CA: Sage.

Darnovsky, Marcy, Barbara Epstein, and Richard Flacks (eds.) (1995) *Cultural Politics and Social Movements*. Philadelphia, PA: Temple University Press.

Davis, Joseph E. (ed.) (2002) *Stories of Change: Narrative and Social Movements*. Albany: State University of New York Press.

Devine, Donald (1972) *The Political Culture of the United States: The Influence of Member Values on Regime Maintenance*. Boston: Little, Brown.

Douglas, Mary (1966) *Purity and Danger*. London: Routledge & Kegan Paul.

——(1973) *Natural Symbols: Explorations in Cosmology*. 2nd ed. London: Barrie & Rockliff.

Eder, Klaus (1985) The "New Social Movements": Moral Crusades, Political Protest Groups, or Social Movements? *Social Research*, 52, 869–901.

Epstein, Barbara (1991) *Political Protest and Cultural Revolution: Nonviolent Direct Action in the 1970s and 1980s*. Berkeley: University of California Press.

Evans, John H. (1997) Multi-organizational Fields and Social Movement Organization Frame Content: The Religious Pro-Choice Movement. *Sociological Inquiry*, 67, 451–69.

Fantasia, Rick (1988) *Cultures of Solidarity: Consciousness, Action, and Contemporary American Workers*. Berkeley: University of California Press.

Fine, Gary Alan (1995) Public Narration and Group Culture: Discerning Discourse in Social Movements. In H. Johnston and B. Klandermans (eds.), *Social Movements and Culture*. Minneapolis: University of Minnesota Press, 127–43.

Gamson, Josh (1989) Silence, Death, and the Invisible Enemy: AIDS Activism and Social Movement "Newness". *Social Problems*, 36, 351–67.

Gamson, William A. (1992) *Talking Politics*. New York: Cambridge University Press.

Geertz, Clifford (1973) *The Interpretation of Cultures*. New York: Basic.

Gerlach, Luther P., and Virginia H. Hine (1970) *People Power and Change: Movements of Social Transformation*. Indianapolis: Bobbs-Merrill.

Giddens, Anthony (1976) *The New Rules of the Sociological Method*. New York: Basic.

——(1984) *The Constitution of Society: Outline of the Theory of Structuration*. Berkeley: University of California Press.

Goffman, Erving (1974) *Frame Analysis: An Essay on the Organization of Experience*. New York: HarperColophon.

Griswold, Wendy (1987) A Methodological Framework for the Sociology of Culture. *Sociological Methodology*, 15, 1–35.

Gurr, Ted Robert (1970) *Why Men Rebel*. Princeton, NJ: Princeton University Press.

Gusfield, Joseph (1986) *Symbolic Crusade*. 2nd ed. Urbana: University of Illinois Press.

——(1994) Reflexivity of Social Movements: Collective Behavior and Mass Society Theory Revisited. In E. Laraña, H. Johnston, and J. R. Gusfield (eds.), *New Social Movements: From Ideology to Identity*. Philadelphia, PA: Temple University Press, 58–78.

Habermas, Jürgen (1981) New Social Movements. *Telos*, 49, 33–7.

Halle, David (1993) *Inside Culture: Art and Class in the American Home*. Chicago: University of Chicago Press.

Hannigan, John H. (1991) Social Movement Theory and the Sociology of Religion: Toward a New Synthesis. *Sociological Analysis*, 52, 311–31.

Hart, Stephen (1996) The Cultural Dimension of Social Movements: A Theoretical Reassessment and Literature Review. *Sociology of Religion*, 57, 87–100.

Haydu, Jeffrey (1999) Counter Action Frames: Employer Repertoires and the Union Menace in the Late Nineteenth Century. *Social Problems*, 46, 313–31.

Huntington, Samuel (1981) *American Politics: The Promise of Disharmony*. Cambridge, MA: Harvard University Press, Belknap Press.

Inglehart, Ronald (1990) Values, Ideology, and Cognitive Mobilization in New Social Movements. In R. Dalton and M. Kuechler (eds.), *Challenging the Political Order*. New York: Oxford University Press, 43–66.

Jasper, James M. (1992) The Politics of Abstractions: Instrumental and Moralist Rhetorics in Public Debate. *Social Research*, 59, 315–44.

——(1997) *The Art of Moral Protest: Culture, Biography, and Creativity in Social Movements*. Chicago: University of Chicago Press.

Jenkins, J. Craig (1983) Resource Mobilization Theory and the Study of Social Movements. *Annual Review of Sociology*, 9, 527–53.

Johnston, Hank, and Bert Klandermans (eds.) (1995) *Social Movements and Culture*. Minneapolis: University of Minnesota Press.

Kane, Anne E. (1997) Theorizing Meaning Construction in Social Movements: Symbolic Structures and Interpretations during the Irish Land War, 1879–1882. *Sociological Theory*, 15, 249–76.

Kniss, Fred (1996) Ideas and Symbols as Resources in Intrareligious Conflict: The Case of American Mennonites. *Sociology of Religion*, 57, 7–23.

Koopmans, Ruud, and Paul Statham (1999) Political Claims Analysis: Integrating Protest Event and Political Discourse Analysis. *Mobilization*, 4, 40–51.

Kriesi, Hanspeter, Ruud Koopmans, Jan Willem Duyvendak, and Marco G. Guigni (eds.) (1995) *New Social Movements in Western Europe: A Comparative Analysis*. Minneapolis: University of Minnesota Press.

Kubal, Timothy J. (1998) The Presentation of the Political Self: Culture, Mobilization, and the Construction of Collective Action Frames. *Sociological Quarterly*, 39, 539–54.

Lamont, Michele (ed.) (1999) *The Cultural Territories of Race: Black and White Boundaries*. Chicago: University of Chicago Press.

——(2000) *The Dignity of Working Men: Morality and the Boundaries of Race, Class, and Immigration*. Cambridge, MA: Harvard University Press.

Lamont, Michele, and Marcel Fournier (eds.) (1992) *Cultivating Differences: Symbolic Boundaries and the Making of Inequality*. Chicago: University of Chicago Press.

Laraña, Enrique, Hank Johnston, and Joseph R. Gusfield (eds.) (1994) *New Social Movements: From Ideology to Identity*. Philadelphia, PA: Temple University Press.

Lipset, Seymour Martin (1996) *American Exceptionalism: A Double-Edged Sword*. New York: W. W. Norton.

McAdam, Doug (1982) *Political Process and the Development of Black Insurgency, 1930–1970*. Chicago: University of Chicago Press.

——(1996) Conceptual Origins, Current Problems, Future Directions. In D. McAdam, J. McCarthy, M. Zald (eds.), *Comparative Perspectives on Social Movements: Political Opportunities, Mobilizing Structures, and Cultural Framings*. New York: Cambridge University Press, 23–40.

McAdam, Doug, John D. McCarthy, and Mayer Zald (eds.) (1996) *Comparative Perspectives on Social Movements: Political Opportunities, Mobilizing Structures, and Cultural Framings*. New York: Cambridge University Press.

McCarthy, John D. (1994) Activists, Authorities, and Media Framing of Drunk Driving. In E. Laraña, H. Johnston, and J. R. Gusfield (eds.), *New Social Movements: From Ideology to Identity*. Philadelphia, PA: Temple University Press, 133–67.

McCarthy, John D., David W. Britt, and Mark Wolfson (1991) The Institutional Channeling of Social Movements in the Modern State. *Research in Social Movements, Conflict and Change*, 13, 45–76.

Maurer, Donna (2002) *Vegetarianism: Movement or Moment?* Philadelphia, PA: Temple University Press.

Melucci, Alberto (1985) The Symbolic Challenge of Contemporary Movements. *Social Research*, 54, 789–816.

——(1989) *Nomads of the Present: Social Movements and Individual Needs in Contemporary Society*. Philadelphia, PA: Temple University Press.

Meyer, David S., and Suzanne Staggenborg (1996) Movements, Countermovements, and the Structure of Political Opportunity. *American Journal of Sociology*, 101, 1628–60.

Mooney, Patrick H., and Scott A. Hunt (1996) A Repertoire of Interpretations: Master Frames and Ideological Continuity in U.S. Agrarian Mobilization. *Sociological Quarterly*, 37, 177–97.

Morris, Aldon D. (1984) *The Origins of the Civil Rights Movement*. New York: Free Press.

Nash, Roderick (1989) *The Rights of Nature*. Madison: University of Wisconsin Press.

Nepstad, Sharon Erickson (1996) Popular Religion, Protest, and Revolt: The Emergence of Political Insurgency in the Nicaraguan and Salvadoran Churches of the 1960s–80s. In C. Smith (ed.), *Disruptive Religion: The Force of Faith in Social Movement Activism*. New York: Routledge, 105–24.

Noonan, Rita (1995) Women against the State: Political Opportunities and Collective Action Frames in Chile's Transition to Democracy. *Sociological Forum*, 10, 81–111.

Offe, Claus (1985) New Social Movements: Challenging the Boundaries of Institutional Politics. *Social Research*, 54, 817–68.

Oliver, Pamela E., and Hank Johnston (2000) What a Good Idea! Ideologies and Frames in Social Movement Research. *Mobilization*, 4, 37–54.

Olson, Mancur (1965) *The Logic of Collective Action*. Cambridge, MA: Harvard University Press.

Park, Robert E., and Ernest Burgess (1967) Collective Behavior. In R. Turner (ed.), *Robert Park on Social Control and Collective Behavior*. Chicago: University of Chicago Press, 225–39.

Pichardo, Nelson A. (1997) New Social Movements: A Critical Review. *Annual Review of Sociology*, 23, 411–30.

Piven, Frances Fox, and Richard A. Cloward (1992) Normalizing Collective Protest. In A. Morris and C. M. Mueller (eds.), *Frontiers in Social Movement Theory*. New Haven: Yale University Press, 301–25.

Platt, Gerald M., and Rhys H. Williams (2002) Ideological Language and Social Movement Mobilization: A Sociolinguistic Analysis of Segregationists' Ideologies. *Sociological Theory*, 20, 328–59.

Polletta, Francesca (1998) "It Was Like a Fever...": Narrative and Identity in Social Protest. *Social Problems*, 45, 137–59.

Polletta, Francesca, and James M. Jasper (2001) Collective Identity and Social Movements. *Annual Review of Sociology*, 27, 283–305.

Rambo, Eric, and Elaine Chan (1990) Text, Structure, and Action in Cultural Sociology. *Theory and Society*, 19, 635–48.

Ramet, S. (1997) *Whose Democracy? Nationalism, Religion, and the Doctrine of Collective Rights in Post-1980 Europe*. Lanham, MD: Rowman & Littlefield.

Rochon, Thomas R. (1998) *Culture Moves: Ideas, Activism, and Changing Values*. Princeton, NJ: Princeton University Press.

Schudson, Michael (1989) How Culture Works: Perspectives from Media Studies on the Efficacy of Symbols. *Theory and Society*, 18, 153–80.

Scott, Alan (1990) *Ideology and the New Social Movements*. London: Unwin Hyman.

Sewell, William H. Jr. (1992) A Theory of Structure: Duality, Agency, and Transformation. *American Journal of Sociology*, 98, 1–29.

Smith, Christian (ed.) (1996) *Disruptive Religion: The Force of Faith in Social Movement Activism*. New York: Routledge.

Snow, David A., and Robert D. Benford (1988) Ideology, Frame Resonance, and Participant Mobilization. In B. Klandermans, H. Kriesi, S. Tarrow (eds.), *International Social Movement Research*. Vol. 1. Greenwich, CT: JAI, 197–218.

——(1992) Master Frames and Cycles of Protest. In A. Morris and C. M. Mueller (eds.), *Frontiers of Social Movement Theory*. New Haven: Yale University Press, 133–55.

Snow, David A., E. B. Rochford Jr., Steven K. Worden, and Robert D. Benford (1986) Frame Alignment Processes, Micromobilization, and Movement Participation. *American Sociological Review*, 51, 464–81.

Steinberg, Marc (1999) The Talk and Back Talk of Collective Action: A Dialogic Analysis of Repertoires of Discourse among Nineteenth Century English Cotton Spinners. *American Journal of Sociology*, 105, 736–80.

Swart, William J. (1995) The League of Nations and the Irish Question: Master Frames, Cycles of Protest, and "Master Frame Alignment." *Sociological Quarterly*, 36, 465–81.

Swidler, Ann (1986) Culture in Action: Symbols and Strategies. *American Sociological Review*, 51, 273–86.

——(1995) Cultural Power and Social Movements. In H. Johnston and B. Klandermans (eds.), *Social Movements and Culture*. Minneapolis: University of Minnesota Press, 127–43.

Tarrow, Sydney (1992) Mentalities, Political Cultures, and Collective Action Frames: Constructing Meaning through Action. In A. Morris and C. M. Mueller (eds.), *Frontiers in Social Movement Theory*. New Haven: Yale University Press, 174–202.

——(1994) *Power in Movement*. New York: Cambridge University Press.

Tilly, Charles A. (1978) *From Mobilization to Revolution*. Reading, MA: Addison-Wesley.

Turner, Ralph H., and Lewis M. Killian (1987) *Collective Behavior*. 3rd ed. Englewood Cliffs, NJ: Prentice Hall.

Walzer, Michael (1965) *The Revolution of the Saints*. Cambridge, MA: Harvard University Press.

Weber, Max (1958/1904) The Protestant Ethic and the Spirit of Capitalism. Translated by Talcott Parsons. New York: Charles Scribner's Sons.

Westby, David L. (2002) Strategic Imperative, Ideology, and Frame. *Mobilization*, 7, 287–304.

Williams, Gwyneth I., and Rhys H. Williams (1995) "All We Want is Equality": Rhetorical Framing in the Fathers' Rights Movement. In Joel Best (ed.), *Images of Issues*. 2d ed. New York: Aldine de Gruyter, 191–212.

Williams, Rhys H. (1994) Movement Dynamics and Social Change: Transforming Fundamentalist Organizations and Ideology. In M. E. Marty and R. S. Appleby (eds.), *Accounting for*

Fundamentalisms: The Dynamic Character of Movements. Chicago: University of Chicago Press, 785–833.

—— (1995) Constructing the Public Good: Social Movements and Cultural Resources. *Social Problems,* 42, 124–44.

—— (1996a) Introduction: The Sociology of Culture and the Sociology of Religion. *Sociology of Religion,* 57, 1–5.

—— (1996b) Religion as Political Resource: Culture or Ideology? *Journal for the Scientific Study of Religion,* 35, 368–78.

—— (1999a) Visions of the Good Society and the Religious Roots of American Political Culture. *Sociology of Religion,* 60, 1–34.

—— (1999b) Public Religion and Hegemony: Contesting the Language of the Common Good. In W. H. Swatos and J. Wellman (eds.), *The Power of Religious Publics: Staking Claims in American Society.* Westport, CT: Praeger, 168–86.

—— (ed.) (2001) *Promise Keepers and the New Masculinity: Private Lives and Public Morality.* Lanham, MD: Lexington.

—— (2002) From the "Beloved Community" to "Family Values": Religious Language, Symbolic Repertoires, and Democratic Culture. In D. S. Meyer, B. Robnett, and N. Whittier (eds.), *Social Movements: Identity, Culture, and the State.* New York: Oxford University Press, 247–65.

Williams, Rhys H., and Susan M. Alexander (1994) Religious Rhetoric in American Populism: Civil Religion as Movement Ideology. *Journal for the Scientific Study of Religion,* 33, 1–15.

Williams, Rhys H., and Robert D. Benford (2000) Two Faces of Collective Action Frames: A Theoretical Consideration. *Research in Social Movements, Conflicts, and Change,* 20, 127–51.

Williams, Rhys H., and Jeffrey Neal Blackburn (1996) Many are Called but Few Obey: Ideological Commitment and Activism in Operation Rescue. In C. Smith (ed.), *Disruptive Religion.* New York: Routledge, 167–85.

Williams, Rhys H., and N. J. Demerath III (1991) Religion and Political Process in an American City. *American Sociological Review,* 56, 417–31.

Williams, Rhys H., and Timothy J. Kubal (1999) Movement Frames and the Cultural Environment: Resonance, Failure, and the Boundaries of the Legitimate. *Research in Social Movements, Conflicts and Change,* 21, 225–48.

Wuthnow, Robert (1987) *Meaning and Moral Order.* Berkeley: University of California Press.

Wuthnow, Robert, and Marsha Witten (1988) New Directions in the Study of Culture. *Annual Review of Sociology,* 14, 49–67.

Young, Michael P. (2002) Confessional Protest: The Religious Birth of U.S. National Social Movements. *American Sociological Review,* 67, 660–88.

Zald, Mayer N., and John D. McCarthy (1987) *Social Movements in an Organizational Society: Collected Essays.* New Brunswick, NJ: Transaction.

—— (1998) Religion as the Crucible for Social Movements. In N. J. Demerath III, P. D. Hall, T. A. Schmitt, and R. H. Williams (eds.), *Sacred Companies: Organizational Aspects of Religion and Religious Aspects of Organization.* New York: Oxford University Press, 24–49.

6

Resources and Social Movement Mobilization

Bob Edwards and John D. McCarthy

Resource: 1a: a new and or reserve source of supply or support: a fresh or additional stock or store available at need: something in reserve or ready if needed. (*Webster's Third New International Dictionary of the English Language, Unabridged*)

Mobilization is a process of increasing the readiness to act collectively... (William A. Gamson, *The Strategy of Social Protest*)

Introduction

The assumption that resource availability enhances the likelihood of collective action is generally taken for granted by contemporary analysts of social movements (see Zald 1992; Cress and Snow 1996). Human time and effort along with money are the most widely appreciated kinds of resources that are more or less available to collective actors. But the simple availability of resources is not sufficient; coordination and strategic effort is typically required in order to convert available pools of individually held resources into collective resources and to utilize those resources in collective action. When movement activists do attempt to create collective action (fielding protests, creating social movement organizations, and the like) through historical time and across geographical locations their successes are consistently related to the greater presence of available resources in their broader environments.

A rich research literature has focused upon a diverse set of movements, times, and places to illustrate this regularity including collective action among the US homeless (Cress and Snow 1996; Snow et al. 2001), shantytown residents in Chile (Schneider 1995), Mexican teachers under the PRI (Cook 1996), liberation theology (Smith 1991) and guerilla movements in Latin America (Wickham-Crowley 1989), the Nicaraguan women's movement (Isbester 2001), the struggle against apartheid in South Africa (Marx 1992), African-American environmental justice mobilization in the US (Edwards 1995), local environmental action in the Czech Republic (Carmin forthcoming), and a cross-national campaign against corporate livestock production in Poland (Juska and Edwards forthcoming). Resource availability has affected the rate and spread of protest (Minkoff 1997; Soule et al. 1999), the founding and mobilization of national women's and minority organizations (Minkoff 1995), environmental organizations in the US (McLaughlin and Khawaja 2000) and Western Europe (Dalton 1994), state-level suffrage organizations in the nineteenth century (McCammon 2001), local Mothers Against Drunk Driving (MADD) groups in the 1980s, as well as participation in transnational social movement organizations (SMOs) in 2000 (Wiest et al. 2002), and the organization of movement music festivals in Western Europe and the US (Eder et al. 1995; Lahausen 1996). These cases provide strong empirical support for the general claims of early research mobilization theorists (McCarthy and Zald 1973, 1977; Jenkins 1985).

In what follows we provide a comprehensive perspective on the nature and role of resources in the mobilization of collective action. First, we want to strongly reemphasize to students of social movements how unequally distributed many kinds of resources are among social groups. Durable patterns of resource inequality in the broader society shape the differential availability of those resources to particular social groups. Efforts by agencies of the state, nongovernmental organizations, and individuals to alter prevailing patterns of resource stratification and redirect resources serve to channel substantial resources to social movements. Nevertheless, middle-class groups remain privileged in their access to many kinds of resources, and, therefore, not surprisingly social movements that resonate with the concerns of relatively privileged social groups predominate and the mobilizations of the poor groups are quite rare in advanced industrial democracies.

Second, we turn to a discussion of resource types. Until the last decade, movement analysts who made resources central to their thinking about mobilization neglected to specify in much detail the concept of resources, and, especially, they developed no clear specification of resource types (McCarthy and Zald 2002). We now have some stronger guidelines for conceptualizing resource forms (Bourdieu 1986; Coleman 1988; Lin 2001) and specifying their primary types among social movements (Oliver and Marwell 1992; Cress and Snow 1996; Lahausen 1996). By synthesizing past work we develop a fivefold typology of moral, cultural, social-organizational, human, and material resources.

Third, clearly defining and specifying resources is a necessary step before theorists and researchers can approach the issues of their use-value to social movements, transferability among groups, and the extent to which access to them can be controlled. Thus resource fungibility and proprietarity is our third line of analysis. While a broader range of resource attributes could be considered, these two are important in analyzing the mobilization of resources from within resource rich social groups, but they are especially important to the processes that shape the transfer of resources between organized social groups. The traditional concern of social movement analysts with movements of the downtrodden, underprivileged, and unrepresented, combined with the importance of resources and the reality of their unequal distribution, brings the analysis of forms of access to resources to central attention.

Fourth, we take up the issue of how social movement actors gain access to crucial resources and the longstanding debate over the extent to which social movements receive material resources from external rather than indigenous sources. This line of analysis inevitably raises the question of the kinds of effects those exchange relationships have on movement goals and activities. We argue that social movements and SMOs rely on multiple means of gaining access to needed resources and discuss specifically four predominant modes: movement self-production, resource aggregation, resource appropriation, and patronage. The four modes of access are discussed in conjunction with the five resource types we specify, and we proceed to argue that longstanding debate over financial patronage represents just one among many distinct exchange relationships by which social movements and SMOs access resources.

Finally, we take up four key resource mobilization processes. Two of them, the mobilization of money and the mobilization of labor, are heavily contingent upon a third, the creation of movement structures, or organization building. This is true because, in general, the most important factor in accounting for whether individuals will contribute money or time and effort to collective enterprises is whether or not they are asked to do so (Klandermans and Oegema 1987; Klandermans 1997). SMOs provide constituents and adherents opportunities to contribute money and labor, resources that would quite likely remain individual unless they were transformed into collective resources through the agency of representatives of SMOs.[1] Lastly, we discuss collective action itself, the deploying of repertoires, as a resource mobilization process. Movement constituents and adherents who take part in movement efforts in turn are more likely to contribute other kinds of resources, and many forms of collective action themselves are resource generating at the same time that they are resource expending. Collective action itself, then, can generate new resources.

SOCIAL MOVEMENTS AND THE DISTRIBUTION AND REDISTRIBUTION OF RESOURCES

Resource Inequality

Even the "simple availability" of resources is actually more complicated, since, in order to be available for use, resources must be both present in a specific sociohistorical context and accessible to potential collective actors. This brings to the fore an assumption implicit in much resource mobilization scholarship. The resources crucial to the initiation or continuation of collective action are unevenly distributed within societies and among them. Moreover, within a society the control of resources varies from one social group to another as it does among the various members of each group. Not all social groups control the same types and amounts of resources, and not all individuals within a given social group have equal access to group resources. It is not our intent, however, to develop a general theory of social stratification. Instead we want to emphasize that the presence of resources and thereby their potential to be mobilized by specific social movement constituencies varies over space, through time, and across constituency. Resource mobilization theory is at root aimed at better understanding how groups are able to overcome prevailing patterns of resource inequality in their efforts to pursue social change goals.

Spatial Variation in Movement Mobilization

Crucial resources are concentrated in core areas and tend to be scarcer and to diffuse more slowly into peripheral zones. This is the case within states and among them. As a consequence, resources important for the mobilization of social movements are more readily accessible to potential collective actors in core zones than is the case in the periphery. Recent research bears this out for transnational SMOs that were founded earlier and at a faster rate in wealthy industrial democracies (Smith and Wiest 2003). A similar dynamic operates within nations like the US between large metropolitan areas and rural ones. Numerous studies have found movements to be more likely to emerge in metropolitan areas as well as large counties where potential activists are in closer proximity to a wide range of resources (Lincoln 1978; McCarthy et al. 1988). The social problems of urban and more recently suburban areas have long commanded more media, philanthropic, and political attention than their rural counterparts. In general, then, we expect the spatial distribution of movement mobilization to correlate more strongly with resource availability than with the spatial distribution of injustice or grievance. McCammon's (2001) analysis of the diffusion of suffrage mobilization finds that state-level mobilizations resulted in large part from the decision of national suffrage leaders to spatially redistribute movement resources across states in the form of organizers, speakers, literature, money, and events.

Historical Variations in Resource Availability

Both the use-value of specific resource types and the amount of resources present in a specific context vary over time. Shifting use-value is clearest with technology as the pace of innovation may hasten the obsolescence of once important techniques or equipment. For example, the telephone lessened the importance of participation in community organizations or events as a means of sharing movement related information, and email is rapidly replacing older techniques, like organizing "phone trees," as a means of contacting large numbers of people. Increases in the discretionary income of movement constituencies over time has been found to increase the likelihood of movement mobilization by middle-class Americans in the 1960s and, under certain circumstances, collective action by West Bank Palestinians between 1976 and 1985 (McCarthy and Zald 1973; Khawaja 1994). The presence and availability of other resources changes over time as well. For example, the number of local feminist organizations and environmental organizations has grown dramatically since the middle 1960s. Many of these groups have evolved into nonprofit service providers and only intermittently become involved in advocacy or collective action. Nevertheless a denser local infrastructure of such groups provides more appropriate forms of social organization available to facilitate mobilization. Demographic trends over time also shape patterns of resource availability. We consider these and other social groupings next.

Social Differences in Resource Availability

A number of scholars with varying theoretical orientations pointed to the rise of a "new middle class" with distinctive social and cultural commitments, similar position in the economy, and similar status as a prime mover in the emergence of the so-called "new" social movements (NSMs) in Europe after the 1960s (Parkin 1968; Inglehart 1977; Melucci 1980; Offe 1985; Kriesi 1989). The NSMs pursued the social change preferences of this increasingly significant and relatively well-resourced social class. During the early 1980s in the US, the African-American tributary of the environmental justice movement emerged to national prominence more rapidly than their white, working-class counterparts. This happened in large part because black environmental justice activists were able to draw upon the substantial civil rights movement infrastructure, seasoned local activists, and a resonant environmental racism issue frame that had already been created. By comparison, working-class white groups "fighting toxics" were resource deprived with a thin national infrastructure, and few seasoned activists and an issue frame their opponents, warped into a caricature of self-interested "not in my backyard" (NIMBY) attitudes that have stuck to this day.[2]

Consider, for instance, the uneven distribution of Internet access and skills and its impact on the mobilization potential of diverse social groups. The Internet is a worldwide social infrastructure widely used to disseminate information and coordinate activities by social movement actors (Gillham 2003). Not only is it widely used; it's use is rapidly becoming the norm among SMOs.[3] Yet use of the web requires access via appropriately equipped computers the distribution of which is highly stratified in the US and worldwide. Recent national research estimates that in September 2001 just over one-half (50.5%) of US households had Internet access at home (NTIA 2002), with substantial disparities by race, income, and education (Wilson et al. 2003). Moreover, putting up and maintaining an effective website requires even better equipment and regular inputs of skilled labor. As Internet competency becomes a marker of legitimacy, which in turn facilitates the acquisition of further resources, the mobilization potential of relatively deprived constituencies may be further constrained.

In general, consistent with our several examples, we expect an inverse relationship between the range of resources that are accessible to specific constituencies and the pace and scope of their mobilization in pursuit of social change preferences. Therefore, the population of currently mobilized social movements in a given society will represent only a subset of its potential social movements. Consequently, currently mobilized movements in any society are more likely to reflect the social change preferences of its better-resourced constituencies than its less well endowed ones.

Resource Redistribution and Social Movements

In neoclassical economics the distribution of resources is treated as the "natural" outcome of market activities and contrasted with the redistribution efforts of states. Resource redistribution by agencies of the state provides significant facilitation to many social movements and even direct patronage to a few. However, individuals and organizations from other sectors (e.g., foundations, religious bodies) also redistribute resources in efforts to redress perceived inequities in the prevailing market driven distribution of goods (Shanahan and Tuma 1994). Such state and nonstate actors are motivated by a number of factors, including altruism, enlightened self-interest, compassion, religious conviction, or ideological commitment. Others may be motivated by the desire to co-opt and thereby to control to some extent the goals and tactics of a movement. Such motives are important considerations, but we emphasize the behavior of such groups in counteracting the existing patterns of resource distribution in ways that support the mobilization of social movements.

Resource Redistribution by the State

States redistribute resources to social movements in three ways, which can be broadly differentiated by the kinds of resources provided and what movement actors must do to gain access to those resources.[4] First, monetary resources and technical assistance are provided directly to organizations that meet specific criteria and agree to operate within government guidelines. Second, in the US, legitimacy and overt fundraising facilitation are provided through the granting of nonprofit status by state governments and tax-exempt status by the IRS in exchange for the group adopting certain constraints upon their activities (McCarthy et al. 1991). Both of these statuses augment organizational legitimacy in the eyes of potential supporters, including foundations that typically require these before making grants. Third, states sometimes allow social movement actors access to state decision-making processes.

US feminist SMOs illustrate the mix of facilitation and constraint that may face groups benefiting directly from the redistribution of state resources. Since the mid-1960s a large number of local women's movement groups have taken on social service functions as federally regulated nonprofits, many often contracting with local government to provide an array of services broadly consistent with feminist goals (Ferree and Martin 1995). Of course, such resources may be accompanied by constraints. Matthews' (1995) analysis of state funded rape crisis centers in the 1970s makes clear that the state and the feminist SMOs they funded agreed that rape crisis work should be done, but eventually clashed over what rape crisis work consisted of and how it should be carried out. Hyde's (1995) analysis of New Right efforts to leverage the government to defund feminist SMOs during the 1980s documents the range of impacts resulting from the withdrawal of state funding. Some of the feminist SMOs retained state funding by emphasizing their identity as human service providers and professionalizing their image. Others became more confrontational and mobilized against the New Right by raising scholarship funds for low-income gynecological services and using the threat of New Right initiatives to broaden and radicalize their membership base.

Third, states provide a variety of mechanisms for organized groups and individual citizens to be included in policy decision-making processes, and these sometimes benefit SMOs. In contrast to "corporatist" mechanisms that are common in some European states, regulatory ones are common in the US. For instance, federal mandates for citizen participation in regulatory processes span a range of social movement issues and have created what amounts to a national infrastructure of loosely coupled, decentralized venues of potential participation or contention for social movement actors. Each step in mandated regulatory review processes offers a potential leverage point at which SMOs or individual activists can exert either positive pressure to support or modify a proposal, or exert negative pressure to resist or halt a given endeavor. For example, environmental and social impact assessments required since the National Environmental Policy Act of 1969 have been used effectively by environmentalists to influence or block a broad range of environmentally damaging endeavors. Nuclear power activists used these kinds of federally mandated venues and regulatory reviews to bring the process of nuclear power plant sitings to a halt in the 1970s (Nelkin and Pollak 1981) as have those opposed to the siting of toxic and hazardous waste facilities in the 1980s and 1990s (Edwards 1995; Peterson 2002).

More recently President Clinton's Executive Order #12898 mandating environmental equity impact assessments has extended this tool into the environmental justice arena. Moreover, that order created and funded the National Environmental Justice Advisory Commission (NEJAC), which has held regular meetings around the country to build a body of related state-level environmental equity regulations and plans. Even though NEJAC's operations have been criticized as autocratic and nonparticipatory, its regular meetings provided an occasion for environmental justice activists in different regions of the country to build movement capacity, develop movement infrastructure, and coordinate activities. Activists used the NEJAC meetings in much the same way that NGOs and SMOs enhanced movement infrastructure and capacity globally by piggy-backing the alternative Earth Summit onto the official United Nations Environment and Development conference in Rio de Janeiro in 1992.

Sirianni and Friedland (2001) argue that the very strong citizen participation mandates in the Clean Water Act of 1972 have since the 1970s spawned a broad range of participatory processes across the US. Some have gone so far as to suggest that such local stakeholder processes are exemplars of a broader movement of civic renewal and cooperation (Bernard and Young 1997; Shutkin 2000), though from our perspective they could just as easily become arenas of local conflict and contention. Regardless, these processes provide potential leverage points, venues of participation, and occasions for movement engagement with state-subsidized transaction costs. The extent to which the state redistributes resources in this way varies dramatically across the range of movement issues. In the US those available to environmentalists, for example, are quite extensive, while those available to peace activists and others who wish to influence US foreign policy are virtually nonexistent. Such differences exert substantial impact on cross-movement variations in the range and types of SMO social change strategies, tactics, and targets.

Redistribution by Organizations

A variety of nonstate organizations act to redistribute resources in ways that facilitate movement mobilization. Formal organizations control vast amounts of wealth and are also rich in other kinds of resources in industrial nations. Here we briefly touch on the role of philanthropic foundations, religious organizations, movement mentoring organizations, movement organizations themselves, as well as profit-making organizations in making their resources available to resource poor movement groups and constituencies.

Foundations. US philanthropic foundations possess vast wealth and are widely known as a source of financial resources for social movements. Yet foundations also provide other important benefits to SMOs, especially including legitimacy and templates for action. Spurred by Federal law in the early 1960s existing foundations greatly increased their giving in general and their aggregate support of groups seeking social change in particular. And since then the number of foundations that do so has steadily increased. A conservative estimate puts that support at close to 90 million dollars in 1990 (Jenkins and Halcli 1999). Nearly one-third of that 1990 total went to women's and environmental groups, and more than half of it went to professionalized advocacy groups and technical support organizations. However, over 40 percent of it went to minority and economic justice groups, so there remains a significant amount of redistribution to groups representing underprivileged constituents in this flow of financial resources.[5] Coalitions of foundations have been formed that aim to expand the extent and level of social change philanthropy, such as the Women's Funding Network and the Neighborhood Funders Group, a caucus of members of the National Council of Foundations.[6]

There is some debate about the intent of foundations in providing such funds, and the possibilities that it may serve to moderate movement goals and tactics (see Jenkins and Eckert 1986), but there is little question that it has shaped the organizational structure of SMOs and, especially, their fiduciary procedures. Only groups that meet minimal standards of organizational structure, usually anchored in formal 501(c)3. Internal Revenue Service charitable registration, and financial responsibility are likely to receive foundation grants (McCarthy et al. 1991). As a result, SMOs typically come into compliance with these formal, and sometimes informal, expectations before they apply for grants.

Receipt of a grant from a prestigious national foundation can serve as an important source of legitimacy for an SMO, and there is evidence suggesting that movement groups receiving support from common foundation sources are more likely to develop other kinds of ties with one another. As well, many foundations provide funds for groups willing to adopt a specific organizational form and social change purpose illustrated by the many health related SMOs that have been spawned through the auspices of the Robert Wood Johnson Foundation.

Religious organizations. Many religious organizations, consistent with their value commitments, are strongly committed to helping the less privileged. Religious groups in the US directly control far fewer monetary resources than do foundations, but high rates of religious participation and extensive infrastructures mean that they are far richer in human and social-organizational resources. The reverse tends to be the case in many European nations where religious participation is lower, but where state tithing mechanisms provide national religious institutions with larger pools of centralized financial resources (Klandermans 1997). The primary forms of religious organization include national level denominational structures, local congregations and "parachurch" organizations that have no formal connections with religious bodies, but claim religious legitimacy and many times mobilize constituents in "blocs" out of religious infrastructures.

Movements for economic and social justice and those opposing war and preparations for war are particularly likely to be the recipients of religious-based resources, as seen in the efforts during the 1960s and 1970s of the US Catholic Bishops and mainline Protestant denominations. Yet their support is not just financial; rather, they provide moral, cultural, social-organizational and human resource as well (Smith 1996; Wuthnow and Evans 2002).[7] Moral legitimacy is perhaps the most valuable resource religious organizations bestow on movement actors. At the local level congregations and parachurch groups regularly contribute access to in-kind resources as well as privileged access to congregational participants (Liebman and Wuthnow 1986; Cress and Snow 1996).

SMOs and movement mentoring organizations. Social movement organizations commonly provide subsidies and, especially, technological advice, to fledgling groups, as well as ongoing support to other SMOs (Walker 1991; Nownes and Neeley 1996). And, as the social movement sector has grown and become professionalized in wealthier nations, a class of organizations has emerged that provide services, sometimes for a fee, but much of the time "pro-bono," to SMOs. Well known as "technical assistance," such services typically include advice about organizational structure, as well as both mobilizing and production technologies. Some of these organizations, social movement "half-way houses" (Morris 1984) and "schools" (Edwards and McCarthy 1992), are far more proactive in attempting to nurture and form organized groups, while working to create and disseminate new social change technologies. In the US a number of these "technical support organizations" (Jenkins and Halcli 1999: 245) serve as significant financial conduits between foundations and less professionalized SMOs.

A note on firms and corporations. Social movement analysts have generally focused more on the support of profit-making organizations for countermovement organizations (Useem and Zald 1982; Switzer 1997) and conservative movements (Sklair 1997), but there are indications of far broader involvement of firms in providing resources for movement groups, especially recent public health movements (e.g., Wolfson 2001). Some such support can be understood as self-interested (e.g., Blue Cross/Blue Shield Health Insurance firms' support of the tobacco control movement and the automobile insurer Allstate Insurance Company's support of anti-drunk driving activists).[8] But many local SMOs successfully seek support from local merchants (as part of their grass-roots fundraising efforts), and such support includes food for volunteers, the purchase of advertisements in SMO publications, the provision of space for movement activities, and contributions of items for raffles. The traditionally heavy emphasis of movement scholars upon progressive and, more recently, "new social movements" has led to an underemphasis upon the extent and variety of resource flows like these to social movements.

Redistribution by Individuals

By providing resources to SMOs and movement activities individuals turn over their control, thereby making the resources collective. Constituents and adherents are a primary source of such resources, usually in the form of small donations of time and money, and less often the bestowal of moral and cultural resources. SMO members may pay regular organizational dues and respond to campaigns for additional support. They may also be asked to volunteer. Many SMOs seek small donations through the modern technologies of direct mail and telemarketing, usually from adherent pools with which they have very tenuous ties (McCarthy 1987). Members of this class of movement constituents have been called "checkbook" members (Skocpol 1999). Many SMOs, at both the local and national level, receive larger financial donations from individual supporters, and such individual supporters can play a crucial role, for instance, in the early stages of SMOs (Walker 1991; Nownes and Neeley 1996). For small local SMOs, individual donations from a few supporters can make up a significant proportion of annual operating budgets (McCarthy and Wolfson 1996). The donation of moral and cultural resources by individuals are less easily accounted for, but can sometimes be of great value, such as the endorsement of a local group by a well-known and highly respected local figure or the volunteering of membership list services by an individual who is adept at that technology.

Typology of Social Movement Resources

Social movement actions many times lay bare existing power relations among constituencies with conflicting interests and competing preferences over the distribution and redistribution of scarce values. The concept of resources is indispensable in any analysis of power and conflict relations.[9] Yet in the early 1980s resources remained "one of the most primitive and unspecified terms in the theoretical vocabulary" of social movement analysts (Gamson et al. 1982: 82). By the mid-1990s Cress and Snow could still argue persuasively that little progress had been made in explicating resources conceptually or anchoring them empirically (1996: 1090). Taking the latter approach Cress and Snow developed an inductive taxonomy of moral, material, informational, and human resources from their analysis of the activities of 15 homeless SMOs in eight US cities. By contrast, we have taken the former, more synthetic, approach to explicate resources more generally. To do so we draw upon other social movement scholarship (Zald and Jacobs 1978; Knoke 1986; Oliver and Marwell 1992; Verba et al. 1995; Lahausen 1996).

Our conceptualization of resources has also been shaped by important efforts in other parts of the discipline to theorize forms of capital in criticism of narrowly economistic approaches (Bourdieu 1986; Coleman 1988; Putnam 1995; Lin 2001). The most significant difference between our resource typology and that of Cress and Snow is our treatment of social-organizational and cultural resources as separate categories, which among other things eliminates their "informational" resource category.[10] Our conceptualization of social-organizational and cultural resources and much of the foregoing discussion of resource inequality and redistribution draws heavily upon our engagement in the evolving debate over social capital and civil society, especially as it relates to social movements and SMOs.[11] Several relatively distinct streams of theorizing have emerged from this debate. In particular, Pierre Bourdieu theorized three forms of capital (economic, cultural, and social) that taken together "explain the structure and dynamics of differentiated societies" (Bourdieu and Wacquant 1992:119). Bourdieu's emphasis on the analytic centrality of unequal access to differing types of resources via the possession of more or less durable relationships has been especially influential here. In what follows we will differentiate between moral, cultural, social-organizational, human, and material resources.

Moral Resources

Moral resources include legitimacy, solidary support, sympathetic support, and celebrity (Snow 1979; Cress and Snow 1996). Of these, legitimacy has received the most theoretical attention. Neo-institutional organizational theorists make strong claims about the importance of legitimacy as a link between macrocultural contexts and meso- and microlevel organizational processes. Thus they claim that collective actors who most closely mimic institutionally legitimated features for their particular kind of endeavor gain an advantage relative to groups that do not reflect that template as well (Meyer and Rowan 1977; Powell and DiMaggio 1992). Moral resources tend to originate outside of a social movement or SMO and are generally bestowed by an external source known to possess them. Nevertheless, some movements succeed in the difficult task of creating moral resources, as was clearly the case with the US Southern civil rights movement of the 1950s and 1960s. A key distinction here is that an outsider possessing these transfers them to a social movement and can retract them as well. The retraction of moral resources could be done through public acts of disavowal, backstage by spreading the word informally to interested parties, or by simple atrophy. Because externally bestowed moral resources can be retracted, they are both less accessible and more proprietary than the cultural resources we discuss next.

Cultural Resources

Cultural resources are artifacts and cultural products such as conceptual tools and specialized knowledge that have become widely, though not necessarily universally, known. These include tacit knowledge about how to accomplish specific tasks like enacting a protest event, holding a news conference, running a meeting, forming an organization, initiating a festival, or surfing the web. This category includes tactical repertoires, organizational templates, technical or strategic know-how encompassing both mobilization and production technologies (Oliver and Marwell 1992). Consistent with Bourdieu's concept of "habitus" as a structural constraint upon access to "cultural capital" and our foregoing discussion of resource stratification, it is worth emphasizing that specific cultural competencies or collective identities, though widely available in a given society, are neither universally available nor evenly distributed. Not every member of a society or group possesses specific competencies or knowledge that could be of value to a social movement or SMO. For example, familiarity with how to navigate the Internet, to point and click a path to useful information, is a rapidly diffusing cultural resource and one that is capable of facilitating movement activities generally. Yet the cultural availability of that resource is distinct from whether or not a specific SMO possesses either the material resource of required equipment, or the human resource of web-competent members.

A key difference between cultural and moral resources is that cultural resources are widely available, less proprietary, and accessible for use independent of favorable judgments from those outside a movement or SMO.[12] For example, Operation Rescue widely employed nonviolent direct-action tactics modeled directly and explicitly upon those used during the heyday of the US civil rights movement without the blessing, and sometimes with the derision, of civil rights organizations and leaders. At a somewhat abstract level this use was possible because that tactical repertoire is a widely accessible cultural resource. At a more operational level the use of this tactical repertoire also depended upon having the human resource of individuals experienced in using the tactics who could train and lead others in doing so. This category of cultural resources includes movement or issue relevant productions like music, literature, magazines, newspapers, and films and videos. Cultural products like these facilitate the recruitment and socialization of new adherents and help movements maintain their readiness and capacity for collective action (see chapter 5 in this volume).

Social-Organizational Resources

This resource category includes both intentional and appropriable social organization (Coleman 1990). Intentional social organization is created specifically to further social movement goals. By contrast, appropriable social organization was created for nonmovement purposes, but movement actors are able to gain access to other types of resources through it. Recruiting volunteers or disseminating information through work, congregation, civic, or neighborhood connections are widely cited examples. The two are further distinguished by the typical means by which movement actors gain access to them. Resources embedded in appropriable social organization must be co-opted, while access to intentional social organization is presumably more collaborative and potentially less problematic. In either case the ease of accessing such resources will vary according to the goodness of fit between the specific legitimacy, organizational form, goals, and tactics of those groups involved. Both forms of social organization have proven crucial in explaining patterns of movement mobilization. Thus presence of social-organizational resources in a particular locale should increase the overall likelihood of movement mobilization and action in that setting. Moreover, we would expect that the social change preferences of those groups with easier access to these resources would be more likely to be mobilized than those of constituencies with constrained access.

There are three general forms of social organizational resources: infrastructures, social networks, and organizations. Clearly, these three forms vary in organizational formality, but we wish to emphasize the extent to which access to them can be controlled, or in other words how proprietary they are. Infrastructures are the social-organizational equivalent of public goods like postal service, sanitation, or civil infrastructures like roads, sidewalks, and traffic lights that facilitate the smooth functioning of everyday life. Infrastructures are nonproprietary social resources. By contrast, access to social networks and especially groups and formal organizations and thereby the resources embedded in them can be controlled. To varying degrees use can be denied to outsiders and hoarded by insiders. Since a chief benefit of any form of social organization is to provide access to other resources, we are here raising the issue of uneven access to social-organizational resources among potential social movement constituencies. Such differential access creates further inequalities in the capacity to access crucial resources of other kinds.

Human Resources

Human resources are both more tangible and easier to appreciate than the three resource types discussed so far. This category includes resources like labor, experience, skills, and expertise. We also include leadership in this category because it involves a combination of other human resources included here. Human resources inhere in individuals rather than in social-organizational structures or culture more generally. Individuals typically have proprietary control over the use of their labor and human resources, except in extreme cases like forced labor or extortion. Through their participation individuals make their labor accessible and usable to specific movements or SMOs. SMOs can aggregate and deploy individuals who are rather portable compared to social-organizational resources, for example. Yet a movement's capacity to deploy personnel is limited by the cooperation of the individuals involved. And their participation is in turn shaped by spatial and economic factors as well as by social relationships, competing obligations, life-course constraints, and moral commitments.

Thus far we have discussed only labor and not any value-added components of human resources like experience, savvy, skills, or expertise, known also as human capital (Becker 1964). The concept of "value-added" may help differentiate between cultural resources generally present in a given society and the specific individuals whose participation puts competencies, skills, or expertise in the service of a movement or SMO. Clearly, not all adherents offer the same mix of capabilities. A savvy and seasoned activist is not directly interchangeable with an eager undergraduate, no matter how effective the student may become with additional experience. SMOs often require expertise of varying kinds, and having access to lawyers, web designers, dynamic speakers, organizers, or outside experts when the need arises can be vitally important. A key issue in whether the availability of skilled individuals will enhance movement mobilization hinges on how their expertise fits with movement or SMO needs. For example, a prominent physician may have little more to offer than a high-school intern if an SMO needs someone to evaluate the methodology of an environmental equity impact assessment, and the high-school intern may be the best choice to recruit six volunteers to distribute fliers (Oliver and Marwell 1992). Similarly, a celebrated musician participating in a blockade contributes no additional human resource to the blockade than either the tone-deaf academic or the grocery clerk with whom she has linked arms. Yet the evaluation would be much different from the standpoint of moral resources contributed by the musician's presence.

Material Resources

The category of material resources combines what economists would call financial and physical capital, including monetary resources, property, office space, equipment, and supplies. Monetary resources have received the most analytic attention and there are good reasons for that. Money is a necessity. No matter how many other resources a movement mobilizes it will incur costs and someone has to pay the bills. Material resources have also received much analytic attention because they are generally more tangible, more proprietary, and in the case of money more fungible than other resource types. We discuss these concepts next.

KEY RESOURCE ATTRIBUTES

In this section we discuss in more detail two important dimensions along which all resource types vary: how fungible they are and how proprietary they are. First, each resource lies somewhere on a continuum between having a use-value to social movements that is fully fungible (context independent) or fully context dependent (idiosyncratic). Second, resources are more or less proprietary, varying in the degree that individual or collective actors can control access to them. The two resource attributes discussed here do not comprise an exhaustive set of potentially useful possibilities. However, they are of central importance to understanding processes of resource redistribution and access and, as a consequence, are central to the broader argument we make here. They are also centrally important for specifying the conditions under which resources have greater or lesser use-value for movement mobilization. Beyond this, however, these particular attributes incorporate aspects of other attributes of resources that we have excluded from attention. Resources that are durable, for example, hold their use-value over time and are, thus, fungible across time. By contrast, perishable resources are time-bound and thus, more context dependent. Similarly, much has been made of the distinction between public and private goods that, in our terms, can be seen to vary greatly in how proprietary they are. In thinking about such attributes it is important to focus on those attributes of specific resources. For instance, as we have discussed above, resources are distributed unevenly, often exhibiting a geographic or social concentration. These are not attributes of the resources per se, but rather attributes of the distribution of resources. We turn now to a discussion of resource fungibility and proprietary.

Fungibility and Context Dependence

All resources can be conceptualized along a continuum ranging from having a fully fungible use-value to those whose use-value is entirely context dependent. A fully fungible resource would be one that could be transferred easily between persons or organizations. The use-value to a social movement of a fully fungible resource would be relatively constant from one sociopolitical context to the next. Money is the most fungible of resources. Yet even its value fluctuates daily depending upon how the vagaries of international currency exchanges affect an SMO's preferred currency.[13] Nevertheless, a highly fungible resource like money can presumably be converted into other resources as needs dictate. Therefore, movement actors with a large proportion of fungible resources at their disposal enjoy greater flexibility in the range of strategies and tactics available to them, while the options of their counterparts rich in context-dependent (localized, spatially bound, issue specific, etc.) resources are more constrained.

The greater fungibility of money compared to other resource types means that money can be converted into other resources through the purchase of equipment, hiring of staff, founding of organizations, organizing events, and even in the production of certain cultural resources. The fungibility of money has limits, especially with respect to moral resources like legitimacy. For example, a celebrity endorsement of an issue campaign can greatly increase public attention, generate media coverage, and open doors to policymakers and resource providers alike. This has been the case with the ongoing engagement of Paul Hewson (aka Bono the well-known leader of the music group U2) on the issue of developing-world debt relief. Celebrity endorsements are especially credible in cases like this one where the celebrity commands the details of the issue, evidences sincere and longstanding commitment, and donates his or her own time. By contrast, a group could convert money into an ersatz moral resource by simply hiring a celebrity spokesperson to endorse a particular issue campaign and derive comparable publicity benefits. The legitimacy of the endeavor, however, would be eroded if it became apparent that the celebrity participated for purely financial reasons.

At the opposite end of the continuum from fungible resources are those with a use-value that is more context dependent and thereby limited to specific movement issues, or is localized in time and place. The use-value of context-dependent resources depends upon a variety of sociocultural and political factors, as well as, the type of endeavor for which they will be used. Among the resource types we have discussed, social-organizational resources and important forms of human capital are quite context dependent. By contrast moral, monetary, and cultural resources are generally more portable, more spatially transferable than social-organizational ones.[14]

For example, in 1999 the Animal Welfare Institute (AWI) collaborated with a coalition of Polish farm organizations to undertake a confrontational direct action campaign to block the plans by Smithfield Foods to establish corporate-owned, industrial-style hog operations in Poland (Juska and Edwards forthcoming). Based in Washington, DC, AWI is an advocacy organization with extensive experience and international connections gained from over 25 years of endangered species work. At different points in the successful campaign against Smithfield Foods AWI provided important resources, including limited financial support and deploying paid and volunteer activists to Poland. AWI also produced a Polish language video entitled *The Trojan Pig*, which proved extremely effective in galvanizing opposition to Smithfield Foods among Polish farmers. Yet prior to this campaign AWI had no operations or connections in Eastern Europe. Despite their ability to provide moral, material, human, and cultural resources, AWI's extensive social-organizational resources embedded in its US and international operations remained relatively inaccessible and of little use-value to the Polish campaign against Smithfield Foods.

The benefits of social organizational resources are confined to the geographical areas in which they are nested. While social-organizational resources would be valuable to social movements in any context, for them to have use-value to a social movement they must be accessible, and access to them is limited to the scope of their operations.[15] Similarly, labor is less context dependent than the human capital represented by skills, specialized knowledge, or technical expertise. For example, an activist with years of effective advocacy experience in Washington on a specific issue (e.g., developing-world debt relief) would find that her knowledge of how that system works, her connections, and command of the issues would be relatively useless if she were to find herself involved in a local environmental justice struggle over a proposed hazardous waste landfill. In much the same way, the professionalized expertise so necessary to run an effective issue advocacy organization at the national level would be of only limited use-value in leading a new congregation-based organizing campaign for an affiliate of the Industrial Areas Foundation (Warren 2001). The use-value of skills and expertise is more context dependent than the use-value of labor per se.

Proprietarity

The resources discussed above also vary in the extent to which they are proprietary. Resources vary on a continuum between being completely proprietary, where access to them can be tightly controlled, to those that are universally accessible in the public domain. Money and human labor are both quite proprietary. The decision to participate in a movement or not is a relatively private one, and individuals control which movement actors, if any, have access to their labor. By contrast, cultural resources are the least proprietary. Tactical repertoires, organizational templates, and other conceptual tools are "culturally available," existing in the public domain usually without proprietary control.[16] Moral resources like formal endorsements or solidary support are proprietary because they are granted from an external source and can be retracted. Social-organizational resources can be highly proprietary, as with those embedded in clandestine organizations or elite social clubs where access is tightly controlled, or they can be widely accessible in the public domain as in the case of dense civic networks. Whether a resource is proprietary or in the public domain will greatly affect social movement efforts to gain access to it and utilize it. As we discuss below, the amount of control a resource provider can exert over a recipient's use of the resource relates directly to how proprietary the specific resource is. All resources may have strings attached, but the strings attached to proprietary resources are likely to be stronger and more numerous.

MECHANISMS OF ACCESS AND SOURCE CONSTRAINTS

Thus far we have emphasized the uneven distribution of resources and efforts to alter that distribution in order to channel resources toward the support of social movements. We turn now to the concept of access. Before resources present in a specific context can be utilized by social movement actors, those resources must first be accessible. For example, certain foundations may redistribute substantial funding to support a specific social movement, yet their largess is not equally accessible to all SMOs within that movement. The process SMOs must go through to obtain and maintain grant funding limits access to those that have already achieved a certain threshold of organizational formality and legitimacy. We discuss here four mechanisms by which social movement actors gain access to resources: aggregation from constituents, self-production, appropriation/co-optation, and patronage.

Four Mechanisms of Resource Access

Table 6.1 cross-classifies the five resource types described above with four mechanisms of resource access. Thus, the 20 cells of table 1 describe distinct exchange relationships movement actors pursue in order to gain access to the range of resources described above. What follows is not intended as an exhaustive discussion of either the mechanisms of resource access or exchange relationships. Rather, we intend them as conceptual tools to help analysts take into account the mix of resource types, means of access, and exchange relations with sources in specific cases of analytic interest. The emphasis we place on mechanisms of access coupled with the broader spectrum of resource types we have specified helps, we believe, to redirect the longstanding debate over the likelihood that receiving money from external sources leads SMOs to displace goals and moderate tactics. We take up that issue in our discussion of source constraints below.

Aggregation

Aggregation refers to mechanisms whereby resources held by dispersed individuals are converted into collective ones that in turn can be allocated by movement actors.

Table 6.1 Means of Social Movement and SMO Resource Access and Resource Types

Means of Access	Moral	Cultural	Resource Types Social-Organizational	Human	Material
Aggregation	• Lists of endorsers • Recruiting celebrity endorsers • Advisory committee members on letterhead • Soliciting statements of support for specific projects	• Social movement schools movement mentoring orgs. • Movement initiated summits and workshops where groups come together to share advice, information, strategy • Working groups	• Building networks • Forming coalitions	• Recruiting constituents	• Member contributions Emily's list • Individual donations from non-members
Self-Production	• Moral authority from the effective use of non-violence (e.g., King, Gandhi)	• Ideas • Frames • Tactical repertoires • Music • History	• Founding SMOs	• Raising and socializing children, • Issue/movement oriented summer camps • Training • Movement Mentors • Women's, Environmental, or Black studies programs	• Grassroots fund raising events • Creating items for sale at events (T-shirts, posters, CDs, coffee mugs, etc.)

Co-optation/ Appropriation	• Allying yourself with a well-respected group • Hiring grassroots supporters to lobby officeholders • Company unions • Listing links to prominent, well respected groups on your webpage	• Providing links on your webpage to materials produced by someone else • Links to someone else's webpage	• Recruiting local affiliates from existing organizations • Gaining access to congregations for solicitation • mesomobilization	• Networked recruitment • Acquiring a mailing list • Organizational members • Bloc recruitment • Drawing on members of coalition partners	• Office space • Buses
Patronage	• A widely respected person or organization recognizing a group or activist in order to call positive attention to their work • Human rights awards • Nobel Pax Prize • An audience with the Pope	• Excellence awards aimed at competence or effectiveness • Accreditation of fiscal procedures to enhance confidence of supporters and donors	• Being loaned the mailing lists and telephone lists of sympathetic individuals	• Providing staff • Providing technical assistance	• Start-up grants • Large donations • Foundation grants • Government grants • Service contracts • Corporate sponsorship

Social movements aggregate privately held resources from beneficiary and conscience constituents in order to pursue collective goals. Social movements aggregate moral resources, for example, by compiling and publicizing lists of individuals and organizations that endorse their goals and actions, as has been the practice of the Mobilization for Global Justice since Seattle (Gillham 2003; Gillham and Edwards 2003). Cultural resources can be aggregated in movement initiated organizing conferences where activists from a range of groups meet to share information, brainstorm strategy, and conduct training.

Self-Production

Self-production of resources refers to those mechanisms whereby SMOs and movement leaders create or add value to resources that have been aggregated, co-opted, or provided by patrons. A fundamental mechanism by which social movements gain access to resources is to produce them internally. Social movements create cultural products like collective-action frames, tactical repertoires, music, literature, and organizational templates for enacting specific types of collective events or issue campaigns. Movements found SMOs, build networks, and form coalitions. Movements self-produce human resources through training rank-and-file activists for leadership, and the socializing of their children into the movement's values and practices. They also produce items to sell such as literature, products with movement symbolic significance like T-shirts, coffee mugs, posters, art, and even cakes and cookies for bake sales.

Co-Optation/Appropriation

Social movements often exploit relationships they have with existing forms of social organization that were not formed for explicit movement purposes. Co-optation refers to the transparent, permitted borrowing of resources that have already been aggregated by such groups. Appropriation refers to the surreptitious exploitation of the previously aggregated resources of other groups. A large proportion of SMOs include other organizations more or less formally among their members. In doing this they are able to some extent to co-opt resources previously produced or aggregated by those other organizations. Co-optation carries with it a transfer of some amount of proprietary control over the resources that are co-opted. The extent of proprietary control varies considerably by resource type. And co-optation usually implies some form of subsequent reciprocity as well as a tacit understanding that the resources will be used for mutually agreeable purposes. Co-optation of resources has received much theoretical attention (McCarthy 1987) because it has been quite common in many consequential movements such as the civil rights (McAdam 1982) and women's liberation (Freeman 1975) movements. Appropriation, on the other hand, has not received as much attention. Selznick (1960) illustrated the process for the American Communist Party, and a number of student groups active in the 1960s that specialized in infiltrating other groups and taking control of their resource base (Isserman 1987; Miller 1987).

Patronage

Patronage refers to the bestowal of resources upon an SMO by an individual or organization that often specializes in patronage. In monetary patronage relationships a patron external to the movement or SMO provides a substantial amount of financial support, but typically exercises some degree of proprietary control over how that money can be used and may well even attempt to exert influence over day-to-day operations and policy decisions. Government contracts, foundation grants, and large private donations are the most common forms of financial patronage as we noted above. Similarly, patronage relationships may involve the provision of some level of human resources, including, especially, the loan of personnel for periods of time. This kind of patronage is common when coalitions of SMOs field large and complex events, usually directed by loosely coupled organizations formed specifically for that purpose. Patronage in moral resources occurs when a widely respected individual or organization recognizes an SMO for positive achievements. Amnesty International's human rights awards and the Nobel Peace Prize are widely known examples, the receipt of which can be an immensely valuable organizational resource.

Source Constraints

Two longstanding debates about resources center on whether social movements obtain their support primarily from indigenous or external sources. This issue leads directly into questions about the extent to which external supporters constrain movement goals and activities (Cress and Snow 1996).[17]

We wish to reframe this debate in several ways. First, we contend that social movements and SMOs typically acquire their resources from a combination of internal and external sources, and all but the very smallest SMOs utilize multiple means of gaining access to resources. Thus the typical SMO simultaneously manages numerous exchange relationships. Even the homeless SMOs studied by Cress and Snow were engaged in multiple exchange relations. Each exchange relationship can be expected to carry a set of expectations and obligations between the parties, with each relationship having widely varying potential for social control. For example, the exchange relationship involved in an SMO aggregating small donations from a range of external conscience constituents is not likely to have the same social control implications for the group as would benefiting from the monetary patronage of a foundation, a single large donor, or a government agency. Given the range of exchange relationships implied in table 6.1, we note that the debate over source and constraint as it has proceeded over the years has been cast very narrowly, focusing almost exclusively on a single exchange relationship – monetary patronage. Even SMOs that benefit from monetary patronage will typically be engaged in a variety of other exchange relationships with various sources. The perspective we advocate here encourages analysts to consider the varying mix of facilitations and constraints across the range of exchange relationships through which specific SMOs, coalitions, issue campaigns, or event organizers mobilize resources.

KEY RESOURCE MOBILIZATION PROCESSES

Leaders and their top aides figure prominently in case studies of social movements (e.g., Sale 1973; Dobofsky 1980; Branch 1988; Binder 2002), yet the role of leaders and the strategic decisions they make typically play a far less central role in social movement theories (see chapter 8 in this volume). The focus upon resource mobilization processes, however, brings the role of strategic leadership to the forefront of analysis (Oliver and Marwell 1992; Ganz 2000). Social change entrepreneurs create social movement organizations, leaders and cadre develop and manage those organizations, and the functionaries of SMOs are responsible for creating the vast majority of opportunities that are available to adherents of the goals of a social movement to contribute time and money to a movement. And while collective action does certainly occur independently of SMOs (Oliver 1989b), during the late twentieth century in Western industrial democracies a substantial proportion of social change oriented collective action is directly fielded by SMOs or proceeds under their auspices.

The initial creation of an SMO requires the mobilization and aggregation of some minimum level of resources, as does its ongoing maintenance. Once in existence, SMOs, like all organizations, can be thought of as more or less rountinized bundles of "ways of doing things." The common patterns of these institutionalized practices come to include preferred repertoire of exchange relationships and means of resource access, and importantly shape the extent and form of the mobilization of material resources and activism within any social movement. And, they, in turn, constrain the choice of forms of collective action. These common practices are in turn shaped by the broader patterns of location and stratification of societal resources.

Creating Organizations and Building Organizational Capacity

Increasingly we live in a world dominated, not by the market, but by large-scale, bureaucratic organizations: multinational firms, the military, governmental agencies. Organizations are more powerful than individuals, and individuals seeking to challenge the practices of powerful organizations have formed their own social movement organizations. SMOs have proliferated at an incredibly rapid pace during the last three or four decades (see chapter 7 in this volume). This trend has been clearly established for national groups in the US (Walker 1991; Minkoff 1995; Baumgartner and Leech 1998) and in a number of European nations (Kriesi et al. 1995), with many indications that it is also the case for local groups (i.e., Edwards and Marullo 1995; Rucht 1999; Kempton et al. 2001).

The organizational structure of the social movement economy mirrors that of the demography of firms such that small, local, mostly volunteer, SMOs are the most common form, while large, financially affluent, heavily professionalized SMOs compose only a tiny proportion of the total population (see Edwards and Foley 2003).[18] Trends in the founding of small and large SMOs are partially responsible for this structure, but so are mortality rates of newly founded SMOs as well as the growth and decline of existing ones. We know more about the entrepreneurial process for large SMOs than for small, local ones. For instance, a significant proportion of larger SMOs were founded with the help of patrons, receiving financial infusions, most importantly, from foundations and wealthy individuals, and sometimes other SMOs (Walker 1991; Nownes and Neeley 1996). If the general process of the founding of SMOs is in most respects similar to that of the founding of firms (Aldrich 1999), most start-ups require very small amounts of capital, and for most of them the entrepreneurs and their friends provide most of it. Some large professionalized national SMOs such as Common Cause (McFarland 1984), for example, began with substantial resources and pretensions to national scope, while others began in local communities and grew into national ones, like MADD (McCarthy 1994).

In any case, when an SMO is initially formed its architects make a variety of strategic choices about the goals, structure, and forms of collective actions that will be embodied in its ways of doing things. Most important for our purposes are decisions about organizational form and "mobilizing technologies."[19] And while SMOs may change and adapt, the choice of templates made at founding are many times very difficult to alter once an organization is up and running, since it has staked its public identity, to some extent, upon them and has begun to invest time and money in acting upon those choices. The templates of structure and mobilizing technology from among which SMO entrepreneurs must choose are part of the stock of available cultural resources, although access to them may be highly stratified as with many forms of knowledge and expertise.[20] Such choices are governed, in part, by typical "organizational means–ends rationality constrained by satisficing" (McCarthy and Zald 2001), but, also importantly, by mimetic, coercive, and normative institutional processes (DiMaggio and Powell 1983).

Adoption of a particular SMO structure may constrain the use of particular mobilizing technologies and facilitate the use of others. A professionalized SMO, like the Children's Defense Fund (Skocpol 1999) that chooses not to enlist individual members, for instance, forgoes a potential source of stable financial support as well as strong ties to a constituency that, potentially, could be mobilized for mass collective actions.

On the other hand, such an SMO may be able to devote greater effort to the use of previously effective fundraising technologies and may, therefore, be in a position to indirectly contribute to mass collective actions by providing subsidies to those groups that directly organize them. This was the case, for example, when Public Citizen provided crucial funding to on-site organizers leading up to the November 1999 WTO protest in Seattle (Gillham 2003). Or an SMO, like one of the local groups associated with the Industrial Areas Foundation (Warren 2001), which chooses to rely upon organizational rather than individual members may, as a result, succeed in stabilizing a large enough financial flow that it can direct more of its effort toward collective action than toward individual membership maintenance. Also SMOs that choose to become officially registered with the US Federal government as nonprofit organizations are expected to adopt certain standard operating procedures and may, as a result, adopt ways of doing things that constrain their choice of certain mobilizing technologies and encourage others (McCarthy et al. 1991; Cress 1997).

The choice of organizational form can have direct implications for the ability of an ongoing SMO to build the organizational capacity for certain types of collective action, such as grass-roots mobilization and litigation. Some SMOs choose to expand their organizational capacity by creating local chapters, such as the suffrage movement (McCammon 2001). Others, like the National Association for the Advancement of Colored People (NAACP), have spun off parallel, but independent, SMOs (The NAACP Legal and Defense Fund) that specialize in litigation tactics. Choices about organizational form like these, pursued for the purpose of building organizational capacity, also can constrain the kinds of mobilizing technologies that are easily accessible to SMO leaders.

Traditional criticisms of the role of SMOs in collective action stress both their conservatizing and their diversionary potential. The former posits that SMOs serve to moderate movement goals and tactics, and the latter that they divert effort from goal accomplishment to organizational maintenance. The greater the share of its resources an SMO devotes to maintaining itself, the less it can invest in production technologies and collective action. Below we will return to the question of SMO overhead costs.

The recent proliferation of SMOs has been accompanied by a trend toward the professionalization of SMO leadership (McCarthy and Zald 1973). The trend reinforces the impact of societal stratification processes upon movement processes. Weed (1995) shows, for instance, that in the US victims movement, paid SMO leaders are increasingly recruited on the basis of professional qualifications rather than on the basis of constituency membership or movement experience. There is also a tendency toward the adoption of professionalized technologies as the locus of SMOs shifts from local to national, to international (McCarthy 1997). To the extent that these trends become even more pervasive, the leadership of movements of disadvantaged groups should be more and more likely to be composed of conscience constituents rather than beneficiary constituents, those for whom the movement speaks.

Mobilizing Money

All money-mobilizing technologies depend, ultimately, upon social movement activists or their representatives asking fellow citizens and/or those in charge of other organizations for financial contributions.[21]

And, under most circumstances, being asked to give is a necessary condition for giving. As a consequence, knowing the volume of requests (the supply side) tells the analyst as much as the rate of positive response (the demand side) about the ebb and flow of money to social movements. Whether the requests for money are directed at beneficiary or conscience constituents defines whether appeals are to internal or external sources, and, as we have noted above, has been the focus of some research attention.

Technologies for mobilizing money can be distinguished between "narrowcast" technologies designed to target a few concentrated deep pockets of money, and "broadcast" ones targeting many widely dispersed shallow pockets. SMOs vary in their typical mix of targets, and hence the technologies they employ, the sources they depend upon, and the various exchange relationships they must negotiate. SMOs with significant annual operating budgets confront dilemmas in choosing, for instance, between whether to seek donations from a few large financial supporters, such as foundations or wealthy philanthropists, or to pursue telemarketing and/or direct mail strategies aimed at gathering large aggregate sums of money in small amounts from many adherents. Choosing the former can create dependencies upon a few large donors, while the latter may create dependencies upon professional marketing firms. Heavy dependence upon a single technology, in general, makes an SMO more vulnerable to short-term fluctuations in revenues.

Once a large-budget SMO is deeply invested in a particular target and associated technology that has been successful for it in the past, that SMO will incur serious organizational costs, and therefore disincentives, for changing. Indeed, we know that those groups that began with extensive financial help from patrons are highly likely to continue to be dependent upon them (Walker 1991). But, sometimes, environmental conditions require SMOs to rethink their money mobilizing technologies. A good example is seen in the national poverty advocacy groups chronicled by Doug Imig (1992, 1996). Three of these SMOs were quite dependent upon financial resource flows from the US Federal Government before 1980. Those subsidies were severely curtailed during the Reagan years, when government funds available to them fell by 58 percent. This forced the groups to diversify their money mobilizing strategies, and to reduce the resources they devoted to advocacy. Walker (1991) chronicles a similar pattern for his sample of citizens' groups based in Washington, DC. Although many suffered severe cutbacks of federal financial support during the Reagan years, almost all survived, and many of them stepped up efforts to generate money from constituents rather than from outside donors.

Money mobilizing technologies can also be distinguished by whether they are typically handled by mainly professionals ("large-donor fund raising, seeking grants and contracts, direct mail solicitation, paid canvassing, and telemarketing") or they are usually carried out by volunteers ("fairs, rummage and bake sales, brunches, car washes, walk- or run-a-thons, volunteer canvassing and telephoning, raffles, ad-books and selling items on commission") (Oliver and Marwell 1992: 259). No inevitable tie exists between the characteristics of a money mobilizing technology and whether or not it has been professionalized, except for the fact that some business entrepreneurs have discovered a profit potential in packaging it and marketing to SMOs. Many large-budget SMOs routinely assess the advantages and disadvantages of keeping a fundraising operation within the organization versus outsourcing it. Take, for instance, direct mail technology. Such services are widely available for purchase from professionalized firms (Godwin 1988), but at the same time the use of direct mail is so incredibly widespread among advocacy organizations that it is safe to say that a substantial amount of it is accomplished by functionaries and volunteers of SMOs themselves (US Postal Rate Commission 1987). Similarly, while many SMO leaders and their cadre can and do write their own grant proposals to foundations for support, this is a function that has been increasingly professionalized and therefore outsourced by leaders of the largest SMOs.

By the same token many fundraising technologies that have traditionally been staffed by volunteers can occasionally be accomplished by organizations that specialize in such services. For example, product sales such as buttons, T-shirts, and hats are a common staple for SMOs small and large, especially at collective-action events. The same is true for production technologies such as large-event management. When the National Organization for Women stage a large rally in Washington, DC (which they have often done during the last several decades), most of the many details of the events are planned and coordinated by National Organization for Women (NOW) staff and local volunteers. In contrast, when the Promise Keepers group held their "Stand in the Gap Rally" in Washington, DC, they hired a number of firms to plan and coordinate aspects of the event such as publicity, security, food service, and the like. As the social movement sector grows in size, more and more of what have been traditionally volunteer money raising technologies can be expected to become available for hire from outside contractors.

Finally, money mobilization strategies can be differentiated by their typical overhead costs, that is, the proportion of total money raised devoted to covering the costs of the fundraising itself. The greater the overhead costs the greater the diversion of the organization's efforts away from its collective-action tasks. Both direct mail and telemarketing technologies are notorious for the many instances of their low yields, so that a substantial proportion of money raised was absorbed by the technology itself rather than becoming available for investment in production technologies that could generate more collective action. The same difficulty has beset the use of paid door-to-door canvassing (Oliver 1989a; Everett 1992) so that the cost of paying canvassers absorbs significant proportions of the money they raise.

Mobilizing Activism

The labor potential of movement constituents is more equitably distributed across locations and social groups than are their financial resources, because clear upper limits exist for how much time any activist can contribute, while the limits on the financial contributions of wealthy citizens are more elastic. Consequently, groups poor in financial resources may be able to compensate by mobilizing in greater numbers. That prospect provides a strong rationale for mobilizing a movement's disadvantaged or beneficiary constituents (Warren 2001). But, as we have noted above, movements or SMOs rarely limit their efforts to mobilize activism exclusively to beneficiary constituents. This is especially the case for consensus mobilization technologies. Mobilizing consensus refers to the process of turning bystanders and opponents into adherents to the goals of a social movement and its associated organizations (see chapter 16 in this volume) (Klandermans 1997). Consensus mobilization technologies contrast with action mobilization ones that pertain to the process of turning constituents of all kinds into adherents. We take up consensus mobilization first, and then turn to action mobilization in general and its specific manifestation, membership mobilization, in particular.

Mobilizing citizens for collective action depends upon available pools of adherents to the goals of a social movement. And movements, in practice, devote extensive effort toward increasing these pools. Their efforts, of course, are not the only, or many times the most important, factor responsible for increasing support. Nevertheless, "public awareness," "public education," and "issue awareness campaigns" are commonly some of the most labor and capital intensive of the technologies employed by SMOs.[22] Gaining media attention to a movement's issues and goals is an important aspect of consensus mobilization. Some evidence indicates that the more material resources an SMO has available and chooses to invest in efforts to achieve such coverage, the more it will obtain (Barker-Plummer 2002). Consensus mobilization outcomes, no matter who produces them, however, are nonproprietary resources and, thus, cannot be hoarded by the SMO that may have produced them.

So, while SMOs pursuing similar goals may be in competition for the money and time of adherents to their causes, any success they have in consensus mobilization generates available human resources for the entire movement.

Action, or production, mobilizing technologies are designed to turn adherents into constituents of a movement – those who engage in collective action and who may or may not become continuing members of the SMOs associated with a movement. It is necessary to distinguish between different kinds of participation in collective action in order to analyze important dimensions of action mobilization, since activists mobilize adherents for diverse kinds of collective action. These may include, for instance, taking part in a demonstration, attending a meeting, taking part in a sit-in occupation of a building, contacting allied organizations to solicit support for an effort to change a law, contributing money, contacting a public official, stuffing envelopes, or representing the group at a table where movement literature is being distributed. Klandermans (1997) has usefully characterized participation in collective action along the independent dimensions of cost and duration, positing that larger numbers of adherents can be mobilized for low-cost activities of short duration, such as attendance at a demonstration, than for higher cost ones that imply ongoing commitment of time and energy, such as agreeing to head an important committee of a local SMO. In other words, an inverse relationship exists between the opportunity costs of participation and the number of people mobilized.

Joining an SMO is a standard form of movement participation that is typically a low cost activity of some duration. There are many meanings of SMO membership, however, that vary from a member being fully engaged on a day-to-day basis with an organization through simply making a small financial contribution to it. For instance, nationally MADD counts all of those who pledge money in response to their telemarketing appeals as members, though that number far exceeds the aggregate number of individuals claimed as members by MADD's local chapters. The rather large research literature on membership recruitment (Lofland 1996) suggests that disembodied recruitment technologies, like direct mail and media appeals, can be successful in generating weaker forms of membership, but that technologies that depend upon social networks and face-to-face interaction are more successful in recruiting adherents into stronger membership roles (see chapter 15 in this volume). That literature also suggests (Lofland 1996: 210) that, in general, those who respond to recruitment appeals by SMOs tend to be the more privileged individuals among the movement's adherents, and that recruiters usually know this and target their appeals to the adherents most likely to participate (the privileged), thereby exacerbating the impact of privilege on who ultimately participates in collective action (Brady et al. 1999). The same pattern holds, but with even greater disparities for those who respond to appeals for money (Brady et al. 1995).

Collective action, of course, includes much more than becoming a member of an SMO (Oliver 1989b). Many adherents who attend mass demonstrations, for instance, do not belong to SMOs. And some forms of collective action develop without much planning or sponsorship by SMOs. Yet for events that do result from some more or less centralized planning and coordination, successful activists extend their appeals for participation far beyond the members of their own organizations. One of the most effective technologies for accomplishing mass mobilization is through the co-optation of social-organizational resources. This is done by exploiting existing relationships with organizations that were not formed for explicit movement purposes, but whose memberships include a large number of adherents who can aid in mobilizing their own constituents.[23] In the US, groups that co-opt social-organizational resources in this way typically enter into these exchange relationships with religious, occupational, or social service organizations. The equivalent technology for enrolling SMO members through cooperating adherent organizations has been called bloc recruitment (Oberschall 1973) and is another example of co-opting social-organizational resources as shown in table 6.1.

Creating Resources and Mobilization Potential Through Collective Action

In order to explore the central role of human and material resources in generating collective action we have had to distinguish between resource mobilization technologies and collective action in a static analysis. But, no doubt, in the dynamic circumstances of social movement development these are reciprocal processes, with people and financial resources being aggregated to facilitate collective action, and that action, in turn, sometimes enhancing subsequent potential for the aggregation of money and people, and sometimes even doing so through a collective action event itself. Such possibilities are most clearly seen in the increasingly popular runs and walk-a-thons (e.g., Klawiter 1999) that engage adherents as participants who may contribute money themselves, probably develop greater commitment to the cause through participation, and extract contributions from nonparticipants that are tied to the event by the participant's own participation.[24] Participation in such an event raises resources through contributions as well as sales of event related merchandise. Similarly, benefit concerts (Lahausen 1996), such as Farm Aid, are collective-action events aimed at raising both money and solidarity among participants, who are probably more likely to contribute to and participate in the movement subsequently if given opportunities to do so.

CONCLUSION

Putting resources at the center of the analysis of social movement processes reemphasizes the inextricable links between broader societal stratification processes and the ability of social groups to mobilize effectively for ongoing collective action. The durable patterns of resource inequality that stratification analysts have identified (Shanahan and Tuma 1994) and the mechanisms that account for those patterns (Tilly 1998) must be taken into account, since specific instances of collective action are always deeply embedded in existing social and economic relations. As a result, the availability of diverse kinds of resources to social actors and privileged access to them are seen to enhance the likelihood of effective collective action. In this way broader social and economic inequalities are replicated in patterns of collective action, making successful mobilization easier for privileged groups (Kim and Bearman 1997). This is seen in the consistent patterns of differential mobilization that characterize social movements in Western democracies where "new" movements based upon privileged constituencies, such as the middle-class supporters of environmental protection, women, gays and lesbians, and college and university students predominated in the latter quarter of the twentieth century. In contrast, groups of the economically marginalized have had far less success in mobilizing for collective action.

In spite of such durable barriers to the mobilization of economically marginalized groups, however, now and then underprivileged groups have successfully overcome them and effectively mobilized constituencies for ongoing campaigns of collective action. A notable example was the unionization of Californian farmworkers in the early 1960s (Jenkins and Perrow 1977; Jenkins 1985; Ganz 2000). And while material resources are not unimportant in cases like that one, it was the creative deployment of human, cultural, and social-organizational resources by movement leaders, what Ganz (2000) has termed "strategic capacity," that appears to account for such an unlikely outcome. That deployment highlights the crucial role of human agency in transcending the durable social and economic barriers to mobilizing underprivileged constituencies. Our explication of diverse resource types, resource attributes, and the mechanisms of access to them provide, we hope, some useful analytic tools for understanding the role of agency in accounting for variation in the successful mobilization of constituencies of all kinds, and especially underprivileged ones.

Notes

The authors wish to thank Mayer Zald, JoAnn Carmin, Pat Gillham, and the editors of this volume for their feedback and criticism of an earlier draft of this manuscript.

1   This argument mirrors the distinction between demand and supply-side accounts of religious vitality clearly articulated by Finke and others (Warner 1993; Finke et al. 1996) for religious groups.
2   The large national environmental groups that might have been expected to support this local movement was composed of many grass-roots groups, but generally ignored them.
3   According to a recent census of 739 local and statewide environmental organizations operating in North Carolina, a majority of them (55.3%) maintain websites (Edwards and Andrews 2002). In Gillham's (2003) census of 1,398 US-based organizations that endorsed, supported, or participated in the November 1999 World Trade Organization protests in Seattle, 75% had websites.
4   We focus here on the redistribution of resources, yet these processes are closely related to aspects of political opportunity. Over time, variations in the extent of this redistribution can contribute to the ebb and flow of political opportunity for the social movement sector as a whole and evidence substantial cross-national variation. However, in a country like the US, for example, uneven state redistribution across issue arenas and constituencies favor some movements over others.
5   Jenkins and Halcli (1999) show that in 1960 almost 95% of the foundation grant dollars flowed to groups pursuing minority or economic justice issues, indicating that there has been a dramatic shift in the intervening years toward support of groups whose own constituents are more rather than less privileged.
6   "The Women's Funding Network is the membership organization of public and private women's foundations, and individual donors. The Network promotes development and growth of women's funds that empower women and girls" (Brilliant 2000: 558).
7   The extensive support of the US Catholic Bishops for the pro-life movement is well known.
8   The increasing involvement of business groups in movements concerned with social problems is highlighted by a new emphasis in funding by the Aspen Institute's Nonprofit Sector research Fund (Nonprofit Sector Strategy Group 2001).

9   Gamson makes a strong case (1968) for the utility of treating the potential of resources through a focus on their capacity rather than upon their use. Evaluating the role of resources in mobilization, as in the exercise of power is quite problematic. Gamson's is the preferred strategy of most analysts, and is the one adopted here.

10 We delete their "informational" category entirely. The provision of connections to outside resources that they call "referrals" and treat as an informational resource fits squarely within recent theorizing of social capital as networked access to resources (Foley et al. 2001; Lin 2001) and is included in our "social-organizational" category below. They include both strategic and technical support as "informational resources," describing them as knowledge that facilitates goal-attainment or organizational development respectively (Cress and Snow 1996: 1095). From the perspective we develop below, each of these conflate a cultural resource (the knowledge per se that exists and is culturally available within a given society) and a human resource (the individuals who command that knowledge and by their participation make it accessible and usable to movements or SMOs). These distinctions are discussed in greater detail below.

11 See, e.g., Foley and Edwards 1996; Edwards and Foley 1997; Foley and Edwards 1999; Edwards and Foley 2001; and Edwards et al. 2001.

12 Clearly, some cultural resources can be made proprietary through copyrighting, patents, and other emerging forms of intellectual property. As the domain of commodified culture becomes larger relative to that of public culture issues of unauthorized access to and use of cultural resources will likely become more problematic for social movements and SMOs.

13 Zelizer (1994) shows how the use of money is in specific instances also quite socially constrained, and hence, sometimes, very context dependent, as for instance the strong norms and legal prohibitions governing the buying and selling of children.

14 While this is generally true for cultural resources within a given society, their portability or transferability cross-nationally or cross-culturally is limited. Professional credentials and tacit knowledge about accomplishing specific organizational tasks, for example, typically do not hold their value well when crossing national or cultural borders

15 Organizations can, of course, grow to a larger scale, encompassing a wider geographic scope of operations, and in the process become a less context-dependent resource, as its use-value to another social movement becomes more widely accessible. As discussed below, organizations expand their scope of operations in a variety of ways, all of which require the mobilization of substantial material and human resources.

16 Some cultural resources in capitalist societies, of course, can be made proprietary. The technology of direct mailing, for instance, the basic techniques of which were invented by movement groups, has been made, in its most elaborated form, into a proprietary mobilization technology.

17 Usually unstated in this debate is that what constitutes "indigenous," and "external" to the movement depends entirely upon how one defines a "social movement" (Diani 1992), and secondarily how one defines an SMO. We do not engage that issue here. Rather, we rely here on the definitions of McCarthy and Zald (1977).

18 This pattern is common for organizations of all types across the nonprofit sector. See Smith (1997).

19 Oliver and Marwell (1992) introduce the distinction between mobilizing technologies, which they define as "sets of knowledge about ways of accumulating the resources necessary for production technologies" (255). Production technologies are "sets of knowledge about ways of achieving goals, such as lobbying, demonstrations, strikes or attending a public hearing" (255).

20 We do not deny that there is an element of innovation and adaptation in this process of cultural borrowing (McCarthy 1996), sometimes even significant innovation (Clemens 1997).

21   Social movements mobilize material resources other than money. These "in-kind" contributions of office space, equipment, or supplies are less fungible than money though equally tangible and proprietary. Money predominates in large part because of its fungibility.

22   SMOs that spend high proportions of the proceeds of direct mailing on carrying out the mailing regularly contend that communicating the content included in their mailings constitutes "public education."

23   What we have termed "co-optation," Gerhards and Rucht (1992) called "mesomobilization."

24   A quite different example of the same process is seen in efforts to generate interaction between liberal philanthropists who make large contributions to community organizing and the community organizers themselves. Silver (1998) suggests that such involvement serves to increase the commitment of donors to the movement groups that they fund. See Ostrander (1995) for a contrasting case of a foundation that sought rather to maintain barriers between donors and the movement leaders it funded.

References and further reading

Aldrich, Howard (1999) *Organizational Evolving*. Thousand Oaks, CA: Sage.

Barker-Plummer, Bernadette (2002) Producing Public Voice: Resource Mobilization and Media Access in the National Organization for Women. *Journalism and Mass Communication Quarterly*, 79, 188–205.

Baumgartner, Frank R., and Beth L. Leech (1998) *Basic Interests: The Importance of Groups in Politics and in Political Science*. Princeton, NJ: Princeton University Press.

Becker, Gary (1964) *Human Capital*. New York: National Bureau of Economic Research, Columbia University Press.

Bernard, Ted, and Jora Young (1997) *The Ecology of Hope: Communities Collaborate for Sustainability*. Philadelphia: New Society.

Binder, Amy J. (2002) *Contentious Curricula: Afrocentrism and Creationism in American Public Schools*. Princeton, NJ: Princeton University Press.

Bourdieu, Pierre (1986) The Forms of Capital. In John Richardson (ed.), *Handbook of Theory and Research for the Sociology of Education*. New York: Greenwood, 241–58.

Bourdieu, Pierre and Loic Waquant. 1992. *Introduction to Reflexive Sociology*. Chicago, IL: University of Chicago Press.

Brady, Henry E., Kay Lehman Schloszman, and Sidney Verba (1999) Prospecting for Participants: Rational Expectations and the Recruitment of Political Activists. *American Political Science Review*, 93, 153–68.

Brady, Henry E., Sidney Verba, and Kay Lehman Schlozman (1995) Beyond SES: A Resource Model of Political Participation. *American Political Science Review*, 89, 271–94.

Branch, Taylor (1988) *Parting the Waters: America in the King Years 1954–63*. New York: Simon & Schuster.

Brilliant, Eleanor L. (2000) Women's Gain: Fundraising and Fund Allocation as an Evolving Social Movement Strategy. *Nonprofit and Voluntary Sector Quarterly*, 29, 554–70.

Carmin, JoAnn (forthcoming) Resources, Opportunities, and Local Environmental Action in the Democratic Transition and Early Consolidation Periods in the Czech Republic. *Environmental Politics*.

Clemens, Elisabeth (1997) *The People's Lobby: Organizational Innovation and the Rise of Interest Group Politics in the United States, 1890–1925*. Chicago: University of Chicago Press.

Coleman, James S. (1988) Social Capital in the Creation of Human Capital. *American Journal of Sociology* (Supplement), 94, S95–S120.

—— (1990) *Foundations of Social Theory*. Cambridge, MA: Harvard University Press.

Cook, Maria Lorena (1996) *Organizing Dissent: Unions, the State, and the Democratic Teachers' Movement in Mexico*. University Park, PA: Pennsylvania State University Press.

Cress, Daniel M. (1997) Nonprofit Incorporation among Movements of the Poor: Pathways and Consequences for Homeless Social Movement Organizations. *Sociological Quarterly*, 38, 343–60.

Cress, Daniel M., and David A. Snow (1996) Mobilization at the Margins: Resources, Benefactors, and the Viability of Homeless Social Movement Organizations. *American Sociological Review*, 61 (6), 1089–109.

—— (2000) The Outcomes of Homeless Mobilization: The Influence of Organization, Disruption, Political Mediation and Framing. *American Journal of Sociology*, 105, 1089–109.

Dalton, Russell (1994) *The Green Rainbow*. Cambridge, MA: Harvard University Press.

Diani, Mario (1992) The Concept of Social Movement. *Sociological Review*, 40, 1–25.

DiMaggio, Paul, and Walter Powell (1983) The Iron Cage Revisited: Institutional Isomorphism and Collective Rationality in Organizational Fields. *American Sociological Review*, 48, 147–60.

DiMaggio, Paul, Eszter Hargittai, W. Russell Neuman, and John P. Robinson (2001) Social Implications of the Internet. *Annual Review of Sociology*, 27, 307–36.

Dobofsky, Melvyn (1980) *We Shall Be All: A History of the Industrial Workers of the World*. Chicago: Quadrangle.

Eder, Donna, Suzanne Staggenborg, and Lori Sudderth (1995) The National Women's Music Festival: Collective Identity and Diversity in a Lesbian-Feminist Community. *Journal of Contemporary Ethnography*, 23 (4), 485–99.

Edwards, Bob (1995) With Liberty and Environmental Justice for All: The Emergence and the Challenge of Grassroots Environmentalism in the USA. In Bron Taylor (ed.), *Ecological Resistance Movements: The Global Emergence of Radical and Popular Environmentalism*. Albany: State University of New York Press, 35–55

Edwards, Bob, and Kenneth T. Andrews (2002) Methodological Strategies for Examining Populations of Social Movement Organizations. Paper presented at the Annual Meetings of the American Sociological Association, Chicago.

Edwards, Bob, and Michael W. Foley (1997) Social Capital and the Political Economy of our Discontent. *American Behavioral Scientist*, 40 (5), 668–77.

—— (2001) Civil Society and Social Capital: A Primer. In Bob Edwards, Michael W. Foley and Mario Diani (eds.), *Beyond Tocqueville: Civil Society and the Social Capital Debate in Comparative Perspective*. Hanover, NH: University Press of New England, 1–14.

—— (2003) Social Movement Organizations beyond the Beltway: Understanding the Diversity of One Social Movement Industry. *Mobilization*, 8 (1), 85–107

Edwards, Bob, and John D. McCarthy (1992) Social Movement Schools. *Sociological Forum*, 7 (3), 541–50.

Edwards, Bob, and Sam Marullo (1995) Organizational Mortality in a Declining Social Movement: The Demise of Peace Movement Organizations in the End of the Cold War. *American Sociological Review*, 60, 908–27.

Edwards, Bob, Michael W. Foley, and Mario Diani (eds.) (2001) *Beyond Tocqueville: Civil Society and the Social Capital Debate in Comparative Perspective*. Hanover, NY: University Press of New England.

Everett, Kevin D. (1992) Opening Doors for Change: Movement Funding and Organizational Transformation. Paper Presented at the Annual Meetings of the American Sociological Association, Washington, DC.

Ferree, Myra Marx, and Patricia Yancey Martin (1995) Doing the Work of the Movement: Feminist Organizations. In Myra Marx Ferree and Patricia Yancy Martin (eds.), *Feminist Organizations: Harvest of the New Women's Movement*. Philadelphia, PA: Temple University Press, 3–26

Finke, Roger, M. Guest Avery, and Rodney Stark (1996) Mobilizing Local Religious Markets: Religious Pluralism in the Empire State, 1855 to 1865. *American Sociological Review*, 61, 203–18.

Foley, Michael W., and Bob Edwards (1996) The Paradox of Civil Society. *Journal of Democracy*, 7 (3), 38–52.

——(1999) Is it Time to Disinvest in Social Capital? *Journal of Public Policy*, 19 (2), 199–231.

Foley, Michael W., Bob Edwards, and Mario Diani (2001) Social Capital Reconsidered. In Bob Edwards, Michael W. Foley, and Mario Diani (eds.), *Beyond Tocqueville: Civil Society and the Social Capital Debate in Comparative Perspective*. Hanover, NH: University Press of New England, 266–80.

Freeman, Jo (1975) *The Politics of Women's Liberation*. New York: McKay.

Gamson, William A. (1968) *Power and Discontent*. Homewood, IL: Dorsey.

——(1975) *The Strategy of Social Protest*. Homewood, IL: Dorsey.

Gamson, William A., Bruce Fireman, and Steven Rytina (1982) *Encounters with Unjust Authority*. Chicago: Dorsey.

Ganz, Marshall (2000) Resources and Resourcefulness: Strategic Capacity in the Unionization of California Agriculture. *American Journal of Sociology*, 14, 1003–62.

Gerhards, Jürgen, and Dieter Rucht (1992) Mesomobilization Contexts: Organizing and Framing in Two Protest Campaigns in West Germany. *American Journal of Sociology*, 98, 555–96.

Gillham, Patrick F. (2003) Social Movement Organization Structure and Action: Three Contentious Episodes in the Global Justice Movement. PhD dissertation, University of Colorado.

Gillham, Patrick F., and Bob Edwards (2003) Global Justice Protesters Respond to the September 11 Terrorist Attacks: The Impact of an Intentional Disaster on Demonstrations in Washington, DC. In Jacki Monday (ed.) *Impacts of and Human Response to the September 11, 2001 Disasters: What Research Tells Us*. Boulder, CO: Natural Hazards Research and Information Center, University of Colorado, 192–229.

Godwin, R. Kenneth (1988) *One Billion Dollars of Influence: The Direct Marketing of Politics*. Chatham, NY: Chatham House.

Hyde, Cheryl (1995) Feminist Social Movement Organizations Survive the New Right. In Myra Marx Ferree and Patricia Yancy Martin (eds.), *Feminist Organizations: Harvest of the New Women's Movement*. Philadelphia, PA: Temple University Press, 306–21.

Imig, Douglas R. (1992) Resource Mobilization and Survival Tactics of Poverty Advocacy Groups. *Western Political Quarterly*, 45, 501–10.

——(1996) *Poverty and Power: The Political Representation of Poor Americans*. Lincoln, NE: University of Nebraska Press.

Inglehart, Ronald (1977) *The Silent Revolution: Changing Values and Political Styles among Western Publics*. Princeton, NJ: Princeton University Press.

Isbester, Katherine (2001) *Still Fighting: The Nicaraguan Women's Movement, 1977–2000*. Pittsburgh, PA: University of Pittsburgh Press.

Isserman, Maurice (1987) *If I Had a Hammer: The Death of the Old Left and the Birth of the New*. New York: Basic.

Jenkins, J. Craig (1985) *The Politics of Insurgency*. New York: Columbia University Press.

Jenkins, J. Craig, and Craig M. Eckert (1986) Channeling Black Insurgency: Elite Patronage and Professional Social Movement Organizations in the Development of the Black Movement. *American Sociological Review*, 51, 249–68.

Jenkins, J. Craig, and Abigail Halcli (1999) Grassrooting the System: The Development and Impact of Social Movement Philanthropy, 1953–1990. In Ellen Condliffe Lagemann (ed.), *Philanthrophic Foundations: New Scholarship, New Possibilities*. Bloomington: University of Indiana Press, 229–56.

Jenkins, J. Craig, and Charles C. Perrow (1977) Insurgency of the Powereless: Farm Workers Movements (1946–72). *American Sociological Review*, 42, 249–67.

Juska, Arunas, and Bob Edwards (forthcoming) Refusing the Trojan Pig: The American–Polish Coalition Against Corporate Pork Production in Eastern Europe. In Joe Bandy and Jackie Smith (eds.), *Coalitions Across Borders: Negotiating Difference and Unity in Transnational Struggles Against Neoliberalism*. Lanham, MD: Rowman & Littlefield.

Kempton, Willett, Dorothy C. Holland, Katherine Bunting-Howarth, Erin Hannan, and Christopher Payne (2001) Local Environmental Groups: A Systematic Enumeration in Two Geographical Areas. *Rural Sociology*, 66, 557–78.

Khawaja, Marwan (1994) Resource Mobilization, Hardship, and Popular Collective Action in the West Bank. *Social Forces*, 73, 191–220.

Kim, Hyojoung, and Peter S. Bearman (1997) The Structure and Dynamics of Movement Participation. *American Sociological Review*, 62, 70–93.

Klandermans, Bert (1997) *The Social Psychology of Protest*. Cambridge, MA: Blackwell.

Klandermans, Bert, and Dirk Oegema (1987) Potentials, Networks, Motivations, and Barriers: Steps towards Participation in Social Movements. *American Sociological Review*, 49, 583–600.

Klawiter, Maren (1999) Racing for the Cure, Walking Women, and Toxic Touring: Mapping Cultures of Action within the Bay Area Terrain of Breast Cancer. *Social Problems*, 46, 104–26.

Knoke, David (1986) Associations and Interest Groups. *Annual Review of Sociology*, 12, 1–21.

Kriesi, Hanspeter (1989) New Social Movements and the New Class in the Netherlands. *American Journal of Sociology*, 94, 1078–116.

Kriesi, Hanspeter, Ruud Koopmans, Jan Willem Duyvendak, and Marco Giugni (1995) *New Social Movements in Western Europe*. Minneapolis: University of Minnesota Press; London: UCL Press.

Lahausen, Christian (1996) *The Rhetoric of Moral Protest: Public Campaigns, Celebrity Endorsement, and Political Mobilization*. Berlin: Walter de Gruyter.

Liebman, Robert, and Robert Wuthnow (eds.) (1986) *The New Christian Right: Mobilization and Legitimation*. Hawthorne, NY: Aldine de Gruyter.

Lin, Nan (2001) *Social Capital: A Theory of Social Structure and Action*. New York: Cambridge University Press.

Lincoln, J. R. (1978) Community Structure and Industrial Conflict. *American Sociological Review*, 43, 199–220.

Lofland, John (1996) *Social Movement Organizations: A Guide to Insurgent Realities*. Hawthorne, NY: Aldine de Gruyter.

McAdam, Doug (1982) *Political Process and the Development of Black Insurgency, 1890–1970*. Chicago: University of Chicago Press.

McCammon, Holly J. (2001) Stirring up Suffrage Sentiment: The Formation of the Women's Suffrage Organizations, 1861–1914. *Social Forces*, 80, 449–80.

McCarthy, John D. (1987) Pro-life and Pro-choice Mobilization: Infrastructure Deficits and New Technologies. In Mayer N. Zald and John D. McCarthy (eds.), *Social Movements in an Organizational Society*. New Brunswick, NJ: Transaction, 49–66.

——(1994) Activists, Authorities, and Media Framing of Drunk Driving. In Enrique Laraña, Hank Johnston, and Joseph Gusfield (eds.), *New Social Movements*. Philadelphia, PA: Temple University Press, 133–67.

—— (1996) Mobilizing Structures: Constraints and Opportunities in Adopting, Adapting and Inventing. In Doug McAdam, John D. McCarthy, and Mayer N. Zald (eds.), *Comparative Perspectives on Social Movements*. New York: Cambridge University Press, 141–51.

—— (1997) The Globalization of Social Movement Theory. In Jackie Smith, Charles Chatfield, and Ron Pagnocco (eds.), *Transnational Social Movements and Global Politics: Solidarity Beyond the State*. Syracuse, NY: Syracuse University Press, 243–59.

McCarthy, John D., and Mark Wolfson (1996) Resource Mobilization by Local Social Movement Organizations: The Role of Agency, Strategy and Structure. *American Sociological Review*, 61, 1070–88.

McCarthy, John D. and Mayer N. Zald (1973) *The Trend of Social Movements in America: Professionalization and Resource Mobilization*. Morristown, NJ: General Learning.

—— (1977) Resource Mobilization and Social Movements: A Partial Theory. *American Journal of Sociology*, 82, 1212–41.

—— (2002) The Enduring Vitality of the Resource Mobilization Theory of Social Movements. In Jonathan H. Turner (ed.), *Handbook of Sociological Theory*. New York: Kluwer Academic/Plenum, 533–65.

McCarthy, John D., David W. Britt, and Mark Wolfson (1991) The Institutional Channeling of Social Movements by the State in the United States. *Research in Social Movements, Conflict and Change*, 14, 45–76.

McCarthy, John D., Mark Wolfson, David P. Baker, and Elaine Mosakowski (1988) The Founding of Social Movement Organizations: Local Citizens' Groups Opposing Drunken Driving. In Glenn R. Carroll (ed.), *Ecological Models of Organizations*. Cambridge, MA: Ballinger, 71–84.

McFarland, Andrew W. (1984) *Common Cause: Lobbying in the Public Interest*. Chatham, NJ: Chatham House.

McLaughlin, Paul, and Khawaja Marwan (2000) The Organizational Dynamics of the U.S. Environmental Movement: Legitimation, Resource Mobilization, and Political Opportunity. *Rural Sociology*, 65, 422–39.

Marx, Anthony W. (1992) *Lessons of Struggle: South African Internal Opposition, 1960–1990*. New York: Oxford University Press.

Matthews, Nancy (1995) Feminist Clashes with the State: Tactical Choices by State-Funded Rape Crisis Centers. In Myra Marx Ferree and Patricia Yancy Martin (eds.), *Feminist Organizations: Harvest of the New Women's Movement*. Philadelphia, PA: Temple University Press, 291–305.

Melucci, Alberto (1980) The New Social Movements: A Theoretical Approach. *Social Science Information*, 19, 199–226.

Meyer, John, and Brian Rowan (1977) Institutionalized Organizations: Formal Structure as Myth Ceremony. *American Journal of Sociology*, 83, 340–63.

Miller, James (1987) *Democracy in the Streets: From Port Huron to the Siege of Chicago*. New York: Simon & Schuster.

Minkoff, Debra (1995) *Organizing for Equality: The Evolution of Women's and Racial-Ethnic Organizations in the America, 1955–1985*. New Brunswick, NJ: Rutgers University Press.

—— (1997) The Sequencing of Social Movements. *American Sociological Review*, 62, 779–99.

Morris, Aldon D. (1981) Black Southern Student Sit-in Movement: An Analysis of Internal Organization. *American Sociological Review*, 46, 755–67.

Morris, Aldon D. (1984). *The Origins of the Civil Rights Movement: Black Communities Organizing for Change*. New York: Free Press.

Nelkin, Dorothy and M. Pollak (1981) *The Atom Besieged*. Cambridge, MA: MIT Press.

Nonprofit Sector Strategy Group (2001) *The Nonprofit Sector and Business: New Visions, New Opportunities, New Challenges*. Washington, DC: Aspen Institute.

Nownes, Anthony J., and Grant Neeley (1996) Public Interest Group Entrepreneurship and Theories of Group Mobilization. *Political Research Quarterly*, 49, 119–46.

NTIA (National Telecommunications and Information Administration) (2002) A Nation Online: How Americans Are Expanding their Use of the Internet <http://www.ntia.doc.gov/ntiahome/dn/index.html>.

Oberschall, Anthony (1973) *Social Conflict and Social Movements*. Englewood Cliffs, NJ: Prentice-Hall.

Offe, Claus (1985) New Social Movements: Challenging the Boundaries of Institutional Politics. *Social Research*, 52, 817–68.

Oliver, Pamela E. (1983) The Mobilization of Paid and Volunteer Activists in the Neighborhood Movement. *Research in Social Movements, Conflict and Change*, 5, 133–70.

——(1989a) Selling the Movement on Commission: The Structure and Significance of Canvassing by Social Movement Organizations. Paper Presented at the Annual meeting of the Society for the Study of Social Problems, San Francisco.

——(1989b) Bring the Crowd Back in: The Nonorganizational Elements of Social Movements. *Research in Social Movements, Conflict and Change*, 5, 133–70.

Oliver, Pamela E., and Gerald Marwell (1992) Mobilizing Technologies for Collective Action. In Aldon D. Morris and Carol McClurg Mueller (eds.), *Frontiers in Social Movement Theory*. New Haven: Yale University Press, 251–72.

Ostrander, Susan A. (1995) *Money for Change: Social Movement Philanthropy at Haymarket People's Fund*. Philadelphia, PA: Temple University Press.

Parkin, Frank (1968) *Middle Class Radicalism: The Social Bases of the British Campaign for Nuclear Disarmament*. Manchester: Manchester University Press.

Peterson, Thomas V. (2002) *Linked Arms: A Rural Community Resists Nuclear Waste*. Albany: State University of New York Press.

Powell, Walter, and Paul J. DiMaggio (eds.) (1992) *The New Institutionalism in Organizational Analysis*. Chicago: University of Chicago Press.

Putnam, Robert D. 1995. Bowling Alone: America's Declining Social Capital. *Journal of Democracy* 6 (1), 65–78.

Rucht, Dieter (1999) Linking Organization and Mobilization: Michel's Iron Law of Oligarchy Reconsidered. *Mobilization: An International Journal*, 4, 151–69.

Sale, Kirkpatrick (1973) *SDS*. New York: Random House.

Schneider, Cathy Lisa. (1995) *Shantytown Protest in Pinochet's Chile*. Philadelphia, PA: Temple University Press.

Selznick, Philip (1960) *The Organizational Weapon: A Study of Bolshevik Strategy and Tactics*. Glencoe, IL: Free Press.

Shanahan, Suzanne Elise, and Nancy Brandon Tuma (1994) The Sociology of Distribution and Redistribution. In N. Smelser and R. Swedborg (eds.), *The Handbook of Economic Sociology*. Princeton, NJ: Princeton University Press, 733–65.

Shutkin, William (2000) *The Land that Could Be: Environmentalism and Democracy in the Twenty-First Century*. Cambridge, MA: MIT Press.

Silver, Ira (1998) Buying an Activist Identity: Reproducing Class through Social Movement Philanthropy. *Sociological Perspectives*, 41, 303–21.

Sirianni, Carmen, and Lewis Friedland (2001) *Civic Innovation in America: Community Empowerment, Public Policy, and the Movement for Civic Renewal*. Berkeley: University of California Press.

Sklair, Leslie (1997) Social Movements for Global Capitalism: The Transformation of the Capitalist Class in Action. *Review of International Political Economy*, 4, 514–38.

Skocpol, Theda (1999) Advocates without Members: The Recent Transformation of American Civic Life. In Theda Skocpol and Morris P. Fiorina (eds.), *Civic Engagement in American Democracy*. Washington, DC: Brookings Institution/Russell Sage Foundation, 461–508.

Smith, Christian. (1991) *The Emergence of Liberation Theology: Radical Religion and Social Movement Theory.* Chicago: University of Chicago Press.

—— (1996) *Disruptive Religion: The Force of Faith in Social Movement Activism.* New York: Routledge.

Smith, David H. (1997) The Rest of the Nonprofit Sector: Grassroots Associations as the Dark Matter Ignored in Prevailing "Flat Earth" Maps of the Sector. *Nonprofit and Voluntary Sector Quarterly,* 26, 114–31.

Smith, Jackie and Dawn Wiest. (2003) The Uneven Geography of Global Civil Society: National and Global Influences on Transnational Association. Unpublished manuscript. State University of New York at Stony Brook.

Snow, David A. (1979) A Dramaturgical Analysis of Movement Accommodation: Building Idiosyncrasy Credit as a Movement Mobilization Strategy. *Symbolic Interactionism,* 2, 23–44.

Snow, David A., Sarah A. Soule, and Daniel M. Cress (2001) Homeless Protest across 17 U.S. Cities, 1980–1991: Assessment of the Explanatory Utility of Strain, Resource Mobilization, and Political Opportunity Theories. Paper presented at the Annual Meeting of the American Sociological Association, Anaheim, CA.

Soule, Sarah A., Doug McAdam, John McCarthy, and Yang Su (1999) Protest Events: Cause or Consequence of State Action? The U.S. Women's Movement and Federal Congressional Activities, 1956–1979. *Mobilization,* 4 (2), 239–55.

Switzer, Jacqueline Vaughn (1997) *Green Backlash: The History and Politics of Environmental Opposition in the U.S.* Boulder, CO: Lynne Rienner.

Tilly, Charles (1998) *Durable Inequality.* Berkeley: University of California Press.

US Postal Rate Commission (1987) *Study of Political Advocacy in Third-Class Nonprofit Mail.* Washington, DC: Postal Rate Commission.

Useem, Bert, and Mayer N. Zald (1982) From Pressure Group to Social Movement: Efforts to Promote Use of Nuclear Power. *Social Problems,* 30, 144–56.

Verba, Sidney, Kay Lehman Schlozman, and Henry E. Brady (1995) *Voice and Equality: Civic Voluntarism in American Politics.* Cambridge, MA: Harvard University Press.

Walker, Jack (1991) *Mobilizing Interest Groups in America: Patrons, Professions and Social Movements.* Ann Arbor: University of Michigan Press.

Warner, R. S. (1993) Work in Progress Toward a New Paradigm for the Sociological Study of Religion in the United States. *American Journal of Sociology,* 98 (5), 1044–93.

Warren, Mark R. (2001) *Dry Bones Rattling: Community Building to Revitalize American Democracy.* Princeton, NJ: Princeton University Press.

Weed, Frank J. (1995) *Certainty of Justice: Reform in the Crime Victim Movement.* Hawthorne, NY: Aldine de Gruyter.

Wickham-Crowley, Timothy P. (1989) Winners, Losers, and Also-Rans: Toward a Comparative Sociology of Latin American Guerrilla Movements. In S. Eckstein (ed.), *Power and Popular Protest: Latin American Social Movements.* Berkeley: University of California Press, 132–81.

Wilson, Kenneth R., Jennifer S. Wallin, and Christa Reiser (2003) Social Stratification and the Digital Divide. *Social Science Computer Review* 21 (3), 133–43.

Wolfson, Mark (2001) *The Fight against Big Tobacco: The Movement, the State and the Public's Health.* Hawthorne, NY: Aldine de Gruyter.

Wuthnow, Robert, and John H. Evans (2002) *The Quiet Hand of God: Faith-Based Activism and the Public Role of Mainline Protestantism.* Berkeley: University of California Press.

Zald, Mayer N. (1992) Looking Backward to Look Forward: Reflections on the Past and Future of the Resource Mobilization Program. In Aldon D. Morris and Carol McClurg Mueller (eds.), *Frontiers in Social Movement Theory.* New Haven, CT: Yale University Press, 326–48.

Zald, Mayer N. and J. Jacobs (1978) Compliance/incentive Classifications of Organizations: Underlying Dimensions. *Administration and Society,* 9 (4), 403–24.

Zelizer, V. A. (1994) *The Social Meaning of Money.* New York: Basic.

Part III

Field of Action and Dynamics

7

Beyond the Iron Law: Rethinking the Place of Organizations in Social Movement Research

Elisabeth S. Clemens and Debra C. Minkoff

In the literature on social movements, "organization" has appeared in two guises. By way of their invocation of Michels's ([1911] 1962) iron law in combination with a critique of the hierarchical mass membership models of the old left, Piven and Cloward (1979) argued that formal organization suppressed the capacity for disruption that threatens elites and extracts concessions. This rejection of formal organization resonated with the sensibilities of the new left with its embrace of participatory democracy. In the stark terms in which their claims were stylized in the literature, Piven and Cloward came to stand for a representation of organization as antithetical to effective mobilization (Cloward and Piven 1984; Gamson and Schmeidler 1984).

During the same period, analyses of collective behavior were largely supplanted by resource mobilization models (Buechler 2000: 34–40) in which organization was foregrounded as the critical element distinguishing ineffective grievances from potentially consequential protest. In elaborating this paradigm, McCarthy and Zald (1977) argued that the resources represented by formal organization facilitated, rather than suppressed, mobilization. Organization was treated as a resource for, or tool of, social movement activists; the more organization, the better the prospects for mobilization and success. This was a powerful conceptualization, easily operationalized in empirical research. Yet "most proponents of the resource mobilization approach did not engage in broader comparative empirical work on the impacts of various organizational forms on protest" (Rucht 1999: 154). "Resources" encompassed a variegated repertoire of organizational forms. The result was a choice between the thin and homogenized sense of organization within resource mobilization research and the distrust of organization that stemmed from an emphasis on disruption and spontaneity.

For the past two decades, resource mobilization theory has been a workhorse of social movement research, fueling an impressive literature in which organization plays a central role. Enriched by attention to political opportunities and cultural frames (McAdam et al. 1996), this tradition of research remains exceptionally vital (Buechler 2000: 52–3; Cress and Snow 2000). From it we've learned about the centrality of local movement centers and other "meso-mobilization" structures for generating and coordinating movement campaigns (Morris 1984; Gerhards and Rucht 1992), as well as the role of formal and informal organizations in protecting and sustaining activists during inhospitable times (Morris 1981, 1984; Evans and Boyte 1986; Taylor 1989; Whittier 1995). Such work has also drawn attention to the importance of organizational diversity for movement stability and innovation (Staggenborg 1988) and the more general processes of the social construction of protest within multiorganizational fields (Klandermans 1992). And with a new nod to Gamson's (1990) seminal work, researchers have started to document the (somewhat mixed) influence of organizational infrastructures and resources on political outcomes (Andrews 2001; McCammon et al. 2001; see also chapter 20 in this volume). But in recent work there are signs of new interest in, indeed affection for, organizations in their own right.

At the heart of these new developments lies a questioning of the equation of organization with the iron law. Explicit in Piven and Cloward's account (1979: 101), the spirit of Michels also infuses resource mobilization arguments through a sort of syllogism: organizations are resources; effective organizations are hierarchies; therefore, hierarchical organizations are valuable resources for movements (Gamson 1990). This assumption effectively "black-boxes" movement organization, rendering it constant, opaque, and static.

In contrast, renewed attention to the varieties of social movement organizations turns assumptions of hierarchy and oligarchy into questions. For some activists, their social location and identity may not elicit the need to "feed the family" that lies at the center of both Michels's iron law and Weber's discussion of the routinization of charisma (Clemens 1993: 764–6). In some cases, formal organization may be associated with more radical actions (Rucht 1999) or even the reinvigoration of organizations that had succumbed to quiescent oligarchy (Voss and Sherman 2000). Within formal organizations, movementlike mobilizations may generate significant change (Katzenstein 1998; Scully and Creed 1999). Across organizations, field-level processes of competition and diffusion may instigate organizational transformations (Minkoff 1994, 1999). In the place of a monolithic model of hierarchical organization, varied and malleable organizational forms populate these studies.

IDENTITY, CULTURE, AND DISCOURSE

As social movement researchers turned from collective behavior theory toward resource mobilization arguments, they discarded symbolic interactionism along with assumptions of the irrationality and spontaneity of mobilization (Buechler 2000: 40). Attention to organization appeared antithetical to analyses of culture and interaction. As organizations were understood instrumentally, as means that enabled mobilization, the cultural content of organizing and the meaning signaled by organizational forms were marginalized as topics for inquiry.

Recently, however, scholars have avidly reached back to recover the insights of symbolic interactionism for social movement research. In a cluster of excellent new studies (Lichterman 1996; Eliasoph 1998; Moore and Hala 2002; Polletta 2002; Stevens 2002), organizations take center stage as arenas of interaction. Rather than being homogenized as a "resource," particular organizations sustain distinctive cultures of interaction and shape trajectories of mobilization. The answer to "how shall we organize?" (Clemens 1996) proves to be consequential for the development of actors as activists and the prospects for organized political action.

Built on rich case studies, either explicitly or implicitly comparative, this new literature foregrounds the diversity of ways of organizing. This emphasis is not necessarily intended. Eliasoph, for example, begins from an interest in "the process of creating contexts for political conversation." Such conversations are governed by "etiquettes" which "implicitly [take] into account a relationship to the wider world: politeness, beliefs, and power intertwine in practice, through this sense of civility." Following Goffman, she uses the concept of "footing" to capture "this constant, unspoken process of assessing the grounds for interaction" (1998: 21). These theoretical sensibilities are quite far from the classics of resource mobilization and, yet, the "contexts for political conversation" are more or less formal organizations – of volunteers or adamantly apolitical country and western dancers or environmental activists. In findings that are both powerfully illuminating and politically depressing, she demonstrates how the interaction rules of many organizational settings suppress political conversation or limit it to the "close to home." Even the environmental activists struggled with organizational settings where the interaction rules relegated conversation to requests for invitation or the self-interested, emotion-laden expressions of "mandatory momism." Only by building networks with other environmental organizations, which then constituted a different audience for conversation, could these activists develop as the democratic citizens they aspired to be. Through such iterative processes, distinctive organizational contexts sustain the development of particular kinds of political selves who then, perhaps, alter their organizational practices as the meanings of political participation are transformed.

Distinctive styles of organizing also make activism attractive to different potential activists. In a comparative ethnography of environmental organizations, Lichterman (1996) contrasts the community-based models championed by communitarian theorists with "personalism," a style of activism understood as self-development. Whereas critics have dismissed such engagement as indulgent and consumerist, Lichterman argues that this talk of self provides a medium for collective action among individuals who share little else, who are disengaged from the communities or major institutions that anchored mobilization in the civil rights or labor movements (1996: 90, 185; Melucci 1996: 9). In his account, formal organizations are nodes of dense interaction in a more fluid network of activists who may shift from group to group and cause to cause:

> Organizations do matter in personalized politics, and organizations are not meant simply to be short-lived sites for self-development. But the individual activist's sense of commitment is highly portable; it can be carried from group to group, in concert with other activists and imagined communities of activists who validate personalized politics. (1996: 34)

Interactions and practices within organizations thus shape the flow of actors through fields of social movement organization.

This rehabilitation of interaction within social movement analysis foregrounds the question of "how people actually manage acting together and becoming a 'we'" (Melucci 1996: 15). Rather than treating social movements as symptomatic of structural strains or configurations of resources, this emphasis restores the creative and generative quality of interaction within movement organizations (Moore and Hala 2002). From this vantage point, the process of formal organization need not entail the suppression of participation and engagement. Exploring the fate of organizations of the homeless, Cress (1997) argues that it is the path by which they come to adopt nonprofit status – rather than the nonprofit form itself – which accounts for the moderation of movement tactics. Formal organization can sustain the development of new forms of solidarity (Stevens 2002) and signal the appropriation of existing identities (Clemens 1993, 1996) or the elaboration of novel ones (Moore 1996; Armstrong 2002a). Unlike Breines (1982) whose conceptualization of "prefigurative politics" presumed that movement aspirations would produce a match between the internal life of movement organizations and some desired future, for these analyses interaction within organizations is consequential in diverse ways that may even undermine the goals explicitly pursued by activists.

ORGANIZATIONAL IDENTITY, STRATEGY, DYNAMICS

With the rehabilitation of symbolic interaction and social constructionism, organizations are recognized as arenas for the development of the practices and identities of activism. The construction of particular kinds of selves or agents is of central interest. For other scholars, however, the inner life of social movement organizations and the symbolic dimensions of organizational form shape specifically organizational outcomes: organizational identity, capacities, strategies, and, ultimately, outcomes. As Jo Freeman argued in her classic essay on "the tyranny of structurelessness" (1972), important consequences flow from the organizational models and practices that are adopted to express particular ideologies or identities. Writing out of her experience in feminist organizations of the 1960s and early 1970s, Freeman traced some of the unintendedly corrosive effects of feminist commitment to participation and rejection of hierarchy. Recent scholarship has returned to this insight with new intensity (Clemens 1993, 1996, 1997; Haydu 1999; Ganz 2000; Voss and Sherman 2000; Stevens 2001; Polletta 2002; Schneiberg 2002), exploring the varieties and consequences of organizational form (Buechler 2000: 204–9).

As with the revitalized analysis of interaction, an appreciation of organizational variety or heterogeneity replaces the homogenizing conception of organization as resource. Echoing Tilly's (1978, 1986) conception of repertoires of collective action, Clemens (1993, 1996) argued that movements were shaped by distinctive organizational repertoires. Comparing labor, agrarian, and women's associations of the late nineteenth century, she documents ongoing debates over alternative models of organization: fraternal, military and union among working men; political party, fraternal, and cooperative among farmers; club, charity, and party among middle-class women (Clemens 1997). Creative transposition of familiar but apolitical models of organization to politics made it possible for relatively disadvantaged groups to mobilize in surprising and novel ways, gaining advantages if only temporarily. Choices of organizational form were simultaneously vehicles of mobilization, signals of identity to opponents and possible coalition partners, and, to use Eliasoph's term, "etiquettes" for collective action.

When combined with close analysis of the internal structure of organizations, this attention to form generates powerful explanations of movement success and collapse. In a study of politically active scientists, Moore (1996) demonstrates how the articulation of a new organizational form (the public interest science organization, e.g. the Union of Concerned Scientists) carved out spaces for political mobilization independent of the dominant associations of professional scientists. Within these new organizations, activism generated innovation in organizational style and political critique (Moore and Hala 2002). Ganz (2000) also argues that new forms provided political advantages, even to the most resource-poor of a trio of groups trying to organize agricultural workers in California in the 1960s. Why did the upstart United Farm Workers succeed where the more experienced and resource-rich Teamsters and AFL-CIO (American Federation of Labor and Congress of Industrial Organizations) failed? "It drew on elements of an ethnic labor association (reminiscent of earlier organizing attempts by farmworkers of color), a union, and community organizing drives in a new synthesis that went far beyond its individual components as its founders engaged environmental challenges by adapting familiar repertoires to new uses" (Ganz 2000: 1041). The mutualistic practices of these models allowed the movement to subsist with minimal resources and encouraged horizontal communication, rather than hierarchy, that enhanced responsiveness to changes in context and opportunity. Practices that signaled an organizational identity as civil rights movement attracted important allies while mobilization in the form of a pilgrimage, or *peregrenacion*, insulated the movement from state repression.

Whereas Clemens (1993, 1997), Moore (1996), and Ganz (2000) use organizational form to explain the comparative success and failure of mobilizations, Stevens (2001), Lo (1990), and Polletta (2002) illuminate the consequences of organizational form for the development and transformation of movement organizations and coalitions. They foreground a theoretical insight common to these studies: structure is constituted as models or schema are embedded in resources and networks (Sewell 1992). In his insightful study of the home-schooling movement, Stevens traces how this "solution" to discontent with the public schools was initially embedded in the networks and organizational practices of the counterculture left. Other parents, who shared this discontent and adopted this solution, were drawn into these organizations despite their commitments to fundamentally different models of organizational practice and etiquette, specifically conservative Protestantism. In time, a full-fledged schism developed. In terms of organizational scale, the conservative Protestant wing was ascendant, sustained by a robust organizational culture (Stevens 2001, 2002), while the countercultural contingent continually faced the coordination problems posed by a commitment to the open, participatory organizational style addressed by Freeman (1972) as "the tyranny of structurelessness."

Choices of organizational form shape alliances as well as fueling schisms. The use of one organizing schema may create power imbalances in subsequent alliances. In an analysis of the California property tax revolt, for example, Lo (1990) illuminates how the initial choice of form by distressed homeowners (community mobilization) was insufficient to build the statewide coalition needed to reform tax law. Consequently, less affluent citizens outraged at the unresponsiveness of government found that their collective action project could be solved by a business-dominated effort to lower taxes (and spending on services valued by homeowners) in a manner that failed to redistribute the burden more equitably. Ultimately, a populist mobilization produced results favorable to big business that had initially opposed the reforms. In a rich study of the Industrial Areas Foundation in Texas, Warren (2001) demonstrates a second effect of organizing models on coalition-building. Here, the reliance on an organizing repertoire grounded in Christianity both strengthened this alliance and created obstacles to extending the coalition to ideologically sympathetic constituencies that were either unmoved or even discomforted by this organizing schema.

In a study of participatory democracy, Polletta (2002) offers a still more fine-grained analysis of how the embedding of organizational practices in social networks shapes the trajectory of social movements. Echoing Eliasoph, she argues that every polity "depends on a sophisticated set of normative understandings that accompany the formal rules, a kind of etiquette of deliberation" (Polletta 2002: 16). This etiquette is jointly constituted by existing social relationships and organizational practices. When adopted by Students for a Democratic Society (SDS) or the Student Nonviolent Coordinating Committee (SNCC), participatory democracy was grounded in particularly intimate relationships, networks of quasi-kinship, friendship, and faith. Consequently, increases in scale produce predictable crises for organizations committed to participatory democracy. At key moments, this decision-making practice comes to be understood as signaling membership in a faction, rather than in an encompassing organizational community: the Prairie People resented how the personal ties among SDS founders were a durable source of political privilege even as formal leadership passed to new cohorts; many of the black members of SNCC embraced a "hard" vision of hierarchical organization as they came to see participatory democracy as enabling the highly verbal white college students from the north. As with Stevens' study of home-schooling, Polletta demonstrates that the sources of schism and change can be identified, indeed anticipated, by close analysis of the organizational relations and practices within movements.

MOVEMENTS INSIDE ORGANIZATIONS

Inverting the lens points to movement practices *within* organizations (Zald and Berger 1978). Organizations not only represent contexts for identity-formation, mobilization, and strategic action in the service of social movements, but they are themselves potential sites and targets of activism. For all of their resistance to formal organizations as vehicles for social movements, Piven and Cloward (1979) astutely note that the disruptive potential of the powerless is conditioned by the organizations and institutions to which they have access. However, their analysis does not take up the important issue of variation in organizational and institutional contexts and the implications for political challenges that take place within them. In addition, a range of sites for "contentious politics" (McAdam et al. 2001) have been left unexplored by the more general emphasis of resource mobilization and political opportunity research on political struggles against national authorities (and the concomitant emphasis on "society" as the target of identity politics in new social movement research).

Recent studies of insider mobilization in such settings as religious and military organizations (Katzenstein 1998), workplaces (Scully and Creed 1999; Raeburn 2001; Scully and Segal 2002), college campuses (Lounsbury 2001), and public schools (Binder 2002), point to the permeability of organizational boundaries to what's happening on the outside, at the same time that such boundaries literally bound (as in constrain) activism within by offering up fairly circumscribed discursive and strategic repertoires. Feminist activism in the Church and the military, for example, takes distinctive forms despite ideological affinities with respect to gender roles and institutional rules that stipulate obedience and conformity in all realms of life ("interaction rules" at the institutional level) (Katzenstein 1998). The key to this difference lies, according to Katzenstein, in each institution's proximity to the state. During the 1970s, the courts rendered a series of decisions that both limited the military's discretion to set its own standards of conduct and privileged the legal norm of gender sameness. This new legal terrain shaped the identities and actions of advocates for women in the military and linked their project to the imperative that jobs and careers be based on individual ability. The result was a politics of influence, seeking to gain the support of other actors in a position to implement change, and an exclusive focus on gender discrimination in the military, divorced from concerns about race, class, and sexual preference there or elsewhere.

In the absence of judicial and legislative oversight, Church-based feminists recognized the limits to structural influence and emphasized a project of meaning-building and reinterpretation in the face of an intransigent hierarchy. At the same time, this enabled them to "talk the talk" of a broader radicalism, taking on radical discourse and identities imported from beyond the institution and creating a new vision of Church and society that integrated social justice issues with women's concerns inside and outside of the organizational structure of the Church. The "footing" in Eliasoph's (1998) terms, was jointly shaped by cultures of activism and the organizational context of mobilization, including "organizational habitats" such as long-established religious orders that created a space for women inclined to challenge the Church hierarchy. Nonetheless, the greater institutional independence of the Catholic Church bolstered its resistance to change, giving women of faith little recourse to anything but a politics of meaning-making. Notably, however, it was a much more radical and inclusive politics than would ever be thinkable in the normative environment of the military.

Diversity activism in the workplace around race, gender, and sexual orientation also highlights the mechanisms by which social movement issues are transmitted into organizations, at the same time that such activism operates as a mechanism of organizational change (Scully and Creed 1999). Scully and Segal's (2002) case study of the software development division of a (nonunion) high-technology firm suggests that social movements in society provide the crucial symbolic material for diversity activists, whereas the organizational context shapes available resources, strategies, and objectives. Their interviews with activists uncovered a symbolic dualism provided by the imagery of social movements in wider society: activists invoke the discourse of broader civil rights struggles (racial, feminist, gay/lesbian), using the language of revolution and grass-roots activism to empower and legitimate their efforts, at the same time as they distance themselves from the militancy of these protest movements. This represents one paradox of workplace activism: the adoption of social movement language provides the impetus and energy for mobilization, while simultaneously enabling activist employees to establish the relatively modest nature of their efforts (although what might look like small gains from the outside, such as designing a group T-shirt with a company logo, may be quite substantial from the vantage point of insiders).

The strategies and activities of workplace activists likewise reflect the organizational setting within which they operate. The groups described by Scully and Segal (2002) were apparently effective at using local knowledge and resources to advance their goals, often in response to specific opportunities or issues. For the most part, it was difficult for diversity groups to maintain activism on a continuous basis (one activist referred to it as "hard slogging work"), which meant that what took place was both sporadic and opportunistic. In one example, the gay employee group was able to mobilize quickly using the electronic network that linked most of its members to persuade the company to move their annual sales meeting from Colorado the year that voters there passed a constitutional amendment barring civil rights protections based on sexual orientation. In terms of more routine organizing, diversity groups took advantage of a readily available repertoire of strategic business techniques: mission statements, memos, electronic billboards, and subcommittee and task force structures familiar to both employees and managers alike. The use of such techniques made the efforts of diversity groups intelligible and nonthreatening, thereby improving the chances of recognition and incorporation at the same time as they risked diluting their initial status as grass-roots and outsider activities.

Raeburn's (2001) analysis of the successful implementation of sexual diversity programs and policies (providing domestic partner benefits, adding sexual orientation in diversity training, and including sexual orientation in corporate nondiscrimination policies), points to a wider set of "institutional opportunities" that promote organizational change. She emphasizes the importance of "structural templates" (the presence of already active "sister networks," access to corporate financial support, official recognition, and inclusion in diversity task forces) that provide both material and symbolic resources for gay and lesbian employee groups; organizational realignments (CEO turnover, changes in the Board of Directors, acquisitions and mergers) that shift the balance of power in favor of activists; and cultural supports such as a prevailing corporate commitment to diversity.

The focus on organizational realignments, not visible in the single case study conducted by Scully and Segal, highlights how workplace activism is constrained by more general organizational dynamics. For example, Raeburn demonstrates that turnover in top managers and executives represent a mechanism for the introduction of new corporate policies and the diffusion of organizational innovations more generally. This study offers a striking example: GLUE (the country's largest gay employee network) mobilized for domestic partner benefits for nine years in a telecommunications company before they were granted. The main impediment was the CEO who, despite vocal support for equitable benefits by a range of corporate officials, refused to even meet with GLUE representatives. Shortly after the CEO retired, the new CEO implemented this policy change. Mergers and acquisitions represent another set of opportunities for realignment, although not always in ways that benefit activists: when Mobil was purchased by Exxon in 1999 it rescinded its domestic partner benefits.

It is clear that movements inside organizations provide a fertile site for the application and development of social movement theories. The impetus for insider mobilizations comes from mass-based social movements, but, once movement ideas and identities hit the workplace (broadly defined), organizational context, culture, and relationships to the environment present activists with distinctive opportunities and constraints. Scully and Segal (2002) suggest that workplace activists are advantaged by a relatively transparent view of how the system works and access to resources and strategies that give them local legitimacy and leverage. Still, such advantages carry the risk of incorporation and routinization in ways that potentially diminish the grass-roots energy that is necessary to sustain them. This is a real dilemma, as the inertial tendencies of organizations and institutions require activists to operate incrementally and opportunistically, taking advantage of grievances as they arise and capitalizing on organizational realignments when they occur (which may be rarely). And, although social movements are a potential source of organizational change, the content of such transformation hinges as much on the broader organizational and institutional context as on internal organizational dynamics.

FIELD LEVEL: STABILITY AND DYNAMICS

Zald and Ash's (1966) early, and relatively overlooked, discussion of SMO transformation provides a foundation for linking social movement development to field level dynamics of stability and change. Presciently arguing against the Weber--Michels model that informs Piven and Cloward's criticism of movement organization, Zald and Ash suggest that there is no necessary trajectory of movement organizations toward goal displacement or institutionalization. Rather, the incentives for organizational transformation, growth, decline, and change, derive from a combination of internal and external pressures, some of which are more easily overcome than others. As a later generation of researches have suggested, such pressures include direct and indirect forms of "institutional channeling" (McCarthy et al. 1991), the degree of "correspondence" between movement organizations and their benefactors (Cress and Snow 1996), and more or less intentional (or invidious) forms of resource dependency (Piven and Cloward 1979; Jenkins and Ekert 1986).

These insights dovetail with a focus in organizational sociology on organization environment relations, a recent synthesis that has proven quite fruitful for social movement researchers and organizational scholars alike (Rao et al. 2000; Lounsbury 2001; Swaminathan and Wade 2001; Lounsbury et al. forthcoming; for more recent work, see Davis et al. forthcoming). Such work is motivated by the dual view that social movement trajectories are influenced by the variety of organizational forms that activists establish and maintain and that such diversity is itself delimited by competitive and institutional pressures, as well as broader political and sociocultural changes (see Zald and McCarthy 1980; Garner and Zald 1987; McCarthy et al. 1991). The larger point is that social movements are embedded in organizational fields, and that their relationships to and with other organizations in the field can take various forms that have implications for their operation and functioning.

A growing group of movement researchers has profited from an evolutionary approach to the study of organizational dynamics that, in its strongest formulation, posits inertia at the organizational level and stability in organizational populations over time (Hannan and Freeman 1984). Rather than locating the dynamism of movement industries and sectors in the actions of organizational (or, in this case, social movement) entrepreneurs, ecological perspectives emphasize selection processes in population growth and change, with those organizations better able to mobilize resources and legitimacy ultimately dominating the sector and establishing the modal forms of organization. In such models, organizational turnover is one mechanism that shapes the contours of social movements as they develop over time.

In one of the earliest applications of ecological models to social movement development, Minkoff (1994) provides an account of the changing "organizational repertoire" (Clemens 1993) available to women and racial and ethnic minorities that emphasizes the competitive mechanisms that contribute to movement change. Studying the trajectory of national organizations since the mid-1950s, she links the post-1970 increase in national advocacy groups to the earlier expansion of more conventional service organizations that established the legitimacy organizational activity by women and minorities and to a somewhat later increase in the number of protest groups that produced a "radical flank" effect (Haines 1984). Her argument is that once advocacy organizations were more successful at monopolizing resources and legitimacy they limited the availability of more traditional *and* more confrontational models of social movement organization through processes of inter-organizational competition (Minkoff 1994).

Minkoff's (1999) more recent work suggests that, at the organizational level, processes of adaptation and selection tend to favor older, more professional, and reform-oriented movement organizations. As such organizations begin to dominate the movement sector, it becomes increasingly difficult for younger, smaller, and more decentralized organizations (presumably those more willing to engage in protest activities) to establish a viable national presence. Edwards and Marullo's (1995) careful analysis of the demise of peace movement organizations at the end of the Cold War era also suggests that groups which are smaller, younger and have less perceived legitimacy were at greater risk of failure as the peace movement declined, with some important differences across movement "domains" (defined in terms of organizational size and scope).

Other researchers have conceptualized movement organizations as carriers of discursive frames and ideological orientations that have their fates linked to organizational processes. In an ambitious study, Robert Brulle (1996, 2000) has examined historical changes in the discourse of the US environmental movement since the early 1800s through an analysis of how such frames have been incorporated into distinctive organizational forms, crystallizing into partially overlapping "discursive communities [that] developed out of the interactions with their external social and natural environments and each other in an evolutionary manner" (Brulle 1996: 79). Starting from a related insight, Marullo et al. (1996) examine frame changes in the US peace movement between 1988 and 1992. Comparing the distribution of organizations that survived the decline of the movement with those that failed, they attribute the shift to a broader and more radical frame of multilateralism and global interdependence to discursive adaptation among surviving groups rather than to the selective mortality of organizations espousing different frames. This "retention frame," which is built on a more complex analysis of the problem, appealed to those members who were likely to stay involved even without the existence of a mass movement, and thereby provided a solution to problems of organizational maintenance.

Population level approaches to social movements, like their resource mobilization counterparts, tend to employ a rather thin concept of organization, differentiating forms with respect to access to resources and conceptualizing legitimacy in cognitive, not cultural, terms. Mirroring debates in organizational sociology, other studies take up the question of field level change by focusing more squarely on the question of how new organizational forms "become imbued with norms, values and beliefs during the process of resource mobilization by entrepreneurs" (Rao 1998: 913). Such work provides both a richer sense of organization and a more multidimensional view of the environment within which organizations operate. The core premise of the "cultural-frame institutional perspective" (Rao 1998) is that the creation of new organizational forms represents an "institutionalization project wherein the theory and values underpinning the form are legitimated by institutional entrepreneurs" (Rao 1998: 914). This approach shifts attention to organizational fields that are constructed by political and cultural processes that constrain individual organizations operating within them. As Rao (1998: 919) notes, "it is in this multiorganizational field that institutional entrepreneurs interpret grievances, exchange evaluations, forge alliances and joust with antagonists." Whereas structural conditions promote the demand or resource space for collective action, new organizational forms represent the outcome of (more or less tentative) "truces" between interested actors regarding which frame will organize activities within the field.

Rao's (1998) case study of the rise of nonprofit consumer watchdog organizations demonstrates how the Consumers Union, which initially sponsored a fairly radical and comprehensive model of consumers-as-workers and sought to regulate business practices by promoting socially responsible buying and equity, succumbed to a "logic of integration" that led to a discarding of its founding mission and its conversion into a "scientific conservative" that promoted the conception of consumers as rational decision makers that emphasized standard-setting as the main goal (the frame sponsored by its main rival, Consumers' Research). More generally, the resolution of this political contest over the identity of the consumer confined future consumer watchdog organizations into a narrow channel of activity (think *Consumer Reports*). An important part of this story is the role that the state and professionals played in both generating and providing a forum for disputes about the boundaries of this organizational form, pointing to more direct forms of "institutional channeling" (McCarthy et al. 1991) that limit organizational diversity and the success of more resistive forms of organization.

Elizabeth Armstrong's (2002a) analysis of changes in San Francisco's lesbian and gay organizations between 1950 and 1994 builds on the cultural-frame institutional perspective, but argues that the emergence of new organizational forms not only requires actors with sufficient resources for, and interests in, promoting new models of organization, but that such activities require a "cultural context that facilitates cultural and organizational creativity" (Armstrong 2002a: 362). The political upheaval associated with new left activism of the 1960s provided exactly such a moment (characterized by the presence of alternative ideas, dense patterns of interaction, and environmental uncertainty) when alternative forms of organization and action became thinkable by gay and lesbian activists who had previously pursued an interest group political logic. Deploying a newly established theory of social change, which located political efficacy in individual, identity-based action and defined "expanding the gay world as the central goal of politics," gay liberationists introduced a novel organizational template, the "Gay + 1" organization (with examples ranging from the San Francisco Tsunami Gay/Lesbian Masters Swim Club to Safe Sex Leather Sluts). This new organizational form combines a positive emphasis on sexual identity and identity-building (the "Gay" part) with specific tasks or functions, such as cultural, political, religious, service, it is intended to accomplish (the "+ 1" part).

In accounting for this relatively abrupt and dramatic change in the gay/lesbian organizational repertoire, Armstrong points to the convergence of new actors and the availability of a new stock of cultural materials that removed barriers to organizational development. On the one hand, the New Left's concern with authenticity resonated for lesbians and homosexuals, especially gay liberationists who began to define the prevailing norm of privacy as a form of inauthentic behavior. At the same time, the logic of identity politics provided a solution to the difficulty that earlier homophile organizations had creating a public constituency; as Armstrong (2002a: 388) notes, "identity politics had to be created before becoming a possible solution to the problem of invisibility." The years 1969–70 represented a critical juncture when the dominance of homophile interest group organizations was ruptured in the context of collective creativity provided by the upheavals of the 1960s. The brief meeting of the New Left and gay liberation set the context for the creation of a new dominant frame of unity in diversity and a novel organizational form that promoted rapid and diverse organizational formation and the crystallization of a gay movement even as political opportunities declined. Although this model glossed important differences within the movement base, it initially served as a catalyst for the formation of a new organizational field (Armstrong 2002b).

At the level of organizational fields, new research is also informed by attention to the varieties of organizational form and how they are embedded in social networks and structures of meaning. Whereas "organization" could once be taken as a simplifying label for collections of actors, the shift toward organizations and organizational fields as contexts of interaction complements renewed attention to the intersections of organizations and networks, the "duality of persons and groups" (Breiger 1974). Rather than being understood unproblematically as a resource for mobilization, formal organization can be viewed as having a variable association with protest depending on political context, identity, and strategy (Osa 2003). In combination with the new emphasis on the diversity of organizing forms and styles, network analysis directs renewed attention to the complex dynamics of coalition-formation and the process of constructing an overarching cultural framework that sustains the identity of *a* social movement comprised of multiple organizations, each with their potentially distinctive culture and inner life (della Porta and Diani 1999; Mische and Pattison 2000).

CONCLUSION

The sheer diversity of research reviewed in this chapter promises to move us "beyond the iron law" toward a richer and more nuanced understanding of the relationships between organizations and social movements. The more we learn about what goes on inside of activist organizations and how such organizations are themselves embedded in complex fields of culture, politics, and action, the more we know about the dynamics of movement development and change. The more widely we define the very object of inquiry (organizations as more or less permeable arenas for the development of practices and identities of activism; organizational practices as a component of strategic action and success; movement fields as sites of cooperation, competition, and creative transformation) the better able we are to move away from the caricatures of organization that have been at once productive and limiting for movement scholarship over the past three decades.

One of the more exciting features of recent work is the creative effort to integrate insights from a broad range of sociological approaches, making for an interesting mix of perspectives drawn from symbolic interactionism to organizational ecology. This renewed attention to organizational variety in social movement scholarship resonates with developments in the world of activism. In response to globalization, novel transnational organizational forms and unexpected "blue-green" coalitions of labor and environmentalists have mobilized. Coverage of mobilizations at global economic summits highlight the distinctive practices of collective decision-making and public protest. At the same time, organized labor, the exemplar of the iron law, is the site of experimentation with new and more politicized forms of organizing. Organizational variety and creativity seem to define this current surge of activism as well as this moment in movement scholarship.

References

Andrews, Kenneth (2001) Social Movements and Policy Implementation: The Mississippi Civil Rights Movement and the War on Poverty, 1965 to 1971. *American Sociological Review*, 66, 71–95.

Armstrong, Elizabeth (2002a) Crisis, Collective Creativity and the Generation of New Organizational Forms: The Transformation of Lesbian/Gay Organizations in San Francisco. In Michael Lounsbury and Marc Ventresca (eds.), *Research in the Sociology of Organizations: Entrepreneurs, Organizations, and Social Change*, 19, 361–95.

——(2002b) *Forging Gay Identities: Organizing Sexuality in San Francisco, 1950–1994*. Chicago: University of Chicago Press.

Binder, Amy (2002) *Contentious Curricula: Afrocentrism and Creationism in American Public Schools*. Princeton, NJ: Princeton University Press.

Breiger, Ronald L. (1974) The Duality of Persons and Groups. *Social Forces* 53, 181–90.

Breines, Wini (1982) *Community and Organization in the New Left, 1962–1968: The Great Refusal*. New York: Praeger.

Brulle, Robert J. (1996) Environmental Discourse and Social Movement Organizations: A Historical and Rhetorical Perspective on the Development of U.S. Environmental Organizations. *Sociological Inquiry*, 66, 58–83.

——(2000) *Agency, Democracy, and Nature*. Cambridge, MA: MIT Press.

Buechler, Steven M. (2000) *Social Movements in Advanced Capitalism: The Political Economy and Cultural Construction of Social Activism*. New York: Oxford University Press.

Clemens, Elisabeth S. (1993) Women's Groups and the Transformation of U.S. Politics, 1892–1920. *American Journal of Sociology*, 98, 755–98.

——(1996) Organizational Form as Frame: Collective Identity and Political Strategy in the American Labor Movement, 1880–1920. In Doug McAdam, John D. McCarthy, and Mayer N. Zald (eds.), *Comparative Perspectives on Social Movements: Political*

Opportunities, Mobilizing Structures, and Cultural Framings. New York: Cambridge University Press, 205–6.

——(1997) *The People's Lobby: Organizational Innovation and the Rise of Interest Group Politics in the United States, 1890–1925.* Chicago: University of Chicago Press.

Cloward, Richard A., and Frances Fox Piven (1984) Disruption and Organization: A Rejoinder. *Theory and Society*, 13, 587–99.

Cress, Daniel M. (1997) Nonprofit Incorporation among Movements of the Poor: Pathways and Consequences for Homeless Social Movement Organizations. *Sociological Quarterly*, 38, 343–60.

Cress, Daniel M., and David A. Snow (1996) Resources, Benefactors, and the Viability of Homeless SMOs. *American Sociological Review*, 61, 1089–109.

——(2000) The Outcomes of Homeless Mobilization: The Influence of Organization, Disruption, Political Mediation, and Framing. *American Journal of Sociology*, 105, 1063–104.

Davis, Gerald, Doug McAdam, W. Richard Scott, and Mayer N. Zald (eds.) (forthcoming) *Social Movements/Organizations: Invigorating the Fields.*

della Porta, Donatella, and Mario Diani (1999) *Social Movements: An Introduction.* Oxford: Blackwell.

Edwards, Bob, and Sam Marullo (1995) Organizational Mortality in a Declining Movement: The Demise of Peace Movement Organizations in the End of the Cold War Era. *American Sociological Review*, 60, 908–27.

Eliasoph, Nina (1998) *Avoiding Politics: How Americans Produce Apathy in Everyday Life.* New York: Cambridge University Press.

Evans, Sara M., and Harry C. Boyte (1986) *Free Spaces.* New York: Harper & Row.

Freeman, Jo (1972) The Tyranny of Structurelessness. *Second Wave* 2 (1). Reprinted in Jane Jaquette (ed.), *Women in Politics.* New York: Wiley, 1974.

Gamson, William A. (1990) *The Strategy of Social Protest.* 2nd ed. Belmont, CA: Wadsworth.

Gamson, William A., and Emilie Schmeidler (1984) Organizing the Poor. *Theory and Society*, 13, 567–84.

Ganz, Marshall (2000) Resources and Resourcefulness: Strategic Capacity in the Unionization of California Agriculture, 1959–1966. *American Journal of Sociology*, 105, 1003–63.

Garner, Roberta Ash, and Mayer N. Zald (1987) The Political Economy of Social Movement Sectors. In Mayer N. Zald and John D. McCarthy (eds.), *Social Movements in an Organizational Society.* New Brunswick, NJ: Transaction, 293–317.

Gerhards, Jürgen, and Dieter Rucht (1992) Mesomobilization: Organizing and Framing in Two Protest Campaigns in West Germany. *American Journal of Sociology*, 98, 1555–95.

Jenkins, J. Craig, and Craig M. Eckert (1986) Channeling Black Insurgency: Elite Patronage and Professional Social Movement Organizations in the Development of the Black Movement. *American Sociological Review*, 51, 812–29.

Haines, Herbert H. (1984) Black Radicalization and the Funding of Civil Rights: 1957–1970. *Social Problems*, 32, 31–43.

Hannan, Michael, and John Freeman (1984) Structural Inertia and Organizational Change. *American Sociological Review*, 49, 149–64.

Haydu, Jeffrey (1999) Counter Action Frames: Employer Repertoires and the Union Menace in the Late Nineteenth Century. *Social Problems*, 46, 313–31.

Katzenstein, Mary Fainsod (1998) *Faithful and Fearless.* Princeton, NJ: Princeton University Press.

Klandermans, Bert (1992) The Social Construction of Protest and Multiorganizational Fields. In Aldon D. Morris and Carol McClurg Mueller (eds.), *Frontiers in Social Movement Theory.* New Haven: Yale University Press, 77–103.

Lichterman, Paul (1996) *The Search for Political Community: American Activists Reinventing Commitment.* New York: Cambridge University Press.

Lo, Clarence Y. H. (1990) *Small Property versus Big Government: Social Origins of the Property Tax Revolt*. Berkeley: University of California Press.

Lounsbury, Michael (2001) Institutional Sources of Practice Variation: Staffing College and University Recycling Programs. *Administrative Science Quarterly*, 46, 29–56.

Lounsbury, Michael, Marc J. Ventresca, Paul M. Hirsch (forthcoming) Social Movements, Field Frames and Industry Emergence: A Cultural-Political Perspective on U.S. Recycling. *Socio-Economic Review*.

McAdam, Doug, John D. McCarthy, and Mayer N. Zald (eds.) (1996) *Comparative Perspectives on Social Movements: Political Opportunities, Mobilizing Structures, and Cultural Framings*. New York: Cambridge University Press.

McAdam, Doug, Sidney Tarrow, and Charles Tilly (2001) *Dynamics of Contention*. New York: Cambridge University Press.

McCammon, Holly, Karen Campbell, Ellen Granberg, and Christine Mowery (2001) How Movements Win: Gendered Opportunity Structures and U.S. Women's Suffrage Movements, 1866 to 1919. *American Sociological Review*, 66, 1, 49–70.

McCarthy, John D., and Mayer N. Zald (1977) Resource Mobilization and Social Movements: A Partial Theory. *American Journal of Sociology*, 82, 1212–34.

McCarthy, John D., David Britt, and Mark Wolfson (1991) The Institutional Channeling of Social Movements by the State in the United States. *Research in Social Movements, Conflict, and Change*, 13, 45–76.

Marullo, Sam, Ron Pagnucco, and Jackie Smith (1996) Frame Changes and Social Movement Contraction: U.S. Peace Movement Framing after the Cold War. *Sociological Inquiry*, 66, 1–28.

Melucci, Alberto (1996) *Challenging Codes: Collective Action in the Information Age*. New York: Cambridge University Press.

Michels, Robert ([1911] 1962) *Political Parties: A Sociological Study of the Oligarchical Tendencies of Modern Democracy*. New York: Free Press.

Minkoff, Debra C. (1994) From Service Provision to Institutional Advocacy: The Shifting Legitimacy of Organizational Forms. *Social Forces*, 72, 943–69.

—— (1999) Bending with the Wind: Strategic Change and Adaptation by Women's and Racial Minority Organizations. *American Journal of Sociology*, 104, 1666–703.

Mische, Ann, and Philippa Pattison (2000) Composing a Civic Arena: Publics, Projects, and Social settings. *Poetics*, 27, 163–94.

Moore, Kelly (1996) Organizing Integrity: American Science and the Creation of Public Interest Organizations, 1955–1975. *American Journal of Sociology*, 101, 1592–627.

Moore, Kelly, and Nicole Hala (2002) Organizing Identity: The Creation of Science for the People. In Michael Lounsbury and Marc Ventresca (eds.), *Research in the Sociology of Organizations: Entrepreneurs, Organizations, and Social Change*, 19, 309–35.

Morris, Aldon (1981) Black Southern Student Sit-in Movement: An Analysis of Internal Organization. *American Sociological Review*, 46, 744–67.

—— (1984) *The Origins of the Civil Rights Movement*. New York: Free Press.

Osa, Maryjane (2003) Networks in Opposition: Linking Organizations Activists in the Polish People's Republic. In Mario Diani and Doug McAdam (eds.), *Social Movements and Networks: Relational Approaches to Collective Action*. Oxford: Oxford University Press, 77–104.

Piven, Frances Fox, and Richard Cloward (1979) *Poor People's Movements: Why They Succeed, How They Fail*. New York: Vintage.

Polletta, Francesca (2002) *Freedom Is an Endless Meeting: Democracy in American Social Movements*. Chicago: University of Chicago Press.

Raeburn, Nicole (2001) Seizing and Creating Institutional Opportunities: Mobilizing for Lesbian, Gay, and Bisexual Rights in the Workplace. Paper presented at the American Sociological Association annual meeting, Anaheim, CA.

Rao, Hayagreeva (1998) Caveat Emptor: The Construction of Nonprofit Consumer Watch-dog Organizations. *American Journal of Sociology*, 103, 912–61.

Rao, Hayagreeva, Calvin Morrill, and Mayer N. Zald (2000) Power Plays: How Social Movements and Collective Action Create New Organizational Forms. *Research in Organizational Behavior*, 22, 239–82.

Rucht, Dieter (1999) Linking Organization and Mobilization: Michels' "Iron Law of Oligarchy" Reconsidered. *Mobilization*, 4, 151–70.

Schneiberg, Marc (2002) Organizational Heterogeneity and the Production of New Forms: Politics, Social Movements and Mutual Companies in American Fire Insurance, 1900–1930. In Michael Lounsbury and Marc Ventresca (eds.), *Research in the Sociology of Organizations: Entrepreneurs, Organizations, and Social Change*, 19, 39–89.

Scully, Maureen, and W. E. Douglas Creed (1999) Restructured Families: Issues of Equality and Need. *Annals of the American Academy of Political and Social Science*, 562, 47–65.

Scully, Maureen, and Amy Segal (2002) Passion with an Umbrella: Grassroots Activists in the Workplace. In Michael Lounsbury and Marc Ventresca (eds.), *Research in the Sociology of Organizations: Entrepreneurs, Organizations, and Social Change*, 19, 125–68.

Sewell, William H. (1992) A Theory of Structure: Duality, Agency, and Transformation. *American Journal of Sociology*, 98, 1–29.

Staggenborg, Suzanne (1988) The Consequences of Professionalization and Formalization in the Pro-Choice Movement. *American Sociological Review*, 53, 585–605.

Stevens, Mitchell (2001) *Kingdom of Children: Culture and Controversy in the Homeschooling Movement*. Princeton, NJ: Princeton University Press.

——(2002) The Organizational Vitality of Conservative Protestantism. In Michael Lounsbury and Marc Ventresca (eds.), *Research in the Sociology of Organizations: Entrepreneurs, Organizations, and Social Change*, 19, 337–60.

Swaminathan, Anand, and James Wade (2001) Social Movement Theory and the Evolution of New Organizational Forms. In Claudia Bird Schoonhoven and Elaine Romanelli (eds.), *The Entrepreneurship Dynamic*. Palo Alto, CA: Stanford University Press, 286–313.

Taylor, Verta (1989) Social Movement Continuity: The Women's Movement in Abeyance. *American Sociological Review*, 54, 761–75.

Tilly, Charles (1978) *From Mobilization to Revolution*. New York: Random House.

——(1986) *The Contentious French*. Cambridge, MA: Harvard University Press.

Voss, Kim, and Rachel Sherman (2000) Breaking the Iron Law of Oligarchy: Union Revitalization in the American Labor Movement. *American Journal of Sociology*, 106, 303–49.

Warren, Mark R. (2001) *Dry Bones Rattling: Community Building to Revitalize American Democracy*. Princeton, NJ: Princeton University Press.

Whittier, Nancy (1995) *Feminist Generations*. Philadelphia, PA: Temple University Press.

Zald, Mayer N., and Roberta Ash (1966) Social Movement Organizations: Growth, Decay and Change. *Social Forces*, 44 (3), 327–41.

Zald, Mayer N., and Michael A. Berger (1978) Social Movements in Organizations: Coup d'Etat, Insurgency, and Mass Movements. *American Journal of Sociology*, 83, 823–61.

Zald, Mayer N., and John D. McCarthy (1980) Social Movement Industries: Co-operation and Conflict among Social Movement Organizations. *Research in Social Movements: Conflict and Change*, 3, 1–20.

8

Leadership in Social Movements

ALDON D. MORRIS AND SUZANNE STAGGENBORG

Leaders are critical to social movements: they inspire commitment, mobilize resources, create and recognize opportunities, devise strategies, frame demands, and influence outcomes. As numerous scholars have noted, however, leadership in social movements has yet to be adequately theorized (cf. Zurcher and Snow 1981; Klandermans 1989; Melucci 1996; Morris 1999; Aminzade et al. 2001; Barker et al. 2001). We argue that this lacuna results from a failure to fully integrate agency and structure in theories of social movements. A focus on great leaders risks neglect of structural opportunities and obstacles to collective action, while an emphasis on structures of opportunity risks slighting human agency. Moreover, an emphasis on leaders seems to unfairly relegate the critical masses of movements to the category of "followers" (cf. Barker et al. 2001). Thus any approach to leadership in social movements must examine the actions of leaders within structural contexts and recognize the myriad levels of leadership and roles of participants.

We define movement leaders as strategic decision-makers who inspire and organize others to participate in social movements. Our goal in this chapter is to show that by taking leadership into account we can improve explanations of key issues in social movement theory. We begin with a brief review of existing approaches to leadership in social movements.[1] We then discuss the social composition of leadership in movements before turning to several areas for which we think leadership is critical.[2]

PERSPECTIVES ON LEADERSHIP IN SOCIAL MOVEMENTS

Early studies of social movement leadership (e.g., Blumer 1951; Lang and Lang 1961; Roche and Sachs 1965) identified the functional roles filled by different types of movement leaders at different stages in movement development (Wilson

1973: 195–6). Gusfield (1966) points to the conflicting requirements for a leader to function both within the movement as a "mobilizer," inspiring participants, and outside the movement as an "articulator," linking the movement to the larger society. More recent work further analyzes the complexity of leadership roles at different levels within movements, the conflicts between different leadership tasks, and changes over time in movement leadership (see Nelson 1971; Turner and Killian 1987; Marullo 1988; Staggenborg 1988; Klandermans 1989; Melucci 1996; Robnett 1997; Herda-Rapp 1998; Aminzade et al. 2001; Goldstone 2001).

Beyond analyzing the various roles and functions of leaders in social movements, researchers have also examined the ways in which leaders gain legitimate authority in social movements. Many draw on Weber's theory of charismatic leadership, a relational approach that assigns a key role to followers in imputing charisma to leaders (Platt and Lilley 1994). Weber (1968) elaborates the movement forms associated with charismatic leadership, including the emotional character of the community and the appointment of officials based on loyalty to the charismatic leader. Despite Weber's focus on the interactional nature of leadership, however, the notion of charisma is commonly used to refer to a personality type, and Weber's insight into the effects of leadership on movement characteristics has been neglected (cf. Wilson 1973: 198–201; Eichler 1977: 101). Melucci (1996: 336) argues that the Weberian theory of charisma leads to the neglect of the social relationship between leaders and followers, who are viewed as giving themselves up to a charismatic leader and therefore lacking agency.

Indeed, in Robert Michels's (1962) theory of political leadership, followers willingly cede agency to their leaders. The masses are grateful to leaders for speaking and acting on their behalf, even though leaders become political elites whose interests conflict with those of their followers. Large bureaucratic organizations, in Michels's view, are necessary to large-scale movements and parties, but they inevitably become oligarchical as leaders are motivated to preserve their own power and positions. Leaders become part of the power elite, more concerned with organizational maintenance than the original goals of the movement. The masses allow this to happen through apathy and a lack of competence in comparison to their skilled leaders. Marx and Engels (1968) and Lenin (1975) shared the view that outside leaders (intellectuals) were required for revolutionary movements because the masses were incapable of developing a theoretical understanding of revolutionary struggle.

Numerous theorists have disputed Michels's argument regarding the inevitable transformation of organizations into oligarchy, arguing that we need to examine the variety of organizational forms that actually constitute movements and the processes that allow some organizations to operate democratically (see Lipset et al. 1956; C. Barker 2001). Zald and Ash (1966) argue that movement organizations change in a variety of ways in response to external environmental factors as well as internal processes. Member apathy, when it occurs, does allow leaders to transform the goals of members, but in some instances leaders transform organizations in a radical rather than conservative direction (Zald and Ash 1966: 339; see also Schwartz et al. 1981). Zald and Ash point to the ways in which organizational characteristics, such as structural requirements for membership, affect the demands placed on leaders. An exclusive organization, for example, would require its leaders to focus on mobilizing tasks, while an inclusive organization would be more likely to have leaders with an articulating style. At the same time, leaders committed to particular goals may also change the structure of an organization (Zald and Ash 1966: 339–40).

Other theorists have detailed both the ways in which leaders influence movement organization and how movement characteristics shape leadership. Expanding on Weber's relational approach, Wilson (1973) distinguishes among charismatic, ideological, and pragmatic types of leaders and associated types of movement organization. Leadership type affects centralization of decision-making, division of labor, and the extent to which the organization is subject to schism. Eichler (1977) similarly associates bases of leadership with organizational characteristics and outcomes. Richard Barker (2001) argues that the right combination of leadership and organizational type will allow movements to defy Michels's predictions and empower participants pursuing radical social change.

Different types of leaders come out of different types of preexisting organizational structures. In the American women's movement, for example, "older branch" leaders came out of experiences in traditional voluntary organizations, unions, and political parties with formalized structures, whereas "younger branch" feminist leaders emerged from experiences in decentralized, participatory civil rights and New Left organizations (Freeman 1975). Leaders from these different types of backgrounds shape organizational structures in accordance with their previous experiences, influencing the mobilization, strategies, and outcomes of movements.

A key theoretical issue is the extent to which the characteristics and actions of leaders, as opposed to structural conditions, matter. Collective behavior theorists have argued that social structural conduciveness is necessary but not sufficient for movement mobilization; leaders create the impetus for movements by providing examples of action, directing action, and defining problems and proposing solutions (Lang and Lang 1961: 517–24). Smelser (1962) argues that leaders are essential to mobilization and can play a role in creating other conditions in the value-added process of collective behavior, but they also need structural strain and conduciveness, generalized beliefs, and precipitating factors to generate collective behavior.

Resource mobilization theorists have viewed leaders as political entrepreneurs who mobilize resources and found organizations in response to incentives, risks, and opportunities; supporters are seen as rational actors who follow effective leaders (see McCarthy and Zald 1973, 1977; Oberschall 1973). Factors such as the availability of outside support and the operation of social control affect the emergence of leaders (Oberschall 1973: 157–9). Political process theorists have analyzed the impacts of structures of political opportunity, but in doing so they have paid little attention to leadership – a problem acknowledged in recent discussions of the role of leaders in recognizing and acting on opportunities (Goldstone 2001; Aminzade et al. 2001).

In our view, the relative neglect of leadership in social movement theory results from a failure to adequately address the importance and limitations of both structure and agency. The political process approach emphasizes structures of political opportunity to the neglect of human agency (see Goodwin and Jasper 1999). The entrepreneurial-organizational version of resource mobilization theory (see McCarthy and Zald 2002) actually overemphasizes agency in arguing that issue entrepreneurs can manufacture grievances. In another sense, however, the theory neglects agency in its treatment of mobilizing structures. Although resource mobilization theory implicitly assumes that leaders are directing movement organizations, analysts have generally not examined the emergence of leadership and the ways in which leaders affect movement strategy and outcomes. As McCarthy and Zald (2002: 543) note in a recent assessment of resource mobilization theory, "[we] were almost silent, at least theoretically, on the issue of strategic decision making."

We argue that social movement theory would benefit greatly from an examination of the numerous ways in which leaders generate social change and create the conditions for the agency of other participants. Although we think that human agency has been neglected by the recent emphasis on structures of opportunity, we do not propose that researchers err in the opposite direction by highlighting agency at the expense of structure. Rather, we need to examine both the structural limitations and opportunities for social movements and the ways in which leaders make a difference within structural contexts.

As this review shows, scholars have produced some general ideas that we can build on in developing theories of leadership in social movements: Leaders operate within structures, and they both influence and are influenced by movement organization and environment. They are found at different levels, performing numerous and varied functions. Leaders sometimes pursue their own interests and maintain organizations at the expense of movement goals, but different organizational structures produce different types of leaders, including some who work to advance movement goals over their own interests. Different types of leaders may dominate at different stages of movement development and sometimes come into conflict with one another.

To get beyond these general ideas about leadership, we need to address the difference that leadership makes for specific processes and issues. In the following sections, we attempt to outline some new directions for the study of movement leadership by showing how leadership is dependent on structural conditions and how leaders matters to the emergence, organization, strategy, and outcomes of social movements.

SOCIAL COMPOSITION OF LEADERSHIP

Leaders of social movements are not a representative assortment of individuals randomly chosen from the populations they lead. V. I. Lenin, Mahatma Gandhi, Martin Luther King Jr., and Betty Friedan were leaders of very different types of social movements, yet they all enjoyed at least middle-class status and were highly educated. Social movement leaders tend to come from the educated middle and upper classes, are disproportionately male, and usually share the race or ethnicity of their supporters (see Brinton 1952; Flacks 1971; Oberschall 1973). Although this assertion is based mainly on research in developed Western countries, studies of movement and revolutionary leaders in poor and non-Western countries also suggest that a majority either come from the middle and upper classes or have more education than their followers (see Rejai and Phillips 1988; Veltmeyer and Petras 2002). Here we seek to understand why this nonrepresentative quality of movement leaders seems to be the rule rather than the exception and what implications the social composition of leadership has for social movements.

It is obvious that privileged class backgrounds provide leaders with financial resources, flexible schedules and social contacts often unavailable to the rank and file. These resources are important because social movements often champion the interests of resource-poor groups. However, we believe that educational capital is the key resource that social movement leaders derive from their privileged backgrounds. To be successful, social movements require that a myriad of intellectual tasks be performed extremely well. A host of social movement activities – framing grievances and formulating ideologies, debating, interfacing with media, writing, orating, devising strategies and tactics, creatively synthesizing information gleaned from local, national, and international venues, dialoguing with internal and external elites, improvising and innovating, developing rationales for coalition building and channeling emotions – are primarily intellectual tasks. The manipulation of language and other symbols is central to these tasks. Formal education, especially at the university level, is the main avenue through which people acquire advanced reading, writing, speaking, and analytic skills, and colleges and universities are settings in which many individuals absorb new ideas from different cultures.

These educational skills enabled Gandhi to develop a weapon for the weak when he formulated the strategy of nonviolent direct action. They were evident in the artistry of King's "I Have a Dream" speech, in which he linked the aspirations of the civil rights movement to those enshrined in the larger American culture. They were apparent in Friedan's *The Feminine Mystique* (1963), which gave voice to women suffering from "the problem that has no name." They shone through in Phyllis Schlafly's debating skills, which helped to defeat the Equal Rights Amendment (Mansbridge 1986). Because we agree with Jasper (1997) that social movements are characterized by creativity, artful experimentation, and improvisation, we argue that educated individuals often land leadership positions because they are best suited to design and preside over social movement tasks.

Social movements spend a great deal of time mobilizing, orchestrating, and dissecting the collective action of social groups. Studies show that contemporary social movement leaders tend to major in the social sciences, humanities, and arts (e.g., Keniston 1968; Zald and McCarthy 1987; McAdam 1988; Pinard and Hamilton 1989). Our view is that these fields of study are highly relevant to movement leaders because they constitute a "science of human action" that imparts movement-appropriate skills. Many activists learn relevant values from their parents (cf. Lipset 1972; Klatch 1999), which are then reinforced by the experiences and skills gained through education.

This does not mean that all movement leaders hail from the privileged classes or receive higher education, which is more common in post–World War II Europe and North America than in earlier times and in less-developed countries. Nor are leaders from privileged classes necessarily the best leaders for all types of movements. Indeed, leaders who emerge from poor and working-class communities are likely to share the interests of their class and to enjoy advantages in mobilizing their social bases that outsiders lack. Yet we believe that even for those who come from working and lower classes, educational capital is crucial. In a study of leadership in the Brazilian rural landless workers' movement, Veltmeyer and Petras (2002) found that a high proportion of leaders of a new wave of rural activism differed from leaders of previous waves of activism in that they had peasant origins rather than coming from the urban middle classes. Nevertheless, a large proportion of these leaders were well educated and committed to continuing education, an asset that, along with their ties to the rural poor, was key to the leaders' ability to carry out successful strategies.

Access to educational capital is a product of both agency and structure. Leaders can advance poor people's movements through their commitment to education for themselves and their followers. Thus Malcolm X was renowned for transforming his jail cell into a "university" and developing the intellectual capital that enabled him to win debates with university-trained scholars. Leaders without much formal education tend to have grown up in "movement families" or to be exposed to movement experiences by significant others, enabling them to acquire skills and knowledge regarding organizing and leadership. Movements that organize poor and uneducated people can develop organizing talents among their constituents when they create educational forums such as the citizenship schools of the civil rights movement. Although the educational capital needed by social movement leaders is more accessible for members of privileged classes and is generally acquired through formal education, it can also be taught by movements and absorbed through hands-on experience.

Large-scale structural trends and the characteristics of institutions also affect access to educational capital and leadership. For example, urban black ministers became leaders of the American civil rights movement after economic changes and subsequent urbanization produced a particular type of black minister who was educated and black churches with sufficient resources to support independent ministers. Large-scale entry of women into universities after World War II increased their presence in social movements such as the student and antiwar movements, and many women became feminist leaders after participating in small groups to discuss new ideas about women's liberation in the universities and movements of the sixties. As we argue below, many social movement leaders acquire leadership positions because of their prior leadership roles and skills acquired in the institutions of challenging groups.

Gender and Leadership

The degree of gender inequality in the community of a challenging group is one of the main determinants of gender inequality in top levels of leadership in social movements. As a result of gender inequalities at the institutional level, the top levels of social movement leadership have often had a male face, with women gaining access to leadership and status through their relationships with men. At the outset of the civil rights movement, for example, over 99 percent of the pastors in black churches were men and that office was one of the primary routes to social movement leadership. In the American New Left, women achieved status as the wives or lovers of important male leaders (Rosen 2000: 120). In revolutionary movements, the few "major female revolutionary leaders all acquired a leadership mantle from martyred husbands or fathers" (Goldstone 2001: 159).

Although men have dominated the top leadership positions in many movements, recent work on gender and leadership shows that social movement leadership is a complex phenomenon consisting of multiple layers (Jones 1993; Robnett 1997; Taylor 1999; Aminzade et al. 2001; Goldstone 2001). Without doubt, women participate widely in social movements and play crucial roles in their activities and outcomes. Robnett (1997) and Jones (1993) demonstrate that women were heavily involved in secondary leadership roles even when they were not involved in the top layers of civil rights movement leadership.

Robnett argues that women often function in the role of "bridge leader," which she defines as "an intermediate layer of leadership, whose task includes bridging potential constituents and adherents, as well as potential formal leaders to the movement" (1997: 191). Such leaders also perform the bulk of a movement's emotional work and may play dominant roles during periods of crisis and spontaneity. In a similar argument, Jones (1993: 119) maintains that women usually engage in leadership activities that establish networks and cement formal ties because of their skills associated with family life and family-like symbols. Robnett and Jones concur that women are usually excluded from the top formal leadership positions of social movement organizations (SMOs), and both tend to view such positions as being occupied by spokespersons of movements. These scholars have pushed us to broaden our conception of movement leadership by not limiting leadership to activities associated with formal roles and masculine activities.

While we welcome this corrective, we worry that this line of analysis could lead to an overly broad definition of leadership and to neglect of power dynamics in movement leadership. In recognizing that leadership is involved in many organizing activities, and that women have been critical to social movements, we do not want to equate all active participation in social movements with leadership. Organizers who create strategy, develop projects, frame issues, or inspire participation are clearly a type of leader. But other participants in organizing projects, who carry out tasks such as fundraising and canvassing (and may be called "organizers" within movements), should not automatically be considered leaders if we want to retain any analytic meaning for the concept of leadership. Moreover, we need to be aware that there is a vertical ordering of leadership in most social movements. When women are excluded from top positions they are separated from a considerable amount of power wielded by top movement leaders.

We are skeptical of arguments that collapse the distinction between formal leadership and movement spokespersons for two different reasons. On the one hand, formal movement leaders like Lenin, Gandhi, King, Castro, Mao, and Nyerere were no mere movement spokespersons: they set movement goals, determined strategies and tactics, and shaped outcomes (Aminzade et al. 2001). On the other hand, some movement "spokespersons" may be individuals who put themselves forward or are selected by the mass media as "stars" but are not accountable leaders at all (cf. Freeman 1975: 120; Gitlin 1980).

Inside and Outside Leaders

The social composition of top leadership positions is important because leaders with different backgrounds and experiences make different strategic choices, which influence movement success. Although members of challenging groups usually provide the majority of leaders for their movements, it is not unusual for members of privileged outside groups to function in leadership positions within movements of oppressed groups. For example, many leaders in the antislavery movement and some in the early civil rights movement were white (see Marx and Useem 1971). Research has shown that a mix of inside and outside leaders brings both advantages and disadvantages to social movement leadership. In terms of advantages, privileged outsiders often bring fresh viewpoints, social contacts, skills, and attention to the leadership circle that would be unavailable otherwise. Such leaders can increase the options open to movement leaders and enrich deliberations that serve as the basis for important decision-making (Marx and Useem 1971; Ganz 2000).

Leaders from outside the challenging group can also bring a host of problems to the leadership table. In a comparison of majority involvement in three very different movements, Marx and Useem (1971) found that mixed leadership teams tend to generate conflicts based on ideological disagreements, prejudices, and hostilities toward the challenging group held by outsiders, differential skill levels that enable outsiders to occupy a disproportionate number of leadership positions, and latent tensions that become highly visible over the course of a movement. Marx and Useem conclude that such conflicts are to be expected given the structural and cultural pressures inherent in insider–outsider interactions. Later, we will return to how the insider–outsider leadership dynamic can affect movement outcomes.

In sum, the composition of social movement leadership matters because it affects access to leadership skills that are crucial to leadership success. Those skills are often acquired through formal education and through knowledge gained in community institutions and prior movement experience. In the following sections, we look at the role of different types of leaders in movement emergence, strategy, and outcomes.

LEADERSHIP AND MOVEMENT EMERGENCE

Research has identified key ingredients for the emergence of social movements, including political and cultural opportunities, organizational bases, material and human resources, precipitating events, threats, grievances, and collective action frames. Although it is doubtful that even the most skilled leaders could mobilize movements in the absence of at least some of these factors, leaders make a difference in converting potential conditions for mobilization into actual social movements. At the same time, structural conditions affect the emergence and effectiveness of leaders. We need to examine how leadership interacts with other influences on movement emergence by looking at how leaders emerge in particular cultural and political contexts and what leaders do to meet the challenges of mobilization.

Cultural and Political Contexts of Leadership

Oberschall (1973) suggests that potential leaders are almost always available, but their emergence depends on political opportunities. He argues that leadership skills "have to be learned through education and the trial and error experience of activists as the movement unfolds" (1973: 158). However, political opportunities are often missed, and leaders play an important role in recognizing and acting on opportunities (Banaszak 1996; Goldstone 2001). If the emergence of movements requires that political leaders recognize structural opportunities, it follows that preexisting organizational and cultural contexts are critical to the emergence of both leaders and movements. The types of preexisting bases vary, however, depending on the type of social movement.

Morris and Braine (2001: 34–7) distinguish three types of movements: "liberation movements" are populated by members of oppressed groups, who draw on the infrastructure of their oppositional culture; "equality-based special issue movements" address specific issues that affect particular oppressed groups; and "social responsibility" movements challenge certain conditions that affect the general population. In a liberation movement such as the civil rights movement, the black churches were a primary source of movement leadership and the participatory tradition and cultural forms of the church were the backbone of the civil rights movement. In a special issue movement like the abortion rights movement, leaders emerged from existing social movements, including the population and family planning movements as well as the women's movement, and they were influenced by the structures and tactics of these movements (Staggenborg 1991).

Social responsibility movements, in contrast to the other two types, may lack such preexisting organizational and structural foundations. "Suddenly imposed grievances" (Walsh 1981), including personal tragedies as well as events such as nuclear accidents and oil spills, may motivate new leaders. For example, the anti-drinking and driving movement took off in the early 1980s in the United States with the founding of Mothers Against Drunk Drivers (MADD) by Candy Lightner after her daughter was killed by a drunk driver. Whereas earlier attempts to raise awareness of drunk driving had attracted little public attention, Lightner's leadership clearly made a difference. Despite her lack of movement experience, Lightner made effective use of the mass media, invoking motherhood and victims' rights in her framing of the problem and spurring the movement with her moral outrage. However, as Reinarman (1988) argues, the cultural and political contexts of the movement were also critical. The crusade thrived in the conservative political context of the 1980s because leaders used the frame of the "killer drunk" and the need for individual responsibility, which resonated with the "just say no" ethos of the Reagan era.

When movements are based on a history of oppression or inequality that generates indigenous institutions and prior social movements, leaders often emerge from preexisting organizations and institutions. When precipitating events create suddenly imposed grievances for individuals and communities, leaders who lack such backgrounds may be more likely to emerge, but their success is nevertheless affected by the political and cultural contexts in which they find themselves. Without doubt, leaders develop their skills in the process of organizing movements and some have no prior experience. However, many bring political and cultural traditions and skills learned in previous social movements, organizations, or institutions to their movement leadership.

Leadership and the Challenges of Mobilization

Social movement analysts have argued that political opportunities such as the presence of allies and divisions among elites encourage movement mobilization because they persuade activists there is a realistic chance for success (see McAdam 1982; McAdam et al. 1996; Tarrow 1998). However, preexisting opportunities, like grievances, do not by themselves convince people to organize and join movements; leaders play an important role in recognizing and interpreting opportunities. Owing to a lack of skilled leadership, opportunities may be missed or, alternatively, mobilization may be attempted under unfavorable conditions (see Goldstone 2001) – although leaders and movements might also help to create political and cultural opportunities.

To understand how leadership affects mobilization, we need to examine the interactive relationships among various types of leaders and movement participants. Leaders do not simply create movements by enthralling followers; rather, the early stages of a movement are typically an "orgy of participation and of talk" in which participants share stories, socially construct meaning, and explore new ideas (Oberschall 1973: 174; Couto 1993; Ospina and Schall 2001). To mobilize movements out of these early interactions, leaders offer frames, tactics, and organizational vehicles that allow participants to construct a collective identity and participate in collective action at various levels. In doing so, leaders rely not only on their personal attractiveness and abilities, but also on previous experiences, cultural traditions, gender norms, social networks, and familiar organizing forms. Insofar as men have traditionally occupied positions of authority and dominated mixed-sex interactions, the gendered character of leadership in many movements is not surprising.

In the early civil rights movement, for example, leaders drew on the participatory tradition, music, narratives, and religious doctrines of the black church to build commitment to the movement and to introduce the strategy of nonviolent protest. King and other ministers who became the formal leaders of the civil rights movement used the resources and organizational model of the black church to create both "local movement centers" and the Southern Christian Leadership Conference (SCLC), which linked local organizations to the larger movement (Morris 1984). This church-based model of organization, and the gender assumptions of male ministers, excluded women from formal leadership positions. Nevertheless, it allowed for numerous tiers of participation from community members, and many women who were previously active in churches and in community organizations became informal leaders who connected other members of the community to the movement (Barnett 1993; Robnett 1997). When black students organized the Student Nonviolent Coordinating Committee (SNCC), Ella Baker, an influential leader who had been excluded from formal power, urged the students to remain independent of the SCLC and to create the kind of decentralized structure that enabled women to become leaders within the SNCC and that attracted a variety of participants to the organization. Later, when the SNCC's ideology changed and the structure became more hierarchical, "the disintegration of the bridging tier" of leadership was at least partly responsible for mobilizing problems (Robnett 1997: 200–1).

As the example of the civil rights movement shows, cultural and political contexts and organizational structures affect the emergence of leaders and movements. At the same time, effective leaders play a critical role in mobilizing movements by engaging potential participants in discussions about movement ideas and strategies and creating organizations in which participants become involved and new leaders and strategies emerge.

AGENCY AND STRUCTURE IN MOVEMENT ORGANIZATION AND STRATEGY

Over the course of a social movement, leaders continue to influence movements by setting goals and developing strategies, creating movement organizations and shaping their structures, and forging connections among activists, organizations, and levels of action. Because organizational structures and networks affect access to leaders, one of the key problems for movements is to organize in ways that facilitate the development of leadership.

Ganz (2000: 1016–18) identifies several features of organizations that generate effective leaders and increase their "strategic capacity": First, organizational structures that permit "regular, open, and authoritative deliberation" give leaders access to information by creating forums for discussion among heterogeneous participants and they motivate leaders by allowing them the authority to act on decisions. Second, "organizations that mobilize resources from multiple constituencies" give leaders flexibility. Finally, organizations that hold leaders accountable to their constituents are likely to have leaders with useful knowledge and political skills. Ganz argues that effective strategy is usually the product of a "leadership team" rather than an individual leader (see also Disney and Gelb 2000), and that diverse leadership teams increase strategic capacity. Teams consisting of both "insiders" with links to constituencies and "outsiders" with normative or professional commitments, of leaders with strong and weak ties to constituencies, and leaders with diverse repertoires of collective action have the greatest strategic capacity (Ganz 2000: 1015).

As Ganz's work demonstrates, analyses of how leaders impact movement strategies need to examine the ways in which organizational structures and networks affect the quality of leadership available to a movement. One of the difficulties of the younger branch of the women's movement, for example, was that many feminist groups shunned leaders and formal structures out of a desire for participatory democracy. As an activist who experienced "the tyranny of structurelessness," Jo Freeman (1972) warned feminists of the impossibility of a truly leaderless, structureless group, arguing that in the absence of a formal structure, an informal structure will develop with unaccountable leaders who are selected through friendship networks. Freeman advocated experimenting with structural forms that encourage maximum participation but also accountability on the part of activists who are delegated authority and responsibilities.

Since the early years of the women's movement, feminist groups have experimented with structures that allow for both participatory democracy and effective and accountable leadership (see Baker 1986; Gottfried and Weiss 1994; Disney and Gelb 2000). Brown (1989) argues that leadership can be seen as "a set of organizing skills" that need not be performed by a minority of participants. Nonhierarchical, "distributed leadership" is possible when the requirements of skilled organizing are recognized and distributed among participants (231). Although she recognizes that "sharing tasks and skills is not an easy process" and that there are often shortages of skilled participants in movement organizations (236), Brown contends that feminist values in support of equality and opposed to hierarchy have resulted in continued attempts to create organizations in which all participants learn leadership skills.

The notions of leadership teams (Ganz 2000), distributed leadership (Brown 1989), and bridge leaders (Robnett 1997) all point to the importance of interactions among participants and networks within movements in the exercise of leadership and organizing skills. Leaders need to obtain information about opportunities, organizational forms, and tactics from one another and from other participants. Connections among leaders create access to a wider repertoire of strategies, promote coordination between national and local strategies, and encourage interorganizational cooperation and coalition work.

In the early civil rights movement, ministers who led the SCLC in different cities knew one another through their activism in the black church, and they shared information about how to organize boycotts and other direct action tactics (see Morris 1984). At the local level, bridge leaders connected members of the community to the movement and they connected leaders to one another (Robnett 1997; Herda-Rapp 1998). Herda-Rapp describes the lifelong leadership of Hattie Kendrick, a local civil rights leader who recruited and inspired young activists to become movement leaders, put new leaders in contact with one another and with older generations of leaders, and introduced them "to a vast network of national, state and grassroots leaders" (1998: 351).

Such connections among levels and generations of leadership are critical to movement strategy. In her comparison of the women's suffrage movements in the United States and Switzerland, Banaszak (1996) argues that the American movement was more successful because it made heavier use of effective organizing techniques and strategies than did the Swiss movement. Although political opportunities were similar in both countries, Banaszak argues, American suffragists perceived these opportunities and used strategies to exploit them much more frequently than did the Swiss suffragists. This superior strategic capacity was the result of connections between national and state suffrage leaders and connections between the American suffrage movement and other movements such as the abolition and temperance movements. For example, the American suffrage movement used paid organizers and lecturers to travel the country and organize the movement, a model that leaders such as Susan B. Anthony learned through their activism in the temperance and abolition movements (Banaszak 1996: 68). The Swiss movement lacked such ties and its decentralized structure also prevented the diffusion of tactics within the movement, whereas the National American Women's Suffrage Association put leaders from different states in contact with one another, helping to spread local innovations.

In addition to influencing organizational models and tactics, connections among leaders also influence interorganizational cooperation and the formation of coalitions. Cooperation among movement organizations is likely to increase under conditions of heightened opportunity or threat (Staggenborg 1986; Zald and McCarthy 1987), but leaders are important in recognizing opportunities for coalition work (Shaffer 2000: 114). Moreover, different types of leaders influence the amount and type of coalition work in a movement. In a study of environmental coalitions, Shaffer (2000) finds that professional leaders, who are employed full time by a movement organization, are more often involved in coalitions than are volunteer leaders, probably because they have more time to cultivate relationships with

other organizations (123). In addition, leaders who are more highly connected
to other organizations in the community and in the movement are most likely to
build coalitions (118–19).

LEADERS AND THE FRAMING PROCESS

A now extensive literature on collective action framing examines the ways in which
social movement actors define grievances and construct social reality to motivate
collective action (see Benford and Snow 2000 for a review). As Snow and Benford
(1992) have argued, collective action frames punctuate the seriousness, injustice,
and immorality of social conditions while attributing blame to concrete actors and
specifying the collective action needed to generate social change. To be effective,
SMOs must engage in highly skilled frame alignment work to create frames that
resonate with the culture and experiences of the aggrieved population or other
relevant actors (see Snow et al. 1986).

The framing perspective has played an important role in revealing how meaning-
generating processes anchored in cultural frameworks propel collective action. Yet
this approach is limited by its own blind spots. Like resource mobilization and
political process theory, its analytical focus is slanted toward structural and organizational factors. The social movement organization (SMO) is depicted as the major
actor, framing its activities, goals, and ideology in a manner congruent with the
interests, values, and beliefs of a set of individuals. In their numerous references to
framers Snow and his colleagues refer to them as organizers, activists, and movement speakers. At times they simply refer to the SMO or the movement as the
framers. The few times they refer to framers as leaders they fail to examine how
movement leaders drive the framing process. This approach discourages analysis of
the factors that enable or prevent social movement leaders from being effective
agents of the framing process.

A second problem is that, in ignoring the role of leaders, framing analyses neglect
the important institutional and social contexts of framers. These actors appear to
operate in the rarefied spaces of SMOs, disembodied from the populations they wish
to lead into collective action. SMOs are portrayed as coherent structures with
developed frames, while potential followers are viewed as culture-bearing individuals operating outside of institutions. We argue that this one-way directional logic
truncates analyses of the framing process, and that these two blind spots divert
attention from the central role that institutionally based leaders play in the framing
process.

SMOs are social structures with a division of labor in which leaders usually
determine organizational goals and design the strategies and tactics for reaching
those goals. Framing is central to these key tasks because it identifies both challenging groups and adversaries and suggests potential allies. Framing specifies the
unjust conditions that must be changed and the appropriate strategies and tactics
to achieve the desired ends. Because they often need to reach multiple targets,
framers must be skilled in using a variety of discourses and identifying a range of
themes appropriate to different audiences (cf. Gerhards and Rucht 1992; McAdam
1996; Evans 1997; Hull 2001). Frame disputes, which arise from the demands of
different constituents and targets, must be carefully mediated (Benford 1993). An

SMO's success or failure is related to its ability to meet the complex demands of framing work.

Because framing work is so important and fraught with difficulty, it is the preserve of social movement leaders and leadership teams who possess the educational capital and necessary skills. Different types of movements and SMOs solve framing needs in various ways. In some SMOs, leaders occupy organizational positions that provide them with privileged access to resources and high-level decision-making, allowing them to exercise a great deal of agency and a virtual monopoly over the framing process. Other organizations find ways to distribute the framing work associated with leadership, as in the case of many early women's liberation groups that rotated public speaking responsibilities – though not all such arrangements are successful. Following Ganz (2000), we suggest that diverse leadership teams that can address a broad range of problems are particularly effective framers for many movements. Leaders with close connections to constituents can produce frames that are credible and salient to aggrieved populations, while outside supporters help reach elite allies. Some organizations are structured to encourage and develop diverse leadership teams that generate ideas for effective frames. Others rely on charismatic leaders capable of reaching diverse audiences.

Effective leaders appeal to heterogeneous supporters and enhance the agency of their supporters as well as their own agency. For example, Martin Luther King mobilized diverse supporters by drawing on a wide variety of themes, including not only religious beliefs, but also the Gandhian philosophy of nonviolence, demo-cratic theory, and pragmatic values (Platt and Lilley 1994; McAdam 1996). Sup-porters interpreted King's messages in light of their own situations, constructing an inclusive collective identity. As Platt and Lilley (1994) show in their analysis of letters written to King, his followers were not passive devotees. They were partici-pants and leaders at different levels of the movement, and many of them offered strategic advice to King. By looking at the interactions of followers and leaders, and the framing work of leaders at multiple levels of movements, we go beyond the focus on elite frames that Benford (1997) identifies as one of the problems with current framing analyses.

Institutions, Leaders, and Framing

In addition to examining the ways in which the internal structures of SMOs and movements affect leadership and framing, we need to look at the effects of other institutions and organizations in the SMO's environment. Current framing theory does not adequately explain where the frames, framing skills, and leaders come from prior to SMO development. Social movements often emerge within indigenous institutions and organizations and social movement leaders often have prior lives that are deeply imbedded in community institutions. These institutions contribute a variety of elements to the leadership and framing of social movements: collective action relevant frames; mass bases of people who share those frames; populations with a collective identity; safe spaces; solidarity and commitment producing rituals; social networks of people imbued with high levels of trust; and skilled leaders who have access to institutionally embedded frames and the legitimacy to set them in motion. In a formulation resonant with our approach, Hart (1996) emphasizes that institutions, especially religious ones, can become central to framing because they house relevant preexisting frames and leaders who can utilize them in framing collective action.

The civil rights movement is a good place to examine the linkage between social movement leaders, framing, and institutional context. A "freedom and justice" frame was deeply embedded in the central black institution of the church and the cultural experiences of black people.[3] This frame was rooted in the church that emerged during slavery and served as the key institutional framework through which slaves fought for freedom and justice. The theology of the black church, largely expressed through the sermons of preachers, emphasized the biblical foundations of freedom and justice and the liberation rhetoric of great biblical personalities, including Jesus, Moses, and Amos. The black church is an interactive institution in which the preacher and congregants come to share cultural frames by engaging in dialogue during the sermon and participating together in prayers and music.

The freedom and justice frame demonstrates that a preexisting institutional frame of a challenging group may emerge as the major collective action frame of a social movement. Of course, preexisting frames are not inelastic, and leaders alter them to frame collective action. To understand this process, we need to shift our analytical focus from the alignment processes of SMOs and professional movement leaders to institutional and cultural processes of challenging groups. At this level, one investigates the presence or absence of historically produced institutional frames and their relevance to the production of collective action. If there exists a mass base of people who share an institutional frame that is conducive to collective action, the difficulty of mobilizing large numbers of people for risky behavior can be reduced considerably. Similarly, when people share a common collective identity as well as an institutional frame, conditions are favorable for the emergence of social movements. In our example, members of the black Christian community saw themselves as an oppressed group of people who desired freedom and justice. Institutionally based frames relevant to the framing of collective action stand a greater chance of being activated if the institutions that generate them also provide safe places where they can be elaborated and enacted and rituals through which solidarity and commitment can be created and maintained among those sharing the frame. Because the potential challenging group controlled it, the black church provided such safe places. It also provided institutionally derived rituals (singing, praying, and the call-and-response dynamic) capable of producing and sustaining solidarity and commitment among the participants.

Earlier we argued that leaders were the main actors in charge of movement framing processes. In our formulation, the institutions of the challenging groups may produce social movement leaders who have the skills and occupy the positions that enable them to frame movements. The freedom and justice frame operated in this manner because it was the pastors and preachers who possessed the authority and leadership skills to lift this institutional frame for collective action purposes. The authority and trustworthiness of the preacher derived from the fact that he and the members of the black church community were co-producers of the institutional frames and were embedded in the same cultural milieu. Rhetorical skills were central to the black preacher, for his prestige and charisma were rooted in his ability to be a virtuoso of language and speaking. As Wills wrote of the preacher, "the entire discipline of these men's lives issued on the eloquence they kept refining for pulpit use. The sermon...was an art form in continual process of refinement, its practitioners skilled critics of each other, improvers of the common state of themes and tropes" (1994: 216). Because of experience, practices, peer criticism, and audience feedback, the preacher established himself as an expert user of symbols.

On the eve of the civil rights movement, the freedom and justice frame was deeply entrenched in the black religious community, as were thousands of preachers who could further refine it to frame collective action. Thus, before the SCLC and SNCC were formed, the mass-based Montgomery Bus Boycott could be organized and framed as a movement for freedom and justice and be led by local ministers because both the frame and the leaders clustered in the church. The job of the leaders was not one of aligning the collective action frame of a SMO with the values and preferences of individual blacks. Rather, the task was to adapt a preexisting institutional frame to collective action. We label this process *frame lifting* because the relevant frame is chosen and lifted from a repertoire of institutional frames by institutional leaders who then alter the frame to accommodate collective action and shape collective action in accordance with the institutionally embedded frame (Morris 2000). This idea of frame lifting differs from McAdam's (1999) concept of appropriation because the latter formulation suggests that outside agents seize sites or ideas from others to use for their own purposes. In contrast, frame lifters are able to use institutional frames because they are inside agents embedded structurally and social psychologically within such frames.

We believe this analysis has general applicability. Although not all institutions are controlled by challenging groups, many serve as sources of leadership and frames.[4] Many leaders of the New Left, for example, were previously student leaders who absorbed frames critical of capitalist society in the universities. The majority of the leaders of the United Farm Workers (UFW) had been organizers and leaders of movements based in the Catholic Church (Ganz 2000). They inherited frames from the Catholic Church, which they utilized in their framing activities of the farmworkers movement. Labor unions and their frames also served as prior organizational and symbolic bases for some organizers who would come to be leaders in the UFW. The modern's women movement was possible in part because militant suffrage leaders continued to keep injustice frames alive within an "elite-sustained" organization (Rupp and Taylor 1987). We conclude, therefore, that many social movement frames are adapted to collective action within organizations and institutions and then lifted by leaders and grafted onto movements. These preexisting organizations and institutions play a major role in producing social movement leaders who perform the bulk of framing work for movements.

Framing and Mass Media

The media is a major channel through which movements recruit members, boost morale of adherents, and convey their importance and messages to the public. Framing work by both movements and media is crucial to how movements are covered and portrayed in the mass media (Motlotch 1979; Gitlin 1980; Ryan 1991; Gamson and Wolfsfeld 1993). Social movement leaders, as the actors most centrally engaged in movement framing, devise media strategy, make judgments regarding information provided to media, conduct press conferences, and are usually sought out by media to serve as movement spokespersons. The ability of leaders to convey movement frames through the mass media is influenced by the organizational and ideological character of both the movement and the media.

News gathering procedures are highly centralized, and media organizations look for authoritative sources of information. Movements such as the New Left and the women's liberation movement, which are ambivalent about leadership because they value democracy and spontaneity, have an extremely difficult time conveying their own frames through the mass media. When movements fail to offer formal spokespersons, the media typically appoint "leaders," often seeking out colorful characters who are not necessarily accountable to movement organizations (cf. Tuchman 1978; Gitlin 1980). Because they can better control their leaders and messages, professionalized movement organizations with centralized structures typically have an advantage in dealing with media organizations. Decentralized organizations with ideological objections to centralized leadership often have difficulty in formulating effective media strategies, and leaders who develop frames may be repudiated by other participants (see chapter 11 in this volume; Gitlin 1980: 104–9).

Movement and media frames compete and often clash, and media decision-makers are usually in a superior position to make their frames stick. One way movements generate favorable media coverage is by utilizing a highly visible charismatic leader, such as Martin Luther King, who attracts media coverage and conveys movement frames to relevant audiences. However, the charismatic leader can lose control of media framing when the effectiveness of the leader becomes the focus rather than the activities and goals of the movement. This happened on the final campaign King led just days before he was assassinated, when the media framed the conflict as an instance of King's inability to prevent demonstrations from becoming violent rather than a battle to empower poor sanitation workers.

The media may withhold coverage of a movement because of the low status of movement participants. In this case movement leaders can alter their strategy by recruiting members of privileged groups or by implementing dramatic tactics. Thus leaders of the 1964 Freedom Summer campaign recruited affluent white students to attract media coverage (McAdam 1988). In the 1963 Birmingham campaign, SCLC recruited young students to confront the dogs and water hoses unleashed by social control agents. While such innovations may attract media coverage and enable leaders to frame movement messages, they can create problems as well. In particular, movements may escalate their tactics and engage in violence as they are caught up in the cycle of needing more and more flamboyant tactics to attract coverage (Gitlin 1980).

In short, movement leaders are essential to the framing process, but they are constrained by the structures of movements and their environments. We have argued that it is leaders who share the disproportionate burden of framing movements because of their institutional positions and skills. It is generally their responsibility to lift frames from their institutional contexts, make any necessary adjustments to the frames, and devise appropriate forms of collective action and media strategies. Organizational and institutional structures, in turn, affect the ability of leaders to perform these tasks.

LEADERSHIP AND MOVEMENT OUTCOMES

Social movement theorists have argued that political and economic structures determine whether social movements fail or succeed (e.g., McAdam 1982; Tarrow

1998). However, social structures cannot deliberate, imagine, strategize or engage in decision-making; human actors, navigating a matrix of social structures, initiate these activities. Strategic decisions figure prominently in determining movement outcomes, and social movement leaders are the primary decision-makers within social movements. Social movement leaders carry out a complex set of activities that are crucial to outcomes because, regardless of structural conditions, there exist a variety of choices to be made regarding these tasks. Because some choices are more effective than others, the quality of the decision-making process can determine success or failure.

A variety of leadership types and styles are required to effectively perform the wide array of tasks inherent to social movements (Robnett 1997; Ganz 2000; Aminzade et al. 2001; Goldstone 2001). Four ideal types of leadership tiers often exist within movements: The first tier consists of leaders who occupy the top formal leadership positions of SMOs. The second tier consists of those who constitute the immediate leadership team of formal leaders. Such leaders often occupy secondary formal positions within SMOs. The third leadership tier consists of bridge leaders. As Goldstone (2001: 158), building on Robnett, writes, "Bridge leaders are those neighborhood and community organizers who mediate between top leadership and the vast bulk of followers, turning dreams and grand plans into on-the-ground realities." The fourth tier of leadership consists of those organizers who, in addition to building connections between members of a challenging group and helping them develop organizations, also routinely engage in leadership activity.

These various tiers of leadership are important in producing different types of movement outcomes. Bridge leaders and organizers affect movement success through their work within the movement, mobilizing the support necessary to carry out collective action tactics, which result in concrete gains for the movement (Robnett 1997). The formal leaders of SMOs are crucial to internal movement dynamics and they are important in influencing elites outside the movement. Successful formal leaders may become "elite challengers" who have connections to elites in other sectors such as political parties, unions, and mass media (Schmitt 1989). Leadership teams are essential in making strategic decisions, and the success of the movement depends on the creativity, imagination, and skill of these leaders.

Movements are more likely to succeed if they attract leadership teams with diverse backgrounds, skills and viewpoints. Quality decisions are likely to emerge from a collective of such leaders who set the creative process in motion through concerted deliberations and brainstorming (Ganz 2000). The civil rights and farmworker movements are cases in point. Both had great charismatic leaders but the overall genius of their decision-making was rooted in the leadership teams in which King and Chavez were embedded. Accounting for King's success, Bennett (1970: 32–3) writes, "King had an unexcelled ability to pull men and women of diverse viewpoints together and to keep their eyes focused on the goal. King demonstrated a rare talent for attracting and using the skills and ideas of brilliant aides and administrators." Ganz reveals that Chavez was embedded in a leadership team whose members were characterized by diverse skills, networks, biographical experiences, and repertoires of collective action (2000: 1026–7). In both of these movements diverse leadership generated creativity, encouraged innovations, and enhanced the possibility of success.

A concrete example of how the creativity of a leadership team can be decisive is provided by the 1963 civil rights campaign in Birmingham, Alabama. The strategy in that setting called for massive direct action to paralyze the city through demonstrations, mass arrests to fill the jails, and an economic boycott. The mobilization and deployment of thousands of protesters was key; without them social order could be maintained and the movement would fail. At a crucial stage King and the SCLC were not able to mobilize enough demonstrators to fill the jails and to create massive disruption. The campaign teetered at the brink of defeat. Meanwhile, King's second tier of leadership mobilized thousands of youth to engage in demonstrations (Garrow 1986; Fairclough 1987; Branch 1988; Morris 1993). The leadership team fiercely debated whether young children should be employed to face the repression sure to be unleashed by social control agents. During a critical weekend King honored an out-of-town engagement only to learn upon his return that members of his leadership team had begun including hundreds of youth in demonstrations while thousands more were en route. Having little choice, King condoned the strategy. The children filled the jails, clogged public spaces and provoked the use of attack dogs, billy clubs, and fire hoses, thereby precipitating the crisis needed to win the struggle. If leadership had failed to act creatively this campaign could have been lost and the entire movement may have stalled. Because of creative leadership, the campaign was a success and served as a model for additional protests that toppled the Jim Crow regime. It was the leadership team rather than an omnipotent and isolated charismatic leader who mobilized a controversial support group and made the decision to deploy them.

Movements led by leadership teams comprising both insiders and outsiders have the greatest chances of success (Marx and Useem 1971; Ganz 2000). Leaders who are members of the challenging group are crucial as they are rooted in the institutional structures and culture of the movement group and enjoy legitimacy given their shared group membership and shared fate. Their biographical experiences provide them with insights into the motives of the challengers and their cultural and organizational resources required for successful mobilization. Thus it was Mexican and Mexican American leaders of the farmworkers who decided to test support for a grape strike "by meeting in the hall of Our Lady of Guadalupe Church in Delano, the religious center of the community on September 16, Mexican Independence Day" (Ganz 2000: 1031). By bringing Mexican history alive and employing the symbols and resources of the farmworkers' religious community, these indigenous leaders ignited a social movement. Similarly, King and other civil rights leaders launched boycotts during the Easter season and engineered arrests on religious holidays because of their understanding of such symbolism (Morris 1984).

Social movement leaders drawn from outside of the challenging group are valuable because they may be anchored in social networks otherwise unavailable to the challenging group and they often bring fresh insights and analyses to the table from cultural sources outside the movement. Especially relevant are collective action repertoires outsiders may have learned from other movements. Thus the civil rights movement drew on leaders who had been active in the Communist, labor and peace movements. Nevertheless, outside leaders often create problems by usurping leadership positions and creating animosity and jealousy, which can lead to disintegration and factionalism (Marx and Useem 1971; McAdam 1988). Even more important, if outsiders dominate the leadership process, they can make poor strategic choices because of their lack of understanding of the challenging group, lower levels of motivation, and the likelihood that they will not be accountable to movement constituencies (Ganz 2000). It appears that movements that employ leaders from the outside but make sure that they are not dominant numerically or strategically are likely to have a greater chance of success.

If creative and innovative leadership emerges from a collective decision-making process, leaders can be effective only if they are able to deliberate collectively. The structure and nature of social movement organizations largely determine whether leaders are provided the latitude to function collectively and creatively. Both classical (Michels 1962) and contemporary analysts (Piven and Cloward 1977; Schwartz et al. 1981) warn that leadership in SMOs can become autocratic and obsessed with narrow self-interests that may limit the chances for movement success or derail the movement altogether. Both bureaucratic and "structureless" forms of organizations tend to stifle creative leadership, for opposite reasons. Bureaucratic SMOs privilege routine decision-making and seek to avoid the uncertainty that usually accompanies mass participation and innovative tendencies (Morris 1984). SMOs that seek to avoid structure and hierarchies run the risk of being ambushed by back-door "invisible" autocratic leadership that operates free of accountability structures (Freeman 1972; Hanisch 2001). Neither of these organizational forms promotes democratic, open-ended deliberations, where numerous options are placed before a collectivity. In contrast, SMOs that have deliberative structures that encourage and promote imaginative and creative collective decision-making avoid these problems (see Ganz 2000).

However, no one structure is appropriate for all types of movements. Some religious movements, for example, succeed under a charismatic leader, with organizational structures that strengthen the leader's charismatic authority. Moreover, mature social movements usually include multiple organizations. We argue that a variety of organizational forms increase the likelihood of social movement success by specializing in different but complimentary work. This dynamic can lead to a leadership team of diverse SMO leaders who propel the movement towards its goals through their cooperation and competition. The same dynamic can degenerate into destructive competition and conflict that leads to failure. On balance, however, we agree with Ganz (2000) that teams of diverse leaders anchored in authoritative organizational structures that are conducive to open and critical debate and challenging deliberations are more likely to succeed because of the creativity and innovation such leaders generate as they execute leadership activities.

Conclusions

This chapter has attempted to show that social movement leadership matters at all levels of social movement activity. We agree with the emerging literature on this topic (Robnett 1997; Aminzade et al. 2001; Barker et al. 2001; Goldstone 2001) that social movement analysts need to open up the black box of leadership and develop theories and empirical investigations of how leadership affects the emergence, dynamics, and outcomes of social movements. Social movement leadership, in our view, is not a residual activity deducible from political and economic structures. We fully agree with political process theorists that a movement's structural context profoundly affects its leadership by creating opportunities and constraints that influence what leaders can and cannot do. At the same time, our approach to leadership suggests that leaders help to create or undermine political and socio-economic realities that influence the trajectories and outcomes of social movements. Leaders interpret relevant structural contexts and identify their weaknesses, strengths, and contradictions and make decisions about how they are to be exploited for movement purposes. In our view social movement theory should avoid the tendency to view political opportunities as part of a structure that is always external to social movements. For example, black leaders had prepared the foundations and developed the connections to exploit the international arena long before the Cold War materialized. Because the groundwork had been established, the leaders of the civil rights movement were positioned to take advantage of Cold War politics.

McAdam et al. (2001) rightly call for the study of mechanisms and processes that drive contentious politics. Yet they fail to analyze leadership itself as a mechanism or a process or even as having explicit bearings on the determination and outcomes of contentious politics. We argue that questions about leadership need to be central to this agenda: Under what conditions and by what means are leaders able to exploit or change structural conditions? How do environmental conditions constrain strategic decision-making, and how does this change with various movement outcomes? How do different types of movements utilize institutionally situated leaders and how are leaders developed within movement organizations? What types of educational forums work to develop educational capital in deprived groups? How do leaders and leadership teams create effective strategies and frames? What types of organizational structures are conducive to democratic leadership and the agency of participants? How are connections among leaders within and across movements created and maintained? How do these connections affect strategies and coalitions? How do movement leaders become elite challengers and how do their connections to leaders in government and other sectors affect movement goals, strategies, and outcomes? Such questions need empirical investigation to develop our understanding of how agency and structure interact in the dynamics of social movements.

Human initiatives and choices guide social movements. Social movement agency is rooted in these initiatives and choices. Social movement leaders are the actors whose hands and brains rest disproportionately on the throttles of social movements. What they do matters and it is the job of social movement analysts to elucidate the dynamics and processes that constrain and enable the work of social movement leaders.

Notes

We are equal co-authors; our names appear in alphabetical order. We are grateful to Marshall Ganz for providing us with in-depth, written insights on social movement leadership. We also thank Francesca Polletta and the editors of this volume for their comments on a previous draft of the chapter.

1 Owing to space constraints, we do not discuss the large organizational and psychological literature on leadership, although we believe that this work is relevant to social movement

theory and it informs our views in general ways. For instance, organizational theorists have stressed the importance of situational context, the ways in which leaders empower others to lead, and the dispersal of leadership in organizations (see Bryman 1996: 283–4). For recent reviews of this literature, see R. A. Barker (2001), Brodbeck (2001), and de Vries (2001).

2   At the risk of bias toward contemporary Western movements, many of our examples are drawn from the civil rights movement because we found this to be an excellent case for understanding leadership dynamics.

3   Influential analyses of framing by the civil rights movement (Snow and Benford 1992; Tarrow 1998) have argued that its guiding frame was one of "rights" and that this frame emerged because early black struggles were waged in courts. The rights frame in this view was adopted by King and other civil rights leaders and aligned to the culture of the black community. In our view, this account is wrong; the leaders of the civil rights movement drew primarily on the "freedom and justice" frame of the black church rather than the "rights" frame of the courts. It is this frame that one encounters in the writings, music, and speeches of the movement. For example, in King's 1963 "I have a Dream" speech the word "freedom" or "free" is mentioned 19 times and "justice" 9 times. "Rights" is mentioned 3 times and not in a prominent manner. Similarly in 1955, at the beginning of the modern movement, King declared that the movement would not accept anything less than freedom and justice and that "we are protesting for the birth of justice in the community." The freedom frame is reflected in the naming of important movement campaigns, events, and cultural activities. Thus there were the "Freedom Rides," "Freedom Summer," Mississippi Freedom Democratic Party," "Freedom Schools," "Freedom Songs," and the "Chicago Freedom Movement." Black people resonated to the message of fighting for freedom and justice and the movement was framed to capture this thrust.

4   See Morris (2000) for a discussion of how "agency-laden" institutions such as the black church, which are controlled by the potential challenging group, play an important role in providing institutionally based collective action frames.

References

Aminzade, Ron R., Jack A. Goldstone, and Elizabeth J. Perry (2001) Leadership Dynamics and the Dynamics of Contention. In Ron R. Aminzade, Jack A. Goldstone, Doug McAdam, Elizabeth J. Perry, William H. Sewell Jr., Sidney Tarrow, and Charles Tilly (eds.), *Silence and Voice in the Study of Contentious Politics*. Cambridge: Cambridge University Press, 126–54.

Baker, Andrea J. (1986) The Problem of Authority in Radical Movement Groups: A Case Study of Lesbian-Feminist Organization. In Louis A. Zurcher (ed.), *Leaders and Followers: Challenges for the Future*. Greenwich, CT: JAI, 135–55.

Banaszak, Lee Ann (1996) *Why Movements Succeed or Fail: Opportunity, Culture, and the Struggle for Woman Suffrage*. Princeton, NJ: Princeton University Press.

Barker, Colin (2001) Robert Michels and "The Cruel Game." In Colin Barker, Alan Johnson, and Michael Lavalette (eds.), *Leadership in Social Movements*. Manchester: Manchester University Press, 24–43.

Barker, Colin, Alan Johnson, and Michael Lavalette (2001) Leadership Matters: An Introduction. In Colin Barker, Alan Johnson, and Michael Lavalette (eds.), *Leadership in Social Movements*. Manchester: Manchester University Press, 1–23.

Barker, Richard A. (2001) The Nature of Leadership. *Human Relations*, 54 (4), 469–94.

Barnett, Bernice McNair (1993) Invisible Southern Black Women Leaders in the Civil Rights Movement: The Triple Constraints of Gender, Race and Class. *Gender & Society*, 7 (2), 162–82.

Benford, Robert D. (1993) Frame Disputes within the Nuclear Disarmament Movement. *Social Forces*, 71 (3), 677–701.

——(1997) An Insider's Critique of the Social Movement Framing Perspective. *Sociological Inquiry*, 67 (4), 409–30.

Benford, Robert D., and David A. Snow (2000) Framing Processes and Social Movements: An Overview and Assessment. *Annual Review of Sociology*, 26, 611–39.

Bennett, Lerone Jr. (1970) When the Man and the Hour Met. In C. Eric Lincoln (ed.), *Martin Luther King, Jr: A Profile*. New York: Hill & Wang, 7–39.

Blumer, Herbert (1951) Collective Behavior. In A. M. Lee, (ed.), *Principles of Sociology*. New York: Barnes & Noble, 166–222.

Branch, Taylor (1988) *Parting the Waters*. New York: Simon & Schuster.

Brinton, Crane (1952) *The Anatomy of Revolution*. New York: Vintage.

Brodbeck, F. (2001) Leadership in Organizations, Psychology of. In Neil J. Smeler and Paul B. Baltes (eds.), *International Encyclopedia of the Social and Behavioral Sciences*. Oxford: Pergamon Press, 8569–73.

Brown, M. Helen (1989) Organizing Activity in the Women's Movement: An Example of Distributed Leadership. *International Social Movement Research*, 2, 225–40.

Bryman, Alan (1996) Leadership in Organizations. In Stewart R. Clegg, Cynthia Hardy, and Walter R. Nord (eds.), *Handbook of Organization Studies*. Thousand Oaks, CA: Sage, 276–92.

Couto, Richard A. (1993) Narrative, Free Space, and Political Leadership in Social Movements. *Journal of Politics*, 55 (1), 57–79.

de Vries, M. F. R. Kets (2001) Leadership in Organizations, Sociology of. In Neil J. Smeler and Paul B. Baltes (eds.), *International Encyclopedia of the Social and Behavioral Sciences*. Oxford: Pergamon Press, 8573–8.

Disney, Jennifer Leigh, and Joyce Gelb (2000) Feminist Organizational "Success": The State of US Women's Movement Organizations in the 1990s. *Women and Politics*, 21 (4), 39–76.

Eichler, Margaret (1977) Leadership in Social Movements. *Sociological Inquiry*, 47 (2), 99–107.

Evans, John H. (1997) Multi-Organizational Fields and Social Movement Organization Frame Content: The Religious Pro-Choice Movement. *Sociological Inquiry*, 67 (4), 451–69.

Fairclough, Adam (1987) *To Redeem the Soul of America: The Southern Christian Leadership Conference and Martin Luther King, Jr*. Athens, GA: University of Georgia Press.

Flacks, Richard (1971) *Youth and Social Change*. Chicago: Markham.

Freeman, Jo (1972) The Tyranny of Structurelessness. In Anne Koedt, Ellen Levine, and Anita Rapone (eds.), *Radical Feminism*. New York: Quadrangle, 285–99.

——(1975) *The Politics of Women's Liberation*. New York: Longman.

Friedan, Betty (1963) *The Feminine Mystique*. New York: Dell.

Gamson, William, and Gadi Wolfsfeld (1993) Movements and Media as Interacting Systems. *Annals of the Academy of Political and Social Science*, 528, 114–25.

Ganz, Marshall (2000) Resources and Resourcefulness: Strategic Capacity in the Unionization of California Agriculture: 1959–1966. *American Journal of Sociology*, 105 (4), 1003–62.

Garrow, David (1986) *Bearing the Cross: Martin Luther King, Jr., and the Southern Christian Leadership Conference*. New York: William Morrow.

Gerhards, Jürgen, and Dieter Rucht (1992) Mesomobilization: Organizing and Framing in Two Protest Campaigns in West Germany. *American Journal of Sociology*, 98 (3), 555–95.

Gitlin, Todd (1980) *The Whole World Is Watching: Mass Media in the Making and Unmaking of the New Left*. Berkeley: University of California Press.

Goldstone, Jack A. (2001) Toward a Fourth Generation of Revolutionary Theory. *Annual Review of Political Science*, 4, 139–87.

Goodwin, Jeff, and James M. Jasper (1999) Caught in a Winding, Snarling Vine: The Structural Bias of Political Process Theory. *Sociological Forum*, 14 (1), 27–54.

Gottfried, Heidi, and Penny Weiss (1994) A Compound Feminist Organization: Purdue University's Council on the Status of Women. *Women and Politics*, 14 (2), 23–44.

Gusfield, Joseph R. (1966) Functional Areas of Leadership in Social Movements. *Sociological Quarterly*, 7 (2), 137–56.

Hanisch, Carol (2001) Struggles Over Leadership in the Women's Liberation Movement. In Colin Barker, Alan Johnson, and Michael Lavalette (eds.), *Leadership in Social Movements*. Manchester: Manchester University Press, 77–95.

Hart, Stephen (1996) The Cultural Dimensions of Social Movements: A Theoretical Reassessment and Literature Review. *Sociology of Religion*, 57 (1), 87–100.

Herda-Rapp, Ann (1998) The Power of Informal Leadership: Women Leaders in the Civil Rights Movement. *Sociological Focus*, 31 (4), 341–55.

Hull, Kathleen E. (2001) The Political Limits of the Rights Frame: The Case of Same-Sex Marriage in Hawaii. *Sociological Perspectives*, 44 (2), 207–32.

Jasper, James M. (1997) *The Art of Moral Protest*. Chicago: University of Chicago Press.

Jones, Kathleen B. (1993) *Compassionate Authority: Democracy and the Representation of Women*. New York: Routledge.

Keniston, Kenneth (1968) *Young Radicals: Notes on Committed Youth*. New York: Harcourt, Brace & World.

Klandermans, Bert (ed.) (1989) Organizing for Change: Social Movement Organizations in Europe and the United States. *International Social Movement Research*, 2, 1–17.

Klatch, Rebecca E. (1999) *A Generation Divided: The New Left, the New Right, and the 1960s*. Berkeley: University of California Press.

Lang, Kurt, and Gladys Engel Lang (1961) *Collective Dynamics*. New York: Thomas Y. Crowell.

Lenin V. I. (1975) *What Is to Be Done?* Peking: Foreign Languages.

Lipset, Seymour Martin (1972) *Rebellion in the University*. Boston: Little, Brown.

Lipset, Seymour Martin, Martin Trow, and James Coleman (1956) *Union Democracy*. Garden City, NY: Anchor.

McAdam, Doug (1982) *Political Process and the Development of Black Insurgency*. Chicago: University of Chicago Press.

——(1988) *Freedom Summer*. New York: Oxford University Press.

——(1996) The Framing Functions of Movement Tactics: Strategic Dramaturgy in the American Civil Rights Movement. In Doug McAdam, John D. McCarthy, and Mayer N. Zald (eds.), *Comparative Perspectives on Social Movements*. Cambridge: Cambridge University Press, 338–55.

——(1999) *Political Process and the Development of Black Insurgency*. Rev. ed. Chicago: University of Chicago Press.

McAdam, Doug, John D. McCarthy, and Mayer N. Zald (eds.) (1996) *Comparative Perspectives on Social Movements*. Cambridge: Cambridge University Press.

McAdam, Doug, Sidney Tarrow, and Charles Tilly (2001) *Dynamics of Contention*. Cambridge: Cambridge University Press.

McCarthy, John D., and Mayer N. Zald (1973) *The Trend of Social Movements in America: Professionalization and Resource Mobilization*. Morristown, NJ: General Learning.

——(1977) Resource Mobilization and Social Movements: A Partial Theory. *American Journal of Sociology*, 82 (6), 1212–41.

——(2002) The Enduring Vitality of the Resource Mobilization Theory of Social Movements. In Jonathan H. Turner (ed.), *Handbook of Sociological Theory*. New York: Kluwer Academic/Plenum, 533–65.

Mansbridge, Jane J. (1986) *Why we Lost the ERA*. Chicago: University of Chicago Press.

Marullo, Sam (1988) Leadership and Membership in the Nuclear Freeze Movement: A Specification of Resource Mobilization Theory. *Sociological Quarterly*, 29 (3), 407–27.

Marx, Gary T., and Michael Useem (1971) Majority Involvement in Minority Movements. *Journal of Social Issues*, 27, 81–104.

Marx, Karl, and Friedrich Engels (1968) *Selected Works*. New York: International.

Melucci, Alberto (1996) *Challenging Codes: Collective Action in the Information Age*. Cambridge: Cambridge University Press.

Michels, Robert (1962) *Political Parties*. New York: Collier.

Molotch, Harvey (1979) Media and Movements. In Mayer Zald and John McCarthy (eds.), *The Dynamics of Social Movements*. Cambridge: Winthrop, 71–93.

Morris, Aldon D. (1984) *The Origins of the Civil Rights Movement: Black Communities Organizing for Change*. New York: Free Press.

——(1993) Birmingham Confrontation Reconsidered: An Analysis of the Dynamics and Tactics of Mobilization. *American Sociological Review*, 58, 621–36.

——(1999) A Retrospective on the Civil Rights Movement: Political and Intellectual Landmarks. *Annual Review of Sociology*, 25, 517–39.

——(2000) Reflections on Social Movement Theory: Criticisms and Proposals. *Contemporary Sociology*, 29, 445–54.

Morris, Aldon, and Naomi Braine (2001) Social Movements and Oppositional Consciousness. In Jane Mansbridge and Aldon Morris (eds.), *Oppositional Consciousness: The Subjective Roots of Social Protest*. Chicago: University of Chicago Press, 20–37.

Nelson, Harold A. (1971) Leadership and Change in an Evolutionary Movement: An Analysis of Change in the Leadership Structure of the Southern Civil Rights Movement. *Social Forces*, 49 (3), 353–71.

Oberschall, Anthony (1973) *Social Conflict and Social Movements*. Englewood Cliffs, NJ: Prentice-Hall.

Ospina, Sonia, and Ellan Schall (2001) Perspectives on Leadership: Our Approach to Research and Documentation for the Leadership for a changing World <http://leadership forchange.org>.

Pinard, Maurice, and Richard Hamilton (1989) Intellectuals and the Leadership of Social Movements: Some Comparative Perspectives. In Louis Kriesberg (ed.), *Research in Social Movements, Conflicts and Change*. Vol. 11. Greenwich, CT: JAI, 73–107.

Piven, Frances Fox, and Richard A. Cloward (1977) *Poor People's Movements: Why They Succeed, How They Fail*. New York: Vintage.

Platt, Gerald M., and Stephen J. Lilley (1994) Multiple Images of a Charismatic: Constructing Martin Luther King Jr.'s Leadership. In Gerald Platt and Chad Gordon (eds.), *Self, Collective Behavior and Society: Essays Honoring the Contributions of Ralph H. Turner*. Greenwich, CT: JAI, 55–74.

Reinarman, Craig (1988) The Social Construction of an Alcohol Problem: The Case of Mothers Against Drunk Drivers and Social Control in the 1980s. *Theory and Society*, 17, 91–120.

Rejai, Mostafa, and Kay Phillips (1988) *Loyalists and Revolutionaries: Political Leaders Compared*. New York: Praeger.

Robnett, Belinda (1997) *How Long? How Long? African-American Women in the Struggle for Civil Rights*. New York: Oxford University Press.

Roche, John P., and Stephen Sachs (1965) The Bureaucrat and the Enthusiast: An Exploration of the Leadership of Social Movements. *Western Political Quarterly*, 8 (2), 248–61.

Rosen, Ruth (2000) *The World Split Open: How the Modern Women's Movement Changed America*. New York: Penguin.

Rupp, Leila, and Verta Taylor (1987) *Survival in the Doldrums: The American Women's Rights Movement, 1945 to 1960*. New York: Oxford University Press.

Ryan, Charlotte (1991) *Prime Time Activism: Media Strategies for Grassroots Organizing*. Boston: South End.

Schmitt, Rudiger (1989) Organizational Interlocks Between New Social Movements and Traditional Elites: The Case of the West German Peace Movement. *European Journal of Political Research*, 17 (5), 583–98.

Schwartz, Michael, Naomi Rosenthal, and Laura Schwartz (1981) Leader–Member Conflict in Protest Organizations: The Case of the Southern Farmers' Alliance. *Social Problems*, 29 (1), 22–36.

Shaffer, Martin B. (2000) Coalition Work among Environmental Groups: Who Participates? *Research in Social Movements, Conflicts, and Change*, 22, 111–26.

Smelser, Neil J. (1962) *Theory of Collective Behavior*. New York: Free Press.

Snow, David A., and Robert D. Benford (1992) Master Frames and Cycles of Protest. In Aldon D. Morris and Carol M. Mueller (eds.), *Frontiers in Social Movement Theory*. New Haven: Yale University Press, 133–55.

Snow, David A., R. Burke Rochford Jr., Steven K. Worden, and Robert D. Benford (1986) Frame Alignment Processes, Micromobilization, and Movement Participation. *American Sociological Review*, 51, 464–81.

Staggenborg, Suzanne (1986) Coalition Work in the Pro-Choice Movement: Organizational and Environmental Opportunities and Obstacles. *Social Problems*, 33 (5), 374–90.

——(1988) The Consequences of Professionalization and Formalization in the Pro-Choice Movement. *American Sociological Review*, 53, 585–605.

——(1991) *The Pro-Choice Movement: Organization and Activism in the Abortion Conflict*. New York: Oxford University Press.

Tarrow, Sidney (1998) *Power in Movement: Social Movements and Contentious Politics*. 2nd ed. New York: Cambridge University Press.

Taylor, Verta (1999) Gender and Social Movements: Gender Processes in Women's Self-Help Movements. *Gender & Society*, 13 (1), 8–33.

Tuchman, Gaye (1978) *Making News*. New York: Free Press.

Turner, Ralph H., and Lewis M. Killian (1987) *Collective Behavior*. 3rd ed. Englewood Cliffs, NJ: Prentice-Hall.

Veltmeyer, Henry, and James Petras (2002) The Social Dynamics of Brazil's Rural Landless Workers' Movement: Ten Hypotheses on Successful Leadership. *Canadian Review of Sociology and Anthropology*, 39 (1), 79–96.

Walsh, Edward J. (1981) Resource Mobilization and Citizen Protest in Communities around Three Mile Island. *Social Problems*, 29 (1), 1–21.

Weber, Max (1968) *Economy and Society*. Berkeley: University of California Press.

Wills, Garry (1994) *Certain Trumpets: The Nature of Leadership*. New York: Simon & Schuster.

Wilson, John (1973) *Introduction to Social Movements*. New York: Basic.

Zald, Mayer N., and Roberta Ash (1966) Social Movement Organizations: Growth, Decay, and Change. *Social Forces*, 44 (3), 327–41.

Zald, Mayer N., and John D. McCarthy (1987) Organizational Intellectuals and the Criticism of Society. In Mayer N. Zald and John D. McCarthy, *Social Movements in Organizational Society*. New Brunswick: Transaction, 97–115.

Zurcher, Louis A., and David A. Snow (1981) Collective Behavior: Social Movements. In Morris Rosenberg and Ralph H. Turner (eds.), *Social Psychology: Sociological Perspectives*. New York: Basic, 447–82.

9

Movement Allies, Adversaries, and Third Parties

DIETER RUCHT

INTRODUCTION

Most students of social movements would agree with the following two observations. First, social movements arise, and, assuming they survive, continue to exist in a situation of conflict; they are involved in struggles with adversaries.[1] Second, social movements are complex social entities with vague and shifting boundaries. They are often composed of networks of groups and organizations. As such, they typically have more or less stable links with other groups which may support or form alliances with them. Indeed, seeking allies can become critical for a movement's survival, particularly when it is in an outsider position. Only by broadening their support can most movements hope to make an impact. Hence challenging an opponent and appealing to potential constituents and allies are both elementary tasks for social movements.

As a conceptual and methodological consequence of their need to both fight an opponent and appeal to potential allies, social movements can be understood only in *relational* terms. While this is widely acknowledged for the analysis of interactions between social movements and their adversaries, most scholars tend to pay less attention to other kinds of relationships, such as alliances with affinity groups, appeals to public bystanders, or interactions with mediators. These linkages, and their interplay with the conflict-ridden relationships that characterize movement adversary relationships, should become part and parcel of social movement studies. It is time to abandon the simplified image of a two-party struggle between a (unified) movement and its (unified) opponent acting in some kind of a social vacuum. Unlike two individuals who may engage in personal struggles without spectators, social movements are internally differentiated actors operating within complex social settings that, in part, consist of public arenas. These settings are not just a kind of neutral background but include different kinds of actors with whom a given social movement engages.

This chapter tries to conceptualize and illustrate the different kinds of linkages a social movements has both internally and with its environment. In the first section, an attempt will be made to clarify the relational character of social movements and to identify their most important external reference groups. The next two sections focus on alliances and adversaries, respectively. The fourth section broadens this perspective by discussing the so far largely neglected aspects of mediators and audiences. Finally, these components are brought together in the concluding section, which also suggests some lines for further research in this area of study.

A Conceptual Approach

The idea that social movements are embedded in a web of relations is not new. From Karl Marx to Herbert Blumer to more recent theorists, scholars have emphasized that social movements emerge and develop through interactions, be they called class struggle, symbolic interactions, exchange processes, or contentious politics. Several works have already attempted to conceptualize these relationships.

Multi-Organizational Fields

Multi-organizational fields are defined as "the total possible number of organizations with which the focal organization might establish linkages" (Curtis and Zurcher 1973: 53). As its very name suggests, the concept focuses attention on *organizations* rather than on broader and more diffuse phenomena such as constituents and sympathizers, thereby corresponding to resource mobilization theory, which emphasizes the role of social movement organizations as the driving force of most movement activity.

Curtis and Zurcher (1973) were among the first to develop an organizational ecology of social movements. As an empirical focus, they chose two social movement organizations (engaged in antipornography) in two different cities. They conducted research based on participant observation of meetings, unstructured interviews, structured questionnaires, documents, and newspaper accounts. Two of Curtis and Zurcher's findings warrant mention here. First, both organizations were enmeshed in multi-organizational fields, though to different degrees. While one group had extensive links to its environment particularly at the organizational level, the other group had more links at the level of individuals. Second, the group with more organizational links, when compared to the other group, had closer and more ordered interaction with its environment, greater recruitment focus, use of organizational rather than extra-organizational contacts, and stability of aligned organizations. Though emphasizing the limitations of their study of two cases only, Curtis and Zurcher (1973: 60) tentatively suggested a more general conclusion:

> The findings indicate that the characteristics of the multi-organizational field, and the degree to which a protest organization is integrated with it, are variables significantly associated with structural and membership characteristics of the organization itself. These findings support the contention that few organizations, unless their purposes include isolation or freedom from exogenous influence or contamination, can operate in an interorganizational void.

In a subsequent article, Curtis and Zurcher (1974) tried to spell out the relationship between different kinds of social movements and their links with their environment in a more systematic, though probably somewhat mechanical, way. Drawing on a classification based on three types of goal orientations (expressive, instrumental, mixed) and three types of membership requirements (exclusive, inclusive, mixed), the authors hypothesized that the different movement organizations, representing different combinations of these features, vary greatly in the degree and kind of their environmental contacts, as well as other factors (e.g., leadership styles). Without going into details, it is important to highlight their discussion of differential effects of two types of movement environments for various kinds of movements: a hostile environment (criticisms, countermovements, organizational operations, etc.) and a reinforcing environment (favorable publicity, increased access to resources, overt citizen support, etc.). Curtis and Zurcher speculate that the hostile environment enhances the existing insulating and solidarity mechanisms of the exclusive-expressive movement organization and the shift of inclusive-instrumental type toward the expressive and exclusive dimension. By contrast, the reinforcing environment, according to the authors, will increase the instrumental orientations of the inclusive-instrumental type and weaken the insulating mechanisms of the exclusive-expressive type (1974: 365–6). While the authors' plea for further elaboration and testing of these assumptions has not sparked the research they anticipated, their idea of two basic kinds of environments was picked up on in subsequent work.

Kriesi (1985: 33), probably unaware of Curtis and Zurcher's concepts, explicitly discussed the role of a "conflict system" and an "alliance system" for social movements. In principle, he argues, the two major conflict parties each can choose between two basic strategies, or a mix of both: confrontation and/or cooperation for the challengers and their alliance partners, repression and/or integration (co-optation) for the control agencies.

A few years later, drawing partly on Curtis and Zurcher's work, Klandermans (1990: 120) distinguished supporting, opposing, and neutral segments of a social movement's environment. By mapping out and identifying their allies, opponents, and those who are indifferent, we might improve our explanations of a social movement organization's ability to mobilize resources, use opportunities, and exert influence. While basically neglecting the indifferent segment, Klandermans concentrated on what he called the movement's alliance and conflict systems.

Della Porta and Rucht (1995) further pursued these ideas and applied them to a study of the social movement sectors in Italy and Germany, focusing mainly on the relationships between new social movements and political parties. For the alliance system, they identified cooperation and competition as two basic strategies, while for the conflict system, bargaining and confrontation were seen as basic strategies. Moreover, this analysis made clear that the distinction between a conflict and an alliance system is variable in that alliances on either side may break apart or some actors may change their position during the course of a struggle.

The System of Social Movements' Reference Groups

Regardless of its utility, the convenient typology of alliance and conflict systems has the disadvantage of neglecting several additional (and important) reference groups of movements: bystander publics, third parties, and mediators. While direct interactions between conflict parties do occur, for the most part social movements and their opponents not only try to influence each other but also appeal to an audience whose attitude may be crucial for the outcome of the conflict. Particularly for social movements that typically lack financial resources and direct access to political decision-makers, getting public attention and support is a major mechanism through which social and political change may be affected. Therefore, it is important to take these aspects of movements' external environment into account. This is all the more critical because in modern societies the mass media play a crucial, and increasingly important, role for movement politics (Turner 1969; Molotch 1979; Kielbowicz and Scherer 1986; Hilgartner and Bosk 1988; Gamson and Wolfsfeld 1993). In their attempt to map the relevant reference groups of a social movement, Neidhardt and Rucht (1991) have integrated these aspects in an interaction model as presented in figure 9.1.

This formal model is closer to reality than the pairing of an alliance and a conflict system. Yet it is still overly crude and one-sided because it suggests that social movements are engaged in the same terrain with a given set of reference groups. A closer look, however, reveals that social movements, along with their allies and opponents, may act in different arenas. Among the latter are the streets, courtrooms, parliaments, referenda, and the mass media. Obviously, these arenas all have their own structures, rules, and roles. They also differ widely in their degree of institutionalization.

For example, access to and interactions in courtrooms are heavily regulated, and the rules are fairly strict and binding for all participants. By definition, the judge plays a crucial role and therefore almost all energies of the conflict parties are devoted to influencing the judge by presenting facts and arguments that are presumed to be admissible and persuasive. Also, engaging in such a judicial procedure usually entails acceptance of its outcome for both conflict parties.

By contrast, street protest is regulated to a lower extent. During the last decades, various techniques of policing street protest have tended to reduce unexpected and/ or illegal forms of protest behavior in Western democracies (della Porta et al. 1998; McCarthy and McPhail 1998). Nevertheless, contrary to many institutionalized channels of expressing dissent such as petitions, litigation, and referenda, street protest may take extremely different forms, ranging from a silent vigil to blockades to severe violence. In addition, street protest certainly does not require the exchange of sophisticated arguments. Nor does it involve an arbiter, as in the case of a juridical court.

Depending on the kind of arena and the situational context, social movements and their reference groups tailor their activities to make an impact. In rare cases, they may also try to modify the institutional setting of the arena to secure a structural advantage. For example, outsider groups have promoted a freedom of information act in several countries to improve their knowledge base when it comes to criticizing their opponents in public campaigns, litigation, and the like. Also, protest groups often call for a widening of the institutionalized form of citizen participation, for example, referenda and urban planning committees.

Things become even more complicated when we consider that some of the reference groups identified in figure 9.1 are not just actors but at the same time represent some sort of arena. This is most obvious with the mass media (see chapter 11 in this volume). On the one hand, the media, when taking a hostile or a

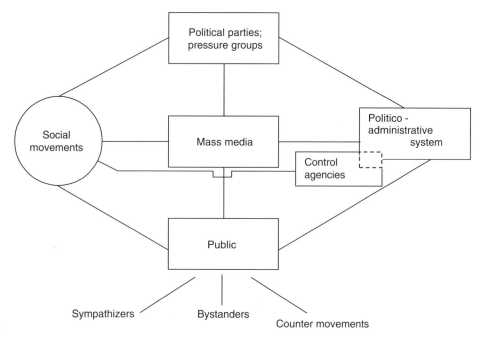

Figure 9.1   Reference groups of social movements.

supportive stance *vis-à-vis* a given social movement, are certainly parties in the conflict. According to many movement organizers, the media tend to neglect, downplay, or distort public protest activities. Therefore, movements try to develop their own media, sometimes even deliberately designed to compensate for the alleged or real failures of the established mass media (Rucht 2003). For example, leftist German protest groups have established the Frankfurt-based Information Service for the Distribution of Suppressed News in the 1980s. Similarly, a short-lived news magazine called *Lies of our Times* was established in the USA in the 1990s. However, there are also examples of mainstream media supporting protest movements. An outstanding example was the so-called White March in Belgium in October 1996 (Walgrave and Manssens 2000). In the absence of an effective mobilization structure, the media served as the driving force to bring together the largest demonstration in the country's history, which was a public outcry against scandalous judicial and political maneuvers to downplay failures in a criminal investigation. Another striking case is the Portuguese media's support for the Pro-East Timor movement in 1999. This Portuguese-based movement tried to prevent further mass killings in the former colony (Cardoso forthcoming).

On the other hand, the media also represent a kind of mirror or platform, though one with gatekeeper roles. Due to the tremendous role of modern mass media in providing information and influencing people's minds, virtually all actors engaged in political struggles try to occupy some space in the media by various techniques, such as distributing press releases or staging events that are particularly designed to attract the media's attention.

Additionally, one has to consider that activities in various arenas are not independent from each other. The street protest of some movement actors may have a radical flank effect for other actors within the same movement industry (Haines 1988). Also, a movement that failed to influence a parliamentary decision may take its cause into the courtroom and, when again unsuccessful, try to block the implementation of both the parliamentary and juridical decisions which then may become an issue in a parliamentary debate. In this case, an interrelated struggle in three arenas unfolds, probably with partly different constellations of allies, opponents, third parties, and attentive publics.

Finally, it is important to consider that many struggles in one or more arenas tend to occur at different levels, ranging from the local to the international. These levels, too, cannot be seen independent from each other. As Keck and Sikkink (1998: 13) have shown in their boomerang model, movement actors who fail to influence their national government can try to target international bodies, which, if supportive to the movement's demands, may then put pressure on the national government under consideration.

From this discussion, it follows that an interactionist conceptualization of social movement activities becomes quite complicated. While parsimony is generally considered to be a virtue in theory building, it should be clear that in the field under discussion it would be inadequate to assume a simple bipolar game with two coherent entities involved. Because complex relationships and processes can only be grasped step by step in a process of gradual disentangling, in the following three sections I will discuss patterns of alliance, opposition, and mediation.

ALLIANCES

It is commonly understood that a set of actors with similar goals strengthen their position when coordinating their activities or even joining forces. This is true for military operations as well as for political struggles. Alliance-building was the rationale for urging "Workers of the world unite!" in the nineteenth century and afterwards. Also, there were numerous attempts in the early twentieth century to bring together groups centered around issues of labor, women, and peace. Similarly, today we can observe that various kinds of groups and movements from many regions attempt to create an overarching global justice movement that, in their view, will overcome neoliberal forces. These examples show that, from an analytical angle, alliances have a twofold meaning with regard to social movements. On the one hand, it is clear that social movements are seldom solitary entities, but are complex webs of individuals, groups, and organizations – "mobilized network(s) of networks," as Neidhardt (1985: 197) aptly put it. Unlike webs of other actors that, for example, are engaged in market exchanges without creating a common identity, the actors comprising a social movement strive for a common cause and, via this and other commonalities, which may be imagined and/or real, create a multilayered collective identity (see chapter 19 in this volume). Yet it remains a collectivity with more or less distinct parts that are not inherently bound together. Rather they entertain more or less friendly, supportive, and competitive relations, or keep distant from each other. As long as these parts deliberately seek to support each other, they form an alliance within or as a social movement.

Apart from this internal bridging and bonding, social movements as whole, or parts of them, may also form alliances with external groups, such as other movements, interest groups, political parties, elites, intellectuals, and media. These different realms of alliance-building are discussed in the following subsections.

Cooperation, Competition, and Conflict within Movements

The term "alliance" is associated with partnership, closeness, and a spirit of mutual support.[2] Nevertheless, alliances tend to remain limited in their purpose and time frame. An alliance is typically formed by actors who want to keep some of their autonomy and distinctiveness, and therefore refrain from merging into a single entity whose prior constituent elements become more or less invisible, or completely dissolve as distinguishable units. Hence an alliance, besides signaling a willingness to cooperate, also implies an insistence on differences between the allied partners. Therefore, alliances should not be idealized as uncomplicated unifications or fusions. Apart from mutual support and close cooperation, alliances also tend to involve, at least in some respects and in some periods, features of competition and even conflict.

Cooperation

Most social movements would not come into existence, let alone survive, if there was no cooperation between the groups and organizations that consider themselves to be parts of a broader entity. Though these components may differ considerably in size, shape, concrete aims, and preferred activities, they tend to exhibit a readiness to participate in joint activities or structures, be it a major protest event, a loosely coordinated but temporary campaign, or a permanent umbrella organization or federation. Such alliances are not a "natural" product of merely sharing the same broad goal. Rather, they require "coalition work" (Staggenborg 1986; Shaffer 2000); in other words, they require more or less constant efforts to create and maintain links, to identify and symbolize common ground, and eventually to act together.

The linkages between these components differ widely in different social movements. Some movements are completely decentralized or even fragmented. In these cases, cooperation occurs mainly on an ad hoc basis without the existence of overarching structures specialized in coordinating the different parts of the movement. Nonetheless, coordinating structures do exist, but these are basically restricted to specific thematic areas and/or to local or regional levels. For example, German feminists established a federal coordination to liberalize abortion (*Bundeskoordination* § *218*) in 1980. Similarly, they also created a federal structure to link the groups that run houses for battered women.

Another example of loose coordination are the groups opposing nuclear power in Germany. While they did not forge a coordinating body at the national level, they had, and still have, occasional federal conferences (*Bundeskonferenzen*). These are open meetings without a system of delegates or formal rules of decision-making. They serve to exchange experiences, to discuss action proposals, and to prepare joint activities. In addition to this informal structure, for many years there existed a more specialized federal coordination on matters of nuclear waste and reprocessing (*Atommüllkonferenz*) as well as similar structures in other regions.

In contrast to the German feminist and antinuclear power movements, the German peace movement established a fairly sophisticated federal coordinating committee (*Koordinationsausschuss*) in the early 1980s. This committee represented, proportional to their estimated size, all relevant streams that took part in the peace activities in that period (see Leif 1985). While in abeyance for many years and having changed its name and structure by the late 1980s, this coordinating mechanism has been revitalized in the advent and during the protests against the military intervention of US and British troops in Iraq in 2003. Also in other countries we would find a great variety of coordinating mechanisms across movements, and, when comparing over time or across countries, even within the same kind of movement (for the environmental movements in France and Germany, see Rucht 1989).

Some movements go even further in building coherent structures by establishing a key organization that is really at the center of most movement activities. This, for example, applied to the German fascist movement in which the Nazi Party gradually assumed the role of a centerpiece and, in a later period, became the ultimate locus of power and control, so that we can no longer speak of a movement but of a full-fledged hierarchical structure, that is, an organization with various suborganizations.

In general, then, it does not appear that there is an ideal way of coordinating the components of a social movement. Some movements seem to fare better with more coherent and formalized structures, others with more loose and informal ties. These structures emerge and develop in response to many factors; both movement characteristics (e.g., a strong belief in grass-roots democracy or, conversely, in strong leadership) and external conditions (e.g., a stick-and-carrot strategy applied by movement opponents or regime structures that are more or less centralized) are important.

Competition

There are several reasons why groups within a given movement are not always mutually supportive but also engage in a competitive struggle. First, these groups differ in their ideological leanings, social bases, experiences, and strategic preferences. Regarding the latter aspect, almost all movements are characterized by the coexistence of more moderate and more radical strands. Second, movement organizations also tend to develop an interest in their own survival and growth, thus creating a potential gap between representatives of social movement organizations and the rank and file who are interested in promoting the cause rather the organization. Third, resources in a given social movement are generally notoriously scarce. Therefore, movement groups compete for support from committed activists for donors, media attention, chairs at the negotiation table, and the like. In some instances, this competition is friendly and more or less latent, probably because organizations from the same movement are basically fishing in different pools of resources or act in an implicit division of labor. Consider, for example, the activities of the moderate World Wide Fund for Nature on the one hand and the more daring Greenpeace on the other hand. Both appeal to the wider public for financial support, but they are targeting fairly different constituencies.

Competition may be more pronounced when it comes to activities in the same issue area or when the target groups are more or less identical. An indicator of a vivid competition is the strategy of Greenpeace to keep its trade mark distinct when it comes to broader public campaigns. In such cases, Greenpeace does not tend to engage in alliances with other environmental groups, but, to the chagrin of the latter, prefers to act on its own (Jamison et al. 1990).

Finally, competition may become direct and fierce in other instances. This was true for two nationwide West German environmental organizations, the Bund für Umwelt und Naturschutz Deutschland and the Naturschutzbund Deutschland, after the fall of the Wall. Being quite similar in their aims and structures, these organizations engaged in a mute but tough competition in the new "market" that had suddenly opened up in East Germany. Both groups tried to recruit as many as members as possible from the dissolving state-controlled nature proctection organization in East Germany, the Gesellschaft für Natur und Umwelt.

Conflict

There is a fine line between direct competition and conflict. Even when groups claim to adhere to the same principles and to belong to the same broader movement, internal conflicts are part and parcel of many movements. The history of the labor movement is ridden with bitter internal struggles between various ideological tendencies, resulting in factionalism, splits, and the like (for a case study, see Ansell 2001). Similarly, fascist movements, particularly in their early phase, were marked by internal struggles that sometimes turned into overt violence, including murder (Reichardt 2002). Also, the history of religious groups provides abundant examples of in-fights, schisms, and the like (for the case of the Hare Krishna, see Rochford 1997). Many sects, for example, result from preceding internal struggles within a broader religious community from which one or several subgroups have split off.

While sharp conflicts within social movements are far from rare, we should not forget that many other cases internal conflict has less severe consequences. Quite often, a sense of solidarity outweighs potential internal dissent. Nevertheless, almost all social movements have some latent or potential internal cleavages, such as a conflict of interest between leaders and staff on the one hand and the rank and file on the other hand, or a conflict between the hard core of "true believers" tending towards ideological purity and those who are less committed to the cause and probably more prone to compromise. Another example of a conflict has been stated with respect to the US environmental movement. According to the analysis of Machlis (1990/1991), there exists a "structural and permanent" tension between the national and local groups. The focus of the former

> will probably continue to shift toward institutional management of environmental issues rather than confrontation and struggle. Since it is confrontation and struggle that energize local groups, the two areas of action will be separated by a lack of common purpose, different styles of action, and even different motivations. The distance between the office of the executive director of a national conservation group and the living room meeting place of a local group of angry citizens can be very, very far. Hence, the central irony of conservation in the democratic regime may be that sometimes conservation groups rob power instead of give power, and thus resemble the architects of dominion and environmental disregard. (1990/ 1991: 278)

Another reason for conflict may be a fundamental disagreement about organizational principles and their underlying broader value. Again Greenpeace is an illustrative case. To secure its coordinated performances, Greenpeace established a strictly hierarchical organization. When Greenpeace Germany was established along these lines in 1980, this soon irked a few members of the founding generation who adhered to principles of grass-roots democracies. When these activists found that their ideas were disregarded or openly rejected by the mainstream of the organization, they decided to create their own group, "Robin Wood," in 1982. This group used essentially the same techniques as Greenpeace but eagerly tried to establish a democratic and participatory structure. Conflicts, though mostly in moderate forms, also occur in movements that explicitly adhere to principles of peace or sisterhood, as a close investigation of peace movements, feminist movements, and religious movements have revealed (see chapter 29 in this volume).

As with competition, the reasons for conflicts within movements can be manifold. They may be rooted in differences in ideology, goal priorities, strategy, and political styles as well as personal rivalries among leaders, organizational patriotism, and struggles for hegemony within the alliance sector. Clearly, conditions external to the movement groups may have a profound impact on the extent, kind, and outcome of conflicts within movements. For example, *agents provocateurs* sent by a governmental agency can contribute to deepen a gap between the moderates and the radicals within a movement organization. Similarly, unjust governmental repression may suddenly unite a movement that was at the brink of breaking apart.

Cooperation, Competition, and Conflict across Movements and with Nonmovement Actors

Almost everything that has been noted above for the different relations within movements also applies to relations across movements and other kinds of actors that, in principle, have some affinities and therefore can potentially be part of an alliance system. Again, we find quite distinct patterns of cooperation, competition, and conflict, though probably with more variation because of the greater heterogeneity of actors that come into play.

Cooperation

Movements, particularly when adhering to the same general principles and goals and targeting the same opponents, tend to have overlaps. At least in some areas and some periods, they may also deliberately join forces. The past and present of social movements exhibits numerous examples of alliances among movements.[3] Liberal and socialist movements occasionally united to fight an authoritarian regime; the free trade and the antislavery movement cooperated; socialist, liberal, and feminist groups allied to promote women's suffrage; and together with pacifist groups, they tried to prevent World War I, albeit unsuccessfully. In a similar vein, the so-called new social movements often united in specific campaigns. They even developed sections that explicitly tied together two or more issue domains. For example, during the 1980s various countries experienced the rise of a "women's peace movement" that developed its own identity and engaged in yearlong struggles, such as the fight against the Greenham Common nuclear weapon base in Great Britain. Another example was the joint struggle against the expansion of the Larzac military training area in southern France during the 1970s. This issue became the focus of a broad alliance of local farmers, environmentalists, peace activists, and regionalist groups. During the struggle, these actors developed more and more overlaps so that they eventually became a small movement in their own right. More recently, we witness an emerging global justice movement, which, upon closer examination, is not yet a movement but rather a rainbow coalition of diverse groups and movements with more specific foci, such as environmental protection, indigenous rights, poverty, and so on. Unlike a more coherent social movement, such a coalition is usually less durable and has not (yet) developed a strong collective identity. Only on given occasions (such as international summits) or with respect to given issue areas (such as the construction of huge dams), do these groups join forces and emphasize their unity, whereas at most other times they tend to act independently from each other.

In a more general perspective, such affinities and convergences are taken into account by the concept of a "movement family," defined as "a set of coexisting movements that, regardless of their specific goals, have similar basic values and organizational overlaps, and sometimes even join for common campaigns" (della Porta and Rucht 1995: 232). Contrary to the concept of a social movement industry that designates all social movement organizations having "as their goal the attainment of the broadest preferences of a social movement" (McCarthy and Zald 1977: 1219), the concept of a social movement family, which is analogous to that of a family of political parties, emphasizes ideological proximity without necessarily stressing the organizational dimension.

While some observers and sympathizers wish that movements belonging to one and the same family come closer together to eventually form one single broad movement, as Touraine's (1968) treatment of the new social movement and Bourdieu's (2001) treatment of the global justice movement illustrate, this is mostly wishful thinking. One could already doubt the existence of a distinct environmental, feminist, or peace movement when looking at the differences within these movements. It becomes all the more questionable that these movements will converge in an overarching entity instead of a rainbow coalition as assumed above. Rather than promoting unifying labels, it would be a matter of empirical investigation to what extent affinity movements are bound together by networks of communication, multiple memberships of activists, organizational overlaps, and joint campaigns.

Movements do not exclusively ally with related movements but may also create alliances with various kinds of nonmovement actors. Aside from the requirement of shared goals, strategies, and/or opponents, such alliances can be attractive because actors other than movements tend to have potential strengths that movements desperately lack. Consider the trade unions with their solid infrastructure and broad membership, the political parties with their access to parliaments and executive power, the media with their great audience, and the elites with their closeness to decision-makers and influence on public opinion. Under certain conditions, these groups, in turn, have an interest in collaborating with movements because the latter may provide fresh ideas, a mass base, and/or a radical mood. These movement assets may be instrumental to nonmovement actors that basically engage in other arenas. For instance, oppositional parties tend to seek linkages to like-minded extraparliamentary groups to strengthen their position *vis-à-vis* the government. This was the case when the German Green Party, an outgrowth of the environmental movement, became established and profited from the support of the movement. But, to the chagrin of a number of movement organizers, the new party also absorbed people and energies for electoral campaigns and parliamentary work so that it is not so clear whether or not the movement, as a whole, was really strengthened by the existence of the party.

Complex relationships between movements and their allies also become obvious when considering the case of Attac, a newly created group that opposes the globalizing neoliberal regime. Attac Germany, which was established in 2000 according to the French model, experienced a rapid growth with some 12,000 members in 2003. What makes Attac interesting to potential allies, however, is not this still relatively modest membership but its public appeal as a creative and vital new player. Thus Attac became attractive to the major trade unions which are strong but also perceived as sclerotic. Not surprisingly, the two biggest unions, those of the steel workers (IG Metall) and the service sector (Ver.di), each with a membership of 2.7 million, joined the dwarf Attac to profit from the latter's fresh image, particularly among youth. Attac, in turn, was pleased to be supported by such big and well-established players. Yet it is still unclear how closely these different groups will collaborate and whether the tail (Attac) can wag the dog (the unions). Gray-haired peace activists of the 1950s and 1960s vividly remember that a strong ally, such as the unions, is an asset only as long as the alliance holds. Yet the peace movement's reliance on the unions became a serious problem for the movement when the unions withdrew, thereby leaving its previous partner deprived of the organizational resources previously provided by the unions.

These examples demonstrate that, in one way or another, social movement mobilization is heavily influenced by the kind and the situation of its allies. As Kriesi et al. (1995: ch. 3) have shown in their comparative analysis of new social movements in four West European countries, the magnitude of these movements' mobilization depended on a number of factors related to the movements' allies, such as the character of the configuration of the parties of the old and new left, whether the left is in or out of government, and the kind of movement with the peace and solidarity movements closer to the parties of the left than other movements. Interestingly, the authors have also stressed that an ally is not always a source of strength but rather a burden. Again, the West German peace movement of the 1950s and 1960s serves as an example. In these decades, the movement suffered more than profited from being supported by communist groups. Given the backdrop of the Cold War, any group applauded by the communist left was met with much suspicion and tended to become politically marginalized.

Allies do not necessarily act side by side but may also act simultaneously, and sometimes quite effectively, in different arenas. For example, established interest groups can strengthen their weight at the negotiation table when loosely allied social movement actors take the streets with claims similar but more radical than those of the interest groups. Conversely, social movement actors who may not be considered as a legitimate actor in the public arena may gain credibility when flanked by more established groups, let alone parts of the political elite.

We should also bear in mind that sometimes social movement groups transform themselves into other kinds of actors, for example a political party, but keep linkages to their origin movement. This, for instance, is the case with many of the green parties, which are no longer genuine parts of environmental movements but nevertheless maintain close bonds to the latter (Dalton 1995). Also, social movements sometimes receive strong support from the mass media (see below).

Competition

The reasons presented for competition within social movements also apply to competitive relations with external actors, both movement and nonmovement alike. It is arguable that nonmovement actors, such as political parties and established pressure groups, are probably more instrumentally orientated than social movements because they have ongoing experience calculating their costs and benefits in routinized power struggles. Because these groups tend to rely on a hierarchical apparatus and have strong interests in their own survival and expansion, their allies may sometimes be regarded as competitors as well. This, for example, becomes obvious when alliances of movement and nonmovement actors seek to present themselves on the public stage. Take the example of a typical mass demonstration or protest march. As a rule, such events are preceded by intense internal debates over questions such as: Which organizations should march in front? Which group or constituency will delegate the keynote speaker? Who will be chosen as a press officer? Should the supporting groups be listed in the leaflet according to alphabetic order or size?

Another field of competitive relations opens when movement and nonmovement groups seek public funds for providing collective goods. When it comes to state subsidies for, say, information campaigns on AIDS, gay movement groups compete with traditional welfare organizations. Similarly, feminist groups running houses for battered women compete with church-related and other welfare organizations that provide the same kind of services for battered women. Also, different movements may seek to get the attention and support of one and the same potential ally or, inversely, different nonmovement actors may court the same movement, provided the latter has something advantageous to offer.

Conflict

Again, competition can easily turn into conflict when the interests of the allied partners diverge or the alliance faces a bifurcation that does not allow for a compromise. In several instances, progressive movements in West Germany had such an experience (Cooper 1996). One case was the discussion on rearmament in the early 1950s. Initially, the Social Democratic Party (SPD) and the trade unions were in line with the autonomous peace groups that strictly opposed the reestablishment of a German army. However, soon the mainstream of the party and the unions changed their mind and quit the alliance. To the extent that they moved closer to the government's position in favor of rearmament, the initial conflict gradually became divisive so that the previous alliance partners were perceived as opponents. A strikingly similar pattern could be observed in the late 1960s when the mainstream of the SPD and the trade unions withdrew from the alliance opposing the emergency laws. Partly based on these experiences, the extraparliamentary opposition became more radical in the late 1960s. It is no wonder that the SPD, at that time in a Grand

Coalition with the conservative parties, became an adversary of the rising student movement. Ironically, at the core of the extraparliamentary opposition was the Socialist Student Alliance, an SPD student organization that had been expelled by the party leaders in 1961.

ADVERSARIES

All social movements strive to achieve certain goals. Therefore, at least implicitly, they reject goals that are incompatible with their own. In this broad sense, social movements always engage in a struggle against something or somebody. Nevertheless, such struggles do not necessarily target specific groups or institutions that are clearly defined as adversaries. Consider an inward-oriented movement (or personal-change movement) that, within or outside its own ranks, seeks to influence people's daily behaviors. In such a case, the movement is not necessarily engaged in a direct fight with a distinct opponent. In most other cases, however, social movements challenge external groups whom they perceive as opponents or adversaries, and vice versa. For most observers, it is this relationship that is a primary characteristic of social movements and, consequently, attracts most attention in terms of theorizing and empirical research. Therefore, I will briefly discuss adversarial relations.

The kinds of adversaries, and the quality of relationships between social movements and their adversaries, can vary greatly. Adversaries range from other social movements (i.e., countermovements) to interest groups, corporations, churches, political parties, and public administrations to distinct political leaders. As in the case of multifaceted alliances involving the challenging movement, the opposite side is not necessarily a single actor but a broader alliance, or a set of actors who, in part, act independently from each other. Consider a government with its various branches, some of which may be supportive toward a movement (say, the environmental department *vis-à-vis* the environmental movement), while others (say, departments of agriculture and industry), remain hostile.

Also the intensity of an adversarial relationship, and thus the kinds of interactions, varies considerably. At one end of the "intensity spectrum" one can situate interactions with relatively low levels of conflict, such as the exchange of arguments or a bargaining situation. At the other, we witness social movements that instigate, or become victims of, severe clashes with destruction of property and killings, as occurs in riots, most revolutions, and repressive measures against movements.[4] Particularly in authoritarian regimes and under dictatorships, adversarial relations tend to be intense and may result in street violence, arrests, kidnapping, torture, and killings. But we should also not forget that severe violence by or against social movements may also occur in democratic regimes, resulting in the death of dozens or even hundreds of people, as in the case of a Mayday demonstration in Berlin in 1929 or in a demonstration of adherents of the Algerian Liberation Front in Paris in 1961.

Given this destructive potential, certain tactics have been developed to prevent or reduce high levels of conflict. For example, the opponents of a social movement can try to co-opt some of the leaders of the movement. Another tactic is to preempt the challengers in order to take the wind out of the latters' sails (Gamson 1975: 29). Still another is to use a stick and carrot, or to threaten the challenger without necessarily engaging in direct confrontation.

When considering that these kinds of interactions can be taken in parallel or subsequently by different actors of an alliance system with respect to different targets in the conflict system, it becomes clear that the patterns of exchange can become very complicated. Complexity further increases when we take into account the role of mediating parties and the reactions of audiences.

MEDIATORS AND AUDIENCES

As mentioned above, the simple juxtaposition of an alliance and a conflict system does not do justice to the reality of most struggles in which social movements are involved. In contemporary societies and particularly in their democratic variants, most societal and political conflicts are mediated in two senses. First, the conflict parties often do not directly speak to each other but communicate via the mass media. A typical exchange occurs when a social movement raises a criticism in the form of a street protest, an open letter, or a press release, which, covered by the media, then triggers a response by the challenged group or institution. This response, in turn, may instigate another media-directed activity of the challengers, or, alternatively, a direct contact between the two parties, which again may be reported by the mass media.

For good reasons, the conflict parties do not consider the mass media just as a neutral mirror. Rather they are aware that the mass media selects, distorts, molds, comments, evaluates, and allies or opposes them during the conflict (Gitlin 1980) (see chapter 11 in this volume). Accordingly, the original actors not only try to get coverage but seek *positive* coverage of their aims and activities and negative coverage of their opponents. This is all the more important as the conflict parties can hardly reach broad audiences without the mass media. Moreover, positive coverage by the mass media is probably more credible than if a conflict party praises itself by its own means of communication.

Second, the media's audiences are not homogenous. In fact, the mass audience is differentiated into various segments. One of these consists of those people who remain indifferent or keep a neutral position on the issue under consideration. As long as they firmly and deliberately hold such a bystander view, they are of no or little interest to the conflict parties (for other instances, see chapter 11 in this volume). The rest can be divided into two segments that are potential sympathizers, or even allies, to one or the other side of the conflict. Because neither the size of these groups nor their level of sympathy or support are set in stone, each side in the conflict tries its best to increase positive reactions to itself and negative reactions to the opponent. To reach this aim, the actors engage in discursive and symbolic struggles to convince the attentive public that their cause is just and worth defending. Research on framing (Snow et al. 1986; Snow and Benford 1988; Gamson 1992) has analyzed such attempts to win support, though still in an unbalanced way. While much attention has been paid to the supply side of frames, the receiving side has been given less attention (see Snow et al. 1986: ch. 17). Potential positive reactions range from increased sympathy to occasional acts of support to continuous and full commitment. Many ways and forms exist to express such reactions. People can defend a movement's cause and action in a daily conversation, applaud a movement speaker, write a letter to the editor, give money, sign a petition, order a newsletter, and the like. Also, isolated supporters may seek to contact a movement group to become engaged with it.

It is arguable that it is at this level of the audience's reactions that most struggles involving social movements are eventually won or lost, at least in democratic societies. While public opinion on a particular issue may not be the decisive factor in a conflict, it certainly becomes crucial when this opinion – actual or potential – is transformed into voting behavior. This is why political elites who wish to come into, or stay in, power are so much interested in both representative population surveys and public opinion, including the actions of protest movements, as expressed in and by the mass media (Neidhardt 1994; Burstein 1999). Whether in the form of a barometer, a stage, a filter, an amplifier, an ally or an opponent, the importance of the media for social movement struggles can hardly be overestimated (see chapter 11 in this volume).

Adversarial exchanges between movements and their opponents are also frequently mediated in another sense, namely by institutionalized third parties, brokers, mediators, and the like. Almost by definition, third parties tend to lower the level of conflict. A clear-cut example is a court case in which the roles of the conflict parties and the outcome of the juridical procedure are under control of one or more judges. The court sentence may not be the final word in the conflict, but those who have engaged in this procedure but do not accept its outcome will have troubles in legitimizing nonjuridical means of resistance.

Conflict mediation also occurs outside courtrooms. In some European countries, it is a standard pattern when struggling to find a compromise in protracted labor conflicts to invite a neutral person. More recently, more or less formalized mediation procedures have also been applied to other policy domains, for example in disputes over large technological projects, environmental struggles, and conflicts over genetic engineering for agriculture. The obvious precondition in these cases is that the conflict parties perceive each other as somehow interdependent, accept the mediator, and have some hope in reaching at least a fair compromise due to this procedural arrangement.

Beyond such formalized mediation, however, the history of social movements offers plenty of examples in which some kind of more informal mediation or brokerage has taken place. According to McAdam et al. (2001: 308), brokerage is of a few key mechanisms that "figured prominently" in a number of empirical cases they studied.

CONCLUSION

In this chapter, a relational approach has been promoted to study social movements. I have argued and empirically illustrated that the crude picture of a fight between two clear-cut antagonistic actors, a social movement and its opponent, is utterly inadequate. Even when a relatively simple bipolar conflict does exist, we rarely find on each side of the conflict line a single and unified actor. Rather, we observe sets of allied actors who entertain complex relationships, ranging from unconditional support to competition to open conflict. Thus, from the viewpoint of a social movement engaged in a struggle with oppositional forces, it is more adequate to speak of a pairing of an internally differentiated alliance and conflict system. In a similar vein, the relations between these two systems can rarely be characterized as just being hostile. Rather, they include various kinds of inter-actions, ranging from bargaining to competition to open and possibly bloody confrontation.

While this has been widely acknowledged by social movement research during the past decades, the role of third parties, such as allies, brokers, mediators, and audiences still remains understudied. Only some of the conflicts involving social movements result in direct encounters with oppositional forces. But many others consist of indirect exchanges mediated by the mass media or by some kind of third party, particularly when occurring in highly institutionalized settings. Notably in modern democracies, the mass publics become an important reference point of all social and political actors who strive for public recognition and support. Hence most of their activities are calculated and designed to impress audiences and to win their support (Ferree et al. 2002: ch. 1). To the extent that research has taken into account the deliberative attempts to address the mass publics, it has mainly concentrated at the supply side, as exemplified by the framing literature. In addition to these useful attempts, more attention should be devoted to the study of the audience that is far from being just an unstructured and passive mass public.

Even when acknowledging the existence of a differentiated actor constellation, this still tends to produce an overly crude picture. In most conflicts involving a social movement, we witness not just a single constellation in a given period. Rather we find a set of constellations depending on the particular arenas (e.g., streets or court rooms) and levels (from local to international) in which interaction takes place. Each of these arenas has its own requirements, rules, and roles. Not every arena includes the same set of actors. And to the extent that the same actors are present in different arenas, they do not necessarily represent the same conflict constellation and exhibit the same behaviors. In addition, these arenas cannot be seen independent from each other. A failure of a given actor in one arena may prompt this actor to carry on the struggle in another and probably more promising arena.

All this leads to a sober conclusion: It is already a difficult task just to empirically *describe* the variety of actor constellations and interactions that typically character-ize a social movement's interactions with its reference groups. If, however, we want to move from description to *explanation*, then the difficulties and complexities tend to become overwhelming. It is not by accident that hitherto most explanatory research in the area of social movements is restricted to case studies. Even then, the focus is rarely on a broad movement and all its relevant reference groups but rather on one or just a small selection of movement issues and the main interactions that evolve around these issues. This chapter, which has mainly served a conceptual purpose and has not engaged in process-oriented and explanatory analysis, has sought to sensitize the reader to some of the complications and limits in studying social movements. When scholars try to explain why social movements act as they do, they too often focus on one or two sets of actors and activities associated with a given movement, on one level of action, and/or on one or two of the arenas in which action takes place. Within these limits, this research may be empirically and theoretically informative. But still, one should not equate such kinds of investiga-tions with a comprehensive analysis that would allow us to fully understand the structure and dynamics of social movement interaction.

Notes

I am grateful to Sarah Soule and David Snow for their helpful comments on an earlier version of this chapter and their careful editorial assistance with my use of English.

1 The conflictual relationship may even be the focal definitional element. For example, following Charles Tilly's lead, Tarrow defines social movements as "collective challenges, based on common purposes and social solidarities, in sustained interaction with elites, opponents, and authorities" (Tarrow 1998: 4). While most scholars, by definition, attribute to social movements an outsider status, some do not share this view and therefore promote a broader concept. For example, Burstein et al. (1995: 278) define social movements "as organized, collective efforts to achieve social change that use noninstitutionalized tactics at least part of the time." It is left open whether or not this effort represents a challenge.

2 To the extent that actors or forces deliberately come together to reach their goals, we can speak of alliances, usually defined as "a union or agreement to cooperate" or "a relationship resulting from affinity in nature or quality" (*Oxford English Reference Dictionary.* 2nd ed. Oxford: Oxford University Press, 1996).

3 On the alliance between the suffragists and the Woman's Christian Temperance Union in the late nineteenth and early twentieth centuries, see McCammon and Campbell (2002).

4 On various techniques used by authorities to help or damage a social movement, see Marx (1979).

References

Ansell, Christopher K. (2001) *Schism and Solidarity in Social Movements: The Politics of Labor in the French Third Republic.* Cambridge: Cambridge University Press.

Bourdieu, Pierre (2001) *Contre-feux 2: pour un mouvement social européen.* Paris: Raison d'agir.

Burstein, Paul (1999) Social Movements and Public Policy. In Marco G. Giugni, Doug McAdam, and Charles Tilly (eds.), *How Social Movements Matter.* Minneapolis: University of Minnesota Press, 3–21.

Burstein, Paul, Rachel L. Einwohner, and Jocelyn A. Hollander (1995) The Success of Social Movements: A Bargaining Perspective. In Bert Klandermans and Craig Jenkins (eds.), *The Politics of Social Protest: Comparative Perspectives on States and Social Movements.* Minneapolis: University of Minnesota Press, 275–95.

Cardoso, Gustavo (with the assistance of Pedro Pereira Neto) (forthcoming) ICTs and the Pro-East Timor movement. In Wim van de Donk, Brian D. Loader, Paul G. Nixon, and Dieter Rucht (eds.), *Cyber Protest: New Media, Citizens and Social Movements.* London: Routledge.

Cooper, Alice Holmes (1996) *Paradoxes of Peace: German Peace Movements Since 1945.* Ann Arbor: University of Michigan Press.

Curtis, Russell L., and Louis A. Zurcher (1973) Stable Resources of Protest Movements: The Multi-Organizational Field. *Social Forces*, 52 (1), 53–61.

—— (1974) Social Movements: An Analytical Exploration of Organizational Forms. *Social Problems*, 21, 356–70.

Dalton, Russell J. (1995) Strategies of Partisan Influence: West European Environmental Groups. In Bert Klandermans and Craig Jenkins (eds.), *The Politics of Social Protest: Comparative Perspectives on States and Social Movements.* Minneapolis: University of Minnesota Press, 296–323.

della Porta, Donatella, and Dieter Rucht (1995) Left-Libertarian Movements in Context: A Comparison of Italy and West Germany, 1965–1990. In Bert Klandermans and Craig Jenkins (eds.), *The Politics of Social Protest: Comparative Perspectives on States and Social Movements*. Minneapolis: University of Minnesota Press, 229–72.

della Porta, Donatella, Olivier Fillieule, and Herbert Reiter (1998) Policing Protest in France and Italy: From Intimidation to Cooperation. In David S. Meyer and Sidney Tarrow (eds.), *The Social Movement Society: Contentious Politics for a New Century*. Lanham, MD: Rowman & Littlefield, 111–30.

Ferree, Myra Marx, Jürgen Gerhards, William Gamson, and Dieter Rucht (2002) *Shaping Abortion Discourse: Democracy and the Public Sphere in Germany and the United States*. Cambridge: Cambridge University Press.

Gamson, William A. (1975) *The Strategy of Social Protest*. Homewood, IL: Dorsey.

——(1992) *Talking Politics*. Cambridge: Cambridge University Press.

Gamson, William, and Gadi Wolfsfeld (1993) Movements and Media as Interacting Systems. In Russell J. Dalton (ed.), *Citizens, Protest, and Democracy*. Annals of the American Academy of Political and Social Science, 529 (July), 114–25.

Gitlin, Todd (1980) *The Whole World Is Watching: Mass Media and the Making and Unmaking of the New Left*. Berkeley: University of California Press.

Haines, Herbert H. (1988) *Black Radicals and the Civil Rights Mainstream, 1954–1970*. Knoxville: University of Tennessee Press.

Hilgartner, Stephen, and Charles L. Bosk (1988) The Rise and Fall of Social Problems: A Public Arenas Model. *American Journal of Sociology*, 94, 53–78.

Jamison, Andrew, Ron Eyerman, and Jacqueline Cramer (1990) *The Making of the New Environmental Consciousness: A Comparative Study of the Environmental Movements in Sweden, Denmark and the Netherlands*. Edinburgh: Edinburgh University Press.

Keck, Margaret E., and Kathryn Sikkink (1998) *Activists beyond Borders: Advocacy Networks in International Politics*. Ithaca, NY: Cornell University Press.

Kielbowicz, Richard B., and Clifford Scherer (1986) The Role of the Press in the Dynamics of Social Movements. In Louis Kriesberg (ed.), *Research in Social Movements, Conflicts and Change 9*. Greenwich, CT: JAI, 71–96.

Klandermans, Bert (1990) Linking the "Old" and "New" Movement Networks in the Netherlands. In Russell J. Dalton and Manfred Kuechler (eds.), *Challenging the Political Order: New Social and Political Movements in Western Democracies*. Cambridge: Polity, 122–36.

Kriesi, Hanspeter (ed.) (1985) *Bewegung in der Schweizer Politik: Fallstudien zu politischen Mobilisierungsprozessen in der Schweiz*. Frankfurt am Main: Campus.

Kriesi, Hanspeter, Ruud Koopmans, Jan Willem Duyvendak, and Marco G. Giugni (1995) *New Social Movements in Western Europe: A Comparative Analysis*. Minneapolis: University of Minnesota Press.

Leif, Thomas (1985) *Die professionelle Bewegung: Friedensbewegung von innen*. Bonn: Forum Europa.

McAdam, Doug, Sidney Tarrow, and Charles Tilly (2001) *Dynamics of Contention*. Cambridge: Cambridge University Press.

McCammon, Holly J., and Karen E. Campbell (2002) Allies on the Road to Victory: Coalition Formation between the Suffragists and the Women's Christian Temperance Union. *Mobilization*, 7 (3), 232–51.

McCarthy, John D., and Clark McPhail (1998) The Institutionalization of Protest in the United States. In David S. Meyer and Sidney Tarrow (eds.), *The Social Movement Society: Contentious Politics for a New Century*. Lanham, MD: Rowman & Littlefield, 83–110.

McCarthy, John D., and Mayer N. Zald (1977) Resource Mobilization and Social Movements: A Partial Theory. *American Journal of Sociology*, 82 (6), 1212–41.

Machlis, Gary E. (1990/1991) The Tension between Local and National Conservation Groups in the Democratic Regime. *Society and National Resources*, 3 (3), 267–97.

Marx, Gary T. (1979) External Efforts to Damage or Facilitate Social Movements: Some Patterns, Explanations, Outcomes, and Complications. In Mayer N. Zald and John D. McCarthy (eds.), *The Dynamics of Social Movements*. Cambridge, MA: Winthrop, 94–125.

Molotch, Harvey (1979) Media and Movements. In Mayer N. Zald and John D. McCarthy (eds.), *The Dynamics of Social Movements*. Cambridge, MA: Winthrop, 71–93.

Neidhardt, Friedhelm (1985) Einige Ideen zu einer allgemeinen Theorie sozialer Bewegungen. In Stefan Hradil (ed.), *Sozialstruktur im Umbruch*. Opladen: Leske & Budrich, 193–204.

——(1994) Öffentlichkeit, öffentliche Meinung, soziale Bewegungen. In Friedhelm Neidhardt (ed.), *Kölner Zeitschrift für Soziologie und Sozialpsychologie*, 34, 7–41.

Neidhardt, Friedhelm, and Dieter Rucht (1991) The Analysis of Social Movements: The State of the Art and Some Perspectives for Further Research. In Dieter Rucht (ed.), *Research on Social Movements: The State of the Art in Western Europe and the USA*. Frankfurt am Main: Campus; Boulder, CO: Westview, 421–64.

Neveu, Eric (1999) Médias, mouvement sociaux, espaces publique. *Reseaux*, 98, 17–85.

Reichardt, Sven (2002) *Faschistische Kampfbünde: Gewalt und Gemeinschaft im italienischen Squadrismus und in der deutschen SA*. Cologne: Böhlau.

Rochford, E. Burke Jr. (1997) Factionalism, Group Defection, and Schism in the Hare Krishna Movement. In Doug McAdam and David Snow (eds.), *Social Movements: Readings on their Emergence, Mobilization, and Dynamics*. Los Angeles: Roxbury, 450–60.

Rucht, Dieter (1989) Environmental Movement Organizations in West Germany and France – Structure and Interorganizational Relations. In Bert Klandermans (ed.), *Organizing for Change: Social Movement Organizations across Cultures*. Greenwich, CT: JAI, S.61–94.

——(2003) Medienstrategien sozialer Bewegungen. *Neue Soziale Bewegungen*, 16 (1), 7–13.

Shaffer, Martin B. (2000) Coalition Work among Environmental Groups: Who Participates? In Patrick G. Coy (ed.), *Research in Social Movements, Conflicts and Change*. Vol. 22. Stamford, CT: JAI, 111–26.

Snow, David A., and Robert D. Benford (1988) Ideology, Frame Resonance, and Participant Mobilization. In Bert Klandermans, Hanspeter Kriesi, and Sidney Tarrow (eds.), *From Structure to Action: Comparing Social Movement Research across Cultures*. Greenwich, CT: JAI, 137–96.

Snow, David A., E. Bourke Rochford, Steven K. Worden, and Robert D. Benford (1986) Frame Alignment Processes, Micromobilization, and Movement Participation. *American Sociological Review*, 51 (4), 464–81.

Staggenborg, Suzanne (1986) Coalition Work in the Pro-Choice Movement: Organizational and Environmental Opportunities and Obstacles. *Social Problems*, 33, 374–90.

Strauss, Anselm (1987) *Qualitative Research for Social Scientists*. Cambridge: Cambridge University Press.

Tarrow, Sidney (1998) *Power in Movement: Social Movements and Contentious Politics*. Cambridge: Cambridge University Press.

Touraine, Alain (1968) *Le mouvement de Mai ou le communisme utopique*. Paris: Seuil.

Turner, Ralph H. (1969) The Public Perception of Protest. *American Sociological Review*, 34 (6), 815–31.

Walgrave, Stefaan, and Jan Manssens, J. (2000) The Making of the White March: The Mass Media as a Mobilization Alternative to Movement Organizations. *Mobilization*, 5 (2), 217–46.

10

Policing Social Protest

Donatella della Porta and Olivier Fillieule

Protest Policing: An Introduction

Social movements have been defined as challengers that address demands to the established members of the polity (Tilly 1978). With their very existence they challenge the given configuration of power that is expressed in the state institutions – and the state is a main interlocutor, if not opponent for them. Moreover, movements mainly rely upon protest, that is, unconventional forms of political participation. Some of these forms are illegal (such as civil disobedience), some even violent. Even legal ones, often disturb the daily routines: marches are, if nothing else, disruptive of traffic routines. For their very use of protest, social movements impact, then, on the state authority to keep public order, eliciting direct state response on the street. In this chapter, we focus on what we consider as a very important aspect of the state response to movements: the *policing of protest*, that is, the police handling of protest events – a more neutral description for what protestors usually refer to as "repression" and the state as "law and order" (della Porta 1995).

Even if the variable repression is included in several models on the preconditions for collective action (among others, Tilly 1978: esp. 101–6; Skocpol 1979; McAdam 1982), empirical research on the relationship between police and protest is still limited (but see Fillieule 1997; della Porta and Reiter 1998b). For a long time, research has been hampered by two concurrent tendencies. On the one hand, the police forces have never been very keen on opening their archives to external researchers (or even to talk with them) – a trend only recently reversed in some, but by no means not all, democracies. On the other hand, researchers often considered the police as a mere "arm of the state," obediently following the orders of the government.

Only more recently, indeed, research started to assess a changeable degree of discretion in police behavior, justifying the study of the police as a specific actor of the state response to social movements. The more research was carried out on the police, the more evident the complexity of the police institutions became. Investigation of the policing of protest therefore became more interesting once it was discovered that the actual functioning of the police does not follow the stereo-type of a single police force with a clear hierarchy, obedient to political orders (Winter 1998a: 13). Attention to protest policing also increased with the under-standing, developed especially in research on terrorism and riots, that the way in which state-controlled movements "on the street" had important consequences for their strategic choices. At their turn, waves of protest also had important effects on police organization.

In what follows, we first provide a typology of protest policing styles and their evolution. Later, we look at the explanations for such an evolution, by looking first at variables internal to the police, such as police organization and culture, and second at external opportunities and constraints. We then focus on the effects of protest policing on the fate of social movements, and conclude with reflections on the directions for future research.

FROM INJUNCTION TO INFLUENCE: A CHANGING PATTERN OF LAW ENFORCEMENT

Research on the police and protest policing produced quite a number of classifica-tions and typologies about policing tactics, strategies, and styles of control. Some relevant dimensions are singled out (della Porta and Reiter 1998a; see also della Porta 1995) as:

- *brutal* versus *lenient*, referring to the degree of force used
- *repressive* versus *tolerant*, referring to the number of prohibited behaviors
- *diffused* versus *selective*, referring to the number of repressed groups
- *illegal* versus *legal*, referring to police respect of the law
- *reactive* versus *preventive*, referring to the timing of police intervention
- *confrontational* versus *consensual*, referring to the degree of communication with the demonstrators
- *rigid* versus *flexible*, referring to the degree of adaptability

A combination of these dimensions describes the *protest policing style* employed by the police forces at protest events. The different dimensions tend to define two coherent protest policing styles, one more opportunist, tolerant, soft, selective, and flexible, the other legalistic, repressive, hard, diffuse, and dissuasive. In fact, a "tough" style usually implies the repression of a large number of protest groups and a wide range of protest activities, via a massive use of force, and sometimes illegal tactics (such as the use of *agents provocateurs*), with low reliance on bargain-ing and a rigid, reactive implementation of the law. On the other hand, a "soft" style usually implies the tolerance of a large number of protest groups and a wide range of protest activities, with low reliance upon the use of force and illegal tactics, and the development instead of prevention and negotiation with a flexible implementation of the law.

In similar vein, McPhail et al. (1998: 51–4) in their research on protest policing in the US distinguished between *escalated force* and *negotiated management*, stressing that "while these two styles are ideal types, they are empirically grounded." The two styles diverge in five ways:

- *First Amendment rights.* If in the escalated force style of policing, First Amendment rights are either ignored or disregarded as mere "cover" for demonstrators, under the negotiated management style of policing, the protection of First Amendment rights is a primary goal of the police.
- *Tolerance for community disruption.* Under the escalated force style of policing, only conventional forms of political protest are tolerated; under the negotiated management style, the police perceives an "acceptable level of disruption," including illegal acts of civil disobedience, as legitimate.
- *Communication.* Communication between police and demonstrators is minimal under the escalated force style of policing; in the negotiated management style communication with demonstrators is considered necessary in order to keep disruption to an acceptable level.
- *Extent and manner of arrests.* Under the escalated force style, violations of the law are immediately followed by mass arrests, while under negotiated management, arrests are considered as a last resort to be used selectively, only against those who violate the law.
- *Extent and manner of using force.* Escalated force style of protest policing relies upon a dramatic show of force, often followed with a progressively escalated force; under the negotiated management style, only the minimum necessary force is used.

Different styles are also defined by the different degree of reliance upon *the power of injunction* (i.e., on the exercise or threat of exercising coercion) or on *the power of influence* (mainly based upon negotiation) (Fillieule 1997).

Most of these typologies converge to distinguish between "hard" police styles, characterized by an escalated use of force in order to implement law and order (with low respect for demonstrators' rights) versus "soft" police styles, where negotiations (and protest rights) prevail.

The two styles of policing originally tended to overlap with the two models of policing historical research has singled out in democratic countries: in Great Britain, a model of "citizens' police" developed, with the "civilized bobby" (unarmed, integrated into the community, and more autonomous from the political power); on the Continent, the French model of a "King's police" (armed, living in barracks and under strict control from the central government) spread to most other countries. These two models were reflected in different styles of protest policing: "softer" in Great Britain; "harder" on the Continent. Nonetheless, more recent research on European countries indicates a progressive uniformity of protest policing.

In Great Britain, the police dealt with the riots at the beginning of the 1980s, as well as policing the miners' strike later on, by "importing" the militarized, continental model of protest policing (Jefferson 1990). The dynamics of modernization were referred to in order to explain why the "soft" style that prevailed in the nineteenth century was replaced by a "harder" style (Reiner 1998).

On the Continent, conversely, a different trend was singled out, with a growing acceptance of forms of direct action and a move towards softer policing, which still, as we will see in what follows, is far from being applied to all social and political groups, and moreover far from being a nonreversible trend (e.g., Waddington 1994; Bruneteaux 1996; Fillieule 1997; della Porta and Reiter 1998a). During the decades from the 1950s to the 1990s, protest control evolved towards more flexible forms based on a more liberal understanding of demonstration rights (see della Porta 1995; Fillieule 1997; and the contributions in della Porta and Reiter 1998b). In parallel to this development in police doctrine and practice, recourse to demonstrations seems to have become institutionalized in a lasting manner since the late 1960s, both in the increasing number of demonstrations and their extension through all levels of society (Tarrow 1994; Dalton 1996; Kriesi et al. 1995; Fillieule 1997; Rucht et al. 1998).

In general, protest policing in democracies in the 1990s seems to be characterized by three tendencies:

- *Under-enforcement of the law.* The strategy used during the 1980s and to date appears to be dominated by the attempt at avoiding coercive intervention as much as possible. Law-breaking, which is implicit in several forms of protest, tends to be tolerated by the police. Law enforcement is usually considered less important than peacekeeping.
- *Search for bargaining.* In order to avoid disorder, complicated procedures of negotiation emerged, and recent research has indicated an increasing formalization of bargaining techniques. Great Britain, France, Germany and Switzerland have witnessed the growth of the role of police officers responsible for "public relations," and acting as mediators between demonstrators and the forces of order, while a sophisticated systems of permits developed in the US (McPhail et al. 1998).
- *Large-scale collection of information.* Although the use of *intelligence* in the control of protestors is not a new trend (see Donner 1990, on the "red squads"), in recent times, the availability of new techniques, as well as increasing professionalization were reflected in an always increasing attention to the collection of information – as is indicated, for instance, in the control of football stadiums (della Porta 1995; De Biasi 1998).[1]

Although the police–demonstrator relationship remains based upon an inherently unequal amount of power, there is a trend from a relationship of *domination* (with the choice, for demonstrators, of either submission or refusal and sanction) to a relationship of *negotiated exchange*, obviously still unequal, but in which bargaining prevails over a straightforward imposition of the rules of the game. The general assumption is, in fact, that preserving law and order in a democracy is always best assured when based upon consensus. The coercive conception poses instead a fundamental problem of credibility in a democratic regime, risking eroding the legitimacy of the governing authorities, and thus remains confined to the register of threats or is exercised with the minimum of publicity.[2]

If these seem to be common general trends, nonetheless, protest policing is *selective*: recent research has indicated the contemporary presence of different police styles, implemented in different situations and towards different actors. As for

France, Fillieule (1997) identified four models of protest policing based on the interactions between and perceptions shared by protestors and the police:

- *Antagonistic*, in which the police, on orders from the political authorities or their own leaders, have a distinctly repressive and/or antagonistic attitude toward nonviolent demonstrators. Most banned and nontolerated demonstrations are here concerned. The use of *agents provocateurs* falls into this category.[3]
- *Opportunistic*, in which the authorities handle illegal protests in a soft manner. The police take a wait-and-see stance with regard to public and private property damage. In the case of the demonstrations by farmers, in particular, both tactical and political necessities often seem to push the police towards tolerating episodes of violence. Indeed, negotiations between the police force and the protestors are oriented to define a "zone of tolerance," "which serves to delimit in advance the type and scale of violence that will be allowed before there is an intervention of the forces of order" (Fillieule 1997: 355–6).
- *Open conflict*, in which protestor and security force commanders alike adopt a position of open conflict, as in the case of demonstrations by leftist radical groups.
- *Cooperative*, which refers to routine demonstrations based on mutual trust and which take place in a climate of mutual cooperation.

The author shows that, apart from a few exemplary cases, differences in policing conflicts do not fall neatly into these four categories, since attitudes during a demonstration are in constant flux and, for instance, a demonstration being handled according to the soft method as long as protest violence remains within certain bounds can turn into an open clash and the dispersion of the protestors as soon as security forces implement repression.

In her research on the Italian case, della Porta singled out four different models of protest policing:

- *Cooperation*, based on a collaboration between the police force and demonstrators, and an inconspicuous police presence.
- *Negotiation*, based on a more active presence by the police with the objective of mediating between the demonstrators and "nondemonstrators" who suffer the disruptive effects of the protest.
- *Ritualistic stand-off*, based on a more "aggressive" police presence, but often at a distance.
- *Total control*, based on a massive presence and close involvement of the police forces.

The principal example of the application of the first model are the large union demonstrations; of the second, direct action by unemployed or homeless people; of the third, demonstrations by the autonomous groups of the radical Left; and of the fourth, the control of football fans going to a match (della Porta 1998).

The recent return of more militarized styles of policing with a growing use of escalating force, especially in the control of the demonstrations of the movement for a "globalization from below," testifies of this selectivity. Not only in Seattle, but also later on when marches were organized to protest against international summits, the police strategies of intervention deviated from the rules of "negotiated manage-ment," often violently charging peaceful demonstrators. The escalation reached its peak in 2001, in Gothenburg and especially in Genoa, when the police fired on demonstrators. The strategies of mediation and negotiation widely applied to the left-libertarian movement of the 1990s do not seem to be automatically transferred to new conflicts (and new movements) (della Porta and Reiter 2001).

Police Characteristics and Policing Styles

How to explain the cross-national and infra-national differences in protest policing, as well as its evolution in time? Two sets of explanations have been offered, the first referring to characteristics of the police and the second to characteristics of the external environment. As for the former, *institutional features* – such as police organization, legal codes, constitutional rights, and police powers – may play an important role in defining the opportunities for, and the constraints on protest policing, as they set the conditions for the actual strategies of protest policing. Also important are aspects of the *police knowledge* of protest, in particular, the police definition of their own role as well as the dangers involved in the protest forms, the judgment about the groups involved in protest, and the assessment about the demands coming from their environment (della Porta and Reiter 1998a).

Institutional Characteristics of the Police

Some institutional variables listed as relevant for police behavior include legislation on civil rights – in particular on civil and political rights (rights of movement, rights of expression); defendants' rights (preventive imprisonment, presence of one's attor-ney at interrogations, right of the police to interrogate a defendant); prisoners' rights (privacy, contact with the external world). The capacity by the police to issue permits or prohibiting and sanctioning behaviors varies cross-nationally. Where police may distribute sanctions without the control of the judiciary, this power is sometimes used in order to blackmail political activists. This was the case, for instance, for Italy in the 1950s, when police sanctions such as *diffida* (cautioning) or *foglio di via* (expulsion from a town) were widely used to intimidate unionists and members of the Communist Party (Reiter 1998). The ease with which the police may declare a demonstration illegal is also relevant – the *prohibition of a demonstration* can set up violent dynamics. Research on disorderly demonstrations in London over 100 years shows that "violence has tended to occur whenever protesters have been castigated as 'subversive', 'unpatriotic', or 'communistic'; when their activities were likely to prove embarrassing to the government, monarchy or 'national reputation', or when the demonstration was technically illegal, occurring in defiance of legal prohibition" (Waddington 1992: 29).

   The understanding of "public order" as well as the ranking of "demonstration rights" has a most important effect on protest policing. As pointed out by the research on the Italian case, a wide perception of "public order," as a moral order "increased the police's authority and limited political and civil rights (della Porta and Reiter 2003). Instead, demonstration rights acquire a higher priority when "public order" is defined in material terms as defense of the life and properties of the citizens. In Germany, in 1985, a turning point for protesters' rights was the constitutional court's decision to uphold their right to demonstrate at an atomic power plant in Broksdorf. The court stated that demonstration rights were strongly protected by the constitution as an expression of democracy, stressing that the authorities had to develop "demonstration-friendly" attitudes and behaviors, and protect the rights of peaceful demonstrators, also *vis-à-vis* the presence of radical groups (Winter 1998a: 197).

Relevant questions about the police *organization* refer to (1) *centralization* (How much power do decentralized units have? How powerful is the central government?); (2) *militarization* (How dependent are police officers on the defense ministry? Do they live in barracks? Are they part of the army? How heavy is the emphasis on "discipline"? What type of armament do they use? Are the police unionized?); (3) *accountability* (Are there special courts for police crimes? What are the legal constraints on police "shoot to kill" policies? What are the mechanisms for citizens to complain against police mistreatment? Are police officers recognizable by identification tags? How far can the parliament investigate police behavior? And what is the power of the judiciary to hold police officers accountable?) (della Porta and Reiter 1998a: 11). Western democracies have very different traditions as far as these institutional features are concerned. As already mentioned, the British model is characterized by higher degrees of decentralization, lower militarization, and higher accountability than in continental Europe. On the Continent the police had autonomous power of interrogations and the sanctioning of suspects, which could be used – and were indeed used – against political opponents.

These models were reflected in protest policing styles. In the British model of citizen policing, decentralization has brought about an emphasis on good relationships with the community, little use of force, and openness to public scrutiny – characteristics that all pushed towards softer strategies.[4] However, the continental model of a King's police granted more power of intervention to the political power, reduced the possibility of democratic controls on police behavior and facilitated the use of force – favoring "tough" policing styles. Not by chance, centralization, lack of accountability and militarization are indeed the main organizational characteristics of the police in authoritarian regimes. In Italy, the militarization of the police with widespread discretional police power (such as the autonomous power of the police to inflict sanctions without judicial proceedings) and low accountability are a legacy of the fascist regime, only partially reformed in the five decades that followed the fall of Mussolini (della Porta and Reiter 2003).

Although an institutional environment in which citizens' rights are protected by law surely discourages repressive intervention by the police, this is insufficient to insure the peaceful enforcement of demonstration rights. In general, decentralization and demilitarization are not, per se, sufficient constraints upon police brutality. Regarding decentralization, "Local control would not guarantee that the police would be employed in ways that liberal and radical critics would like" (Waddington 1991: 134). In particular, as the Northern Ireland conflict indicates, in an ethnically divided society a decentralized local police force can become the long arm of the ethnically dominant group upon the ethnic minority (Ellison and Smyth 2000). As for demilitarization, Robert Reiner (1991: 54–5) remarked:

In violent confrontations, a "non-militaristic" response by police (i.e., without adequate training, manpower, coordination, and defensive or even offensive equipment) could mean that injuries will be multiplied. This doesn't just mean injuries to the police, but also to others who will suffer from undisciplined and excessive violence from constables who lose their cool or their courage.

Moreover, the effects of the long-lasting trend of police professionalization on the above-mentioned characteristics are ambivalent. In general, professionalization went hand in hand with demilitarization – in fact, even in countries with recent experiences with authoritarian regimes, such as Italy and Spain, at least some branches of the police are by now "demilitarized" and police unions legalized (often after long-lasting struggles from within the police). The effects of unionization on police accountability nonetheless vary in different countries and in different movements. In Germany, the strong Gewerkschaft der Polizei, part of the Deutscher Gewerkschafts Bund, often opposed measures of tough policing (Winter 1998a). In France, the 1977 police reforms and CRS (Compagnie Républicaines de Sécurité) discontent drove some unions to incite disturbances at demonstrations to prove, via the media, the ineffectiveness of reforms which had reduced them to a subordinate role. In the 1990s high-school student movement, the astonishingly high number of police injuries and the alarmist statements of the unions to the press about "new threats" developing supported a lobbying offensive to the authorities for a renewal of defensive and offensive equipment (electric truncheons, flash balls) (Fillieule 1997). After the Genoa demonstrations, the dozens of Italian police unions (with the only exception of the left-wing one) used various forms of protest in order to channel into the media their criticism of the "campaigns against the police" (della Porta and Reiter 2001, 2003).

Equally complex are the effects of police specialization, a trend systematically singled out in police research in the last three decades (Funk et al. 1980). If on the one hand specialization implies the development of negotiating skills (among others, the formation of officers with special training in bargaining), on the other hand the deployment in public order policing of special units created for antirioting, anti-terrorism, and/or anti-organized crime emergencies have an escalating effect. In federal countries the use of these special squads has often allowed for a centralization of policing (usually a matter of the single states) (Winter 1998a: 277ff.). In countries like Italy, with a large presence of organized crime, the deployment of special anti-Mafia units in the control of mass demonstrations spread the "tough" styles developed against the Mafia to political activities, as the experience of the anti-G8 demonstrations in Genoa in 2001 dramatically indicated (Andretta et al. 2002).

Last but not least, professionalization brought about an increasing *Verrechtlichung* (legal definition) of police intervention that sometimes constrains "tough" styles (Lüdtke 1992: 17), but at other times reduces the possibility for the police to implement deescalating strategies "under enforcing" the law. For example, German police officers perceived the *Vermummungsverbot* (the prohibition to disguise oneself during public marches), introduced by conservative governments, as an unwelcome imposition on the use of force even at the risk of producing disorders (Winter 1998a: 279). Developments in the recruitment of the rank and file, improvement in the in-service training they are offered, modification of crowd containment

techniques, all have ambivalent effects on police strategies, allowing for deescalation, but also increasing police efficacy in crowd control by force (Waddington
1994; Bruneteaux 1996; Fillieule 1997; della Porta and Reiter 1998a, 1998b).[5]

Police Culture and Knowledge

In the analysis of police behavior, sociological research has developed the concept of
police knowledge, that is, the police's perception of their role and of the external
reality (della Porta and Reiter 1998a). As Manning observed, "Policing tends to be
shaped by adaptations made by actors to structural patterns, to the reality they
perceive, construct and maintain" (1979: 48–9). As other fields of policing, protest
policing is influenced first of all by the *professional culture*, or the police images
about their own role, that is, "a set of assumptions that is widely shared among
officers, and includes a 'cause' to which they are expected to adhere" (Worden 1989:
674). Moreover, protest policing is influenced by the *environmental culture*, that is,
a set of assumptions about the external reality – especially, but not only, the public
order "problem" they are called to control (della Porta and Reiter 1998a: 22–3).
Some hypotheses can be discussed at this point.

In the search for an explanation of policing styles, past research on the police,
based mainly on an ethnographic approach to the urban subdivision of police at
work, emphasized some characteristics of the professional culture widespread
among officers. In general, the social background as well as working conditions
facilitate the spread of a sense of isolation and *macho attitudes* that brings especially
rank-and-file policemen to privilege crime fighting over peacekeeping (Lipset 1971;
Cain 1973; Benyon 1984). In the police culture, negotiated strategies are usually
reflected in a conception of the police as a "citizens' police," with respect
for professionalism in crime-fighting and high importance given to peacekeeping.
Instead, repression often went hand in hand with a conception of the police as the
"King's police," the long branch of the government, mainly oriented towards
the repression of political opposition.

Trends such as a demilitarization of the police and their professionalization tend
to be reflected in a higher-class background, as well as in an increasing integration in
society. Although policemen still tend to consider themselves as "craftsmen," an
increasing emphasis on training, and a shift in its content, may also have produced
changes in police culture. Political reforms, as in the South African case, set the
ground for a (slow) change in police attitudes. In Italy, the reform of the Polizia di
Stato, introducing unionization and opening the police to women, contributed to a
change in the culture of the police, often stressed in police literature through the
frame of a "police among the people" (della Porta and Reiter 2001). Similar trends in
police culture have been signaled for Germany, in the 1960s, and Spain in more
recent times (Jaime-Jiménez and Reinares 1998; Winter 1998b).

As for police environmental culture, police studies indicated some *stereotypes
about disorders and disordered behavior*: "Police commonly develop a 'shorthand'
by which they can more easily identify individuals with whom they anticipate
difficulty. The shorthand may consist of generalizations about people with certain
skin color, hair length or clothing style" (Lipsky 1970: 4). Stereotypes about protestors may overlap with those of other groups usually included in the (socially constructed) definition of public disorders. Recurring themes in the police definition of

those who produce disorders are references to *"young, 'outsiders'* such as immi-grants, ethnic minority members or *agents provocateurs,* of those whose *lifestyle deviates from the norm,* and of *disadvantaged socio-economic groups* as being especially implicated in public disorder or as posing a special threat of it" (Lacey et al. 1990: 71; emphasis added).

Recent research has indicated a complex, and selective, image of protestors, with a legitimation of some political and social actors and the stigmatization of others (see, again, Fillieule 1997: ch. 8; della Porta and Reiter 1998a: 24–7). In police percep-tion, "peaceful demonstrators" tend to be opposed to "hooligans." According to a research on German police officers, in their images, "Peaceful demonstrators have a pragmatic interest, and a clear aim, for which they engage themselves with a lot of involvement and credibility. They make use of their basic right to demonstrate. Normally, they are peaceful demonstrators...with a direct interest in the con-flict...They are available to discuss, they are well informed" (Willems et al. 1988: 153). The violent hooligans, instead,

> are not interested in the topic of the conflict, but only in rioting, to reduce their aggression in the struggle with the police. They are described as destructive and misin-formed. They travel from demonstration to demonstration, are probably supported and financed by wire-pullers...In comparison with the peaceful demonstrators, they are a relatively small group, many of them are very young, and for this reason are easy to influence. Normally, they are not interested in the discussion. (153–4)

Police distinction between "good" and "bad" demonstrators is based on their conception of "legitimate" protest. Legitimate protest, linked to social problems and organized by those who want to make themselves heard in order to solve the problems, is distinguished from that of "professional demonstrators," who upset public order because they enjoy provocation and revolt. A similar distinction exists between "good" or "genuine" protestors (those interested in a single objective that they mobilize around) and "the opposition" (characterized for instance by the image of the London police). The former are considered to be demonstrating in good faith, protesting for good reasons; the latter are troublemakers. "'Genuine protesters' consisted of ordinary people who rarely protest, but felt strongly about a specific issue and wished to express their grievance. 'The opposition' were the 'rent-a-mob' of the extreme left, who protested about virtually everything, which, in police eyes, disqualified them from genuinely feeling strongly about anything" (Waddington 1994: 112–13; see also Fillieule 1997: 311–28; della Porta 1998).

Stereotypes become a kind of *guideline* for police intervention (McClintock et al. 1974: 102). Explaining police repression of disorders during the 1968 Democratic Convention in Chicago, Donner (1990: 116) observed that the police believed an army of demonstrators planned to invade the city, and misinterpreted as "true" the provoking "threats" disseminated by hippies as a sort of theater provocation to "burn the city down" or to flood the city sewers with gasoline or dump LSD in the water supply (Donner 1990: 116–17). During the anti-G8 demonstrations in Genoa in July 2001, police strategies were influenced by unreliable information provided by the secret services, indicating that the demonstrators were going to spread HIV-infected blood and take policemen hostage (della Porta and Reiter 2001). On the other hand, the development of deescalating strategies derived from an understanding that within the mass of good demonstrators and a few bad ones a significant component exists of demonstrators reactive to police strategies: although not looking for trouble, these groups of demonstrators are nonetheless willing to respond with force to police use of force (Winter 1998a: 315ff.; della Porta and Reiter 2003).

We can add that police strategy is a function not only of the images the police have of the actors involved in a protest, but also of the image they have about other social actors, considered to be relevant to the question of public order: the police themselves, political powers, and public opinion as it is expressed through the media. In particular, the legal frame is filtered via police knowledge. In some cases, legal constraints on police behavior are disregarded in practice, but in other cases they become a focal point for the choice of police strategy. As mentioned, in Germany the Brokdorf decision of the constitutional court, stating the prevalence of demonstration rights, had a long-lasting impact on police strategies. The tradition of police respect for the legal system, as well as the relevance of a legal issue in the public sphere and its resonance with police culture seems to influence the police acknowledgment of some legal constraints and disregard for others. Moreover, police strategies are influenced by police perception of the legitimate protest in the political system and the public opinion. For instance, as Nigel Fielding observed, "Few mothers and children have been prosecuted for disrupting traffic while demanding pedestrian crossings, a very common protest in the 1970s and the 1980s. Obstruction and even conspiracy charges could have been applied, if the group were not one to whom the police judged most people to be sympathetic" (1991: 77).

CONFIGURATION OF POWER AND PROTEST POLICING

If internal characteristics of the police have relevant impacts on police behavior, research did not nonetheless disregarded the environmental conditions for police intervention. Various collective actors put forward their interests or opinions, forming what Kriesi (1989) refers to as *configuration of power*. First of all, the governments define some general lines about how to deal with protest. Moreover, social movements intervene on the issue related to citizens' rights and police work, they organize protest actions to denounce police brutality, they ask for more democracy. Political parties, interest groups, trade unions, and voluntary associations conflict or cooperate with them on the issue of how to police protest. Like-minded actors on each side of the issue form coalitions upholding, on the one hand, "law and order," and on the other, "civil rights" (della Porta 1998). The *media* intervene in this picture, partially as a "spokesperson" of the one or the other coalition, and partially following an "autonomous" logic.

Protest Policing and the Government

The *degree of political control* on protest policing, which varies cross-nationally and in time, strongly influences police methods. As Geary (1985: 125–6) noticed:

Of course, constitutionally the police are supposed to be a neutral law enforcement agency independent of political influence. However, there seems little doubt that the

Government does influence the policing of industrial disputes both in terms of the overall approach and in terms of particular operational decisions.

If, in general, the police strongly assess their "technical" autonomy in the implementation of public order, in practice, there is a varying degree of intervention of the political authorities: "As a general rule, the more politically sensitive and visible in the public sphere a police intervention is, the higher the probability that the politicians in government...intervene" (Winter 1998a: 295). As Fillieule and Jobard (1998: 86) observed for France:

> Differential police perceptions of demonstrators are not enough to explain differences in styles of protest handling. Political involvement has yet to be taken into account. As we have already noted, calling in any sort of security force is always the result of a decision on the part of the administrative authorities (the Prefect). This state of legal subordination suggests that we should examine both the instructions given by the civil authorities and how they are implemented in the field. We will first see that the intransigence displayed at times by the political authorities makes the outbreak of violence highly probable. Conversely, government representatives sometimes handle conflicts in a patrimonialistic manner.

The political control on the police can, still, play in different directions. If in the US there are several examples of conflicts between a liberal city mayor and his or her more conservative police, there are nonetheless also several examples in which political authorities asked a reluctant police for more repression. It is fair to say that the inputs from the political system vary with the *political orientation of the government*. Shifts in the policing of protest – or techniques of repression – have often been traced to changes in the makeup of the government.

In his explanatory model of repression in the United States, Goldstein (1978) considered the party affiliation of the American president as the most important determinant of police strategies. Several historical examples indicate that the policing of protest is an issue on which parties tend to polarize along the traditional Left–Right cleavage. Left-wing parties, with vivid memories of state repression of the labor and socialist movements, tend to rally in favor of civil liberties; conservative parties, fearful of losing votes to parties further to their right, often advocate law and order. In Italy, the center-left governments of the 1960s broke the tradition of allowing the police to shoot at demonstrators (della Porta 1995). In France, mortal incidents during demonstrations systematically increased each time the Right was in power in the 1980s and 1990s (Fillieule 1997: 335–40). In Germany, the first SPD-FDP Brandt government developed a more tolerant style of protest policing, and also liberalized laws concerning public marches and citizens' rights (Busch et al. 1988). In his study on the policing of the industrial disputes in Great Britain, Roger Geary attributed the shift from a "hard style" to a "soft style" of protest policing – a shift he located around 1910 – to political considerations that constrained the behavior of the authorities (Geary 1985: 117). In the 1980s, a partial rollback to a harder protest policing was instead connected with the neoliberalist political choices of the conservative government led by Margaret Thatcher (Geary 1985: ch. 7). Many observers, even from within the police, explained the brutal intervention of the Italian police during the above-mentioned anti-G8 protest against the political influence of the post-fascist Alleanza Nazionale (AN) in the government (and in particular the presence in the operational center of the Carabinieri of the leader of AN and Vice-Prime Minister Gianfranco Fini) (della Porta and Reiter 2003a). Although rarely via direct orders, also in Germany the influence of the political parties in government on policing styles, often expressed via the police chief (appointed by the state government and often with more or less explicit party affiliation), is evident in the different approaches to protest policing adopted in Christian-Democratic versus Social-Democratic states – that is, respectively, the Bayerische Linie versus the Nord-Rhein/Westfalischen Linien (Winter 1998a: 294ff.; 377ff.).

It would be, nonetheless, inaccurate to state that left-wing governments are *always* more tolerant of protest than conservative governments. In fact, there seem to be periods in which the main parties do *not* differ much from each other in their position on internal security police and public order styles (Funk 1990). One of the possible reasons for this is that protest policing is, in fact, a tricky issue for left-wing governments. A comparative research on Italy and Germany (della Porta 1995) indicated that left-wing governments often have to face aggressive law and order campaigns launched by the conservative opposition (as happened in Germany under Chancellor Brandt). Especially when the Left feels the need to legitimate itself as "fit to govern," it makes concessions to the hardline proponents of law and order. These compromises not only inevitably disappoint social movement activists (usually to the advantage of the most radical wings); they also elicit internal criticism. About one year before the Genoa demonstration, Amnesty International had criticized police brutality in the policing of another march on globalization, this time in Naples and this time under center-left national and local governments (della Porta and Reiter 2003). Again in the policing of the protest against neoliberalist forms of globalization, the traditionally "soft" policing styles of social-democratic Sweden were abandoned during the protest in Gothenburg in 2001, resulting in a dramatic escalation in violence (Peterson and Oskarsson 2001). Just as left-wing governments are not automatically lenient towards protest, so conservatives in power do not always implement repressive policies. Strategies of deescalation in the conflict with the squatter movement in Berlin survived, for instance, the shift of the state government from center-left to center-right (Busch et al. 1988).

In general, research stresses selective strategies of protest policing. Old movements tend to be legitimized, in shorter or longer time span, but new movements emerge and the established political actors tend to be, at least initially, closed to their emerging demands. As the case of the movement for a globalization from below clearly indicates, the rise of a new actor is perceived as a dangerous challenge not only by the right-wing parties, against which the movement protests, but also by the movement's potential allies on the Left (della Porta and Reiter 2003a and b). The brutal repression of the demonstrations in Genoa, but also earlier in Gothenburg, has been facilitated by the delegitimation of the movement in institutional politics. Moreover, escalation is very likely during ethnic conflicts, especially when police forces recruit mainly in one community. In Northern Ireland, the British style of community policing was hard to implement with a police body – the Royal Ulster Constabulary – overwhelmingly composed of Protestant Unionists. The radicalization of the civil rights movement was triggered by a military police intervention with escalated force against the Catholic community, with strategies that resonated more with the colonial policing strategy than with the British tradition of citizens' policing (Ellison and Smyth 2000).

Protest Policing and the Public Sphere

Government choices on protest policing are sensitive to the pressures of various actors. Political parties, interest groups, and movement organizations express their preferences on protest policing, addressing either their constituency, the public, or the policymakers directly. Their discourses are then filtered through the media, and form public opinion.

Ethnographic observation of protest policing suggests in particular a central role of the relationship linking the media and police forces. Television and newspapers have catalyzed changes in the strategies used by demonstrating groups – which Patrick Champagne (1990) defines as "paper demonstrations." Research on the police is starting to address some parallel questions: Has media presence at sites of social conflict modified the nature of demonstrations by imposing changes in police practices, or, on the contrary, do the latter remain indifferent to the "power of the media"? Moreover, what is the role of the police in the "co-construction" of the news, both as an actor in the field and, more traditionally, as a source of information?

Herbert Gans was one of the first to describe the softening effect of the media on protest policing in his analysis of social disorder news before and after the Chicago Democratic Convention in 1968, when the media denounced a "police riot" (Gans 1979: 53ff.). In his afterword to della Porta and Reiter's book on policing protest, Gary Marx (1998: 257) remarks, "the presence of the mass media is an important factor here, serving to moderate police behavior. The symbolic importance of being always under control is given lesser importance than ... the longer negative consequences that might flow from media accounts of police violence." The expression "mediatization of preserving law and order" comes from a perspective that sees changes in the handling of demonstrations as being a factor of media influence. A variant of this view argues that, henceforth, police–demonstrator interactions cannot be reduced to on-site interactions: "paper demonstrations" would have become as much an issue for the police forces as for the demonstrators. As Wisler and Tackenberg (forthcoming) argue, "the portrayals of the police practices, as they are depicted in the mass media and within the political field ... may be even more crucial for the development of major occurrences of public disorders than the 'actual' police action in the streets."

Although most authors have agreed with this point of view,[6] the situation seems more complex. The idea of "mediatization of the policing of protest" risks over-emphasizing "mediacentrism," hiding, rather than explaining, the roots of the development it claims to describe. What is presented as a result of autonomous action by the media, is due to the various causal sequences we have described in the previous sections and, of course, the development of the kinds of action taken by the demonstrating groups themselves. In this complex process, the media appears more as an intervening variable than as a cause.[7] Similarly, as della Porta and Reiter have noted (1998a: 18), "the mere presence of journalists, in fact, appears to have a de-escalating effect on the police, although the fact that this presence does not always discourage the police from a 'hard' style of intervention is testified by the very existence of media coverage of such interventions." Additionally, media coverage of events may often "cover up" police behavior.

It does not mean that the police forces are structurally insensitive to the media. On the contrary, they generally seek, in a variety of ways, to influence the media for their own ends, among other things by using their power as a main source of information. Although this is a field of research largely unexplored in the sociology of social movements, much groundwork has been done, for example, on the construction of the crime news (Crandon 1992), and several scholars have noted the extent to which the media have tended to privilege accredited sources.[8] Studies on media coverage of violent protest events also pointed to the use by journalists of police categories with derogatory or discrediting connotations, such as "zulus," "vandals," "people foreign to the student movement," "gangs," "wild hordes" that "swarm into" the city, "take" it, "set it ablaze" (see also Murdock 1984: 83–4; Waddington 1992: 177). As Schlesinger (1990: 68) pointed out, the category of "primary definers" is extremely loose and, among institutional actors, the chances for access to the media vary unequally according to the resources but also to situations. In this game, the police forces certainly play an important role.

In particular, the police sometimes develop strategies for maintaining public order in view of expected media coverage, particularly by recourse to the whole spectrum of provocation techniques (Fillieule 1997): the waiting game in front of demonstrator violence, *agents provocateurs* (Marx 1979), encouragement of resistance to better quash rebellion,[9] and so on. However, there are also forms of cooperation between demonstrator groups and police forces during the event with the declared aim of "coproducing" a spectacle that will attract media attention. As Sommier (1990: 50) points out in the case of France:

> Cooperation with police forces can even be a personalized service exchange between leaders on both sides or even a bargaining. Like a union representative who, to end an occupation of a public location without loosing their face, call with its "direct line" the *commissaire* X: "Listen, it could be OK if you come with 200 guys, but not in a drag queen fashion!" This is a special idiom for experts to mean guys [some CRS–Compagnie Républicaine de Sécurité)] with riot helmets, with many tricks on them, so that they can be impressive. And we will say to our fellows: "The only way is to get out". Our honor is safe, we retreat under the pressure of the bayonets and my comrades are happy, you know. Everybody saw it, broadcasts were at the place, we could not escape but go out!

In many cases, the police forces openly use the media with the objective of reducing tension during the event and avoiding any outbreak of violence. Fillieule (1997) gives many examples where, under the benevolent eyes of the police, demonstrators are allowed to set fire to a bus-shelter or a truck with the sole objective of allowing photographs to be taken by the media, before everyone packs up and peacefully goes home.

MORE PROTEST OR ACQUIESCENCE? THE CONSEQUENCES OF PROTEST POLICING

We can turn now to the effects of protest policing on social movements. First of all, protest policing is a relevant, and delicate, task for the police. As Winter observed, "during protest policing the police enters the public sphere. The police intervention inevitably takes a political dimension" (1998a: 17). In research in Germany, Helmut Willems and his collaborators (1988) noticed that the interaction with protestors "became problematic for the policemen when they have to represent interests and impose decisions whose legitimacy is put into question by the mass resistance and the protest of the population, and that, therefore, they cannot anymore interpret as a common interest." In particular, reliance upon the political power for legitimacy is a risky attitude for the police. The more involved in political repression, the less the police will be able to raise support by the citizens, even to fulfill their tasks in crime fighting. Especially in authoritarian regimes, the delegitimation of the police brings about the creation of alternative, informal institutions to keep peace and punish crime. For instance, in South Africa, in the 1980s:

> defense structures arose, both as a response to state harassment by the security forces, as well as to inadequate, partisan policing, and the perceived illegitimate justice system . . . These structures were simultaneously responsible for both the organization of insurrectionary activities, and for identifying and punishing individuals or groupings believed to have committed such crimes as theft, murder, and rape. (Marks and McKenzie 1995: 10; see also Brogden and Shearing 1993: 145–8)

During transitions to democracy, as the regime loses credibility and support, a usually unprofessional and underpaid police will find it harder and harder to justify their own role. In democratic regimes, in order to avoid delegitimation, the police can disregard political orders to stand firm given by the political authorities (prefect, minister) and aim primarily to satisfy the ends pursued by professional order-keeping forces: not to fight, not to wound and not to be wounded – in sum, avoid "on-the-job troubles" (Waddington 1994).

In fact, protest policing plays a most important role in the self-understanding of the police. It is no surprise, consequently, that research indicates that protest cycles affect police organization and strategies. In France, the constitution of police knowledge, police practices, and legal tools to deal with demonstrations were mostly initiated as a reaction to the changing tactics of demonstrators – the reforms of 1893–8, 1934, 1968, 1990–3 being major examples in that respect (Fillieule 1997). In Britain, the development of the decentralized police and of the conception of a "citizens' police" followed waves of protest (Morgan 1987; Reiner 1998). In Germany, the "new line" on protest policing – with, among others, the import-ance given to negotiation and psychological skills – emerged from the weaknesses of police intervention in 1968, a year police officers, over three decades later, still consider to be a turning point (Winter 1998a: 310–11). In Italy, the demilitariza-tion of the Polizia di Stato was one of the most unexpected consequences of the long protest cycle that had started in the mid-1960s (della Porta and Reiter 2003: ch. 4).

Policing styles also have important effects on protest tactics. "Police," Michael Lipsky (1970: 1) stated, "may be conceived as 'street-level bureaucrats' who 'repre-sent' government to people. And at the same time as they represent government policies, police forces also help defining the terms of urban conflict by their actions." Police intervention has very important effects on protestors' perceptions of the state reaction to them.

The social science literature provides us with some, not always coherent, hypotheses on the direction of these interactions. Some scholars have first of all stated that a reduction in repression facilitates the development of social movements (Skocpol 1979; McAdam 1982). The policing of protest is a particularly relevant issue not only in long established democracies, but also in regime transition and authoritarian regimes that use repression in an attempt to silence opposition. Yet, even in the most repressive regimes, protest survives in more or less visible forms, with the range going from sporadic mass demonstration to atomized individual resistance (Johnston 1996; Pickvance 1996; Bennani and Fillieule 2001). Most of these forms of protest meet with police attempts at controlling them, the most brutal of which are often followed by waves of outrage both inside the country as well as at the international level.

Moreover, a higher degree of repression was often associated with radical behavior on the part of the challengers. Goldstein concluded his comparative analysis on political repression in nineteenth-century Europe by observing that "those countries that were consistently the most repressive, brutal, and obstinate in dealing with the consequences of modernization and developing working-class dissidence reaped the harvest by producing opposition that was just as rigid, brutal, and obstinate" (Goldstein 1983: 340; see also Benanni and Fillieule 2001 on Islamic movements). Repression also often produces a shift in the aims of the protest itself that focuses on the very issue of policing – as Edward Escobar noticed in a study on the Chicano movement in Los Angeles (Escobar 1993: 1485). The reaction to police repression is the change of protest focus from single issue to the meta-issue of protest rights. Research on South Africa between 1970 and 1984 demonstrated that "high levels of repression increase the likelihood of future collective action" (Olivier 1991: 115).

Other scholars, however, have reported less clear-cut outcomes. In a review of studies on the American protest movements in the 1960s and 1970s, Wilson (1976) observed that the empirical results sometimes indicate a radicalization of those groups exposed to police violence, at other times their retreat from unconventional actions. In the comparison of Italy and Germany (della Porta 1995: ch. 3), it emerged that more repressive and diffuse techniques of policing tend, at the same time, to discourage the mainly peaceful protesters while fueling the more radical fringe.

In order to explain the complex relations between repression and social movement activities we have to take into account the fact that protest policing influences both costs and (expected) benefits of collective action. First, state repression represents one of the most relevant (potential) costs of taking part in collective behavior (Tilly 1978). Even if other costs and benefits are taken into account – and even if collective behavior is not always "rational" – the weight of the cost defined by state repression would be difficult to overstate. But the form of repression influences the same grievances that spark protest in the first place, for example, by creating "injustice frames" (Gamson et al. 1982). The more "repressive" the state, therefore, the higher the potential benefits of collective action, since the "punishment" of the unfair state would become part of the expected rewards, and the need to "do something" would appear all the more urgent to some activists. As indicated in research on the radicalization of the New Left, cases of brutal repression (in particular, the death of demonstrators) tended to produce among the activists images of an "unfair state," delegitimating the political institutions as nondemocratic (della Porta 1995).

Moreover, we have to consider the characteristics of specific social movements. Material and cultural resources available for challengers contribute to determine when episodes of high repression are likely to trigger waves of moral protest, and when instead they will demobilize movements. The development of spirals of violent action–reaction is facilitated in movements with a radical ideology and semiclandestine structures. However, escalation is more difficult the less the legitimacy of the violent repertoire and the more open and decentralized the organizational structure. For the Italian social forums that followed the Genoa Social Forum, for instance, the experience of repression did not justify violent reactions, and much attention was paid to avoid escalation in the numerous mass demonstrations that followed the anti-G8 protest (della Porta 2003).

Besides the directions of large historical trends, researchers pointed at the dynamics of escalation or deescalation in specific police protestors' encounters via the *reciprocal adaptation of police and protestors' tactics*. The relationship between protestors and the police does not have a unique causal determination: protest tactics influenced the police tactics through interactive processes. On the other hand, adaptations to police tactics affects protest organizational structures and strategies. As for the former, the development of *servizi d'ordine* (marshal bodies) was the militant response to a militarization of the interactions between demonstrators and police forces (della Porta 1995). As for the movement repertoires, the escalation of the antinuclear protest in Germany involved the ritualization of the conflict between an increasing militant wing of activists and an increasingly aggressive police. On one side of the conflict, in fact, a militant group began to organize, appearing at all the various protest events and pushing for direct confrontation; on the other side, the state police, bolstered by police units from different states, used massive intervention. A similar ritualization of physical confrontations – although at a larger scale – nowadays involves movement against neoliberalist globalization and the American and European police forces, in particular during the policing of countersummit protest (della Porta and Reiter 2001). These interactive processes have to be taken into account to explain the dynamics of escalation (see also McAdam 1983).

In general, some internal dynamics of protest policing *facilitated* escalation. In particular, the main instrument of coercive police intervention – the baton charge – easily leads to escalation.

> The reason why baton charges are difficult to control is known colloquially in the Metropolitan Police as "the red mist". This refers to a potential cocktail of psychological conditions which diminishes any person's self-control, and from which the police are not exempt. Baton charges require officers to act aggressively in conditions of relative anonymity...they may be wearing protective clothing with visors to obscure their facial features; and they will almost certainly be acting, not as individuals, but as a group. The target of their actions will not be other individuals, but an equally anonymous collective – "the crowd", "Them" – who will have insulted and physically attacked "Us" – the police. Officers' anger and frustration will thus have been aroused, and a baton charge will allow retaliation in conditions which minimize individual responsibility. The violence that the police employ in response is seen, certainly by the police themselves, as justified – upholding the law – a feeling that inhibits restraint. Baton charge is also physically arousing because of the exertion involved. In striking members

of the crowd officers are likely to experience pleasure, not because they are sadists, but because they will undergo a reduction in physical stress which is experienced as pleasurable and which will encourage them to repeat the aggressive action. Psychologically, these are conditions virtually designed to encourage aggression and violence. Added to this volatile mixture, the human physique makes it extremely difficult to strike in a manner other than that which will inflict serious injury. Whilst officers are instructed to strike people with their batons only on the arms, legs and torso, and are forbidden to hit people on the head, this is an unnatural action which is likely to be forgotten in the heat of the moment. The natural inclination is to strike downwards. (Waddington 1991: 177–8)

Escalation can also derive from *organizational dynamics*. As Monjardet observes (1990: 217ff.), at least three main organizational mechanisms in police intervention favor escalation: the dialectic of centralization and autonomy in police units, the difficulties of coordinating the different groups, and uncertainty about the aims of the intervention. Although a police force may have well-developed techniques for controlling large masses, it may be ill prepared to isolate and control small groups operating within larger, peaceful crowds (Monjardet 1990: 233; see also della Porta 1995; Fillieule 1997: 252–81).

Some Conclusions and Perspectives for Further Research

In *Demonstration Democracy* (1970), Etzioni observed, at the beginning of the 1970s, that recourse to direct expression of opinions was becoming increasingly common in democratic countries, visible both in the growing number of demonstrations and their diffusion through all levels of society. Ten years later, in the last chapter of *Political Action* (1979), Barnes et al. observed that demonstrations are now established as a normal aspect of political participation. These accounts of the growing institutionalization of street action seem timelier than ever for the 1980s and 1990s. Recourse to demonstrations in Europe seems to have become an everyday event involving most social actors (Kriesi et al. 1995; Fillieule 1997; Rucht et al. 1998). In a parallel way, the analysis of the doctrine and practice of maintaining public order seems to indicate that today cooperation, or at least tolerance, takes precedence over direct confrontation.

This movement, though, embodies a paradox that is also to be found in the history of other modes of protest actions: to the extent that demonstrations have become widespread, acceptable, and more predictable, they seem to have lost political effectiveness. From this point of view, Piven and Cloward are undoubtedly right to prefer the term "normalization" to that of institutionalization to describe this kind of development (Piven and Cloward 1992). This tendency to normalization has entailed at least two consequences.

On one hand, it has shifted the priority of protest movements from the need to "make trouble" to the need to "make up the numbers," which clearly means that the resources that may contribute to the success of a demonstration have changed in nature and are, above all, accessible to groups with strong organization and powerful backing. The same would apply to strikes whose revolutionary potential has weakened as they have become institutionalized (Piven and Cloward 1977;

McCammon 1990). In general, the protest policing style based upon negotiation reduces disruption and therefore the visibility of protest (della Porta and Reiter 2003).

On the other hand, the dominant political discourse developed around the notion of "a communications society" aims at eliminating all traces of social conflict in favor of negotiation and dialogue (Neveu 1994). In this world, conflict is increasingly perceived as pathology, and the rules of "good demonstrating" increasingly exclude the legitimacy of recourse to violence, or even civil disobedience. Radical protest is more and more considered as not only illegitimate, but even unpolitical (della Porta and Reiter 1998a). The fact that demonstrations are increasingly perceived as a peaceful and legitimate mode of expressing opinions effectively reinforces the exclusion of groups poor in other resources and for whom disruption is a last resource, justifying by the same token the selective resurgence of repression. In fact, the distribution of resources that allows one to adapt to the new rules of the game of "opinion-geared democracy" is neither equally nor randomly distributed among social groups.

This last observation warns us against the idea of a continual process of pacification of nonconventional participation that would fit into a process of euphemization of violence, inspired – often without much rigor – by the Elias school of sociology and for which one finds the exact counterpart in the idea of a civilizing process on the agents of state violence, due to the effect of greater transparency. Everything indicates that the forms of demonstrations, from the decision to hold one to the forms it can take in action, are the product of a number of variables of which it is difficult to say if they have followed, are following or will follow, even tendentiously, a continuous process of institutionalization and routinization. The legitimacy of protest is always subject to contingent historical processes, and a return to a radicalization of street action and/or of repression cannot be excluded.

More research is needed, especially on the selectivity of protest policing, with "soft" treatment of "good demonstrators" and "tough" treatment of "bad ones." The events of September 11, 2001, prompt further investigation into how a change in geopolitical circumstances affects the policing of internal turmoil. In both the US and Europe, the reaction to the threat of fundamentalism and terrorism has resulted, in the short term, in a reduction of democratic freedoms in the so-called "advanced democracies," but it has also stifled liberalization processes in some Southern countries. New trends seem all the more important to study, since protest is becoming increasingly global, constructing a new public sphere.

Notes

1 Gary Marx (1979: 112–14) observes that agencies that deal with intelligence gathering and the prevention of crime or subversion have an *inherent tendency to expand*. Control agencies would consequently produce political deviants. A similar point is raised by David Garret, in a study of the FBI involvement against Martin Luther King (Garret 1981: 224–5).

2 This last point highlights the role of the mass media in the practical management of social conflicts in the field (more on this point later).

3 On the use of the *agent provocateur*, see Marx (1979) and, for an analysis of a contemporary case in France, Fillieule (1997: 340–51).
4 An important factor in pushing towards "soft" policing is, for instance in the US, the fear
   that financially strapped governments face lawsuits from citizens claiming to have been
   mistreated (Marx 1998: 267). On the deescalating role of lawsuits, see also McCarthy and
   McPhail (1998: 103) about Act Up in the US.
5 Mainly, a whole set of techniques based on the idea of a necessary distance between
   demonstrators and officers has been progressively implemented (Fillieule and Jobard
   1998).
6 See, e.g., Geary (1985: 129–30) on Great Britain; della Porta et al. (1998: 127–8) on Italy
   and France; Favre (1990: 161–2) on France; McCarthy and McPhail (1998) and McPhail
   et al. (1998) on the US.
7 E.g., it is because policing techniques have moved towards keeping demonstrators at a
   distance (with the aim of protecting police officers from attack) that television and
   newspapers, sheltered by the police barricades, can cover the event live and close-up.
8 There are – e.g., in Marx (1979) and Gans (1979: 269, 274) – numerous details of the
   ways the police seek to feed disinformation to the media; Gitlin (1980: 27ff.), regarding
   the political power's strategies to discredit the Students for a Democratic Society, suggests
   a typology, several elements of which refer to police action. Systematic disagreements
   about the number of demonstrators – the police figures as against those provided by the
   organizers (Fillieule 1997), or the official releases about the number of injured policemen
   (Fillieule 1997: 122–3) – are part of this problematic (also Hall et al. 1978; Murdock
   1984; Waddington 1990; Fielding 1991; Anderson 1997: 38–72; della Porta and Reiter
   1998a; Fillieule and Jiménez forthcoming).
9 This is an age-old technique, as indicated by Le Roy Ladurie's work on the troubles of a
   Roman carnival at the turn of the sixteenth century, during which a coalition of notables
   fueled a tax revolt only to bloodily repress it (Le Roy Ladurie 1979).

References and further reading

Anderson, Alison (1997) *Media, Culture and the Environment*. Berkeley: University of Cali-
   fornia Press.
Andretta, Massimiliano, Donatella della Porta, Lorenzo Mosca, and Herbert Reiter (2002)
   Global, noglobal, new global: La protesta contro il G8 a Genova. Roma-Bari: Laterza.
Barnes, Samuel, Max Kaase, et al. (1979) *Political Action: Mass Participation in Five Western
   Democracies*. Beverley Hills, CA: Sage.
Bennani, Mounia, and Olivier Fillieule (eds.) (2001) *Les mouvements sociaux dans le monde
   musulman*. Paris: Presses de Sciences Po.
Benyon, John (1984) The Policing Issue. In John Benyon (ed.), *Scarman and After*. Oxford:
   Pergamon, 99–113.
Brogden, Mike, and Clifford Shearing (1993) *Policing for a New South Africa*. London:
   Routledge.
Bruneteaux, Patrick (1996) *Maintenir l'ordre*. Paris: Presses de Sciences Po.
Busch, Heiner, Albrecht Funk, Udo Kauss, Wolf-Dieter Narr, and Falco Werkentin (1988) *Die
   Polizei in der Bundesrepublik*. Frankfurt am Main: Campus.
Cain, Maureen E. (1973) *Society and the Policeman's Role*. London: Routledge & Kegan
   Paul.
Champagne, Patrick (1990) *Faire l'opinion*. Paris: Minuit.
Crandon, Garth (1992) *The Police and the Media: Information Management and the Con-
   struction of Crime News*. Bradford, Horton.

Dalton, Russell (1996) *Citizen Politics*. Chatham, NJ; Chatham House.

De Biasi, Rocco (1998) The Policing of Hooliganism in Italy. In Donatella della Porta and Herbert Reiter (eds.), *The Policing of Mass Demonstrations in Contemporary Democracies*. Minneapolis: University of Minnesota Press, 213–27.

della Porta, Donatella (1995) *Social Movements, Political Violence and the State: A Comparative Analysis of Italy and Germany*. New York: Cambridge University Press.

——(1998) Police Knowledge and Protest Policing: Some Reflections on the Italian Case. In Donatella della Porta and Herbert Reiter (eds.), *The Policing of Mass Demonstrations in Contemporary Democracies*. Minneapolis: University of Minnesota Press, 228–52.

——(1999) Protest, Protesters and Protest Policing. In Marco Giugni, Doug McAdam, and Charles Tilly (eds.), *How Movements Matter*. Minneapolis: University of Minnesota Press, 66–96.

——(2003) New Global. Chi sono e cosa vogliono I critici della globalizzazione. Bologna: Il Mulino.

della Porta, Donatella, and Herbert Reiter (1998a) The Policing of Protest in Western Democracies. In Donatella della Porta and Herbert Reiter (eds.), *The Policing of Mass Demonstrations in Contemporary Democracies*. Minneapolis: University of Minnesota Press, 1–34.

——(eds.) (1998b) *The Policing of Mass Demonstrations in Contemporary Democracies*. Minneapolis: University of Minnesota Press.

——(2001) Protesta noglobal e ordine pubblico. *Il Mulino*, 397, 871–82.

——(2003a) *"You are the G8, we're Six billion"*: The Genoa Demonstrations. In Paolo Bellucci and Martin Bull (eds), *Italian Politics: The Return of Berlusconi*. New York: Berghahn Books, 105–24.

——(2003b) *Protesta e ordine pubblico*. Bologna: Il Mulino.

della Porta, Donatella, and Mario Diani (1999) *Introduction to Social Movements*. Oxford: Blackwell.

della Porta, Donatella, Olivier Fillieule, and Herbert Reiter (1998) Policing Protest in France and Italy: From Intimidation to Cooperation? In Sidney Tarrow and David Meyer (eds.), *The Social Movement Society: Contentious Politics for a New Century*. Boulder, CO: Rowman & Littlefield, 111–30.

Donner, Frank (1990) *Protectors of Privilege*. Berkeley: University of California Press.

Ellison, Graham, and Jim Smyth (2000) *The Crowned Harp: Policing Northern Ireland*. London: Pluto.

Escobar, Edward J. (1993) The Dialectic of Repression: The Los Angeles Police Department and the Chicano Movement, 1968–1971. *Journal of American History*, 79 (March), 1483–1514.

Etzioni, Amitai (1970) *Demonstration Democracy*. New York: Gordon & Breach.

Favre, Pierre (1990) La manifestation, Paris, Presses de la Fondation Natianale des Sciences Politiques.

Fielding, Nigel (1991) *The Police and Social Conflict*. London: Athlone.

Fillieule, Olivier (1997) *Stratégies de la rue: Les manifestations en France*. Paris: Presses de Sciences Po.

Fillieule, Olivier, and Manuel Jiménez (forthcoming) Media Bias and Environmental Protest Event Analysis. In Chris Rootes (ed.), *Environmental Mobilization in Comparative Perspectives*. Oxford: Oxford University Press.

Fillieule Olivier, and Fabien Jobard (1998) The Maintenance of Order in France: Towards a Model of Protest Policing. In Donatella della Porta and Herbert Reiter (eds.), *The Policing of Mass Demonstrations in Contemporary Democracies*. Minneapolis: University of Minnesota Press, 70–90.

Funk, Albrecht (1990) Innere Sicherheit: Symbolische Politik und exekutive Praxis. In B. Blanke and H. Wollmann (eds.), *40 Jahre Bundesrepublik*. Special issue of *Leviathan*, 367–88.

Funk, Albrecht, Udo Kauss, and Thomas von Zabern (1980) Die Ansätze zu einer neuen Polizei – Vergleich der Polizeientwicklung in England/Wales, Frankreich und der Bundesrepublik Deutschland. In E. Blankenburg (ed.), *Politik der Inneren Sicherheit*, Frankfurt am Main: Suhrkamp, 16–90.

Gamson, William, and David S. Meyer (1993) The Framing of the Political Opportunities, European/American Perspectives on the Dynamics of Social Movements. Proceedings of the conference on Social Movementsheld in Washington, on August 13–15, 1992.

Gamson, William, Bruce Fireman, and Steven Rytina (1982) *Encounters with Unjust Authorities*. Homewood, IL: Dorsey.

Gans, Herbert, J. (1979) *Deciding what's News: A Study of CBS Evening News, NBC Nightly News, Newsweek and Time*. London: Constable.

Garret, David (1981) *The FBI and Martin Luther King Jr.* New York: Norton.

Geary, Roger (1985) *Policing Industrial Disputes: 1893 to 1985*. Cambridge: Cambridge University Press.

Gitlin, Todd (1980) *The Whole World Is Watching*. Berkeley: University of California Press.

Goldstein, Robert J. (1978) *Political Repression in America*. Cambridge, MA: Schenkman.

——(1983) *Political Repression in Nineteenth Century Europe*. London: Croom Helm.

Hall, S., C. Chricher, T. Jefferson, J. Clark and B. Roberts (1978) *Policing the Crisis: Mugging, the State, and Law and Order*. London: Macmillan.

Jaime-Jiménez, Oscar, and Fernando Reinares (1998) The Policing of Mass Demonstrations in Spain. In Donatella della Porta and Herbert Reiter (eds.), *The Policing of Mass Demonstrations in Contemporary Democracies*. Minneapolis: University of Minnesota Press, 166–87.

Jefferson, Tony (1990) *The Case against Paramilitary Policing*. Milton Keynes: Open University Press.

Johnston, Hank (1996) Mobilization and Structure of Opposition in Repressive States. Paper presented at the Second European Conference on Social Movements, Vitoria-Gasteiz, October 2–5.

Kitschelt, Herbert (1986) Political Opportunity Structures and Protest: Anti-Nuclear Movements in Four Democracies. *British Journal of Political Science*, 16, 57–85.

Kriesi, Hanspeter (1989) The Political Opportunity Structure of the Dutch Peace Movement. *West European Politics*, 12, 295–312.

Kriesi, Hanspeter, R. Koopmans, J. W. Duyvendak, and M. G. Giugni (1995) *The Politics of New Social Movements in Western Europe*. Minneapolis: University of Minnesota Press.

Lacey, Nicola, Celia Wells, and Dirk Meure (1990) *Reconstructing Criminal Law: Critical Perspectives on Crime and the Criminal Process*. London: Weidenfeld & Nicolson.

Le Roy Ladurie, Emmanuel (1979) *Carnival in Romans*. New York: Georges Braziller, [1st ed. in French: *Le carnaval de Romans, De la Chandeleur au mercredi des Cendres 1579–1580*. Paris: Gallimard, 1979].

Lipset, Seymour Martin (1971) Why Cops Hate Liberals – And Vice Versa. In William J. Bopp (ed.), *The Police Rebellion: A Quest for Blue Power*. Springfield, IL: Thomas, 23–39.

Lipsky, Michael (1970) Introduction. In Michael Lipsky (ed.), *Law and Order: Police Encounters*. New York: Aldine, 1–7.

——(1980) *Street Level Bureaucracy: Dilemmas of the Individual in Public Services*. New York: Russell Sage Foundation.

Lüdtke, Alf (1992) Einleitung: "Sicherheit" und "Wohlfahrt": Aspekte der Polizeigeschichte. In Alf Lüdtke (ed.), *"Sicherheit" und "Wohlfahrt": Polizei, Gesellschaft und Herrschaft im 19. und 20. Jahrhundert*. Frankfurt am Main: Suhrkamp, 7–33.

McAdam, Doug (1982) *Political Process and the Development of Black Insurgency, 1930–1970*. Chicago: University of Chicago Press.

——(1983) Tactical Innovation and the Pace of Insurgency. *American Sociological Review*, 48, 735–54.

McCammon, H. J. (1990) Legal Limits on Labor Militancy: Labor Law and the Right to Strike since the New Deal. *Social Problems*, 37 (2), 206–29.

McCarthy, John, D., and Clark McPhail (1998) The Institutionalization of Protest in the United States. In David S. Meyer and Sidney Tarrow (eds.), *The Social Movement Society: Contentious Politics for a New Century*. Rowman & Littlefield, 83–111.

McClintock, Frederick, André Normandeau, Robert Philippe, and Jérome Skolnick (1974) Police et violence collective. In Denis Szabo (ed.), *Police, culture et société*. Montréal: Les Presses de l'Université de Montreal.

McPhail, Clark, Davis Schweingruber, and John McCarthy (1998) Policing Protest in the United States, 1960–1995. In Donatella della Porta and Herbert Reiter (eds.), *The Policing of Mass Demonstrations in Contemporary Democracies*. Minneapolis: University of Minnesota Press, 49–69.

Manning, Peter K. (1979) The Social Control of Police Work. In S. Holdaway (ed.), *British Police*. London: Edward Arnold, 41–65.

Marks, Monique, and Penny McKenzie (1995) *Political Pawns or Social Agents: A Look at Militarized Youth in South Africa*. Cape Town: Centre for the Study of Violence and Reconciliation.

Marx, Gary T. (1979) External Efforts to Damage or Facilitate Social Movements: Some Patterns, Explanations, Outcomes and Complications. In John McCarthy and Mayer N. Zald (eds.), *The Dynamics of Social Movements*, Cambridge, MA: Winthrop, 94–125.

——(1998) Some Reflections on the Democratic Policing of Demonstrations. In Donatella della Porta and Herbert Reiter (eds.), *Policing Protest: The Control of Mass Demonstrations in Western Democracies*. Minneapolis: University of Minnesota Press, 253–70.

Monjardet, Dominique (1990) La manifestation du coté du maintien de l'ordre. In Pierre Favre (ed.), *La Manifestation*. Paris: Fondation Nationale des Sciences Politiques, 229–44.

Morgan, Jane (1987) *Conflict and Order: The Police and Labor Disputes in England and Wales, 1900–1939*. Oxford: Clarendon.

Murdock, Graham (1984) Reporting the Riots: Images and Impact. In John Benyon (ed.), *Scarman and After*. Oxford: Pergamon, 73–95.

Neveu, Eric (1994) *Une société de communication?* Paris: Montchrestien.

Olivier, Johan L. (1991) State Repression and Collective Action in South Africa, 1970–84. *South African Journal of Sociology*, 22, 109–17.

Peterson, Abby, and M. Oskarsson (2001) Policing Political Protest: A Study of Police Handling of Protest Events in Conjunction with EU Summit Meeting in Goteburg. Unpublished manuscript.

Pickvance, Chris (1996) Regime Change and Social Movements: A Comparative Approach. Paper presented at the Second European Conference on Social Movements, Vitoria-Gasteiz, October 2–5.

Piven, Frances Fox, and Richard Cloward (1977) *Poor People Movements: When They Succeed, How They Fail*. New York: Vintage.

——(1992) Normalizing Collective Protest. In Aldon Morris and Carol McClurg Muller (eds.), Frontiers in Social Movement Theory. New Haven: Yale University Press, 301-25.

Reiner, Robert (1991) *The Politics of the Police*. 2nd ed. Hempstead, UK: Harvester Wheatsheaf.

——(1998) Policing, Protest, and Disorder in Britain. In Donatella della Porta and Herbert Reiter (eds.), *The Policing of Mass Demonstrations in Contemporary Democracies*. Minneapolis: University of Minnesota Press, 35–48.

Reiter, Herbert (1998) Police and Public Order in Italy, 1944–1948: The Case of Florence. In Donatella della Porta and Herbert Reiter (eds.), *The Policing of Mass Demonstrations in Contemporary Democracies*. Minneapolis: University of Minnesota Press, 143–65.

Rucht, Dieter, Ruud Koopmans, and Friedhelm Neidhart (eds.) (1998) *Acts of Dissent: New Development of the Study of Protest*. Berlin: Sigma.

Schlesinger, P. (1990) Rethinking the Sociology of Journalism: Source Strategies and the Limits of Media Centrism. In M. Ferguson (ed.), *Public Communicatio: The New Imperatives*. London: Sage, 61–83.

Skocpol, Theda (1979) *States and Social Revolutions*. New York: Cambridge University Press.

Skolnick, Jerome H. (1966) *Justice without Trial: Law Enforcement in Democratic Society*. New York: John Wiley.

Sommier, Isabelle (1990) Analyse des services d'ordre CGT et CFDT: mémoire de DEA. M.A. dissertation, Ecole des Hautes Etudes en Sciences Sociales, Paris.

Tarrow, Sidney (1994) *Power in Movement: Social Movements, Collective Action and Mass Politics in the Modern State*. New York: Cambridge University Press.

Tilly, Charles (1978) *From Mobilization to Revolution*. Reading, MA: Addison-Wesley.

Waddington, David (1992) *Contemporary Issues in Public Disorders*. London: Routledge.

Waddington, P. A. J. (1991) *The Strong Arm of the Law: Armed and Public Order Policing*. Oxford: Clarendon.

——(1994) *Liberty and Order: Policing Public Order in a Capital City*. London: UCL Press.

——(1998) Controlling Protest in Contemporary, Historical and Comparative Perspective. In Donatella della Porta and Herbert Reiter (eds.), *The Policing of Mass Demonstrations in Contemporary Democracies*. Minneapolis: University of Minnesota Press, 117–41.

Willems, Helmut, Roland Eckert, Harald Goldbach and Tony Losen, (1988) *Demonstranten und Polizisten: Motive, Erfahrungen und Eskalationsbedingungen*. Munich: Juventa.

Wilson, James Q. (1968) *Varieties of Police Behavior: The Management of Law and Order in Eight Communities*. Cambridge, MA: Harvard University Press.

Wilson, John (1976) Social Protest and Social Control. *Social Problems*, 24, 469–81.

Winter, Martin (1998a) *Politikum Polizei: Macht und Funktion der Polizei in der Bundesrepublik Deutschland*. Münster: LIT.

——(1998b) Police Philosophy and Protest Policing in the Federal Republic of Germany. 1960–1990. In Donatella della Porta and Herbert Reiter (eds.), *The Policing of Mass Demonstrations in Contemporary Democracies*. Minneapolis: University of Minnesota Press, 188–212.

Wisler, Dominique, and Marco Tackenberg (forthcoming) The Role of the Police in Public Disorders: Image or Reality? In Richard Bessel and Clive Emsley (eds.), *Patterns of Provocation*. New York: Berghahn.

Worden, R. E. (1989) Situational and Attitudinal Explanations of Police Behavior: A Theoretical Reappraisal and Empirical Reassessment. *Law and Society Review*, 23 (4), 667–711.

11

Bystanders, Public Opinion, and the Media

WILLIAM A. GAMSON

THE SCOPE OF CONFLICT

"If a fight starts, watch the crowd," E. E. Schattschneider told us in 1960. Political contention is centrally about scope, and bystanders don't necessarily stay bystanders but can become engaged as new players in ways that alter the power dynamics among the existing players. Or players can become disengaged and turn into bystanders with similar implications for power dynamics.

Schattschneider's insights about the importance of the scope of conflict are especially meaningful for students of social movements. When the contest is limited to those with ample resources and established access, marginalized groups are unlikely to prevail. It is typically to the advantage of weaker groups to expand the scope. Some of the bystanders may be drawn into the conflict in support of one's adversaries but weak groups have little to lose by shaking up the present power constellation.

As Schattschneider (1960) put it, "Private conflicts are taken into the public arena precisely because someone wants to make certain that the power ratio among the private interests shall not prevail." It is an interesting sign of the times that neither "social movements" nor "mass media" appear in any form in the index to this classic. Nevertheless, contemporary work on movements and media relies heavily on his insights, whether acknowledged or not.

The Role of the Mass Media

What does it mean to take something into the public arena? Actually, public discourse is carried out in various *forums*.[1] A forum includes an *arena* in which individual or collective actors engage in public speech acts, an active audience or *gallery* observing what is going in the arena, and a back-stage *production center* where the would-be speakers in the arena work out their ideas and strategize over how they are to be presented, make alliances, and do the everyday work of cultural production.

There are different forums in which public discourse takes place: mass media, parliaments, courts, party conventions, town hall assemblies, scientific congresses, and the like. The more specialized forums have more specialized galleries – lawyers, for example, predominate in the gallery for legal discourse. But in the current era, there is one central arena that overshadows all others, making them sideshows. For various reasons, general audience mass media provide a master arena.

First, the players in every other arena – that is, the individual or collective actors who engage in public speech acts – are all part of the gallery for the mass media arena. Some of them may well become important players in the mass media as well. But whether they do or not, all collective actors must assume that their own constituents are part of the mass media gallery. Hence, the messages that their supporters hear cannot be ignored, no matter how extensive the actors' own alternative media may be.

Second, the mass media arena is *the* major site of contests over meaning because all of the players in the policy process *assume* its pervasive influence – whether it is justified or not. Something that players in a more specialized arena say may be quoted in the mass media – often in a highly selective and simplified way. They look to the mass media to assess their effectiveness, measuring success by whether a speech in parliament, for example, makes it into the leading newspapers and whether it draws favorable commentary from journalists.

Finally, the mass media are not simply a site that an observer can use to assess relative success or failure in cultural contests. They are not merely an indicator of broader cultural changes in the civil society but they also spread changes in language use and political consciousness to the workplace and other settings in which people go about the public part of their daily lives. When a social movement challenges a cultural code, a change in the media arena both signals and spreads the change. To have one's preferred labels used, for example, is both an important outcome in itself and carries a strong promise of a ripple effect.

Journalists play a dual role in this arena. By including quotations and paraphrases from various spokespersons, journalists decide which collective actors should be taken seriously as important players. They are not *merely* gatekeepers in this process but are themselves players who comment on the positions of other players, shaping and framing the discussion in their interpretations and analyses.

The Nature of Bystanders

A term like "bystanders" has an individualistic bias. Like the term "audience," it conjures up an image of atomized individuals or perhaps families, who in aggregate make up a public. Watch "the crowd," says Schattschneider, conjuring up collective behavior images of the unattached.

It makes more sense to assume that the gallery for the mass media is composed of people who carry around with them various collective identities – solidarity groups with whom they personally identify. Anderson (1991) captures the idea best with his concept of *imagined communities*. Examples would include women, workers, Christians, greens, conservatives, Latinos, progressives, and many others. Since people have multiple identities, they are potentially part of many imagined communities.

Imagined communities are not collective actors. They can only speak through some form of organization or advocacy network that attempts to generate, aggregate, transform, and articulate their concerns (see Rucht 1995). These carriers attempt to represent and make claims on behalf of the interests and values of particular imagined communities that become their constituencies. Often rival players compete for the same constituency offering different and even contradictory claims about the "real" interests of the general public or of some more specific constituency such as women or Christians.

On some issues, however, large portions of the gallery may be less engaged by their identification with imagined communities than by the incidental personal injury or inconvenience they may suffer from the continuation of conflict. As Turner and Killian (1987: 216–17) point out, a *bystander perspective* may permeate the gallery. "The bystander public defines the primary issue as restoration of order and elimination of danger and inconvenience by bringing *any* end to the conflict. The bystanders slogan is 'a plague on both your houses!'" For such a gallery, the issues being debated by the contestants in the arena are unimportant relative to the collateral damage and inconvenience they produce.

Ferree et al. (2002: 255–285) describe how many US journalists have come to embrace this bystander perspective toward the abortion issue. In 1990, David Shaw of the *Los Angeles Times*, wrote a four-part series on "Abortion and the Media." In preparing it, he interviewed a number of high-ranking media executives and discussed with them their coverage of the abortion issue.

Many expressed the wish that the issue would simply go away. Paul Friedman, executive producer of ABC's "World News Tonight," told Shaw that he was "stunned the way this intensely personal issue has taken over the public debate. I'm profoundly tired of the story. As a citizen, I just resent the fact that it is taking so much time and attention away from other issues that are so critical." Turner and Killian (1987: 217) suggest the general principle that "all publics tend to become bystander publics when oppositions remain active over a long period of time."

The Nature of Public Opinion

In the late 1940s, Herbert Blumer (1948) first raised the question of whether public opinion polls measured public opinion and concluded that they did not. Polling techniques have become more sophisticated in the interim but, with certain qualifications, the conclusion stands. The central issues are both theoretical and methodological.

In the tradition represented by Blumer, the term "public" has a quasi-collective quality. Turner and Killian (1987: 158) define it as "a dispersed group of people interested in and divided about an issue, engaged in discussion of that issue, with a view to registering a collective opinion which is expected to affect the course of action of some decision-making group or individual." We might call such a public a discursive community.

This is not the way the term "public" is used in popular discourse. Typically, it is used to mean the aggregation of individual opinions in a population with no implications that they form a public in the sense above. Neidhardt (1996) suggests the term "population opinion" to avoid confusion with the more collective nature of the term "public." The answer to Blumer's question is that public opinion polls clearly do not measure public opinion; but what about population opinion?

Do polls measure population opinion? One can, of course, solve this problem tautologically by defining population opinion operationally as that which is measured by polls and surveys. In the current constructivist conception of public opinion, this simply evades the question. One must unpack the process involved in producing opinion statements in response to survey questions.

As Zaller (1992: 5) puts it, "citizens do not typically carry around in their heads fixed attitudes on every issue on which a pollster may happen to inquire; rather they construct 'opinion statements' on the fly." It is not a random process by any means but depends on many situational cues, some flowing from the issue framing suggested by question wording and order, others flowing from the relevance of a particular issue to such attributes of the interviewer as class, race, and gender. The process is about the construction of meaning by a respondent in contrast to a "file drawer" model (Wilson and Hodges 1991) in which a person accesses and reports the contents of a preexisting mental file.

Today, we recognize contests over meaning as framing contests. The concept of frames and framing has been part of the vocabulary of social movement theory since the 1970s and I have no desire to repeat the many useful discussions of it (see, e.g., chapter 17 in this volume; Tuchman 1978; Gitlin 1980; Gamson and Modigliani 1987, 1989; Gamson 1992; Snow and Benford 1988, 1992; Ryan 1991). I use it here to mean a thought organizer. Like a picture frame, it puts a border around something, distinguishing it from what is around it. A frame spotlights certain events and their underlying causes and consequences, and directs our attention away from others. Like a building frame, it gives shape and support. A frame organizes and makes coherent an apparently diverse array of symbols, images, and arguments, linking them through an underlying organizing idea that suggests what is at stake on the issue.

Ideally, what we would like to know about population opinion is the relative prominence of different frames as predispositions in the population and whether and how these predispositions are changing over time. But there are three major problems in using polls to measure such predispositions: (1) Constructed opinion statements are contingent on the particular frames that are invoked by the survey questions and situation; (2) ambivalent frames do not provide clear guidance on what policies should be followed; and (3) bystander frames render issue disagreements secondary to whatever policies will get the issue off the agenda.

Multiple Frames

With rare exceptions, surveys of population opinion generally rely on closed-ended questions to get at positions on particular issues. They presume a frame in formulating questions and provide precoded categories of answers. This all works very well when there is a dominant frame and the respondent is using it to understand the issue. But when the frames are heavily contested, respondents may be using different frames and their answers conceal this. Many respondents switch frames and can think about the same issue in different ways, depending on which one is triggered by the question. "If different frames or different question orders produce different results," Zaller (1992: 95) writes, "it is not because one or the other has distorted the public's true feelings; it is, rather, because the public, having no fixed true opinion, implicitly relies on the particular question it has been asked to determine what exactly the issue is, and what considerations are relevant to settling it."

Ambivalent Frames

In addition to the problem of survey questions framing the issue for respondents, thereby leading them to contruct opinions consistent with the frame invoked, some frames are intrinsically ambivalent about what policies make sense. There are examples from virtually every issue, but let me use nuclear power for illustration. Imagine a US respondent who generally uses a Devil's Bargain frame to understand the issue: "Nuclear power turns out to be a bargain with the Devil. There are clear benefits such as inexhaustible electricity and an energy supply that doesn't depend on the whims of OPEC. But sooner or later there will be a terrible price to pay. We are damned if we do and damned if we don't."

Now assume that this respondent is asked a typical survey question on nuclear power: "In general, do you favor or oppose the building of more nuclear power plants in the United States?" Does she answer "favor," "oppose," or "not sure"? Any of these alternatives is consistent with this ambivalent frame and none of them reveals how this respondent is actually thinking about the issue.

Bystander Frames

A final problem for measuring population opinion flows from the bystander perspective described above. If an issue has gone on for some time and has provoked some disorder and inconvenience, large portions of the population may be adopting a frame that says, "I don't want to hear any more about that problem" (Turner and Killian, 1987: 217). In this frame, the policies being contested by the partisans on both sides really are not what matters since the main issue is the collateral damage being caused by the conflict. "Win or get out" was the bystander frame on the Vietnam War and it did not make it easy for respondents who felt this way to answer survey questions about being for or against specific policies.

Not only do polls fail to measure public opinion, but their ability to measure population opinion is fundamentally problematic. It is most useful to think of public opinion on any issue – in either sense of public – as a claim made by players in a framing contest, based on whatever evidence they can muster on its behalf. We rightfully give more credence to claims based on carefully conducted probability samples or systematic focus groups than we do to claims based on conversations with one's taxi drivers. But on contested issues, we are frequently left with competing claims based on equally plausible survey evidence – and unable to determine what the respondents who answered the questions were actually thinking. The perception of public opinion by officials who will be making policy decisions is the outcome of a framing contest in which certain claimants have succeeded in getting their particular interpretation of "what the public thinks" accepted.

Burstein (1999: 9) argues that advocacy groups[2] frequently "fail to get what they want because a majority of the *public* wants something else." Elected officials want to be reelected and they pay attention to public opinion. Advocacy groups typically speak for minorities who care what happens on a particular issue and they often offer offsetting opinions. While Burstein recognizes that the public has a limited attention span and that issue salience and importance vary, elected officials are likely to do what the majority prefers rather than what advocacy groups want.

The concept of public opinion is largely taken for granted and unproblematic in Burstein's argument. Implicitly, he uses a file-drawer conception of the process by which people produce opinion statements. He recognizes that advocacy groups engage in claims that try to persuade elected officials that they have strong public support, but legislators are more likely to rely on surveys by disinterested polling organizations. Public opinion exists as an independent force that political leaders take into account rather than the outcome of a framing contest.

This understanding of public opinion contrasts with the constructionist model described above. Quoting Zaller (1992: 96) again:

> Political leaders are seldom the passive instruments of majority opinion. Nor, as it seems to me, do they often attempt openly to challenge public opinion. But they do regularly attempt to play on the contradictory ideas that are always present in people's minds, elevating the salience of some and harnessing them to new initiatives while downplaying or˙ignoring other ideas – all of which is just another way of talking about issue framing.

Movements as Carriers of Symbolic Interests

In current usage, social movements are fields of collective actors. The actors in this field – organizations and advocacy networks – may be carriers for different preferred frames. Or, if the various actors in the movement share a general frame, particular actors may offer special versions, emphasizing aspects of an issue that other versions ignore. So it is useful to think of movements as typically having multiple preferred frames rather than a single one. In fact, the competition among frames within a movement about which one should be promoted and emphasized is one major component of a frame-critical analysis of movements.

Whatever their preferred frames, movement actors are only one of multiple actors operating in a complex system of what Schmitter (1977) and Rucht (1995) call "political interest mediation." Political parties, corporations, associations of many sorts, as well as movement actors, are attempting to generate, aggregate, transform, and articulate the interests of some underlying constituencies.

To call this a mediation system, Rucht points out, implies the linking of at least two external elements that, for a variety of reasons, cannot or do not communicate directly. They "obey conflicting logic and principles which permit no direct link" (Rucht, 1995: 105) or, more metaphorically, they do not speak the same language. But the mediation system discussed here does more than simply translate inputs and outputs into a common language. It takes on a life of its own with its own operating logic and interests and transforms and shapes what is being communicated; indeed, its processes often override the intentions of actors in the external systems being linked.

Social movements, then, are one part of a complex mediation system that carries the political interests of a constituency of imagined communities; but what is the other end of this mediation system? This is more problematic and forces us to take a closer look at what is meant by "interests." Consider, for example, that the constituency whose interests are being mediated is "farmers." The term "interests" conjures up images of crop subsidies, regulations, and other agricultural policies that will operate to the advantage or disadvantage of this group. Or perhaps of power arrangements that will increase or decrease the political influence of those who carry the political interests of farmers. In this narrow sense of policy interests, the other end of the mediation system is the set of authorities who are able to make binding decisions on policies and how they are implemented.

In considering cultural change, however, the term "interests" seems too narrow and restrictive. Farmers also have certain "interests" in the nature of public discourse and these include both interests in promoting desired policy frames in various forums and also more subtle ones that do not relate to any specific policy contests. As an example of the former, support for policies favoring farmers is likely to be greater in the US if the image of farmers in public discourse emphasizes the small, independent family farm rather than the agribusiness that is, in fact, the dominant "farmer" in the production and distribution of most crops.

But aside from this instrumental and strategic use of public discourse to further policy interests, some groups of farmers may have concerns about the degree of respect they receive in the broader culture – for example, about the disparaging depiction of white farmers in the South as "rednecks" or "hillbillies" in movies and in television entertainment forums. In short, the various constituencies whose interests are being mediated have *symbolic interests*, and furthering these is a central strategic goal for many movements.

For the mediation of symbolic interests, the other end of the mediation system is less clear than for policy interests. Authorities do not make binding decisions about language use nor does anyone else. Their decisions about usage may or may not be adopted by others, and often authorities may simply follow the lead of various parts of the mediation system – especially the dominant usage in mass media discourse. Hence, for symbolic interests, it is the outputs of the mass media system, rather than the decisions of authorities, that are being linked to constituencies via the mediation system.

We can recognize the dual role of the media discussed earlier in the following distinction: When the media are a site in which various carriers compete to further the symbolic interests of their constituencies, they are the output end of the mediation system. But when we examine how their structure and practices shape the outputs and how journalists articulate the symbolic interests of particular constituencies, we are considering them as part of the mediation system in their own right.

The mass media system also has autonomous interests of its own, beyond the varying organizational interests of the field of actors that comprise it. Again, these system-wide interests may or may not be engaged in a given issue but cannot be ignored. We should begin with the working assumption that the mass media system is not neutral among different types of carriers – for example, between members and challengers. Rather, the openness varies from issue to issue and must therefore be part of a movement's framing strategy.

MOVEMENT FRAMING STRATEGY

The Discursive Opportunity Structure

Social movements engaged in collective action aimed at influencing policy outcomes shape and adapt their strategies in light of the structure of opportunities and constraints that they face. What the political opportunity structure is to policy outcomes, the discursive opportunity structure is to the outcome of framing contests.[3]

Distinctions applied to the political opportunity structure more generally also apply to the discursive opportunity structure. Structure implies stability but it is useful to treat stability as a variable element, running from highly inert components that are more or less permanent features of the terrain to windows of opportunity that may be open only briefly (see Gamson and Meyer 1996). Agents who are attempting to shape the discourse can influence the more volatile components of opportunity. Some aspects of opportunity apply across many issues and are general features of the playing field, while others are issue specific or are relevant for only a limited range of framing contests. Finally, structure includes both cultural (e.g., values, belief systems, symbols) and institutional (e.g., electoral and party systems) elements. Ferree et al. (2002) organize the components of discursive opportunity under three rubrics: sociocultural, political, and mass media.

The discursive opportunity structure is the playing field in which framing contests occur. The mass media arena is not the flat, orderly and well-marked field in a soccer stadium but one full of hills and valleys, sinkholes, promontories, and impenetrable jungles. To make matters even more complicated, the contours of the playing field can change in an Alice-in-Wonderland fashion in the middle of the contest because of events that lie beyond the control of the players; and players can themselves sometimes change the contours through actions that create new discursive opportunities. This complex playing field provides advantages and disadvantages in an uneven way to the various contestants in framing contests.

The discussion here focuses on four especially difficult problems that social movements face in adapting their strategies and tactics to the discursive opportunity structure: (1) the depth of challenge dilemma, (2) the access dilemma, (3) the need for validation dilemma, and (4) the weak control dilemma.

The Depth of Challenge Dilemma

The ubiquitous nature of the mass media gallery creates strategic problems for social movements. First, it contains the imagined communities whose symbolic interests they claim to be promoting. But this target of mobilization is surrounded by two other targets that also need to be part of a successful framing strategy.

One significant part of the gallery are the bystanders who, though not currently engaged or part of the primary target constituency, can become potential allies if they adopt preferred movement frames. A successful framing strategy may increase what Klandermans and Oegema (1987) call the movement's *mobilization potential* by creating sympathy, support, and goodwill that may convert into useful, practical resources of various sorts.

Another part of the gallery consists of actual and potential adversaries and rivals. What is an effective framing strategy with one's constituency, and perhaps even with many bystanders, may leave one open and vulnerable to counterattack and discrediting. When a group uses the mass media to rally its target constituency, it cannot keep its messages from the rest of the gallery.

A full-fledged framing strategy for the mass media, then, should try to reach three separate goals: (1) Increase the readiness to act collectively on the part of one's primary constituencies; (2) increase mobilization potential among bystanders who are possible supporters; and (3) neutralize and discredit the framing efforts of adversaries and rivals, keeping their potential supporters passive. Since they are all part of the mass media gallery, every framing effort must perforce try to reach all three goals simultaneously, often a formidable task.

Herein lies the *depth of challenge* dilemma that most movements face, a dilemma that often animates internal arguments among different movement actors. Some movement actors challenge deeply held, taken-for-granted assumptions of the dominant frame. The danger in doing so is marginalization and dismissal as irrelevant – thereby making the frame invisible and effectively silencing its carriers. Other movement actors leave problematic and vulnerable assumptions unchallenged, taking on the dominant frame only on narrow grounds. The danger here that is by accepting the assumptions underlying the dominant frame, one is effectively reinforcing them and allowing them to constrain the terms of the discourse.

Take, for example, the Central American solidarity movement of the 1980s. The official frame in support of US military aid to El Salvador and Honduras and sponsorship of the contra war against the Sandinista government in Nicaragua was a Cold War frame. The US, in this frame, was facing a concerted Soviet challenge in the heart of the US sphere of influence. The Sandinista regime was depicted as a Soviet-Cuban proxy in the larger Cold War game and US policy should be directed at defeating this broader challenge.

Some actors in the movement challenging US Central American policy offered an alternative framing that challenged Cold War assumptions. In this counterframe, the governments of El Salvador and Honduras were depicted as brutal military dictatorships, kept in power by the US government, contingent on their willingness to serve as US client states in the Cold War game. The Sandinista government was depicted as the outgrowth of an indigenous nationalist movement that overthrew a brutal and unpopular US-supported military regime, accepting help in its battle to survive wherever it could find it. Those actors who offered such a frame were vulnerable to red-baiting attacks and to being disregarded by mainstream media for not being a serious player (see Croteau and Hoynes 1994).

Other actors opposed US Central American policy without challenging Cold War assumptions. The official depiction of the Sandinista government was tacitly accepted while challenging the depiction of the contras as "freedom fighters." US military support for El Salvador was opposed on the basis of the undemocratic nature of the regime and its sorry human rights record. But with the Cold War frame intact, each battle over a specific appropriation had to be fought within the confines of a larger framing in which the basic issue was about the most effective way of meeting the larger Soviet challenge in Central America.

There is no formula or right answer to the depth of challenge dilemma. An effective movement strategy must do its best to avoid both horns – to find a way to challenge fundamental aspects of the dominant frame while still being taken seriously as a player by the mass media.

The Access Dilemma

A second set of dilemmas flow from mass media norms and practices.

Some of these practices are double-edged, offering opportunities as well as obstacles. The practices concern the rules journalists use for granting *standing*.

"Standing" means having a voice in the media. The concept comes from legal discourse where it refers to the right of a person or group to challenge in a judicial forum the conduct of another. Rather than a matter of clear definition, legal standing is a battleground. By analogy, media standing is also contested terrain. In news accounts, it refers to gaining the status of a media source whose comments are directly or indirectly quoted.

Standing is not the same as being covered or mentioned in the news. A movement actor may be in the news in the sense that its actions are described or criticized without it having any opportunity to provide interpretation and meaning to the events in which it is involved. Standing refers to a group being treated as an agent, not merely as an object being discussed by others.

From the standpoint of most journalists, the granting of standing is anything but arbitrary. Sources are selected, in this view, because they speak for serious players in any policy domain: Individuals or groups who have enough political power to make a difference in what happens. Most journalists would insist that their choice of sources has nothing to do with whether they personally like or dislike or agree or disagree with them.

Having standing in certain media forums, however, also creates power. Being visible and quoted defines for other journalists and a broader public who really matters. Many journalists recognize that their choices also enhance or diminish the power of those to whom they offer or deny standing. Gaining standing, then, is both a strategic goal in its own right for a movement and provides it with a platform for increasing the prominence of its preferred frames.

Most reporting is the product of ongoing news routines. Standing is not granted *de novo* for each new article but flows from these routines. Certain sources have routine standing on a given set of issues or, in the case of leading government officials, across the board. When reporters are given continuing assignments or beats, it is rare for them to be assigned to cover a social movement. Hence, it is rare for them to develop routine relationships with movement sources. Movement actors must not only compete with officials and spokespersons for political parties, corporations, and other heads of large organizations, but they must struggle to gain any standing at all.

The tactics they use to gain entry can create problems for conveying their messages once they have gained standing. As Gamson and Wolfsfeld (1993: 121–2) put it:

> Members of the club enter the media forum through the front door when they choose, they are treated with respect, and they are given the benefit of the doubt. Challengers must contend with other would-be claimants for attention at the back door, finding some gimmick or act of disorder to force their way in. But when they do so, they enter

defined as upstarts and the framing of the groups may obscure any message it carries. Those who dress up in costume to be admitted to the media's party will not be allowed to change before being photographed.

Movements can solve this dilemma in part through an intentional or unintentional division of labor among actors. When this occurs, those who engage in actions designed to gain standing do not themselves attempt to be the main carriers of the issue frame. For this, they defer to partners who do not carry the baggage of deviance but can articulate a shared preferred frame. In the case of nuclear power, for example, the most common spokesperson for the antinuclear movement in the United States was the Union of Concerned Scientists (UCS). The actions of anti-nuclear demonstrators and site occupiers across the country, created standing for other movement actors. When demonstrators were arrested at Seabrook, phones rang at UCS.

Internal rivalries between movement actors can undermine such convenient divisions of labor. Those whose actions create standing for other actors may find that their preferred frame is poorly represented by those who become the media-designated spokespersons. They may attack and attempt to undercut their rivals within the movement. This internal movement contest can easily become the media's story, thereby distracting attention or blurring the preferred issue frame. A division of labor is likely to work only if there is a common frame and a willingness to subordinate who gets credit for being the messenger.

The Need for Validation Dilemma

When demonstrators chant "The whole world is watching," it means that they matter, that they are making history. The media spotlight validates their importance. Conversely, a demonstration with no media coverage at all is a nonevent, unlikely to have any positive influence either on mobilizing followers or influencing the target. No news is bad news.

There is a danger that mere coverage becomes an end in itself rather than a means to gaining standing and greater prominence for one's preferred frame. Since the commercial media emphasize entertainment values relative to journalistic values, media strategies may try to satisfy these entertainment needs. Gitlin (1980: 153) describes this effect for the New Left movement in the United States in the 1960s: "The all-permeating spectacular culture insisted that the movement be identified through its celebrities; naturally it attracted personalities who enjoyed performance, who knew how to flaunt some symbolic attribute, who spoke quotably." The result was the creation of leaders who rose to glory as spokespersons without accountabil-ity to a movement base.

To avoid the media's awarding of celebrity status, some movement participants rejected the idea of having any movement spokespersons. Sales (1973: 235) describes how Paul Booth, as national secretary of Students for a Democratic Society, was attacked for making statements to the media on behalf of the organization. One member suggested he should have referred reporters to local chapters, who would tell them what was going in their particular area. Such a strategy simply compounds the dilemma, since, by failing to provide its own spokespersons, it is inviting the media to designate who will speak for the movement.

Some movements have found ways of making the media interest in celebrities and spectacle work for them as part of a larger media strategy. Celebrities can be used to draw the attention of journalists. They can then share the spotlight with accountable movement leaders or act themselves as articulators of preferred frames. Shortly after 1960s celebrity-activist Abby Hoffman surfaced from the underground – where he had been active in the environmental movement under the name Barry Freed – he agreed to speak at a rally for an environmental group in Bucks County, Pennsylvania. His celebrity brought a strong media turnout, complete with television cameras. But instead of performing or giving a speech, he simply introduced a spokesperson for the local group and disappeared from camera and interview range. Having lost the celebrity story that drew them, the assembled media had to settle for covering the message from local movement leaders.

Guerilla theater and other uses of drama can embody preferred frames in the symbolism they use – in effect *performing* the frame through costume, props, puppets, and other visual images. United for a Fair Economy has been especially creative in this regard, using its affiliated street theater group Class Act to dramatize the increasing gap between rich and poor in the US since the 1970s. Its satirical group Billionaires for Bush stalked the electoral campaign appearances in 2000 of the presidential candidate, enacting their preferred frame in the guise of especially enthusiastic supporters. Such tactics use spectacle to achieve broader strategic goals.

The Weak Control Dilemma

Bureaucratic organizations can do strategic planning and, although there are always some implementation problems, they have employees who are expected to carry out the plan. If these paid agents fail or are unwilling to do so, they are subject to sanctions and replacement by other agents. Movements, for the most part, rely heavily on those whose commitments are normative and voluntary. If some participants are unwilling to follow directions, one can try to persuade them but there is little to prevent them from trying their own version of what they think will be more effective.

The weak control that movements have over followers and adherents undercuts the ability of a movement to have any coherent or coordinated framing strategy at all. The organizers of a demonstration may decide on certain approved slogans that embody the preferred frame, but a group that disagrees may choose other slogans and use tactics that contradict and undermine the chosen strategy.

The global justice movement that acquired media visibility with the Seattle demonstrations against the WTO in November, 1999, illustrates the problem. Within the field of actors, there is a faction (the "Black bloc") that uses vandalism against particular corporate targets as a protest tactic. Their actions have been repudiated and criticized as counterproductive by more mainstream actors in the movement, who, while making heavy use of political theater, see vandalism as undermining their chosen strategy of nonviolent direct action. They also fear that the vandalism tactic will make the movement as a whole more vulnerable to repressive social control.

Ultimately, movements lack an authority structure for enforcing *any* strategic plan and must rely on persuading others to adopt it in the name of unity and achieving their larger shared objectives, even if they are unconvinced by the plans to achieve them.

Movements that attempt to engage in strategic planning must do so with the understanding that their plans always run the risk of being undermined by dissidents who go their own way, or perhaps even by *agents provocateurs* (see Marx 1974).

MEDIA AS A SOURCE OF POWER

Advocacy groups that are relatively poor in conventional resources and limited in access to decision-makers can still influence policy by various means. One means of influence – *persuasion* – involves changing the orientation of decision-makers, essentially through reframing the issue. The other two means – *inducements* and *constraints* – involve changing the situation in which the target of influence operates. Constraints involve the addition of new disadvantages or the threat to do so; inducements are the addition of new advantages or the promise to do so.[4] Tactics using each of these means depend on using the mass media as a central instrument to make it work. We consider below a central tactic of advocacy groups using each of the three means of influence.

Tapping Cultural Resonances

Persuasion works through increasing the prominence of one's preferred frame in the mass media. By changing the way various publics and bystanders understand an issue, those who are opposed or neutral may redefine how their interests and values are affected. This can increase the flow of resources to those organizations and networks that make claims on their behalf and perhaps even influence decision-makers directly.

Worldviews and values, and the more specific norms, ways of thinking, practices, resources, and rules that support them, provide a pool of potential legitimizing devices for particular ways of framing an issue. "In all public arenas," Hilgartner and Bosk (1988: 71) argue, "social problems that can be related to deep mythic themes or broad cultural preoccupations have a higher probability of competing successfully." Some frames have a natural advantage because their ideas and language resonate with the broader culture.

Resonances increase the appeal of a frame by making it appear natural and familiar. "Those who respond to the larger cultural theme will find it easier to respond to a frame with the same sonorities," writes Gamson (1992: 135). Snow and Benford (1988: 210) make a similar point in discussing the concept of "narrative fidelity." Some frames, they write, "resonate with cultural narrations, that is, with stories, myths, and folk tales that are part and parcel of one's cultural heritage."

Frames on specific issues gain power by resonating with cultural themes and counterthemes. Sometimes there is competition for the power of particular symbols. Gamson and Modigliani (1987) describe the contest over the symbolism of equal opportunity in affirmative action discourse. Originally, this potent symbol was owned by sponsors of a Remedial Action frame. "Equal opportunity" was the banner of the civil rights movement and affirmative action was presented as a program to achieve it.

In the 1970s, a neoconservative advocacy network opposing affirmative action programs sponsored a Reverse Discrimination frame that made its own claim to the equal opportunity theme. Affirmative action programs were framed as racially based, preferred treatment programs. Some people, they argued, were being given less than equal opportunity because of their race. With both sides waving the banner of equal opportunity, its resonances were effectively neutralized. The Reverse Discrimination framing strategy by opponents of affirmative action deprived the supporters of affirmative action of one of their most potent symbols.

Cultural resonances, then, are a source of potential influence but do not flow automatically from the content of a frame. They must be activated in a contested process by sponsors. Movements often find that dominant frames have a firm hold on themes and they must rely on their resonances with counterthemes. There is no theme without a countertheme. Themes are safe, conventional, and normative; one can invoke them as pieties on ceremonial occasions with the assumption of general social approval, albeit some private cynicism. Counterthemes are adversarial, contentious, oppositional. Themes and counterthemes are coupled so that whenever one is invoked, the other is always present in latent form, ready to be activated with the proper cue.

To illustrate, on issues with a strong technological dimension, the theme of Progress through Technology is paired with the countertheme Harmony with Nature (see Gamson 1992). The countertheme is skeptical of, or even hostile to, technology. The countertheme has as deep cultural roots as the theme. To quote Emerson, "Things are in the saddle and ride mankind." Much of popular culture reflects the countertheme: Chaplin's *Modern Times*, Huxley's *Brave New World*, Kubrick's *2001*, and countless other films and books about mad scientists and technology gone wild, out of control, a Frankenstein's monster turning on its creator.

On the issue of nuclear power, supporters made heavy use of the Progress through Technology theme. But opponents were able to neutralize its power by emphasizing the countertheme of a technology that was out of control. During the 1970s, frames emphasizing the countertheme became more prominent in media discourse than those emphasizing the theme. This example highlights the battle over cultural resonances as a contested *process* in which framing strategy focuses on activating one's potential and neutralizing the resonances of the dominant frame being challenged.

Marketing a Constituency

Advocacy groups with lots of money can offer inducements directly to the relevant decision-makers, without using the mass media; indeed, publicity may undercut their effectiveness. Few social movements have the surplus resources necessary to compete in the system of legalized inducements by which US elections are financed, although they may gain some leverage from bundling the contributions of their constituents. They are rarely in the position of being able to offer much of a quid pro quo in an exchange relationship with decision-makers.

A number of movements, however, find themselves faced with a tempting opportunity of an exchange relationship with commercial enterprises, and particularly with commercial media companies who make their profit by selling an audience to advertisers. By marketing their constituency, they can offer something of considerable value in exchange for the money they need to fight the good fight. Marketing one's constituency involves exchanging its buying power for much-needed funding.

"It takes money...to construct any alternative to the society predicated on the community of money. This is the essential truth that social movements have to confront; otherwise, it confronts and destroys them," warns David Harvey (1989: 185). One can see how the executive director of a struggling nonprofit (spending inordinate amounts of time on fundraising that could be used to push their campaigns and programs forward) might see a win-win situation in some corporate partnerships.

Chasin (2000: 201) describes a "particularly sophisticated" form of corporate sponsorship: cause-related marketing. In these marketing campaigns, "corporations publicize a partnership with a discrete non-profit cause related to a very specific goal." This is especially tempting when the short-term goal is a concrete step toward achieving the group's long-term goals. In such circumstances, it is easy to convince oneself that the sponsor's interests and values do not and will not influence what actions or frames the organization will pursue.

Stauber and Rampton (1995: 68) give us a glimpse of how such partnerships are viewed from the corporate side, quoting an industry source, *O'Dwyer's PR Services Report*. O'Dwyer advises his subscribers how to "test the waters" when entering into a relationship with an environmental group. "Help them raise money. Offer to sit on their board of directors. That can open up a good symbiotic relationship." He also suggests financing a conference on a topic of mutual interest and funding a specific publication for the group. "The company gets substantial input into the product because the publication has its name on it."

Purism in such matters is a luxury only available to those in the ivory tower. The problems with this marketing tactic, however, go deeper than the hidden strings and compromises attached to the bargain. Specific problems arise from the more subtle ways in which it (1) mainstreams the movement in both its collective identity and politics, and (2) reduces accountability to the movement. At an even more fundamental level, it transforms the constituents from collective agents into individual consumers.

Mainstreaming

Chasin explores how the marketing of the gay and lesbian constituency has affected the movement's advocacy organizations. Most of the mechanisms for funding these organizations, she argues, "in one way or another, promote a liberal political agenda; a white, male, middle-class leadership; and the growth of large national organizations. By contrast the same mechanisms effectively diminish the resources available for smaller, local, grassroots, and/or politically off-center organizations" (Chasin 2000: 26).

Movements typically struggle with issues of collective identity. Much internal movement discussion concerns who "we" are. The marketing tactic has a heavy impact on this collective identity process. Dávila (2001: 15) examines the phenomenon of "Hispanic marketing," noting the business preference for the officially census-sanctioned category of "Hispanic" over "Latino," a term of self-designation more connected to social struggles and activism.

"The commercial representation of US Latinos," she suggests (Dávila 2001: 20) "has sustained particular hierarchies of representation that are indicative of wider dynamics affecting Latino cultural politics." Instead of the racial diversity actually present in the Latino community, the Hispanic advertising world presents "blanquitos who look polished," where blanquito stands "not only for a person's whiteness but also for speech, demeanor, and ability to keep ethnicity 'in its place'" (2001: 141). Ricky Martin is who "we" are.

Similarly, in gay and lesbian marketing, the advertising image is one of assimilated, normal looking and sounding, gay men and lesbians with money. Chasin (2000) calls it an unintended disenfranchisement, not only on the basis of race and class, but also of bisexuals and transgendered folks who are included in the broader political community. It strengthens the voice of those whose message is "we are just like you except for our sexual preference" and silences those whose message is "We're here. We're queer. Deal with it."

Accountability

Media organizations targeting a particular constituency are less and less accountable to it. The gay media world has seen the emergence of PlanetOut Partners, "a single dominant company, merging with and acquiring media properties old and new, controlled by a single board of directors, owned and answering to a handful of corporate and individual investors, aiming to be ground zero of the gay and lesbian cultural and informational system" (Gamson 2003).

Those high up in the company believe in a community mission but they "resist any notion that they are *accountable* to 'the community,' which is neither their primary network nor their primary concern" (Gamson 2003). Gamson quotes executive vice-president Susan Schuman, former managing director of the Human Rights Campaign: "People want to treat us as a nonprofit organization representing the community and we're not. We're a business and we provide goods and services" (Gamson 2003). The consequence is that activists, especially in less mainstream movement organizations, are out of the loop.

Consumers Versus Citizens

Ultimately, marketing one's constituency reduces citizens to consumers, a mass of individuals who exercise consumer sovereignty by pulling a product off a shelf, pulling a voting lever, or writing a check. This follows, Chasin (2000: 182) argues, "from the belief that acts of private consumption can serve as political participation. Such a form of participation may be inevitable, but it narrows the range of possibilities for social change." Dávila (2001: 138) describes her skepticism about the increasing visibility of Latinas: "Yes, Latinas are undoubtedly gaining visibility... but only as a market, never as a people, and 'markets' are vulnerable; they must be docile; they cannot afford to scare capital away."

Creating a sense of collective agency is central to the idea of collective action frames. It can hardly be encouraged by treating potential participants as objects to be manipulated. The marketing tactic leads one to look for emotional hot buttons that will trigger the desired response. The problem with the hot button approach is not that it doesn't work but that it directly undermines the goal of increasing people's sense of agency. It provides a good reason to extend the pervasive cynicism about those who run the society to include those who supposedly challenge their domination.

Boycotts

Boycotts employ the marketing tactic as a constraint, rather than an inducement. They are typically employed or threatened to limit the presentation of content that the movement finds offensive or against the interests of its constituency. While the means of influence being used is different, the logic of treating a constitutency as a market remains the same – and with it all of the attendant problems of mainstreaming, accountability, and treating potential agents of collective action as, above all, consumers.

Embarrassing the Target

Some movement targets deal directly with the public, either as elected or accountable public officials or as corporations that sell goods and services directly to the public. They have a brand to protect. Favorable publicity or embarrassing publicity that reaches the whole mass media gallery translates into good or bad will among bystanders. This in turn may lead to gained or lost votes or sales.

The potential to embarrass may be the single most important tactic available to a movement that is poor in resources and routine access. Typically, CEOs or other high-ranking corporate officers are personally targeted, with the boundaries of their private lives transgressed, to hold them accountable for the policies and public actions of their organizations.

Saul Alinsky pioneered the technique. In his Rules for Radicals (1972: 130–1) he pinpoints the problem for organizers:

> In a complex urban society, it becomes increasingly difficult to single out who is to blame for any particular evil. There is a constant, and somewhat legitimate, passing of the buck.... One big problem is a constant shifting of responsibility from one jurisdiction to another – individuals and bureaus one after another disclaim responsibility for particular conditions, attributing the authority for any change to some other force.

More recent examples include the mischievous filmmaker Michael Moore (*Roger and Me*) who has targeted General Motors and Nike executives to publicize their respective roles in plant closures in Flint, Michigan, and sweatshops in Southeast Asia. A recent film, *Bread and Roses*, dramatizes the use of the embarrassment tactic in an effort to organize janitors in California.

This tactic is heavily media dependent. If the mass media fail to cover the attempt to embarrass the target, then no embarrassment is produced. One can, à la Michael Moore, bring one's own camera crew along to film a scene but it helps to have a bona fide journalist along to legitimize its use. The effectiveness and newsworthiness of the action involves the breaking of unspoken rules about invading private space – the deliberate blurring of public and private life. It is embarrassing to have pickets outside of one's suburban home carrying signs labeling one a slumlord or a sweatshop owner, drawing the attention of the media with its camera crews and journalists asking embarrassing questions and interviewing the neighbors. For movements in democracies, it is relatively low risk and low cost but likely to reach a point of diminishing return with overuse.

Conclusion

Bystanders, public opinion and the media are central to understanding the scope of conflict and efforts to change the balance of power from the current set of participants. A mass media-directed framing strategy provides the central mechanism for affecting scope. A full-fledged symbolic strategy aims not only at increasing the mobilization potential among bystanders but also at increasing the readiness of one's primary constituency to act collectively and thereby neutralizing the framing efforts of one's adversaries. The ultimate goals of a media framing strategy are to increase or maintain media standing and increase the prominence of one's preferred frames.

Given these multiple goals, movement framing strategy must cope with difficult dilemmas. Should movement actors challenge embedded and heavily defended beliefs in dominant frames or tacitly accept these while challenging on narrower grounds? One path leads to marginalization; the other to a continuing battle on unfavorable terms.

Lack of routine access produces a second dilemma. Access can be had by staging media spectacles or other tactics that draw the spotlight, but this may blur or distract from one's preferred frames. A third dilemma involves allowing media coverage to become an end in itself, regardless of whether it increases standing or frame prominence. Finally, weak control over one's followers and adherents can make the whole effort of strategic planning inoperable because some of one's allies undermine it by going their own way.

Despite these obstacles and a mass media playing field tilted against them, challengers to dominant frames often are able to use the media to generate power. Some do this by using frames that resonate with broader themes and counterthemes while neutralizing the resonances of their competitors. Some use their marketing power to gain resources for their cause and the threat of withdrawing it (i.e., boycotts) as a constraint on their adversaries. Finally, some movements use publicity that embarrasses their adversaries as a means of changing their policies.

All of these tactics are centrally dependent on an effective mass media strategy. That there are many dilemmas and no easy formulas for solving them only makes strategic planning more important. And the importance is not diminished by the fact that the best-laid plans may be subverted by participants who don't accept them or by *agents provocateurs* who set about to subvert them.

Notes

The author is indebted to Charlotte Ryan and the participants in the Media Research and Action Project (MRAP) at Boston College, to Joshua Gamson, and to the editors of this volume for many helpful comments and suggestions on earlier drafts of this chapter.

1   The model outlined here is elaborated more fully in Ferree et al. (2002).
2   Burstein uses the term "interest organizations" to include both interest groups and social movement organizations, arguing that "it is impossible to distinguish among them in terms of the characteristics usually used to define them" (1999: 8). He reasons that organizations vary on such dimensions as degree of institutionalization, state of mobilization, institutional versus extra-institutional strategies of collective action, ease of access, etc. Since

these are continua, there is no clear boundary and, hence, treating social movement organizations as a separate category is not meaningful. At one point he asserts categorically that "there is no theoretical justification for distinguishing between social movement organizations and interest groups" (19). This seems to me something of a non sequitur. Some organizations are at a stable peak in mobilization and others are in a low and rising state or are declining; some organizations use only institutional means of action, while others use only extra-institutional means or a mix of both; some organizations have easy and regular access to policymakers while others are completely excluded or included only with great effort and risk. To ignore these differences because there is no clear demarcation makes little sense when their theoretical relevance has been so well established. The criteria allow us to form ideal types against which to judge actual organizations. However, it is useful to have a general category that includes the full range of members and challengers who are attempting to influence the policy process. "Advocacy groups" seems preferable to "interest organizations" as a term since many such organizations are more concerned about values than interests in any material sense and some are more like networks than formal organizations.

3 The concept has been around longer than the term. With the cultural turn in social movement theory, many scholars have suggested or implied that there are "cultural" or "symbolic" opportunities and constraints. A number of scholars (Koopmans and Statham 2000; Ferree et al. 2002) have recently begun using "discursive opportunity structure" as the term of choice.

4 This discussion of means of influence is elaborated in Gamson (1968).

References

Alinsky, Saul (1972) *Rules for Radicals*. New York: Random House.

Anderson, Benedict (1991) *Imagined Communities*. New York: Verso.

Blumer, Herbert (1948) Public Opinion and Public Opinion Polling. *American Sociological Review*, 13, 542–54.

Burstein, Paul (1999) Social Movements and Public Policy. In Marco Giugni, Doug McAdam, and Charles Tilly (eds.), *How Social Movements Matter*. Minneapolis: University of Minnesota Press, 3–21.

Chasin, Alexandra (2000) *Selling Out: The Gay and Lesbian Movement Goes to Market*. New York: Palgrave.

Croteau, David, and William Hoynes (1994) *By Invitation Only: How the Media Limit Political Debate*. Monroe, ME: Common Courage.

Dávila, Arlene (2001) *Latinos, Inc.: The Marketing and Making of a People*. Berkeley: University of California Press.

Ferree, Myra Marx, William A. Gamson, Jürgen Gerhards, and Dieter Rucht (2002) *Shaping Abortion Discourse: Democracy and the Public Sphere in Germany and the United States*. New York: Cambridge University Press.

Gamson, Joshua (2003) Gay Media, Inc.: Media structures, the New Gay Conglomerates and Collective Sexual Identities. In Martha McCaughey and Michael D. Ayers (eds.), *Cyberactivism: Online Activism in Theory and Practice*. New York: Routledge.

Gamson, William A. (1968) *Power and Discontent*. Homewood, IL: Dorsey.

——(1992) *Talking Politics*. New York: Cambridge University Press.

Gamson, William A., and David Meyer (1996) Framing Political Opportunity. In Doug McAdam, John McCarthy, and Mayer Zald (eds.), *Current Perspectives on Social Movements*. New York: Cambridge University Press, 275–90.

Gamson, William A., and Andre Modigliani (1987) The Changing Culture of Affirmative Action. In Richard D. Braungart (ed.), *Research in Political Sociology*. Vol. 3. Greenwich, CT: JAI, 137–77.

——(1989) Media Discourse and Public Opinion on Nuclear Power: A Constructionist Approach. *American Journal of Sociology*, 95, 1–37.

Gamson, William A., and Gadi Wolfsfeld (1993) Movements and Media as Interacting Systems. *Annals of the American Academy of Political and Social Science*, 528, 114–25.

Gitlin, Todd (1980) *The Whole World Is Watching*. Berkeley: University of California Press.

Harvey, David (1989) *The Urban Experience*. Baltimore: Johns Hopkins University Press.

Hilgartner, Stephen, and Charles L. Bosk (1988) The Rise and Fall of Social Problems: A Public Arenas Model. *American Journal of Sociology*, 94 (1), 53–78.

Klandermans, Bert, and Dirk Oegema (1987) Potentials, Networks, Motivations, and Barriers: Steps toward Participation in Social Movements. *American Sociological Review*, 52, 519–31.

Koopmans, Ruud, and Paul Statham (2000) Migration and Ethnic Relations as a Field of Political Contention: An Opportunity Structure Approach. In Ruud Koopmans and Paul Statham (eds.), *Challenging Immigration and Ethnic Relations Politics: Comparative European Perspectives*. Oxford: Oxford University Press, 13–56.

Marx, Gary T. (1974) Thoughts on a Neglected Category of Social Movement Participant: The *Agent Provocateur* and the Informant. *American Journal of Sociology*, 80, 402–42.

Neidhardt, Friedhelm (1996) Offentliche Diskussion und politische Entscheidung: Der deutsche Abtreibungskonflikt 1970–1994. In Wolfgang van den Daele and Friedhelm Neidhardt (eds.), *Kommunikation und Entscheidung*. Berlin: Sigma, 53–82.

Rucht, Dieter (1995) Parties, Associations, and Movements as Systems of Political Interest Mediation. In J. Thesing and W. Hofmeister (eds.), *Political Parties in Democracy*. Sankt Augustin: Konrad-Adenauer-Stiftung, 103–25.

Ryan, Charlotte (1991) *Prime Time Activism*. Boston: South End.

Sales, Kirkpatrick (1973) *SDS*. New York: Random House.

Schattschneider, E. E. (1960) *The Semi-Sovereign People*. New York: Holt, Rinehart, & Winston.

Schmitter, Philippe C. (1977) Modes of Interest Mediation and Models of Societal Change in Western Europe. *Comparative Political Studies*, 10.

Snow, David, and Robert D. Benford (1988) Ideology, Frame Resonance, and Participant Mobilization. In Bert Klandermans, Hanspeter Kriesi, and Sidney Tarrow (eds.), *From Structure to Action: Comparing Social Movement Research across Cultures*. Greenwich, CT: JAI, 197–217.

——(1992) Master Frames and Cycles of Protest. In Aldon Morris and Carol Mueller (eds.), *Frontiers in Social Movement Theory*. New Haven: Yale University Press, 133–55.

Stauber, John, and Sheldon Rampton (1995) *Toxic Sludge Is Good for you: Lies, Damn Lies, and the Public Relations Industry*. Monroe, ME: Common Courage.

Tuchman, Gaye (1978) *Making News*. New York: Free Press.

Turner, Ralph H., and Lewis M. Killian (1987) *Collective Behavior*. 3rd ed. Englewood Cliffs, NJ: Prentice-Hall.

Wilson, Timothy, and Sara D. Hodges (1991) Attitudes as Temporary Constructions. In A. Tesser and L. Martin (eds.), *The Construction of Social Judgment*. Hillsdale, NJ: Erlbaum.

Zaller, John R. (1992) *The Nature and Origins of Mass Opinion*. New York: Cambridge University Press.

12

"Get up, Stand up": Tactical Repertoires of Social Movements

Verta Taylor and Nella Van Dyke

Tactical Repertoires, Action, and Innovation

One Tuesday afternoon in November 2002, a group of 50 women of all ages from West Marin, California, lay down naked in a light rain to spell out "PEACE" with their bodies. A photographer captured the scene from the top of a ladder, and the resulting image sped around the world via the internet. This innovative protest, organized just the day before by a group that took the name "Unreasonable Women," was intended to shock the Bush administration into paying attention to the grass-roots opposition to the threat of a war against Iraq and to express solidarity with the women, children, and men of Iraq, thousands of whom had already died as a result of US bombing and sanctions. Some of the protestors had not been involved in a demonstration since the 1960s; others had long been pondering a way to make women's voices heard (or, in this case, bodies seen). Disrobing, they decided, would outdo the normally "predictable, mechanized, boring" protests of today (Pogash 2003). If this might seem at first glance a very Californian protest, what is especially interesting is that the women adopted the idea from a Nigerian women's demonstration against corporate exploitation the preceding summer. In that protest, 600 mostly elderly women occupied the facilities of Chevron Texaco, took 1,000 oil workers hostage, and threatened to cast shame on corporate executives by stripping in front of them. Using a tribal shaming ritual, they demanded health care, education, and jobs for their families. The Nigerian women succeeded, while the West Marin women's protest, which did catch the attention of the national media as planned and spread rapidly over the internet, met with mixed responses. Some focused on the women's nudity, calling it variously lewd, erotic, or an affront to Islam. Others clamored for a copy of the photograph and expressed solidarity with the women's goals and tactics. Certainly people paid attention.

"*Get Up, Stand Up.*" Words and Music by Bob Marley and Peter Tosh. 1973.

Protest – or the collective use of unconventional methods of political participation to try to persuade or coerce authorities to support a challenging group's aims – is perhaps the fundamental feature that distinguishes social movements from routine political actors. Protest can encompass a wide variety of actions, ranging from conventional strategies of political persuasion such as lobbying, voting, and petitioning; confrontational tactics such as marches, strikes, and demonstrations that disrupt the day-to-day life of a community; violent acts that inflict material and economic damage and loss of life; and cultural forms of political expression such as rituals, spectacles, music, art, poetry, film, literature, and cultural practices of everyday life. Protest is occasionally used by institutionalized political actors such as political parties and interest groups, and social movements frequently adopt the same means of political expression used by political parties and interest groups. If there is a single element that distinguishes social movements from other political actors, however, it is the strategic use of novel, dramatic, unorthodox. and noninstitutionalized forms of political expression to try to shape public opinion and put pressure on those in positions of authority. Social movements, as McAdam and Snow (1997: 326) so aptly describe them, "eschew politics through proper" channels, often because their participants lack access to political institutions and other conventional means of influence or because they feel that their voices are not being heard.

The tactics of protest used by social movements are so integral to popular views of social movements that sometimes a movement is remembered more for its tactics than for its goals (Wilson 1973). For example, the second wave of the US women's movement is still often denounced as a group of "bra-burners" based on a single demonstration in 1968 against the Miss America pageant. In this case, no bras were actually burned. Rather, women staged several guerilla theater actions, including crowning a sheep Miss America, mopping the boardwalk holding pots and pans, and throwing objects of female oppression – high-heeled shoes, girdles, bras, curlers, and tweezers – into a "freedom trash can." The goal was to protest the male chauvinism, commercialization of beauty, racism, and oppression of women symbolized by the pageant, but the participants' rejection of dominant symbols of beauty is what caught the media's attention.

From a scholarly standpoint, the study of protest events is a defining feature of the resource mobilization and political process traditions that have dominated the study of social movements over the past several decades (Tilly 1978; McAdam 1982; Tarrow 1989; Gamson 1990). Tilly (1999) has gone so far as to argue that social movements are best understood not as groups or organizations but as clusters of contentious interactive performances or protest events. So central are protest tactics to the scholarly research on social movements that measurement of variations in the number and timing of protest events such as strikes, riots, violent incidents, and other contentious gatherings has emerged as a major means of assessing the state of mobilization of social movements (Tilly 1978; McAdam 1982; Jenkins and Eckert 1986; Tarrow 1988; Olzak 1989; Kriesi et al. 1995; McCarthy et al. 1996). Given this development, it is remarkable that social movement scholarship lacks any agreed-upon definition that can be used to identify a tactic of protest. In this chapter we draw on relevant research in order to develop a clearer conceptual and empirical understanding of social movement tactics.

Our discussion takes up three questions. First, how have scholars interested in social movements conceptualized social movement tactics? We build on and extend existing conceptualizations to offer a theoretical definition that specifies three features common to all tactical repertoires: contestation, intentionality, and collective identity. Second, what factors influence a social movement's selection of tactics? Theorists of contentious politics suggest that macrohistorical factors as well as internal movement processes influence tactical repertoires and innovations. The third question we address is what kinds of tactics are more likely to achieve successful outcomes? Here we distinguish between political and cultural outcomes, noting that the limited research that has examined this question suggests that certain tactical repertoires might be better suited to one type of outcome rather than the other.

REPERTOIRES OF CONTENTION AND TACTICAL REPERTOIRES

The specific tactics of public protest used by social movement activists take a myriad of forms. Rochon (1998: 1) describes the following tactics used by the New Left in the late 1960s:

> petitioning, rock throwing, canvassing, letter writing, vigils, sit-ins, freedom rides, lobbying, arson, draft resistance, assault, hair growing, nonviolent civil disobedience, operating a free store, rioting, confrontations with cops, consciousness raising, screaming obscenities, singing, hurling shit, marching, raising a clenched fist, bodily assault, tax refusal, guerilla theater, campaigning, looting, sniping, living theater, rallies, smoking pot, destroying draft records, blowing up ROTC buildings, court trials, murder, immolation, strikes, and writing various manifestoes or platforms.

This list is by no means exhaustive of the novel and innovative tactics used by social movement actors in the United States, as the scholarly research on protest tactics reveals.

Scholars interested in social movement tactics have paid considerable attention to the nonviolent direct action tactics used by the US civil rights movement, such as organized boycotts of public transportation and white owned businesses, student sit-ins at white lunch counters, voter registration drives, freedom schools, and mass demonstrations (Morris 1984; McAdam 1986). The literature on labor movements points to the widespread use of sit-down strikes, labor walkouts, and secondary boycotts as weapons of political coercion (Fantasia 1988; Fonow 1998; Lichtenstein 2002). Young (2002) examines the confessional forms of protest that swept the US in the 1830s in which thousands of men and women gathered to bear witness against the sins of drinking and slavery and to demand that religious and civil institutions take heed, revealing that movements have often combined personalized strategies with social change oriented strategies. Researchers of the women's movement have added greatly to our understanding of the way movements combine tactics oriented to political and personal change by demonstrating how feminist movements meld mass demonstrations and other forms of direct action with consciousness-raising, self-help, and embodied forms of resistance to critique and transgress dominant conceptions of heterosexualized femininity (Staggenborg 1991; Taylor and Rupp 1993; Whittier 1995; Taylor 1996). Social movement scholars studying right-wing movements have chronicled their use of coercive and violent forms of protest.

Anti-abortion activists, organized hate groups, and patriot and militia groups have bombed abortion clinics, black churches, and federal buildings, and have lynched and assassinated perceived enemies in an attempt to influence public opinion and public policy (Soule 1992; Blee 2002; Van Dyke and Soule 2002). Contemporary right-wing movements also use tactics that challenge state intrusion into the life worlds of individuals. Snow and Clarke-Miller (2003) reveal that one right-wing group used "constitutional confrontations" (e.g., the violation of gun laws) and "registration refusals or boycotts" (e.g., the destruction of driver's licenses) to resist the identification-tracking power of the government.

Recently, scholars have turned their attention to the cultural forms of political expression adopted by social movements, for example the use of street perform-ances, cross-dressing, gender transgression, and alternative underground magazines ("zines") by the modern gay and lesbian movement (Gamson 1995; Bernstein 1997; D'Emilio 1998; Rupp and Taylor 2003). Modern feminist movements, too, have relied extensively on discursive forms of political protest to increase women's status and political power, focusing on institutional targets such as the medical system (Taylor 1996), the Catholic Church and the US military (Katzenstein 1998), as well as state level policies and legislation, such as those curtailing women's reproductive rights (Staggenborg 1991; Ferree et al. 2002). Cultural repertoires are as central to right-wing as left-wing movements. Public spectacles and rituals such as cross-burnings have served as major tactics of the Ku Klux Klan, and contemporary organized hate movements, such as the skinheads and neo-Nazis, rely heavily upon racist music, literature, graffiti, and personalized political strategies including wearing swastikas, insignias, tattoos, shaven heads, Doc Martens, and combat fatigues to promote their racist ideas (Blee 2002). Faith-based social movements also rely heavily on public performances, such as parades, mass celebrations, public chanting, and prayer to spread the word and secure recruits (Snow 1979; Pattillo-McCoy 1998; Heath 2003). Social movement groups historically have incorporated new technologies into their tactical repertoires, whether newspaper, radio, televi-sion, film, magazines, or newsletters. The emergence of political activism on the Internet – referred to as "hactivism" (McCaughey and Ayers 2003) – has resulted in important tactical innovations such as strategic voting (Earl and Schussman 2002), hacking, online sit-ins, defacing Web pages, email floods, viruses and worms, and data theft or destruction (McCaughey and Ayers 2003; Costanza-Chock forthcoming).

These examples may suggest that protest possibilities are virtually unlimited. However, social movement researchers interested in understanding the factors that influence a movement's choice of particular tactics point out that tactics of protest are, to the contrary, fairly predictable, limited, and bounded by the repertoires that protestors have learned. Scholars use the term "repertoires of contention" (Tilly 1978, 1995; Traugott 1995; Tarrow 1998) to describe the distinctive constellations of tactics and strategies developed over time and used by protest groups to act collectively in order to make claims on individuals and groups. Like its theatrical counterpart, the term "repertoire" implies that the interactions between a movement and its antagonists can be understood as strategic performances or "established ways in which pairs of actors make and receive claims bearing on each other's interests" (Tilly 1995: 43). Tilly introduced the repertoires concept to identify important historical variations in forms of protest and to explain the rise of the national social movement as a form of claims-making used by subordinate groups in modern capitalist democratic societies (Tilly 1986; Tarrow 1998).

In addition to being *historically specific*, protest repertoires are *modular* in the sense that similar tactics may be borrowed by different groups of activists pursuing different targets without face-to-face interaction (Tarrow 1993). Activists pick up on and adapt the tactics used by other groups so that they do not have to "reinvent the wheel at each place and in each conflict" (McAdam and Rucht 1993: 58). As a result, *tactical innovations occur slowly*. Because of linkages between activist networks and movement organizations, the same protest tactics spread from one campaign to another (Meyer and Whittier 1994). Soule (1997) illustrates this process by showing how US students protesting the South African system of apartheid introduced shacks or makeshift structures, known as "shantytowns," to call attention to the oppressive living conditions of South Africans. Because the shanties were successful in gaining media attention, they were adopted by student activists on campuses across the United States. Repertoire transformations such as this do not come easily, and Beckwith (2000) introduces the idea of a "hinge in collective action" as a way of understanding significant changes in tactical repertoires.

Social movement scholars use the concept of repertoires of contention to refer to the recurrent, predictable, and fairly narrow "toolkit" of specific protest tactics used by a set of collective actors in a particular campaign (Taylor 1996; McAdam and Snow 1997; della Porta and Diani 1999; Mueller 1999; Beckwith 2000). The tactics or specific forms of collective claims-making used by social movements, as Mueller (1997) points out, are increasingly examined in terms of their place in a larger repertoire of collective action. In this chapter, we provide a more delimited concept of tactical repertoires to describe and understand the features and implications of particular forms of collective protest. We are interested in *tactical repertoires* as interactive episodes that link social movement actors to each other as well as to opponents and authorities for the intended purpose of challenging or resisting change in groups, organizations, or societies.

Types of Tactical Repertoires

Scholars interested in understanding why a challenging group chooses a particular form of protest have generally used two different criteria to distinguish the different types of tactics. Some writers classify social movements on the basis of fundamental differences in their tactics (Rucht 1988). Early formulations defined movements either as instrumental or expressive based on whether a group's actions and strategies were oriented toward social change or personal change (Gusfield 1963; Breines 1982; Jenkins 1983). More recently, this dichotomy of movement types is reflected in the work of scholars who differentiate between "strategy-oriented" and "identity-oriented" movements (Touraine 1981; Cohen 1985) or between movements that use instrumental, externally oriented tactics and movements engaged in what Bernstein (1997: 531) terms "identity deployment" that is internally oriented (Duyvendak and Giugni 1995). This dichotomous model reveals fundamental differences in the way new social movement theorists (Touraine 1981, 1985; Melucci 1989, 1996) and resource mobilization and political process theorists view contemporary forms of collective action. Reflecting this debate, Tilly (1995) excludes collective claims-making focused on affirmation of identity from his definition of repertoires of contention.

Numerous studies call into question the bifurcation of movement types by demonstrating that social movements combine both instrumental and expressive action (Steinberg 1995; Bernstein 1997; Goodwin and Jasper 1999; Buechler 2000). This work suggests that we should distinguish tactics on the basis of the type of interaction taking place between the movement and its target. Using this criterion, Turner and Killian (1987) identify four basic tactics: *persuasion*, which appeals to the values or self-interest of the target; *facilitation*, which assists the target group in acquiring knowledge or resources to support the movement, for example, through consciousness raising; *bargaining*, such as when a movement exchanges electoral and other kinds of cooperation with the target group for support of the movement; and *coercion*, which punishes the target group for failure to support the movement's goals. Recent formulations tend to differentiate between two modes of action: one category subsumes nonconfrontational or *insider tactics*, such as boycotts, dramaturgy, lawsuits, leafleting, letter-writing campaigns, lobbying, petitions, and press conferences. The second includes confrontational or *outsider tactics*, such as sit-ins, demonstrations, vigils, marches, strikes, motorcades, symbolic actions, boycotts of classes, blockades, and other illegal actions such as bombings (Soule et al. 1999; Van Dyke et al. 2001). Some scholars introduce violence as a third and separate category. For example, Tarrow (1998) differentiates three types of protest actions: *conventional*, *disruptive*, and *violent*, acknowledging that contentious politics frequently combines all three elements.

Protest Events as Tactical Repertoires

These classificatory schemes have produced important new advances in our understanding of how different tactical repertoires influence social movement outcomes, a topic that we take up in the last section. Much of the recent work on social movement tactics comes out of what is referred to as "protest event" research. This term refers to the content coding of newspaper accounts of collective action events pioneered by Tilly and his colleagues (Shorter and Tilly 1974; Tilly et al. 1975) that has since developed into a routine method for studying social movements (Jenkins and Perrow 1977; McAdam 1982; Olzak 1989, 1992; Tarrow 1989; Koopmans 1993; Duyvendak 1995; Kriesi et al. 1995; Andrews 1997; Mueller 1997; Soule et al. 1999; Van Dyke 2003a, 2003b). Our conception of collective action repertoires builds on but extends the event count method of studying collective action to overcome two problems with the way protest tactics have been studied by scholars who have used data on the timing and sequence of events to analyze social movements.

The first is that the formalized rules and conventions for coding information on collective events using records from newspapers are biased toward a standard set of mainly public protest forms – marches, demonstrations, boycotts, sit-ins, strikes, and attacks – that emerged in the nineteenth century (McCarthy et al. 1996; Mueller 1997; Oliver and Myers 1999). The unit of analysis is generally the collective action event, which is defined using three criteria: the event must be *collective*, involving more than one person; the actors must be making a *claim or expressing a grievance* either to change or preserve the system; and the event must be *public* (Tilly 1978;

McAdam and Su 2002). The criterion that the event be "public" results inevitably in the counting of "reported" events. In addition to the ideological biases inherent in using mainstream newspaper reports to identify protest (Mueller 1997), this research strategy vastly underestimates the incidence of protest. Newspaper event counts ignore the cultural and discursive tactics used by social movements, protest that takes place inside institutions (Katzenstein 1998; Kurtz 2002; Raeburn forthcoming), what James Scott calls "everyday forms of resistance" (1985), and other less publicly conspicuous tactics such as those used by identity-based struggles (Taylor and Whittier 1992; Gamson 1995), terrorist groups, and right-wing movements (Blee 2002; Snow and Clarke-Miller 2003).

Second, McAdam et al. (2001: 5) suggest that we limit the definition of contentious politics to claims-making that involves the "government as a claimant, target, or mediator." Research using the event count method does not restrict the counting of events to collective action that targets the government (Kriesi et al. 1995; Van Dyke et al. 2002). However, media sensitivity to these types of protest actions and the theoretical preference of some theorists of contentious politics for studying political movements more narrowly limits our understanding of the significant role played by social movements and other forms of contention in shaping social institutions and cultural codes (Zald 2000). We adopt the view of scholars who define the institutional locus of social movements more broadly as targeting systems of authority in institutional structures, such as religion, medicine, the military, education, the mass media, as well as in the political arena (see in particular Snow 2002, as well as Epstein 1996; Taylor 1996; Chaves 1997; Katzenstein 1998; Goodwin and Jasper 1999; Zald 2000; Jenness and Grattet 2001; Young 2002). This more general conceptualization of authorities as targets of protest requires a broader definition of what constitutes a protest tactic.

Our conception of tactical repertoires adapts the three criteria used in protest event research to define a collective action event in ways that will encompass a wider range of contentious actions. We propose that the essential features of all protest events are contestation, intentionality, and the construction of collective identity. Our definition complements but improves upon protest event research by offering a definition that is amenable to the closer engagement and in-depth examination of the making and receiving of claims possible through the use of qualitative and historical methods.

A Definition of Tactical Repertoires: Contestation, Intentionality, and Collective Identity

To return to the episode of protest with which we began this chapter, the West Marin women's embodiment of "PEACE" was staged to oppose President Bush's threat of war with Iraq and to express solidarity with the people of Iraq. This protest action, which subsequently spread to other communities around the United States, embodies what we consider to be the three main features of all tactical repertoires: contestation, intentionality, and collective identity.

First, tactical repertoires are sites of *contestation* in which bodies, symbols, identities, practices, and discourses are used to pursue or prevent changes in institutionalized power relations. A major tactic used by the US antiwar movement in the Vietnam War era was to register potential draftees for a deferment or exemption from the draft using "conscientious objection," traditionally a category for members of certain religions, as a rationale (McAdam and Su 2002). Snow and his colleagues (1986) contend that social movements typically mobilize by drawing upon identities, practices, beliefs, and symbols that are already meaningful from the standpoint of dominant ideologies and frameworks and placing them in another framework so that they are, as Goffman (1974: 43–4) put it, "seen by the participants to be something quite else." The West Marin women's peace protest also illustrates the way a movement's oppositional tactics exhibit this process of cultural borrowing.

There is general consensus that the *raison d'être* of social movements is to pursue or prevent change, and tactical repertoires in all their variants are interactions that embody contestation between groups with different and competing interests. If tactical repertoires involve strategic interactions between a set of challengers and their external targets, however, the West Marin women's peace protest also illustrates that protest is rarely enacted as face-to-face interaction. Rather, in modern information-driven societies, protest operates to influence decision-makers primarily through indirect channels, such as the mass media and the Internet (Lipsky 1968; Melucci 1996). As a result, social movements frequently use dramatic and unorthodox tactics to draw the attention of the mass media in hope of winning the sympathies of more powerful groups able to exert influence on institutionalized decision-makers (Gitlin 1980; Gamson and Modigliani 1989).

We view *intentionality* as the second component of collective action repertoires. We share the view of resource mobilization and political process theorists that strategic decision-making is one of the essential aspects of the social psychology of collective claims-making (Jenkins 1983; Gamson 1992; Klandermans 1997). Even participants in seemingly spontaneous uprisings such as urban riots may be acting strategically with conscious intention to produce or prevent change. One indication of the strategic nature of protests is what della Porta and Diani (1999: 174) call "the logic of numbers." Even when groups are small, they try, through marches, strikes, petitions, letter-writing campaigns, and referenda, to convey numerical strength. Rupp and Taylor (1987) describe, for example, how prior to the resurgence of a mass US women's movement in the mid-1960s, feminists in the National Woman's Party formed state branches of only one or two members and then printed up stationary to use in letter-writing campaigns to press for the Equal Rights Amendment. Similarly, male leaders in organized hate movements bestow on themselves "ostentatious titles" such as Grand Dragon, Imperial Wizard, and Commander to give the impression of a large hierarchical organization when, in reality, these men typically enjoy the allegiance of only a handful of committed group members (Blee 2002: 134).

Cultural performances are also intentionally staged as part of the larger repertoire of contention of social movements. Stockdill (2002) describes the Divas from Viva, three gay Latino men from Southern California, who use teatro – short political skits historically performed in Latino/a communities – to raise people's consciousness about AIDS and mobilize individual and collective action. By examining the intentions of the performers, Rupp and Taylor (2003) find that drag shows in gay commercial establishments can serve as both entertainment and serious political protest by calling attention to the role of cultural markers and practices in constructing gender and sexual difference. Whittier (2001: 238) recounts how the child sexual abuse survivors' movement organizes public events, such as media campaigns, demonstrations, theatrical performances and art exhibits where participants deploy oppositional emotions of trauma (grief, fear, shame, and helpless anger) and resistance (pride, happiness, love, safety, confidence, and righteous anger) as a strategy to bring about social change. Religious movements such as the Buddhist Nichiren Shoshu of America sponsor large parades and public chanting sessions in order to spread the word and secure recruits (Snow 1979). As these examples illustrate, in examining whether any form of collective action serves as part of a tactical repertoire, we should not make a priori judgments about what constitutes a protest event. Rather, we should be asking what are the intentions of the actors and whether a particular set of actors are consciously and strategically promoting or resisting change in dominant relations of power.

Acting collectively requires the development of solidarity and an oppositional consciousness that allows a challenging group to identify common injustices, to oppose those injustices, and to define a shared interest in opposing the dominant group or resisting the system of authority responsible for those injustices. Protest actions are one of the means by which challenging groups develop an oppositional consciousness and *collective identity* (Melucci 1989; Gamson 1992; Taylor and Whittier 1992; Jasper 1997; Klandermans and de Weerd 2000; Poletta and Jasper 2001; Snow 2001). In his analysis of three distinct cases of grass-roots labor action in the United States, Fantasia (1988) illuminates the way strikes express a culture of solidarity embodying a set of values and practices that makes it possible for workers to resist and challenge the repression of corporate anti-unionism. Blee (2002) finds that participating in cross burnings, terrorist harassment, and political rallies, as well as adopting cultural markers such as tattoos and shaved heads, is central to women's development of a racist identity in male-dominated hate groups. Recent studies of activism on the Internet suggest that one of the main functions of online tactical repertoires is to create solidarity and collective identity (McCaughey and Ayers 2003).

To consider the construction of collective identity as one of the defining features of a tactical repertoire means recognizing that a movement's particular forms of protest are not only directed to *external* targets, but they also have an *internal* movement-building dimension (della Porta and Diani 1999). One of the major tasks of any movement is to create opportunities and incentives for participation in protest that outweigh the costs by facilitating the creation of new forms of solidarity. A movement's repertoire of tactics typically supplies a range of levels of participation, varying from low risk and low effort actions such as donating money, writing a letter, signing a petition, participating in a peaceful demonstration, or constructing a quilt to what McAdam (1986) has termed "high risk" and high effort actions such as bombing a building, registering Southern Black voters, sitting in a tree to defend a National Forest from loggers, acting as a suicide bomber, or engaging in self-burning to protest government injustice (Kim 2002). Defining collective identity construction as a feature of all public displays of protest accentuates the collective and the interactional elements of political contention. A social movement's tactical repertoires serve as sites for negotiating the relationship and the boundaries between a set of political actors and those explicitly opposed to them.

We offer this conceptual definition of collective action repertoires as engaged in contestation, intentionality, and collective identity work because it will allow us to analyze the common features and processes of the myriad of strategies used by social movements – whether cultural or more traditionally political, embodied or discursive, emotional or rational, disruptive or legitimate, violent or nonviolent.

FACTORS THAT INFLUENCE TACTICAL REPERTOIRES: PROTEST ACTION AND INNOVATION

Theorists of contentious politics (Tilly 1978, 1986, 2002; Tarrow 1989, 1998; Traugott 1995; McAdam et al. 1996, 2001) have used the concept of repertoires of contention as part of a larger framework for analyzing differences in types of contention in particular historical periods and identifying the factors that lead to new and innovative forms of collective action. The basic tenet of this approach is that repertoires of contention are created out of a group's prior experience of making and receiving claims, and that specific forms of collective action are determined by the degree and type of political opportunity, the form of organization adopted by subordinate groups, and a subordinate group's cultural framing of its grievances. In this section, we take up research by social movement scholars interested in understanding how these various factors influence a movement's selection of particular tactics. We proceed by discussing, first, the *external* sociopolitical factors that shape tactical repertoires; second, we examine the *internal* movement processes that influence a challenging group's selection of tactics.

External Macrohistorical Conditions

Discussions of the external factors that influence the tactical repertoires of contemporary social movements have sought to explain an apparent shift in forms of political contention in Western nations by linking these changes to macrohistorical factors in the larger sociopolitical environment. We can think of this work as focusing on three processes: modernization, the rise of postindustrial society, and the development of cycles of collective action.

Tilly (1978, 1986, 1995) contends that the forms of protest that we have come to associate with modern social movements are part of a larger repertoire of contention that emerged in the nineteenth century with the rise of the nation-state and centralized decision-making, the development of capitalist markets, and the emergence of modern forms of communication. Examining contentious repertoires in the United States, Britain, and France between the eighteenth and nineteenth centuries, Tilly provides empirical evidence of fundamental changes in the forms of protest used by subordinated groups. Older or "traditional" repertoires included actions such as grain seizures, field invasions, barricades, and the use of music, irreverent costumes, and other performances that ridiculed local authorities. What all of these political performances had in common is that they were *particular*, in that participants were drawn from a limited geographic area, protest addressed local actors or elites, the tactics were specific to the grievances, collective action repertoires drew on existing social relations, and collective actors often took advantage of official occasions, public celebrations, and other routine activities to convey grievances. For instance, Traugott's (1995) examination of the use of the barricade in popular protest in the French Revolution illustrates how forms of protest originated out of the disputes of everyday life, since the erection of barricades was a routinely used method of neighborhood protection in sixteenth-century Paris.

By the mid-nineteen century, contentious politics had changed drastically. The geographic scale of claims-making increased, with national authorities serving as the target of an ever increasing number of claims and special interest groups emerging for the express purpose of challenging authorities. As political contention became national in focus, the tactical repertoires shifted to actions such as strikes, marches, electoral rallies, public meetings, petitions, insurrections, and public demonstrations. What we recognize today as the social movement that brought together ordinary citizens in new and relatively stable networks to act on behalf of their own interests in the national arena had emerged as a distinctively modern repertoire of contention. The social movement provides a repertoire of contention that can be adapted by a variety of groups in different localities to stage protests around different grievances (Tilly 1995). Recently, Tilly and his collaborators (McAdam et al. 2001) have extended their model beyond Western societies and nineteenth-century social movement repertoires to analyze twentieth-century rebellions, revolutions, nationalism, and contentious democratization outside of the Western world. Tilly and his colleagues identify three macrohistorical factors that are important in shaping modern tactical repertoires: *the nature of political authority, the geographical reach of political authorities*, and *technology*. With respect to the role of political authority, Fraser (1997) argues that a new repertoire of contention that she terms "recognition struggles," emerged in response to the misrecognition of identities (e.g., multiracial, sexual, racial, gender, etc.) and status subordination (e.g., of women, gays and lesbians, ethnic and racial minorities) encoded in formal law, government policies, administrative codes, and professional practices, as well as in social practices in civil society. These recognition struggles challenge structures of authority by combining claims for respect and recognition with claims for social justice and redistribution. The role of discourse and identity in the tactical repertoires of groups challenging dominant cultural codes is linked, then, to the nature of political authority in modern societies (Ferree et al. 2002).

Secondly, the geographic reach of political power has also continued to expand, with the last half of the twentieth century marked by increasing globalization and the development of international governing structures such as the World Trade Organization, the European Union, the International Monetary Fund, the United Nations, and international legal bodies such as the International Court for Human Rights and the European Court of Justice. These developments have been accompanied by the expansion of transnational protest repertoires that combine direct action, radical democracy, street performance, and the Internet (see chapter 14 in this volume, as well as Imig and Tarrow 1999).

Technology and the rise of new forms of mass communication is the third macrohistorical factor that influences protest repertoires. During the eighteenth century, the development of the print media enabled the rapid diffusion of information and facilitated the formation of geographically dispersed networks of collective actors (Goody 1968; Gouldner 1975; Chartier 1991; Tarrow 1998). Social movement researchers are beginning to explore how the Internet as a recent technological innovation is emerging as an important mobilizing tool, as well as a means and target of protest action (Carty 2002; Earl and Shussman 2002; McCaughey and Ayers 2003; Costanza-Chock forthcoming). Groups such as the Zapatistas in Mexico are now able to mobilize rapid international support to apply pressure on targeted regimes and authorities (Garrido and Halavais 2003). At the same time, social movements are increasingly using the Internet as a means of communicating grievances. In 2000, protestors effectively sabotaged the campaign website of George W. Bush by gaining control of the campaign's web domain name and posting an anti-Bush site in its place.

A competing paradigm to the political process and contentious politics approach, sometimes grouped under the rubric of new social movement theory (Habermas 1981, 1984; Touraine 1981; Cohen 1985; Offe 1985; Melucci 1989, 1996) also emphasizes the role of macrohistorical factors in explaining tactical repertoires and innovations. New social movement theorists see fundamental changes in the repertoires of contemporary social movements as resulting from the shift from an industrial to a postindustrial economy. Postindustrial society has brought new forms of social control resulting from the intervention of capitalism and the state into private areas of life including the self and the body (Habermas 1987; Fraser 1995, 1997); increased structural differentiation, especially the autonomy of cultural institutions from political and economic institutions (Cohen 1985; Melucci 1995); and a transition from materialist to postmaterialist values (Inglehart 1981). These macrohistorical changes, they argue, have resulted in a new form of mainly middle-class activism that is distinct from earlier forms of class-based protest centered in the working class. The core thesis is that new social movements, such as the women's, peace, gay and lesbian, environmental, animal rights, disability rights, mental health, antiglobalization movements, and even the New Christian Right and contemporary hate movements, are unique in that they are less concerned with economic redistribution and policy changes than with issues of the quality of life, personal growth and autonomy, and identity and self-affirmation. Some scholars classify these struggles as "life politics" (Giddens 1991; Taylor and Whittier 1992; Taylor 1996; Bernstein 1997; Young 2002). The evidence for the hypothesis that contemporary movements are a product of the postindustrial society remains questionable (Tarrow 1988; Pichardo 1997). In addition, some studies have taken issue with the notion of "newness" by arguing that these cultural and identity-based repertoires of protest appeared much earlier than the limited historical period identified by new social movement theorists (Brand 1990; Calhoun 1993; Young 2002).

To explain how repertoires evolve, broaden, and get refined, Tarrow (1989, 1993, 1998) advances the notion of "protest cycles," which turns our attention to another way that the larger sociopolitical environment influences collective action repertoires (see chapter 2 in this volume). According to this view, protest tends to follow a recurrent cycle in which collective mobilizations increase and decrease in frequency, intensity, and formation. The notion that protest occurs in cycles or waves allows us to recognize how the ebb and flow that characterizes protest determines the tactics adopted by social movements. In the early stages of a cycle, for example, the use of disruptive tactics predominates. McAdam (1983) shows how civil rights activists developed a series of major tactical innovations in the early 1960s that were highly successful because of their capacity for disruption and the effect they had on stimulating subsequent protest. As a protest wave develops, interaction between protestors and authorities stimulates the use of increasingly disruptive tactics. For example, the 1963 protest campaign of the civil rights movement in Birmingham, which provoked violence by whites and the intervention of the federal government, deployed multiple strategies of disruption including an economic boycott, sit-ins, and mass demonstrations (Morris 1993).

Several studies demonstrate that over the course of a protest cycle, a process of both increasing radicalization and institutionalization occurs (Tarrow 1989; Koopmans 1993; Kriesi et al. 1995). Over time as they are repeated, disruptive tactics lose their shock value so that a demonstration that might have at first frightened authorities loses some of its original punch, taking on a ritualized quality. Frustration with the limited effectiveness of routine tactics, as well as competition for members and media attention between different movement organizations, leads to the increasing use of disruptive tactics and even violence over the course of a protest cycle. For example, at the height of the suffrage campaign, when the United States entered World War I and the mainstream suffrage organization supported the war effort, the National Woman's Party, in contrast, launched a picket of the White House to criticize President Wilson's hypocrisy in fighting to make the world safe for democracy (Rupp and Taylor 1987). As McCammon et al. (2001) have argued, picketing and other public demonstrations were bold and innovative tactics that defied gender prescriptions and the ideology of separate spheres governing the lives of middle- and upper-class women. Cooperation and coalition formation between social movement organizations can also influence tactical repertoires (Meyer and Whittier 1994). Jenness and Broad (1997) find, for example, that tactics emanating from the women's movement's struggles to combat violence were critical in shaping the repertoires of gay and lesbian antiviolence campaigns that emerged in the United States in the late 1980s and into the 1990s.

In assessing the repertoires of contention model, the postindustrial society thesis, and the cycles of protest argument, scholars of social movements suggest that there is more empirical support for the repertoires of contention and the cycles of protest argument than for new social movement theory's hypothesis that protests focused principally on personal and social change are unique to the postindustrial age (see Mueller 1999 on the repertoires of contention model and Pichardo 1997 on new social movement theory). However, Young (2002) has recently presented evidence that challenges both the repertoires of contention and the new social movement models. He demonstrates that the temperance and antislavery movements, which were the first national social movements to emerge in the United States in the 1830s, were not the result of interactions with national states, as Tilly (1978, 1995) advanced, but rather with religious institutions. Further, these campaigns engaged in a form of life politics by pursuing goals that combined personal and social transformation in a period that precedes the time frame when new social movement theorists see a historical rupture in Western patterns of protest.

Internal Movement Processes

A significant amount of research on protest tactics has explored how the characteristics of collective actors influence the particular tactics used in political contention. This work focuses on three internal features that influence a social movement's tactical choices: the *level of organization* among collective actors; the *cultural frames* of meaning used to justify collective action; and the *structural power of the participants*. Research on how internal movement processes relate to tactical repertoires has been dominated by a debate over whether the level of organization among a set of collective actors is related to the use of confrontational and disruptive tactics rather than more conventional tactics. On one side are scholars who assert that organizations are necessary for collective action and that, under certain circumstances, organizations facilitate disruptive protest. On the other side are those who argue that the involvement of organizations inevitably leads to the use of conventional pressure group tactics and the institutionalization of a movement. Piven and Cloward's (1979) research on workers' movements, the Southern civil rights movement, and the welfare rights movement in the United States suggests that the increased involvement of organizations in "poor people's movements" led to a channeling of energy away from mass defiance and the use of disruptive tactics into organization building and institutionalized forms of political action. These findings support Michels' (1962) argument that the leaders of large political organizations inevitably come to value their own interests and the security of their positions over the goals and interests of the organization's membership.

Several studies report empirical support for Piven and Cloward's thesis. In her research on abortion rights organizations in the United States, Staggenborg (1988) finds that the processes of professionalization and institutionalization among abortion rights organizations, such as the National Abortion Rights Action League and the National Organization for Women, resulted in greater reliance on conventional pressure group tactics, such as lobbying and political campaign work. Kriesi et al. (1995) and Koopmans (1993) examine the relationship between the use of different types of tactics and the development of movement organizations over the course of an entire protest wave. They find that the involvement of mainstream movement organizations has the effect of institutionalizing movement actors and decreasing the use of confrontational forms of protest.

While the debate over the way organization affects the mobilization of disruption has continued for nearly three decades, recent research suggests that the link between organization and strategy is more complex than a simple one-to-one relationship (Cress and Snow 2000). One set of studies (Rucht 1999; Van Dyke et al. 2001) agrees with Piven and Cloward, finding evidence that formal organizations are more likely than informal groups to use conventional tactics of protest. However, they find variation among movement organizations, and that an organization's goals and constituency influence tactical choices (Van Dyke et al. 2001). Student organizations and groups explicitly focused on social change rather than personal transformation frequently engage in disruptive collective action. In their study of the homeless movement in eight US cities, Cress and Snow (1996, 2000) find that sustained and effective protest by impoverished constituencies requires strong organizations capable of mobilizing resources and representing the voice of homeless people in policy discussions. However, organization-building does not always result in moderation; rather, about half of the local homeless organizations in their sample combined disruptive tactics with political mediation in the struggle to protect homeless people from discriminatory practices.

Others focus on the ways that particular decentralized and participatory democratic organizations give rise to the use of confrontational direct action tactics. Examining the radical wing of the US abortion rights movement, Staggenborg (1988) shows how decentralized and informalized organizational structures encouraged individuals' input and collective decision-making and generated innovative and confrontational actions. For example, activists attracted media and public attention by staging "funeral marches" to protest the deaths of women killed by back-alley abortionists and made media appearances carrying blown-up photographs of women lying lifeless on motel room floors after illegal abortions. Jasper (1997) traces the dramatic turn in the antinuclear movement beginning in 1975 toward site occupations, encampments, the sabotage of buildings and equipment, and large rallies at nuclear power plants to the affinity group structure of groups such as the Clamshell Alliance that opposed the Seabrook plant in New Hampshire. Polletta (2002) explains the way egalitarian organizational forms contribute to the use of innovative and disruptive tactics by using "deliberative" talk that reinforces the group's solidarity and commitment to direct action.

The tactical repertoires used by a set of collective actors are also influenced by social movement culture (Darnovsky et al. 1995). Frequently activists adopt strategies and tactics not simply because they have been shown to be effective, but because they resonate with the beliefs, ideas, and *cultural frames of meaning* people use to make sense of their situation and to legitimate collective action (Snow and Benford 1988; Gamson 1992; Morris and Mueller 1992; Taylor and Whittier 1995; Jasper 1997; Benford and Snow 2000). In her study of the Irish women's movement for reproductive rights, Taylor (1998) shows how tactical decisions and innovations are linked to a challenging group's framing of their grievances. To attract attention to the illegality of abortion in Ireland, the movement launched an abortion boat decorated with flags reading "Our Right to Choose" to carry women on the journey to England that thousands of women had taken to secure a legal abortion.

A considerable body of scholarship demonstrates the significance of gender ideology and symbolism in a movement's selection of tactics (Naples 1992; Robnett 1996; Taylor 1996; Gamson 1997; Taylor and Whittier 1998, 1999; Klatch 1999; Blee 2002). Radical feminists, for example, adopted collectivist organizational forms and emotional expressiveness as part of a larger repertoire of direct action, justifying these strategies on the basis of fundamental differences between women and men and a rejection of masculinist styles (Taylor and Rupp 1993; Whittier 1995; Polletta 2002). The language of gender difference and power is also pervasive in women's self-help movements in medicine and mental health and serves as a rationale for the use of tactics such as consciousness-raising, empowerment, and woman-to-woman support in addition to traditional pressure group tactics geared toward social and institutional change (Taylor 1996; Taylor and Van Willigen 1996; Whittier 2001). Gender specific ideology and appeals also serve as a basis for the use of violent tactics by nationalist movements such as the Palestine Liberation Organization (Nagel 1998), male-dominated left-wing movements such as the Black Panthers (Brown 1992), and right-wing movements such as Christian Identity (Blee 2002).

In devising tactical repertoires, collective actors also draw on established cultural schemas that structure social life, according to Sewell (1996: 842), by providing the "meanings, motivations, and recipes for social action." Social movements appropriate conventional symbols and modify them in ways that allow them to take on new meaning. This is one means by which collective actors create new and innovative forms of protest. Clemens (1993) argues that alternative models of organization should themselves be understood as distinctive "organizational repertoires" of contention shaped by participants' collective identities and established cultural schemas.

The American women's movement of the late nineteenth and early twentieth century, for example, drew on a culturally available model of organization – the women's club – and used it as a template to legitimate lobbying as one of the few models of political influence available to women. Taylor (1996) contends that in the US self-help is a distinctive organizational repertoire, and Polletta treats participatory democratic organizational forms in similar terms. Van Dyke (2003a) also emphasizes the importance of beliefs and ideas to a group's organizational repertoires by demonstrating that multi-issue movement organizations formed around broad ideological principles are more likely to participate in coalition formation and collaborative forms of protest.

Collective actors choose among tactical repertoires, then, not simply on the basis of strategic decision-making. Rather, activists choose options that conform to their ideological visions, are congruent with their collective identities, and embody the cultural schemas that provide meanings, motives, and templates for action. In her study of the Direct Action Network (DAN), which emerged out of the 1999 Seattle World Trade Organization demonstrations, Polletta (2002) finds that the group, which blatantly rejected "masculinist" styles, embraced emotional expressiveness, and drew on the language of the self, nevertheless sought to dissociate itself from tactics – for example, vibes watching and group hugs – that they associated with "touchy-feely" Californian styles of protest.

The *structural power of protestors* also influence a group's tactical repertoires (Schwartz 1976; Tilly 1978, 1986; Gamson 1989; Taylor 1996). Participants' relative position in the larger social structure, their sense of justice and "rights," their prior experiences with collective action, their everyday routines and cultures of subordination, and their relative position in social movement organizations all figure into the specific tactics used in a struggle. Several studies find that actors who occupy subordinate positions economically and socially and who lack access to institutionalized political and economic power are more likely to engage in disruptive protest, as are constituencies that have less to lose when faced with the costs or negative consequences of protest (Piven and Cloward 1979; Scott 1985; Van Dyke et al. 2001). Piven and Cloward (1979) find that in the US, the unemployed are most likely to participate in riots and actions that present a threat to public order because they lack institutional alternatives for expressing their grievances. Although the relationship between constituency and protest tactics is more complex with respect to racial and ethnic groups in the United States, a recent study by Van Dyke et al. (2001) finds that, on the whole, members of less powerful ethnic and racial groups are also more likely to use confrontational tactics. Students are also more likely to participate in disruptive protest because they are available for "high risk" forms of protest, have fewer countervailing ties to the constraints of adulthood, and have limited access to politics through other means (McCarthy and Zald 1973; Snow et al. 1980; McAdam 1988; White 1989; Soule 1997; Zhao 1998; Van Dyke et al. 2001).

A movement's tactical repertoires can also be fed by participants' cultural resources, skills, and sense of justice and "rights" (Tilly 1978; Mansbridge and Morris 2001). Bourdieu (1990) defines the cultural meanings, scripts, and know-how that motivate action as "habitus," and Swidler (1986) thinks of these templates as a cultural "tool kit" from which movements borrow. Crossley (2002) analyzes the way habitus influenced the specific repertoires used by different branches of

the psychiatric survivors' movement in its campaign to ban electroconvulsive ther-
apy in the UK. Activists who had a "radical habitus" and possessed "protest capital"
as a result of prior participation in radical forms of community activism were cynical
with respect to the use of tactics relying on persuasion. They therefore used public
demonstrations and performances – for example, peaceful candlelight vigils that did
not play into the public's notion of their status as "mental patients" – to command
public sympathy and support. By contrast, the habitus of activists in another branch
of the movement was based on an establishment orientation and participants'
competence in academic fields, psychiatry, and the media. These activists embraced
a different set of tactics, using their skills and cultural capital to pursue campaigns in
their respective fields, for example through publishing books and articles and
making films and documentaries about the mental health system and psychiatric
survivors.

This example illustrates, as other studies have found, that prior participation in
protest has a significant impact on the subsequent tactics adopted by protest participants (Evans 1979; Van Dyke 1998). However, as Morris and Braine (2001)
contend, opposition is also present in the daily routines and cultural practices that
promote submission among marginalized groups such as African Americans (Morris
1984; Patillo-McCoy 1998; Harris 2001), women (Bosco 2001), people with
disabilities (Groch 2001), Mexican Americans (Rodriguez 2001), and gays and
lesbians (Stockdill 2001). Patillo-McCoy (1998) analyzes the way participation in
the black church (specifically prayer, song, and call-and-response interaction) shows
up in the tactics used in collective political organizing in the civil rights movement.
Social movement networks, organizations, and communities are also sites of inequality and subordination. A growing body of research documents the way gender,
racial and ethnic, class, and sexual inequalities within a movement constrain
the tactical choices available to participants (McAdam 1992; Robnett 1996;
Klatch 1999). When they participate in male-dominated movements, women are
often restricted to protest forms that draw on traditionally feminine roles, such
as clerical work, reproducing and socializing children, kitchen duty, and other
forms of caretaking (Fonow 1998; Blee 2002). Scholars have also examined how
activists' attempts to reduce discrimination on the basis of race, ethnicity, gender,
and class within social movements produce tactical innovations. The AIDS and the
modern gay and lesbian movements have initiated strategies such as the formation
of separate caucuses for women and people of color, constructive dialogue, empowerment initiatives, and spotlighting marginalized groups' indigenous culture as a
means of undermining inequalities (Gamson 1995; Adam et al. 1999; Stockdill
2001).

How Tactical Repertoires Shape Movement Outcomes

The tactics used by oppositional groups have implications for movement success.
Political protest can have a multitude of consequences, both intended and unintended (see chapter 20 in this volume). Our discussion follows Staggenborg's (1995)
categorization of three types of movement outcomes: political and policy outcomes,
mobilization outcomes, and cultural outcomes. Because most research on the effectiveness of different tactics focuses on political or policy changes, we present only

limited evidence of how tactics relate to mobilization and cultural outcomes (but see chapters 22 and 23 in this volume).

Researchers who have been interested in whether and how social movements produce social and political change identify several characteristics of protest related to effectiveness: *novelty, militancy, variety, size,* and *cultural resonance.* Because movements are indirect forms of political persuasion, their impact depends in large measure on getting the message to the intended audience. The use of innovative, militant, and a variety of tactics, along with the mobilization of large numbers, increases the likelihood that the media will cover protest events (Snyder and Kelly 1977; Molotch 1979; McCarthy et al. 1996; Oliver and Myers 1999). Public displays of protest that tap into prevailing beliefs about democratic practices also increase the likelihood of positive outcomes (Kriesi and Wisler 1999).

Novelty

Protestors typically choose from a fairly limited tactical repertoire when deciding on forms of collective action. Although social movements are more likely to select tactics with which they are familiar (Tarrow 1998), empirical studies suggest that innovative tactics are more successful in achieving policy changes. For example, McAdam (1983) demonstrates that tactical innovations on the part of civil rights activists such as sit-ins and freedom rides were effective because they caught authorities off guard. McCammon et al. (2001) provide evidence that suffrage activists were successful in winning the vote in part as a result of the invention of the suffrage parade. The parades put hundreds of women on the streets both to publicize the demand for the vote and resist the ideology of separate spheres that precluded women from participating in political life. Kurtz (2002) attributes the success of the Columbia clerical strike of 1991–2 to a series of protests intended to embarrass Columbia's board of directors, such as demonstrating at posh department stores and office buildings in Manhattan, disrupting elegant fundraising events for alumni, and eventually threatening to disrupt commencement. Movements that are primarily engaged in symbolic struggles for the recognition of different identities can also transform social policy by posing symbolic challenges, as Taylor (Taylor 1996; Taylor and Van Willigen 1996) shows with respect to women's self-help movements in medicine and mental health.

The use of novel tactics, such as music, theater, art, poetry, speak-outs, and street performances, are among the ways social movements gain a hearing to serve as vehicles of cultural change. Two recent studies suggest that cultural performances that meld politics with entertainment may have a range of cultural effects, including transformation in beliefs, identities, and ideologies. In their analysis of the pattern of diffusion of the textile strikes of 1929 to 1934 that swept the US South, Roscigno and Danaher (2001) find that protest music played on local radio stations served as an important tactical repertoire to articulate grievances and construct solidarity among workers. Rupp and Taylor (2003), using focus group data with heterosexual and gay audiences of drag shows, reveal that drag performances, which are part of the larger repertoire of the gay and lesbian movement, transform heterosexual audience members' beliefs about gender and sexuality.

Militancy

Tactical innovations are often successful because of the uncertainty and disruption they bring about. Several early studies led to the conclusion that groups using disruptive tactics are more successful than those that opt for quieter institutional options (Tilly et al. 1975; Piven and Cloward 1979; Steedly and Foley 1979; Mirowsky and Ross 1981; McAdam 1983). Examining the tactics of 53 challenging groups in the US, Gamson (1990) finds that activists that used violence were more likely to achieve both policy gains and access to political power. Soule et al. (1999) report the opposite finding: in the US, when women's groups have used conventional *insider* tactics, they have been more likely to win Congressional support than when they engaged in disruptive outsider tactics. Recent research suggests, however, that the picture is more complicated. Cress and Snow (2000) find that political context influences whether disruptive tactics have successful outcomes in local campaigns to improve the conditions of homeless people. Disruptive tactics, such as blockades, sit-ins, housing takeovers, and unauthorized encampments, were more effective in cities where the movement had allies in city councils and the city had not previously been responsive to the interests of the homeless population. However, in cities that had shown signs of prior support for the homeless issue, nondisruptive tactics such as petitions, rallies, and demonstrations yielded more success. Based on their analysis of the impact of antiwar protest on Congressional support for US involvement in the Vietnam War, McAdam and Su (2002) argue that, for movements to be effective in the US, they must combine threat and disruption with a commitment to democratic politics of persuasion.

The use of militant tactics also has consequences for mobilization. Participation in high-risk collective action increases activists' commitment to social movement networks and organizations and can also lead to participation in other forms of political protest over the life course. For example, militant suffragists who took part in pickets of the White House and went on hunger strikes in the 1920s when they were arrested were more likely to maintain their commitment to feminism in the hostile political climate of the antifeminism and McCarthyism of the 1950s (Taylor 1989). There has been limited research on the immediate and long-term impact of threatening and disruptive protest on cultural transformation. Schuman (1972; cited in McAdam and Su 2002) reports that increasingly disruptive protests against the Vietnam War had contradictory effects, contributing both to growing opposition to the war as well as to a backlash of public opinion against the antiwar movement.

Variety

Morris's (1993) study of the 1963 Birmingham, Alabama, campaign against racial segregation suggests that using a *variety* of tactics may yield the best results in terms of policy change. Civil rights activists simultaneously staged an economic boycott against the city's businesses, held sit-in demonstrations at local lunch counters, and staged large-scale demonstrations. Morris concludes that neither novelty nor militancy can explain the success of the Birmingham campaign. Rather, activists' use of multiple tactics that resulted in a community-wide crisis that authorities were unable to contain explains the gains of the civil rights movement in Birmingham. Scholars of feminism also provide evidence that when the women's movement's repertoire of contention has included a variety of protest forms – both conventional and unconventional – the movement has been more likely to achieve policy changes (Rupp and Taylor 1987; Staggenborg 1991; Gelb and Hart 1999).

Increases in the rate and variety of forms of collective action are also linked to what Tarrow (1993) terms "moments of madness" or protest waves that bring about increases in the number of organizations and other mobilizing structures engaged in collective action (Tarrow 1989; Koopmans 1993; Kriesi et al. 1995). There is some evidence that increased movement mobilization, in turn, is linked to cultural change or changes in collective consciousness. A number of empirical studies report that the organizational proliferation of the US women's movement in the late 1980s and 1990s, when new groups embraced a variety of tactics to address wide-ranging issues such as economic equity, violence, women's health, rape, sexuality, and reproductive rights, brought about changes in public consciousness and values (Mueller 1987; Ferree and Hess 1994; Gelb and Hart 1999). Meyer (1999) reports that the range of tactics used by the nuclear freeze movement in the US in 1982 was responsible for winning broad public support in public opinion polls, town meetings, and state and local referenda.

Size

The civil rights movement's ability to mobilize large numbers of participants in Birmingham was another ingredient in the campaign's success (Morris 1993). Staging protest performances that display a movement's numerical strength is one way that social movements exercise influence. Large demonstrations capture media attention and follow the logic of democratic principles by demonstrating a strong surge of public and electoral support. Perhaps just as important, numerical strength increases a collective action's disruptive potential by overburdening law enforcement's capacity to repress the protest. Widespread mobilization may also be effective by virtue of that fact that it severely disrupts a community's daily routines, as well as its economic, institutional, and political infrastructures. In the Birmingham campaign, nearly half of the city's population boycotted local businesses, causing severe economic crisis for business owners, and a series of demonstrations involving hundreds of protestors left the city's jails filled beyond capacity: this garnered a great deal of national media attention.

Participation in large-scale protests involving thousands of people can be an exhilarating and empowering experience that functions both to mobilize individual commitment and strengthen movement organizations. In his research on the Dutch peace movement Klandermans (1997) found that individuals who participated in the first mass peace demonstrations were more likely to take part in subsequent peace actions. Several studies link sustained commitment to feminism to participation in demonstrations, such as "Take Back the Night Marches" (Taylor and Whittier 1992) and cultural forms of political expression such as women's musical festivals, alternative women-only institutions, and other feminist rituals (Taylor and Rupp 1993; Whittier 1995; Staggenborg 2001). Raeburn (forthcoming) traces the founding of the first gay employee network in what later emerged as a nationwide multi-organizational movement to combat discrimination against lesbians and gays in the workplace to activist networks formed at the 1986 National Gay and Lesbian March on Washington. Although researchers have rarely examined the direct effects of large-scale demonstrations on changes in cultural beliefs and values, Nagel (1995) argues that shifting identification with ethnic identities, as measured in the significant increase in the number of Americans reporting an American Indian race in the US census, provides evidence of the cultural impact of large-scale protests by Native Americans.

Cultural Resonance

Snow and his colleagues (1986, 1988) suggest that movement success and failure depends, in part, on a group's ability to frame collective actions in ways that link participants' grievances to mainstream beliefs and values. In the US, protest is more likely to be met with favorable government action if collective actors convey a commitment to democratic practices and the politics of persuasion (McAdam and Su 2002). Koopmans and Statham (1999) suggest that differences in the cultural meaning of collective action explain the greater policy gains that resulted from neo-Nazi demonstrations and other right-wing mobilizations in Germany as compared with Italy in the mid-1990s. They attribute these favorable outcomes in Germany to the resonance of the extreme Right's ethnic-cultural framing of national identity with the dominant German discourse on ethnic nationalist identity.

Cultural resonance not only mediates the policy impact of collective action, but it also determines the mobilization outcome of particular types of tactical repertoires. Taylor and her colleagues (Taylor and Whittier 1992; Taylor and Rupp 1993) suggest that the tactical repertoire of lesbian feminism, which included separate women's organizations, the valorization of relationships between women, and organizing around feminist rituals, tapped into traditional women's cultures of subordination. This resistance culture and style of politics operated to sustain the movement in a hostile political context.

Cultural resonance may be fundamental to understanding how a movement's tactical repertoires affect its ability to achieve changes in values, belief systems, and identities. Contemporary welfare movements in the US and Western Europe, using self-help tactics and strategies based on recognition politics, have been instrumental in creating a new empowered welfare subject who contrasts with the older passive recipient of benefits (Martin 2001). Williams attributes this success to activists' articulation of people's needs on the basis of race, class, gender, and age rather than material need, a cultural interpretation that is consistent with the fragmentation and specialization of postindustrial welfare provision and discourse (Williams 1992; Fraser 1995; Naples 1998). Perhaps one of the clearest cases of a movement that met with success because its repertoire of tactics appropriated familiar symbols, ideas, and elements in ways that resonated with both indigenous groups and national and international elites is the Rastafarian movement. Buffonge (2001) analyzes how the movement was able to mobilize support and alter mainstream political discourse about the poverty of rural and urban Jamaicans by using elements of Jamaican myth, story, religion, and music in novel ways. The movement's use of reggae music to communicate a political message and the popularity of musicians such as Bob Marley who wrote the song "Get Up, Stand Up" – which we took as the title of this chapter – resulted in widespread adoption of activists' ideas about the nature of Jamaican social and economic problems.

CONCLUSION

Public protest and the use of unconventional means of political persuasion is a fundamental feature of democratic societies, and certainly the average person equates protest with social movements. Repertoires and tactics of protest are also, as Mueller (1999) points out, the theoretical building blocks of all of the major theories constructed over the past three decades to understand social movements and other forms of contentious politics. Yet, as much as we have learned about the tactics and strategies of social movements, we, surprisingly, still have more to learn.

We began and end this chapter with two examples that are typical of the innovative protests used by modern groups and that help to expand current thinking about the variety of public performances of protest used by contemporary activists. The West Marin women's peace protestors relied on the Internet to communicate their performance, and the Rastafarians used music to convey their message. We have explored the ways that social movement scholars have conceptualized and categorized a wide range of protest forms and, drawing from this body of work, we propose a definition of tactical repertoires that is broad enough to encompass them all and avoids the bifurcation of expressive and instrumental politics that has dominated the study of social movement tactics.

Our definition proposes that we treat tactical repertoires as involving contestation, intentionality, and collective identity, and we offer this definition for several reasons. First, it is consistent with the conceptualization of collective action used by proponents of the protest event approach to studying social movements which will allow cumulative work but will hopefully stimulate more qualitative in-depth analyses of collective action events. Second, we think this model will provide a better understanding of some previously unexamined questions pertaining to the interactive dimensions of protest. For example, how do different tactical repertoires link challenging groups and their targets in episodes of contention? Are some tactical repertoires more successful than others in engaging authorities in sustained interaction? How do tactical repertoires create solidarity among a set of challengers? And how do tactical repertoires articulate boundaries and competing interests between members of challenging groups as well as between challengers and target groups?

In addition to offering conceptual clarification, our discussion also considered the external macrohistorical factors, as well as the internal movement processes, that determine a movement's choice of tactics. Evaluating the repertoires of contention model, the postindustrial society thesis, and the cycles of protest argument, we find studies that challenge all of these explanations of the way large-scale social, political, and economic processes constrain the tactical options available to collective actors. Even if tactical repertoires evolve slowly, protest innovations do come onto the scene. We need further research on the impact of external sociopolitical factors on tactical repertoires. Considering the way internal movement processes relate to forms and repertoires of protest, we conclude that scholars' disagreement about the role of organization in the deployment, innovation, and effective use of tactics suggests the need for still more research.

Ultimately, of course, the question that activists and scholars alike would most like to have answered is what kinds of tactics are the most effective? We, therefore, find considerable literature on this question, but we discover that scholars have learned more about the impact of militant than nonmilitant tactics. Further, the small but growing body of literature on protest outcomes has been more concerned with political and policy outcomes than the cultural consequences of social movement actions. Following Gusfield (1991), who advances a "fluid" concept of social movements, we have taken a broader definition of movement outcomes. We think there is need for further attention to the way different tactical repertoires result in changes in belief systems, identities, and cultural practices. We think that ultimately this may be the most powerful consequence of public performances of protest.

Note

We thank Dick Flacks for suggesting the song that is the title of this chapter and other valuable insights. In addition, we are grateful to Jennifer Earl, Lisa Leitz, Leila Rupp, Sarah Soule, David Snow, and members of the Social Movements Pro-seminar at the University of California at Santa Barbara for their comments on various drafts of this chapter.

References and further reading

Adam, Barry D., Jan Willem Duyvendak, and Andre Krouwel (eds.) (1999) *The Global Emergence of Gay and Lesbian Politics*. Philadelphia: Temple University Press.

Andrews, Kenneth T. (1997) The Impacts of Social Movements on the Political Process: The Civil Rights Movement and Black Electoral Politics in Mississippi. *American Sociological Review*, 62, 800–19.

——(2001) Social Movements and Policy Implementation. *American Sociological Review*, 66, 71–95.

Beckwith, Karen (2000) Hinges in Collective Action: Strategic Innovation in the Pittston Coal Strike. *Mobilization*, 5, 179–99.

Benford, Robert D., and David A. Snow (2000) Framing Processes and Social Movements: An Overview and Assessment. *Annual Review of Sociology*, 26, 611–39.

Bernstein, Mary (1997) Celebration and Suppression: Strategic Uses of Identity by the Lesbian and Gay Movement. *American Journal of Sociology*, 103, 531–65.

Blee, Kathleen M. (2002) *Inside Organized Racism: Women in the Hate Movement*. Berkeley, CA: University of California Press.

Bosco, Fernando J. (2001) Place, Space, Networks, and the Sustainability of Collective Action. *Global Networks*, 1, 307–29.

Bourdieu, Pierre (1990) *The Logic of Practice*. Stanford, CA: Stanford University Press.

Brand, Karl-Werner (1990) Cyclical Aspects of New Social Movements: Waves of Cultural Criticism and Mobilization Cycles of New Middle-class Radicalism. In Russell J. Dalton and Manfred Kuechler (eds.), *Challenging the Political Order: New Social and Political Movements in Western Democracies*. Cambridge: Polity, 24–42.

Breines, Wini (1982) *The Great Refusal: Community and Organization in the New Left: 1962–1968*. New York: Praeger.

Brown, Elaine (1992) *A Taste of Power: A Black Woman's Story*. New York: Pantheon.

Buechler, Steven M. (1995) New Social Movement Theories, *Sociological Quarterly*, 36, 441–64.

—— (2000) *Social Movements in Advanced Capitalism: The Political Economy and Cultural Construction of Social Activism.* New York: Oxford University Press.

Buffonge, A. E. Gordon (2001) Culture and Political Opportunity: Rastafarian Links to the Jamaican Poor. *Research in Social Movements, Conflict and Change,* 23, 3–35.

Calhoun, Craig (1993) "New Social Movements" of the Early Nineteenth Century. *Social Science History,* 17, 385–427.

—— (1995) "New Social Movements" of the Early Nineteenth Century. In Mark Traugott (ed.), *Repertoires and Cycles of Collective Action.* Durham, NC: Duke University Press, 173–215.

Carty, Victoria (2002) Technology and Counter-hegemonic Movements: The Case of Nike Corporation. *Social Movement Studies,* 1, 129–46.

Castells, Manuel (1997) *The Power of Identity.* Oxford: Blackwell.

Chartier, Roger (1991) *The Cultural Origins of the French Revolution.* Durham, NC: Duke University Press.

Chaves, Mark (1997) *Ordaining Women: Culture and Conflict in Religious Organizations.* Cambridge, MA: Harvard University Press.

Clemens, Elisabeth S. (1993) Organizational Repertoires and Institutional Change: Women's Groups and the Transformation of US Politics, 1890–1920. *American Journal of Sociology,* 98, 755–98.

Cohen, Jean (1985) "Strategy or Identity"? New Theoretical Paradigms and Contemporary Social Movements. *Social Research,* 52, 663–716.

Costanza-Chock, Sasha (forthcoming) Mapping the Repertoire of Electronic Contention. In Andrew Opel and Donnalyn Pompper (eds.), *Representing Resistance: Media, Civil Disobedience, and the Global Justice Movement.* Westport, CT: Greenwood.

Cress, Daniel M., and David A. Snow (1996) Mobilization at the Margins: Resources, Benefactors, and the Vitality of Homeless Social Movement Organizations. *American Sociological Review,* 61, 1089–109.

—— (2000) The Outcomes of Homeless Mobilization: The Influence of Organization, Disruption, Political Mediation, and Framing. *American Journal of Sociology,* 105, 1063–104.

Crossley, Nick (2002) Repertoires of Contention and Tactical Diversity in the UK Psychiatric Survivors Movement: The Question of Appropriation. *Social Movement Studies,* 1, 47–71.

Darnovsky, Marcy, Barbara Epstein and Richard Flacks (eds.) (1995) *Cultural Politics and Social Movements.* Philadelphia: Temple University Press.

D'Emilio, John (1998) *Sexual Politics, Sexual Communities: The Making of a Homosexual Minority in the United States, 1940–1970.* 2nd ed. Chicago: University of Chicago Press.

della Porta, Donatella, and Mario Diani (1999) *Social Movements: An Introduction.* New York: Blackwell.

Duyvendak, Jan Willem (1995) *The Power of Politics: New Social Movements in France.* Boulder, CO: Westview.

Duyvendak, Jan Willem, and Marco G. Giugni (1995) Social Movement Types and Policy Domains. In Hanspeter Kriesi, Ruud Koopmans, Jan Willem Duyvendak, and Marco G. Giugni (eds.), *New Social Movements in Western Europe: A Comparative Anlaysis.* Minneapolis: University of Minnesota Press, 82–110.

Earl, Jennifer, and Alan Schussman (2002) The New Site of Activism: On-line Organizations, Movement Entrepreneurs, and the Changing Location of Social Movement Decision-Making. *Research in Social Movements, Conflicts and Change,* 24, 155–87.

Epstein, Steven (1996) *Impure Science: AIDS, Activism, and the Politics of Knowledge.* Berkeley: University of California Press.

Evans, Sara (1979) *Personal Politics: The Roots of Women's Liberation in the Civil Rights Movement and New Left.* New York: Knopf.

Fantasia, Rick (1988) *Cultures of Solidarity: Consciousness, Action, and Contemporary American Workers*. Berkeley: University of California Press.

Ferree, Myra Marx, and Beth Hess (1994) *Controversy and Coalition: The Feminist Movement across Three Decades of Change*. New York: Twayne.

Ferree, Myra Marx, and Silke Roth (1998) Gender, Class, and the Interaction between Social Movements: A Strike of West Berlin Day Care Workers. *Gender and Society*, 12, 626–48.

Ferree, Myra Marx, William A. Gamson, Jürgen Gerhards, and Dieter Rucht (2002) *Shaping Abortion Discourse: Democracy and the Public Sphere in Germany and the United States*. New York: Cambridge University Press.

Fonow, Mary Margaret (1998) Protest Engendered: The Participation of Women Steelworkers in the Wheeling-Pittsburgh Steel Strike of 1985. *Gender and Society*, 12 (6), 710–29.

Fraser, Nancy (1995) Clintonism, Welfare, and the Antisocial Wage: The Emergence of a Neoliberal Political Imaginary. In Antonio Callari, Stephen Cullenberg, and Carole Biewener (eds.), *Marxism in the Postmodern Age: Confronting the New World Order*. New York: Guilford, 493–505.

——(1997) *Justice Interruptus*. New York: Routledge.

Freeman, Jo (1973) *The Politics of Women's Liberation*. Chicago: University of Chicago Press.

Gamson, Joshua (1989) Silence, Death and the Invisible Enemy: AIDS Activism and Social Movement "Newness." *Social Problems*, 36, 351–65.

——(1995) Must Identity Movements Self-Destruct? A Queer Dilemma. *Social Problems*, 42: 390–407.

——(1997) Messages of Exclusion: Gender, Movements, and Symbolic Boundaries. *Gender and Society*, 11, 178–99.

Gamson, William A. (1990) *The Strategy of Social Protest*. 2nd ed. Belmont, CA: Wadsworth.

——(1992) *Talking Politics*. New York: Cambridge University Press.

Gamson, William A., and Andre Modigliani (1989) Media Discourse and Public Opinion on Nuclear Power: A Constructionist Approach. *American Journal of Sociology*, 95 (1), 1–37.

Gamson, William A., and Emilie Schmeidler (1984) Organizing the Poor: An Argument with Frances Fox Piven and Richard A. Cloward's *Poor People's Movements*. *Theory and Society*, 13, 567–85.

Garrido, M., and A. Halavais (2003) Mapping Networks of Support for the Zapatista Movement: Applying Social Networks Analysis to Study Contemporary Social Movements. In Martha McCaughey and Michael D. Ayers (eds.), *Cyberactivism: Critical Practices and Theories of Online Activism*. New York: Routledge, 165–84.

Gelb, Joyce, and Vivien Hart (1999) Feminist Politics in a Hostile Environment: Obstacles and Opportunities. In Marco Giugni, Doug McAdam, and Charles Tilly (eds.), *How Social Movements Matter*. Minneapolis: University of Minnesota Press, 149–81.

Giddens, Anthony (1984) *The Constitution of Society*. Berkeley: University of California Press.

——(1991) *Modernity and Self-Identity*. Stanford: Stanford University Press.

Gitlin, Todd (1980) *The Whole World Is Watching: Mass Media in the Making and Unmaking of the New Left*. Berkeley: University of California Press.

Goffman, Erving (1974) *Frame Analysis: An Essay on the Organization of Experience*. New York: Harper & Row.

Goodwin, Jeff, and James M. Jasper (1999) Caught in a Winding, Snarling Vine: The Structural Bias of Political Process Theory. *Sociological Forum*, 14, 27–54.

Goodwin, Jeff, James M. Jasper, and Francesca Polletta (2000) The Return of the Repressed: The Fall and Rise of Emotions in Social Movement Theory. *Mobilization*, 5, 65–84.

Goody, Jack (ed.) (1968) *Literacy in Traditional Societies*. Cambridge: Cambridge University Press.

Gouldner, Alvin W. (1975) Prologue to a Theory of Revolutionary Intellectuals. *Telos*, 26, 3–36.

Groch, Sharon (2001) Free Spaces: Creating Oppositional Consciousness in the Disability Rights Movement. In Jane Mansbridge and Aldon Morris (eds.), *Oppositional Consciousness: The Subjective Roots of Social Protest*. Chicago: University of Chicago Press, 65–98.

Gusfield, Joseph R. (1963) *Symbolic Crusade: Status Politics and the American Temperance Movement*. Urbana, IL: University of Illinois Press.

——(1991) Social Movements and Social Change: Perspectives of Linearity and Fluidity. *Social Movements, Conflict, and Change*, 4, 317–39.

Habermas, Jürgen (1981) New Social Movements. *Telos*, 49, 33–7.

——(1984) *The Theory of Communicative Action: Reason and the Rationalization of Society*. Vol. 1. Translated by Thomas McCarthy. Boston: Beacon.

——(1987) *The Theory of Communicative Action: Lifeworld and System*, Volume 2, translated by Thomas McCarthy. Boston: Beacon.

Harris, Fredrick C. (2001) Religious Resources in an Oppositional Civic Culture. In Jane Mansbridge and Aldon Morris (eds.), *Oppositional Consciousness: The Subjective Roots of Social Protest*. Chicago: University of Chicago Press, 38–64.

Heath, Melanie A. (2003) Soft-Boiled Masculinity: Renegotiating Gender and Racial Ideologies in the Promise Keepers Movement. *Gender and Society*, 17, 423–44.

Imig, Doug, and Sidney Tarrow (1999) The Europeanization of Movements? A New Approach to Transnational Contention. In Donatella della Porta, Hanspeter Kriesi, and Dieter Rucht (eds.), *Social Movements in a Globalizing World*. New York: St. Martin's, 112–33.

Inglehart, Ronald (1981) Post-Materialism in an Environment of Insecurity. *American Political Science Review*, 75, 880–900.

——(1990) Values, Ideology, and Cognitive Mobilization in New Social Movements. In Russell J. Dalton and Manfred Kuechler (eds.), *Challenging the Political Order: New Social and Political Movements in Western Democracies*. Cambridge: Polity, 43–66.

Jasper, James (1997) *The Art of Moral Protest: Culture, Biography, and Creativity in Social Movements*. Chicago: University of Chicago Press.

Jenkins, J. Craig (1983) Resource Mobilization Theory and the Study of Social Movements. *Annual Review of Sociology*, 9, 527–53.

Jenkins, J. Craig, and Craig Eckert (1986) Channeling Black Insurgency: Elite Patronage and the Development of the Civil Rights Movement. *American Sociological Review*, 51, 812–30.

Jenkins, J. Craig, and Charles Perrow (1977) Insurgency of the Powerless: Farm Worker Rights Movements (1946–1972). *American Sociological Review*, 42, 249–68.

Jenness, Valerie, and Kendal Broad (1997) *Hate Crimes: New Social Movements and the Politics of Violence*. Hawthorne, NY: Aldine de Gruyter.

Jenness, Valerie, and Ryken Grattet (2001) *Making Hate a Crime: From Social Movement to Law Enforcement*. New York: Russel Sage.

Jennings, M. Kent, and Ellen Ann Anderson (1996) Support for Confrontational Tactics among AIDS Activists: A Study of Intra-Movement Divisions. *American Journal of Political Science*, 40, 311–34.

Johnston, Hank, and Bert Klandermans (eds.) (1995) *Social Movements and Culture*. Minneapolis: University of Minnesota Press.

Johnston, Hank, Enrique Laraña, and Joseph R. Gusfield (1994) Identities, Grievances, and New Social Movements. In Enrique Laraña, Hank Johnston, and Joseph R. Gusfield (eds.), *New Social Movements: From Ideology to Identity*. Philadelphia, PA: Temple University Press, 3–35.

Katzenstein, Mary Fainsoid (1998) *Faithful and Fearless: Moving Feminist Protest inside the Church and Military*. Philadelphia, NJ: Princeton University Press.

Kim, Hyojoung (2002) Shame, Anger, and Love in Collective Action: Emotional Consequences of Suicide Protest in South Korea, 1991. *Mobilization*, 7, 159–76.

Klandermans, Bert (1997) *The Social Psychology of Protest*. New York: Blackwell.

Klandermans, Bert, and Marga de Weerd (2002) Group Identification and Political Protest. In Sheldon Stryker, Timothy Owens, and Robert W. White (eds.), *Self, Identity, and Social Movements*. Minneapolis: University of Minnesota Press, 68–90.

Klatch, Rebecca (1999) *A Generation Divided: The New Left, the New Right, and the 1960s*. Berkeley, CA: University of California Press.

Koopmans, Ruud (1993) The Dynamics of Protest Waves: West Germany, 1965 to 1989. *American Sociological Review*, 58, 637–58.

Koopmans, Ruud, and Dieter Rucht (2002) Protest Event Analysis. In Bert Klandermans and Suzanne Staggenborg (eds.), *Methods of Social Movement Research*. Minneapolis: University of Minnesota Press, 231–59.

Koopmans, Ruud, and Paul Statham (1999) Ethnic and Civil Conceptions of Nationhood in the Differential Success of the Extreme Right in German and Italy. In Marco Giugni, Doug McAdam, and Charles Tilly (eds.), *How Social Movements Matter*. Minneapolis: University of Minnesota Press, 225–54.

Kriesi, Hanspeter, and Dominique Wisler (1999) The Impact of Social Movements on Political Institutions: A Comparison of the Introduction of Direct Legislation in Switzerland and the United States. In Marco Giugni, Doug McAdam, and Charles Tilly (eds.), *How Social Movements Matter*. Minneapolis: University of Minnesota Press, 42–65.

Kriesi, Hanspeter, Ruud Koopmans, Jan Willem Duyvendak, and Marco G. Giugni (1995) *New Social Movements in Western Europe: A Comparative Analysis*. Minnesota: University of Minnesota Press.

Kurtz, Sharon (2002) *Workplace Justice: Organizing Multi-identity Movements*. Minneapolis: University of Minnesota Press.

Lichtenstein, Nelson (2002) *State of the Union: A Century of American Labor*. Princeton, NJ: Princeton University Press.

Lipsky, Michael (1968) Protest as a Political Resource. *American Political Science Review*, 62, 1144–58.

McAdam, Doug (1982) *Political Process and the Development of Black Insurgency, 1930–1970*. Chicago: University of Chicago Press.

——(1983) Tactical Innovation and the Pace of Insurgency. *American Sociological Review*, 48, 735–54.

——(1986) Recruitment to High-Risk Activism: The Case of Freedom Summer. *American Journal of Sociology*, 92, 64–90.

——(1988) *Freedom Summer*. New York: Oxford University Press.

——(1992) Gender as a Mediator of the Activist Experience: The Case of Freedom Summer. *American Journal of Sociology*, 97, 1211–40.

——(1994) Culture and Social Movements. In Enrique Laraña, Hank Johnston, and Joseph R. Gusfield (eds.), *New Social Movements: From Ideology to Identity*. Philadelphia, PA: Temple University Press, 36–57.

McAdam, Doug and Dieter Rucht (1993) The Cross-National Diffusion of Movement Ideas. *The Annals of the American Academy of Political and Social Research*, 528, 56–74.

McAdam, Doug, and David Snow (eds.) (1997) *Social Movements: Readings on their Emergence, Mobilization, and Dynamics*. Los Angeles: Roxbury.

McAdam, Doug, and Yang Su (2002) The War at Home: Anti-War Protests and Congressional Voting, 1965–73. *American Sociological Review*, 67, 696–721.

McAdam, Doug, Sidney Tarrow, and Charles Tilly (1996) To Map Contentious Politics. *Mobilization*, 1, 17–34.

——(2001) *Dynamics of Contention*. New York: Cambridge University.

McCammon, Holly J., Karen E. Campbell, Ellen M. Granberg, and Christine Mowry (2001) How Movements Win: Gendered Opportunity Structures and U.S. Women's Suffrage Movements, 1866–1919. *American Sociological Review*, 66, 49–70.

McCarthy, John D. and Mayer N. Zald (1973) *The Trend of Social Movements in America: Professionalization and Resource Mobilization*. Morristown, NJ: General Learning.

——(1977) Resource Mobilization and Social Movements: A Partial Theory. *American Journal of Sociology*, 82, 1212–41.

McCarthy John D., Clark McPhail, and Jackie Smith (1996) Images of Protest: Dimensions of Selection Bias in Media Coverage of Washington Demonstrations, 1982 and 1991. *American Sociological Review*, 61, 478–99.

McCaughey, Martha, and Michael D. Ayers (eds.) (2003) *Cyberactivism: Online Activism in Theory and Practice*. New York: Routledge.

Mansbridge, Jane, and Aldon Morris (eds.) (2001) *Oppositional Consciousness: The Subjective Roots of Social Protest*. Chicago: University of Chicago Press.

Martin, Greg (2001) Social Movements, Welfare, and Social Policy: A Critical Analysis. *Critical Social Policy*, 21, 361–83.

Melucci, Alberto (1980) The New Social Movements: A Theoretical Approach. *Social Science Information*, 19, 199–226.

——(1989) *Nomads of the Present: Social Movements and Individual Needs in Contemporary Society*. Philadelphia, PA: Temple University Press.

——(1995) The Process of Collective Identity. In Hank Johnston and Bert Klandermans (eds.), *Social Movements and Culture*. Minneapolis: University of Minnesota Press, 41–63.

——(1996) *Challenging Codes: Collective Action in the Communication Age*. Cambridge: Cambridge University Press.

Meyer, David S. (1999) How the Cold War Was Really Won: The Effects of the Antinuclear Movements of the 1980s. In Marco Giugni, Doug McAdam, and Charles Tilly (eds.), *How Social Movements Matter*. Minneapolis: University of Minnesota Press, 182–203.

Meyer, David S., and Nancy Whittier (1994) Social Movement Spillover. *Social Problems*, 41, 277–91.

Michels, Robert (1962) *Political Parties*. New York: Collier.

Minkoff, Debra C. (1997) The Sequencing of Social Movements. *American Sociological Review*, 62, 779–99.

Mirowsky, John, and Catherine Ross (1981) Protest Group Success: The Impact of Group Characteristics, Social Control, and Context. *Sociological Focus*, 14, 177–92.

Molotch, Harvey (1979) Media and Movements. In Mayer N. Zald and John D. McCarthy (eds.), *The Dynamics of Social Movements*. Cambridge: Winthrop, 71–93 .

Morris, Aldon (1981) Black Southern Sit-in Movements: An Analysis of Internal Organization. *American Sociological Review*, 45, 744–67.

——(1984) *The Origins of the Civil Rights Movement*. New York: Free Press.

——(1993) Birmingham Confrontation Reconsidered: An Analysis of the Dynamics and Tactics of Mobilization. *American Sociological Review*, 58, 621–36.

Morris, Aldon, and Naomi Braine (2001) Social Movements and Oppositional Consciousness. In Jane Mansbridge and Aldon Morris (eds.), *Oppositional Consciousness: The Subjective Roots of Social Protest*. Chicago: University of Chicago Press, 20–37.

Morris, Aldon, and Carol McClurg Mueller (1992) *Frontiers in Social Movement Theory*. New Haven: Yale University Press.

Mueller, Carol McClurg (1987) Collective Consciousness, Identity Transformation, and the Rise of Women in Public Office in the United States. In Mary Fainsod Katzenstein and Carol McClurg Mueller (eds.), *The Women's Movements of the United States and Western Europe*. Philadelphia, PA: Temple University Press, 89–108.

——(1992) Building Social Movement Theory. In Aldon Morris and Carol McClurg Mueller (eds.), *Frontiers in Social Movement Theory*. New Haven: Yale University Press, 3–25.

——(1997) International Press Coverage of East German Protest Events, 1989. *American Sociological Review*, 62, 820–32.

——(1999) Escape from the GDR, 1961–1989: Hybrid Exit Repertoires in a Disintegrating Leninist Regime. *American Journal of Sociology*, 105, 697–735.

Nagel, Joane (1988) Masculinity and Nationalism: Gender and Sexuality in the Making of Nations. *Journal of Ethnic and Racial Studies*, 21, 242–69.

——(1995) Politics and the Resurgence of American Indian Ethnic Identity. *American Sociological Review*, 60, 947–65.

——(1998) Masculinity and Nationalism: Gender and Sexuality in the Making of Nations. *Journal of Ethnic and Racial Studies*, 21, 242–69.

Naples, Nancy (1992) Activist Mothering: Cross-generational Continuity in the Community Work of Women from Low-income Urban Neighborhoods. *Gender & Society*, 5, 478–94.

——(ed.) (1998) *Community Activism and Feminist Politics*. New York: Routledge.

Offe, Claus (1985) The New Social Movements: Challenging the Boundaries of Institutional Politics. *Social Research*, 52, 817–68.

Oliver, Pamela, and Gerald Marwell (1992) Mobilizing Technologies for Collective Action. In Aldon Morris and Carol McClurg Mueller (eds.), *Frontiers of Social Movement Theory*. New Haven: Yale University Press, 251–72.

Oliver, Pamela E., and Daniel J. Myers (1999) How Events Enter the Public Sphere: Conflict, Location and Sponsorship in Local Newspaper Coverage of Public Events. *American Journal of Sociology*, 105, 38–87.

Olzak, Susan (1989) Analysis of Events in the Study of Collective Action. *Annual Review of Sociology*, 15, 119–41.

——(1992) *The Dynamics of Ethnic Competition and Conflict*. Stanford: Stanford University Press.

Pattillo-McCoy, Mary (1998) Church Culture as a Strategy of Action in the Black Community. *American Sociological Review*, 63, 767–84.

Pichardo, Nelson A. (1997) New Social Movements: A Critical Review. *Annual Review of Sociology*, 23, 411–30.

Piven, Frances Fox, and Richard Cloward (1979) *Poor People's Movement*. 2nd ed. New York: Vintage.

Pogash, Carol (2003) A Naked Plea for Peace Gets Legs as Protest Draws Imitators: Northern California Women Bare All in their Opposition to War with Iraq. *Los Angeles Times*, January 14, 2003.

Polletta, Francesca (2002) *Freedom Is an Endless Meeting: Democracy in American Social Movements*. Chicago: University of Chicago Press.

Polletta, Francesca, and James M. Jasper (2001) Collective Identity and Social Movements. *Annual Review of Sociology*, 27, 283–305.

Raeburn, Nicole C. (forthcoming) *Inside out: The Struggle for Lesbian, Gay, and Bisexual Rights in the Workplace*. Minneapolis: University of Minnesota Press.

Robnett, Belinda (1996) African-American Women in the Civil Rights Movement, 1954–1965: Gender, Leadership, and Micromobilization. *American Journal of Sociology*, 101, 1661–93.

Rochon, Thomas R. (1998) *Culture Moves: Ideas, Activism, and Changing Values*. Princeton, NJ: Princeton University Press.

Rodriguez, Marc Simon (2001) Cristaleno Consciousness: Mexican-American Activism between Crystal City, Texas, and Wisconsin, 1963–80. In Jane Mansbridge and Aldon Morris (eds.), *Oppositional Consciousness: The Subjective Roots of Social Protest*. Chicago: University of Chicago Press, 146–69.

Roscigno, Vincent J., and William F. Danaher (2001) Media Mobilization: The Case of Radio and Southern Textile Worker Insurgency, 1929 to 1934. *American Sociological Review*, 66, 21–48.

Rucht, Dieter (1988) Themes, Logics and Arenas of Social Movements: A Structural Approach. *International Social Movement Research*, 1, 305–28.

——(1990) The Strategies and Action Repertoires of New Movements. In Russell J. Dalton and Manfred Kuechler (eds.), *Challenging the Political Order: New Social and Political Movements in Western Democracies*. Cambridge: Polity, 156–75.

——(1999) Linking Organization and Mobilization: Michels' Iron Law of Oligarchy Reconsidered. *Mobilization*, 2, 151–69.

Rupp, Leila J., and Verta Taylor (1987) *Survival in the Doldrums: The American Women's Rights Movement, 1945 to the 1960s*. New York: Oxford University Press.

——(2003) *Drag Queens at the 801 Cabaret*. Chicago: University of Chicago Press.

Schuman, Howard (1972) Two Sources of Anti-war Sentiment in America. *American Journal of Sociology*, 78, 513–36.

Schwartz, Michael (1976) *Studies in Social Discontinuity*. New York: Academic.

Scott, James C. (1985) *Weapons of the Weak: Everyday Forms of Peasant Resistance*. New Haven: Yale University Press.

Sewell, William H. (1996) Historical Events as Transformations of Structures: Inventing Revolution at the Bastille. *Theory and Society*, 25, 841–81.

Shorter, Edward, and Charles Tilly (1974) *Strikes in France: 1830–1968*. New York: Cambridge University Press.

Snow, David A. (1979) A Dramaturgical Analysis of Movement Accommodation: Building Idiosyncrasy Credit as a Movement Mobilization Strategy. *Symbolic Interaction*, 2, 23–44.

——(2001) Collective Identity and Expressive Forms. In N. J. Smelser and P. B. Baltes (eds.) *International Encyclopedia of the Social & Behavioral Sciences*. Oxford: Pregamon Press, 2212–19.

——(2002) Social Movements as Challenges to Authority: Resistance to an Emerging Conceptual Hegemony. Presented at the Conference on Authority in Contention, Notre Dame University, South Bend, IN.

Snow, David A., and Robert D. Benford (1988) Ideology, Frame Resonance and Participant Mobilization. *International Social Movement Research*, 1, 197–217.

Snow, David A., and Jason Clarke-Miller (2003) Frame Articulation and Elaboration in a Right-Wing Group: An Empirical Examination of Framing Processes. Unpublished manuscript.

Snow, David A., Louis A. Zurcher Jr., and Sheldon Ekland-Olson (1980) Social Networks and Social Movements: A Micro-Structural Approach to Differential Recruitment. *American Sociological Review*, 45, 787–801.

Snow, David A., E. Burke Rochford Jr., Steven K. Worden, and Robert D. Benford (1986) Frame Alignment Processes, Micromobilization, and Movement Participation. *American Sociological Review*, 51, 464–81

Snyder, David, and William R. Kelly (1977) Conflict Intensity, Media Sensitivity and the Validity of Newspaper Data. *American Sociological Review*, 42, 105–23.

Soule, Sarah A. (1992) Populism and Black Lynching in Georgia: 1890–1900. *Social Forces*, 71, 431–49.

——(1997) The Student Divestment Movement in the United States and Tactical Diffusion: The Shantytown Protest. *Social Forces*, 75, 855–83.

Soule, Sarah A., Doug McAdam, John McCarthy, and Yang Su (1999) Protest Events: Cause or Consequence of State Action? The U.S. Women's Movement and Federal Congressional Activities, 1956–1979. *Mobilization*, 4, 239–55.

Staggenborg, Suzanne (1988) Consequences of Professionalization and Formalization in the Pro-Choice Movement. *American Sociological Review*, 53, 585–606.

——(1991) *The Pro-Choice Movement: Organization and Activism in the Abortion Conflict*. New York: Oxford University Press.

—— (1995) Can Feminist Organizations Be Effective? In Myra Marx Ferree and Patricia Yancey Martin (eds.), *Feminist Organizations: Harvest of the New Women's Movement*. Philadelphia, PA: Temple University Press, 339–55.

—— (2001) Beyond Culture versus Politics: A Case Study of a Local Women's Movement. *Gender and Society*, 15 (4), 505–28.

Steedly, Homer R., and John W. Foley (1979) The Success of Protest Groups: Multivariate Analyses. *Social Science Research*, 8, 1–15.

Steinberg, Stephen (1995) *Turning Back: The Retreat from Racial Justice in American Thought and Policy*. Boston: Beacon.

Stockdill, Brett (2001) Forging a Multidimensional Oppositional Consciousness: Lessons from Community-Based AIDS Activism. In Jane Mansbridge and Aldon Morris (eds.), *Oppositional Consciousness: The Subjective Roots of Social Protest*. Chicago: University of Chicago Press, 204–37.

Swidler, Ann (1986) Culture in Action: Symbols and Strategies. *American Sociological Review*, 51, 273–86.

Tarrow, Sidney (1988) The Oldest New Movement. In Bert Klandermans, Hanspeter Kriesi, and Sidney Tarrow (eds.), *From Structure to Action: Comparing Social Movements across Cultures*. International Social Movement Research. Vol. 1. Greenwich, CT: JAI, 281–304.

—— (1989) *Democracy and Disorder: Protest and Politics in Italy, 1965–1975*. Oxford: Oxford University Press.

—— (1993) Cycles of Collective Action: Between Moments of Madness and the Repertoire of Contention. *Social Science History*, 17, 281–307.

—— (1998) *Power in Movement: Social Movements and Contentious Politics*. New York: Cambridge University Press.

Taylor, Judith (1998) Feminist Tactics and Friendly Fire in the Irish Women's Movement. *Gender & Society*, 12, 674–91.

Taylor, Verta (1989) Social Movement Continuity: The Women's Movement in Abeyance. *American Sociological Review*, 54, 761–75.

—— (1996) *Rock-a-by Baby: Feminism, Self-Help, and Postpartum Depression*. New York: Routledge.

Taylor, Verta, and Leila J. Rupp (1993) Women's Culture and Lesbian Feminist Activism: A Reconsideration of Cultural Feminism. *Signs*, 19, 32–61.

Taylor, Verta, and Marieke Van Willigen (1996) Women's Self-Help and the Reconstruction of Gender: The Postpartum Support and Breast Cancer Movements. *Mobilization: An International Journal*, 2, 123–43.

Taylor, Verta, and Nancy E. Whittier (1992) Collective Identity in Social Movement Communities: Lesbian Feminist Mobilization. In Aldon D. Morris and Carole McClurg Mueller (eds.), *Frontiers in Social Movement Theory*. New Haven: Yale University Press, 104–29.

—— (1995) Analytical Approaches to Social Movement Culture: The Culture of the Women's Movement. In Hank Johnston and Bert Klandermans (eds.), *Social Movements and Culture*. Minneapolis: University of Minnesota Press, 163–87.

—— (1998) Guest Editors' Introduction: Special Issue on Gender and Social Movements: Part 1. *Gender & Society*, 12, 622–5.

—— (1999) Guest Editors' Introduction: Special Issue on Gender and Social Movements: Part 2. *Gender & Society*, 13, 5–7.

Tilly, Charles (1978) *From Mobilization to Revolution*. New York: Random House.

—— (1986) *The Contentious French*. Cambridge, MA: Harvard University Press, Belknap Press.

—— (1995) Contentious Repertoires in Great Britian, 1758–1834. In Mark Traugott (ed.), *Repertoires and Cycles of Collective Action*. Durham, NC: Duke University Press, 15–42.

—— (1999) From Interactions to Outcomes in Social Movements. In Marco Giugni, Doug McAdam, and Charles Tilly (eds.), *How Social Movements Matter*. Minneapolis: University of Minnesota Press, 253–70.

—— (2002) *Stories, Identities, and Political Change*. Lanham, MD: Rowman & Littlefield.

Tilly, Charles, Louise Tilly, and Richard Tilly (1975) *The Rebellious Century 1830–1930*. Cambridge: Harvard University Press.

Touraine, Alain (1981) *The Voice and the Eye: An Analysis of Social Movements*. New York: Cambridge University Press.

—— (1985) An Introduction to the Study of Social Movements. *Social Research*, 52, 749–87.

Traugott, Mark (ed.) (1995) Barricades as Repertoire: Continuities and Discontinuities in the History of French Contention. In Mark Traugott (ed.), *Repertoires and Cycles of Collective Action*. Durham, NC: Duke University Press, 43–56.

Turner, Ralph H., and Lewis M. Killian (1987) *Collective Behavior*. Englewood Cliffs, NJ: Prentice-Hall.

Valocchi, Steve (1990) The Unemployed Workers Movement of the 1930s: A Reexamination of the Piven and Cloward Thesis. *Social Problems*, 37, 191–205.

—— (1993) External Resources and the Unemployed Councils of the 1930s: Evaluating Six Propositions from Social Movement Theory. *Sociological Forum*, 8, 451–70.

Van Dyke, Nella (1998) Hotbeds of Activism: Locations of Student Protest. *Social Problems*, 45, 205–19.

—— (2003a) Crossing Movement Boundaries: Factors That Facilitate Coalition Protest by American College Students, 1930-1990. *Social Problems*, 50, 226–50.

—— (2003b) Protest Cycles and Party Politics: The Effect of Elite Allies and Antagonists on Student Protest in the United States, 1930–1990. In Jack Goldstone (ed.), *Parties, Politics and Movements*. Cambridge: Cambridge University Press, 226–45.

Van Dyke, Nella, and Sarah A. Soule (2002) Structural Social Change and the Mobilizing Effect of Threat: Explaining Levels of Patriot and Militia Mobilizing in the United States. *Social Problems*, 49, 497–520.

Van Dyke, Nella, Sarah A. Soule, and John D. McCarthy (2001) The Role of Organization and Constituency in the Use of Confrontational Tactics by Social Movements. Paper presented at the Annual Meeting of the American Sociological Association, Anaheim, CA.

Van Dyke, Nella, Verta Taylor, and Sarah A. Soule (2002) Cultural Targets and Confrontation: "New" Versus Old Social Movements, 1968–1975. Paper presented at the Annual Meeting of the American Sociological Association, Chicago.

White, Robert W. (1989) From Peaceful Protest to Guerrilla War: Micromobilization of the Provisional Irish Republican Army. *American Journal of Sociology*, 94, 1277–1302.

Whittier, Nancy E. (1995) *Feminist Generations: The Persistence of the Radical Women's Movement*. Philadelphia, PA: Temple University Press.

—— (2001) Emotional Strategies: The Collective Reconstruction and Display of Oppositional Emotions in the Movement against Child Sexual Abuse. In Jeff Goodwin, James M. Jasper, and Francesca Polletta (eds.), *Passionate Politics: Emotions and Social Movements*. Chicago: University of Chicago Press, 233–50.

Williams, Fiona (1992) Somewhere over the Rainbow: Universality and Diversity in Social Policy. In N. Manning and R. Page (eds.), *Social Policy Review*. Canterbury: Social Policy Association, 200–19.

Wilson, James Q. (1973) *Political Organizations*. New York: Basic.

Young, Michael P. (2002) Confessional Protest: The Religious Birth of U.S. National Social Movements. *American Sociological Review*, 67, 660–88.

Zald, Mayer N. (2000) Ideologically Structured Action: An Enlarged Agenda for Social Movement Research. *Mobilization*, 5, 1–16

Zald, Mayer N., and Roberta Ash (1966) Social Movement Organizations: Growth, Decay and Change. *Social Forces*, 40, 327–40.

Zhao, Dingxin (1998) Ecologies of Social Movements: Student Mobilization during the 1989 Prodemocracy Movement in Beijing. *American Journal of Sociology*, 103, 1493–529.

13

Diffusion Processes within and across Movements

Sarah A. Soule

Introduction

The field of social movements has historically been an area upon which the diffusion literature has had a significant impact. Early thinkers considered contagion to be a central, albeit negative, component of most collective action. Implicit in the works of LeBon (1897), Tarde (1903), and Blumer (1939) is the idea that the contagion of maladaptive and aggressive impulses drives collective action. Scholars writing somewhat more recently also viewed collective action and its diffusion as something to be feared, perhaps because they based their assumptions on their observations of race riots, lynching, Nazism, fascism, Stalinism, and McCarthyism (Garner 1997). In all of these early works, individuals are seen as nonrational and as "functioning outside of normative constraints and propelled by high levels of strain" (Morris 1981: 745). And, collective action is viewed as a spontaneous and somewhat random occurrence that had the potential to spread through simple contagion processes.[1]

In recent years, references to diffusion have reappeared in the literature on social movements and collective action, but no longer is the process considered negative or pathological. The revisitation of diffusion and diffusion processes was originally motivated by scholars such as Goertz (1994) and McAdam and Rucht (1993) who noted that mobilization campaigns in different locales are rarely isolated and independent from one another. And, more recently, the study of diffusion of collective action has been motivated by an interest in globalization and the increasing interdependencies among actors and events in disparate locations (della Porta and Kriesi 1999).

More generally, scholars working in this area have tried to better specify the *mechanisms* by which innovations diffuse, rather than merely arguing for the contagion of collective action. These changes occurred with the development of resource mobilization theory and the accompanying focus on the social movement as an organized, rational, and goal-oriented entity. Once scholars began to see social movement organizations in this manner, it became possible to consider diffusion as a function of connections between different organizations and individuals. It is now recognized that social movement organizations are rarely bounded entities; rather, they are most often linked to other movement organizations that may be either within the same social movement or in different social movements, within the same nation or in different nations. As well, it is now widely recognized that movement actions do not occur in a vacuum and that movement actors are highly attuned to the actions of other actors, borrowing or imitating tactics, frames, slogans, and so forth when deemed advantageous.

When social scientists speak of diffusion they very broadly mean the "flow of social practices among actors within some larger system" (Strang and Meyer 1993: 488). The term "social practices" refers to anything from child-rearing to agricultural practices, religious practices to welfare policies, urban riots to aircraft hijacking. According to Rogers (1983), diffusion occurs when some "innovation is communicated through certain channels over time among members of a social system" (1983: 14). The diffusion of an innovation follows an S-shaped curve where the process is initially slow, then rapidly increases, then tapers off as fewer and fewer actors are left to adopt the innovation. Most definitions of diffusion include the following four elements: a *transmitter*, an *adopter*, an *innovation* that is being diffused, and a *channel* along which the item may be transmitted. The transmitter is often referred to as the "previous adopter" while the adopter is sometimes called the "potential adopter" (Soule and Zylan 1997).

It is generally recognized that there are two basic types of models of diffusion, the *hierarchical* and the *proximal* (Collier and Messick 1975; della Porta and Kriesi 1999). Hierarchical models posit that diffusion occurs in a "top-down" fashion from actors of high status to actors of lower status, or that the actions of high status members will be emulated by lower status members (see Wejnert 2002 for a discussion of status characteristics and how these affect diffusion). For example, Soule (1995) examines (but finds no support for) the "Harvard Effect," whereby the tactics of activists at Harvard were closely copied by students at other, less prestigious, universities. Proximal models posit that actors mimic others who are spatially or culturally relevant to them. These models examine the effects of regional diffusion and/or diffusion among culturally constructed categories (Soule 1997).

Diffusion between social movement organizations can be mediated by two primary types of linkages or channels: *direct* or *indirect* (Soule 1997). Direct channels of diffusion are akin to cohesion models used by network analysts which hold that ideas diffuse most rapidly when individuals are in direct and frequent contact. In other words, the rate at which items diffuse varies with the level of interaction between actors: at high levels of interaction between individuals, we expect to see higher rates of adoption of innovations. Thus, with respect to direct channels of diffusion, the primary mechanism of diffusion are the network ties that facilitate the direct (or point to point) spread of an innovation. (See chapter 15 in this volume for a discussion of the role of direct network ties in collective action.)

Despite the intuitive nature of this process, direct channels of diffusion fail to account for the fact that *unconnected* actors and organizations frequently display high degrees of homogeneity in form, structure, ideology, and practice. In other words, at times it appears that items diffuse between actors that are not at all

connected. When this happens, it is common to consider the effects of indirect
channels or "nonrelational" channels of diffusion (McAdam and Rucht 1993).
There are two primary mechanisms associated with indirect channels of diffusion.
The first is a sense of shared identification between activists, or as McAdam and
Rucht note, this type of diffusion depends "on a minimal identification of adopter
and transmitter" (1993: 60). The higher the level of identification with a shared
social or cultural category, the more extensive the transmission of an innovation.[2]
The second mechanism of indirect diffusion is the media that can both broadcast the
actions of the transmitter to potential adopters *and* connect otherwise unconnected
individuals via a shared response to events covered (Oliver and Myers 2000). The
following section provides a brief review of the role of direct and indirect diffusion
channels in the social movements literature.

DIFFUSION RESEARCH IN THE FIELD OF SOCIAL MOVEMENTS

Direct Ties

Several studies of direct network ties have looked at their effect on the diffusion of
collective action and other elements of social movements.[3] A classic example of
work in this area is Rudé's (1964) examination of the diffusion of collective action
along transportation routes in England and in France between 1730 and 1848. He
argues that information about rebellions diffused through communication networks
of travelers along transportation routes. In a similar vein, Bohstedt and Williams
(1988) analyze the spread of rioting in Devonshire in the late eighteenth century.
Through their qualitative historical analysis, these authors find that food riots at the
community level were far more common when a neighboring community previously
experienced a riot. Further, they argue that dense community networks formed
through market transactions facilitated the imitation of food riots across communities. Finally, and more recently, Hedström et al. (2000) found that the diffusion of
the Swedish Social Democratic Party between 1894 and 1911 followed the travel
routes of political agitators at that time.

   Another study of the role of direct ties in diffusion is that by Petras and Zeitlin
(1967) who examine political rebellion in Chile and the role that communication
networks had in the dissemination of radical ideology. Arguing that the mining
industry in Chile tended to spawn high levels of radical, Marxist ideology and
activism, Petras and Zeitlin (1967) attempt to demonstrate that radical ideology
spread from mining to agricultural municipalities in Chile. Specifically, these authors
find that the propensity of an agricultural municipality to vote for Salvadore Allende
in the elections of 1958 and 1964 was directly related to the number of mining
municipalities to which the agricultural municipality was connected. The implication is clear; ideology diffuses via communication networks between mining and
agricultural municipalities.

   In another historical account, Gould (1991) studies the strength of network ties
between different districts of the Paris Commune of 1871. He argues that overlapping enlistment in the National Guard (i.e., people belonging to battalions outside
their own districts) produced interdependencies across districts in the commitment
to resistance of the Versailles army. More specifically, insurrection against the

impeding Versailles army in one district depended on the levels of resistance in other districts to which the district was directly linked.

Through his event history analysis of data on the mobilization of Swedish trade unions from 1890 to 1940, Hedstrom (1994) also shows that direct network ties are important to the mobilization of individuals. He argues that "an individual's decision to join a social movement is influenced not only by the actor's own situation but also by the behavior of other actors included in the decision maker's immediate social network" (Hedstrom 1994: 1176). Hedstrom's conclusions are quite similar to those drawn by McAdam and Paulsen (1993) who argue that the strength of decision ties of applicants to the 1964 Mississippi Freedom Summer Project is one of the more important factors predicting eventual participation by applicants to the project.

In his study of the Detroit riot of 1967, Singer (1970) interviewed 500 African-American men about where they received information about where, in that city, looting, rioting, and police presence were located. The chief source of information, according to his informants, was personal communication. Apparently, direct network ties were an important source of information during this particular riot. These findings resonate with those reported by Feagin and Hahn (1973) and Wilson and Orum (1976) who note that intracity diffusion of information on riots was facilitated by interpersonal or direct ties.

Not only are direct ties important to the mobilization of individuals, but they may also facilitate the transmission of information between already mobilized groups of collective actors. For example, Meyer and Whittier (1994) argue that ideological frames, tactical innovations, and organizational structures can "spill over" from one social movement to another. Their study of the impact that the women's movement had on the peace movement shows that social movements are not bounded and discrete entities and that direct and indirect ties between movements facilitate the diffusion of ideas, tactics, and organizational structures.[4]

Direct network ties have also been shown to facilitate the diffusion of protest tactics. Morris (1981) studies the diffusion of the sit-in protests in the late 1950s and early 1960s during the civil rights movement and argues that direct network ties facilitated their spread. By emphasizing the role that organizational and personal networks played in the diffusion of sit-ins, Morris (1981) shows that sit-ins were not spontaneous and uncoordinated activities but that preexisting organizational and personal ties "provided the sit-ins with resources and communication networks needed for their emergence and development" (Morris 1981: 765).[5] In related work, Morris (1984) discusses the way in which attendees at church services learned about (and were drawn to action in) the Montgomery Bus Boycott.

Indirect Ties

Like direct network ties, indirect network ties are also important to the diffusion of collective action, as well as social movement ideology, symbols, and tactics. One important mechanism of indirect network ties is the collective identity or shared cultural understanding of activists who are not directly connected. Perhaps one of the first empirical analyses of diffusion through indirect channels is Pitcher et al.'s (1978) study of collective violence in several nation states over a century and a half.[6] Beginning with the criticism of previous analyses of collective violence that assumed independence among violent events, the authors argue to the contrary. Collective violence events are very much influenced by previous events. Further, the authors state that "units of the population which generate...[collective violence] are seldom, if ever, in direct communication with one another" (Pitcher et al. 1978: 24). More likely, units are indirectly linked, which nonetheless provides for a very salient means of diffusion of innovation.

McAdam and Rucht (1993) also discuss the tendency for different tactics of protest to diffuse throughout the world system. For example, the 1976 mass demonstrations at the nuclear site of Seabrook were inspired by the 1974 protests at another nuclear site in Germany, which were, in turn, inspired by a similar demonstration earlier in that year in France. McAdam and Rucht (1993) trace antinuclear demonstrations of similar magnitude that used similar protest tactics to the non-violent collective action in South France in 1971. Implicit in their analysis is the notion of a socially constructed identity between social movement actors in one country and actors in other countries during different time periods. In other words, membership in the category "social movement activist" enhances the likelihood of the diffusion of tactics among members. Similarly, we may observe that the protest events of the peace movement of the early 1980s followed a similar pattern. For example, there was an international wave of protest in November 1981 over NATO's decision to station cruise missiles in several Western European countries. Protests began in Germany, the country most adversely affected by the NATO decision, but rapidly spread to Great Britain, France, Belgium, and the Netherlands (Kriesi et al. 1995). Interestingly, several countries not directly affected by the decision also witnessed protest (i.e., Switzerland, Finland, Norway, Sweden, and Denmark).

Soule and Tarrow (1991) study the protest events that took place in Europe between 1847 and 1849. The authors claim that the years of their study mark the first modern cycle of protest. By comparing the temporal incidence of collective action and some of the symbols used by activists in logical pairs of countries (France and Germany, and Italy and Austria), it is shown that certain types of collective action diffused across national boundaries seemingly in the absence of direct ties (Soule and Tarrow 1991).

Soule (1995, 1997), by applying the institutionalist approach, shows that innovative student protest tactics diffused among educational institutions that were similar along certain dimensions. The construction of categories of similarity served as indirect channels between colleges and universities in the mid-1980s, leading to the diffusion of the shantytown protest tactic during the student anti-apartheid movement.

Conell and Cohn (1995), in their historical analysis of the French coal mining industry, examine the effect strikes have on subsequent strikes. These authors argue that it was *not* the objective bargaining conditions or level of organizational resources that led French miners to strike between 1890 and 1935. Rather, it was the rate of strikes in other labor movements. Conell and Cohn (1995) posit that strikes stimulate subsequent strikes by raising the consciousness of oppressed workers, by setting a date or an occasion for collective action, and by providing a tactical template for others to follow. Although Conell and Cohn (1995) do not cast their arguments in terms of indirect ties, the implication is that strikes affect the probability of subsequent strikes via shared cultural understandings.

The mass media is another important mechanism for indirect channels of diffusion. In a well-known series of studies on race riots, Spilerman (1970, 1971) found that the structural characteristics of metropolitan areas were seemingly unrelated to whether or not the metropolitan area experienced a riot in the late 1960s. In particular, Spilerman (1970, 1971) argues that a number of objective conditions (e.g., education, employment, housing conditions, etc.) of urban blacks were *not* related to riot violence. Instead, noting that riot incidences appeared to cluster in time, Spilerman (1976) hypothesized that riots diffused throughout urban, black areas. Spilerman points to the crucial role that televised civil rights activism had on creating a "black solidarity that transcended boundaries of communities" (1976: 790). To Spilerman (1976), then, the media served as an indirect channel of diffusion by creating a cultural linkage between African Americans in different metropolitan areas. Television, he argues, familiarized individuals all over the country with the "details of rioting and with the motivations of rioters" (1976: 790). Singer's aforementioned (1970) work on the Detroit riot of 1967 points to the media (as well as interpersonal or direct communication) as a leading source of information on the riot in their city.

Recently, Myers (1997) has reanalyzed Spilerman's (1976) data using event historical analysis and diffusion models. Myers (1997) demonstrates first that the structural characteristics of Spilerman's cities actually *do* lead to riots; in particular, Myers (1997) finds support for competition and strain theories. Additionally, Myers (1997) finds evidence for both Spilerman's (1976) hypothesis that riots diffused both regionally and nationally. In more recent treatments, Myers (2000) finds evidence for the claim that riots that received national media attention increased the subsequent national level of riots, while smaller riots that only received local media attention only increased riot propensities in their local area. Myers (2000) stresses the importance of the mass media in sustaining collective violence.

THEORETICAL DEVELOPMENTS IN THE AREA OF DIFFUSION AND SOCIAL MOVEMENTS

With the recent growth in interest in diffusion in social movements has come a series of theoretical contributions to this area. Perhaps Tarrow (1998) has made the most central and important link to diffusion theory by relating to the concept of *cycles of protest*. A cycle of protest is a period of increased conflict, across many sectors of a social system, in which we are likely to see the diffusion of new tactical forms, identities, frames, and so forth. Work on cycles of protest has long recognized that, in social movements, actions by one group affect subsequent actions by other groups. The focus of work on cycles has been on the interrelations between various actors, including movement participants, the state or other targets, and counter-movements.

Building on Tarrow's work, McAdam (1995) makes the distinction between "initiator" and "spin-off" movements. Noting the recent trend in the social movements literature to recognize that social movements are not discrete, independent entities, but rather are typically affected by other social movements, McAdam (1995) seeks to specify the differences between initiator movements, which set a protest cycle in motion, and spin off movements, which are sparked by the initi-ators.[7] In particular, McAdam (1995) specifies the important role that diffusion processes have in the rise of spin-off movements. He disputes the classic notions of the contagion of collective behavior (LeBon 1897; Tarde 1903; Blumer 1939) and argues that the diffusion process is far from irrational and pathological; rather, it is "thought to reflect normal learning and influence processes as mediated by the network structures of everyday social life" (McAdam 1995: 231). Closely akin to this is the observation made by Snow and Benford (1992) and Tarrow (1994) that innovative "master frames" are developed early on in the cycle of protest and diffuse to later movements within the cycle.

Related to work on cycles of protest are two other key concepts that are important to work on tactical diffusion: Tilly's (1978) notion of the *repertoire of contention* and Tarrow's (1993, 1998) concept of *modularity*. The repertoire of contention is the complete set of protest tactics available to a social movement at any given time (Tilly 1978). Historically and culturally specific, the repertoire is what actors "know how to do and what others expect them to do" (Tarrow 1993: 70). Social movement actors frequently employ a *flexible repertoire of contention* that allows for the observation of other groups' tactics and for the adoption of tactics believed to be effective. Social movement actors "do not have to reinvent the wheel at each place and in each conflict. Rather, they often find inspiration in the ideas and tactics espoused and practiced by other activists" (McAdam and Rucht 1993: 58). Imitation of protest tactics leads to their diffusion and to "waves" of certain forms of protest (Tilly 1978; Soule and Tarrow 1991).

According to Tilly (1978) and Tarrow (1993, 1998), the modern repertoire of contention is quite different from the traditional repertoire. The traditional reper-toire often consisted of what Hobsbawm (1959) calls "primitive rebellion." Tactics found in the traditional repertoire tended to be directed at the cause of the grievance, were very specific in nature, and were rather inflexible; examples include food riots and banditry. The modern repertoire is far more flexible and includes tactics that are easily imported by actors to various settings; examples include the boycott and the strike (Tarrow 1998). Once the tactics of the modern repertoire are used and understood, they can be readily employed by virtually any movement actor in virtually any situation; in other words, these tactics become *modular*. The result of the shift to the modern repertoire is that "activists in disparate locations with minimal organization and without direct linkages are able to unite in national social movements" (Soule 1997: 859).

Another important theoretical development in this area attempts to better specify the role of agency in the diffusion process, particularly as it applies to the study of social movements. Snow and Benford (1999) criticize research on diffusion for failing to adequately define whether or not the transmitter and the adopter are active or passive agents. They argue that in the recent studies reviewed above, the agency of the actors is ignored or taken for granted. These authors discuss four types of diffusion and discuss the role of agency within each of these types.

First, "reciprocation," includes cases of diffusion when both the transmitter and the adopter are interested in the item being diffused and have an interest in promot-ing the diffusion process. An example of this is Soule's (1997) work on the diffusion of the protest tactic of the shantytown where activists at colleges and universities were interested in this new and innovative tactic of protest and benefited from its diffusion. Hence both previous and potential student activist-adopters are interested in the item and gain from its diffusion.

The "adaptation" form of diffusion includes the case of an active adopter and a passive transmitter such as when the adopter intentionally selects an item or items to copy from the transmitter, who remains passive. Here, the adopter deliberately and strategically selects an innovation that is then adapted to fit the new situation or context. In Soule's (1999) work on the shantytown protests, she describes how students borrowed from their predecessors the tactic of the "sit-in," but modified it in important ways to become the shantytown tactic.

The "accommodation" form of diffusion includes cases of diffusion where the transmitter promotes the diffusion of a relatively alien practice by tailoring the innovation to the needs of a fairly passive adopter. In this case, the item being diffused is strategically fit to the adopter's culture or context by the transmitter. Snow and Benford (1999) provide the useful example of the spread of the Sokagakkai/Nichiren Shoshu Buddhist movement to the United States and other countries from Japan. Part of the reason that this movement has been so successful worldwide is its ability to cloak its beliefs in culturally specific traditions and symbols that resonate with the particular society that the leaders are targeting.

Simple contagion is the final case discussed by Snow and Benford (1999), who argue this form makes little sense in the context of the diffusion of social processes. Here, neither the adopter nor the transmitter have any interest in the item being diffused; both are passive and/or uninterested in the item and its diffusion. This type might best be exemplified by biological processes of the diffusion or contagion of an illness, which is nonagentic. Despite the fact that a number of early scholars have argued that collective behavior diffuses in this manner (LeBon 1897; Tarde 1903; Blumer 1939) there has been scarce empirical support for this notion.

Finally, Oliver and Myers (1998, 2000), in a series of unpublished papers, have outlined a theory of social movements that focuses on diffusion as the central process. To these authors, a social movement is a set of interrelated events and actions by a number of actors who are oriented toward a broad goal or issue. Movement actions and actors affect others that, in turn, set in motion the cycle of protest. These authors begin with three basic observations. First, much (if not all) collective action is mobilized via networks and then diffuses. Second, the diffusion of protest leads to cycles, as discussed by Tarrow and others. Finally, these authors note (as I do here) that networks are important to diffusion. Thus the work of Oliver and Myers has better specified the role of networks in the process of diffusion. And these authors have been instrumental in developing formal models of protest diffusion within cycles of protest.

Some Suggestions for Future Research

Thus far I have reviewed the important empirical work that has been done on diffusion in the field of social movements and I have discussed some of the recent theoretical work that impacts the study of diffusion in this field. It is now time for scholars of social movements interested in diffusion processes to expand on what has already been done. To this end, there are a number of questions that should be examined.

First, scholars might begin to ask how a particular movement innovation comes to dominate other possible innovations in a particular period. To date, work on diffusion in social movements has focused more on charting the process of diffusion of items, not on asking why it is that certain innovations diffuse over, other possibilities. With respect to tactical innovations, there has been some work done on *how* new innovations come about (McAdam 1983; Tarrow 1989),[8] but less work done on the question of *which* innovation will be chosen, given a set of innovations from which to choose.

Certainly, the decision to adopt an innovation has something to do with the success (or perceived success) of the choices available at a given time. And it probably has something to do with whether or not the innovation strikes a chord with the social movement actors and/or leaders. But, it might also have something to do with decision structure within the social movement, and it might have something to do with how repressive the state is. In other words, there are a great many factors that might affect which innovations are actually adopted; these should be explored in more detail by movement scholars.

Related to the issue of the choice of innovation is the notion that innovations with certain characteristics are more likely to be adopted (or be adopted at a higher rate). The broader diffusion literature points to five important characteristics of the innovation that should affect the rate of adoption. Perhaps scholars of social movements should begin to examine some of these five characteristics with respect to innovations in movements.

First, innovations perceived as better than other existing options will be more likely to be adopted; the *relative advantage* of an innovation, according to the diffusion literature, is central. Questions about whether or not a new tactic will bring success or spur extreme repression speak to the relative advantage of a new tactic, as do questions about the cost of an innovation (Wejnert 2002). Or, questions about whether a new frame is likely to resonate with social movement actors, or a new identity likely to mobilize more people, also speak to the relative advantage of innovations.

Second, innovations *compatible* with the experiences, values, ideas, and needs of activists are said to be more likely to diffuse. For example, when considering the use of a new and violent tactic, movement organizers will be more likely to adopt it if they, in the past, have used violence. Or, when considering adopting a "Pro-Life" frame, for example, movement leaders should be certain that this frame is consistent with the values of its members who may be in favor of the death penalty, despite their disdain for abortion. The importance of choosing a frame that resonates with the experiences and culture of the subject of the frame has been called the "narrative fidelity" by Snow and Benford (1988).

A third characteristic of the innovation that affects its diffusion is its *complexity*. If an innovation is difficult to use, it may be less likely to diffuse. In the early 1990s, activists associated with the Lesbian Avengers began to eat fire at various demonstrations, a dramatic and dangerous protest tactic to say the least. While the tactic has been used on many occasions by members of this organization, there is not much evidence that this tactic has diffused to other social movements or movement organizations. Perhaps the failure of this tactic to diffuse widely has something to do with the fact that fire-eating is not easily implemented and is dangerous if not done correctly.

A fourth characteristic of an innovation closely related to this is its *triability*, or whether or not there is a low-cost or easy way for activists to try out the innovation, without necessarily committing to it. With respect to the shantytown protest tactic discussed earlier, at many universities, students erected day-long, temporary shantytowns that were not actually slept in (Soule 1995). At several of these universities, students subsequently built more permanent structures that were, in fact, slept in. The triability of the shantytown may have made its eventual adoption easier by allowing activists to gauge the response of the university and other students.

Finally, whether or not the *results* of an innovation are *observable* to potential adopters is another characteristic that ought to impact the diffusion of an innovation. With respect to movement actions, the most observable result may be police or state response to a particular protest (see Chapter 10 in this volume). The question of how repression affects protest has long been studied and there is some evidence that, in some contexts, repression can stimulate protest (Van Dyke et al. 2001). But, other observable responses may be in concessions granted by the target. If, for example, a university divests of its South African holdings because students are building shantytowns, students at other colleges and universities who observe this action may be more inclined to build shantytowns as well (Soule 1999, 2001).

Perhaps scholars of diffusion of social movements could gain purchase on questions about the attributes of innovations and the diffusion process by studying innovations that failed to diffuse. Scholars have scarcely looked at these, as they are most often considered mistakes. For example, in May of 1978, environmentalists in the United States attempted to popularize "Sun Day," modeled after Earth Day (Hollie 1978). The purpose of the demonstrations that these activists sponsored was to promote solar power. However, unlike Earth Day, "Sun Day" never really caught on. What is it about innovations that fail to catch on? Careful comparisons within a movement of two innovations, one that diffused and one that did not, would likely yield a great understanding about why it is that some innovations diffuse, while others do not.

Related to the issue of innovations that fail to diffuse is the idea of failed innovation. Often, as noted above, it is assumed that innovations that diffuse are successful. While this makes intuitive sense, it is not always the case empirically. In fact, the diffusion literature is rife with examples of failed innovations that diffused, nonetheless. In the medical literature, for example, elective hysterectomies, tonsilectomies, bleeding as a treatment for disease (Bikhchandani et al. 1998), and an ineffective herpes treatment (Lipton and Hershaft 1985) all diffused across communities of physicians. Outside of the medical literature, a classic example of a failure that diffused is Project DARE, an educational program designed to deter drug use among children, which diffused across US cities in the late 1990s. Research on the effectiveness of DARE has shown that the actual effectiveness at preventing drug use has been quite small (Ennett et al. 1994). In the field of social movements, Soule (1995, 1999) shows that the shantytown protest tactic was not actually effective at causing university divestment, yet diffused across college campuses at a very rapid rate in the 1980s. As movement scholars begin/continue to ask questions about the efficacy of particular movements or campaigns (see chapters on outcomes earlier in this volume), questions about how the efficacy affects diffusion should also be addressed.

Another area for future research relates to Snow and Benford's (1999) discussion of the role of agency in the diffusion process, as discussed above. These authors have provided a useful typology of different types of diffusion, based on the agency of the transmitter and the adopter. I would like to suggest that diffusion scholars now start to empirically examine these types of diffusion by comparing and contrasting each along certain dimensions. For example, does the rate of diffusion differ between these types of diffusion? Or, are certain types of diffusion more or less likely to occur in repressive regimes? And, are direct and indirect ties, as discussed earlier, more or less likely to facilitate certain types of diffusion? Questions about the role of agency in the diffusion process are obviously not limited to these questions; however, it is time for researchers to begin to empirically investigate the similarities and differences between the types of diffusion described by Snow and Benford.

Scholars should also begin to compare the effectiveness of indirect and direct channels of diffusion for spreading elements of social movements. Recently Oliver and Myers (2000) have pointed out that there is an often overlooked distinction between *communication* and *influence*. Both of these processes may convey information; thus both have the potential to impact the actions of others. However, communication, as exemplified by the mass media, is less likely to change opinions and perhaps cause others to act than is the influence of direct, personal ties. Thus we might expect that, at least in certain contexts, direct ties may be better or more effective channels than are indirect ties. Most studies of diffusion in social movements have tended to focus on either direct *or* indirect ties and their role in the diffusion process; however, there is a need to carefully examine the differences between these two conduits of diffusion, because, as Oliver and Myers (2000) correctly note, there are differences between these with respect to potential for changing opinions and presumably for diffusion.

Finally, scholars interested in expanding what we understand about framing processes and diffusion would be well served to examine the concept of *theorization* as advanced by diffusion scholars (Strang and Meyer 1993). Theorization is the "self-conscious development and specification of abstract categories and the formulation of patterned relationships such as chains of cause and effect". It is a "strategy for making sense of the world" (Strang and Meyer 1993: 492, 493). In many ways, the concept of theorization is similar to the way in which "frames" are used by scholars of social movements. Building on the early work of Goffman (1974: 21) who defined frames as "schemata of interpretation" that enable people to "locate, perceive, identify, and label" events and issues in their world, scholars of social movements argue that frames "render events or occurrences meaningful and thereby function to organize experience and guide action" (Benford and Snow 2000: 614).

The way that frames have been talked about with respect to diffusion assumes that, in most cases, it is the innovation or practice (or "diffusing object" in the words of Snow and Benford 1999) that is being framed. For example, Benford and Snow have recently hypothesized that framing activity may be "most relevant to social movement diffusion processes when only one party in the process ... takes the active role" (2000: 627). Here, an innovation (idea, tactic, slogan, set of religious beliefs, and so on) may be strategically framed in such a way as to improve the chances for adoption. Thus, in the example discussed earlier, the spread of the Sokagakkai/

Nichiren Shoshsu set of beliefs was made possible through the efforts of the movement to tailor the stated beliefs to fit a variety of different national contexts.

This discussion resonates with the ideas articulated by diffusion theorists who speak of theorization. According to these scholars, most often, theorization "documents the many virtues involved" with the innovation (Strang and Meyer 1993: 497). However, the way in which diffusion scholars talk about theorization is somewhat broader. For example, to Strang and Meyer (1993), it is not merely the innovation or practice that is theorized, but also the adopters and transmitters. While the adopters and transmitters may differ greatly on many dimensions, often one dimension is theorized as similar; thus social practices flow because of this one dimension of similarity. In other words, while the diffusing practice may be theorized or framed to fit different adopters and transmitters, the adopters and transmitters are *also* theorized (or framed) as similar on some dimension or set of dimensions. This culturally constructed homogeneity (or, as discussed above, indirect channel of diffusion) facilitates the diffusion process, just as strategically framing the diffusion object does.

CONCLUSION

In this chapter, I have discussed the existing theoretical and empirical literature on diffusion in social movements with an eye to suggesting some areas for future research. I have categorized the empirical work based on the type of diffusion channel relevant to the study at hand, direct or indirect. And, I have noted some of the important theoretical advances in recent years that have dealt with the topic of diffusion. While we have come quite a distance since some of the original work in this area that conceived of diffusion as a pathological and disturbing phenomenon, there are still questions that might be addressed by those interested in diffusion of social movements.

In particular, this review has suggested that scholars need to examine more carefully the content of the innovation being diffused. By this, I mean that we ought to begin to ascertain what sorts of characteristics of innovations are likely to speed the process of adoption. I have suggested some characteristics of innovations that may be relevant to diffusion within social movements. But, I have also suggested that scholars would be well served to investigate innovations that do *not* diffuse as a way to gain purchase on why certain innovations spread very rapidly. Related to the call for research on innovations that fail to diffuse, I have also suggested that scholars examine unsuccessful innovations that diffuse nonetheless.

A second broad suggestion for future research was a call for empirical tests of Snow and Benford's (1999) potentially useful typology of diffusion based on the role of agency in the diffusion process. These scholars based their typology on some of the existing research on diffusion; thus the typology is quite grounded and makes a great deal of sense. However, like any good typology, it is now time to use it to generate new questions about the differences and similarities of the diffusion types suggested.

A third broad suggestion for future research that I have discussed is a comparison between the two types of diffusion channels (direct and indirect) with respect to the influence versus communication. In particular, it would be useful to understand the effectiveness of both of these types of diffusion in various contexts.

Finally, I have suggested that those interested in the role of frames in the diffusion process examine the concept of theorization that is used by diffusion scholars. I have suggested that the concept of theorization is broader and has been applied (at least in theoretical work) to adopters and transmitters, and not merely to the object of diffusion.

Notes

1   The idea that collective action is "contagious" is revisited by Lichbach (1985), who models protest in the postwar United Kingdom.

2   The concept of collective identity is important to the concept of indirect channels of diffusion. Klandermans (1992) argues that, at the most general level, individuals belong to groups and "to the extent that they identify with these categories, they come to share the beliefs of others within the same category" (Klandermans 1992: 94). Activists in one locale, then, may come to identify with activists elsewhere or even in a different movement altogether. Via the formation of this collective identity, ideas and beliefs (and even tactics) are more readily transferred.

3   Throughout this chapter I will discuss research on riots and crowds as well as on social movements. While it is important to note that these phenomena differ in important ways, it is interesting to note that some of the findings with regard to diffusion are similar.

4   It is important to note, however, that Meyer and Whittier (1994) discuss both direct and indirect ties between the women's movement and the peace movement.

5   Oberschall (1989) disagrees with Morris's (1981) assertion that direct ties led to the diffusion of sit-ins used in the 1959–60 period of the civil rights movement. Instead, Oberschall (1989) uses a diffusion model based on collective behavior theory to demonstrate that the sit-ins were actually not planned but were unorganized and spontaneous. Also see Killian's (1984) article for a conclusion similar to that of Oberschall (1989).

6   See Diekmann (1979) for an elaboration on Pitcher et al.'s (1978) mathematical model.

7   Initiator movements are such movements as Solidarity in Poland and the American civil rights movement (McAdam 1995), while spin-off movements are those that are set in motion by these initiators.

8   McAdam (1983) has examined how new tactics are employed as a response to how the state has dealt with previous tactics. In other words, we might think of tactical innovation as a game of chess between movement actors and the state; as each makes its move, the other changes tactics and strategy. Tarrow (1989) discusses how, during a cycle of protest, we are likely to see the radicalization of tactics, as a function of competition between different movement organizations. As each organization attempts to compete for support, organizations employ more radical tactics.

References and further reading

Benford, Robert D., and David A. Snow (2000) Framing Processes and Social Movements: An Overview and Assessment. *Annual Review of Sociology*, 26, 611–39.

Bikhchandani, Sushil, David Hirshleifer, and Ivo Welch (1997) Learning from the Behavior of Others: Conformity, Fads, and Informational Cascades. *Journal of Economic Perspectives*, 12 (3), 151–70.

Blumer, Herbert (1939) Collective Behavior. In R. E. Park (ed.), *Principles of Sociology*. New York: Barnes & Noble, 219–88.

Bohstedt, John, and Dale Williams (1987) The Diffusion of Riots: The Patterns of 1766, 1795, and 1801 in Devonshire. *Journal of Interdisciplinary History*, 19, 1–24.

Coleman, James S., Elihu Katz, and Herbert Menzel (1966) *Medical Innovation*. New York: Bobbs-Merrill.

Collier, David, and Richard E. Messick (1975) Prerequisites Versus Diffusion: Testing Alternative Explanations of Social Security Adoption. *American Political Science Review*, 69, 1299–1315.

Conell, Carol, and Cohn, Samuel (1995) Learning from Other People's Actions: Environmental Variation and Diffusion in French Coal Mining Strikes, 1890–1935. *American Journal of Sociology*, 101, 366–403.

Curtis, Russell L., and Louis A. Zurcher (1973) Stable Resources of Protest Movements: The Multi-Organizational Field. *Social Forces*, 52, 53–61.

Davis, Gerald F. (1991) Agents without Principles? The Spread of the Poison Pill through the Intercorporate Network. *Administrative Science Quarterly*, 36, 583–613.

della Porta, Donatella, and Hanspeter Kriesi (1999) Social Movements in a Globalizing World: An Introduction. In Donatella della Porta, Hanspeter Kreisi, and Dieter Rucht (eds.), *Social Movements in a Globalizing World*. London: Macmillan, 3–22.

Denton, Frank, and Warren Phillips (1967) Some Patterns in the History of Violence. *Journal of Conflict Resolution*, 12, 182–95.

Diekmann, Andreas (1979) A Dynamic Stochastic Version of the Pitcher-Hamblin-Miller Model of "Collective Violence." *Journal of Mathematical Sociology*, 6, 277–82.

Ennett, Susan T., Nancy S. Tobler, Christopher L. Ringwalt, and Robert L. Flewelling (1994) How Effective Is Drug Abuse Resistance Education? A Meta-Analysis of Project DARE Outcome Evaluations. *American Journal of Public Health*, 84 (9), 1394–401.

Feagin, Joe R., and Harlan Hahn (1973) *Ghetto Revolts: The Politics of Violence in American Cities*. New York: Macmillan.

Fischer, Claude S., and Glenn R. Carroll (1987) Telephone and Automobile Diffusion in the United States, 1902–1937. *American Journal of Sociology*, 93, 1153–78.

Galaskiewicz, Joseph, and Ronald S. Burt (1991) Interorganization Contagion in Corporate Philanthropy. *Administrative Science Quarterly*, 36, 88–105.

Garner, Roberta (1997) Fifty Years of Social Movement Theory. In Roberta Garner and John Tenuto (eds.), *Social Movement Theory and Research*. Lanham, MD: Scarecrow, 1–60.

Goertz, Gary (1994) *Contexts of International Politics*. New York: Cambridge University Press.

Goffman, Erving (1974) *Frame Analysis: An Essay on the Organization of the Experience*. New York: HarperColophon.

Gould, Roger (1991) Multiple Networks and Mobilization in the Paris Commune, 1871. *American Sociological Review*, 56, 716–29.

Greve, Henrich (1995) Jumping Ship: The Diffusion of Strategy Abandonment. *Administrative Science Quarterly*, 40, 444–73.

Hagerstrand, Torsten ([1953] 1967) *Innovation Diffusion as a Spatial Process*. Chicago: University of Chicago Press.

Hedstrom, Peter (1994) Contagious Collectivities: On the Spatial Diffusion of Swedish Trade Unions, 1890–1940. *American Journal of Sociology*, 99, 1157–79.

Hedstrom, Peter, Rickard Sandell, and Charlotta Stern (2000) Mesolevel Networks and the Diffusion of Social Movements: The Case of the Swedish Social Democratic Party. *American Journal of Sociology*, 106 (1), 145–72.

Hobsbawm, Eric J. (1959) *Primitive Rebels*. New York: Norton.

Holden, Robert T. (1986) The Contagiousness of Aircraft Hijacking. *American Journal of Sociology*, 91, 874–904.

Hollie, Pamela G. (1977) Energy Plea on Sun Day: Convert Dream to Reality. *New York Times*, May 4.

Huff, David, and James Lutz (1974) The Contagion of Political Unrest in Independent Black Africa. *Economic Geography*, 50, 352–367.

Jackson, Maurice, Elenora Peterson, James Bull, Sverre Monsen, and Patricia Richmond (1960) The Failure of an Incipient Social Movement. *Pacific Sociological Review*, 3, 35–40.

Katz, Elihu (1967) Diffusion (Interpersonal Influence). In David L. Shils (ed.), *International Encyclopedia of the Social Sciences*. London: Macmillan; New York: Free Press, 78–85.

Killian, Lewis M. (1984) Organization, Rationality and Spontaneity in the Civil Rights Movement. *American Sociological Review*, 49, 770–83.

Klandermans, Bert (1990) Linking the "Old" and "New" Movement Networks in the Netherlands. In Russell J. Dalton and Manfred Kuechler (eds.), *Challenging the Political Order: New Social Movements in Western Democracies*. Cambridge: Polity, 122–36.

——(1992) The Social Construction of Protest and Multiorganizational Fields. In Aldon D. Morris and Carol McClurg Mueller (eds.), *Frontiers in Social Movement Theory*. New Haven: Yale University Press, 77–103.

Kornhauser, William (1959) *The Politics of Mass Society*. New York: Free Press.

Kriesi, Hanspeter, Ruud Koopmans, Jan Willem Duyvendak, and Marco G. Giugni (1995) *New Social Movements in Western Europe*. Minneapolis: University of Minnesota Press.

Land, Kenneth, Glenn Deane, and Judith Blau (1991) Religious Pluralism and Church Membership: A Spatial Diffusion Model. *American Sociological Review*, 56, 237–49.

LeBon, Gustave (1897) *The Crowd*. London: Unwin.

Lichbach, Mark (1985) Protest: Random or Contagious? *Armed Forces and Society*, 11, 581–608.

Lipton, Jack P., and Alan M. Hershaft (1985) On the Widespread Acceptance of Dubious Medical Findings. *Journal of Health and Social Behavior*, 26, 336–51.

McAdam, Doug (1982) *Political Process and the Development of Black Insurgency, 1930–1970*. Chicago: University of Chicago Press.

——(1983) Tactical Innovation and the Pace of Insurgency. *American Sociological Review*, 48, 735–54.

——(1987) *Freedom Summer*. New York: Oxford University Press.

——(1995) "Initiator" and "Spin-off" Movements: Diffusion Processes in Protest Cycles. In Mark Traugott (ed.), *Repertoires and Cycles of Collective Action*. Durham, NC: Duke University Press, 217–39.

McAdam, Doug, and Ronnelle Paulsen (1993) Specifying the Relationship between Social Ties and Activism. *American Journal of Sociology*, 3, 640–67.

McAdam, Doug, and Dieter Rucht (1993) The Cross National Diffusion of Movement Ideas. *Annals of the American Academy of Political and Social Science*, 528, 36–59.

Meyer, David S., and Nancy Whittier (1994) Social Movement Spillover. *Social Problems*, 41, 277–98.

Morris, Aldon (1981) Black Southern Sit-in Movement: An Analysis of Internal Organization. *American Sociological Review*, 46, 744–67.

——(1984) *The Origins of the Civil Rights Movement: Black Communities Organizing for Change*. New York: Free Press.

Myers, Daniel J. (1997) Racial Rioting in the 1960s: An Event History Analysis of Local Conditions. *American Sociological Review*, 62, 94–112.

——(2000) The Diffusion of Collective Violence: Infectiousness, Susceptibility, and Mass Media Networks. *American Journal of Sociology*, 106 (1), 173–208.

Oberschall, Anthony (1973) *Social Conflict and Social Movements*. Englewood Cliffs, NJ: Prentice-Hall.

——(1989) The 1960 Sit-ins: Protest Diffusion and Movement Takeoff. *Research in Social Movements, Conflict, and Change*, 11, 31–3.

Oliver, Pamela E., and Daniel J. Myers (1997) Diffusion Models of Cycles of Protest as a Theory of Social Movements. Paper presented at the Congress of the International Sociological Association, Montreal, July.

—— (2000) Networks, Diffusion, and Cycles of Collective Action. Paper presented at the Workshop for Social Movement Analysis: The Network Perspective, Scotland, June.

Petras, James, and Maurice Zeitlin (1967) Miners and Agrarian Radicalism. *American Sociological Review*, 32, 578–86.

Pitcher, Brian, Robert Hamblin, and Jerry Miller (1977) The Diffusion of Collective Violence. *American Sociological Review*, 43, 23–35.

Rogers, Everett M. (1983) *Diffusion of Innovations*. New York: John Wiley.

Rude, George (1964) *The Crowd in History, 1730–1848*. New York: John Wiley.

Shorter, Edward, and Charles Tilly (1974) *Strikes in France: 1930–1968*. London: Cambridge University Press.

Singer, Benjamin D. (1970) Mass Media and Communication Processes in the Detroit Riot of 1967. *Public Opinion Quarterly*, 34 (2), 236–45.

Snow, David A., and Robert D. Benford (1988) Ideology, Frame Resonance, and Participant Mobilization". In Bert Klandermans, Hanspeter Kriesi, and Sidney Tarrow (eds.), *From Structure to Action: Social Movement Participation Across Cultures*. Greenwich, CT: JAI Press.

—— (1992) Master Frames and Cycles of Protest. In Aldon D. Morris and Carol McClurg Mueller (eds.), *Frontiers in Social Movement Theory*. New Haven: Yale University Press, 133–55.

—— (1999) Alternative Types of Cross-National Diffusion in the Social Movement Arena. In Donatella della Porta, Hanspeter Kreisi, and Dieter Rucht (eds.), *Social Movements in a Globalizing World*. London: Macmillan, 23–39.

Snyder, David, and William Kelly (1976) Industrial Violence in Italy, 1878–1903. *American Journal of Sociology*, 82, 131–62.

Soule, Sarah A. (1995) The Student Anti-Apartheid Movement in the United States: Diffusion of Protest Tactics and Policy Reform. PhD dissertation, Cornell University.

—— (1997) The Student Divestment Movement in the United States and Tactical Diffusion: The Shantytown Protest. *Social Forces*, 75, 855–83.

—— (1999) The Diffusion of an Unsuccessful Innovation. *Annals of the American Academy of Political and Social Sciences*, 566, 120–31

—— (2001) Situational Effects on Political Altruism: The Student Divestment Movement in the United States. In Marco Giugni and Florence Passy (eds.), *Political Altruism? Solidarity Movements in International Perspective*. Lanham, MD: Rowman Littlefield, 161–76.

Soule, Sarah A., and Sidney Tarrow (1991) Acting Collectively, 1847–1849: How Repertoires of Collective Action Changed and where it Happened. Paper presented at the Annual Meeting of the Social Science History Association, New Orleans, Louisiana.

Soule, Sarah A., and Yvonne Zylan (1997) Runway Train? The Diffusion of State-Level Reform to A(F)DC Eligibility Requirements, 1950–1967. *American Journal of Sociology*, 103 (3), 733–62.

Spilerman, Seymour (1970) The Causes of Racial Disturbances: A Comparison of Alternate Explanations. *American Sociological Review*, 35, 627–49.

—— (1971) The Causes of Racial Disturbances: A Test of Alternate Explanations. *American Sociological Review*, 36, 427–42.

—— (1976) Structural Characteristics of Cities and the Severity of Racial Disorders. *American Sociological Review*, 41, 771–93.

Strang, David, and Nancy Brandon Tuma (1993) Spatial and Temporal Heterogeneity in Diffusion. *American Journal of Sociology*, 99, 614–39.

Strang, David, and John W. Meyer (1993) Institutional Conditions for Diffusion. *Theory and Society*, 22, 487–511.

Strang, David, and Sarah A. Soule (1997) Diffusion in Organizations and Social Movements: From Hybrid Corn to Poison Pills. *Annual Review of Sociology*, 24, 265–90.

Tarde, G. (1903) *The Laws of Imitation*. New York: Holt.

Tarrow, Sidney (1993) Modular Collective Action and the Rise of the Social Movement: Why the French Revolution Was not Enough. *Politics and Society*, 21, 69–90.

——(1989) *Struggle, Politics, and Reform: Collective Action, Social Movements, and Cycles of Protest*. Cornell Studies In International Affairs, Western Societies Paper Number 21.

——(1998) *Power in Movement*. 2nd ed. Cambridge: Cambridge University Press.

Tilly, Charles (1977) *From Mobilization to Revolution*. Reading, MA: Addison-Wesley.

Tolbert, Pamela S., and Lynne G. Zucker (1983) Institutional Sources of Change in the Formal Structure of Organizations: The Diffusion of Civil Service Practices. *Administrative Science Quarterly*, 28, 22–39.

Turner, Ralph, and Lewis Killian (1987) *Collective Behavior*. Englewood Cliffs, NJ: Prentice-Hall.

Van Dyke, Nella, Sarah A. Soule, and John D. McCarthy (2001) The Role of Organization and Constituency in the Use of Confrontational Tactics by Social Movements. Unpublished Paper.

Wejnert, Barbara (2002) Integrating Models of Diffusion of Innovations: A Conceptual Framework. *Annual Review of Sociology*, 28, 297–326.

Wilson, Kenneth, and Anthony M. Orum (1976) Mobilizing People for Collective Political Action. *Journal of Political and Military Sociology*, 4, 187–202.

14

Transnational Processes and Movements

Jackie Smith

Global integration of various types has been occurring for hundreds of years, but recent decades have witnessed an especially rapid increase in the scope and scale of transnational interactions that significantly impact local conditions. The close of World War II ushered in a new set of international institutions designed to advance international political and economic cooperation, and those institutional frameworks have expanded into hundreds of new international organizations and have encouraged the formation of many thousands of transnational nongovernmental associations (Chatfield 1997; Boli and Thomas 1999). International cooperation, moreover, has grown beyond the more traditional realms of economic exchange and military security to include a growing array of issues that transcend national boundaries such as the environment, health, and crime. All of these changes have significant implications for the structures of political opportunities that activists face, including the formal structures governing national and international political participation, the configurations of movement allies and opponents, and the prospects for favorable or repressive government responses to movement pressure (della Porta and Kriesi 1999; Marks and McAdam 1999). Nevertheless, scholars have only recently begun to explore the consequences of these changes for social movements. This chapter examines the ways that transnational and global processes affect the conditions under which social movement actors seek to advance their claims and how activists have responded to the opportunities and challenges accompanying global integration. It also considers how social movements' interventions in transnational political processes have served to shape this evolving global political arena.

Pol. Opp.
Dynamics
Outcomes.

Globalization Processes and Social Movements

The World System and the National State

An appreciation for the institutional and cultural contexts of international politics must not ignore the underlying structural factors that define relations among states. Specifically, as world systems theory claims, the system of states is highly stratified between the "core" or early-industrializing states and the "periphery" states that were, through colonization or through some other form of unequal economic relations, relegated to a tertiary role in the world economic system. Economic globalization serves to institutionalize and reinforce this inequality (see Korzeniewicz and Moran 1997; Bello 2000a; Sklair 2001). "Semi-peripheral" states lie somewhere in the middle, as they have substantial enough resources to influence world market relations but they lack enough influence to play a leadership role in this system (see, e.g., Chase-Dunn 1998). This global hierarchy is reflected in global financial and political institutions, and although it does not always account for policy outcomes, it clearly impacts institutional dynamics. For instance, one of the major critiques by both protesters against the World Trade Organization and by governments of the global South is that this organization is largely controlled by the wealthy countries of the North, and in particular by the "Quad": the US, the European Union, Japan, and Canada (Wallach and Sforza 1999; Khor 2000). A state's position in the world-system hierarchy, therefore, will impact the opportunities for social movement mobilization both domestically and internationally.

A key assumption in world systems theory is that the hegemony of the core states in the world economic system depends upon the extraction of labor and other resources from the periphery to support both high levels of consumption among core workers as well as the maintenance of core hegemony in the world economy (Chase-Dunn 1998: 42–3). Thus structural features of the world economy give citizens in core states comparatively higher levels of political opportunity and resources for collective action. In contrast, while citizens in periphery countries do mobilize protests, they are far more likely than their counterparts in core countries to be violently repressed by their governments (Arrighi and Drangel 1986; Jenkins and Schock 1992). Contrast, for instance, the ten reported protester deaths in four periphery countries (Argentina, Paraguay, Pakistan, and Guyana) during the summer months of 2002 with the wave of protests against neoliberal globalization in the global North between 1999 and 2002, in which a single protester died.[1] Repression of citizens on the periphery alone does not maintain the inequalities of the global system, but the high standard of living for citizens of the core also helps sustain the legitimacy of the system by which core states exploit the periphery: "Perhaps even a stronger statement is warranted. It may be that the democratization of the core of the world economy owes a great deal to the control of sufficient resources to pay for the extension of rights, while that extension helped secure democratic popular assent for global domination" (Markoff 1999: 255).

The demand of the capitalist world economy for cheap labor from the periphery contributes to the political exclusion and repression of lower- and working classes in those states.[2] The repressive and exclusive character of many periphery states can be traced back to their colonial origins. Whereas European state development was an outcome of the interplay between military-coercive agents, the bourgeoisie, and the broader populace, the geographic and institutional dimensions of states on the periphery were defined by imperialist states for the purposes of economic exploitation. As a consequence of this history and of the Cold War politics of military aid, states on the periphery tend to be highly coercive and to have an inordinate coercive capacity in comparison with other actors in society (Tilly 1990: ch. 7). As contemporary experience shows, countries where the military is the strongest social institution face tremendous obstacles to democratization.

Further contributing to the limited opportunities for political mobilization on the periphery is the fact that core states intervene in the domestic political processes of key periphery states in order to support regimes that are favorable to their economic interests. Ironically, such activity is often legitimated by a claim that it is helping to support democratic development in a subject country. William Robinson (1996) refers to this intervention as the promotion of "low intensity democracy" or "poly-archy," where electoral competition and governance is restricted to those alterna-tives that do not threaten the economic interests of the core. Such a dynamic is evidenced, for instance, in the need for Brazil's popular presidential candidate – Luis Inacio Lula da Silva – to convince US officials that he would not substantially alter international financial arrangements in his country, and, more recently, in the favorable US response to an attempted coup and subsequent uprisings against Hugo Chavez, the democratically elected president of Venezuela. In order to suc-ceed, democratically "elected" politicians outside the core must agree to open their nation's markets to foreign goods and investments, to continue making payments on international debts, and not to threaten the economic interests of the United States.

Not only are domestic political opportunity structures for social movements limited on the periphery, but also those political opportunities as well as grievances are more strongly determined by global-level processes than are the domestic oppor-tunities of core activists. In other words, it is much harder for activists on the periphery to ignore global processes and institutions than it may be for activists in the core. Arrighi notes how the advance of neoliberal economic policies under Thatcher and Reagan exacerbated existing core–periphery inequalities. He notes that Thatcher-Reaganism used "a bloated state to deflate the social power of first world workers and third world peoples in an attempt to regain confidence and support of [the owners of transnational capital]." The important shift in this time period was not the rising power of transnational corporations *vis-à-vis* states, but rather of "differences in power relations ... between western states and non-western peoples" (Arrighi 1999: 129). Thus many analysts trace the origins of contemporary resistance to neoliberal forms of economic globalization not to the 1999 World Trade Organization meeting in Seattle, but rather to the countless "IMF riots," or protests in the global South beginning in the 1980s to oppose the economic policies imposed on their governments by the World Bank and International Monetary Fund (IMF) (Walton and Seddon 1994).

At the same time, the world-system hierarchy makes both elite and social movement actors on the periphery (or the "global South") far less able to affect the global economic and political decisions that shape their environments than their counterparts in the core (or the "global North"). Numerous scholars have docu-mented how the United States worked systematically since the 1980s to marginalize the role of the UN General Assembly in global policy processes while it enhanced the powers of the global financial institutions (see Bennis 1997; Bello 1999, 2000b; Bruno and Karliner 2002: chs. 1–2). By doing so, it weakened the more democratic (i.e., one country, one vote) decision-making structures in the United Nations and ensured that it would maintain its ability to control key decisions and debates in the international arena. This process produces what we might call a dual disenfranchising of Third World citizens: they generally lack effective means for democratic input within their countries, and their states are comparatively voiceless in global arenas. Several respondents to a survey I conducted of affiliates of a transnational organization, EarthAction, captured this sentiment, complaining that they lack access to their domestic political leaders, while their governments were also marginalized in international arenas by US domination of global institutions (Smith 2002).

Global Institutions and the National State

Most social movement research takes for granted the assumption that the national state defines the relevant political space for political contenders. However, if globalization is indeed amplifying the importance of remote decision-making arenas for local actors, then we must consider how global factors shape the political contests within states.

The proliferation of social interactions that cross national boundaries requires expanded attempts to address collectively the problems arising from these transactions. National states have turned to international institutions increasingly throughout the twentieth century as a means of coordinating responses to problems that cross national boundaries. The quickening pace of global integration, combined with the demise of the Cold War, has helped strengthen attempts by states to both govern international exchanges and to address shared problems through multilateral institutions at the regional (i.e., European Union, NAFTA) and global levels (i.e., United Nations, World Trade Organization).

The expansion of intergovernmental agencies that address substantive issues creates both challenges and opportunities for social movement actors. On the one hand, when governments relinquish part of their authority to global institutions, they undermine the traditional channels of democratic accountability. This leads to what is called the "democratic deficit" of international institutions, which are typically staffed by appointed rather than elected officials who have few if any ties to local or national constituencies. In some instances, particularly within the global financial institutions, international officials are selected for their technical expertise alone, and institutional cultures either ignore or disdain democratic values (see Stiglitz 2000). In fact, the World Trade Organization (WTO) even posts on its website a "top ten list" of the main benefits of the WTO which includes the supposed "benefit" of "protecting governments from the influences of special interests."

On the other hand, the fact that international institutions are charged with addressing global problems relating to peace, the environment, and human rights means that within these organizations social movements can find important allies as well as material and symbolic resources. In fact, because international agencies lack natural constituencies that can provide them with political support, international officials see a need to build direct links between their agencies and popular groups. The fact that governments have signed international declarations and treaties indicating their support for the values movements advance provides both international and legal legitimacy for activists' claims as well as political leverage.[4] (Although governments may sign treaties with no intention of actually implementing them, no government welcomes – and most actively resist – attempts to bring international attention to their violations of these treaties.[5]) In his study of factors promoting the formation of human rights NGOs, Patrick Ball concludes that the most important cross-national predictor is the presence of some state commitment to human rights, reflected either by a liberal constitutional tradition or by participation in international human rights treaties. He posits a "hypocrisy hypothesis" to account for this phenomenon:

> state hypocrisy led to the formation of human rights NGOs. Activists exploited the weakness of the hypocritical position required by the international public sphere in order to strengthen claims for justice. (In this use of hypocrisy lies an insight: although noble international agreements made by brutal state leaders may seem cynical or meaningless, in the context of a globalizing regime of international human rights, activists have learned how to hold states accountable for these promises. (Ball 2000: 74)

International negotiating forums such as the UN General Assembly, Human Rights Commission, and other treaty monitoring bodies provide key opportunities for confronting the gaps between governments' normative commitments and practices. Kathryn Sikkink and her colleagues have collected substantial evidence to support a model of institutional change highlighting the ways that international negotiation processes themselves help socialize states into increasing levels of compliance with emergent international norms. They use the metaphor of a "norms cascade" or a "spiral model" of normative change, noting that evidence of a state's internalization of international human rights norms can be observed in its movement from repression, to denial of violations, to gradual changes in its behavior and legal structures. Evidence about the actual work of social change advocates in international institutions shows that, in many issue areas, it is these actors who are the catalysts that prompt movement along this spiral.[6] They do so primarily through "information politics" (Keck and Sikkink 1998), that is, by collecting information about violations of international norms or other threats to broader values of peace, security, and human rights and deploying this information in strategic ways in both the public arenas as well as in more limited intergovernmental arenas.

There is a tendency within social movement research to conceptualize social movement actors as opponents of the state. But a comparative and global perspective demands that we abandon this a priori assumption and conceptualize the state as one of several actors within a field, and there are times when the state (or elements thereof) will be allies of social movements in their struggles against other actors in the broader political field. For instance, Macdonald's study of civil society actors in Central America (1997) highlights the ways that social change advocates had to alter their strategic approach to the state as military dictatorships succumbed to newly democratizing regimes during the 1980s. And Guidry's study of children's rights advocacy in Brazil found a blurring of the boundary between the state and social movements. In that case, claims-making was based on notions of citizenship rights to protections that were defined largely in transnational contexts, making the state a "fulcrum between conflicting globalizations" (2000: 162). Maney (2001) contends that movement alliances with elements of the state are important in determining the outcomes of conflicts over indigenous rights. (Similarly, Seidman (2002) maintains that contemporary labor struggles must seek to reinforce state authority to protect traditional citizenship rights against global capital.) Within the US, McAdam (1982) demonstrates the ways that civil rights activists in the Southern US cultivated ties with federal authorities in their efforts to gain leverage against state and local authorities.

This same dynamic can be seen at the international level when, for instance, human rights activists within a country appeal to international treaties and institutional mechanisms to bring pressure against a given state. Thus activists from the United States working to oppose the death penalty and police brutality routinely draw attention to US policy at the United Nations Human Rights Commission. To the extent that they can convince a broad public that their demands are consistent with both the Universal Declaration of Human Rights and with the views of other governments, these activists gain greater legitimacy and symbolic leverage in their struggle to end capital punishment. Keck and Sikkink (1998) use the metaphor of a "boomerang effect" to describe this strategy of using international arenas in attempts to alter the behaviors of particular governments. A key point to remember, however, is that in many areas activists need to defend the state against other rising actors that threaten the aims of social movements, such as militia groups that violate human rights or transnational corporations that fail to observe labor rights or environmental regulations. Without a state that is capable of enforcing domestic and international law, no rights or regulations can exist (Tilly 1995). And neoliberal policies have made it easier for private actors to acquire enough resources to make them a threat to the state while they have reduced the state's regulatory and redistributive (but not its coercive) capacities.

While international institutions can serve as allies and opportunities for social movement actors, they nevertheless remain agents of governments, which ultimately control their budgets, agendas, and leadership. Powerful minorities or single states often have substantial influence over these institutions. So having access to some international officials and finding legitimation in international treaties that proclaim support for the values a movement advocates does not neatly translate into real influence. Many activists argue that the limited access provided to international arenas reflects an attempt by states to co-opt movement organizations and to channel movement pressure in directions that limit its capacity for achieving fundamental social change. And the fact that states govern the rules of NGO access to international institutions means that the more radical critics are kept outside of this institutional arena (Nelson 1995; Fox and Brown 1998).

Scholars who have examined the ways that social movements make use of international political arenas in their struggles have used a variety of concepts to capture the dynamics involved. Marx and McAdam (1996: 119) describe it as a system of "multi-level governance,"

> European integration combines elements of continued state authority, with the creation of decentralized sub-national power and the development of supranational decision making bodies.... Whereas the classic nation-state tended to define the "structure of political opportunities" for *all* challenging groups, the emergence of a multi-level polity means that movements are increasingly likely to confront highly idiosyncratic opportunity structures defined by that unique combination of governmental bodies (at all

levels) which share decision making authority over the issues of interest to the move-ment. So instead of the rise of a single new social movement form, we are more apt to see the development and proliferation of multiple movement forms keyed to inherited structures and the demands of mobilization in particular policy areas.

Rothman and Oliver (1999: 43) use the notion of "nested political opportunity structures," where "local political opportunity structures are embedded in national political opportunity structures, which are in turn embedded in international polit-ical opportunity structures" (see also Boyer and Hollingsworth 1997: 470), creating possibilities for complex patterns of relations among actors seeking political influ-ence. Tarrow (2001: 241) extends to the European level Wayne te Brake's notion of the "composite" national state as a setting where subjects act in a context of "overlapping, intersecting, and changing political spaces defined by often competi-tive claimants to sovereign authority over them." Similarly, as states enter new arrangements with other sovereign national governments, they add another overlap-ping layer to this already existing composite polity. This "opens opportunities for coalitions of actors and states to formulate common positions and overcome their diversity and dispersion to exploit its political opportunities" (Tarrow 2001: 243–4). In summary, existing work on global institutions and movements sees national polities as nested within a much broader system of institutional relations that will vary across issue, time, and place. Scholars must consider the extent to which this influences any given political conflict by providing sources of alliances, symbolic or material resources, and/or political leverage for both challengers and authorities.

It is also important to emphasize how, through their challenges, social movement actors contribute to institution-building at the international level. Histories of international organizations reveal important influences of social movement actors, such as peace or human rights activists, on the League of Nations and later the United Nations (Robbins 1971; Chatfield 1997). As noted above, they have also been crucial to the articulation, institutionalization, and implementation of inter-national norms (Smith 1995; Finnemore 1996; Wapner 1996). Wielding "soft power" in the form of knowledge and communication networks, social change advocates have helped advance a global system of norms and have developed a variety of mechanisms for pressing states to conform to these norms (Sikkink 2002).

Globalization, States, and Citizens

The systemic and institutional changes described above have tremendous impacts on the character of political participation and governance at national and local levels. This, in turn, affects the opportunities (or lack thereof) for social movement mobil-ization. When national boundaries give way to transnational flows of goods and capital, and national governments relinquish some of their authority to international institutions and privatize state functions, what remains of our notions of citizenship and the protections that it implies (Tilly 1995; Boyer and Hollingsworth 1997; Markoff 1999)?

Global integration can be conceptualized in a variety of ways (see Held and McGrew 2000; Scholte 2000). One approach that helps highlight the democratic dilemma described above identifies two competing forms of global integration: (1) "Globalization" or "the global economic integration of formerly national economies into one global economy...the effective erasure of national boundaries for economic purposes"; and (2) "Internationalization," or "the increasing importance of relations between nations [or other democratically governed subsidiary entities]: international trade, treaties, alliances, protocols, etc." With internationalization, "The basic unit of community and policy remains the nation, even as relations among nations, and among individuals in different nations, become increasingly necessary and important" (Daly 2002: 1; see also Sklair 2002). Underlying and enabling both of these forms of global integration is sociocultural globalization, or the transnational interactions among individuals and groups that generate the ideologies, identities, and cultures that transcend national boundaries. Since much social movement activity involves the articulation of collective identities, this aspect of global integration is key; but with Sklair I want to emphasize that this realm can be mobilized to support either of the two other types of global integration.

While the globalization view is most consistent with the world-systems or structural perspective discussed above, internationalization emphasizes the role that interactions taking place within global political institutions play in shaping global relations and policies. The distinction between these types of globalizations helps us conceptualize the ways that transnational conflicts are articulated and processed, thereby enhancing our capacities to identify how citizens and social movements are involved in shaping these processes. For instance, the contemporary global justice movement has articulated a critique of economic globalization, or the governance of the world system by market principles. A key element of this critique is that this system has undermined democratic institutions at the national level while strengthening unaccountable and nontransparent institutions at the global level.

Activists within this movement engage in serious debates about whether stronger or new political institutions can remedy the inadequacies of markets or whether attempts to build local cultural, economic, and political alternatives from the grass roots up are most likely to effectively challenge global capital (International Forum on Globalization 2002). Many see both institutional and grass-roots approaches as necessary, although individual organizations may emphasize one or the other approach. Sklair (2001) demonstrates how the transnational capitalist class has used global political institutions to promote its interests. He argues that resistance to a globalized capitalist class must target both the political institutions that enable and enhance capital accumulation while also challenging the culture-ideology of consumerism that underpins this economic order. Some speak of this approach as "globalization from below" (Brecher et al. 2000), emphasizing that, by enhancing popular participation in economic decision-making and in global processes, movement actors both democratize global institutions (shaping internationalization) and transform global sociocultural relations as they challenge economic globalization.

Proponents of neoliberalism have advanced the "globalization" model of global market governance, and this produced over the 1980s and 1990s a shift within the global financial institutions (i.e., the World Bank, IMF, and WTO) towards policies that reduced the regulatory capacities of governments in favor of unregulated markets. While the states of the core largely adopted these policies out of a desire to make their companies more competitive in the global economy (Moody 1997; Sklair 2001), the states of the global South were compelled to do so under the conditions attached to their World Bank and IMF loans as well as international aid packages (Walton and Seddon 1994; Bello 1999).

As they promoted neoliberal practices through international financial institutions, proponents of economic globalization also worked to marginalize the United Nations and other international institutions that subordinated market considerations to other values and identities – that is, ones that operated under the "internationalization" model. By the time the WTO came into being in the mid-1990s, social movement activists who had worked to strengthen international treaties for human rights, peace, and the environment were beginning to realize that the financial institutions were capable of trumping many of the political agreements for which they had fought so long and hard. The protests in Seattle and elsewhere reflect this recognition of a fundamental "institutional contradiction" (cf. Friedland and Alford 1991) between the internationalization reflected in the UN and its various treaties and the globalization emphasis of the international financial institutions.

Social movement scholars must consider how these changes affect future prospects for social change activism. While the proliferation of international regimes for human rights, environmental protection, and equitable development both focus transnational movements and expand their opportunities for participation, the neoliberal emphasis on market governance and the expanding influence of international financial institutions has reduced the political power of citizens as it excludes them from decision-making arenas that have increasingly significant implications for their lives. Is it possible to overcome the democratic deficit of global institutions? And can the political community of a nation coexist alongside emerging transnational communities? What role will social movements play in the process of reconciling the need for transnational governance structures with the desire to preserve local democracy? These are all crucial questions for social movement research to address. The historical analyses of the role of social movements in shaping the modern democratic state and the processes of representation should provide important guidance for attempts to answer these questions (see Tilly 1984; Clemens 1996; Markoff 1996, 2004; Tarrow 1998).

This reflection on transnational processes suggests that our understandings of social movements in an increasingly global era must continue to account for a role of the national state. Whereas many discussions of globalization highlight the ways globalization weakens the state, it is more plausible to acknowledge that the role of states is changing, and that other actors – including transnational corporations, intergovernmental organizations, and social movements – are struggling to define their places in a globalizing society. States continue to affect the mobilization and strategic prospects for social movements and other actors. But their capacities for doing so vary. Scholars must differentiate among states to consider how a state's location within a global system of institutions and structural relations shape movement opportunities and constraints (see Maney 2002).

At the same time, we should consider the specific ways in which the interstate system conditions and channels activism by helping to define a global public sphere (see Guidry et al. 2000). Drawing from observations of transnational activism to end apartheid in South Africa, Seidman found that activists self-consciously "shifted the ground" upon which they framed their struggle, selecting global or national/local frames according to their strategic calculations. Her conversations with participants revealed that they had a strong sense of belonging to a *global* community rather than a local or national one. Seidman's and other case studies reveal that activists work deliberately to make connections between global processes and local contexts. But the institutional circumstances in which activists find themselves do not always favor the mobilization of transnational identities: "the institutional fact that international bodies are generally composed of national representatives forces potentially global identities into national frames. But it need not blind us to the possibility that activists might under other circumstances frame their concerns more globally" (Seidman 2000: 347). Under what conditions are activists likely to adopt global as opposed to national frames and identities? If global frames are indeed more common today than they were in the past, what factors best account for this? And how have the global framing of identities and conflicts affected transnational political processes and institutional dynamics? Answers to these types of questions require more systematic investigation of particular interactions between social movements and global institutions.

Transnational Movement Dynamics

While global integration has altered dramatically the arenas of political struggle, there are tremendous continuities in how social movements operate and interact with authorities. Indeed, we should view transnational processes as a continuation of previous forms of contention between power holders and challengers (Tilly 1984; Smith 1995; Passy 1999; Markoff 2004). In many ways, the movement forms and dynamics we see in the transnational arena resemble their national and local predecessors, even as they are adapted to fit a transnational political context.

As was true within national states, we see that an increasingly integrated global political environment has brought a proliferation of transnationally organized social movement organizations, or TSMOs, which combine activists from multiple countries around common social change goals (Smith 1997; Sikkink and Smith 2002; Smith 2002). In addition, we increasingly find that national groups are participating in more informal transnational networks or coalitions as they discover that achieving their organizational aims requires engagement at the transnational level. Internationalization has contributed to this by supporting the global conferences and international agencies that provide resources and otherwise facilitate networking among national and even local associations with transnational groups working for change. This section examines how movement actors have engaged in transnational political action, emphasizing the continuities they share with national and localized social movements.

Movement Issues

Not all issues generate social movements, either nationally or transnationally. Interestingly, the issues that have generated the most transnational activity are also those that have also achieved wide support among national groups in Western democracies. For instance, we did not see a substantial transnational environmental movement until after the 1970s, when strong national environmental movements began to emerge. And the most populous transnational movement has consistently been that for human rights. In the wake of a surge of "IMF-riots" in Third World countries, and coupled with new attention in the global North to the negative consequences of trade liberalization for the environment and labor rights, we saw during the 1990s a rise in the numbers of TSMOs focused on global economic justice. Women's and peace issues are the focus of a consistent percentage of TSMOs, but they remain a relatively small (around 10 percent) segment of the total population of transnational groups (Smith 2002). This remains despite the fact that both movements grew substantially in many countries after the 1960s, lending support to the argument of Ferree and Gamson (1999) that different national cultural and political structures can limit the possibilities for a convergence among national policy debates on some issues.

In some instances, claims defined within national struggles may need to be "reframed" in order to fit within transnational discourses. For instance, Alison Brysk demonstrates how indigenous rights groups shifted the emphasis of their grievances from cultural preservation and human rights to environmental preservation (Brysk 1996, 2000; see also Rothman and Oliver 2002). Clifford Bobb (2001) analyzes why certain Third World organizations and causes gain the attention of transnational SMOs while others that have equally or even more pressing grievances do not. A key factor in this selection process is the presence of leaders who can articulate the claims of Southern groups in ways that resonate with major transnational issue campaigns.

While the organization of the population of TSMOs may indeed shape the ways that local and national activists frame their struggles, research into the workings of transnational organizations and campaigns suggest that the process is more complex and two-way than this conclusion suggests. For instance, Snyder (2003) analyzes how women's groups managed their conflicts as they participated in the 1995 World Conference on Women in Beijing. She found important divisions between activists from the global North and South, but she also found that the TSMOs she analyzed devoted extensive amounts of organizational resources and energies to providing space for promoting dialogue about these conflicts and for finding ways to resolve conflicts within the group. Her analysis shows that Northern activists often changed their interpretations of problems as a result of these dialogues. Nevertheless, Southern activists had to learn to "speak the language" (literally and figuratively) of the global conferences in order to effectively bring their issues onto the transnational agenda. Often this meant escalating conflict within the group in order to attract attention and dialogue on matters of difference. But *how* groups escalated a conflict, or how they framed their issues with regard to the preexisting debates, affected their chances of winning transnational allies. Frames that reinforced other widely shared norms and that identified connections between one region's or group's concerns and those of a broader transnational coalition were most successful.

Inequalities among movement actors in the transnational context matter, but they are not strictly reproduced. Many movement actors aim not to reproduce inequality, but to transform it, and thus they are sensitive to claims of exclusion made by less powerful groups. The interactions among actors from rich and poor countries that are central to the process of building transnational alliances do transform the ways that groups frame issues and structure their interactions.

Arenas of Engagement

Many studies of transnational social movement activity point to the importance of the United Nations-sponsored intergovernmental conferences and transnational conferences of civil society groups to the development of transnational social movements. Much recent scholarship points especially to the UN global conferences held in rapid succession during the 1990s. But here, too, we find more historical continuity than novelty in this form of social movement engagement. For instance, Chatfield (1997) describes numerous international conferences in which movement actors participated at the turn of the twentieth and in the early twentieth century, showing how citizens' groups working for peace used these meetings to press for changes in how the interstate system was organized. Keck and Sikkink's (1998) study of "transnational issue networks" and the examination of women's organizational networks by Rosenthal et al. (1985) illustrate how international conferences helped foster cooperation among various groups, including missionary groups, women's suffragists, abolitionists, and labor groups. The main difference we should expect between these historical conferences and more recent ones is that technological advances and stronger national social movement sectors make such meetings more accessible to those from less elite circles.

Global conferences provide opportunities and some resources for activists to gather at the sites of international government meetings to consider strategies for addressing global problems. They served as "training grounds" in global politics, as networking arenas, as spaces for information exchange and dialogue, and as targets for local and national political campaigns (Archer 1983; Willetts 1996; Clark et al. 1998). Moreover, in seeking to address shared global problems, global conferences explicitly cultivate international community by generating common understandings of problems and their causes and a shared set of objectives and commitments to address them. By fostering commitments to a peculiar set of transnational organizing forms, skills, and activities, they cultivate global identities. As Riles concluded from her work on transnational organizing for the 1995 UN Womens' conference in Beijing, "more than any place or society, what the persons and institutions described here share is a set of informational practices [that include attending meetings, networking, coordinating, fundraising, organizing information, and drafting and re-drafting international texts]" (Riles 2001: xv).

Transnational and now, increasingly, national or local associations send representatives to these global conferences to participate in NGO "parallel conferences" on the problem at hand, to network with other NGOs, and to gather information about government positions and decisions. Because the UN conference structure provides limited time and space for civil society actors to address government delegations, NGOs have been forced to develop routines for developing consensus statements. These common positions require extensive amounts of work before the conference itself to identify the shared goals of NGO representatives, but they help convey more unified demands from civil society while providing focal points for advocacy work in different countries. Accounts from observers, participants, and from a survey of NGOs participating in global conferences document the importance of global conferences as spaces where activists develop their agendas as well as cultivate transnational strategic frames and the collective identities that underlie them (Krut 1997; Foster and Anand 1999).

Many transnational organizations use global conferences to network and hold meetings of their own organizational leadership. Groups can more readily raise funds for travel to United Nations conferences from a variety of private and government sources, whereas travel to a site for an organizational meeting is less likely to be funded. Thus "piggy-backing" meetings is a common organizational strategy, and it suggests that global conferences have a "multiplier effect" on global civil society by focusing strategic planning and discourse around a set of problems and policy proposals as well as by structuring opportunities for transnational consensus-building and organizing work.

But not all social movement organizations can attend or actively participate in international conferences. Among respondents to a survey of transnational human rights organizations, fewer than half (47 percent) of all groups attended the global conference on Human Rights in 1993.[7] And far fewer attended conferences on issues less central to these organizations' missions. We would expect large gaps between participation from relatively wealthier Northern regions and that of Southern groups, and in absolute terms that is what we see. However, a larger percentage of transnational groups based in the global South attended the United Nations Conferences on Children (New York, 1990) (12 percent vs. 7 percent), Human Rights (Vienna, 1993) (52 percent vs. 45 percent), Population (Cairo, 1994) (25 percent vs. 13 percent), and Women (Beijing, 1995) (45 percent vs. 37 percent). This may be due in part to the presence of funding from the United Nations and other bodies to help overcome inequities in North–South representation at global conferences.

The significance of global conferences extends far beyond the groups that actually attend them. Many groups work to develop positions regarding the conference agenda, or they sign the common statements, often using these statements to shape their own advocacy agendas. Many delegates from NGOs return home from global conferences energized and eager to report back to their colleagues at home about the outcomes of global meetings and the new networks that they cultivated at the conferences. Through this process, the strategic thinking and campaigns taken up by many local and national groups are infused with ideas from transnational dialogues taking place alongside global conferences. Such dialogues help identify variations in interests and the objections that people from different regions of the world bring to the topic, contributing to an ongoing process of building relationships and new identities among diverse activist groups.

Riles's study of women's organizing around the UN conference in Beijing provides a useful examination of the social processes behind global conferences. Her work shows how Fijian organizers came to internalize organizational practices and forms that were largely defined within global settings. The conference process allowed groups to become socialized in the skills of international conferencing: For instance, she found that activists from Pacific countries learned at the 1992 conference on Environment and Development that they needed to focus more on the process of drafting the intergovernmental conference documents than on the content of the issues themselves. They also learned through the conferencing process and through attempts to raise funds from international agencies and private foundations that they needed to cultivate networks and to present information in particular ways if they were to be successful in global settings:

> form generates consensus where content and doctrine could never do so. . . . On the one hand . . . the UN conferences subvert critique of the aesthetics of politics by rendering it impossible to imagine a political life without "aesthetics." Conversely, in the world conferences and the designs described in this book, we find design already "politicized" and even generating political commitment from within. (Riles 2001: 182)

But while global conferences encourage activists to adopt transnational organizing forms, they also encourage conscious efforts to develop connections between global processes and local practices. Thus when Fijian activists left the Beijing conference, their transnational networks provided templates and encouragement for them to work locally to harmonize the practices of the Fijian government with the set of government commitments made in Beijing. Guidry and his colleagues describe this phenomenon as the emergence of a "transnational public sphere," or a

> space in which both residents of distant places (states or localities) and members of transnational entities (organizations or firms) elaborate discourses and practices whose consumption moves beyond national boundaries.... the transnational public sphere is realized in various localized applications, potentially quite distant from the original production of the discourse or practice in question. (2000: 6–7)

Mobilizing Resources and Leverage

Although the preceding argument suggests plenty of reasons why activists might turn to transnational organizing forms in order to pursue their aims, we must not forget that transnational organizing is considerably more difficult and costly than more localized work. What leads activists, then, to globalize their political struggles? Analysts of transnational advocacy campaigns and movements have identified important linkages between social movement actors and global institutions, such as the United Nations or European Union, that encourage transnational activism. These mechanisms are not terribly different from those identified in research on national movements, and often they work in very similar ways. McAdam and his colleagues have worked to specify relationships among authorities and contenders that affect the dynamics of a conflict in terms of "mechanisms" (McAdam et al. 2001). Tarrow's work (2001) looks specifically at international institutions to specify four such mechanisms – brokerage, certification, modeling, and institutional appropriation – that can enhance the material, knowledge, and symbolic resources available for transnational as well as national activism. Examining these relations between institutional and movement actors, we see that as national governments have turned increasingly to international institutions to address problems of governance, they have created opportunities for challengers to mobilize new allies and resources within a broader, interstate polity.

Brokerage refers to the making of connections between otherwise unconnected domestic and/or international actors that generate new understandings or identities. Brokers are networkers and translators; they help bridge diverse ideologies and interpersonal networks in order to stimulate and shape joint actions. The mechanism is apparent in many studies of national and local movements, particularly studies that emphasize networks (Rosenthal et al. 1985; Caniglia 2002) and frame-bridging activities (Snow et al. 1986). Most studies of coalitions highlight the work of key groups or individuals who help "bridge" differences among groups (e.g., Rose 2000; Bandy 2003; Cullen 2004). Similarly, brokers provide important relational resources for transnational movement actors, often at international conferences and through international agencies and TSMOs. International agencies' need to collect specialized information brings them into regular contact with nongovernmental actors, including social movement groups. Occasionally, individuals working within international institutions may use their positions to facilitate connections among social change groups as a means of addressing some broader, officially recognized goal. TSMOs may also serve as brokers, helping link local groups with international institutions and with other activist networks.

Certification refers to the recognition and legitimation of actors and activities by authorities or other groups in society. Certification by international actors (either transnational citizens' groups and international agencies) has important effects on national political struggles, as it demonstrates that activists' struggles are supported by the international community or that a movement's claims are seen as appropriate by those outside the country in question. It can enhance activists' sense of efficacy by suggesting that its efforts will be supported by other groups. Whereas groups lacking transnational contacts might find themselves either ignored or repressed by their own national governments, those whose struggles are somehow recognized by international actors can gain political leverage in their domestic contexts. For instance, Reimann (2001) found that Japanese environmental groups gained new access to their national officials only when their government hosted the global Climate Change treaty negotiations and was thereby pressed to abide by UN norms of allowing citizens' groups a voice in such international conferences. Certification by the UN or other international bodies can help protect local groups from repression by their own governments, and it helps them attract allies among the transnational activist community. Bob's work (2001) reminds us, however, that the process of certification by international civil society groups and – I would add – by intergovernmental organizations privileges groups that relate most readily to predominant global norms and strategies, such as groups with English-speaking leaders and familiarity with Western democratic traditions.

Modeling refers to the adoption of norms or forms of collective action or organization in one setting that have been developed and used in another. We might also speak of this mechanism as "diffusion" (see chapter 13 in this volume). We see diffusion at work in national movements, as in the spread of the sit-in tactic from a single university campus across the United States (Oberschall 1989). Transnational diffusion is evident in the flow of ideas between movements in different countries, such as between the US and European student protest movements in the 1960s (McAdam and Rucht 1993) and between Gandhians and US civil rights organizers (Chabot 2002). We also see the diffusion or modeling of organizing forms. Riles's work (2001), for instance, shows how organizing templates developed for international conferences were readily transferred to new groups and activists, allowing them to more quickly assimilate understandings of interstate political processes and the appropriate strategies for influencing these. Moreover, because these templates were modeled after intergovernmental forms, they helped maximize the potential political impact of groups by making their aims more legible or transparent to those familiar with these institutional contexts. Adopting ideas and strategies from other movements and organizations reduces the start-up costs for activists. Moreover, it contributes to innovation as forms are adapted to fit different spacial or temporal contexts. TSMOs and more informal transnational networks are also important places where modeling, or the diffusion and adaptation of organizational and action forms can happen, since these groups make an explicit effort to help members find ways to engage in effective political action in their diverse locales.

Finally, institutional appropriation – or the co-optation of social infrastructures – refers to the use of an institution's resources or reputation to serve the purposes of affiliated groups. Activists work within organizations such as churches or universities to win these institutions over to their cause (Zald and Garner 1987). Or they might seek to work with government or international agencies that share their social change goals in order to gain access to information, legitimacy, or other resources that such agencies can provide (see McCarthy forthcoming). On the other hand, these agencies of governments and international organizations may welcome (or even seek out) ties to social movements and other civil society groups as a means of enhancing their own position in intragovernmental power struggles. For instance, groups working to promote broad access to medications for the treatment of HIV/AIDS appealed to the United Nations in pressing their claims against multinational pharmaceutical companies. This appropriation of international agencies highlighted the contradictions between international humanitarian norms and the practices of multinational corporations. Similarly, social movement actors cultivate ties with international treaty bodies, and sometimes these ties produce funding for activism in support of a treaty's environmental or humanitarian goals.

Cooperation and Conflict

Within transnational organizations and campaigns, we find considerable evidence to support the notion that transnational activism generates new leadership skills and identities among activist populations. This also parallels findings from national studies (e.g., McAdam 1988). Transnational meetings and seminars help cultivate "'the technology to unite us' [...such as] techniques for speaking in groups, listening to each other, forming networks around a concrete issue, [and] thinking strategically at the grassroots level about specific actions" (Sperling et al. 2001: 1172). Given the complexities of the multilevel political arenas described above, such knowledge and skills sharing is an important resource for many groups, particularly those from countries with fewer opportunities for political participation. Transnational SMOs can help provide information about global policymaking processes and guidance about how activists can seek to influence these processes. Many transnational groups sponsor formal training sessions to help reduce the costs of mobilizing around transnational issues. In doing so, they contribute to the socialization of activists for both international political participation and for democratic politics more generally. The experience of transnational activists, moreover, can lead to their appointments in international agencies or on national delegations, where they become key resources for movement actors as they provide access to information and other resources.

Case studies suggest that we should not view the resource flows within transnational alliances as only moving from the wealthier, more established democracies of the North to the global South. Often it is information or analyses provided by activists in the global South that flows to the North rather than vice versa. Macdonald (1997), for instance, demonstrates learning by international groups working in Latin America that derives from the work of local activists to help them better appreciate the ways that international aid affected their countries. Rothman and Oliver (1999) document a similar phenomenon as environmental activists from the global North were challenged by Brazilian activists to transform their environmental thinking in ways that paid greater attention to human rights and to the ways that political inequalities affected decision-making on the environment. Markoff's (2003) analysis of the historical progression of women's suffrage indicated that the innovators in this movement tended to come from outside the core areas of concentrated wealth and power. He found this pattern within countries as well as transnationally. While globalizing processes provide various new sources of resources, just as is true in national social movements, they also encourage competition among a growing array of social movement actors (cf. Zald and McCarthy 1980). Important sources of funding for transnational social change campaigns can come from international agencies charged with promoting certain international treaties or their implementation; national governments and their international aid agencies, which might fund transnational advocacy groups as a means of promoting particular foreign policy goals; and private foundations or corporations. Competition for public or private funding is enhanced as more activists gain the skills needed to compete for grants. Observers also found that the same people and groups tend to receive funding, while those outside these developed networks have difficulties gaining access (Riles 2001). Finally, the grant-proposal-writing process itself encourages hierarchy within organizations, and it also tends to emphasize projects whose effects can be readily documented. This serves to drain resources from grassroots level organizing and from educational and mobilizing work that is most needed in many areas. On the other hand, Cullen's (2004) work shows how EU-level funding encouraged transnational cooperation among European civil society groups.

Transnational Strategies

Globalization has altered the playing field on which many social movements operate. Even within countries, movements may find it difficult to mobilize for major social changes without considering the transnational sources of a policy or condition. Thus we are increasingly aware that activists have adopted new strategies as they try to influence this globalized polity. I discussed above the ways that movement actors have used global institutions to gain leverage in their efforts to change state behaviors, and I noted the common and important strategy of the "boomerang" effect, whereby groups can use international norms as a lever to try to change state behavior. And we found that social movement actors have served as key catalysts in the process of developing and promoting international norms in the first place.

Given this notion of the relationships between global institutions and social movements, we must consider whether this mutually supportive relationship is likely to continue, especially in light of more recent and very confrontational protests *against* the global financial institutions.

In his broad overview of NGO relations with global institutions, Charnovitz (1997) observes a cyclical pattern of NGO mobilization around international organizations that corresponds with governments' and IGO needs for the information or popular legitimacy that NGOs provide. He and other analysts have anticipated a decline in NGO access as governments respond to the overwhelming expansion of NGO involvement in IGOs during the 1990s (Otto 1996). I suspect that the trend since the 1990s is towards greater restrictions on NGO access to global institutions, and this is partly a response of governments to the earlier success of NGO participation.

A 1995 survey of NGOs active in international arenas concluded that, while a substantial proportion of groups attending intergovernmental conferences actively engaged in efforts to lobby governments and/or international officials: a "competing characteristic of the new global system is that NGOs are more interested in creating direct citizen to citizen links at and around international events than in attempting to alter what apparently is perceived to be the relatively weak or weakening existing intergovernmental machinery" (Benchmark Environmental Consulting 1996: 54).[8] Some of the tension and rationales dividing the two approaches is manifest in more recent debates among NGOs. For instance, some activists have become increasingly critical of "NGOs" – by which they mean formalized organizations that generally have large budgets and focus on lobbying global institutions as opposed to grassroots mobilization:

> Seattle marked the end of a period. [People's Global Action's initial focus was on the WTO and free trade. But t]he discourse is easily recuperated [*sic*] by the NGO reformist community which goes hand in hand with governments playing the trick of "dialogue with civil society." Most agree we need to extend our discourse and analysis if we don't want to end up contributing to the stabilization and modernization of capitalism. (People's Global Action 2000: 23)

Activists with some experience in global politics have recognized that "summit hopping" – or focusing a substantial amount of organizational energies on international conferences – can limit their achievement of their goals. Also, younger activists in the global arena may have little patience for the slow, polite, and politically limited tactics of international diplomacy. In electronic discussion lists, some activists have derided the "CONGOs," or "co-opted NGOs," for losing touch with the needs of people at local levels and for seeking agreements with authorities that do little to resolve the movement's broader concerns about inequity and exclusion.

This tension between more radical and militant activists and those seeking to "work the system" parallels divisions within national movements. As is also true within countries, in practice, these two models may not be mutually exclusive, and often groups explicitly engage in both strategies: they lobby to gain access to information they need to mount effective protests against these complex, secretive institutions (cf. Minkoff 1995). There may be a "radical flank effect" at work here, whereby the militancy of some activists opens new channels of access for more moderate groups (Haines 1988). Remaining questions are whether sufficient consensus exists for groups to make effective use of the lobbying skills of some groups, while maximizing the pressure for change by groups seeking new forms of political and economic representation, and whether the goal of promoting multilateralism will sustain the lobbying efforts of a substantial number of activists.[9]

Conclusion

A key argument in this chapter is that global political processes are in many ways a continuation or reiteration of the same kind of contentious dynamics that contributed to the formation of the modern national state. While the actors and institutional frameworks obviously differ, the processes have many similarities. We can thus draw from the rich body of theoretical work on national social movements to understand transnational political processes and movements.

Global economic and political integration alters the political context in which activists operate by creating a multilevel system of governance. National governments continue to be important focal points for movement efforts, but change at the national level may be sought by first influencing the international normative or legal structures and then seeking national government compliance with these. Movements might also find allies among some national governments in their efforts to promote changes in others. A global perspective demands that we recognize that there are instances when social movements will form alliances with governments or international agencies as they pursue social change goals, and where movements will seek to enhance state authority *vis-à-vis* other actors in the course of advancing their interest in things like human rights or environmental protections. This perspective also sensitizes us to the vast differences in the power that individual states have to influence their own domestic policies, and these differences are often magnified in terms of state impact on international processes.

Transnational movement strategies and processes parallel developments of national social movements, and indeed they may be seen as a continuation of the same processes of contention between popular groups and state authorities. We identified parallels between national and transnational movements in the process of framing issues, developing organizational templates, and cultivating relational mechanisms. Strategic tensions over questions of whether to work within or outside the system plague transnational as well as national movements. And a substantial number of activists frequently cross over this boundary to engage in both insider and outsider strategies of influence. While it may be difficult to predict the future course of relations between social movements, international institutions, and national governments, what we can say is that it is the interactions among these actors that will help determine the future structure of the global political arena.

Notes

I am grateful to the editors and to Pauline P. Cullen, John Markoff, John D. McCarthy, Ivana Eterovic, Sidney Tarrow, and Dawn Wiest for their comments on an earlier draft of this chapter.

1   Reports of protester deaths from Lexis-Nexis search, December 19, 2002.
2   Gregory M. Maney (2001) provides a thorough review of world-systems research along with an assessment of what this literature tells us about the opportunities for social movement mobilization in different world regions.
3   The World Bank and IMF have a weighted voting system whereby those countries with the largest investments exert the most control over decisions. The US has roughly a 17% share in that system. And while the WTO technically allows for majority decisions, in practice the economic strength of core countries prevents significant challenges to their interests from poor countries.
4   This parallels Markoff's findings about the historical development of democracies. In exchange for legitimacy, governments yielded certain rights and accepted certain

responsibilities to "citizens" (however defined). These legally defined rights provided resources for emerging challenger groups to press claims for expanded democracy (see Markoff 1994, 1996)

5 Note, e.g., the outrage of the US government over its failure to be elected to the United Nations Human Rights Commission in 2001 and the extensive lobbying of the People's Republic of China to block the Commission's introduction of resolutions critical of China's human rights practices.

6 See, e.g., the case studies in Willetts (1982, 1996); Smith et al. (1997); Keck and Sikkink (1998); Risse et al. (1999); O'Brien et al. (2000); Khagram et al. (2002).

7 Following the human rights conference, the next highest percentage of groups (40%) reported attending the Beijing conference on Women's rights in 1995. For details on the survey, see Smith et al. 1998; Smith 2002.

8 The nonrandomized survey yielded 500 responses, 54% of which were from organizations in the global South, while 62% were from organizations that did not have formal Consultative Status with any United Nations agency.

9 Even among groups that have focused on supporting multilateral initiatives as a means of promoting changes in the behaviors of governments, there is growing discontent with the UN. Many in the activist community have grown wary of a growing corporate influence in the UN, which began during the mid-1990s, and the International Forum on Globalization articulated this fear most directly when it hosted a meeting to parallel the UN Millennium Forum entitled, "Can the UN be Salvaged?" These groups are especially critical of a recent initiative called the "Global Compact," which seeks to augment the UN budget from private sources and ostensibly seeks to gain voluntary cooperation from corporations with UN environmental, labor, and human rights principles. In practice, however, the neoliberal mantra of deregulation has prevailed, and the Compact has deliberately excluded provisions for monitoring the behavior of corporate "Partners."

References

Archer, Angus (1983) Methods of Multilateral Management: The Interrelationship of Inter-governmental Organizations and NGOs. In T. T. Gati (ed.), *The United States, the UN and the Management of Global Change*. New York: New York University Press, 303–25.

Arrighi, Giovanni (1999) Globalization and Historical Macrosociology. In J. L. Abu-Lughod (ed.), *Sociology for the Twenty-First Century*. Chicago: University of Chicago Press, 117–33.

Arrighi, Giovanni, and Jessica Drangel (1986) The Stratification of the World-Economy: An Exploration of the Semiperipheral Zone. *Review*, 10, 9–74.

Ball, Patrick (2000) State Terror, Constitutional Traditions, and National Human Rights Movements: A Cross-National Quantitative Comparison. In J. A. Guidry, M. D. Kennedy, and M. N. Zald (eds.), *Globalizations and Social Movements: Culture, Power, and the Transnational Public Sphere*. Ann Arbor: University of Michigan Press, 54–75.

Bandy, Joe (2003) Laboring against Liberalization in North America: Emerging Coalitions between U.S. and Mexican Unions. Unpublished Manuscript.

Bello, Walden (1999) *Dark Victory: The United States and Global Poverty*. London: Pluto.

——(2000a) Building an Iron Cage: Bretton Woods Institutions, the WTO, and the South. In S. Anderson (ed.), *Views from the South: The Effects of Globalization and the WTO on Third World Countries*. Chicago: Food First, 54–90.

——(2000b) UNCTAD: Time to Lead, Time to Challenge the WTO. In K. Danaher and R. Burbach (eds.), *Globalize This! The Battle against the World Trade Organization and Corporate Rule*. Monroe, ME: Common Courage, 163–74.

Benchmark Environmental Consulting (1996) Democratic Global Civil Governance Report of the 1995 Benchmark Survey of NGOs. Royal Ministry of Foreign Affairs, Oslo.

Bennis, Phyllis (1997) *Calling the Shots: How Washington Dominates Today's UN*. New York: Olive Branch.

Bob, Clifford (2001) Marketing Rebellion: Insurgent Groups, International Media, and NGO Support. *International Politics*, 38, 311–34.

Boli, John, and George Thomas (eds.) (1999) *Constructing World Culture: International Nongovernmental Organizations Since 1875*. Stanford: Stanford University Press.

Boyer, Robert, and J. Rogers Hollingsworth (1997) From National Embeddedness to Spatial and Institutional Nestedness. In J. R. Hollingsworth and R. Boyer (eds.), *Contemporary Capitalism: The Embeddedness of Institutions*. New York: Cambridge University Press, 433–84.

Brecher, Jeremy, Tim Costello, and Brendan Smith (2000) *Globalization from Below: The Power of Solidarity*. Cambridge: South End.

Bruno, Kenny, and Joshua Karliner (2002) *Earthsummit.biz: The Corporate Takeover of Sustainable Development*. Oakland: Food First.

Brysk, Allison (1996) Turning Weakness into Strength: The Internationalization of Indian Rights. *Latin American Perspectives*, 23, 38–58.

——(2000) *From Tribal Village to Global Village: Indigenous Peoples Struggles in Latin America*. Stanford: Stanford University Press.

Caniglia, Beth Schaefer (2002) Informal Alliances Vs. Institutional Ties: The Effects of Elite Alliances on Environmental TSMO Networks. In J. Smith and H. Johnston (eds.), *Globalization and Resistance: Transnational Dimensions of Social Movements*. Lanham, MD: Rowman & Littlefield, 153–72.

Chabot, Sean (2002) Transnational Diffusion and the African American Reinvention of Gandhian Repertoire. In J. Smith and H. Johnston (eds.), *Globalization and Resistance: Transnational Dimensions of Social Movements*. Lanham, MD: Rowman & Littlefield, 65–79.

Charnovitz, Steve (1997) Two Centuries of Participation: NGOs and International Governance. *Michigan Journal of International Law*, 18, 183–286.

Chase-Dunn, Christopher (1998) *Global Formation*. Rev. ed. Boulder, CO: Rowman & Littlefield.

Chatfield, Charles (1997) Intergovernmental and Nongovernmental Associations to 1945. In J. Smith, C. Chatfield, and R. Pagnucco (eds.), *Transnational Social Movements and World Politics: Solidarity beyond the State*. Syracuse, NY: Syracuse University Press, 19–41.

Clark, Ann Marie, Elisabeth J. Friedman, and Kathryn Hochstetler (1998) The Sovereign Limits of Global Civil Society: A Comparison of NGO Participation in UN World Conferences on the Environment, Human Rights, and Women. *World Politics*, 51, 1–35.

Clemens, Elisabeth (1996) *The People's Lobby*. Chicago: University of Chicago Press.

Cullen, Pauline P. (2004) Obstacles to Transnational Cooperation in the European Social Policy Platform. In Joe Bandy and Jackie Smith (eds.), *Coalitions across Borders: Transnational Protest in a Neoliberal Era*. Lanham, MD: Rowman & Littlefield, 71–94.

Daly, Herman E. (2002) Globalization Versus Internationalization, and Four Economic Arguments for why Internationalization Is a Better Model for World Community. <www.bsos.umd.edu/socy/conference/newpapers/daly.rtf>.

della Porta, Donatella, and Hanspeter Kriesi (1999) Social Movements in a Globalizing World: An Introduction. In D. della Porta, H. Kriesi, and D. Rucht (eds.), *Social Movements in a Globalizing World*. New York: St. Martin's, 3–23.

Ferree, Myra Marx, and William Gamson (1999) The Gendering of Abortion Discourse: Assessing Global Feminist Influence in the United States and Germany. In D. della Porta,

H. Kriesi, and D. Rucht (eds.), *Social Movements in a Globalizing World*. New York: St. Martin's, 40–56.

Finnemore, Martha (1996) *National Interests in International Society*. Ithaca, NY: Cornell University Press.

Foster, John, and Anita Anand (eds.) (1999) *Whose World Is it Anyway? Civil Society, the United Nations, and the Multilateral Future*. Ottawa: United Nations Association of Canada.

Fox, Jonathan A., and L. David Brown (1998) Introduction. In J. A. Fox and L. D. Brown (eds.), *The Struggle for Accountability: The World Bank, NGOs, and Grassroots Movements*. Cambridge: MIT Press, 1–48.

Friedland, Roger, and Robert R. Alford (1991) Bringing Society Back in: Symbols, Practices, and Institutional Contradictions. In W. W. Powell and P. J. DiMaggio (eds.), *The New Institutionalism in Organizational Analysis*. Chicago: University of Chicago Press, 232–63.

Guidry, John A. (2000) The Useful State? Social Movements and the Citizenship of Children in Brazil. In J. A. Guidry, M. D. Kennedy, and M. N. Zald (eds.), *Globalizations and Social Movements: Culture, Power, and the Transnational Public Sphere*. Ann Arbor: University of Michigan Press, 147–80.

Guidry, John A., Michael D. Kennedy, and Mayer N. Zald (eds.) (2000) *Globalizations and Social Movements: Culture, Power, and the Transnational Public Sphere*. Ann Arbor: University of Michigan.

Haines, Herbert (1988) *Black Radicals and the Civil Rights Mainstream 1954–1970*. Knoxville, TN: University of Tennessee Press.

Held, David, and Anthony McGrew (eds.) (2000) *The Global Transformations Reader: An Introduction to the Globalization Debate*. Malden, MA: Blackwell.

International Forum on Globalization. (2002) *Alternatives to Economic Globalization: A Better World Is Possible*. New York: Berrett-Kohler.

Jenkins, Craig J., and Kurt Schock (1992) Global Structures and Political Processes in the Study of Domestic Political Conflict. *Annual Review of Sociology*, 18, 161–85.

Keck, Margaret, and Kathryn Sikkink (1998) *Activists beyond Borders*. Ithaca, NY: Cornell University Press.

Khagram, Sanjeev, James V. Riker, and Kathryn Sikkink (2002) *Restructuring World Politics: Transnational Social Movements, Networks, and Norms*. Minneapolis: University of Minnesota Press.

Khor, Martin (2000) How the South Is Getting a Raw Deal at the WTO. In S. Anderson (ed.), *Views from the South: The Effects of Globalization and the WTO on Third World Countries*. Chicago: Food First, 7–53.

Korzeniewicz, R. Patricio, and Timothy P. Moran (1997) World Economic Trends in the Distribution of Income, 1965–1992. *American Journal of Sociology*, 102, 1000–39.

Krut, Riva (1997) *Globalization and Civil Society: NGO Influence on International Decision Making*. Geneva: United Nations Research Institute for Social Development.

McAdam, Doug (1982) *Political Process and the Development of Black Insurgency*. Chicago, IL: University of Chicago Press.

——(1988) *Freedom Summer*. New York: Oxford University Press.

McAdam, Doug, and Dieter Rucht (1993) The Cross-National Diffusion of Movement Ideas. *Annals of the American Academy of Political and Social Science*, 528, 56–74.

McAdam, Doug, Sidney Tarrow, and Charles Tilly (2001) *Dynamics of Contention*. New York: Cambridge University Press.

McCarthy John D. (2002) Teflon Triangles: The Mobilization of Issue Coalitions by Government, Business and Foundations. Paper presented at Conference on Social Movements, Public Policy and Democracy, University of California, Irvine, January 11–13.

Macdonald, Laura (1997) *Supporting Civil Society: The Political Role of Non-Governmental Organizations in Central America*. New York: St. Martin's.

Maney, Gregory M. (2001) Rival Transnational Networks and Indigenous Rights: The San Blas Kuna in Panama and the Yanomami in Brazil. *Research in Social Movements, Conflicts and Change*, 23, 103–44.

——(2002) Transnational Structures and Protest: Linking Theories and Assessing Evidence. In J. Smith and H. Johnston (eds.), *Globalization and Resistance: Transnational Dimensions of Social Movements*. Lanham, MD: Rowman & Littlefield, 31–50.

Markoff, John (1994) *The Great Wave of Democracy in Historical Perspective*. Ithaca, NY: Institute for European Studies.

——(1996) *Waves of Democracy: Social Movements and Political Change*. Thousand Oaks, CA: Pine Forge.

——(1999) Globalization and the Future of Democracy. *Journal of World-Systems Research*, 5, 242–62 <http://csf.colorado.edu/wsystems/jwsr.html>.

——(2003) Margins, Centers, and Democracy: The Paradigmatic History of Women's Suffrage. In *Signs: Journal of Women in Culture and Society*, 29, 85–116.

——(2004) Who Will Construct the Global Order? In Bruce Williamson (ed.), *Transnational Democracy*. London: Ashgate.

Marx, Gary, and Doug McAdam (1996) Social Movements and the Changing Structure of Political Opportunity in the European Community. In G. Marx, F. W. Scharpf, P. C. Schmitter, and W. Streeck (eds.), *Governance in the European Union*. Thousand Oaks, CA: Sage, 95–120.

——(1999) On the Relationship of Political Opportunities to the Form of Collective Action: The Case of the European Union. In Donatella della Porta, Hanspeter Kriesi, and Dieter Rucht (eds.), *Social Movements in a Globalizing World*. New York: St. Martin's, 97–111.

Minkoff, Deborah (1995) *Organizing for Equality: The Evolution of Women's and Racial Ethnic Organizations in America, 1955–1985*. New Brunswick, NJ: Rutgers University Press.

Moody, Kim (1997) *Workers in a Lean World: Unions in the International Economy*. New York: Verso.

Nelson, Paul (1995) *The World Bank and Nongovernmental Organizations: The Limits of Apolitical Development*. New York: St. Martin's.

O'Brien, Robert, Anne Marie Goetz, Jan Aard Scholte, and Marc Williams (2000) *Contesting Global Governance: Multilateral Economic Institutions and Global Social Movements*. New York: Cambridge University Press.

Oberschall, Anthony (1989) The 1960s Sit-ins: Protest Diffusion and Movement Take-off. *Research in Social Movements Conflicts and Change*, 11, 31–53.

Otto, Dianne (1996) Nongovernmental Organizations in the United Nations System: The Emerging Role of International Civil Society. *Human Rights Quarterly*, 18, 107–41.

Passy, Florence (1999) Supranational Political Opportunities as a Channel of Globalization of Political Conflicts. The Case of the Conflict around the Rights of Indigenous Peoples. In D. della Porta, H. Kriesi, and D. Rucht (eds.), *Social Movements in a Globalizing World*. New York: St. Martin's, 148–69.

People's Global Action (2000) *Worldwide Resistance Roundup: Newsletter "Inspired by" People's Global Action*. London: People's Global Action.

Reimann, Kim D. (2001) Building Networks from the Outside In: International Movements, Japanese NGOs, and the Kyoto Climate Change Conference. *Mobilization: An International Journal*, 6, 69–82.

Riles, Annelise (2001) *The Network inside out*. Ann Arbor: University of Michigan Press.

Risse, Thomas, Stephen C. Ropp, and Kathryn Sikkink (eds.) (1999) *The Power of Human Rights: International Norms and Domestic Change*. New York: Cambridge University Press.

Robbins, Dorothy B. (1971) *Experiment in Democracy: The Story of U.S. Citizen Organizations in Forging the Charter of the United Nations*. New York: Parkside.

Robinson, William (1996) *Promoting Polyarchy: Globalization, U.S. Intervention and Hegemony*. Cambridge: Cambridge University Press.

Rose, Fred. (2000) *Coalitions across the Class Divide: Lessons from the Labor, Peace, and Environmental Movements*. Ithaca: Cornell University Press.

Rosenthal, Naomi, Meryl Fingrutd, Michele Ethier, Roberta Karant, and David McDonald (1985) Social Movements and Network Analysis: A Case Study of Nineteenth-Century Women's Reform in New York State. *American Journal of Sociology*, 90, 1022–55.

Rothman, Franklin Daniel, and Pamela E. Oliver (1999) From Local to Global: The Anti-Dam Movement in Southern Brazil 1979–1992. *Mobilization: An International Journal*, 4, 41–57.

—— (2002) From Local to Global: The Anti-Dam Movement in Southern Brazil 1979–1992. In J. Smith and H. Johnston (eds.), *Globalization and Resistance: Transnational Dimensions of Social Movements*. Lanham, MD: Rowman & Littlefield, 115–31.

Scholte, Jan Aart. 2000. *Globalization: A Critical Introduction*. New York: St. Martin's.

Seidman, Gay W. (2000) Adjusting the Lens: What Do Globalizations, Transnationalism, and the Anti-apartheid Movement Mean for Social Movement Theory? In J. A. Guidry, M. D. Kennedy, and M. N. Zald (eds.), *Globalizations and Social Movements: Culture, Power, and the Transnational Public Sphere*. Ann Arbor: University of Michigan Press, 339–58.

—— (2002) Deflated Citizenship: Labor Rights in a Global Era. Paper presented at American Sociological Association annual meeting, Chicago.

Sikkink, Kathryn (2002) Restructuring World Politics: The Limits and Asymmetries of Soft Power. In S. Khagram, J. V. Riker, and K. Sikkink (eds.), *Restructuring World Politics: Transnational Social Movements, Networks, and Norms*. Minneapolis: University of Minnesota Press, 301–17.

Sikkink, Kathryn, and Jackie Smith (2002) Infrastructures for Change: Transnational Organizations, 1953–1993. In S. Khagram, J. Riker, and K. Sikkink (eds.), *Restructuring World Politics: The Power of Transnational Agency and Norms*. Minneapolis: University of Minnesota Press, 24–44.

Sklair, Leslie (2001) *The Transnational Capitalist Class*. Cambridge, MA: Blackwell.

—— (2002) *Globalization and its Alternatives*. New York: Oxford University Press.

Smith, Jackie (1995) Transnational Political Processes and the Human Rights Movement. In L. Kriesberg, M. Dobkowski, and I. Walliman (eds.), *Research in Social Movements, Conflict and Change*. Vol. 18. Greenwich, CT: JAI, 185–220.

—— (1997) Characteristics of the Modern Transnational Social Movement Sector. In J. Smith, C. Chatfield, and R. Pagnucco (eds.), *Transnational Social Movements and World Politics: Solidarity beyond the State*. Syracuse, NY: Syracuse University Press, 42–58.

—— (2002) Organizing for Global Change: Organizational Strength and Strategic Framing in Transnational Social Movement Organizations. Unpublished paper, Stony Brook, NY.

Smith, Jackie, Charles Chatfield, and Ron Pagnucco (eds.) (1997) *Transnational Social Movements and Global Politics: Solidarity beyond the State*. Syracuse, NY: Syracuse University Press.

Smith, Jackie, Ron Pagnucco, and George Lopez (1998) Globalizing Human Rights: Report on a Survey of Transnational Human Rights NGOs. *Human Rights Quarterly*, 20, 379–412.

Snow, David, E. B. Rochford, S. Warden, and Robert Benford (1986) Frame Alignment Processes, Micromobilization and Movement Participation. *American Sociological Review*, 51, 273–86.

Snyder, Anna (2003) *Setting the Agenda for Global Peace: Conflict and Consensus Building*. Burlington, VT: Ashgate.

Sperling, Valerie, Myra Marx Ferree, and Barbara Risman (2001) Constructing Global Feminism: Transnational Advocacy Networks and Russian Women's Activism. *Signs: Journal of Women in Culture and Society*, 26, 1155–86.

Stiglitz, Joseph (2000) What I Learned at the World Economic Crisis. *New Republic*, April 17, <http://www.tnr.com/041700/stiglitz041700.html>.

Tarrow, Sidney (1998) *Power in Movement: Social Movements, Collective Action and Politics*. 2nd ed. New York: Cambridge University Press.

——(2001) Contentious Politics in a Composite Polity. In D. Imig and S. Tarrow (eds.), *Contentious Europeans: Protest and Politics in an Emerging Polity*. Boulder, CO: Rowman & Littlefield, 233–51.

Tilly, Charles (1984) Social Movements and National Politics. In C. Bright and S. Harding (eds.), *Statemaking and Social Movements: Essays in History and Theory*. Ann Arbor: University of Michigan Press, 297–317.

——(1990) *Coercion, Capital and European States AD 990–1990*. Cambridge, MA: Blackwell.

——(1995) Globalization Threatens Labor Rights. *International Labor and Working Class History*, 47, 1–23.

Wallach, Lori, and Michelle Sforza (1999) *Whose Trade Organization? Corporate Globalization and the Erosion of Democracy*. Washington, DC: Public Citizen.

Walton, John, and David Seddon (1994) *Free Markets and Food Riots: The Politics of Global Adjustment*. Cambridge, MA: Blackwell.

Wapner, Paul (1996) *Environmental Activism and World Civic Politics*. New York: City University of New York Press.

Willetts, Peter (1982) The Impact of Promotional Pressure Groups on Global Politics. In P. Willetts (ed.), *Pressure Groups in the International System*. New York: St. Martin's, 179–200.

——(1996) *The Conscience of the World: The Influence of NGOs in the United Nations System*. London: C. Hurst.

Zald, Mayer N., and Roberta Garner (1987) Social Movements in Organizations. In John D. McCarthy and Mayer N. Zald (eds.), *Social Movements in an Organizational Society*. New Brunswick, NJ: Transaction, 121–42.

Zald, Mayer N., and John D. McCarthy (1980) Social Movement Industries: Competition and Cooperation among Movement Organizations. In L. Kriesberg (ed.), *Research in Social Movements, Conflict and Change*. Vol. 3. Greenwich, CT: JAI, 1–20.

Part IV

Microstructural and Social-Psychological Dimensions

15

Networks and Participation

Mario Diani

Introduction

Social movement scholars usually treat social networks as predictors of individual participation. Networks may increase individual chances to become involved, and strengthen activists' attempts to further the appeal of their causes. There is a dynamic, diacronic element to this process: while people often become involved in specific movements or campaigns through their preexisting links, their very participation also forges new bonds, which in turn affect subsequent developments in their activist careers (and, indeed, in their lives at large). There is, however, at least another fruitful way of conceiving the relationship between networks and participation, namely, as a particular instance of the duality of the link between individuals – in particular, their identity – and group memberships (Simmel 1955; Breiger 1974). While the identities of social movement activists are determined by the particular combination of their multiple group memberships, by being members of different groups and organizations, individuals create linkages between the latter. This perspective enables us to better recognize that social movement activities are usually embedded in dense relational settings, and to explore in greater detail the web of multiple ties that ultimately make up a social movement.[1]

In the following pages, I elaborate on these basic ideas. After tracing the origins of the interest in social networks as facilitators of participation, I chart developments in our understanding of how social structure affects individual and collective behavior, and how structure is generated and reproduced through action. I then move on to illustrate the relationship between multiple memberships and social movement structure, before concluding with some suggestions for future research. In this chapter, "structure" largely coincides with social networks, and structural effects on the intensity and forms of participation are mainly conceptualized in terms of actors' locations in specific webs of exchanges. The main themes addressed here relate to a recurrent, much broader discussion of the relationship between structure and action, which since the 1990s has attracted many contributions from scholars with a specific interest in collective action (Sewell 1992; Emirbayer and Goodwin 1994; Emirbayer 1997; Emirbayer and Mische 1998; Livesay 2003).

This chapter also overlaps with recent discussions of the role of social ties as sources of individual as well as collective opportunities (Coleman 1990; Putnam 1995a, 1995b, 2000; Edwards et al. 2001; Prakash and Selle 2003). From that particular angle, networks facilitating involvement in social movement activities may be regarded as one particular version of social capital (Diani 1997). They may conveniently be compared to similar mechanisms taking place in organizations with no explicit political goals, and/or reluctant to include protest and direct action among their tactical options (Wilson 2000). When looking at processes of individual recruitment and participation, the boundary between social movements and other forms of collective action is even thinner than usual. Decisions on whether to commit one's time and resources to a collective activity may surely be affected by the characteristics of the organizations one is considering joining, or the activities one might get to support. However, differences in those criteria only partially overlap with conventional wisdom about the real or presumed (mainly presumed, in my view: Diani 1992, 2003) distinctions between social movements "proper" and other instances of collective action. As it happens, many studies of recruitment to social movements refer to organizations, such as environmental or solidarity groups, that other scholars would regard as "public interest groups" (Jordan and Maloney 1997; Leech 2001; Passy 2001, 2003). Accordingly, it is advisable, and consistent with other reviews of this field (Knoke and Wisely 1990; Kitts 2000; Oliver and Marwell 2001), to approach the issue by considering network mechanisms with reference both to radical, grass-roots organizations and other types of associations (Wilson 2000; Ray et al. 2001).

BACKGROUND AND EARLY DEVELOPMENTS OF NETWORK APPROACHES

When the interest in protest politics and grassroots activism restarted in the 1960s, prompted by the spread of contentious collective action across Western democracies (and not only there), scholars willing to account for phenomena such as the civil rights or antiwar movements in America, anticolonial mobilizations, student movements, working class action, and so on, found themselves to be badly equipped intellectually. As late as the early 1970s, established academic views still regarded individual involvement in social movements as the result of a "mix of personal pathology and social disorganization" (McAdam 2003: 281). At the microlevel, collective action was explained by the marginal location of the individuals involved in protest activity, and the lack of integration in their social milieu; at the macrolevel, by the disruption of routine social arrangements, brought about by radical processes of change and modernization. Both explanations posited a fundamental opposition between protest politics and democratic politics (Kornhauser 1959; Lipset 1960; see also chapter 3 in this volume).

Scholars who were often involved in the 1960s movements, and even more frequently sympathetic to them, challenged those interpretations. They refused first of all the equation between grass-roots politics and the radical movements of the extreme right and left. To them, protest and contentious collective action was ultimately "politics by other means," and social movements were merely one of the options that challengers could draw upon to pursue their policy outcomes and their quest for membership in the polity (Tilly 1978). In contrast to accounts of movement participation in social movements as dysfunctional behavior, social movement activists and sympathizers were portrayed as rich in both cognitive resources and entrepreneurial and political skills (Oberschall 1973; McCarthy and Zald 1977). Most important to us, they also were rich in relational resources, that is, they were well integrated in their communities, and strongly involved in a broad range of organizations, from political ones to voluntary associations and community groups.

Mass society theorists posited that associations would discourage radical collective action because of their capacity to integrate elites and ordinary citizens, socialize their members to the rules of the game, give them a sense of political efficacy, and provide them with primary attachments and a more satisfactory life. Critics objected that organizational participation could work as well in the opposite direction: for example, membership in associations could also socialize people to orientations critical of the status quo rather than supportive of it; it could put people, sympathizing with a certain cause, in touch with fellow members with the necessary political skills; it could generate group loyalties and social pressures, which sanctioned not radicalism, but rather *free riding* and passivity when your fellow members were active in a given cause (Pinard 1968: 683). Mobilization in social movements frequently occurred through mechanisms of "bloc recruitment" (Oberschall 1973): cells, branches, or simply significant groups of members of existing organizations were recruited as a whole to a new movement, or contributed to the start of new campaigns. The mass society argument was also disputable in its assumption that organizations would necessarily be the most important reference group for their members; primary groups and social networks within small communities would often play that role (Pinard 1968: 684; see also Bolton 1972; Pickvance 1975).

Another important development, made possible by the attention to networks, was a critique of structuralist (and Marxist) theories of collective action that explained it as the result of the shared attributes of a given population (whether a class, a nation, or an otherwise defined group). In contrast, collective action was associated with CATNETs, that is, with the co-presence in a given population of *cat*(egorical traits) and *net*(works). While the former provided the criteria on the basis of which recognition and identity-building would take place, the latter constituted the actual channels of communication and exchange which enabled the mobilization of resources and the emergence of collective actors (Tilly 1978).

Theoretical arguments prompted several empirical investigations of networks and participation in protest activities, which paralleled similar explorations focusing on voluntary organizations of any kind (Booth and Babchuk 1969). In one of the first studies of the topic, Snow et al. (1980) showed social networks to account for the adhesion of a large share (60 percent to 90 percent) of members of various religious and political organizations, with Hare Krishna being the only exception. Stark and Bainbridge (1980) pointed at strong personal bonds with leaders and influential members as powerful predictors of recruitment to, and long-lasting membership in religious sects. Networks also emerged as important facilitators of adhesion to denominations and conventional faiths. Only sects, overtly hostile to their social environment, seemed to attract a significant share of people with personal difficulties. Looking at nonreligious organizations, Diani and Lodi (1988) found 78 percent of environmental activists in Milan to have been recruited through private or associational networks.

Moreover, the more costly and dangerous the collective action, the stronger and more numerous the ties had to be in order to support decisions to participate. Studying recruitment to the civil rights project Freedom Summer, aimed at increasing blacks' participation in politics in the southern states of the US in the 1960s, McAdam (1986) suggested that joining was not correlated with individual attitudes but rather with three factors: the number of organizations individuals were members of, especially the political ones; the volume of previous collective action experiences; and the links to other people who were also involved with the campaign. In her study of a similarly risky, though very different, type of activism, della Porta (1988) found that involvement in violent left-wing groups in Italy was facilitated by strong interpersonal linkages, many to close friends or family.[2]

Studies of organizations as diverse as fast-food ones (Krackhardt and Porter 1985) and monasteries (Sampson 1969) have long suggested that embeddedness in social networks not only matters for recruitment, but also discourages leaving, and supports continued participation. Focusing on memberships in voluntary associations in America, McPherson et al. (1992) showed their extension over time to be longer for individuals with a high proportion of ties to other organization members, than for those with a greater share of connections to nonmembers. In his study of dropouts from Swedish temperance organizations, Sandell (1999) also discovered substantial positive and negative bandwagon effects, as people both tended to join and leave in clusters, and to be affected more heavily by their closest links.[3]

The empirical evidence demonstrating the role of networks in recruitment processes has been questioned from different angles. Advocates of malintegration/breakdown theory (in particular Piven and Cloward 1992) have challenged the network argument in the context of a broader critique of the resource mobilization and political process perspectives. In their view, breakdown theory is being dismissed for a claim it never made, namely, that rapid social change brought about by urbanization processes, large-scale economic crises, and so on, generates collective action. But breakdown theory actually focused on collective violence and disruptive behavior, and not on the broader range of forms of contention that theorists like Tilly include in their studies. The network thesis would also be inconsistent with the overwhelming presence among activists of young people, biographically available because their original family ties no longer bind them as they used to do, and new family and professional ties are still developing (Piven and Cloward 1992: 308–9). Most fundamentally, the network thesis would also be largely tautological, given the spread of ties across groups and individuals: "lateral integration, however fragile, is ubiquitous, thus making opportunities for protest ubiquitous" (Piven and Cloward 1992: 311). Rather than highlighting exclusively those cases in which ties are found to predict involvement, analysts should also look at those cases when networks are there, yet participation does not occur.

We actually have several instances of mobilization occurring both largely outside social networks, or not occurring despite the presence of social networks. For example, only one-fifth of participants in anti-abortion mobilizations in California had been recruited through networks (Luker 1984); members of Hare Krishna also joined largely independently from their previous connections (Snow et al. 1980). Conversely, Mullins (1987) showed that the wealth of interpersonal contacts in a Brisbane local community did not result in mobilizations against plans for a freeway crossing the neighborhood. Even when network effects are discovered, findings are sometimes ambiguous. For example, although Oliver (1984) found people acquainted with their neighbors to be more likely to become involved in neighborhood associations, network effects were overall mixed in her analysis. More recently, Nepstad and Smith (1999) duplicated McAdam's study of Freedom Summer by looking at participants and dropouts in the Nicaragua Exchange Brigade in the 1980s. In that case, ties to people directly involved were the most powerful predictor of participation, but the number of prospective participants' ties to other organizations did not matter. However, the relationship was reversed for people who joined after the organization's third year in existence, with the number of organizational links being important and ties to actual participants no longer helping.

According to yet another line of criticism (Jasper and Poulsen 1993), focusing on networks diverts attention away from the really crucial process for mobilization, namely, the transmission of cognitive cultural messages. Although this may happen through networks, it may also take place through other channels, such as the media. Campaigners may have to resort to "moral shocks" with strong emotional impact in order to recruit strangers whom they cannot access via personal networks. This may be particularly true for movements trying to bring new issues on the political agenda, and/or led by people without a significant political background:

> The use of condensing symbols without social networks may mean that a movement is more likely to employ extreme moralistic appeals that demonize its opponents. It may be more likely to rely on professional or highly motivated bands to do much of its work, as with animal rights activists who break into labs. In contrast . . . movement organizers [who] can tap into an active subculture of politically involved citizens . . . can rely on earlier framing activity . . . They have correspondingly less need of moral shocks administered to the public. (Jasper and Poulsen 1993: 508)

BROADENING AND SPECIFYING NETWORK EFFECTS

Individual effects

The critiques addressed at network explanations of recruitment and participation processes have encouraged their proponents to further qualify their points. I use the word "further" on purpose, for questions such as "Which networks explain what?" and "Under what conditions do specific networks become relevant?" were already behind early, admittedly unsophisticated, explorations of the networks-participation link. Snow et al. (1980) discussed why Hare Krishna recruits only marginally joined through networks, in contrast to other religious groups such as Nichiren Shoshu, or to political organizations. This was due to the exclusive nature of Hare Krishna, which made it more difficult to recruit people who were involved in broader networks, rather than isolated individuals. Along similar lines, Stark and Bainbridge (1980) illustrated how involvement in religious practices fairly close to market activities such as individual meditation required less support from networks than conversion to more demanding religious cults or sects. Diani and Lodi (1988) found a different weight of organizational versus private networks as facilitators of adhesion to political ecology and conservation groups. Recruitment to organizations in the more established conservation sector depended more on private networks than recruitment to more critical groups, which largely took place through ties developed in previous experiences of collective action.

Instead of looking at the role of different networks in different organizations, others have focused on how differential location in specific networks could affect chances of participation in specific organizations or campaigns. In one of their explorations of participation in Freedom Summer, Fernandez and McAdam (1989) looked at individual centrality in the network, which consisted of all the activists who had applied to take part in the campaign in Madison, Wisconsin. Joint memberships in social organizations of all sorts represented the links between individuals. Those who were more central in that network (i.e., who were either linked to a higher number of prospective participants, and/or were connected to people who were also central in that network) were more likely to go through the training process undeterred, and eventually to join the campaign. In that case, past activism did not matter directly: it affected one's current organizational memberships, and thus one's location in the network, but it was the latter who ultimately influenced decisions to get involved.

Several empirical investigations have also focused on the context in which mobilization attempts take place, and on how local conditions affect the way social networks operate. Kriesi (1988) studied recruitment to the 1985 People's Petition campaign, which opposed the deployment of SS-20 cruise missiles in the Netherlands, in different areas of the country. Where countercultural networks were weak, people who mobilized in the campaign were in most cases already members of local organizations; where countercultural networks were strong, more people were recruited through personal friendship networks or even in other forms, not based on networks, such as self-applications (Kriesi 1988: 58). Strong countercultural networks seemed to have an autonomous capacity to motivate people, which in turn made specific organizational links less necessary. Along similar lines, McAdam and Fernandez (1990) found that recruitment to the Freedom Summer campaign depended more strongly on membership in organizational networks on a campus with a weak tradition of activism like Madison, Wisconsin, than on a campus with a strong tradition of alternative politics like Berkeley.

The form of prospective participants' ego-networks, that is, the distribution and density of the ties between the actors that one is connected to, has also been regarded as a significant explanatory factor. In their study of adhesion to temperance organizations in Sweden, Sandell and Stern (1998) focused on the role of social pressures within small groups in recruitment processes. They assumed the number of relevant others, who may be expected to affect individual decisions on whether or not to join collective action, to fall between five and ten. The greater the share of ego-network members already active in temperance organizations, the more important the role of social incentives, and the higher the chance that individuals would eventually get involved in mobilization.

Increasingly, researchers have recognized that people are involved in multiple ties, and that while some may facilitate participation, others may discourage it (Kitts 2000). Taking this possibility into account, McAdam and Paulsen (1993) tried to determine what dimensions of social ties are most important, and how different types of ties shape decisions to participate. Their conclusions substantially qualified

earlier arguments (including their own: McAdam 1986) on the link between participation and former organizational memberships. As such, embeddedness in organizational links did not predict activism, nor did strong ties to people who already
volunteered. What mattered most was, instead, a strong commitment to a particular
identity, reinforced by ties to participants, whether of an organizational or private
type. Having been a member of, say, left-wing groups in the past did not represent a
predictor of participation in Freedom Summer unless it was coupled with a strong,
subjective identification with that milieu.

Being directly linked – mostly via organizational ties – to people who already
participate may thus not be an essential precondition for recruitment. Lack of
direct ties may be overcome if prospective participants are embedded in organizational networks, compatible with the campaign/organization they are considering
joining (Kriesi 1988; McAdam and Fernandez 1990; McAdam and Paulsen 1993).
However, we can also think of the reverse situation, with people mobilizing through
contacts developed in contexts not directly associated with participation. By "social
relays" (Ohlemacher 1996) we refer to organizations or groups where membership
does not generate collective action per se, but creates opportunities for people
with similar presuppositions to meet, and eventually develop joint action. Research
on opposition to low-flying military jets in two German villages (Ohlemacher 1996)
showed that recruitment attempts were far more successful for the committee,
whose members were mostly part of neutral organizations in their village
rather than of explicitly political ones. Membership in apparently innocuous organizations such as parent–teacher associations or sports clubs enabled members of the
committee to reach, and gain the trust of, a broader range of people than they could
have, had they been members of organizations with a more clear-cut political
identity. Similar mechanisms may also influence involvement in nonprotest actions.
For example, Becker and Dhingra (2001) illustrated how membership in religious
congregations, and the resulting ties to fellow members, enabled people to engage
in a variety of activities in the community, yet without any bearing on levels of
involvement in the congregational activities. Congregations offered individuals
the opportunity to form close links of friendship and support, but the resulting
social capital seemed to exert its effects mainly beyond the boundaries of
the congregation.

Over the last few years it has been increasingly argued that we ought to look for
mechanisms rather than correlations, that is, we should clarify how networks really
operate, and what impact they have on participation. Kitts (2000) differentiated
between *information*, *identity*, and *exchange* mechanisms. Information refers to the
capacity of networks to create opportunities for participation; identity, to the fact
that social ties to significant others create and reproduce solidarity; exchange, to the
informal circulation of social approval, rewards and sanctions through networks.
Along similar lines, McAdam (2003) identified four crucial mechanisms: recruitment attempts, identity-movement linkages, positive and negative influence attempts (see also Klandermans 1984; della Porta 1988; Opp 1989; Opp and Gern
1993; Passy 2001). In a most recent empirical application of this line of analysis,
Passy drew a distinction between *socialization*, *structural-connection*, and *decision-
shaping* functions of networks in the mobilization process (2003: 41). She showed
how these functions take different forms, depending on the traits of the organization
trying to recruit, and its visibility in the public space.[4]

Population and Organization Effects

For all claims to the contrary, most of the analyses mentioned in the previous section still treat network location as an individual attribute among others, sharing the same methodological ground with mainstream, individual-level analyses of participation (Dalton 1996; Norris 2002). The amount and type of ties that people are involved in are included – along with education, age, profession, status – among the factors facilitating or discouraging participation. However, we have to go beyond that and focus on global network properties if we are to offer a genuinely structural account of participation. Our task becomes then to consider how individual ties combine into broader and more complex network patterns (Gould 1991). This enables us to explain not only individual behavior, but also the overall patterns of mobilization in a given population.

Questions such as the proportion of people willing to contribute to a cause, or the intensity of participation, have been approached through both formal modeling and the empirical analysis of specific cases. Among the proponents of the former approach, Marwell and Oliver (1993; Oliver and Marwell 2001) deserve special mention.[5] They started with a criticism of Mancur Olson's (1963) well-known claim that only small groups, where individual members can estimate their personal gains from getting involved, will actually be capable of generating collective action. Olson defined a "large group" as a group where no individual gives a noticeable contribution to the collective good, but then inferred that groups with many members be automatically "large groups." As an alternative, Marwell and Oliver emphasized the crucial role of a critical mass of people ("organizers"), prepared to face the costs of starting collective action, regardless of the size of the group taken as a whole. They also assessed the properties of networks in which organizers operate. Simulations suggested a strong positive relationship between centralization of a group and its propensity to become involved in collective action (Marwell and Oliver 1993: 101–29). What matters is not so much the number of ties that organizers are involved in, as their selectivity, that is, the quantity of resources controlled by potential participants they are connected to. On the other hand, the presence of *cliques* – that is, of strongly connected subgroups – within a population does not seem to have an impact on its mobilization levels, if not in the sense that an excessive number of cliques may discourage the formation of a critical mass. In another study based on simulations, Kim and Bearman (1997) also qualified the role of network centrality. They found that collective action occurs only if interest in specific issues and actors' network centrality are positively correlated; a negative correlation reduces chances of collective action.

Network heterogeneity also seems to matter. In highly heterogeneous networks, selective mobilization attempts, targeting specific subgroups of a population, may prove more effective. The opposite seems to apply to homogeneous networks (Marwell and Oliver 1993: 130–56). This line of argument is consistent with the more general point that recruitment strategies differ in how they balance *reach* and *selectivity*. The more mobilizing messages will attempt to reach a broad and diversified group of prospective participants, thus enlarging the pool from which to recruit, the more vague and encompassing such messages will have to be; conversely, selective messages with sharp focus and clear content will be more likely to raise the spirits of those already sympathetic to a cause, but this very fact will alienate the movement from a broader, more distant, and more diversified constituency (Friedman and McAdam 1992).

Explorations of collective action dynamics from this particular, systemic angle also discuss the mechanisms accounting for the fact that networks ultimately do matter. Some stress that network ties enable people to calculate the impact of their actions. For example, Kim and Bearman (1997) identified a double mechanism in that regard. On the one hand, people are likely to respond to decisions taken by other people if they have network ties to them; on the other hand, being connected to other people facilitates the assessment of the impact that one's actions will have on them. Gould (1993b) stressed the importance of norms of fairness in determining collective outcomes. As people do not wish to be viewed as exploiters, once someone has started contributing to a collective good, others are likely to follow, if just by adding a fraction of the original contribution. Collective action then results from an iterative, interdependent process, not from independent individual decisions. In his models, Gould also assumed that principles of fairness only apply to people to whom one has network ties. His simulations suggested that the denser a network, the higher the levels of collective action. The network position of original contributors also matters, with rates of participation increasing much more steeply if those who started collective action in the first place are centrally located in the overall network.

Roger Gould (1991, 1993a, 1995) also pioneered the empirical study of the relationship between collective performance and network variables. In particular, he explained levels of resistance by different Parisian neighborhoods in the Commune uprising of spring, 1871, in the light of organizational and informal relations between neighborhoods. He suggested that contacts between neighborhoods would stimulate emulation mechanisms across them and that battalions of the Communards National Guard would be more prepared to face losses and continue resistance to the Versailles government troops if they were linked to similar units based in neighborhoods with high levels of resistance. The intensity of resistance expressed by different districts was actually found to be related not only to non relational properties such as levels of wealth in the neighborhood, percentage of resident salaried workers, and percentage of resident middle-class white collars, but also to relational variables. The stronger the link between two neighborhoods,[6] the more similar the levels of resistance in the two areas; both sustained mobilization and demobilization appeared to be significantly affected by network properties.

Another important illustration of how links between territorial units may affect mobilization processes comes from the investigations that Peter Hedström and his associates devoted to the spread of trade union and social democratic party organizations in Sweden from the late 1800s to the mid-1900s (Hedström 1994; Hedström et al. 2000; Sandell 2001). Their point of departure was Granovetter's (1978) idea of collective action threshold, that is, the notion that a certain number of people have to be active for individuals to decide to contribute themselves to collective action, and that this number varies across situations. They also drew on Hägerstrand's (1967) model of spatial diffusion, which posits an innovation to spread, dependent on density of links between areas, and spatial proximity. Their units of analysis were 371 administrative districts in Sweden. Looking at the diffusion of trade union branches between 1890 and 1940, they suggested that spatial proximity, and the resulting increased likelihood of personal acquaintances, has an important influence over the spread of collective action (Hedström 1994).

An expansion of this line of inquiry paid special attention to the role of specific activists (that Hedström et al. [2000] call "socialist agitators") in creating a macronetwork between otherwise disjointed groups of actors and regions. The role of traveling activists in bonding local groups and individuals, thus facilitating the emergence of broader movements, had long been noticed (Gerlach and Hine 1970). Here, it found a more formal and systematic treatment. The timing of the founding of a labor movement organization in each of 365 Swedish districts was related to properties of the district such as density of population and working class presence, as well as to network factors. The visit of an agitator made a difference along with the strength of ties between regions, given by geographical proximity, or the number of social democratic members in other districts. This suggested the opportunity of elaborating a multilevel network approach, recognizing the importance of both macro- and micro-networks.

OVERLAPPING NETWORKS AND AFFILIATIONS

So far we have focused on networks as predictors of participation, measured both at the individual and the collective level. However, we can also meaningfully look at how activists connect groups, and how groups create links between their members. We just noticed that Hedström et al.'s "socialist agitators" and other types of traveling activists operated as bridges between movement milieus in different localities. Although with varying levels of theoretical elaboration, these and related concepts have long inspired the analysis of social movements. In some cases, emphasis has been on the contribution of these linkages to the strengthening of subcultural dynamics. By going places, being connected to several groups or associations, patronizing specific venues, cafes, or bookshops, individuals create and reproduce dense webs of informal exchanges. These help to maintain collective identities alive even when open challenges to state authority may not be taking place (when, in Melucci's [1989, 1996] words, movements are going through phases of "latency"). In this sense, networks provide the structure of social movements "free-spaces" (Polletta 1999), that is, areas of social interaction in which holders of specific worldviews reinforce mutual solidarity and experiment with alternative lifestyles. This view of movement networks has generated a wealth of studies, usually little formalized but rich in qualitative insight and ethnographic data, focusing mostly on movements with strong emphasis on identity dynamics, such as the women's movement (Rupp and Taylor 1987; Taylor and Whittier 1992, 1995; Mueller 1994; Whittier 1995) or religious and ethnic movements (Gerlach and Hine 1970).

Other studies have mostly emphasized the role of multiple memberships as channels for the circulation of information, resources, expertise – as well as of course solidarity – among organizations mobilizing on issues of common concern. Already in the early 1970s, Curtis and Zurcher (1973) regarded individual activists as interorganizational links, and thus as a basic structural feature of movement "organizational fields." Along similar lines, Bolton (1972) talked of "chains of group affiliations" in relation to the structure of overlapping memberships in voluntary organizations. Many empirical investigations have followed, adding details to the broad picture. Diani and Lodi (1988) documented multiple commitments in Italian environmentalism, with 28 percent of activists being involved in several other environmental organizations, and the same percentage active in both environmental and other political or social groups. Looking at Dutch environmentalism, Kriesi (1993: 186) found 43 percent of core activists to have personal links to other movement activists (there were 25 percent in Italy according to Diani and Lodi), and 67 percent to be connected to other new social movements participants.

Patterns of multiple participation seem to be affected by organizational features. Investigating members of voluntary associations in the US, McPherson (1983) found that bigger organizations not only were able to secure their members' commitment for a longer time, but could also rely on more ties to other groups, generated by their members' overlapping affiliations. However, other data (e.g., Diani 1995: 113) suggest a more ambiguous relationship between one organization's size and its members' propensity to engage in multiple activities.

Looking at how individuals link organizations through their memberships generates useful insights on the structure of social movement milieus. This approach may be conveniently applied to groups and organizations dealing with a specific set of issues and/or sharing the same collective identity – for example, women's or environmental organizations (Philips 1991). It may also refer, though, to larger sets of organizations, covering broad ranges of issues from a similar or at least compatible perspective – for example, the organizations addressing women's, environmental, human rights, development, gay and lesbian issues, often referred to as "new social movements" (Kriesi et al. 1995), or "left-libertarian movements" (Kitschelt 1990).

In their study of the organizational affiliations of 202 leading feminists in New York State between 1840 and 1914, Rosenthal and her associates (Rosenthal et al. 1985, 1997) provided one of the earliest and most systematic treatments of overlapping memberships as interorganizational links. Access to data spread over time enabled them to chart not only the map of connections, provided by individuals at a single point in time, but its transformations at different historical periods. They identified three phases: one from 1840 to the late 1860s, when early women's organizations displayed high mobilizing capacity and strong overlaps with antislavery and temperance organizations; a period of "latency" until the late 1880s, featuring limited public collective action and limited chances to establish national organizations; and a phase, until 1914, characterized by a restart of activities, mainly about voting rights, and the emergence of new organizations in central positions.

In another exploration of the same data, Rosenthal et al. (1997) looked at multiple memberships in women's organizations in four different milieus (three local communities, plus one network of women active at state level in NY state) between 1840 and 1920. They highlighted the different roles played by national and local women's organizations (e.g., in terms of their different relationship to other radical movements), the division of labor between a few multi-issue organizations and the multiplicity of groups operating on a smaller scale and in semi-isolation, and the limited contacts between suffrage organizations and charitable ones.

Guided by the same principle, Carroll and Ratner (1996) investigated overlapping networks in the social movement sector in Vancouver. They related structural positions in networks of multiple memberships to the activists' frames and social representations. They identified three different views of injustice and domination, labelled "political economy/injustice," "liberal," and "identity" and showed how they could be linked with specific positions within intermovement networks. Activists adopting a political-economy injustice frame were most likely to be embedded in linkages involving different types of movements. Those who framed injustice in terms of identity politics were least embedded in ties and most likely to be "localists."

While most studies of the duality of individuals and groups focus on rank-and-file activists, it is also possible to apply this perspective to relationships between movement leaders, eventually extending the analysis to the ties involving members of other sectors of the elites. For example, Schmitt-Beck (1989) explored the connections between central figures in the German peace movement of the 1980s. Data about the overlapping memberships linking core activists of peace movement organizations to members of other political groups documented the strong integration of the movement leadership with churches, trade unions, university, media, and other established social and political organizations.

CONCLUSIONS

Studies of the relationship between networks and participation have gone a long way toward specifying its terms. Questions such as "What networks account for what type of participation?" have been addressed from a variety of perspectives (Opp 1989; McAdam and Paulsen 1993; Diani 1995: ch. 3; Passy and Giugni 2000; Tindall 2000; McAdam 2003; Passy 2003). Although findings are not always consistent, nor necessarily comparable, it is possible to identify some recurring themes:

- The role of networks seems to vary, depending on the costs attached to the action that they are supposed to facilitate. If costs are defined in terms of personal risks, or of the energy and commitment required to join a specific action or organization, more demanding forms of action have usually been backed by stronger and more specific networks. Number and intensity of ties to other participants have been found to play a role in recruitment to dangerous actions, of the violent (della Porta 1988) as well as of the peaceful (McAdam 1986, 1988) kind. A central position in the networks, linking prospective participants, has also been identified as an important predictor of actual participation (Fernandez and McAdam 1989).
- The extent to which the mobilizing messages and the cultural orientation of a movement differ from, and are at odds with, the dominant orientations in society also seems to make certain networks more effective than others. Private networks, consisting, for example, of ties to friends or acquaintances without involvement in specific organizations or subcultural milieus, have been found to matter most in cases when the message of a movement was well accepted in the social milieus in which prospective participants lived and operated – whether conservation styles of environmental activism in 1980s Milan (Diani and Lodi 1988), radical civil rights action in 1960s Berkeley subcultures (McAdam and Fernandez 1990), or peace campaigns in cities with strong countercultures in

1980s Netherlands (Kriesi 1988). Networks more directly embedded in political and sometimes radical organizations and subcultures seemed to count relatively more for recruitment to organizations whose message was less mainstream, although not necessarily antagonistic, in their specific context (such as political ecologists in Milan, civil rights activism in Madison, or peace action in Dutch cities with a weak presence of alternative cultures).

- Not only do different networks matter in different contexts, they also perform different functions, ranging from socialization to the creation of concrete opportunities to become involved, and to influencing prospective participants' decisions at crucial points in time (Kitts 2000; Passy 2001, 2003; McAdam 2003). The relevance of such functions may change at different points in time, depending on whether we are looking at recruitment rather than at the strengthening of commitment and the extension of militancy over time. The different public exposure of different organizations may also affect the relative weight of specific types of networks over others (Passy 2003).

- It is important to take into account the properties of networks taken as a whole, and not only individual location within a network. The dependent variable, then, is no longer individual recruitment or intensity of participation, but the overall level of collective action in a given population. Simulations have suggested that more centralized networks are more likely to overcome free-riding problems and generate higher amounts of collective action; degrees of network heterogeneity and homogeneity have also been found to play a role (Marwell and Oliver 1993).

- Notable empirical studies have focused on the flows of communication and the links between different territorial areas. They have illustrated how levels of collective performance in one area depend on levels of performance in other areas (Gould 1991, 1995), and how diffusion of new forms of collective action are also facilitated by previous connections between different territorial locations (Hedström et al. 2000; Sandell 2001).

While all the strands of research I have just recalled are likely to generate additional important work in the near future, I would like to point at three research directions I consider particularly urgent. The first relates to the growing awareness of the "duality of individuals and organizations" (Breiger 1974). This perspective enables us to take the analysis of networks and participation beyond classic questions of individual recruitment and collective performance, towards recognition of the nature of social movements as complex social systems. We have to pay greater attention to how participation in multiple organizations as well as in different personal networks creates webs of links that connect different instances of collective action, political protest, and countercultural activity to each other. Here, networks are no longer primarily the source of opportunities and incentives for individuals pondering their choices; they become indicators of the connections between individuals, organizations, and events. While movements undoubtedly consist of participating individuals, of strings of protest events, and of organizations, it is the connections between those components that differentiate social movements from atomized, isolated instances of political behavior. The more individuals link through their involvement in organizations and/or events, which could as well reflect mobilizations on specific issues, disconnected from broader political projects (Mische 2003), and the more activists get to identify with wider causes through their multiple involvements in organizations and protest events, the more we have genuine social movement dynamics in progress (Diani 1992, 2000a, 2003).[7]

We also need to introduce the time dimension more explicitly into our analyses of movement networks. Some notable exceptions notwithstanding (in particular, Rosenthal et al. 1985, 1997; see also McPherson and Rotolo 1996), most studies of networks and participation are still based on data collected at one single point in time. It is far rarer to find illustrations of how networks evolve over time, and how those changes affect persistence or interruption of activism. Moreover, looking at the evolution of networks from the perspective of overlapping memberships would also provide us with a valuable clue to interpret the evolution of the structure of critical milieus.[8]

Finally, research on networks and participation will have to explore the impact of virtual links, in particular those originating from computer-mediated communication, on recruitment processes. It is widely recognized that the spread of new forms of communication is likely to affect social organization in depth, and that this requires a reformulation of sociological concepts, including that of social relations (Castells 1996, 1997; Cerulo 1997; Cerulo and Ruane 1998). However, it is more problematic to assess the substantive impact of changes in communication technology on specific milieus, or types of behavior. In the case of social movements, the main question is whether "virtual," computer-mediated ties may replace "real" ties in the generation not only of the practical opportunities, but of the shared understandings and – most important – the mutual trust, which have consistently been identified as important facilitators of collective action (Calhoun 1998; Diani 2000b). Available evidence (Hampton and Wellman 2001; Norris 2002: ch. 10; Quan y Haase et al. 2002) is still too rare to be conclusive, and much more work is required to achieve conclusions that are at least as sound as those achieved, for all their limitations, in the study of the link between participation and "real" social networks.

Notes

1 I have discussed the network nature of social movements in several recent, and not so recent, pieces (Diani 1992, 2000a, 2000b, 2003).

2 The relevance of these findings is not restricted to recruitment to social movement or religious organizations. E.g., Knoke (1990) studied the impact of networks on conventional forms of political participation, such as getting involved with national elections and local community action. He found that people, who are connected to other people strongly involved with party politics, and have the opportunity to discuss political matters regularly with them, are more likely to participate in national elections; likewise, members of voluntary organizations are more likely to become active on local issues if they interact regularly with other organization members.

3 Sandell's criteria for measuring ties are different from McPherson and associates': following Hägerstrand's (1967) suggestion that the structure of a social network depends on social and/or spatial distance between actors, he estimates the probability of ties between pairs of individuals on the basis of how close they are on variables such as age, class position, or geographical location. This renders the bandwagon argument particularly robust.

4 E.g., the social-connection function is more important for adhesion to organizations that are not very visible in the public space, like the Third World solidarity group Bern Declaration, than for organizations with a strong public presence, like the Swiss World Wildlife Fund.

5 Other systematic attempts to apply formal modeling to the investigation of collective action dynamics include Macy's (1990, 1991, 1993) and Heckathorn's (1989, 1990, 1993, 1996). Although applications of formal theories to the analysis of concrete empirical cases are relatively rare (Gould 2003), the works cited above have actually also inspired empirical research. E.g., Heckathorn's has been adopted by Brown and Boswell (1995) in order to account for interracial solidarity as opposed to strikebreaking behavior in the 1919 steel strike in the US.

6 Network links between neighborhoods were measured as the number of residents of district *i* enlisted in the battalion of district *j*, divided by the overall number of i residents enlisted anywhere else. Other indicators of linkages included rates of marriages between residents of different districts.

7 Unfortunately, scarcity of systematic data, covering all the important actors in a network, may drastically affect the interpretation of a given network structure (Kitts 2000). One way to face this problem is to adopt some kind of snowball sampling, starting with activists that for some reasons were deemed important, then interviewing their direct contacts, and so forth (e.g., Carroll and Ratner 1996). However, we have no guarantee that the resulting sample will bear any resemblance to the unknown population, and that the actors close to the original interviewees reflect more general network patterns. A possible alternative is to get a representative sample of activists in a population and count the number of joint memberships for any organization pair, where the strength of a tie is proportional to the number of shared memberships (Kitts 2000: 251).

8 One obvious problem with the implementation of this strategy is the rarity of data charting the evolution of personal networks over time. However, if it is difficult to identify the direct ties in which individuals were involved at different points in time, it may be easier to trace their past and present organizational memberships, and then to posit that all members of a relevant population, sharing the same past memberships (as well as, for that matter, participation in certain activities, such as protest events), are somehow related. This approach would enable us to map changes in the overall structure of a movement sector, and to link those changes to the evolution of networks within civil society at large.

References and further reading

Anheier, Helmut (2003) Movement Development and Organizational Networks: The Role of "Single Members" in the German Nazi Party, 1925–1930. In M. Diani and D. McAdam (eds.), *Social Movements and Networks*. Oxford: Oxford University Press, 49–74.

Barkan, Steven E., Steven F. Cohn, and William H. Whitbaker (1995) Beyond Recruitment: Predictors of Differential Participation in a National Antihunger Organization. *Sociological Forum*, 10, 113–33.

Becker, Penny Edgell, and Pawan Dhingra (2001) Religious Involvement and Volunteering: Implications for Civil Society. *Sociology of Religion*, 62, 315–35.

Bolton, Charles D. (1972) Alienation and Action: A Study of Peace Group Members. *American Journal of Sociology*, 78, 537–61.

Booth, A., and N. Babchuk (1969) Personal Influence Networks and Voluntary Association Affiliation. *Sociological Inquiry*, 39, 179–88.

Breiger, Ronald L. (1974) The Duality of Persons and Groups. *Social Forces*, 53, 181–90.

Brown, C., and Terry Boswell (1995) Strikebreaking or Solidarity in the Great Steel Strike of 1919: A Split Labor Market, Game-Theoretic, and QCA Analysis. *American Journal of Sociology*, 100, 1479–1519.

Calhoun, Craig (1998) Community without Propinquity Revisited: Communication Technology and the Transformation of the Urban Public Sphere. *Sociological Inquiry*, 68, 373–97.

Carroll, William K., and Robert S. Ratner (1996) Master Framing and Cross-Movement Networking in Contemporary Social Movements. *Sociological Quarterly*, 37, 601–25.

Castells, Manuel (1996) *The Rise of the Network Society*. Oxford: Blackwell.

——(1997) *The Power of Identity*. Oxford: Blackwell.

Cerulo, Karen (1997) Reframing Sociological Concepts for a Brave New (Virtual?) World. *Sociological Inquiry*, 67, 48–58.

Cerulo, Karen, and Janet M. Ruane (1998) Coming Together: New Taxonomies for the Analysis of Social Relations. *Sociological Inquiry*, 68, 398–425.

Coleman, James (1990) *Foundations of Social Theory*. Cambridge, MA: Harvard University Press, Belknap Press.

Curtis, Russell L., and Louis A. Zurcher Jr. (1973) Stable Resources of Protest Movements: The Multi-organizational Field. *Social Forces*, 52, 53–61.

Dalton, Russell (1996) *Citizen Politics in Western Democracies*. Chatham, NJ: Chatham House.

della Porta, Donatella (1988) Recruitment Processes in Clandestine Political Organizations: Italian Left-Wing Terrorism. In B. Klandermans, H. Kriesi, and S. Tarrow (eds.), *From Structure to Action*. Greenwich, CT: JAI, 155–72.

della Porta, Donatella, and Mario Diani (1999) *Social Movements*. Oxford: Blackwell.

Diani, Mario (1992) The Concept of Social Movement. *Sociological Review*, 40, 1–25.

——(1995) *Green Networks: A Structural Analysis of the Italian Environmental Movement*. Edinburgh: Edinburgh University Press.

——(1997) Social Movements and Social Capital: A Network Perspective on Movement Outcomes. *Mobilization*, 2, 129–47.

——(2000a) Simmel to Rokkan and Beyond: Elements for a Network Theory of (New) Social Movements. *European Journal of Social Theory*, 3, 387–406.

——(2000b) Social Movement Networks Virtual and Real. *Information, Communication, and Society*, 3, 386–401.

——(2003) Networks and Social Movements: A Research Programme. In M. Diani and D. McAdam (eds.), *Social Movements and Networks*. Oxford: Oxford University Press, 299–318.

Diani, Mario, and Giovanni Lodi (1988) Three in One: Currents in the Milan Ecology Movement. In B. Klandermans, H. Kriesi, and S. Tarrow (eds.), *From Structure to Action*. Greenwich, CT: JAI, 103–24.

Diani, Mario, and Doug McAdam (eds.) (2003) *Social Movements and Networks*. Oxford: Oxford University Press.

Edwards, Bob, Michael W. Foley, and Mario Diani (eds.) (2001) *Beyond Tocqueville: Social Capital, Civil Society, and Political Process in Comparative Perspective*. Hanover, NH: University Press of New England.

Emirbayer, Mustafa (1997) A Manifesto for a Relational Sociology. *American Journal of Sociology*, 103, 281–317.

Emirbayer, Mustafa, and Ann Mische (1998) What Is Agency? *American Journal of Sociology*, 103, 962–1023.

Emirbayer, Mustafa, and Jeff Goodwin (1994) Network Analysis, Culture, and the Problem of Agency. *American Journal of Sociology*, 99, 1411–54.

Fernandez, Roberto, and Doug McAdam (1988) Social Networks and Social Movements: Multiorganizational Fields and Recruitment to Mississippi Freedom Summer. *Sociological Forum*, 3, 357–82.

——(1989) Multiorganizational Fields and Recruitment to Social Movements. In B. Klander-mans (ed.), *Organizing for Change*. Greenwich, CT: JAI, 315–44.

Friedman, Debra, and Doug McAdam (1992) Collective Identity and Activism: Networks, Choices, and the Life of a Social Movement. In A. D. Morris and C. Mueller (eds.), *Frontiers in Social Movement Theory*. New Haven: Yale University Press, 156–73.

Gerlach, Luther, and Virginia Hine (1970) *People, Power, Change: Movements of Social Transformation*. Indianapolis: Bobbs-Merrill.

Gould, Roger V. (1991) Multiple Networks and Mobilization in the Paris Commune, 1871. *American Sociological Review*, 56, 716–29.

——(1993a) Trade Cohesion, Class Unity, and Urban Insurrection: Artisanal Activism in the French Commune. *American Journal of Sociology*, 98, 721–54.

——(1993b) Collective Action and Network Structure. *American Sociological Review*, 58, 182–96.

——(1995) *Insurgent Identities: Class, Community, and Protest in Paris from 1848 to the Commune*. Chicago: University of Chicago Press.

——(2003) Why Do Networks Matter? Rationalist and Structuralist Interpretations. In M. Diani and D. McAdam (eds.), *Social Movements and Networks*. Oxford: Oxford University Press, 233–57.

Granovetter, Mark (1978) Threshold Models of Collective Behavior. *American Journal of Sociology*, 83, 1420–43

Hägerstrand, Torsten (1967) *Innovation Diffusion as a Spatial Process*. Chicago: University of Chicago Press.

Hampton, Keith, and Barry Wellman (2001) Long Distance Community in the Network Society. *American Behavioral Scientist*, 45, 477–96.

Heckathorn, Douglas D. (1989) Collective Sanctions and the Creation of Prisoners' Dilemma Norms. *American Journal of Sociology*, 94, 535–62.

——(1990) Collective Sanctions and Compliance Norms: A Formal Theory of Group-Mediated Social Control. *American Sociological Review*, 55, 366–84.

——(1993) Collective Action and Group Heterogeneity: Voluntary Provision versus Selective Incentives. *American Sociological Review*, 58, 329–50.

——(1996) The Dynamics and Dilemmas of Collective Action. *American Sociological Review*, 61, 250–77.

Hedström, Peter (1994) Contagious Collectivities: On the Spatial Diffusion of Swedish Trade Unions, 1890–1940. *American Journal of Sociology*, 99, 1157–79.

Hedström, Peter, and Richard Swedberg (eds.) (1998) *Social Mechanisms: An Analytical Approach to Social Theory*. Cambridge: Cambridge University Press.

Hedström, Peter, Rickard Sandell, and Charlotta Stern (2000) Mesolevel Networks and the Diffusion of Social Movements: The Case of the Swedish Social Democratic Party. *American Journal of Sociology*, 106, 145–72.

Jasper, James (1997) *The Art of Moral Protest: Culture, Biography, and Creativity in Social Movements*. Chicago: University of Chicago Press.

Jasper, James M., and Jane Poulsen (1993) Fighting Back: Vulnerabilities, Blunders, and Countermobilization by the Targets in Three Animal Campaigns. *Sociological Forum*, 8, 639–57.

Jordan, Grant, and William Maloney (1997) *The Protest Business*. Manchester: Manchester University Press.

Kim, Hyojoung, and Peter S. Bearman (1997) The Structure and Dynamics of Movement Participation. *American Sociological Review*, 62, 70–93.

Kitschelt, Herbert (1990) New Social Movements and the Decline of Party Organization. In R. J. Dalton and M. Kuechler (eds.), *Challenging the Political Order*. Cambridge: Polity, 179–208.

Kitts, James (2000) Mobilizing in Black Boxes: Social Networks and SMO Participation. *Mobilization*, 5, 241–57.

Klandermans, Bert (1984) Mobilization and Participation. Social-Psychological Expansions of Resource Mobilization Theory. *American Sociological Review*, 49, 583–600.

Knoke, David (1990) Networks of Political Action: Toward Theory Construction. *Social Forces*, 68, 1041–63.

Knoke, David, and Nancy Wisely (1990) Social Movements. In D. Knoke (ed.), *Political Networks*. Cambridge: Cambridge University Press, 57–84.

Kornhauser, William (1959) *The Politics of Mass Society*. Glencoe, IL: Free Press.

Krackhardt, David, and Lyman W. Porter (1985) When Friends Leave: A Structural Analysis of the Relationship between Turnover and Stayer's Attitudes. *Administrative Science Quarterly*, 30, 242–61.

Kriesi, Hanspeter (1988) Local Mobilization for the People's Petition of the Dutch Peace Movement. In B. Klandermans, H. Kriesi, and S. Tarrow (eds.), *From Structure to Action*. Greenwich, CT: JAI, 41–82.

——(1993) *Political Mobilization and Social Change*. Aldershot: Avebury.

Kriesi, Hanspeter, Ruud Koopmans, Jan Willem Duyvendak, and Marco Giugni (1995) *New Social Movements in Western Europe*. Minneapolis: University of Minnesota Press.

Leech, Beth L. (2001) Social Movements and Interest Groups: Same Message, Different Frequencies. Paper presented at the First General Conference, European Consortium for Political Research, University of Kent at Canterbury, England, September 6–8.

Lipset, Seymour Martin (1960) *Political Man*. New York: Anchor.

Livesay, Jeff (2003) The Duality of Systems: Networks as Media and Outcomes of Movement Mobilization. *Current Perspectives in Social Theory*, 22, 185–224.

Luker, Kristin (1984) *Abortion and the Politics of Motherhood*. Berkeley: University of California Press.

McAdam, Doug (1986) Recruitment to High Risk Activism: The Case of Freedom Summer. *American Journal of Sociology*, 92, 64–90.

——(1988) Micromobilization Contexts and Recruitment to Activism. In B. Klandermans, H. Kriesi, and S. Tarrow (eds.), *From Structure to Action*. Greenwich, CT: JAI, 125–54.

——(2003) Beyond Structural Analysis: Toward a More Dynamic Understanding of Social Movements. In M. Diani and D. McAdam (eds.), *Social Movements and Networks*. Oxford: Oxford University Press, 281–98.

McAdam, Doug, and Roberto Fernandez (1990) Microstructural Bases of Recruitment to Social Movements. In L. Kriesberg (ed.), *Research in Social Movements, Conflict and Change*. Vol. 12. Greenwich, CT: JAI, 1–33.

McAdam, Doug, and Ronnelle Paulsen (1993) Specifying the Relationship between Social Ties and Activism. *American Journal of Sociology*, 99, 640–67.

McCarthy, John D., and Mayer N. Zald (1977) Resource Mobilization and Social Movements: A Partial Theory. *American Journal of Sociology*, 82, 1212–41.

McPherson, Miller (1983) An Ecology of Affiliation. *American Sociological Review*, 48, 519–32.

McPherson, Miller, and Thomas Rotolo (1996) Testing a Dynamic Model of Social Composition: Diversity and Change in Voluntary Groups. *American Sociological Review*, 61, 179–202.

McPherson, Miller, Pamela Popielarz, and Sonja Drobnic (1992) Social Networks and Organizational Dynamics. *American Sociological Review*, 57, 153–70.

Macy, Michael W. (1990) Learning-Theory and the Logic of Critical Mass. *American Sociological Review*, 55, 809–26.

——(1991) Chains of Cooperation: Threshold Effects in Collective Action. *American Sociological Review*, 56, 730–47.

——(1993) Backward-Looking Social-Control. *American Sociological Review*, 58, 819–36.

Marwell, Gerald, and Pamela Oliver (1993) *The Critical Mass in Collective Action*. Cambridge: Cambridge University Press.

Melucci, Alberto (1989) *Nomads of the Present*. Philadelphia, PA: Temple University Press.

——(1996) *Challenging Codes*. Cambridge: Cambridge University Press.

Mische, Ann (2003) Cross-talk in Movements: Reconceiving the Culture-Network Link. In M. Diani and D. McAdam (eds.), *Social Movements and Networks*. Oxford: Oxford University Press, 258–80.

Mueller, Carol M. (1994) Conflict Networks and the Origins of Women's Liberation. In E. Laraña, H. Johnston, and J. R. Gusfield (eds.), *New Social Movements: From Ideology to Identity*. Philadelphia, PA: Temple University Press, 234–63.

Mullins, Patrick (1987) Community and Urban Movements. *Sociological Review*, 35, 347–69.

Nepstad, Sharon E., and Christian Smith (1999) Rethinking Recruitment to High-Risk/Cost Activism: The Case of Nicaragua Exchange. *Mobilization*, 4, 25–40.

Norris, Pippa (2002) *Democratic Phoenix*. New York: Cambridge University Press.

Oberschall, Anthony (1973) *Social Conflict and Social Movements*. Englewood Cliffs, NJ: Prentice-Hall.

Ohlemacher, Thomas (1996) Bridging People and Protest: Social Relays of Protest Groups against Low-Flying Military Jets in West Germany. *Social Problems*, 43, 197–218.

Oliver, Pamela (1984) If you Don't Do it, Nobody Else Will: Active and Token Contributors to Collective Action. *American Sociological Review*, 49, 601–10.

Oliver, Pamela, and Gerald Marwell (2001) Whatever Happened *to* Critical Mass Theory? A Retrospective and Assessment. *Sociological Theory*, 19, 292–311.

Olson, Mancur (1963) *The Logics of Collective Action*. Cambridge, MA: Harvard University Press.

Opp, Karl-Dieter (1989) *The Rationality of Political Protest*. Boulder, CO: Westview.

Opp, Karl-Dieter and Christiane Gern (1993) Dissident Groups, Personal Networks, and Spontaneous Cooperation: The East German Revolution of 1989. *American Sociological Review*, 58, 659–80.

Passy, Florence (2001) Socializing, Connecting, and the Structural Agency/Gap: A Specification of the Impact of Networks on Participation in Social Movements. *Mobilization*, 6, 173–92.

——(2003) Social Networks Matter: But How? In M. Diani and D. McAdam (eds.), *Social Movements and Networks*. Oxford: Oxford University Press, 21–48.

Passy, Florence, and Marco Giugni (2000) Life-Spheres, Networks, and Sustained Participation in Social Movements: A Phenomenological Approach to Political Commitment. *Sociological Forum*, 15, 117–44.

Pearce, Jone (1993) *Volunteers*. London: Routledge.

Philips, Susan (1991) Meaning and Structure in Social Movements: Mapping the Network of National Canadian Women's Organizations. *Canadian Journal of Political Science*, 24, 755–82.

Pickvance, Chris (1975) On the Study of Urban Social Movements. *Sociological Review*, 23, 29–49.

Pinard, Maurice (1968) Mass Society and Political Movements: A New Formulation. *American Journal of Sociology*, 73, 682–90.

Piven, Frances F., and Richard Cloward (1992) Normalizing Collective Protest. In A. Morris and C. Mueller (eds.), *Frontiers in Social Movement Theory*. New Haven: Yale University Press, 301–25.

Pizzorno, Alessandro (1996) Decisioni o interazioni? La micro-decisione del cambiamento sociale. *Rassegna italiana di sociologia*, 37, 107–32.

Polletta, Francesca (1999) Free Spaces in Collective Action. *Theory and Society*, 28, 1–38.

Prakash, Sanjeev, and Per Selle (eds.) (2003) *Investigating Social Capital*. New Delhi: Sage.

Putnam, Robert (1995a) Bowling Alone: America's Declining Social Capital. *Journal of Democracy*, 6, 65–78.

——(1995b) Tuning in, Tuning out: The Strange Disappearance of Social Capital in America. *PS: Political Science and Politics*, 28, 664–83.

——(2000) *Bowling Alone*. New York: Simon & Schuster.

Quan y Haase, Anabel Wellman, and Barry Wellman, with James Witte and Keith Hampton (2002) Capitalizing on the Internet: Social Contact, Civic Engagement, and Sense of Community. In B. Wellman and C. Haythornthwaite (eds.), *Internet in Everyday Life*. Oxford: Blackwell, 291–324.

Ray, Kathryn, Mike Savage, Gindo Tampubolon, Brian Longhurst, Mark Tomlison, and Alan Warde (2001) An Exclusive Political Field? Membership Patterns and Networks in Social Movement Organizations. Paper presented at the Social Movements Stream, European Sociological Association Conference, August 26 to September 1, Helsinki.

Rosenthal, Naomi, Meryl Fingrutd, Michele Ethier, Roberta Karant, and David McDonald (1985) Social Movements and Network Analysis. *American Journal of Sociology*, 90, 1022–54.

Rosenthal, Naomi, David McDonald, Michele Ethier, Meryl Fingrutd, and Roberta Karant (1997) Structural Tensions in the Nineteenth Century Women's Movement. *Mobilization*, 2, 21–46.

Rupp, Leila, and Verta Taylor (1987) *Survival in the Doldrums: The American Women's Rights Movement, 1945 to the 1960s*. Columbus: Ohio State University Press.

Sampson, S. (1969) Crisis in a Cloister. PhD dissertation, Cornell University.

Sandell, Rickard (1999) Organizational Life aboard the Moving Bandwagons: A Network Analysis of Dropouts from a Swedish Temperance Organization, 1896–1937. *Acta Sociologica*, 42, 3–15.

——(2001) Organizational Growth and Ecological Constraints: The Growth of Social Movements in Sweden, 1881 to 1940. *American Sociological Review*, 66, 672–93.

Sandell, Rickard, and Charlotta Stern (1998) Group Size and the Logic of Collective Action: A Network Analysis of a Swedish Temperance Movement 1896–1937. *Rationality and Society*, 10, 327–45.

Schmitt-Beck, Rüdiger (1989) Organizational Interlocks between New Social Movements and Traditional Elites. *European Journal of Political Research*, 17, 583–98.

Sewell, William J. Jr. (1992) A Theory of Structure: Duality, Agency, and Transformation. *American Journal of Sociology*, 98, 1–29.

Simmel, Georg (1955) The Web of Group Affiliations. In R. Bendix (tr.), *Conflict and the Web of Group Affiliations*. New York: Free Press, 125–95.

Smelser, Neil J. (1962) *Theory of Collective Behavior*. New York: Free Press.

Snow, David A, Louis A. Zurcher, and Sheldon Ekland-Olson (1980) Social Networks and Social Movements: A Microstructural Approach to Differential Recruitment. *American Sociological Review*, 45, 787–801.

Stark, Rodney, and William S. Bainbridge (1980) Networks of Faith: Interpersonal Bonds and Recruitment to Cults and Sects. *American Journal of Sociology*, 85, 1376–95.

Tarrow, Sidney (1998) *Power in Movement*. Cambridge: Cambridge University Press.

Taylor, Verta, and Nancy Whittier (1992) Collective Identity in Social Movement Communities: Lesbian Feminist Mobilization. In A. Morris and C. Mueller (eds.), *Frontiers in Social Movement Theory*. New Haven: Yale University Press, 104–32.

——(1995) Analytical Approaches to Social Movement Culture: The Culture of the Women's Movement. In H. Johnston and B. Klandermans (eds.), *Social Movements and Culture*. Minneapolis: University of Minnesota Press; London: UCL Press, 163–87.

Tilly, Charles (1978) *From Mobilization to Revolution*. Reading, MA: Addison-Wesley.

Tindall, David (2000) Personal Networks, Identification, and Movement Participation over Time. Paper presented at the conference Social Movement Analysis: The Network Perspective, Ross Priory, Loch Lomond, Scotland, June 22–24.

Wasserman, Stanley, and Katherine Faust (1995) *Social Network Analysis*. Cambridge: Cambridge University Press.

Whittier, Nancy (1995) *Feminist Generations: The Persistence of the Radical Women's Movement*. Philadelphia, PA: Temple University Press.

Wilson, John (2000) Volunteering. *Annual Review of Sociology*, 26, 215–40.

Zald, Mayer N., and John D. McCarthy (1987) *Social Movements in an Organizational Society*. New Brunswick, NJ: Transaction.

16

The Demand and Supply of Participation: Social-Psychological Correlates of Participation in Social Movements

Bert Klandermans

Participation in social movements is a multifaceted phenomenon. Indeed, there are many different forms of movement participation. Two important dimensions to distinguish forms of participation are *time* and *effort*. Some forms of participation are limited in time or of a once-only kind and involve little effort or risk – giving money, signing a petition, or taking part in a peaceful demonstration. Examples in the literature are the demonstration and petition against cruise missiles in the Netherlands (Klandermans and Oegema 1987; Oegema and Klandermans 1994). Other forms of participation are also short-lived but involve considerable effort or risk – a sit-in, a site occupation, or a strike. Participation in the Mississippi Freedom Summer (McAdam 1988) and participation in the Sanctuary movement (Nepstad and Smith 1999) are cases in point. Participation can also be indefinite but demanding little – paying a membership fee to an organization or being on call for two nights a month. Pichardo et al. (1998) studied a variety of such forms of participation in the environmental movement. Finally, there are forms of participation that are both enduring and taxing, like being a member on a committee or a volunteer in a movement organization. Examples are the members of neighborhood committees (Oliver 1984) and the members of underground organizations (della Porta 1988, 1992). From a social-psychological viewpoint taxonomies of participation are relevant because one may expect different forms of participation to involve different motivational dynamics. This is indeed what Passy (2001) found in one of the rare comparative studies of types of movement participation.

In this chapter I will try to develop a social psychology of movement participation that takes these intricacies into account. In doing so I borrow the "demand and supply" metaphor from economics. Demand refers to the potential in a society for protest; supply refers, on the other hand, to the opportunities staged by protest organizers. Mobilization brings a demand for political protest that exists in a society together with a supply of opportunities to take part in such protest. The demand-side of participation requires studies of such phenomena as socialization, grievance formation, causal attribution, and the formation of collective identity. The study of the supply-side of participation concerns such matters as action repertoires, the effectiveness of social movements, the frames and ideologies movements stand for, and the constituents of identification they offer. Mobilization is the process that links demand and supply. Mobilization is the marketing mechanism of the social movement domain, and thus the study of mobilization concerns such matters as the effectiveness of (persuasive) communication, the influence of social networks, and the perceived costs and benefits of participation.

Studies of participation tend to concentrate on mobilization and to neglect the development of demand and supply factors. Yet, there is no reason to take either for granted. To be sure, grievances abound in a society, but that does not mean that there is no reason to explain how grievances develop and how they are transformed into a demand for protest. Nor does the presence of social movement organizations in a society mean that there is no need to understand their formation and to investigate how they stage opportunities to protest and how these opportunities are seized by aggrieved people.

THE DYNAMICS OF MOVEMENT PARTICIPATION

My treatment of the dynamics of movement participation builds on the assumption that we can distinguish three fundamental reasons why movement participation is appealing to people: people may want to change their circumstances, they may want to act as members of their group, or they may want to give meaning to their world and express their views and feelings. I suggest that together these three motives account for most of the demand for collective political action in a society. Social movements may supply the opportunity to fulfil these demands, and the better they do, the more movement participation turns into a satisfying experience. In order to refer in brief to these three types of transactions of demand and supply I will use as shortcuts instrumentality, identity, and ideology. *Instrumentality* refers to movement participation as an attempt to influence the social and political environment; *identity* refers to movement participation as a manifestation of identification with a group; and *ideology* refers to movement participation as a search for meaning and an expression of one's views. Different theories are associated with these three angles (see Klandermans 1997 and Tarrow 1998 for overviews). Instrumentality is related to resource mobilization and political process theories of social movements and at the psychological level to rational choice theory and expectancy-value theories; identity is related to sociological approaches that emphasize the collective identity component of social movement participation and to the social-psychological social identity theory; and ideology is related to approaches in social movement literature that focus on culture, meaning, narratives, moral reasoning, and emotion, and in psychology to theories of social cognition and emotions. I am not suggesting that these are mutually exclusive motives, or competing views on social movement participation, I do hold, however, that approaches that neglect any of those three motives are fundamentally flawed.

I know of no study that has attempted to assess the relative weight of all three motives in their effect on participation. Simon and his students (Simon et al. 1998) have studied the relative influence of identity and instrumentality and shown that both instrumentality and identity play an independent role in the explanation of participation (see also Kelly and Breinlinger 1996; de Weerd 1999; Stürmer 2000). In her study of farmer's protest in the Netherlands (1999), de Weerd showed that feelings of injustice, identity, and agency – the three dimension of the collective action frame – independently contributed to the explanation of why farmers participate in protest. But other than that, we are bound to speculation. Based on these studies I would at the very least propose an additive model. If all three motives apply participation it is more likely than if only one or two apply. An additive model, of course, implies that the motives may compensate one another perhaps even to the extent that in an individual case one or two motives may be irrelevant altogether. To complicate matters further, the three motives may interact. For example, a strong identification or ideology might alter cost-benefit calculations. Similarly, a strong ideology may reinforce levels of identification. These are thorny issues and robust results from empirical studies are lacking.

The Demand-Side of Collective Political Action

Marwell and Oliver (1993) once observed that in view of significant changes in their environment most people continue to do what they were doing, namely, nothing. This observation suggests that the demand for collective political action in a society is usually low. On the other hand, it has been argued that collective political action has become more common over the last decades (Meyer and Tarrow 1998; Klandermans 2001). In this section, I will further elaborate on the issue and discuss the demand side of instrumentality, identity, and ideology.

Instrumentality

A demand for change begins with dissatisfaction, be it the experience of illegitimate inequality, feelings of relative deprivation, feelings of injustice, moral indignation about some state of affairs, or a suddenly imposed grievance (Klandermans 1997). Social-psychological grievance theories such as relative deprivation theory, or social justice theory, have tried to specify how and why grievances develop (see Hegtvedt and Markovsky 1995; Tyler et al. 1997; Tyler and Smith 1998 for overviews). Despite the fact that grievances are at the root of collective political action, they have not featured prominently in social movement literature since the early 1970s. Resource mobilization theory and political process theory, the two approaches that have dominated the field in that period, have always taken as their point of departure that grievances are ubiquitous and that the key-question in movement participation research is not so much why people are aggrieved, but why aggrieved people participate. However, a focus on the demand-side of participation will bring grievances back to center stage (Neidhardt and Rucht 1993; Klandermans et al. 2001b).

In the 1970s, in reaction to approaches that tended to picture movement participation as irrational (Hoffer 1951; Kornhauser 1959; Le Bon 1960), social movement scholars began to emphasize the instrumental character of movement participation. No longer was it depicted as behavior out of resentment by marginalized and isolated individuals, or as aggressive reaction to frustration, or as politics of impatience, but as politics with other means. It was especially the resource mobilization (Oberschall 1973; McCarthy and Zald 1976) and political process approaches (Tilly 1978; McAdam 1982) that took the assumed rationality of movement participants as their point of departure. According to these authors, movement participation is as rational or irrational as any other behavior. Movement participants are people who believe that they can change their political environment to their advantage and the instrumentality paradigm holds that their behavior is controlled by the perceived costs and benefits of participation. It is taken for granted that they are aggrieved, but it is not so much the grievances per se but the belief that the situation can be changed at affordable costs that make them participate. They have the resources and perceive the opportunities to make an impact.

From an instrumental perspective a solution must be found for the dilemma of collective action. Olson (1968) argued that rational actors will *not* contribute to the production of a collective good unless selective incentives persuade them to do so. Olson's argument helped to explain why so often people do not participate in social movements despite the interest they have in the achievement of the movement's goals. Movement scholars argued that movement goals typically are collective goods. If the goal is achieved, people will enjoy the benefits irrespective of whether or not they have participated in the effort. In view of a goal for which achievement is uncertain, but for which benefits – if materialized – can be reaped anyway, rational actors will take a free ride (so the Olsonian reasoning). Selective incentives are supposedly the solution to the dilemma of collective action. Such incentives are typically supply-factors. Therefore, we will return to the issue when we discuss the supply-side of participation.

However, social movement scholars quickly discovered that reality is more complex than Olson's reasoning suggested. The problem with Olson's logic is that indeed it provides an explanation for why people do *not* participate, but fares poorly in explaining why people *do* participate. Moreover, Oliver (1980) argued that Olson's solution that selective incentives make people participate is fundamentally flawed, as it does not give a satisfactory answer to the question of where the resources needed to provide selective incentives come from. If these must be collected from individual citizens, the same collective action dilemma arises again. This is not to say that selective incentives are irrelevant, but that in the final instance they cannot solve the collective action dilemma. Kim and Bearman (1997) have argued that the failure of rational choice models to explain collective action is rooted in the assumption that interests are fixed. They develop a far more complex model that relaxed the assumptions of fixed interests and assumes that interactions shape interests. "Interests are sensitive to history," they hold, "actors are interdependent, and activism is enhanced through increasing embeddedness in activist networks" (72). They conclude that interest and embeddedness in dense activist network accounts for the occurrence of collective action. This relates to a recurring criticism that Olson's model assumes that individuals make their decisions in isolation, as if there are no other people with whom they consult, with whom they feel solidarity, and by whom they are kept to their promises. This pointed to the significance of collective identity as a factor in movement participation.

Identity

Soon it became clear that instrumentality was not the only motive to participate. After all, much of the movement goals are only reached in the long run if at all. Similarly, when it comes to material benefits, costs often outweigh benefits. Apparently, there is more in being a movement participant than perceived costs and benefits. Indeed, one of those motives relates to belonging to a valued group.

Simon (1998, 1999) succinctly described identity as a place in society. People occupy many different places in society. They are students, unemployed, housewives, soccer players, politicians, farmers, and so on. Some of those places are exclusive, occupied only by a small number of people. The members of a soccer team are an example. Others are inclusive, encompassing large numbers of people such as Europeans. Some places are mutually exclusive, such as male–female, or employed–unemployed; some are nested, for example, French, Dutch, German versus European; and some are cross-cutting, such as female and student (Turner 1999; Hornsey and Hogg forthcoming). All these different roles and positions a person occupies form his or her *personal identity*. At the same time, every place a person occupies is shared with other people. I am not the only professor of social psychology, nor the only Dutch person or European. I share these identities with other people – a fact that turns them into collective identities. Thus a *collective identity* is a place shared with other people. This implies that personal identity is at the same time always collective identity. Personal identity is general, referring to a variety of places in society, whereas collective identity is specific, referring to a specific place (see chapter 19 in this volume for an elaborate discussion of collective identity).

Most of the time collective identities remain latent. Self-categorization theory hypothesizes that depending on contextual circumstances an individual may act as a unique person, that is, display his personal identity *or* as a member of a specific group, that is, display one of the many collective identities he has (Turner et al. 1994; Turner 1999). Contextual factors may bring personal or collective identity to the fore. Obviously, this is often no matter of free choice. Circumstances may force a collective identity into awareness whether people like it or not, as the Yugoslavian and South African histories have illustrated dramatically. But also in less extreme circumstances collective identities can become significant. Take for example the possible effect of an announcement that a waste incinerator is planned next to a neighborhood. Chances are that within a very short time the collective identity of the people living in that neighborhood becomes salient.

The basic hypothesis regarding collective identity and movement participation is fairly straightforward: a strong identification with a group makes participation in collective political action on behalf of that group more likely (Huddy 2001; see Stryker et al. 2000 for a comprehensive treatment of the subject). The available empirical evidence overwhelmingly supports this assumption. Kelly and Breinlinger (1996) found that identification with a labor union and its members made it more likely for workers to participate in industrial action; while gender identification made participation in the women's movement more likely. Simon et al. (1998) and Stürmer (2000) observed that identification with other gay people, but especially with other members of the gay movement, reinforced involvement in the gay movement. Finally, Klandermans and his colleagues (de Weerd and Klandermans

1999; Klandermans et al. 2002) reported that farmers who identified with other farmers were more likely to be involved in farmers' protest than those who did not display any identification with other farmers.

Ideology

The third motive, wanting to express one's views, refers at the same time to a long-standing theme in the social movement literature and to a recent development. In classic studies of social movements the distinction was made between instrumental and expressive movements or protest (see Searles and Williams 1962; Gusfield 1963). In those days, instrumental movements were seen as movements that aimed at some external goal, for example, the implementation of citizenship rights. Participation in expressive movements, on the other hand, was a goal in itself, for example, the expression of anger in response to experienced injustice. Movement scholars felt increasingly uncomfortable with the distinction, because it was thought that most movements had both instrumental and expressive aspects and that the emphasis on the two could change over time. Therefore, the distinction lost its use. Recently, however, the idea that people might participate in movements to express their views has received new attention, this time from movement scholars who were unhappy with the overly structural approach of resource mobilization and political process theory. These scholars put an emphasis on such aspects as the creative and cultural aspects of social movements, narratives, emotions, and moral indignation (see chapters 17 and 18 in this volume). People are angry, develop feelings of moral indignation about some state of affairs or some government decision and they want to make that known. They participate in a social movement not only to enforce political change, but to gain dignity in their lives through struggle and moral expression.

Goodwin et al. argue that emotions are socially constructed, but that "some emotions are more [socially] constructed than others, involving more cognitive processes" (2001: 13). In their view, emotions that are politically relevant are more than other emotions located at the social construction end of the scale. For these emotions, cultural and historical factors play an important role in the inter-pretation of the state of affairs by which they are generated. Emotions, these authors hold, are important in the growth and unfolding of social movements and political protest. Obviously, emotions can be manipulated. Activists work hard to create moral outrage and anger and to provide a target against which these can be vented. They must weave together a moral, cognitive, and emotional package of attitudes. Also, in the ongoing activities of the movements emotions play an important role (Jasper 1997, 1998). Anger and indignation are emotions related to a specific appraisal of the situation. At the same time, people might be puzzled by some aspects of reality and try to understand what is going on. They may look for others with similar experiences and a social movement may provide an environment to exchange experiences, to tell their stories and to express their feelings.

THE SUPPLY-SIDE OF PARTICIPATION

Social movement organizations are more or less successful in satisfying demands for collective political participation and we may assume that movements which supply what potential participants demand, gain more support than movements which fail to do so. Movements and movement organizations can be compared in terms of their effectiveness in this regard.

Instrumentality

Instrumentality presupposes an effective movement that is able to enforce some wanted changes or at least to mobilize substantial support. Making an objective assessment of a movement's impact is not easy (see Giugni 1998; Giugni et al. 1999; see also chapters 20 to 23 in this volume), but of course movement organizations will try to convey the image of an effective political force. They can do so by pointing to the impact they have had in the past, or to the powerful allies they have. Of course, they may lack all this, but then, they might be able to show other signs of strength. A movement may command a large constituency, as witnessed by turnout at demonstrations, or by membership figures, or large donations. It may comprise strong organizations with charismatic leaders who have gained respect, and so on. Instrumentality also implies the provision of selective incentives. The selective incentives of participation that can be made available may vary considerably between movement organizations. Such variation depends on the resources a movement organization has at its disposal (McCarthy and Zald 1976; Oliver 1980). Surprisingly, little systematic comparison of the characteristics of movements, movement organizations, and campaigns in view of the supply-side of participation can be found in the literature (but see Klandermans 1993). The political system and the alliance and conflict system movement organizations are embedded in may also show considerable variation that influences the supply-side of movement participation. Indeed, Tilly (1978) coined the terms "repression" and "facilitation" to distinguish between political systems that increase or decrease the costs of participation. Repressive political environments may increase the costs of participation considerably: people may lose friends, they may risk their jobs, or otherwise jeopardize their sources of income, they may be jailed, and they may even lose their lives.

An important element of the supply-side of participation is the provision of information about the behavior of others. Social networks are of strategic importance in this respect, because it is through these networks that people are informed about the behavior or intentions of others (Oegema and Klandermans 1994; Kim and Bearman 1997; Chwe 1999; Passy 2001). As discussed, the importance of such information differs depending on the type of participation. Building on the argument that individuals hold different thresholds, Rule (1988, 1989) argued that seeing that increasing numbers take part in a collective action in itself motivates growing numbers of people to join, because their individual thresholds to participation are passed. In his paper on the Chinese student movement of 1989, Zhao (1998) gives a striking illustration of this mechanism. He describes how the ecological circumstance that most students in Beijing live in the same part of town made the success of the movement in terms of mobilization literally visible in the streets in front of the dormitories.

Identity

Movements offer the opportunity to act on behalf of one's group. This is most attractive if people identify strongly with their group. The more farmers identify with other farmers, the more prepared they are to take part in farmers' protests (de Weerd and Klandermans 1999; Klandermans et al. 2002). The more women identify with other women, the more prepared they are to take part in the women's movement (Kelly and Breinlinger 1996); and the more gay people identify with other gay people, the more prepared they are to take part in the gay movement (Simon et al. 1998; Stürmer 2000). Interestingly, all these studies show that identification with the more exclusive group of movement participants is far more influential than identification with the more inclusive category. Indeed, in addition to the opportunity to act on behalf of the group, collective political action participation offers further constituents of identification: the movement's cause; the people in the movement; the movement organization; or the group one is participating in; and the leader of the movement. Not all these sources of identification are always equally appealing. Movement leaders can be more or less charismatic, or the people in the movement or in someone's group can be more or less attractive. Moreover, movements and movement organizations may be, and in fact often are, controversial. Hence, becoming a participant in a movement organization does not mean taking upon oneself a respected position. Within the movement's framework this is, of course, completely different. There the militant does have the status society is denying him or her. And, of course, for an activist ingroup–outgroup dynamics may turn the movement organization or group into a far more attractive group than any other group "out there" that is opposing the movement. Indeed, it is not uncommon for militants to refer to the movement organization as a second family, a substitute for the social and associative life society no longer offers them (Tristan 1987; Orfali 1990). Movement organizations not only supply sources of identification; they also offer all kinds of opportunities to enjoy and celebrate the collective identity: marches, rituals, songs, meetings, signs, symbols, and common codes (see Stryker et al. 2000, and chapter 19 in this volume).

A complicating matter when it comes to the supply-side of participation is the fact that people have multiple identities, while movements emphasize a collective identity, and therefore by definition refer to a single place in society. This may imply competing loyalties as Oegema and Klandermans (1994) demonstrated with regard to the Dutch peace movement. The movement's campaign against cruise missiles brought many a citizen who sympathized with the movement but was affiliated to the Christian Democratic Party, which in regard to cruise missiles stood opposite the movement, under cross-pressure. Movement organizations are more or less successful in coping with multiple identities. Sharon Kurtz (2002) describes how clerical workers of Columbia University struggled but succeeded to reconcile gender, ethnic, and class identities. Karen Beckwith (1998), on the other hand, explains how women in the Pittston Coal Strike were denied the possibility to act on their gender identity. Very little systematic attention has been given in the social movement literature to the issue of multiple identities, yet every movement must deal with the problem and, depending on how this is accomplished, it succeeds in appealing to various constituencies. Gerhards and Rucht (1992), for example, describe how the organizers of two demonstrations in Berlin went to great lengths to make it possible for various constituencies to identify with goals of the demonstration. Similar observations can be found in the first studies on the antiglobalization movement (Smith 2001; Levi and Murphy 2002).

There is evidence that identity processes have both an indirect and a direct effect on protest participation (Stürmer 2000). They are *indirect* when collective identity influences instrumental reasoning such that it makes it less attractive to take a free ride. Hirsch's (1990) study of the Columbia divestment protest is a good example of how solidarity with the group as it developed on the doorstep of the administration of Columbia University make it difficult for participants to drop out. Indeed, collective identity appears to be a way to overcome the social dilemma built into the instrumental route to movement participation (see also Klandermans 2000). High levels of group identification increase the costs of defection and the benefits of cooperation. In other words, collective identity impacts on the instrumental pathway to protest participation. *Direct* effects occur when collective identity creates a shortcut to participation. People participate not so much because of the outcomes associated with participation but because they identify with the other participants.

Ideology

Social movements play a significant role in the diffusion of ideas and values (Eyerman and Jamison 1991). Rochon (1998) makes the distinction between "critical communities," where new ideas and values are developed, and "social movements," which are interested in winning social and political acceptance for those ideas and values. Since "in the hands of movement leaders, the ideas of critical communities become ideological frames" (31), Rochon argues that social movements are not simply extensions of critical communities. After all, not all ideas developed in critical communities are equally suited to motivate collective action. Social movement organizations, then, are carriers of meaning. Through processes such as consensus mobilization (Klandermans 1984), framing (Snow et al. 1986), or dialogue (Steinberg 1999) they seek to disseminate their definition of the situation to the public at large. Gerhards and Rucht's study (1992) of flyers produced by the various groups and organizations involved in the protests against the IMF and the World Bank in Berlin is an excellent example in this respect. These authors show how links are constructed between the ideological frame of the organizers of the demonstration and those of the participating organizations in order to create a shared definition of the situation. Such definitions of the situation have been labeled "collective action frames" (Gamson 1992; Klandermans 1997; see also chapter 17 in this volume). Collective action frames can be defined in terms of injustice (i.e., some definition of what is wrong in the world); identity (i.e., some definition of who is affected and who is responsible); and agency (i.e., some beliefs about the possibilities to change society). We may assume that people who join a movement come to share some part of the movement's action frame and that, in the process of sharing, meaning is given to their world.

Social movements do not invent ideas; they build on an ideological heritage as they relate their claims to broader themes and values in society (see also chapter 17 in this volume for elaboration). In so doing they relate to societal debates that have a history of their own, and that history is usually much longer than that of the movement itself. Gamson (1992), for example, refers to the "themes" and "counterthemes" that in his view exist in every society. One such pair of a theme and countertheme he mentions, is "self-reliance" versus "mutuality," that is, the belief that individuals must take care of themselves versus the belief that society is responsible for its less fortunate members. In a study of the protests about disability payment in the Netherlands we demonstrated how in the Netherlands these two beliefs became the icons that galvanized the debates (Klandermans and Goslinga 1996). While "self-reliance" became the theme of those favouring restrictions in disability payment, "mutuality" was the theme of those who defended the existing system. Another example is what Tarrow (1998) calls "rights frames": human rights, civil rights, women's rights, animal rights, and so on. In other words, collective action frames that relate a movement's aims to some fundamental rights frame. For decades Marxism has been such an ideological heritage from the past movements identified with it: positively, by embracing it, or negatively, by distancing themselves from it. In a similar vein, fascism and Nazism form the ideological heritage rightwing extremism must comes to terms with either by identifying with it or by keeping it at a distance. Some of those ideas from the past are more useful than others are. For example, Kitschelt (1995) has argued that parties of the new radical right that identify too much with Nazism or fascism are doomed to be unsuccessful (see also Ignazi and Ysmal 1992)

It is not just the cognitive component of ideology that social movements are the conduits of. Emotions, that is, the affective component of ideology are equally important. After all, people are angry, morally outraged, and movement organizations provide the opportunity to express and communicate those feelings. Scholarly attention to the role of emotions in the realm of movement participation is only in its infancy. In an edited volume Goodwin et al. (2001) have brought work on the subject together. As a chapter by the same authors in this volume is devoted to the subject of emotion, passion, and participation, I will be brief. Obviously, movements differ in regard to how they deal with emotions, feelings, or passion, both in terms of the passion that spurs participation and in terms of how they deal with emotion and affection inside the movement. The better they do this, the more committed to the movement people will become; but if they fail, this may become a reason for a movement to collapse, as Goodwin's (1997) study of the Huk Rebellion illustrates. The failure of that rebellious movement to deal with affective and sexual relations within the movement and between movement participants and outsiders eventually undermined the movement.

MOBILIZATION

When an individual participates in collective political action staged by a social movement organization, this is the result of a sometimes lengthy process of mobilization. Successful mobilization gradually brings demand and supply together. If substantial proportions of the population are aggrieved, and if movement organizations stage collective action to voice those grievances, a massive protest movement may develop. Mobilization is a complicated process that can be broken down into several, conceptually distinct steps. In the early 1980s I proposed breaking the process of mobilization down into consensus and action mobilization (Klandermans 1984). Consensus mobilization refers to dissemination of the views of the movement organization, and action mobilization refers to the transformation of those who adopted the view of the movement into active participants. Thus defined, action

mobilization is constrained by the results of consensus mobilization, as I demonstrated in my own work (1997). Indeed, action mobilization attempts tend to
concentrate on people with an attitudinal disposition to participate, rightly so, as
Marwell and Oliver's (1993) computer simulation suggests. An interesting recent
illustration of the strategic importance of consensus mobilization can be found in
Walgrave and Manssens' (2000) study of the "White March" in Brussels in response
to the government's failure to deal with the Dutroux kidnappings and killings.
Moral outrage brought hundreds of thousands of people onto the streets of Brussels.
The authors demonstrate that the mass media played a crucial role in mobilizing
consensus on the issue. Consensus mobilization has been elaborated much further by
Snow and Benford and their colleagues in their frame alignment approach to
mobilization (see chapter 17 in this volume, and Benford 1997 for a critical review).

In my own work, I focused on the process of action mobilization, which I broke
down into four separate steps (Klandermans and Oegema 1987). Each step brings
the supply and demand of collective political action closer together until an individual takes the final step toward participation in an instance of collective political
action. As action mobilization builds on the results of consensus mobilization, the
first step accounts for the results. It distinguishes the general public into people who
sympathize with the cause and people who do not. The more successful consensus
mobilization has been, the larger the pool of sympathizers a mobilizing movement
organization can draw from. A large pool of sympathizers is of strategic importance,
because for a variety of reasons many a sympathizer never turns into a participant.
The second step is equally crucial: it divides the sympathizers into those who have
been a target of mobilization attempts and those who have not. In addition to the
question of whether people have been targeted, we can distinguish qualitative and
quantitative differences in targeting. People can be targeted more or less frequently
and in more or less insistent ways. The third step concerns the social-psychological
core of the process. It divides the sympathizers who have been targeted into those
who are motivated to participate in the specific activity and those who are not.
Finally, the fourth step differentiates the people who are motivated into those who
end up participating and those who do not (see figure 16.1).

In our research on the mobilization campaign for a peace demonstration (Klandermans and Oegema 1987) we found that three quarters of the population of a small
community south of Amsterdam felt sympathy for the movement's cause. Of these
sympathizers, three-quarters were somehow targeted by mobilization attempts. Of
those targeted, one-sixth were motivated to participate in the demonstration. And
finally, of those motivated, one-third ended up participating. The net result of these

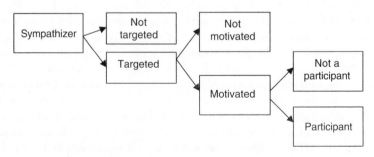

Figure 16.1 Four steps toward participation.

different steps is some (usually small) proportion of the general public that partici-pates in collective action.[1] With each step smaller or larger numbers drop out. The smaller the number of dropouts the better the fit between demand and supply. This can be illustrated with the following queries related to the subsequent steps: (1) Does the cause of the movement appeal to concerns of individual citizens? (2) Do the movement's networks link to the individuals' networks? (3) Is the activity the movement is mobilizing for appealing to individual citizens? (4) Is the movement able to eliminate any remaining barrier for individual citizens?

In a motivational model of movement participation (Klandermans 1984, 1997) I have tried to account for the third step. The model takes as its point of departure that movement goals are public goods. It belongs to the expectancy-value family and links the supply of collective political action as perceived by the individual to his or her demands. In doing so, it combines insights from rational choice theory with those from collective action theory. The model makes a distinction between collect-ive and selective incentives. Put simply, it poses that people are motivated by the possibility to support the production of an attractive public good – such as clean air, peace, or equal rights (collective incentives) to be achieved by participation in attractive action means – for example, a rally where their favourite music group performs (selective incentives). Collective incentives are further broken down into the value of the public good and the expectation that it will be produced. A key element of that expectation is expectations about the behaviour of others. This is what makes collective behaviour different from individual behaviour. The theory supposes an optimum: too many expected participants makes it unnecessary for the individual to participate; too few expected participants makes it useless for the individual to participate. Perceived selective incentives add to the explanation, especially so-called social incentives, which, in Klandermans' model, consist of the expected reaction of significant others if the individual decides to participate. Since its publication, the model has found convincing empirical support (Klandermans 1984; Briet et al. 1987; Klandermans and Oegema 1987; White 1989, 1993; Klandermans 1993; Kelly and Breinlinger 1996; Simon et al. 1998; Stürmer 2000).

I am not aware of much research into the last step. Obviously, we may assume that at this stage barriers interact with strength of motivation. The stronger someone's motivation, the more likely that she will overcome the last barriers. Our own research suggests that friendship networks play a crucial role in this respect: it is your friends who keep you to your promises (Oegema and Klandermans 1994). The second step is about networks. Networks to a large extent determine whether someone becomes a target of mobilization attempts: they are the conduits of all kinds of information processed during a mobilization (Ohlemacher 1992; Chwe 1999; Passy 2001). An extensive literature exists on the role of networks in movement mobilization (see Kitts 2000 and chapter 15 in this volume for overviews).

THE DYNAMICS OF DISENGAGEMENT

The dynamics of participation in social movements have an obvious counterpart, namely, the dynamics of disengagement. Why do people defect from the movement for which they have worked so very hard? Surprisingly little attention has been given to that question. Compared to the abundant literature on why people join movements, literature on why they exit is almost nonexistent. Elsewhere, I have discussed extensively the social-psychological dynamics of disengagement (Klandermans 2003). The guiding principle of that discussion was the following simple model (figure 16.2).

Insufficient gratification in combination with declining commitment produces a growing intention to leave. Eventually, some critical event tips the balance and makes the person quit. Obviously, the event itself only triggers the final step. Against that background its impact may be overestimated. It is the decline in gratification and commitment that causes defection – the critical event only precipitates matters.

Insufficient Gratification

In the previous sections I distinguished three fundamental motives to participate. In each of these motives a movement may fall short. Most likely, movements fall short in terms of instrumentality. Although it is difficult to assess the effectiveness of social movements, it is obvious that many a movement goal is never reached. Opp (1989) has argued that people are well aware of the fact that movement goals are not always easy to achieve, but that they reason that nothing happens in any event if nobody participates. Yet, sooner or later some success must be achieved for the instrumentality motive to continue to fuel participation (Schwartz 1976). In addition to not being achieved, movement goals may lose their attraction to people. They may lose their urgency and end up lower on the societal agenda scale. Finally, the individual costs or risks of participation may be too high compared to the attraction of the movement's goals. Repression adds to the costs and might make participation too costly for people (Tilly 1978).

Movements offer the opportunity to act on behalf of one's group. This is most attractive if people identify strongly with their group. But the composition of a movement may change and, as a consequence, people may feel less akin to the others in the movement (Klandermans 1994; Whittier 1997). Indeed, I have shown how activists from other movements flocked in increasing numbers into the Dutch peace movement, and thus estranged the original activist who had a church background. Schisms are another reason why movements fail to satisfy identity motives. Schisms are not uncommon in the social movement domain (Gamson 1975). Sani

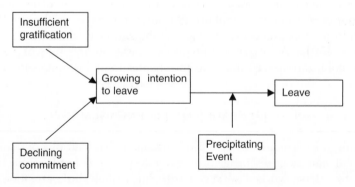

Figure 16.2   The dynamics of disengagement.

and Reicher (1998) demonstrate that schisms result from fights over the core identity of a movement and that people who leave no longer feel that they can identify with the movement. Finally, people occupy a variety of positions in society. Each position is shared with other people and therefore comes with a (most of the time) latent collective identity. A change in context may make the one collective identity more and the others less salient, and therefore identification with a movement may wither. For example, in our study of a farmers' protest in the Netherlands and Spain we observed that in Spain during a campaign for local and provincial elections the identification with farmers declined (Klandermans et al. 2002).

Social movements provide the opportunity to express one's views and feelings. This is not to say that they are always equally successful in that regard. Obviously, there is not always full synchrony between a movement's ideology and a person's beliefs. Indeed, many a movement organization ends in fights between ideological factions and schisms, and consequently in defection (Gamson 1975). Movements also differ in regard to how they deal with emotions, feelings, or passion, both in terms of the passion that spurs participation and in terms of how they deal with emotion and affection inside the movement.

Declining Commitment

The concept of commitment is rooted in the fields of organizational psychology and the social psychology of union participation, where a lively debate on commitment has taken place since the 1980s (Goslinga 2002). Movement commitment does not last by itself. It must be maintained via interaction with the movement, and any measure that makes that interaction less gratifying helps to undermine commitment. Downton and Wehr (1991, 1997) discuss mechanisms of social bonding that movements apply to maintain commitment. Leadership, ideology, organization, rituals, and social relations that make up a friendship network all contribute to sustaining commitment, and the most effective is, of course, a combination of all five. These authors refer to the "common devotion" that results from shared leadership; to group pressure as the primary means of maintaining a social movement's ideology; to "taking on a role within the organization itself" as a way of increasing people's investment in the organization; to rituals as patterns of behavior repeated over time to strengthen core beliefs of the movement; and to circles of friends who strengthen and maintain individual commitment by putting an individual's beliefs and behavior under greater scrutiny and social control.

Although not all are equally well researched, each of these five mechanisms is known from the literature on union and movement participation as a factor that fosters people's attachment to movements. For example, it is known from research on union participation that involving members in decision-making processes increases commitment to a union (Klandermans 1986, 1992). For such different groups as the lesbian movement groups (Taylor and Whittier 1995) and a group called Victims of Child Abuse Laws (Fine 1995) it was demonstrated how rituals strengthen the membership's bond to the movement. Unions and other movement organizations have developed all kind of services for their members to make membership more attractive. Selective incentives may seldom be sufficient reasons to participate in a movement, but they do increase commitment.

The Role of Precipitating Events

When gratification falls short and commitment declines, an intention to leave develops. Yet this intention to leave does not necessarily turn into defection. Many participants maintain a marginal level of participation for extended periods until some event makes them quit. For example, Goslinga (2002) calculated that a stable 25 percent of the membership of Dutch labour unions considered leaving. As the event is the immediate cause of disengagement, it draws disproportionate attention as an explanation of exit behavior, but the event has this impact only in the context of an already present readiness to leave. Such critical events can have many different appearances. When some decades ago Dutch labour unions changed to a different system of dues collection and members had to sign to agree with the new system quite a few members chose not to sign. Changing address may be seized as an opportunity to leave the movement, simply by not renewing contact in the new place of residence. More substantial reasons might be a conflict with others in the organization, disappointing experiences in the movement, a failed collective action, and so on. Such events function as the last drop that makes the cup run over.

CONCLUSIONS

Participation in a social movement is not just a matter of people who are pushed to act by some internal psychological state (the demand-side of participation), nor is it a matter of movement organizations pulling people into action (the supply-side of participation). Demand, supply, *and* mobilization account for instances of participation. The reason why often no collective action takes place despite widespread discontent, is that there is no viable movement organization to stage any action. At the same time, when present a movement organization does not get very far if there are no people who are concerned about the issues the organization tries to address. Finally, without effective mobilization campaigns supply and demand may never meet. Understanding the supply-side of participation involves theories from sociology and political sciences about the development and dynamics of social movements; understanding the demand-side requires models from social and political psychology about grievance formation, the formation of identity, and social cognition and emotion. As in economics, there is an intriguing interplay of demand and supply. Sometimes an attractive, well-timed action attracts an enormous turnout, that is to say, the supply reinforces the demand. Sometimes massive discontent generates a strong movement: demand triggers supply. But, of course, most of the time demand and supply reinforce each other. Mobilization is the process that makes the two meet. Theories of persuasion and network analysis are relevant in this realm.

Different motives come into play in the exchange between a movement and its participants. Instrumentality, identity, and ideology have been proposed as possible motives that contribute to the individual's motivation to participate. I suggested that the three can compensate one another. Participation may not immediately be effective in bringing about changes. Participants understand that and will not expect government to give in at the first sign of contention. On the other hand, it may suffice for many a participant to have the opportunity to meet with other like-minded people and to express an opinion. Collective political action is not only about effectiveness but also about passionate politics. This is not to say that effectiveness is likely to become altogether irrelevant. Obviously, sooner or later something should change. If nothing ever happens, a movement of change will collapse, fade, or turn into a social club or self-help organization.

Note

1 A small proportion does not necessarily mean a negligible event. E.g., although only 4% of the population participated in the peace demonstration, this amounted nevertheless to a demonstration with 500,000 participants – the largest demonstration the country had ever seen.

References

Beckwith, Karen (1998) Collective Identities of Class and Gender: Working-Class Women in the Pittston Coal Strike. *Political Psychology*, 19, 147–67.

Benford, Robert, D. (1997) An Insider's Critique of the Social Movement Framing Perspective. *Sociological Inquiry*, 67, 409–30.

Briet, Martien, Bert Klandermans, and Frederike Kroon (1987) How Women Become involved in the Women's Movement. In Carol Mueller and Mary Katzenstein (eds.), *The Women's Movements of Western Europe and the United States: Changing Theoretical Perspectives*. Philadelphia, PA: Temple University Press, 44–67.

Chwe, Michael Suk-Young (1999) Structure and Strategy in Collective Action. *American Journal of Sociology*, 105, 128–56.

de Weerd, Marga (1999) Social Psychologische Determinanten van Boerenprotest: Collectieve Actie Frames, Identiteit en Effectiviteit. PhD dissertation, Free University, Amsterdam.

de Weerd, Marga, and Bert Klandermans (1999) Group Identification and Social Protest: Farmers' Protest in the Netherlands. *European Journal of Social Psychology*, 29, 1073–95.

della Porta, Donatella (1988) Recruitment into Clandestine Organizations: Leftwing Terrorists in Italy. In Bert Klandermans, Hanspeter Kriesi, and Sidney Tarrow (eds.), *From Structure to Action: Comparing Movement Participation across Cultures*. Greenwich, CT: JAI, 155–72.

——(1992) On Individual Motivations in Underground Political Organizations. In Donatella della Porta (ed.), *Social Movements and Violence: Participation in Underground Organizations: International Social Movement Research*. Vol. 4. Greenwich, CT: JAI, 3–28.

Downton, James, and Paul Wehr (1991) Peace Movements: The Role of Commitment and Community in Sustaining Member Participation. *Research in Social Movements, Conflicts and Change*, 13, 113–34.

——(1997) *The Persistent Activist: How Peace Commitment Develops and Survives*. Boulder, CO: Westview.

Eyerman, Ron, and Andrew Jamison (1991) *Social Movements: A Cognitive Approach*. Oxford: Polity.

Fine, Gary Alan (1995) Public Narration and Group Culture: Discerning Discourse in Social Movements. In Hank Johnston and Bert Klandermans (eds.), *Social Movements and Culture*. Minneapolis: University of Minnesota Press; London: UCL Press, 127–43.

Gamson, William A. (1975) *The Strategy of Social Protest*, Homewood, IL: Dorsey.

——(1992) The Social Psychology of Collective Action. In Aldon Morris and Carol McClurg Mueller (eds.), *Frontiers in Social Movement Theory*. New Haven: Yale University Press, 53–76.

Gerhards, Jürgen,and Dieter Rucht (1992) Mesomobilization: Organizing and Framing in Two Protest Campaigns in West Germany. *American Journal of Sociology*, 98, 555–96.

Giugni, Marco (1998) Was it Worth the Effort? The Outcomes and Consequences of Social Movements. *Annual Review of Sociology*, 24, 371–93.

Giugni, Marco, Doug McAdam, and Charles Tilly (1999) *How Social Movements Matter*. Minneapolis: University of Minnesota Press.

Goodwin, Jeff (1997) The Libidinal Constitution of a High-Risk Social Movement: Affectual Ties and Solidarity in the Huk Rebellion. *American Sociological Review*, 62, 53–69.

Goodwin, Jeff, James Jasper, and Francesca Polletta (2001) Why Emotions Matter. In Jeff Goodwin, James Jasper, and Francesca Polletta (eds.), *Passionate Politics: Emotions and Social Movements*. Chicago: University of Chicago Press, 1–24.

Goslinga, Sjoerd (2002) Binding aan de Vakbond: Union Commitment. PhD dissertation, Free University, Amsterdam.

Gusfield, J. R (1963) *Symbolic Crusade: Status Politics and the American Temperance Movement*. Urbana, IL: University of Illinois Press.

Hegtvedt, Karen A., and Barry Markovsky (1995) Justice and Injustice. In Karen S. Cook, Garry A. Fine, and James S. House (eds.), *Sociological Perspectives in Social Psychology*. Boston: Allyn & Bacon, 257–80.

Hirsch, Eric L. (1990) Sacrifice for the Cause: The Impact of Group Processes on Recruitment and Commitment in Protest Movements. *American Sociological Review*, 55, 243–54.

Hoffer, E. (1951) *The True Believer*. New York: Harper.

Hornsey, Matthew J., and Michael A. Hogg (forthcoming) Intergroup Similarity and Subgroup Relations: Some Implications for Assimilation. *Personality and Social Psychology Bulletin*.

Huddy, Leonie (2001) From Social to Political Identity: A Critical Examination of Social Identity Theory. *Political Psychology*, 22, 127–56.

Ignazi, Piero, and Colette Ysmal (1992) New and Old Extreme Right Parties: The French Front National and the Italian Movimento Sociale. *European Journal of Political Research*, 22, 101–21.

Jasper, James M. (1997) *The Art of Moral Protest: Culture, Biography, and Creativity in Social Movements*. Chicago: University of Chicago Press.

—— (1998) The Emotions of Protest: Affective and Reactive Emotions in and around Social Movements. *Sociological Forum*, 13, 397–424.

Kelly, Caroline, and Sarah Breinlinger (1996) *The Social Psychology of Collective Action*. Basingstoke: Taylor & Francis.

Kim Hyojoung, and Peter S. Bearman (1997) The Structure and Dynamics of Movement Participation. *American Sociological Review*, 62, 70–93.

Kitschelt, Herbert (1995) *The Radical Right in Western Europe*. Ann Arbor: Michigan University Press.

Kitts, James, A. (2000) Mobilizing in Black Boxes: Social Networks and Participation in Social Movement Organizations. *Mobilization*, 5, 241–57.

Klandermans, Bert (1984) Mobilization and Participation: Social Psychological Expansions of Resource Mobilization Theory. *American Sociological Review*, 49, 583–600.

—— (1986) Psychology and Trade union Participation: Joining, Acting, Quitting. *Journal of Occupational Psychology*, 59, 189–204.

—— (1992) The Social Construction of Protest and Multi-organizational Fields. In Aldon Morris and Carol McClurg Mueller (eds.), *Frontiers in Social Movement Theory*. New Haven: Yale University Press, 77–103.

—— (1993) A Theoretical Framework for Comparisons of Social Movement Participation. *Sociological Forum*, 8, 383–402.

——(1994) Transient Identities? Membership Patterns in the Dutch Peace Movement. In Enrique Laraña, Hank Johnston, and Joseph R. Gusfield (eds.), *New Social Movements: From Ideology to Identity*. Philadelphia, PA: Temple University Press, 168–84.

——(1997) *The Social Psychology of Protest*. Oxford: Blackwell.

——(2000) Identity and Protest: How Group Identification Helps to Overcome Collective Action Dilemmas. In M. van Vugt, M. Snyder, T. R. Tyler, and A. Biel (eds.), *Cooperation in Modern Society: Promoting the Welfare of Communities, States, and Organizations*. London: Routledge, 162–83.

——(2001) Why Movements Come into Being and Why People Join Them. In Judith Blau (ed.), *The Blackwell Companion to Sociology*. Oxford: Blackwell, 268–81.

——(2003) A Social Psychology of Disengagement. Working Paper. Free University, Amsterdam.

Klandermans, Bert, and Sjoerd Goslinga (1996) Media Discourse, Movement Publicity and the Generation of Collective Action Frames: Theoretical and Empirical Exercises in Meaning Construction. In Doug McAdam, John McCarthy, and Mayer Zald (eds.), *Opportunities, Mobilizing Structures, and Frames: Comparative Applications of Comtemporary Movement Theory*. Cambridge: Cambridge University Press, 312–37.

Klandermans, Bert, and Dirk Oegema (1987) Potentials, Networks, Motivations and Barriers: Steps toward Participation in Social Movements. *American Sociological Review*, 52, 519–31.

Klandermans, Bert, Marlene Roefs, and Johan Olivier (2001a) *The State of the People: Citizens, Civil Society and Governance in South Africa, 1994–2000*. Pretoria: Human Science Research Council.

——(2001b) Grievance Formation in a Country in Transition: South Africa 1994–1998. *Social Psychology Quarterly*, 64, 41–54.

Klandermans, Bert, Jose Manuel Sabucedo, and Mauro Rodriguez (2002) Politicization of Collective Identity: Farmers' Identity and Farmers' Protest in the Netherlands and Spain. *Political Psychology*, 23, 235–52.

Kornhauser, William (1959) *The Politics of Mass Society*. Glencoe, IL: Free Press.

Kurtz, Sharon (2002) *All Kinds of Justice: Labor and Identity Politics*. Minneapolis: University of Minnesota Press.

Le Bon, G. (1960) *The Crowd: A Study of Popular Mind*. New York: Viking.

Levi, Margaret, and Gillian Murphy (2002) Coalitions of Contention: The Case of the WTO Protests in Seattle. Paper presented at the Fifteenth World Congress of Sociology, Brisbane, Australia, July 9–13.

Marwell, Gerald, and Pamela Oliver (1993) *The Critical Mass in Collective Action: A Micro-Social Theory*. Cambridge: Cambridge University Press.

McAdam, Doug (1982) *Political Process and the Development of Black Insurgency*. Chicago: University of Chicago Press.

——(1988) *Freedom Summer*. New York: Oxford University Press.

McCarthy, John D., and Mayer Zald (1976) Resource Mobilization and Social Movements: A Partial Theory. *American Journal of Sociology*, 82, 1212–41.

Meyer, David, and Sidney Tarrow (1998) The Social Movement Society: Contentious Politics for a New Century. Boulder, CO: Rowman & Littlefield.

Neidhardt Friedhelm, and Dieter Rucht (1993) Auf dem Weg in die Bewegungsgesellschaft? Uber die Stabilisierbarkeit sozialer Bewegungen. *Sozialer Welt*, 44, 305–26.

Nepstad, Sharon Erickson, and Christian Smith (1999) Rethinking Recruitment to High-Risk/Cost Activism: The Case of Nicaragua. *Mobilization*, 4, 25–40.

Oberschall, Anthony (1973) *Social Conflict and Social Movements*. Englewood Cliffs, NJ: Prentice-Hall.

Oegema, Dirk, and Bert Klandermans (1994) Non-Conversion and Erosion: The Unwanted Effects of Action Mobilization. *American Sociological Review*, 59, 703–22.

Ohlemacher, Thomas (1992) *Social Relays: Micro-Mobilization via the Meso-Level. An Empirical Study of Protest Groups against Low-flying Military Jets in West Germany.* Berlin: Wissenschaftszentrum Berlin für Sozialforschung.

Oliver, Pamela E. (1980) Rewards and Punishments as Selective Incentives for Collective Action: Theoretical Investigations. *American Journal of Sociology,* 85, 1356–75.

——(1984) If you Don't Do it, Nobody Else Will: Active and Token Contributors to Local Collective Action. *American Sociological Review,* 49, 601–10.

Olson, Mancur (1968) *The Logic of Collective Action: Public Goods and the Theory of Groups.* Cambridge, MA: Harvard University Press.

Opp, Karl-Dieter (1989) *The Rationality of Political Protest. A Comparative Analysis of Rational Choice Theory.* Boulder, CO: Westview.

Orfali B. (1990) *L'adhésion au Front national: De la minorité au mouvement Social.* Paris, Kimé.

Passy, Florence (2001) Socialization, Connection, and the Structure/Agency Gap: A Specification of the Impact of Networks on Participation. *Mobilization,* 6, 173–92.

Pichardo, Nelson A., Heather Sullivan Catlin, and Glenn Deane (1998) Is the Political Personal? Everyday Behaviors as Forms of Environmental Movement Participation. *Mobilization,* 3, 185–206.

Rochon, Thomas R. (1998) *Culture Moves: Ideas, Activism, and Changing Values.* Princeton, NJ: Princeton University Press.

Rule, James B. (1988) *Theories of Collective Violence.* Berkeley: University of California Press.

——(1989) Rationality and Non-Rationality in Militant Collective Action. *Sociological Theory,* 7, 145–60.

Sani, Fabio, and Stephen Reicher (1998) When Consensus Fails: An Analysis of the Schism within the Italian Communist Party. *European Journal of Social Psychology,* 28, 623–45.

Schwartz, Michael (1976) *Radical Protest and Social Structure.* New York: Academy.

Searles, Ruth, and J. Allen Williams Jr. (1962) Negro College Students' Participation in Sit-ins. *Social Forces,* 40, 215–20.

Simon, Bernd (1998) Individuals, Groups, and Social Change: On the Relationship between Individual and Collective Self-Interpretations and Collective Action. In C. Sedikides, J. Schopler, and C. Insko (eds.), *Intergroup Cognition and Intergroup Behavior.* Mahwah, NJ: Lawrence Erlbaum, 257–82.

——(1999) A Place in the World: Self and Social Categorization. In T. R. Tyler, R. M. Kramer, and O. P. John (eds.), *The Psychology of the Social Self.* Mahwah, NJ: Lawrence Erlbaum, 47–69.

Simon, Bernd, Michael Loewy, Stefan Stürmer, Ulrike Weber, Claudia Kampmeier, Peter Freytag, Corinna Habig, and Peter Spahlinger (1998) Collective Identity and Social Movement Participation. *Journal of Personality and Social Psychology,* 74, 646–58.

Smith, Jackie (2001) Globalizing Resistance: The Battle of Seattle and the Future of Social Movements. *Mobilization,* 6, 1–19.

Snow, David A., Rochford, E. Burke Jr., Steve K. Worden, and Robert D. Benford (1986) Frame Alignment Processes, Micro-Mobilization and Movement Participation. *American Sociological Review,* 51, 464–81.

Steinberg, Marc W. (1999) The Talk and Back Talk of Collective Action: A Dialogic Analysis of Repertoires of Discourse among Nineteenth-Century English Cotton Spinners. *American Journal of Sociology,* 105, 736–80.

Stryker, Sheldon, Timothy J. Owens, and Robert W. White (eds.) (2000) *Self, Identity, and Social Movements.* Minneapolis: University of Minnesota Press.

Stürmer, Stefan (2000) Soziale Bewegungsbeteiligung: Ein psychologisches Zwei-Wege Modell. PhD dissertation, University of Kiel.

Tarrow, Sidney (1998) *Power in Movement: Social Movements, Collective Action and Mass Politics in the Modern State*. 2nd ed. Cambridge: Cambridge University Press.

Taylor, Verta, and Nancy E. Whittier (1995) Analytical Approaches to Social Movement Culture: The Culture of the Women's Movement. In Hank Johnston and Bert Klandermans (eds.), *Social Movements and Culture*. Minneapolis: University of Minnesota Press; London: UCL Press, 163–87.

Tilly, Charles (1978) *From Mobilization to Revolution*, Reading, MA: Addison-Wesley.

Tristan, A. (1987) *Au Front*. Paris: Gallimard.

Turner, John C. (1999) Some Current Issues in Research on Social Identity and Self-Categorization Theories. In Naomi Ellemers, Russell Spears, and Bertjan Doosje (eds.), *Social Identity*. Oxford: Blackwell, 6–34.

Turner, John C., P. J. Oakes, A. Haslam, and C. McGarty (1994) Self and Collective: Cognition and Social Context. *Personality and Social Psychology Bulletin*, 20, 454–63.

Tyler, Tom R., Robert R. Boeckmann, Heather J. Smith, and Yuen J. Huo (1997) *Social Justice in a Diverse Society*. Boulder, CO: Westview.

Tyler, Tom R., and Heather Smith (1998) Social Justice and Social Movements. In D. Gilbert, S. T. Fiske, and G. Lindzey (eds.), *Handbook of Social Psychology*. 4th ed. New York: McGraw-Hill, 595–626.

Walgrave, Stefaan, and Jan Manssens (2000) The Making of the White March: The Mass Media as a Mobilization Alternative to Movement Organizations. *Mobilization*, 5, 217–40.

White, Robert, W. (1989) From Peaceful Protest to Guerilla War: Micromobilization of the Provisional Irish Republican Army. *American Journal of Sociology*, 94, 1277–303.

——(1993) *Provisional Irish Republicans: An Oral and Interpretive History*. Westport: Greenwood.

Whittier, Nancy (1997) Political Generations, Micro-Cohorts, and the Transformation of Social Movements. *American Sociological Review*, 62, 760–78.

Zhao, Dingxin (1998) Ecologies of Social Movements: Student Mobilization During the 1989 Prodemocracy Movement in Beijng. *American Journal of Sociology*, 103, 1493–1529.

17

Framing Processes, Ideology, and Discursive Fields

DAVID A. SNOW

In this chapter, I examine ideational factors and interpretive processes associated with the operation of social movements by drawing on the framing perspective and related constructs such as ideology and discursive fields. However, I focus most heavily on collective action frames and framing processes, in part because these topics have figured prominently in theorizing about and empirical analyses of social movements in recent years, and in part because framing processes focus attention on the actual interpretive work engaged in by movement actors and other relevant parties. However, I am keenly aware of the broader conceptual arsenal associated with the analysis of interpretive processes and work, and thus seek to elaborate the overlapping linkages among these various interpretive concepts as they relate to social movement processes and dynamics.

There have been a number of recent review essays summarizing the range of literature pertaining to framing processes and social movements (Benford and Snow 2000) and, more narrowly, the methodologies and procedures associated with frame analysis (Johnston 2002). Not wanting to reproduce either these works or the discussion of aspects of the framing perspective in several chapters in this volume (see, in particular, chapters 5, 8, and 11), I proceed by elaborating a number of issues not fully covered by these other works. I begin with an overview of how mobilizing ideas and beliefs have been dealt with historically in relation to social movements in order to contextualize the development of the framing perspective. I then turn to a conceptual overview of the framing perspective, first focusing attention on collective action frames and the ways in which they are similar to and different from everyday interpretive frames. This distinction is important inasmuch as it underscores the relevance of interpretive framing processes to social movements. Next, I provide a summary categorization of the scholarship on framing and then highlight a number of empirical and theoretical implications of selected research on framing processes for achieving a fuller understanding of both the framing perspective and various aspects and dimensions of the dynamics of social movements. And last, I elaborate the connection of framing to such related constructs as ideology and discursive fields and opportunity structures, arguing that these are different, albeit overlapping, concepts that, considered together, yield a more thoroughgoing understanding of the ideational factors and interpretive processes associated with the emergence and operation of social movements.

Historical Overview of the Treatment of Mobilizing Beliefs and Ideas

Dating back to at least Destutt de Tracy and his coinage of the concept of ideology (1797), mobilizing ideas and beliefs have been associated with scholarship on social movements and related phenomena, but such scholarship has neither been of one mind nor progressed in a continuous, accretive fashion. Rather, it has been characterized historically by debate and division regarding the relevance and sources of mobilizing ideas and beliefs in relation to social movements, and often by a kind of analytic interruptus with respect to assessing and demonstrating empirically that relationship. Indeed, the theoretical and conceptual centrality of mobilizing ideas and beliefs, traditionally conceptualized as ideology, to explanations of movement mobilization and dynamics, has, just as protest itself, waxed and waned historically.

Marxists, for example, once debated contentiously about the relevance and source of mobilizing ideas and beliefs (e.g., Lenin 1929; Lukacs 1969; Korsch 1970; Marx and Engels 1970; Gramsci 1971). One group argued in a historicist fashion that the mobilizing ideas signaling the development of revolutionary class consciousness would arise spontaneously when the material conditions were right; another group contended that such consciousness and its associated ideas and beliefs had to be stimulated, nurtured, and even molded because the hegemony of capitalist ideology rendered the working class falsely conscious, or at least masked the link between their interests and class situation. This established the contours for a debate as to whether ideology is best conceived in terms of its "masking" or "remedial" functions, a debate that manifested itself in Mannheim's (1936) distinction between "ideology" and "utopia" and that still simmers unresolved today and hints at the politically laden character of the concept.

Years later, following the two major wars of the twentieth century, scholarly attention shifted from interest in the sources and character of mobilizing ideas and beliefs to the psychology of individuals presumably drawn to such ideas and beliefs. Underlying this switch in focus was the assumption that movement participation could be explained largely in terms of a psychofunctional linkage between individual predispositions and movement appeals (e.g., Adorno et al. 1950; Hoffer 1951; Kornhauser 1959; Toch 1965). From this vantage point, mobilizing ideas and beliefs constituted a category of movement appeals that functioned almost magnetically for susceptible individuals. Attention focused more on identifying the character and sources of individual vulnerability than on mobilizing ideas and beliefs per se.

Immediately subsequent and more sociologically oriented work abandoned the focus on individual susceptibility, and reasserted the prominence of mobilizing ideas and beliefs in relation to social movements (e.g., Turner and Killian 1957, 1972; Smelser 1963; Wilson 1973). But such work distinguished between the beliefs and ideas associated with everyday life and those associated with social movements by emphasizing that the latter are "akin to magical beliefs" (Smelser 1963: 8) that "provide a simplifying perspective" given to "the universal creation of villains" and conspiratorial thinking (Turner and Killian 1972: 270–1; see also Wilson 1973: 99–104), and that are totalistic, "all-embracing," and "consistent" modes of orientation (Wilson 1973: 94–5). Thus, while ideology was reasserted as central to the emergence and operation of social movements, not only was the "strangeness" previously associated with susceptible individuals transferred to the realm of mobilizing ideas, but the conceptualization and character of these ideas suggested a view of ideology that neither squares with many social movements nor, as will be discussed later, with research on the coherence and consistency of systems of beliefs and values more generally.

But these flaws in the conceptualization and treatment of ideology were rendered relatively inconsequential when, in the wake of the civil rights, free speech, and antiwar movements of the 1960s, a new wave of scholars rejected the notions of psychologically susceptible individuals and magical or out-of-the-ordinary mobilizing beliefs and ideas, both of which were seen as marginalizing movement participants and their causes. Additionally, this new wave of scholars accented the importance of resources (McCarthy and Zald 1977; see also chapter 6 in this volume) and political opportunity (Tilly 1978; McAdam 1982; see also chapter 4 in this volume) in relation to the emergence and operation of social movements, with mobilizing ideas and beliefs not just placed on the back burner but metaphorically taken off the stove. This was due largely to the presumption that grievances are ever-present features of everyday life, and therefore are relatively inconsequential in relation to the dynamics of social movements. Grievances, much like weeds, were thought to flourish naturally and abundantly, thus making the mobilizing beliefs and ideas some scholars associated with their interpretation relatively insignificant. McCarthy and Zald (1977: 1214–15), in their elaboration of the key elements of their resource mobilization approach, took a strong position with respect to the omnipresence of grievances, arguing, for example, that "there is always enough discontent (grievance) in any society to supply the grass-roots support for a movement."

In some respects, this position harkened back to the classical Marxist argument that mobilizing grievances arose spontaneously from nurturant social conditions, but with the qualification that such conditions are omnipresent rather than historically intermittent. However, cursory examination of the relationship between such assumptions and the flow of events, both historically and in any immediate present, quickly reveals their error. History is replete with examples of aggregations of individuals who are deprived relative to their neighbors, who are exploited economically, or who are objects of stigmatization and differential treatment, but who have not mobilized in order to collectively challenge the appropriate authorities regarding their situation. The progenitors of the resource mobilization and political process theories understood this well, with their emphasis, respectively, on the salience of resource availability and accumulation and political opportunities to the process of mobilization. However, the proponents of these perspectives not only privileged these factors initially, but failed to appreciate the extent to which material conditions like economic deprivation or unemployment are themselves subject to differential interpretation and therefore do not automatically constitute or generate mobilizing grievances.

The importance of the differential interpretation of conditions in relation to the generation of mobilizing grievances was clearly hinted at, several years prior to the development of the resource mobilization and political process/opportunity perspectives, by Turner's observation that the evolution of a major social movement is partly dependent on its ability to define some existing problem, annoyance, or condition as an "injustice" that demands correction or elimination rather than as a "misfortune" that warrants only charitable consideration (1969: 391). Today, of course, few students of social movements would take exception with the importance of a revised sense of what is just and unjust in relation to the development and operation of many significant social movements. It was a central theme in Gamson, Fireman, and Rytina's (1982) experimental examination of the conditions leading to the challenge of unjust authority. And even Piven and Cloward (1977: 12), whose approach to social movements is quite different than Turner's, understood that "the social arrangements that are ordinarily perceived as just and immutable must come to seem both unjust and mutable" if some movements are to get off the ground. Implied in the recognition of the importance of a revised sense of what is just or unjust to some mobilizations is a view of social movements as being embroiled in conflict over competing claims about aspects of reality, a view that was concretized in Lofland's (1996: 3) conceptualization of the study of social movements and movement organizations as "a special case of the study of contention among deeply conflicting realities."

But this aspect of the dynamic of social movements did not figure prominently in the dominant perspectives on social movements that emerged in the 1970s, as the relationship between meaning and mobilization, and the role of interpretive processes in mediating that relationship, was glossed over. Additionally, those few works that suggested the importance of symbolic transformations in what is seen as just and unjust (e.g., Turner 1969; Moore 1978; Piven and Cloward 1977) did not provide a conceptual and processually sensitive handle for theorizing and examining empirically the interpretive processes through which extant meanings are debated and challenged and new ones are articulated and amplified. When these dual oversights were coupled with the politically laden, often rigid or inelastic, and marginalizing conceptions of ideology associated with earlier work on social movements, there was little in the way of conceptual scaffolding or discursive space for exploring the relevance of interpretive processes to mobilization either empirically or theoretically.

It was in response to this conceptual and theoretic void, coupled with the growing realization among a handful of social movement scholars that grievances can't be taken for granted and that interpretive processes matter for some purposes and under some conditions, that the framing perspective on social movements emerged. Ideology has since been rediscovered and brought back into the analysis of social movements (e.g., Garner 1996; Oliver and Johnston 2000; Zald 2000), but without having been fully cleansed of some of the ambiguities and shortcomings associated with the concept and its application. I explore the link between framing and ideology within the context of discursive fields later in the chapter, but first provide an overview of the framing perspective.

SUMMARIZING AND ELABORATING THE FRAMING PERSPECTIVE

The framing perspective is rooted in the symbolic interactionist and constructionist principle that meanings do not automatically or naturally attach themselves to the objects, events, or experiences we encounter, but often arise, instead, through interactively based interpretive processes.[2] Consistent with this orienting principle, the framing perspective, as it has evolved in the social movement arena since the mid-1980s (see Snow et al. 1986; Snow and Benford 1988, 1992; Gamson 1992; Tarrow 1998; Benford and Snow 2000; Williams and Benford 2000; Johnston 2002), focuses attention on the signifying work or meaning construction engaged in by social-movement activists and participants and other parties (e.g., antagonists, elites, media, countermovements) relevant to the interests of social movements and the challenges they mount. In contrast to the traditional view of social movements as carriers of extant, preconfigured ideas and beliefs, the framing perspective views movements as signifying agents engaged in the production and maintenance of meaning for protagonists, antagonists, and bystanders. Like local governments, the state, representatives of other authority structures, the media, and interested publics, social movements are regarded as being embroiled in "the politics of signification" (Hall 1982). The verb "framing" is used to conceptualize this signifying work, which is one of the activities that social movement adherents and their leaders do on a regular basis. That is, "they frame, or assign meaning to and interpret relevant events and conditions in ways that are intended to mobilize potential adherents and constituents, to garner bystander support, and to demobilize antagonists" (Snow and Benford 1988: 198). The resultant products of this framing activity within the social movement arena are referred to as "collective action frames."

Distinguishing Collective Action Frames from Everyday Interpretive Frames

Collective action frames, like picture frames, focus attention by punctuating or specifying what in our sensual field is relevant and what is irrelevant, what is "in frame" and what is "out of frame," in relation to the object of orientation. But frames also function, perhaps even more importantly, as articulation mechanisms in the sense of tying together the various punctuated elements of the scene so that one set of meanings rather than another is conveyed, or, in the language of narrativity, one story rather than another is told. Additionally, frames may also perform a transformative function in the sense of altering the meaning of the object(s) of attention and their relationship to the actor(s), as in the transformation or reconfiguration of aspects of one's biography, as commonly occurs in the contexts of some movements, or in the transformation of routine grievances or misfortunes into injustices or mobilizing grievances in the context of collective action.

Given the focusing, articulation, and transformative functions of frames, it is arguable that they are fundamental to interpretation, so much so that few, if any, utterance, gesture, action, or experience could be meaningfully understood apart for the way it is framed. Indeed, one student of discourse and interaction has claimed as much, noting that "in order to interpret utterances in accordance with the way in which they are intended, a hearer must know what frame s/he is operating in, that is, whether the activity being engaged in is joking, imitating, chatting, lecturing, or performing a play..." (Tannen 1993: 18). This, of course, is the central theme of Goffman's *Frame Analysis* (1974), wherein he argues that frames function to organize experience and guide action by enabling individuals "to locate, perceive, identify, and label" occurrences and events within their life spaces (21). Collective action frames also perform this interpretive work via the focusing, articulation, and transformative functions of frames, but in ways intended to activate adherents, transform bystanders into supporters, exact concessions from targets, and demobilize antagonists. Thus collective action frames not only perform an interpretive function in the sense of providing answers to the question "What is going on here?", but they also are decidedly more agentic and contentious in the sense of calling for action that problematizes and challenges existing authoritative views and framings of reality.

Because of the agentic and contentious character of collective action frames, it is arguable that they also are likely to be more thoroughly linked to interpretive processes than is the case with everyday interpretive frames. In seeking "to isolate the basic frameworks of understanding available in our society for making sense out of events," Goffman (1974: 10) suggests that these frames are not so much constructed or negotiated *de novo* as individuals go from one situation or activity to another, but exist, instead, as elements of the individual's or group's enveloping culture and thus contain within them the situation-relevant meanings. As he stated explicitly in response to Denzin and Keller's (1981) critical reading of *Frame Analysis*, "frames are a central part of culture and are institutionalized in various ways" (Goffman 1981: 63). When such observations are coupled with parallel ideas regarding the routinization or "sedimentation" of meaning (Berger and Luckmann 1966), there is good reason for presuming that the primary frameworks of everyday life are indeed culturally embedded. But one can easily glean from Goffman's *Frame Analysis*, as well as from social life itself, numerous direct and indirect ambiguities and situations calling for a more interpretive and contextual approach to frames and framing. Not only is some interpretive work required when reading a new situation or encounter, and deciding, however instantaneously, what extant frame should be invoked or applied, but these primary frames are themselves subject to transformation through, in Goffman's language, various "keyings" and "fabrications." In turn, these transformations can be fleeting or enduring, thus suggesting that frames are "subject to change historically" (Goffman 1981: 63) rather than static cultural entities.

Additionally, there are moments and situations in social life in which the relevance or fit of extant cultural frames is likely to be ambiguous or open to question, and thus contestable, as is often the case in the contexts in which social movements arise. Indeed, it can be argued that it is in such contexts that the kind of interpretive work associated with collective action frames is most likely to flourish. To note the kinds of contexts and moments that appear to call for interpretive framing activity associated with collective action is not to suggest, however, that collective action framing is a purely unconstrained constructionist activity.[3] As noted in chapter 5 of this volume, and as we will discuss more fully, collective action frames and the framing processes through which they are derived are variously embedded in and bounded by aspects of the broader culture and political context.

Categories of Scholarship

As suggested earlier, there were a number of works scattered throughout the social movement literature between the late 1960s and the mid-1980s that noted in one fashion or another that grievances can't be taken for granted and that interpretative processes matter in relation to movement mobilization (e.g., Turner 1969; Piven and Cloward 1977; Moore 1978; Zurcher and Snow 1981; Gamson et al. 1982; McAdam 1982; Ferree and Miller 1985). But it wasn't until 1986, when these and related works and empirical observations were joined under the rubric of "frame alignment processes" (Snow et al. 1986), that a framing perspective on social movements began to evolve. Since then, there has been an abundance of scholarship on aspects of the relationship between framing processes, collective action frames, and social movements. Generally, this work clusters into five focal categories: (1) enlargement and clarification of the conceptual architecture of collective action frames and framing processes, as with the conceptual elaboration of core framing tasks (e.g., diagnostic, prognostic, and motivational framing), the determinants of frame resonance (e.g., credibility and salience), the components of collective action frames (e.g., injustice, agency, and identity), and the character and functions of master frames (e.g., Snow and Benford 1988, 1992; Gamson 1992; Tarrow 1992; Benford and Snow 2000; Williams and Benford 2000); (2) empirical research investigating the application and analytic utility of various framing concepts (e.g., core framing tasks, master frames) and processes (e.g., frame alignment, frame contests or debates, counterframing) for understanding various social movements or episodes of collective action (e.g., Johnston 1991; Ryan 1991; Capek 1993; McCarthy 1994; Jenness 1995; Meyer 1995; Babb 1996; Mooney and Hunt 1996; Zdravomyslova 1996; Cornfield and Fletcher 1998; Shupe 1998; Klandermans et al. 1999; Taylor 2000; Rohlinger 2002); (3) exploration of the link between framing processes and other factors relevant to the dynamics of social movements, such as political opportunity, discursive fields and opportunity structures, the media, ideology, narratives, identity, and emotion (e.g., Hunt et al. 1994; Gamson and Meyer 1996; Jasper 1997; Koopmans and Statham 1999; Steinberg 1999; Oliver and Johnston 2000; Snow and McAdam 2000; Kemper 2001; Ferree et al. 2002; Polletta 2002; Westby 2002); (4) methodological issues and techniques relevant to conducting framing research (Donati 1992; Gerhards 1995; Johnston 1995, 2002); and (5) critical assessment of the framing perspective, and some work employing it, for various neglects and oversights (e.g., Fine 1995; Hart 1996; Benford 1997; Fisher 1997; Jasper 1997; Steinberg 1998, 1999; Oliver and Johnston 2000).

There is neither sufficient space nor need – in light of the previously mentioned reviews on collective action frames and framing processes (Benford and Snow 2000) and on alternative methodologies for studying framing and related discursive practices (Johnston 2002) – to review the work associated with each of the above focal categories. However, since two assessments of framing scholarship published in the mid-1990s noted that it was insufficiently empirical (McAdam et al. 1996: 19; Benford 1997: 411), and since the bulk of scholarship on collective action frames and framing processes is now clearly empirically based and thus falls within the second above-mentioned category, I turn to an examination of a sample of this work in order to provide a sense of its empirical breadth and its conceptual and theoretical implications for various aspects of social movements.

Empirical Research and Conceptual Elaborations

A cursory review of the research on collective action frames and framing processes quickly reveals that it has been conducted with respect to a broad range of movements in a variety of contexts and countries, that it has drawn on a variety of data and employed a variety of methodologies, and that it has assessed the relevance of various framing concepts and processes to illuminating a host of movement-related issues and processes. All of this can be seen in table 17.1, which provides summary information on 15 studies, selected not only because they empirically explore, among other things, aspects of the link between framing and social movements, but also because they refine and extend, directly or indirectly, understanding of various framing concepts and processes. The refinements and extensions I elaborate below do not exhaust the conceptual and theoretical implications that can be culled from the empirical research on framing processes, but they do effectively illustrate how research on framing has moved beyond the initial identification of specific collective action frames associated with specific movements.

Collective Action Frames as Properties of Organizations

One of the interesting features of a number of the studies included in table 17.1 is their focus on framing processes and consequences or outcomes at the meso-organizational level of analysis. For example, Benford's analysis of frame disputes within the nuclear disarmament movement in Texas focuses on interorganizational conflict within a segment of the movement; Ellingson's examination of the dialect-ical relationship between collective action frames and collective action events in the debate over abolitionism in antebellum Cincinnati locates the debate at the inter-group level, focusing on the discursive contention among anti-abolitionists, aboli-tionists, and a law and order faction; Gerhards and Rucht's analysis of the protest campaigns against US President Reagan's visit to Berlin in 1987 and the IMF and World Bank congress in Berlin in 1988 focuses on the role of framing in the mobilization of an assortment of groups rather than on individuals per se, that is, on what they term "mesomobilization" rather than micromobilization; and McCaffrey and Keys's study of the efforts of the New York State branch of the National Organization for Women (NOW) to neutralize or disparage the counterframings of the "pro-life" movement concentrates on conflict between movement and countermovement. A characteristic feature of these four studies, considered together, is that in examining framing processes at the meso-organizational level of analysis, they invite reconsid-eration of the conceptualization of frames as purely individual cognitive structures or mental schemata. Clearly frames can be operationalized and studied as individual cognitive structures (see Johnston 1995, 2002; Oliver and Johnston 2000), but the above studies, as well as others, suggest that they can also be properties of organiza-tions, and thus located in their records, brochures, fliers, and placards rather than merely in the heads of individuals. And some research has even argued that organiza-tional forms can constitute frames themselves, functioning to influence subsequent

Table 17.1 Selected empirical studies of collective action frames and framing processes in relation to social movements

Authors	Soc. Mov. Protest Location and dates	Data/methods	Movement issue	Framing issue/process
Benford (1993)	Nuclear disarmament movement in Austin, Texas, 1982–3	Ethnography, interviews, documents	Intramovement, interorganizational conflict	Framing contests/debates
Berbrier (1998)	Contemporary white separatist movement in the US, 1980s–1990s	Media, political speeches, newspapers	Movement respectability/ legitmacy	Frame transformation
Cadena-Roa (2002)	Asamblea de Barrios in Mexico City, 1993	Newspapers, magazines, books	Mobilization via dramatic arousal of emotions	Mediating affect of emotions on strategic framing
Cress and Snow (2000)	15 homeless SMOs in 8 US cities, 1989–1992	Ethnography, interviews, documents	Outcomes	Diag./prognostic-frames as independent variables
D'Anjou (1996)	First abolition campaign in Great Britain, 1787–92	Historical documents	Mobilizing public opinion against slavery	Diagnostic framing and resonance
Diani (1996)	Regional populism in Italy, 1990–1993	Analysis of secondary data sources	Relationship between political contexts and framing	Structural constraints on development of master frames
Ellingson (1995)	Abolitionist movement and rioting in antebellum Cincinnati, 1830s	Textual analysis of newspapers	Relation between events and frames, and movement/ countermovement dynamics	Frame debates and reframing or frame transformation

Study	Case	Method	Factors affecting success (standing and framing) in mass media	Effect of discursive opport. structure on framing and framing contests
Ferree et al. (2002)	Abortion discourse in Germany and US, 1970–94	Comp. content analysis of newspapers, survey of organizations	Factors affecting success (standing and framing) in mass media	Effect of discursive opport. structure on framing and framing contests
Gerhards and Rucht (1992)	Protest against Reagan visit and IMF and WB meeting in Berlin, 1987/1988	Textual analysis of two distributed leaflets	Mesomobilization of protest groups	Master frames and frame bridging
McCaffery and Keys (2000)	NY State NOW response to abortion countermov., 1970–88	Analysis of NY State NOW archives	Movement/ countermovement dynamics	Frame alignment in relation to countermovements
McCammon (2001)	Formation of US state suffrage organizations, 1866–1914	Event history analysis of state organizations	Variation in organizational mobilization	Contribution of framing to organizational formation
Noonan (1995)	Women's movement against the state in Chile, 1913–1978	Historical case study	Mobilization in relation to democratic transition	Frame transformation and master frames
Rothman and Oliver (1999)	Anti-dam movement in southern Brazil, 1979–92	Field interviews, documents	Changes from local to global frames, identities and POS	Frame alignment and change
Snow and Clark-Miller (2003)	Right-wing group in Tucson, Arizona, 1990s	Ethnography, analysis of discourse	Process through which frames are developed and maintained	Frame articulation and elaboration
Zuo and Benford (1995)	Chinese student democracy movement, Beijing, 1989	Participant observation, interviews, documents	Rapid mobilization in the face of a repressive political regime	Frame alignment, resonance, and neutralization of counterframings

collective actions (Clemens 1996). Thus studies of framing processes and outcomes at the meso-organizational level of analysis have, wittingly or unwittingly, broadened understanding of the conceptualization of frames and the sites in which they can be tracked and studied.

Elaboration of the functions of master frames

Master frames were originally conceptualized as collective action frames that have expanded in scope and influence such that they color and constrain the orientations and activities of other movements within cycles of protest (Snow and Benford 1992). Since that initial conceptualization a number of works have applied and refined the concept of master frames in ways that broaden its analytic relevance beyond cycles of protest (e.g., Gerhards and Rucht 1992; Carroll and Ratner 1996; Noonan 1995; Swart 1995; Mooney and Hunt 1996). Noonan (see table 17.1), for example, applied the concept of master frames in her historical case study of the mobilization of women against the state in Chile. In particular, she found that while the "leftist" master frame of the 1950s and 1960s did not accommodate feminism because of its narrow focus on working-class issues, its subsequent repression and the emergence of a more elaborated democracy frame in the 1980s created space for a variety of movement-specific frames, including the reemergence of feminism. She also reports that during the era of authoritarian military rule women mobilized under the rubric of a "maternal" frame that provided them with a measure of immunity and safety because of its resonance with the traditions and discourse of both Catholicism and the state as regards women. These findings show that, among other things, master frames do indeed vary in terms of how restrictive or exclusive they are, and that this variation can significantly affect the mobilizability of some aggregations or potential constituencies in comparison to others.

Similarly, Gerhards and Rucht's (see table 17.1) analysis of two protest campaigns in Berlin in the late 1980s revealed how two congruent master frames functioned to facilitate mobilization by "bridging" the sometimes different views and concerns of numerous heterogeneous groups. The two master frames – one emphasizing world imperialism symbolized by the IMF and the World Bank, and the other accenting US hegemonic power symbolized by President Reagan – were sufficiently inclusive, and yet focused in terms of the diagnostic, prognostic, and motivational framing tasks, to suggest common ground and muster the support of 140 groups for the anti-Reagan demonstration, and 133 groups for the anti-IMF campaign. As with Noonan's findings, Gerhards and Rucht's analysis reveals the functionality of relatively inclusive and elaborated master frames for broad-based mobilization, especially when there is heterogeneity among the groups and interests targeted for mobilization.

Such findings appear to be especially relevant to recent large-scale mobilizations and protest events constituted by an alliance or coalition of a multitude of heterogenous groups, as in the case of the November 1999 anti-World Trade Organization (WTO) protest in Seattle and the July 2002 protest against the summit of G8 industrial nations in Genoa. Insofar as such large-scale, coalition-based mobilizations are becoming a more common feature of collective action landscape worldwide, it is arguable that effective coordinating master frames will become even more critical in the dynamics of tomorrow's social movement activity, functioning as an important integrative mechanism across groups and movements at particular moments in time as well as during broader cycles of protest.

Frames as both Dependent and Independent Variables

In a social-psychologically oriented discussion of cognitive perspectives on social movements, Snow and Oliver (1995: 582–9) juxtaposed rational choice and constructionist perspectives, suggesting that the two perspectives could be partly distinguished in terms of the language of variable analysis. "The 'independent variable' group," which includes rational choice theory, "takes cognitions more or less as givens and attempts to predict behavior from cognitions." In contrast, "the 'dependent variable' group," they wrote, "seeks to explain the processes whereby the cognitions themselves are created" and "rejects the notion that cognitions can ever be treated as unproblematic givens and stresses that behavior and cognitions are interconnected in a dynamic and reflexive fashion" (Snow and Oliver 1995: 583).

Included in the constructionist group was work on framing processes and collective action frames and on collective identity, all of which had been conducted in the early 1990s or before. Given the focus of most of the framing work at that point in time, perhaps it seemed reasonable to think of framing processes primarily from the vantage point of dependent variables. Now, in 2003, however, such a view is clearly misguided, as research on collective action frames and framing processes has proceeded to examine frames as both dependent and independent variables, even though the language of variable analysis is not always used.

Assessment of collective action processes and frames, or dimensions of them, as independent variables has focused on their effects, that is, on their consequences or implications for various social movement processes, such as recruitment and mobilization, resource acquisition, and outcome attainment. A number of such analyses have proceeded primarily in terms of conceptual or theoretical extension and assertion, as in the case of Gamson and Meyer's (1996) argument that the extent to which political opportunity structures facilitate or constrain social movement activity is affected by how they are framed by movement actors and others. As well, Hunt, Benford, and Snow (1994), and Snow and McAdam (2000), have argued that framing processes and personal and movement collective identities are linked, with the former playing a critical role in the development and maintenance of the latter. But these arguments have been based more on theoretical argumentation and anecdotal evidence than systematic investigation.

There are, however, numerous studies that have examined systematically how variation in one or more dimensions of collective action frames have affected movement processes or outcomes. An example is provided by Cress and Snow's (see table 17.1) examination of variation in the local outcomes of 15 homeless social movement organizations active in eight US cities (Boston, Denver, Detroit, Houston, Minneapolis, Oakland, Philadelphia, and Tucson) during the 1980s. Using the technique of qualitative comparative analysis (Ragin 1987), they assessed ethnographically derived data on how organizational, tactical, political, and framing variables interacted and combined to account for variation in the outcomes (representation, resources, rights, and/or relief) attained by the 15 homeless social movement organizations. Of the four sets of independent variables examined, framing variables (articulate and focused diagnostic and prognostic frames) were operative in all but one of the six pathways leading to the attainment of one or more of the four types of outcomes. The other variables were also of influence, particularly organizational viability, but none were as persistently present across all six pathways as the framing variables. McCammon's (see table 17.1) event history analysis of the factors that affected the emergence of state suffrage movement organizations in the US from 1866 to 1914 similarly revealed that the way in which pro-suffrage arguments were framed was critical in mobilizing support for suffrage. Not only were some framings more effective than others, but the more effective (resonant) ones were found to "have an independent influence on movement emergence" (McCammon 2001: 470).

Among other things, these two studies show not only that framing variables can be studied and operationalized like many other variables, but that they may also affect certain movement processes and outcomes. Similar findings are provided by Gerhards and Rucht's (table 17.1) previously mentioned study of the mesomobilization effects of two master frames with respect to two mass protest events in Berlin in 1987/1988, D'Anjou's (table 17.1) historical analysis of the significant role played by resonant diagnostic framing in the abolition of the slave trade in Great Britain in the 1780s and 1790s, McCaffery and Keys's (table 17.1) analysis of the of the New York State's NOW chapter's crafting and deployment of three counterframing strategies – polarization/vilification, frame debunking, and framing saving – in their efforts to neutralize the challenges launched by the anti-abortion countermovement, and by Zuo and Benford's (table 17.1) examination of the contribution of frame alignment strategies, in conjunction with political and organizational factors, to the rapid emergence of the 1989 Chinese democracy movement.

Regarding the treatment of collective action frames and master frames as dependent variables, much of the initial work, as previously indicated, focused on the identification and development of collective action frames, with analytic attention focused on conceptual, rather than empirical, specification of the conditions under which or the processes through which frames developed and/or changed. In contrast, more recent work has provided greater empirical specification of those conditions or processes. Cadena-Roa (table 17.1), in his analysis of protest among the urban poor in Mexico City, shows how the public's response to SMO framing, and the character of that framing, was affected by the mediating role played by emotions aroused by "the emergence of Superbarrio, a masked crusader for justice who used honor and drama" to command and focus the attention of targeted constituents. In their study of an anti-dam movement in southern Brazil from 1979 to 1992, Rothman and Oliver (table 17.1) analyze how a change in the framing of the issues – from a struggle over peasants' right to land to a struggle about the destruction of the natural habitat – was precipitated by a confluence of events: "the weakening of the regional power company... the crisis of the Left after the fall of the Berlin Wall, the defeat of the agrarian reform movement, the rise of national and international ecology movements, and the anti-dam movement's need for a broader political and financial base" (1999: 41). This set of findings is congruent with Ellingson's (table 17.1) finding, derived from his historical analysis of public debate and rioting over abolitionism in Cincinnati, Ohio, in the 1830s, that collective action events (in this case riots) can force movement actors to modify exiting framings or create new ones that enhance the mobilization of adherents and resources.

Taken together, such studies underscore the dynamic rather than static character of collective action frames, and remind us that the flow of events – biographical, local, national, and international – have a way of intruding into our realities and forcing us either to incorporate them into our current understandings or modify those understandings accordingly.

Elaborating Frame Transformation

Changes in collective action frames or master frames of the kind noted above can be construed as a form of frame transformation, but they are quite different than the kinds of ideational and orientational transformations emphasized in the initial discussion of frame transformation as a type of alignment process (Snow et al. 1986). In each of above cases, attention is focused on, among other things, how various events affected change in either a collective action or master frame. Additionally, the change described constituted a refinement or elaboration of the exiting frame. In contrast, the initial formulation of frame transformation encompassed fairly dramatic reconstitutions in the way in which the object of orientation – be it an activity, one's self, or a group – is seen. Additionally, in the initial formulation, the transformation was discussed primarily as being agent-based rather than event-based – that is, as the result of movement or group effort. Thus, these two different sets of discussions suggest two different strands of frame transformation: one that tends to be event-initiated or -based and that results in a modification or partial transformation of an extant frame; and one that tends to be agent-initiated or -based and that results in a more dramatic or radical transformation in the way in which the object of orientation is seen or regarded.

As a variant form of frame alignment processes, it is interesting to note that the more dramatic and systematic form of frame transformation has received less explicit attention than other strategic alignment processes (e.g., frame bridging, amplification, and extension) (Benford and Snow 2000: 625). This is somewhat puzzling in light of the importance attached to the transformation of misfortunes into more severe problems in relation to mobilization and the fact that social movements are in the business of affecting change, not only structurally or culturally, but also in terms of orientation or "hearts and minds." Turner (1983: 177) accented this point when he observed that although many of the great movements of the past several centuries – such as those seeking the abolition of slavery, women's suffrage, and the termination of child labor – sought major legislative changes, those changes or initiatives were "unthinkable until a tremendous task of altering people's views of reality had been accomplished," which depended "upon reaching the hearts and minds of vast numbers of people."

Affecting changes in hearts and minds is, of course, the stuff of the more sweeping kind of frame transformation in that the objects of orientation, to paraphrase Goffman (1974: 43–4), come to be seen by the participants or other relevant parties as something quite different from the way in which they were previously viewed and regarded. Heuristically, such transformations can vary in terms of at least two dimensions: whether the change occurs at the individual or group level, and whether it is domain-specific, in the sense of being confined to a bounded aspect of social life, or more generalized and pervasive, in the sense of transcending specific contexts.

The cross-classification of these two dimensions yields four generic types of transformation, as diagramed in table 17.2.

The transformations captured in both cells A and B encompass significant change in individual consciousness about and perspective on some issue or problem, but they vary in terms of whether the change is limited to a particular segment or domain of social life or is more pervasive in the sense of being generalized across situations and domains. Both kinds of transformations can be usefully conceptualized and analyzed as conversions, but one involves a transformation in thinking and feeling about a particular set of activities or domain of life (such as health, schooling, self-esteem, and use of substances), whereas the more generalized transformation, while being anchored in a particular domain such as religion or politics, entails conversions that transcend any single domain and affect one's perspective with respect to a range of issues and situations. Studies of conversion to religious movements provide numerous examples of both kinds of conversions,[4] but they are hardly peculiar to just the religious realm. This is made clear, for example, by the consciousness-rasing activities associated with the women's movement (Bird 1969; see also chapter 25 in this volume), the process through which women in racist hate groups acquire "racial awareness" and develop a "racist self" (Blee 2002), and by the accounts of various European intellectuals who, upon leaving the Communist Party, attempted to reconstruct their conversion experiences, which tended to be take the form of generalized, global transformations (Crossman 1952). In recounting his own experience, for instance, the Italian writer Ignazio Silone noted how his "own internal world, the 'middle ages,' which [he] inherited and which were rooted in [his] soul" was not only "shaken to [its] foundations, as though by an earthquake," but "*[e]verything was thrown into the melting-pot, everything became a problem*" (Crossman 1952: 87; emphasis added).

Turning to cells C and D of table 17.2, we move to the group or collective level of frame transformation. Cell C encompasses transformations in the way in which a

Table 17.2 Typology of frame transformations

Scope of change/ Level of change	Domain-specific change	Generalized change
Individual transformation	(A) Conversion to some self-help and religious movements (e.g., Erhard Seminar Training, Alcoholics Anonymous, Transcendental Meditation)	(B) Conversion to some religious and political movements (e.g., Hare Krishna, "Moonies," racist hate movements, Communism)
Group/collective transformation	(C) Redefining the domain-specific status of a social category or status group (e.g., Mothers Against Drunk Driving, NIMBY movements)	(D) Generalized change in the conception of a category (e.g. New Racist White Separatist movement, women's movement, civil rights movement)

specific status group is defined, such that they are constituted or reconstituted as a social problem and are thus the target for social movement activity. Examples of status groups that have been framed or reframed as legitimate targets for movement protest include drunk drivers, cigarette smokers, the homeless, the mentally ill, persons affected by HIV/AIDS, various immigrant groups, and advocates for memory recovery, with various antagonistic social movement organizations, such as Mothers Against Drunk Driving (MADD) and a diversity of not-in-my-backyard (NIMBY) movements, taking the lead in the constitution or reconstitution of these groups as "troublesome" (McCarthy 1994; Ofshe and Watters 1994; Takahashi 1998; Wright 1997; see chapter 19 in this volume).

In contrast to these domain- or niche-specific transformations in the conception of a specific status group are the more generalized and pervasive transformations in the projected image or collective identity of a category of social actors, as with the different views of women and blacks promulgated respectively by the women's movement and the civil rights movement (e.g., "Black is Beautiful"). In these and other cases, the movement itself plays a central role in this reframing activity. This variety of frame transformation is amply illustrated by Berbrier's analysis of framing strategies of the New Racist White Separatist movement (NRWS), a US-based movement that seeks to advance the interests of a new form of racism and white separatism in which both are "redefined as normative and positive, an expression of love and preservation, rather than one of hatred and destruction" (1998: 437). The framing strategy, according to Berbrier's analysis, is to transform traditional white supremacist rhetoric, which is perceived as being "antithetical to contemporary values and mores...into one better aligned with the authoritative pluralist frame of contemporary American culture" (1998: 437). Thus the objective of the new white supremacist rhetoric is to transform the stigma of white supremacy by reframing the movement and its activities in terms of love, pride, heritage-preservation, and victimage. This transformative work is done by pursuing two metatransformative strategies: equivalence and reversal. The equivalence strategy portrays whites as equivalent to ethnic minority groups by articulating and amplifying claimed commonalities, as when former Ku Klux Klansman David Duke urged European Americans to "band together as a group the same way African Americans do, the same way as other minorities do" (Associated Press 2000). Since other ethnic groups have organized in collective action organizations, such as the Student Nonviolent Coordinating Committee (SNCC), La Raza Unida, and the Jewish Defense League, it is appropriate for whites to organize along similar lines. Hence the National Association for the Advancement of White People. The reversal strategy portrays whites as victims, as objects of discrimination and/or elimination, as exhibited in Duke's contention that European Americans face "massive discrimination" from the country's rapidly growing population of minorities and that they soon will be "outnumbered and outvoted in [their] country" (Associated Press 2000).

Considered together, the four types of frame transformation sketched in table 17.2 and discussed above indicate that frame transformation is more variegated and complex than portrayed in some of the literature. Not only does it vary in terms of the level and scope of change, but the role of movement organizations and actors in relation to each type can vary as well, sometimes attempting to affect conversion among prospective adherents or members, other times constructing or reconstituting an object or target of protest, and at other times reframing the image or identity of the movement itself. The similarities and differences in the character of each of these transformative processes is not well understood and thus invites further empirical investigation. Nor is there a clear and consensual answer to questions concerning the generation of the frames that evolve.

Connecting Ideology, Frames, and Discursive Fields

Questions concerning the generation of collective action and master frames raise questions about their derivation, which, in turn, beg questions concerning the relationship between collective action frames and the broader culture, and particularly ideology. As noted earlier, the relevance of ideology to discussions of the emergence and mobilization of social movements has waxed and waned historically. After a number of years in which ideational matters and issues were glossed over by movement scholars, the concept of ideology has been resuscitated and brought back into the discussions of emergence and mobilization. Ideology was not totally ignored by the initial discussions of framing and social movements, but it was not prominently featured in that work either, in large part because of the previously discussed issues associated with its use and application. However, in a context of resurgent interest in the concept of culture and its discursive elements within the social sciences (see chapter 5 in this volume), coupled with questions about the derivation of collective action frames, a number of works have suggested that the concept of ideology (Steinberg 1998; Oliver and Johnston 2000) and related cultural constructs, such as discursive fields (Steinberg 1999) and discursive opportunity structures (Koopmans and Statham 1999; Ferree et al. 2002), can illuminate understanding of the link between ideational and interpretive factors, including framing processes, and social movement dynamics. Thus, in this final section of the chapter, I proceed in an integrative fashion by elaborating the way(s) in which these various constructs are connected and how these connections yield a more complete picture of movement-relevant interpretive processes and work. I begin with the concept of ideology, deconstructing and problematizing its use in the social movement literature, and then turn to amplifying the connection between collective action frames and ideology via the processes of frame articulation and elaboration within the context of discursive fields.

Problematizing Ideology

In the study of social movements, ideology is generally invoked as a cover term for a relatively stable and coherent set of values, beliefs, and goals associated with a movement or a broader, encompassing social entity, and is assumed to provide the rationale for defending or challenging various social arrangements and conditions (see Wilson 1973; Turner and Killian 1987; Garner 1996; Oliver and Johnston 2000; Zald 2000). Because of the presumably overarching interpretive and motivational functions of ideology, some scholars have suggested that social movements can be best conceptualized as "ideologically structured action" (Zald 2000). Although few scholars would quibble with the contention that there is an ideological dimension to much social movement activity, there clearly are other dimensions that are equally, if not more, important in determining the course and character of social movements.

As well, it can be argued, according to some conceptualizations of ideology (e.g., Geertz 1973; Gouldner 1976; Seliger 1976), that most social action is structured or influenced in some way by ideology. If so, then there seems to be little, if any, analytic purchase in claiming that social movements can be best understood as ideologically structured action in contrast to social action outside of the context of the social movement arena.[5]

But to note that social movement activity is hardly uniquely ideological is not to suggest that ideology is irrelevant to social movements. The problem is that most treatments of social movements that accent the influence of ideology rarely unpack and elaborate the character of the ideology or how it is used and affects the ebb and flow of movement activity. Instead, the concept is typically applied or asserted in too blunt a fashion, as when it is claimed that social movement activity is ideologically structured, social movement participants are ideologically driven or subscribe to the same set of beliefs and ideas, or that collective action frames are simply derived from an extant ideology or existing cultural stock. Such arguments are not only too mechanistic, but they foster four kinds of overlapping errors. One is the tendency to assume greater ideological coherence and integration than often exists, the second is the tendency to assume greater ideological unanimity among participants than is often the case, the third is the tendency to assume greater correspondence between ideology and behavior than is often the case, and the fourth is the tendency to see movement-related framing activity as merely ideologically derived.

The first error is reflected in the difficulty of reconciling the view that ideology in general or a movement-specific ideology is a fairly coherent and integrated set of values and beliefs with various contradictory strands of research. For example, research shows, at least for the US, that not only do individuals acknowledge a range of values and beliefs that are often contradictory or in conflict, but that they rarely cohere in an integrated, systematic fashion (Williams 1970; Rokeach 1973). As Williams found in his examination of values in American society, there is neither "a neatly unified 'ethos' [nor] an irresistible 'strain toward consistency'"(1970: 451). The findings of recent research on the "cultural wars" thesis in the US makes this point as well (Davis and Robinson 1996; DiMaggio et al. 1996): American political opinions, attitudes, and values do not cluster neatly or tightly together at any one ideological pole, thus suggesting that the American "public does not seem to be divided into warring camps as the culture war metaphor might suggest" (Kniss 1997: 259). Even when attention is focused at the religious conservative/orthodox or political right-wing end of the hypothesized ideological continuum, there is greater ideological variation among both the groups and individuals that fall under these categorical umbrellas than often presumed (Aho 1990; Williams and Blackburn 1996; Woodberry and Smith 1998). As Blee (2002: 114) found in her in-depth study of women in four racist hate movements (Christian Identity, Ku Klux Klan, neo-Nazi, and white-power skinheads) in the US, "most racist groups simultaneously advocate gender and racial subjugation, but often the two impulses combine in complex ways," such that these groups harbor views "as disparate as a belief in alien invasions, faith in homeopathic healing, and concern for animal rights. In such an ideological stew, a variety of ideas about Aryan women can coexist with dedication to hard-core racism." And it appears that there is similar variation among the so-called "left" with respect to specific issues. As Ferree et al. (see table 17.1) note in their study of abortion discourse in Germany and the United States:

The definition of what "the left" stands for with regard to abortion is neither simple nor unidimensional. The imagined community of those who identify with the left has cast abortion variously as a matter of the inalienable rights of citizens to control their private lives, the state's responsibility to care for and protect the needy, and social justice for those who face structural inequalities. (2002: 199)

What's more, they note, "each of these themes has shifted over time in both countries" (2002: 199). The point, then, is that ideology probably is rarely as coherent or stable as often presumed. Overlapping with this coherence assumption is the corollary assumption of ideological unanimity, which can give rise to the kind of "illusion of homogeneity" that Turner and Killian (1987: 20–1) warned of in respect to crowd behavior. Their point is that crowds are rarely composed of participants who share identical characteristics, demographic or motivational, or who engage in identical behaviors, even though they are often portrayed as being homogeneous in one or both of these ways. Applying Turner and Killian's caveat to social movements suggests that there is probably greater ideological diversity within movements than is often presumed. Such diversity surfaced repeatedly in Snow and Clark-Miller's (see table 17.1) ethnographic study of a far right-wing group in Tucson, Arizona. Most of the group's collective activity consisted of talking, listening to presentations, and talking some more during two-hour, weekly meetings. While there were clearly shared beliefs and ideas among the participants, particularly regarding the federal government's perceived violation of the Constitution, there were also striking differences in the governmental influence attributed to different groups, such as the Masons, Jews, and minorities, with some members insisting on accenting the role of one group over another. Because of these differences, the group sometimes seemed to be on the cusp of fractionalization, but such schism was averted by shifting attention away from ideological differences to commonalities. Westby (2002: 290–1) succinctly summarizes such axes of ideological diversity when he observes, in his insightful analysis of the complexity of the relationship between ideology and framing, that "movements frequently have internal schismatic struggles over ideology," they sometimes engage in "various forms of collaboration" that "engender contentious ideological variants," they sometimes differ internally "regarding the primacy of particular aspects of the ideology," and they occasionally "march under an eclectic banner of more than a single distinct ideology," as appears to have been the case with the previously mentioned anti-WTO protest gathering in Seattle in 1999 and subsequent anti-globalization demonstrations.

Regarding the issue of correspondence between ideology and behavior, whether individual or collective, there is good reason to believe that this relationship is just as untidy as the relationship between attitudes and behavior (Deutscher et al. 1993). Research conducted by Berger (1981) and Rochford (1985) suffice to make the point. One of the conundrums Berger (1981) encountered in his study of rural communards in upstate California in the 1970s was the glaring disjunction between some of their ideological beliefs and some of their behaviors, as when their child-raising practices contradicted basic tenets of their communal ideology. In order to get a conceptual handle on the remedial discourse the communards engaged in so as to "maintain some semblance of consistency, coherence, and continuity" between their beliefs and actions, Berger (1981: 22) coined the concept of "ideological work." In examining change and adaptation within the Hare Krishna movement in the US in the later half of the 1970s, Rochford (1985: 192) similarly found the movement was confronted with a number of contradictions "between its professed beliefs and day-to-day practices of its members," which it attempted to repair through engagement in various forms of ideological work specific to the movement. Such remedial discourse or ideological work is likely to be called forth not only (1) when ideological beliefs and behavior contradict each other, as both the Berger and Rochford studies indicate, but also (2) when beliefs and events in the world are discordant, and (3) when the existence of competing or conflicting beliefs within a group threatens its coherence and increases the prospect of schism or factionalization.

The final error that reveals itself in many discussions of ideology, and particularly its relationship to collective action frames, is the presumption that movement-related discourse and/or frames are merely and simply ideologically derived. Gramsci's (1971) distinction between "non-organic" and "organic" ideologies, and Rudé's (1980) parallel distinction between "inherent" and "derived" ideologies, raise serious questions about the generality of such an assumption, as does Westby (2002: 292, 299), who notes that while some movement frames are "clearly derived from movement ideology," there is "a substantial range of framing that transcends the confines of this model." He discusses a number of such examples, including situations wherein "ideology is absent or not implicated in framing," suggesting the Three Mile Island mobilization as one such instance; situations in which framing activity "goes beyond ideological limits," citing the case of European socialism; and the appropriation of some broader cultural ideology, in the case of the civil rights movement's appropriation of liberal democratic ideology (Westby 2002: 294–8). Also contraindicating the simple derivation presumption are two related observations: that movement ideologies and collective action frames often include strands of multiple cultural ideologies or clusters of beliefs and values; and, when this is the case, these various ideologies may be associated with strikingly different cultures or "critical communities" (Rochon 1998). Finally, the call of a number of scholars to attend more closely to the processes through which collective action frames develop and evolve, and particularly the discursive nature of those processes (Fine 1995; Johnston 1995; Fisher 1997; Steinberg 1998, 1999), further calls into question the analytic utility of ideological-derivation models of collection action frames in particular and collective action more generally. This emphasis on discursive processes does not imply that extant ideologies and movement discursive activities are unrelated. Rather, what Rudé (1980: 29) observed regarding the relationship between inherent and derived ideologies also holds for the relationship between existing ideologies and other cultural stuff and movement discourse, including framing: "there is no one way traffic but constant interaction between them." And, as Steinberg (1999) emphasized in his dialogic analysis of the discourse of nineteenth-century English cotton spinners, much of this interaction is discursive, with the resultant connections generally worked out or worked up through multivocal discourse or "talk and back talk".[6]

Taken together, the foregoing sets of considerations suggest a number of sensitizing directives regarding ideology and its relationship to collective action frames and collective action. The first directive concerns the conceptualization of ideology: rather than conceptualize it as a fairly pervasive and coherent set of beliefs and values that functions in a programmatic and doctrinaire fashion, it would appear to be closer to the mark if ideology is conceived as a variable phenomenon that ranges on a continuum from a tightly and rigidly connected set of values and beliefs at one end to a loosely coupled set of values and beliefs at the other end, and that can function, in either case, as both a constraint on and a resource for the kind of sense-making, interpretive work associated with framing. The second directive follows: both ideology and its relationship to collective action frames should be problematized and explored empirically rather than assumed or theorized in a simple, mechanistic fashion. The third directive focuses attention on the flow of events, many of which have to be interpreted or framed because they are inconsistent, or not obviously consistent, with extant movement frames or because they introduce new elements of relevance to the issues being discussed and contested. And the fourth directive, flowing from both the discussion of the above questionable tendencies and the foregoing directives is the imperative of attending closely to the discursive processes through which ideologies are used, modified, challenged, and even generated.

The Discursive Process of Frame Articulation and Elaboration

Attending to these directives requires consideration of the discursive processes of frame articulation and elaboration, and the overlapping concepts of discursive fields and opportunities. Frame articulation involves the connection and coordination of events, experiences, and strands of one or more ideologies so that they hang together in a relatively integrated and meaningful fashion. It constitutes a kind of collective packaging device that assembles and collates slices of observed, experienced, and/or recorded "reality." Frame elaboration refers to the process in which some events, issues, and beliefs or ideas are accented and highlighted in contrast to others, with the result that they become more salient in an array or hierarchy of group-relevant issues, perhaps coming to function as significant coordinating symbols or mechanisms.

Although these articulation and elaboration processes have rarely been the object of systematic inquiry by movement scholars, examples of both processes are readily discernible in the oral discourse and textual documents (e.g., placards, pamphlets, books, and speeches) of movement members and leaders. Consider, for example, the framings of such historically prominent movement leaders as Gandhi and Martin Luther King, as well as those of more rank-and-file participants, as in the case of the 1989 Chinese democracy movement. In the case of Gandhi, it is said that his guiding principles of "satyagraha" and "ahimsa," which evolved into what can be construed as a mobilizing master frame for much of the world, were based on a mixture of beliefs derived from Hinduism, Buddhism, and Christianity, and his spiritual mentors included Jesus, Buddha, Socrates, and his mother. As noted in one biographical sketch: "While studying in England to be a lawyer, he first read the *Bible* and the *Bhagavad Gita*," which provided him with "a clarion call to the soul to undertake the battle of righteousness. It taught him to renounce personal desires not by withdrawal from the world but by devotion to the service of his fellow man. In the Christian New Testament, he found the stirring of passive resistance in the words of the Sermon on the Mount" (McGeary 1999: 121).

In the case of Martin Luther King, we find the same kind of frame articulation in his blending and weaving together strands of Gandhism, Christianity, and the US

Constitution into a powerful "rights" master frame (but see chapter 8 in this volume). As one student of the civil rights movement observed in explaining King's media-staying power and the appeal of his speeches and arguments:

> no black leader ever sounded like King before. In the *unique blending of familiar Christian themes, conventional democratic theory, and the philosophy of nonviolence,* King brought an unusually compelling, yet accessible, frame to the struggle.... while singling out this or that theme in King's thought, it should be noted that the very variety of themes granted those in the media (and the general public) multiple points of ideological contact with the movement. So, secular liberals might be unmoved by King's reading of Christian theology, but resonate with the application of democratic theory. And so on. In short, the sheer variety of themes invoked by King combined with their substantive resonance to give his thought (and the movement he came for many to symbolize) an ideational appeal unmatched by many other movement figures. (McAdam 1996: 347–8; emphasis added)

In a similar vein, Zuo and Benford (see table 17.1), in their analyses of mobilization processes in relation to the Chinese democracy movement, suggest that the framings and claims of student mobilizers were grounded in a blend of ideas about democracy and freedom along with traditional Chinese cultural ideologies or narrations associated with Confucianism, communism, and nationalism. By incorporating strands of all three cultural traditions in the movement's collective action frames, activists, according to Zuo and Benford (1995: 139), were not only able to "win sympathy and active support from bystander audiences," but they "were able to deflect any state attempts to impugn their collective character, particularly attributions regarding their patriotism."

Such examples ground empirically the argument that insofar as collective action frames are connected to extant ideologies, they probably are rarely determined by or isomorphic with them (Snow and Benford 2000). Instead, they often, and perhaps more typically, appear to constitute innovative articulations and elaborations of existing ideologies or sets of beliefs and ideas, and thus function as extensions of or antidotes to them. This makes collective action frames somewhat akin to what the historian George Mosse (1985: 134) has called "scavenger ideolog(ies)." But I would argue, based on the foregoing observations, that this scavenging metaphor applies to the ideational work of social movements in general, and thus cuts to the heart of the frame articulation and elaboration processes. The above examples also suggest that the relative appeal or resonance of proffered framings is linked to cultural traditions and narratives (see Benford and Snow 2000: 619–22; Davis 2002; also chapter 5 in this volume). However, the processes of frame articulation and elaboration are not only facilitated and constrained by the broader cultural context or stock, which often extends beyond national or societal borders as the above cases illustrate (see chapter 14 in this volume), but also are affected by the discursive contexts in which they are embedded.

Discursive Fields and Opportunity Structures

Since the late 1990s scholars oriented to the analysis of social movements from cultural and political/structural perspectives have come to argue almost simultaneously that a thoroughgoing understanding of movement-related processes, such as

framing, cannot be adequately understood apart from the broader enveloping contexts in which those processes are embedded. Culturalists have conceptualized these
contexts as "discursive fields" (Steinberg 1999); structuralists have dubbed them
"discursive opportunity structures" (Koopmans and Statham 1999; see also chapters
2 and 4 in this volume). Both concepts, like the kindred concept of organizational
fields (DiMaggio and Powell 1983) and multi-organizational fields (see chapter 9 in
this volume), fall into the genre of concepts in the social sciences that can be thought
of as "embedding" concepts in the sense that they reference broader enveloping
contexts in which discussions, decisions, and actions take place.

Discursive fields are conceptualized broadly as the "discursive terrain(s) in which
meaning contests occur" (Spillman 1995: 140–1; Steinberg 1999: 748). Drawing on
the work of various cultural and semiotic theorists, Steinberg (1999) in particular
has suggested the relevance of the concept of discursive fields to understanding
movement-related discourse and framing activities. Such fields emerge or evolve in
the course of discussion of and debate about contested issues and events, and
encompass not only cultural materials (e.g., beliefs, values, ideologies, myths and
narratives, primary frameworks) of potential relevance, but also various sets of
actors whose interests are aligned, albeit differentially, with the contested issues or
events, and who thus have a stake in what is done or not done about those issues and
events. These various sets of actors include, in addition to the social movement in
question, one or more countermovements, the targets of action or change, the
media, and the larger public, which includes clusters of individuals who may side
with the protagonists or antagonists as well as those who are indifferent and thus
constitute bystanders (see chapter 11 in this volume). The ways in which any
particular set of actors' interests are aligned with the issues or events in question is
not always self-evident or clear, however. As noted earlier, ideologies can "mask" or
"obfuscate" as well as "illuminate" and "crystalize." Additionally, the stream of
events that flows or cuts through any particular discursive field can quickly affect its
shape and the relationships among the relevant sets of actors. It is because of such
considerations that framing processes and contests figure prominently within discursive fields related to social movements and the collective actions with which they
are associated.

Snow and Clark-Miller's (see table 17.1) previously mentioned ethnography of a
far-right-wing group provides an "on the ground" illustration of how the flow of
events and issues (in this case the topics referred to or questions raised) within a
discursive context (consisting mainly of several leaders, an invited speaker, and 30 to
40 participants attending a group meeting) are taken into account and articulated
and elaborated, not only in a fashion consistent with existing frames, but in a
manner that constitutes and reproduces these frames. At one meeting, for example,
they observed conversation flow from the topic of (1) teaching the Constitution in
American schools, to (2) the President's involvement in "the new world order," to (3)
the courts forcing fathers to pay alimony for their children, to (4) the government
confiscating land in Utah. While the connection among these issues is not automatically evident, they were eventually linked together in a "jurisdictional frame" in the
commentary by one of the leaders during a multivoiced discussion. The basic
problem in each instance was that the federal government was violating its constitutional obligations either by failing to abide by it or reaching beyond its limits
or confines.

Such observations suggest that framing is an ongoing process in that frames are continuously articulated and elaborated during the course of conversation and debate among the interactants within a discursive field as they go about the business of making sense of the events and issues with which they are confronted. Thus, rather than being static, reified entities, collective action frames are the product of ongoing interaction that involves both frame articulation and frame elaboration within discursive fields. That is to say, borrowing from Steinberg's paraphrasing (1998) of Bakhtin, these are dynamic, interindividual, recursive processes that organize and interpret discourse or talk within concrete interactional contexts.

The kindred concept of discursive opportunity structures suggests, however, that the shape and life course or history of discursive framing processes and the fields in which they are embedded are not only a function of the stream of events coursing through them and the cultural resources, interactants, and framing debates that constitute them, but are also influenced by the enveloping political context. Thus Duyvendak and Koopmans (chapter 6 in Kriesi et al. 1995) found that varying political conditions across western European countries affected the influence of movement framing efforts with respect to nuclear energy in the wake of the Chernobyl disaster in April 1986. In the case of France, they write:

> the strong French state even successfully denied the existence of a problem, and in the absence of any competing version among the country's political elites, was able to convince the population that radiation had somehow halted at the country's borders, and that the unsafe nature of Soviet reactors was of no relevance to superior French technology....Conversely, antinuclear movements that were confronted with more favorable opportunity structures and were able to successfully block or slow down the construction of nuclear power stations were also able to win the discursive battle, and to convince a majority of the public of the problematic nature of nuclear energy. (Duyvendak and Koopmans in Kriesi et al. 1995: 163)

Similarly, Diani's (see table 17.1) assessment of the electoral success of the populism of the Northern League in Italy in comparison to a number of competing groups in the same region in the early 1990s suggests a link between different configurations of political opportunity structure and different master frames, implying a kind of elective affinity between the two. Although Koopman and Statham's (1999) comparison of the relative success of the German extreme right in contrast to its Italian equivalent does not indicate such a neat fit between proffered framings and political opportunity, the findings do suggest that the greater impact of the German right on official politics was due in part to a more conducive discursive opportunity structure. In a similar vein, Ferree et al.'s comparative study of abortion discourse in Germany and the US (see table 17.1) shows how differences in the abortion frames in the two countries can be explained in part by differences in their respective discursive opportunity structures.

Such findings clearly suggest that a more thorough understanding of the character and influence of movement framing processes is likely to be gained when considering the political contexts in which those processes occur. Yet it is also important to keep in mind that political contexts and opportunities do not so much determine either the occurrence or substance of framing processes as delimit the spaces in which oppositional framing occurs and affects its public character. The overlapping concepts of submerged networks (Melluci 1989), abeyance structures (Taylor 1989), subcultures of accommodation (Johnston and Snow 1998), and free spaces (Evans and Boyte 1986; Groch 2001), and the dramaturgical distinctions between front stage and back stage (Goffman 1959) and public and hidden transcripts (Scott 1990), remind us that framing processes and ideological work can and often do proceed in the face of repressive political structures, albeit cautiously and in private, hidden, or submerged rather than public contexts. Thus the analytic utility of the concept of discursive opportunity structures resides in its focus of attention on the ways in which broader political contexts affect framing processes and the discursive fields in which they are embedded.

Summary

Since our actions depend in part on the meanings attached to our objects of orientation, differences in imputed meanings can yield differences in action, *ceteris paribus*. Additionally, these imputed or constructed meanings are not fixed or static but are subject to change as the social context changes. Shifting patterns of inter-action, discourse, and identification are especially likely to alter the meanings one attaches to persons, groups, nations, events, experiences, material objects, and even to one's biography and self, and thus the course of social action, be it individual or collective. Rooted theoretically in these symbolic interactionist and contextual constructionist principles, the framing perspective on social movements, as it has evolved, not only focuses attention on matters of meaning and the interpretive processes through which movement-relevant meanings are generated, debated and contested, diffused, and altered, but contends that the collective action and master frames that are the product of these interpretive processes are central to understand-ing the course and character of social movements. That this is indeed the case is suggested by the proliferation of research on collective action frames and framing processes in relation to social movements.

In this chapter, I have elaborated a number of issues regarding collective action frames and framing processes not covered or adequately discussed in recent substan-tive and methodological reviews of the extensive literature (e.g., Benford and Snow 2000; Johnston 2002). In particular, I have sought to contexualize the development of the framing perspective by providing a historical overview of the place of idea-tional and interpretive factors in the study of social movements; to clarify conceptu-ally collective action frames and how they are similar to and different from everyday, interactional frames; to provide a summary categorization of the scholarship on framing; to selectively highlight a number of empirical and theoretical implications of the research on collective action frames; and to elaborate the connection of framing to the kindred concepts of ideology, discursive fields, and discursive oppor-tunity structures.

Based on these various explorations and elaborations, I conclude with the following generalizations regarding the issues addressed. First, while framing processes are relevant to understanding everyday social life, they are particularly relevant to understanding the course and character of social movements in that such collective action flourishes in contexts of interpretive ambiguity and contested meanings. Second, collective action frames are not only cognitive structures located in the minds of individuals, but they also are properties of organizations or collectivities and can be examined as such. Third, the concept of master frames becomes increasingly important as the scale of protest and mobilization expands to involve coalitions of groups and movement organizations, as with the recent globalization or transnationalization of protest. Fourth, in the language of variable analysis, collective action frames and master frames can be examined not only as dependent variables, but also profitably as independent variables in relation to a host of movement issues and processes. Fifth, processes of frame transformation are more complex than often presumed, varying not only in terms of the level and scope of change, but also in terms of whether the transformations are event-based or agent-based. And finally, the concepts of ideology, collective action frames and master frames, and discursive fields and opportunity structures can best be regarded as different words not for the same thing but for different aspects and dimensions of the complex of symbolic, ideational, and intersubjective factors associated with movement mobilization and dynamics. Furthermore, these constructs not only bear a family resemblance in Wittgenstein's (1967) sense, but they are highly interconnected, in part via the discursive framing processes of articulation and elaboration, in a fashion that is mutually constraining and facilitating.

Notes

I am indebted to Daniel Cefai, Marc Steinberg, and Danny Trom for their intellectual counsel regarding ideology and its relationship to framing. Although my discussion of these topics and their connections may not accord exactly with their views, their discussions of these topics with me were most edifying. As well, I want to thank Hanspeter Kriesi, Sarah Soule, and Rhys Williams for their comments on the initial draft of this chapter.

1   McAdam's inclusion of "cognitive liberation" in the development of the political-process model in his analysis of the black insurgency between 1930 and 1970 constitutes a major exception, of course. But as the model was applied and elaborated, political opportunity became the focal concern, both empirically and theoretically, with the idea of cognitive liberation receiving relatively little attention (1982: 48–51).
2   For a discussion of the connection between symbolic interactionism, constructionism, and the framing perspective, see Snow (2003) and Rohlinger and Snow (2003).
3   Given that constructionism encompasses a variety of interpretive perspectives, I find it useful to view constructionism on a continuum, with unconstrained interpretation at one extreme to highly constrained and contextualized interpretation at the other. Work associated with the more solipsistic variants of postmodernism would be skewed toward the unconstrained end of the continuum, with most work on framing, with its emphasis on the importance of issues of resonance and discursive opportunity structures, skewed toward the contextual end of the continuum. This distinction parallels Best's (1995) division of work within the constructionist perspective on social problems into "strict construction-ism" and "contextual constructionism."
4   For summary overviews of research on conversion to religious movements, see Robbins (1988) and Snow and Machalek (1984). See also chapter 29 in this volume.
5   For other critiques of the conceptualization of movements in terms of ideology, see Diani (2000) and Klandermans (2000). For further discussion and debate regarding the

conceptualization of ideology more generally, see Fine and Standstrom (1993), Steinberg (1993, 1994) and Thompson (1990).

6 The dialogical approach advocated by Steinberg is derived in large part from the theorizing of Bakhtin and his circle (see Todorov 1984). The basic idea is that talk or discourse, and their products (e.g., meanings, frames), are highly interactive phenomena in that they occur within multivocal contexts that are constrained and facilitated by the discursive fields in which they are embedded. Thus Steinberg argues that "repertoires of discourse" qua frames "are *relational products of contention* between challengers and powerholders" that are embedded in "dynamic, conflict-ridden cultural terrain" (1999: 748, 750, passim; emphasis added). Given the rediscovery of culture, it is not surprising that other scholars interested in social movements and related collective actions have made similar observations regarding the highly dynamic and interactive character of movement-related discourse and its connection to broader ideologies or cultural systems of meaning. Thus, in his analysis of the origins of the discourse of Islamic modernism in India, Egypt, and Iran, Moaddel (2001) proposes an "episode discourse model" to account for the production of ideas. It is important to note that his model, like Steinberg's, is not only inspired in part by Bakhtin, but portrays ideological development as highly contentious and interactive rather than simply derivative. In a similar vein, Eyerman and Jamison (1991), who draw their inspiration from Gramsci rather than Bakhtin, invoke the concept of "cognitive praxis" to capture the interactive process through which mobilizing ideas are developed. And Rochon (1998), with his concept of "critical communities," which can be construed as a niche for Gramsci's "organic intellectuals" and for cognitive praxis, also highlights the interactive character of the generation of ideas and values relevant to social movements.

References

Adorno, Theodore, E. Frenkel-Brunswik, D. J. Levinson, and R. N. Samford (1950) *The Authoritarian Personality.* New York: Harper.

Aho, James (1990) *The Politics of Righteousness: Idaho Christian Patriotism.* Seattle: University of Washington Press.

Associated Press (2000) Duke Group Is Pushing White's Rights. <http://www.azstarnet.com/public/dnews/080-5049.html>.

Babb, Sarah (1996) True American System of Finance: Frame Resonance in the U.S. Labor Movement, 1866 to 1886. *American Sociological Review,* 61, 1033–52.

Benford, Robert D. (1993) Frame Disputes within the Nuclear Disarmament Movement. *Social Forces,* 71, 677–701.

——(1997) An Insider's Critique of the Social Movement Framing Perspective. *Sociological Inquiry,* 67, 409–30.

Benford, Robert D., and David A. Snow (2000) Framing Processes and Social Movements: An Overview and Assessment. *Annual Review of Sociology,* 26, 611–39.

Berbrier, Mitch (1998) "Half the Battle": Cultural Resonance, Framing Processes, and Ethnic Affectations in Contemporary White Separatist Rhetoric. *Social Problems,* 45, 431–50.

Berger, Bennett M. (1981) *The Survival of the Counterculture: Ideological Work and Everyday Life among Rural Communards.* Berkeley: University of California Press.

Berger, Peter L., and Thomas Luckmann (1966) *The Social Construction of Reality.* Garden City, NY: Doubleday.

Best, Joel (1995) Constructionism in Context. In Joel Best (ed.), *Images of Issues: Typifying Contemporary Social Problems.* New York: Aldine de Gruyter, 337–54.

Bird, Caroline (1969) *Born Female.* New York: Pocket.

Blee, Kathleen M. (2002) *Inside Organized Racism: Women in the Hate Movement*. Berkeley: University of California Press.

Cadena-Roa, Jorge (2002) Strategic Framing, Emotions, and Superbarrio – Mexico City's Masked Crusader. *Mobilization*, 7, 201–16.

Capek, Stella M. (1993) The "Environmental Justice" Frame: A Conceptual Discussion and Application. *Social Problems*, 40, 5–24.

Carroll, William K. and R. S. Ratner (1996) Master Framing and Cross-Movement Networking in Contemporary Social Movements. *Sociological Quarterly*, 37, 601–25.

Clemens, Elisabeth A. (1996) Organizational Form as Frame: Collective Identity and Political Strategy in the American Labor Movement. In Doug McAdam, John D. McCarthy, and Mayer N. Zald (eds.), *Comparative Perspectives on Social Movements*. New York: Cambridge University Press, 205–26.

Cornfield, Daniel B., and Bill Fletcher (1998) Institutional Constraints on Social Movement "Frame Extension": Shifts in the Legislative Agenda of the American Federation of Labor, 1881–1995. *Social Forces*, 75, 1305–21.

Cress, Daniel M., and David A. Snow (2000) The Outcomes of Homeless Mobilization: The Influence of Organization, Disruption, Political Mediation, and Framing. *American Journal of Sociology*, 105, 1063–1104.

Crossman, Richard (ed.) (1952) *The God that Failed*. New York: Bantam.

D'Anjou, Leo (1996) *Social Movements and Cultural Change: The First Abolition Campaign Revisited*. New York: Aldine de Gruyter.

Davis, Joseph E. (ed.) (2002) *Stories of Change: Narrative and Social Movements*. Albany: State University of New York Press.

Davis, Nancy J., and Robert V. Robinson (1996) Are the Rumors of the War Exaggerated? Religious Orthodoxy and Moral Progressivism in America. *American Journal of Sociology*, 102, 756–87.

Denzin, Norman K., and Charles M. Keller (1981) Frame Analysis Reconsidered. *Contemporary Sociology*, 10, 52–60.

Deutscher, Irwin, Fred P. Pestello, and H. Frances G. Pestello (1993) *Sentiments and Acts*. New York: Aldine de Gruyter.

Diani, Mario (1996) Linking Mobilization Frames and Political Opportunities: Insights from Regional Populism in Italy. *American Sociological Review*, 61, 1053–69.

——(2000) Comments on Zald: The Relational Deficit of Ideologically Structured Action. *Mobilization*, 5, 17–24.

DiMaggio, Paul J., and Walter W. Powell (1983) The Iron Cage Revisited: Institutional Isomorphism and Collective Rationality in Organization Fields. *American Sociological Review*, 48, 147-60.

DiMaggio, Paul J., John Evans, and Bethany Bryson (1996) Have Americans' Attitudes Become More Polarized? *American Journal of Sociology*, 102, 690–755.

Donati, Paulo R. (1992) Political Discourse Analysis. In Mario Diani and Ron Eyerman (eds.), *Studying Collective Action*. Newbury Park, CA: Sage, 136–67.

Ellingson, Stephen (1995) Understanding the Dialectic of Discourse and Collective Action: Public Debate and Rioting in Antebellum Cincinnati. *American Journal of Sociology*, 101, 100–44.

Evans, Sara M., and Harry C. Boyte (1986) *Free Spaces: The Sources of Democratic Change in America*. New York: Harper & Row.

Eyerman, Ron, and Andrew Jamison (1991) *Social Movements: A Cognitive Approach*. Cambridge: Polity.

Ferree, Myra Marx, and Frederick D. Miller (1985) Mobilization and Meaning: Toward an Integration of Social Psychological and Resource Perspectives on Social Movements. *Sociological Inquiry*, 55, 38–61.

Ferree, Myra Marx, William A. Gamson, Jürgen Gerhards, and Dieter Rucht (2002) *Shaping Abortion Discourse: Democracy and the Public Sphere in Germany and the United States.* New York: Cambridge University Press.

Fine, Gary Alan (1995) Public Narration and Group Culture: Discerning Discourse in Social Movements. In Hank Johnston and Bert Klandermans (eds.), *Social Movements and Culture.* Minneapolis: University of Minnesota Press, 127–43.

Fine, Gary Alan, and Kent Sandstrom (1993) Ideology in Action: A Pragmatic Approach to a Contested Concept. *Sociological Theory*, 11, 21–38.

Fisher, Kimberly (1997) Locating Frames in the Discursive Universe. *Sociological Research Online*, 2 (3) <http://www.socresonline.org.uk/socresonline/2/3/4.html>.

Gamson, William A. (1992) *Talking Politics.* New York: Cambridge University Press.

Gamson, William A., and David S. Meyer (1996) The Framing of Political Opportunity. In Doug McAdam, John D. McCarthy, and Mayer N. Zald (eds.), *Comparative Perspectives on Social Movements.* New York: Cambridge University Press, 275–90.

Gamson, William A., Bruce Fireman, and Steven Rytina (1982) *Encounters with Unjust Authority.* Homewood, IL: Dorsey.

Garner, Roberta (1996) *Contemporary Movements and Ideologies.* New York: McGraw-Hill.

Geertz, Clifford (1973) Ideology as a Cultural System. In Clifford Geertz, *The Interpretation of Cultures.* New York: Basic, 193–233.

Gerhards, Jürgen (1995) Framing Dimensions and Framing Strategies Contrasting Ideal- and Real-type Frames. *Social Science Information*, 34, 225–48.

Gerhards, Jürgen, and Dieter Rucht (1992) Mesomobilization: Organizing and Framing in Two Protest Campaigns in West Germany. *American Journal of Sociology*, 98, 555–95.

Goffman, Erving (1959) *The Presentation of Self in Everyday Life.* New York: Anchor/ Doubleday.

——(1974) *Frame Analysis.* New York: HarperColphon.

——(1981) A Reply to Denzin and Keller. *Contemporary Sociology*, 10, 60–8.

Gouldner, Alvin W. (1976) *The Dialectic of Ideology and Technology: The Origins, Grammar, and Future of Ideology.* New York: Seabury.

Gramsci, Antonio (1971) *Selections from the Prison Notebooks.* New York: International.

Groch, Sharon (2001) Free Spaces: Creating Oppositional Consciousness in the Disability Rights Movement. In Jane Mansbridge and Aldon Morris (eds.), *Oppositional Consciousness: The Subjective Roots of Social Protest.* Chicago: University of Chicago Press, 65–98.

Hall, Stuart (1982) The Rediscovery of Ideology: Return of the Repressed in Media Studies. In M. Gurevitch, T. Bennet, J. Curon, and J. Woolacott (eds.), *Culture, Society and the Media.* New York: Methuen, 56–90.

Hart, Steven (1996) The Cultural Dimension of Social Movements: A Theoretical Assessment and Literature Review. *Sociology of Religion*, 57, 87–100.

Hoffer, Eric (1951) *The True Believer.* New York: Harper & Row.

Hunt, Scott A., Robert D. Benford, and David A. Snow (1994) Identity Fields: Framing Processes and the Social Construction of Movement Identities. In Enrique Laraña, Hank Johnston, and Joseph Gusfield (eds.), *New Social Movements: From Ideology to Identity.* Philadelphia, PA: Temple University, 185–208.

Jasper, James M. (1997) *The Art of Moral Protest.* Chicago: University of Chicago Press.

Jenness, Valerie (1995) Social Movement Growth, Domain Expansion, and Framing Processes: The Gay/Lesbian Movement and Violence against Gays and Lesbians as a Social Problem. *Social Problems*, 42, 145–70.

Johnston, Hank (1991) *Tales of Nationalism.* New Brunswick, NJ: Rutgers University Press.

——(1995) A Methodology for Frame Analysis: From Discourse to Cognitive Schemata. In Hank Johnston and Bert Klandermans (eds.), *Social Movements and Culture.* Minneapolis: University of Minnesota Press, 217–46.

—— (2002) Verification and Proof in Frame and Discourse Analysis. In Bert Klandermans and Suzanne Staggenborg (eds.), *Methods of Social Movements Research*. Minneapolis: University of Minnesota Press, 62–91.

Johnston, Hank, and David A. Snow (1998) Subcultures and Social Movements: The Emergence of the Estonian Nationalist Opposition. *Sociological Perspectives*, 41, 473–97.

Kemper, Theodore D. (2001) A Structural Approach to Social Movement Emotions. In Jeff Goodwin, James M. Jasper, and Francesca Polletta (eds.), *Passionate Politics: Emotions and Social Movements*. Chicago: University of Chicago Press, 58–73.

Klandermans, Bert (2000) Comments on Zald: Must we Define Social Movements as Ideological Structured Action? *Mobilization*, 5, 25–30.

Klandermans, Bert, M. de Weerd, J. M. Sabucedo, and M. Costa (1999) Injustice and Adversarial Frames in a Supranational Political Context: Farmers' Protest in the Netherlands and Spain. In Donatella della Porta, Hanspeter Kriesi, and Dieter Rucht (eds.), *Social Movements in a Globalizing World*. London: Macmillan, 134–47.

Kniss, Fred (1997) Culture Wars: Remapping the Battleground. In Rhys H. Williams (ed.), *Cultural in American Politics: Critical Reviews of a Popular Myth*. New York: Aldine de Gruyter, 259–80.

Koopmans, Ruud, and Paul Statham (1999) Ethnic and Civic Conceptions of Nationhood and the Differential Success of the Extreme Right in Germany and Italy. In Marco Giugni, Doug McAdam, and Charles Tilly (eds.), *How Social Movements Matter*. Minneapolis: University of Minnesota Press, 225–51.

Kornhauser, William (1959) *The Politics of Mass Society*. New York: Free Press.

Korsch, Karl (1970) *Marxism and Philosophy*. New York: MR.

Kriesi, Hanspeter, Ruud Koopmans, Jan Willem Duyvendak, and Marco Giugni (1995) *New Social Movements in Western Europe: A Comparative Analysis*. Minneapolis: University of Minnesota Press.

Lenin, V. I. (1929) *What Is to Be Done? Burning Questions of our Movements*. New York: International.

Lofland, John (1996) *Social Movement Organizations: Guided to Research on Insurgent Realities*. New York: Aldine de Gruyter.

Lukacs, Georg (1969) *History and Class Consciousness: Studies in Marxist Dialectics*. Cambridge, MA: MIT Press.

McAdam, Doug (1982) *Political Process and the Development of Black Insurgency: 1930–1970*. Chicago: University of Chicago Press.

—— (1996) The Framing Function of Movement Tactics: Strategic Dramaturgy in the American Civil Rights Movement. In Doug McAdam, John D. McCarthy, and Mayer N. Zald (eds.), *Comparative Perspectives on Social Movements: Political Opportunities, Mobilizing Structures, and Cultural Framings*. New York: Cambridge University Press, 338–55.

McAdam, Doug, John D. McCarthy, and Mayer N. Zald (eds.) (1996) *Comparative Perspectives on Social Movements: Political Opportunities, Mobilizing Structures, and Cultural Framings*. New York: Cambridge University Press.

McCaffrey, Dawn and Jennifer Keys (2000) Competitive Framing Processes in the Abortion Debate: Polarization-vilification, Frame Saving, and Frame Debunking. *Sociological Quarterly*, 41, 41–61.

McCammon, Holly J. (2001) Stirring up Suffrage Sentiment: The Formation of the State Women Suffrage Organizations, 1866–1914. *Social Forces*, 80, 449–80.

McCarthy John D. (1994) Activists, Authorities, and Media Framing of Drunk Driving. In Enrique Laraña, Hank Johnston, and Joseph R. Gusfield (eds.), *New Social Movements: From Ideology to Identity*. Philadelphia, PA: Temple University Press, 133–67.

McCarthy, John D., and Mayer N. Zald (1977) Resource Mobilization and Social Movements: A Partial Theory. *American Journal of Sociology*, 82, 1212–41.

McGeary, Johanna (1999) Mohandas Gandhi. *Time*, 154, December 31, 118–23.

Mannheim, Karl (1936) *Ideology and Utopia: An Introduction to the Sociology of Knowledge*. San Diego: Harcourt Brace Jovanovich.

Marx, Karl, and Friedrich Engels (1970) *The German Ideology*. New York: International.

Melucci, Alberto (1989) *Nomads of the Present: Social Movements and Individual Needs in Contemporary Society*. Philadelphia, PA: Temple University Press.

Meyer, David. S. (1995) Framing National Security: Elite Public Discourse on Nuclear Weapons During the Cold War. *Political Communication*, 12, 173–92.

Moaddel, Mansoor (2001) Conditions for Ideological Production: The Origins of Islamic Modernism in India, Egypt, and Iran. *Theory and Society*, 30, 669–731.

Mooney, Patrick H., and Scott A. Hunt (1996) A Repertoire of Interpretations: Master Frames and Ideological Continuity in U.S. Agrarian Mobilization. *Sociological Quarterly*, 37, 177–97.

Moore, Barrington (1978) *Injustice: The Social Bases of Obedience and Revolt*. White Plains, NY: Sharpe.

Mosse, George L. (1985) *Nationalism and Sexuality: Middle-Class Morality and Sexual Norms in Modern Europe*. Madison: University of Wisconsin Press.

Noonan, Rita K. (1995) Women against the State: Political Opportunities and Collective Action Frames in Chile's Transition to Democracy. *Sociological Forum*, 19, 81–111.

Ofshe, Richard, and Ethan Watters (1994) *Making Monsters: False Memories, Psychotherapy, and Sexual Hysteria*. Berkeley: University of California Press.

Oliver, Pamela E., and Hank Johnston (2000) What a Good Idea! Ideology and Frames in Social Movement Research. *Mobilization*, 5, 37–54.

Piven, Frances Fox, and Richard A. Cloward (1977) *Poor People's Movements*. New York: Vintage.

Polletta, Francesca (2002) Plotting Protest: Mobilizing Stories in the 1960 Student Sit-ins. In Joseph E. Davis (ed.), *Stories of Change: Narrative and Social Movements*. Albany, NY: State University of New York Press, 31–51.

Ragin, Charles C. (1987) *The Comparative Method*. Berkeley: University of California Press.

Robbins, Thomas (1988) *Cults, Converts, and Charisma*. Newbury Park, CA: Sage.

Rochford, E. Burke Jr. (1985) *Hare Krishna in America*. New Brunswick, NJ: Rutgers University Press.

Rochon, Thomas R. (1998) *Culture Moves: Ideas, Activism, and Changing Values*. Princeton, NJ: Princeton University Press.

Rohlinger, Deana (2002) Framing the Abortion Debate: Organizational Resources, Media Strategies, and Movement–Countermovement Dynamics. *Sociological Quarterly*, 43, 479–507.

Rohlinger, Deana, and David A. Snow (2003) Social Psychological Perspectives on Crowds and Social Movements. In John Delamater (ed.), *Handbook of Social Psychology*. New York: Kluwer Academic/Plenum, 503–27.

Rokeach, Milton (1973) *The Nature of Human Values*. New York: Free Press.

Rothman, Franklin Daniel, and Pamela E. Oliver (1999) From Local to Global: The Anti-Dam Movement in Southern Brazil, 1979–1992. *Mobilization*, 4, 41–58.

Rudé, George (1980) *Ideology and Popular Protest*. New York. Pantheon.

Ryan, Charlotte (1991) *Prime Time Activism: Media Strategies for Grassroots Organizing*. Boston: South End.

Scott, James C. (1990) *Domination and the Arts of Resistance*. New Haven: Yale University Press.

Seliger, M. (1976) *Ideology and Politics*. New York: Free Press.

Shupe, Anson (1998) Frame Alignment and Strategic Evolution in Social Movements: The Case of Sun Myung Moon's Unification Church. In Anson Shupe and Bronislaw Misztal (eds.), *Religious Mobilization and Social Action*. Westport, CT: Praeger, 197–215.

Smelser, Neil (1963) *Theory of Collective Behavior*. New York: Free Press.

Snow, David A. (2001) Analyse de cadres et mouvements sociaux. In Daniel Cefaï and Danny Trom (eds.), *Les Formes de l'action collective: mobilisations dans les arènes publiques*. Paris: Éditions de l'École des Hautes Études en Sciences Sociales, 27–49.

——(2003) Social Movements. In Larry T. Reynolds and Nancy J. Herman-Kinney (eds.), *Handbook of Symbolic Interaction*. Walnut Creek, CA: Altamira, 811–33.

Snow, David A., and Robert D. Benford (1988) Ideology, Frame Resonance, and Participant Mobilization. *International Social Movement Research*, 1, 197–217.

——(1992) Master Frames and Cycles of Protest. In Aldon D. Morris and Carol M. Mueller (eds.), *Frontiers in Social Movement Theory*. New Haven: Yale University Press, 133–55.

——(2000) Comment on Oliver and Johnston: Clarifying the Relationship between Framing and Ideology. *Mobilization*, 5, 55–60.

Snow, David A., and Jason Clark-Miller (2003) Frame Articulation and Elaboration in a Right-Wing Group: An Empirical Examination of Framing Processes. Unpublished manuscript.

Snow, David A., and Doug McAdam (2000) Identity Work Processes in the Context of Social Movements: Clarifying the Identity/Movement Nexus. In Sheldon Stryker, Timothy J. Owens, and Robert W. White (eds.), *Self, Identity, and Social Movements*. Minneapolis: University of Minnesota Press, 41–67.

Snow, David A., and Richard Machalek (1984) The Sociology of Conversion. *Annual Review of Sociology*, 10, 167–90.

Snow, David A., and Pamela E. Oliver (1995) Social Movements and Collective Behavior: Social Psychological Considerations and Dimensions. In Karen S. Cook, Gary Alan Fine, and James S. House (eds.), *Sociological Perspectives on Social Psychology*. Boston, MA: Allyn & Bacon, 571–99.

Snow, David A., R. Burke Rochford Jr., Steven K. Worden, and Robert D. Benford (1986) Frame Alignment Processes, Micromobilization, and Movement Participation. *American Sociological Review*, 51, 464–81.

Spillman, Lyn (1995) Culture, Social Structures and Discursive Fields. *Current Perspectives in Social Theory*, 15, 129–54.

Steinberg, Marc W. (1993) Rethinking Ideology: A Dialogue with Fine and Sandstrom from a Dialogic Perspective. *Sociological Theory*, 11, 314–20.

——(1994) The Dialogue of Struggle: The Contest of Ideological Boundaries in the Case of London Silk Weavers in the Early Nineteenth Century. *Social Science History*, 18, 505–41.

——(1998) Tilting the Frame: Considerations on Collective Framing from a Discursive Turn. *Theory and Society*, 27, 845–72.

——(1999) The Talk and Back Talk of Collective Action: A Dialogic Analysis of Repertoires of Discourse among Nineteenth-Century English Cotton-Spinners. *American Journal of Sociology*, 105, 736–80.

Swart, William J. (1995) The League of Nations and the Irish Question: Master Frames, Cycles of Protest, and "Master Frame Alignment." *Sociological Quarterly*, 36, 465–81.

Takahashi, Lois M. (1998) *Homelessness, AIDS, and Stigmatization: The Nimby Syndrome in the Unites States at the End of the Twentieth Century*. New York: Oxford University Press.

Tannen, Deborah (1993) What's in a Frame? Surface Evidence for Underlying Expectations. In Deborah Tannen (ed.), *Framing in Discourse*. New York: Oxford University Press, 14–56.

Tarrow, Sidney (1992) Mentalities, Political Cultures, and Collective Action Frames: Constructing Meanings through Action. In Aldon D. Morris and Carol M. Mueller (eds.), *Frontiers in Social Movement Theory*. New Haven: Yale University Press, 174–202.

——(1998) *Power in Movement: Social Movements, Collective Action and Politics*. New York: Cambridge University Press.

Taylor, Dorcetta E. (2000) The Rise of the Environmental Justice Paradigm: Injustice Framing and the Social Construction of Environmental Discourses. *American Behavioral Scientist*, 43, 508–80.

Taylor, Verta (1989) Social Movement Continuity: The Women's Movement in Abeyance. *American Sociological Review*, 54, 761–75.

Thompson, John B. (1990) *Ideology and Modern Culture: Critical Social Theory in the Era of Mass Communication*. Stanford: Stanford University Press.

Tilly, Charles (1978) *From Mobilization to Revolution*. Reading, MA: Addison-Wesley.

Toch, Hans (1965) *The Social Psychology of Social Movements*. Indianapolis: Bobbs-Merrill.

Todorov, Tzvetan (1984) *Mikhail Bakhtin: The Dialogic Principle*. Minneapolis: University of Minnesota Press.

Turner, Ralph H. (1969) The Theme of Contemporary Social Movements. *British Journal of Sociology*, 20, 390–405.

——(1983) Figure and Ground in the Analysis of Social Movements. *Symbolic Interaction*, 6, 175–81.

Turner, Ralph H., and Lewis M. Killian (1957) *Collective Behavior*. Englewood Cliffs, NJ: Prentice-Hall.

——(1972) *Collective Behavior*. 2nd ed. Englewood Cliffs, NJ: Prentice-Hall.

——(1987) *Collective Behavior*. 3rd ed. Englewood Cliffs, NJ: Prentice-Hall.

Westby, David L. (2002) Strategic Imperative, Ideology, and Framing. *Mobilization*, 7, 287–304.

Williams, Rhys H., and Robert D. Benford (2000) Two Faces of Collective Action Frames: A Theoretical Consideration. *Current Perspectives in Social Theory*, 20, 127–51.

Williams, Rhys H., and Jeffrey Neal Blackburn (1996) Many Are Called but Few Obey: Ideological Commitment and Activism in Operation Rescue. In Christian Smith (ed.), *Disruptive Religion: The Force of Faith in Social Movement Activism*. New York: Routledge, 167–85.

Williams, Robin M. (1970) *American Society: A Sociological Interpretation*. 3rd ed. New York: Alfred A. Knopf.

Wilson, John (1973) *Introduction to Social Movements*. New York: Basic.

Wittgenstein, Ludwig (1967) *Philosophical Investigations*. Oxford: Blackwell.

Wright, Talmadge (1997) *Out of Place: Homeless Mobilizations, Subcities, and Contested Landscapes*. Albany: State University of New York Press.

Woodberry, Robert D., and Christian S. Smith (1998) Fundamentalism et al.: Conservative Protestants in America. *Annual Review of Sociology*, 24, 25–56.

Zald, Mayer N. (2000) Ideological Structured Action: An Enlarged Agenda for Social Movement Research. *Mobilization: An International Journal*, 5: 1–16.

Zdravomyslova, Elena (1996) Opportunities and Framing in the Transition to Democracy: The Case of Russia. In Doug McAdam, John D. McCarthy, and Mayer N. Zald (eds.), *Comparative Perspectives on Social Movements: Political Opportunities, Mobilizing Structures, and Cultural Framings*. New York: Cambridge University Press, 122–37.

Zuo, Jiping, and Robert D. Benford (1995) Mobilization Processes and the 1989 Chinese Democracy Movement. *Sociological Quarterly*, 36, 131–56.

Zurcher, Louis A., and David A. Snow (1981) Collective Behavior: Social Movements. In Morris Rosenberg and Ralph H. Turner (eds.), *Social Psychology: Sociological Perspectives*. New York: Basic, 447–82.

18

Emotional Dimensions of Social Movements

Jeff Goodwin, James M. Jasper, and Francesca Polletta

Emotions are a part of all social action, yet they have been given little or no place in most social-scientific theories. They have been considered too personal, too idiosyncratic, too inchoate, or too irrational to be modeled or measured properly. This neglect has characterized the study of social movements since the 1970s. In the structural and organizational paradigm that has dominated research, emotions have been dismissed as unimportant, epiphenomenal, or invariable, providing little explanatory power. Even cultural analysts of movements have largely ignored emotions. Since the 1990s, however, the silence has been broken by a rising chorus of researchers describing emotions in protest, social movements, and political conflict (Taylor 1995; Groves 1997; Fernández 2000; Aminzade and McAdam 2001; Goodwin et al. 2001; Petersen 2002).

Emotions have been inadequately studied for several reasons. For one, the term and concept emotion has been used to cover a number of distinct entities, which have different sources and affect action differently (Griffiths 1997). For this reason, we have structured this chapter to highlight the different types of emotions. The reflex fear of being struck has little in common with the love one feels for family or nation or with moods such as resignation or joy. We distinguish between immediate reflex emotions, longer-term affective commitments, moods, and emotions based on complex moral and cognitive understandings. These categories should help to clear up some of the confusion surrounding emotion as a general phenomenon. Second, as the following section argues, a generation of researchers, eager to establish the rationality of participants as a way of rejecting earlier crowd theories, associated strong emotions with irrational behavior (just as their predecessors had). They took a handful of sudden, reflex emotions as the exemplar of all emotions. Most categories of emotion, however, do not especially encourage irrational acts, and even reflex emotions do so only occasionally. More strategic errors arise from cognitive mistakes or missing information, we suspect, than from emotions.

Both of these problems stem from a tendency to reduce emotions to biology, the body, and the brain. Only after the cultural turn in the social sciences in recent decades has the path been opened to a more cultural approach to emotions. In different ways and to varying degrees, most emotions are shaped by cultural understandings and norms, a point emphasized in the dramaturgical approach to emotions (Zurcher 1982; Hochschild 1983). We no longer need to link them entirely to biology (Darwin [1872] 1965) or to social-structural relationships (Kemper 1978). The former approach is of little interest to sociologists, while the latter (which concentrates on positions in social hierarchies) has less relevance to social movements than to families and workplaces (cf. Kemper 2001).

For this reason, we take a cultural approach to emotions in this chapter. Most of the time, we believe, emotions can be analyzed with the same theoretical and methodological tools that have been used to understand cognitive beliefs and moral visions (Jasper 1997). There is the same tension, and potential conflict, between socially accepted emotions and individual embodiments. There are public displays of emotions that may be more or less sincere (and judged that way by others), like declared allegiances to publicly shared beliefs and morals. Individual deviations from dominant emotions or from beliefs can be explained in part through biographical histories. Methodologically, interpretation can proceed from either individual or more public expressions of emotions. To view emotions as part of culture is not to deny their physiological correlates (just as cognitive activity can be traced neurologically) or to insist that emotions are purely cultural constructions (this no doubt varies across emotions, and at any rate requires further research). It is to recognize that emotions are simultaneously creative and conventional.

Political activists often use emotions strategically to signal things about themselves to each other and to outsiders. And in doing so, they depend on cultural rules about how, when, and where to experience and express different emotions (Hochschild 1975, 1979, 1983). We can talk, then, about emotions operating in protest at multiple levels, from the microlevel processes by which bystanders become participants (Wood 2001), to the emotional repertories that activists draw upon when pitching their case in different settings (Groves 1997; Whittier 2001), to the organizational mechanisms through which particular emotions are managed (Epstein 1991), to the macrostructural shifts responsible for making certain emotions legitimate motivations for protest (Haskell 1985; Baker-Benfield 1992). Some protesters also seek to alter the emotional state of broad publics as one of their main strategic goals (Taylor 1995). Indeed, one important repertory of collective action – terrorism – takes its very name from the emotional state that its perpetrators try to induce among its intended audience.

EMOTIONS IN SOCIAL MOVEMENT THEORY

The field of collective behavior, under whose rubric social movements were studied until the 1960s, placed a central emphasis on emotions, especially those thought (not always correctly) to characterize crowds or mobs. When gathered in large numbers, individuals were thought to become impressionable, angry, and violent, easily led by demagogues to regress, doing things that they would normally not consider or which were against their long-run self-interests (LeBon [1895] 1960; Freud [1921] 1959).

Rationality and emotionality were sharply contrasted, with the former attributed to politics through normal channels and the latter to extra-institutional activity. Some authors saw certain kinds of individuals as particularly susceptible to emotionality, including those with a need to belong (Hoffer 1951) or with other problems of personal identity (Klapp 1969). Others at least blamed certain social structures for making people vulnerable to the emotional appeals of demagogues (Kornhauser 1959; Smelser 1962). Campus unrest in the 1960s further convinced many scholars that protestors were immature and unduly emotional, perhaps as a result of unresolved Oedipal issues (Smelser 1968). The putative contrast between emotion and rationality continues to haunt the social sciences (Massey 2002).

The generation of scholars who came of age in the 1960s were more sympathetic to the social movements they saw around them, viewing them as a fully rational type of politics by other means. In order to demonstrate that these mobilizations were rational, however, scholars began to deny – or simply ignore – that participants were emotional, thereby accepting the contrast laid down by the earlier crowd theorists whose work they otherwise rejected. The frustration that led protestors away from institutional channels and into more radical ones reflected a reasoned judgment of what would work rather than an emotional process (Kitschelt 1986). Issues of motivation and grievance formation disappeared from the agenda in resource-mobilization research, in part because they were viewed as ubiquitous and constant rather than varying (Jenkins and Perrow 1977; McCarthy and Zald 1977).

As this structural paradigm evolved into political process theory, incorporating greater attention to the impact of states and elites on social movements, emotions remained conspicuously absent. McAdam's (1982) concept of cognitive liberation, meant to capture the subjective dynamics of participation, was presented and interpreted as an instrumental calculation of the odds of repression and the costs of action (also Klandermans 1984). Strategic rationality, which also dominated game theory, seemed to preclude strong (or even weak) emotions. Without admitting it, political process theorists had at the heart of their models the coolly calculating actors of rational choice theory.

Social movement scholars were not totally oblivious to emotions during the 1980s and 1990s. Zurcher and Snow (1981), for example, complained that the resource-mobilization approach deflected attention from the importance of passion in movements. Lofland (1981, 1982) suggested that the elementary forms of collective action were based on joy, anger, and fear. Della Porta (1995) argued that affective bonds were especially important for holding together underground terrorist organizations (also Snow and Phillips 1980). And Snow and Oliver (1995) examined affective dimensions as one of the key social-psychological aspects of social movements. These claims, however, had little influence on other scholars. The analysis of emotions and social psychology generally was undoubtedly tarnished by its association with crowd theorists and collective behavior. And the emphasis on rationality continued to preclude treating emotions seriously.

Dissatisfaction with the narrow rationalism of political process theory encouraged attention to the cultural aspects of social movements beginning in the late 1980s. However, the framing processes through which recruiters appealed to potential recruits (Snow et al. 1986) were seen as almost entirely cognitive by researchers who used the concept (Benford 1997). One exception was Gamson et al.'s (1982) injustice frame, in which righteous anger was central. In experiments that exposed ordinary people to transgressions by authority figures, the authors found that suspicion, anger, and other emotions often arose even before blame was allocated through more cognitive processes. Yet this insight was not taken up by other students of framing. The concept of collective identity, for its part, became popular in part because it promised to get at the passions behind the culture, but it too was often defined as a cognitive issue of boundary formation with little attention to the strong emotions that protected those boundaries (with the work of Melucci [1995]) an exception). Nor have discourse approaches, with roots in structural literary theory, readily integrated emotions into their research.

Nonetheless, the cultural turn in the social sciences opened the way to incorporating emotions into our explanations of social movements, as much of the work that organizers and leaders do to animate movements involves emotion work. Organizers reinforce group loyalties (Hirsch 1986, 1990), inspire pride (Gould 2001), and calm fears (Goodwin and Pfaff 2001), among other activities that we will examine below. Once we see emotions as, for the most part, cultural accomplishments rather than automatic physiological responses, we can treat them as normal variables or mechanisms in our models of social movements. (For a more detailed history of how social-movement scholars have treated emotions, see Goodwin et al. 2000.)

In the rest of this chapter, we discuss several types of emotions and their relation to movement processes. Distinguishing among these types can help us to identify the different resources that emotions give to movements – as well as the practical challenges they create.

REFLEX EMOTIONS

Certain emotions (six, to be precise: fear, surprise, anger, disgust, joy, and sadness) seem to arise suddenly, without conscious cognitive processing, in an involuntary fashion. They involve a complex but regular cluster of physiological changes, including facial expressions. They are like muscle reflexes, only more coordinated and complex. They involve the processing of information through mechanisms different than our normal cognition: quicker, more primitive neurological routes that allow us to respond immediately. They feel like reflexes precisely because they are not routed through our regular cognitive systems, through which we could talk ourselves out of them in inappropriate circumstances. In this, they are not only like reflexes but like perception. There is considerable evidence that the expression of these emotions is similar across cultures (see Ekman 1972, who later added contempt to his list of these emotions).

For most people, reflex emotions are the exemplar of all emotions: out of control, with attendant bodily changes, causing us to act in ways that feel automatic and irrepressible, and passing quickly. Because these emotions launch us into programs of action without our thinking about them, they have the potential to cause irrational actions, in the sense of causing us to do things we later regret, for instance. We may reveal emotions that we had been trying to hide. Because of fear we may fail to act in ways that we wish or think we should. Paradigmatically, anger may cause us to say things or act violently in ways that ultimately hurt us.

We need to be wary, however, of linking reflex emotions to irrationality. Beside the fact that they involve complex evaluative processes, they can also make us more alert and focused on the problem at hand and therefore more rather than less rational (Solomon 1976; de Sousa 1987; Frank 1993; Barbalet 1998). It was crazy not to be scared, a participant later observed of the 1961 Freedom Rides, in which volunteers integrating Southern buses were subjected to brutal attacks (*New York Times*, November 11, 2001). Those who were *not* fearful were probably more likely to be attacked. Nor is it irrational to make mistakes; it is irrational to be unable to learn from them, to keep making the same mistakes over and over. Even the proverbial sheriff in the American South who was caught on tape striking peaceful civil rights demonstrators was not necessarily acting irrationally. After all, that sort of violence had kept African Americans down effectively for three hundred years. His mistake was not in lashing out, but in getting caught on television film that would be shown to millions of viewers nationally (a new audience that helped change the balance of civil rights politics) – in other words, in continuing to strike demonstrators when the context had changed. His anger may have led him to overlook the new circumstances, but he no doubt learned quickly to control his anger (on historical changes in the control of anger see Elias [1939] 1978; Stearns and Stearns 1986).

Whether or not we use a framework of rationality, we can certainly analyze reflex emotions as strategic tools. As with all strategic choices, mistakes can be made. Protestors try to goad the forces of order into discrediting themselves through actions like that of the angry sheriff, or through the expression of feelings they normally keep hidden. In the latter case, for instance, politicians may be tricked into expressing contempt or disgust for voters. Terrorists often attempt to provoke angry officials into overreacting, hoping that their repression will undermine their authority. Each side in a conflict tries to surprise the other into an inappropriate response. Scholars have puzzled over why state repression decreases or even eliminates protest in some cases while increasing it in others. The answer almost certainly lies partly in the management of emotions, especially fear. How great is the fear of police weapons? How strong is the indignation over the repression? Does moral outrage spread to new parts of a population in response to state repression? At what point does loyalty to a collective outweigh the risk of individual harm? How do insurgent leaders manage the emotions of their forces?

In high-risk situations, fear may threaten to cripple collective action. Goodwin and Pfaff (2001) show that fear was very much on the minds of activists in the US civil rights movement and the East German opposition movement. The political opportunities for protest were not particularly broad in either case. But Goodwin and Pfaff also show how factors such as intimate social networks, mass meetings, strong collective identities, shaming, and (for some) a belief in divine protection directly or indirectly helped mitigate fears of police repression. These factors encouraged people to protest despite and even because of the risks involved.

There is asymmetry to emotional management in conflicts. Your opponents are trying to frighten your supporters; you must defuse their efforts. They are trying to goad you into a mistake made out of anger, and you are trying to do the same to them. Each side works to surprise the other with an unexpected move. There is thus an element of psychological warfare – or emotional warfare – in many conflicts. But do social-movement leaders use the same techniques as political, military, or corporate leaders? Do differences in the kind of formal organization which each side uses matter? Only individuals have emotions, so how are their reflex actions controlled from above? It would seem to be primarily (especially?) in the heat of strategic interaction that reflex emotions play a role in the study of social movements.

Sudden joy or elation is also relevant to social movements, helping to form those moments of madness that Zolberg (1972) described. Although we discuss moods below, the sudden joy of victory (especially unexpected victory) would seem to affect the sense of efficacy of participants and potential participants, providing a cognitive liberation for many. But it also is a direct and enticing pleasure in its own right (Lofland 1982).

The example of joy suggests that many emotions come in different forms. The sudden fear of a lunging figure differs from the permanent dread of nuclear winter. The quick anger we exhibit when we drop something on our toe differs from the permanent anger, shading into outrage, we feel toward our government's foreign policy. The latter cases, in both examples, fall under the category of a complex cognitive and moral emotion, examined below. The fact that we use the same term to cover rather different feelings does not mean they have the same causes and effects. Expressions of reflex emotions may be similar across cultures, furthermore, but their causes are not. What disgusts or frightens members of one culture may have little effect on another. Think of the foods eaten in different cultures, or responses to magical or religious symbols. Medieval aristocrats were expected to fly into a rage over slights to their honor; modern citizens are not. Other forms of emotion are even more strongly linked to culture and cognition, making them even more important to the study of social movements.

Affective Bonds

If reflex emotions come upon us suddenly and subside quickly, affective emotions such as love and hate, respect and trust normally persist over a long period of time. Affects are positive and negative commitments or investments – cathexes, in psychoanalytic language – that we have toward people, places, ideas, and things. Commitment to a group or cause may be based on instrumental calculations and morality, but it is also based on affection (Kanter 1972; Zurcher and Snow 1981; see also chapter 19 in this volume).

Our affects give us our basic orientations toward the world, especially telling us what we care most deeply about. They are the reason we bother to participate in movements at all rather than sit on the sidelines: the costs of participation are lower if participation entails spending time with those we like or love; the benefits are higher if they extend to those we love as well as ourselves. Friends and foes, Schmitt ([1932] 1996) pointed out, are the stuff of politics. We do not simply organize to pursue our material interests, but to help those we love and punish those we hate – affects that can arise during the course of a conflict as well as instigating it (e.g., Fernández 2000). Petersen (2002) has shown that the fear, hatred, or resentment of others explains much ethnic violence – specifically, fear of suddenly threatening groups, hatred of traditional enemies, and resentment of others' heightened status (or fear of suddenly losing one's own). Rhetorically demonizing one's foes can change people's basic affects (Vanderford 1989).

We also protest in order to protect a coastline or historic building that we love, or the honor of a nation or group to which we feel loyal. Collective identities, in fact, are nothing more or less than affective loyalties (see also chapter 19 in this volume). This is most obvious in the fondness we feel for fellow members of our collectivity, but also in our negative feelings for those outside it. As Anderson (1991) points out, our loyalty can be to the idea of the collectivity as much as to its reality, just as nationalism was founded on fanciful ideas of national traits and histories. Organizers not only try to link their groups to existing identities, but they seek to create an identity for the movement itself. The feelings which participants have toward each other have been labeled the reciprocal emotions of the movement (Jasper 1998).

Respect and trust are crucial factors in politics. At a cognitive level, we tend to believe the statements of those individuals and organizations toward whom, at the emotional level, we have positive affects: We trust those we agree with, and agree with those we trust (Jasper 1997: 112). The affective emotions often come first. Trust is a kind of shortcut through which we can avoid processing a lot of information for ourselves. It is an emotional equivalent of a cognitive schema, simplifying the world in useful ways. We know little, though, about how trust operates in social movements – for instance, how a general trust in one's political system may discourage participation in protest – or encourage it.

Conversely, how does trust in the movement and its leaders lead people to participate or to employ certain tactics? Community organizers have long argued that they are more effective when they come onto the scene as outsiders (Alinsky 1945). People are less likely to see the outside organizer as aligned with particular subgroups within the community and more likely to see her as trustworthy – one reason Martin Luther King Jr. was chosen to head the Montgomery Improvement Association (Morris 1984). Like Simmel's ([1908] 1971) stranger, she can navigate among the competitive groups that make up any community. This argument points to the structural conditions facilitating leadership, but also to its emotional components.

Efforts to portray the relations between leaders and followers as an exchange, with various costs and benefits going to each (Melucci 1996), always feel flat, as though they had missed the essence of leadership. Successful leaders embody the moral ideals of a group, crafting a way of living that resonates with their followers. There is both identification with and admiration for leaders, who are both similar to their followers and at the same time superior (although some leaders emphasize their common attributes, others their unique qualities). Although Freud's group psychology ([1921] 1959) and Weber's analysis of charisma ([1922] 1978) touched on these issues, only recently have sociologists begun to reexamine the relationship between leaders and their constituencies as emotionally complex and variable (Selbin 1993; Aminzade et al. 2001; see also chapter 8 in this volume).

Whether leadership within a movement organization tends toward the hierarchical or the egalitarian, trust among the parties is essential. As research on for-profit organizations has shown, trust and the positive affect that comes from a collective identity are necessary for cooperation (Dawes and Thaler 1988; Mishra 1996). This is even more true of social movement organizations, which usually lack institutionalized sanctions against breaches of trust. Organizational processes such as agenda-setting, decision-making, factionalization, and the development of internal oligarchies are affected by the level and kinds of trust operating within the group. If this suggests that we should be paying more attention to the organizational conditions for trust, we should also recognize that an emotional stance of trust may be adopted self-consciously by activists as part of a positive political identity (Kramer et al. 1996).

Emotions have been prominent in analyses of one kind of movement organization: the egalitarian collective. The feminist collectives of the women's liberation movement, the cooperatives of the late 1960s, and the affinity groups of the antinuclear movement, to name but a few, promise their members relationships that are emotionally more satisfying than those characteristic of mainstream institutions (Rothschild-Whitt 1979; Mansbridge 1980; Epstein 1991; Whittier 1995; Polletta 2002). Such groups devote real energy to developing bonds of trust, love, and mutual respect among group members, who sometimes refer to each other as brothers and sisters. The emotional work is demanding, and scholars have described the tensions generated by activists' competing commitments to developing personal relations within the group and effecting political changes outside it (Breines 1989; Epstein 1991). It is important to note, though, that such conflicts are shaped by activists' views of what emotional work entails and who should do it. In the alternative health center Kleinman (1996) studied, men's participation was viewed as altruistic and self-sacrificial – and rewarded for that – in a way that women's was not. And where men's grievances were viewed as properly addressed through policy change, women's grievances were seen as purely interpersonal.

Of course, we should not assume that because emotions are frequently center stage in collectivist organizations, they are not operating in more conventionally bureaucratic groups. The emotional performances are simply different. Trust may be generated by cool displays of authority and collective identity may be affirmed by ritualized assertions of the group's difference from unserious or more emotional groups. As Weber emphasized, there are emotional components of bureaucratic authority as well as charismatic and traditional authority (Herzfeld 1993; Bandes 1999). Seemingly affectless self-presentations may be quite effective in certain contexts, and they may be self-consciously performed. One of the most popular – some might even say charismatic – figures on the US left is Noam Chomsky, who is famous for his phlegmatic self-presentation and monotone speech. Members of violent underground groups, moreover, who are presumably motivated by deep wells of anger and resentment, must work hard to control those emotions lest they expose themselves. Documents left behind by the terrorists who attacked the United States in September 2001 suggest that they were vigilant about appearing normal and strove hard to suppress their own fears and misgivings.

Affective ties can undermine social movements as well as reinforcing them. While scholars have emphasized the role of traditional institutions like churches and fraternal organizations in grass-roots mobilization among disadvantaged groups, they have paid less attention to how the relations of *deference* that often characterize such organizations shape, and sometimes impede, mobilization (Polletta 1999; Wood 1999). Within ongoing movements, in addition, feelings can focus on subgroups rather than the whole. Striking workers, for instance, may feel more solidarity with their immediate companions or union local than with the industry-wide union and its efforts. The most striking case of this kind of defection, though, are the dyads which so often form within collective action, the couples who meet and become involved and decide they would rather spend more time with each other than in pursuit of broader collective goals. Drawing on the work of Slater (1963),

Goodwin (1997) has explored how the dyadic withdrawal and familial withdrawal of activists weakened the Communist-led Huk Rebellion in the Philippines.

Psychoanalytic traditions have examined the transferences, fantasies, compulsions, and so on that give sparkle to our understandings and actions. Although Smelser (1968) focused too exclusively on unresolved Oedipal complexes (making it seem as though only certain individuals have psychodynamic responses), he recognized the complex feelings, possibly based on childhood identifications, that shape our attitudes toward others, including political leaders on both sides of a conflict. Basic affective commitments need not be conscious to influence our actions and beliefs.

MOODS

Most emotions take a direct object – we are afraid of something, we love someone – but moods do not. Moods are modular or transportable emotions. We typically carry a mood from one situation to the next, in part because most moods are apparently correlated with biochemical changes (Griffiths 1997: ch. 10). Thus, a mood formed in one context may affect how we think and act in another. Good moods make us more optimistic and give us more positive feelings about others; bad ones do the opposite.

Movement leaders often try to arouse in participants feelings of hope or optimism, a sense that they can have a positive, transformative effect through their collective action. Optimism is associated with a heightened sense of individual and collective efficacy. When political-process theorists talk about the cognitive liberation that flows from a recognition that the system is newly vulnerable to protest, one can imagine that optimism is the dominant emotion. But the mood in some movements, especially those operating in highly repressive situations, is more one of grim determination and firm resolve than of optimism or even hope (Aminzade and McAdam 2001). Participants do not necessarily believe that the movement's goals will be realized. Rather, their satisfaction comes in acting *now*, in the face of those who deny their capacities for courage, dignity, and coordination (Wood 2001). And it comes from acting on behalf of their children, and their children's children, on the basis of the possibility – not the certainty – that they will eventually win (Jasper 1997; Polletta 2000).

Movements differ in their capacities to stimulate those moods, in part because of the cultural materials they have available. Activists with a fund of culturally resonant stories about endurance and struggle may be better able to stimulate feelings of resolve and determination, to create a mood of "keep on keeping on" than those whose culturally dominant stories emphasize brief struggle and uncomplicated triumph (Polletta 1998; Voss 1998). What some scholars call cultures of opposition or cultures of resistance (Foran 1997) are important both because they provide people with models or repertories of protest and because they stimulate these emotions. Yates and Hunter (2002: 129) argue that different religious traditions may provide broad postures of withdrawal, accommodation, or resistance to the world around them.

The moods or emotional climates (Barbalet 1998) of movement organizations influence whom they attract and how they operate. Movement organizations that combine support with advocacy, as for example rape crisis centers and battered women's clinics, may work to create a supportive, caring mood as a counter to the traumatic experiences participants have had outside the organization (Morgen 1995). Staffers must withstand the feelings of anxiety, anger, sorrow, and fear that accompany work with traumatized groups. This may be exacerbated by the emotional intensity characteristic of collectivist organizations – which rape crisis centers and battered women's clinics often are. People frequently burn out. Conversely, of course, movement organizations that create an emotional climate of neutral professionalism may find themselves losing members to organizations whose passions are more up-front.

MORAL EMOTIONS

Perhaps the largest group of emotions arise out of complex cognitive understandings and moral awareness, reflecting our comprehension of the world around us and sometimes of our place in it. They reflect cultural variations and constructions much more than reflex emotions do. Some of these moral emotions reflect judgments, often implicit, about our own actions. We feel pride when we follow what we take to be sound moral rules, shame or guilt when we do not. We even feel pride or shame about our own emotions – even our pride or shame (Elster 1999). Other emotions entail judgments about the actions of others, such as outrage or jealousy. That so many of our evaluative words are based on emotions (awful, stunning, proud, contemptible, disgusting, lovely, shameless) suggests that we see normative assessments as more emotional than we do strategic assessments (Jagger 1989).

Compassion is a complex cultural feeling especially important to those altruistic movements with little overlap between activists and beneficiaries (Jasper and Nelkin 1992; Allahyari 2001). Without compassion, the transnational movements against slavery, sweatshops, the World Trade Organization, or the US war against Iraq would not have become so broad. If compassion is crucial to these movements, indignation is at the core of far more. It is a component of the moral shocks that often lead individuals to search out protest groups (Luker 1984; Jasper and Poulsen 1995; Jasper 1997), as well as providing the dynamic propulsion for whistleblowers (Bernstein and Jasper 1996). Jasper (1997: 140) has enumerated some of the moral aspirations and expectations that can be shocked, leading to indignation and outrage: professional ethics, religious beliefs, community allegiances, a sense of security in one's physical surroundings, economic security, and political ideologies. Some kind of moral intuition or principle would seem to lie behind most recruitment into activism.

Movement organizers work hard to inspire and spread moral emotions, which often define a movement. Gay rights movements often highlight pride, animal rights groups focus instead on compassion, and dignity may be key in other movements of the oppressed. Feminists have seen one of their chief tasks as helping women turn their feelings of shame and inadequacy into feelings of anger and potency (Frye 1983). Against opponents who call their anger bitterness, and therefore without effective expression or moral legitimacy, they struggle to assert its moral character (Campbell 1994).

Indignation interferes with even the most calculating social interaction, as rational-choice and game theorists have discovered to their chagrin. It turns out that experimental subjects are willing to pay significant amounts to punish those they perceive as cheating (Hoffman et al. 1994). This willingness varies across cultures (Henrich et al. 2001).

As cultural accomplishments, moral emotions are especially closely tied to cognition, and narratives and discourse prove central in creating and reinforcing them. Analyzing the trials of Jack Kevorkian, Tatum (2002: 183) comments that narratives can bestow moral legitimation through pathos. Testimony was aimed at arousing compassion in jurors for those in extreme pain. To get a bed in many battered-women's shelters, applicants need to frame their stories in the right way, presenting themselves as victims with no alternatives or resources, thus conforming to feminist ideologies about abuse (Rothenberg 2002). Personal stories of conversion undergo a similar process of emotional construction (Davis 2002). The strategic aim is to appeal to widespread moral emotions, to apply them to new cases, and sometimes to reshape them.

STRATEGY

Activists strategize about what kinds of emotions to display, as well as what kinds of emotions to try to stimulate in movement participants, targets, and opponents. In a recent debate, philosophers Martha Nussbaum (1999) and Dan Kahan (1999) squared off about the merits of *disgust* for movement groups. Nussbaum argued that the persistent historical association of disgust with powerless groups – Jews, women, homosexuals, and untouchables – has made that emotion dangerous and unuseable for disadvantaged groups. Disgust rests on the notion that the other is contaminated, inhuman: it makes relations of mutual respect, even in the long term, impossible. Kahan disagreed. Gay and lesbian activists should encourage disgust for the hate-monger; women, disgust for the wife-abuser. In a kind of emotional ju-jitsu, activists can appropriate disgust and turn it around: it is those who accuse gays and lesbians of being disgusting who are themselves disgusting.

The debate illustrates a key conceptual and political problem: can emotions be invested with new meanings? Can they be extended to groups widely seen as incapable of them, for example, women in the case of anger or gays in the case of romantic love? Should activists fight for those kinds of emotional recodings? Calhoun (1999) argues that judges accepted flimsy legal arguments against homosexual marriage because they, like much of the public, assumed that gays and lesbians were incapable of romantic love. Our emotional scripts reserve such bonds of affection for heterosexual couples and, accordingly, homosexual unions could not be perceived as anything but narcissistic, competitive, and unworthy of being legitimated through marriage. The same thing that made securing a legal right to homosexual marriage difficult was what made it so important: its validation of gays' and lesbians' emotional competency. Calhoun makes another point, though: even as they were fighting for the right to homosexual marriage, lesbian and gay activists failed to challenge head-on the script that reserved romantic love for heterosexual couples.

Activists are often strategic in their displays of emotion. They may seek to elicit and transform emotions in their followers and in their targets, and to appeal to common emotions to secure support for their cause. They sometimes express uncommon, outlaw emotions (Jagger 1989) – emotions that are seen as inappropriate for particular groups – in order to secure a hearing for their cause. Activists thus exploit widespread rules for expressing emotions (Hochschild 1983). But their calculations of strategy depend also on assumptions they share with the public about how emotions work: about who has what kinds of emotions and what effects emotions have (Polletta 2001). Gordon (1989) calls these epistemologies of emotion, and they are influential in movement strategizing. For example, the animal rights activists whom Groves (1997, 2001) studied believed that men were better equipped than women to make rational arguments against cruelty to animals. Women were seen as prone to the kind of emotional accounts that would cost the movement credibility. For that reason, they were rarely made spokespeople and leaders of the movement (when male activists displayed sorrow or empathy, however, they were seen as admirably sensitive). Activists were being strategic in projecting animal rights claims made by men rather than women. But their notions of strategy depended on emotional gender rules. One can question on strategic grounds – but from outside the movement's frame of reference – the merits of passing women over as leaders and spokesmen of the movement, as well of basing opposition to animal cruelty on rights rather than compassion (Jasper 1999). The latter might be served by just the kinds of emotional stories associated with women.

In her study of activist survivors of child abuse, Whittier (2001) shows that activists urged each other to experience and express strong emotions when they participated in movement conferences and meetings: anger, grief, and shame, but also pride at overcoming their victimization. However, when survivors told their stories in court to press claims for crime victims' compensation, they were urged to demonstrate grief, fear, and shame, but not anger or pride. This made them seem properly crime victims. But it may also have reproduced a commonplace view of the victim as passive, powerless, and shameful – and discouraged other victims from similarly giving up their sense of autonomy in order to press legal claims (see Bumiller [1988] on the unwillingness of victims of discrimination to press legal cases for these reasons). Justified as strategy, the emotional performances described by Groves and Whittier also reveal normative assumptions about reason, emotion, and gender. Such assumptions conceal the fact that what seem like strategic imperatives may in fact be strategic trade-offs.

CONCLUSION

We have suggested in this chapter that various types of emotions that matter for movements can be analyzed with the same theoretical tools that have been used by scholars to understand cognitive beliefs and moral visions. The methodological approaches that have been used to study beliefs and morality can also be employed to gather data on emotions. Surveys and in-depth interviews, for example, may be used to accumulate systematic information about the emotions of movement participants or the emotional strategies of leaders (Nepstad and Smith 2001; Stein 2001; Wood 2001). Informants may be asked directly about their feelings, or scholars can see if certain questions or cues elicit talk of particular emotions – or emotional talk. Participant observation is another method that can be used to study the everyday emotional culture of movements (Allahyari 2001; Groves 2001; Whittier 2001).

Scholars may also carry out more or less formal content analyses of historical records (newspapers, government documents, court records, organizational archives, diaries, memoirs) in order to analyze the emotional displays and strategies of past movements (Barker 2001; Berezin 2001; Goodwin and Pfaff 2001; Kane 2001). The discourse and frames produced by movements in their documents, rituals, banners, and slogans can be plumbed for emotional content (Gould 2001; Young 2001). And visual sociology (photography and videotape) can be employed to capture the range of emotional displays evident in protest events – the emotional repertory of protest.

Bringing emotions back in will not only result in thicker descriptions of social movements and a better understanding of their microfoundations. Because emotion, like culture generally, is a dimension of all social action, attending to emotions will illuminate more clearly all of the key issues that have exercised scholars of movements: Why do people join or support movements? Why do movements occur when they do? Why and how are movements organized the way they are? Why do some people remain in movements, while others drop out? What strategies and tactics do movements employ? What ends do movements attempt to realize? Why do movements decline? After years of neglect, the study of emotions is experiencing a resurgence among social movement scholars. It should become a routine aspect of movement analysis.

Note

The authors would like to thank the editors for their helpful comments on an earlier draft of this chapter.

References and further reading

Adorno, Theodore W., Else Frenkel-Brunswik, Daniel J. Levinson, and R. Nevitt Sanford (1950) *The Authoritarian Personality*. New York: Harper & Row.

Alinsky, Saul (1945) *Rules for Radicals*. New York: Random House.

Allahyari, Rebecca Ann (2001) The Felt Politics of Charity: Serving "the Ambassadors of God" and Saving "the Sinking Classes." In Jeff Goodwin, James M. Jasper, and Francesca Polletta (eds.), *Passionate Politics: Emotions and Social Movements*. Chicago: University of Chicago Press, 195–211.

Allport, Floyd (1924) *Social Psychology*. Boston: Houghton Mifflin.

Aminzade, Ronald R., and Doug McAdam (2001) Emotions and Contentious Politics. In Ronald R. Aminzade, Jack A. Goldstone, Doug McAdam, Elizabeth J. Perry, William H. Sewell Jr., Sidney Tarrow, and Charles Tilly (eds.), *Silence and Voice in the Study of Contentious Politics*. New York: Cambridge University Press, 14–50.

Aminzade, Ronald R., Jack A. Goldstone, and Elizabeth J. Perry (2001) Leadership Dynamics and Dynamics of Contention. In Ronald R. Aminzade, Jack A. Goldstone, Doug McAdam, Elizabeth J. Perry, William H. Sewell Jr., Sidney Tarrow, and Charles Tilly (eds.), *Silence and Voice in the Study of Contentious Politics*. New York: Cambridge University Press, 126–54.

Anderson, Benedict (1991) *Imagined Communities*. Rev. ed. London: Verso.

Ashmore, Richard D., and Lee Jussim (eds.) (1997) *Self and Identity*. New York: Oxford University Press.

Baker-Benfield, G. J. (1992) *The Culture of Sensibility: Sex and Society in Eighteenth-Century Britain*. Chicago: University of Chicago Press.

Bandes, Susan A. (1999) Introduction. In Susan A. Bandes (ed.), *The Passions of Law*. New York: New York University Press, 1–15.

Barbalet, J. M. (1998) *Emotion, Social Theory, and Social Structure: A Macrosociological Approach*. Cambridge: Cambridge University Press.

Barker, Colin (2001) Fear, Laughter, and Collective Power: The Making of Solidarity at the Lenin Shipyard in Gdansk, Poland, August 1980. In Jeff Goodwin, James M. Jasper, and Francesca Polletta (eds.), *Passionate Politics: Emotions and Social Movements*. Chicago: University of Chicago Press, 175–94.

Bartky, Sandra (1990) *Femininity and Domination: Studies in the Phenomenology of Oppression*. New York: Routledge.

Benford, Robert D. (1993) Frame Disputes within the Nuclear Disarmament Movement. *Social Forces*, 71, 677–701.

——(1997) An Insider's Critique of the Social Movement Framing Perspective. *Sociological Inquiry*, 67, 409–30.

Benford, Robert D., and Scott A. Hunt. (1992) Dramaturgy and Social Movements: The Social Construction and Communication of Power. *Sociological Inquiry*, 62, 36–55.

Berezin, Mabel (2001) Emotions and Political Identity: Mobilizing Affection for the Polity. In Jeff Goodwin, James M. Jasper, and Francesca Polletta (eds.), *Passionate Politics: Emotions and Social Movements*. Chicago: University of Chicago Press, 83–98.

Bernstein, Mary, and James M. Jasper (1996) Whistleblowers as Claims-Makers in Technological Controversies. *Social Science Information*, 35, 565–89.

Blee, Kathleen M. (1991) *Women of the Klan: Racism and Gender in the 1920s*. Berkeley: University of California Press.

Blumer, Herbert (1939) Collective Behavior. In Robert E. Park (ed.), *Principles of Sociology*. New York: Barnes & Noble, 221–80.

Breines, Wini (1989) *Community and Organization in the New Left, 1962–68: The Great Refusal*. New Brunswick, NJ: Rutgers University Press.

Browning, Frank (1993) *The Culture of Desire: Paradox and Perversity in Gay Lives Today*. New York: Crown.

Bumiller, Kristin (1988) *The Civil Rights Society*. Baltimore: Johns Hopkins University Press.

Calhoun, Craig (2001) Putting Emotions in their Place. In Jeff Goodwin, James M. Jasper, and Francesca Polletta (eds.), *Passionate Politics: Emotions and Social Movements*. Chicago: University of Chicago Press, 45–57.

Calhoun, Cheshire (1999) Making up Emotional People: The Case of Romantic Love. In Susan A. Bandes (ed.), *The Passions of Law*. New York: New York University Press, 217–40.

Campbell, Sue (1994) Being Dismissed: The Politics of Emotional Expression. *Hypatia*, 9 (3), 46–65.

Collins, Randall (2001) Social Movements and the Focus of Emotional Attention. In Jeff Goodwin, James M. Jasper, and Francesca Polletta (eds.), *Passionate Politics: Emotions and Social Movements*. Chicago: University of Chicago Press, 27–44.

Crane, Diana (ed.) (1994) *The Sociology of Culture*. Cambridge, MA: Blackwell.

Darwin, Charles ([1872] 1965) *The Expression of Emotion in Man and Animals*. Chicago: University of Chicago Press.

Davis, Joseph (2002) Narrative and Social Movements: The Power of Stories. In Joseph E. Davis (ed.), *Stories of Change: Narrative and Social Movements*. Albany: State University of New York Press, 3–39.

Dawes, R. M., and R. Thaler (1988) Anomalies: Cooperation. *Journal of Economic Perspectives*, 2, 187–97.

della Porta, Donatella (1995) *Social Movements, Political Violence, and the State*. Cambridge: Cambridge University Press.

de Sousa, Ronald (1987) *The Rationality of Emotion*. Cambridge, MA: MIT Press.

Dobbin, Frank (2001) The Business of Social Movements. In Jeff Goodwin, James M. Jasper, and Francesca Polletta (eds.), *Passionate Politics: Emotions and Social Movements*. Chicago: University of Chicago Press, 74–80.

Ekman, Paul (1972) *Emotions in the Human Face*. New York: Pergamon.

Elias, Norbert ([1939] 1978) *The Civilizing Process*. New York: Urizen.

Elster, Jon (1999) *Alchemies of the Mind: Rationality and the Emotions*. Cambridge: Cambridge University Press.

Epstein, Barbara (1991) *Political Protest and Cultural Revolution: Nonviolent Direct Action in the 1970s and 1980s*. Berkeley: University of California Press.

Fernández, Damián (2000) *Cuba and the Politics of Passion*. Austin: University of Texas Press.

Flax, Jane (1993) *Disputed Subjects*. New York: Routledge.

Foran, John (1997) The Comparative-Historical Sociology of Third World Social Revolutions: Why a Few Succeed, Why Most Fail. In John Foran (ed.), *Theorizing Revolutions*. London: Routledge, 227–67.

Frank, Robert H. (1993) The Strategic Role of the Emotions: Reconciling Over- and Under-socialized Accounts of Behavior. *Rationality and Society*, 5, 160–84.

Freud, Sigmund ([1921] 1959) *Group Psychology and the Analysis of the Ego*. New York: Norton.

Fromm, Erich (1941) *Escape from Freedom*. New York: Farrar & Rinehart.

Frye, Marilyn (1983) A Note on Anger. In Marilyn Frye, *The Politics of Reality: Essays in Feminist Theory*. Trumansburg, NY: Crossing, 84–94.

Gamson, William A. (1975) *The Strategy of Social Protest*. Homewood, IL: Dorsey.

—— (1992) *Talking Politics*. Cambridge: Cambridge University Press.

Gamson, William A., Bruce Fireman, and Steven Rytina (1982) *Encounters with Unjust Authority*. Homewood, IL: Dorsey.

Goodwin, Jeff (1997) The Libidinal Constitution of a High-Risk Social Movement: Affectual Ties and Solidarity in the Huk Rebellion. *American Sociological Review*, 62, 53–69.

Goodwin, Jeff, and James M. Jasper (1999) Caught in a Winding, Snarling Vine: The Structural Bias of Political Process Theory. *Sociological Forum*, 14, 27–54.

Goodwin, Jeff, and Steven Pfaff (2001) Emotion Work in High-Risk Social Movements: Managing Fear in the U.S. and East German Civil Rights Movements. In Jeff Goodwin, James M. Jasper, and Francesca Polletta (eds.), *Passionate Politics: Emotions and Social Movements*. Chicago: University of Chicago Press, 282–302.

Goodwin, Jeff, James M. Jasper, and Francesca Polletta (eds.) (2001) *Passionate Politics: Emotions and Social Movements*. Chicago: University of Chicago Press.

Gordon, S. L. (1989) The Socialization of Children's Emotions. In Carolyn Saarni and Paul L. Harris (eds.), *Children's Understanding of Emotion*. New York: Cambridge University Press, 319–49.

Gould, Deborah (2001) Rock the Boat, Don't Rock the Boat, Baby: Ambivalence and the Emergence of Militant AIDS Activism. In Jeff Goodwin, James M. Jasper, and Francesca Polletta (eds.), *Passionate Politics: Emotions and Social Movements*. Chicago: University of Chicago Press, 135–57.

Griffiths, Paul E. (1997) *What Emotions Really Are: The Problem of Psychological Categories*. Chicago: University of Chicago Press.

Groves, Julian McAllister (1997) *Hearts and Minds*. Philadelphia, PA: Temple University Press.

—— (2001) Animal Rights and the Politics of Emotion: Folk Constructions of Emotion in the Animal Rights Movement. In Jeff Goodwin, James M. Jasper, and Francesca Polletta (eds.),

Passionate Politics: Emotions and Social Movements. Chicago: University of Chicago Press, 212–29.

Haskell, Thomas L. (1985) Capitalism and the Origins of the Humanitarian Sensibility, Parts I and II. *American Historical Review*, 90 (2), 339–61, (3), 547–66.

Henrich, Joseph, Robert Boyd, Samuel Bowles, Colin Camerer, Ernst Fehr, Herbert Gintis, and Richard McElreath (2001) Cooperation, Reciprocity and Punishment in Fifteen Small-scale Societies. *American Economic Review*, 91, 73–8.

Herzfeld, Michael (1993) *The Social Production of Indifference: Exploring the Symbolic Roots of Western Bureaucracy*. Chicago: University of Chicago Press.

Hirsch, Eric L. (1986) The Creation of Political Solidarity in Social Movement Organizations. *Sociological Quarterly*, 27, 373–87.

——(1990) Sacrifice for the Cause: Group Processes, Recruitment, and Commitment in a Student Social Movement. *American Sociological Review*, 55, 243–54.

Hochschild, Arlie Russell (1975) The Sociology of Feeling and Emotion: Selected Possibilities. In Marcia Millman and Rosabeth Moss Kanter (eds.), *Another Voice: Feminist Perspectives on Social Life and the Social Sciences*. Garden City, NY: Anchor, 280–307.

——(1979) Emotion Work, Feeling Rules, and Social Structure. *American Journal of Sociology*, 85, 551–75.

——(1983) *The Managed Heart: Commercialization of Human Feeling*. Berkeley: University of California Press.

Hoffer, Eric (1951) *The True Believer*. New York: Harper & Row.

Hoffman, Elizabeth, Kevin McCabe, Keith Shachat, and Vernon L. Smith (1994) Preferences, Property Rights, and Anonymity in Bargaining Games. *Games and Economic Behavior*, 7, 346–80.

Huntington, Samuel P. (1968) *Political Order in Changing Societies*. New Haven: Yale University Press.

Jagger, Alison (1989) Love and Knowledge: Emotion in Feminist Epistemology. *Inquiry*, 32, 151–76.

Jasper, James M. (1992) The Politics of Abstractions: Instrumental and Moralist Rhetorics in Public Debate. *Social Research*, 59, 315–44.

——(1997) *The Art of Moral Protest: Culture, Biography, and Creativity in Social Movements*. Chicago: University of Chicago Press.

——(1998) The Emotions of Protest: Affective and Reactive Emotions in and around Social Movements. *Sociological Forum*, 13, 397–424.

——(1999) Sentiments, Ideas, and Animals: Rights Talk and Animal Protection. In Peter A. Coclanis and Stuart Weems Bruchey (eds.), *Ideas, Ideologies, and Social Movements*. Columbia: University of South Carolina Press, 147–57.

Jasper, James M., and Dorothy Nelkin (1992) *The Animal Rights Crusade*. New York: Free Press.

Jasper, James M., and Jane Poulsen (1995) Recruiting Strangers and Friends: Moral Shocks and Social Networks in Animal Rights and Anti-Nuclear Protests. *Social Problems*, 42, 493–512.

Jenkins, J. Craig, and Charles Perrow (1977) Insurgency of the Powerless: Farm Worker Movements (1946–1972). *American Sociological Review*, 42, 249–68.

Johnson, Claudia L. (1995) *Equivocal Beings: Politics, Gender, and Sentimentality in the 1790s*. Chicago: University of Chicago Press.

Johnston, Hank, and Bert Klandermans (1995) The Cultural Analysis of Social Movements. In Hank Johnston and Bert Klandermans (eds.), *Social Movements and Culture*. Minneapolis: University of Minnesota Press, 3–24.

Johnston, Hank, Enrique Laraña, and Joseph R. Gusfield (1994) Identities, Grievances, and New Social Movements. In Enrique Laraña, Hank Johnston, and Joseph R. Gusfield (eds.), *New Social Movements: From Ideology to Identity*. Philadelphia, PA: Temple University Press, 3–35.

Kahan, Dan M. (1999) The Progressive Appropriation of Disgust. In Susan A. Bandes (ed.), *The Passions of Law*. New York: New York University Press, 63–79.

Kane, Anne (2001) Finding Emotion in Social Movement Processes: Irish Land Movement Metaphors and Narratives. In Jeff Goodwin, James M. Jasper, and Francesca Polletta (eds.), *Passionate Politics: Emotions and Social Movements*. Chicago: University of Chicago Press, 251–66.

Kanter, Rosabeth Moss (1972) *Commitment and Community*. Cambridge, MA: Harvard University Press.

Kemper, Theodore (1978) *A Social Interactional Theory of Emotions*. New York: John Wiley.

——(2001) A Structural Approach to Social Movement Emotions. In Jeff Goodwin, James M. Jasper, and Francesca Polletta (eds.), *Passionate Politics: Emotions and Social Movements*. Chicago: University of Chicago Press, 58–73.

Kitschelt, Herbert (1986) Political Opportunity Structures and Political Protest: Anti-Nuclear Movements in Four Democracies. *British Journal of Political Science*, 16, 57–85.

Klandermans, Bert (1984) Mobilization and Participation: Social-Psychological Expansions of Resource Mobilization Theory. *American Sociological Review*, 49, 583–600.

Klapp, Orrin (1969) *Collective Search for Identity*. New York: Holt, Rinehart & Winston.

Kleinman, Sheryl (1996) *Opposing Ambitions: Gender and Identity in an Alternative Organization*. Chicago: University of Chicago Press.

Kornhauser, William (1959) *The Politics of Mass Society*. Glencoe, IL: Free Press.

Kramer, Roderick M., Marilynn B. Brewer, and Benjamin A. Hanna (1996) Collective Trust and Collective Action: The Decision to Trust as a Social Decision. In Roderick M. Kramer and Tom R. Taylor (eds.), *Trust in Organizations: Frontiers in Theory and Research*. Thousand Oaks, CA: Sage Publications.

Lamont, Michèle, and Marcel Fournier (eds.) (1992) *Cultivating Differences: Symbolic Boundaries and the Making of Inequality*. Chicago: University of Chicago Press.

Laraña, Enrique, Hank Johnston, and Joseph R. Gusfield (eds.) (1994) *New Social Movements: From Ideology to Identity*. Philadelphia, PA: Temple University Press.

Lasswell, Harold D. (1930) *Psychopathology and Politics*. Chicago: University of Chicago Press.

——(1948) *Power and Personality*. New York: W. W. Norton.

LeBon, Gustave ([1895] 1960) *The Crowd*. New York: Viking.

Leidner, Robin (1993) *Fast Food, Fast Talk: Service Work and the Routinization of Everyday Life*. Berkeley: University of California Press.

Lewicki, Roy J., and Barbara Benedict Bunker (1996) Developing and Maintaining Trust in Work Relationships. In Roderick M. Kramer and Tom R. Tyler (eds.), *Trust in Organizations: Frontiers of Theory and Research*. Thousand Oaks, CA: Sage, 114–39.

Lichterman, Paul (1996) *The Search for Political Community: American Activists Reinventing Commitment*. New York: Cambridge University Press.

Lofland, John (1981) Collective Behavior: The Elementary Forms. In Morris Rosenberg and Ralph H. Turner (eds.), *Social Psychology*. New York: Basic, 278–446.

——(1982) Crowd Joys. *Urban Life*, 10, 355–81.

——(1985) Social Movement Culture. In John Lofland, *Protest: Studies of Collective Behavior and Social Movements*. New Brunswick, NJ: Transaction, 219–39.

——(1996) *Social Movement Organizations*. New York: Aldine de Gruyter.

Luker, Kristin (1984) *Abortion and the Politics of Motherhood*. Berkeley: University of California Press.

McAdam, Doug (1982) *Political Process and the Development of Black Insurgency, 1930–1970*. Chicago: University of Chicago Press.

——(1994) Culture and Social Movements. In Enrique Laraña, Hank Johnston, and Joseph R. Gusfield (eds.), *New Social Movements: From Ideology to Identity*. Philadelphia, PA: Temple University Press, 36–57.

McCarthy, John D., and Mayer N. Zald (1977) Resource Mobilization and Social Movements: A Partial Theory. *American Journal of Sociology*, 82, 1212–41.

Mansbridge, Jane (1980) *Beyond Adversary Democracy*. Chicago: University Chicago Press.

Massey, Douglas S. (2002) A Brief History of Human Society: The Origin and Role of Emotion in Social Life. *American Sociological Review*, 67, 1–29.

Melucci, Alberto (1995) The Process of Collective Identity. In Hank Johnston and Bert Klandermans (eds.), *Social Movements and Culture*. Minneapolis: University of Minnesota Press, 41–63.

——(1996) *Challenging Codes*. Cambridge: Cambridge University Press.

Miller, Neal, and John Dollard (1941) *Social Learning and Imitation*. New Haven: Yale University Press.

Mishra, Aneil K. (1996) Organizational Response to Crisis: The Centrality of Trust. In Roderick M. Kramer and Tom R. Tyler (eds.), *Trust in Organizations: Frontiers of Theory and Research*. Thousand Oaks, CA: Sage, 261–87.

Morgen, Sandra (1995) "It Was the Best of Times, It Was the Worst of Times": Emotional Discourse in the Work Cultures of Feminist Health Clinics. In Myra Marx Ferree and Patricia Yancey Martin (eds.), *Feminist Organizations: Harvest of the New Women's Movement*. Philadelphia: Temple University Press, 234–47.

Morris, Aldon D. (1984) *The Origins of the Civil Rights Movement: Black Communities Organizing for Change*. New York: Free Press.

Mueller, Carol McClurg (1992) Building Social Movement Theory. In Aldon Morris and Carol McClurg Mueller (eds.), *Frontiers in Social Movement Theory*. New Haven: Yale University Press, 3–25.

Munt, Sally R. (1998) *Butch/Femme: Inside Lesbian Gender*. London: Cassell.

Nepstad, Sharon Erickson, and Christian Smith (2001) The Social Structure of Moral Outrage in Recruitment to the U.S. Central America Peace Movement. In Jeff Goodwin, James M. Jasper, and Francesca Polletta (eds.), *Passionate Politics: Emotions and Social Movements*. Chicago: University of Chicago Press, 158–74.

Nussbaum, Martha C. (1999) "Secret Sewers of Vice": Disgust, Bodies, and the Law. In Susan A. Bandes (ed.), *The Passions of Law*. New York: New York University Press, 19–62.

Oberschall, Anthony (1973) *Social Conflict and Social Movements*. Englewood Cliffs, NJ: Prentice-Hall.

Payne, Charles (1995) *I've Got the Light of Freedom: The Organizing Tradition and the Mississippi Freedom Struggle*. Berkeley: University of California Press.

Petersen, Roger D. (2002) *Understanding Ethnic Violence: Fear, Hatred, and Resentment in Twentieth-Century Eastern Europe*. Cambridge: Cambridge University Press.

Pierce, Jennifer L. (1995) *Gender Trials: Emotional Lives in Contemporary Law Firms*. Berkeley: University of California Press.

Polletta, Francesca (1998) Contending Stories: Narrative in Social Movements. *Qualitative Sociology*, 21, 419–46.

——(1999) Free Spaces in Collective Action. *Theory and Society*, 28, 1–38.

——(2000) The Structural Context of Novel Rights Claims: Rights Innovation in the Southern Civil Rights Movement, 1961–1966. *Law and Society Review*, 34, 367–406.

——(2001) The Laws of Passion. *Law and Society Review*, 35, 467–93.

——(2002) *Freedom Is an Endless Meeting: Democracy in American Social Movements*. Chicago: University of Chicago Press.

Polletta, Francesca, and James M. Jasper (2000) Collective Identity and Social Movements. *Annual Review of Sociology*, 27, 283–305.

Riesman, David (1950) *The Lonely Crowd*. New Haven: Yale University Press.

Robnett, Belinda (1997) *How Long? How Long? African-American Women in the Struggle for Civil Rights*. New York: Oxford University Press.

Rorty, Amelie O. (1980) Introduction. In Amelie Oksenberg Rorty (ed.), *Explaining Emotions*. Berkeley: University of California Press, 103–26.

Rothenberg, Bess (2002) Movement Advocates as Battered Women's Storytellers. In Joseph E. Davis (ed.), *Stories of Change*. Albany: State University of New York Press, 203–25.

Rothschild-Whitt, Joyce (1979) The Collectivist Organization: An Alternative to Rational-Bureaucratic Models. *American Sociological Review*, 44, 509–27.

Scheff, Thomas J. (1994a) *Bloody Revenge*. Boulder, CO: Westview.

——(1994b) Emotions and Identity: A Theory of Ethnic Nationalism. In Craig Calhoun (ed.), *Social Theory and the Politics of Identity*. Cambridge, MA: Blackwell, 277–304.

Scheman, Naomi (1980) Anger and the Politics of Naming. In Sally McConnell Ginet, Ruth Borker, and Nelly Foreman (eds.), *Women and Language in Literature and Society*. New York: Praeger, 174–87.

Schmitt, Carl ([1932] 1996) *The Concept of the Political*. Chicago: University of Chicago Press.

Searles, Ruth, and J. Allen Williams Jr. (1962) Negro College Students' Participation in Sit-ins. *Social Forces*, 40, 215–20.

Selbin, Eric (1993) *Modern Latin American Revolutions*. Boulder, CO: Westview.

Shils, Edward A. (1954) Authoritarianism: "Right" and "Left." In Richard Christie (ed.), *Studies in the Scope and Method of the Authoritarian Personality*. Glencoe, IL: Free Press, 24–49.

Simmel, Georg ([1908] 1971) The Stranger. In Donald Levine (ed.), *Georg Simmel, Individuality and Social Forms*. Chicago: University of Chicago Press, 143–9.

Slater, Philip (1963) On Social Regression. *American Sociological Review*, 28, 339–64.

Smelser, Neil J. (1962) *Theory of Collective Behavior*. New York: Free Press.

——(1968) Social and Psychological Dimensions of Collective Behavior. In Neil J. Smelser, *Essays in Sociological Explanation*. Englewood Cliffs, NJ: Prentice-Hall, 92–121.

Snow, David A., and Pamela E. Oliver (1995) Social Movements and Collective Behavior: Social Psychological Dimensions and Considerations. In Karen S. Cook, Gary Alan Fine, and James House (eds.), *Sociological Perspectives on Social Psychology*. Boston: Allyn & Bacon, 571–99.

Snow, David A., and Cynthia L. Phillips (1980) The Lofland-Stark Conversion Model: A Critical Assessment. *Social Problems*, 27, 430–47.

Snow, David A., E. Burke Rochford Jr., Steven K. Worden, and Robert D. Benford (1986) Frame Alignment Processes, Micromobilization, and Movement Participation. *American Sociological Review*, 51, 464-81.

Solomon, Robert C. (1976) *The Passions: Emotions and the Meaning of Life*. Garden City, NY: Anchor.

——(1996) *Rock-a-by Baby: Feminism, Self-Help, and Postpartum Depression*. New York: Routledge.

Stearns, Carol Zisowitz, and Peter N. Stearns (1986) *Anger: The Struggle for Emotional Control in America's History*. Chicago: University of Chicago Press.

Stein, Arlene (2001) Revenge of the Shamed: The Christian Right's Emotional Culture War. In Jeff Goodwin, James M. Jasper, and Francesca Polletta (eds.), *Passionate Politics: Emotions and Social Movements*. Chicago: University of Chicago Press, 115–31.

Tatum, Jeffery D. (2002) Compassion on Trial. In Joseph E. Davis (ed.), *Stories of Change*. Albany: State University of New York Press, 179–202.

Taylor, Verta (1995) Watching for Vibes: Bringing Emotions in the Study of Feminist Organizations. In Myra Marx Ferree and Patricia Yancey Martin (eds.), *Feminist Organizations: Harvest of the New Women's Movement*. Philadelphia, PA: Temple University Press.

Taylor, Verta, and Nancy Whittier (1995) Analytical Approaches to Social Movement Culture: The Culture of the Women's Movement. In Hank Johnston and Bert Klandermans (eds.), *Social Movements and Culture*. Minneapolis: University of Minnesota Press, 163–87.

Thoits, Peggy A. (1989) The Sociology of Emotions. *Annual Review of Sociology*, 15, 317–42.

Tilly, Charles (1978) *From Mobilization to Revolution*. Reading, MA: Addison-Wesley.

Turner, Ralph H., and Lewis M. Killian (1957) *Collective Behavior*. Englewood Cliffs, NJ: Prentice-Hall.

Vanderford, Marsha L. (1989) Vilification and Social Movements: A Case Study of Pro-Life and Pro-Choice Rhetoric. *Quarterly Journal of Speech*, 75, 166–82.

Voss, Kim (1998) Claim Making and the Framing of Defeats: The Interpretation of Losses by American and British Labor Activists, 1886–1895. In Michael P. Hanagan, Leslie Page Moch, and Wayne te Brake (eds.), *Challenging Authority: The Historical Study of Contentious Politics*. Minneapolis, University of Minnesota Press, 136–48.

Walsh, Edward J. (1981) Resource Mobilization and Citizen Protest in Communities around Three Mile Island. *Social Problems*, 29, 1–21.

Weber, Max ([1922] 1978) The Nature of Charismatic Domination. In W. G. Runciman (ed.) and Eric Matthews (tr.), *Weber: Selections in Translation*. Cambridge: Cambridge University Press, 226–50.

Whittier, Nancy (1995) *Feminist Generations: The Persistence of the Radical Women's Movement*. Philadelphia, PA: Temple University Press.

—— (2001) Emotional Strategies: The Collective Reconstruction and Display of Oppositional Emotions in the Movement Against Child Sexual Abuse. In Jeff Goodwin, James M. Jasper, and Francesca Polletta (eds.), *Passionate Politics: Emotions and Social Movements*. Chicago: University of Chicago Press, 233–50.

Wiley, Norbert (1994) *The Semiotic Self*. Chicago: University of Chicago Press.

Williams, Raymond (1977) *Marxism and Literature*. Oxford: Oxford University Press.

Wood, Elisabeth Jean (2001) The Emotional Benefits of Insurgency in El Salvador. In Jeff Goodwin, James M. Jasper, and Francesca Polletta (eds.), *Passionate Politics: Emotions and Social Movements*. Chicago: University of Chicago Press, 267–81.

Wood, Richard L. (1999) Religious Culture and Political Action. *Sociological Theory*, 17, 307–32.

Yates, Joshua J., and James Davison Hunter (2002) Fundamentalism. In Joseph E. Davis (ed.), *Stories of Change*. Albany: State University of New York Press, 123–48.

Young, Michael P. (1999) Confessional Protest: The Evangelical Origins of Social Movements in the United States, 1800–1840. PhD dissertation, New York University.

—— (2001) A Revolution of the Soul: Transformative Experiences and Immediate Abolition. In Jeff Goodwin, James M. Jasper, and Francesca Polletta (eds.), *Passionate Politics: Emotions and Social Movements*. Chicago: University of Chicago Press, 99–114.

Zolberg, Aristide R. (1972) Moments of Madness. *Politics and Society*, 2, 183–207.

Zurcher, Louis A. (1982) The Staging of Emotion: A Dramaturgical Analysis. *Symbolic Interaction*, 5, 1–10.

Zurcher, Louis A., and David A. Snow (1981) Collective Behavior: Social Movements. In Ralph H. Turner and Morris Rosenberg (eds.), *Social Psychology: Sociological Perspectives*. New York: Basic, 447–82.

19

Collective Identity, Solidarity, and Commitment

Scott A. Hunt and Robert D. Benford

Collective identity is a widely used concept. It is evoked in social scientific studies of and social commentaries on gender, multiculturalism, sexuality, identity politics, ethnicity, nationalism, and social movements (Phelan 1989; Calhoun 1994, 1997; Kelly-Fikohazi 1997; Lichterman 1999; Ryan 2001; Armstrong 2002). As Snow (2001) suggests, collective identity may well be a concept that captures the "animating spirit" of the "latter quarter of the twentieth century."

In the social science literature on movements, the use of collective identity is extensive. It is seen as both a necessary precursor and product of movement collective action. Researchers have used collective identity in various theories and at all levels of analysis (Stryker et al. 2000). Collective identity has been central in accounts of movement "emergence, trajectories, and impacts" (Polletta and Jasper 2001: 283). It has also been incorporated into analyses of grievance constructions and framing processes (Hunt et al. 1994; see also chapter 17 in this volume), motivations for participation (see chapter 16 in this volume), activists' tactical choices (see chapter 12 in this volume), life-course outcomes (McAdam 1988; Whittier 1995), and emotions (Goodwin et al. 2001). Collective identity seems to be either a central concept or a residual category for nearly every theoretical perspective and empirical question associated with contemporary studies of social movements.

Reviewing a concept with a scope as immense as collective identity, especially one that encompasses various kindred concepts such as solidarity and commitment, is a task requiring some defining parameters to make the task more manageable. We thus situate our analytic essay in the context of "micromobilization and participation," particularly focusing on the relationships between collective identity, solidarity, and commitment. The purpose of this chapter is to assess the social scientific literature on collective identity in terms of three general questions. How can solidarity and commitment help to illuminate the multifaceted nature of collective identity? How can these collective identity constructs help to illuminate the multifaceted nature of participation? How have recent empirical studies on collective identity illuminated our understanding of social movement micromobilization dynamics?

Our purpose in asking and answering these questions is one of conceptual development. Accordingly, as well as being mindful of several recent reviews of the collective identity literature (Polletta and Jasper 2001; Snow 2001; Snow and McAdam 2000), we are selective in terms of the literature reviewed most closely. We proceed by providing a brief sketch of the classical and underpinnings of collective identity, focusing on Continental and North American contributions. We follow this with some orienting definitions of micromobilization, participation, solidarity, commitment, and collective identity. The definitions provide the groundwork for our more detailed review of contemporary theoretical and empirical treatments of collective identity that depict its relationships to solidarity and commitment.

THEORETICAL UNDERPINNINGS OF COLLECTIVE IDENTITY

Contemporary treatments of collective identity build upon classical and social-psychological underpinnings. The classical theories of Marx, Durkheim, and Weber provide a foundation for understanding the structural-cultural bases for group identity formation. Social psychology provides insights on individuals' group identifications and motivations to engage in collective action. To elaborate, we provide a brief review of classical and social-psychological influences.

Classical Roots

The conceptual precursors of movement collective identity can be found in Marx's work, particularly his emphasis on class consciousness and revolution (Avineri 1968; Cohen 1978). The development of revolutionary class consciousness depends upon the realization of class interests and collective agency – a shift from being a class "in-itself" to a class "for itself" (Marx and Engels 1970; Lukacs 1971). Marx's focus on class consciousness as a necessary condition for revolutionary action is similar to contemporary understandings of collective identity and social movements. For both, collective action involves the *identification of* a collectivity (e.g., a class) with common values, interests, goals, and sentiments (i.e., collective consciousness) as well as the *identification with* a collectivity that includes a sense of mutuality and solidarity. Another important characteristic of Marx's perspective on class consciousness is that it is brought into being via the ongoing dialectics between social context, human interpretation, and social interaction (Fantasia 1988: 3–24). In an epistemological shift followed by many contemporary scholars interested in movement collective identity, Marx "cojoined" "objectivity" and "subjectivity," rather than abstracting them from each other (Fantasia 1988: 9).

Similar to Marx, consciousness and solidarity are central for Durkheim (1964, 1965). Solidarity gives rise to social cohesion and depends upon an awareness of and identification with a collectivity. Cohesion revolves around individuals developing normative frameworks based on a group perspective (i.e., a collective conscience). Collective consciousness provides a mutuality, enabling individuals to relate in terms of shared morals and goals. The most dramatic way solidarity develops is via "collective effervescence" (Durkheim 1965). With this concept, Durkheim (1965) suggests the importance of affect for group identity. Additionally, collective consciousness, solidarity, and group identity are objectified as "collective representations," symbols of shared cognitive and emotional meanings (Durkheim 1965). A collective representation is the embodiment of the spirit of a collective identity in time and space, giving a sense that the collective, as such, lives, thinks, feels, and acts.

Weber (e.g., see 1978) explores some of the same themes. From Weber's view, Marx overemphasizes the point of production, thereby neglecting other bases for group identification and social action. In contrast to Marx, Weber suggests that collective action stems from three distinct sources of group identification: class, status, and party (cf. Wright 2002). For Weber, a class exists when a category of people have similar specific and significant components of their life chances determined by commodity and labor markets. Similar to Marx, Weber believed that objective class interests do not create a class for itself. Class-based collective action requires the development of collective identification. The characteristics of social groups that an economic class often lacks are found in status associations. Status groups have normative expectations of "proper" lifestyles and a collective sense of we-ness that revolves around social esteem or "honor" (either positive or negative). While the connection between status identity and movement activity is implied, Weber's most explicit treatment of collective action involves his concept of party. A party is a social group with a shared identity that is concerned with power, the ability to influence others, even against their will. Parties are associations with a collective identity that seek to influence the hearts, minds, and actions of others.

Social Psychological Foundations

In addition to classical treatments, social-psychological approaches to identity have formed a "critical cornerstone within modern sociological thought" (Cerulo 1997: 385). This has been particularly the case within the field of social movements where there has been a longstanding interest in the social-psychological concepts of self and identity (Stryker et al. 2000).

Much of the work on identity is indebted to Mead's (1934) theorizing on self and society. He not only provides a social-psychological foundation for understanding the connection of personal identities to social groups, but also furnishes a basis for conceptualizing collective identity construction. Mead implies a dialectical relationship between the self and society. Preexisting social structures, meanings, and contexts condition the development of the self, and the self, interacting with others, shapes emerging social structures, meanings, and contexts. His approach and the work of his symbolic interactionist followers flow from three guiding assumptions: (1) individual identity is accomplished or imputed via process of symbolic interaction, (2) language is central to interaction processes, and (3) identity construction conditions and is conditioned by social structures, meanings, and contexts (Blumer 1969).

In addition to the symbolic interactionism tradition, Berger and Luckmann's (1966) constructionist perspective has had considerable influence. Berger (1966: 110–11) sums up this perspective on identity:

The relationship between a society and its world is a dialectic one because, once more, it cannot be adequately understood in terms of a one-sided causation. The world though socially constructed, is not a mere passive reflection of the social structure within which it arose. In becoming "objective reality" for its inhabitants it attains not only a certain autonomy with respect to the "underlying" society but even the power to act back upon the latter. Men invent a language and then find that its logic imposes itself upon them. And men concoct theories, even theories that may start out as nothing but blatant explications of social interests, and then discover that these theories themselves became agencies of social change. It may be seen, then, that there is a theoretically significant similarity between the dialectics of social psychology and sociology of knowledge, the dialectic through which society generates psychological reality and the dialectic through which it engages in world-building. Both dialectics concern the relationship between objective and subjective realities, or more precisely, between socially objectivated reality and its subjective appropriation. In both instances, the individual internalizes facticities that appear to him as given outside himself and, having internalized them to become given contents of his own consciousness, externalizes them again as he continues to live and act in society.

From this view, collective identity is the social construction of a facticity – that is, the objectivated reality of an identity assigned to a group, organization, or movement.

Berger and Luckmann's (1966) treatise and later works such as Giddens's (1991) exposition on self in the "late modern age" exemplify European interests in situating social-psychological concerns within larger sociocultural and historical frameworks (see Jones 1985; Farr 1996; Hogg and Abrams 1999). Contemporary European social cognition studies have focused on "language and communication, the role of affect, and the articulation of basic cognitive processes and structures with interpersonal, group, and societal processes (Hogg and Abrams 1999: 6). Of particular interest are examinations of ideology. Billing's (1991, 1992), Augoustinos's (1995), and Moscovici and Doise's (1994) rhetorical approach to social psychology highlights the social processes of persuasion and thinking, linking them to cultural representations that are foundations for personal and collective identities (e.g., the Royal Family). According to Moscovici (1981: 181), representations are "a set of concepts, statements, and explanations originating in daily life in the course of inter-individual communication" (see also Farr and Moscovici 1984). While there are significant differences between European and North American social psychology, both suggest that collective identities are products of and are produced by interaction and sociocultural structures.

CONTEMPORARY CONCEPTUALIZATION

The Continental and North American perspectives reviewed above provide conceptual and empirical bases for the identification and development of the concept of collective identity. A few early efforts by Chicago School theorists used classical and social-psychological insights to develop perspectives akin to collective identity. Blumer (1939), for instance, argued that a movement must develop an *esprit de corps* among its members by constructing in-group-out-group relationships, providing occasions for informal interactions, and organizing formal ceremonies and rituals. Blumer's (1939) work anticipates later formulations of collective identity by calling attention to the need for movements to construct ideologies and foster morale or feelings of enthusiasm and energy. Klapp (1969) likewise relied upon classical sociological approaches and symbolic interactionism to formulate his views on social movements. Klapp maintained that US society suffers from considerable anomie, alienation, estrangement, and symbolic poverty, suggesting that a central concern for movement actors is to develop meaningful identities. As a whole, Klapp's work suggests that collective behavior is intimately involved in the construction of collective identities to communicate dramas replete with heroes, heroines, villains, and fools. Along slightly different lines, Gusfield (1963, 1981) uses Weber's notions of status and party politics to examine social movements that emerge on the basis of and as reactions to constructed group identities. Also, Turner and Killian's (1987: 341) "emergent norm" approach implies that actors' commitments to movements revolve around identities that emerge from actions taken on behalf of the group: "activity in the movement contributes toward anchoring the self-conception when it gives the individual a part to play in a drama that highlights the movement's goals and when it supplies successful experience that builds self-confidence."

New Social Movements

These efforts notwithstanding, the most focused and sustained effort to examine collective identity *per se* emerged in Europe in the wake of the wave of social protest culminating in 1968. Disillusioned by the lack of a proletarian revolutionary consciousness and undemocratic tendencies in socialist states, scholars pointed to non-class based movements (e.g., feminist, environmental, and civil rights movements) as the new historical agents of democratic change (e.g., see Pizzorno 1978; Melucci 1980, 1985, 1988, 1989, 1995, 1996; Habermas 1981, 1984, 1987; Cohen 1982, 1985; Eder 1982; Mainwaring and Viola 1984; Kitschelt 1985; Offe 1985; Touraine 1985; Tarrow 1986; Dalton and Kuechler 1990; Giddens 1994; Kriesi et al. 1995). New social movements in postindustrial societies differ from their class-based-movements predecessors in terms of "ideology, origins, structure, [political] style, and goals" (Dalton and Kuechler 1990: 10).

In a sense, collective identity replaced class consciousness as the factor that accounts for mobilization and individual attachments to new social movements. The new social movement perspectives "hold that the collective search for identity is a central aspect of movement formulation" (Johnston et al. 1994: 10). As Melucci (1988: 343) explains:

> The propensity of an individual to become involved in collective action is thus tied to the differential capacity to define an identity, that is, to the differential access to resources that enable him to participate in the process of identity building.... Circumstantial factors can influence the structure of opportunities and its variations. But the way in which the opportunities are perceived and used depends on the differential access of individuals to identity resources.

As Klandermans (chapter 16 in this volume) points out, collective identity and participation's hypothesized relationship, which is "overwhelmingly supported" by extant empirical evidence, is straightforward: a strong identification with a collectivity makes participation on behalf of that collectivity more likely. Despite the rather straightforward relationship between collective identity and participation, some fundamental questions remain. Specifically, exactly *how* do the various aspects of collective identity shape the different dimensions and kinds of participation, and exactly *how* do the diverse dimensions and kinds of participation shape the many aspects of collective identity?

Micromobilization, Solidarity, Commitment, and Collective Identity

To address these issues, it is necessary to provide some working definitions of our concepts of interest: micromobilization, solidarity, commitment, and collective identity.

Micromobilization

We believe that "micromobilization" is a term that came into existence to highlight the rather normal work in which activists engage to produce a "movement," for example, the assembling and activating of material resources, cultural capital, and labor. Efforts such as those by McCarthy and Zald (1977) go beyond "black box" theories that seem to suggest that movements wondrously appear out of social structural conditions or the confluence of individuals with psychological predispositions for activism. Instead, they insist that the study of collective action is the examination of the processes, products, and consequences of human labor.

Informed by this view, we understand micromobilization as the collaborative work individuals do on behalf of a social movement or social movement organization to muster, ready, coordinate, use, and reproduce material resources, labor, and ideas for collective action. Viewed in this light, micromobilization refers to the totality of social movement work. A grounding orientation is that collective identity shapes and is shaped by micromobilization.

This dialectic relationship between collective identity and micromobilization might best be understood by examining participation. By definition, micromobilization work requires the coordinated participation of individuals. Indeed, a central component of micromobilization work is the production of the coordination of participation. Four other pivotal aspects of micromobilization that pertain to participation include the (1) production of new participation, (2) reactivation of lapsed participation, (3) sustaining of current participation, and (4) enhancement of existing participation. As these four aspects of micromobilization suggest, participation itself is a complex, multifaceted concept (see chapter 16 in this volume).

Participation has been extensively studied in a variety of forms, including conversion, recruitment, participation/nonparticipation, mobilization, rebellion, protest, activism, commitment, weak/strong support, volunteerism, biographical consequences, as well as commitment and solidarity. In an attempt at conceptual clarification, Hunt (2000) identifies eight aspects of social movement participation: onset or initial involvement with a movement, frequency of participation, range of participation in movement activities, dispersion of activities across movements or organizations, risk-intensity of participation, persistence of participation across time, disengagement from participation, and drift in-and-out of participation.

Solidarity

Participation often emerges out of a sense of solidarity. For Fireman and Gamson (1979: 21), "solidarity is rooted in the configuration of relationships linking the members of a group to one another." Another useful way to understand solidarity is in terms of Blumer's (1939) notion *of esprit de corps* – feelings of devotion and enthusiasm for a group that is shared by its members (see also Hunt 1991). *Esprit de corps* suggests that solidarity has two major facets: a body of confederates that can be identified as a collectivity and a spirit that involves feelings of identification with that group. Put differently, solidarity requires the *identification of* and *identification with*: the identification of a collective entity and participant's identification with a body of affiliated actors (cf. Foote 1951; Stone 1962). While solidarity is conceptually distinct from collective identity, the two constructs are intertwined. Similar to Melucci (1996: 23) we define solidarity as "the ability of actors to recognize others, and to be recognized, as belonging to the same social unit." Solidarity has two fundamental foci: internal and external. Internal solidarity is focused on the group to which one belongs and to the members within that group (della Porta and Diani 1999: 141). External solidarity is the identification of and identification with groups to which one does not belong. The construction of internal and external solidarity depends a great deal upon the framing of worldviews or ideologies (Benford and Snow 2000).

Concerning the *corpus* feature of solidarity, a related line of scholarship suggests that because the physical body is the vehicle for experiencing reality, it is an essential component of personal and social identities (Stone 1962; Goffman 1963; Douglas 1973; Foucault 1980; Glassner 1992; Bordo 1993; Becker 1995; Turner 1996). However, since collectivities do not literally have a single, united corporeal form, collective identity depends upon the identification of a body of associated actors (Stone 1962). For some groups, the identification of a body of actors entails projecting an image of an actual corporal entity. Military organizations, for example, convey such a notion by wearing uniforms and marching in formation as a homogeneous mass. Other groups, such as social movements, use other methods to mark membership boundaries, relying on decals, T-shirts, bumper stickers, and other "tie signs" (Goffman 1971: 188–237).

Concerning the *spiritus* feature of solidarity, Blumer (1939), in the late 1930s, argued that solidarity involved *feelings* of belonging to a collectivity. Nearly 50 years later, a scholar examining new social movements made a similar point, asserting that one dimension of collective identity is the "making of emotional investments, which enable individuals to recognize themselves" (Melucci 1988: 343). Solidarity implies a sense of loyalty and emotional interest (Benford and Hunt 1992; Gamson 1992; Taylor and Whittier 1992). Further, solidarity includes the notion that the well-being of the group and/or the well-being of members of the group are of such a concern that potential threats to or opportunities to advance that well-being will produce nearly unqualified participation (cf. Fantasia 1988). This sense of solidarity is captured by the International Workers of the World rallying cry "An injury to one is an injury to all" (cf. Fantasia 2001). In sum, solidarity is an identification with a collectivity such that an individual feels as if a common cause and fate are shared.

Commitment

In addition to solidarity, commitment is a concept seen as key to explaining social movement participation. Zurcher and Snow (1981: 458), for example, note:

> The staying power is largely a function of the extent to which the individual's dispositions, interests, and world view become linked to the goals, ideology, and internal requirements of the movement as an organized collectivity. In other words, whether the new recruit leaves or stays is largely dependent on whether he or she becomes committed to the movement.

As Zurcher and Snow (1981) also point out, commitment is relative, varying from one movement to another as well as within the same movement (cf. Lichterman 1996; Downton and Wehr 1997). In a classic statement on commitment, Becker (1960) defines it in terms of "side bets." That is, actors are committed when their investment in a consistent line of action (e.g., volunteering to participate in a movement) constrains future activities; a committed individual pursues a consistent line of activity even at the expense of other potential activities and interests. Kanter (1972: 66) offers a slightly different perspective, suggesting that commitment is the "attachment of self to the requirements of social relations." For Kanter (1968: 502) "commitment refers to a person's willingness to carry out the requirements of a pattern of social action because he or she sees it as stemming from his or her own basic nature as a person." It is possible to conceive of Kanter's perspective as suggesting that the salience and centrality of a movement identity is key in understanding the degree to which an individual is committed to a collectivity. She further implies that salience and centrality are based on three forms of rationality: instrumental, affective, and moral (Kanter 1972). In this light, commitment can be seen as an individual's identification with a collectivity that leads to instrumental, affective, and moral attachments that lead to investments in movement lines of activity.

Collective Identity

At its most basic level, collective identity is a shared sense of "we-ness" and "collective agency" (Snow 2001). In their review of collective identity, Polletta and Jasper (2001: 284) define it as

> an individual's cognitive, moral, and emotional connections with a broader community, category, practice, or institution. It is a perception of a shared status or relation, which may be imagined rather than experienced directly, and it is distinct from personal identities, although it may form part of a personal identity. A collective identity may have been first constructed by outsiders (for example, as in the case of "Hispanics" in this country), who may still enforce it, but it depends on some acceptance by those to whom it is applied. Collective identities are expressed in cultural materials – names, narratives, symbols, verbal styles, rituals, clothing, and so on – but not all cultural materials express collective identities. Collective identity does not imply the rational calculus for evaluating choices that "interest" does. And unlike ideology, collective identity carries with it positive feelings for other members of the group.

This definition highlights the multidimensional character of collective identity – for example, it includes cognitive, moral, and emotional elements (cf. Kuumba and Ajanaku 1998). It also suggests that collective identity is related to and yet distinct from such concepts as ideology, personal identity, and motivation. Finally, Polletta and Jasper's definition identifies several empirical referents or indicators of collective identity.

EMPIRICAL CONTRIBUTIONS

To date, the lion's share of the social movement literature pertaining to collective identity, solidarity, and commitment has been conceptual rather than empirical. More often than not, scholars who employ the terms "collective identity," "solidarity," or "commitment" appear to take for granted their existence without offering compelling evidence that such phenomena exist outside the minds of the social movement analysts. Although social movement scholars invoke the concepts frequently, there has been little in the way of systematic empirical work that sheds additional light on the various dynamics associated with these concepts that might be generalizable across social movements, movement organizations, participants, and time. What little we know about collective identity has been derived primarily from case studies of specific movements or social movement organizations typically situated in one culture during one relatively brief period of time. Yet, as the foregoing conceptual summary of the literature suggests, there are sound theoretical reasons for believing that collective identity, solidarity, and commitment are empirically accessible and that systematic studies of these movement processes are warranted.

To assert that there has been a dearth of systematic empirical studies of collective identity, solidarity, and commitment is not to claim that there have been no empirical studies related to the topic. As is more generally the tendency in the area of social movement studies, the bulk of the research has involved case study methods. And while the almost exclusive reliance on the case study method for studying collective identity and its kindred concepts may have stunted the development of a corpus of generalizable knowledge, especially at the meso- and macrolevels, it has also yielded richly textured insights regarding micromobilization dynamics. We turn now to an analytic summary of those insights that we have organized into two general categories: collective identity formation or construction and the effects or accomplishments of collective identity.

Collective Identity Construction

The bulk of social movement research on collective identity addresses questions pertaining to its formation or construction. The disproportionate focus of attention directed toward identity construction processes is not surprising particularly in view of its centrality to social movements. As William Gamson (1991: 27) concludes, "any movement that seeks to sustain commitment over a period of time must make the construction of collective identity one of its most central tasks."

Taylor and Whittier (1992) posited three analytical tools for understanding collective identity construction: boundaries, consciousness, and negotiation. *Boundaries* refer to "the social, psychological, and physical structures that establish differences between a challenging group and dominant groups" (111). In their studies of lesbian feminist mobilization, Taylor and Whittier observed that boundary markers served to "heighten awareness of a group's commonalities and frame interaction between members of the in-group and the out-group" (111). *Consciousness* refers to "the interpretive frameworks that emerge out of a challenging group's struggle to define and realize its interests" (111). In the context of most social movements, this means the development of "political consciousness" (Morris 1992) or an "oppositional consciousness" (Mansbridge 2001). Taylor and Whittier found that lesbian feminists' consciousness yielded a "reevaluation of lesbianism as feminism," at least for many of the movement's activists (1992: 117). By "removing lesbian behavior from the deviant clinical realm and placing it in the somewhat more acceptable feminist arena," this newly constructed collective identity "establishes lesbian identity as distinct from gay identity" (117). Finally, the third analytical tool, *negotiation*, entails "the symbols and everyday actions subordinate groups use to resist and restructure existing systems of domination" (Taylor and Whittier 1992: 111). They add that "the concept of negotiations points to the myriad of ways that activists work to resist negative social definitions and demands the others value and treat oppositional groups differently" (118). In the case of the lesbian feminist movement, activists engaged in a variety of identity negotiation actions ranging from the "politicization of everyday life" to constructing lesbian feminist organizations based on consensus decision making and other nonhierarchical forms (119).

Although boundaries, consciousness, and negotiation are analytically distinct, they can be empirically fused and often interact, sometimes in unintended ways. Taylor and Whittier elaborate, again by drawing upon their case study materials:

> Using these factors to analyze lesbian feminist identity suggests three elements that shape the social construction of lesbian feminism. First, lesbian feminist communities draw boundaries that affirm femaleness and separate them from a larger world perceived as hostile. Second, to undermine the dominant view of lesbianism as perversion, lesbian feminists offer identity accounts that politicize sexuality. Finally, by defining lesbians as the vanguard of the women's movement, lesbian feminists valorize personal experience, which, paradoxically, further reifies the boundaries between lesbians and nonlesbians and creates the impression that the differences between women and men and between lesbian and heterosexual feminists are essential. (1992: 121)

The explicit recognition of such dialectical forces and the resultant sociological ironies enhances the appeal of Taylor and Whittier's analytic framework. Morever, their schema provides a useful way of organizing the empirical literature pertaining to collective identity construction.

Boundaries

Boundaries mark the social territories of group relations by accentuating putative moral, cognitive, affective, behavioral, and other attributed differences between social movement participants and the web of others in the contested social world (Taylor and Whittier 1992). Boundary work thus constitutes a central dynamic of collective identity construction. By virtue of constructing an elaborated sense of who they are, movement participants and adherents also construct a sense of who they are not. In other words, boundary work entails constructing both a collective self and a collective other, an "us" and a "them" (Taylor 1989; Taylor and Whittier 1992; Hunt et al. 1994; Gamson 1997; Sanders 2002).

Social movement researchers have identified a variety of internal and external forces and practices associated with boundary demarcation. Robnett's (2002) examination of the US civil rights movement, for example, shows how the influx of educated whites into the Student Nonviolent Coordinating Committee (an internal factor), the passage of the 1964 Civil Rights Act (an external factor), and the movement's defeat at the 1964 Democratic National Convention in Atlantic City (an external factor) each contributed to dramatic reformulations of collective identities. Kuumba and Ajanaku (1998) found that the practice of growing dreadlocks, a hairstyle traditionally associated with the Rastafarian movement, has become a global identity marker for people of African decent. Dreadlocks have become "a symbolic accompaniment to oppositional collective identities associated with the African liberation/Black Power movements" and have also spread among African liberationists, womanists, and radical artists of African descent as a reflection of "counterhegemonic politics" (1998: 227).

Boundary demarcation and maintenance activities not only occur in opposition to imputed movement antagonists in a struggle to overcome extant systems of domination, but activists mark boundaries within movements in an attempt to distinguish their particular social movement organization (SMO) from others within the movement. Research on the peace, women's, Nichiren Shoshu Buddhist, and various other new social movements indicate that social movement actors locate their movement organization and its views within a collective action field or context (Benford and Zurcher 1990; Hunt 1991; Taylor and Whittier 1992; Benford 1993; Snow 1993; Kriesi et al. 1995). As Hunt et al. (1994: 193) note, this "entails making in-group/out-group distinctions and assigning other organizations to ideological, geographical and tactical 'turfs'," a process they refer to as "boundary framing" (also see Silver 1997). Their research further suggests that "framings that mark and bound a movement and its activities in space and time are central to the construction and maintenance of SMO actors' collective and personal identities" (Hunt et al. 1994: 195).

Evidence suggests that once an SMO has constructed fairly clear boundaries, it is not unusual for its activists to engage in efforts to maintain and enforce those boundaries. Such enforcement efforts can range from subtle to heavy-handed controlling tactics. In his study of social control within the peace movement, Benford (2002) reports that peace activists employed gossip, rumor, ridicule, censorship, and ostracism in order to enforce socially constructed, identity boundaries associated with the movement's narrative. Benford (2002: 71) offers an explanation for the emergence of such intramural dynamics:

> Having carefully constructed a clear demarcation between the "good" folks and the "bad," movement adherents seek to preserve those distinctions. If it is suddenly revealed that the antagonist is actually good or that the protagonist is really not all that good, the movement story lacks narrative fidelity (Fisher 1984, 1987) and thus loses its "frame resonance" (Snow and Benford 1988). With these considerations in mind, it is apparent why collective identity is often the object of intramovement social control efforts.

Other researchers have arrived at similar conclusions. In his ethnographic study of the animal rights movement, Jagger (1992) found that in order to sustain the constructed collective identity, certain behaviors were required of the group's members. For example, movement members were expected to practice veganism (strict vegetarianism). Veganism helped to create solidarity in the movement by serving as a boundary marker between in-group and out-group members. This consumption practice not only united the members in their collective struggle against the dominant culture; it also served as a distinctive status marker within the movement by distinguishing between the truly committed and the less committed. Consistent with Kanter's (1968, 1972) earlier findings, Jagger concluded that long-term commitment to a movement will be greatest when participants are required to behave in ways that clearly distinguish them from nonmembers.

Joshua Gamson's (1997) research on two intramovement disputes involving the expulsion of some members provides additional evidence of the contested nature of collective identity construction processes. The International Lesbian and Gay Association expelled members of the North American Man/Boy Love Association from their group. Similarly, organizers of the Michigan Womyn's Music Festival excluded transsexuals from their annual event. Gamson (1997: 180) notes that such boundary contestation is part and parcel of identity construction processes: "The *us* is solidified not just against an external *them* but also against *thems* inside, as particular subgroups battle to gain or retain legitimate *us* standing." He concludes that "the 'achievement' of collective identity is inevitably tied to some degree of boundary patrol" (1997: 181). He asserts that there are sound sociological and strategic reasons for movements to engage in inclusion/exclusion practices:

> All social movements, and identity movements in particular, are thus in the business, at least sometimes, of exclusion. Their reasons, in addition to the general advantages of group solidarity, are good ones at both the strategic and expressive levels. In political systems that distribute rights and resources to groups with discernable boundaries, activists are smart to be vigilant about those boundaries; in cultural systems that develop so many identities, a movement with clarity about who belongs can better provide its designated members with the strength and pride to revalue their identities. (1997: 179)

Reger's (2002) research on the New York City chapter of the National Organization for Women (NOW) suggests that such exclusionary practices are not always necessary. She identifies the importance of interorganizational boundaries in collective identity construction. The NYC NOW chapter developed an organizational structure and culture that accommodated both the "political feminists" and the "empowerment feminists." Reger concludes that groups can avoid divisive factionalism by accommodating diverse ideologies and identities via structural and cultural adjustments that provide a legitimate role and space for the coexistence of disparate collective identities. Hunt's (1991) research on the peace movement in Nebraska during Gulf War I yielded similar conclusions. Nebraskans for Peace, a statewide peace and justice coalition, constructed a collective identity that emphasized "unity with diversity" (1991: 151).

Consciousness

"Boundaries locate persons as members of a group," Taylor and Whittier (1992: 114) point out, "but it is group consciousness that imparts a larger significance to a collectivity." Research indicates that group consciousness is constructed through a variety of mechanisms including talk, narratives, framing processes, emotion work, and interactions with antagonists among others. Before turning to the research pertaining to how group consciousness is constructed, it is worth pausing to ask "*which* group consciousness?"

Several social movement researchers have observed that collective identities are multilayered (Hunt 1991; Stoecker 1995; Jasper 1997; Rupp and Taylor 1999; Snow 2001; Reger 2002). William Gamson (1991), for example, identifies three layers. The broadest is the social movement community or solidary group – for example, all women as in relation to the women's movement. The next level is the movement layer – for example, as in the case of the women's movement as such. The third level is the organizational level – for example, the National Organization for Women in relation to the women's movement. While this distinction is useful, it is not exhaustive of all the layers to collective identities. For instance, a layer beneath national NOW could be a state organization, and under that might be a local chapter, and underneath that might be a steering committee. Drawing on her in-depth case study of the women's movement in Columbus, Ohio from 1969 to 1992, Whittier (1997) provides evidence to suggest that collective identities within a movement or movement organization might be based on cohort identification. The crucial point here is that any particular movement, indeed, probably any movement organization, has a multiplicity of collective identities.

The multiplicity of collective identities has special implications for "identity correspondence" – the alignment of personal and collective identities (Snow and McAdam 2000). Given the multiplicity of collective identities, the question is not simply is there a correspondence between an individual's personal identity and a collective identity. Rather, which collective identities among a constellation correspond with which personal identities? And how are these identity correspondences negotiated, managed, and experienced?

Although little research has been done that takes into account the multiplicity of collective and personal identities associated with social movement participation, scholars have sought to identify and elaborate various ways in which group consciousness is formed. Fundamentally, collective identities are *talked* into existence. In our research on the peace and justice movement (Hunt and Benford 1994), we found that personal and collective identities shape and are shaped by collective action and the subsequent identity talk (cf. Snow and Anderson 1987). In the course of engaging in and talking about various micromobilization activities, meanings are produced that facilitate the alignment of personal and collective identities, identity constructions, and convergences that condition future micromobilization efforts. Our research suggests that, in a variety of movement contexts, participants frequently engaged in identity talk that tended to revolve around four moments of identity construction: becoming aware, active, committed, and weary. These identity accounts accomplished several practical objectives, not the least of which was the development and maintenance of an oppositional consciousness.

In a similar vein, several researchers have studied how oppositional consciousness and solidarity can be constructed and sustained via movement narratives (Polletta 1998; Gongaware 2001; Nepstad 2001; Steward et al. 2002). Based on an in-depth study of participant narratives from the metaphysical movement, Steward et al. (2002) identified narratives of conversion, continuity, connection, and conflict that served to mark boundaries, identify out-groups, and create and sustain collective consciousness among adherents. Gongaware's (2001) research on Native American social movements reveals that various collective memory processes, most of which involve narratives or storytelling, augmented the construction of collective identities and also provided unity and continuity within the movements he studied. Still other researchers have gathered data on the use of narratives in creating transnational solidarity. Nepstad (2001), for instance, relates how the story of Salvadorian Archbishop Romero fostered solidarity between the progressive Central American Church and US Christians which in turn stimulated the construction of a transnational collective identity, one that prioritized religious identity over national allegiance. Finally, Diani (2000) studied the impact of computer-mediated communication on political activism and social movements. He found that such new technologies were more effective at enhancing existing bonds and solidarities than they were at creating new ones.

Another recurrent empirical finding is that collective identity can be imposed by outsiders and thus lead to the development of oppositional dynamics (Castells 1997; Kuumba 2001; Wieloch 2002). As Mansbridge (2001: 4–5) states, "oppositional consciousness is an empowering mental state that prepares members of an oppressed group to act to undermine, reform, or overthrow a system of human domination" (see also Morris 1992). However, as Whittier (2002: 302) reminds, collective identity is "shaped by forces external to the movement, but it is never a straightforward result of a shared location" (see also Taylor and Whittier 1995). This notion was reaffirmed by Joshua Gamson (1995) in his study of the lesbian and gay movements as well as queer politics. According to Gamson (1995: 390), the dialectic of the oppression and power of imposed identities is that "fixed identity categories are both the basis for oppression and the basis for political power."

Emphasizing an oppositional consciousness is to take a "relational approach" to collective identity construction (Robnett 2002). It suggests that collective identities emerge in conflictual interactional contexts and that collective identity functions as cultural capital to be deployed for personal as well as collective hegemonic resistance (Taylor and Raeburn 1995; Robnett 2002). From this view, Bernstein (1997) suggests that identity can be for empowerment, a goal in itself, and a strategy – a pattern that was apparent in the four lesbian and gay rights campaigns she studied.

A growing body of research suggests that both solidarity and commitment not only need to be conceived and enacted; they must be *felt* (e.g., Jasper 1997; Klatch 1999; Barker 2001; Berezin 2001; Goodwin et al. 2001; Goodwin and Pfaff 2001; Kane 2001; Young 2001). The dialectic constituting process between commitment, solidarity, and collective identity – a reciprocal shaping and being shaped by – is largely a matter of emotion work. Emotion work, which goes hand in hand with collective identity construction, is not a one-way street with only the movement participant making emotional investments. Rather, for solidarity and commitment to be realized, the impression that the collectivity is also emotionally invested must be conveyed. Kane (2001), for example, shows how metaphors of humiliation, shame, and sorrow were combined to raise consciousness among peasants in the Irish Land War of 1879–82, thereby contributing to the construction of solidarity and collective identity and subsequently inspiring militant actions. Young's (2001) historical analysis of the abolitionist (antislavery) movement in the 1830s further highlights the crucial role that emotions played, taking the form of moral shocks conveyed via religious revivals against "the sin of slavery," in transforming the consciousness of young evangelicals. Other researchers have found that loathing, shame, moral repulsion and indignation are not the only cluster of emotions relevant to collective identity construction and micromobilization. Nor are emotions fixed. In his study of the making of Solidarity at the Lenin Shipyard in Gdansk, Barker (2001: 193) found that, over the course of two weeks in August 1980 when Polish workers organized occupation strikes, emotional tones changed: "fear then laughter, doubt and pleasure, solidarity and contempt, solemn silences and fierce shouting, moments of panic and idylls."

Negotiation

Suffice it to say that the research reported thus far supports the general contention that collective identity is an interactional accomplishment. Reflecting this view, Melucci (1989: 34–5) elaborates on the interactive and thus negotiated dimensions of collective identity:

> Collective identity is an interactive and shared definition produced by several interacting individuals who are concerned with the orientations of their action as well as the field of opportunities and constraints in which their action takes place. The process of construct-ing, maintaining, and altering a collective identity provides the basis for actors to shape their expectations and calculate the costs and benefits of their action.... Collective identity is thus a process in which actors produce the common cognitive frameworks that enable them to assess their environment and to calculate the costs and benefits of their action. The definitions which they formulate are in part the result of negotiated interactions and relationships of influence and in part the fruit of emotional recognition.

Collective identity is not strictly an individual attribute. Rather, it is a cultural representation, a set of shared meanings that are produced and reproduced, negoti-ated and renegotiated, in the interactions of individuals embedded in particular sociocultural contexts.

Research indicates that collective identity not only emerges from the interactions of activists within a specific movement or movement organization, but it is also produced from the relationships between allies, those opposed to the movement in some fashion, and bystander audiences such as print and electronic news media (e.g., Einwohner 2002; Meyer 2002). These interactions have been conceptualized by Benford and Hunt (forthcoming) as "framing," "counterframing," and "reframing" processes between protagonist, antagonist, and audience "identity fields" (Hunt et al. 1994).

Einwohner's (2002) study of the animal rights movement, is illustrative. She concludes that the identity attacks by movement opponents and other outsiders helped shape activists' identity. Criticisms that they were "overly emotional" and "irrational" lead activists to engage in various "identity disconfirmation" and identity recasting" activities, responses that contributed to the negotiation of the movement's identity. We (Benford and Hunt forthcoming) report similar reactions by peace and justice movement activists in response to opponents' counterframing tactics. Antagonists' attacks frequently took the form of impugning the character of movement supporters, a direct attack on the collective identity initially fostered by the movement (e.g., "aiding and abetting the enemy," "dupes," "naive," etc.). Peace activists employed a variety of reframing techniques in response, including ignoring, keying, embracing, distancing, and counter-maligning. Such techniques served to sustain and repair apparently "spoiled or discredited movement identities (cf. Goffman 1963). Taken together, the findings from these studies support Taylor and Whittier's (1992) assertions that collective identities are negotiated, in part, as participants seek to resist negative definitions imposed by opponents.

Collective identity is not only negotiated by way of protagonist–antagonist interactions; it is also negotiated during the course of collective action and over the life course of a social movement (Taylor and Whittier 1992; Klandermans 1994; Melucci 1995; Klandermans and de Weerd 2000). Fantasia's (1988) research on grass-roots labor organizing in the United States indicates that various solidarity practices help to shape collective identity. In his study of the peaceful revolution that toppled East Germany's Communist regime in 1989, Pfaff (1996) acknowledges that collective identities situated in small-scale social networks can precede the formal organization of movements and are thus often antecedent to collective action. However, he also found that collective identity can be transformed by movement participation itself (1996: 99). He notes that risky collective action is greater when a relatively small group has a strong collective identity. But collective identity is also strengthened in the course of engaging in risky movement activities, a finding confirmed by Gould (1995) in his study of protest in Paris during the mid-nineteenth century.

Effects/Accomplishments of Collective Identity

As is the case with the wider social movement literature in general, we know far less about the effects of collective identity than we know about its emergence and maintenance. What little we know about the outcomes of collective identity is based on case studies and remains at a fairly speculative level. Nevertheless, there is some suggestive evidence indicating that movement collective identities increase commitment and solidarity, yield biographical consequences, and contribute to a backlash and social control.

Building Commitment and Solidarity

One rather consistent finding is that collective identities facilitate commitment by enhancing the bonding to leadership, belief systems, organizations, rituals, cohorts, networks, and localities (Harrison 1977; Oliver 1983; Hirsch 1986, 1990; Downton and Wehr 1991, 1997; Gould 1995; Whittier 1997; Passy and Giugni 2000). In their study of persistent peace activists, Downton and Wehr (1997) found that persisters (i.e., those who remained active for five or more years) creatively and actively managed commitment, in part by shaping the circumstances of their lives for long-term peace work. The fostering of deep and enduring commitment to a cause and thus sustained participation is more likely to occur when activists remain imbedded in social networks relevant to the cause, especially when they develop and maintain a symbolic linkage between their activism and their personal lives (Passy and Giugni 2000). Gould (1995) reiterates the importance of one's immediate lifeworld, concluding that even when large-scale coalitions are formed between informal community networks and formal organizations, the primary solidarity of most movement actors is local. Finally, Jagger's (1992) previously cited work on the animal rights movement also suggests that commitment results from the construction of a distinctive collective identity.

Biographical Consequences

A significant body of evidence indicates that participation in social movements can lead to enduring changes in personal identities, transformations that persist after the movement, or at least its heyday, has ended (Rupp and Taylor 1987; McAdam 1988; Whalen and Flacks 1989; Klandermans 1994; Taylor and Raeburn 1995; Whittier 1995, 1997; Downton and Wehr 1997; Robnett 1997; Young 2001; see chapter 21 in this volume). Former movement participants change not only the way they see themselves, but also the way they view the world, the occupations they pursue, their consumption patterns, and the friends they make. According to Polletta and Jasper (2001: 296), such movement-generated biographical transformations not only occur among "people whose active participation was of long duration or high intensity," but also among "many casual participants."

Backlash and Social Control

As we noted above, the construction and deployment of collective identities often generates a counter response from movement opponents. This backlash can in turn spawn renewed attempts by dominant groups to reassert their power and to institute new forms of social control. Zuo and Benford (1995), for example, found that when students in the 1989 Chinese democracy movement constructed a resonant collective identity grounded in traditional Chinese values, a collective identity that seemed resilient to state attempts to counter it rhetorically, the authorities responded with massive lethal force. Other backlashes take the form of active countermovements. For instance, a series of victories by the animal rights movement lead the biomedical community to construct a new public identity, one that emphasized its contributions to helping find cures for and relieving the suffering of sick people, especially children, rather than focusing on the less resonant abstraction of scientific progress (Jasper and Poulsen 1993; Jasper 1997; Polletta and Jasper 2001). Similar backlash dynamics have been observed in reaction to the peace, women's, and antinuclear power movements (Faludi 1991; Jasper 1997; Benford and Hunt forthcoming). For instance, pro-nuclear citizens in the Oak Ridge, Tennessee, community developed a collective identity in response to the antinuclear movement's attacks on Oak Ridge Laboratory (Shriver et al. 2000). Shriver and his colleagues show how the counter-movement's collective identity successfully suppressed the movement's health grievances and inhibited future mobilization on the part of the antinuclear movement.

CONCLUSION

In this chapter we have sought to provide an analytical review of collective identity in the context of micromobilization of participation, including discussion of its relationships to solidarity and commitment. Collective identity is conceptualized as individuals' identifications of, identifications with, and attachments to some collectivity in cognitive, emotional, and moral terms. Rooted in and shaped by particular sociocultural contexts, collective identities are produced and reproduced in ongoing interactions between allies, oppositional forces, and audiences who can be real or imagined. While providing a sense of we-ness and collective agency, collective identities also create a sense of other via boundary identification, construction, and maintenance. Collective identities, as shared meanings, provide cultural contexts for planning, enabling, carrying out, and evaluating individual participation and collective actions. Collective identity is closely related to but yet distinct from other concepts such as ideology, personal identity, participation, solidarity, and commitment.

Our review suggests that notions of collective identity can be traced to classical late nineteenth and early twentieth century theorists as well as pioneering social-psychological work in Europe and the United States. Also, interest in collective identity has intensified in the last two decades, yielding scores of theoretical and empirical studies. In our assessment, we believe that despite the longstanding intellectual interest in collective identity and related concepts, despite the recent deluge of work exploring and refining collective identity concepts, and despite our own scholarly pursuits revolving around collective identity, much work remains to be done. For instance, while significant progress has been made, a great deal of conceptual haziness is still associated with collective identity, solidarity, and commitment. What is needed is the advancement of comprehensive, systematic theories of collective action that incorporate and distinguish such concepts as collective identity, solidarity, and commitment. The literature suggests that this trio of concepts presents some intriguing possibilities in terms of developing a comprehensive perspective. To elaborate, commitment focuses attention on individuals' investments in personal lines of action that are consistent with lines of action advanced by a collectivity. Commitment helps to illuminate the individual-collectivity nexus by concentrating primarily on individual activists. In contrast, solidarity calls attention to the degree to which social cohesion exists within and between groups. Solidarity explores the individual-collectivity nexus by focusing primarily on collectivities as such. Collective identity suggests that a group of individuals with common interests, values, feelings, and goals exist in time and space beyond the here and now. Collective identity therefore includes commitment's emphasis on individuals, solidarity's accent on collectivities, as well as highlighting broader, macrosocial structures and dynamics that go beyond movement collectivities, including those that help shape and/or provide interests, political contexts, cultural symbols, goals, and so forth. We believe that this trio of concepts could form the basis of a systematic, comprehensive theory that synthesizes psychological, social-psychological and macrosociological perspectives.

We suggest that the emergence of theories with greater conceptual clarity and comprehensiveness will occur in conjunction with further empirical contributions. Our review of extant empirical contributions supports this claim. While there has been a wealth of research contributions, some broad empirical questions still need to be explored. For instance, some research, particularly studies of new social movements, suggests that movement collective action grows directly from collective identities. Others show that collective identities emerge from movement collective action. From our view, we suspect that both sets of findings are accurate. However, there has not been research that examines the reciprocal relationships between movement collective action and collective identity construction. Indeed, the case study data suggest clear associations between movement collective action and collective identities, but they have not revealed empirically the causal mechanisms at work. Similarly, while there is agreement and some evidence that the alignment of personal and collective identities is crucial for individual participation, there are insufficient data to illuminate exactly how and why this occurs.

In sum, collective identity and related concepts, such as solidarity and commitment, have been at the center of some of the most intriguing advances in recent social movement scholarship. Perhaps more importantly, collective identity and related constructs can help fashion answers to psychological, social-psychological, and macrosociological questions pertaining to social movements.

References

Armstrong, Elizabeth A. (2002) *Forging Gay Identities: Organizing Sexuality in San Francisco, 1950–1994*. Chicago: University of Chicago Press.

Augoustinos, Martha (1995) Social Representations and Ideology: Towards the Study of Ideological Representations. In U. Flick (ed.), *The Psychology of the Social: Language and Social Knowledge in Social Psychology*. Reinbek: Rowohlt, 156–69.

Avineri, Shlomo (1968) *The Social and Political Thought of Karl Marx*. Cambridge, MA: Cambridge University Press.

Barker, Colin (2001) Fear, Laughter, and Collective Power: The Making of Solidarity at the Lenin Shipyard in Gdansk, Poland, August 1980. In J. Goodwin, J. M. Jasper, and F. Polletta (eds.), *Passionate Politics: Emotions and Social Movements*. Chicago: University of Chicago Press, 175–94.

Becker, Anne E. (1995) *Body, Self, and Society: The View from Fiji*. Philadelphia: University of Pennsylvania Press.

Becker, Howard S. (1960) Notes on the Concept of Commitment. *American Journal of Sociology*, 66, 32–40.

Benford, Robert D. (1993) Frame Disputes within the Nuclear Disarmament Movement. *Social Forces*, 71, 677–701.

——(2002) Controlling Narratives and Narratives as Control within Social Movements. In J. E. Davis (ed.), *Stories of Change: Narrative and Social Movements*. Albany: State University of New York Press, 58–79.

Benford, Robert D., and Scott A. Hunt (1992) Dramaturgy and Social Movements: The Social Construction and Communication of Power. *Sociological Inquiry*, 62, 36–55.

——(forthcoming) Interactional Dynamics in Public Problems Marketplace: Movements and the Counterframing and Reframing of Public Problems. In G. Miller and J. A. Holstein, *Constructionist Controversies*. Hawthorne, NY: Aldine.

Benford, Robert D., and David A. Snow (2000) Framing Processes and Social Movements: An Overview and Assessment. *Annual Review of Sociology*, 26, 611–39.

Benford, Robert D., and Louis A. Zurcher (1990) Instrumental and Symbolic Competition among Peace Movement Organizations. In S. Marullo and J. Lofland (eds.), *Peace Action in the Eighties: Social Science Perspectives*. New Brunswick, NJ: Rutgers University Press.

Berezin, Mabel (2001) Emotions and Political Identity: Mobilizing Affection for the Party. In J. Goodwin, J. M. Jasper, and F. Polletta (eds.), *Passionate Politics: Emotions and Social Movements*. Chicago: University of Chicago Press, 83–98.

Berger, Peter L. (1966) Identity as a Problem in the Sociology of Knowledge. *European Journal of Sociology*, 7, 105–15.

Berger, Peter L., and Thomas Luckmann (1966) *The Social Construction of Reality: A Treatise in the Sociology of Knowledge*. New York: Doubleday.

Bernstein, Mary (1997) Celebration and Suppression: The Strategic Uses of Identity by the Lesbian and Gay Movement. *American Journal of Sociology*, 103, 537–65.

Billing, Michael (1991) *Ideology, Rhetoric, and Opinions*. Thousand Oaks, CA: Sage.

——(1992) *Talking of the Royal Family*. London: Routledge.

Blumer, Herbert G. (1939) Collective Behavior. In R. E. Park (ed.), *An Outline of the Principles of Sociology*. New York: Barnes & Noble, 221–80.

——(1969) *Symbolic Interactionism*. Englewood Cliffs, NJ: Transaction.

Bordo, Susan (1993) *Unbearable Weight: Feminism, Western Culture, and the Body*. Berkeley: University of California Press.

Calhoun, Craig (ed.) (1994) *Social Theory and the Politics of Identity*. Oxford: Blackwell.

——(1997) *Nationalism*. Minneapolis: University of Minnesota Press.

Castells, Manuel (1997) *The Power of Identity*. Oxford: Blackwell.

Cerulo, Karen A. (1997) Identity Construction: New Issues, New Directions. *Annual Review of Sociology*, 23, 385–409.

Cohen, G. A. (1978) *Karl Marx's Theory of History: A Defence*. Oxford: Clarendon.

Cohen, Jean L. (1982) Between Crisis Management and Social Movements: The Place of Institutional Reform. *Telos*, 52, 21–40.

——(1985) Strategy or Identity: New Theoretical Paradigms and Contemporary Social Movements. *Social Research*, 52, 663–716.

Dalton, Russell J., and Manfred Kuechler (eds.) (1990) *Challenging the Political Order: New Social and Political Movements in Western Democracies*. Oxford: Oxford University Press.

della Porta, Donatella, and Mario Diani (1999) *Social Movements: An Introduction*. Malden, MA: Blackwell.

Diani, Mario (2000) Social Movement Networks Virtual and Real. *Information, Communication, and Society*, 3, 386–401.

Douglas, Mary (1973) *Natural Symbols: Explorations in Cosmology*. New York: Vintage.

Downton, James Jr., and Paul Wehr (1991) Peace Movements: The Role of Commitment in Sustaining Member Participation. *Research in Social Movements, Conflicts and Change*, 13, 113–34.

——(1997) *The Persistent Activist: How Peace Commitment Develops and Survives*. Boulder, CO: Westview.

Durkheim, Emile (1964) *The Division of Labor*. New York: Free Press.

——(1965) *The Elementary Forms of Religious Life*. New York: Free Press.

Eder, Klaus (1982) A New Social Movement? *Telos*, 52, 5–20.

Einwohner, Rachel L. (2002) Bringing the Outsiders in: Opponents' Claims and the Construction of Animal Rights Activists' Identity. *Mobilization: An International Journal*, 7, 253–268.

Faludi, Susan (1991) *Backlash*. New York: Crown.

Fantasia, Rick (1988) *Cultures of Solidarity*. Berkeley: University of California Press.

——(2001) The Myth of the Labor Movement. In Judith R. Blau (ed.), *The Blackwell Companion to Sociology*. Malden, MA: Blackwell, 450–63.

Farr, Robert M. (1996) *The Roots of Modern Social Psychology: 1872–1954*. Oxford: Blackwell.

Farr, Robert M., and Serge Moscovici (eds.) (1984) *Social Representations*. Cambridge: Cambridge University Press.

Fireman, Bruce, and William A. Gamson (1979) Utilitarian Logic in the Resource Mobilization Perspective. In M. N. Zald and J. D. McCarthy (eds.), *The Dynamics of Social Movements*. Cambridge, MA: Winthrop, 8–45.

Foote, Nelson N. (1951) Identification as the Basis for a Theory of Motivation. *American Sociological Review*, 16, 14–21.

Foucault, Michel (1980) *A History of Sexuality*. New York: Vintage.

Gamson, Joshua (1995) Must Identity Movements Self-Destruct? A Queer Dilemma. *Social Problems*, 42, 390–407.

——(1997) Messages of Exclusion: Gender, Movements, and Symbolic Boundaries. *Gender and Society*, 11, 178–99.

Gamson, William (1991) Commitment and Agency in Social Movements. *Sociological Forum*, 6, 27–50.

——(1992) Social Psychology of Collective Action. In A. D. Morris and C. M. Mueller (eds.), *Frontiers in Social Movement Theory*. New Haven, CT: Yale University Press, 53–76.

Giddens, Anthony (1991) *Modernity and Self-Identity: Self and Society in the Late Modern Age*. Cambridge: Polity.

——(1994) *Beyond Left and Right: The Future of Radical Politics*. Cambridge: Polity.

Glassner, Barry (1992) *Bodies: Overcoming the Tyranny of Perfection*. Los Angeles: Lowell House.

Goffman, Erving (1963) *Stigma: Notes on the Management of Spoiled Identities*. Englewood Cliffs, NJ: Prentice-Hall.

——(1971) *Relations in Public*. New York: Basic.

Gongaware, Timothy Brooks (2001) Finding the Memory in Identity: Native American Social Movements Challenging Educational Institutions. PhD dissertation, University of Nebraska.

Goodwin, Jeff, and Steven Pfaff (2001) Emotion Work in High-Risk Social Movements: Managing Fear in the U.S. and East German Civil Rights Movements. In J. Goodwin, J. M. Jasper, and F. Polletta (eds.), *Passionate Politics: Emotions and Social Movements*. Chicago: University of Chicago Press, 282–300.

Goodwin, Jeff, James M. Jasper, and Francesca Polletta (2001) Why Emotions Matter. In J. Goodwin, J. M. Jasper, and F. Polletta (eds.), *Passionate Politics: Emotions and Social Movements*. Chicago: University of Chicago Press, 1–24.

Gould, Roger V. (1995) *Insurgent Identities: Class, Community, and Protest in Paris from 1848 to the Commune*. Chicago: University of Chicago Press.

Gusfield, Joseph R. (1963) *Symbolic Crusade: Status Politics and the American Temperance Movement*. Urbana: University of Illinois Press.

——(1981) *The Culture of Public Problems: Drinking-Driving and the Symbolic Order*. Chicago: University of Chicago Press.

Habermas, Jürgen (1981) New Social Movements. *Telos*, 49, 33–7.

——(1984) *The Theory of Communicative Action*. Vol. 1, *Reason and Rationalization of Society*. Cambridge: Polity.

——(1987) *The Theory of Communicative Action*. Vol. 2, *The Critique of Functionalist Reason*. Cambridge: Polity.

Harrison, Michael (1977) Dimensions of Involvement in Social Movements. *Sociological Focus*, 10, 353–66.

Hirsch, Eric L. (1986) The Creation of Political Solidarity in Social Movement Organizations. *Sociological Quarterly*, 27, 372–87.

——(1990) Sacrifice for the Cause: The Impact of Group Processes on Recruitment and Commitment in Protest Movements. *American Sociological Review*, 55, 243–55.

Hogg, Michael A., and Dominic Abrams (1999) Social Identity and Social Cognition: Historical Background and Current Trends. In D. Abrams and M. A. Hogg (eds.), *Social Identity and Social Cognition*. Oxford: Blackwell, 1–25.

Hunt, Scott A. (1991) Constructing Collective Identity in a Peace Movement Organization. PhD dissertation, University of Nebraska.

——(2000) Social Psychology and Narrative Concepts: Explaining Individual Movement Participation. *Perspectives on Social Problems*, 12, 255–90.

Hunt, Scott A., and Robert D. Benford (1994) Identity Talk in the Peace and Justice Movement. *Journal of Contemporary Ethnography*, 22, 488–517.

Hunt, Scott A., Robert D. Benford, and David A. Snow (1994) Identity Fields: Framing Processes and the Social Construction of Movement Identities. In E. Laraña, H. Johnston, and J. R. Gusfield (eds.), *New Social Movements: From Ideology to Identity*. Philadelphia, PA: Temple University Press, 185–208.

Jagger, Lake J. S. (1992) Collective Identity at an Animal Rights Sanctuary. Paper presented at the Annual Meetings of the American Sociological Association.

Jasper, James M. (1997) *The Art of Moral Protest: Culture, Biography, and Creativity in Social Movements*. Chicago: University of Chicago Press.

Jasper, James M., and Jane Poulsen (1993) Fighting Back: Vulnerabilities, Blunders, and Countermobilization by the Targets in Three Animal Rights Campaigns. *Sociological Forum*, 8, 639–57.

Johnston, Hank, Enrique Laraña, and Joseph R. Gusfield (eds.) (1994) Identities, Grievances, and New Social Movements. In E. Laraña, H. Johnston, and J. R. Gusfield (eds.), *New Social Movements: From Ideology to Identity*. Philadelphia, PA: Temple University Press, 5–35.

Jones, Edward E. (1985) Major Developments in Social Psychology During the Past Five Decades. In G. Lindzey and E. Aronson (eds.), *Handbook of Social Psychology*. Vol. 1. New York: Academic, 47–107.

Kane, Anne (2001) Finding Emotion in Social Movement Processes: Irish Land Movement Metaphors and Narratives. In J. Goodwin, J. M. Jasper, and F. Polletta (eds.), *Passionate Politics: Emotions and Social Movements*. Chicago: University of Chicago Press, 251–66.

Kanter, Rosabeth M. (1968) Commitment and Social Organization: A Study of Commitment Mechanisms in Utopian Communities. *American Sociological Review*, 33, 499–517.

——(1972) *Commitment and Community: Communes and Utopias in Sociological Perspective*. Cambridge, MA: Harvard University Press.

Kelly-Fikohazi, Christine (1997) No Map, No Compass, No Dime. *Peace Review*, 9, 481–7.

Kitschelt, Herbert (1985) New Social Movements in West Germany and the United States. *Political Power and Social Theory*, 5, 273–324.

Klandermans, Bert (1994) Transient Identities? In E. Laraña, H. Johnston, and J. R. Gusfield (eds.), *New Social Movements: From Ideology to Identity*. Philadelphia, PA: Temple University Press, 168–84.

Klandermans, Bert, and Marga de Weerd (2000) Group Identification and Political Protest. In S. Stryker, T. J. Owens, and R. W. White (eds.), *Self, Identity, and Social Movements*. Minneapolis: University of Minnesota Press, 68–90.

Klapp, Orrin E. (1969) *Collective Search for Identity*. New York: Holt, Rinehart, & Winston.

Klatch, Rebecca E. (1999) *A Generation Divided: The New Left, the New Right, and the 1960s*. Berkeley: University of California Press.

Kriesi, Hanspeter, Ruud Koopmans, Jan Willem Duyvendak, and Marco G. Giugni (1995) *New Social Movements in Western Europe: A Comparative Analysis*. Minneapolis: University of Minnesota Press.

Kuumba, M. Bahati (2001) *Gender and Social Movements*. Walnut Creek, CA: Alta Mira.

Kuumba, M. Bahati, and Femi Ajanaku (1998) The Hair Aesthetics of Cultural Resistance and Collective Identity Formation. *Mobilization*, 3, 227–43.

Lichterman, Paul (1996) *The Search for Political Community*. Cambridge: Cambridge University Press.

——(1999) Talking Identity in the Public Sphere: Broad Visions and Small Spaces in Sexual Identity. *Theory and Society*, 28, 101–41.

Lukacs, Georg (1971) *History and Class Consciousness*. London: Merlin.

McAdam, Doug (1988) *Freedom Summer.* New York: Oxford University Press.

McCarthy, John D., and Mayer Zald (1977) Resource Mobilization and Social Movements: A Partial Theory. *American Journal of Sociology,* 82, 1212–41.

Mainwaring, Scott, and Eduardo Viola (1984) New Social Movements, Political Culture, and Democracy: Brazil and Argentina. *Telos,* 61, 17–52.

Mansbridge, Jane (2001) The Making of Oppositional Consciousness. In J. Mansbridge and A. Morris (eds.), *Oppositional Consciousness: The Subjective Roots of Social Protest.* Chicago: University of Chicago Press, 1–19.

Marx, Karl, and Friedrich Engels (1970) *The German Ideology.* New York: International.

Mead, George Herbert (1934) *Mind, Self, and Society.* Chicago: University of Chicago Press.

Melucci, Alberto (1980) The New Social Movements: A Theoretical Approach. *Social Science Information,* 19, 199–226.

—— (1985) The Symbolic Challenge of Contemporary Movements. *Social Research,* 52, 789–816.

—— (1988) Getting Involved: Identity and Mobilization in Social Movements. *International Social Movements Research,* 1, 329–48.

—— (1989) *Nomads of the Present.* Philadelphia, PA: Temple University Press.

—— (1995) The Process of Collective Identity. In E. Laraña, H. Johnston, and J. R. Gusfield (eds.), *New Social Movements: From Ideology to Identity.* Philadelphia, PA: Temple University Press, 101–30.

—— (1996) *Challenging Codes: Collective Action in the Information Age.* New York: Cambridge University Press.

Meyer, David S. (2002) Opportunities and Identities: Bridge Building in the Study of Social Movements. In D. S. Meyer, N. Whittier, and B. Robnett (eds.), *Social Movements: Identity, Culture, and the State.* New York: Oxford University Press, 3–21.

Morris, Aldon D. (1992) Political Consciousness and Collective Action. In A. D. Morris and C. M. Mueller (eds.), *Frontiers in Social Movement Theory.* New Haven: Yale University Press, 351–73.

Moscovici, Serge (1981) On Social Representations. In J. P. Forgas (ed.), *Social Cognition: Perspectives on Everyday Understandings.* London: Academic, 181–209.

Moscovici, Serge, and W. Doise (1994) *Conflict and Consensus: A General Theory of Collective Decisions.* London: Sage.

Nepstad, Sharon Erickson (2001) Creating Transnational Solidarity: The Use of the Narrative in the U.S. Central America Peace Movement. *Mobilization,* 6, 21–36.

Offe, Claus (1985) New Social Movements: Challenging the Boundaries of Institutional Politics. *Social Research,* 52, 817–68.

Oliver, Pamela (1983) The Mobilization of Paid and Volunteer Activists in the Neighborhood Movement. *Research in Social Movements, Conflicts and Change,* 5, 133–70.

Passy, Florence, and Marco Giugni (2000) Life-Spheres, Networks, and Sustained Participation in Social Movements: A Phenomenological Approach to Political Commitment. *Sociological Forum,* 15, 117–44.

Pfaff, Steven (1996) Collective Identity and Informal Groups in Revolutionary Mobilization: East Germany in 1989. *Social Forces,* 75, 91–118.

Phelan, Shane (1989) *Identity Politics: Lesbian Feminism and the Limits of Community.* Philadelphia, PA: Temple University Press.

Pizzorno, Alessandro (1978) Political Exchange and Collective Identity in Industrial Conflict. In C. Crouch and A. Pizzorno (eds.), *The Resurgence of Class Conflict in Western Europe since 1968.* New York: Holmes & Meier, 277–98.

Polletta, Francesca (1998) "It Was Like a Fever...": Narrative and Identity in Social Protest. *Social Problems,* 45, 137–59.

Polletta, Francesca, and James M. Jasper (2001) Collective Identity and Social Movements. *Annual Review of Sociology,* 27, 283–305.

Reger, Jo (2002) More than One Feminism: Organizational Structure and the Construction of Collective Identity. In D. S. Meyer, N. Whittier, and B. Robrett (eds.), *Social Movements: Identity, Culture, and the State*. New York: Oxford University Press, 241–86.

Robnett, Belinda (1997) *How Long, How Long? African American Women in the Struggle for Civil Rights*. New York: Oxford University Press.

——(2002) External Political Change, Collective Identities, and Participation in Social Movement Organizations. In D. S. Meyer, N. Whittier, and B. Robrett (eds.), *Social Movements: Identity, Culture, and the State*. New York: Oxford University Press, 287–301.

Rupp, Lelia, and Verta Taylor (1987) *Survival in the Doldrums: The American Women's Rights Movement, 1945 to the 1960s*. New York: Oxford University Press.

——(1999) Feminist Identity in an International Movement: A Collective Identity Approach to Twentieth-Century Feminism. *Signs*, 24, 363–86.

Ryan, Barbara (ed.) (2001) *Identity Politics in the Women's Movement*. New York: Widener.

Sanders, Jimmy (2002) Ethnic Boundaries and Identity in Plural Societies. *Annual Review of Sociology*, 28, 327–57.

Shriver, Thomas E., Sherry Cable, Lachelle Norris, and Donald W. Hastings (2000) The Role of Collective Identity in Inhibiting Mobilization: Solidarity and Suppression in Oak Ridge. *Sociological Spectrum*, 20, 41–64.

Silver, Ira (1997) Constructing "Social Change" through Philanthropy: Boundary Framing and the Articulation of Vocabularies of Motive for Social Movement Participation. *Sociological Inquiry*, 67, 488–503.

Snow, David A. (1993) *Shakubuku: A Study of the Nichiren Shoshu Buddhist Movement in America, 1960–1975*. New York: Garland.

——(2001) Collective Identity and Expressive Forms. In N. J. Smelser and P. B. Baltes (eds.), *International Encyclopedia of the Social and Behavioral Sciences*. London: Elsevier Science, 196–254.

Snow, David A., and Leon Anderson (1987) Identity Work among the Homeless: The Verbal Construction and Avowal of Personal Identities. *American Journal of Sociology*, 92, 2212–19.

Snow, David A., and Robert D. Benford (1988) Ideology, Frame Resonance, and Participant Mobilization. *International Social Movements Research*, 1, 197–217.

Snow, David A., and Doug McAdam (2000) Identity Work Processes in the Context of Social Movements: Clarifying the Identity/Movement Nexus. In S. Stryker, T. J. Owens, and R. W. White (eds.), *Self, Identity, and Social Movements*. Minneapolis: University of Minnesota Press, 41–67.

Steward, Gary A. Jr., Thomas E. Shriver, and Amy L. Chasteen (2002) Participant Narratives and Collective Identity in a Metaphysical Movement. *Sociological Spectrum*, 22, 107–35.

Stoecker, Randy (1995) Community, Movement, Organization: The Problem of Identity Convergence in Collective Action. *Sociological Quarterly*, 36, 111–30.

Stone, Gregory P. (1962) Appearance and the Self. In A. M. Rose (ed.), *Human Behavior and Social Processes*. Boston, MA: Houghton Mifflin, 86–118.

Stryker, Sheldon, Timothy J. Owen, and Robert W. White (eds.) (2000) *Self, Identity, and Social Movements*. Minneapolis: University of Minnesota Press.

Tarrow, Sidney (1986) Comparing Social Movement Participation in Western Europe and the United States: Problems, Uses, Examples, and a Proposal for Synthesis. *Journal of Mass Emergencies and International Disasters*, 4, 145–70.

Taylor, Verta (1989) Social Movement Continuity: The Women's Movement in Abeyance. *American Sociological Review*, 54, 761–75.

Taylor, Verta, and Nicole C. Raeburn (1995) Identity Politics as High-Risk Activism: Career Consequences for Lesbian, Gay, and Bisexual Sociologists. *Social Problems*, 42, 252–73.

Taylor, Verta, and Nancy E. Whittier (1992) Collective Identity in Social Movement Communities: Lesbian Feminist Mobilization. In A. D. Morris and C. M. Mueller (eds.), *Frontiers in Social Movement Theory*. New Haven: Yale University Press, 104–29.

——(1995) Analytical Approaches to Social Movement Culture: The Culture of the Women's Movement. In H. Johnston and B. Klandermans (eds.), *Social Movements and Culture*, Minneapolis: University of Minnesota Press, 163–87.

Touraine, Alain (1985) An Introduction to the Study of Social Movements. *Social Research*, 52, 749–88.

Turner, Bryan (1996) *The Body and Society: Exploration in Social Theory*. Thousand Oaks, CA: Sage.

Turner, Ralph, and Lewis M. Killian (1987) *Collective Behavior*. 3rd ed. Englewood Cliffs, NJ: Prentice-Hall.

Weber, Max (1978) *Economy and Society*. Berkeley: University of California Press.

Whalen, Jack, and Richard Flacks (1989) *Beyond the Barricades: The Sixties Generation Grows up*. Philadelphia, PA: Temple University Press.

Whittier, Nancy (1995) *Feminist Generations: The Persistence of the Radical Women's Movement*. Philadelphia, PA: Temple University Press.

——(1997) Political Generations: Micro-Cohorts and the Transformation of Social Movements. *American Sociological Review*, 62, 760–78.

——(2002) Meaning and Structure in Social Movements. In D. S. Meyer, N. Whittier, and B. Robnett (eds.), *Social Movements: Identity, Culture, and the State*. New York: Oxford University Press, 24–48.

Wieloch, Neil (2002) Collective Mobilization and Identity from the Underground: The Deployment of Oppositonal Capital in the Harm Reduction Movement. *Sociological Quarterly*, 43, 45–72.

Wright, Erik Olin (2002) The Shadow of Exploitation in Weber's Class Analysis. *American Sociological Review*, 57, 832–53.

Young, Michael P. (2001) A Revolution of the Soul: Transformative Experiences and Immediate Abolition. In J. Goodwin, J. M. Jasper, and F. Polletta (eds.), *Passionate Politics: Emotions and Social Movements*. Chicago: University of Chicago Press, 99–114.

Zuo, Jiping, and Robert D. Benford (1995) Mobilization Processes and the 1989 Chinese Democracy Movement. *Sociological Quarterly*, 36, 131–56.

Zurcher, Louis A., and David A. Snow (1981) Collective Behavior: Social Movements. In M. Rosenberg and R. H. Turner (eds.), *Social Psychology: Sociological Perspectives*. New York: Basic Books, 131–56.

Part V

Consequences and Outcomes

20

The Legislative, Organizational, and Beneficiary Consequences of State-Oriented Challengers

Edwin Amenta and Neal Caren

After years of neglect, scholars have now turned their attention to the consequences of social movements (compare the reviews of McAdam et al. 1988 with Giugni 1998; see also Amenta et al. 1999; Cress and Snow 2000; Earl 2000; Amenta et al. 2002; Meyer forthcoming). Much of this work has focused on the external consequences of social movements, especially those relating to states and struggles over legislation. This is not surprising as many challengers come into being to alter the relationship between states and specific groups, and other challengers often require some state action in order to further their cultural or other goals that are not mainly state related. Despite this recent work, a recent review (Giugni 1998) suggests that research findings have yet to accumulate at the same pace as in other areas in social movement research.

Perhaps part of the reason is that there are many different potential consequences of social movements and trying to make sense of the state-related consequences alone raises specific and difficult conceptual, theoretical, and methodological issues. Conceptually speaking, scholars have to address the meaning of "success" or "influence" for challengers that make state-related claims. It may be more difficult to forge agreement on this issue than on other concepts movement scholars address, such as resource mobilization, participation, or collective identity. The possible consequences of social movements are many, and scholars' understandings of them have tended to be broad and not tailored to fit state-related circumstances. Theoretically, scholars need to address what matters – beyond some degree of mobilization and plausible claims-making – in explaining the state-related impacts of challengers. Each is necessary, but neither seems sufficient to realize gains for challengers addressing states. In comparison to mobilizing supporters, fashioning identities among them, or achieving recognition from targets, most state-related consequences of challengers are not as directly related to the efforts expended by challengers;

explaining challengers' state-related consequences requires addressing and under-standing other actors inside and outside states who may be pressing in similar or different directions, considerably complicating the issue. Methodologically, scholars need to assess the individual impact of challengers or their impact in interaction with the other many potential influences on state outcomes. Causal arguments in this area can be complicated, making assessing them more difficult. Yet because it is already difficult to study phenomena as evanescent and often poorly recorded as social movements, scholars often engage in case studies that place informational restrictions on the appraisal of their arguments.

In this chapter we review the literature on state-oriented and legislative consequences of social movements as they apply to a variety of beneficiary groups and movement organizations. In doing so we address the ways that scholars of social movements have approached the peculiar conceptual, theoretical, and methodological issues in understanding these state-related consequences. In our review we also refer to the comparative academic literature on policymaking – which indicates that social movements usually play a minor role, with other factors, such as political institutions, party systems and actors, and public opinion, held to be more important (see Baumgartner and Jones 1993; Burstein 1998; Hicks 1999; Huber and Stephens 2001; reviews in Amenta et al. 2001; Amenta 2003). These studies are often comparative or follow policy for long periods of time, or both, whereas most studies about social movements concern one country or one movement or challenger over a relatively brief period of time. Complicated though the issues surrounding the state-related consequences of challengers are, we offer suggestions for ways of addressing them.

Before going further, it is worth saying that we see the impact of states on social movements as a recursive process (Amenta et al. 2002; Meyer forthcoming; see also Soule et al. 1999). States influence social movements, which always are begun in a political context that favors action in some times and places rather than others, that favors certain forms of organization and lines of actions over others, and certain types of political identities over others. States, and some other longstanding political institutions like political parties, tend to dwarf social movements in terms of size, resources, and power, and the structure and activities of states influence lines of organization and action among movements by making some more likely to be productive than others. Social movements in turn attempt to influence states by mobilizing people and resources and claims around specific strategic lines of action. Challengers contest state policies, laws, bureaucracies, rules, and institutions in order to make gains for those whom they represent. This collective action in turn often influences the state through legislation. For analytical reasons and the purposes of this volume we mainly discuss the second process below.

STATE-RELATED CONSEQUENCES OF SOCIAL MOVEMENTS: CONCEPTUAL ISSUES

Despite the fact that many challengers are mainly state-oriented or have important goals or claims that require state action, states are not typically well conceptualized as a target of social movement activity. For the most part, the academic literature on the consequences of social movements concerns either the successes or failures of challengers, as they perceive them and in a broad way. These successes and failures generally refer to new benefits and recognition generated from various targets. In what follows, we discuss this literature as it applies to states and the political process and refer explicitly to new advantages through states, especially through legislative activity relating to the beneficiary groups of challengers, as well as recognition or representation through states as they apply to movement organizations. These conceptual issues are important to making sense of what scholars seek to explain regarding the state-related consequences of social movements.

"Success," "New Advantages," "Acceptance," "Power," and "Collective Goods"

In designating the consequences of social movements, William Gamson's (1975, 1990) two types of success greatly influenced later studies and have since been modified by scholars focusing on state-related consequences of social movements. Gamson considers success in new advantages, his first type, as meaning whether a challenger's goals or claims were mainly realized. Burstein et al. (1995) modify this program-based understanding of new advantages by applying it to state action. They see a state-oriented challenger as being successful in this way according to the degree to which it gets its legislation based on its program on the political agenda, influences its passage into policy, or helps to ensure its enforcement, as well as the degree to which the legislation has intended effects (see also Banaszak 1996). Acceptance, Gamson's second type, was gained when a challenger was recognized as a legitimate representative of a constituency by the target of collective action, altering the relationship between a challenging organization and the groups it attempts to influence. For Gamson's state-oriented challengers, this meant some basic acknowledgment by governmental officials that the challenger was legitimate. Other scholars have pressed further in specifically addressing access to the state, including specifying "procedural" gains (Kitschelt 1986) and "representation" (Cress and Snow 2000). Yet others propose an additional dimension of "structural" gains (Kitschelt 1986; Burstein et al. 1995) to address more substantial and long-term gains in access. In general, these more substantial gains in access to states concern ongoing connections between states and social movement organizations or other organizations related to movements.

Despite these modifications, each definition of success has liabilities. Gamson's concept of new advantages places limits on the consideration of possible impacts of challenges. It may be possible, notably, for a challenger to fail to achieve its stated program – and thus be deemed a failure – but still to win substantial new advantages for its constituents. This is especially likely for challengers with far-reaching goals. There may also be unintended consequences that influence beneficiary groups, and challengers may do worse than fail. In addition, in democratic states some form of basic recognition or acceptance of challenging organizations is highly probable. What is more, the understanding of acceptance as constituting a success – given that it may lead to nothing for the challenger's constituency – has been contested (Piven and Cloward 1977). As a result scholars focusing on the impact of challengers on states have not as frequently dealt with acceptance as an object of explanation (see Gamson 1990: appendix) or have seen it mainly as a potential means of gaining new advantages (Ragin 1989; Amenta et al. 1992).

Some scholars of the impact of social movements have addressed the state explicitly by addressing gains in power. For the most part, however, these do not go beyond the limited ideas of new benefits and access. Craig Jenkins (1982) suggests a three-part scheme based on short-term changes in political decisions, alterations in decision-making elites, and long-term changes in the distribution of goods. The first and third are different forms of new benefits, while the second is connected to the idea of access or acceptance. Herbert Kitschelt (1986) argues social movements can achieve substantive, procedural, and structural gains, with the first two analogous to Gamson's categories. The third type is a "transformation of political structures," which suggests more fundamental change, including that provided by a new political party, but is not well specified. These ideas need to be better connected to specific state structures and processes to make sense of the impact of challengers on the state.

To address some of these issues other scholars start with an alternative based on the concept of *collective goods*, or group-wise advantages or disadvantages from which nonparticipants in a challenge cannot be easily excluded (Olson 1965; Hardin 1982). Collective goods can be material, such as categorical social spending programs, but can also be less tangible, such as new ways to refer to members of a group. Social movement organizations almost invariably claim to represent a group extending beyond the leaders and adherents of the organization and most make demands that would provide collective benefits to that larger group (Tilly 1999). According to the collective benefit standard, a challenger can have considerable impact even when it fails to achieve what it is seeking. It also can address the possibility that challengers would have negative consequences (collective bads) or negligible ones, such as achieving a program that did not realize its intended effect to benefit constituents (Amenta and Young 1999a). Scholars working from this standard tend to refer to the "consequences" or impacts of social movements rather than successes or failures.

New Advantages as State-Related Collective Benefits

We build on these approaches by employing some of the ideas regarding new benefits and collective goods and connecting them to political sociology concepts of the state, employing a three-level approach (Amenta and Young 1999a; Amenta et al. 2002). From this perspective, the greatest sort of impact is the one that provides a group, not necessarily organizations representing that group, continuing leverage over political processes. These sorts of gains increase the returns to routine collective action of a challenger. These gains are usually at a structural or systemic level of state processes. Most collective action, however, is aimed at a more medium level – benefits that will continue to flow to a group unless some countering action is taken. These generally involve major changes in policy and the bureaucratic enforcement and implementation of that policy. The most minor impact is to win a specific state decision or legislation with no long-term implications for the flows of benefits to the group. In each case, new legislation is required to secure the benefits. The difference is in the content of the legislation and what it means regarding the flow of collective benefits to groups represented by challengers. Although collective action in practice may be aimed at different levels simultaneously, these distinctions offer a basis for analyses of state-related gains by social movements for constituent groups.

These levels of collective benefits can be related back to the characteristics of states (Amenta et al. 2002), including the structure of the polity, state bureaucracies, and policies. Social movements may have an impact on the structure of the polity, on the degree to which authority is centralized or divided among levels of government or according to functions at the central and other levels of government. Social movements may also contest other system-wide features of states, such as their democratic practices and electoral rules. At a more middle level, both in terms of the likely stability of the change and its effects across groups are changes in state bureaucracies. The creation or major alteration of a state domestic bureaucracy has great implications for the implementation of all policy under its purview and the development of future policies. Finally, there are new state policies. These can range quite dramatically, however, from those that are short-term and apply to few people and at one point in time to others that may apply to large numbers of people and groups and backed with legislation and bureaucratic authority. The levels of influence do not line up perfectly with the most structural and systemic aspects of the state, but there is a rough correspondence.

At the highest level, a challenger may gain structural reforms of the state that give the represented group increased influence over political processes. These gains are a kind of metacollective benefit, as they increase the productivity of all future collective action of the group. For instance, challengers sometimes demand the devolution of political authority, which can aid territorial minorities, and have also pressed for various direct democratic devices, with notable results achieved in many US states and in Switzerland. Gains in the democratization of state processes are perhaps the most important that social movements can influence and have the greatest systemic effects. Winning the right to vote or the protection of that right for low-income or other disfranchised groups increases the productivity of future state-directed collective action by such groups (Piven and Cloward 1989; Tilly 1998). Many of the most prominent social movements and challengers have sought this basic goal, including movements of workers, women, and, in the United States, the civil rights movement (McAdam 1982; Rueschemeyer et al. 1992; Banaszak 1996).[1]

By contrast, state policies are institutionalized benefits that provide collective goods in a routine fashion to all those meeting specified requirements. Once enacted and enforced with bureaucratic means, categorical social spending programs, notably, provide benefits in such a manner (Amenta 1998). The beneficiaries gain rights of entitlement to the benefits, and legal changes and bureaucratic reinforcement of such laws help to ensure the routine maintenance of such collective benefits. Under these circumstances, the issue is privileged in politics, is effectively removed from the political agenda, and the political system becomes biased in favor of the group. For the situation to change some other person or group must challenge the institutionalized benefits. A bureaucracy would have to be targeted and altered, if not captured, or new legislation would have to be passed rescinding benefits – a process that becomes more difficult as time passes as bureaucracies are reinforced and people organize their lives around the programs (Pierson 1994). Regulatory bureaucracies that are products of challenger mobilizations may push on their own to advance mandates in the absence of new legislation, as in the case of state labor commissions (Amenta 1998) or in affirmative action (Skrentny 1996; Bonastia

2000). Policies, however, vary widely in their implications. At a low level, challengers may win something specific and minor for their constituency group, such as a short-run or one-time benefit – which is often criticized as insubstantial (Lipsky 1968; Piven and Cloward 1977) and designed more to assure a public audience than to aid the beneficiaries of a challenger. Such minimal benefits imply limited rights for the groups to which the benefits pertain.

Through their policies states can ratify or attempt to undermine potential collective identities or help to create new ones, sometimes on purpose, often inadvertently. To be valuable a new identity should aid in elevating and defining group members, in relation to other members of the group and those outside, and the identity must receive a kind of societal endorsement or recognition. Insofar as a challenger constructs a new collective identity that extends to a beneficiary group and provides psychological rewards such as pride, winning affirmations of this identity is a potentially important accomplishment (for a review, see Polletta and Jasper 2001). Although states do not hold a monopoly on recognizing new identity claims, states do provide many influential and authoritative communications that can greatly influence identities, and state actors are often in the vanguard of recognizing new identity claims, frequently recognizing these claims by way of changes in policy (Amenta and Young 1999a). These results can range from a challenger's constituency gaining greater respect through official governmental representations to having the group recognized as such in state policies. The state's role in defining racial categories, for instance, has been at times the target of social movements. In the United States, activists attempting to legitimate a multiracial identity were able to alter questions in the 2000 census. Similarly, activists in Brazil fought successfully for the inclusion in the 1991 census of racial questions in the hopes of achieving greater recognition of the special status of black Brazilians (Nobles 2000). However accomplished, gains in collective identity may influence later attempts to gain collective benefits taking other forms, such as pecuniary rewards or legal rights, or may reinforce existing ones.

Dividing the process of creating new laws containing collective benefits into the agenda setting, legislative content, passage, and implementation of legislation simplifies analysis and also makes it easier to judge the impact of challengers (Kingdon 1984; Burstein et al. 1995; Baumgartner and Jones 1993; Amenta and Young 1999b). If a challenger, for instance, inserts its issue onto the political agenda, it can be seen as having increased its probability of winning some collective benefits for its larger constituency. This has been called "sensitizing" the "institutional agenda" (Kriesi et al. 1995).[2] The value of the benefits would be unknown, however, until legislative alternatives had been developed. As far as legislative content is concerned, a challenger can work to increase the value of collective benefits included in any bill that makes it onto the agenda. Once the content has been specified, moreover, challengers can influence individual legislators to vote for the bill and thus influence the probability of gaining specified collective benefits. From there the program must be implemented, and the more secure the implementation the greater the probability of collective benefits over the long run.

To put it another way, if a challenger has an impact on any one of these processes it would increase the expected value of collective benefits for the beneficiary group. Unless all processes are negotiated successfully – placing the issue on the agenda, writing a bill with collective benefits, passing the bill, *and* seeing its implementation

– no collective benefits will result. Influence in implementation depends on successfully negotiating these other steps. It seems that it will be only very rarely that a challenger can influence all of these processes. That said, for a challenger to influence the placement of an issue on the agenda, to increase the collective benefits in legislation, to affect the probabilities that elected officials might support such legislation, or to reinforce the implementation of legislation, each of these is a kind of beneficial impact in itself. Often, though, challengers have to bid to influence policies once they are already institutionalized in ways that harm the interests of their constituents.

State-Related Benefits to and Connections with Social Movement Organizations

A second sort of consequence, the "acceptance" (Gamson 1975) or "representation" (Cress and Snow 2000) achieved by challenging organizations, can also be related systematically back to states and collective benefits. These consequences apply specifically to challenging organizations, and to the extent that state action recognizing these organizations influences the form or resources of challenger organizations, they also influence their potential to gain future collective benefits for their constituents. This of course assumes that organized challengers effectively represent some group; this may not always be the case, as organizational leaders may form different interests from broader constituencies (Piven and Cloward 1977; cf. Gamson 1975). Even for challenging organizations that do faithfully press in the interests of a larger constituency, gaining official representations remains one step removed from gaining collective benefits through the state.

Gamson's idea of acceptance may, however, be too broadly drawn to capture the sorts of representation sought by challengers attempting to influence democratic states. According to Gamson's understanding, a state-oriented challenging group was accepted if it was invited to testify before Congress, which is a fairly minimal connection to politics. More advanced forms of acceptance included negotiations, formal recognition, and inclusion, which meant placing members of the challenging organization in the organization of the antagonist. Although challenging organizations and interest groups can gain access to politicians and may receive various sorts of certification, very rarely do states and their leaders directly negotiate with challengers or other organized actors for that matter over the creation of policy – which is the purview of elected officials and their appointees. In addition, most democratic states are formally open to challenging groups; there is no analogous situation to having an employer refusing to recognize a union organization. Organizations that accept the legitimacy of democratic states are not best described as their antagonists. Frequently challengers seek to gain attention from states regarding an ignored issue, attempting to have their voice heard among competing claims. The claims that many challengers make, such as demands for social spending, regulation, or enforcement, may have societal opponents that are highly diffuse, such as taxpayers or automobile owners.

More important and plausible for state-oriented challengers is a version of Gamson's inclusion, which would amount to the placing of challengers in state positions. The two main ways that challengers can gain such inclusion are through election or appointment. Challengers can become candidates for office, riding the backing of the challenging organization to election, or can stand as representatives of new political parties. More likely in the American setting, given the inability of third political parties to gain a footing in the US polity, is for challenging organizations' representatives to be appointed to state positions. The most likely scenario here is to be selected for study commissions designed to address a specific issue or problem. More influential are positions in regular governmental bureaucracies. As is the case for other, better politically situated groups, it is possible for social movement organizations to capture bureaucracies and run them in favor its constituency. Although most bureaucracies are staffed by long-term civil-service employees, social movement representatives can be appointed as political employees at the top of state bureaucracies and guide their ruling-making and enforcement procedures. In assessing the representation of challengers in bureaucracies, care is needed to distinguish among actual participants in challenges and those who are largely members of the challenger's target constituency. Also, any members of these groups are liable to be captured by the mission of the bureaucracy, which is not necessarily going to be the same as the interests or preferences of the challenger's constituency. By gaining representation in legislative offices and bureaucracies, challengers can influence policies for their constituencies throughout the process, including placing programs on the agenda, helping to specify their content, aiding their passage, and supporting their enforcement.

State policies can also aid challenging organizations, just as policies may aid their constituencies. Policies that aid challenging organizations can often be seen as flows of resources and rights between states and challenger organizations, including everything from rights to organize to taxation exemptions and funding, with the more important legislation insuring long-term flows of resources or recognition to organized challengers. Movements may also attempt to gain recognition and legitimation for altered or new movement organizations, which might include political parties, political lobbying, or educational organizations (see discussions in Clemens 1997; Burstein 1999). The formation by movements of political parties is something like the structural change discussed by Kitschelt (1986) (see also Dalton 1995; Schwartz 2000), but the creation of political parties or other organizations with established relationships with states remains one step removed from structural change in the state itself.

Collective action may be intended to win or may result in winning higher-order rights through the state that advantage a group in its conflicts with other groups (Skocpol 1985). The state may be used as a "fulcrum" in this sense (Tarrow 1998) by groups not mainly state-oriented. The general way to differentiate this sort of benefit from the other types is that it increases the probability of the impact of collective action by a group with regard to its targets outside the state. Labor movements, notably, often focus on the state to ensure rights to organize and engage in collective bargaining with businesses and business associations. In the United States equal employment opportunity laws provided advantages for the civil rights movements in fighting discrimination by private corporations (Burstein 1991, 1998). By outlawing a set of practices and providing a legal remedy for class of employees, they created another channel for protest, and by creating a bureaucracy that has influenced the outcomes of these legal cases, they have provided additional resources and legitimation for the movement. A second way the state may be used as a fulcrum is in transnational protest (Keck and Sikkink 1998). Challengers blocked in one country may appeal to sympathetic organizations in other countries. These other actors can apply pressure on their governments in order to change the policies of the original state. This "boomerang pattern" of activism can be found in the Latin American human rights advocacy network, which includes Latin American organizations appealing to solidarity groups around the world, resulting in international pressure on Latin American governments.

ACCOUNTING FOR THE STATE-RELATED CONSEQUENCES OF CHALLENGERS

There are four main arguments designed to explain the impact of social movements on states. The claims that stand out most in the literature are the following: (1) the simple hypothesis that mobilization or collective action in itself is likely to be effective (Jenkins 1982; McCarthy and Zald 2002); (2) that once mobilized certain forms of challenger organization or strategies, including framing strategies, are more effective than others (Gamson 1990; cf. Piven and Cloward 1977; see also Cress and Snow 2000; Ganz 2000; Andrews 2001); (3) that political opportunities or favorable political contexts result in benefits for mobilized challengers (Jenkins and Perrow 1977; Goldstone 1980; Kitschelt 1986); (4) that the collective action of mobilized challengers is politically mediated – combinations of specific forms of mobilization, action, and political conditions determine whether movements have consequences (Piven and Cloward 1977; Amenta et al. 1992; Skocpol 1992; Amenta et al. 1994; Kriesi et al. 1995; Amenta et al. 1999). Like other arguments in the literature on social movements, the arguments about the impacts of social movements have not always been clearly geared toward specific outcomes. Thus scholars link these various factors to all manner of different "successes" or "outcomes" of social movements relatively indiscriminately. In what follows we discuss the various perspectives and some of the evidence regarding their claims with respect to state-related outcomes.

The first argument is that whatever aids a group's mobilization will lead to its making gains, as mobilization of various sorts will aid movements in whatever they do. To look at it another way, the mobilization of various resources is needed to engage in collective action, and collective action, wherever aimed, is designed and expected to bring a certain amount of collective benefits (Tilly 1978). This line of argumentation is consistent with rational choice discussions of collective action problems, in that they view the main issue for social movements as overcoming free-rider disincentives to participation (Olson 1965; Chong 1991). The ability to mobilize different sorts of resources is key for the impact of movements and mobilization of resources and membership has been shown to influence some state-related consequences in different research (Rucht 1999; see review in McCarthy and Zald 2002). However, mobilization seems to be necessary to have influence over states, as there seems to be no connection between size of a mobilized challenger and gaining new benefits (Kitschelt 1986; Gamson 1990). This does not seem surprising in that bids to influence the state and other political institutions through legislation require several steps to be negotiated, and many additional actors and institutions bear on the process.

A second point of view addresses the impact of relatively well mobilized challengers and focuses on conditions largely under the control of challengers.

Associated with Gamson (1990), this line of argumentation is that specific strategies and goals of collective action and forms of challenger organization are more likely to produce success. In his study of 53 randomly selected social movement organizations spanning American history before World War II, Gamson (1990) found notably that limited goals, the use of "constraints," selective incentives, and bureaucratic forms of organization (see also Staggenborg 1991) were more likely to produce new advantages. In contrast, goals and strategies aiming at "displacement" – in which a movement seeks to destroy or replace its opponent – were likely to fail. Most other scholars following Gamson's lead and employing the data from his remarkable research project have also focused on relative merits of different sorts of strategies or forms of challenger organization, but because of the nature of Gamson's study their ability to examine the role of various political contexts is limited. What is more, the efforts of Gamson and others employing his data do not distinguish between states and other targets of challengers. Also, the arguments are based on the US case and thus may be geared explicitly to the contexts facing US challengers before World War II.

Other scholars have focused on aspects of either the social movement's form of organization or its strategies. One famous statement was Piven and Cloward's (1977) argument that organization in poor people's movements undermines their ability to gain concessions (see also Button 1989; review of research in Skocpol and Amenta 1986). Others have advanced Gamson's opposing argument about the importance of organization in social movement success by focusing on the sorts of "mobilizing structures" (McAdam et al. 1996) or social movement organizations likely to produce gains. It has been argued that resourceful movement infrastructures led to gains in policy implementation for the civil rights movement in the South (Andrews 2001), that innovative organizational forms can lead to gains for challengers and transformations of political institutions (Clemens 1997), and that movement organizations with greater strategic resources are likely to prevail over others (Ganz 2000).

Part of a challenger's strategy singled out for special attention among scholars in this area concerns claims-making and framing – which have been deemed essential by some to making gains for state-oriented challengers. Cress and Snow (2000) argue notably that for a challenger to have an impact it is necessary for it to employ resonant "prognostic" and "diagnostic" frames (see also Snow and Benford 1988). This means that to gain results challengers need to identify problems and pose credible solutions to those problems that play to state actors and other third parties as well as to be able to mobilize participants. Tilly (1999) argues in a somewhat similar vein that a movement's public displays of "worthiness" are critical to a movement's impact, along with its unity, numbers, and commitment, which he refers to as WUNC. Worthiness incorporates aspects of Gamson's (1992) "injustice frame," but also encompasses aspects of appearance and moral standing. Suffering should be shown to be "undeserved" because social movements rarely achieve goals as a direct result of their actions. Political identities need to be created and recognized, and the ability to produce WUNC increases the likelihood of recognition from state actors. There remains, however, the difficulty of assessing the plausibility of frames independent of their apparent influence in convincing policymakers.

Additionally, through various framing devices, a challenger may be able to elicit general support by sensitizing "public attitudes" (Kriesi et al. 1995). An issue that becomes framed, either by the social movement or others, as part of high-profile policy domain may become more difficult for social movements to influence, however (Burstein 1999). Issues in these policy domains are those that are closely tied to the national cleavage structure, involve high levels of material resources, contest current power relations, involve the 'national interest,' or have electoral relevance (Kriesi et al. 1995). In these areas, there are more likely to be powerful nonstate actors working in opposition and state actors may be able to expend more resources to block movement demands. Additionally, where public opinion in opposition to the movement is strong and deeply held, elected officials may be reticent to offend constituents and accede to demands (Burstein 1998, 1999).

A third argument attempts to take into account contextual influences by claiming that once a challenger is mobilized the main thing influencing its impact is the political context or "opportunity structure" (Jenkins and Perrow 1977; Kitschelt 1986; Kriesi 1995; for a general review of this literature, see chapter 4 in this volume). This line of argumentation has both systemic and dynamic components to it, and sometimes it is also argued that systemic political contexts greatly influence or determine the strategies of challengers. Kriesi et al. (1995) take the most systemic view, arguing that the openness and capacity of states largely determines whether a state-related movement will have an impact and whether or not it will be proactive or reactive. When states have both inclusive strategies and strong capacities, challengers are most likely to achieve "proactive" impacts. Under weak states, by contrast, reactive impacts are more probable, as the state lacks the capacity to implement policies. These arguments build on Kitschelt (1986), who argued that the varying impacts of antinuclear power challengers in four countries depended on a state's "implementation capacities" – the ability of the state's bureaucratic infrastructure to carry out policy. These capacities would presumably vary, however, from issue to issue. In an open polity, as in the case of a federal system, the multiplicity of targets may increase the likelihood that a challenger will be recognized by at least one state actor, and thus there may be less reliance on disruptive protest (Kitschelt 1986). Rucht (1989) found a wider variety of protest tactics in the environmental movement in federalist Germany than in centralized France.[3]

These analyses of the role of systemic political contexts have the advantage of being applicable in comparative studies. The more overarching arguments have been criticized, however, on the grounds that all manner of social movements with different strategies have developed within similar countries (Dalton 1995; Tarrow 1996) and that within any country differences in impacts have varied over time. Arguments regarding systemic political contexts have also been criticized on the grounds that they take a too abstract view of states and political opportunity structures. Notably, focusing on the overall openness of polities and strength of states ignores conceptual and theoretical developments in political sociology literatures that have addressed the influence of polities and states in more fine-grained ways (Amenta et al. 2002).

Along these lines, others argue that longstanding characteristics of states and political institutions influence the prospects of challenges generally and encourage certain forms and strategies, but do not completely determine them. Important factors include the polity structure, the democratization of state institutions, electoral rules and procedures, and state policies (see review in Amenta et al. 2002). These aspects of states influence forms of challenger representation, as well as the tactics of challengers. These arguments tend to drop the weak/strong state and open/closed polity dichotomies and refer to specific aspects of polity and political actors.

The centralization and division of power between each branch of government also has an impact on social movement organizations. An autonomous court system with veto power over the legislative branch, for example, may lead to an emphasis on legal mobilizations, which may either increase the overall level of protest or shift focus away from more mass-based protests. Multiple points of access is a two-edged sword, however, as multiple points of access also means multiple points of veto. The level of democracy has important consequences for the forms that mobilization will take place. Specifically, the greater the exclusion from the democratic process, the more likely noninstitutional forms of protest will take place (Amenta and Young 1999a). This is not always the case, however, as groups may instead transform and extend the definition of institutional behavior. The presuffrage women's movement, for example expanded the organizational repertoire for protest groups by adopting a multiplicity of legitimate, but previously nonpolitical organizational forms (Clemens 1993). The basis for exclusion from the democratic process increases the likelihood that groups will form along these identities, such as the African American civil rights in the American context (McAdam 1982) and workers in the European one (Katznelson 1981).

Electoral rules may have the greatest impact on the relationship between social movements and the party system. Winner-take-all systems, such as in the US, discourage the formation and legitimacy of new political parties (Lipset and Rokkan 1967) and discourage party movements (Schwartz 2000). Initiative and referendum procedures increase the likelihood that organizations will be single-focused. In addition, states can also provide a variety of resources for specific social movements that can vary from concrete items, such as a desk and phone (Cress and Snow 2000) to more abstract resources, such as legitimacy (Edwards and Marullo 1995).

On the dynamic side, the political opportunity argument focuses on alterations in political conditions that improve the productivity of collective action of challengers (Goldstone and Tilly 2001). In their study of farmworkers' mobilization and collective action, Jenkins and Perrow (1977) found that changes in the political context influenced their growth and impact, through the rise to power of favorable political regimes and through the support of liberal organizations like organized labor. In his reanalysis of Gamson's data, Goldstone (1980) argued that challengers' success was determined by the timing of national crises. In his study of the civil rights movement, McAdam (1982, 1983, 2000) argued that favorable political conditions were necessary for its gains – which were based on tactical innovations. Once political conditions turned against the movement, however, no further advances were possible. Amenta et al. (1994) found that Share Our Wealth had an impact on US taxation policy, but only when both the president and Congress were sympathetic to reform, understood as being a super-majority of Democrats (see also Jenkins and Perrow 1977; Costain 1992). In short, according to the strongest form of this argument, mobilized challengers have impacts largely because they engage in collective action at the right time.

This line of argumentation has the advantage of addressing some of the problems faced by the systemic views – that challengers have varied over time in making state-related gains. This argumentation has suffered, however, in comparison with the systemic view of political contexts in being able to specify what constitutes a favorable context. The main candidates – polity openness, instability of elite alliances, the presence of elite allies for challengers, declines in capacities and propensities for repression (McAdam 1996; see also Tarrow 1996) – are drawn so widely as to be difficult to operationalize (Amenta et al. 2002). It is difficult to show beforehand whether political contexts are becoming definitely more favorable or not and to compare different contexts across time and place with respect to their friendliness to challengers. And without being able to specify in advance what would constitute evidence of a favorable change in the political context, scholars can point to almost anything in the political background as constituting evidence of such a favorable change.

Finally, many scholars have developed different political mediation models of social movement consequences, which build on arguments concerning strategy, organizational form, and political contexts (Piven and Cloward 1977; Amenta et al. 1992; Skocpol 1992; Amenta et al. 1994; Amenta et al. 1999; Lipset and Marks 2000). The basic point of this argument is that the collective action of challengers is politically mediated. In a democratic political system, mobilizing relatively large numbers of committed people is probably necessary to winning new collective benefits for those otherwise under-represented in politics. So, too, are making plausible claims regarding the worthiness of the group and the usefulness of its program. Yet challengers' action is more likely to produce results when institutional political actors see benefit in aiding the group the challenger represents. To secure new benefits, challengers will typically need help or complementary action from like-minded state actors, including elected officials, appointed officials, and state civil servants. And so challengers need to engage in collective action that changes the calculations of relevant institutional political actors, such as elected officials and state bureaucrats, and challengers need to adopt organizational forms that fit political circumstances. State actors need in turn to see a challenger as potentially facilitating or disrupting their own goals – which might range from augmenting or cementing new electoral coalitions, to gaining in public opinion, to increasing the support for the missions of governmental bureaus.

Political mediation arguments are generally less concerned to identify individual organizational forms, strategies, or long-term or short-term political contexts that will always or usually help challengers to win collective benefits. Instead the idea is that certain organizational forms and collective action strategies will be more productive in some political contexts rather than others. Some examples may help to underscore the logic behind this sort of argument – which often relies on quite different mechanisms of influence. Taking a dynamic view of political contexts, Piven and Cloward (1977) argue that the disruptive and spontaneous collective action by poor people in times of electoral instability would produce concessions in their classic treatment of US challenges in the mid-twentieth century. A specific sort of action (mass turmoil) for challengers with a specific constituency (the poor) is likely to gain results (increased social spending) in a specific, short-term political context (electoral instability). In her examination of organized groups throughout US history, Skocpol (1992) argues that to have influence the forms of challengers and other mass-based interest organizations need to fit the divided nature of the American political context, a systemic condition. US organizations need to have a wide geographical presence to influence Congress, which is based on district representation. In this manner challengers and other groups relying on large numbers can overcome the obstacles to policy change in the American polity. Lipset and Marks (2000) argue that the failure of socialist movements in the United States resulted from a combination of difficult systemic political conditions for the establishment of new parties and flawed strategies. Kriesi et al. (1995) highlight the importance of the "interaction context" between political opportunity structures and mobilization. Here, political authorities react to the opportunity structure to create a system of incentives for social movements. These "concrete opportunities" created by elites influence movement strategy, size, and outcomes.

The most extensive discussion of this sort suggests that challengers need to moderate strategies and forms to address political circumstances widely. The standard distinction between disruptive and assimilative strategies is dropped in favor of addressing variations in assertiveness of action (Amenta 2002; Amenta et al. 1999), with assertive meaning the use of increasingly strong sanctions, something akin to Gamson's "constraints." If the political regime is supportive and the domestic bureaucrats are professionalized and supportive, limited protest based mainly on the evidence of mobilization is likely to be sufficient to provide increased collective benefits. The challenger needs merely to demonstrate that it has support, through time-honored activities such as writing letters, rallies, or petitioning, as well as public awareness campaigns. Members of a reform-oriented regime are likely to use the evidence of mobilization and modest protest as a confirmation of the beneficiary group's relative importance in an electoral coalition. Domestic bureaucrats are likely to portray the mobilization as indicating the need for the augmentation or greater enforcement of its program. If the regime hopes to add to its coalition or if domestic bureaucrats have a mission that is not yet realized, those groups best mobilized are likely to win the greatest benefits in public policy for their constituencies.

By contrast, achieving collective benefits through public policy is likely to be more difficult if neither a supportive regime nor administrative authority exists. Although this understanding of the political context is a dynamic one that takes into account short-run and medium-term changes in political contexts, it can also be related back to systemic and structural characteristics of political systems, notably political institutional conditions that make the establishment of a reform-oriented regime or bureaucratic capacities difficult. When the regime is opposed to the challenger or sees no benefit in adding its beneficiary group to its coalition and when state bureaucracies in the area are hostile or absent, the sorts of limited protest listed above are likely to be ignored or have a limited effect. As political circumstances become more difficult, more assertive or bolder collective action is required to produce collective benefits. Sanctions in assertive institutional collective action threaten to increase or decrease the likelihood of gaining or keeping something valuable to political actors – often positions – or to take over their functions or prerogatives. The institutional collective action of challengers works largely by mobilizing large numbers of people behind a course of activity, often one with electoral implications. This collective action may be designed to convince the general public of the justice of the cause and influence elected and appointed officials in that manner, but may also demonstrate to these officials that a large segment of the electorate is willing to vote or engage in other political activity mainly on the basis of a single key issue.

Challengers also benefit by targeting their actions to fit the administrative or legislative context. If the relevant state bureaucratic actors are present and either supportive or neutral and the political regime is not supportive of the challenger's group, collective action will be most productive if it focuses on elected officials. Such action might induce those who would otherwise be indifferent or hostile to legislation to support it or at least not to challenge it. If the political regime is supportive or neutral and domestic bureaucrats are either absent or hostile to the challenger's constituency, bureaucratic capabilities must be created or existing bureaucratic actors must be sanctioned. They might respond by providing feasible proposals that increase the collective benefits to the group represented by the challenger. These theoretical claims are more flexible than those based mainly on strategies and political conditions alone, and have the advantage of specifying political conditions and making links between systemic political contexts and more short-term ones. But they are somewhat more complex than one or two factor approaches, and thus more difficult to appraise, and like the others require specifying the strategies likely to work in different political contexts.

Methodological Issues

Analyzing the state-related consequences of social movements often provides a series of methodological problems that can hinder empirical appraisals of theoretical claims, whatever form they take. Establishing a challenger's impact on states is straightforward in principle. It means to demonstrate that state-related collective goods would not have appeared in the way that they did in the absence of the challenger. To determine why a movement had consequences often means determining first whether it had any consequences and which ones – not an easy task. Where the state is concerned usually more than one set of actors is making claims and taking action in areas of concern to social movements, making it difficult to sort out causal influence. This problem is aggravated by the fact that scholars typically study individual movements or organizations, making it difficult to rule out plausible, but alternative explanations. In part because of the great scarcity of information on social movements, no one has followed Gamson in examining a random sample of movements or movement organizations. Often neglected, too, even by Gamson, are means to ascertain whether and the degree to which the mobilization and action of any challenger had an impact on collective goods. The researcher has to show that the challenger has caused the collective benefits and address the surrounding issues (see Amenta et al. 1992; Kriesi et al. 1995; Giugni 1998; Amenta and Young 1999b; Tilly 1999; Earl 2000).

Because actors aside from challengers are influencing the state and other conditions may also influence outcomes of interest to the constituencies of challengers, collective benefits may result for reasons that have little to do with challengers. This is troublesome in that many theoretical claims apply both to the rise of challengers and what they are expected to influence. Alterations in political contexts are often claimed to influence the rise of challengers (McAdam et al. 1988; McAdam 1996) as well as what they attempt to effect. Similarly, shifts in public opinion may influence both the rise of social movements and what they may be explaining (Burstein 1999). Research indicates, for instance, that various economic and political conditions and actors aside from challengers, as well as public opinion, influence social spending policy (reviews in Amenta et al. 2001; Amenta 2003). These other determinants have to be taken into account in assessing the impact of challengers on achieving collective benefits.

The ways that establishing impact has been handled in the literature on social movements have not been completely satisfactory. Gamson (1990) counted a challenger as having achieved new advantages merely if its agenda was mainly fulfilled within 15 years of the challenge's demise. Calling a realized agenda a success or claiming that other pro-social movement collective benefits demonstrate the impact of a challenger without demonstrating that the challenger made them happen, however, risks overstating the influence of a challenger. A premature declaration of success or impact disregards the potential that other conditions have influenced both social protest and the collective benefits – or that some combination of outside actors and social movement influenced the effect. Other researchers do worse by merely assuming that anything that happens somewhere close in time to a collective action campaign was a result of it (see review in Burstein 1993).

The tendency of researchers in this area to attribute results to collective action without demonstrating them is probably due to the fact that researchers are engaged in case studies (see Ragin and Becker 1992). Case studies in turn are typically beset by the so-called identification problem – too many potential causes chasing too few pieces of information (Lieberson 1992). For that reason researchers of movement impacts need to employ techniques current in social science to extend case studies in order to make their claims more plausible. Most of these techniques employ histor-ical or other comparisons to increase the leverage of studies (Giugni 1998; Amenta and Young 1999b; Earl 2000). Researchers with information on a smaller number of cases or with questions that cannot be easily addressed by large-scale research can always employ time-honored ways of making the most of these empirical materials (Amenta 1991). Like any research involving causal statements, research on the impacts of challenges should be designed to appraise specific claims, either those devised by a researcher or those extant in the literature. To do that requires maxi-mizing variation in the conditions deemed to be most influential (King, Keohane, and Verba 1994). Alternatively, scholars can attempt to explain positive cases, by appraising alternative paths or combinations of causes that might lead to them (Ragin 2000). Theoretical arguments on the impact of challengers have lagged behind theoretical arguments concerning their mobilization, making precise meth-odological prescriptions is difficult.

The most systematic way to ascertain the potential impact of challengers and to appraise alternative arguments is by way of gaining information from a large number of ecological units (Snyder and Kelly 1979). This is possible because chal-lengers typically attempt to have an influence in more than one place at a time; movements have been increasingly national and international in their scope. This approach relies on gaining information on variation in a movement organization's presence and activities, other potential determinants of collective benefits, and the benefits themselves. If information on each of these is available, all important potential causal conditions can be taken into account in attempting to explain variations in outcomes. This has been the approach of many researchers, who sometimes employ cross-national and over-time analyses, especially regarding strike activity (Hicks and Misra 1993) or examine one movement across a series of polities (Dalton 1995). But scholars mainly rely on examining campaigns of one challenger across subnational units, such as states (Amenta et al. 1992; Amenta et al. 1994;

McCammon et al. 2001), provinces (Banaszak 1996), counties (Amenta et al. 1999; Andrews 2001), or over-time analyses of one country alone (Soule et al. 1999). Employing inferential statistical methods on these units makes it possible to assess the impact of a challenger relative to those of other relevant conditions and to appraise specific arguments about forms of challenge and outcome. For causal claims that are interactive or combinational, such as those described above, interactive specifications should be employed or like means.

To appraise propositions, any number of other small-N comparisons might be made. Interactions can be readily modeled by way of qualitative comparative analysis (QCA). This technique has the advantage of being usable in the absence of large numbers of cases and can address combinational and multiple causation (Ragin 1987; Amenta and Poulsen 1994). This has been used to good effect in re-analyses of Gamson's data (Ragin 1989). It has also been employed in other studies of state-oriented consequences of social movements across US states (Amenta et al. 1992; Amenta and Poulsen 1996) and cities (Cress and Snow 2000). In each case, combinations of determinants were found to lead to new gains for challengers. This form of analysis can also incorporate a time dimension, by employing time-sensitive measures (see also Caren and Panofsky 2002). Needless to say, scholars have also employed small-N cross-national comparisons (Kitschelt 1986; della Porta 1996) to appraise or develop arguments, with these small-N comparisons sometimes buttressed by quantitative analyses (Banaszak 1996). Some other likely sorts of comparisons are made between challengers mobilized in different ways in a given place and time (Clemens 1997), and between places in which challengers are and are not mobilized, or are mobilized in different ways (Amenta et al. 1999). Making a choice among these sorts of comparisons depend on the propositions being appraised.

In historical inquiries of the impact of one challenger or a few challengers, researchers have options that go beyond assuming that challengers always have impacts. Standard techniques include juxtaposing the trajectory of the challenger's mobilization and different forms of collective action to outcomes of interest and, like Gamson, examining the views of participants, contemporary observers, and historians. A lack of a correlation between action and outcome probably would indicate a lack of impact. So, too, might a historical consensus that a challenger was ineffective. However, a positive correlation would not necessarily mean causation, and witnesses can be divided or biased in opinion. Analysts can go further than these preliminary historical analyses. Most arguments about the impact of collective action specify theoretical mechanisms, indicating linkages between various causes and effects. Scholars can take advantage of this by tracing historical processes to address whether hypothesized theoretical mechanisms occur and thus appraise specific lines of argument (Bennett and George 1997; Tilly 1999; Andrews 2001). Although these analyses may not make it possible to discount alternative explanations, they can be buttressed by making comparisons of processes across movements (McAdam et al. 2001) or collective action campaigns (Marwell and Oliver 1988; Amenta 2002).

Analyses of the political process in the development of legislation can be useful, particularly in ascertaining whether a challenger had an impact or not. To make a convincing claim, any historical analysis would need to demonstrate that the challenger achieved one or more of the following: changed the plans and agendas of political leaders; had an impact on the content of the proposals as devised by executives, legislators, or administrators; or influenced disinterested representatives key to the passage of proposed legislation (Amenta et al. 1999; see also Burstein et al. 1995). Making such a case would require understanding political leaders' agendas and the content of legislative programs prior to the challenge as well as assessing how legislators might have voted in its absence. New legislation must also be implemented, and movements can influence the speed and nature of this process as well. This sort of technique is possible in settings where these processes are often quite separate, as in the US polity, but would require some modification for use in other polities.

Conclusion

Scholars have pursued issues surrounding the impact of social movements, especially state-related impacts. As we have seen, however, understanding the state-related consequences of social movements poses several difficult conceptual, theoretical, and methodological problems. The problems stem mainly from the fact that to have an impact on states, challengers depend on many actors inside and outside states and are further removed from these processes than most outcomes of concern to movements. For that reason scholars need to think specifically about the state-related consequences of social movements. This means conceptualizing these impacts beyond the standard ideas of new advantages and acceptance. It also means theorizing in ways that take into account other key actors and institutions. From there scholars need to devise methodological strategies to ascertain the impact of challengers and appraise often complex arguments about their influence.

Despite the fact that much social movement activity is aimed at states, conceptualizations of the potential consequences of this collective action have not relied enough on conceptual developments in political sociology scholarship on states. Instead, social movement scholars have focused on broad notions of new advantages and the acceptance of social movement organizations, as might be applied to any target of a challenge. Progress has been made, however, in connecting the standard concepts of new advantages and acceptance to conventionally understood aspects of states. Thinking about state related new advantages as collective benefits in particular makes it possible to connect possible consequences of challengers with transformations in state structures and policies. Similarly, because states only rarely negotiate with challengers, it is useful thinking about the different ways that connections can be forged between challengers and the state, including challenger representation in state institutions.

Making sense of potential impacts of challengers on states is necessary for constructing theoretical arguments as they constitute what is to be explained. As we have seen, theoretical arguments regarding the consequences of social movements tend to assume a certain level of resource mobilization. Some arguments focus on the strategies of social movement organizations, as well as their form and goals. Key among these strategies are claims-making and framing. Other scholars have argued that mobilized challengers have impacts based on systemic, structural, or changing political opportunities or contexts. Yet others have attempted to combine issues of strategy, organization form, and political context by examining the politically mediated effects of movements. These theoretical arguments attempt to take into account actors other than social movement organizations that are often found to be influential in the literature on the determinants of public policy and other alterations in the relations between states and societies.

Because of the many potential causal factors connected to state-related outcomes, the complexity of theoretical arguments concerning the influence of challengers on them, and information limitations that often lead to small-N studies, methodological difficulties have constrained research in this growing area of study. Yet there are a number of ways out, and these are being employed by scholars. Standard means for sorting out competing arguments include employing cross-national or subnational units for quantitative analyses. Scholars with medium-N research designs can employ Boolean techniques, which also allow for the appraisal of multiple and combinational causation and can be altered to take time into account. Small-N studies can analyze in detail one movement across polities or similar challengers within a given polity to appraise arguments. A variety of over-time and historical techniques can be employed to appraise the mechanisms of theoretical arguments, addressing whether linkages occur and in hypothesized order. It may be true that there has been a relative lack of progress in this area, despite all the recent attention to it (Giugni 1998), and perhaps this is due to the conceptual, theoretical, and methodological obstacles facing scholarship on the state-related consequences of challengers. Yet recent conceptual, theoretical, and methodological developments provide great promise, and there seem to be few major hurdles standing in the way of accumulating knowledge in this growing area of study.

Notes

1 It seems less likely that struggles over other aspects of electoral processes would increase the leverage of groups in this way. For instance, challengers seeking to gain direct democratic devices, such as the initiative, referendum, and recall, would not automatically provide groups a greater likelihood of achieving collective benefits through the state. Whatever gains that might be made along these lines would likely be situational. In the US case, these reforms were designed to break the power of the major political parties over political processes and their control over the development of state bureaucracies and policies. American parties were hierarchically organized and more oriented toward patronage and economic advantages than to issues, which were kept off political agendas (Mayhew 1986). The results of these mobilizations were uneven, with some western states and scattered municipalities gaining reforms (Shefter 1977; Finegold 1995; Clemens 1997). The advantages of such mobilizations for groups would seem to come only where patronage-oriented parties had a stranglehold over politics; mobilizations over electoral processes otherwise would not seem likely to provide political leverage for politically uninfluential groups.

2 This can be contrasted with sensitizing the "systemic agenda" (Kriesi et al. 1995), which is bringing an issue to the public's attention, or raising its "salience" (Burstein 1998, 1999).

3 Some scholars have proposed other "opportunity structures," such as the cultural ones (Banaszak 1996) and economic and gender-based opportunities (McCammon et al. 2001), that are also held to promote the productivity of collective action by challengers.

References and further reading

Amenta, E. (1991) Making the Most of a Case Study: Theories of the Welfare State and the American Experience. *International Journal of Comparative Sociology*, 32, 172–94.

——(1998) *Bold Relief: Institutional Politics and the Origins of Modern American Social Policy*. Princeton, NJ: Princeton University Press.

——(2002) Political Contexts, Strategies, and the Impact of Challengers on Public Policy: The Townsend Plan and U.S. Social Spending Challengers. In Conference on Social Movements, Public Policy, and Democracy, Jan. 11–13, 2002.

——(2003) What we Know about Social Policy: Comparative and Historical Research in Comparative and Historical Perspective. In D. Rueschemeyer and J. Mahoney (eds.), *Comparative and Historical Analysis*. New York: Cambridge University Press, 91–130.

Amenta, E., and J. D. Poulsen (1994) Where to Begin: A Survey of Five Approaches to Selecting Independent Measures for Qualitative Comparative Analysis. *Sociological Methods and Research*, 23, 21–52.

——(1996) Social Politics in Context: The Institutional Politics Theory and Social Spending at the End of New Deal. *Social Forces*, 75, 33–60.

Amenta, E., and M. P. Young (1999a) Democratic States and Social Movements: Theoretical Arguments and Hypotheses. *Social Problems*, 46, 153–68.

——(1999b) Making an Impact: The Conceptual and Methodological Implications of the Collective Benefits Criterion. In M. Giugni, D. McAdam, and C. Tilly (eds.), *How Movements Matter: Theoretical and Comparative Studies on the Consequences of Social Movements*. Minneapolis: University of Minnesota Press, 22–41.

Amenta, E., B. G. Carruthers, and Y. Zylan (1992) A Hero for the Aged? The Townsend Movement, the Political Mediation Model, and U.S. Old-Age Policy, 1934–1950. *American Journal of Sociology*, 98, 308–39.

Amenta, E., K. Dunleavy, and M. Bernstein (1994) Stolen Thunder? Huey Long's "Share our Wealth," Political Mediation, and the Second New Deal. *American Sociological Review*, 59, 678–702.

Amenta, E., D. Halfmann, and M. Young (1999) The Strategies and Contexts of Social Protest: Political Mediation and the Impact of the Townsend Movement. *Mobilization*, 56, 1–25.

Amenta, E., C. Bonastia, and N. Caren (2001) U.S. Social Policy in Comparative and Historical Perspective: Concepts, Images, Arguments, and Research Strategies. *Annual Review of Sociology*, 27, 213–34.

Amenta, E., N. Caren, T. Fetner, and M. P. Young (2002) Challengers and States: Toward a Political Sociology of Social Movements. *Research in Political Sociology*, 10, 47–83.

Andrews, K. T. (1997) The Impacts of Social Movements on the Political Process: The Civil Rights Movement and Black Electoral Politics in Mississippi. *American Sociological Review*, 62, 800–91.

——(2001) Social Movements and Policy Implementation: The Mississippi Civil Rights Movement and the War on Poverty, 1965–1971. *American Sociological Review*, 66, 21–48.

Balser, Deborah B. (1997) The Impact of Environmental Factors on Factionalism and Schism in Social Movement Organizations. *Social Forces*, 76, 199–228.

Banaszak, Lee Ann (1996) *Why Movements Succeed or Fail: Opportunity, Culture and the Struggle for Woman Suffrage*. Princeton, NJ: Princeton University Press.

Banaszak, Lee Ann, Karen Beckwith, and Dieter Rucht (eds.) (forthcoming) *Women's Movements Facing a Reconfigured State*. Cambridge: Cambridge University Press.

Barkan, S. E. (1984) Legal Control of the Southern Civil Rights Movement. *American Sociological Review*, 49, 552–65.

Barnes, D. A., and C. Connolly (1999) Repression, the Judicial System, and Political Opportunities for Civil Right Advocacy During the Reconstruction. *Sociological Quarterly*, 40, 327–45.

Baumgartner, F., and B. Jones (1993) *Agendas and Instability in American Politics*. Chicago: University of Chicago Press.

Baumgartner, Frank R., and Beth L. Leech (1998) *Basic Interests: The Importance of Groups in Politics and in Political Science*. Princeton, NJ: Princeton University Press.

Bennett, A., and A. George (1997) Process Tracing in Case Study Research. Paper presented at the MacArthur Foundation Workshop on Case Study Methods, October 17–19.

Bonastia, C. (2000) Why Did Affirmative Action in Housing Fail During the Nixon Era? Exploring the "Institutional Homes" of Social Policies. *Social Problems*, 47, 523 ff.

Brockett, C. D. (1991) The Structure of Political Opportunities and Peasant Mobilizations in Central America. *Comparative Politics*, 23, 253–74.

Brooks, Rachelle (1997) Feminists Negotiate the Legislative Branch: The Violence Against Women Act. In Cynthia R. Daniels (ed.), *Feminists Negotiate the State*. New York: University Press of America, 65–82.

Burnham, W. D. (1970) *Critical Elections and the Mainsprings of American Politics*. New York: W. W. Norton.

Burstein, P. (1991) Legal Mobilization as a Social Movement Tactic: The Struggle for Equal Employment Opportunity. *American Journal of Sociology*, 96, 1201–25.

—— (1993) Explaining State Action and the Expansion of Civil Riots: Passage of the Civil Riots Act of 1964. *Research in Political Sociology*, 6, 117–37.

—— (1998) *Discrimination, Jobs, and Politics*. Chicago: University of Chicago Press.

—— (1999) Social Movements and Public Policy. In Marco Giugni, Doug McAdam, and Charles Tilly (eds.), *Why Social Movements Matter*. Minneapolis: University of Minnesota Press, 3–21.

Burstein, Paul, and Marie Bricher (1997) Problem Definition and Public Policy: Congressional Committees Confront Work, Family and Gender, 1945–1990. *Social Forces*, 75, 135–69.

Burstein, Paul, and April Linton (2002) The Impact of Political Parties, Interest Groups, and Social Movement Organizations on Public Policy: Some Recent Evidence and Theoretical Concerns. *Social Forces*, 81, 380 ff.

Burstein, P., R. L. Einwohner, and J. A. Hollander (1995) The Success of Political Movements: A Bargaining Perspective. In J. C. Jenkins and B. Klandermans (eds.), *The Politics of Social Protest: Comparative Perspectives on States and Social Movements*. Minneapolis: University of Minnesota Press, 275–95.

Bush, Diane Mitsch (1992) Women's Movements and State Policy Reform Aimed at Domestic Violence against Women: A Comparison of the Consequences of Movement Mobilization in the U.S. and India. *Gender & Society*, 6, 587–608.

Button, J. (1989) *Blacks and Social Change: Impact of the Civil Rights Movement in Southern Communities*. Princeton, NJ: Princeton University Press.

Calman, Leslie J. (1989) Women and Movement Politics in India. *Asian Survey*, 29, 940–58.

Caren, N., and A. Panofsky (2002) HQCA: Adding Temporality to Ragin's Qualitative Comparative Analysis. Paper presented at the 2002 American Sociological Association Conference.

Cauthen, N. K., and E. Amenta (1996) Not for Widows Only: Institutional Politics and the Formative Years of Aid to Dependent Children. *American Sociological Review*, 60, 427–48.

Chong, D. (1991) *Collective Action and the Civil Rights Movement*. Chicago: University of Chicago Press.

Clemens, E. S. (1993) Organizational Repertoires and Institutional Change: Women's Groups and the Transformation of U.S. Politics, 1890–1920. *American Journal of Sociology*, 98, 755–98.

——(1997) *The People's Lobby: Organizational Innovation and the Rise of Interest Group Politics in the United States, 1890–1925*. Chicago: University of Chicago Press.

——(1999) Securing Political Returns to Social Capital: Women's Associations in the United States, 1880s–1920s. *Journal of Interdisciplinary History*, 29, 613–38.

Clemens, E. S., and J. M. Cook (1999) Politics and Institutionalism: Explaining Durability and Change. *Annual Review of Sociology*, 25, 441–66.

Conell, Carol, and Kim Voss (1993) Formal Organization and the Fate of Social Movements: Craft Association and Class Alliance in the Knights of Labor. *American Sociological Review*, 55, 255–69.

Costain, A. (1992) *Inviting Women's Rebellion: A Political Process Interpretation of the Women's Movement*. Baltimore: Johns Hopkins University Press.

Costain, A. N., and W. D. Costain (1987) Strategy and Tactics of the Women's Movement in the United States: The Role of Political Parties. In M. F. Katzenstein and C. McClurg Mueller (eds.), *The Women's Movements of the United States and Western Europe: Consciousness, Political Opportunity, and Public Policy*. Philadelphia, PA: Temple University Press, 196–214.

Costain, A. N, and S. Majstorovic (1994) Congress, Social Movements and Public Opinion: Multiple Origins of Women's Rights Legislation. *Political Research Quarterly*, 47, 111–35.

Cress, D. M., and D. A. Snow (2000) The Outcomes of Homeless Mobilizations: The Influence of Organization, Disruption, Political Mediation, and Framing. *American Journal of Sociology*, 105, 1063–104.

Dahl, R. (1971) *Polyarchy: Participation and Opposition*. New Haven: Yale University Press.

Dalton, R. (1988) *Citizen Politics in Western Democracies: Public Opinion and Political Parties in the United States, Great Britain, West Germany, and France*. Chatham, NJ: Chatham House.

——(1995) Strategies of Partisan Influence: West European Environmental Groups. In J. Craig Jenkins and Bert Klandermans (eds.), *The Politics of Social Protest*. Minneapolis: University of Minnesota Press, 296–323.

Daniels, R. (1971) *The Bonus March: An Episode of the Great Depression*. Westport, CT: Greenwood, 296–323.

——(1999) Protest, Protesters, and Protest Policing: Public Discourses in Italy and Germany from the 1960s to the 1980s. In M. Giugni, D. McAdam, and C. Tilly (eds.), *How Social Movements Matter*. Minneapolis: University of Minnesota Press, 66–96.

Deitch, Cynthia (1993) Gender, Race and Class Politics and the Inclusion of Women in Title VII of the 1964 Civil Rights Act. *Gender & Society*, 7, 183–203.

della Porta, D. (1996) Social Movements and the State: Thoughts on the Policing of Protest. In D. McAdam, J. D. McCarthy, and M. N. Zald (eds.), *Comparative Perspectives on Social Movements: Political Opportunities, Mobilizing Structures, and Cultural Framings*. Cambridge: Cambridge University Press, 62–92.

Diani M. (1997) Social Movements and Social Capital: A Network Perspective on Movement Outcomes. *Mobilization*, 2, 129–47.

Duerst-Lahti, G. (1989) The Government's Role in Building the Women's Movement. *Political Science Quarterly*, 104, 249–68.

Earl, J. (2000) Methods, Movements and Outcomes: Methodological Difficulties in the Study of Extra-Movement Outcomes. *Research in Social Movements, Conflicts and Change*, 22, 3–25.

Edwards, B., and S. Marullo (1995) Organizational Mortality in a Declining Social Movement: The Demise of Peace Movement Organizations in the End of the Cold War Era. *American Sociological Review*, 60, 908–27.

Ferree, M. M. (1987) Equality and Autonomy: Feminist Politics in the U.S. and the Federal Republic of Germany. In M. Katzenstein and C. Mueller (eds.), *The Women's Movements of the United States and Western Europe.* Philadelphia, PA: Temple University Press, 172–95.

Fetner, Tina (2001) Working Anita Bryant: The Impact of the Christian Antigay Movement on Lesbian and Gay Movement Claims. *Social Problems*, 48, 411–28.

Finegold, K. (1995) *Title Experts and Politicians: Reform Challenges to Machine Politics in New York, Cleveland, and Chicago.* Princeton, NJ: Princeton University Press.

Fowler, Linda L., and Ronald Shaiko (1987) The Grass Roots Connection: Environmental Activists and Senate Roll Call Votes. *American Journal of Political Science*, 31, 484–510.

Gamson, W. A. (1975) *The Strategy of Social Protest.* Homewood, IL: Dorsey.

——(1990) *The Strategy of Social Protest.* 2nd ed. Belmont, CA: Wadsworth.

——(1992) *Talking Politics.* Cambridge: Cambridge University Press.

Ganz, M. (2000) Resources and Resourcefulness: Strategic Capacity in the Unionization of California Agriculture, 1959–1966. *American Journal of Sociology*, 105, 1003–62.

Gentile, Pierre (1998) Radical Right Protest in Switzerland. In Dieter Rucht, Ruud Koopmans, and Friedhelm Neidhard (eds.), *Acts of Dissent: New Developments in the Study of Protest.* Berlin: Edition Sigma, 227–52.

Giugni, M. (1998) Was it Worth the Effort? The Outcomes and Consequences of Social Movements. *Annual Review of Sociology*, 24, 371–93.

——(1999) How Social Movements Matter: Past Research, Present Problems, Future Developments. In M. Giugni, D. McAdam, and C. Tilly (eds.), *How Social Movements Matter.* Minneapolis: University of Minnesota Press, xiii–xxxiii.

Goldstone, J. (1980) The Weakness of Organization: A New Look at Gamson's *The Strategy of Social Protest. American Journal of Sociology*, 85, 1017–42.

Goldstone, J., and C. Tilly (2001) Threat (and Opportunity): Popular Action and State Response in the Dynamics of Contentious Action. In Ronald Aminzade (ed.), *Silence and Voice in the Study of Contentious Politics.* Cambridge: Cambridge University Press, xv, 179–94.

Goodwin, J., and J. M. Jasper (1999) Caught in a Winding, Snarling Vine: The Structural Bias of Political Process Theory. *Sociological Forum*, 14, 27–54.

Gurr T. R. (ed.) (1983) Group Protest and Policy Responses: New Cross-National Perspectives. *American Behavioral Scientist*, 26, entire issue.

Halman, L., and N. Nevitte (eds.) (1996) *Political Value Change in Western Democracies.* Tilburg: Tilburg University Press.

Hansen, John Mark (1991) *Gaining Access: Congress and the Farm Lobby, 1919–1981.* Chicago: University of Chicago Press.

Hardin, R. (1982) *Collective Action.* Baltimore: Johns Hopkins University Press.

Hattam, V. C. (1993) *Labor Visions and State Power: The Origins of Business Unionism in the United States.* Princeton, NJ: Princeton University Press.

Hicks, A. (1999) *Social Democracy and Welfare Capitalism: A Century of Income Security Politics.* Ithaca, NY: Cornell University Press.

Hicks, A., and J. Misra (1993) Political Resources and the Growth of Welfare Effort: The Case of Affluent Capitalist Democracies, 1960–1982. *American Journal of Sociology*, 99, 668–710.

Huber, E., and J. D. Stephens (2001) *Political Choice in Global Markets: Development and Crisis of Advanced Welfare States.* Chicago: University of Chicago Press.

Huber, E., C. Ragin, and J. D. Stephens (1993) Social Democracy, Christian Democracy, Constitutional Structure and the Welfare State: Towards a Resolution of Quantitative Studies. *American Journal of Sociology*, 99, 711–49.

Huntington, S. P. (1968) *Political Order in Changing Societies.* New Haven, CT: Yale University Press.

Jenkins, J. C. (1982) Why Do Peasants Rebel: Structural and Historical Theories of Peasant Rebellion. *American Journal of Sociology*, 88, 487–512.

——(1983) Resource Mobilization Theory and the Study of Social Movements. *Annual Review of Sociology*, 9, 527–53.

——(1995) Social Movements, Political Representation, and the State: An Agenda and Comparative Framework. In J. C. Jenkins and B. Klandermans (eds.), *States and Social Movements*. Minneapolis: University of Minnesota Press, 14–35.

Jenkins, J. C., and C. Perrow (1977) Insurgency of the Powerless: Farm Worker Movements (1946–1972). *American Sociological Review*, 42, 249–68.

Jenness, Valerie, and Ryken Grattet (2001) *Making Hate a Crime*. New York: Russell Sage Foundation.

Joppke, Christian (1992–3) Decentralization of Control in U.S. Nuclear Energy Policy. *Political Science Quarterly*, 107, 709–25.

Katzenstein, M. F. (1987) Comparing the Feminist Movements of the United States and Western Europe: An Overview. In M. F. Katzenstein and C. McClurg Mueller (eds.), *The Women's Movements of the United States and Western Europe: Consciousness, Political Opportunity, and Public Policy*. Philadelphia, PA: Temple University Press, 3–20.

——(1998) *Faithful and Fearless: Moving Feminist Protest inside the Church and Military*. Princeton, NJ: Princeton University Press.

Katznelson, I. (1981) *City Trenches*. New York: Pantheon.

Keck, M., and K. Sikkink (1998) *Activists beyond Borders: Advocacy Networks in International Politics*. Ithaca, NY: Cornell University Press.

King, G., R. Keohane, and S. Verba (1994) *Designing Social Inquiry: Scientific Inference in Qualitative Research*. Princeton, NJ: Princeton University Press.

Kingdon, J. (1984) *Agendas, Alternatives and Public Policies*. Boston: Little, Brown.

Kitschelt, H. P. (1986) Political Opportunity Structures and Political Protest: Anti-Nuclear Movements in Four Democracies. *British Journal of Political Science*, 16, 57–85.

——(1988) Left-Libertarian Parties: Explaining Innovation in Competitive Party Systems. *World Politics*, 40, 195–234.

Klarman, Michael J. (1994) How *Brown* Changed Race Relations: The Backlash Thesis. *Journal of American History*, 81, 81–118.

Kousser, J. M. (1974) *The Shaping of Southern Politics: Suffrage Restriction and the Establishment of the One-Party South, 1880–1910*. New Haven: Yale University Press.

Kriesi, H. (1995) The Political Opportunity Structure of New Social Movements: Its Impact on Their Mobilization. In J. C. Jenkins and B. Klandermans (eds.), *States and Social Movements*. Minneapolis: University of Minnesota Press, 167–98.

——(1996) The Organizational Structure of New Social Movements in a Political Context. In D. McAdam, J. D. McCarthy, and M. N. Zald (eds.), *Comparative Perspectives on Social Movements: Opportunities, Mobilizing, Structures, and Cultural Framings*. New York: Cambridge University Press, 152–84.

Kriesi, Hanspeter, and Domnique Wisler (1999) The Impact of Social Movements on Political Institutions: A Comparison of the Introduction of Direct Legislation in Switzerland the United States. In M. Giugni, D. McAdam, and C. Tilly (eds.), *How Movements Matter: Theoretical and Comparative Studies on the Consequences of Social Movements*. Minneapolis: University of Minnesota Press, 42–65.

Kriesi, H., R. Koopmans, J. W. Duyvendak, and M. Guigni (1995) *New Social Movements in Western Europe: A Comparative Analysis*. Minneapolis: University of Minnesota Press.

Lieberson, S. (1992) Small *N*'s and Big Conclusions: An Examination of the Reasoning in Comparative Studies Based on a Small Number of Cases. In Charles C. Ragin and Howard S. Becker (eds.), *What Is a Case? Exploring the Foundations of Social Inquiry*. New York: Cambridge University Press, 105–18.

Lijphart, A. (1997) Unequal Participation: Democracy's Unresolved Dilemma. *American Political Science Review*, 91, 1–14.

Lipset, S. M., and G. Marks (2000) *It Didn't Happen Here: Why Socialism Failed in the United States*. New York: W. W. Norton.

Lipset, S. M., and S. Rokkan (1967) Cleavage Structures, Party Systems, and Voter Alignments. In S. M. Lipset and S. Rokkan (eds.), *Party Systems and Voter Alignments: Party Systems and Voter Alignments*. New York: Free Press, 1–66.

Lipsky, M. (1968) Protest as Political Resource. *American Political Science Review*, 62, 1144–58.

Lo, C. Y. H. (1990) *Small Property versus Big Government: The Social Origins of the Property Tax Revolt*. Berkeley: University of California Press.

Lowi, Theodore J. (1964) American Business, Public Policy, Case Studies, and Political Theory. *World Politics*, 6, 677–715.

McAdam, D. (1982) *Political Process and the Development of Black Insurgency, 1930–1970*. Chicago: University of Chicago Press.

——(1983) Tactical Innovation and the Pace of Insurgency. *American Sociological Review*, 48, 735–54.

——(1996) Conceptual Origins, Current Problems, Future Directions. In D. McAdam, J. D. McCarthy, and M. N. Zald (eds.), *Comparative Perspectives on Social Movements: Political Opportunities, Mobilizing Structures, and Cultural Framings*. New York: Cambridge University Press, 23–40.

McAdam, D., J. McCarthy, and M. N. Zald (1988) Social Movements. In Neil J. Smelser (ed.), *The Handbook of Sociology*. Beverly Hills, CA: Sage, 695–737.

——(1996) Introduction: Opportunities, Mobilizing Structures, and Framing Processes – Toward a Synthetic, Comparative Perspective on Social Movements. In D. McAdam, J. D. McCarthy, and M. N. Zald (eds.), *Comparative Perspectives on Social Movements: Political Opportunities, Mobilizing Structures, and Cultural Framings*. New York: Cambridge University Press, 1–22.

McAdam, D., S. Tarrow, and C. Tilly (2001) *Dynamics of Contention*. New York: Cambridge University Press.

McCammon, H., K. Campbell, E. Granberg, and C. Mowery (2001) How Movements Win: Gendered Opportunity Structures and U.S. Women's Suffrage Movements, 1866 to 1919. *American Sociological Review*, 66 (1), 47–70.

McCarthy, John D., and Clark McPhail (1998) The Institutionalization of Protest in the United States. In David S. Meyer and Sidney Tarrow (eds.), *The Social Movement Society*. Boulder, CO: Rowman & Littlefield, 83–110.

McCarthy, J. D., and M. Wolfson (1992) Consensus Movements, Conflict Movements, and the Cooptation of Civic and State Infrastructures. In A. D. Morris and C. McClurg Mueller (eds.), *Frontiers in Social Movement Theory*. New Haven: Yale University Press, 273–97.

McCarthy, J. D., and M. N. Zald (2002) The Enduring Vitality of the Resource Mobilization Theory of Social Movements. In Jonathon H. Turner (ed.), *Handbook of Sociological Theory*. New York: Kluwer Academic/Plenum, 533–65.

McCarthy, John D., David Britt, and Mark Wolfson (1991) The Institutional Channeling of Social Movements by the State in the United States. *Research in Social Movements, Conflicts and Change 13*. Oxford: JAI.

MacDougal J., S. D. Minicucci, and D. Myers (1995) The House of Representatives' vote on the Gulf War, 1991: Measuring Peace Movement Impact. *Research in Social Movements, Conflicts and Change*, 18, 255–84.

Mann, M. (1986) The Autonomous Power of the State: Its Origins, Mechanisms, and Results. In J. A. Hall (ed.), *States in History*. Oxford: Basil Blackwell.

Marwell, G., and P. Oliver (1988) The Paradox of Group Size in Collective Action: A Theory of the Critical Mass II. *American Sociological Review*, 53, 1–8.

Mayhew, David (1986) *Placing Parties in American Politics: Organization, Electoral Settings, and Government Activity in the Twentieth Century.* Princeton, NJ: Princeton University Press, 109–36.

Mettler, Suzanne (1998) *Dividing Citizens: Gender and Federalism in the New Deal.* Ithaca, NY: Cornell University Press.

Meyer, D. S. (forthcoming) Social Movements and Public Policy: Eggs, Chicken, and Theory. In H. Ingram, V. Jenness, and D. S. Meyer (eds.), *Routing the Opposition: Social Movements, Public Policy and Democracy.*

Meyer, D. S. (1993). Institutionalizing Dissent: The United States Structure of Political Opportunity and the End of the Nuclear Freeze. *Sociological Forum*, 8, 157–79.

Meyer, D. S., and S. Staggenborg (1996) Movements, Countermovements, and the Structure of Political Opportunities. *American Journal of Sociology*, 101, 1628–60.

Meyer, David S., and Sidney Tarrow (1998) *The Social Movement Society.* Boulder, CO: Rowman & Littlefield.

Minkoff, Debra C. (1994) From Service Provision to Institutional Advocacy: The Shifting Legitimacy of Organizational Forms. *Social Forces*, 72, 943–69.

Moore, Kelly (1999) Political Protest and Institutional Change: The Anti-Vietnam War Movement and American Science. In Marco Giugni, Doug McAdam, and Charles Tilly (eds.), *How Social Movements Matter.* Minneapolis: University of Minnesota Press, 97–118.

Nagel, J., and S. Olzak (1982) Ethnic Mobilization in New and Old States: An Extension of the Competition Model. *Social Problems*, 30, 127–43.

Nobles, M. (2000) *Shades of Citizenship: Race and the Census in Modern Politics.* Stanford: Stanford University Press.

Oestreicher, R. (1988) Urban Working-Class Political Behavior and Theories of American Electoral Politics, 1870–1940. *Journal of American History*, 74, 1257–86.

Olson, M. (1965) *The Logic of Collective Action.* Cambridge, MA: Harvard University Press.

Orloff, A. S., and T. Skocpol (1984) Why not Equal Protection? Explaining the Politics of Public Social Welfare in Britain and the United States, 1880s–1920s. *American Sociological Review*, 49, 726–50.

Oxhorn, Philip (1994) Where Did All the Protests Go? Popular Mobilization and the Transition to Democracy in Chile. *Latin American Perspectives*, 82, 49–68.

Pierson, P. (1994) *Dismantling the Welfare State? Reagan, Thatcher, and the Politics of Retrenchment.* New York: Cambridge University Press.

Piven, F. F., and R. A. Cloward (1977) *Poor People's Movements: Why They Succeed, How they Fail.* New York: Random House.

——(1989) *Why Americans Don't Vote.* New York : Pantheon.

Plotke, D. (1996) *Building a Democratic Political Order: Reshaping American Liberalism in the 1930s and 1940s.* New York: Cambridge University Press.

Polletta, F. (1999) Snarls, Quacks, and Quarrels: Culture and Structure in Political Process Theory. *Sociological Forum*, 14, 63–70.

Polletta, F., and J. M. Jasper (2001) Collective Identity and Social Movements. *Annual Review of Sociology*, 27, 283–305.

Quadagno, J. (1992) Social Movements and State Transformation: Labor Unions and Racial Conflict in the War on Poverty. *American Sociological Review*, 57, 616–34.

Ragin, C. C. (1987) *The Comparative Method: Moving beyond Qualitative and Quantitative Strategies.* Berkeley: University of California Press.

——(1989) The Logic of the Comparative Method and the Algebra of Logic. *Journal of Quantitative Anthropology*, 1, 373–98.

——(2000) *Fuzzy Set Social Science.* Chicago: University of Chicago Press.

Ragin, C., and H. Becker (1992) *What Is a Case? Exploring the Foundations of Social Inquiry.* Cambridge, MA: Cambridge University Press.

Ray, R., and Korteweg, A. C. (1999) Women's Movements in the Third World. *Annual Review of Sociology*, 25, 47–71.

Reese, Ellen (1996) Maternalism and Political Mobilization: How California's Postwar Child Care Campaign Was Won. *Gender & Society*, 10, 566–89.

Rochon T., and D. A. Mazmanian (1993) Social Movements and the Policy Process. *Annals of the American Academy of Political and Social Science*, 528, 75–87.

Rohrschneider, Robert (1993) New Party versus Old Left Realignments: Environmental Attitudes, Party Policies, and Partisan Affiliation in Four West European Countries. *Journal of Politics*, 55, 682–701.

Rucht, D. (1989) Environmental Movement Organizations in West Germany and France. In B. Klandermans (ed.), *Organizing for Change: Social Movement Organizations in Europe and the United States*. Greenwich, CT: JAI, 69–94.

——(1999) The Impact of Environmental Movements in Western Societies. In M. Giugni, D. McAdam, and C. Tilly (eds.), *How Movements Matter: Theoretical and Comparative Studies on the Consequences of Social Movements*. Minneapolis: University of Minnesota Press, 204–24.

Rueschemeyer, D., E. H. Stephens, and J. D. Stephens (1992) *Capitalist Development and Democracy*. Cambridge: Polity; Chicago: University of Chicago Press, 1992.

Schwartz, M. A. (2000) Continuity Strategies among Political Challengers: The Case of Social Credit. *American Review of Canadian Studies*, 30, 455–77.

Shefter, M. (1977) Party and Patronage: Germany, England and Italy. *Politics and Society*, 7, 403–52.

——(1986) Trade Unions and Political Machines: The Organization and Disorganization of the American Working Class in the Late Nineteenth Century. In I. Katznelson and A. Zolberg (eds.), *Working-Class Formation: Nineteenth-Century Patterns in Western Europe and the United States*. Princeton, NJ: Princeton University Press, 197–298.

Skocpol, T. (1980) Political Response to Capitalist Crisis: Neo-Marxist Theories of the State and the Case of the New Deal. *Politics and Society*, 10, 155–201.

——(1985) Bringing the State Back In: Strategies of Analysis in Current Research. In P. B. Evans, D. Rueschemeyer, and T. Skocpol (eds.), *Bringing the State Back In*. Cambridge: Cambridge University Press, 3–37.

——(1992) *Protecting Soldiers and Mothers: The Political Origins of Social Policy in the United States*. Cambridge, MA: Harvard University Press.

Skocpol, T., and E. Amenta (1986) States and Social Policies. *Annual Review of Sociology*, 12, 131–57.

Skrentny, J. D. (1996) *The Ironies of Affirmative Action: Politics, Culture and Justice in America*. Chicago: University of Chicago Press.

Snow, D. A., and R. D. Benford (1988) Ideology, Frame Resonance, and Participant Mobilization. *International Social Movement Research*, 1, 197–217.

Snyder, D., and W. R. Kelly (1979) Strategies for Investigating Violence and Social Change: Illustrations from Analysis of Racial Disorders and Implications for Mobilization Research. In Mayer N. Zald and John D. McCarthy (eds.), *The Dynamics of Social Movements*. Cambridge, MA: Winthrop, 212–37.

Soule, Sarah (forthcoming) Divestment by Colleges and University in the United States: Institutional Pressures toward Isomorphism. In Walter W. Powell and Daniel L. Jones (eds.), *How Institutions Change*. Chicago: University of Chicago Press.

Soule, S., D. McAdam, J. D. McCarthy, and Y. Su (1999) Protest Events: Cause or Consequence of State Action? The U.S. Women's Movement and Federal Congressional Activities, 1956–1979. *Mobilization*, 42 (2), 239–56.

Staggenborg, S. (1991) *The Pro-Choice Movement: Organization and Activism in the Abortion Conflict*. New York: Oxford University Press.

Steinmo, S., K. Thelen, and F. Longstreth (eds.) (1992) *Structuring Politics: Historical Institutionalism in Comparative Analysis*. New York: Cambridge University Press.

Steson, D. M., and A. G. Mazur (2000) Women's Movements and the State: Job-training Policy in France and the U.S. *Political Research Quarterly*, 53, 597–623.

Stone, Deborah (1989) Causal Stories and the Formation of Policy Agendas. *Political Science Quarterly*, 104, 281–300.

——(1997) *Policy Paradox: The Art of Political Decision Making*. New York: W. W. Norton.

Suh, D. (2001) How Do Political Opportunities Matter for Social Movements? Political Opportunity, Misframing, Pseudosuccess, and Pseudofailure. *Sociological Quarterly*, 42, 437–60.

Tarrow, S. (1996) States and Opportunities: The Political Structuring of Social Movements. In D. McAdam, J. D. McCarthy, and M. N. Zald (eds.), *Comparative Perspectives on Social Movements: Opportunities, Mobilizing, Structures, and Cultural Framings*. New York: Cambridge, 41–61.

——(1998) *Power in Movement: Social Movements, Collective Action, and Politics*. 2nd ed. Cambridge: Cambridge University Press.

Thelen, K. (1999) Historical Institutionalism in Comparative Politics. *Annual Review of Political Science*, 2, 369–404.

Tilly, C. (1978) *From Mobilization to Revolution*. Reading, MA: Addison-Wesley.

——(1986) *The Contentious French*. Cambridge, MA: Harvard University Press.

——(1998) Regimes and Contention CIAO Working Paper. New York.

——(1999) Conclusion: From Interactions to Outcomes in Social Movements. In D. McAdam, J. D. McCarthy, and M. N. Zald (eds.), *Comparative Perspectives on Social Movements: Political Opportunities, Mobilizing Structures, and Cultural Framings*. Cambridge: Cambridge University Press, 253–70.

Valocchi, Steve (1990) The Unemployed Workers' Movement: A Reexamination of the Piven and Cloward Thesis. *Social Problems*, 37, 191–205.

Wald, Kenneth D., James W. Button, & Barbara A. Rienzo. (1996) The Politics of Gay Rights in American Communities: Explaining Anti-discrimination Ordinances and Policies. *American Journal of Political Science*, 40, 1152–78.

Walker, Jack (1991) *Mobilizing Interest Groups in America: Patrons, Professions and Social Movements*. Ann Arbor: University of Michigan Press.

Walton, J. (1992) *Western Times and Water Wars: State, Culture, and Rebellion in California*. Berkeley: University of California Press.

Weed, Frank (1995) *Certainty of Justice: Reform in the Crime Victim Movement*. New York: Aldine de Gruyter.

Werum, R., and B. Winders (2001) Who's "In" and Who's "Out": State Fragmentation and the Struggle over Gay Rights, 1974–1999. *Social Problems*, 48, 386–410.

Western, B. (1993) Postwar Unionization in Eighteen Advanced Capitalist Countries. *American Sociological Review*, 58, 266–82.

Wilson, James Q. (1995) *Political Organizations*. 2nd ed. Princeton, NJ: Princeton University Press.

Wolfson, Mark (2001) *The Fight against Big Tobacco: The Movement, the State and the Public's Health*. New York: Aldine de Gruyter.

21

Personal and Biographical Consequences

Marco G. Giugni

Personal, Biographical, and Other Consequences of Social Movements

Personal and biographical consequences of social movements are effects on the life course of individuals who have participated in movement activities, effects that are at least in part due to involvement in those activities. At stake is not the impact of movements as a whole, but the effect of individual involvement in movement activities on the life course of participants, especially – but not exclusively – those who are strongly involved, as well as on aggregate-level life-course patterns. Thus defined, personal and biographical consequences of social movements exclude a number of related but distinct phenomena. First, since we speak of *personal and biographical* consequences, it excludes all kinds of movement effects that do not bear upon the individual life of participants in movement activities. Social movements have consequences on different areas of human affairs (political, cultural, social) and are located at different levels of analysis (micro, meso, macro). Researchers have tended to focus quite narrowly on the political impact of movements, both for theoretical and methodological reasons. Even more narrowly, policy and legislative effects form the bulk of existing work (see Giugni 1998 for a review; see further chapter 20 in this volume and Burstein 1999). Moreover, and related to this analytic focus, scholars have primarily studied the intended consequences of protest activities. Yet, as Tilly (1999: 270) among others has underscored, we must consider seriously "the possibility that the major effects of social movements will have little or nothing to do with the public claims their leaders make." In spite of recent efforts in this direction (Deng 1997), the unintended consequences of movement actions remain an understudied aspect of this field. Individual or life-course effects of social movement activities certainly belong to this category.

Second, since we speak of personal and biographical *consequences*, the above definition excludes other aspects of social movements related to the individual and the life course. A fair amount of work on social movements and contentious politics since the 1970s has dealt with the microsociological question of individual participation in social movements, in particular by stressing the social-structural factors that account for activism, that is, social networks (e.g., Snow et al. 1980; Rosenthal et al. 1985; McAdam 1986, 1988; Fernandez and McAdam 1988; McAdam et al. 1988; Gould 1993, 1995; Kriesi 1993; McAdam and Paulsen 1993; McCarthy 1996; Kim and Bearman 1997). A lower but nevertheless significant number of studies have stressed the attitudinal or psychological determinants of activism (e.g., Hardin 1982; Opp 1989; Chong 1991; Macy 1991; Sandler 1992) as well as, closer to our present focus, the role of "biographical availability" (e.g., McAdam 1986; Wiltfang and McAdam 1991; Passy and Giugni 2000). Finally, some scholars have attempted to combine both perspectives within a more integrated approach (e.g., Klandermans 1984, 1997; Marwell and Oliver 1993; Passy 1998; Passy and Giugni 2001). In the face of so many works focusing on the factors that account for individual participation in and recruitment to social movements (see further the contributions to Part IV of this volume), the literature on the consequences of activism and participation on the personal lives of participants is little more than a marginal part of this field of study.

The analysis of the personal and biographical consequences of social movements lies at the crossroad of two major fields in the social sciences: (1) studies of life course and the life cycle (see Hareven 1994 for a review), and (2) work on processes of political socialization and participation (see Milbrath 1981 and Johnston Conover 1991 for reviews). A recent essay by Goldstone and McAdam (2001) helps us to locate our subject matter within the more specific context of scholarly work on the demographic and personal dimensions of contentious politics. They provide a map of the literature on demography, life course, and contention in an attempt to redress what they see as two major lacunae in this literature: (1) the lack of a sustained demographic/life-course perspective on contention in favor of a piecemeal approach to the topic, and (2) a general asymmetry whereby "most work by social movement scholars is pitched at the *microlevel* and concerned with life-course outcomes, while students of revolutions reverse the two emphases, focusing on the *macrodeterminants* of contention" (Goldstone and McAdam 2001: 196–7).

Table 21.1 shows the conceptual map laid out by Goldstone and McAdam. It distinguishes between four discrete literatures in the study of demography, life course, and contention. These literatures differ according to their thematic focus (movement emergence/development or decline/outcomes) and according to their analytic focus (macro- or microlevels of analysis). A first set of studies has looked at the origin of contention from a macrosociological point of view, for example by inquiring about the impact of demographic pressures for the emergence of contention, after the relationship between land pressures and peasant rebellion, or about the role of migration processes to account for the rise of ethnic competition. A second set of studies, following a microsociological perspective, has looked at the biographical availability or other life-course factors that facilitate or prevent movement activism. A third kind of work, concerned with the demographic and life-course dimensions of social movements, less common than the other three, has analyzed contention as a force for aggregate change in life-course patterns. As I

Table 21.1   Silence and voice in the study of demography, life course, and contention

	Emergence/development	*Decline/outcomes*
Macro	Demographic pressures and the emergence of contention Land pressure and peasant rebellion Migration and the rise of ethnic competition	Contention as a force for aggregate change in life-course patterns
Micro	"Biographical availability" or other life-course factors mediating entrance into activism	Biographical consequences of individual activism

Source: Goldstone and McAdam (2001)
(Copyright: Cambridge University Press, 40 West 20th Street, New York, NY 10011-4211)

will argue in more detail below, this macrolevel analysis represents a particularly promising avenue for grasping the long-term impact of social movements on contemporary society. Finally, a fourth specific literature geared at the microlevel of analysis has focused on the biographical consequences of individual activism. The important point for our present purpose is that we should distinguish clearly between two different types of demographic impact (third column of the table): the *biographical consequences of individual activism* and the *aggregate-level change in life-course patterns* (see further McAdam 1999). While the former concerns the microlevel effects of sustained participation in social movements, the latter deals with the broader, macrolevel consequences of social movements. Needless to say, the broader perspective potentially has more to say about social change.

My review deals exclusively with the third column of table 21.1. I consider studies both of the biographical consequences of activism and work on the aggregate-level change in life-course patterns that has a wide impact on society. However, since the former represents the bulk of work in this subfield of the social movement's literature, I pay special attention to it. The main part of the chapter is formed by the next four sections. In the next section, I review a number of studies that have focused on activists involved in protest activities – often high-risk activities – within the New Left. I then report on work that has dealt with less risky activities and less committed participants. The still sporadic work on aggregate-level change in life-course patterns is discussed in the following section. Finally, I mention certain methodological problems shared by most of the existing studies of the personal and biographical consequences of activism.

FOLLOW-UP STUDIES OF NEW LEFT ACTIVISTS

The cycle of contention of the 1960s inspired a number of systematic follow-up studies of people who were involved in protest activities during that period. In line with the main ideological orientation of that period, all these studies have examined former activists in movements of the New Left. Many of them, furthermore, have looked at participants in the US civil rights movement, both because this is one of the major social movements of that period and because some of the researchers were themselves involved in this movement. If work on the policy consequences of social movements yields ambivalent findings (see Giugni 1998), these *follow-up studies of New Left activists* provide a more consistent picture of the biographical impact of participation on movement activities: in general, they all point to a strong and durable impact on the personal lives of activists. Table 21.2, which adapts a table presented in McAdam's (1989) article on the biographical consequences of activism, offers a schematic overview of the follow-up studies of movement activists.[1] With the help of this table, I first review the main existing works (including the principal resulting publications) in chronological order and then summarize their main findings.

James Fendrich is among those who have inquired most thoroughly into the personal consequences of movement participation. He studied a sample of 100 activists involved in the civil rights movement in Tallahassee, Florida, in the early 1960s. The data were gathered in 1971, and included 72 black and 28 white activists. Although some of the published materials focus on the subsample of white activists (Fendrich and Tarleau 1973; Fendrich 1974), this is a methodological advantage of Fendrich's study, as thus he was able to compare the two groups (Fendrich 1977). Another advantage of his approach as compared to other work lies in the fact that he returned to 85 of his subjects at a later stage, in 1986, in order to assess the impact of their involvement in the long run (Fendrich and Lovoy 1988; Fendrich 1993).[2]

If Fendrich is one of the most prominent students of the personal and biographical consequences of social movements, the first major follow-up study of New Left activists was done by Jay Demerath, Gerald Marwell, and Michael Aiken. In 1969, they interviewed 40 of the 223 volunteers they had surveyed four years earlier before and after the latter took part in a voter registration effort sponsored by the Southern Christian Leadership Conference (Demerath et al. 1971). Much later, and similarly to the approach followed by Fendrich, they again surveyed 145 of the volunteers in order to gauge the long-term effects of their participation (Marwell et al. 1987).

One of the most thorough and methodologically sound follow-up studies of New Left activists was conducted by Kent Jennings and Richard Niemi in 1973, when they surveyed 216 former activists (Jennings and Niemi 1981). Unlike other works, their study concerned subjects whose involvement in movement activities varied greatly. In addition, previous involvement spanned a longer time frame, namely, an 8-year period. This double feature gives their study a clear methodological advantage as compared to most of the other studies reviewed here.

This is certainly true for the study conducted by Alberta Nassi and Stephen Abramowitz, which, in chronological order, is the next major piece of research. In 1977, these researchers surveyed 30 activists who, ten years earlier, got involved in demonstrations in Berkeley, California (Nassi and Abramowitz 1979; Abramowitz and Nassi 1981). Not only is the period of involvement in this case much shorter (as it is limited to participating in a series of episodes of contention), but the number of subjects in the sample was significantly lower than in Jennings and Niemi's work.

The sample was even smaller in the well-known study by Jack Whalen and Richard Flacks, which included only 11 subjects. These were student radicals who

Table 21.2 Major follow-up studies of movement activists

Investigator(s)	Year of participation	Year of follow-up	Activists in sample	Control group?	Before and after data?	Selected resulting publications
Demerath et al.	1965	1969	40	no	yes	Demerath et al. 1971
Fendrich	1960–3	1971	28/100[a]	yes	no	Fendrich 1974, 1977; Fendrich and Krauss 1978; Fendrich and Tarleau 1973
Fendrich and Lovoy	1960–3	1986	23	yes	no	Fendrich 1993[b]; Fendrich and Lovoy 1988
Jennings and Niemi	1964–72	1973	216	yes	yes	Jennings and Niemi 1981; Jennings 1987
Maidenberg and Meyer	1967	1969	230	no	no	Maidenberg and Meyer 1970
Marwell et al.	1965	1984	145	no	yes	Marwell et al. 1987
McAdam	1964	1983–84	330	yes	yes	McAdam 1988, 1989
Nassi and Abramowitz	1967	1979	15/30[c]	no	no	Abramowitz and Nassi 1981; Nassi and Abramowitz 1979
Whalen and Flacks	1970	1980	11	no	no	Whalen and Flacks 1980, 1984, 1989

[a]Fendrich's 1977 article is based on comparative data on 28 white and 72 black activists.
[b]Fendrich's 1993 book summarizes the overall thrust of his work on this topic.
[c]Nassi and Abramowitz (1979) relied on 15 subjects; Abramowitz and Nassi (1981), on 30.
Source: Adapted from McAdam (1989: 747).

were arrested in relation to the burning of a bank in Santa Barbara, California, in 1970. The researchers interviewed these activists ten years later to assess the long-term impact of their involvement in that event (Whalen and Flacks 1980, 1984, 1989).

The last follow-up study of New Left activists I would like to mention in my brief review was conducted by Doug McAdam. In 1983 and 1984, this author collected data on 212 participants in the 1964 Mississippi Freedom Summer project in order to assess both the short-term and long-term political and personal consequences of movement participation (McAdam 1988, 1989). An important feature of McAdam's study lies in the comparison he was able to make with 118 "no-shows," that is, individuals who applied, were accepted, but did not take part in the project. As I will argue in more detail below, this gave him a crucial methodological advantage as compared to other work, as thus he had at his disposal a control group (but see the studies by Fendrich and Lovoy 1988, and Jennings and Niemi 1981).

What do these follow-up studies of New Left activists tell us about the personal and biographical consequences of participation in social movements? As McAdam (1999; see further Goldstone and McAdam 2001) has stressed in his own review, and as I mentioned earlier, taken together, they point to a powerful and enduring impact of participation in movement activities on the biographies of participants. Specifically, activism had a strong effect both on the political and personal lives of the subjects. On the political side, former activists (1) had continued to espouse leftist political attitudes (e.g., Demerath et al. 1971; Fendrich and Tarleau 1973; Whalen and Flacks 1980; Marwell et al. 1987, 1989); (2) had continued to define themselves as "liberal" or "radical" in political orientation (e.g., Fendrich and Tarleau 1973); and (3) had remained active in contemporary movements or other forms of political activity (e.g., Fendrich and Krauss 1978; Jennings and Niemi 1981; Fendrich and Lovoy 1988; McAdam 1989). On the personal side, former activists (1) had been concentrated in teaching or other "helping" professions (e.g., Maidenberg and Mayer 1970; Fendrich 1974; McAdam 1989); (2) had lower incomes than their age peers; (3) were more likely than their age peers to have divorced, married later, or remained single (e.g., McAdam 1988, 1989); and (4) were more likely than their age peers to have experienced an episodic or nontraditional work history (e.g., McAdam 1988, 1989).

In sum, participation in social movement activities appears to have profoundly affected the biographies of former activists and to have left a strong imprint on their personal lives. However, the subjects of the studies reviewed above are in many respects quite peculiar. On the one hand, they were all involved in New Left movements, in particular in the US civil rights movement. On the other hand, most of them belonged to the core activists of these movements and hence were strongly committed to their cause. The question remains open whether similar results would be found for other types of movements (for example, right-wing movements) or less strongly committed participants. Concerning movements, very little work has been done so far. A significant example is Klatch's (1999) study of longstanding personal and biographical consequences of people "on the left" and people "on the right" of the political spectrum. Yet, work on the New Left still dominates the existing literature. Concerning participants, some efforts have recently been made to redress the present bias toward the impact of activities that imply a strong commitment. I address this issue next.

BEYOND NEW LEFT ACTIVISM

Existing work on the personal and biographical consequences of social movements has focused mainly on a specific type of movement participants, namely, activists, those who strongly identify with a movement and its cause or objectives, and who devote considerable time and energy to movement activities, including engagement in high-risk activism.[3] Other researchers, in addition to those mentioned earlier, have examined the consequences of being involved in risky or at least costly political activities. Involvement in "identity politics" is a case in point. For example, Taylor and Raeburn (1995) have looked at the career consequences of high-risk activism by lesbian, gay, and bisexual sociologists. Following a broader perspective, Whittier (1995) has shown in her study of the radical women's movement in Colombus, Ohio, that social movements may alter their social context, leading successive generations of participants to develop new perspectives. Looking at another kind of movement, Nagel (1995) has also addressed the impact of identity-based activism. In her study of the Native American Movement, she argues that Native American activism in the 1960s and 1970s led to an increased tendency of Native Americans to self-identify as such. Thus the apparent demographic trend of an increase in Native Americans can be partly explained by the increase in ethnic pride associated with the movement.

While focusing on a specific type of political activism is not a weakness in itself and, in a way, is even a reasonable methodological choice, it certainly limits the possibility for generalizing the findings, especially if the number of subjects is small, like in some of the works reviewed above. A number of more recent studies, using survey data, have tried to avoid this pitfall by looking at the *personal consequences of more "routine," low-risk forms of participation*. For example, Sherkat and Blocker (1997) have analyzed data from the Youth–Parent Socialization Panel Study to inquire into the political and personal consequences of participation in antiwar and student protests of the late 1960s. They found that ordinary involvement in these movements had an impact on the lives of those who had participated. Comparing participants with people who were not involved in those protests, they could show that demonstrators differed from nonactivists both shortly after their movement experiences and some ten years later, when they were in their mid-30s. Specifically, they found former protesters held more liberal political orientations and were more aligned with liberal parties and actions, selected occupations in the "new class," were more educated, held less traditional religious orientations and were less attached to religious organizations, married later, and finally, were less likely to have children.

Similarly, research conducted by McAdam and a number of collaborators aims to go beyond a specific focus on strongly committed activists to provide a broader perspective on the personal and biographical consequences of participation in social movements (McAdam 1999; see further McAdam et al. 1998; Wilhelm 1998; Van Dyke et al. 2000). The main goal of this study is "to assess the relationship between people's 'political experiences and orientations' during the 1960s and 1970s and their subsequent life-course choices" (McAdam 1999: 122). Recognizing that students of contentious politics have rarely inquired systematically into the unintended and long-term impact of movements, to focus instead on short-term political effects, McAdam and his colleagues have conducted a random national survey of US residents born between 1943 and 1964 to study the impact of movement participation in America, both on the lives of those who participated in those struggles and on the structure of the American society at the end of the 1990s. Similar to what Sherkat and Blocker (1997) have found, and consistent with the results of follow-up studies of New Left activists, their research shows among other things that movement participants are more likely to have been divorced, to have been married later, to have cohabited outside of marriage, and to have experienced an extended period of unemployment since completing their education, and, conversely, were less likely to have had children and to have married (see further Goldstone and McAdam 2001). In short, people who have been involved in social movement activities, even at a low level of commitment, carry the consequences of that involvement throughout their life.

Unlike the follow-up studies of New Left activists reviewed above, which relied on relatively small to very small samples of individuals, these more recent studies make use of large-scale survey data. In doing so, the authors were able to show that the personal and biographical consequences of participation in social movements are not limited to the most committed activists who are involved in high-risk actions, but also affect the lives of people who participate in more "routine," lower-level activities. Of course, this is not to say that the use of survey data is exempt from certain methodological limitations. The data created by McAdam and collaborators, just to mention one major study, indeed present some important flaws. For example, as they are ready to admit (see McAdam 1999), the response rate of 53 percent is only marginally acceptable by usual social-science standards and raises questions concerning the sample's representativeness. This is obviously a major handicap for research that arguably has among its aims to go beyond the limited possibility for generalization offered by the small samples used in earlier work. Similarly, the comparison of their sample with the overall distributions of certain social character-istics among the general population is sometimes problematic. For example, the share of women and whites in the sample is larger than in the US population at large. The overestimation of certain characteristics is even greater with regard to educa-tion. Their findings should thus be weighed in the light of these discrepancies. Yet, as compared to earlier work, these more recent studies move us a step forward toward a better understanding of the personal and biographical consequences of participa-tion in social movements. This leads me to discuss the issue of the broader social and cultural significance of movement participation and the role of social movements as a force for aggregate change in life-course patterns.

SOCIAL MOVEMENTS AND AGGREGATE-LEVEL CHANGE

The follow-up studies on former activists as well as other work on life-course changes resulting from sustained participation in social movements, although inter-esting in themselves, have little to say about contemporary society as a whole. This is especially true to the extent that researchers have most of the time examined a particular type of activist usually involved in high-risk activities. Work that has looked at more "routine," lower-level forms of involvement in social movements partly avoids this limitation. Nevertheless, the question remains open whether these findings have broader implications for the population at large and the aggregate patterns of life-course events. Work on aggregate-level change in life-course patterns is much more informative about processes of political, cultural, and social change.

The recent study conducted by McAdam and his colleagues mentioned earlier (McAdam et al. 1998; Wilhelm 1998; McAdam 1999; Van Dyke et al. 2000) tries to transcend the individual-level consequences of activism to embrace a broader perspective that provides insights into the role of contention for social change. I briefly touched upon the first part of their study in the previous section. Here I would like to say a bit more about its second part, that concerned with *aggregate-level changes in the life course*, the most important one with respect to the relationship between social movements and cultural change.

The research by McAdam and his collaborators points to the role of the turbulence of the 1960s in shaping aggregate-level changes in the life course. The point of departure is represented by the cultural shift associated with the people born during the period of the so-called "baby boom" after the end of World War II, a shift that can be observed among other things in deviations from the normal life-course sequence (Rindfuss et al. 1987) or in the transformation from a materialist to a postmaterialist value system (Inglehart 1977). The question, then, is how to explain these deviations and shift.

We know Inglehart's (1977, 1990) answer to this question. He points to the role of economic growth and development of the welfare state after World War II in producing a "silent revolution" that, through socialization processes, has transformed the core values of Western societies. According to his well-known thesis, postwar cohorts in Western Europe have different value priorities from older cohorts, because people born during that historical phase grew up under far more secure formative conditions. While the cohorts that had experienced the two world wars and the Great Depression gave priority to economic and physical security, a growing proportion of the younger cohorts privilege self-expression and the quality of life. Thus, in this perspective, postwar prosperity would have contributed to spreading postmaterialist values. Since fundamental value change takes place as younger birth cohorts replace older ones in the adult population of a society, this long period of growing economic and physical security led to a substantial difference in the value priorities of older (mainly materialist) and younger (mainly postmaterialist) groups, who have been shaped by different experiences in their formative years. Following this reasoning, the deviations from life-course norms may be seen as a result – indeed, an indicator – of this fundamental value shift.

A different answer to the question of what accounts for the changes in the organization of the life course was provided by Easterlin (1980; see further Pampel and Peters 1995; Macunovich 1997). His explanation stresses economic and demographic factors. According to him, the deviations from the normal life course observed among the baby boomers depend to a large extent on the size and sequence of the baby boom cohorts. The early baby boomers took advantage of unprecedented occupational opportunities created by a rapidly expanding economy and the relatively small size of the Depression and World War II cohorts. This, in turn, led them to conform to the normative path of getting into adulthood. In contrast, the younger baby boomers faced an increasingly stagnant economy and intense competition on the labor market, which prevented them from finding full-time employment. This delayed their entrance into other adult roles.

Easterlin's explanation came under explicit attack by McAdam (1999; see further Goldstone and McAdam 2001). Criticizing the incompleteness and demographic determinism of Easterlin's account, he argues for a greater role of the broader political, cultural, and social dynamics of the period in question. He suggests that "the effects of cohort size were mediated by the values and the political and cultural experiences of the baby boomer" (McAdam 1999: 136). To explain the link between the movements of the 1960s and 1970s and the changes in life-course patterns associated with the baby boom cohorts, he hypothesizes a three-stage process "by which the broad social movement dynamics of the period came to reshape the normative contours of the life-course" (McAdam 1999: 138). In the first stage, activists in the political and countercultural movements of the period (whose value system, as Inglehart would argue, leaned strongly toward postmaterialism) rejected normal life-course trajectories in favor of newer alternatives. Life-course deviations such as cohabitation, childlessness, and an episodic work track were consciously chosen as alternatives to traditional patterns. In the second stage, these alternatives became embedded in a number of geographic and subcultural locations that were the principal centers of the "1960s experience" and of New Left activism, above all college campuses and self-counsciously countercultural neighborhoods. Thus, upper-middle-class suburbs gradually came to embody the new alternatives through socialization processes. Finally, in the third stage, these alternative life-course patterns became available to increasingly heterogeneous strata of young Americans through processes of diffusion and adaptation. At the same time, these alternatives were largely stripped of their original political or countercultural content to be experienced as simply new life-course norms.

McAdam has thus proposed a model of demographic diffusion in which new lifestyle patterns spread with each passing cohort (joining Inglehart on this point). Again, the findings of his team's research must be read in the light of the methodological problems mentioned above concerning the representativeness of their sample. In addition, one might question the kind of variables used in their analysis as well as the relationship established between prior activism and demographic outcomes. For example, while Inglehart (1977, 1990) looked at a general shift in value orientations among European populations, McAdam and his colleagues focus on a limited number of variables, such as the age at marriage or the age of birth of the first child. While the diminished impact of prior activism and the greater effect of some mediating factors (such as attendance at an "activist college" and church attendance) on these measures of demographic change over subsequent cohorts shows that these behavioral patterns became stripped from their original embeddedness in participation in movement activities, this remains at best a very limited empirical measure of demographic outcomes of social movements. In spite of this necessary caution, the important point from the perspective of the analysis of the personal and biographical consequences of social movements is that this approach contributes to the sociological literature on the demographic significance of broader historical events and process (e.g., Elder 1974; Buchman 1989; Elder and Caspi 1990), but at the same time stresses the role of the political and cultural movements of the 1960s in this process. In so doing, it suggests an impact of these movements that goes well beyond the individual life histories of those who took part in the struggles to affect the entire structure of American society. It remains to determine whether one would find similar processes and mechanisms in other social and cultural contexts, and hence whether these findings can be generalized beyond the specific case of the US. The challenge, both theoretical and methodological, for other researchers is launched.

METHODOLOGICAL ISSUES

I already hinted at some methodological shortcomings of existing works in the previous discussion. Here I would like to address them in a more systematic fashion. As far as the follow-up studies of movement activists reviewed above are concerned, we can do so by taking another look at table 21.2 (see further McAdam 1999). Generally speaking, these studies share two kinds of methodological problems: one related to timing and the cause-effect nexus, the other to sampling and the generalization of empirical findings.

Concerning *timing*, four main problems can be mentioned that make the attribution of causality from empirical data problematic or at least more difficult. This, indeed, is an issue too often overlooked in social science in general, not only in the study of the biographical consequences of activism. The first and perhaps most important problem lies in the lack of *"before/after" data* on activists (Pierce and Converse 1990). Researchers have often inferred the effects of movement participation from information gathered "after the fact." Among the studies of New Left activists reviewed above, this important methodological tool has been used by Demerath et al. (1971), Jennings and Niemi (1981), Marwell et al. (1987), and McAdam (1988, 1989). In the absence of measures taken both before and after involvement, the researcher must rely entirely on retrospective data (i.e., data collected by looking backward in time), an approach that raises a number of methodological problems. Retrospective data are especially problematic and potentially biased when they rely on people's recollection of previous attitudes or opinions. This bias can be reduced, although not eliminated entirely, by focusing on behavioral rather than attitudinal data, that is, by looking at the subjects' recollection of previous events and actual behaviors. Yet, without a measure of the dependent variable prior to involvement in movement activities, one cannot draw any firm conclusion about the real impact of activism on life course.

The three other methodological shortcomings related to timing are less crucial, but they nevertheless weaken the findings and explanations proposed. One problem is that most work was carried out during a period of turmoil during which non-institutional mobilization and participation in social movements were particularly strong. This *focus on the 1960s cycle of contention* makes it hard to determine to what extent the life-course characteristics observed in follow-up interviews are due to individual involvement in political activities rather than being a product of the special era that forms the background of the research. In addition, such a narrower focus prevents one from drawing empirical generalizations, an issue I address in more detail below.

Another problem can derive from the *time span separating activism from its consequences*. A sufficient amount of time should have elapsed between activism and follow-up investigation in order to be able to determine the extent to which the former has had a durable influence on life course. Not all the studies mentioned above fulfill this criterion. Notable exceptions are provided by Fendrich and Lovoy (1988), Marwell et al. (1987), and McAdam (1988). Fendrich re-interviewed his subjects 15 years after his first study and nearly a quarter of a century after their involvement in civil rights activities. Marwell and colleagues in 1965 not only conducted the first major study of the impact of participation in social movements, but returned to the field about 20 years later to assess the longer-term effects of participation. McAdam made his study of former applicants to the 1964 Mississippi Freedom Summer nearly 20 years after the fact. In both cases, the research design yields stronger findings about the long-term consequences of activism.

A final problem, related to the previous point, is that prior activism has often been measured at a *single point in time*. In other words, we do not know whether the subjects had been activists for a fairly long period or whether their commitment was rather short-lived and they were defined as activists only at the time the research was conducted. This issue has been discussed in some research on conversion to and participation in religious movements (e.g., Snow and Phillips 1980; Snow and Machalek 1984), but research that does not take it into account is weaker. It is not a major problem, but repeated measures of the consequences of activism would strengthen the explanation, as it would provide information on the relationship between the duration of activism and its long-term consequences on the lives of the people involved. Of course, a panel design, which allows the researcher to follow the same subjects over time, is the best methodological choice in this case. However, such a design is costly, and one is usually forced to use the existing national panel studies (where they exist), which do not necessarily include the research questions interesting from the point of view of the analysis of the personal and biographical consequences of participation in social movements.

As I have said, these four methodological weaknesses are all related to timing issues. In a way, they all concern the relationship between time and social change as well as the interpretation of longitudinal effects. In fact, causes of long-term changes are often difficult to disentangle, as at least three time-related processes can be at work. Briefly put, observed attitudinal or behavioral changes in life course may be attributed to aging, cohort, or period effects. This is a familiar distinction to demographers and life-span specialists (see Hardy 1997 for a discussion in the social sciences). Aging or life-cycle effects refers to changes in the subjects due to their maturation. In other words, these are shifts linked to the fact of "getting older" and thus being in different phases of life. For example, it could be argued that people become more conservative in their value orientations as they get older. Cohort or generational effects refer to changes within an age group of people who share a significant experience during a given period at about the same time in their lives. In other words, these are shifts linked to the year of birth. For example, according to Inglehart (1977, 1990), the generation that grew up in the postwar period benefited from a favorable social and economic environment to develop a postmaterialist value orientation.[4] Finally, period effects refer to changes that can be observed across all age groups. In other words, these are shifts linked to a specific period or year and often to a specific event. For example, the accident that occurred at the Chernobyl nuclear plant in 1986 might have produced an increase in the awareness toward and opposition against nuclear energy among European populations at large.

These three processes are interrelated, and although cohort effects are most directly linked to the personal and biographical consequences of social movements, it is nevertheless important to assess the role of each in order to reach an accurate understanding of the impact of activism on life course. Researchers must carefully examine the possibility that shifts in individual attitudes or behaviors result from getting older, from sharing with the other members of the same cohort a significant experience at about the same time in life, or from living in a particular historical era. Again, a panel design is the most efficient – and perhaps only – way to really disentangle these three processes empirically.

Four further methodological problems, in part related to the ones just mentioned and concerning *sampling*, undermine many of the existing studies of New Left activists, in particular by limiting the possibilities for a generalization of their findings. The most general and important one concerns the *representativeness of the sample* used. As Goldstone and McAdam (2001) have pointed out, most of the follow-up studies of former movement activists reviewed above (including McAdam's early study) share a major weakness: the subjects were drawn from nonrepresentative samples of the population. On the one hand, researchers have focused mainly on a specific type of activists, namely, New Left activists. Other protest sectors have not been subject to the same detailed scrutiny. A few researchers have begun to look at other movements, such as right-wing movements, but the existing literature remains heavily flawed in the direction of leftist activism. On the other hand, apart from a few exceptions, even within this specific group, most studies have looked only at those movement participants who are most strongly involved. This narrow focus has the great disadvantage of preventing one from generalizing the results to the whole social movement sector and makes generalizations even within the New Left quite problematic. As I said, recent work that has used survey data to create representative samples of the population is an important further step in this direction.

Another important problem stems from the lack of a *control group* made of people who did not participate in movement activities. Control groups were present in the studies by Fendrich, Fendrich and Lovoy, Jennings and Niemi (1981), and McAdam (1989). This is indeed a major weakness of certain follow-up studies of former activists. In the absence of a comparison of the subject under study with a nonactivist control group, one lacks a baseline against which to judge the impact of participation. In the worst case, the relationship between activism and attitudinal or behavioral changes observed in the group of activists may well be spurious, as nonactivists may display similar changes as well.

A third shortcoming lies in the *small number of subjects*. The number of activists in the samples used in the follow-up inquiries reviewed above range from a low 11 in Whalen and Flacks's study to a high 330 in McAdam's Freedom Summer study. Many studies involved fewer that 40 subjects. While this is not a problem in itself, especially if the aim of the research is theory building rather than theory testing, it is indeed a major obstacle to generalization. Again, the use of survey data provides a satisfactory answer to this problem, although the price to pay might be the loss of detail and "thick" analyses of the processes and mechanisms involved. Thus perhaps a combined quantitative and qualitative approach would serve the purpose best.

Finally, often researchers drew their subjects from *narrow geographical areas*. For example, Whalen and Flacks (1980) examined activists from a single city, Santa Barbara, which furthermore belongs to an atypical area as regards involvement in social movements and protest activities. In such cases, of course, generalizations become even more problematic. Here, if this is the aim and if one wants to keep the small-sample, more detailed approach, the subjects should be selected from different locations or at least from a larger area, although attention should be paid to the criteria for comparing different groups of activists.

In sum, many – although not all – existing studies of the impact of individual participation in social movements on the subsequent life choices and attitudes of former activists suffer from a number of methodological problems, above all, the use of nonrepresentative samples (a problem avoided by those who have analyzed survey data) and the lack of control comparisons (either cross-sectional, over time, or both) that allow researchers to check and possibly rule out plausible rival hypotheses. In order to avoid the problems linked to the lack of control comparisons, the ideal research design should have the following features: "before/after" measures of the dependent variable, experimental and control conditions, multiple groups for both experimental and control conditions, time sampling of the variables under study, and time-series of the "before/after" measures (Pettigrew 1996: ch. 3). Such an ideal design, of course, is extremely difficult to obtain, and is often possible only in quasi-experimental settings, in which the researcher keeps control over the timing and form of the independent variable. Yet researchers should aim to approximate it as much as possible. As can be seen in table 21.2, among the earlier studies of New Left activists, McAdam's work on Freedom Summer is the one that gets closer to this ideal design. Together with Jennings and Niemi's work, his is the only study of New Left activists that has a sufficiently large sample of activists, makes use of a control group, and has "before/after" data. In addition, McAdam has also examined his subjects well after they were involved in movement activities.

Summary and Prospective Look

After having been long neglected, the study of the outcomes and consequences of social movements today seems to have found its way into the scholarly literature. However, most work still deals with the political and institutional outcomes of movement challenges, often measured through policy or legislative changes. Much less attention has been paid to unintended social or cultural effects related to activism, both at the micro- or macrolevel of analysis. To be sure, individual-level variables have indeed received much attention from students of social movements, but the main focus of the analysis here has been on recruitment to activism and the microsociological factors that account for participation in social movements and protest activities, rather than the personal and biographical consequences of participation.

Among the latter, we may distinguish between two types of effects: the biographical consequences that follow from individual involvement in social movements and the broader, aggregate-level change in life-course patterns. Existing work has focused mainly on the biographical impact of activism, but researchers have recently begun to look at the broader societal effects of movements. Findings quite consistently point to a strong and enduring impact of participation on the life course of activists. Similarly, more rare but equally important studies have shown activism to have a significant effect on the social and cultural patterns of contemporary Western society. Looking at other sociocultural and institutional domains, these studies represent a first step toward a more general and balanced understanding of the personal and biographical consequences, in a literature weighted in the direction of political activism and movements. More generally, these aggregate-level studies are important because they provide important insights into the relationship between social movements and processes of social change. In addition to addressing the effects of movements on policy or other political variables, we would gain much knowledge about our societies by looking at the ways activism translate into broader processes of change.

In spite of their consistent – and therefore encouraging – findings, many of the studies reviewed in this chapter are undermined by a number of methodological shortcomings related to timing and sampling issues, which make it problematic to establish causal relationships and to generalize the empirical findings beyond the specific group under investigation. The most general and important of such weaknesses comes from the fact that former activists in follow-up studies were drawn from nonrepresentative sectors of the population. Other problems include the failure to collect "before/after" data on the activists, the lack of a control group of non-activists, and often too small a number of cases in the sample. While it would be quite difficult to have the perfect study, which would include sample representativeness, pre- and post-measures of the dependent variable, as well as control groups for comparisons, further work should aim to approach this ideal as far as possible.

The small sample and the representativeness problems are avoided in research that has analyzed survey data, especially that addressing the aggregate-level consequences of participation in social movements. In the end, however, while methodological improvements are both desirable and necessary, not only our knowledge of the personal effects of activism, but also our understanding of the consequences of social movements in general will gain much from nesting the microsociological study of the biographical impact of activism within a broader reflection about the causes of social and cultural change. In this regard, Goldstone and McAdam's (2001) recent attempt to bring together a microfocus on the life course with a macrofocus on demographic change related to contentious politics provides a good example of the kind of intellectual endeavor we should aim at.

Notes

This chapter draws extensively from the work of Doug McAdam (1989, 1999; see further Goldstone and McAdam 2001), who has published previous useful reviews of work on the personal and biographical consequences of social movements.

1 I adapted this table by adding one more publication by Fendrich (1993), two more publications by Whalen and Flacks (1984, 1989), and two publications resulting from McAdam's own study (1988, 1989). The table focuses on follow-up studies of movement activists and thus excludes work on aggregate-level effects of participation using survey data, which are reviewed in the next section.
2 Fendrich's 1993 book, in fact, summarizes the overall thrust of his two-decades-long work on this topic.
3 High-risk activism can be defined as activism that implies danger to those involved, stemming either from the action itself (e.g., a hunger strike, trespassing a dangerous zone) or the reaction of other actors (e.g., strong repression by the policy, confrontation with a countermovement). Of course, what constitutes risky or nonrisky activity is in part a matter or perspective and is thus subject to differential interpretation.
4 A number of authors have analyzed the role of a significant event experienced by cohorts in creating political generations (e.g., Mannheim 1952; Braungart 1971, 1984; DeMartini 1983). The concept of generation is close to – although distinct from – that of cohort. In

his influential work, Mannheim (1952) maintained that specific events decisively shape the political orientation of particular birth cohorts, giving rise to what he called a "political generation." E.g., the 1960s cycle of contention would be among those events that would have influenced an entire generation (several cohorts, in a strict sense) throughout their lives.

References

Abramowitz, Stephen I., and Alberta J. Nassi (1981) Keeping the Faith: Psychological Correlates of Activism Persistence into Middle Adulthood. *Journal of Youth and Adolescence*, 10, 507–23.

Braungart, Richard G. (1971) Family Status, Socialization and Student Politics: A Multivariate Analysis. *American Journal of Sociology*, 77, 108–29.

——(1984) Historical and Generational Patterns of Youth Movements: A Global Perspective. *Comparative Social Research*, 7, 3–62.

Buchmann, Marlis (1989) *The Script of Life in Modern Society*. Chicago: University of Chicago Press.

Burstein, Paul (1999) Social Movements and Public Policy. In M. Giugni, D. McAdam, and C. Tilly (eds.), *How Social Movements Matter*. Minneapolis: University of Minnesota Press, 3–21.

Chong, Dennis (1991) *Collective Action and the Civil Rights Movement*. Chicago: University of Chicago Press.

DeMartini, Joseph R. (1983) Social Movement Participation: Political Socialization, Generational Consciousness and Lasting Effects. *Youth and Society*, 15, 195–233.

Demerath, N. Jay, III, Gerald Marwell, and Michael T. Aiken (1971) *Dynamics of Idealism*. San Francisco: Jossey-Bass.

Deng, Fang (1997) Information Gaps and Unintended Outcomes of Social Movements: The 1989 Chinese Student Movement. *American Journal of Sociology*, 102, 1085–1112.

Easterlin, Richard A. (1980) *Birth and Fortune*. New York: Basic.

Elder, Glen H. (1974) *Children of the Great Depression*. Chicago: University of Chicago Press.

Elder, Glen H., and A. Caspi (1990) Studying Lives in a Changing Society: Sociological and Personalogical Explorations. In A. I. Rabin, R. A. Zucker, R. Emmons, and S. Frank (eds.), *Studying Persons and Lives*. New York: Springer, 201–47.

Fendrich, James M. (1974) Activists Ten Years Later: A Test of Generational Unit Continuity. *Journal of Social Issues*, 30, 95–118.

——(1977) Keeping the Faith or Pursuing the Good Life: A Study of the Consequences of Participation in the Civil Rights Movement. *American Sociological Review*, 42, 144–57.

——(1993) *Ideal Citizens*. Albany: State University of New York Press.

Fendrich, James M., and Ellis M. Krauss (1978) Student Activism and Adult Left-Wing Politics: A Causal Model of Political Socialization for Black, White and Japanese Students of the 1960s Generation. *Research in Social Movements, Conflict and Change*, 1, 231–56.

Fendrich, James M., and Kenneth L. Lovoy (1988) Back to the Future: Adult Political Behavior of Former Political Activists. *American Sociological Review*, 53, 780–4.

Fendrich, James M., and Alison T. Tarleau (1973) Marching to a Different Drummer: Occupational and Political Correlates of Former Student Activists. *Social Forces*, 52, 245–53.

Fernandez, Roberto M., and Doug McAdam (1988) Social Networks and Social Movements: Multiorganizational Fields and Recruitment to Mississippi Freedom Summer. *Sociological Forum*, 3, 357–82.

Giugni, Marco (1998) Was it Worth the Effort? The Outcomes and Consequences of Social Movements. *Annual Review of Sociology*, 24, 371–93.

Goldstone, Jack, and Doug McAdam (2001) Contention in Demographic and Life-Course Context. In R. R. Aminzade, J. A. Goldstone, D. McAdam, E. J. Perry, W. H. Sewell Jr., S. Tarrow, and C. Tilly (eds.), *Silence and Voice in the Study of Contentious Politics.* Cambridge: Cambridge University Press, 195–221.

Gould, Roger V. (1993) Collective Action and Network Structure. *American Sociological Review,* 58, 182–96.

——(1995) *Insurgent Identities.* Chicago: Chicago University Press.

Gusfield, Joseph R. (1981) Social Movements and Social Change: Perspectives of Linearity and Fluidity. *Research in Social Movements, Conflict and Change,* 4, 317–39.

Hardin, Russell (1982) *Collective Action.* Baltimore: Johns Hopkins University Press.

Hardy, Melissa (ed.) (1997) *Studying Aging and Social Change: Conceptual and Methodological Issues.* Thousand Oaks, CA: Sage.

Hareven, T. K. (1994) Aging and Generational Relations: A Historical and Life Course Perspective. *Annual Review of Sociology,* 20, 437–61.

Inglehart, Ronald (1977) *The Silent Revolution.* Princeton, NJ: Princeton University Press.

——(1990) *Cultural Shift in Advanced Industrial Society.* Princeton, NJ: Princeton University Press.

Jennings, M. Kent (1987) Residues of a Movement: The Aging of the American Protest Generation. *American Political Science Review,* 81, 367–82.

Jennings, M. K., and R. G. Niemi (1981) *Generations and Politics.* Princeton, NJ: Princeton University Press.

Johnston Conover, P. (1991) Political Socialization: Where's the Politics? In W. Crotty (ed.), *Political Science: Looking to the Future.* Vol. 3, *Political Behavior.* Evanston, IL: Northwestern University Press, 125–52.

Kim, Hyojoung, and Peter S. Bearman (1997) The Structure and Dynamics of Movement Participation. *American Sociological Review,* 62, 70–93.

Klandermans, Bert. (1984) Mobilization and Participation: Social-Psychological Expansions of Resource Mobilization Theory. *American Sociological Review,* 49, 583–600.

——(1997) *The Social Psychology of Protest.* Cambridge, MA: Blackwell.

Klatch, Rebecca. (1999) *A Generation Divided: The New Left, The New Right, and the 1960s.* Berkeley: University of California Press.

Kriesi, Hanspeter (1993) *Political Mobilization and Social Change.* Aldershot: Avebury.

Macunovich, D. J. (1997) A Conversation with Richard Easterlin. *Journal of Population Economics,* 10, 119–36.

Macy, Michael. (1991) Chains of Cooperation: Threshold Effects of Collective Action. *American Sociological Review,* 56, 730–47.

Maidenberg, M., and P. Meyer (1970) The Berkeley Rebels Five Years Later: Has Age Mellowed the Pioneer Radicals? *Detroit Free Press,* February 1–7.

Mannheim, Karl (1952) The Problem of Generations. In P. Kecskemeti (ed.), *Essays on the Sociology of Knowledge.* London: Routledge & Kegan Paul, 276–322.

Marwell, Gerald, Michael Aiken, and N. Jay Demerath III (1987) The Persistence of Political Attitudes among 1960s Civil Rights Activists. *Public Opinion Quarterly,* 51, 359–75.

Marwell, Gerald, and P. Oliver (1993) *The Critical Mass in Collective Action.* Cambridge: Cambridge University Press.

McAdam, Doug (1986) Recruitment to High-Risk Activism: The Case of Freedom Summer. *American Journal of Sociology,* 92, 64–90.

——(1988) *Freedom Summer: The Idealists Revisited.* New York: Oxford University Press.

——(1989) The Biographical Consequences of Activism. *American Sociological Review,* 54, 744–60.

——(1999) The Biographical Impact of Social Movements. In M. Giugni, D. McAdam, and C. Tilly (eds.), *How Social Movements Matter.* Minneapolis: University of Minnesota Press, 117–46.

McAdam, Doug, and Ronnelle Paulsen (1993) Specifying the Relationship between Social Ties and Activism. *American Journal of Sociology*, 99, 640–67.

McAdam, Doug, John D. McCarthy, and M. N. Zald (1988) Social Movements. In N. J. Smelser (ed.), *Handbook of Sociology*. Beverly Hills, CA: Sage, 695–737.

McAdam, Doug, Nella Van Dyke, A. Munch, and J. Shockey (1998) Social Movements and the Life-Course. Unpublished paper, Department of Sociology, University of Arizona.

McCarthy, John D. (1996) Constraints and Opportunities in Adopting, Adapting and Inventing. In D. McAdam, J. D. McCarthy, and M. N. Zald (eds.), *Comparative Perspectives on Social Movements*. Cambridge: Cambridge University Press, 141–51.

Milbrath, Lester W. (1981) Political Participation. In S. Long (ed.), *Handbook of Political Behavior*. Vol. 4. New York: Plenum, 197–240.

Nagel, Joane (1995) American Indian Ethnic Renewal: Politics and the Resurgence of Identity. *American Sociological Review*, 60, 947–65.

Nassi, Alberta J., and Stephen I. Abramowitz (1979) Transition or Transformation? Personal and Political Development of Former Berkeley Free Speech Movement Activists. *Journal of Youth and Adolescence*, 8, 21–35.

Opp, Karl-Dieter (1989) *The Rationality of Political Protest*. Boulder, CO: Westview.

Pampel, F. C., and H. E. Peters (1995) The Easterlin Effect. *Annual Review of Sociology*, 21, 163–94.

Passy, Florence (1998) *L'action altruiste*. Geneva: Droz.

Passy, Floernce, and Marco Giugni (2000) Life-Spheres, Networks, and Sustained Participation in Social Movements: A Phenomenological Approach to Political Commitment. *Sociological Forum*, 15, 117–44.

——(2001) Social Networks and Individual Perceptions: Explaining Differential Participation in Social Movements. *Sociological Forum*, 16, 123–53.

Pettigrew, Thomas F. (1996) *How to Think Like a Social Scientist*. New York: HarperCollins.

Pierce, R., and Philip E. Converse (1990) Attitudinal Sources of Protest Behavior in France: Differences between Before and After Measurement. *Public Opinion Quarterly*, 54, 295–316.

Rindfuss, Ronald R., C. Gray Swicegood, and Rachel A. Rosenfeld (1987) Disorder in the Life Course: How Common and Does it Matter? *American Sociological Review*, 52, 785–801.

Rosenthal, Naomi, M. Fingrutd, M. Ethier, R. Karant, and D. McDonald (1985) Social Movements and Network Analysis: A Case Study of Nineteenth Century Women's Reform in New York State. *American Journal of Sociology*, 90, 1022–55.

Sandler, T. (1992) *Collective Action*. Ann Arbor: University of Michigan Press.

Sherkat, Darren E., and T. Jean Blocker (1997) Explaining the Political and Personal Consequences of Protest. *Social Forces*, 75, 1049–70.

Snow, David A., and Richard Machalek (1984) The Sociology of Conversion. *Annual Review of Sociology*, 10, 167–90.

Snow, David A., and Cynthia Phillips (1980) The Lofland-Stark Conversion Model: A Critical Reassessment. *Social Problems*, 45, 430–47.

Snow, David A., Louis A. Zurcher Jr., and Sheldon Ekland-Olson (1980) Social Networks and Social Movements: A Microstructural Approach to Differential Recruitment. *American Sociological Review*, 45, 787–801.

Taylor, Verta, and N. C. Raeburn (1995) Identity Politics as High-Risk Activism: Career Consequences for Lesbian, Gay, and Bisexual Sociologists. *Social Problems*, 42, 252–73.

Tilly, Charles (1999) From Interactions to Outcomes in Social Movements. In M. Giugni, D. McAdam, and C. Tilly (eds.), *How Social Movements Matter*. Minneapolis: University of Minnesota Press, 253–70.

Van Dyke, Nella, Doug McAdam, and Brenda Wilhelm (2000) Gendered Outcomes: Gender Differences in the Biographical Consequences of Activism. *Mobilization*, 5, 161–77.

Whalen, Jack, and Richard Flacks (1980) The Isla Vista "Bank Burners" Ten Years Later: Notes on the Fate of Student Activists. *Sociological Focus*, 13, 215–36.

——(1984) Echoes of Rebellion: The Liberated Generation Grows up. *Journal of Political and Military Sociology*, 12, 61–78.

——(1989) *Beyond the Barricades*. Philadelphia, PA: Temple University Press.

Whittier, Nancy (1995) *Feminist Generations*. Philadelphia, PA: Temple University Press.

Wilhelm, Brenda (1998) Changes in Cohabitation across Cohorts: The Influence of Political Activism. *Social Forces*, 77, 289–310.

Wiltfang, Greg, and Doug McAdam (1991) Distinguishing Cost and Risk in Sanctuary Activism. *Social Forces*, 69, 987–1010.

22

The Cultural Consequences
of Social Movements

JENNIFER EARL

It was not long ago that women did not sweat or perspire, but instead only "glistened." Women did not play major professional sports, were not seen as competent by most to hold important elected offices and were depicted in demeaning and/or humorous ways in high art and popular media. Women were "Miss" or "Mrs." Few were "Dr." Fewer still of those women who were medical doctors or PhDs were addressed as such.

It was also not long ago that African Americans were thought by most to be inferior to whites, legally and informally separated from whites in their use of public facilities, and satirized and caricatured in the visual arts. Indeed, one could sum up these examples and many more quite simply: we live in a somewhat different nation and world today than existed several decades ago. Such a simple observation belies two fundamentally vexing questions from the standpoint of most social scientific researchers: (1) To what extent and in what precise ways is the world we confront today different? (2) *Why* is the world we confront today different?

Social movement scholarship is largely built on the assumption that the world we live in today is different and that part of the answer to "why" is that social movements have exerted direct and indirect pressure on key civil and political decision-makers, resulting in cultural and political changes. Unfortunately, as virtually every study of social movement consequences and outcomes notes, this fundamental assumption has not been well researched (Burstein et al. 1995; Kriesi et al. 1995; Staggenborg 1995; Giugni 1998; Amenta and Young 1999; Cress and Snow 2000; Earl 2000).[1] In fact, we know too little about what has changed and even less about the causal processes that could tie social movements to those changes.

Even still, in what Cress and Snow (2000) accurately term "lacunae" in social movements research, there are still areas where more progress has been made. For instance, Amenta and Caren (see chapter 20 in this volume) discuss research on the political and organizational consequences of social movements, which according to

Earl (2000) have received a relatively large share of research attention when compared to other types of movement outcomes. Similarly, Giugni (see chapter 21 in this volume) reviews the growing literature on personal and biographical consequences to activism. In contrast to these areas, the paucity of research on cultural outcomes has been readily evident to most researchers in the field (Burstein et al. 1995; Earl 2000).

This chapter treads down the less worn path of cultural outcomes research in order to address three questions: (1) What challenges have scholars interested in cultural outcomes faced in defining cultural outcomes? (2) What kinds of cultural outcomes have social movement scholarship uncovered? (3) What explanations of cultural change have been suggested in cultural outcomes research? In answering these three questions, I hope to both shed light on where cultural outcomes scholarship stands presently and also suggest where future research may productively develop.

CHALLENGES IN IDENTIFYING THE CULTURAL CONSEQUENCES OF SOCIAL MOVEMENTS

Social movement consequences are notoriously hard to define. Even within the relatively more settled area of political outcomes, numerous scholars have bemoaned the difficulty of defining outcomes and created typologies meant to resolve such problems. Perhaps the most important of such scholars is Gamson ([1975] 1990), who led the field by identifying acceptance and new advantages as two key social movement outcomes (see chapter 20 in this volume for more detail). More recently, Kriesi et al. (1995) delineate between 14 different types of movement outcomes, Amenta and Young (1999) argue that we should study "collective goods" gained by movements, Earl (2000) suggests differentiating between internal movement outcomes and external outcomes, and Cress and Snow (2000) build on Gamson's initial conceptualization to study four types of consequences. The examples could continue. The ultimate conclusion would be the same: the field lacks a consensual definition of, or classification of, movement outcomes.

Students of cultural outcomes face two additional barriers. First, most studies of movement consequences (and reviews of that literature) have relatively ignored cultural outcomes (Earl 2000). As well, many of the numerous typologies of movement outcomes lack conceptual space for cultural outcomes, leaving this area of research even farther away from finding some common conceptual vocabulary. With some notable exceptions, such as Gamson (1998), the methodological difficulties associated with studying cultural outcomes have been assumed to be so difficult that few have devoted much theoretical attention to laying the conceptual groundwork and fewer still have applied what tools do exist to the actual study of cultural outcomes.

The second issue facing researchers involves the conceptualization of culture itself (readers interested in a thorough, independent discussion of culture should see chapter 5 in this volume). As Williams (1976) notes, culture has meant many things to many scholars across time. This has been as true for students of culture as it has been for students of social movements and culture. According to Hart (1996), contemporary scholarship has focused on three dimensions of culture.[2]

First, Hart (1996) notes that scholars have argued that culture is social-psychological: it is the set of values, beliefs, and meanings that individuals carry. For example, as we will see more fully below, studies of cultural consequences guided by this definition would look to changes in opinion polls over time to determine whether people's viewpoints on particular movement-related issues had changed (Rochon 1998). To the extent to which opinion does change, one would affirm that cultural outcomes have been achieved.[3]

A second dimension of culture identified by Hart (1996) is constituted by a web of signs and the signified meaning of those signs. That is, culture from this viewpoint is "not in people's head" (Polletta 2002). Polleta explains this perspective in the following manner:

> An alternative conception of culture views it as the symbolic dimension of all structures, institutions, and practices (political, economic, educational, etc.). Symbols are signs that have meaning and significance through their interrelations. The pattern of those relations is culture. Culture is thus patterned and patterning; it is enabling as well as constraining; and it is observable in linguistic practices, institutional rules, and social rituals rather than existing only in people's minds. (1999: 66–7)

This view of culture has frequently been related to "production of culture" approaches and discussions of cultural products such as the visual arts or music. However, practices should also be considered within this domain to the extent to which a practice (or "routine") has an associated meaning (Hart 1996).

In this second view of culture, changes in signs or practices would be clear examples of cultural change. For instance, many would assert that changes in the relationship between signs and their audiences, such as the re-appropriation of symbols, are important cultural changes (Schudson 1989, 1997). To the extent to which one could tie social movement activity to these cultural changes, one could again affirm that cultural outcomes were achieved.

Hart (1996) argues that a third dimension of culture focuses on more macro elements, which is in line with the way that many anthropologists and social historians have understood culture. In this third view, culture frames the worldview and social situation of entire communities or subcultures. Put most simply, culture denotes "a particular way of life" (Williams 1976: 90). This way of life may be represented in totems à la Durkheim or in cockfights à la Geertz. Whether or not there is a focal practice or product that is used to shed light on a culture, the focus is nonetheless on social practices and beliefs shared by an entire community that together uniquely distinguishes that community from other "cultures" (read: places and time periods). Put differently, Mary Douglas did not want to understand dirt (Douglas 1966) or jokes (Douglas 1991) for their own sake, and Darnton (1991) was not solely interested in explaining how cruelty to cats could be comedic; Douglas and Darnton were both using these particular social occurrences to gain leverage over the rich meanings that infused everyday life within particular communities and subcultures.

Further, this dimension of cultural research acknowledges the importance of large constellations of interconnected values and beliefs by focusing on the totality of those beliefs. Culture in this sense is not reducible without remainder to the individual beliefs and values that compose it, and this approach to culture is thus distinguishable analytically from the social-psychological dimension of culture addressed above. Indeed, in this view the sum is greater than the parts such that an isolated change in any particular value or belief would not create cultural change of theoretical concern for this group of scholars.

Applying this vision of culture to social movement consequences requires that social movements are tied to changes in the basic fabric of communities or the creation of new communities that share fundamentally new ways of life. Since some religious and self-help movements attempt to create exactly this type of new culture and community, it is important to note that whether one regards the creation of small communities as cultural change should be a question about the degree of cultural change, but not its presence or absence. That is, if a small but distinct new religious community is formed, it is clear that some cultural change has occurred from this perspective.

It is worth noting that some social movement scholars have also blended the symbolic view of culture with a view of culture that examines collective identities and new communities or subcultures. These researchers argue that identity and community exists, for instance, only in practice (Fantasia 1988) and are represented by (and perhaps even identified by) cultural symbols (Taylor and Whittier 1992). Nonetheless, I will review such works as if they address more stable, holistic communities because the thrust of the theoretical inquiry is on the collective group, identification with that group, and relations to that group; their central theoretical interest is not in the symbols and/or practices themselves or changes in those symbols and/or practices.

As one might suspect from the foregoing review of the meaning of "outcomes" and the dimensions of "culture," when these terms are wed, the result is a harrowingly enigmatic dependent variable. In fact, as the next section will reveal, existing scholarship on the cultural consequences of social movements has been spread broadly and thinly. That is, of the small number of studies on cultural consequences, there is not a tremendous amount of overlap in conceptualizations of cultural outcomes. As the third section will show, the way in which cultural outcomes have been conceptualized has also affected the causal explanations for cultural change offered by researchers.

IDENTIFYING CULTURAL CONSEQUENCES

In this section, I review the different types of movement consequences that have been studied, organizing that review according to the three major perspectives on culture outlined above. Table 22.1 summarizes the categories of outcomes that this section covers as well as leading studies on each type of outcome.

Social Psychological Studies of Cultural Outcomes

Several recent studies of the cultural outcomes of social movements have focused on changes in values, beliefs, and opinions. In particular, three lines or research stand out.[4] First, d'Anjou examines the abolitionist movement in England (d'Anjou 1996; d'Anjou and Van Male 1998) and its role in turning opinion against the slave trade.

Table 22.1 Conceptualizing the cultural consequences of social movements

Conceptualization of culture	Consequence	Research traditions and projects
Social-psychological approach	Values, beliefs and opinions	Rochon (1998), d'Anjou (1996), d'Anjou and Van Male (1998), NSM research, Gamson and Modigliani (1989)
Cultural production and practices	Literature	Children's literature: Pescosolida et al. (1997) Magazines: Farrell (1995)
	Media coverage	Gamson (1998)
	Visual culture	Oldfield (1995)
	Music	Eyerman and Jamison (1995, 1998), Eyerman and Barretta (1996)
	Fashion	McAdam (1988, 1994)
	Science and scientific practices	Epstein (1996), Moore (1999)
	Language	McAdam (1988), Rochon (1998)
	Discourse	Gamson and Modigliani (1989), Gamson (1998), Katzenstein (1995)
Worldviews and communities	Collective identity	Taylor and Whittier (1992), Polleta and Jasper (2001), NSM research
	Subcultures	Within movements: Kanter (1968), Fantasia (1988), Bordt (1997) As distinct subcultures: Birmingham Center of Cultural Studies including Hall and Jefferson (1976) and Hebdige (1979)

In the book length treatment of this issue, d'Anjou adopts a more social-psychological view of culture by arguing that "changes in the symbolic realm such as changes in definitions, views, beliefs, and values" (d'Anjou 1996: 45) constitute cultural change. The book then seeks to understand how British abolitionists were able to change the hearts and minds of Britons where the slave trade was concerned. In other works he continues this emphasis: "Although the first abolition campaign did not reach its goal – prohibition of the slave trade – the public discourse it initiated affected the way slavery and the slave trade were collectively defined in British society from then on" (d'Anjou and Van Male 1998: 214). In particular, the abolitionist view that the slave trade was immoral became "definitive" and "unassailable" (d'Anjou and Van Male 1998: 214).

Second, Rochon (1998) examines a wide array of changes in opinion, values, and beliefs through a series of case studies, attempting to tie these changes to "critical communities" and social movement inspired diffusion of critical ideas. Rochon is quite clear about his take on culture: "Culture consists of the linked stock of ideas that define a set of commonsense beliefs about what is right, what is natural, what works" (Rochon 1998: 9). Accordingly, he seeks to study cultural change by examining changes in discrete beliefs, noting that his unit of analysis is a "single cultural value" (Rochon 1998: 48).

Because each of these works tie changes in beliefs and values to changes in language and/or discourse, some might be tempted to argue that each study also casts language and/or discourse as the subject(s) of inquiry. However, this view is not actually consistent with either authors' arguments. As will be discussed more fully below, both d'Anjou and Rochon are centrally interested in explaining changes in beliefs, values and opinions. Although discourse and/or language may also change, the authors' focus is on more social-psychological phenomena.

Work by new social movements (NSM) scholars also has implications for this dimension of cultural outcomes research (in addition to other dimensions, as will be discussed below). Since a full review of the NSM literature is beyond the scope of this chapter, I will only briefly note that many leading theorists have argued that NSMs are less directed toward policy outcomes and instead are more concerned with contesting cultural values and beliefs (Cohen 1983, 1985; Melucci 1985, 1989, 1994; Offe 1985; Touraine 1985; Pichardo 1997).[5] For instance, Melucci (1994) argues that movements such as the women's movement, the environmental movement, and the youth movement have been centrally concerned with contesting values, opinions, and beliefs.

Despite the salience of this cultural theme in NSM theorizing, research has largely focused on establishing that large-scale changes in values, opinions, and beliefs have occurred, with less emphasis on establishing the clear empirical role of social movements in that change process. Across a large body of work, Inglehart (1977, 1981, 1990; Inglehart and Appel 1989) has been able to show that younger cohorts across numerous nations have endorsed less materialist, and more "postmaterialist" values, opinions, and beliefs. Such postmaterialist values include concerns for freedom, self-actualization, and esthetics, among others. While there are good reasons to believe that some of Inglehart's findings may be attributable to NSMs (Kriesi 1993), scholars have not yet pinpointed what aspects of NSM activity produce these cultural changes. Further, it is likely that NSMs have a reciprocal relationship with value change: as Inglehart (1981) reports, increases in postmaterialist values may both result from and contribute to NSM activity.

Finally, Gamson and Modigliani (1989) propose a multidimensional view of culture in their study of media discourse and opinion on nuclear power. Specifically, they blend a social-psychological view of culture (i.e., culture as opinions) with a more symbolic view of culture (i.e., culture as discourse itself). Although they explicitly term discourse "cultural" and term opinion "cognitive", they nonetheless argue that both discourse and opinion "involve the social construction of meaning" (Gamson and Modigliani 1989: 2). Further, in terms of the causal relationship between discourse and opinion, they assert:

> We do not, in this paper, argue that changes in media discourse *cause* changes in public opinion. Each system interacts with the other: media discourse is part of the process by which individuals construct meaning, and public opinion is part of the process by which

journalists and other cultural entrepreneurs develop and crystallize meaning in public discourse. (Gamson and Modigliani 1989: 2; emphasis in original)

In this way, Gamson and Modigliani suggest that changes in opinion are important, but not the only meaning-related outcomes of social movements.

Symbolic Studies of Cultural Outcomes: Sign and Signified

A larger (although still not large) number of studies have examined cultural change from a more symbolic standpoint. As table 22.1 suggests, the changes that have been explored include both cultural products and cultural practices.[6] In terms of cultural products, literature has been the focus of limited inquiry. For example, Pescosolida et al. (1997) examine changing representations of African Americans in children's literature. They find that when the civil rights movement was highly mobilized, and thus contention over racial issues was high, that there were fewer black characters in children's books. They argue that their finding resulted from caution on the part of publishers: publishers were afraid to include black characters that might be criticized by the civil rights movement, but publishers were also afraid to include black characters that would be endorsed by the civil rights movement, because such characters could offend whites.

Farrell (1995) examines the production of *Ms.* Magazine as a widely distributed feminist magazine. Farrell argues that *Ms.* grew directly out of the women's movement, with influential women's activists such as Gloria Steinem playing a key role in its founding. However, just as Pescosolida found that market pressures interacted with movement mobilization, Farrell shows that *Ms.* struggled to keep its feminist editorial style while attempting to generate sufficient advertising revenue. Ultimately, this juggling act could not be sustained and *Ms.* was forced to switch to an ad-free format that uses high subscription fees, instead of advertising revenue, to fund the magazine. In doing so, *Ms.* also moved out of the mass-distribution magazine market and into the more specialized subscription market, effectively limiting its ability to reach out to nonmovement members.

Gamson (1998) moves away from books and magazines to address the media more generally, arguing that that media coverage and representations of movements are critical cultural movement outcomes. Further, he devises an approach to studying movement success in the cultural sphere. He adapts his definition of movement success from *The Strategy of Social Protest* (Gamson [1975] 1990) to focus on cultural acceptance and new cultural advantages, arguing that "acceptance" as a cultural outcome is defined by having media standing (e.g., being a regularly quoted news source), whereas "new advantages" are gained when a challenger's frame is more prominent than an antagonist's frame (Gamson 1998: 70).

Oldfield (1995) focuses on visual culture. In his study of the British abolitionist movement, he discusses the ways in which abolitionists created visual culture, most famously represented by the image of a black slave kneeling with the phrase "Am I not a Man and a Brother" attached. Oldfield shows that a number of pro-abolition products were produced and sold in Britain, including work by Wedgwood, penny and half-penny producers, printmakers, and other artists. This art was both a part of abolitionist mobilization and an enduring outcome of the campaign to end the slave trade. That is, art produced in this period was created by abolitionists to popularize and diffuse support for abolition, but the art was also clearly produced to literally capitalize on the growing pro-abolition sentiment in Britain. In particular, this type of art was marketed to middle class and aspiring upper class members as a symbol of their up and coming class status.

Eyerman and Jamison (1995, 1998) and Eyerman and Barretta (1996) show that movements have also played a role in shaping music. Eyerman and Jamison (1995) argue that music and movements are mutually constitutive of one another, using US folk music in the 1960s as an example. Folk music in this period inspired young people to participate in movements and allowed singer-songwriters to serve as movement intellectuals who framed movement issues in powerful and provocative ways. However, movements acted back upon folk music by inspiring new visions of folk music that radically changed the genre. Coupled with a new and booming youth market, folk music became more commercial and ultimately pulled away from the mooring of its Old Left roots.

Eyerman and Barretta (1996) also focus on folk music, but they examine folk music's development in the 1930s and its transformation in the 1960s using a more elaborated theoretical model. They show that folk music developed from a policy of the Communist Party of the USA (CPUSA) that sought to promote the representation of common people's lives through music. While initially the CPUSA had focused on the biographies of artists and to a lesser extent the instruments played, the Party ultimately adopted a stance the allowed folk music to grow into a kind of common person's truth-telling.

Building on Eyerman and Jamison's (1995) study of folk music in the 1960s, Eyerman and Barretta (1996) argue that folk music was reinvigorated and altered by its association with the civil rights movement and then with the antiwar movement. Most notable in their explanation is the way in which old left politics ceased to influence folk music in the 1950s because of McCarthy-era blacklisting. As Communist notables and influences pulled back from folk music, broader visions of political interests came to be represented within folk music. Of course, many folk artists in the 1950s and 1960s shared the prior belief in a music formed around truth-telling and everyday people, but these artists shifted their attention from labor politics to concerns raised by the new left, particularly racial and peace politics. Eyerman and Jamison's (1998) book length treatment of this subject extends these arguments, examines the relationship between soul music and the civil rights movement, and discusses the development of the progressive music movement in Sweden.

Finally, to the extent to which music festivals reoccur over time, they can serve as lasting culture consequences of movement activity. For instance, Staggenborg (1995) discusses the success and failure of women's music festivals in the United States (although her focus is on repercussions of collectivist organizational forms). The Michigan Womyn's Music Festival (Taylor and Whittier 1992), and more recently, the Lilith Fair, which featured female and feminist musicians, suggest that the women's movement has created and continues to create cultural events of independent significance.

Still within the world of cultural production, McAdam (1988, 1994) shifts the focus to the ways in which fashion can be inadvertently affected by social movements. McAdam (1988) argues that the Northern, white, middle- and upper-class youth who participated in Freedom Summer sought to emulate Student Non-Violent Coordinating Committee (SNCC) leaders and activists through their dress. For example, Freedom Summer participants replaced their chinos with jeans as a way of signifying their association with Freedom Summer and the civil rights movement more generally. McAdam argues that this privileged conduit to elite Northern colleges and communities allowed jeans to diffuse into Northern mainstream culture. Just as Oldfield argued that some Britons consumed abolitionist products in order to demonstrate their aspiring class position, McAdam asserted that young whites were attempting to use consumption and fashion to demonstrate their connection to the civil rights struggle.

As mentioned earlier, a symbolic view of culture can also include cultural practices that are imbued with meaning. Polletta, a major proponent of this position, argues that culture can be understood to include sets of rules, routines, and schemas (Polletta 2002). This view of culture allows some work to be labeled cultural even when the researchers conducting that work have not cast their studies in such lights.

In this vein, Moore (1999) examined the relationship between antiwar protest and science in the United States during and after Vietnam. She argues that science as an institution was altered by antiwar protest, in large part because of the actions of influential mediators who held dual-identities as scientists and antiwar activists. Moore does point out that it was not only these influential movement-related actors that mattered: science had become a vulnerable target for change as a result of massive growth, extensive ties to the state, a developing association with a clientele that demanded more responsible scientific practices, and dispersed (and hence weak) internal authority structures.

Epstein's (1996) study of AIDS activism similarly shows how movements can affect scientific practices. His study examines the confrontation between lay activists and scientists over the search for the cause of AIDS and over the procedures used in clinical trials. He ultimately concludes that while AIDS activists where not very influential in affecting the search for a cause of AIDS, AIDS activists were very influential in critiquing and ultimately changing the model used in clinical trials for HIV and AIDS medication. By changing treatment protocols and drug testing protocols, AIDS activists challenged core institutional practices within medicine and in some ways the meaning of clinical trials.

By way of further example, one could also imagine that movements could affect more general cultural routines. For instance, forms of address (e.g., the Miss, Mrs., Ms. example discussed in the introduction) and certain social practices (such as men always paying for dates or opening doors) may have changed over time as a result of movement efforts. However, a wide search through the movements literature was unable to locate systematic studies conducted on such changes in mainstream culture.

Language and discourse, which blend symbol and practice, are also argued to have been affected by social movements. As was discussed above, Rochon (1998) argues that social movements can produce linguistic changes. McAdam's (1988) discussion of Freedom Summer participants' emulation of SNCC activists extended beyond just the fashion of jeans; McAdam also argued that Freedom Summer participants adopted language and linguistic styles from SNCC activists.

Focusing specifically on discourse, Gamson and Modigliani (1989) and Gamson (1998) discuss the ways in which movements may seek to shape discourse by advocating particular interpretive frames. Gamson and Modigliani (1989), for instance, show the way in which the antinuclear movement attempted to insert new framings of nuclear power into public discussions and portrayals of nuclear power. Gamson (1998) highlights the importance of framing by arguing that movements achieve new cultural advantages to the extent to which they are successful at having their frames adopted over alternatives.

Similarly, Katzenstein (1995) discusses the way in which Catholic women have challenged religious discourse (and doctrine) within the Church. Although she does not argue that her research is a study of cultural outcomes, she does show that religious women have been able to place feminist issues on the agenda for discussion at lower church levels (e.g., bishops conferences) and have been able to create a discourse about feminism within the church. Further, she shows the importance of the cultural changes by applying Gaventa's (1980) definition of power.

According to Gaventa, power partly involves the ability to keep insurgent or contentious issues off of the public agenda (i.e., "the mobilization of bias"). The women that Katzenstein studies have been able to overcome that mobilization of bias and have forced the Catholic Church into discussions about feminism and the role of women in the Church. Another facet of power, according to Gaventa, involves control over language, discourse, and symbols, which Katzenstein also argues are challenged by these religious women. Again, while Katzenstein does not cast these changes in discourse as a cultural outcome, to the extent to which they endure, they should be considered cultural outcomes within the institution of the Catholic Church.

Communities and Cultures as Cultural Outcomes

Most work on more macrocultural outcomes examines the creation of new collective identities and new communities. Even though collective identities and subcultures are often mutually constitutive of one another in practice, I separate collective identity creation and subculture formation for analytic ease.

As well, I do not address much of the work on collective identity, referring readers instead to chapter 19 of this volume. It is sufficient to note three things here. First, collective identities can be thought of as important cultural movement outcomes. For instance, Polletta and Jasper (2001) suggest the following where collective identity outcomes are concerned: (1) movements can have identity change as a goal, as is the case with some self-help and religious movements; (2) movement participation can change people's individual biographies and hence values and ideals; (3) movements can create broad identities that persist in abeyance structures until later mobilization revives them; (4) by attaching certain symbols to specific movement identities, movements can affect what cultural symbols are available for use by other movements; and (5) movements can create or legitimize new identities that result in subsequent backlash. Of particular importance to this review is the first class of identity-related outcomes: movements that have identity change as a goal (Kanter 1968; Breines 1989; Melucci 1989; Epstein 1991; Lichterman 1999).[7]

Second, this focus on identity has been an animating concern of NSM theorists and researchers (see Cohen 1985 for a thorough theoretical discussion on this point). Melucci (1985, 1989, 1994), in particular, has elaborated on the connection between NSMs and collective identity, casting the collective identity work of NSMs as integral to both their existence and their success.

Third, collective identity is often explicitly constructed in social movement activity (Snow 2001). For instance, Taylor and Whittier (1992) examine the explicit creation of a lesbian-feminist social movement community in the US, arguing that lesbian feminists created a culture where personal politics were central and lesbianism was rendered inherently political. Importantly, according to their analysis, a lesbian-feminist identity did not automatically arise from common structural positioning. Instead, three processes were key to the creation of a collective lesbian-feminist identity: (1) the creation and maintenance of community boundaries; (2) the creation of a self-reflexive group consciousness; and (3) negotiation with and resistance to dominant culture.

Where the creation of subcultures, countercultures, and communities is concerned, this review limits itself to scholarship that explicitly focuses on the generative role of social movements, even while acknowledging that a great deal of work in cultural studies (e.g., by members of the Birmingham Center of Cultural Studies, such as Hall and Jefferson 1976), the sociology of religion (see Sherkat and Ellison 1999 for a brief review) and the sociology of youth (see Bucholtz 2002 for a review) have focused on the creation, meaning, and implications of subcultures, countercultures, and communities.[8] Within movement-centered scholarship, there are a number of influential studies that examine the ways in which movements themselves can form important communities with distinct cultures. For instance, Kanter's (1968, 1972) work on commitment in utopian communities examines the types of movement/community created structures that are likely to result in strong and distinct utopian subcultures (see Hall 1988 for a re-analysis of Kanter's original findings). Zablocki's (1971) work on utopian communities studies the way in which the resolution of recurrent community crises can strengthen some utopian communities. Moving away from utopian communities, Yinger focuses on "contracultures" (1960) and "countercultures" (1977, 1982), arguing that movements as well as more demographically-oriented social changes set the stage for the creation of some countercultural communities (as did some of his contemporaries, see Berger 1983 for a brief review).

More recently, Fantasia (1988) used a practice-oriented approach to culture and consciousness to argue that communities, ideology, and consciousness are made and remade in the process of contention. When contention is high, entire communities can be remade around an axis of ideological contention. For instance, in discussing the strike against Clinton Corn, Fantasia argues that the ideology of pro-strike forces became much more radical such that all areas of social life – from religion, to politics, to family, to work – were read through class lines and motives. Indeed, in summarizing his major contributions in the book, he discusses exactly the kind of collective identity and insular sense of community that one would expect from a study with this view of culture: "workers then engaged in new forms of activity (militant, direct action), created new associational bonds in practical forms (essentially emergent social movements), and developed new-found values of mutual solidarity (a new sense of 'us', a new sense of 'them', and emergent moral sensibilities about the values associated with each)" (Fantasia 1988: 232–3).

Bordt (1997) studies transformations of communities at a slightly smaller level: she examines the way in which feminist collectives came to be dominant and, in many ways, identifying forms of organizing in the women's movement and women's communities. While she also argues that collectives were later deinstitutionalized, at a more microlevel the predominance of this form of social organization represents the kind of coupling between social organization and worldview represented in this view of culture.

Finally, Hebdige's (1979) study of British youth subcultures suggests that movements broadly construed can create and be recreated by subcultures, as subcultures engage dominant culture in contention over signs, signification, and material conditions. Work in cultural sociology by other scholars associated with the Birmingham Center of Cultural Studies such as Stuart Hall (Hall and Jefferson 1976) also examines the ways in which subcultures can use style and signification in contention, and in doing so constantly recreate their own subcultures.

Explaining Cultural Consequences

As one might expect, given the variety of ways in which cultural outcomes have been conceptualized and studied, scholars have also produced different causal explanations for cultural outcomes. As was the case with the last section, I will review these causal explanations according to the dimension of culture on which researchers have focused. Table 22.2 summarizes this discussion.

Explanations in Social-Psychological Studies of Culture

Studies that conceive of culture in a social-psychological manner have shared a fairly common casual explanation: framing (Snow et al. 1986). That is, most studies that fall within this category of work on cultural outcomes suggest that well-framed arguments are more likely to lead to large-scale changes in values, beliefs, and opinions. Of course, the specifics and terminology of each argument, propositions about what makes an effective frame, and factors beyond framing that may affect cultural change all vary slightly between researchers.

In their studies of the British abolitionist movement, d'Anjou (1996) and d'Anjou and Van Male (1998) argue that movement success depends on a movement's ability to reframe issues in familiar yet still challenging manners. By developing "interpretative packages" that identify and explain problems as well as suggesting how problems can be rectified, movements attempt to reshape the cultural terrain.[9] However, the tools that movements draw upon in the construction of interpretative packages must have some preexisting cultural currency to be effective.

Specifically, d'Anjou and Van Male (1998) identify three paths for successful reframing: (1) connecting movement issues with culturally accepted values; (2) connecting movement issues with existing oppositional cultural themes; and (3) connecting movement issues with rising cultural themes (i.e., themes that are neither hegemonic nor completely oppositional and are gaining popularity independent of the movement). No matter what path a movement follows, it is the successfulness of the interpretative package that determines the extent of cultural (read: value) change. According to d'Anjou and Van Male (1998), the British abolitionist movement largely succeeded because it was able to frame opposition to the slave trade both in terms of oppositional themes and newly rising cultural themes.

In addition, d'Anjou and Van Male argue that the successfulness of an interpretative package will, in part, also depend on the conduciveness of the cultural context: "movement actors produce new meanings but not exactly as they wish. They are free

Table 22.2 Explaining the cultural consequences of social movements

Conceptualization of culture	Explanation	Research traditions and projects
Social-psychological approach	Framing	Rochon (1998), d'Anjou (1996), d'Anjou and Van Male (1998), Gamson and Modigliani (1989)
	Cultural opportunities	d'Anjou and Van Male (1998)
	Media practices	Gamson and Modigliani (1989)
Cultural production and practices	Framing and movement mobilization	Rochon (1998)
	Movement institutional insiders	Moore (1999), Epstein (1996), Katzenstein (1995)
	Network connections	McAdam (1994, 1988)
	Movements and markets	Pescosolida et al. (1997), Farrell (1995), Oldfield (1995), Eyerman and Jamison (1995)
	Media practices	Gamson and Modigliani (1989), Gamson (1998)
	Production of culture	Eyerman and Barretta (1996), Eyerman and Jamison (1998)
Worldviews and communities	Internal movement dynamics	Kanter (1968), Taylor and Whittier (1992), NSM research
	Contentious interactions	Fantasia (1988), Taylor and Whittier (1992), Birmingham Center of Cultural Studies including Hall and Jefferson (1976) and Hebdige (1979)

to choose neither the elements from which they produce them nor the circumstances under which production takes place. The situation in which they act is a given that is handed down to them" (d'Anjou and Van Male 1998: 223). In this way, effective frames can only be created or forwarded by movements in some historical moments.

Instead of being concerned with a specific movement, such as the abolitionist movement, Rochon (1998) is primarily interested in explaining rapid cultural change (read: rapid changes in values). He argues that many values do not change steadily over time by consistently adding converts to a position each year. Instead, values tend to be fairly stable and then experience rapid changes only to once again stabilize at new and different points. In order for values to change rapidly, Rochon argues that issues have to named and raised, issues have to be discussed, that discussion has to diffuse, and finally the new ideas that the discussion carries have to become normalized (or, in some senses, institutionalized). Rochon (1998) forwards two key players in these tasks: critical communities and social movements.

Critical communities identify and name issues and problems. Movements take the "conceptual innovations" produced by critical communities and repackage or reframe these ideas for mass appeal. In doing so, movements attempt to diffuse the new value and eventually normalize the perspective.[10] In many ways, Rochon's arguments about critical communities and movements parallel work discussed above on the role of NSMs and value change.

Rochon also makes clear that discourse is the driving force behind value change: to the extent to which movements can properly package new conceptual innovations, they will better compete in the marketplace of ideas. The linkage he draws between values and discourse is so strong that Rochon uses changes in language to diagnose value change. That is, according to Rochon ideas are so tightly linked to language and discourse that changes in culture (read: ideas) can be read from linguistic changes: "The connection between language and culture is so close that changing use of language is one of our primary signals that culture is being re-formed. Cultural change is invariably accompanied by innovations in the language..." (Rochon 1998: 16). In this way, one can determine when movement discourse has successfully changed values: if linguistic innovations become normalized, movements have succeeded.

Finally, Gamson and Modigliani (1989) studied the way in which media packages affect opinion. Media packages are frames that imply "a range of positions... allowing for a degree of controversy among those who share a common frame" (3) and offer "a number of different condensing symbols that suggest the core frame and positions in shorthand" (3). They argue that three things shape the life course (and success) of media packages: (1) the cultural resonance of the package; (2) the actions of sponsors of those packages; and (3) internal media norms and practices. Movements, as sponsors of certain packages, change public opinion by effectively advocating for specific frames. Applying these ideas to their study of opinions on nuclear power, they argue that shifts in public opinion were complicated and far from stable because of the intense competition between different pro- and anti-nuclear power frames and media packages.

Explanations in Symbolic Studies of Cultural Outcomes

A range of theoretical explanations has been proposed by movement researchers studying changing cultural products and practices. Some of these explanations tie movement outcomes fairly directly to movement action (although not necessarily just to the level of mobilization attained by a movement). One such explanation, offered by Rochon (1998), mirrors the framing explanation just discussed. Specifically, Rochon (1998) argues that language changes as a result of ideational changes, thereby constituting almost a secondary cultural effect of movement framing. Put simply, the better movements are at framing, the more likely values are to change, and, consequently, the more likely language is to change.

Researchers who have examined institutional practice and discourse have also had movement-centered explanations of cultural change. For example, Katzenstein's religious women are argued to have directly altered discourse by using their insider roles and connections to generate discussions about the place of women in the Catholic Church. Similarly, Epstein (1996) argues that direct action by AIDS activists was critical to the cultural and institutional outcomes that were achieved, as was action by doctors who played a bridging role between the movement and medicine. Moore (1999) offers a similar although slightly more elaborated model in which movement-friendly insiders still figure prominently. In her model, changes exogenous to science occurred that rendered military-related sciences vulnerable. After protest against the Vietnam War grew, scientists who were both marginally connected scientists and marginally connected protesters began to pressure military-related sciences to change. As external pressure grew from the antiwar movement, internal and external pressure mounted until scientific practices and, in some senses, the meaning of science were altered.

Others have examined direct diffusion routes from the movement to subcultures and the general public. In explaining the diffusion of jeans and linguistic practices associated with the South and the civil rights movement, McAdam (1988) suggests that Northern white students who participated in Freedom Summer began emulating SNCC workers. When these students returned to their privileged institutions the following year, these new forms of dress and speech diffused through those campus bodies and into popular culture. McAdam (1994) extends this argument to suggest that network connections to cultural elites are important to explaining cultural outcomes. While not examining culture outcomes, Diani (1997) proposes that networks often play an important role in movement outcomes. In fact, he suggests that networks are so influential that scholars should consider the development of social capital (understood by Diani in terms of network connections) to constitute an important mesolevel outcome of social movements.

Other researchers have tried to blend movement-centered explanations of changes with cultural markets and production systems. For instance, Pescosolida et al. (1997), Farrell (1995), Oldfield (1995) and Eyerman and Jamison (1995) all make use of market dynamics in their explanations of cultural movement outcomes. As discussed above, Pescosolida et al. (1997) attribute a decline in the number of black characters featured in children's books during the peak of the civil rights movement to countervailing market forces produced by civil rights protest. Publishers thought that blacks were increasingly less likely to purchase books that depicted black characters in traditional or unaffirming ways. Further, even if black consumers would still purchase these books, the civil rights movement would be likely to generate bad press around books that included questionable characterizations of blacks. Publishers also feared that white consumers would not purchase books that featured characters acceptable to the African-American community and to the civil rights movement. Facing market pressures that made any portrayal of black characters a hazardous bet, publishers simply omitted black characters all together.

Similarly, Farrell (1995) shows movements and movement organizations may have to reinvent themselves overtime to adjust to market pressures. According to Farrell, *Ms.* Magazine was unable to overcome the pressures of advertisers, who did not always bend to the feminist editorial policy of the magazine and who expected free and supportive editorial copy to accompany advertisements. After over more than a decade of struggle with advertisers, *Ms.* ultimately reissued itself as an ad-free, subscription-based magazine so that it could avoid continuing pressure from advertisers.

Instead of market pressures affecting cultural outcomes, Oldfield (1995) suggests a way in which markets can create opportunities for movements and facilitate cultural outcomes.[11] His research shows that consumption was used as a marker for social standing in Britain. Thus once abolition began to be seen as a social cause of the middle and upper classes, entrepreneurial abolitionists created art for profit that at once conveyed pro-abolitionist perspectives and the rising class affiliations of the owners.

Eyerman and Jamison's (1995) research suggests that folk music was in part altered in the 1950s and 1960s because of the massive youth music market that had been created by the baby boom. The large market created interest among recording labels and generated new venues for performers. In turn, this helped to decrease the importance of Old Left influence on folk music, allowing some folk music to become commercialized and other folk music to focus on political issues of the New Left. This is not to suggest that markets were the only influence in Eyerman and Jamison's explanation. As is true of many of the works that consider the role of markets, social movements were integral in inspiring and actualizing cultural change.

Other researchers look to the cultural production processes, instead of more narrowly at nexus of movement action and market forces and/or opportunities. For instance, both Gamson (1998) and Gamson and Modigliani (1989) argue that media practices and routines are critical to explaining changes in media coverage and changes in discourse. As Gamson and Modigliani summarize: "packages succeed in media discourse through a combination of cultural resonances, sponsor activities, and a successful fit with media norms and practices" (1989: 9). Media norms of interest would be such preferences as tastes for official sources and more institutional sources. As noted above, social movements play key roles as sponsors of certain packages, hoping to effectively advance a preferred package.

Finally, some have advocated for a more full-blown production of culture approach that considers movement influences, market influences, and production-related influences. Eyerman and Barretta (1996) outline such an approach in their explanation of the development and change of folk music, suggesting the following:

> The production of culture perspective analyzes forms of cultural expression as products of organized "worlds" or "fields." Rather than discussing artistic works or other symbolic goods as the product of an isolated creator, or alternatively, as mirroring "society," this perspective explains them in terms of their location in a social and organizational context. Integrated into an art world or market for symbolic goods, the object (a cultural good) is explained in relation to a social organization of production, distribution, and recognition. (Eyerman and Barretta 1996: 503–4)

In applying this approach to the case of folk music, they show that a burgeoning youth market, new production processes (e.g., the popularization of the cassette tape), and changing interests of recording labels combined with movement action to fundamentally change folk music:

> In attempting to account for both this continuity and change in the two waves of folk revival we have drawn from both the cognitive approach to the study of social movements, which calls attention to the creative role of social-movement actors in the production of knowledge, and the production of culture perspective, which

highlights the effects of institutional arrangements in the production of cultural goods. From the former, we have focused on the changing character of "movement intellectuals" ... from the latter, we have noted how, among other things, the changing nature of the recording industry helped recast the folk music revival. (Eyerman and Barretta 1996: 536)

Explaining Communities and Cultures

Research on collective identity and subcultures suggests two important casual mechanisms. First, many researchers have stressed the importance of internal movement dynamics to the development of collective identities and insular subcultures. For instance, Kanter's (1968, 1972) and Zablocki's (1971) studies suggest where insular movements are concerned (e.g., utopian and some religious groups), the actual structure and process of group participation shapes the level of commitment and identification that members share. Instead of focusing on group processes, NSM scholars, such as Melucci (1989), have argued for the importance of submerged, internal NSM networks and communities in the (re)creation of collective identity.

Showing a similar interest in internal movement dynamics, Taylor and Whittier (1992) attribute the development of lesbian feminist collective identity and community to disputes within the feminist movement. As was noted above, many prominent heterosexual feminists shunned lesbian feminists, fearing that an association between feminism and lesbianism would hurt the women's movement. In response, lesbian feminists developed a related but nonetheless importantly distinct collective identity. In part, this collective identity was built around a reinterpretation of lesbians' role in feminism that cast lesbians as a feminist vanguard. This positioning owed to lesbians seemingly unique ability to wholly reject the masculine world and ties to men. Heterosexual women could join this vanguard only if they considered themselves to be "political lesbians," which were women who were not sexually attracted to other women but who nonetheless wholly rejected the masculine world and ties to men.

Other researchers have suggested that collective identities and subcultures are produced through interaction with and conflict between social movement groups and mainstream culture and institutions. Yinger (1960, 1977, 1982), Hall and Jefferson (1976), Hebdige (1979), and Fantasia (1988) would fall within this camp. Illustratively, Fantasia suggests that conflict forges identities and that the lived experience of that conflict creates ties between participants. Importantly, practice is so critical to the creation of collective identities that such identities are necessarily ephemeral. Fantasia notes quite clearly that class consciousness and solidarity (read: collective identity) are not traits, characteristics, or attitudes; they are emergent properties of conflictual or oppositional encounters and are created out of opposition itself.[12]

CONCLUSION

As this review has made evident, students of social movement outcomes have not reached consensus over what outcomes can be appropriately considered cultural, or even on the meaning of culture. Analyzing three dimensions of culture, social movement researchers have instead identified a number of potential social movement outcomes over a broad area of social life, ranging from value and opinion change, to changes in art, to the development of new and distinct collective identities and communities. That is, in a somewhat ironic manner, the polysemic character of culture itself as an analytic concept has produced a diverse set of research projects on cultural movement outcomes.[13]

Further, cultural outcomes have been explained in very different ways. Even though most work on value and opinion change focuses on framing and most work on collective identity and subcultures focuses on movement activity and conflict, research on cultural production and practices have relied on a number of different explanatory approaches. Such diversity has some advantages. For instance, it should increase the depth at which researchers understand the processes surrounding movement-related cultural changes and ensure that important theoretical contributors to cultural change are not overlooked. However, the wide array of theoretical perspectives coupled with very different conceptualizations of culture also makes evaluating different theoretical propositions and support for those propositions difficult.

Perhaps as important as the theoretical issues of conceptualization and explanation are issues of causation that have not been raised in this chapter. As prior reviews of movement outcomes research stress (Giugni 1998; Giugni et al. 1999; Earl 2000), moving from plausible explanations to evidence of causal relations can be much harder than expected where social movement outcomes are concerned. This is arguably even more the case where cultural outcomes are concerned. For instance, to ultimately build a rich and powerful explanation of cultural outcomes, researchers need to be able to move beyond simply identifying correlations in time and/or space between movement action and cultural changes. Scholars must work toward identifying mechanistic links between movements and possible outcomes, identifying and examining the plausibility of causal contenders, and defending against claims of spuriousness (Earl 2000).

Since the primary goal of this chapter was to review the existing literature on cultural outcomes, a more detailed discussion of issues surrounding causality is not warranted here. Nonetheless, it is essential to note that even if the number of research projects on cultural outcomes were to expand dramatically and/or coalesce around specific visions of culture and definitions of cultural outcomes, the literature would still face the significant challenge of demonstrating that the causal explanations underlying various approaches are clearly supported by available data. Thus scholars interested in cultural outcomes research should also consult methodological (Earl 2000) and review (Burstein et al. 1995) pieces that confront concerns over causality more directly.

In sum, researchers interested in the cultural consequences of social movements have faced, and will continue to face, a number of concerns in the areas of conceptualization and theoretical explanation. To varying extents, though, a growing pool of scholars have attempted to address these issues and demonstrate that social movements do matter and that movements can shape culture. As this review has shown, the fruits of that labor are thus far varied and interesting.

Notes

I would like to thank David Snow, Sarah Soule, Hanspeter Kriesi, Jenny Irons, Saylor Breckenridge, and Verta Taylor for their comments and suggestions.

1   I will use "consequences" and "outcomes" interchangeably throughout this review.

2   While Hart (1996) describes these three dimensions of culture as separate meanings for the concept of culture, I use dimensions instead to emphasize the interrelationships between the three views of culture.

3   While I adopt Hart's labeling of "social-psychological" research, I acknowledge that much of the research that focuses on this cultural dimension has examined cognitive factors such as beliefs, values, and meanings, while less research has focused on more affective sentiments.

4   Other researchers have discussed or alluded to cultural changes in terms of changing values, beliefs, or opinions, but their research has not been centrally concerned with explaining cultural outcomes. For instance, Jenness (1990) and Weitzer (1991) both examine the political goals of the prostitutes' rights movement. However, both also conclude that opinions about prostitution have not fundamentally changed in the US. Relatedly, Bush (1992) examines the policy outcomes of two women's movements and argues that while policy aims were not achieved, the US battered women's movement was able to transform domestic abuse from a private to public issue. Since these projects, and others like them, do not directly demonstrate the extent or cause of reported cultural changes, they are not reviewed here.

5   I use the term "movement" here in a more singular manner than many NSM theorists, given that NSM theorists contest the "reification" of social movements, arguing that movements are too heterogeneous, multivocal, and dynamic to be captured by any single description or characterization. This, for instance, is why Melucci (1994) is so clear in arguing that some segments of new social movements may be concerned with policy and the distribution of state resources even while other segments are fundamentally concerned with more cultural contestation.

6   One could argue that theorists have suggested that NSM contest meaning, logics, and practices. However, since the bulk of NSM theory attempts to tie these changes to the larger development of collective identity and subcultures, I do not review that work separately here. Instead, I discuss NSM work again in the discussion of collective identity later in the chapter.

7   Other work has been done in this area but has a less exclusive view identity. For instance, Gould's (1995) study of identity demonstrated the ways in which multiple sources of identity are available in mobilization. Theoretically, his study made clear that the salience and activation of particular identities within a larger set of available identities is of critical importance and should be the subject of study. However, I do not review his work or other work similar to his because it focuses on mobilization, not outcomes.

8   Certainly some of the works excluded from this review focus on the relationship between resistance and subcultural creation and identity. Nonetheless, because social movements are not centrally important to the explanations, interested readers are referred to the pieces cited in the main text for more detail on this topic.

9   D'Anjou and Van Male (1998) adopt the language of "interpretative packages" instead of frames, drawing in part on Gamson's and his collaborators prior use of this terminology (Gamson and Lasch 1983; Gamson and Modigliani 1989). While later work by Gamson (1998) predominately uses the language of frames, earlier work by Gamson argued that interpretive packages were distinguishable from frames. D'Anjou and Van Male (1998) extend Gamson's use of interpretive packages, arguing the interpretative packages include

three components: a cognitive frame, justificatory reasoning, and discussions of "the effects of what is being framed as an issue" (211). In terms of this review's discussion of discourse and framing, any distinction between a frame and interpretative package is not consequential to this paper's arguments.

10   Rochon (1998) also considers the relationship between political change and cultural change, but concludes that there is not necessarily a directional relationship between the two. At times political changes create cultural changes, as he argued occurred with equal employment opportunity for women, while at other times cultural changes cause political changes, as he argued occurred with the failure of the Equal Rights Amendment.

11   It is interesting to note that studies of other types of movement outcomes also show that market opportunities and forces can shape the success of movements. For instance, Rosenberg's (1991) research on social movements and legal change suggests that movements are much more likely to achieve social change when some sort of market implementation of legal decisions is possible. In his examination of abortion-related decisions, for instance, he found the market forces strongly shaped both the immediate provision of abortion services to women after Roe v. Wade and that these same forces accounted for a constriction in abortion services in the 1980s.

12   When conflict over rhetoric between movement insiders and opponents is considered, Hunt et al. (1994) suggest that framing is integrally related to the creation of collective identities.

13   As Earl (2000) points out, even once issues of conceptualization are resolved, cultural outcomes researchers also face major difficulties in the operationalization of the changes they seek to study. Earl (2000) reviews these additional methodological burdens in more detail and suggests approaches designed to overcoming some of these conceptual and methodological obstacles.

References

Amenta, Edwin, and Michael P. Young (1999) Making an Impact: Conceptual and Methodological Implications of the Collective Goods Criterion. In Marco G. Giugni, Doug McAdam, and Charles Tilly (eds.), *How Social Movements Matter*. Minneapolis: University of Minnesota Press, 22–41.

Berger, Bennett M. (1983) Still Thinking about the Sixties. *Contemporary Sociology*, 12, 482–5.

Bordt, Rebecca L. (1997) How Alternative Ideas Become Institutions: The Case of Feminist Collectives. *Nonprofit and Voluntary Sector Quarterly*, 26, 132–55.

Breines, W. (1989) *Community and Organization in the New Left 1962–1968*. New Brunswick, NJ: Rutgers University Press.

Bucholtz, Mary (2002) Youth and Cultural Practice. *Annual Review of Anthropology*, 31, 525–52.

Burstein, Paul, Rachel L. Einwohner, and Jocelyn A. Hollander (1995) The Success of Political Movements: A Bargaining Perspective. In J. Craig Jenkins and Bert Klandermans (eds.), *The Politics of Social Protest: Comparative Perspectives on States and Social Movements*. Minneapolis: University of Minnesota Press, 275–95.

Bush, Diane Mitsch (1992) Women's Movements and State Policy Reform Aimed at Domestic Violence against Women: A Comparison of the Consequences of Movement Mobilization in the U.S. and India. *Gender & Society*, 6, 587–608.

Cohen, Jean (1983) Rethinking Social Movements. *Berkeley Journal of Sociology*, 28, 97–113.

——(1985) Strategy or Identity: New Theoretical Paradigms and Contemporary Social Movements. *Social Research*, 52, 663–716.

Cress, Daniel M., and David A. Snow (2000) The Outcomes of Homeless Mobilization: The Influence of Organization, Disruption, Political Mediation, and Framing. *American Journal of Sociology*, 105, 1063–1104.

d'Anjou, Leo (1996) *Social Movements and Cultural Change: The First Abolition Campaign Revisited*. New York: Aldine de Gruyter.

d'Anjou, Leo, and John Van Male (1998) Between Old and New: Social Movements and Cultural Change. *Mobilization*, 3, 207–26.

Darnton, Robert (1991) Workers Revolt: The Great Cat Massacre of the Rue Saint-Séverin. In Chandra Mukerji and Michael Schudson (eds.), *Rethinking Popular Culture: Contemporary Perspectives in Cultural Studies*. Berkeley: University of California Press, 97–120.

Diani, Mario (1997) Social Movements and Social Capital: A Network Perspective on Movement Outcomes. *Mobilization*, 2, 129–47.

Douglas, Mary (1966) *Purity and Danger: An Analysis of the Concepts of Pollution and Taboo*. New York: Routledge.

——(1991) Jokes. In Chandra Mukerji and Michael Schudson (eds.), *Rethinking Popular Culture: Contemporary Perspectives in Cultural Studies*. Berkeley: University of California Press, 291–310.

Earl, Jennifer (2000) Methods, Movements, and Outcomes: Methodological Difficulties in the Study of Extra-Movement Outcomes. *Research in Social Movements, Conflicts, and Change*, 22, 3–25.

Epstein, Barbara (1991) *Political Protest and Cultural Revolution*. Berkeley: University of California Press.

Epstein, Steven (1996) *Impure Science: AIDS, Activism, and the Politics of Knowledge*. Berkeley: University of California Press.

Eyerman, Ron, and Andrew Jamison (1995) Social Movements and Cultural Transformation: Popular Music in the 1960s. *Media, Culture, and Society*, 17, 449–68.

——(1998) *Music and Social Movements: Mobilizing Traditions in the Twentieth Century*. Cambridge: Cambridge University Press.

Eyerman, Ron, and Scott Barretta (1996) From the 30s to the 60s: The Folk Music Revival in the United States. *Theory and Society*, 25, 501–43.

Fantasia, Rick (1988) *Cultures of Solidarity: Consciousness, Action and Contemporary American Workers*. Berkeley: University of California Press.

Farrell, Amy (1995) "Like a Tarantula on a Banana Boat": Ms. Magazine, 1972–1989. In Myra Marx Ferree and Patricia Yancey Martin (eds.), *Feminist Organizations: Harvest of the New Women's Movement*. Philadelphia, PA: Temple University Press, 53–68.

Gamson, William A. ([1975] 1990) *The Strategy of Social Protest*. Homewood, IL: Dorsey.

——(1998) Social Movements and Cultural Change. In Marco G. Giugni, Doug McAdam, and Charles Tilly (eds.), *From Contention to Democracy*. Lanham, MD: Rowman & Littlefield, 57–77.

Gamson, William A., and Kimberly E. Lasch (1983) The Political Culture of Social Welfare Policy. In S. E. Spiro and E. Yuchtman-Yaar (eds.), *Evaluating the Welfare State: Social and Political Perspectives*. New York: Academic, 397–415.

Gamson, William A., and Andre Modigliani (1989) Media Discourse and Public Opinion of Nuclear Power: A Constructionist Approach. *American Journal of Sociology*, 95, 1–37.

Gaventa, John (1980) *Power and Powerlessness: Quiescence and Rebellion in an Appalachian Valley*. Chicago: University of Illinois Press.

Giugni, Marco G. (1998) Was it Worth the Effort? The Outcomes and Consequences of Social Movements. *Annual Review of Sociology*, 98, 371–93.

Giugni, Marco G., Doug McAdam, and Charles Tilly (eds.) (1999) *How Social Movements Matter*. Minneapolis: University of Minnesota Press.

Gould, Roger V. (1995) *Insurgent Identities: Class, Community, and Protest in Paris from 1848 to the Commune*. Chicago: University of Chicago Press.

Hall, John R. (1988) Social Organization and Pathways of Commitment: Types of Communal Groups, Rational Choice Theory, and the Kanter Thesis. *American Sociological Review*, 53, 679–92.

Hall, Stuart, and Tony Jefferson (eds.) (1976) *Resistance through Rituals: Youth Subcultures in Post-War Britain*. New York: Holmes & Meier.

Hart, Stephen (1996) The Cultural Dimension of Social Movements: A Theoretical Assessment and Literature Review. *Sociology of Religion*, 57, 87–100.

Hebdige, Dick (1979) *Subculture: The Meaning of Style*. New York: Routledge.

Hunt, Scott A., Robert D. Benford, and David A. Snow (1994) Identity Fields: Framing Processes and the Social Construction of Movement Identities. In Enrique Laraña, Hank Johnston, and Joseph R. Gusfield (eds.), *New Social Movements: From Ideology to Identity*. Philadelphia, PA: Temple University Press, 185–208.

Inglehart, Ronald (1977) *The Silent Revolution: Changing Values and Political Styles among Western Publics*. Princeton, NJ: Princeton University Press.

——(1981) Post-Materialism in an Environment of Insecurity. *American Political Science Review*, 75, 880–900.

——(1990) *Culture Shift in Advanced Industrial Society*. Princeton, NJ: Princeton University Press.

Inglehart, Ronald, and David Appel (1989) The Rise of Postmaterialist Values and Changing Gender Roles and Sexual Norms. *International Journal of Public Opinion Research*, 1, 4575.

Jenness, Valerie (1990) From Sex as Sin to Sex as Work: Coyote and the Reorganization of Prostitution as a Social Problem. *Social Problems*, 37, 403–20.

Kanter, Rosabeth Moss (1968) Commitment and Social Organization: A Study of Commitment Mechanisms in Utopian Communities. *American Sociological Review*, 33, 499–517.

——(1972) *Commitment and Community: Communes and Utopias in Sociological Perspectives*. Cambridge, MA: Harvard University Press.

Katzenstein, Mary Fainsod (1995) Discursive Politics and Feminist Activism in the Catholic Church. In Myra Marx Ferree and Patricia Yancey Martin (eds.), *Feminist Organizations: Harvest of the New Women's Movement*. Philadelphia, PA: Temple University Press, 35–52.

Kriesi, Hanspeter (1993) *Political Mobilization and Social Change: The Dutch Case in Comparative Perspective*. Brookfield, VT: Ashgate.

Kriesi, Hanspeter, Ruud Koopmans, Jan Willem Dyvendak, and Marco G. Giugni (1995) *New Social Movements in Western Europe*. Minneapolis: University of Minnesota Press.

Lichterman, Paul (1999) Talking Identity in the Public Sphere: Broad Visions and Small Spaces in Sexual Identity Politics. *Theory and Society*, 28, 101–41.

McAdam, Doug (1988) *Freedom Summer*. New York: Oxford University Press.

——(1994) Culture and Social Movements. In Enrique Laraña, Hank Johnston, and Joseph R. Gusfield (eds.), *New Social Movements: From Ideology to Identity*. Philadelphia, PA: Temple University Press, 36–57.

Melucci, Alberto (1985) The Symbolic Challenge of Contemporary Movements. *Social Research*, 52, 790–816.

——(1989) *Nomads of the Present: Social Movements and Individual Needs in Contemporary Society*. London: Hutchinson Radius.

——(1994) A Strange Kind of Newness: What's New in New Social Movements. In Enrique Laraña, Hank Johnston, and Joseph R. Gusfield (eds.), *New Social Movements: From Ideology to Identity*. Philadelphia, PA: Temple University Press, 101–30.

Moore, Kelly (1999) Political Protest and Institutional Change: The Anti-Vietnam War Movement and American Science. In Marco G. Giugni, Doug McAdam, and Charles

Tilly (eds.), *How Social Movements Matter*. Minneapolis: University of Minnesota Press, 97–115.

Offe, Claus (1985) New Social Movements: Challenging the Boundaries of Institutional Politics. *Social Research*, 52, 817–68.

Oldfield, John R. (1995) *Popular Politics and British Anti-Slavery: The Mobilization of Public Opinion against the Slave Trade, 1784–1807*. Manchester: Manchester University Press.

Pescosolida, Bernice A., Elizabeth Grauerholz, and Melissa A. Milkie (1997) Culture and Conflict: The Portrayal of Blacks in U.S. Children's Picture Books through the Mid- and Late-Twentieth Century. *American Sociological Review*, 62, 443–64.

Pichardo, Nelson A (1997) New Social Movements: A Critical Review. *Annual Review of Sociology*, 23, 411–30.

Polletta, Francesca (1999) Snarls, Quacks, and Quarrels: Culture and Structure in Political Process Theory. *Sociological Forum*, 14, 63–70.

—— (2002) Authority in Movements. Paper presented at the Authority in Contention Conference, Notre Dame, August.

Polletta, Francesca, and James M. Jasper (2001) Collective Identity and Social Movements. *Annual Review of Sociology*, 27, 283–305.

Rochon, Thomas R. (1998) *Culture Moves: Ideas, Activism, and Changing Values*. Princeton, NJ: Princeton University Press.

Rosenberg, Gerald N. (1991) *The Hollow Hope: Can Courts Bring about Social Change?* Chicago: University of Chicago Press.

Schudson, Michael (1989) How Culture Works: Perspectives from Media Studies on the Efficacy of Symbols. *Theory and Society*, 18, 153–80.

—— (1997) Paper Tigers: A Sociologist Follows Cultural Studies into the Wilderness. *Lingua Franca*, August, 49–56.

Sherkat, Darren, and Christopher Ellison (1999) Recent Developments and Current Controversies in the Sociology of Religion. *Annual Review of Sociology*, 25, 363–94.

Snow, David A. (2001) Collective Identity and Expressive Forms. In Neil Smelser and Paul B. Baltes (eds.), *International Encyclopedia of the Social and Behavioral Sciences*. Oxford: Pergamon, 2212–19.

Snow, David A., E. Burke Rochford, Steven K. Worden, and Robert D. Benford (1986) Frame Alignment Processes, Micromobilization, and Movement Participation. *American Sociological Review*, 51, 464–81.

Staggenborg, Suzanne (1995) Can Feminist Organizations Be Effective? In Myra Marx Ferree and Patricia Yancey Martin (eds.), *Feminist Organizations: Harvest of the New Women's Movement*. Philadelphia, PA: Temple University Press, 339–55.

Taylor, Verta, and Nancy E. Whittier (1992) Collective Identity in Social Movement Communities: Lesbian Feminist Mobilization. In A. Morris and C. Mueller (eds.), *Frontiers of Social Movement Theory*. New Haven: Yale University Press, 104–29.

Touraine, Alain (1985) An Introduction to the Study of Social Movements. *Social Research*, 52, 749–87.

Weitzer, Ronald (1991) Prostitutes' Rights in the United States: The Failure of a Movement. *Sociological Quarterly*, 32, 23–41.

Williams, Raymond (1976) *Keywords: A Vocabulary of Culture and Society*. New York: Oxford University Press.

Yinger, J. Milton (1960) Contraculture and Subculture. *American Sociological Review*, 25, 625–35.

—— (1977) Countercultures and Social Change. *American Sociological Review*, 42, 833–53.

—— (1982) *Countercultures: The Promise and the Peril of a World Turned Upside Down*. New York: Free Press.

Zablocki, Benjamin (1971) *The Joyful Community*. Baltimore: Penguin.

23

The Consequences of Social Movements for Each Other

Nancy Whittier

The US women's movement of the late 1960s and 1970s emerged at the height of a cycle of protest, when many constituencies were mobilized, engagement with the state and other targets was high, and activists around the world expected that social transformation, if not revolution, was around the corner. Why did feminist activism grow at that time? Women had been organizing on their own behalf for at least a century previously, and some persistent activists and organizations from earlier eras remained on the scene in the 1960s (Rupp and Taylor 1987; Weigand 2001). These predecessors made important organizational, ideological, and tactical contributions to the emerging feminist mass mobilization (Rupp and Taylor 1987; Weigand 2001), as did structural changes in women's position (Buechler 1990). Yet the other movements of the 1960s, arguably, made it possible for large-scale feminist activism to emerge by training and mobilizing the women who would staff the movement, providing an organizational infrastructure from which activists could draw recruits and resources, innovating tactics that feminist activists could adapt, and constructing ideologies and frames that activists combined with earlier feminist analyses to create a new and compelling account of the causes of women's subordination and the promise of women's liberation.

In turn, the women's movement reshaped the larger movements of the New Left with a broad-based critique of male dominance within activist circles and of the links between patriarchy and racism, capitalism, and militarism (Meyer and Whittier 1994; Whittier 1995). The women's movement itself helped to spawn other challenges around gay and lesbian liberation, child sexual abuse, and intersections of race, class, and gender. Its frames, discourses, and collective identity were enormously influential on the range of movements on the Left over the next several decades. Feminist activism in the US shaped and was shaped by women's activism transnationally (Mueller and Katzenstein 1987; Morgan 1996), and it established a base from which feminism could endure and change over subsequent decades and waves (Taylor 1989; Walker 1995; Whittier 1995; Baumgardner and Richards

2000). It also produced substantial opposition, galvanizing activists on the Right to oppose abortion rights, gay and lesbian families, employed mothers, prosecution of alleged sex offenders, and sex education and birth control in the schools, to name a few. These opponents not only emerged in response to the successes and visibility of feminist protests, but in many cases they adopted similar tactics, using sit-ins and direct action in front of abortion clinics, or even adapted feminist ideology and collective identity, calling themselves "feminist" and claiming to support gender equity (Roiphe 1993; Sommers 1994).

As the example of the women's movement shows, movements can generate both allied and opposed movements and can influence their form and content, sometimes through direct contact and sometimes indirectly through changes in the social movement sector and effects on external institutions. There are several related literatures that deal with what Staggenborg (1986) calls "mobilization outcomes." First, a small body of work addresses the influences between movements directly, including "social movement spillover" (Meyer and Whittier 1994), how influential movements can generate new "spin-off movements" (McAdam 1995), and the diffusion of tactics or ideologies from one movement organization or locale to another (Soule 1997; see also chapter 13 in this volume). Second, a closely related body of work deals with protest cycles. (See also chapter 2 in this volume for a detailed discussion.) Work on cycles of protest rests on the notion that diffusion from a first movement to others sparks the growth of widespread protest. It thus provides useful tools for conceptualizing the interrelations among movements within the cycle, particularly between "early risers" – the first to emerge in a protest cycle – and later movements and for analyzing how influential movements can reshape political opportunities and the social movement sector (Tarrow 1998). Third, organizational ecology approaches analyze the various factors, including social movements themselves, that shape social movement sectors, showing how changes in the social movement sector in turn affect individual movements (Edwards and Marullo 1995; Minkoff 1995, 1997). Fourth, scholars have studied several specific kinds of movement–movement interactions: between partners in coalitions (Hathaway and Meyer 1994; Meyer and Whittier 1994; Meyer and Rochon 1997; Tarrow 1998: 144), between opposing movements (Meyer and Staggenborg 1996), and between earlier and later waves of an ongoing challenge (Isserman 1987; Rupp and Taylor 1987; Whittier 1995; Weigand 2001).

In sum, movements have a variety of *kinds* of effects on each other. They may alter the form that another movement takes – its frames, discourses, collective identity, goals, tactics, and organizational structure (Meyer and Whittier 1994). They may give rise to other social movements by creating new opportunities or through inspiration or factionalization (McAdam 1995), or they may give rise to opposing movements (Meyer and Staggenborg 1996). They may persist through abeyance structures and survive to spark a new wave of an ongoing struggle (Taylor 1989). All of these effects can occur either between movements that are contemporaries or over time; and all can be reciprocal. Movements exert these influences through both direct and indirect *routes*. The personnel or organizations of one movement may affect another movement through direct contact, or the changes that one movement brings about in the larger social movement sector, culture, or political opportunities may indirectly affect other movements.

In this chapter, I draw from all of these approaches to examine the consequences of social movements for other social movements. Examples are drawn from my research on feminist, lesbian, and gay movements, and movements against the sexual abuse of children, as well as from secondary literature, primarily on US movements since the 1960s protest cycle (Taylor and Whittier 1992; Whittier 1995, 1997, 2000, 2001). Following Meyer and Whittier (1994), I first discuss the kinds of effects that movements have on each other, and then turn to a detailed discussion of the routes and determinants of movement–movement effects.

Types of Effects

The variety of ways that movement–movement influence can take shape can be broken down into two broad categories. First, movements can have *generative effects*, that is, creating new challenges, changing the overall level of protest, shaping later waves of the same challenge, or sparking countermovements (Isaacs et al. 2001). Second, they can alter the form of other protests through social movement *spillover* that shapes frames, collective identities, organizational structures, and relations with authorities (Meyer and Whittier 1994).

Generative Effects

Generative effects are quite varied. Social movements can produce new challenges that "spin off" directly through relationships within a social movement sector (McAdam 1995). They can affect later waves of the same movement, and they can give rise to countermovements. Following Isaacs et al. (2001), I term all of these ways that activists foster new movements "generative effects."[1]

Cycles of Protest and Movement Spin-off

The fact that mobilization occurs in waves – in cycles that grow, peak, and decline (see chapter 2 in this volume) – suggests the significance of the generative effects of movements on each other. To be sure, cycles of protest are partially the result of shifts in political opportunities that make their emergence possible and, ultimately, redirect them or shut them down (except in the case of revolutions) (Tilly 1978, 1993; McAdam 1995; Tarrow 1998: 141). But they are just as much the result of the cognitive, organizational, cultural, and tactical effects of "early risers," the influential movements that emerge first in the cycle, on later movements (McAdam 1995; Minkoff 1995; Tarrow 1998; chapter 2 in this volume). When activists begin to organize, they are inspired by their observation of or knowledge about other challengers. They may draw on the frames that are already in use by influential movements (Snow and Benford 1992), gain concrete assistance from other movement organizations, or recruit members from within the ranks of other challenges. They adopt tactics that are familiar from previous use, or that they have observed to be effective for others. And they take advantage of any openings in political opportunities or mainstream culture that their predecessors create (Tilly 1978, 1993; Meyer and Whittier 1994; McAdam 1995; Tarrow 1998). For these reasons, one of the major outcomes of social movements is the creation and facilitation of other social movements (Staggenborg 1986).

The first movements to emerge in a cycle, the "early risers," emerge as a result of a complicated set of contextual and indigenous factors. Once influential challenges emerge, they facilitate the emergence of subsequent movements by creating a pool of trained and interested potential recruits, an organizational infrastructure from which other mobilizations can draw resources and support, and a sense of possibility or efficacy. In these ways, the US civil rights movement, for example, facilitated subsequent mobilizing around a host of issues (Evans 1979; McAdam 1995; Minkoff 1995, 1997). As the numbers of challenges, campaigns, organizations, protest actions, and participants rise, they also diversify, addressing a wider range of targets, using varied tactics, and ultimately constituting a protest cycle. Tactics that are appealing to activists either because they seem to be successful or because they are consistent with movement ideology or culture can readily diffuse from one movement locale to another through either strong or weak ties (Morris 1981; Soule 1997; see also chapter 13 in this volume). Such diffusion is most likely to occur when activists see themselves as similar to those from whom they adopt new forms of collective action (Soule 1997 and chapter 13 in this volume). But movements can continue to spin off new challenges or factions even after a cycle of protest declines.

For example, an important spin-off of the second-wave women's movement was activism against child sexual abuse. Initially framed in feminist terms, as a problem of patriarchal male abuse against children, the movement rose to prominence in the mid-1980s, after the 1960s/1970s cycle of protest that spawned the women's movement had died down. As its feminist progenitors lost influence, the movement against child sexual abuse sparked its own spin-offs, factions that departed sufficiently from the feminist theme to form their own organizations and networks. These include organizing around child sexual abuse prevention and treatment within medical, psychiatric, and religious organizations, and movements of protective parents (Whittier 2001).

Spin-off movements do not simply mirror the form of their progenitors. By definition, they organize in new ways as they depart from the initial mobilization. Indeed, spin-off movements may organize partly as a challenge to conditions in the progenitor movement, as the women's movement did when it challenged sexism in the New Left (Evans 1991; Rosen 2000). Valocchi (2001) argues that spin-off movements do cultural work, adapting the ideology of the initiator movement through a dialectical process that grows in part from the contradictions between individual identities and interests and those of the initiator movement. For example, the first homophile activists cut their political teeth in the Old Left, but their identities could not be reconciled with the Communist Party's condemnation of homosexuality as bourgeois; thus they spun off from the CP to form the autonomous Mattachine Society, carrying lessons from their Old Left experience with them (Valocchi 2001). Thus activists may spin off new challenges both out of an enthusiastic desire to expand the reach of the originating movement and out of dissatisfaction with its limits; in doing so, they simultaneously adopt and adapt previous approaches.

Yet, in order for a new movement to emerge from a previous one, it must either change the existing movement (spillover) or factionalize from it (spin-off). The characteristics of initiator movement organizations shape which of these courses the spin-off movement takes (Valocchi 2001). More flexible movement organizations, which have more mechanisms to deal with and address internal dissent, are more likely to change in response to internal challenges, while less flexible movement organizations that seek to suppress internal dissent are more likely to spawn factions. For example, although early homophile activists had participated in the US Communist Party (CP), the CP could not expand its focus to address gay and lesbian rights, nor could it accommodate internal diversity over the issue, and so the nascent homophile movement organized autonomously. Conversely, the more flexible organizational structure of the New Left allowed it to accommodate the nascent gay liberation movement in the early 1970s (Valocchi 2001).

New challenges can emerge as an outcome of other movements, even when the activists that organize them do not have experience in the earlier movement. In fact, a thriving social movement sector can spark protest or organization among far-flung groups by establishing channels through which resources can flow, creating a widely visible example, and legitimizing social movement actors (Meyer and Whittier 1994; McAdam 1995; Minkoff 1997; Isaacs et al. 2001). Thus, for example, the growth and success of AIDS activists in the late 1980s prompted breast cancer activists to mobilize for similar goals (increased federal research funding and visibility) using similar tactics (Taylor and Van Willigen 1996).

Continuity and Abeyance

Challengers can also generate long-term movements; that is, an earlier wave of a movement can shape later waves of organizing around the same grievances or by the same constituency. During periods of mass mobilization, activists construct organizations, collective identities, frames, and tactics that can persist after mobilization declines. These mobilization outcomes are significant not so much for the fairly minimal gains they can make during abeyance periods, but because they facilitate and shape the emergence of later mobilization around the same issue (Taylor 1989). Their organizational infrastructure may contribute resources to an emerging movement, as the National Woman's Party did by providing meeting space to some feminist activists in the mid-1960s (Rupp and Taylor 1987). Their veterans may have become potentially powerful members of institutions as with the elections of civil rights leaders to state and federal office in the 1970s and 1980s after the movement had died down (Meyer 2000). The issues they hatched may provide an impetus for later organizing, as the Equal Rights Amendment, promoted by feminists since 1921, did for liberal feminists in the 1960s (Rupp and Taylor 1987). As with any spin-off movement, later waves do not simply adopt their predecessors' forms of organizing unquestioningly. In fact, activists usually depart from earlier approaches as they reshape the movement to fit their own experiences and changed political and cultural contexts (Whittier 1995, 1997). As in spin-off movements, continuity is a dialectical process of influence and reinterpretation (Valocchi 2001).

Countermovements

Countermovements are not "spin-offs" of their opponents, but they are a case of mobilization that is generated or intensified by another movement. Unlike spin-off movements, however, they emerge not because they are supported by the other movement's organizational infrastructure, but in response to its gains. Their origins, thus, are largely interpretive, as a movement's successes and visibility galvanize opposition. Arguably, activists on all sides of an issue may feel greater efficacy when they see others mobilize successfully. Activists do not simply join counter-movements because a movement's success threatens or outrages them, however, but because movement gains provide both a concrete target and an arena in which to mount challenges (Zald and Useem 1987). When abortion was legalized in the US in 1973, for example, opponents mobilized on a large scale with a newly clear goal; their efforts and gains, in turn, continued to rally abortion rights activists (Meyer and Staggenborg 1996).

Spillover Effects

Even when movements do not directly generate new mobilizations, they may still influence each other. Social movements that exist alongside each other can, and often do, change each other. Activists define themselves, frame their issues, develop tactics, and establish organizations with reference to what other collective actors have done. Movements can spill over onto each other over time, as in the influence of an earlier movement on a later one, or across contemporaries. In fact, spin-off movements may turn around and reshape their parent movements, as the women's movement did with much of the New Left (Meyer and Whittier 1994). Like genera-tive effects, spillover effects travel through shared personnel (as a result of biograph-ical and generational outcomes), organizational and movement community overlap and coalition, and reflected influence from external contexts and shifts in the social movement sector (Meyer and Whittier 1994). A range of movement characteristics can spill over from one challenge to another, including frames, collective identities, tactics, and movement culture (Meyer and Whittier 1994).[2] I will discuss these next, illustrating the ways that movements can change in response to one another.

Frames

Activists promote particular ways of understanding the world. When movements are influential within the social movement sector, their frames and discourses affect how other activists frame their issues and the discourses they draw on to justify their claims. When movements are influential in the larger world, they reshape discourses and frames in mainstream culture and thus receptiveness to claims by other activists. Movements, then, affect each others' frames in several ways.

First is the influence of *master frames* (see chapter 17 in this volume). Part of what characterizes a new cycle of protest are the distinctive frames that activists in early movements construct. These frames serve as "a kind of master algorithm that colors and constrains the orientations and activities of other movements" (Benford and Snow 2000). The master frames of early risers set the terms for the frames of subsequent movements in a cycle of protest (Snow and Benford 1992). Influential master frames also can affect how activists in movements that are not part of the same cycle of protest frame their causes; they may even influence opposing move-ments. For example, the civil rights frame was originated by advocates of African-American civil rights, and shaped how allied activists framed demands for student rights, women's rights, and gay and lesbian rights (Snow and Benford 1992). A civil rights frame turned up later as religious fundamentalists argued for the right to pray in schools and the anti-abortion group Operation Rescue talked about defending the civil rights of fetuses. Similarly, the frame of "community control," originated by community activists in an effort to gain self-determination and improve city schools, was later adopted by advocates of vouchers and charter schools (Naples 2002). Although some feminists, for example, adopted a civil rights frame because they had direct contact with the civil rights movement and saw themselves as similar in orientation, Operation Rescue, in contrast, adopted the frame because of its media prominence and apparent success. Clearly, both direct and indirect channels of influence are important (Soule 1997 and chapter 13 in this volume). Indirect channels are plausibly particularly important for diffusion across unrelated or even opposing movements.

The idea of master frame suggests a frame that emerges early in a cycle and is adopted – perhaps with modifications – by later movements. Second, in addition, activists in movements that coexist in a cycle of protest, including latecomers, can reshape each others' frames. For example, the women's movement developed a "capitalist patriarchy" frame that drew on both earlier New Left and newer feminist frames to explain not only women's oppression, but militarism, imperialism, racism, and class inequality as the result of the intersection of male dominance and capitalism (Whittier 1995). This frame then influenced how peace activists conceptualized and protested war and nuclear buildup, sparking protests like the Women's Pentagon Action and analyses that saw militarism as an expression of phallocentrism (Meyer and Whittier 1994).

Third are the results of movement gains in changing mainstream frames, because mainstream culture limits the kinds of frames that other movements are inclined to, and indeed are able to, advocate. For example, the early movement against child sexual abuse, couched in feminist terms, simultaneously sought changes in laws against child sexual abuse and prosecution of offenders, and more sweeping changes in patriarchal domination of women and children within the nuclear family. They achieved far more promoting frame (and policy) changes related to the first goal than the second, successfully changing the understanding of child sexual abuse from a very rare psychiatric *pathology* for which children were as much to blame as offenders, to a *crime* for which offenders should be punished. As a result, later waves of activism against child sexual abuse tended to frame the problem in terms of legal and criminal causes and solutions. These later waves include parents' advocacy of "Megan's Law," a set of federal and state laws that require that convicted sex offenders register with the police and that communities be notified of sex offenders who live in their areas. Activists in this latter effort framed child sexual abuse as a criminal offense committed by nonfamily members. This frame would not have been possible without the success of early feminist activists in changing mainstream understandings, and their concurrent failure to promulgate the patriarchy frame on child sexual abuse (Whittier 2000).

Collective Identities

Activists create collective identities when they participate in movements (see chapter 19 in this volume). Individuals who adopt these collective identities can carry them into other social movements, influencing the latter challenges. For example, participants in Freedom Summer changed how they thought about themselves and politics as a result of their experiences, and they carried this perspective into other New Left movements (McAdam 1988). In addition, the collective identities that emerge from collective action can become independently available for adoption, modification, or influence on other activists. Collective identities are in this sense a cultural product of movements, similar to frames, that can influence contemporaneous or subsequent movements. The collective identity of "feminist," for example, has entered the mainstream lexicon, and while its value is rather low in mainstream contexts, in progressive movement contexts labeling oneself or one's organization "feminist" carries considerable cultural capital. Thus the US Green Party, in an effort to build a broad coalition, identifies itself as feminist, among other things. Declaring its alliance with feminist collective identity shapes its frames and goals, as members pressure the group to be consistent with its avowed feminism (personal interview, Green Party activist).

Subsequent movements need not claim preexisting collective identities to be influenced by them. Activists may also shape their collective identities in contrast to preexisting collective identities. For example, third-wave feminist activists define a collective identity that is distinguished largely by its attempts to depart from second-wave feminist collective identity despite similarities in ideology and goals (Walker 1995; Baumgardner and Richards 2000). When third-wave feminists declare their focus on intersections of gender with race, class, and sexuality, for example, they emphasize how this focus departs from the "white feminism" of the second wave in a process that Lynn (2001) calls "anti-spillover." Here, generational divisions within social movements reflect an indirect influence – by contrast – of earlier collective identities on later ones. In more extreme cases, activists who seek to contrast their collective identity with that of other movements may actually mount opposing movements. Antifeminist activists, for example, advocate a collective identity as women that emphasizes their differences from feminists such as their love of husband, home, and children over careers (Marshall 1995).

Tactical and Cultural Repertoires

One of the central ways that movements affect each other is through their tactical and cultural repertoires. Activists draw from the relatively limited menu of actions developed by previous movements that Tilly (1978, 1993) calls repertoires of contention (Tarrow 1998). Major tactics such as the demonstration, sit-in, civil disobedience and mass arrest, street theater, and political lobbying outline the possibilities for activists from quite different movements. Thus one of the outcomes of early risers in a protest cycle is the establishment of a tactical repertoire from which a host of later movements draw. Tactical repertoires can shape the actions of activists that are not part of the same cycle of protest, but are quite distant in time. They can affect tactics in contemporaneous movements that are only loosely allied, as in the case of growing labor militancy during the 1960s and 1970s, which Isaacs et al. (2001) find was influenced by New Left organizing during the same period. Tactics can also diffuse across locales within a movement as with the spread of shantytown protests on US college campuses during the 1980s anti-apartheid movement (Soule 1997, 1999). This spread is facilitated by activists' direct connections to each other and by indirect means such as media coverage. One movement's tactics may even influence opposing movements. For example, the direct action tactics pioneered by the civil rights movement in the 1960s included sit-ins and mass arrest. These tactics revolutionized activists' sense of possible actions and were adopted by participants in many other left movements of the 1960s and later. But they were also adopted by movements of the right, notably the anti-abortion group Operation Rescue, which used sit-ins and mass arrests to great effect in closing or obstructing access to abortion providers (Blanchard 1994).

On a more micro level, the specific ways that activists deploy and interpret tactics and the *content* of those tactics may be influenced by other social movements. Not every demonstration or street theater protest is the same in its slogans, performances, level of militancy, and so forth; activists do not frame or prepare for every sit-in or mass arrest in the same way; and lobbyists use a range of approaches and arguments. For example, peace and antinuclear activists often relied on direct action tactics in the 1980s. These were part of a tactical repertoire initiated in the civil rights movement 20 years earlier and disseminated by the range of New Left movements of the 1960s and 1970s. But because participants in the 1980s movements were profoundly influenced by the women's movement, they practiced direct action in new ways, developing complex means of assuring equal participation by all group members in consensus decision-making, and emphasizing both logistical and emotional connections among participants (Epstein 1991; Meyer and Whittier 1994). Similarly, the street theater of the late 1990s and early 2000s antiglobalization protests uses some of the tropes of earlier repertoires – giant puppets, satirical masks, what one commentator called a "carnival against capital" (Kaufmann 2001a) – but it slants these in innovative ways, often as a result of broad coalition participation in protests.

For example, protests at the 2001 presidential inauguration of George W. Bush drew a range of groups such as the National Organization for Women and labor unions committed to moderate, nonviolent tactics, along with anarchists and others committed to radical, disruptive, sometimes violent tactics. Yet when police threatened mass arrests of the more disruptive protesters, the large groups of peaceful marchers marched upon the police, forcing the release of the others (Kaufmann 2001a). In fact, demonstrations that include violent and nonviolent factions and a range of constituencies and cultural styles addressing shared opposition to globalization constitute an innovative combination of tactics drawn from previously-separate movements. They are in themselves an example of spillover. These protests show the influence of recent movements such as third-wave feminism, women of color feminism, international feminism and new worker militancy, and reflect the cultural work of the antiglobalization movement as it adapts earlier traditions to its own purposes.

Movements' actions go beyond tactics, per se, to encompass cultural forms and productions more broadly. As with tactics, activists develop cultural practices from within existing cultural repertoires that overlap with and influence tactical repertoires. The combination of playfulness and militancy in the antiglobalization protests, for example, is as much an expression of that movement's emerging culture as it is a matter of tactical attempts to influence targets. Protest songs, literature, and art spread from one movement to another. Early riser movements may produce influential cultural products, such as the rich lode of protest music that the civil rights movement developed, often drawing on folk and religious songs with new, politicized words or meanings (Horton 1998). Songs such as "We Shall Overcome" inspired activists who sang them at demonstrations for peace, women's, gay and lesbian, and, later, even anti-abortion causes, all of which modified the lyrics to suit their cause. Later rising movements can also develop influential cultural products. For example, Holly Near's song "Singing for Our Lives" emerged in the early 1980s feminist-left and spread throughout the movement family. The song could tolerate many adaptations, since the first line of each verse followed the template of "we are ___ and ___ together," allowing activists to declare that they were black and white together, or gay and straight, or women and men, emphasizing the identities and inequalities salient to the movement at hand (Near 1990).

Popular performers may in fact provide a bridge between movements through which influence can travel. Pete Seeger, for example, a singer who got his start in the Old Left, remained popular in the New Left and throughout progressive movements of the 1980s and 1990s. By singing union songs in later movements, Seeger helped carry a particular ideology about class – a model of protest as originating in the mass revolt and daily lives of those at the bottom – into later movements that were not mobilized around class issues. The Bread and Puppet Theater, which constructed large and colorful puppets and dramatized political issues and stances, had its origins in the 1960s protest cycle, but was even larger and more visible during the antiglobalization protests of the late 1990s and early 2000s. It was clearly a part of the tactical and cultural repertoire of earlier protests that survived to shape the actions of the later ones. Other cultural products are also important in cultural spillover, such as influential publications *Mother Jones*, the *Progressive*, or *Ms.* Magazine, that bridge multiple movements, synthesizing their messages in new ways and then disseminating those messages to activists.

Activists' cultural styles indicate social movement spillover at the same time as they show how organizers innovate when they adopt cultural repertoires. For example, activist and writer L. A. Kaufmann (2001b) describes how antiglobalization protesters planned to wear gas masks at a protest against the World Bank in Washington.[3] In doing so, they not only sought to protect themselves against tear gas (an instrumental purpose), but symbolically referred to the history of police brutality during protests against the Vietnam War, and to the police brutality directed against antiglobalization protesters in Seattle in 1999 and Quebec City in the spring of 2001. As they gathered gas masks, however, organizers decorated them, painting them with bright colors, adding glitter, in order to project the sense of play that characterized at least some factions of this movement, which reflected in part the influence of flamboyantly visible queer protest in the preceding decade (Kaufmann 2001b). Thus they expressed their similarity with earlier movements, attempted to evoke the condemnation of past police brutality against any police actions in the planned demonstration, and linked these with the unique characteristics of their own movement.

Activists adopt tactics used by others not just because they expect those tactics to be effective, but to "express their identification with the earliest of risers and signal a more inclusive and broader definition of the emerging struggle" (McAdam 1995: 236). Thus, the use of similar tactics and cultural expressions does not simply reflect a connection between movements, but may actually effect or cement such a connection. Broad movement communities are tied together in part through a shared cultural and tactical repertoire. Yet, although a sense of identification or commonality fosters spillover, it is not a prerequisite, as evidenced by the way that opposing movements also sometimes adopt parallel tactics, be it following an opponent into the legislative or judicial arena, adopting direct action or mounting counterprotests (Meyer and Staggenborg 1996).

Spillover effects can shape organizational structure, ideology, identification of targets, and numerous other characteristics of movements in a similar way (Meyer and Whittier 1994; Ferree and Roth 1998; Rosen 2000; Isaacs et al. 2001). Rather than expanding on these examples, however, I turn next to a consideration of the routes and processes that foster movements' effects on each other.

ROUTES OF INFLUENCE

Biographical and Generational

One major outcome of mobilization is the formation of a political generation, a cohort of activists who are committed to the cause in enduring ways (Mannheim [1928] 1952; Whittier 1995; Klatch 1999). Core activists remain politicized over time because they construct a collective identity through movement participation. Considerable evidence suggests that core activists retain their commitments years later and continue to act on them, in various ways, throughout their lives (Jennings 1987; Fendrich and Lovoy 1988; McAdam 1989; Whalen and Flacks 1989; Sherkat and Blocker 1994; Whittier 1995; see chapter 21 in this volume). There are many "biographical effects" of activism (McAdam 1989). Most relevant to us is the consistent finding that movement veterans continue to participate in social movements at greater rates than nonveterans (Jennings 1987; Fendrich and Lovoy 1988; McAdam 1989; Sherkat and Blocker 1994). In doing so, they can carry the lessons of earlier movements into the other movements that they join. They thus carry the political lessons and perspectives of the movement that shaped their enduring collective identity into other movements (Whittier 1995, 1997). They do so under various conditions.

First, an initial movement or cycle of protest may die down altogether, leaving veterans casting about for political outlets. This was the case with the 1960s wave of protest. Veterans of these movements, particularly men (who did not, by and large, enter the women's movement, which thrived longer), sought other political activities after the New Left, student, antiwar, and civil rights movements declined. Many entered local community activism, environmental, and antinuclear movements during the later 1970s and 1980s (McAdam 1988; Whalen and Flacks 1989). When they did so, they shaped those movements' beliefs and frames. They also brought with them the tactics of earlier protests; thus, for example, the spread of direct action in the antinuclear movement (Epstein 1991). Of course, they did not simply transfer New Left movement tactics, frames, or goals into later movements unmodified. They were influenced by other movements, particularly the women's movement, by changes in the larger culture, by innovations and learning and lore about effective tactics, and by shifts in political opportunities (Meyer and Whittier 1994).

Second, even when an initial movement does not die down, participants may leave for other causes. White activists in the civil rights movement of the 1960s, for example, left in large numbers as the ideology of integrationism declined in favor of Black Power in the mid- to late 1960s (Robnett 2002). They did not abandon activism, however, but went on to form large and influential movements of students, against the war in Vietnam, and for women's liberation. These movements, as many analysts have noted, were indelibly marked by the frames, tactics, ideologies, and culture of the civil rights movement (Evans 1979; Gitlin 1987; Miller 1987; Rosen 2000). For different reasons, women left mixed-sex New Left groups in the late 1960s. Protesting women's treatment within those groups and extending demands for liberation to women, feminist activists were nevertheless influenced by the New Left in which they cut their political teeth. They analogized women's oppression to that of African-Americans, called for revolution and liberation and criticized those in power drawing on discourses similar to the New Left, and used similar kinds of direct action, street theater, mass protest, and alternative media to disseminate their message (Evans 1979; Rosen 2000). In both cases, activists left ongoing movements to establish new ones that were strongly influenced by the former movement.

Finally, activists may enter additional movements without leaving their initial commitments. For example, Raeburn (forthcoming) finds that when members of corporate caucuses of lesbian/gay/bisexual employees entered caucuses for women or people of color, in what she calls "organizational seeding," they were able to win allies for their efforts. Decline of a movement, factors promoting participant departure from a movement, and networks that promote simultaneous participation in more than one movement, then, promote transmittal of movement influence through biological and generational routes. This kind of contact and influence is also an important outcome of coalitions between movements and is a regular feature of the overlapping causes and institutions that make up broad-based social movement communities (Meyer 2002). These contacts between movement organizations are the second major route of influence.

Networks and Organizational Contact

In addition to the entry of individuals into one challenge from another, participants in social movements have direct and indirect contact with each other in a variety of relationships. Movement organizations, activists, protest events, and related institutions (such as publications, bookstores, cultural institutions) are connected to each other within social movement communities (Buechler 1990). Movement communities often contain activists and organizations working on different issues or identified with different social movements (Whittier 1995). In this context, they come into contact with each other's frames, ideologies, collective identities, tactics, and organizational styles (Meyer and Whittier 1994). For Tarrow (1998), the diffusion that results is the central dynamic driving protest cycles. Diffusion easily occurs where there is a strong and dense network of internal ties (within a given movement or perhaps movement community) and where there are weak bridging ties that connect one movement to another (McAdam 1995). The kinds of overlaps that occur within movement communities foster such weak bridging ties, through, for example, several different movement organizations using a shared community center for meeting space, using each other's email lists to publicize a petition drive, placing announcements in each other's newsletters, or organizing joint "umbrella" demonstrations to address shared targets. As a cycle of protest grows, these network ties increase, facilitating more and faster spillover effects and spawning more spin-off movements (McAdam 1995).

Yet direct ties are by no means the only route of influence. Indirect ties and cultural observation through the media can also serve as routes of transmission (McAdam and Rucht 1993; Soule 1997, and chapter 13 in this volume). For example, even when there is relatively little day-to-day overlap in a social movement community, organizations may form coalitions to work on a shared issue. These coalitions are an important route by which influence travels (Meyer and Rochon 1997; Tarrow 1998: 51). At a most basic level, agreeing to work in coalition often entails adopting a shared goal. For example, many peace groups adopted the Nuclear Freeze as a goal, partly because of its rapid success, but partly because their lobbying coalitions with other organizations required a shared agenda (Hathaway and Meyer 1994). Influence through coalitions is not unidirectional; rather, both sides reshape each other, leading in some cases to a broadened focus on the part of both groups as they incorporate each others' issues and emphases. For example, Raeburn (forthcoming) shows that as groups promoting the interests of women, people of color, and lesbians and gay men within corporations began to work together, they increasingly addressed the issues facing the other constituencies, and Obach (1999) shows that unions and environmental organizations adopted each others' issues as they worked together.

The mere existence of coalitions or network connections between movements is not sufficient to generate mutual influence, however. McAdam (1995) and Soule (1997 and chapter 13 in this volume) point out that activists adopt the approaches or lessons of others when they see those others as similar to themselves. This "attribution of similarity" is a "process of social construction in which the adopters define both themselves and the situation they face as essentially similar to that of the innovators" and is what "makes the actions and ideas of the innovators relevant to the adopter" (McAdam 1995: 233). Attribution of similarity depends on framing one's own problems as similar to another's (McAdam 1995) and on kindred collective identity – identifying oneself as similar in kind, in group, or in position, to another (Soule 1997, 1999, and chapter 13 in this volume). So, while a rowdy public demonstration, with kiss-ins, eating fire, and civil disobedience might have worked as well to publicize the goals of groups of "ex-gays" promoting the idea that gays can and should become heterosexual, as it did to publicize the pro-gay goals of groups like Queer Nation and Lesbian Avengers, the ex-gay groups would be unlikely to adopt strategies that signify similarity with a group that they see themselves as different from. Because the use of similar tactics signifies allegiance or solidarity, spin-off movements pattern themselves after early risers in part to indicate that they are part of the same struggle (McAdam 1995: 236). Student activists of the 1960s, for example, used sit-ins because they felt themselves to be part of a larger struggle that included the civil rights movement which had originated the sit-in tactic. Coalitions and overlapping movement communities, in addition to providing a network by which groups are connected, may facilitate the attribution of similarity and thus further accelerate influence.

The characteristics of a movement's organizations and community affect the way they change in response to contact with other social movements. If movement leaders forge coalitions, they can spread the resulting innovations within their constituencies only when there are sufficiently strong internal organizational ties between leaders and rank-and-file (Obach 2001; Valocchi 2001). Valocchi (2001) shows, for example, that the Mattachine Society, an early homophile group whose organizers had been involved in the Communist Party, had a cell-type structure in which only the highest levels were aware of the group's ties to the Left. When those ties were revealed during McCarthy's persecutions, the mass membership, who had never developed a collective identity that entailed allegiance to Left causes, purged the group's founders and the organization no longer reflected the influence of the CP. This is a case of "failed diffusion" (Soule, chapter 13 in this volume).

Finally, the mass media are a central route through which otherwise-unconnected movement organizations can influence each other (Soule 1997, and chapter 13 in this volume). As with other routes of diffusion, adopter movements must see themselves as similar to the initiators (Soule 1997, 1999). As the structure of mass media changes, we would expect to see the emergence of new routes of influence and the contraction of old ones. Certain kinds of events and frames, particularly those that are consistent with mainstream discourses, receive more media coverage than others (Ryan 1991; McCarthy et al. 1996). Protest against a US war with Iraq in 2002/3, in the US and worldwide, for example, received relatively little media coverage from increasingly consolidated and monopolistic print and visual media in the US. At the same time, the Internet provides a steadily expanding and less-regulated means by which activists can connect with and learn from each other.

In sum, movement–movement influence is promoted by networks and coalitions, indirect ties and media observation, shared collective identity or attribution of similarity, and internal ties that disseminate and foster new approaches or that force factionalization.

Social Movement Sector

While movements may produce spin-offs as a result of the information activists gain from direct and indirect exposure to others' tactics and approaches, they also affect other challenges as a result of the changes they produce in the social movement sector, in an organizational effect (Minkoff 1995, 1997).[4] As movements develop and gain support (or, conversely, as they decline), they change the size, composition, and dynamics of the social movement sector. These changes in the social movement sector are both a product of mobilization and an indirect route through which different movements affect each other. Activists pursue resources and supporters, define collective identities, and frame issues in relationship to other movements, seeking to differentiate themselves and stake a unique and compelling claim to legitimacy and action on their issue. Thus shifting levels of mobilization within different movements affect each other (Edwards and Marullo 1995; Minkoff 1997). In response to increased competition (i.e., to the emergence of a larger number of movements addressing related issues), activists may shift their structures, targets, or frames to emulate successful movements; conversely, they may differen-tiate themselves by adopting distinct frames, strategies, or targets, emphasizing the ways that they are distinct from other movements in order to compete for supporters (Staggenborg 1986; Hathaway and Meyer 1994; Minkoff 1995).

Initial growth in the number of movement organizations encourages further growth, as early rising movements establish an "enduring organizational niche" into which later activists can move, gaining access to established routes, sources of resources, and a pool of recruits for other causes (Tarrow 1998; Minkoff 1997: 795). In addition, established organizations provide a measure of legitimacy, which "affects the willingness of funders to support new constituencies, of authorities to tolerate their dissent, and of the media to broadcast their claims in a favorable light." As movement organizations increase, they thus support both protest and additional organizations, providing resources even when political opportunities are less favorable (Minkoff 1997: 795). Activists for related emerging causes can recruit supporters from within these organizations (Meyer and Whittier 1994; McAdam 1995; Whittier 1995; Minkoff 1997: 782).

Minkoff finds empirical support for the idea that rising levels of organization in one movement foster higher levels of mobilization in another movement in an examination of the impact of the civil rights movement on women's movement organizations. Increasing levels of protest in one movement can also increase the level of protest in another movement, but only under favorable political opportunity conditions. In fact, under hostile political opportunities, increased protest by one movement actually decreases the amount of protest by the other, presumably because of competition (Minkoff 1995: 791) In addition, Minkoff (1997: 796) suggests that as national organizations increase, coalitions among movements also increase. She sees this as primarily important for positioning allies in the political system, but coalitions also increase the possibilities for other kinds of spillover, shaping the content (not just the level) of protest.

As the social movement sector enlarges during a cycle of protest, however, it becomes more competitive. After a point, the organizational niche becomes crowded; competition between organizations mitigates against the founding of new organizations and can threaten the growth and survival of existing ones. The more crowded a niche in the sector becomes, the more these issues are heightened. As a cycle of protest declines, the niche becomes tighter as resources decrease. Edwards and Marullo (1995: 909) suggest that organizations in the peace movement dealt with the resulting increasing competition by differentiating and developing specialized niches within the peace movement industry. They do not find that the decline of the peace movement entailed massive organizational demise. Minkoff (1997) also finds that early risers in particular enjoy a protected status within their niche – that is, even as spin-off movements proliferate, early risers are not forced to disband. Similarly, Whittier (1997) finds that during movement decline, the size of the movement sector remained relatively stable, while both organizational births and deaths decreased and existing organizations maintained themselves in diminished form in a kind of movement stasis.

Growth in the social movement sector may also affect the *kinds* of tactics activists employ. As movement organizations seek to differentiate in order to deal with competition, they may adjust their tactics. Tarrow (1989, 1998) argues that competition increases at the height of protest cycles, leading both early risers and newcomers to adopt more militant tactics in order to compete for supporters and attention. This pattern is not consistently borne out empirically, however. Minkoff (1999: 1688) finds that heightened overall protest activity does not increase, and in some cases actually decreases, the amount of organizational change in tactics and focus. Similarly, Koopmans (1993: 653) found that competition among organizations is less influential in producing militancy than are the effects of repression and facilitation by the state. Nevertheless, while activists may not be inevitably driven to militancy by competition within the social movement sector, they do assess their tactics in light of comparisons to other groups.

Social movement sector features can also promote or hinder spillover. In a study of the influence of the New Left on labor militancy, Isaacs et al. (2001) argue that protest and level of organization in the social movement sector promote spillover in different ways and to different degrees. They argue that increasing levels of *protest* promote diffusion or spillover through a demonstration effect, that is, by making frames and tactics visible to other activists who may then adopt them (Soule 1999). They note that such demonstration effects are more likely when potential adopters are receptive to the initial movement's approach, the attribution of similarity that McAdam (1995) refers to. Increasing *organizational* density in the social movement sector, in contrast, influences other activists both through demonstration effects and by providing an infrastructure for mobilizing (Meyer and Whittier 1994; McAdam 1995; Minkoff 1997; Isaacs et al. 2001). In sum, the social movement sector is a route through which movements influence each other. Up to a point, increasing levels of organization and protest promote additional mobilization and spillover by providing legitimacy, an infrastructure, and visible examples of protest that can diffuse to other collective actors (Meyer and Whittier 1994; Edwards and Marullo 1995; Minkoff 1997; Soule 1999; Isaacs et al. 2001). Increasing organizational density may, under different external conditions, promote either movement decline or differentiation as competition increases (Edwards and Marullo 1995; Minkoff 1997; Whittier 1997; Isaacs et al. 2001). These processes vary according to external political opportunities and contexts, which I will discuss next.

External Political and Cultural Contexts

Finally, movements affect other movements through the changes they make in political and cultural contexts. As activists produce change in policy or political alignments, they alter the political opportunities that are available to other social movements, both present and future. As they change frames and discourses in mainstream culture, they alter the cultural context with which other social movements engage. In doing so, they can facilitate other movement's emergence or demise, increase or decrease their likelihood of influence, or shape their direction. Political contexts can channel movements' impact to other movements in several ways. Activists in early rising movements create or make visible new political opportunities, including alliances with elites, that can spur others to organize and spark a protest cycle (Tarrow 1998: 24). Such successes can sustain a wide range of related challenges over considerable time. The entry of allies into institutions and legislative bodies is an important outcome of movements that fosters additional mobilization both by the initial movement and related causes (Minkoff 1997: 795). For example, feminist activists in the 1970s pushed for the establishment of women's studies programs in colleges and universities. As the academy restructured itself in response, it provided new sources of support, resources, knowledge, and influential allies for third-wave feminists (Baumgardner and Richards 2000). Political and institutional allies can promote legislation or policy that channels resources to ongoing movements or provides them with openings. As participants in the women's movement entered state and local government and bureaucracies in the 1980s, for example, they were able to structure programs that addressed women's interests, funding rape prevention training or child assault prevention training, special programming for elderly women within local Councils on Aging, or training in nontraditional careers as part of work training offered to women on public assistance (Matthews 1995; Whittier 1995).

On the other hand, McAdam (1995) argues that political opportunities do not change significantly during reform protest cycles.[5] Thus it is not increasing vulnerability of the state that makes spin-off movements proliferate. Instead, activists in later movements *see* the state as more vulnerable, and themselves as more efficacious, because they can observe the gains of earlier activists. The effect, in his view, is thus primarily cognitive, rather than based on improvements in policy or opportunity. But even if early risers in reform cycles do not radically weaken the state, they may make more limited policy gains that affect the emergence and direction of their successors in the same country. For example, the 1964 Civil Rights Act, primarily lobbied for by civil rights groups, included prohibitions against sex discrimination; that policy change proved very significant in shaping the direction of feminist challenges against discrimination (Gelb and Palley 1987).

Changes in the larger culture are another route through which movements influence each other. When activists change the dominant culture, activists in other movements are constrained from some kinds of frames and encouraged towards others. For example, the feminist movement of the 1960s and 1970s wrought profound changes in how the larger culture viewed gender and the position of women. Subsequent movements had to engage with those changed views. Movements on the left were constrained from overt displays of sexism: it would be unthinkable for a male movement leader on the left in the 2000s to declare, as civil rights leader Stokely Carmichael did in 1964, that the only position of women in the movement was prone (Meyer and Whittier 1994). Even conservative movements pay discursive attention to feminism and antiracism even as they simultaneously oppose the changes gained by both movements. Organizers opposing referenda on gay and lesbian rights, for example, have attempted to appeal to African Americans by using rhetoric supporting "civil rights," while opposing "special rights" for gays and lesbians. In general, cultural gains that are widespread, or that are influential in arenas that other movements wish to change, are the most likely to reshape other movements.

More directly, cultural representations and news coverage of protest shape the practices of activists through diffusion (Soule 1997, 1999, and chapter 13 in this volume). Even when activists share no network connections and do not see themselves as similar to other protesters, they can learn about movement innovations, actions, and successes through mass media. For example, the public demonstration is a routine form of protest, adopted even by groups of neophyte activists who have no significant contact with experienced activists. These neophytes know about demonstrations, and conceptualize protest in that form, because of media depictions. In a different kind of example, opponents of abortion may not have had network connections to participants in progressive movements who used sit-ins or passive resistance, yet they knew about these tactics and employed them themselves. As Tarrow (1998:145) argues, the "demonstration effect of a challenge that succeeds" can spur unrelated groups and opponents to adopt similar forms of collective action (Meyer and Staggenborg 1996). But even tactics that are unsuccessful can diffuse if media represent them as effective and if they resonate with activists' existing beliefs and tactical repertoires, as Soule (1999) argues was the case for the widespread use of student shantytowns in US protests against apartheid.

Cross-national diffusion of collective action with similar issues and tactics during the 1960s cycle of protest provides another example of the impact of visible movements on activists who see themselves as similar, but may not have direct network ties (McAdam and Rucht 1993).

CONCLUSION

Many questions remain about the nature and mechanisms of movements' effects on other movements. For example, are there differences in the routes by which movements influence each others' tactics, frames, or collective identities? What are the conditions under which changes in the dominant culture wrought by one movement have more or less influence on various aspects of other movements? What are the outcomes of coalitions, in terms of mutual influence, and how do they vary with different kinds of coalitions and under different external circumstances? What are the interpretive processes by which movements analyze, adopt, and modify the lessons or approaches of other movements? What are the limits on these processes; that is, what are the conditions under which spillover does not occur?

Surprisingly little empirical work focuses on these questions, and there is a particular dearth of comparative research. Nevertheless, we know that movements often produce new mobilizations and change existing ones. This is one of the fundamental outcomes of social movements: to alter the political landscape and thus to alter how other activists see themselves and how they attempt to make change.

Notes

1   Isaacs et al. (2001) do not include countermovements and movement continuity in their definition of generative effects.
2   The concepts of diffusion and spillover are very similar. For a detailed consideration of diffusion, see chapter 13 in this volume.
3   The protest was scheduled for September, 2001, and was canceled by most participating groups following the terrorist attacks of September 11. Kaufmann reports that activists donated the gas masks, stripped of their decorations, to rescue workers in New York City.
4   Minkoff's focus (unlike examinations of spin-off and spillover (Meyer and Whittier 1994; McAdam 1995) is on how the level of organization or protest in a late-rising movement is affected by the level of organization or protest in an early riser, not on the content of protest or organization.
5   In revolutionary cycles, in contrast, the initiator movement greatly weakens the state, which is then more vulnerable to challenge from multiple spin-off movements.

References

Baumgardner, Jennifer, and Amy Richards (2000) *Manifesta: Young Women, Feminism, and the Future*. New York: Farrar, Straus, & Giroux.
Benford, Robert D., and David A. Snow (2000) Framing Processes and Social Movements: An Overview and Assessment. *Annual Review of Sociology*, 26, 611–39.

Blanchard, Dallas A. (1994) *The Anti-Abortion Movement and the Rise of the Religious Right*. New York: Twayne.

Buechler, Steven (1990) *Women's Movements in the United States*. New Brunswick, NJ: Rutgers University Press.

Edwards, Bob, and Sam Marullo (1995) Organizational Mortality in a Declining Social Movement: The Demise of Peace Movement Organizations in the End of the Cold War Era. *American Sociological Review*, 60, 908–27.

Epstein, Barbara (1991)*Political Protest and Cultural Revolution*. Berkeley: University of California Press.

Evans, Sara (1979) *Personal Politics*. New York: Knopf.

——(1991) *Born for Liberty*. New York: Free Press.

Fendrich, James, and Kenneth Lovoy (1988) Back to the Future. *American Sociological Review*, 53, 780–84.

Ferree, Myra Marx, and Silke Roth (1998) Gender, Class, and the Interaction among Social Movements: A Strike of West Berlin Daycare Workers. *Gender & Society*, 12 (6), 626–48.

Gelb, Joyce, and Marian Lief Palley (1987) *Women and Public Policies*. 2nd ed. Princeton, NJ: Princeton University Press.

Gitlin, Todd (1987) *The Sixties*. New York: Bantam.

Hathaway, Will, and David S. Meyer (1994) Competition and Cooperation in Social Movement Coalitions: Lobbying for Peace in the 1980s. *Berkeley Journal of Sociology*, 38, 157–83.

Horton, Myles, with Judith Kohl and Herbert Kohl (1998) *The Long Haul*. New York: Teachers College.

Isaacs, Lawrence, Gina Carreno, Johnny Johnson, Rachel LaCroix, Greg Lukasik, and Steve McDonald (2001) Engendering Militancy at Work: New Left Social Movement Spillover on Labor Militancy in Postwar America. Paper presented at the Annual Meeting of the American Sociological Association, Anaheim, CA.

Isserman, Maurice (1987) *If I Had a Hammer: The Death of the Old Left and the Birth of the New Left*. New York: Basic.

Jennings, M. Kent (1987) Residues of a Movement. *American Political Science Review*, 81, 367–82.

Kaufmann, L. A (2001a) Militants and Moderates. *Free Radical*, 15 (January). Online journal <http://www.free-radical.org/issue15.shtml

——(2001b) The DC Masquerade. *Free Radical*, 18 (September). Online journal <http://www.free-radical.org/issue15.shtml

Klatch, Rebecca (1999) *A Generation Divided*. Berkeley: University of California Press.

Koopmans, Ruud (1993) The Dynamics of Protest Waves: West Germany, 1965 to 1989. *American Sociological Review*, 58 (5), 637–58.

Lynn, Morgan (2001) (In)Visible Privilege: An Examination of Whiteness in Social Movement Organizations. Honors thesis, Smith College.

McAdam, Doug (1988) *Freedom Summer*. Chicago: University of Chicago Press.

——(1989) The Biographical Consequences of Activism. *American Sociological Review*, 54, 744–60.

——(1995) "Initiator" and "Spin-off" Movements: Diffusion Processes in Protest Cycles. In Mark Traugott (ed.), *Repertoires and Cycles of Collective Action*. Durham: Duke University Press, 217–39.

McAdam, Doug, and Dieter Rucht (1993)The Cross-National Diffusion of Movement Ideas. *Annals of the American Academy of Political and Social Sciences*, 528, 56–74.

McCarthy, John D., Clark McPhail, and Jackie Smith (1996) Images of Protest: Estimating Selection Bias in Media Coverage of Washington Demonstrations, 1982–1991. *American Sociological Review*, 61 (3), 478–99.

Mannheim, Karl ([1928] 1952) The Problem of Generations. In P. Kecskemeti (ed.), *Essays on the Sociology of Knowledge*. London: Routledge & Kegan Paul, 276–332.

Marshall, Susan (1995) Confrontation and Cooptation in Antifeminist Organizations. In Myra Marx Ferree and Patricia Yancey Martin (eds.), *Feminist Organizations*. Philadelphia, PA: Temple University Press, 323–35.

Matthews, Nancy (1995) *Confronting Rape: The Feminist Anti-Rape Movement and the State*. London: Routledge.

Meyer, David S. (2000) Claiming Credit. Paper presented at the Annual Meeting of the American Sociological Association, Washington, DC.

——(2002) Introduction. In David S. Meyer, Nancy Whittier, and Belinda Robnett (eds.), *Social Movements: Identity, Culture, and the State*. New York: Oxford University Press, 3–21.

Meyer, David S., and Tom Rochon (1997) Towards a Coalitional Theory of Social and Political Movements. In Tom Rochon and David S. Meyer (eds.), *Coalitions and Political Movements: The Lessons of the Nuclear Freeze*. Boulder, CO: Lynn Rienner, 237–51.

Meyer, David S., and Suzanne Staggenborg (1996) Movements, Countermovements, and the Structure of Political Opportunity. *American Journal of Sociology*, 101 (6), 1628–60.

Meyer, David S., and Nancy Whittier (1994) Social Movement Spillover. *Social Problems*, 41 (2), 277–98.

Miller, James (1987) *Democracy Is in the Streets*. New York: Simon & Schuster.

Minkoff, Debra C. (1995) *Organizing for Equality: The Evolution of Women's and Racial-Ethnic Organizations in America, 1955–1985*. New Brunswick, NJ: Rutgers University Press.

——(1997) The Sequencing of Social Movements. *American Sociological Review*, 62 (October), 779–99.

——(1999) Bending with the Wind: Strategic Change and Adaptation by Women's and Racial Minority Organizations. *American Journal of Sociology*, 104 (6), 1666–703.

Morgan, Robin (ed.) (1996) *Sisterhood Is Global: The International Women's Movement Anthology*. New York: Feminist.

Morris, Aldon (1981)The Black Southern Sit-in Movement. *American Sociological Review*, 46, 744–67.

Mueller, Carol, and Mary Katzenstein (eds.) (1987) *The Women's Movements of the U.S. and Western Europe*. Philadelphia, PA: Temple University Press.

Naples, Nancy (2002) Materialist Feminist Discourse Analysis and Social Movement Research: Mapping the Changing Context for Community Control. In David S. Meyer, Nancy Whittier, and Belinda Robnett (eds.), *Social Movements: Identity, Culture, and the State*. New York: Oxford University Press, 226–46.

Near, Holly (1990) *Fire in the Rain . . . Singer in the Storm*. New York: William Morrow.

Obach, Brian (1999) The Wisconsin Labor-Environmental Network: A Case Study of Coalition Formation among Organized Labor and the Environmental Movement. *Organization and Environment*, 12 (1), 45–74.

——(2001) A Model of Social Movement Coalition Formation. Paper presented at the Annual Meeting of the American Sociological Association, August 19–21, Anaheim, CA.

Raeburn, Nicole (forthcoming) *Inside out: The Struggle for Lesbian, Gay, and Bisexual Rights in the Workplace*. Minneapolis: University of Minnesota.

Robnett, Belinda (2002) External Political Events and Collective Identity. In David S. Meyer, Nancy Whittier, and Belinda Robnett (eds.), *Social Movements: Identity, Culture, and the State*. New York: Oxford University Press, 266–85.

Roiphe, Katie (1993) *The Morning after: Sex, Fear, and Feminism on Campus*. Boston: Little, Brown.

Rosen, Ruth (2000) *The World Split Open: How the Modern Women's Movement Changed America*. New York: Penguin.

Rupp, Leila, and Verta Taylor (1987) *Survival in the Doldrums*. New York: Oxford University Press.

Ryan, Charlotte (1991) *Prime-Time Activism*. Boston: South End.

Sherkat, Darren, and T. Jean Blocker (1994) The Political Development of Sixties Activists. *Social Forces*, 72, 821–42.

Snow, David, and Robert Benford (1992) Master Frames and Cycles of Protest. In Aldon Morris and Carol Mueller (eds.), *Frontiers of Social Movement Theory*. New Haven: Yale University Press, 133–55.

Sommers, Christina Hoff (1994) *Who Stole Feminism?* New York: Simon & Schuster.

Soule, Sarah (1997) The Student Divestment Movement in the United States and the Shantytown: The Diffusion of a Protest Tactic. *Social Forces*, 75, 855–83.

——(1999) The Diffusion of an Unsuccessful Innovation. *Annals of the American Academy of Political and Social Science*, 566 (November), 120–31.

Staggenborg, Suzanne (1986) Coalition Work in the Pro-Choice Movement: Organizational and Environmental Opportunities and Obstacles. *Social Problems*, 33 (5), 374–89.

Tarrow, Sidney (1989) *Democracy and Disorder: Protest and Politics in Italy 1965–1975*. Oxford: Clarendon.

——(1998) *Power in Movement*. 2nd ed. New York: Cambridge University Press.

Taylor, Verta (1989) Sources of Continuity in Social Movements. *American Sociological Review*, 54, 761–75.

Taylor, Verta, and Nancy Whittier (1992) Collective Identity and Lesbian Feminist Mobilization. In Aldon Morris and Carol Mueller (eds.), *Frontiers of Social Movement Theory*. New Haven: Yale University Press, 104–29.

Taylor, Verta, and Marieke Van Willigen (1996) Women's Self-Help and the Reconstruction of Gender: The Postpartum Support and Breast Cancer Movements. *Mobilization*, 2, 123–43.

Tilly, Charles (1978) *From Mobilization to Revolution*. Reading, MA: Addison-Wesley.

——(1993) Contentious Repertoires in Great Britain, 1758–1834. *Social Science History*, 17, 253–80.

Valocchi, Steve (2001) Individual Identities, Collective Identities, and Organizational Structure: The Relationship of the Political Left and Gay Liberation in the United States. Paper presented at the Annual Meeting of the American Sociological Association, August 19–21, Anaheim, CA.

Walker, Rebecca (ed.) (1995) *To Be Real*. New York: Anchor.

Weigand, Kate (2001) *Red Feminism*. Baltimore, MD: Johns Hopkins University Press.

Whalen, Jack, and Richard Flacks (1989) *Beyond the Barricades*. Philadelphia, PA: Temple University Press.

Whittier, Nancy (1995) *Feminist Generations: The Persistence of the Radical Women's Movement*. Philadelphia, PA: Temple University Press.

——(1997) Political Generations, Micro-Cohorts, and the Transformation of Social Movements. *American Sociological Review*, 62 (October), 760–78.

——(2000) Changing Culture and Policy: Child Sexual Abuse, Collective Identity, and Discourse. Paper presented at the Annual Meeting of the American Sociological Association, Washington, DC.

——(2001) Emotional Strategies. In Francesca Polletta, Jeff Goodwin, and James Jasper (eds.), *Political Passions*. Chicago: University of Chicago, 145–57.

Zald, Mayer, and Bert Useem (1987) Movement and Countermovement Interaction. In Mayer Zald, and John McCarthy (eds.), *Social Movements in an Organizational Society*. New Brunswick, NJ: Transaction, 247–71.

Part VI
Major Social Movements

24

The Labor Movement in Motion

RICK FANTASIA AND JUDITH STEPAN-NORRIS

Labor movements are fundamental social formations whose effects on society run deep and reverberate broadly. Though not a common occurrence, when labor rises it can shake a social order to its very core, exposing basic fault lines, unsettling deeply rooted social hierarchies, and revealing the degree of social power that can be realized in collective action. Consider South Korea, one of the four Asian "tigers" that saw "miraculous" economic growth in the 1960s and 1970s (Deyo 1989). In the early 1990s there emerged a remarkable labor movement whose membership quickly doubled as workers flowed into newly combative organizations, galvanized by waves of strikes and factory occupations, a volcanic reaction to the social damage left by the so-called economic "miracle" (McNally 1998: 150). Though it seems quiescent in the context of the current economic crisis, for the coming generation, and perhaps two, the labor movement will be treated as the (sleeping) "tiger" in Korean society.

The same is also true in France where, in 1995, after a seemingly mundane protest strike by French railway workers against proposed pension "reforms," a massive social upheaval was sparked whose spirit will likely haunt the French establishment for at least as long as May '68 has. The strikes of 1995 brought millions into the streets in remarkable demonstrations of solidarity across the country, and forged direct organizational and symbolic links between the labor movement and various groups of the "excluded," including "illegal" immigrants, unemployed workers, and the homeless, as well as *lycée* and university students and an intelligentsia that had been widely dismissed as apathetic and uninterested.[1] Though they lasted but a short two months, "the strikes of December 1995" not only created new external bonds between the labor movement and other social groups, but created important new organizational forms and led to important reconfigurations among the traditional organizations of the French labor movement itself.[2]

Although their symbolic reverberations can be felt internationally, and for generations to come, labor rebellions such as these are rare events indeed. Nowhere are they as rare or as unlikely than in the United States, where employers are exceptionally strong, and where, in consequence, the labor movement is weak.) However, although labor unions, when they were at the peak of their power and influence, once received a reasonable amount of attention from social scientists, more recently, in much leaner times, they have generally not been central objects of analysis for scholars who study social movements in the United States. Although the purpose of this chapter is to demonstrate why labor movements are analytically important and interesting as social movements, we might begin by asking why it is that the labor movements have been out of the range of vision of social movement analysts.

Mostly, we think that the official US labor movement has been disregarded because it has not behaved very much like a social movement since the 1950s.[3] In fact, for much of the past half-century its most visible leaders and its most powerful organizations have eschewed ideas, practices, and representations that might appear too social movement-like, at times giving the labor movement the appearance of an "antimovement." Thus it has been difficult for sociologists to imagine labor as a social movement in the US, because labor's dominant representations of itself throughout most of the postwar period have consciously sought to obscure any such view.

Second, however, we think that the labor movement has received relatively sparse attention because scholars have oftentimes been predisposed by their own autobiographical experiences of social movement activism to study those movements that are similar to those in which they have worked, or those that have played a role in the development of their own intellectual stance and career trajectory, as well as those movements that embody their own political values.[4] Similarly, an increase in labor movement activism in recent years has been accompanied by a renewed intellectual interest, and we would therefore expect a new generation of social movement scholars, perhaps with experience in innovative unions and affinities with labor struggles, to begin working with social movement theories to understand the contemporary labor movement.

We are certain that social movement theory will be able to provide them with useful concepts, approaches, and ways of seeing the labor movement. However, we also think that the labor movement is based on a set of practices and is embedded in a set of institutional relationships that may sometimes require a different analytical lens than is normally provided by social movement theoretical frameworks.

While we indicated above that the mainstream labor movement has consciously shunned the adoption of most social movement characteristics since the 1950s, it is also true that the labor movement has not been monolithic and that there have been labor groups and organizations that have demonstrated a progressive and militant unionism throughout this same period. In particular, there have been various individual unions, and dissident movements within unions that have maintained an ideological orientation challenging the dominant relations of power in American society, while drawing upon tactics and forms of mobilization that very much resembled those of a radical social movement (and, indeed, can even be seen as having directly borrowed from it).[5]

To adequately understand the twists and turns of labor in the US, we must consider not only struggles *between* the main protagonists (the labor movement and employers), but the social and institutional struggles *within* the ranks of each of the camps of the protagonists (and the interactions between them). Internal differ-

why study labor ?

ences over goals, tactics, and an overall vision of the world are just as important analytically as the larger struggle between the main protagonists. Conflict between the protagonists therefore involves the concerted actions of both groups in pursuit of goals that are contested by factions and forces within each domain, while at the same time these struggles inform and impact those in the other. As we discuss below, and show through a series of brief cases and examples, the character of the labor movement at any point in time is the result of a complex set of decisions, actions, and struggles both within the movement itself (often including struggles over questions of inclusion and exclusion) and between labor and employers and the organizations that represent them.

Part of the difficulty in analyzing the labor movement as a social movement has to do with the heavily institutionalized character of certain of its dimensions and practices. The organizations that constitute a labor movement are not simply (or even frequently) organizations mobilized to engage in direct action or social combat. Unions also bargain and negotiate with employers, they help to regulate economic activity, and they serve a brokerage function as employment agents, stabilizing labor markets on behalf of their members. In these ways unions restrain social combat and collective action, and thus a significant part of the labor movement can be seen as not only institutionalized, but institutionalizing.

It is for this reason that although we think that labor movements are very fruitful sites for social movement analysis, we must resist the impulse to treat the labor movement as a clear and simple case of a "social movement," a bounded thing in itself, in favor of a broader, more relational analysis. This is also why we resist a formal definition of the labor movements and of social movements, for adopting a formal definition might foreclose our ability to view the labor movement as a fluid and multidimensional social formation that is produced and reproduced relationally, along the continuum between direct action and institutionalized power, between democracy and bureaucracy. What we mean is that the extra-institutional cannot be so easily disentangled from institutional practices. They must be analyzed in relation to one another, because they have been produced in relation to one another and because they can only be properly understood in such a reciprocally generating form.

Our view would seem to be in accord with recent criticisms that have argued for a more relational, more dynamic, and less "movement-centric" perspective on "contention" (and against social movements as things-in-themselves) (McAdam et al. 2001). Our perspective has also been informed by Pierre Bourdieu's theoretical method, an approach to the study of social practices that has a radically relational perspective and methodology at its analytical core. By eschewing the conceptual divisions that organize (and dichotomize) our ways of seeing the social world (objectivity/subjectivity, micro/macro, material/symbolic) Bourdieu's approach can offer a penetrating analytical method for understanding the social life of the labor movement and its representations.[6]

In certain respects bureaucracies and social movements are expressions of important strategic and historical oppositions, and for the purposes of this brief chapter we will tend to sustain the opposition for purposes of clarity. However, we recognize, as do recent social movement theorists, that there is considerable fluidity between the polarities, as social movements are often bureaucratic and frequently utilize a mix of institutional and extra-institutional tactics. Moreover, if we consider the relations between bureaucracies (both as organizations and practices) and social movements (both as organizations and practices), we see that they are not separate phenomena, but tend to represent the reciprocally opposing products of the unequal and shifting relationships that prevail within unions (between workers and the union leadership), and in society (between labor and capital). If ideal-typical bureaucracies can be seen to represent the congealed power of a social group, its interests realized, codified, and institutionalized (in rules, in procedural order and organizational segmentation, and in an enforced individuation), so ideal-typical social movements can be seen to represent the organized and organizational embodiment of institutional powerlessness, a mobilized expression of challenge to "the powers that be," displaying the sorts of tactics and resources that can be mobilized by those without institutional resources (i.e., organizing people to act in concert rather than as individuals, causing the disruption of bureaucratic routine, the breaking of rules and of established procedures, etc.). Whereas bureaucracies compel by bringing the weight of legal rules, regulations, and the "proper channels" down on an opponent, social movements compel with the use or threat of collective force and disruption, and the circumvention of those channels. Because their power is not institutionalized, the powerless can hope only to change things extra-institutionally (Schwartz 1976; Piven and Cloward 1977). In reality, of course, there can be a blending or reversal of these oppositions, and the literature has demonstrated that social movement organizations are sometimes powerful enough to be able to effect institutional change (Staggenborg 1988; Amenta, et al. 2002). As long as the work process is characterized by relations of domination and subordination, workers will have a strong incentive to participate in what Fitch called "an instinctive movement, and it is a movement for something more than the possession of a larger portion of the world's goods" (Fitch 1924, cited in Roberts 1966: 267). Through the doctrine of "managerial prerogative," US labor law locates control over production in the hands of management, and, without union representation, workers have no institutional power to confront problems and issues that directly affect their everyday lives. Collective action and union representation represent practical solutions to the daily problems of workers, yet, as social movement theorists have emphasized, grievances alone don't account for the initiation of movements, and challengers often face enormous obstacles to mobilization. There are stable features of the state (e.g., its strength and propensity to repress insurgents) (Kriesi et al. 1995), as well as more unstable factors like the structuring of existing power relations that give insurgent groups the incentive or disincentive to act (McAdam 1982; Tarrow 1998).

In response to conditions during different periods in US history, the labor movement has developed institutions that seemed to engender unambiguous social movement characteristics and practices, as in the 1930s when the labor movement seemed to come alive with insurgency. During other periods, labor bureaucracies have tended to dominate on the surface, while generating various expressions of internal union dissent and insurgency below.

The labor movement is more than the individual institutions that have arisen in various periods to accommodate workers' needs and interests. Some organizations have been radical and nonbureaucratic, like the Industrial Workers of the World (IWW) and certain unions of the Congress of Industrial Organizations (CIO), and others very conservative and bureaucratic, like many of the unions of the American Federation of Labor (AFL). It makes a difference, for when labor organizations have resembled social movements, workers have been afforded structured access to social movement activities that solicit their participation, that give them a voice in the articulation of their concerns, and that generate an ethos of solidarity. When labor organizations have been overly bureaucratic, workers play little or no role in the life of the union, which comes to appear as a lifeless appendage to the employer, generating cynicism and leaving a labor movement that is powerless to respond to corporate power. At times, in such situations, workers' everyday experiences have prompted them to eschew ineffective union procedures and engage in extra-institutional actions (such as wildcat strikes or democratization movements within their unions) generating social movement activities within unions and against union leaders.

We should not misunderstand the situation, for in any given period in US history the vast majority of workers have remained unorganized. Some workplaces remain unorganized because, for a variety of reasons (fear being prominent among them), workers oppose unionization. Other workplaces have never been the object of a union organizing drive. But unorganized workers may and often do venture to engage in collective behavior. Some such efforts may win minor victories, and others may congeal into a larger labor action (e.g., the unionization of a plant). Elsewhere, militancy may remain dormant until some catalyzing event (a new work rule that makes the job more onerous, or a new technology that intrudes on customary practices, an imposed austerity, or any such assault on what is perceived as a basic sense of collective dignity) prompts workers to throw caution to the wind and engage the employer collectively. The web of everyday social relationships among friends and co-workers may serve as the building blocks for solidarity and for the organized activities that unionism requires. *Network*

Oftentimes, before workers even enter a workplace, the employer personifies a collective and institutional entity whose interests are directly opposed to the collective organization of workers. While unions might be viewed as more or less effective social movements, and employers' organizations as "counter movements" (see Griffin et al. 1986), the very term would seem to understate their ability to deploy massive resources to counteract both local union activity as well as the labor movement as a whole. Employers do not only seek to weaken unions, but to create a "union-free environment" in which to do business. As we've indicated, employers in the US have been extremely effective in shaping the terrain on which unions operate, constraining the range of possible union actions, and reducing the social power of unions. We would suggest that the sheer institutional (and institutionalized) weight of corporate power in US society, both materially and symbolically, makes the actions of employer anti-unionism appear more than just "countermovement" activity.

At the same time, Meyer and Staggenborg (1996) have suggested theoretical propositions about the movement – countermovement relationship that could be useful in considering the situation of labor. For example, they suggest that countermovements will tend to emerge where successful movements threaten a population that has strong potential political allies.

The labor movement in the US would seem to offer an obvious case. Relative to European societies, where collective bargaining tends to be centralized, where the state bears a larger portion of the costs of nonmonetary social benefits, and where the benefits of unionization tend to accrue to all workers, regardless of union membership status, US employers have much more of a financial incentive, as well as all the necessary legal machinery to destroy unions (Fantasia and Voss 2003). Because the benefits of de-unionization can be immediately realized by individual employers in the US, they have mobilized their considerable political resources to create a situation of enormous obstacles to the mobilization of new members and to the maintenance of existing union organizations (Goldfield 1987; Human Rights Watch 2000).

This is not to say that labor movements in other societies have not been the object of much more severe employer hostility and state repression. After all, throughout the 1980s an entire generation of labor leaders in the agricultural and export sectors of El Salvador, Guatemala, and Honduras were systematically pursued and killed, intimidated into silence, or forced into exile by government-assisted death squads. Though the murder rate has subsided throughout Central America, employer anti-unionism and intimidation persist throughout the region's export processing zones (Krupat 1997).

Even in Europe, where the notion of "social partnership" still generally characterizes the relationship between employers and labor movements, the past decade has witnessed an erosion of union power and a rise in employer intransigence. This is true not only in Britain where, first under Thatcher and now under Blair, the state authorized and assisted a sustained employer assault on trade unionism, but elsewhere as well. For example, while both Sweden and the Netherlands retain the image of welfare state beneficence, the capitalist class in both societies have mobilized aggressively on behalf of a neoliberal agenda of deregulation, cuts to public expenditures, and against the collaborative model of employment security that once represented the foundation of the welfare state "model" that once characterized Northern Europe; while a politically demobilized German labor movement has provided employers the "opportunity to break many of the restrictions imposed on them by the partnership model" (Albo and Roberts 1998: 171; Visser 1990). If so, such developments suggest that, like the longer-term effects of bureaucratic unionism in the US, while the European social partnership model still offers considerable social benefits, its pacifying qualities may also have a soporific effect, in political terms, leaving workers ill-prepared for aggressive mobilization by their erstwhile partners.

As we mentioned above, social movement theory helps to elucidate such developments, but we must also continue to utilize other theoretical lenses. For example, as we've suggested, the political opportunity perspective may be quite helpful for locating the permissive factors that create the openings for labor militancy, but may not necessarily be helpful for analyzing the social production of the labor bureaucrat, who may be predisposed to a faceless social conformity that avoids confrontation like the plague. And we can certainly see where the concept of social movement "abeyance" (Rupp and Taylor 1987; Taylor 1989) might be employed to good analytical use, where, say, the defeat of a union drive has led to a hunkering down, while informal workplace social networks become strengthened, over time, in the wait for another chance to revive the campaign. But, in fact, workplace networks may be just as likely, if not more so, to become frayed after a defeat, and understanding the dynamics of demoralization is rarely the focus of social movement theory ("political opportunity" is the focus, not political "foreclosure"; "abeyance," but not defeat).[7] A social analysis of the logic of the labor movement (as against an analysis of a specific union drive as a thing in itself) really seems to demand an analysis of a much wider configuration of institutions and practices than most social movement theories tend to allow. Concepts like "abeyance" and "countermovement" (designating the anti-union actions of employers, for example) and even "framing" have their analytical uses,[8] but they seem wholly insufficient as a distillation of an entire social edifice of institutions (economic, legal, political) as well as the vast symbolic apparatus arrayed against collective practices and solidarity in the United States.

Having expressed these qualifications, in what follows, we draw upon five brief historical vignettes, five "moments" in the life of the labor movement in the United States that allow us to demonstrate why we think the labor movement represents an exemplary case for understanding social movement dynamics. Succinctly, without providing a great deal of historical detail, we indicate that it has been the mutually constituting process of mobilization and countermobilization that has shaped not only the relations between labor and the employers, but relations within the ranks of labor as well. Among other things, these examples indicate that one cannot fully comprehend the logic of social movement mobilization without simultaneously considering it in relation to the forces of countermobilization, very broadly considered.

RADICALS, EMPLOYERS, AND THE RELATIONAL ROOTS OF LABOR "PRAGMATISM"

Emerging in the late nineteenth century, the Knights of Labor can be seen as an early organizational expression of what is now often termed "social" or "social movement" unionism. A remarkably egalitarian organization whose goal was to organize all workers, regardless of skill level, race, or gender, the Knights experienced several years of remarkable growth, and by 1886, a year of widespread labor militancy nationally, the Knights had formed local assemblies in every state and had organized over 700,000 members, almost 10 percent of the industrial labor force. However, the fall of the Knights was about as dramatic as its emergence, for within five years the Knights were virtually destroyed by a ferocious employer counteroffensive, and ironically it was the rapid rise of the Knights that precipitated the mobilization of the powerful employers' organizations which would proceed to destroy them (Voss 1993: 2). As Meyer and Staggenborg suggest,[9] militant working class political mobilization was derailed for several generations by the countermobilization of employers, thus narrowing the field of the possible to the kinds of organizations that least resembled (revolutionary) social movements.

Such an organization was the AFL, founded in 1886.[10] Defining itself in contrast to revolutionary syndicalism with the slogan "pure and simple unionism," it became the organizational template for American business unionism for more than a century. One would not be able to adequately understand the relentless pragmatism of its leader, Samuel Gompers, however, without a consideration of the radical unionism to which it was a reaction and in relation to which it defined itself. Indeed, according to Buhle (1999: 34), young Samuel Gompers, a London-born immigrant of Dutch ancestry, was frightened into his conservative labor pragmatism after having been caught up in the Tompkins Square police riot in New York City in 1874. Having narrowly escaped having his head bashed by a policeman's nightstick, Gompers reportedly blamed not the police who had charged the peaceful demonstrators but the radical socialists who had organized the demonstration against unemployment in the first place (Madison 1962: 78). Despite his having been inspired by an early reading of the *Communist Manifesto*, and despite the many socialists he had had as acquaintances in his early trade union days, Gompers developed and maintained a deep loathing for the labor radicalism of the revolutionary Left, and this perspective was at the heart of the so-called "pragmatic ideology" that was inscribed into the American Federation of Labor. As an organization attempting to supplant revolutionary unionism, the AF of L must be understood in terms of it.

Radical social unionism, on the other hand, could not be fully understood outside of its own relational logic either, and in important ways the Industrial Workers of the World, the "Wobblies," were a relational product of the "pure and simple trade unionism" of Gompers' AF of L, for they were largely produced in reaction to it (Buhle 1999: 66). The Wobblies were about as far from conservative pragmatism as any labor organization could be, essentially refusing the status of a responsible "labor organization." They rode the rail lines from conflict to conflict organizing among the most marginal workers (immigrants, seasonal laborers, the unskilled), while rejoicing in their marginal status ("Halleluja, I'm a Bum" was their theme song), and, as Rothenbuhler (1988) has noted, the membership dues of the IWW were too low to maintain a budget, they kept no strike fund, refused to sign collective bargaining agreements, and rotated their officials to prevent fixed organizational hierarchies (under the slogan "We are all leaders!"). It was in the context of a heavily bureaucratic and conservative AF of L unionism that such a remarkable "anti-organization" like the anarcho-syndicalist Wobbly movement took such a form, before it was routed by ferocious state repression at the close of World War I. As we've suggested, organizational relations within the labor movement and between labor and capital ought to be viewed from the perspective of the mutually constituting actions of each, in relation to the other.

CIO UNIONISM, AND THE EMPLOYER OFFENSIVE

The CIO was mobilized in a period of large-scale insurgency that followed in the wake of a decade of labor repression and union decline. It was initially constituted as the *Committee* for Industrial Organizations, in an experiment on behalf of eight AFL unions to pursue industrial unionism in several mass-production industries that seemed ripe for this form of organization (including steel, auto, rubber, and radio). The AFL initially opposed the idea, and soon took steps to halt the endeavor. However, once it was clear that the CIO union campaigns were unstoppable, the AFL suspended the (now) ten unions involved in the effort, and the *Congress* of Industrial Organizations was formed. The CIO represented a new, more socially inclusive type of unionism. It sought to organize workers by industries, rather than by craft (which, by definition, had eliminated the majority of American workers in the 1930s). This strategy of focusing on semi- and unskilled industrial workers reflected the changes in the structure of the labor force since the turn of the century. But the CIO was also cognizant of the fact that in order to be successful, it required organizing all workers, regardless of sex, race, religion, and national origin, since most industrial workers didn't have the skills that made them irreplaceable in the workplace. The CIO's political stance tended to be much more left wing than that of the AFL, whose social and political vision was reflected in the call to workers to "reward your friends and punish your enemies" at the ballot box. In contrast to the AFL, many of the leaders of the CIO had been recruited from the ranks of various socialist and communist parties and movements that were active in the struggles surrounding the Great Depression. As part of its all-encompassing strategy of representation, the CIO supported legislation to improve the lot of working people overall, and encouraged militant tactics, like the sit-down strike, which were spontaneously adopted by workers in the formation of CIO unions.

The founding of the CIO can be seen as having occurred following a crucial opening in the political opportunity structure: namely, significantly improved labor legislation in the form of the National Labor Relations Act. At the same time, however, this legislation, in turn, is arguably related to the actions of left-wing and radical organizers (through the Unemployed Councils and other organizations) who had mobilized massive demonstrations that put pressure on the government to pass such legislation (see Goldfield 1987). Coming at a crucial historical moment, that legislation served to tilt the balance of power with regard to union organizing away from employers and toward unions, facilitating the effectiveness of the CIO's strategy of industrial organization within the mass production industries.

Once free from AFL domination, CIO President John L. Lewis found it necessary to invite all willing participants to help in the new organizing efforts. Whereas the AFL unions had commonly prohibited Communists from holding positions of union leadership and even from being union members, the CIO unions had no such restrictions on participation. That allowed Communists with recent union experience in the Trade Union Educational League (where they had attempted to "bore from within" the AFL unions) and the Trade Union Unity League (where they had organized "dual unions" mainly to complement AFL unions), along with Socialists, Trotskyists, and other radicals with labor experience to heed the call to assist in the massive organizing drives being planned by the CIO.

Although the CIO was already predisposed toward a form of social movement unionism, this invitation unintentionally set the organization decisively on that course. We say unintentionally because Lewis initially believed he could prevent the radicals from gaining a base of support within the emerging CIO unions by closely monitoring their actions and frequently moving them from site to site, and thereby preventing them from gaining a base in any one locale. But the scope of the CIO's effort, along with the effectiveness of the radicals, thwarted Lewis's strategy, and Communists and their sympathizers rose to the leadership of roughly half of all CIO unions, and maintained operating factions in several others (Stepan-Norris and Zeitlin 2003).

Communist leadership had important implications for the ways the CIO unions would come to represent the workers as well as for the kinds of political stances they would support. In an analysis of CIO union collective bargaining contracts, Stepan-Norris and Zeitlin (2003) show that in contrast to other unions, the left-wing unions were more likely to fight for and win enhanced worker control on the shop floor, by reserving workers' right to strike, by refusing to cede management prerogatives, and by establishing effective and timely grievance procedures. In addition, the left-wing unions were also more prone to uphold the practices of internal union democracy and to support the rights of women and minority workers both inside and outside the workplace. Moreover, by offering an oppositional voice against the more mainstream CIO leadership, the presence of Communist leaders and their sympathizers significantly enhanced the overall level of democracy within the CIO.

At the same time, the success of Communist leaders in representing workers' shop floor interests, along with a huge postwar strike wave, inflamed the ire of corporate management, who played a primary role in the passage of the Taft-Hartley Act. This was legislation that constrained the rights of all unions by weakening union security and severely restricting the use of the strike. The Taft-Hartley Act also expressly targeted the Communist union leadership by requiring that all union leaders sign a non-Communist affidavit. In the context of the burgeoning hysteria of McCarthyism and with the entire labor leadership on the defensive, the CIO opted to sacrifice its left wing by pushing all labor leaders to sign the non-Communist affidavits, while expelling 11 "Communist dominated" unions from its midst. With this act, the CIO eliminated a substantial core of progressive and energetic voices from its organization, men and women who considered their positions as union leaders a "calling" rather than just a "vocation." The CIO shifted decisively from the practices of a social movement unionism toward a more bureaucratic unionism, and could for the first time consider merging with its former nemesis, the AFL. Whereas earlier employer repression decisively crushed the Knights of Labor, employer repression of the 1940s effectively accomplished the transmogrification of the CIO. From a social movement unionism that embodied a frontal challenge to American capitalism, the CIO embraced a form of business unionism that was a practical accommodation to it.

This moment in the American labor movement can be seen to exemplify the relational dynamic. Social movement activities initiated favorable labor legislation, which, in turn, led to enhanced union mobilization. The enhanced opportunities for union organization then sparked internal political struggles within the union movement itself (represented by the split between the AFL and the CIO), which, in turn, had ramifications (within the CIO) for the form of social movement unionism that would emerge. Later, at the close of World War II, the countermobilization of capital against labor had the effect of moving the CIO back in the opposite direction, toward a more bureaucratic unionism, and of dissolving the social movement forces within the labor movement. This set the terms for the postwar US labor movement that we consider below.

ROUTINIZATION AND ITS DISCONTENTS

As we indicated above, employer countermovements are sometimes visible and direct. In other instances, employers draw upon their institutional power through state structures to narrow the unions' room for maneuvering, to weaken their "political opportunity structure." Drafted by a team of corporate lawyers and passed in 1947, the Taft–Hartley Act served, in many respects, as a repeal of the "Wagner Act" of 1935, which had played such a key role in the establishment of industrial unionism. As we've indicated, it was designed to accomplish several longstanding goals of American employers. First, it substantially weakened union security by outlawing the closed shop, by making the union shop subject to an election supervised by the Federal labor board (the National Labor Relations Board [NLRB]), rather than by the force of collective mobilization, and by establishing mechanisms by which union members could arrange to have their union officially "decertified." The Act allowed states to restrict union security even further, creating a region of anti-union "right to work" states that came to encompass a huge part of the US.

Second, under the Taft-Hartley Act, (the most effective forms of industrial action were declared illegal.) Sympathy strikes and secondary boycotts, forms of action through which working class solidarity had been successfully expressed in communities throughout the United States, were now forbidden. The President was given the newfound power to impose a temporary 60-day halt to any strike deemed likely "to imperil the national health or safety," a provision that was invoked 7 times in the first year of its passage, and 29 times over the next two decades (United States Department of Labor 1969). The Act further strengthened employers' ability to respond to strikes by allowing strikebreakers the right to vote in union representation elections and to participate in the decertification of existing unions, and gave employers the opportunity to seek injunctions against mass picketing.

For unions forced to operate within such a framework of strict "bureaucratic" constraints, the mobilization of collective action still represented an important dimension of trade union activity. Although contemporary unions normally trade away their right to strike during the course of the contract period, they maintain the right to strike *between* contracts. On one level, this has made strikes more predictable, to the extent that employers could better prepare for them, thus making strikes less of a threat. Indeed, the strike, which has historically represented the union movement's tour de force, has a long process of routinization in the United States, in which its form became fairly standardized, it was officially recognized, adjudicated, and monitored, and generally underwent a process of domestication that molded it into more of a pressure tactic than a weapon of industrial warfare (see Ross and Hartman 1960; Tilly 1978; Fantasia 1988). On the other hand, even the most routinized strikes are quite extraordinary social phenomena, requiring that workers mobilize to act in concert to disrupt normal production and the flow of profits to corporations. Spontaneous action can occur in the process, while at the same time, in order for strikes to be successful, they require a high degree of coordinated discipline. This is why C. Wright Mills (1948) commented that unions are simultaneously expected to be both "town halls" and "armies."

The postwar union leadership, purged of radicals, while presiding over huge bureaucracies themselves, was clearly predisposed to embrace the new bureaucratic order. As mentioned above, the left-wing unions of the CIO era, faced with bureaucratization themselves, tended to negotiate more effective grievance procedures, thus demonstrating that they were often able to operate more effectively against the constraints of the system than were the moderate industrial unions that expelled them. For example, they normally required the union steward's presence at the first stage of the grievance procedure (which put the union's collective strength behind the complaint), had a limited number of steps, and included time limits on each step (together, these two stipulations ensured that the grievances would be settled in a timely fashion). These grievance procedures encouraged workers' involvement in settling their disputes and allowed them to see the effectiveness of workers' collective power.

In contrast, later AFL-CIO union contracts tended to exclude these clauses specifying worker-oriented grievance procedures. The procedures became further removed from the shop floor, and, most importantly, from the observation of the
workers involved. Aronowitz (1973: 253–4) locates the beginning of this process in
the 1946 United Auto Workers agreement with each of the major auto producers,
in which the union steward was replaced by a "committeeman," who was paid by
the company to handle union members' grievances. According to Aronowitz, the
"committeeman is perceived as the 'man in the middle,' having interests that are
neither those of the rank and file nor those of management." And most importantly,
the committeeman was helpless to deal with issues such as "the speedup of production, introduction of labor-saving machinery, plant removal, and disciplinary layoffs
that do not result in immediate discharge." The Taft-Hartley Act further enfeebled
the shop steward system by making union leaders liable for not acting as disciplin-
arians of the membership, as strikes during the term of a contract suddenly became
the responsibility of union leaders.

With the purge of radicals from the unions, the practitioners of social movement
unionism were out of the way, and a thoroughgoing bureaucratization of postwar
labor relations was now possible. Bureaucratization was not the fulfillment of some
organizational "iron law," nor was it a neutral process, but was a clear victory for
employers, serving as a true pacification program that, secondarily, generated a
stability that benefited careerist-oriented labor leadership as well (Stepan-Norris
and Zeitlin 1996).

However, in response to the blunting of the strike weapon and to the growing
distance between the leadership and the membership in most unions, union militants
came to rely on new forms of industrial action. Thus did the wildcat strike come to
play an important symbolic role in postwar industrial relations, representing an
extra-institutional mechanism that could preserve for workers on the shop floor
some of the very elements of surprise, of spontaneity, and of democratic participation that had been stripped from the official strike. Moreover, such strikes essentially
represented a practical critique of an often ineffective system of grievance resolution
that tended to individuate collective grievances and that removed, spatially and
temporally, the settlement of grievances from the site of their occurrence as well as
from the aggrieved. They also implicitly drew the worker away from the union
leader (required by law to oppose all strikes during the term of the contract) and
from the company who, together, served as partners of this arrangement.

Wildcat strikes were not only significant on a symbolic level, but in quantitative
terms as well. Though notoriously difficult to quantify, since union leaders and
employers alike had a stake in discounting them (for the very reasons we indicated
above), and though government data sources only offer a hint of their magnitude,
studies of specific industries (mining, auto, electrical, rubber) indicate that wildcats
were substantial in quantitative terms in the decades following passage of the Taft-
Hartley Act (Sayles 1954: 54; Mangum 1960a, 1960b: 19; Slichter et al. 1960;
Green 1978; Kassalow 1979; Zetka 1995). Until 1979, the Bureau of Labor Statistics (BLS) collected an annual census of strikes "involving six or more workers and
lasting a full shift or longer," but case studies actually indicate that many wildcats
were less than a full shift long, so would not have been captured by the BLS.
But between 1961 and 1978 the BLS did record strikes occurring "During Term
of Agreement," and since 94 percent of labor-management agreements contained

a no-strike clause (Baer 1975: 85), this can serve as a rough but reasonable estimate of wildcat ("unofficial") strikes during a period when business unionism was dominant in the United States (Edwards 1981: 180–3) (see table 24.1).

Although ours should not be considered anything other than a very rough estimate of unofficial strike activity, in many respects the same characterization could be made about the BLS's "official" statistics on strikes, which, since 1979 record only those strikes involving 1,000 workers or more and no longer even tries to measure "unofficial" strike activity (Jacobs 1998). If the qualifications and assumptions that we indicate above are at all reasonable, and we believe that they are, then the wildcat strike would have been the preponderant form of strike action in the postwar period. At the very least, it can be asserted with confidence that relatively spontaneous, direct actions were quantitatively and qualitatively significant during a period when the labor movement would have seemed as far from being a social movement as an organization could have been.

Indeed, it must be recalled that bureaucratic reforms were instituted in an attempt to eliminate the social movement character of the American labor movement, and therefore can be seen as having been a form of countermobilization themselves. As we see, however, workers and union militants sought to circumvent the bureaucratic channels with mechanisms of direct action that represented extra-institutional forms of grievance resolution.

"COUNTERSTRIKES"

As we indicated, the wildcat strike was largely a response by rank and file workers to the routinization of industrial relations and to the domestication of the strike weapon, and served as a more or less effective form of industrial action, at least while unions had a relatively firm institutional place in the Fordist political economic order. However, both the cause and the effect of subsequent union decline can be seen to have hinged, paradoxically, on employers' ability to take possession of the official strike, and to turn what had become a blunt instrument in labor's hands into a rather sharp weapon in their own. In other words, in their latest countermovement strategy, employers increasingly turned the strike around, training it against the labor movement itself. Relying upon legal mechanisms that had been furnished by the Taft-Hartley Act, employers quickly discovered that they could rid their companies of their unions altogether and begin to remake American society as a "union-free environment."

Thus employers in the 1970s embarked on a sustained campaign of union busting that would continue for over two decades, largely hinging on the ability of employers to hire permanent replacement workers during strikes, thus effectively nullifying the right to strike in the United States (Jackson 1981; United States House of Representatives 1988; United States Senate Subcommittee on Labor 1990; Schnell and Gramm 1994). Once strikers are replaced, employers have often maneuvered replacements into petitioning the National Labor Relations Board for an election to have the union decertified. The number of decertification elections increased sharply as both cause and effect of the employer assault, rising from 239 in 1968 to a plateau of between 800 to 900 annually between 1977 and 1986 (and thereafter leveling off at 400 to 500 decertification elections annually, at least through the year 1998) with

Table 24.1   Estimated occurrence of wildcat strikes in the United States, 1961–78

Year	Official no. of strikes (a)	Official no. of strikes during term of agreement) (b)	Estimated no. of wildcats (c)	No. of added wildcats (d)[*]	Estimated total (all strikes) (e)	Wildcats as a percentage of all strikes (f)
1961	3,367	1,041(30.9)	2,776	1,735	5,102	54.4
1962	3,614	1,035(28.6)	2,760	1,725	5,339	51.7
1963	3,362	1,156(34.4)	3,083	1,927	5,289	58.3
1964	3,655	1,264(34.6)	3,371	2,107	5,762	58.5
1965	3,963	1,319(33.3)	3,517	2,198	6,161	57.1
1966	4,405	1,864(42.3)	4,971	3,107	7,511	66.2
1967	4,595	1,495(32.5)	3,987	2,492	7,087	56.2
1968	5,045	1,522(30.2)	4,059	2,537	7,582	53.5
1969	5,690	1,876(33.1)	5,003	3,127	8,817	56.7
1970	5,716	1,834(32.1)	4,891	3,057	8,773	55.7
1971	5,138	1,631(31.7)	4,349	2,718	7,856	55.3
1972	5,010	1,914(38.2)	5,104	3,190	8,200	62.2
1973	5,353	1,739(32.5)	4,637	2,898	8,251	56.2
1974	6,074	1,553(25.6)	4,141	2,588	8,662	47.8
1975	5,031	1,664(33.1)	4,437	2,773	7,804	56.8
1976	5,648	1,872(33.1)	4,992	3,128	8,768	56.9
1977	5,506	1,403(25.5)	3,741	2,338	7,844	47.7
1978	4,203	657(16.0)	1,750	1,093	5,323	32.9

[*]Projections are extrapolated from data on the Westdale Steel Plant collected from 1944 to 1958 as part of a Brookings Institution study of collective bargaining in 100 corporations (Slichter et al. 1960). The accuracy of the extrapolations depends upon the following assumptions: that the rates of wildcat strikes did not change significantly between the late 1950s and the early 1960s, that Westdale was representative of other steel plants in the period, and that steel was representative of other manufacturing industries (not entirely unreasonable since a broad range of industries were surveyed by Mangum for the Brookings Institution study, and since over half of the corporate respondents to the study claimed wildcat strikes to be an important management problem), and that manufacturing was representative of other sectors.

a   Total number of officially recorded work stoppages by year.

b   This statistic was recorded in BLS data as work stoppages during term of agreement. I have adjusted this figure to reflect the fact that 94% of all labor agreements had a no-strike clause in this period, putting them within the general definition of wildcat strikes. Bracketed percentages are in relation to the official number of strikes.

c   Extrapolated from Mangum's Westdale data. Adjusted to show the total number of wildcats that took place, assuming (1) that the proportion of strikes that were less than a full shift at Westdale were the same for all industrial settings; and (2) that company records had the same error rate in recording wildcats across the industry as at Westdale, where the supervisor of labor relations admitted that two stoppages were taking place for every one recorded in company records. This would then allow us to assume that twice as many wildcats (including those that were less than a full shift long) were taking place than were being recorded in company records, as was the case at Westdale.

d   The difference between the number of official wildcats (b) and our estimated number of wildcats (c).

e   The sum of official strikes (a) and our projected number of added wildcats (d). Estimated number of wildcats (c) as a percentage of our new estimated total of all strikes (e).

Sources: United States Department of Labor, Bureau of Labor Statistics Analysis of Work Stoppages, 1961–78 , and Mangum (1960b)

unions consistently losing between two-thirds and three-quarters of the elections (Fantasia 2001b).

Throughout the decade of the 1980s and 1990s a series of epic strikes were provoked by employers fully prepared to "fight to the finish." These included nationwide strikes of air traffic controllers and bus drivers, militant regional conflagrations like International Paper Company in Maine, and a group of companies in Decatur, Illinois, whose provocations toward their respective workforces prompted union supporters everywhere to rename Decatur "the war zone" for the intensity and simultaneity of the labor battles waged there. These were in addition to the scores of lesser-known "counterstrikes" that, for two decades, punctuated the industrial landscape with struggles for union survival and that time after time resulted in defeat for the labor movement.

In the US the employer offensive was both relentless and multidimensional, with the right to organize reduced to the same status as the right to strike in the US (Bronfenbrenner 2000). Thus, in every year since 1975 (to at least 2000) 20,000 Unfair Labor Practice charges filed against employers were "deemed to have merit" by the NLRB, with 10,000 of these specifically for the illegal discharge of workers during union organizing campaigns (Fantasia 2001b). In the context of employer aggression, the bureaucratic mechanisms of union representation and certification are widely recognized by unions as deliberately sclerotic. These are increasingly regarded as forms of official sabotage that mostly provide the legal "cover" for disruption of the process of union representation (Human Rights Watch 2000).

New Voices for a New Unionism

In the same way that sustained crisis provoked the organizational changes that produced the CIO, so the situation of sustained employer assault against unions has sparked important changes in the more recent period as well. After a half-century in which union membership in the private sector fell from over 30 percent to less than 10 percent (in 2003), the first contested union election in the Federation's history was held in 1995, displacing a long-entrenched top leadership of the AFL-CIO with the triumvirate of reformers, Sweeney, Trumka, and Chavez-Thompson, calling themselves a "New Voice" (Clawson forthcoming).

The prospect of internal change has continuously aroused contention within labor organizations, and dissidence has too often been treated as treason. When reformers have proposed change and renovation, some leaders (and some members) have vigorously defended the status quo. The victory of the New Voice leadership was essentially a "palace coup" and the changes it has sought have had to be forced and cajoled from the top down and demonstrated in those unions where the leaders have maintained a constituency or have been able to exert influence. This has been an excruciatingly difficult job to accomplish, since the rules, the budgets, the existing structures of bureaucracy, as well as the various leadership hierarchies remain intact, and therefore continue to serve as a base of organized resistance to change.

Just as the new vision for industrial unionism arose in the industrial sectors in an earlier era, the source and strength of the AFL-CIO's new vision has been germinated in the service sector unions, which have initiated many of the labor movement's most aggressive and effective union organizing campaigns since the early 1990s. In particular, the massive Service Employees Industrial Union (SEIU) and the Hotel Employees and Restaurant Employees (HERE) are unions that have often been effective in applying new and militant organizing tactics, and have become important sources of tactical experimentation. In the process, labor's geographic compass can be seen to have shifted from the industrial belt to the sun belt, from Detroit and Pittsburgh to Las Vegas and Los Angeles, as formerly low-waged service workers, many recent immigrants, have more and more become an important focus of labor organizing activity (Milkman 2000; Fantasia and Voss 2003).

So, whereas the CIO impetus came largely from the ground up, with the added push from the economic woes of the Great Depression and the social movements that were organized in response to them, the current AFL-CIO innovations have been accomplished from the top down. The Sweeney leadership has initiated new organizing efforts, using new and innovative strategies and tactics. These include the AFL-CIO's attempt to incorporate various nonlabor activists in its organizing campaigns, and to forge alliances with other social movements, including the struggle for a living wage. And in contrast to the CIO initiative, the Sweeney revolution does not have the privilege of being accompanied by favorable labor legislation, nor has it occurred in the context of a particularly favorable political opportunity structure. Rather, it comes after several decades of failed attempts to liberalize labor laws and in the midst of a conservative political climate.

What is the New Voice strategy? To organize. The AFL-CIO leadership is vigorously encouraging its member unions to dramatically increase the profile of organizing activity within their unions, by increasing their budgets for organizing to 30 percent (from the 5 percent that unions typically spend), and therefore to put less attention on "servicing" the needs of existing union members as well as those parts of the existing bureaucracy. Implementation of what some call an "Organizing Model" of unionism has brought new militant leaders to the fore. They are increasingly willing to circumvent the existing and largely ineffective union representation process, in favor of what is called "card check recognition," wherein instead of submitting to the deliberately slow and overly bureaucratic NLRB election procedures, labor organizers simply demand immediate union recognition from the employers, once over 50 percent of employees have signed union membership cards (sometimes accompanied by a demonstration or march to the employers' offices). While employers are already having legislation drafted that would forbid union recognition to be achieved without an NLRB election, the significance of this really lies in the increasing willingness of union leaders to circumvent the channels that they upheld for so long. Unlike its stance for the past half-century, such actions increasingly recommend the AFL-CIO leadership as a purveyor of social movement action rather than as an obstruction to it.

A crucial focus of the new orientation is to initiate more aggressive organizing strategies that utilize confrontational tactics, like corporate campaigns that bring "third party" pressure on intransigent companies, that build community solidarity for union struggles by incorporating community and religious groups, and that reach out to other social movements. While only a small number of unions have enthusiastically and fully responded to these initiatives, one might say that "it takes one to know one" in the sense that as they are being encouraged by the top leadership of the Federation to embrace other social movements and to engage in the tactics of mobilization that we have noted, unions are increasingly coming to resemble social movements themselves.

It is impossible to know whether or not a new labor movement will actually be reconstructed, for the factors pushing against it are enormous ones, internally as well as externally. At the same time, it is important to recognize the relational character of the attempt. For it was largely the actions of employers that helped to ready the terrain for a change in leadership of the AFL-CIO, by having successfully lobbied for an antilabor and pro-company legal and regulatory climate, and by successfully executing a long-term assault on unionism in the US. Such changes, along with changes in the composition of the labor force, created a situation of crisis that forced a reassessment and that allowed a challenge.

CONCLUSION

It may very well be, as we speculated at the outset, that the labor movement has been understudied by social movement analysts because it has acted in such an unmovementlike fashion for so long, and because of the predisposition of scholars to study those movements that they know. But there may be a third reason why the labor movement has been understudied by social movement scholars, having to do with the limits to a conceptual/methodological approach that until recently, has underappreciated the mutually constituting relations that exist between mobilization and countermobilization, between a social movement and its converse, the exercise of institutionalized power. As we have tried to demonstrate, the reasons why labor has not acted as a social movement has a good deal to do with the actions of organized employers, the state, as well as those within the labor movement itself who have had a stake in bureaucratically imposed stability. Developments within labor movement organizations are thus constrained by the social relations they are ensconced within, by the visible and not-so-visible actions (and the effectiveness of those actions) of their unusually powerful opponents, and by internal conflicts over various interests and practices, often expressed by debates over strategic differences.

On the basis of what we have learned about the labor movement, we would recommend that analysts of social movements focus less on the bounded social movement group per se, and more on the group's relationship to the larger configuration of institutional relations of power from which the movement develops and to which the movement therefore owes a good deal of its shape and character.

Notes

1   For short recapitulations of these remarkable events, see Bensaid (1996) and Fantasia (2001a).
2   The strikes gave rise to two new militant trade union groups among postal and telecommunications workers and among schoolteachers, and led to a historic rapprochement between the leaders of two rival union federations (one communist-led and the other anticommunist). See, for example, Aguiton and Bensaid (1997), Duval et al. (1998), and Leneveu and Vakaloulis (1998) for analyses (in French) of the strikes and some of their social and political effects.

3 This was not true of the American labor movement during earlier times, and during its most recent period of revitalization.

4 As Meyer has noted, "people usually study movements they like," though their views may be altered by what they learn (Meyer et al. 2002: 17). We would add that although they would seem to contradict Meyer's assertion, those who study countermovements, including fascist and other extreme rightist movements, also tend to be motivated by ideological predispositions (on behalf of the victims or the opponents of such movements) and thus are no less animated by strong political allegiances.

5 While there is evidence of a "spillover" effect (Meyer and Whittier 1994) from the Black Power and the civil rights movement into the labor movement (Georgakas and Surkin 1975; Geschwender 1977; Ganz 2000), and of a reignition (of labor militancy by the civil rights movement) (Isaac and Christiansen 2002), the labor movement also contains self-generating sources of revitalization (Voss and Sherman 2000).

6 Bourdieu and the labor movement are considered briefly in Fantasia (2001a), with his approach informing a fuller treatment in Fantasia and Voss (2003).

7 In an exceptionally thoughtful exception Barker and Lavallette (2002) recommend a consideration of "cycles of containment" in order to view the troughs on the other side of the peaks of protest activity.

8 See Steinberg (1998) for an extended critique of the framing perspective, and see Fantasia (2001a: 454–7) for a brief consideration of the limits of the framing perspective in relation to labor movements. (But see chapter 17 in this volume.)

9 Meyer and Staggenborg (1996: 1652) propose that "movements that face strong opposing movements will be unable to take advantage of favorable political conditions after victories because countermobilization preempts the development of new claims."

10 The AFL was initially founded in 1881 as the Federation of Organized Trade and Labor Unions. It formalized its structure and changed its name to the American Federation of Labor in 1886.

References

Aguiton, Christophe, and Daniel Bensaid (1997) *Le retour de la question sociale*. Lausanne, Switzerland: Editions Page deux.

Albo, Gregory, and Chris Roberts (1998) European Industrial Relations: Impasse or Model? In Ellen Meiksins Wood, Peter Meiksins, and Michael Yates (eds.), *Rising from the Ashes? Labor in the Age of Global Capitalism*. New York: Monthly Review, 164–79.

Amenta, Edwin, Bruce G. Carruthers, and Yvonne Zylan (1997) A Hero for the Aged? The Townsend Movement, the Political Mediation Model, and U.S. Old-Age Policy, 1934–1950. In Doug McAdam and David A. Snow (eds.), *Social Movements: Readings on their Emergence, Mobilization, and Dynamics*. Los Angeles: Roxbury, 494–510.

Andrews, Kenneth T. (2002) Creating Social Change: Lessons from the Civil Rights Movement. In David S. Meyer, Nancy Whittier, and Belinda Robnett (eds.), *Social Movements: Identity, Culture, and the State*. New York: Oxford University Press, 105–17.

Aronowitz, Stanley (1973) *False Promises*. New York: McGraw-Hill.

Baer, Walter (1975) *Strikes: A Study of Conflict and How to Resolve it*. New York: AMACOM.

Barker, Colin, and Michael Lavalette (2002) Strategizing and the Sense of Context: Reflections on the First Two Weeks of the Liverpool Docks Lockout. In David S. Meyer, Nancy Whittier, and Belinda Robnett (eds.), *Social Movements: Identity, Culture, and the State*. New York: Oxford University Press, 140–56.

Bensaid, Daniel (1996) Neo-Liberal Reform and Popular Rebellion. *New Left Review*, 215, 109–16.

Bronfenbrenner, Kate (2000) Uneasy Terrain: The Impact of Capital Mobility on Workers, Wages and Union Organizing. Report for the U.S. Trade Commission. Ithaca, NY: New York State School of Industrial Relations, Cornell University.

Buhle, Paul (1999) *Taking Care of Business*. New York: Monthly Review.

Clawson, Dan (2003) *The Next Upsurge: Labor and the New Social Movements*. Ithaca, NY: ILR.

Deyo, Frederic C. (1989) *Beneath the Miracle: Labor Subordination in the New Asian Industrialism*. Berkeley: University of California Press.

Duval, J. C. Gaubert, F. Lebaron, D. Marchetti, and F. Pavis (1998) *Le decembre des intellectuals francais*. Paris: Editions Raisons D'Agir.

Edwards, P. K. (1981) *Strikes in the United States, 1881–1974*. New York: St. Martin's Press.

Fantasia, Rick (1988) *Cultures of Solidarity*. Berkeley: University of California Press.

——(2001a) The Myth of the Labor Movement. In Judith R. Blau (ed.), *The Blackwell Companion to Sociology*. Oxford: Blackwell.

——(2001b) Dictature sur le Proletariat. *Actes de la Recherche en Sciences Sociales*, 138, 3–18.

Fantasia, Rick, and Kim Voss (2003) *Des syndicates domestiqués: répression patronale et résistance syndicale aux États-Unis*. Paris: Raisons D'Agir [English edition forthcoming, University of California Press].

Fitch, John (1924) *Causes of Industrial Unrest*. New York: Harper & Brothers.

Ganz, Marshall (2000) Resources and Resourcefulness: Strategic Capacity in the Unionization of California Agriculture, 1959–1966. *American Journal of Sociology*, 105, 1003–62.

Georgakas, Dan, and Marvin Surkin (1975) *Detroit, I Do Mind Dying*. New York: St. Martin's.

Geschwender, James (1975) *Class, Race and Worker Insurgency: The League of Revolutionary Black Workers*. New York: Cambridge University Press.

Goldfield, Michael (1987) *The Decline of Organized Labor in the U.S.* Chicago: University of Chicago Press.

Green, James R. (1978) Holding the Line: Miners' Militancy and the Strike of 1978. *Radical America*, 12 (3), 3–27.

Griffin, Larry, Beth Rubin, and Michael Wallace (1986) Capitalist Resistance to the Organization of Labor before the New Deal: Why? How? Success? *American Sociological Review*, 51, 147–67.

Human Rights Watch (2000) *Unfair Advantage: Workers' Freedom of Association in the U.S.* New York: Human Rights Watch.

Isaac, Larry, and Lars Christiansen (2002) How the Civil Rights Movement Revitalized Labor Militancy. *American Sociological Review*, 67, 722–46.

Jackson, Gordon E. (1981) *When Labor Trouble Strikes: An Action Handbook*. Englewood Cliffs: Prentice-Hall.

Jacobs, Eva E. (1998) *Handbook of U.S. Labor Statistics*. Lanham, MD: Berman.

Kassalow, Everett M. (1979) Labor-Management Relations and the Coal Industry. *Monthly Labor Review*, 102 (5), 23–7.

Kriesi, Hanspeter, R. Koopmans, J. W. Duyvendak, and M. G. Giugni (1995) *The Politics of New Social Movements in Western Europe*. Minneapolis: University of Minnesota Press.

Krupat, Kitty (1997) From War Zone to Free Trade Zone. In Andrew Ross (ed.), *No Sweat: Fashion, Free Trade and the Rights of Garment Workers*. New York: Verso.

Leneveu, Claude, and Michel Vakaloulis (eds.) (1998) *Faire movement: Novembre–Decembre 1995*. Paris: Presses Universitaires de France.

McAdam, Doug (1982) *Political Process and the Development of Black Insurgency, 1930–1970*. Chicago: University of Chicago Press.

McAdam, Doug, Sidney Tarrow, and Charles Tilly (2001) *Dynamics of Contention*. Cambridge: Cambridge University Press.

McNally, David (1998) Globalization on Trial: Crisis and Class Struggle in East Asia. In Ellen Meiksins Wood, Peter Meiksins, and Michael Yates, *Rising from the Ashes? Labor in the Age of Global Capitalism*. New York: Monthly Review, 142–52.

Madison, Charles (1962) *American Labor Leaders: Personalities and Forces in the Labor Movement*. New York: Ungar.

Mangum, Garth (1960a) Taming Wildcat Strikes. *Harvard Business Review*, 38 (2), 88–96.

——(1960b) Wildcat Strikes and Unions Pressure Tactics in American Industry. PhD dissertation, Harvard University.

Meyer, David S., and Suzanne Staggenborg (1996) Movements, Countermovements, and the Structure of Political Opportunity. *American Journal of Sociology*, 101, 1628–60.

Meyer, David S., and Nancy Whittier (1994) Social Movement Spillover. *Social Problems*, 41, 277–98.

Meyer, David S., Nancy Whittier, and Belinda Robnett (eds.) (2002) *Social Movements: Identity Culture, and the State*. New York: Oxford University Press.

Milkman, Ruth (2000) *Organizing Immigrants: The Challenge for Unions in Contemporary California*. Ithaca, NY: ILR.

Mills, C. Wright (1948) *The New Men of Power*. New York: A. M. Kelley.

Piven, Frances Fox, and Richard A. Cloward 1977. *Poor People's Movements: Why They Succeed, How They Fail*. New York: Pantheon.

Roberts, Harold (1966) *Robert's Dictionary of Industrial Relations*. Washington, DC: Bureau of National Affairs.

Ross, Arthur, and Paul Hartmann (1960) *Changing Patterns of Industrial Conflict*. New York: Wiley.

Rothenbuhler, Eric W. (1988) The Liminal Fight: Mass Strikes as Ritual and Interpretation. In Jeffrey Alexander (ed.), *Durkheimian Sociology: Cultural Studies*. Cambridge: Cambridge University Press.

Rupp, Leila J., and Verta Taylor (1987). *Survival in the Doldrums: The American Women's Rights Movement, 1945 to the 1960's*. New York: Oxford University Press.

Sayles, Leonard (1954) Wildcat Strikes. *Harvard Business Review*, 32 (6), 42–52.

Schnell, John F., and Cynthia Gramm (1994) The Empirical Relations between Employers' Strike Replacement Strategies and Strike Duration. *Industrial and Labor Relations Review*, 47, 189–206.

Schwartz, Michael (1976) *Radical Protest and Social Structure*. New York: Academic.

Slichter, Sumner, James Healy, and Robert Livernash (1960) *Impact of Collective Bargaining on Management*. Washington, DC: Brookings Institution.

Staggenborg, Suzanne (1988) The Consequences of Professionalization and Formalization in the Pro-Choice movement. *American Sociological Review*, 53, 585–605.

Steinberg, Marc (1998) Tilting the Frame: Considerations on Collective Action Framing from a Discursive Turn. *Theory and Society*, 27 (6), 845–72.

Stepan-Norris, Judith, and Maurice Zeitlin (1996) Insurgency, Radicalism, and Democracy in America's Industrial Unions. *Social Forces*, 75, 1–32.

——(2003) *Left Out: Reds and America's Industrial Unions*. Cambridge: Cambridge University Press.

Tarrow, Sidney (1998) *Power in Movement*. Cambridge: Cambridge University Press.

Taylor, Verta (1989) Social Movement Continuity: The Women's Movement in Abeyance. *American Sociological Review*, 54, 761–75.

Tilly, Charles (1978) *From Mobilization to Revolution*. New York: McGraw-Hill.

United States Department of Labor, Bureau of Labor Statistics (BLS) (1969) National Emergency Disputes: Labor Management Relations [Taft-Hartley] Act 1947–68. BLS Bulletin Number 1633.

——1962–80. Analysis of Work Stoppages.

United States House of Representatives (1988) Hearings before the Subcommittee on Labor Management Relations of the Committee on Education and Labor HR 4552 and the Issue of Strike Replacement. Serial number 100–107.

United States Senate Subcommittee on Labor (1990) Committee on Labor and Human Resources, Hearings Conducted June 6, 1990. Hearings on S.2112.

Visser, Jelle (1990) Continuity and Change in Dutch Industrial Relations. In Guido Baglioni and Colin Crouch (eds.), *European Industrial Relations: The Challenge of Flexibility*. London: Sage.

Voss, Kim (1993) *The Making of American Exceptionalism: The Knights of Labor and Class Formation in the Nineteenth Century*. Ithaca, NY: Cornell University Press.

Voss, Kim, and Rachel Sherman (2000) Breaking the Iron Law of Oligarchy: Union Revitalization in the American Labor Movement. *American Journal of Sociology*, 106, 303–49.

Zetka, James Jr. (1995) *Militancy, Market Dynamics and Workplace Authority*. Albany: State University of New York Press.

25

Feminism and the Women's Movement: A Global Perspective

Myra Marx Ferree and Carol McClurg Mueller

The women's movement is not new, not only Western, and not always feminist. Since the early 1800s, women have been organizing as women to confront a variety of problems that reflect systematic inequalities of class, status, and power. The organizations women have built, campaigns women have led and events women have staged to challenge these relationships of domination have had an enormous impact on societies worldwide. The legacies of such organizing also continue to contribute to women's ongoing mobilization potential.

In this chapter we suggest that understanding feminism in relation to contemporary women's specific local activism demands a perspective that is comparative, historical and transnational. Women's movements are among the most enduring and successful of all social movements of the modern period.[1] Along with liberalism and socialism, democratization and nationalism, mobilizations by and for women have shaped what we think of as modernity itself. Contemporary collective actions taken by women are rooted in structures of opportunity that are themselves the products of women's past organizing efforts as well as of present-day social relations. Women and men, together and in opposition, produce definitions of women and women's interests that serve as a discursive framework for making appeals to women to organize collectively. Both the organizational and the discursive resources available to women are used not only to challenge gender inequalities but also to mobilize women as a particular constituency to work for and against a variety of other changes in the political and economic status quo.

We present our argument in two major sections. In the first, we look at the macrosociological basis of women's movements and their remarkable level of historical success. We focus here on defining what women's movements are, what they do, and how they relate to other social movements today and in the past two centuries. In this section our goals are to offer some general typologies, to highlight some of the dynamic elements in women's mobilizations, and to show what contemporary movements owe to their predecessors. Such a broad overview demands a wide lens, and the specificity of particular women's movement organizations and actions over so many different places and periods can only be superficially sketched.

In the second section, we narrow our focus to pick out instances of and processes in specific women's movement mobilizations that particularly challenge and extend current theories of social movements. Women's movements remain on the fringes of most theoretical efforts to understand "social movements" generically, meaning that most theories still approach male-led movements as if they represented the normative case. Instead, we argue that bringing women's movements, feminist and otherwise, equally into the formulation of basic concepts poses interesting new theoretical challenges. Social movement theories that take gender relations into account from the outset will provide a more dynamic, long-term, and less state-centered approach to power, protest, and change.

MOVEMENTS OF WOMEN AND FEMINISM

Definitions

For most Americans, the women's movement seems to be synonymous with organized feminism, where feminism is defined as efforts to challenge and change gender relations that subordinate women to men. However, in much of the world women are conspicuously organizing as women to contest or support other social relations as well. We refer to all organizing of women explicitly as women to make any sort of social change as "women's movements" regardless of the specific targets of their change efforts at any particular time.[2] This broader definition takes explicitly into account that many mobilizations of women as women start out with a nongender directed goal, such as peace, antiracism, or social justice and gradually acquire explicitly feminist components; other, originally feminist mobilizations, expand their goals to challenge racism, colonialism, and other oppressions. To restrict our analysis to those temporary phases in which women's movements have chosen to focus exclusively on changing gender relations would be to remove this important dynamic element.[3]

This dynamism works in both directions. We define *women's movements* as mobilizations based on appeals to women as a *constituency* and thus as an organizational strategy. Women's movements address their constituents as women, mothers, sisters, daughters. Regardless of their particular goals, they bring women into political activities, empower women to challenge limitations on their roles and lives, and create networks among women that enhance women's ability to recognize existing gender relations as oppressive and in need of change. We define *feminism* as the *goal* of challenging and changing women's subordination to men. Feminist mobilizations are informed by feminist theory, beliefs, and practices, and also often encourage women to adopt other social change goals. Autonomous forms of feminist mobilization are based on organizations and campaigns directed by and to women, and thus take the specific form of feminist women's movements.

Defining feminism has never been simple (Delmar 1986; Offen 1988; Davidson 2001). For some feminists, feminism means simultaneously combating other forms of political and social subordination, since for many women, embracing the goal of equality with the men of their class, race, or nation would mean accepting a still-oppressed status. For some feminists, it means recognizing ways in which male-dominated institutions have promoted values fundamentally destructive for all people, such as militarism, environmental exploitation, or competitive global capitalism, and associating the alternative values and social relations with women and women-led groups. To insist on a definition of feminism that limits its application to those mobilizations that *exclusively* focus on challenging women's subordination to men would exclude these types of feminism. When analysts do this, they discover that the groups that are left within their purview are largely limited to mobilizations of relatively privileged women who are seeking access to existing social, political, and economic institutions and to the opportunities enjoyed by males of their social group (e.g., Chafetz and Dworkin 1986; Margolis 1993; see critiques in Gluck et al. 1998; Buechler 2000).

This, we suggest, is a definitional problem rather than an inherent limit on what feminists do in real political contexts. By acknowledging the diversity of women's movements that address feminist goals, whether or not such goals are primary or exclusive, we make central to our analysis the actual *intersectionality* of social movements.[4] By intersectionality we mean that oppressions, and movements to combat them, are not apportioned singularly; of necessity, organizations as well as individuals are multiply positioned in regard to social relations of power and injustice. This is not always acknowledged theoretically. As Ferree and Roth (1998) argue, scholars of social movements have tended to construct ideal-typical movements that they envision as composed of ideal-typical constituents: thus the "worker's" movements are imagined as organizations of and for white men, "nationalist" movements as of and for indigenous men, "feminist" movements as of and for white middle-class women. At any given historical moment in a particular country their organizations might appear feminist or not, as the immediate focus of their efforts shifted.

The Scope and Range of Women's Movements

Women's movements are ubiquitous in contemporary societies. Women mobilize as women to demand equal rights from Fiji to Finland, but women also mobilize as women to confront authoritarian rule (e.g., Mothers of the Disappeared in Argentina and El Salvador), to demand peace (e.g., Women in Black in Bosnia and in Israel), to call for handgun control (the Million Moms March in the US), and to address a variety of social problems across their communities. As examples of the latter, consider Mothers of East Los Angeles, a Chicana group fighting drug abuse and environmental contamination (Pardo 1995) and Women's Light, a group in Tver, Russia, that fights alcohol abuse and fosters women's political participation with explicitly feminist rhetoric (Ferree et al. 1999).[5]

Addressing women as women can be a strategy to focus attention on problems that women face distinctively or to a greater degree than men do, as in India the Women's Equality Initiative (MSK) does with regard to low-caste women's illiteracy and the Self-Employed Women's Association (SEWA) does with regard to the economic issues of the informal economy (Subramaniam 2000). But mobilizing women as women may also be a response to gendered political opportunity structures for addressing problems that affect the entire community. The political opportunity for mobilizing women may be distinctively advantageous, as in Chile or East

Germany, where women's domestic networks offered them greater protection and moral leverage in challenging the dictatorships in power than did men's (Noonan 1995; Miethe 1999). Alternatively, opportunities to mobilize women may be more limited by restrictive laws (Jacobin France and Prussia in the nineteenth century forbade all political gatherings or associations of women, and *purdah* in parts of the Islamic world achieves a similar result) or by a political culture that makes gender-specific claims problematic (a commitment to "gender-blindness" in US law, for example).

In stressing that all women's movements are rooted in gendered structures of oppression and of opportunity, we stress that they all have some actual or potential relation to feminism, whether this is currently a primary goal for them or not. But we explicitly refrain from defining all women's movements as feminist. Maxine Molyneux (1985) takes a different approach to the complex and varying relations between women's movements and feminism. She extends the concept of feminism to encompass all women's organizing, using the term "pragmatic gender interests" for those women's groups whose objectives "are given inductively and arise from the concrete conditions of women's positioning within the gender division of labor" and are formulated "by the women who are themselves within these positions rather than through external interventions" (233). In contrast, "strategic gender interests" designate those that reflect an "extra-local," theoretically based "deductive" approach to challenging gender relations. Molyneux sees only this latter, strategic approach as the one "usually termed 'feminist'" but argues for politicizing the former demands as contributing to "the level of consciousness required" to take this more advanced position (233). This pragmatic/strategic distinction is not only frequently cited in the literature (see Peterson and Runyon 1999; Chassen-Lopez and Udvary (2000) but has also become widespread within women's own political organizations. For example, Seidman (1999, 2001) shows how the South African Gender Commission used this distinction to discuss and direct their own work with local women and women's groups at the beginning of the post-apartheid state.

However, this strategic/pragmatic model is problematic in three important regards. First, it assumes that there is some external, overarching theoretical model that will permit judging the "correctness" of the analysis that guides the movement and makes it "strategically" address the roots of gender inequality or not. In that sense, it replaces the grand theoretical claims of Marxist social analysis with equally comprehensive, but competing, claims for objective feminist truth (Phelan 1989). Second, it establishes a hierarchy between the strategic and the pragmatic, in which it is better when knowledge comes from theory rather than experience, and when extra-local experts lead and direct local activists (Tripp 2000). Particularly for feminists who found locally situated direct experience to be a potent source of criticism of established theoretical paradigms, the value system ("vanguardism") thus imbedded in these analytic categories is troubling. Finally, it suggests a single direction of change, in which "pragmatic" movements grow more "strategic" over time as they "learn" to adopt more explicit and exclusive claims about gender inequality. This disallows the alternative dynamic, where feminist women's movements learn to address gender issues in more locally specific, pragmatic ways or adopt a more intersectional and less exclusively gendered analysis over time, as post-suffrage feminists did in the US (Cott 1987).

By distinguishing women's movements (a constituency and organizational strategy) from feminism (a belief system and political goal that many movements may share), we open up the question of how women's movements relate to feminism as an empirical issue. This has several concrete implications for research.

First, because the relationship between feminism and women's movements may vary over time and place, historical/comparative approaches are especially important, paralleling studies of the relation between worker's movements and socialism (Thompson 1964; Taylor 1983; Calhoun 1993). The very diversity of women's movements globally offers a rich field for developing empirical generalizations about women's organizing and when and how such organizing makes use of feminist concepts (e.g., Basu 1995; Miles 1996; Bystydzienski and Sekhon 1999). Women's movements currently exist in virtually every country of the world and in multiple forms within each. Where and how specific feminist goals play a role in these mobilizations should be more systematically investigated, as well as the routes by which feminist ideas "travel" between them (Sperling et al. 2001; Gal forthcoming). Heitlinger (1999) points, for example, to the role of emigré feminists in linking the movements of their natal countries and their current homelands. Exiled women who fled civil war in Rwanda and Cambodia have played a similar role (Kumar 2001). How feminist theories are constructed and spread is important not only as a matter of philosophy, but to understand the relationships among women's movements transnationally and over time.

Second, in this approach "women's interests" are no longer assumed to be known a priori by some privileged theory, but are examined as social constructions that are discursively produced by actual political struggles over how needs are to be defined (Melucci 1989, 1996; della Porta and Diani 1999). As Fraser (1989) argues, "need definition" is often the prior stage of politics to struggles over the satisfaction of needs thus defined, and as such it is often the focus of social movement mobilization rather than the exclusive domain of institutional policymaking (see also Stone 2003). Bringing issues of women's oppression into the realm of politics at all is a key aspect of women's self-definition of their needs (e.g., by defining rape as a "crime against humanity," and wife-battering and "honor killings" as social practices that states should work to eliminate). Need definition is a political struggle over whose version of reality will be translated into public policy and social practices.

The rhetoric that defines women as a distinctive constituency, instead of, within or against their other potentially competing allegiances and identities, is a critical element of what creates women's movements. Defining who "women" are said to be is a political process (Bacchi 1999), and the inclusions and exclusions created in these definitional struggles are important for understanding the course of specific movements over time. Women of color in the United States, for example, have pointed out the ways in which "women" is often equated in practice with "white women," where whiteness is treated as an "unmarked category" and normative claims are made as if this category represented the whole (e.g., Hull et al. 1982; Spelman 1988; Collins 1990). Who "women" are understood to be will always be central in defining what "women" need.

Third, this approach also brings women's movement organizations with diverse goals into the center of the analysis, where their work as "bridge-builders" figures in coalition formation (Meyer and Whittier 1994; Bordt 1997; Roth 2003) and their focus on multiple, concrete needs in their communities makes them central in grass-roots mobilizations for social and political change, whether in American cities (Naples 1998) or African villages (Tripp 2000). The practical work of organizing concrete women and the obstacles and opportunities encountered in this process become a basis for theory, as much as the reverse. Rather than positing any certain relation between these grass-roots women's groups and feminism as a goal, movement analysts need to explore and explain their reciprocal contributions to each other. Overviews of women's mobilizations around the world (e.g., Miles 1996) suggest that many local women's movements adopt a "strategic essentialism" that allows them to focus on politically recognizing women's differences in their current experiences and perspectives without claiming any fundamental gender differences in character or rights (cf. Sturgeon 1997). Specific women's movements may be in a more or less explicit struggle with abstract liberal individualist definitions of "rights" that make being treated as a "rights-bearer" contingent on disavowing gender-specificity (for a simultaneously gendered and raced perspective, see Roberts 1997).

In sum, therefore, a model of women's movements that treats them as contingently and variably related to feminism, and women's interests as the objects of definitional struggle rather than dichotomously "strategic" or "pragmatic," opens up such relationships for empirical examination.[6] Changes over time both toward and away from a primary emphasis on challenging gender relations as a goal need to be explained, as well as differences among women's movements in their definitions of who "women" are, the exclusivity of the racial/national/ethnic communities to which "women" are loyal, and the relative priority they give to feminist goals in meeting their needs. Because "women's interests" are the object of social movement negotiations, making a women's movement feminist (or not) is always going to reflect struggle on the part of participants. Such active struggles over defining needs, constituencies, and politics itself become more prominent as elements of all social movement agendas, since it is in such struggles that movements grow, divide, exclude, multiply, and splinter (Mueller 1994). What has sometimes been described as "spillover" of ideas from one movement to another (Meyer and Whittier 1994) looks therefore more like a tug-of-war within and among necessarily heterogeneous movement groups.

The Historical Context for Feminism and Women's Movement Mobilization

Contemporary collective actions taken by women are rooted in structures of opportunity that are in part the products of women's past organizing efforts. Taking a comparative-historical approach to feminist women's movements suggests that it would be problematic to describe them as "new social movements." Even though autonomous feminist mobilization in the early 1970s received a major impetus from the anti-authoritarian student movements of Europe in the 1960s (Kaplan 1992), from the civil rights movement in the US in the 1950s and 1960s (Evans 1979), from movements for social justice in Latin America (Stephen 1997), and from movements of national liberation in Asia and Africa (Jayawardena 1986), these were by no means the only sources of their identities, organizations, or political analyses.

Contemporary feminist movements draw on rich lodes of organization as well as political theory in their mobilizing efforts. Some of these organizations were embedded within states and international bodies, such as the Inter-American Commission of Women (since the 1920s), the Women's Bureau in the US Department of Labor (since the 1930s) and the UN's Commission on the Status of Women (since the 1940s). Others, such as the International Association of University Women and its constituent national organizations, exist within civil society. Many in the US were organized on racial/ethnic lines, including those that maintained an exclusionary white-only identity (Gluck et al. 1998). The League of Women Voters (itself a descendant of the National American Women's Suffrage Association) excluded black women from membership in the South in the 1950s and 1960s, for example, prompting black women to form the Women's Political Council and support emergent civil rights actions in Alabama (Barnett 1993). Other political and educational associations for women of color also trace their origins to racially exclusionary practices as well as to recognition of the special needs of their communities (Giddings 1984). In Europe, socialist politics from the late nineteenth century on made class rather than race the dividing line for organizing women and defining women's interests (Evans 1987; Ferree 2002). Thus, even to understand contemporary groups, a wider historical lens is necessary.

Feminist Women's Movements are not New Social Movements

Feminism emerged forcefully in the eighteenth century in the writings of such political theorists as Mary Wollstonecraft and Olympe de Gouges, who in Karen Offen's words "claimed the Enlightenment" for women (2000: 29). By the nineteenth century this was no mere intellectual argument, but also was a framework for actual mobilizations of women. Campaigns for women's education as well as increasingly for the right to vote, to retain their identity and property in marriage, and to participate more fairly and equally in the emerging wage economy animated the mobilization of women in Europe and the United States (Flexner 1959; Offen 2000). These campaigns were contemporary with and often connected to the emergence of socialism, liberalism, nationalism, and democratization, mobilizations that brought women into the sphere defined as "political" (and thus as male by nature and right). Feminism provided a rationale for women to mobilize as women in relation to the emergent social relations being constructed in and through markets, educational institutions, political parties, and civic associations (Gerhard 2000).

Yet as women seized the opportunity to be political actors in their own right, they also asserted a variety of social and political objectives that extended beyond challenging gender relations. Women in the nineteenth century mobilized to end slavery and the slave trade, to obtain more just and humane relations of paid employment for themselves and others, to spread Christian doctrine and European social values in the expanding empires of increasingly influential nation-states, and to protect such weak and marginalized groups as the physically and mentally ill, prisoners, children, and paupers. The close association between feminism and all sorts of women's mobilization in the nineteenth century, a period in which any political activity by women was inherently controversial, makes it tempting to bring all women's organizations together under the rubric of "social justice feminism," whatever their specific goals (Offen 1988; Sklar et al. 1998).

This approach obscures the debates of the period about the relative priority to be given in practice to women's rights demands and advocacy of other social changes. American feminists after the Civil War were divided, for example, over whether this was "the Negro's hour" in which the rights of both White and Black women were to be deferred in favor of gaining constitutional protection for Black men (Flexner 1959). In the 1880s and 1890s, German feminists divided between those who supported the right to vote for women on the same class-based system as men and those who advocated universal suffrage for men and women (Evans 1976; Gerhard 2000). The rise of nation-states, imperial claims and nationalist thinking throughout Europe from the French Revolution to World War I gave rise to debates over whether, as the Czech suffragist Josefa Zeman argued, women were "first patriots and then women" (Offen 2000: 213) or whether, in the words of Virginia Woolf, "as a woman, I have no country... As a woman, my country is the whole world." (Woolf 1938).

Such debates of the nineteenth and early twentieth century, in which both women and men engaged, make clear that the division between "old" and "new" social movements that sometimes emerges in the literature is deeply misleading (see critique in Calhoun 1993). The "old" distributive, class-based politics that became institutionally established in Europe in the form of socialist and social democratic parties at the turn of the century was energetically involved from its very origins in active "needs definition" work.[7] There is simply no modern period in which public debate over economic relations, class interests, and redistributive politics failed to include claims about the gender identities and gendered interests of "workers" and "citizens" (Kontos 1979; Offen 2000; Glenn 2002). "Old" social movements had to work to construct a sense of shared fate among workers in a diversity of occupations; appeals to their common manhood (and in the US to whiteness) created *exclusionary* forms of solidarity that still have consequences in specific organizing campaigns among women workers (Johnson 1994; Beckwith 1996; Ferree and Roth 1998).

A politics of gender, asserting men's interests as men as well as women's interests as women, is therefore just as "old" as class politics. It is institutionalized in male-led groups and "women's auxiliaries" within class, race, and other movements, no less than in those autonomous feminist organizations that put their primary emphasis on what women want economically and socially as women. The emergence of the workplace (as a site distinct from the home), the mobilization of men in workplace-based politics, and the organization of political parties centered on unions and class relations are also forms of institutionalizing gender-based repertoires of contentious politics for men that marginalize women. The struggle between class-based and gender-based priorities remains visible today in the different gender mobilizations and issues emphasized in places where socialist party politics have shaped the political field and those where the political field follows other lines of conflict (cf. Ray's comparison of Calcutta and Bombay, 1999; Hobson's comparison of Sweden and Ireland, forthcoming; Ferree's comparison of Germany and the US, 2002).

International feminism has also been long enmeshed in struggles over nationalism, racism, colonialism, and popular self-determination, sometimes in conjunction with international socialism and sometimes not (Molyneux 1985; Seidman 1993; Tétreault 1994; Yuval Davis 1997). Women's gains in insurrectionary periods were often pushed back by the newly institutionalized states, albeit not without resistance. Because women are charged with the reproduction of peoples (both biologically and in the sense of cultural reproduction via maintaining language and customs and early socialization of children), defining "proper" gender relations is often an explicit part of the national project (Kandiyoti 1991; Yuval Davis 1997). National women's movements in many countries have long histories both of collaborating with the subordination of other racial/ethnic groups at home and abroad, but also of organizing antiracist and anti-imperialist efforts (Burton 1994; Twine and Blee 2001). The effort to define feminism as "foreign" or "Western" (as with the label "bourgeois") is an act of political resistance to women's claims, one that attempts to deny local women's movements national legitimacy. Maria Sierra's 1917 appeal to "study, study our history, Spanish ladies and gentlemen, before accusing a feminist of being foreign" (cited in Offen 2000: 6) is much like the contemporary plea made by Russian and other Eastern European feminists who are attempting to recover their own nineteenth and early twentieth century feminist forebears (see Sperling 1999; Gal and Kligman 2000).

Overall, across classes and countries, the history of feminist claims and women's movement mobilizations stretches back into the earliest formation of nation-states, political parties, and democratic institutions. Attacks on the naturalness of patriarchy, as well as defenses of men's "traditional" right to govern, animate the earliest theorists of the state (Pateman 1988). Gender politics continue to be centrally involved in all efforts to think about nature, the person and the citizen, not only in debates over veiling in the Middle East (Kandiyoti 1991) or genital surgery in Africa (Keck and Sikkink 1998), but in Western Europe and the United States, as ongoing debates over issues such as abortion, prostitution, and women's military service show (see, e.g., Katzenstein 1998; Outshoorn 2001; Ferree et al. 2002).

Feminist Women's Movements Have Long Been Transnational

Just as feminist women's movements are not new, they are also not newly transnational. The current tendency to define globalization as a new process and transnational organizations as creating unprecedented linkages among previously separate movements is misleading in two respects. First, the historical trajectory for many contemporary developments might better be understood as a pendulum swing rather than a monotonic line of development. Second, the already existing international women's movement was part of the institutional structure that contributed to the creation and revitalization of local and national movements. Separately existing women's movements did not simply come together; in both the nineteenth and twentieth centuries transnational groups and conferences created regional interests in mobilization and pushed the development of national and local movements in certain directions, particularly in embracing a transnational discourse of citizenship, equality, and rights.

In the late nineteenth century, the predominant form of women's autonomous feminist mobilization was the suffrage organization. Individual national organizations pressing for the right to vote were already widespread when they came together in the International Women Suffrage Alliance in 1902 (Rupp 1997). From the 1890s to the 1930s, women's mobilizations were deeply concerned with issues of citizenship and nationhood, partly expressed in their focus on the vote, but also evident in women's involvement in nation-building and democratization struggles around the world (Jayawardena 1986; Sinha et al. 1999). Ruling elites in countries such as Iran, Turkey, and China also saw the demands of "modernity" as including increasing individual rights for women. Suffrage organizations pressed their case for women's citizenship so effectively within the world community that although virtually no state extended women the right to vote in 1900, virtually all did by 1950 (Ramirez et al. 1997). The equation of citizenship with men ended; no newly independent state after 1950 failed to include women in the franchise. However, the value of modernity, its equation with classical liberal values of individualism, independence, and democracy, and the extension of such values to include women, continues to be debated. Often a "fundamentalist" form of religion stands in active opposition to women's rights (whether among the Christian Right in the US or the Islamic Right globally; see Kandiyoti 1991; Sered 1998).

The International Council of Women, the Inter-American Commission of Women, the International Women Suffrage Alliance, and the Women's International League for Peace and Freedom formed an organizational infrastructure for national mobilizations of women in the early part of the century, but perhaps more importantly, these and other transnational women's organizations provided a bridge to the remobilization of women in the 1970s (Rupp and Taylor 1999). In contrast to the 1960s, women in the early decades of the twentieth century formed international organizations that had hundreds of thousands of members; international socialist congresses also brought women activists together despite the enormous costs that distance imposed; colonial relationships fostered travel and trade relations in which women also became internationally knowledgeable and experienced actors. It was the disruptions of two world wars and the subsequent division of the world into two hostile blocs that brought internationalism to an atypical low point by the 1950s, and which also, and not coincidentally, marked the low ebb of women's activism in Europe and the United States (Rupp and Taylor 1987; Rupp 1997; Lenz 2001).

Our short historical memory offers the 1950s as the epitome of traditional values and practices in family and gender relations in the United States. Actually, the 1950s are the bottom of a curvilinear path taken by many diverse social indicators in the twentieth century: Women's age at marriage, likelihood of not marrying at all, participation in higher education, formation of women's social organizations, and explicitly feminist activism are all higher in the 1920s and 1980s than in the 1950s. Rates of international trade, formation of international organizations, and immigration also hit bottom in the 1950s and are just now equaling or in some cases surpassing the rates that were typical of the early twentieth century. Thus we might better understand the current globalization of women's movements as the resumption of a temporarily suppressed process than as a wholly new development.

From this perspective, the linkages and legacies of the transnational women's movement of the early twentieth century demand particular attention. One such direct connection runs through the United Nations, which on the urging of long-established international women's groups, established its own internal offices to deal with women's affairs (Meyer and Prügl 1999; Moghadam 2000). The International Women's Year, celebrated by a worldwide conference in Mexico City in 1975, gave rise to the declaration of the UN's 1976–85 "Decade for Women" (Fraser 1987).

As participants soon discovered, women's movement representatives at the NGO Tribunes and Forums that paralleled the UN assemblies had quite varied interpretations of women's interests (Fraser 1987). Sharp debates about the gender dimensions of issues such as development, poverty, colonialism, and wars of independence characterized the meetings. Delegates from more affluent countries listened and responded to the critiques raised by women from the global South, and began a process of reevaluation of their exclusive focus on narrowly defined gender interests (Booth 1998; Catagay et al. 1986). Women from the global South also found the conference an impetus to challenge their own governments on issue of gender equality and to mobilize in their own national and regional organizations (Ashworth 1982). Women in Latin America, in particular, developed an extensive and diverse network of organizations across the countries in this region, and many of these networks became important in resistance to the dictatorships that spread in the late 1970s and early 1980s (Alvarez 1990; Jaquette 1994; Stephen 1997).

Subsequent UN conferences in Copenhagen, Nairobi and Beijing drew ever widening circles of women's NGO participation, and continued to foster debate among the participants as well as spur mobilization at home both in preparation for the conference and in response to ties established there (Ashworth 1982; Catagay et al. 1986). A strong effect of women's mobilization on the agenda of other transnational organizations became evident. For example, population groups took up a discourse of gender, in which women's education was seen as the key to birth control, thus giving recognition to women as agents and individuals with rights in a way that earlier, more coercive population control discourses had not (Ferree and Gamson 1999; Greenhalgh 2001). Other feminist issues, such as objections to clitoridectomy, revulsion at the use of rape in war, and questions of coercion in prostitution and the international trafficking in women for sex, also came increasingly onto the agenda of other UN conferences, under the rubric of "women's rights are human rights." (Correa and Reichmann 1994; Booth 1998; Keck and Sikkink 1998). Women in the global South found this use of a human rights frame for feminist demands to be empowering and useful for local and regional mobilization as well (Keck and Sikkink 1998; Ray and Korteweg 1999).

Overall, a strong current of support for rights talk in the transnational arena reflected an increasing willingness to include women in the definitions of citizenship grounded in classical liberal political theory. This reflects both a long-term trend toward the expansion of liberal discourse transnationally (Meyer et al. 1997) and a victory of women's movements in having their concerns incorporated in how liberalism defines its constituency of "individuals" with rights. For example, Berkovich (1999) shows how the mobilizations of women in and around international labor organizations throughout the twentieth century pushed a redefinition of women and their needs; the "mothers" who were seen in the early twentieth century to need special protections and benefits from the state in the workplace were redefined in the late twentieth century as "citizens" who had rights to representation in labor organizations and to participate in the definition of their own needs. Increasingly, women were represented as a resource for economic development that should not be wasted, and whose progress toward equality was an indicator of modernity. Nation-states therefore had a growing obligation to produce measures of "women's status" in education and in the economy, for which they were held internationally accountable. The women's movement, Berkovich demonstrates, both helped to produce the demand from international organizations for such statistics and continues to use such statistical data to push for changes in women's opportunities in specific nation-states, a classic example of what Keck and Sikkink call a "boomerang" effect (1998).

In sum, the connection between feminist women's mobilizations of the early twentieth century and those of the latter part of the century is direct and organizationally based. Women's movements institutionalized in civil society in a variety of formal organizations that survived and spanned "the doldrums" of the middle of the century (Rupp and Taylor 1987; Stienstra 1994; Meyer and Prügl 1999). Women's movements also created direct access into government through winning the suffrage and the right to hold public office. Although the structures of opportunity in workplaces and other nonstate political organizations continued to favor men, women continued to be active internationally in civic organizations and movements. Local and transnational women's movements have each spurred on the other's mobilization, and feminist discourses circulate through them. Women's movement demands challenged gender relations in expanding the concepts of citizenship and human rights, but also brought gendered analyses into national and international forums on development, poverty, race, urbanization, aging, and other issues.

Having established a conceptual scaffolding for examining women's movements in relation to feminism, other social movements, institutional forms of politics, and state policy and practices transnationally, we turn now to examine what social movement theory can learn from studies of women's movements. Most "general" movement theory has developed to date with primary reference to movements led by and directed toward men. In this section we ask not only whether these models apply well to women's movements but also how the analysis we have derived above from the study of women's movements can add significant questions and insights to these frameworks.

WOMEN'S MOVEMENTS AND SOCIAL MOVEMENT THEORY

We begin with the theoretical framing that McAdam et al. (2001: 14–15) characterize as the "classic social movement agenda" since the early 1970s (see also McAdam et al. 1996; Tarrow 1998). In this basic model, social changes initiate (1) new political opportunities and threats, (2) shifts in mobilizing structures of communication, coordination, and commitment among potential actors, and (3) reframing of claims, identities, and culturally resonant meanings. Activities encompassed by these three clusters of concepts (political opportunity, mobilizing structures, and meaning work) influence each other as well as create integrated repertoires of contention, the forms of claims-making that are transmitted between organizations and generations and adapted for specific interactions in concrete historical moments of opportunity (Clemens 1993; Tilly 1995). Although we organize our look at concrete women's movements in terms of these three clusters of concepts, in conclusion, we integrate all three into the overall idea of *gendered repertoires of contention* in movements that address gendered opportunities through gendered structures of mobilization with gendered rhetorics of meaning. We stress that social/political structures, opportunities, organizations, and frames are gendered. Thus in this section we argue that analysts need to study not only women's movements as defined above with attention to gender, but to make all social movement theory attentive to the gender dynamics that shape mobilization. Not all feminist mobilization is autonomous, in the form of women's movements, but all social movements in a gendered society perforce use gendered repertoires of contention. We indicate how women's movements theoretically raise issues for all movements. We particularly argue that a long-term view of history and social change is essential for understanding the origins, outcomes, and dynamics of women's movements (cf. Buechler 2000; Offen 2000), and that most social movement theories have taken an approach that is too short term – one in which gender-specific relations and repertoires appear to be stable, "natural" facts rather than variable aspects of contentious politics for both women and men.

Political Opportunity Structures

Political opportunity structures were initially conceptualized as the given alignments of potential allies and opponents faced by a potential social movement within a single nation; opportunities that were thus more or less available to social movements were understood as chances (at best) to seize and (at a minimum) to influence state decision-making institutions (McAdam 1982). Increasingly criticizing this as an excessively static and state-centered view of politics, current social movement theorists define opportunity structures as comprising temporally stable elements, both formal institutional arrangements as well as cultural patterns and expectations, in addition to dynamic elements of shifting alignments and "policy windows" interpreted through issue cultures, public discourse, and media frames (Gamson and Meyer 1996; Ferree et al. 2002). This more expansive view of both politics and of opportunities is helpful in considering which elements support and which undercut the emergence and/or effects of women's movements. Yet it still fails to consider when and how political opportunity structures are specifically gendered (McCammon et al. 2001).

Looking specifically at women's movements suggests that political opportunity is not gender neutral, either for individuals or for groups. Rita Noonan (1995), for instance, shows how women under the Pinochet dictatorship in Chile had opportunities not open to men to take to the streets and demand protection and support for their families because their needs and their protests were defined as less "political," and therefore less threatening, than similar acts by men would have been.

Such mobilization appears to be timeless, as women have long drawn on a political tradition of gendered opportunity that connects women's responsibility to feed and protect their families to women's rights to make claims on state and society for the means to do so (Molyneux 1985; Miles 1996). The women's march to Versailles in 1789 demanding bread "captured the imagination of contemporaries as well as subsequent commentators" and was one of the opening salvos of the French Revolution (Offen 2000: 53). Other mobilizations of women have also drawn on similar imagery of maternal care to legitimize challenging political actions that also became more widespread: The Mothers of the Plaza de Mayo spurred a more general human rights campaign in Argentina (Keck and Sikkink 1998) and US mothers' activism around Love Canal and other sites spurred more general environmental mobilizations (Kaplan 1997). Studies of Black women in the American civil rights movement emphasize their role as early innovators of resistance strategies, such as the Montgomery Bus Boycott, and point to the significance of their own gender-specific organizations as forerunners for later mobilization, as well as grass-roots leadership (Payne 1990; Barnett 1993; Robnett 1997).

Some analysts (e.g., Miles 1996) understand this sort of gendered mobilization as inherent in the position of women, across societies and periods, as the universal caregivers. Instead, we would ask, why women are apparently overrepresented in both early and informal forms of resistance and rebellion. Why are women's movement organizations among the "early risers" in many cycles of protest? We suggest that women's movements respond to a long-term organization of political opportunity by gender that is part of the organization of state and nonstate forms of authority. The factors that privilege access to modern state and party systems (workplace-based connections, control over wealth, "paying one's dues" in the bureaucratic organizations and networks in which favors are traded) among men and male-led organizations are strongly gendered in their social organization (Chapman 1993; Sturgeon 1997). As an outgrowth of the way nation-states constructed their politics on gendered lines, women are institutionally disadvantaged in contests waged on "men's" terrain. Women thus are more likely to organize outside the formal polity, in those community and grass-roots contexts that are gendered female.[8]

Such domestic-based politics is less likely to be recognized as "political," which may provide protective coloration in a wide variety of dictatorships and other conditions of marginal opportunity for male mobilization, as Noonan (1995), Miethe (1999), and others have found. These examples suggest that women will mobilize as women, and frequently in the absence of men, when the risks are exceedingly high and when women's maternal role and existing networks render their political roles invisible. Ingrid Miethe's studies of women peace activists before and after the collapse of the East German state points to a conscious use of the separation of public and private in state socialism to pursue dissident "politics around the kitchen table," a locale in which women were already present and legitimate actors (1999). In recently unified Germany, where "politics" now means reliance on political parties in which women are organizationally disadvantaged, women have lost their former leadership roles.

Even women activists themselves, however, may be slow to define grass-roots community organizing and "bridge leadership" as being really "politics," which they may define as the male-dominated formal institutions – electoral office, bureaucratic positions, and even official leadership roles in movement organizations. Local women activists in Russia (Gottlick 1999; Sperling et al. 2001), grass-roots organizers in Africa and India (Tripp 2000; Subramaniam 2000) and community organizers in poor communities in Canada and the US (Christiansen-Ruffman 1995; Naples 1998; Robnett, 1997) all seem to distance themselves and their "work for their community" from what they call "politics," which they frequently define as corrupt, self-serving, and male-dominated. Their disavowal of politics in favor of some other rhetoric is striking. Quite unlike Molyneux's assumption that such activism springs spontaneously or naturally from women's position in the gender division of labor (pragmatic gender interests), we argue that it is constructed as nonfamilial but also as nonpolitical community work – quintessentially bridging these domains (Stall and Stoecker 1998).[9] A rhetoric of male-dominated politics as untrustworthy, corrupt, self-serving, unresponsive may be an important factor creating the space for women to do such "antipolitics." This gender division of labor flows from the definition of formal politics as male no less than from the idea that women are the ones who are domestic/private/responsible for the home.

Such gendered dichotomies, like the distinction between paid work and housework, obscure the essential political labor being done by women in their local communities, the "housework of politics" (Ferree 1997). Grass-roots organizing faces a structure of opportunity that differs from ephemeral forms of street-level protest as well as from the creation of more formal social movement organizations, particularly but not only on gender lines (Stall and Stoecker 1998). Payne (1990) has noted that Ella Baker, the first "Acting" Director of the Southern Christian Leadership Conference, distinguished between "mobilizing" (for short-term events) and "organizing" (for the long-term), and that women more readily serve as activists in the latter type of work. Moreover, as opportunities arise for community groups to gain public recognition and become more "conventionally political," women and women's groups tend to lose or withdraw from public leadership roles (see Bookman and Morgen 1988).

Because gender segregation leaves an alternative geography of opportunity open to women more than to men, women's political openings and allies are more to be found in the institutional domains defined as "apolitical": communities, grass-roots civic organizations, social work, and social services. From this perspective, maternalist mobilizations are not merely outpourings of "natural" grievances, but organized efforts to mobilize the power of civil society against "politics as usual," which is still defined as male. Particularly when states are inaccessible or irresponsible in general, and fear of challengers makes them hostile to male mobilization, women have a structural and cultural opportunity to play a significant role.

Nonetheless, any issues that can be defined as "women's" can offer an entré for women's groups and networks to make inroads in formal politics, as German women legislators found for the abortion debate in the early 1990s (Ferree et al. 2002) and women's pacifist groups demonstrated in international relations debates about resolving conflict via arbitration in the early 1900s (Hoganson 1998). Defining building democratic community groups as something at which women excel has given women's groups a means to appeal for support from international donors throughout former Yugoslavia (Bagic 2002). At the World Bank, women have achieved their greatest success in bringing gendered concerns to bear on bank policies where they support conventional understandings of women's reproductive responsibilities for health, population, and education, and less success with arguments based on gender equality (O'Brien et al. 2000).

In sum, studies of women's movements point to the analytic usefulness of (1) acknowledging a relationship between gender and political opportunity that may vary systematically between states and in state institutions relative to civil societies, giving either women or men different advantages in mobilizing at any given point; (2) linking gendered leadership, gender-specific organization, location in party-based or community-networked political systems to opportunities for long-term organizing; and (3) finding out how change in gendered opportunity arises out of and affects the actions of women and men throughout the entire cycle of protest, including both incentives to engage in "antipolitics" and new chances to enter the formal political system.

Forms of Mobilization

Women's movements do not only arise in gendered structures of opportunity; women respond to opportunity through mobilizing structures and strategies that at times may differ systematically from men's. Such gender differences may actually not be great, and may appear more pronounced than they in fact are because of the difference in emphasis among scholars of women's and men's movements. For example, the role of emotion has only recently come to be studied in nonfeminist movements (see Ferree and Merrill 2000; Goodwin et al. 2001; Aminzade and McAdam 2002) but was previously recognized in women's movement mobilizations (Morgen 1995; Taylor 1995, 1996). Women's movements also rarely if ever attempt to organize political parties, to seize direct control of the state, or to use political violence as a tool, perhaps because these are strategies severely disfavored by the gendered political opportunity structure discussed above.

In this section, we consider the interplay between opportunity and mobilization strategy, particularly as it affects the nature of organizations that movements develop. We argue that specific studies of how women's movements do politics suggest general ideas about the interplay between more and less formal organizational strategies. Rather than thinking of movement organizations as preexistent collective actors, we highlight questions about why organizations take the form they do and what consequences such strategic choices may have.

Mary Katzenstein (1998) argues that only in the later part of the twentieth century did social movements seek to move collectively into institutional structures and change them from the inside out. Patricia Yancey Martin (1990) describes this as the move from "standing outside and casting blame" to "moving inside and occupying space." The move inside institutions is different from that of establishing alternative institutions, be they political parties, schools, colleges and universities, benevolent associations, hospitals, or churches, which was still the more typical approach of collective actors in the late nineteenth and early twentieth centuries (Katzenstein, 1998). It is also different from the revolutionary impulse to conquer, destroy, and replace states and institutions (Halliday 1999). When social movements move into institutions, they move not as individuals trying to "make it" as tokens for the success of their groups, but as organized collective entities that are trying to change the institution's goals, decision-making or modes of operation, whether or not they end up successful, expelled, or co-opted.

Katzenstein (1998), comparing feminist mobilizations within two of the most explicitly male-dominated and hierarchical institutions in American society, the Catholic Church and the US military, finds that they adopt quite different strategies for social change. Each reflects the different contexts of opportunity and resources available in the institution. Catholic feminists, lacking access to outside leverage in the form of court decisions or institutionalized rights, have adopted a strategy of discursive politics, in which the values of hierarchy and authority are called into question and empowering the grass-roots "people in the pews" is a key strategy for changing power relations. In contrast, the women in the US military can use rights discourse as a resource in the courts and in administrative rule-setting to leverage access to the same entitlements that men have. Their strategy explicitly does not involve a discursive challenge to the hierarchical principles of the organization, and they do not advocate either "empowering" the ordinary soldier in the ranks or challenging the centrality of combat in military careers. Katzenstein argues that both groups have chosen strategies adapted to the institutional terrain in which they are struggling.

Similarly, Ferree et al. (2002) argue that feminist adaptation to institutionalized opportunities in the political culture of Germany and the US has led to differences in their mobilization strategies and types of success in abortion politics in each country. For American feminists, the combination of universalistic individual rights discourses affirmed by the Supreme Court and a weak welfare state offer an opportunity to mobilize male allies to support "privacy" for women's abortion decision, yet leave poor women's childbearing needs out. US abortion rights mobilization is thus dominated by mixed-gender groups who campaign for the "right to choose" abortion without stigma or sanction. German feminists face a constitutional court decision affirming the fetus's right to life and a strong welfare state, which give them the opportunity for a specifically gendered mobilization to empower women, using women legislators to represent "women's demands" that the state protect the fetus "with the woman and not against her" by offering the social supports that would allow her to raise a child and permitting the woman herself to decide whether she is able to do so or not. But quietly accepting the continuing stigmatization of abortion by criminal law is the price feminists in Germany pay for their strategic choice, no less than American feminists see the loss of state abortion funding for the poor as a painful part of the cost that liberal individualism extracts for the abstract "right to choose" (cf. Solinger 1998; R. Roth 2000).

The interweaving of strategic choice and perceived opportunity in these cases is not accidental, and highlights the difficulty of neatly separating mobilization processes from opportunity structure. As these two examples show, opportunity structures already anchored in institutions provide powerful incentives to movements to choose certain types of strategies and these differ dramatically between institutional contexts. Since opportunities, as perceived, affect choices of strategy and over the longer term strategies affect the types of gains that movements can make, there can be no question that mobilization practices institutionalize opportunity. Given the variability in institutional contexts, it should not be at all surprising that women's movements adopt quite different strategies from time to time and place to place; what is more surprising are the commonalities. The contrast that Katzenstein draws between a discursive politics about values (in the Church) and a politics of rights and access (in the military) is a common strategic distinction between those who would define themselves as "radical" and others, variously defined as pragmatic or liberal within Western societies (Ryan 1992).[10] Explicitly naming women as women as a constituency with distinctive experiences and interests, as German but not American feminists do on abortion, frequently vies with strategies that focus on downplaying differences of gender (Cott 1987; Offen 2000).

Among feminists, strategies that adapt to institutions and their constraints are often in conflict with strategies that entail staying "outside and casting blame" (Ferree and Martin 1995). This strategic debate is often pronounced initially, for example as the battered women's movement and the rape crisis movement debated the move toward more professionalized and state-supported forms of intervention in the late 1970s (Bevacqua 1999). Later, when the institutionalization of once-radical feminist goals seems commonplace (e.g., higher education for women, equal pay, or the criminalization of rape in marriage), debates within feminist organizations may focus on how they do their practical work, such as racial inclusivity in staffing and services (Scott 1998). What remains constant is the fact that women's choices of mobilization strategies and tactics are deeply embedded in institutional practices. How this applies to men's choices of organizational strategy appears to have been less studied, perhaps because studies of men's movements have been more sharply divided into competing theoretical schools in which specific organizational types were postulated as the normative standard case.

The resource mobilization approach initially took the language of corporate organization (entrepreneurs, franchises, etc.) as its dominant metaphor for thinking about movement organizations (McCarthy and Zald 1977). Useful as these analogies have been, we suggest that they also have guided social movement thinking in the US toward theorizing the hierarchical, centralized, formalized organization as the normative "SMO." Juxtaposed to this, often in a gendered and dichotomous way, were the nonhierarchical, decentralized, branching networks that were more typical of some women's movements and some "new social movements" in Europe, as well as in the "participatory democracy" mode of organizing among a younger generation on the Left in the US within the civil rights, antiwar, feminist, peace, and environmental movements (Miller 1988; Meyer and Whittier 1994; Polletta 2002). When the NSM approach postulated this specific organizational form as defining the movements of interest, it made it difficult to see when and how transitions between organizational types might be occurring.

The synthesis into a comparative political process model seems to have resolved the tension between the two schools, but at the cost of not considering historical transformations in strategy as something to be explained. The institutionalization of class politics (but not their nineteenth and early twentieth century feminist competitors) in Europe and the emergence of lobbying forms of movement organizations in the US in the early twentieth century to express both class and gender demands (Clemens 1997) laid the groundwork for movement organizing to follow different institutional tracks in each context. For example, network-like informal groups have remained more common for longer among feminists in Europe, while American feminist groups – like those of other movements – shifted to more conventional lobby-like structures (Ferree 1987). The basic lobby form was already part of the institutional repertoire of the US, even if the fully-professionalized SMO and "checkbook activism" that McCarthy and Zald (1977) saw emerging were innovative developments within it. In contrast, the NSM groups emphasized a style of decentralized organizing that was not in the corporate model, and that focused on identitization and "lifestyle" politics in daily life (Lichterman 1996). Some of these persist among American feminists (e.g., Whittier 1995) although less significantly today than in the 1970s. As the history of women's movements makes clear, using lifestyle to challenge social exclusion and subordination is not a new strategy (cf. the nineteenth century dress reform of "Bloomerism" in the US and cross-dressing "Georgesandisme" in France). But it competes with strategies that are more adapted to gaining access and influence within formal, state-centered politics. Working-class organizations, especially in Europe where class-based politics is institutionalized in the formal party system, have moved far away from a politics of daily life, and this makes the "new" (nonclass-based) movements appear more "radical" by contrast. As feminist politics become more anchored in party caucuses and electoral systems in Europe, one could predict a shift away from discursive and toward more access-oriented strategies there as well, in which formal organizations would have advantages over collectives and networks.

While they compete for members, the formal-bureaucratic and collectivist-lifestyle organizational types do not necessarily conflict within a movement, but may offer synergistic advantages (Lofland 1995). Levitsky (2001) offers an example of how organizers themselves see the potential "division of labor" among groups between pursuing more formal organizational strategies (e.g., those focused on elections, legislation, courts, and rights) or more localized, community-based challenges to norms in the gay rights movement. She also suggests that the least advantaged sub-groups in the movement have the most to gain by not narrowing the repertoire of contention to more formally political strategies. Particularly when the analysis of oppressive relations focuses on institutions other than the state (such as feminist critiques of organized medicine, the Catholic Church or the media), discursive and informal repertoires of contention may be especially suitable (see Taylor 1996).

But it would be a mistake to view such strategic choices of organizational form as necessarily dichotomous or exclusionary. Bordt (1997) surveyed a variety of women's movement organizations in NYC and found not only a melding of more collectivist and bureaucratic structures had become typical, but that *networks* were a particularly valued and useful organizational structure in their own right. Keck and Sikkink's important study of transnational social movement influence processes particularly indicates the suitability of the "principled advocacy network" as an organizational form for working across borders (1998). Students of women's move-ments have also looked critically at the use of the advocacy network as a form of taking movements inside institutions (on "NGO-ization" see Alvarez 1990; Silliman 1999), contrasting this both with the model of mass movements on the streets (using numbers as a resource rather than access or expertise) and the more lifestyle approaches (focused on discourse as a resource). The differences between and transitions among these three broad types of organizational forms may be clearest when one looks at women's movements, since all three types of mobilizing strategies have been commonly found there since the nineteenth century.

One location where the significance of all three types of organizing can be seen is the *conference* as a specific type of movement activity. Women's movement cam-paigns based on conferences as a movement tool were a significant part of the organizational basis of first-wave feminist mobilization (Rupp 1997; Meyer and Prügl 1999); and they formed a spur to mass mobilization in the second-wave as well (cf. Rossi 1982; West 1999). Conferences are a resource for building networks regionally around the globe among contemporary women's movements: such "encuentros" have been particularly important in Latin America (Alvarez 1990; Alvarez et al. 2003; Stephen 1997). Because conferences are both organizational and interpersonal, they offer a particularly useful melding of advocacy network and lifestyle politics, as Rupp and Taylor's argument about social construction of affec-tional ties of sisterhood suggests (1999).

Conferences have been a major part of the international feminist women's move-ment, not only as mobilizing structures but also as elements in the repertoire of contention in their own right (see chapter 14 in this volume, for more general coverage of international conferences). As events, not merely sites where something else happens, conferences punctuate and focus organizing that has become less episodic and more regularized, giving a concrete form to an otherwise dispersed network (see Sperling [1999], on Russian; Hercus [1999a, 1999b, forthcoming], on Australian; and Stephen [1997], on Latin American conferences). Although conferences are events in the same way that a strike, a demonstration or an urban insurrection is, they have been less readily recognized as important by social movement researchers, perhaps because women have relied on them as mobilizing tools disproportionately more than men.

In sum, studies of women's movements, their differences, and changes over time suggest that organizational repertoires may be broader, more strategic, and more interconnected than dominant ways of conceptualizing social movements suggest. The long time span of feminist movements and the variety of their organizational forms has encouraged women's studies scholars to pay more attention to the transitions between types of organization and the strategic implications of organizational form than is found in the mainstream of social movement research. Taking full account of scholarship on women's movements would tend to direct the social movement research agenda toward acknowledging a more diverse and varying organizational repertoire, including mobilization within institutions in addition to autonomous movement groups in bureaucratic, collectivist, and hybrid organizational styles; conferences as well as confrontations as significant events; and interpersonal networks as well as advocacy networks among NGOs as strategically important links sustaining activists over the long run.

Ideologies and Frames for Women's Movements

The so-called "cultural turn" in social movement theory has placed increasing emphasis on discourses rather than organizations as the critical carriers of movement intentions, without always making careful distinctions between terms such as ideologies, beliefs, frames, and grievances (Oliver and Johnston 2000). Still, giving attention to ideas provides a useful point of entry into considering both micro (social psychological) and macro (institutional cultural) dynamics that the mesolevel organizational emphasis of the 1980s had neglected. Research on women's movements additionally points to blind spots at each of these levels that have been produced by taking men and male experience as the standard case for thinking about people and cultures (Ferree and Merrill 2000).

At the cultural level of institutions, the organization of public and private as gendered spheres in modern societies creates specific contradictions that are often the locus of movement debates. Especially as notions of a world polity with norms that are negotiated in transnational venues (Meyer et al. 1997) begin to challenge "realist" visions of states acting on narrow self-interest, the underlying value structures of democracy and market economies are increasingly recognized as important to what movements do and claim. Normative political theory offers useful insights into the nature of these values.

While liberal democracy defined the "rights of man," it also premised the exercise of these formal rights on a social position as a head of a household, one who was autonomously able to enter into contracts, participate in labor markets, and exercise free choice. Even when property qualifications for such a vision of autonomous citizenship were discarded, the anchoring of concepts of modernity and democracy in a marketized and gendered vision of autonomy (freedom from family dependency and rejection of moral claims that would interfere with self-interest) made it inconceivable to some that women could or should be included as appropriate political actors. If women are free citizens on these terms, the family and morality seem to be at risk, and resistance to feminism has been framed as the "decline of the family," "women's selfishness," and the "natural" demands of eugenics/sociobiology. Gender politics is therefore misunderstood by focusing only on feminist women's movements, and not recognizing those men's movements that raise reactionary claims, from the Boy Scouts to the Promise Keepers (Kimmel 1996; Schwalbe 1996).

Despite the expansion of the franchise and women's political participation around the globe, discourses of familial domesticity and religious fundamentalism continue to cast women as the preservers of "tradition" and reservoirs of moral values on whose subordination the good of the nation depends (Yuval Davis 1997; Sered 1998). Such deeply gendered ways of thinking pervade specific claims about liberalism, modernity, nationalism, and globalization, and continue to offer ways of articulating resistance to the state-building, science, and secularism that are seen as characteristic of contemporary public life, particularly as associated with the West. Gender ideologies, no less than those of race, class and nation, are core arguments that movements develop and on which they depend for frames that will resonate with socially institutionalized values. Antifeminist and antimodernist goals can thus logically be used to mobilize reactionary women's movements, too.

Thus as current events drive social movement analysts to consider right-wing mobilizations, antimodernization ideologies, and religious fundamentalisms as important aspects of political culture, feminist theorizing about gender and the state offers significant conceptual tools for understanding these changes and conflicts transnationally. The mobilization of racist visions of the nation often combine with masculinist discourses of humiliation and the loss of honor, whether in the US militia and Christian Identity movements (Kimmel and Ferber 2000; Blee 2002), Hindu nationalism (Sehgal 2002), or Islamic fundamentalisms (Kandiyoti 1991; Moghadam 1992). Such antimodernist movements have often been the opponents of organized feminism, and have made gender relations (along with race and nation) an explicit target of movement mobilization. Understanding gender ideologies and frames as pervasive elements in political struggles around the globe is now inescapably part of the challenge facing movement theorists.

At the social psychological level, the gendering of rationality as male has led to a dichotomization of reason and emotion, leaving emotionality, the "female half," both understudied and undervalued (Taylor 1996; Ferree and Merrill 2000). Without positing women as actually any more emotional than men, studies of women's movements have challenged the idea that emotions interfere with reason rather than complementing and enhancing narrowly cognitive responses. Issues of will (motivation) and of values are especially poorly understood by a model that posits unemotional calculation of expected outcomes.

Producing activists who have long-term, even lifetime, commitments to social change and the communities that sustain and support such enduring identities is one dimension of movement organizing that demands an analysis of "passions" in protest (Goodwin et al. 2001; McComiskey, 2001). This also suggests the usefulness of biographical models (Andrews 1991; Stryker et al. 2000; Miethe and Roth 2001). Social movement organizations exist beyond the lifetimes of single individuals. They transmit ideologies over time and space, and not only recruit participants but sustain their involvement and help them to transmit values to new generations, as Roth's discussion of political socialization in the Congress of Labor Union Women (2003) and Whittier's cohort analysis of radical feminist groups in Columbus Ohio (1995) point out. Understanding such "social movement communities" (Buechler 2000) offers a less state-centered view of how social change comes to be institutionalized.

Organizational behavior is another significant dimension of movement activities that can hardly be analyzed without understanding how emotions are used to frame political action. Groves's (2001) analysis of the gendered understandings of "scientific objectivity" as valued and "empathetic identification" as suspect bases for making claims about animal rights shows why and how men came to be preferred (even by women) as spokespeople for the movement, despite its majority female membership (cf. Einwohner 1999). Similarly, women's attempts to challenge World Bank priorities have been stifled by neo-liberal economistic frameworks that reduce gender change to "the business case for gender" or "the economic rationale for investing in gender" (O'Brien et al. 2000). Cohn (1987) shows how the discourse of "defense intellectuals" makes peace talk seem "emotional" and "uniformed" while disguising nuclear planners' own emotional investments in "beautiful" weapons and in "winning" a masculinity-testing game.

While "outlaw emotions" such as rage over inequality may be important for movements to generate passion among both women and men (Jaggar 1989), the expression of emotions may be regulated by gender codes that specifically associate irrationality and "tender-heartedness" to women, and can discredit the force of their claims to speak for peace, social justice, or the needy if this is defined as an "emotional" rather than a "realistic" appeal. But because emotionality is ascribed to women, women may be more aware of their emotions and more able to use them strategically, while men in movements may suffer under the illusion that they are dispassionate and fail to recognize their own visceral responses.

Overall, drawing from feminist democratic theory as well as studies of women's and men's movements to recognize that emotions and emotion work (Hochschild 1983) are part of the framing process for all movements should enrich our models of political culture and its discontents. It should also expand the model of the social movement actor from a narrowly cognitive rational actor to a more historically and biographically situated person with attachments and emotions that can be intrinsically motivating (but also open to manipulation by others). Such actors are part of communities with historically developed traditions and acquire commitments and a sense of entitlement through processes of political socialization, within movement communities as well as in mainstream, possibly patriarchial cultures. Social movement organizations, no less than individual actors, are shaped by emotion norms in the culture as well as by the personal passions of participants.

CONCLUSION

Looking at feminism and women's movements as a lens on social movement theory has suggested that formal and informal political opportunities, organizational structures and strategies, and frames and feelings carry gender meanings that have often been disregarded by purportedly general theories that have in practice studied men. By making gender salient and visible, feminist women's movements in particular expose dynamics that are in play in many if not all movements. Political action, whether women's or men's, occurs within systems that have deeply institutionalized gender in their structures of formal policymaking. Gender relations are also power relations. They are therefore important for organizations and individuals that are attempting to mount political challenges on a variety of issues. Gendered repertoires of contention are strategic responses to institutions that structure oppression and opportunity along lines of gender and are therefore found in all movements that attempt to navigate such political terrain.

Making gender salient, or conversely, concealing or denying the gender dynamics that are part of institutional structures, is part of what movements do. Constructing solidarity based on gender is a dynamic process that requires work, but so also is the construction of solidarities among women and men based on other identities that are defined as more significant than gender. The intersectionality of gender, race, class, nation, and other potential identities creates specific opportunities and obstacles for collective action. Understanding these boundaries, and when and how they shift historically, poses a challenge for social movement theories that take group interests for granted and focus on explaining only what predefined groups demand of the state. Social movement theories that instead take gender relations into account from the outset suggest a more dynamic, long-term, and less state-centered approach to power, protest, and change.

While women's movements are not to be confused with specifically feminist claims, it is also clear that there will be a relationship between mobilizing women as women and challenging existing gender relations that still situate women as "outside" politics and the public. The forms that women's movements take are widely variable, as are the goals they adopt, and this variety helps to illuminate the range of ways in which opportunities, organizations, and frames are all gendered. Changing these gender relations, the objective of feminism, is one of the ongoing struggles associated with the realization of the modernist project, along with democratization, and thus a core feature of what many social movements struggle for or against. Bringing the analysis of feminist women's movements into the center of social movement theory is therefore an essential corrective to the gender blinders that have limited its vision, and will contribute to constructing more historically and geographically inclusive thinking about social movements as central to social change in modern society as well. With issues around modernization, democratization, and gender privilege animating many of the social movements that are of most concern today, the centering of a gender analysis in a long-term, historically grounded understanding of social movements, states, and societal change is more pressing and potentially fruitful than ever.

Notes

1   This assertion is based on a wide scholarship in history, political science, and political sociology as well as women's studies. Studies that have focused more narrowly may arrive at different conclusions, particularly if indicators of the women's movement are restricted to public protest events.
2   Some would call these women's activism, or mobilizations, or movements of women rather than "women's movements," but we find such a subtle linguistic distinction confusing.

Our definition implies that women's movements are to be found on both the left and the right; indeed, it has been empirically the case that mobilizing women as a constituency for some goals (e.g., nationalism, moral reform) brings together left and right as "strange bedfellows." To limit the term "women's movements" to those that are feminist or those that are on the left obscures the indeterminacy and struggle involved in defining what women's interests are in any particular time or place. See Meera Sehgal (2002) on Hindu nationalist women's movements.

3   Such transformations have been particularly dramatic in Latin America where women's participation in socialist and anti-authoritarian movements for social justice in the 1980s eventually took a more feminist turn (see Stephen 1997).

4   Of course, not all women's movements by our definition will adopt feminist goals of any sort at any time, and then the empirically interesting question is why they do not.

5   Racism and nationalism, cast as community defense, are also goals used to mobilize women's movements, as in Boston's antibusing campaign of the 1970s or the Hindu nationalist women's movement in India.

6   Molyneux's own reassessment of her model (1998) also stresses the variable relation between strategic and pragmatic interests in practice and the need to examine the process of making connections between them, but continues to define each type as intrinsically given by the situation or the theory.

7   E.g., the "woman question" was one of the earliest and most contentious issues within socialism. German (and other) socialists divided between those who wanted better wages for women and those who wanted women excluded from the labor force to improve men's wages. Achieving a definition of "the worker" and "his family" as the proper constituency for socialist organization went hand in hand with the victory of the latter strategy in the union movement (Pinl 1977; Cockburn; 1983, Kessler-Harris 2001).

8   Note as well that the emergence of a politically active male citizen in a nation-state was not prior to but enmeshed in debates over whether political activity belonged to humanity, women as well as men. The separation of spheres that created formal politics for men also created the mother-educator-civilizer role for women in informal politics; in this it is precisely parallel to the division of labor into "paid work" for men in physically separate factories and mills, and newly devalued "domestic" labor without pay for women. Both housework as such and the housework of politics, civic activism, emerge together in the nineteenth century (Offen 2000, provides a good overview of the source materials and debates).

9   The currently fashionable rhetoric of "civil society" focuses on this liminal area between public and private. As an arena in which movements typically work, civil society is constructed with and through rhetorical contests about gender: is (this part of) civil society "really" politics? If so, then it belongs to men. Or is it "really" just an extension of "family responsibilities"? Then it can be "civic housekeeping" and legitimate for women. As Gal and Kligman (2000) show with regard to Eastern Europe, an important area in which the rhetoric of "civil society" has been deployed, these are framing debates about the boundaries of the political, not the essence of the domain itself.

10   This emphasis is also evident in the distinction made between "queer politics" and the politics of access for gays and lesbians on the "ethnic group model" (see Gamson 1995; and Vaid 1995).

References and further reading

Alvarez, Sonia (1990) *Engendering Democracy in Brazil: Women's Movements in Transition Politics*. Princeton, NJ: Princeton University Press.

——(1997) Dilemmas of Gendered Citizenship in Post-Authoritarian Latin America. Paper presented at the Conference on Gendered Citizenships: European and Latin American Perspectives, Minda de Gunzburg Center for European Studies, Harvard University, March 14–17.

Alvarez, Sonia, Elizabeth Friedman, Erika Beckman, Maylei Blackwell, Norma Chinchilla. Nathalie Lebon, Marysa Navaro, and Marcela Rios (2003) Encountering Latin American and Carribbean Feminisms. *Signs*, 28 (2), 537–80.

Aminzade, Ron, and Doug McAdam (2002) Emotions and Contentious Politics. Special issue. *Mobilization*, 7 (2).

Andrews, Molly (1991) *Lifetimes of Commitment: Aging, Politics, Psychology*. New York: Cambridge University Press.

Ashworth, Georgina (1982) The United Nations' Women's Conference and International Linkages in the Women's Movement. In Peter Willets (ed.), *Pressure Groups in the Global System*. New York: St. Martin's.

Bacchi, Carol (1999) *Women, Policy, and Politics: The Construction of Policy Problems*. Thousand Oaks, CA: Sage.

Bagic, Aida (2002) International Assistance for Women's Organizing in South Eastern Europe: From Groups and Initiatives to NGOs. Paper presented at Women's Worlds Conference, Makerere University, Kampala Uganda.

Barnett, Bernice McNair (1993) Invisible Southern Black Women Leaders in the Civil Rights Movement: The Triple Constraints of Gender, Race and Class. *Gender & Society*, 7, 162–82.

Basu, Amrita (1995) *The Challenge of Local Feminisms: Women's Movements in Global Perspective*. Boulder, CO: Westview.

Beckwith, Karen (1996) Lancashire Women against Pit Closures: Women's Standing in a Men's Movement. *Signs*, 21, 1034–68.

——(2001) Women's Movements at Century's End: Excavation and Advances in Political Science. *Annual Review of Political Science*, 4, 371–90.

Berkovich, Nitza (1999) *From Motherhood to Citizenship: Women's Rights and International Organizations*. Baltimore: Johns Hopkins University Press.

Bevacqua, Maria (1999) *Rape on the Public Agenda: Feminism and the Politics of Sexual Assault*. Boston: Northeastern University Press.

Blee, Kathleen (2002) *Inside Organized Racism: Women in the Hate Movement*. Berkeley: University of California Press.

Bookman, Ann, and Sandra Morgen (1988) *Women and the Politics of Empowerment*. Philadelphia, PA: Temple University Press.

Booth, Karen M. (1998) National Mother, Global Whore, and Transnational Femocrats: The Politics of AIDS and the Construction of Women at the World Health Organization. *Feminist Studies*, 24 (1), 115–39.

Bordt, Rebecca (1997) *The Structure of Women's Nonprofit Organizations*. Bloomington: Indiana University Press.

Buechler, Steven (2000) *Social Movements in Advanced Capitalism*. New York: Oxford University Press.

Burton, Antoinette (1994) *Burdens of History: British Feminists, Indian Women, and Imperial Culture, 1865–1915*. Chapel Hill: University of North Carolina Press.

Bystydzienski, Jill, and Joti Sekhon (1999) *Democratization and Women's Grassroots Movements*. Bloomington: Indiana University Press.

Cagatay, Nilufer, Caren Grown, and Aida Santiago (1986) Commentary. The Nairobi Women's Conference: Toward a Global Feminism? *Feminist Studies*, 12 (2), 401–12.

Calhoun, Craig (1993) "New Social movements" of the Early Nineteenth Century. *Social Science History*, 17 (3), 385–428.

Chafetz, Janet, and Anthony Dworkin (1986) *Female Revolt: Women's Movements in World and Historical Perspective*. Totowa, NJ: Rowman & Allanheld.

Chapman, Jenny (1993) *Politics, Feminism, and the Reformation of Gender*. New York: Routledge.

Chassen-Lopez, Francie, and Monica Udvary (2000) Theorizing Women's Collective Forms of Action: Comparative and Critical Perspectives. Paper presented at Gender and Globalization Symposium, University of Illinois.

Christiansen-Ruffman, Linda (1995) Women's Conception of the Political: Three Canadian Women's Organizations. In Myra Marx Ferree and Patricia Yancey Martin (eds.), *Feminist Organizations: Harvest of the New Women's Movement*. Philadelphia, PA: Temple University Press, 372–93.

Clemens, Elisabeth (1993) Organizational Repertoires and Institutional Change: Women's Groups and the Transformation of U.S. Politics, 1890–1920. *American Journal of Sociology*, 98 (4), 755–98.

——(1997) *The People's Lobby: Organizational Innovation and the Rise of Interest Group Politics*. Chicago: University of Chicago Press.

Cockburn, Cynthia (1983) *Brothers: Male Dominance and Technological Change*. London: Pluto.

Cohn, Carol (1987) Sex and Death in the Rational World of Defense Intellectuals. *Signs*, 12 (4), 687–718.

Collins, Patricia Hill (1990) *Black Feminist Thought: Knowledge, Consciousness, and the Politics of Empowerment*. Boston: Unwin Hyman.

Correa, Sonia, and Rebecca Reichmann (1994) *Population and Reproductive Rights: Feminist Perspectives from the South*. Atlantic Highlands, NJ: Zed.

Cott, Nancy (1987) *The Grounding of Modern Feminism*. New Haven: Yale University Press.

Davidson, Denise (2001) Decentering Twentieth-Century Women's Movements. *Contemporary European History*, 10 (3), 503–12.

della Porta, Donatella, and Mario Diani (1999) *Social Movements*. Malden, MA: Blackwell.

Delmar, Rosalind (1986) What Is Feminism? In Juliet Mitchell and Ann Oakley (eds.), *What Is Feminism? A Re-examination*. New York: Pantheon, 8–33.

Einwohner, Rachel L. (1999) Gender, Class, and Social Movement Outcomes: Identity and Effectiveness in Two Animal Rights Campaigns. *Gender & Society*, 13 (1), 56–76.

Evans, Richard (1976) *The Feminist Movement in Germany, 1894–1933*. Thousand Oaks, CA: Sage.

——(1987) *Comrades and Sisters: Feminism, Socialism and Pacifism in Europe, 1870–1945*. New York: St. Martin's.

Evans, Sarah (1979) *Personal Politics: The Roots of Women's Liberation in the Civil Rights Movement and the New Left*. New York: Vintage.

Ferree, Myra Marx (1987) Equality and Autonomy: Feminist Politics in the United States and West Germany. In Mary Katzenstein and Carol McClurg Mueller (eds.), *The Women's Movements of Western Europe and the United States*. Philadelphia, PA: Temple University Press, 172–95.

——(2002) Thinking Globally, Acting Locally: German and American Feminism in the World System. In Silke Roth and Sara Lennox (eds.), *Feminist Movements in a Globalizing World*. Washington, DC: American Institute for Contemporary German Studies, 13–29.

——(forthcoming) The Gendering of Governance and the Governance of Gender. In Barbara Hobson (ed.), *Recognition Struggles*. New York: Cambridge University Press.

Ferree, Myra Marx, and William A. Gamson (1999) The Globalization of Feminism: Abortion Discourse in the US and Germany. In Donatella della Porta, Hanspeter Kriesi, and Dieter Rucht (eds.), *The Globalization of Social Movements*. New York: St. Martin's, 40–56.

Ferree, Myra Marx, and Patricia Yancey Martin (1995) *Feminist Organizations: Harvest of the New Women's Movement*. Philadelphia, PA: Temple University Press.

Ferree, Myra Marx, and David Merrill (2000) Hot Movements, Cold Cognition: Thinking about Social Movements in Gendered Frames. *Contemporary Sociology*, 29 (3), 454–62.

Ferree, Myra Marx, and Silke Roth (1998) Gender, Class and the Interaction among Social Movements: A Strike of West Berlin Daycare Workers. *Gender & Society*, 12 (6), 626–48.

Ferree, Myra Marx, William A. Gamson, Jürgen Gerhards, and Dieter Rucht (2002) *Shaping Abortion Discourse: Democracy and the Public Sphere in Germany and the United States*. New York: Cambridge University Press.

Ferree, Myra Marx, Barbara Risman, Valerie Sperling, Tatyana Gurikova, and Katherine Hyde (1999) The Russian Women's Movement: Activists' Strategies and Identities. *Women and Politics*, 20 (3), 83–109.

Flexner, Eleanor (1959) *Century of Struggle*. Cambridge, MA: Harvard University Press.

Fraser, Arvonne S. (1987) *The U.N. Decade for Women: Documents and Dialogue*. Boulder, CO: Westview.

Fraser, Nancy (1989) *Unruly Practices: Power, Discourse, and Gender in Contemporary Social Theory*. Minneapolis: University of Minnesota Press.

Gal, Susan (forthcoming) Movements of Feminism: The Circulation of Discourses about Women in East-Central Europe. In Barbara Hobson (ed.), *Recognition Struggles*. New York: Cambridge University Press.

Gal, Susan, and Gail Kligman (2000) *The Politics of Gender after Socialism*. Princeton, NJ: Princeton University Press.

Gamson, Joshua (1995) Must Identity Movements Self-destruct? A Queer Dilemma. *Social Problems*, 42 (3), 390–408.

Gamson, William A., and David Meyer (1996) Framing Political Opportunity. In Doug McAdam, John D. McCarthy, and Mayer Zald (eds.), *Comparative Perspectives on Social Movements*. New York: Cambridge University Press, 275–90.

Gerhard, Ute (2000) *Debating Women's Equality*. New Brunswick, NJ: Rutgers University Press.

Giddings, Paula (1984) *When and Where I Enter: The Impact of Black Women on Race and Sex in America*. New York: Bantam.

Glenn, Evelyn Nakano (2002) *Unequal Freedom: How Race and Gender Shaped American Citizenship and Labor*. Cambridge, MA; Harvard University Press.

Gluck, Sherna, with Maylei Blackwell, Sharon Cotrell, and Karen Harper (1998) Whose Feminism, Whose History? Reflections on Excavating the History of (the) US Women's Movements. In Nancy Naples (ed.), *Community Activism and Feminist Politics*. New York: Routledge, 31–56.

Goodwin, Jeffrey, James Jasper, and Francesca Polletta (2001) *Passionate Politics: Emotions and Social Movements*. Chicago: University of Chicago Press.

Gottlick, Jane Berthusen (1999) From the Ground Up: Women's Organizations and Democratization in Russia. In Jill Bystydzienski and Joti Sekhon (eds.), *Democratization and Women's Grassroots Movements*. Bloomington: Indiana University Press, 239–61.

Greenhalgh, Susan (2001) Fresh Winds in Beijing: Chinese Feminists Speak out on the One-Child Policy and Women's Lives. *Signs*, 26 (3), 847–87.

Groves, Julia McAllister (2001) Animal Rights and the Politics of Emotion: Folk Constructions of Emotion in the Animal Rights Movement. In Jeff Goodwin, James M. Jasper, and Francesca Polletta (eds.), *Passionate Politics: Emotions and Social Movements*. Chicago: University of Chicago Press, 212–29.

Halliday, Fred (1999) *Revolution and World Politics*. Durham, NC: Duke University Press.

Heitlinger, Alena (1999) *Émigré Feminism: Transnational Perspectives*. Toronto: University of Toronto Press.

Hercus, Cheryl (1999a) Identity, Emotion, and Feminist Collective Action. *Gender & Society*, 13 (1), 34–55.

——(1999b) Stepping out of Line: A Study of Involvement in Feminist Collective Action. PhD dissertation, School of Psychology and Sociology, James Cook University of North Queensland.

——(forthcoming) *Becoming a Feminist*. New York: Routledge.

Hobson, Barbara (forthcoming) Recognition Struggles in Universalistic and Gender Distinctive Frames: Ireland and Sweden. In Barbara Hobson (ed.), *Recognition Struggles*. Cambridge: Cambridge University Press.

Hochschild, Arlie (1983) *The Managed Heart: Commercialization of Human Feeling*. Berkeley: University of California Press.

Hoganson, Kristin (1998) *Fighting for American Manhood: How Gender Politics Provoked the Spanish-American and Philippine-American Wars*. New Haven: Yale University Press.

Hull, Gloria, Patricia Bell-Scott, and Barbara Smith (1982) *All the Women Are White, and All the Blacks Are Men, but Some of us Are Brave: Black Women's Studies*. Old Westbury, NY: Feminist Press.

Jackson, Cecile, and Ruth Pearson (eds.) (1998) *Feminist Visions of Development: Gender, Analysis and Policy*. New York: Routledge.

Jacquette, Jane (1994) *The Women's Movement in Latin America: Participation and Democracy*. 2nd ed. Boulder, CO: Westview.

Jaggar, Alison (1989) Love and Knowledge: Emotion in Feminist Epistemology. *Inquiry*, 32, 161–76.

Jayawardena, Kumari (1986) *Feminism and Nationalism in the Third World*. London: Zed.

Johnson, Paul (1994) *Success while Others Fail: Social Movement Unionism and the Public Workplace*. Ithaca, NY: ILR.

Kandiyoti, Deniz (ed.) (1991) *Women, Islam and the State*. Philadelphia, PA: Temple University Press.

Kaplan, Gisela (1992) *Contemporary Western European Feminism*. New York: New York University Press.

Kaplan, Temma (1997) *Crazy for Democracy*. New York: Routledge.

Katzenstein, Mary Fainsod (1998) *Faithful and Fearless: Moving Feminist Protest inside the Church and Military*. Princeton, NJ: Princeton University Press.

Keck, Margaret, and Kathryn Sikkink (1998) *Activists beyond Borders: Advocacy Networks in International Politics*. Ithaca, NY: Cornell University Press.

Kessler-Harris, Alice (2001) *In Pursuit of Equity: Women, Men, and the Quest for Economic Citizenship in the Twentieth Century*. New York: Oxford University Press.

Kimmel Michael (1996) *Manhood in America: A Cultural History*. New York: Free Press.

Kimmel, Michael, and Abby L. Ferber (2000) "White Men are this Nation": Right-Wing Militias and the Restoration of Rural American Masculinity. *Rural Sociology*, 65 (4), 582–604.

Klatch, Rebecca (1999) *A Generation Divided: The New Left, the New Right and the 1960s*. Berkeley: University of California Press.

Kontos, Sylvia (1979) *Die Partei kämpft wie ein Mann: Frauenpolitik der KPD in der Weimarer Republik*. Frankfurt am Main: Roter Stern.

Kumar, Krishner (ed.) (2001) *Women and Civil War: Impact, Organizations and Action*. Boulder, CO: Lynne Rienner.

Leidner, Robin (1991) Stretching the Boundaries of Liberalism: Democratic Innovation in a Feminist Organization. *Signs*, 16, 263–89.

Lenz, Ilse (2001) Neue Frauenbewegung, Feminismus und Geschlechterforschung. In Bettina Fritsche, Claudia Nagoda, and Eva Schäfer, *Geschlechterverhältnisse im sozialen Wandel*. Opladen: Leske & Budrich.

Levitsky, Sandra (2001) Narrow but Not Straight: Professionalized Rights Strategies in the Chicago GLBT Movement. MA thesis, University of Wisconsin-Madison.

Lichterman, Paul (1996) *The Search for Political Community: American Activists Reinventing Commitment*. New York: Cambridge University Press.

Lofland, John (1995) Charting Degrees of Movement Culture: Tasks of the Cultural Cartographer. In Hank Johnston and Bert Klandermans (eds.), *Social Movements and Culture*. Minneapolis: University of Minnesota Press, 188–216.

McAdam, Doug (1982) *Political Process and the Development of Black Insurgency, 1930–1970*. Chicago: University of Chicago Press.

McAdam, Doug, John McCarthy, and Meyer Zald (1996) *Comparative Perspectives on Social Movements: Political Opportunities, Mobilizing Structures, Cultural Frames*. New York: Cambridge University Press.

McAdam, Doug, Sidney Tarrow, and Charles Tilly (2001) *The Dynamics of Contention*. New York: Cambridge University Press.

McCammon, Holly, Karen E. Campbell, Ellen M. Granberg, and Christine Mowery (2001) How Movements Win: Gendered Opportunity Structures and United States Women's Suffrage Movements, 1866 to 1991. *American Sociological Review*, 66, 49–70.

McCarthy, John, and Mayer Zald (1977) Resource Mobilization and Social Movements: A Partial Theory. *American Journal of Sociology*, 82 (6), 1212–41.

McComiskey, Marita (2001) Passionately Political Peace-Activist Parents: Nurturing the World while Politicizing the Family. PhD dissertation, University of Connecticut.

Margolis, Diane R. (1993) Women's Movements around the World – Cross-Cultural Comparisons. *Gender & Society*, 7 (3), 379–99.

Martin, Patricia Yancey (1990) Rethinking Feminist Organizations. *Gender & Society*, 4, 182–206.

Melucci, Alberto (1989) *Nomads of the Present*. Philadelphia, PA: Temple University Press.

——(1996) *Challenging Codes*. Cambridge, NY: Cambridge University Press.

Meyer, David, and Nancy Whittier (1994) Social Movement Spillover. *Social Problems*, 41, 277–98.

Meyer, John W., John Boli, George Thomas, and Francisco Ramirez (1997) World Society and the Nation-State. *American Journal of Sociology*, 103, 144–81.

Meyer, Mary K., and Elisabeth Prügl (eds.) (1999) *Gender Politics in Global Governance*. Boulder, CO: Rowman & Littlefield.

Miethe, Ingrid (1999) From "Mother of the Revolution" to "Fathers of Unification": Concepts of Politics among Women Activists Following German Unification. *Social Politics*, 6 (1), 1–22.

Miethe, Ingrid, and Silke Roth (eds.) (2001) *Politische Biografien und sozialer Wandel*. Giessen: Psychosozial.

Miles, Angela (1996) *Integrative Feminisms: Building Global Visions, 1960s–1990s*. New York: Routledge.

Miller, James (1988) *Democracy Is in the Streets: From Port Huron to the Siege of Chicago*. New York: Simon & Schuster.

Moghadam, Valentine (1992) Patriarchy and the Politics of Gender in Modernizing Societies: Iran, Pakistan and Afghanistan. *International Sociology*, 7 (1), 35–53.

——(2000) Transnational Feminist Networks – Collective Action in an Era of Globalization. *International Sociology*, 15 (1), 57–85.

——(2002) Transnational Feminist Networks and the Financing for Development Conference. *Critical Mass Bulletin*, 27 (1), 3–7.

Molyneux, Maxine (1985) Mobilization without Emancipation? Women's Interests, the State and Revolution in Nicaragua. *Feminist Studies*, 11, 225–54.

——(1998) Analyzing Women's Movements. *Development and Change*, 29, 219–45.

Morgen, Sandra (1995) It Was the Best of Times, It Was the Worst of Times: Emotional Discourse in the Work Cultures of Feminist Health Clinics. In Myra Marx Ferree and Patricia Yancey Martin (eds.), *Feminist Organizations*. Philadelphia, PA: Temple University Press, 234–47.

Mueller, Carol (1994) Conflict Networks and the Origins of Women's Liberation. In Enrique Laraña, Hank Johnston, and Joseph Gusfield (eds.), *New Social Movements*. Philadelphia, PA: Temple University Press, 234–63.

——(2002) International Women's Year Conferences as Social Movement Events: English Language Media Coverage. Paper presented at the World Women's Conference, Kampala, Uganda.

Naples, Nancy (1998) *Grassroots Warriors: Activist Mothering, Community Work and the War on Poverty*. New York: Routledge.

Noonan, Rita (1995) Women against the State: Political Opportunities and Collective Action Frames in Chile's Transition to Democracy. *Sociological Forum*, 10, 81–111.

O'Brien, Robert, Ann Marie Goetz, Jan Aart Scholte, and Marc Williams (2000) *Contesting Global Governance: Multilateral Economic Institutions and Global Social Movements*. New York: Cambridge University Press.

Offen, Karen (1988) Defining Feminism: A Comparative Historical Approach. *Signs*, 14 (1), 119–57.

——(2000) *European Feminisms 1700–1950: A Political History*. Stanford: Stanford University Press.

Oliver, Pamela E., and Hank Johnston (2000) What a Good Idea! Ideologies and Frames in Social Movement Research. *Mobilization*, 5 (1), 37–54.

Outshoorn, Joyce (2001) Debating Prostitution in Parliament: A Feminist Analysis. *European Journal of Women's Studies*, 8 (4), 472–90.

Pardo, Mary (1995) Doing it for the Kids: Mexican American Community Activists, Border Feminists? In Myra Marx Ferree and Patricia Yancey Martin, *Feminist Organizations*. Philadelphia, PA: Temple University Press, 356–71.

Pateman, Carol (1988) *The Sexual Contract*. Stanford: Stanford University Press.

Payne, Charles (1990) Men Led, but Women Organized: Movement Participation of Women in the Mississippi Delta. In Guida West and Rhoda Blumberg (eds.), *Women and Social Protest*. New York: Oxford University Press, 156–65.

Peterson, V. Spike, and Anne Sisson Runyan (1999) *Global Gender Issues*. Boulder, CO: Westview.

Phelan, Shane (1989) *Identity Politics: Lesbian-Feminism and the Limits of Community*. Philadelphia, PA: Temple University Press.

Pietilea, Hilkkä, and Jean Vickers (1990) *Making Women Matter: The Role of the United Nations*. London: Zed.

Pinl, Claudia (1977) *Das Arbeitnehmerpatriarchat: Die Frauenpolitik der Gewerkschaften*. Cologne: Kiepenheuer & Witsch.

Polletta, Francesa (2002) *Freedom Is an Endless Meeting: Democracy in American Social Movements*. Chicago: University of Chicago Press.

Ramirez, Francisco, Yasmin Soysal, and S. Shanahan (1997) The Changing Logic of Political Citizenship: Cross-National Acquisition of Women's Suffrage Rights, 1890 to 1990. *American Sociological Review*, 62 (5), 735–45.

Ray, Raka (1999) *Fields of Protest: Women's Movements in India*. Minneapolis: University of Minnesota Press.

Ray, Raka, and A. C. Korteweg (1999) Women's Movements in the Third World: Identity, Mobilization, and Autonomy. *Annual Review of Sociology*, (25), 47–71.

Roberts, Dorothy (1997) *Killing the Black Body: Race, Reproduction, and the Meaning of Liberty*. New York: Vintage.

Robnett, Belinda (1997) *How Long? How Long? African American Women in the Struggle for Civil Rights.* New York: Oxford University Press.

Rossi, Alice (1982) *Feminists in Politics: A Panel Analysis of the First National Women's Conference.* New York: Academic.

Roth, Rachel (2000) *Making Women Pay: The Hidden Costs of Fetal Rights.* Ithaca, NY: Cornell University Press.

Roth, Silke (2000) Developing Working Class Feminism: A Biographical Approach to Social Movement Participation. In Sheldon Stryker, Timothy Owens, and Robert White (eds.), *Self, Identity and Social Movements.* Minneapolis: University of Minnesota Press, 300–23.

——(2003) *Building Movement Bridges: The Coalition of Labor Union Women.* Boulder, CO: Westview.

Rupp, Leila (1997) *Worlds of Women: The Making of an International Women's Movement.* Princeton, NJ: Princeton University Press.

Rupp, Leila, and Verta Taylor (1987) *Survival in the Doldrums: The American Women's Rights Movement, 1945 to the 1960s.* New York: Oxford University Press.

——(1999) Forging Feminist Identity in an International Movement: A Collective Identity Approach to Twentieth-Century Feminism. *Signs,* 24 (2), 363–86.

Ryan, Barbara (1992) *Feminism and the Women's Movement.* New York: Routledge.

Schwalbe, Michael (1996) *Unlocking the Iron Cage: The Men's Movement, Gender Politics, and American Culture.* New York: Oxford University Press.

Scott, Ellen (1998) Creating Partnerships for Change: Alliances and Betrayals in the Racial Politics of two Feminist Organizations. *Gender & Society,* 12 (4), 400–23.

Sehgal, Meera (2002) The Gendered Mobilization of Collective Fear in Right Wing Movements: The Emotional Socialization of Female Activists at Hindu Nationalist Paramilitary Camps in India. Paper Presented at Gendered Citizenship conference, Center for Advanced Feminist Studies, University of Minnesota, May.

Seidman, Gay (1993) "No Freedom without the Women": Mobilization and Gender in South Africa, 1970–1992. *Signs: Journal of Women in Culture and Society,* 18 (2), 291–320.

——(1999) Gendered Citizenship: South Africa's Democratic Transition and the Construction of a Gendered State. *Gender & Society,* 13 (3), 287–307.

——(2001) Feminist Interventions: The South African Gender Commission and "Strategic" Challenges to Gender Inequality. *Ethnography,* 2 (2), 219–42.

Sered, Susan (1998) "Woman" as Symbol and Women as Agents: Gendered Religious Discourses and Practices. In Myra Marx Ferree, Judith Lorber, and Beth B. Hess (eds.), *Revisioning Gender.* Thousand Oaks, CA: Sage, 193–221.

Silliman, J. (1999) Expanding Civil Society, Shrinking Political Spaces: The Case of Women's Nongovernmental Organizations. *Social Politics,* 6 (1), 23–53.

Sinha, Mrinalini, Donna Guy, and Angela Woollacott (1999) *Feminisms and Internationalism: Gender and History.* Special Issue. Oxford: Blackwell.

Sklar, Kathryn Kish, Anja Schüler, and Susan Strasser (eds.) (1998) *Social Justice Feminists in the United States and Germany: A Dialogue in Documents, 1885–1933.* Ithaca, NY: Cornell University Press.

Solinger, Rickie (1998) *Abortion Wars: A Half-Century of Strugle, 1950–2000.* Berkeley: University of California Press.

Soule, Sarah A., Doug McAdam, John McCarthy, and Yang Su (1999) Protest Events: Cause or Consequence of State Action? The U.S. Women's Movement and Federal Congressional Activities, 1956–1979. *Mobilization,* 4 (2), 239–56.

Spelman, Elisabeth (1988) *Inessential Woman: Problems of Exclusion in Feminist Thought.* Boston: Beacon.

Sperling, Valerie (1999) *Organizing Women in Contemporary Russia: Engendering Transition.* New York: Cambridge University Press.

Sperling, Valerie, Myra Marx Ferree, and Barbara J. Risman (2001) Constructing Global Feminism: Transnational Advocacy Networks and Russian Women's Activism. *Signs*, 26 (4), 1155–86.

Stall, Susan, and Randy Stoecker (1998) Community Organizing or Organizing Community? Gender and the Crafts of Empowerment. *Gender & Society*, 12 (6), 729–56.

Stephen, Lynn (1997) *Women and Social Movements in Latin America*. Austin: University of Texas Press.

Stienstra, Deborah (1994) *Women's Movements and International Organizations*. London: St. Martin's.

Stone, Deborah (2003) *Policy Paradox: The Art of Political Decision Making*, 3rd ed. New York: W. W. Norton.

Stryker, Sheldon, Timothy Owens, and Robert White (2000) *Self, Identity and Social Movements*. Minneapolis: University of Minnesota Press.

Sturgeon, Noël (1997) *Ecofeminist Natures: Race, Gender, Feminist Theory and Political Action*. New York: Routledge.

Subramaniam, Mangala (2000) Translating Participation in Informal Organizations into Empowerment: Women in Rural India. PhD dissertation, University of Connecticut.

Tarrow, Sidney (1998) *Power in Movement*, 2nd ed. New York: Cambridge University Press.

Taylor, Barbara (1983) *Eve and the New Jerusalem: Socialism and Feminism in the Nineteenth Century*. London: Virago.

Taylor, Verta (1995) Watching for Vibes: Bringing Emotions into the Study of Feminist Organizations. In Myra Marx Ferree and Patricia Yancey Martin (eds.), *Feminist Organizations: Harvest of the New Women's Movement*. Philadelphia, PA: Temple University Press, 223–33.

——(1996) *Rock-a-by Baby: Feminism, Identity and Post-Partum Depression*. New York: Routledge.

Tétreault, Mary Ann (1994) *Women and Revolution in Africa, Asia and the New World*. Columbia, SC: University of South Carolina Press.

Thompson, E. P. (1964) *The Making of the English Working Class*. New York: Pantheon.

Tilly, Charles (1995) To Explain Political Processes. *American Journal of Sociology*, 100, 1594–1610.

Tinker, Irene (1990) The Making of a Field: Advocates, Practioners, Scholars. In I. Tinker (ed.), *Persistent Inequalities*. New York: Oxford University Press, 27–53.

Tripp, Aili Mari (2000) Women's Mobilization and Societal Autonomy in Comparative African Perspective. In Aili Tripp (ed.), *Women and Politics in Uganda*. Madison: University of Wisconsin Press, 1–28.

Twine, France Windance, and Kathleen Blee (2001) *Feminism and Antiracism: International Struggles for Justice*. New York: New York University Press.

Vaid, Urvashi (1995) *Virtual Equality: The Mainstreaming of Gay and Lesbian Liberation*. New York: Anchor.

West, Lois A. (1999) The United Nations Women's Conferences and Feminist Politics. In Mary K. Meyer and Elisabeth Prügl (eds.), *Gender Politics in Global Governance*. Boulder, CO: Rowman & Littlefield, 177–93.

Whittier, Nancy (1995) *Feminist Generations: The Persistence of the Radical Women's Movement*. Philadelphia, PA: Temple University Press.

Woolf, Virginia (1938) *Three Guineas*. London: Hogarth.

Yuval Davis, Nira (1997) *Gender and Nation*. Thousand Oaks, CA: Sage.

26

Environmental Movements

CHRISTOPHER ROOTES

INTRODUCTION

The environmental movement has been described as "the most comprehensive and influential movement of our time" (Castells 1997: 67). Indeed, "it is entirely possible that when the history of the twentieth century is finally written, the single most important social movement of the period will be judged to be environmentalism" (Nisbet 1982: 101).

Grand claims have been made for the centrality of the environmental movement to processes of macrosocial and political change. Thus Touraine et al. (1983) saw in the ecology movement of the late 1970s the embryo of the transformative social movement that would be to the "postindustrial" society what the working-class movement promised to be for industrial society. Robert Brulle (2000: 101) suggests that, because it is able "to mobilize a wide variety of symbolic and material resources over a sustained period," the environmental movement is capable of the scarcely less ambitious task of recreating civil society, an undertaking that is essential if humankind is to be saved from the destructive logics of the market and the state. Moreover, the environmental movement is often regarded as a uniquely global social movement and one that is pioneering the development of a global civil society (Wapner 1996).

Certainly, environmental movements are the great survivors of the wave of new social movements that arose throughout the industrialized Western democracies from the 1960s through the 1980s. Despite fluctuations in the salience of environmental issues over the years, they and the organizations that arose from them enjoy widespread public support. Moreover, in most industrialized countries, the public is more inclined to trust what environmental movement organizations (EMOs) tell them about environmental issues than what they are told by governments or corporations (Worcester 1999: 40; Christie and Jarvis 2001: 141).

EMOs are supported by millions of citizens in Western industrialized countries. In the US, in 1995 over 10,000 environmental organizations, with a combined membership of over 41 million, annual income of $2.7 billion and assets of $5.8 billion, had registered as tax-exempt bodies with the Internal Revenue Service (Brulle 2000: 102–4). The density of EMO membership is at least as high in several Western European countries.

Many EMOs in many countries have become substantial operations and have acquired many of the characteristics of formal, bureaucratized organizations (Jordan and Maloney 1997; van der Heijden 1997; Rawcliffe 1998: 23; Diani and Donati 1999). Externally, too, environmentalism has become institutionalized. Ecology has become established as an academic discipline, and universities and colleges now routinely offer programs and courses dealing with environmental issues. Environmental journalism, which has become a recognized specialism, and mass media not only carry programs, sections, or columns dedicated to the environment, but routinely report on environmental issues as part of their general coverage. Environmental protection agencies have become nearly universal, and environment ministries have been established and have moved from the margins of government closer to the centers of power.

Environmental issues have moved up the political agenda to become embedded in the programs of mainstream political parties. Green parties have become established in most liberal democratic states of the industrialized world and collectively constitute the most significant new "party family" to emerge since the rise of social democracy in the first half of the twentieth century (Richardson and Rootes 1995). Greens have achieved representation in the European Parliament and in the parliaments and local assemblies of most European and Australasian states, have held government office in three of the four largest Western European states (Germany, France, and Italy) as well as in Belgium and Finland, and have come to appear to be indispensable electoral allies of social democratic parties unable to secure parliamentary majorities in their own right (Müller-Rommel and Poguntke 2002).

Yet, intriguingly, despite all this evidence of institutionalization, environmental movements appear in a number of countries to have escaped many of its negative consequences. Environmental issues have not lost their capacity to stimulate popular mobilizations, environmental protest has not disappeared, and recurrent waves of environmental mobilization revitalize the movement by introducing thematic and organizational innovation.

DEFINING ENVIRONMENTAL MOVEMENTS

Conceptions of the environmental movement are as various as those of social movements in general. The chief difference has been between a mainly American tradition that adopts a catholic, nominalist, and empirical approach, and a European macrosociological tradition that conceives of social movements restrictively as agents of profound structural change or, at least, as extraordinary phenomena of periods of dramatic social change. From the perspective of the latter, the continuing existence of an environmental movement is problematic.

Thus Eyerman and Jamison (1991: 103–8) conceive of the modern environmental movement as that relatively brief period between the constitution of the "knowledge interests" that define the movement and their institutionalization. The movement has all but ceased to exist now that "its movement intellectuals have grown into new kinds of established intellectuals" (Eyerman and Jamison 1991: 66). For Jamison et al. (1990: 197–8), "to be a social movement, a collection of organizations, groups, and individual activists must develop and attempt to realize a collective project, based on specific knowledge interests. It is that which gives identity to a movement and which makes it a potential force for fundamental social change." The fragmentation of the movement into specialized groups with problematic relationships to one another, and the incorporation of movement intellectuals and concerns, make it questionable whether it is any longer a social movement. For Eyerman and Jamison, the institutionalization of a social movement is a contradiction in terms.

Such a restrictive approach sits uncomfortably with common usage in which those inside and outside environmentalist circles continue to refer to "the environmental movement" as a present reality. Nevertheless, a social movement is not a natural object but a social construct and, for the social scientist, it is a theoretical construct whose purpose is to assist understanding and explanation. Following Weber, it is best conceived as an ideal type, an abstraction from social reality whose relation to that reality is necessarily not one of precise identity. Adapting what Diani (1992) describes as the consensual definition of a social movement that emerges from recent literature, an environmental movement may be defined as a loose, noninstitutionalized network of informal interactions that may include, as well as individuals and groups who have no organizational affiliation, organizations of varying degrees of formality, that are engaged in collective action motivated by shared identity or concern about environmental issues (cf. Diani 1995: 5).[1]

The advantage of the network approach over the cognitive approach is that the former focuses attention upon the linkages among the putative constituents of a social movement. Whether they do indeed constitute a movement is then an empirical question to be settled by scrutiny of the network links, collective action, and evidence of shared identity, all of which are essential to the identification of a movement. From this perspective, modern semi-institutionalized environmental movements are not abolished by definition but may be analyzed and compared. The chief disadvantage of this approach is that it is not clear how much networking, collective action, or shared concern is required to constitute a movement. Clearly these are not black and white but matters of degree, points on a continuum. The forms and intensity of both action and concern, and the degree of integration of the network, may vary considerably from place to place and from time to time.

It is, nevertheless, important to distinguish the movement from its most visible manifestations. An environmental movement is identical neither with environmental movement organizations (nor any one of them) nor with episodes of environmental protest. Although there may be many formal environmental organizations and many environmental protests, it is only when such organizations (and other actors) are networked one with another and engaged in collective action that an environmental movement can sensibly be identified. Doherty (2002) proposes that the employment of direct action methods of protest is a defining characteristic of a social movement and that, therefore, those more institutionalized environmental organizations that do not characteristically resort to protest lie outside the "green" movement. That, however, appears to privilege forms of action over identity and networks, and it omits to consider the extent to which hitherto radical forms of protest are no longer unconventional but instead form part of the extended repertoire of political action in liberal democracies. For that reason it seems preferable to construe collective action broadly and to consider variations within a broad environmental movement rather than to define that movement narrowly at the outset (cf. della Porta and Diani 1999: 15).

Some observers contend that such is the specialization and fragmentation of activity among organizations concerned with environmental issues that it no longer makes sense to speak of an environmental "movement" (Bosso 2000: 73; Jamison 2001).[3] Bosso, writing of the US at the end of the 1990s, suggests that environmentalism has become an "interest group community," but it is by no means clear why an interest group community and an environmental movement should not coexist.

The question whether environmentalism is any longer a movement is an empirical one, and the answer – in terms of networks, collective action, and shared identity or concern – may not be the same in all countries at any one point in time. One major obstacle to answering the question definitively is that the linkages amongst the constituent actors and organizations of an increasingly mature environmental movement are not always readily visible. Now that they are well past the first flush of novelty, the balance of environmental movement actions has shifted from highly visible protest to lobbying and "constructive engagement" with governments and corporations, much of which is publicly invisible but which, no less than more public forms of protest, contests established economic and social relationships and cultural understandings. As a result, in the countries where environmentalism has become most entrenched, the full range of movement activities is unlikely any longer to be visible to those whose knowledge of the movement is dependent entirely upon reports in mass media. The more established EMOs are generally engaged in less public activities; new, less formally organized, often local groups proliferate; and there are many informal and "subterranean" linkages among groups and organizations. As a result, arguments about the persistence or decline of environmental movements cannot be settled by the evidence of media reports, the casual empiricism of newspaper readers is apt to mislead, and statements about trends must be treated with caution.[4]

There are particular difficulties in ascertaining the extent of network links and shared identity in a country like the US which is geographically extensive and politically decentralized. Network structures will be different, and network links easier to identify, in geographically compact and politically centralized states. Nevertheless, research in Western Europe suggests that, even at the end of the 1990s, at a time when in many countries the environmental movement might be considered at least as mature as that in the US, there was, within countries, sufficient evidence of network links among EMOs, sufficient engagement in collective action, and sufficient shared concern to warrant continued use of the term "environmental movement" (Rootes 2003b). Already by the mid-1980s, relations among European EMOs were predominantly cooperative (Dalton 1994: 170), even across the mostly rhetorical divide between environmental and ecological groups. With the greater maturity of the movement during the 1990s, linkages and cooperation among its diverse constituents appear to have increased rather than declined, even if collective action has in some cases become less visible. In Britain, which has perhaps the most organizationally specialized and diverse environmental movement in Europe, national EMOs do not regard one another as competitors but instead practice a division of labor that recognizes the particular competences and styles of the various organizations (Rootes 1999a).

THE EVOLUTION OF ENVIRONMENTALISM: CONSERVATION, PRESERVATION, AND REFORM ENVIRONMENTALISM

The history of environmentalism and EMOs has most often been represented as one of the succession of conservationism, environmentalism, and ecologism (Rucht 1989; Mertig et al. 2002). Any such typologization is necessarily a simplification, and its presentation as a universal historical sequence is in some respects misleading,[5] but it will serve to organize this discussion.

In many countries, including the US, hunting was an important initial stimulus to nature conservation. Thus the forests and parks of European royalty and nobility were the precursors of reserved areas that in due course became state or national parks. Hunters, conscious of the depletion of the populations of the game they hunted, developed knowledge of and interest in the preservation of its habitat, and were prominent in efforts to establish reserves where game species might be protected. As a result, late into the twentieth century, pro-hunting and antihunting groups coexisted within broad environmental organizations. The predominantly utilitarian concerns of hunters were shared by early conservationists who saw forests as a precious natural resource to be conserved.

Preservationists reasserted a spiritual relationship between humankind and nature. Already informing the Romantic movement in Europe, such ideas were firmly established in the US by the mid-nineteenth century in the Arcadianism of Thoreau and the celebration of wilderness as an alternative to the ills of urban industrial civilization. So long as conservationists were concerned principally with the protection of land from exploitation, there was little or no conflict between them and preservationists, but when it was proposed to exploit the resources so conserved, differences became apparent. In the US these came to a head in the first decade of the twentieth century with the decision to dam the wild Hetch Hetchy Valley, within the Yosemite Park, to provide water for San Francisco. Never accepted by preservationists, this propelled groups such as the Sierra Club to campaign for the more secure protection of National Parks (Brulle 2000: 167–8).

Although preservationism has been effective in securing the protection of wildlife and substantial wilderness areas, it is "a limited discourse" that has not sought wide-ranging social change as a condition of the protection of the natural environment (Brulle 2000: 172). As a result, preservationists have tended to limit themselves to short-term pragmatic politics and have generally employed conventional political strategies and the oligarchical organizational structures appropriate to them.

During the nineteenth and early twentieth centuries, campaigns were waged for clean water, safe disposal of sewage and other waste, clean air, and better public health in the industrialized areas of Europe, the US and Australia. This "reform environmentalism" recognized that humankind is part of nature and that the health of human populations is intimately bound up with the health of ecosystems, but it remained a discourse apart from those of conservation and preservation. Indeed, until the latter half of the twentieth century, reform environmentalism appears to have been a discrete series of campaigns mounted by distinct and separate interest groups rather than a single coherent social movement (Hutton and Connors 1999: 86; Brulle 2000: 181). Only with further advances in scientific knowledge and the development of ecology as a discipline did reform environmentalism acquire coherence and become established as the dominant discourse of environmentalism.

On both sides of the Atlantic, demands for environmental protection were fed both by increasing scientific understanding of the unintended consequences of rampant industrialization and by individuals' personal experience of environmental degradation. Even before postwar reconstruction restored prosperity in Europe, measures were taken to improve environmental conditions believed to impact adversely upon human health. In England, the Clean Air Act of 1956 was a direct response to the 4,000 deaths attributed to the London smog of December 1952. In the US, environmental reform restarted under the Kennedy administration of the early 1960s and gained momentum with the publication of Rachel Carson's *Silent Spring* in 1962. As a consensus issue at a time when the US was bitterly divided over Vietnam, it prospered under the administrations of Presidents Johnson and, especially, Nixon. The process of reform thereafter was continuous if not always steady, following a logic of development that interacted with but was not simply dependent upon the social movement mobilization and political critique of the late 1960s. Indeed, reform environmentalism has been limited in its interest in and capacity for political mobilization, let alone sharp political critique. Because it is based upon arguments within a natural scientific framework, it does not extend to an analysis of the social origins of environmental problems, and it has generally sustained oligarchic organizations often substantially dependent upon the economic support of foundations (Dowie 1995; Brulle 2000: 191–3).

The Formation of the Modern Environmental Movement

Although environmentalism has a long history, the developments in and since the late 1960s mark a step change in the mobilization of environmental movements. Remarkably, it was, as with many developments associated with the student revolt, an innocent beginning: "the modern environmental movement set out on a path it thought to be wholly novel, the subsequent discovery of precursors being an unlooked for surprise" (Hay 2002: 26).

Increasing scientific understanding of environmental impacts and the extension of higher education to ever larger proportions of the population contributed to increasing public awareness of and concern about environmental degradation that had itself accelerated as a result of the increasingly effective technological exploitation of scientific knowledge. The development of the movement was facilitated too by the development of mass media that transmitted images and information more effectively and made communication and travel cheaper and easier. The dramatic growth in the numbers of "members" and supporters of EMOs was made possible by their effective exploitation of new techniques of polling and direct mail marketing (Mitchell et al. 1992: 16–17). But, crucially, the emergence of the environmental movement was made possible by the new political space opened up by the student revolt and the New Left.

Although criticism of the degradation of the natural environment was part of the New Left's critique of consumerist capitalism, it was seldom central to it, and the idealism and utopianism that came to characterize environmentalism in and from the 1960s, particularly in the US, also had other sources. Moreover, to the extent that the New Left emphasized the systemic sources of environmental ills rather than individual responsibility, it came into conflict with the reformist environmentalism of established environmental groups (Gottlieb 1993: 97) and with some counter-cultural elements. The sudden implosion of the US New Left in 1970 curtailed its influence on environmentalism. The countercultural movement that coexisted with and outlasted the New Left was perhaps more influential. Although the communes so characteristic of the counterculture in the early 1970s mostly disappeared during the following decade, diffuse countercultural environmentalism – "part cultural expression, part social dissatisfaction, part search for new environmental values" – had a more enduring impact. Differing "in both language and focus" from earlier manifestations of environmentalism, "the counterculture, along with the New Left, served as a transition to a new environmental politics in which the question of Nature could no longer be separated from the question of society itself" (Gottlieb 1993: 105). The Los Angeles smogs and major pollution incidents such as the 1969 Santa Barbara oil spill were critical in demonstrating that it was not only the urban poor who were vulnerable to environmental degradation (Rothman 1998: 102).

Earth Day 1970, in which 20 million Americans participated in a wide variety of actions designed to highlight environmental issues, can be seen both as the culmination of the environmental critique that developed during the 1960s and as a critical point in the transition toward the institutionalization of environmentalism in the US (Dowie 1995). The organizers of Earth Day drew on the radical activism of the 1960s but attempted to transcend it by forging a new environmentalist consensus. In this it was at best partially successful but it probably did encourage the Nixon administration to proceed with environmental protection measures, including the foundation of the Environmental Protection Agency.

The student revolt, the New Left and the critique of capitalism's assault on the environment were not confined to the US but had parallels in Western Europe (Dalton 1994: 36–7; Doherty 2002: 33–8) and in Australia (Hutton and Connors 1999: 126). The students and young graduates who raised the critique of consumerist capitalism were mostly schooled in the humanities and social sciences, but the development of the environmental movement was often associated with students and graduates of the natural sciences, and so reflected an early stage in the social as well as intellectual diffusion of New Left ideas.[7] Another interwoven strand was that of the peace movement. Its development, from the late 1970s, into a movement focused especially upon opposition to the deployment of nuclear weapons was paralleled by the development of campaigns against the civil uses of nuclear energy. Particularly in Germany, but also in Australia, the conjunction of these strands was a powerful driver to political innovation and, ultimately, to the formation of Green parties. In the US, however, in the 1970s campaigns against nuclear power conjoined with those against toxic industrial waste to produce a movement against the dumping of hazardous military and industrial waste that later developed into the environmental justice movement.

Although the development of the modern environmental movement was undoubtedly influenced by the ideas and campaigns of 1960s New Leftism, it was by no means simply a product of them. Quite independently, increasing awareness of the environmental depredations of economic development was generating increasing dissatisfaction with the social conservatism and political timidity of established conservation organizations. In the US, David Brower, forced from office in the Sierra

Club, founded Friends of the Earth (FoE). Recognizing the global character of environmental issues, Brower encouraged the formation of FoE organizations in France and England, but neither their local autonomy nor the nominally participatory structures that were to become characteristic of FoE were part of Brower's original plan. Brower's vision collided – productively – with the spirit of the times and so a distinctive and highly adaptable organizational dimension was added to modern environmentalism. Greenpeace, too, developed out of urgent concerns to act and to bear witness but, unlike FoE, it had, outside the US, little time for the other legacies of the New Left, becoming instead a professionalized campaigning organization distinguished by its skillful use of mass media.[8] Although the new ecology groups such as FoE and Greenpeace were radical in their self-image and, by comparison with older environmental organizations, in their tactics, their agenda and strategies were generally moderate and, though highly critical of existing social and political arrangements, did not usually envisage fundamental systemic change (Dalton 1994: 131, 145–9). They thus appear less a radical departure from reform environmentalism than a revitalization of it.

Dissatisfaction with the philosophical and political shortcomings of reform environmentalism led, in both Europe and North America, to the development of various strands of political ecologism. The most radical of this "fourth wave" (Dowie 1995: ch. 8), deep ecology, starts from the proposition that all living things are part of a single natural system in which no part is of more intrinsic value than any other. It prioritizes the defense of wilderness and is radically critical of the impact of human activity upon the natural environment. Unlike reform environmentalism, which in at least some of its manifestations is anthropocentric, deep ecology is resolutely ecocentric even to the point of hostility to humankind as the perpetrator of greatest damage to other elements of the ecosystem. Their mistrust of humankind has led deep ecologists to prioritize direct action in defense of the natural environment rather than the building of social movement organizations. Accordingly, their organizations are typically small and command few resources and, in the US, are almost uniformly oligarchic, tend to be dominated by charismatic individuals, and have no capacity for conventional political action (Brulle 2000: 203–7). Less surprisingly, deep ecology has attracted more followers in those countries where there is still wilderness to preserve than in countries where valued landscapes are more obviously human artifacts. This probably explains why Earth First!, the best known incarnation of deep ecology in the US, has in Britain been from the outset much less obviously ecocentric and more involved with reformist environmental campaigns even if for more than merely reformist reasons.

Although issues of equity in the distribution of environmental burdens informed the early stages of reform environmentalism, environmental justice emerged as a distinct discourse and prominent strand of environmentalism only in the 1980s. From this perspective, it is existing structures of social organization that are the ultimate causes of environmental degradation, and the remedy for that degradation requires fundamental social change and the empowerment of local communities (Brulle 2000: 207–8). In the US, because the communities that host or neighbor waste dumps and noxious industries are disproportionately the homes of people of color and perhaps, too, because in the post–civil rights era, the charge of racism has such profound political resonance, proponents of environmental justice have often framed the problem as one of environmental racism (Cole and Foster 2001).

Although the US environmental justice movement is the best known exemplar of this discourse, it has also and increasingly been articulated by environmentalists in other countries, particularly in the Third World where poverty has been increasingly identified as the immediate cause of the deforestation and unsustainable agricultural and industrial practices that contribute to environmental degradation further afield.[9] One of the most interesting developments of the last decade of the twentieth century, particularly after the 1992 Rio Earth Summit, was the increasingly close relationship between aid and development NGOs and internationally oriented EMOs, many of the latter having expanded their remit to encompass issues of sustainable development.

Another strand of the "fourth wave," ecofeminism, has emphasized the special affinity between women and women's roles in society and interests in environmental protection (Shiva 1989; Mellor 1997; Salleh 1997). Although women and their concerns have been prominent in less formally organized local environmental campaigns (Mertig et al. 2002: 471), ecofeminism has developed principally as a critical discourse within environmental philosophy and has given rise to few and relatively small organizations in Western industrialized countries. In such less-industrialized countries as India and Kenya women have played important roles in environmental activism.

The most recent development and, at the beginning of the twenty-first century, perhaps the fastest growing strand of environmentalism in the US, ecotheology develops themes of the major religious traditions as critiques of the degradation of the natural environment. It invests the natural world with spiritual value and treats environmental degradation as an offense against divine creation and a dereliction of sacred duty (Brulle 2000: 229–35). Although ecotheology can be found in most societies, its significance is greatest in societies in which religious observance is still widespread. It is potentially most subversive where, as in the US, it is invoked as a critique of the previously dominant Christian view that human dominion over the natural world was divinely ordained and justified unlimited human exploitation of the natural environment.[10]

The "fourth wave" of environmentalism is philosophically and organizationally diverse. It remains an open question how well these concerns and the organizations that carry them can be integrated either one with another or with discourses and organizations that developed in the course of previous waves of environmentalism, but the environmental movement has in the past proved remarkably syncretic and pragmatic. Indeed, its history, on both sides of the Atlantic, has been one of successive waves of critique, innovation, and incorporation. Greenpeace and Friends of the Earth arose in response to the perceived inadequacies of conservationism, and radical ecologist groupings and the environmental justice movement (EJM) have in turn grown out of dissatisfaction with increasingly institutionalized reform environmentalism.

Many of the organizations formed in those previous waves not only survive but they have, to varying degrees, adapted to accommodate more recent concerns and developments in ecological consciousness. In the US, observers doubt that established, "wilderness obsessed" EMOs are capable of accommodating the concerns of the EJM (Dowie 1995) but recent changes within the Sierra Club and the local efforts of Greenpeace in California suggest that some at least take the environmental justice agenda seriously. In Western Europe, established EMOs such as the World Wildlife

Fund (WWF) and the national bird protection societies have developed a more inclusive ecological perspective and have broadened the range of their campaigns to include issues of habitat and the welfare of human populations (Rootes et al. 2000). Moreover, even in the US, local environmental campaigners often "discover" neglected issues that better resourced national EMOs then take up (Carmin 1999). The rhetoric of conflict and critique may give a misleading impression of the divisions within environmental movements whose existence can be demonstrated by the persistence, despite such differences, of network links of varying degrees of strength and intensity (Dalton 1994: 168–76; Rootes and Miller 2000; Rucht and Roose 2001).

THE SOCIAL BASES OF ENVIRONMENTAL ACTIVISM

Most research on the social backgrounds of environmental activists and the members of national EMOs has concluded that they are disproportionately highly educated and employed in the teaching, creative, welfare, or caring professions (Cotgrove 1982; Kriesi 1989) and, especially, the sons and daughters of the highly educated (Rootes 1995). As a result, environmentalism has sometimes been interpreted as the self-interested politics of a "new class" of traffickers in culture and symbols, opposed or indifferent to the interests of those whose labor involves the manipulation of material things. However, such arguments must reckon with the fact that environmental activists are by no means exclusively drawn from such backgrounds, and they founder on the abundant evidence that support for or approval of EMOs and environmental activism, as well as pro-environment attitudes, are much more widely socially distributed and extend to most segments of society (Mertig and Dunlap 2001).

Grassroots environmental movements also appear to involve a much broader cross-section of society than do the major national EMOs (Freudenberg and Steinsapir 1992). This is in part because locally unwanted land uses are more often imposed upon the poor than upon the affluent, with the result that even a relatively lower incidence of community resistance among the former results in relatively large numbers of campaigns. The fact that women play more prominent roles in grass-roots mobilizations than in national EMOs may reflect women's greater attachment to and confidence in acting in the local community than in the wider public sphere, but it also reflects the fact that the barriers to entry to the local political sphere are lower and confer fewer lasting advantages upon those in possession of the resources relevant to participation in national politics. Thus grass-roots environmental activism is, as well as an important means of social learning about environmental issues and a school for participation generally, an entry point for new activists and new issues. For that reason, it is also a source of revitalization of the environmental movement and a means by which it may be made more socially representative (cf. Carmin 1999).

VALUES

The work most frequently invoked to characterize and explain values and attitudes favorable to environmentalism is that of Ronald Inglehart (1977). Inglehart purported to identify a revolution in values in advanced industrialized states in which postmaterial values that prioritized aesthetic, intellectual, and self-actualization needs were gradually becoming more widely held at the expense of materialist values that placed a higher priority on economic and security needs. Inglehart proposed that this value change was occurring chiefly because new, younger generations raised in relative affluence and security were replacing older generations more likely to have experienced economic privation and the insecurities of war during their formative years. Inglehart included the rise of environmentalism as one of the consequences of the increasing prevalence of post-materialism, but the correlation between the environmental item in Inglehart's battery and the index of postmaterialism was weak. In fact, it fell neatly in the middle between the materialist and postmaterialist clusters (Inglehart 1977: 43–8). This suggests that postmaterialism may not be as good a predictor of environmentalism as has been supposed. Environmental concerns embrace both postmaterialist esthetic and principled concerns with environmental protection *and* essentially materialist concerns with safety and security. Even global environmental concern, so often portrayed as unproblematically postmaterialist, might be represented as a materialist concern. It is, then, not surprising that those who have explored the various dimensions of environmental concern have painted a more complex picture.

Pakulski and Crook (1998) distinguished between concern with the "brown" issues of pollution and environmental hazards, and the "green" concern with the preservation of relatively pristine natural environments. Examining Australian survey evidence, they found that postmaterialism was correlated positively with "green" but negatively with "brown" concerns. "Brown" concerns were more wide-spread in the population, but were much less likely than "green" concerns to be associated with environmental activism. This finding may help to make sense of the patterns of environmental concern and action elsewhere. In both Southern and Eastern Europe large majorities profess concern about the environment, but their concern more often than in Northern Europe takes the form of "personal complaint" about the possible effects of environmental degradation upon the health and welfare of respondents and their families, rather than "global concern" (Hofrichter and Reif 1990). Despite high levels of concern about the environment, EMOs in these countries generally attract only small numbers of supporters.

"Global green awareness" appears to be associated with "postmaterialism," and "materialism" with "personal complaint" and fear of environmental hazards. The connection appears to be education. As well as being less likely than the less educated to suffer the exigencies of pressing material concerns that make green issues less immediately compelling, the highly educated are more knowledgeable, better able to comprehend complex environmental issues, to assess risks, and to conceive of practical remedial action, either individual or collective. In Britain, the simpler and less sophisticated forms of environmental concern were most often found among the less educated while attitudes approximating an ecological worldview were more often found among the highly educated (Witherspoon and Martin 1993)

Postmaterialism appears to be a poor predictor of support for environmentalism because concerns for the environment are held both by highly educated "postma-terialist" ecologists, who are not so much fearful for their own security as concerned about global environmental problems whose effects are relatively remote, as well as people, usually less well educated, who are more exercised by fear of the threats that pollution poses to their own immediate material security. Postmaterialism is a better predictor of environmental *activism* because it is highly correlated with higher education which is itself an antecedent of most forms of political activism (Rootes 1995).

VALUES AND FORMS OF ACTION

Sharp distinctions have been made between traditional conservationism, modern environmentalism, and ecologism, but it is unusual for such clear philosophical distinctions to be precisely mirrored in divisions among movement organizations, their members, and supporters. True, in Germany, at the founding congress of Die Grünen, conservative environmentalists split from radical leftists to form a separate Democratic Ecological Party. Nevertheless, such organizational formalizations of ideological division are more likely in the formal political sphere, where membership tends to be exclusive, than in the movement milieu, where organizations are more fluid, overlapping memberships are common, and where the flexibility of the network structure is better able to accommodate differences without their becoming overtly conflictual.

Brulle (2000) contends that the discursive frames adopted by environmentalists have consequences for the ways in which they campaign and the forms of organization they adopt. Because of their common recourse to direct action, Greenpeace is often bracketed with radical ecologist groups such as Earth First! (DeLuca 1999; Mertig et al. 2002: 472). However justifiable that may be in the US, consideration of European cases reveals the limits of the putative link between ideology and strategy and tactics. Whereas Greenpeace employs (often spectacular) direct action to attract media attention in order to put pressure on governments and corporations to change their practice, Earth First!ers more often take direct action as a means of directly disrupting the activities they oppose (Rucht 1995; Seel and Plows 2000).[11] Earth First! is thus quite fundamentalist about the relationship between strategy, tactics, and ultimate aims, whereas Greenpeace, despite employing superficially similar direct action tactics, is quite pragmatic, a professionalized campaigning organization that employs instrumentally efficient means and whose agenda falls squarely within the ambit of reform environmentalism.

As Dalton (1994) discovered, contrary to his expectations, even by the mid-1980s, whether European EMOs had been originally committed to conservationism or ecologism made surprisingly little difference to their choices of strategies, tactics, and styles of action. The apparent convergence within the broad environmental movement sector was by no means simply a matter of the progressive institutionalization and incorporation of more radical organizations such as Friends of the Earth and Greenpeace. If FoE and Greenpeace were learning the etiquette necessary to smooth dealings with the powerful, so more traditional conservationist organizations were becoming more ecological in their worldviews and, occasionally, more radical in their tactics.

Although Dalton found evidence of the effects of EMOs' values upon their strategy and tactics, there was more evidence of the effects of the pattern of opportunities and constraints inherent in the structures of the national political systems within which those organizations operated (cf. Rootes 1997a).

ISSUES AND FORMS OF ACTION

As befits a mature and substantially institutionalized movement, the forms of environmental activism in advanced industrial societies are overwhelmingly moderate. Even when environmental issues give rise to protest, it is relatively conventional forms of action that predominate in most countries most of the time. Indeed, given the relative lack of news value attached to conventional actions, and the media's preoccupation with spectacle, violence, and confrontation, the moderation of most reported environmental protest is striking. Thus, in Western Europe during the decade 1988–97, only in Germany and Britain did as many as one-third of reported environmental protests involve actions more disruptive than street demonstrations; violence was rare everywhere (Rootes 2003b). With the exception of some animal rights and antinuclear protests, even where environmentalists resorted to direct action, they almost always confined themselves to nonviolent direct action, the form of action most consistent with the philosophical principles of environmentalism and ecologism.

Why, then have environmental movements that have been overwhelmingly moderate and peaceful in most countries sometimes been disruptive, even violent in others?

Part of the answer may lie in the character of the issues. The issues that have stimulated the most disruptive protests in Australia and the US have concerned the preservation of wilderness, especially forests. Wilderness protection, unlike most urban environmental issues, has been represented as a zero-sum game – either wilderness is preserved or it is lost for ever. No compromise is possible and the urgency of action is extreme. In this respect, wilderness preservation resembles the issue that has stimulated the most disruptive protests in Western Europe – nuclear energy and the disposal of nuclear waste. In this case too, half measures were not considered enough. Absolute rejection of nuclear power appeared essential, and the struggle was given special urgency by the imminence of the initiation or expansion of nuclear energy systems and/or their associated reprocessing or waste disposal facilities. In other respects, however, the wilderness and antinuclear issues were quite different: antinuclear campaigns drew support from the far left because of the association of nuclear energy with nuclear weapons and the authoritarian implications of the high levels of security necessary to protect nuclear plants, whereas wilderness and other conservation issues were generally disparaged by the left as preoccupations of the privileged.

Perhaps surprisingly in view of what has been written about the institutionalization and domestication of environmentalism in Germany (Blühdorn 1995; Brand 1999), reported environmental protest there was, in aggregate, more disruptive, even violent, during the 1990s than anywhere else in Western Europe. In Britain, although the incidence of confrontational protests rose dramatically during the 1990s, violent actions were largely confined to animal rights protests that were at best marginal to the environmental movement (Rootes 2000). In Germany, by contrast, confrontational protest, present throughout the decade, rose and fell with the general waves of environmental protest; violent protests increased sharply from 1994 to 1997 (Rucht and Roose 2003).

What explains the patterns of protest repertoires? Aside from the fact that France was the country where environmental protest most commonly involved demonstrations, the patterns in Western Europe during the 1990s do not conform with the usual stereotypes of national political cultures. Violent protest was relatively more common in supposedly moderate Britain and Sweden than in reputedly more volatile France, Greece, and Spain. However, these anomalies largely disappear if animal rights protests are distinguished from more strictly environmental protests. Indeed, it appears that repertoires may be reflections less of national cultures than of movement cultures, the culture of environmentalism being overwhelmingly nonviolent everywhere whereas those of the antinuclear and, especially, the animal rights movements have significant (minority) strains of violence.

The character of issues does not, however, simply determine the repertoire of environmental movements. Wilderness preservation was the original *raison d'être* of the US environmental movement, but until very recently it was an issue pursued by overwhelmingly conventional and peaceful means, even to the extent that organizations such as the Sierra Club came to be regarded as conservative and establishment-dominated. Just as the repertoire of action associated with particular issues has varied over time so too it has varied cross-nationally. Most strikingly, the antinuclear movement was much more disruptive and had much more enduring political consequences in Germany and France than in Britain. Indeed, the violence of the massive antinuclear protests in Germany and France discouraged British antinuclear protesters from continuing with their own campaign of nonviolent direct action (Welsh 2000). Reported environmental protest in Germany was, moreover, much more confrontational and/or violent during 1994–7 than it had been during the 1988–9 peak of environmental mobilization. Yet it was the same issue – nuclear energy – that dominated both periods.

Movement cultures do not exist in a social and political vacuum. Violent environmental protests in Italy and Spain were carry-overs to the environmental issue arena from other wider political ructions – in Italy, the tail end of the political violence of the 1970s and 1980s, and in Spain, the temporary association of militant Basque nationalism with environmentalist struggles. Similarly, the dramatic rise of confrontational environmental protest in Britain in the 1990s was the crest of a wave of more general confrontational protest that rose with the campaign against the poll-tax (Rootes 2003a). National political cultures appear to explain less than political conjunctures.

The tactical and strategic choices of protesters cannot be reduced to the character of the issues about which they mobilize. Much depends on how the issues are framed, and on the political cultural and institutional contexts in which mobilization occurs. Much also depends on the nature of the immediate political conjuncture as well as the historical dynamics of protest and on the interactions among them.

FORMS OF ACTION AND ORGANIZATION: THE IMPACT
OF POLITICAL CONTEXT

The institutional structures of states have clearly influenced the organizational structures, forms of action, and courses of development of environmental movements. Although authoritarian regimes have generally tolerated environmental activists more than human rights or pro-democracy campaigners, it is only where liberal democratic institutions are well established that fully developed environmental movements have flourished. Even among liberal democracies, different structures of the state have different impacts. Thus centralized and strong states have tended to produce strong, centralized movements, whereas decentralized states, with their several levels of governmental authority and avenues of redress, have tended to produce more decentralized movements. States that are structurally open to challengers have tended to produce more consensual environmental movements, whereas those more closed to challengers have experienced more confrontational movements (Kitschelt 1986; Diani and van der Heijden 1994). However, the structure of political institutions cannot explain the temporal variation in the forms of environmental movement repertoires within states. States are not merely structurally open or closed but contingently open or closed to particular issues and movements at different times (cf. Dryzek et al. 2002, 2003). Thus Britain, reputedly relatively open to environmentalists before 1980, became closed as government prioritized economic development in general and, in the 1990s, road-building in particular (Rootes 1997a). France, famously closed to antinuclear activists, has latterly been surprisingly open to environmentalists in respect of water policies (Hayes 2002). Even temporary closure of access has tended to incite confrontational responses whereas openness has encouraged moderation.

The forms of movements are not, however, simply products of political opportunities.

In one respect, the impact of national political cultures appears persistent. In Italy, and especially Spain and Greece, the characteristic localism of southern European political cultures has been fully reflected in the character of environmental protest. In Greece, 90 percent of protests during 1988–97 were local mobilizations around local issues, albeit that half of them were targeted at national authorities (Kousis 1999, 2003).

Recent trends in Greece and Spain away from localism and toward national levels of organization and translocal, perhaps even global, environmental concerns, may be attributed to the stabilization of national democratic politics. This has been reflected even in the disconnection of environmentalism from nationalism in the Basque Country. Another factor has been the impact of the EU and the increasing connectedness of environmentalists in these countries, through the EU itself and through involvement in organizations developed to lobby EU institutions, with those countries of northern Europe where EMOs and environmental consciousness were already highly developed. Localism appears to have declined because consciousness of environmental issues has become more sophisticated, and because awareness has increased that the structures of political opportunity have changed. Paradoxically, the degree of localism or regionalism of French environmental activism has increased for the same reason. What is peculiar about France, formerly so central-ized administratively, is that, at least insofar as environmental matters are con-cerned, the structures of political opportunity have been so markedly decentralized (Hayes 2002; Fillieule 2003).

Differences in fiscal regimes also affect the character of environmental move-ments. Concern to retain the tax and other benefits of nonprofit status has tended to constrain US EMOs to moderation and has propelled them into ever greater professionalism (Mitchell et al. 1992: 21–2). The generous taxation concessions to charitable giving in the US have encouraged the development of a plethora of charitable foundations, and foundation funding has encouraged EMOs to tailor their styles and concerns to harmonize with the preferences of their actual or potential benefactors (Dowie 1995: 49–53).[12] Brulle (2000) distinguishes between participatory grass-roots organizations and nonparticipatory "astroturf" organiza-tions that are dependent upon foundation funding and constrained by their eco-nomic sponsors. Only the former, he suggests, are capable of contributing to the revitalization of the public sphere and the democratic empowerment of the presently dispossessed. Even if participatory organizations, such as the Sierra Club, accept foundation funding, it is possible for members to counter its more pernicious effects.

Yet oligarchic organizations may sometimes be precisely the kinds of organiza-tions most capable of making timely interventions. The directors of Greenpeace International, for example, have made a clear-eyed choice to maintain its oligarchic structure because they calculate that this is the organizational form best suited to the successful prosecution of Greenpeace's environmental objectives. Although there are undoubtedly tensions and problems arising from such choices, there is not the neat correlation between democratic structures and effectiveness in promoting environ-mentalist goals that some theorists suppose.

GREEN PARTIES

One of the more distinctive aspects of the institutionalization of environmentalism has been the development of Green parties and the consolidation of their position in the politics of most Western democratic states. Here the impact of political oppor-tunity structures been less ambiguous. Whereas Greens have prospered in states whose legislatures are elected by proportional representation, they have found it altogether more difficult to become established where majoritarian electoral systems prevail, as they do in the US and Britain (Rootes 1997a: 326–35; Bosso 2000: 65–7).

Their rise was undoubtedly predicated upon the increase in environmental con-cern and activism, but Green parties were never simply or consistently extensions of the environmental movement into the arena of parliamentary politics. In countries such as Sweden and Britain where environmental groups already enjoyed a measure of access to policymakers, the formation of Green parties was greeted with suspi-cion, hostility or indifference by the leaders of established EMOs who feared that the party politicization of environmental issues might reduce rather than increase their influence. Indeed, it was unusual for leading environmentalists to be prominent in the formation of Green parties, although in some cases they later became members, and it remains the case that the numbers of members of EMOs almost everywhere exceeds by a considerable margin the number of voters for, let alone members of, Green parties. In fact, the origins of Green parties in most Western European countries lay less in the broad environmental movement than in the antinuclear movement, a movement that, while it has generally been assimilated to the environmental movement, was distinct from the broad environmental movement in several important respects, including its appeal to the Left.

Nevertheless, where they have achieved parliamentary representation, Green parties have become one vehicle by which environmentalists might influence policy. Thus in Germany, while the Greens are by no means dominant players in the environmental movement, they are well networked to all the prominent EMOs (Rucht and Roose 2001, 2003). Where they remain marginal to the formal political system, as they do in Britain, Greens find it easier to represent themselves as part of the environmental movement but are less able to serve the environmental movement as a conduit into formal politics.

As Green parties have approached power, so relationships between them and environmental movements have become more complicated. Concerned to enhance their credibility and to escape the allegation that they are "single-issue" parties, Greens have sought to develop policies across the broad range of political agenda. While, on the one hand, this is a logical extension of the green critique, on the other it tends to distance Green parties from environmental movement activists who remain more focused upon more strictly environmental concerns. This distance should not be exaggerated. Greens, especially in government, have, in addition to the environment, emphasized policy areas such as health, food, and consumer affairs, and overseas aid and development, issues that are directly cognate to the central concerns of environmentalists and that are increasingly taken up by the larger national and international EMOs themselves.

INSTITUTIONALIZATION AND ITS DISCONTENTS

On any of several dimensions – size, income and degree of formality of organizations, number and professionalization of employees, frequency and kind of interaction with established institutional actors – environmental movements in most highly industrialized countries are relatively highly institutionalized.[13] However, while such institutionalization might be seen as a sign of the success of the environmental movement, it is also a possible source of weakness, and certainly it has been a major source of discontent.

The most dire tales are told of the consequences of institutionalization for EMOs in the US. While the increased use of direct mail produced impressive numbers in the reports and balance sheets of organizations, it also produced an unprecedentedly large number of passive "check book / credit card" supporters (Mitchell et al. 1992: 16). The ease with which this "conscience constituency" could, at least initially, be tapped for funds has been blamed for the subsequent loss of direction and demobilization of some of the organizations that were its principal beneficiaries (Dowie 1995: 42–9). Moreover, EMOs' increasing dependence on funding from charitable foundations led them to diminish their efforts to mobilize their grass-roots constituencies and influenced them away from protest, and from criticism of corporations, and towards "noncontroversial positions and nonconfrontational practices" (Dowie

1995: 49–53; Brulle 2000: 261–3). The increased receptiveness of legislators and administrations to environmental lobbyists encouraged EMOs to focus more of their activities in Washington, a move that led to the homogenization of their styles and increased the pressures to be "reasonable" in order to ensure continued access (Dowie 1995: 86; Bosso 2000: 68–70).

Worries are widely shared that the increasing professionalization of EMOs' staffs and the responsibilities that come with the ownership of assets may fatally distance EMOs from their mass constituencies, since it is EMOs' potential to mobilize those constituencies that is their ultimate sanction in their unequal struggles with the powerful (van der Heijden 1997; Diani and Donati 1999; Rootes 1999a). Yet such institutionalization does not appear everywhere to have entailed the deradicalization of the movement or the loss of shared identity.

In Germany, a substantially institutionalized movement has coexisted with the revival of highly confrontational, at times violent, antinuclear protest. Moreover, established EMOs have given assistance to local antinuclear groups. In Britain, even though the 1990s was, for EMOs, a period of steady growth as well as increased access to and influence upon the mass media, politicians, government agencies, and business corporations, it was also a period in which reported environmental protest increased and became more confrontational. Although the rise of new, more radical EMOs such as Earth First! can be traced to dissatisfaction with the apparent moderation of more established organizations such as Friends of the Earth (FoE) and Greenpeace, shared identity survived differences, and networks of advice and support connected even the "disorganizations" most committed to direct action to more established organizations. Indeed, the sense of identity among the constituent parts of the movement has not dissolved with the rise of increasingly formally institutionalized organizations, but has instead grown as groups realized that there was much to be gained by cooperation. Moreover, if organizations such as FoE and Greenpeace have been constrained to caution by their increased vulnerability to litigation, their rise encouraged yet more established conservation organizations not previously known for their activism to broaden their repertoires and agenda and become more actively critical in their engagement with government and industry.[14]

British and German experience shows that it is possible for an environmental movement to maintain many of the characteristics of an informal movement while taking advantages of the opportunities presented by a measure of institutionalization, and that institutionalization is no barrier to the mobilization of protest. While some writers have referred to the "self-limiting radicalism" of Green parties, it is no less important to recognize the self-limiting institutionalization of environmental movements.

ENVIRONMENTAL MOVEMENTS COMPARED

The International Social Science Programme (ISSP) survey in 1993 found that over 10 percent of respondents claimed membership of an environmental group in countries as diverse as New Zealand, the Netherlands, the Philippines, and the USA, nearly 10 percent in Australia, and over 5 percent in Canada, Israel, Germany, Great Britain, and Norway (Pakulski and Crook 1998: 3). However, the ISSP surveys may substantially have underestimated environmental group membership.

A national survey in Britain in 2000 found that, as in 1993, fewer than 6 percent of respondents to the standard ISSP question claimed to be members of any group whose "main aim is to preserve or protect the environment" (Christie and Jarvis 2001: 147). Yet, in another section of the same survey, when respondents were asked whether they belonged to any of ten listed environmental groups / kinds of groups, almost one-fifth said they did (Johnston and Jowell 2001: 178). The way questions are asked clearly makes a difference; general, abstract questions produce lower figures for membership than questions that remind respondents of the kinds of groups that might be considered environmental.

Similarly, studies of the declared membership of environmental organizations produce higher estimates of EMO membership than do ISSP survey questions. Thus, whereas the 1995 US General Social Surveys found under 10 percent of Americans claimed to be members of environmental organizations, an implied aggregate membership of 19 million, Brulle (2000: 104–5), using US Internal Revenue Service data, estimated the total membership of US environmental organizations at 41 million. Overlapping memberships are unlikely to account for all the discrepancy.

Comparing the strength of environmental movements cross-nationally is difficult. Attempts to compare levels of public opinion favorable to environmental protection have been bedeviled by problems concerning the wording and meaning of questions that derive from the peculiarities of different languages and national or local cultures as well as the varying enthusiasms of pollsters. The less frequent attempts to compare levels of "environmentally friendly" activity and "mobilization potential" in different countries have been similarly problematic. In any case, both attitudes and "environmentally friendly" activity are necessarily only very indirect indicators of the strength of environmental movements.

Measures of the density of EMO membership are also complicated by idiosyncrasies in the way "membership" has been defined both by the EMOs themselves and by researchers, and by difficulties in deciding which organizations should be included and which excluded from the national environmental movement in a particular country. Thus Bosso (2000: 64) puts the aggregated membership of 15 selected national US environmental organizations at 9.5 million in 1998, whereas Mertig et al. (2002: 463) calculate the aggregate membership of the 12 leading US national environmental lobbying organizations – excluding WWF, the Natural Resources Defense Council and Greenpeace – at under 3.9 million in 2000, the difference being mostly attributable to the latter's exclusion of WWF, the Natural Resources Defense Council and Greenpeace (total 2 million), and the inclusion by the former of over 3 million associate members ("mainly schoolchildren") in the figures for the National Wildlife Federation.

Only rarely has cross-nationally comparative research employing systematically common criteria of inclusion or exclusion been attempted. Even in Western Europe, the diversity of national political structures and cultures is such that comparison of the strengths of national environmental movements remains qualitative. In Britain, the aggregated membership of national EMOs exceeded 5 million by the late 1990s (Johnston and Jowell 2001: 179). In the Netherlands, the per capita rate of EMO membership was even higher: the combined membership of national EMOs in 2001 was 3.7 million in a country with a population of 16 million, the membership of WWF, Greenpeace, and the Dutch affiliate of FoE together amounting to more than

1.5 million (van der Heijden 2002). These figures are not, however, strictly comparable, not least because while those for the Netherlands include animal welfare groups, those for Britain do not, because in Britain, but not in the Netherlands, the animal rights movement appears to be quite distinct from the environmental movement (Rootes 2000: 28–30; Rootes and Miller 2000; Doherty et al. 2002: 33).

Although the per capita membership of major national EMOs appears to be greater in the Netherlands and in Britain than in Germany or the US, such comparisons fail to take account of the varying levels of subnational group activity. Membership of subnational groups is likely to be considerably greater in territorially extensive and politically decentralized states such as the US or Germany than in relatively compact, densely settled and politically centralized countries such as the Netherlands or Britain, hence the disparity between Bosso's figures for the membership of US *national* environmental groups and Brulle's much higher estimates of the aggregate number of members of *all* US environmental groups.

DEVELOPMENT . . . AND DECLINE?

Despite the difficulties in estimating and comparing the sizes of the environmental movements, it is clear that the numbers and memberships of EMOs have grown everywhere throughout the industrialized West, and that there have been two nearly universal surges in membership – in the early 1970s and in 1989–90 – closely following surges in environmental concern among the public. However, it is also apparent that there are nationally idiosyncratic patterns that, against the backdrop of the great international waves of concern, reflect variations in local political circumstances.

In the US, the environmental movement declined during the 1970s as gains were institutionalized and as progress was made in dealing with problems such as urban air quality, but there was a marked upsurge in support for and membership of national EMOs during the 1980s as a reaction against attempts by the Reagan and Bush administrations to roll back environmental protection regimes established under previous administrations. Growth continued, in aggregate, during the 1990s (Mertig et al. 2002: 463). However, it appears that organizations with local chapters and that attended to local concerns fared better than did those with centralized structures and global concerns (Bosso 2000: 63). The most remarkable loser from this localization was Greenpeace. By far the most widely supported US EMO in 1990, with 2.35 million "members," Greenpeace had shrunk by 1998 to just 350,000 "members" and its income from $40 million to $21 million. (Bosso 2000).

In Britain, between 1971 and 1981, the membership of several of the longest established EMOs grew fourfold; between 1981 and 1991, it doubled again, and it went on increasing, albeit more slowly, through the 1990s. New organizations were established at such a rate that well over half of all national EMOs identified in 1999 had been founded since 1980 (Rootes and Miller 2000). During the 1980s the most spectacular growth was in organizations newly established during the 1970s, the numbers of members or supporting donors of FoE growing sixfold and those of Greenpeace tenfold. Both these new campaigning organizations became and remain substantial operations, although their numbers of members / supporters and income have fallen somewhat from their early 1990s peaks. In numbers of employees and income, national EMOs grew significantly during the 1980s and 1990s, and the overall fairly steady rise in aggregate EMO membership balanced a more episodic pattern of environmental protest (Rootes 2000).

Nature protection organizations in Germany date from the late nineteenth century (Brand 1999; Rucht and Roose 1999). New groups emerged in and after the early 1970s; almost half the national EMOs active in 1999 were created after 1980 and almost a fifth after 1989. Older groups responded to new debates by moving gradually away from traditional conservationist and apolitical stances. The combined membership of the large national groups increased little from 1988 to 1994 but grew significantly during the next two years, to reach 4.4 million. At the end of the 1990s, the German environmental movement was a decentralized network of some 120 national EMOs and more than 9,000 local groups. Greenpeace Germany had 90 local groups and the number of regular donors was stable at around 530,000. Surprisingly, German unification did not much affect aggregate EMO membership. Few East German EMOs created during or shortly after the 1989 upheaval survived, but in major East German cities the numbers of environmental groups doubled or tripled between 1989 and 1993. Overall, the German movement was stable in numbers and grew in resources during the 1990s, and local groups remained important (Rucht and Roose 2001). What most distinguished the German movement from others in Western Europe during the 1990s was the remarkable rise of sometimes violent antinuclear protest sustained by a highly decentralized network of local and regional groups (Rucht and Roose 2003) and by the major national EMOs (Hunold 2001: 56).

In the Netherlands, an already strongly institutionalized environmental movement grew dramatically during the 1990s. Between 1991 and 2001 the total number of national groups rose from 30 to 68, and their total membership increased by over 75 percent to 3.7 million. However, almost all the growth was in numbers and memberships of conservation and animal welfare groups. The environmentalist sector, which includes Greenpeace and FoE, shrank slightly. Nevertheless, with 700,000 regular donors, Greenpeace Netherlands remains the strongest national Greenpeace organization. Although scarcely reflected in any rise in confrontational activism, there was some evidence of increasing radicalism in the rise of animal rights and alternative-exemplary EMOs. Numbers of the latter increased fivefold (to 15) and their combined membership almost doubled to 31,000 (van der Heijden 2002).

The development of environmental movements during the 1990s in other Western European countries responded to nationally peculiar circumstances. While national EMOs began to be consolidated in Spain and Greece, in France, where they had always been weak by comparison with regional or local associations, they became weaker still. In Sweden, already well-institutionalized EMOs became increasingly professionalized and have played a central role in sustainable development programs, including technology and product innovation, ecolabeling, and environmental management and assessment, often in cooperation with corporations and governmental authorities at national, local, and European levels. During the 1990s, environmental protests, especially by established EMOs, appear to have declined, as did the memberships of the more activist groups. However, the traditional conservation organization, the Swedish Association for the Protection of Nature (SNF), gained members and, as the government cut expenditure and transferred responsibility to the private sector in many areas of environmental policy and research, so the SNF, after much soul-searching, took on a new consultative role, while seeking to maintain its traditional "people's movement" character and a presence in local politics (Jamison and Ring 2003). The result is that environmentalism in Sweden has now become so institutionalized that it retains few movement characteristics (Jamison 2001).

In Australia, national EMOs lost ground dramatically during the 1990s. They had developed increasingly close relationships with the Labor Party during its years of federal government in and since the 1980s. As a result, when Labor lost office in 1996, the national EMOs lost influence (Doyle 2000). Public concern about the environment declined as easily understood, concrete and universally acknowledged urban environmental issues were tackled but were succeeded by less easily understood, apparently abstract and contested issues such as climate change and soil salination. However, in response to the urgency of these new issues as well as the perceived shortcomings of the conservative government, membership of practical environmental groups such as those concerned with landcare soared, and by 2001 the numbers of members of environmental advocacy groups had more than recovered from their mid-1990s slump (Miller and Wroe 2001).

Clearly the relationship between environmental issues, public opinion, and the development of EMOs is complex. As environmentalism has achieved a large measure of institutionalization, so EMOs are less directly dependent on mass public opinion, and other, less publicly visible forms of environmentalist action have developed, including a variety of practical measures aimed at environmental conservation or restoration.

LOCAL, COMMUNITY-BASED ENVIRONMENTAL ACTION GROUPS

Local, community-based environmental action groups, linked loosely if at all to established EMOs, proliferated in most countries during the 1980s. Often referred to dismissively as "NIMBY" (Not in my backyard) groups, they have taken up a wide range of issues, many of them focusing upon the siting of waste dumps, incinerators, and noxious industries. It is, however, only in the US that they have cohered to form a clearly distinct strand to the environmental movement (Szasz 1994). Although they have resisted formal organization at the national level, these groups, together comprising what has become known as the "environmental justice movement" (EJM), have become increasingly effectively networked through the Citizens' Clearinghouse for Hazardous Waste (latterly Center for Environment, Health and Justice) (Schlosberg 1999).

Why should such a network have developed in the US but not elsewhere? The most plausible explanation is in terms of the character of established US EMOs and the US political structure. Established EMOs were generally focused upon wilderness and wildlife protection issues and, constrained by their limited resources, their anxiety to preserve their privileged political access, and their socially circumscribed interests, they showed little interest in extending their ambit to the kinds of environmental issues raised by urban and rural working class communities. The very openness of national institutions to established EMOs had the effect of co-opting them (Dryzek et al. 2002: 666). Moreover, in a decentralized political system with a bipolar party system in which one party or other is frequently locally entrenched, with many possible points of political access but where local political boundaries frequently isolate communities with environmental grievances, the attractions of translocal networking are obvious. The closest European parallel was the development in the late 1960s in West Germany of the Citizens' Initiative movement which, in similarly uncongenial political circumstances, sought to stimulate and to network local political initiatives, many of which were focused upon urban environmental issues and which led to the formation of the BBU. In Britain, such networks have thus far been issue-specific, as with the formation of ALARM UK to foster links among local antiroads protests.

It has been claimed that because local environmental activism is participatory and empowering, it has the potential to transform the environmental movement as a whole (Gottlieb 1993: 320; Mertig et al. 2002: 472). However, empirical investigation in the US suggests that the relationship between informal local groups and formally organized national EMOs is more enduringly complex, with waves of local protest and national campaigning succeeding one another in a (so far) endless procession (Carmin 1999).

There is nothing inevitable about the networking of local environmental protests. In Spain, Portugal, and especially Greece, although there was a great deal of local, community-based environmental activism, most of it remained local (Kousis 1999). Only with the belated emergence in the late 1980s and 1990s of national EMOs, most of them inspired by foreign exemplars in a top-down rather than bottom-up way, did southern European community environmental protests begin to be effectively networked.

It is perfectly possible for there to be a great deal of local environmental protest – and widespread environmental concern – without there being an environmental movement. In most Western European countries, networking and common concern have been supplied in large part by existing national EMOs. In southern Europe – and in many places beyond the industrialized West – national EMOs have either been absent or until very recently too weak to perform such a networking role, with the result that local protests have generally remained unnetworked or have been linked by transnational EMOs.

Environmental Movements beyond the Industrialized West

As in the most recently industrialized parts of southern Europe, in the countries of central and eastern Europe ravaged by rapid industrialization under Communist regimes, environmental concern has more often articulated personal complaint than global environmental consciousness. As a result, environmentalist action there has usually taken the form of intense local campaigns, and national EMOs have been weak. Environmental movements are often credited with a major role in the popular mobilizations that accompanied the collapse of Communist regimes, but their subsequent weakness in central and eastern Europe suggests either that green was often adopted as protective camouflage by antiregime activists who subsequently turned to more mainstream political roles, or that the political and economic urgencies of posttransition states sidelined environmental concerns (Rootes 1997a: 335–42; Pickvance 1998).

In the less industrialized countries of the Third World, environmental issues are so intimately bound up with those surrounding the distribution of social, economic and political power and resources that struggles to protect the environment, although they sometimes involve large numbers of people, rarely take the form of straightforward environmental movements. The lack of safeguards for democratic political activity and judicial redress of grievances and the corresponding underdevelopment of civil society more often than not conspire to defeat the most desperate efforts of the world's most impoverished people to defend their habitat (Haynes 1999). Comparison of environmentalism in east Asia and in southern Africa suggests that it is the stronger states in east Asia with their more developed channels for the articulation of civil society, as well as their greater affluence, that have fostered more vigorous development of environmental movements there than in sub-Saharan Africa (Mittelman 1998: 867–8).

In east Asia, the development of environmental movements has, in some respects, paralleled that in Central and Eastern Europe. Environmental movements have often been used as cover by activists concerned to promote democratization (Lee and So 1999: 290). In South Korea and Taiwan, environmentalists' protests against pollution were among the few forms of popular mobilization tolerated by military regimes. Environmental campaigns, which enjoyed widespread popular support and so were less easily suppressed than those for democracy, legitimated repertoires of collective action and created a public sphere within which political dissidents could act. Thus in these countries environmental movements were significant forces for democratization and, during the liberalization process, environmental and democracy movements were partners. By contrast, in Hong Kong, under a liberal colonial regime there was little interpenetration between the democracy and environmental movements. In the Philippines, however, where governments were intermittently more repressive but where the foundations of the democracy movement were stronger, environmental demands were subsumed by those of the democracy movement, with the result that the environmental movements that developed in the 1980s attributed ecological abuses to authoritarianism, lack of opportunities for public participation, and to the concentration of economic power in a few hands (Lee et al. 1999).

In the less industrialized states of Asia and Africa, as in the recently democratized societies of central and eastern Europe, success for environmentalists' campaigns often depends upon their ability to secure the support of First World EMOs and human rights organizations. The danger is that dependence on foreign assistance may displace local agenda in favor of those of donors, and may divert the energies of activists away from efforts to mobilize local people (Yanitsky 1999). Perhaps for this reason, environmental movements have had greatest impact where they have become indigenized in the course of mobilizing local people and incorporating local cultural values and rituals, because then they have empowered local activists and enabled them to challenge authoritarian states (Lee and So 1999: 291).

A GLOBAL ENVIRONMENTAL MOVEMENT?

Despite frequent references to "the" environmental movement, even to "the global environmental movement," there is in fact such variation among and within local and national environmental movements that to speak of a global environmental movement is a triumph of abstraction or of aspiration over experience. The many obstacles to the formation of a global environmental movement include the wide diversity of material circumstances, cultures, and languages that divide the world's people, and the variety of political circumstances that they must negotiate. Just as national environmental movements have flourished under conditions of stable democracy in strong states, not the least obstacle to the development of a *global* environmental movement is the absence of a developed democratic global polity. Although the advent of international agreements and agencies, including those of the United Nations and the World Bank, has encouraged the development of transnational environmental NGOs, the latter are not mass participatory organizations and their representativeness is at best problematic (Yearley 1996: 91). They would appear to be unlikely agents of the construction of a democratic global polity or a global civil society (Rootes 2002b).

Yet, because international organizations themselves are so lacking in democratic procedures and accountability, it can be argued that the efforts of transnational EMOs make an important contribution to the democratization of global politics. For example, EarthAction, a transnational organization that works to help its affiliates participate in global arena and that, rather than mounting its own campaigns, identifies campaigns consonant with its goals, and provides affiliates with "action kits" to encourage them to mobilize around those campaigns. Even allowing for the risk that, in encouraging EMOs to recognize the global dimensions of their particular struggles, such organizations may disproportionately broadcast the perspectives of environmentalists in the industrialized North, there is evidence that EarthAction's affiliates in the global South derive sustenance from their transnational ties and, confident that they are part of a transnational movement, are better able to resist repression locally and to acquire the skills necessary to participate effectively in global arena (Smith 2002).

It is possible that more substantial global organizations may, for a relatively ill-resourced constituency, require more energy and resources to construct and to maintain than could be justified by the results (Sklair 1995). If so, then the present loose form of transnational environmental movement networks may, given existing resources, be optimal, even within such relatively well-developed supranational political arena as the European Union (Rootes 2002a). It may be that the facilitation of exchanges of information is sufficient to maintain the coordination of activists' efforts across the globe while action is mostly limited to bringing pressure to bear where it may be most effective – at the national level and on national governments. It is nevertheless the case that even the coordination of separate national actions would be more effective if transnational movement networks were more dense and more active (Rootes 2002b).

However, if the prospects for an effective and genuinely democratic global environmental movement appear limited today, they are likely to improve as better and cheaper means of communication make the global village ever better connected and as increasing access to higher education gives more people the personal skills and resources necessary to make common cause with their counterparts in other countries and regions.

Conclusion

Throughout the history of environmentalism, the concerted actions of groups and individuals have been crucial to the achievement of progress in environmental protection. Campaigns have succeeded in bringing particular issues to the notice of the public and policymakers alike, and have often been essential to ensure effective legislative and administrative action. However, at least in the most affluent industrialized countries, the modern environmental movement that has developed since 1970 is qualitatively different from its predecessors insofar as it has achieved a level of maturity, organizational development, and cooperative interaction among its constituent parts that enables it to maintain the visibility of environmental issues even in the absence of spectacular crises and to ride out the troughs of public indifference and official neglect.

Contrary to what sociologists have often assumed about the inevitable fates of social movements – bureaucratization, institutionalization, ossification and, ultimately, death – environmental movements appear so far to have beaten the odds. In most countries where conditions have enabled them to develop, they – or large parts of them – remain vital and resist the complete co-optation that would render them toothless. Indeed, there is evidence of a cycle of regeneration that maintains the dynamism of the movements. Overall, it appears that, contrary to the assumptions of the Weberian and Michelsian theoretical traditions, the institutionalization of EMOs has not thus far entailed their sclerosis and marginalization, nor their loss of all their movement characteristics, nor yet a systematic decline or deradicalization of protest.

In the many decisions, great and small, that they have influenced, environmental movements have had a whole series of substantive impacts. There have been many great battles, and many defeats, but it is difficult to imagine that so much of the Californian redwood forests or the Alaskan wilderness, the Great Barrier Reef, the Australian wet tropics or the Tasmanian forests would have been saved without the efforts of environmentalists. No less important have been the countless small victories to preserve locally valued but internationally unknown sites, and the many successful efforts to prevent the dumping of waste or the construction of incinerators where they might harm local populations. Greenpeace's campaign against the dumping at sea of the Brent Spar oil storage buoy changed the corporate policies of major oil companies as well as perceptions of the sea as a limitless waste repository, and there can be little doubt that Greenpeace's campaign to promote ozone-friendly refrigerators advanced the phasing out of CFCs by several years.

The broader and more diffuse impact of environmental movements is difficult to determine with precision, not least because they have both stimulated and mediated the concerns of the wider public, and reflected and amplified concerns originating in scientific and policy communities. Nevertheless, it seems clear that they have at least intermittently succeeded in sensitizing mass publics, politicians, and other decision-makers to environmental issues that would not otherwise have been so salient. For the most part, it is EMOs that have set the agenda of environmental reform and succeeded in framing the issues as matters of global collective responsibility. As a result, governments that now resist such framing, as those of the US and Australia do with respect to climate change, do so in defiance of majority public opinion.

Environmental movements have impacted, too, upon the structures of government insofar as the institutionalization of environment ministries and agencies can be attributed to their demands. By ensuring that environmental groups as well as affected populations are consulted when environmentally consequential decisions are proposed, they have also had procedural impacts at local, national, and international levels (Carter 2001: 150–3). Above all, environmental movements have opened the space in which EMOs have been able to play constructive roles in the formation of policy and its implementation, as they have done in some European countries with Agenda 21 and other sustainability projects. Where their impact upon policy has been limited, it is principally a reflection of the limitations of the resources of which EMOs dispose. Even those EMOs that are now substantial organizations are minnows by comparison with governments and corporations. Limited resources constrain them to selectivity in the projects they undertake and, where they have relatively broad ranges of concerns, limit their capacity to influence policy in detail or to engage continuously with policymakers.

It may be a reflection of the success of the environmental movement in the US, as well as of the peculiar strength there of possessive individualism, that from the late 1980s a vigorous countermovement arose, committed to the defense of the rights of private property against the collectivist claims of environmentalists (Switzer 1997; Mertig et al. 2002: 459–61). Yet, despite support from the deep pockets of conservative interest groups, this "Wise Use" movement has so far made little impression; American public opinion remains in favor of more rather than less environmental protection. The fact that comparable countermovements have not developed in other industrialized countries is, however, less a sign that environmental movements are weaker there than that their struggles for the hearts and minds of the public and for the ears of the powerful have been more completely won. Western governments may sometimes speak with forked tongues about their commitment to environmental protection, but none now dares to refuse at least to pay lip service to environmental concerns. The power of environmental movements may be mainly countervailing power, but it is power nonetheless.

Yearley (1994) argued that the environmental movement was distinctive in three respects: its intimate relationship to science, its practical claims to international solidarity, and its ability to offer a critique of and an alternative to industrial capitalism. These remain good reasons for environmental movements to make a special claim on our attention. No other movement so convincingly challenges the hubris of modern science, or uses scientific expertise so effectively. No movement makes a more convincing claim to being truly global in the scope of its concerns. And no existing movement makes a more convincing critique of the costs of capitalist industrialism to people and planet, or so persistently burns the candle of hope that there is a better way.

Notes

I am indebted to Robert Brulle, Neil Carter, Mario Diani, and Brian Doherty, as well as the editors, for their helpful comments on an earlier draft of this chapter.

1   Eyerman and Jamison accept that social movements are networks but operate with a restrictive conception of collective identity as "knowledge interests." For Diani, for collective identity to exist, it is sufficient that actors "define themselves as part of a broader movement and, at the same time, be perceived as such, by those within the same movement, and by opponents and/or external observers" (Diani 1992: 8–9). Diani suggests that there are many environmental protests that are not part of a social movement because the protesters do not recognize their shared identity with other such protesters. Yet the social scientific observer might detect the latent connections that the actors themselves at any point in time do not.

2   Less clear is the centrality of conflict to the identification of a social movement. Della Porta and Diani (1999: 15) include as one element of their definition of a social movement that it involves "collective action focusing upon conflicts." "Social movement actors are," they suggest, "engaged in political and/or cultural conflicts, meant to promote or oppose social change at either the systemic or non-systemic level. By conflict we mean an oppositional relationship between actors who seek control of the same stake." Particularly because these stakes may be symbolic, cultural, political or material, the requirement of "conflict" does not seem to be sufficiently demanding or discriminating to warrant its inclusion as an essential element of the definition.

3   Reassuringly, Bosso appears to contradict himself on the very next page: "The environmental movement has become a mature and very typical American interest group community, albeit one with a greater array of policy niches and potential forms of activism" (Bosso 2000: 74). Bosso draws attention to the institutionalization and organizational specialization of environmentalism in the US without exploring the extent of networking among environmental organizations.

4   For an attempt to systematically address these issues using press reports for eight Western European countries, see Rootes (2003b).

5   Thus Mertig et al. (2002) are led to classify as instances of ecologism developments such as the environmental justice movement, apparently because it is recent, and to overlook the precursors of modern environmentalism and ecologism in nineteenth- and early twentieth-century urban hygiene movements.

6   Indeed, some would argue that in Britain it still does in the form of the Countryside Alliance, which in 1998 and 2002 organized the biggest demonstrations London had ever seen.

7   As, e.g., in the development of the environmentalist group NOAH in Denmark (Jamison et al. 1990: ch. 3).

8   On the peculiarities of Greenpeace USA, see Shaiko (1993).

9   On the construction of an environmental justice agenda in Britain, see Agyeman (2002).

10 The website http://www.nrpe.org gives an overview of religious environmentalism in the US.

11 DeLuca (1999: 6) argues that in the US Earth First! activists, no less than Greenpeace, have been practitioners of "image politics."

12 In Western Europe, by contrast, foundations are less significant; even the foundations associated with German political parties, including the Greens, are funded from the public purse. It was precisely to avoid prohibitions on political activity that, in Britain, FoE and Greenpeace, unusually among EMOs, declined to apply for charitable status, although both subsequently formed separate charitable trusts.

13 Another dimension of the institutionalization of environmental movements is the frequency with which EMO activists move between one organization and another and, especially, the frequency with which they move between government and state agencies and EMOs. In the US, both the Carter and Clinton administrations drew on the environmental movement to fill important positions (Mertig et al. 2002: 467), and in Britain, prominent EMO personnel have been recruited to senior policy advice positions under

both Conservative and Labour governments, and some have retraced their paths to senior EMO posts. In Sweden, the rise of environmental concern prompted all the major political parties to recruit activists from EMOs.

14 In fact, although Greenpeace has become more focused upon "solutions campaigning" it has not become markedly more moderate. FoE may appear less protest-prone because many actions of its local groups use campaign-specific names.

References and further reading

Agyeman, Julian (2002) Constructing Environmental (In)justice: Transatlantic Tales. *Environmental Politics*, 11 (3), 31–53.

Blühdorn, Ingolfur (1995) Campaigning for Nature: Environmental Pressure Groups in Germany and Generational Change in the Ecology Movement. In Ingolfur Blühdorn, Frank Krause, and Thomas Scharf (eds.), *The Green Agenda: Environmental Politics and Policy in Germany*. Keele: Keele University Press, 167–222.

Bosso, Christopher J. (2000) Environmental Groups and the New Political Landscape. In Norman J. Vig, and Michael E. Kraft (eds.), *Environmental Policy*. 4th ed. Washington, DC: CQ, 55–76.

Brand, Karl-Werner (1999) Dialectics of Institutionalisation: The Transformation of the Environmental Movement in Germany. In Christopher Rootes (ed.), *Environmental Movements*. London: Frank Cass , 35–58, and *Environmental Politics*, 8 (1), 35–58.

Brulle, Robert (2000) *Agency, Democracy and Nature: The U.S. Environmental Movement from a Critical Theory Perspective*. Cambridge, MA: MIT Press.

Carmin, JoAnn (1999) Voluntary Associations, Professional Organisations and the Environmental Movement in the United States. In Christopher Rootes (ed.), *Environmental Movements*. London: Frank Cass, 101–21, and *Environmental Politics*, 8 (1), 101–21.

Carter, Neil (2001) *The Politics of the Environment: Ideas, Activism, Policy*. Cambridge: Cambridge University Press.

Castells, Manuel (1997) *The Power of Identity*. Oxford: Blackwell.

Christie, Ian, and Lindsey Jarvis (2001) How Green Are our Values? In Alison Park, John Curtice, Katarina Thomson, Lindsey Jarvis, and Catherine Bromley (eds.), *British Social Attitudes: The Eighteenth Report*. London: Sage, 131–57.

Cole, Luke W., and Sheila R. Foster (2001) *From the Ground Up: Environmental Racism and the Rise of the Environmental Justice Movement*. New York: New York University Press.

Cotgrove, Stephen (1982) *Catastrophe or Cornucopia: The Environment, Politics and the Future*. Chichester: Wiley.

Dalton, Russell J. (1994) *The Green Rainbow: Environmental Groups in Western Europe*. New Haven: Yale University Press.

della Porta, Donatella, and Mario Diani (1999) *Social Movements: An Introduction*. Oxford: Blackwell.

DeLuca, Kevin (1999) *Image Politics: The New Rhetoric of Environmental Activism*. New York: Guilford.

Diani, Mario (1992) The Concept of Social Movement. *Sociological Review*, 40, 1–25.

——(1995) *Green Networks: A Structural Analysis of the Italian Environmental Movement*. Edinburgh: Edinburgh University Press.

Diani, Mario, and Paolo Donati (1999) Organisational Change in Western European Environmental Groups: A Framework for Analysis. In Christopher Rootes (ed.) *Environmental Movements*. London: Frank Cass , 13–34, and *Environmental Politics*, 8 (1), 13–34.

Diani, Mario, and Hein-Anton van der Heijden (1994) Anti-nuclear Movements across States: Explaining Patterns of Development. In Helena Flam (ed.), *States and Anti-nuclear Movements*. Edinburgh: Edinburgh University Press, 355–82.

Doherty, Brian (2002) *Ideas and Action in the Green Movement*. London: Routledge.

Doherty, Brian, Alex Plows, and Derek Wall (2002) Comparing Radical Environmental Activism in Manchester, Oxford and North West Wales. Unpublished paper, SPIRE (School of Politics, International Relations and Environment), Keele University.

Dowie, Mark (1995) *Losing Ground: American Environmentalism at the Close of the Twentieth Century*. Cambridge, MA: MIT Press.

Doyle, Timothy (2000) *Green Power: The Environment Movement in Australia*. Sydney: University of New South Wales Press.

Dryzek, John, Christian Hunold, David Schlosberg, David Downes, and Hans-Kristian Hernes (2002) Environmental Transformations of the State: The USA, Norway, Germany and the UK. *Political Studies*, 50, 659–82.

Dryzek, John, Christian Hunold, David Schlosberg, David Downes, and Hans-Kristian Hernes (2003) *Green States and Social Movements: Environmentalism in the United States, United Kingdom, Germany and Norway*. Oxford: Oxford University Press.

Dunlap, Riley E., and Angela G. Mertig (eds.) (1992) *American Environmentalism: The US Environmental Movement, 1970–1990*. Bristol, PA: Taylor & Francis.

Eyerman, Ron, and Andrew Jamison (1991) *Social Movements: A Cognitive Approach*. Oxford: Polity.

Fillieule, Olivier (2003) France. In Rootes 2003b, 59–79.

Freudenberg, Nicholas, and Carol Steinsapir (1992) Not in our Backyards: The Grassroots Environmental Movement. In Dunlap and Mertig 1992, 27–37.

Gottlieb, Robert (1993) *Forcing the Spring: The Transformation of the American Environmental Movement*. Washington, DC: Island.

Hay, Peter (2002) *Main Currents in Western Environmental Thought*. Sydney: University of New South Wales Press.

Hayes, Graeme (2002) *Environmental Protest and Policymaking in France*. Basingstoke: Palgrave.

Haynes, Jeff (1999) Power, Politics and Environmental Movements in the Third World. In Christopher Rootes (ed.), *Environmental Movements*. London: Frank Cass, 222–42 , and *Environmental Politics*, 8 (1), 222–42.

Hofrichter, Jürgen, and Karlheinz Reif (1990) Evolution of Environmental attitudes in the European Community. *Scandinavian Political Studies*, 13, 119–46.

Hunold, Christian (2001) Environmentalists, Nuclear Waste, and the Politics of Passive Exclusion in Germany. *German Politics and Society*, 19 (4), 43–63.

Hutton, Drew, and Libby Connors (1999) *A History of the Australian Environmental Movement*. Cambridge: Cambridge University Press.

Inglehart, Ronald (1977) *The Silent Revolution: Changing Values and Political Styles among Western Publics*. Princeton, NJ: Princeton University Press.

Jamison, Andrew (2001) *The Making of Green Knowledge Environmental Politics and Cultural Transformation*. Cambridge: Cambridge University Press.

Jamison, Andrew, and Magnus Ring (2003) Sweden. In Christopher Rootes (ed.), *Environmental Protest in Western Eruope*. Oxford: Oxford University Press, 216–33.

Jamison, Andrew, Ron Eyerman, Jacqueline Cramer, and Jeppe Læssøe (1990) *The Making of the New Environmental Consciousness*. Edinburgh: Edinburgh University Press.

Jiménez, Manuel (1999) Consolidation through Institutionalisation? Dilemmas of the Spanish Environmental Movement in the 1990s. In Christopher Rootes (ed.), *Environmental Movements*. London: Frank Cass, 149–71, and *Environmental Politics*, 8 (1), 149–71.

Johnston, Michael, and Roger Jowell (2001) How Robust Is British Civil Society? In Alison Park, John Curtice, Katarina Thomson, Lindsey Jarvis, and Catherine Bromley (eds.), *British Social Attitudes: The Eighteenth Report*. London: Sage, 175–97.

Jordan, Grant, and William Maloney (1997) *The Protest Business? Mobilizing Campaign Groups*. Manchester: Manchester University Press.

Kitschelt, Herbert (1986) Political Opportunity Structures and Political Protest: Anti-nuclear Movements in Four Democracies. *British Journal of Political Science*, 16, 57–85.

Kousis, Maria (1999) Sustaining Local Environmental Mobilisations: Groups, Actions and Claims in Southern Europe. In Christopher Rootes (ed.), *Environmental Movements*. London: Frank Cass, 172–98, and *Environmental Politics*, 8 (1), 172–98.

——(2003) Greece. In Christopher Rootes (ed.), *Environmental Protest in Western Europe*. Oxford: Oxford University Press, 109–34.

Kriesi, Hanspeter (1989) New Social Movements and the New Class. *American Journal of Sociology*, 94, 1078–1116.

Lee, S., H. Hsiao, H. Liu, O. Lai, F. Magno, and A. So (1999) The Impact of Democratization on Environmental Movements. In Y. F. Lee and A. Y. So (eds.), *Asia's Environmental Movements*. Armonk, NY: M. E. Sharpe, 230–51.

Lee, Yok-Shiu, and Alvin So (1999) Conclusion. In Yok-Shiu Lee and Alvin So (eds.), *Asia's Environmental Movements*. Armonk, NY: M. E. Sharpe, 287–308.

Mellor, Mary (1997) *Feminism and Ecology*. Cambridge: Polity.

Mertig, Angela G., and Riley E. Dunlap (2001) Environmentalism, New Social Movements, and the New Class: A Cross-national Investigation. *Rural Sociology*, 66 (1), 113–36.

Mertig, Angela G., Riley E. Dunlap, and Denton E. Morrison (2002) The Environmental Movement in the United States. In Riley E. Dunlap and William Michelson (eds.), *Handbook of Environmental Sociology*, Westport, CT: Greenwood, 448–81.

Miller, Claire, and David Wroe (2001) Green at Heart. *The Age*, Melbourne, June 25.

Mitchell, Robert C., Riley E. Dunlap, and Angela G. Mertig (1992) Twenty Years of Environmental Mobilization: Trends among National Environmental Organizations. In Riley E. Dunlap and Angela G. Mertig (eds.), *American Environmentalism: The U.S. Environmental Movement, 1970–1990*. Bristol, PA: Taylor & Francis, 11–26.

Mittelman, James H. (1998) Globalisation and Environmental Resistance Politics. *Third World Quarterly*, 19 (5), 847–72.

Müller-Rommel, Ferdinand, and Thomas Poguntke (eds.) (2002) *Green Parties in National Governments*. London: Frank Cass [also published as *Environmental Politics*, 11 (1) 2002].

Nisbet, Robert N. (1982) *Prejudices: A Philosophical Dictionary*. Cambridge, MA: Harvard University Press.

Pakulski, Jan, and Stephen Crook (1998) The End of the Green Cultural Revolution? In Jan Pakulski and Stephen Crook (eds.), *Ebbing of the Green Tide? Environmentalism, Public Opinion and the Media in Australia*. Hobart: School of Sociology and Social Work, University of Tasmania, 1–20.

Pickvance, Katy (1998) *Democracy and Environmental Movements in Eastern Europe: A Comparative Study of Hungary and Russia*. Boulder, CO: Westview.

Rawcliffe, Peter (1998) *Environmental Pressure Groups in Transition*. Manchester: Manchester University Press.

Richardson, Dick, and Chris Rootes (eds.) (1995) *The Green Challenge: The Development of Green Parties in Europe*. London: Routledge.

Rootes, Christopher (1995) A New Class? The Higher Educated and the New Politics. In Louis Maheu (ed.), *Social Movements and Social Classes: The Future of Collective Action*. London: Sage, 220–35.

——(1997a) Environmental Movements and Green Parties in Western and Eastern Europe. In Michael Redclift and Graham Woodgate (eds.), *International Handbook of Environmental Sociology*. Cheltenham: Edward Elgar, 319–48.

——(1997b) Shaping Collective Action: Structure, Contingency and Knowledge. In Ricca Edmondson (ed.), *The Political Context of Collective Action*. London: Routledge, 81–104.

——(1999a) The Transformation of Environmental Activism: Activists, Organisations and Policy-making. *Innovation: The European Journal of Social Sciences*, 12 (2), 155–73.

——(ed.) (1999b) *Environmental Movements: Local, National and Global.* London: Frank Cass.

——(2000) Environmental Protest in Britain 1988–1997. In Ben Seel, Mathew Paterson, and Brian Doherty (eds.), *Direct Action in British Environmentalism.* London: Routledge, 25–61.

——(2002a) The Europeanisation of Environmentalism. In Richard Balme, Didier Chabanet, and Vincent Wright (eds.), *L'action collective en Europe/Collective Action in Europe.* Paris: Presses de Sciences Po, 377–404.

——(2002b) Global Visions: Global Civil Society and the Lessons of European Environmentalism. *Voluntas*, 13 (4), 411–29.

——(2003a) The Resurgence of Protest and the Revitalization of British Democracy. In Pedro Ibarra (ed.), *Social Movements and Democracy.* New York: Palgrave, 137–68.

——(ed.) (2003b) *Environmental Protest in Western Europe.* Oxford: Oxford University Press.

Rootes, Christopher, and Alexander Miller (2000) The British Environmental Movement: Organisational Field and Network of Organisations. Paper presented at European Consortium for Political Research Joint Sessions, Copenhagen <http://www.essex.ac.uk/ ecpr/jointsessions/Copenhagen/papers/ ws5/rootes_miller.pdf>.

Rootes, Christopher, Ben Seel, and Debbie Adams (2000) The Old, the New and the Old New: British Environmental Organisations from Conservationism to Radical Ecologism. Paper presented at European Consortium for Political Research Joint Sessions, Copenhagen <http://www.essex.ac.uk/ ecpr/jointsessions/Copenhagen/ papers/ws5/rootes.pdf>.

Rothman, Hal K. (1998) *The Greening of a Nation? Environmentalism in the US Since 1945.* Fort Worth, TX: Harcourt Brace.

Rucht, Dieter (1989) Environmental Movement Organisations in West Germany and France. Structure and Interorganisational Relations. In Bert Klandermans (ed.), *Organizing for Change: Social Movement Organisations in Europe and the United States, International Social Movement Research.* Vol. 2. Greenwich, CT: JAI, 61–94.

Rucht, Dieter, and Jochen Roose (1999) The German Environmental Movement at a Crossroads? In Rootes 1999b, 59–80, and *Environmental Politics*, 8 (1), 59–80.

——(2001) Neither Decline nor Sclerosis: The Organisational Structure of the German Environmental Movement. *West European Politics*, 24 (4), 55–81.

——(2003) Germany. In Christopher Rootes (ed.), *Environmental Protest in Western Europe.* Oxford: Oxford University Press, 80–108.

Salleh, Ariel (1997) *Ecofeminism as Politics.* London: Zed.

Schlosberg, David (1999) Networks and Mobile Arrangements: Organisational Innovation in the US Environmental Justice Movement. In Christopher Rootes (ed.), *Environmental Movements.* London: Frank Cass, 122–48, and *Environmental Politics*, 8 (1), 122–48.

Seel, Ben, and Alex Plows (2000) Coming Live and Direct: Strategies of Earth First! In Ben Seel, Matthew Paterson, and Brian Doherty (eds.), *Direct Action in British Environmentalism.* London: Routledge, 112–32.

Shaiko, Ronald (1993) Greenpeace USA: Something Old, New, Borrowed. *Annals of the American Academy of Political and Social Science*, 528, 88–100.

Shiva, Vandana (1989) *Staying Alive.* London: Zed.

Sklair, Leslie (1995) Social Movements and Global Capitalism. *Sociology*, 29, 495–512.

Smith, Jackie (2002) Bridging Global Divides? Strategic Framing and Solidarity in Transnational Social Movement Organizations. *International Sociology*, 17 (4), 505–28.

Switzer, Jacqueline Vaughn (1997) *Green Backlash: The History and Politics of Environmental Opposition in the U.S.* Boulder, CO: Lynne Reinner.

Szasz, Andrew (1994) *EcoPopulism: Toxic Waste and the Movement for Environmental Justice.* Minneapolis: University of Minnesota Press.

Taylor, Bron (ed.) (1995) *Ecological Resistance Movements: The Global Emergence of Radical and Popular Environmentalism*. Albany: State University of New York Press.

Touraine, Alain, Zsuzsa Hegedus, François Dubet, and Michel Wieviorka (1983) *Anti-nuclear Protest: The Opposition to Nuclear Energy in France*. Cambridge: Cambridge University Press.

van der Heijden, Hein-Anton (1997) Political Opportunity Structure and the Institutionalisation of the Environmental Movement. *Environmental Politics*, 6 (4), 25–50.

——(1999) Environmental Movements, Ecological Modernisation and Political Opportunity Structures. In Rootes 1999b, 199–221, and *Environmental Politics*, 8 (1), 199–221.

——(2002) Dutch Environmentalism at the Turn of the Century. *Environmental Politics*, 11 (4), 120–30.

Wapner, Paul (1996) *Environmental Activism and World Civic Politics*. Albany: State University of New York Press.

Welsh, Ian (2000) *Mobilising Modernity: The Nuclear Moment*. London: Routledge.

Witherspoon, Sharon, and Jean Martin (1993) Environmental Attitudes and Activism in Britain. *JUSST Working Paper* 20. Oxford: SCPR and Nuffield College.

Worcester, Robert (1999) Public and "Expert" Opinion on Environmental Issues. In Joe Smith (ed.), *The Daily Globe: Environmental Change, the Public and the Media*. London: Earthscan, 33–45.

Yanitsky, Oleg N. (1999) The Environmental Movement in a Hostile Context: The Case of Russia. *International Sociology*, 14 (2), 157–72.

Yearley, Steven (1994) Social Movements and Environmental Change. In Michael Redclift and Ted Benton (eds.), *Social Theory and the Global Environment*. London: Routledge, 150–68.

——(1996) *Sociology, Environmentalism, Globalization*. London: Sage.

27

Antiwar and Peace Movements

SAM MARULLO AND DAVID S. MEYER

INTRODUCTION

States make wars, often opposed by the people within them. Citizens' struggles against war have as long a history as the practice of war. The simplest reasons for opposing war are perhaps the most powerful: people see the potential benefits of violent conflict as far outweighed by the costs and risks of fighting, and preparing to fight, wars. Opponents of war in general, and of particular wars, have employed the full arsenal of social movement tactics to try to get what they want, ranging from public education and moral suasion to sabotage, assassination, and self-immolation, and featuring a full spectrum of tactics in between, including conventional political activity and more disruptive political actions such as demonstrations and civil disobedience.

Peace activists usually lose – at least in terms of preventing their nation from going to war. But their actions often have significant consequences in terms of altering public opinion, forcing policymakers to alter their goals, or undermining the institutional or political infrastructure that supports war-making. Nevertheless, by the time a state has engaged in war, using the full range of its material and ideological resources to shape or stifle opinion and mobilize nationalist fervor in support of war, activists face not only an uphill struggle, but one in which their opponents are already easily mobilizable, and even democratic states enjoy broad support in confining or marginalizing antiwar activists. Usually during wars, antiwar efforts are confined to a small group of committed activists associated with a range of marginal political positions, and willing to endure great costs to make moral witness against evil. As the costs of ongoing wars mount, the processes of legitimation by the state become more costly and difficult, such that opponents can build broad support for their position, as in the campaign against the American war in Vietnam. Likewise, sustained arms buildups that become so costly as to threaten the quality of life of citizens, due to vast diversion of resources toward war-making infrastructure, can provide opportunities for peace activists to mobilize against war and the preparations for war.

World War II changed not only the international political order and the possibilities and conduct for war, but also the opportunities for activists to fight against it. At once, the introduction of nuclear weapons into the calculus of international politics meant that the declared policies of the superpowers maintained a constant threat of imminent war, and the potential for catastrophic global destruction. The permanence of the threat and preparation for war meant that activists found cause to challenge governments even in the absence of actual fighting, such that the possibility of peace mobilization was also always imminent.

In this chapter, we focus primarily on movements against nuclear weapons in the United States, the most consistent demand of the peace movement since the end of World War II. Although these efforts are surely not the whole of the peace movement, this approach allows an analytical focus that speaks to the development of our understanding of social movements and contentious politics. We draw on examples from the Western European peace movement to help us illustrate our analytical claims. The focus on opposition to nuclear weapons limits our historical scope to the period after World War II and the dropping of atomic bombs on Hiroshima and Nagasaki. Since then, the antinuclear weapons movement has waxed and waned, even as American declaratory doctrine has remained relatively constant (Wittner 1984; Kleidman 1993; Marullo 1993). During most of the second half of the twentieth century, the movement was largely invisible, sustained by a core of pacifist, anti-interventionist, and international humanitarian organizations with relatively small constituencies. Occasionally, however, opposition to US nuclear weapons policies has spread beyond these relatively marginal groups to engage large sectors of the population and mainstream politics. In explaining the timing and magnitude of crests and troughs in peace mobilization, we come to a deeper understanding of the relationships among protest, policy, and politics.

Our argument is based on a paradox: *peace movements are most likely to mobilize extensively when they are least likely to get what they want.* When there is a relatively open moment in American policy, when the conduct and content of American foreign policy is under review, as in the period after the end of the Cold War, for example, peace movements are generally invisible. At times when movements are facing the most difficult challenges, that is, when policy appears to be becoming more aggressive, expensive, and dangerous, mobilization is most likely to be extensive. The effect that peace movements have, at least over the short and medium term then, is to preserve the status quo that they struggle against. They do so by preventing or slowing more escalatory policies or military expansion, but not typically by winning actual reductions in militarism.

Periods of high peace movement mobilization have occurred when there is widespread public concern about international and foreign policy, such as during times of impending war, new developments in weapons technology, or when military interventions abroad are being undertaken (Peace 1991; Chatfield 1992; Meyer and Marullo 1992). Opportunities for peace movement mobilization are characterized by visible splits among policy makers and strategic experts that spill outside the boundaries of political institutions. The peace movement takes advantage of splits among elites and stokes anxieties in the broader public by appealing to survival concerns, decrying the high costs and further risks of pursuing current policies, and promoting alternative, less risky (and less militaristic) policies.

Because foreign and military policies are only intermittently on the public agenda (Page and Shapiro 1992), peace activists fight an uphill battle in trying to get attention to the issues that concern them. International events can set the public agenda, offering opportunities to try to mobilize activists. Additionally, out-of-power elites sometimes choose to make public their opposition to policy reforms, again, creating an opportunity for activists to respond to the governmental agenda (Meyer and Imig 1993). During the relatively brief episodes of extensive mobilization, public concern with nuclear weapons and national security policy spreads broadly, and policy reforms seem possible. As movement actors mobilize broadly, they forge coalitions with more institutionally oriented actors. Although these alliances make it easier for a movement to get alternative perspectives out to a broad public, they also limit the extent of how alternative those perspectives will be. These periods end when government makes some kind of accommodation with public concerns, often by moderating the policy disputes that provoked mobilization in the first place (Solo 1988).

We begin with a brief history of the peace movement in the United States, noting some of the philosophical roots of modern day antiwar, antinuclear, and anti-interventionist movements. We next explore in some detail the episodes of extensive mobilization against nuclear weapons policy in the United States since World War II, noting connections and contacts with movements in allied countries. In conclusion, we summarize the workings of the peace movement as a movement and elaborate our analytical findings with respect to social movement theory. Specifically, we offer nine findings based on our analysis of the peace movement, which we summarize here:

1   Political opportunities are critical for successful mobilization. Despite the best efforts of committed organizers, broad peace movement mobilization is contingent upon peculiar constellations of institutional politics and public policy that provoke and create a space for mobilization. Such mobilization, in turn, alters those political opportunities. For this reason, it's appropriate to start any analysis of the peace movement with its expressed grievances: government policy and politics about national security.

2   The consistency of the threat of nuclear annihilation presents a challenge to peace activists that becomes increasingly difficult as it becomes more and more taken for granted. Since the risk of global destruction is no longer new, activists are dependent upon changes in military strategy to provide an opportunity for activists to direct new attention to the nuclear threat and put forward an alternative vision.

3   For the peace movement to mobilize sufficient support to affect policy, organizers must craft very simple yet broad movement goals in order to attract very diverse constituencies. These coalitions are quite tenuous and generally easily undermined by opponents in government.

4   Successful movement coalitions need to link far broader constituencies than movement theories would suggest. The role of scientists and strategic policy experts is critical for the success of the peace movement, yet they are fairly easily reintegrated into mainstream institutional politics.

5 Successful mobilizations rely on the co-optation of substantial resources from other movements typically not involved in peace politics.
6 Radical tactics such as civil disobedience and direct action enliven the broader movement during times of movement resurgence. During times of quiescence, however, they are easily ignored by mass media and the public and repressed by the government.
7 Activists and dissident intellectuals attempt to open the political decision-making process during times of heightened mobilization. However, both movement opponents and even scientific and policy intellectuals that support movement goals seek to retain and restore limited participation in this policymaking arena.
8 Even when the heightened peace mobilization ends, the infrastructure of a core remains in a sort of abeyance structure (Rupp and Taylor 1989), through which more radical and multipurpose critiques of American foreign and military policy are supported (Marullo et al. 1996). This infrastructure proves critical during subsequent opportunities for remobilization.
9 Reforms in policy and shifts in political alignments, in response to the disruption created by the movement, are generally limited in scope, far narrower than what activists demand. At the same time, they may have long-term consequences beyond what is apparent in the immediate wake of a movement.

HISTORIC ROOTS OF THE US PEACE MOVEMENT

The groups that have comprised the peace movement in American history, defined primarily by opposition to some elements of war and preparations for war, have varied dramatically in how they conceptualize peace. Whereas the vast majority of peace groups emphasize the absence of war – although effective mobilization has been contingent upon negotiating alliances with actors with less ambitious goals – a much smaller set of groups views peace as including not just the absence of large-scale physical violence ("negative peace") but also the presence of just domestic and/or international structures ("positive peace") (Galtung 1969; Joseph 1993; Marullo et al. 1996). An even smaller subset of movement organizations combines advocacy for justice with a principled adherence to nonviolence as a means of achieving political ends. These few radical pacifist groups have comprised the consistent core of peace movement activism since before World War II, but are consistently eclipsed by groups with more moderate aims during periods of high mobilization.

Dating back to the 1600s, the historic peace churches – Quakers, Church of the Brethren, and Mennonites – advocated social justice as well as nonviolence (DeBenedetti 1980; Chatfield 1992). Quakers and others worked for the abolition of slavery, fair treatment of Native Americans, and the rights of women, as well as the abolition of war. Stopping war was only one part of the faith-based reform agenda. Many of the groups that advocated for peace on the basis of faith promoted nonviolence at the interpersonal level as well as the international level. Beginning in the 1800s, secular peace societies focused on the issue of international war and its prevention, some downplaying other injustices in the process.

At the beginning of the twentieth century, opponents of war began calling for a new international framework that could prevent the outbreak of war, sometimes including world government. Academic and political intellectuals developed plans for global institutions, providing a set of goals that activists could advocate, pursuing the development of organizations like the League of Nations, the World Court, and later the United Nations. The political exigencies of the two world wars undermined faith in alternatives to war, such that the primary opposition to US participation in these wars was the pacifists.

WORLD WAR II AND ITS AFTERMATH: THE SEA CHANGE IN PEACE ORGANIZING

The use of the atomic bomb in World War II changed the calculus of United States foreign and military policy. Many of the atomic scientists who worked on developing the bomb had grave misgivings about the actual use of the weapon, even to stop Hitler (Rhodes 1986; Herken 1987). Many of the scientists agreed that the weapon should not be treated as merely another instrument of foreign policy, to be wielded as the "big stick" to back the national interests of its owner. During the war, a number of the scientists, led by Danish physicist Neils Bohr, promoted a plan to share information about the development of nuclear weapons with their allies in order to build an international atomic weapons control regime after the war. In 1945 the Franck Report called for a demonstration blast of the bomb rather than its actual use against Japan, hoping to convince the all-but-beaten nation to surrender. The Administration dismissed both alternatives, viewing more outspoken proponents with suspicion – and sometimes surveillance – in the immediate aftermath of the war (Smith 1965; Gaddis 1987; Powaski 1987). But unleashing the destructive power of the atomic bomb opened a debate over the uses, and even the possession, of nuclear weapons.

Initially, the mass media focused debate on the weapons' destructiveness and potential applications. Norman Cousins' influential essay "Modern Man is Obsolete," published in the *Saturday Review* just a week after the bombing of Nagasaki, helped to frame the debate and critique of atomic weapons. For Cousins, nuclear weapons represented a new problem for which there was only one solution: "In the absence of world control as part of world government, [the atomic bomb] will create universal fear and suspicion." Cousins, along with numerous other writers, called for moral consideration and unspecified political action (Divine 1978; Wittner 1984; Boyer 1986).

The use and development of atomic weapons was hotly debated in both academia and mass culture. Magazines and academic journals published special issues, academic and cultural organizations sponsored symposia, and politicians inside and outside of government called for mass education on atomic weapons (Boyer 1986; Inglis 1991). There were two essential components to the American response to atomic weapons – fear, and an sense of urgency that something had to be done about these weapons (Lifton and Falk 1982). However, what that response might be was often unspecified or proposed in vague terms. Peace movement organizations were themselves unclear, agreeing only that the public had to become educated about atomic weapons. The most frequently articulated alternative policies were those Cousins proposed: international control of nuclear weapons and world government. Several local groups of scientists formed by the end of 1945 to focus on public education about nuclear weapons, most notably the Federation of Atomic Scientists, which published *The Bulletin of the Atomic Scientists*, featuring the famed "doomsday clock" on its cover. These groups joined the call of the United World Federalists, also formed shortly after the war, to press for international cooperation and political action. What was lacking, however, in these calls was a blueprint for government policy or citizen action. The lack of specific strategies for peace aided the movement's growth, but also allowed the government to manage the movement's agenda.

Public education campaigns fueled public concern over nuclear weapons, without leading to purposive action or policy change. Inside the government, the debate was over whether the US would cede any control over the development and use of atomic weapons to any international body. The State Department created a special commission to create the Acheson-Lilienthal "Report on International Control of Atomic Energy," which called for the United Nations to establish an international atomic control regime. The administration divided on the issue of whether the Soviet Union, or any of the UN Security Council members, would have veto power over nuclear weapons issues. By all accounts, President Harry Truman's appointment of Bernard Baruch as special ambassador on international atomic weapons control, foreclosed any possibility of movement on these issues. By early 1948, the UN proposal was dead and division within the administration prevented bilateral agreements with the Soviet Union. The administration, and most Americans, ascribed this breakdown, with some justice, to Soviet intransigence.

This debate set the tone for the next half century of nuclear weapons development. Truman commenced the building of a permanent military establishment, buttressed by the growth of defense and security agencies and budgets, and supported outside government by contracts to companies who would build weapons (Mills 1956). At the same time, the United States also engaged in substantial efforts to rebuild the economies of Western Europe, postponing, in effect, challenge to its policies. Debates within the US Congress turned on how rapidly the United States would pursue new weapons systems and technological breakthroughs, as the nuclear arsenal diversified, and the potential uses to which it could be put increased. Within European states, the initial debates were about the vigor with which US policies would be supported, particularly whether to join NATO, and whether to allow nuclear weapons to be based in Europe. The public was rarely part of these technical and policy debates, and would only engage when some new threshold was about to be crossed, and divisions within government spilled out. Domestic affairs dominated government and public attention in the United States, and nuclear weapons seemed too horrifying to take seriously (Lifton and Falk 1982). As the escalating arms race reached new thresholds, prompting public attention, the initial public response was fear and anxiety and an unspecified call for something to be done. Typically, the peace movement organizations themselves were divided as to what the alternative policies should be, ranging from the most radical pacifist calls for disarmament, to the world order framework adherents call for international control of weapons, to the great powers framework adherents calling for bilateral arms control between the two superpower (Marullo et al. 1996). Government competed with peace movement organizations to provide political and policy answers to the problem of nuclear anxiety, and the costs and threats of the arms race.

Soviet repression internally, and then in Eastern Europe, in conjunction with a harsh domestic political environment provided little maneuvering room for advocates of either the internationalist or bilateralist alternative policy approaches within the United States (Lebow and Stein 1994). A new obsession with internal security quashed domestic debate over alternative policies, particularly preventing the scientists working on weapons development from speaking out on their dangers. As the Cold War developed, internationalist perspectives gave way to unilateralism, with some peace activists, notably including Cord Meyer Jr., who went from cofounding the United World Federalists to working in the CIA, which he viewed as the best strategy to promote peace. Many supporters of international control also supported the Korean War, imagining a new era of international cooperation springing from the multilateral military effort. Fear of nuclear weapons was outstripped by fear of the Soviet Union, and ameliorated with optimism about the promise of atomic energy (Boyer 1986). Antinuclear activism disappeared from public debate as a Cold War political order emerged.

THE TEST BAN

While the first expressions of peace protest in the immediate aftermath of World War II led by scientists engaged in the war effort, were relatively quickly stilled, their efforts resumed in the 1950s, and were augmented by radical pacifists. The test ban campaign marked the emergence of the peace movement in the nuclear era. This effective mobilization was the result of a coincidence of a new provocation, demonstrable evidence of harm (in this case, of atmospheric radiation), and enhanced political opportunity. It is a pattern that would repeat itself later, over the Anti-Ballistic Missile (ABM) Treaty debate and the Nuclear Freeze Campaign (Kleidman 1993; Meyer 1993). Antinuclear protest would come from leaders internationally, expert scientists in the United States and Europe, and radical pacifists at the grass roots.

The end of the Korean War, in conjunction with the censure of Senator Joseph McCarthy and the death of Joseph Stalin, opened a space for political debate inside and outside government in the United States. Lessened fear of repression allowed dissidents to question government policy openly and to propose new alternatives. At the same time, the conduct of the arms race provoked more criticism and the search for alternatives. In March 1954, the BRAVO tests in the Bikini Islands catapulted nuclear weapons and the arms race to mass public attention. Radioactive fallout from one test covered "The Lucky Dragon," a Japanese tuna trawler, contaminating its crew and catch, and drawing international attention to the hazards of atomic testing. International leaders, including Pope Pius XII, Jawaharlal Nehru, the British Labour Party, and the Japanese Diet, immediately appealed to the United States to stop testing and negotiate a test ban. Activists in Japan and Great Britain marched in opposition to nuclear testing specifically, and the arms race more generally. In the United States, activists echoed and amplified the international calls; hundreds of letters arrived daily at the White House supporting a test ban, and doctors and scientists debated the dangers of radioactive fallout in both specialized journals and mass market magazines (Divine 1978).

The Eisenhower administration, internally divided, temporized on test ban proposals and on the public debate more generally. Activists seized control of defining the agenda, and focused on radioactive fallout. In February 1955, physicist Ralph

Lapp published detailed information on the atmospheric consequences of BRAVO tests in the *Bulletin of the Atomic Scientists*, nearly a week before the Atomic Energy Commission released its own report. Shortly afterward, a group of international scientists issued the "Einstein–Russell Manifesto," calling for an end to both testing and the arms race. The manifesto directly led to a series of more than 200 Pugwash international meetings of scientists that continues to this day, through which atomic scientists have continually reinforced the importance of nongovernmental and international action on nuclear weapons.

Public recognition of the dangers of nuclear fallout provided an opening for peace activists to lodge claims against the nuclear arms race and the US's role in it. Fear of fallout, coupled with increased anxiety about US preparations for war with the Soviet Union, especially a large domestic civil defense campaign, provided a fertile base of support upon which activists could draw. The federal government's neglect of growing public concern opened political space for dissent, space first claimed by pacifist activists in opposition to civil defense efforts. On June 15, 1955, when New York City conducted its first annual air raid drill, several members of the *Catholic Worker* refused to participate, sitting on park benches and waving placards instead. Police arrested 29 protesters, and the trial judge, denouncing the activists as "murderers," set a very heavy bail. In 1956, British citizens staged an Easter demonstration in Aldermaston, where Britain was developing its own nuclear weapons. The newly founded British CND would stage annual marches from Aldermaston to London to protest the arms race generally, and Britain's participation in it. Activists in Canada, Australia, and New Zealand formed sister CND groups that staged protests and marches as well (Wittner 1997).

Governmental responses to opposition to the arms race and nuclear testing focused ultimately on more effective management of the arms race. The US Senate held hearings on testing in 1956, further opening the door to press for alternative policies through legitimate political avenues. The public demonstrations, massive education campaigns, and civil disobedience so extended the realm of possible policy alternatives that pursuit of a test ban seemed a sane and moderate option. Peace activists pressed Democratic presidential candidate Adlai Stevenson to support a test ban, and Stevenson made the issue a central point in his campaign. Although personally ambivalent about a test ban, President Eisenhower refused to discuss it, probably as part of his own campaign strategy, and argued against politicizing matters of national security. Shortly after winning reelection, however, Eisenhower instructed his staff to explore the possibilities for negotiated limits on testing more aggressively.

Stevenson's defeat spurred further antitesting activism, as it dashed hopes that meaningful reform could be achieved through the electoral process. Test ban advocates sought other routes for influence, as two broad wings of a movement emerged. One called for international agreements coupled with unilateral restraint, and pressed its claims through public education efforts. Its adherents issued appeals, staged international conferences, including the first Pugwash meeting, organized rallies, and ran newspaper and television advertisements. SANE, the National Committee for a Sane Nuclear Policy, founded in 1957, typified this liberal internationalist approach (Cortright 1993). Concurrently, several groups drawing from smaller left wing and pacifist bases of support launched a campaign of civil disobedience and direct action aimed at raising the political costs of continued testing.

Activists again disrupted civil defense exercises in New York City and similar protests against civil defense spread to other cities over the next five years. Pacifist leader A. J. Muste organized a series of trespass campaigns at the Nevada test site. Other activists repeatedly attempted to disrupt atomic testing in the Pacific by sailing into the restricted area, creating much visibility for antinuclear protest.

The US press covered these efforts extensively, effectively encouraging a more politically moderate public education campaign, as dramatic nonviolent direct action efforts expanded the boundaries of legitimate public discourse. Subsequently, pacifist activists organized peace walks, sit-in demonstrations, and other acts of civil disobedience. Activists believed that two wings of the movement working in concert would heighten the visibility and effectiveness of both. Thus, for example, some of SANE's founders also simultaneously organized the Committee for Nonviolent Action to coordinate more radical pacifist efforts.

By the middle of 1957, officials in the US and Great Britain, responding to domestic political fallout and what Secretary of State John Foster Dulles described as the "propaganda drubbings" the US was taking on the issue, moved toward negotiations on a test ban. Public opposition was particularly visible in the UK, where the first British nuclear tests, in the aftermath of the Suez Crisis of 1956, drew attention not only to British testing, but the arms race more generally. Eisenhower and Khrushchev presided over a testing moratorium 1958 to 1960. In the 1960 presidential campaign both Richard Nixon and John Kennedy promised, if elected, to secure an arms control agreement on testing, a substantive shift from only four years earlier.

Formal negotiations stalled however, and Eisenhower urged incoming President Kennedy to resume testing. Increased testing on both sides early in Kennedy's term spurred protest and activism, including trespass at military sites as well as rallies and demonstrations. Nobel prize winning scientist Linus Pauling was a visible antinuclear activist, pressed the issue both at a White House dinner in 1962 and outside the White House in protest the following evening. Meanwhile, antinuclear activism spread throughout Western Europe. In the Nordic countries, activists focused on preventing their own states from developing nuclear weapons, and on refusing to base American weapons. In West Germany, the transformation of the Social Democratic Party from a worker's party into a mass party pushed activists against nuclear weaponry into the streets, as left and pacificist activists organized Easter marches against the arms race (Cooper 1996; Wittner 1997).

The Cuban missile crisis underscored the urgency of managing the nuclear rivalry with the Soviet Union, and accentuated the administration's drive to establish an arms control regime. Kennedy used antinuclear activist Norman Cousins to open a back channel for negotiations with Khrushchev, securing an agreement, joined immediately by British Prime Minister Harold Macmillan, to ban atmospheric testing. The agreement stopped the immediate dangers of atmospheric testing, but it also effectively ended this surge of antinuclear mobilization. Having won the victory of ending atmospheric testing, activists had a more difficult time making claims against the arms race in general, and many turned to other issues. At the same time, the US increased the number of nuclear tests, even if limiting the political and atmospheric fallout by moving them underground. Although protest marches continued in Europe, they became less a call for programmatic reform than an expression of commitment to peace. In an era of superpower *détente* and arms control, it was more difficult to direct attention to the dangers of the arms race, especially, as the decade continued, in comparison with an actual war in Vietnam.

Increased testing was the price President Kennedy agreed to pay in securing military support for treaty ratification. Accelerated underground testing programs allowed the technological modernization of US nuclear weapons, and the development of multiple warhead missiles. The end of superpower atmospheric testing and the establishment of an ongoing arms control process also restored a new elite consensus, institutionalizing both arms control and an arms race. It effectively protected the arms race from strong criticism both within and outside the nuclear power. Peace activists in the US turned to civil rights, economic justice, or against the war in Vietnam for their political efforts, reflecting a social movement spillover (Meyer and Whittier 1994).

AGAINST THE VIETNAM WAR

Opposition to nuclear weaponry was the most consistent issue for the postwar peace movement, but opposition to the war in Vietnam was the most volatile. Following the ratification of the Test Ban Treaty, SANE locals dissipated, and many activists turned to other issues, among these, student democracy (Miller 1987). Students for a Democratic Society found its roots in campus-based SANE chapters, and Tom Hayden's Port Huron Statement pointed to the arms race as both a severe problem, and a symptom of larger social problems. Opposition to the Vietnam War came to organize much SDS activity, contributing to the organization's extraordinarily rapid growth (Gitlin 1980; Miller 1987) and, understandably, was the most visible face of the peace movement.

The initial commitment of US military advisors to Vietnam in the early 1960s prompted little attention and very limited opposition. As the numbers of troops deployed increased, media coverage of casualties, particularly on television, drew public attention to the risks and costs of war (DeBennedetti and Chatfield 1990). Expanded American commitment to the war, under circumstances that would prove to be far more adverse than the government suggested, was demonstrated by increased spending and by a vastly expanded military draft, and ultimately the end of student deferments. This enabled the antiwar mobilization to expand quickly in terms of numbers and visibility, and encouraged an escalation of tactics. In this case, there was a very direct constituency for the movement to be mobilized, and college campuses became the hotbed for antiwar mobilizing. Civil rights and free speech advocates on campuses turned their attention to the war, and reached a far larger audience on campus and beyond. Once again, civil disobedience grew, as increasing numbers of young men refused to register for the draft, burned their draft cards, or fled the country, most commonly to Canada. Opposition to the war, in a context of increasing activism, stoked a radical wing of the movement that included fringe groups that would use violence. Attacks and vandalism against selective service centers disrupted the ability of the government to conduct the draft and hold draft resisters liable for their noncompliance. The large scale campus teach-ins and protests, supported by civil disobedience and a radical fringe that would resort to violence, raised the stakes considerably for sustaining commitment to fighting the war in Vietnam.

By 1968, the presidency of Lyndon Johnson was in shambles, bitterly divided, and Johnson himself refused to run for reelection. The Democratic Party nominated Johnson's vice-president Hubert H. Humphrey for president, although Humphrey had not entered any primaries and had embraced conflicting positions on the war. The Democratic convention in Chicago that year, rather than unifying the party, demonstrated its divisions, as local party leaders kept antiwar activists out of the convention hall, while Chicago police beat, gassed, and generally terrorized activists outside the hall. Democratic dissarray allowed Republican candidate Richard Nixon to run successfully on a campaign pledge to restore law and order to the streets.

Movement opposition continued to build, particularly as the war dragged on and student deferments ended. Although the breadth of the antiwar coalition expanded throughout the Democratic party once Nixon and the Republicans were running the war, antiwar opponents were unable to run their 1972 challenge on the war. Increased antiwar mobilization, including violent protest, produced a backlash against the movement (Schuman 1972). Polarized public opinion allowed Nixon's reelection campaign to rely on a promise of a "secret" plan to end the war as an alternative to Democratic candidate George McGovern's proposal to withdraw the troops. Nixon's plan, such as it was, was to convince the leadership of North Vietnam to believe that he was crazy enough to use nuclear weapons against them, leading them to make concessions at the negotiating table. According to Nixon (1978: 396–404), however, the antiwar movement undermined his plan, making the use of nuclear weapons unthinkable.

By 1972, the US Congress had effectively legislated the end of the war by withholding funding to continue the draft and provide supplies to continue fighting the war. The antiwar movement can claim substantial credit for provoking opposition to the war, raising the costs of conducting the war, and serving an agenda-setting role in which the merits of US foreign policy received an unusual degree of scrutiny (McAdam and Su 2002). The difficulties of conducting the war, both abroad and at home, eventually led to US withdrawal. Once again, the peace movement dissipated, after an apparent victory, but also like the earlier episodes, the movement left behind an enlarged residue of peace movement organizations, trained activists, and sympathetic middle-class adherents who could be mobilized more rapidly during the next cycle of antiwar protest.

Indeed, many of these antiwar activists turned to the burgeoning women's movement (Rupp and Taylor 1987; Meyer and Whittier 1994) and the newly emerging environmental movement, to further realize their growing commitment to participatory democracy and social justice. Some continued with peace issues (Solo 1988).

The Antiballistic Missile Debate

The emergence of an effective campaign against the development and deployment of antiballistic missiles, in the midst of the even more heated politics surrounding the war in Vietnam, demonstrated the power of an expert/citizen coalition. Soviet deployment of a primitive ABM system outside Moscow in 1966 provoked a policy debate within the Johnson administration; although less interested in deploying a system in the US, they did not want not to respond to a development that could easily be portrayed as a threat or provocation internationally. Secretary of Defense McNamara, responding largely to political considerations, antagonistic to the costs and effects of an American ABM system, and dubious about the prospects for an effective system in any case, proposed a "light" defensive system, ostensibly to protect the US from nuclear weapons from China and other small nuclear powers.

Hawkish opponents of the Johnson administration charged McNamara with leaving the US undefended against the Soviet threat. At the same time scientific opponents of the ABM publicized their differences with the administration through articles in scientific journals and testimony before Congress, and sought to exert pressure on elected officials by mobilizing citizen activists, nationally in groups like SANE, and locally in cities slotted to be protected. Unable to achieve their goals through conventional politics, institutionally oriented scientists turned to mass politics (Primack and Von Hippel 1974).

Upon taking office, President Nixon called for speeding the development of ABM systems to defend both US weapons and major metropolitan areas, provoking a wave of activism from both atomic scientists and from local residents who opposed deployment of nuclear weapons near their homes. Activists sponsored teach-ins and rallies in cities where ABMs were to be deployed, including Chicago, Seattle, and Boston. Coordinated by groups like the new Union of Concerned Scientists, formed to organize scientific opposition to the war in Vietnam, ABM opponents testified before Congress, giving cover to Congressional opponents, and conducted public education campaigns to buttress opposition at the grass roots.

Surprised that it was facing criticism from the cities due to be "protected," rather than those left "undefended," the Nixon administration redefined the ABM's mission to defend weapons rather than cities. This meant relocating missile sites from metropolitan areas, with resistant populations, to more remote locations in less politically risky places like Grand Forks, North Dakota. He also began negotiations to limit ABM systems as a precursor to the 1972 SALT (Strategic Arms Limitation Talks) treaty. (The ABM treaty stayed in effect for nearly 30 years, until President Bush announced the US's withdrawal from the accord.)

This redefinition of mission and deployment strategy, in conjunction with active bilateral negotiations, reduced the salience of the nuclear weapons issue and made it difficult for activists to build a broad movement. The eventual treaties effectively managed the size of an ABM effort and defused public opposition in the process. Although ignoring potentially more destabilizing weapons, especially multiple warhead missiles (MIRVs), the ABM and SALT treaties continued the institutional arms control process and kept the public profile of nuclear weapons relatively low. Nixon's political management of ABM, in the context of a broader strategic *détente* with the Soviet Union, allowed the administration to recapture control of the issue. Nuclear weapons issues moved to the back burner of most activist agendas around the world.

The political reception of ballistic missile defenses in Europe differed markedly from that in the US. Whereas American activists questioned the cost and effectiveness of missile defense, European political leaders questioned the effect of a potentially effective strategic defense system on tactical realities in Europe. Specifically, NATO, pressed by German Chancellor Helmut Schmidt, called for a sign of a strategic US commitment to European defense (Cooper 1996). The resultant "dual track decision" taken in 1977, provided a target for peace activists that ultimately unified European and American activists, and refocused activist attention on peace issues.

European Nuclear Disarmament and the Nuclear Freeze Campaign

In the mid-1970s, in the wake of the end of the Vietnam War, peace activists sought a vehicle for unifying their efforts and reaching a broader public. The American Friends Services Committee, an historic pacifist organization, commissioned Randall Forsberg to draft a proposal that might serve as a political strategy and rallying point for diverse strands of the peace movement; including arms control advocates fighting for the ratification of SALT II, local groups active against nuclear power; small campaigns against particular weapons systems, notably the MX missile and the B-1 bomber; and longtime pacifist groups. The nuclear freeze emerged in 1979 both as a political strategy and as an arms control objective. Forsberg's "nuclear freeze" proposal, by advocating a "bilateral" halt to the deployment, production, and testing of nuclear weaponry, would have remained one idea among many competing for attention among mostly marginal groups, had not political circumstances shifted dramatically at the end of the decade.

Even as President Jimmy Carter's administration adopted a more bellicose posture in response to both world events (especially the Nicaraguan and Iranian revolutions and the Soviet invasion of Afghanistan), he was attacked from the "right" by Republican presidential candidate, Ronald Reagan. Reagan's landslide election, bringing Republicans to control of the Senate, ushered in efforts to implement a dramatically more aggressive and expensive security posture, eschewing arms control efforts to focus instead on an aggressive military buildup (Meyer 1990).

At the same time, the 1980 election offered one bit of good news for activists; in three Western Massachusetts electoral districts (carried by Reagan), voters endorsed a referendum supporting the nuclear freeze. At once, activists established the freeze as a viable vehicle for organizing against the new president and his policies. The Reagan administration provided an opportune target for peace activists. Reagan's explicit commitment was to rebuild what he saw as America's neglected armed forces, which emphasized that institutional routes for influence were not open to activists. Administration officials were also candid in their assessments of the prospects of limited nuclear wars, the necessity of strategic superiority, and the futility of arms control; their rhetoric was untempered by qualifiers or guarded language about "options." Reagan appointees spoke cavalierly about fighting and winning nuclear wars, and worked to deploy the weapons to do so (Scheer 1982).

The Reagan administration came into office with a ready-made conflict with European allies about nuclear force modernization. NATO's "dual track" decision, to begin preparations for deploying intermediate range forces in Europe while simultaneously engaging in negotiations to eliminate them – and Soviet SS-20 missiles – was already controversial when Carter announced the decision. In contrast, under Reagan's presidency, the possibility of deploying Pershing II and ground launched cruise missiles in five European countries now seemed a promise, for the Reagan administration publicly disparaged arms control. In this light, nuclear force modernization in Europe, and the governments that supported it, generated unprecedented opposition from European publics (Thompson and Smith 1981; Johnstone 1984; Cooper 1996).

Activists in Western Europe, particularly, used the planned modernization as a vehicle for criticizing superpower politics that threatened European security and sovereignty. As in the ABM case, citizens were understandably critical of talk of limited nuclear wars when their governments made preparations to host the weapons that would fight such wars. New antinuclear movements in Western Europe emerged strongly in 1981, focusing specifically on stopping the so-called "Euromissiles," but offering broader criticisms of the conduct of the Cold War. Demonstrations in Amsterdam, Brussels, Paris, London, Rome, and Bonn each attracted hundreds of thousands of activists. European activists, most notably historian E. P. Thompson, appealed explicitly to their counterparts in the US for help. Peace activists surrounded NATO bases and threatened to physically disrupt the introduction of these new weapons onto the bases. The deployment issue set off massive protests and a new generation of peace organizations in the Federal Republic of Germany, Great Britain, the Netherlands, and Italy, forcing new national elections and party realignment. Although the conservative parties won reelection and the intermediate range missiles were deployed, the decision took its toll on the alliance. Further modernization plans were abandoned as previously allied Western European conservative parties became unwilling to risk further opposition. Grass-roots movements in Western Europe, along with their allies in Liberal, Labor, left, and green parties, played a role in preventing further NATO modernization.

Meanwhile, the Reagan administration had purged from the State and Defense Departments moderate scientists and strategists unconvinced of the possibility or desirability of a war winning strategic posture or interested in arms control at all. Many experts, who lost access to the administration, sought a broader public audience. Mass media followed this elite criticism of the Reagan program, subjecting the President's policies and advisers to an unusual degree of scrutiny (Rojecki 1997).

The nuclear freeze proposal, which the Reagan administration had made suddenly salient and viable, provided a vehicle for organizing around. Activists used the proposal, frequently offered in state and local referenda and town meetings, as an opportunity to conduct public education campaigns. By 1982, the freeze movement had succeeded in commanding broad public attention, winning numerous referenda, demonstrating overwhelming support in public opinion polls, and rallying one million people in Central Park (Lofland and Marullo 1993). Public opinion support for a nuclear freeze fluctuated between 60 and 80 percent, depending on the wording of the questions (Meyer 1990; Rojecki 1997).

Although activists espoused a broad variety of ultimate goals and means, the mass media grouped virtually all opponents of the Reagan administration's security policies under the banner of the "nuclear freeze." As articulated by Randall Forsberg in 1984, a freeze proposal was the first step in a complicated and comprehensive program to remake world politics (Forsberg 1984). As generally explained in mass media, it was an unfocused cry for arms control. The broad movement coalition made this struggle particularly important, and activist efforts to control it especially difficult. As the movement grew, activists were increasingly divided on the meaning of the proposal that so many supported. The administration's announcement of resumed arms control talks with the Soviet Union, immediately following this peak, signaled the beginning of the end for the movement (Meyer 1990).

Broad public mobilization, punctuated by dramatic acts of civil disobedience, brought the movement serious attention from mass media and political leaders. At the same time, the prospects of influence, represented by inroads in mainstream political institutions, exacerbated tensions within the freeze coalition. Institutionally oriented arms control groups cultivated their Washington connections and tried to influence Congress on "pragmatic" policy goals, including a variety of budget issues, curtailing the Strategic Defense Initiative ("Star Wars"), and pushing the resurrection of an arms control regime. Public education and mobilization had brought them what seemed like the prospects for meaningful influence. At the same time, many pacifist and left-liberal groups continued their activities, but grew disaffected with the nuclear freeze, now redefined as a rallying cry for moderation rather than a policy alternative, and shifted to more salient issues, such as supporting economic sanctions against South Africa or preventing US military intervention in Nicaragua.

As the peace movement changed American politics, the freeze came to mean less and less. Endorsed in some way by six of seven Democratic aspirants for the presidential nomination in 1984, the freeze came to be little more than shorthand for a more moderate approach than that offered by the incumbent administration. President Reagan worked to ensure the election would not be a referendum on either the freeze or his own national security policies. In January of 1984, Reagan announced a new commitment to arms control negotiations, and to restoring summit meetings with the Soviet Union, offering conciliatory rhetoric to both freeze supporters and the Soviets. At the same time, a somewhat strengthened Congressional opposition prevented the most aggressive aspects of the Reagan buildup, limiting growth of the budget, and effectively mandating arms control. European allies, while endorsing the deployment of the intermediate range missiles, made it clear that they would not tolerate a subsequent round of nuclear modernization. Reagan declared his landslide reelection, in November 1984, as a mandate for arms control. Similarly, elections of the early 1980s in Western Europe installed conservative and center-right governments that were similarly committed to the arms control process.

For all its limitations, the freeze movement rescued the previous bipartisan policy consensus, restricting the Reagan administration's military initiatives, and returned legitimacy and institutional access to advocates of arms control and nuclear restraint. Clearly, the nuclear freeze movement affected US policy – which ultimately produced a new round of strategic arms control agreements with the Soviet Union, later Russia – albeit in ways that it did not intend or anticipate (Meyer and Marullo 1992; Knopf 1997). On one level, a return to an arms control regime and a technological arms race seems a meager achievement. At the same time, Reagan's arms control proposals, however, offered more for domestic political reasons than international response, and had extensive unexpected effects. The new posture offered incoming Soviet General Secretary Gorbachev a lever with which to reopen *détente*. When Gorbachev accepted the disproportionate cuts in nuclear forces Reagan had proposed, the administration was cornered: it could not reject its own proposals. This forced flexibility on arms control proved to be critical in ending the Cold War (Kaldor 1990; Meyer and Marullo 1992). The movements won far less than they hoped, yet turned out to be far more significant than anyone involved would have guessed, playing a critical role in precipitating and shaping the events that marked the end of the Cold War.

Organizing for Peace after the Cold War: Persian Gulf Wars and Beyond

The peace movement of the 1950s onward had a dramatic effect on American foreign policy, ensuring the maintenance of tempered rhetoric and an arms control regime. Possible breakouts from this regime, such as that represented by the first Reagan administration, were restrained, and advocates of such positions were forced to reform or pay a political price. The movement against US participation in the Vietnam War effectively ended the draft, and constrained the use of military force abroad, the so-called "Vietnam syndrome." Acknowledging the importance of public support, and the risks of opposition, Reagan's first Secretary of Defense, Caspar Weinberger (1990) articulated a doctrine sharply altering the possibilities and parameters for American use of force abroad: all deployment of American forces had to be easily explainable to the public, extremely likely to succeed, limited in time, and with easy and quick exit strategies. Ironically supported in effect by the anti-intervention movement of the 1980s, the Weinberger doctrine confined US military efforts in Central America to covert activities and the support of proxies – less costly, less visible, and less provocative to the US public.

The Persian Gulf War, conducted by Reagan's former vice-president, George Bush, who was now president, and Weinberger's protégé, Colin Powell, as Chair of the Joint Chiefs of Staff, demonstrated both the influence and the limitations of the peace movement. Bush's military buildup in the Gulf, a response to Iraq's invasion of Kuwait in 1990, quickly generated an antiwar response, organized by the longtime pacifist core of the peace movement. The immediate threat of war afforded groups with different ideologies – pacifist, anti-interventionist, and multilateralist – to join forces quickly in opposition to pending military hostilities. Activists directed the resources they had developed in support of the nuclear freeze (such as skilled and knowledgeable organizers, networks among peace groups, and the communication capacities of movement organizations) toward opposing the Gulf War military buildup (Marullo 1993). They organized national and regional demonstrations that turned up thousands of demonstrators before forces were even deployed, and pressed for an alternative policy of economic sanctions, rather than a quick resort to force.

Despite such a rapid mobilization by the peace movement, President George Bush's administration organized a military and political response in accord with what Powell and others had learned from Vietnam, one that effectively marginalized the peace movement. The administration effectively negotiated support from European allies, and once battle started, overwhelmed the severely outmatched Iraqi armed forces through air attacks. The US-led international coalition sought minimal policy gains, allowing Saddam Hussein's regime to remain in power, and employed insurmountable forces, deploying more than 500,000 troops in the Persian Gulf in a period of a few months, minimizing casualties to the volunteer US forces in the process, and reducing American presence in the region almost immediately. The peace movement virtually disappeared as soon as bombing began, and full-scale war lasted little over a month.

As we are completing this chapter in the fall of 2002, the US government led by George W. Bush is apparently relearning lessons learned by the first President Bush in the conduct of the Persian Gulf War. Initially, President Bush engaged in months of sabre-rattling and talk of "regime change," in conjunction with threats to remove Saddam Hussein from power unilaterally. Responses from US allies, neutral countries, and indeed, foreign policy experts outside of government (e.g., Fallows 2002; Lemann 2002), were almost uniformly negative on both the substance and process of US policy toward Iraq. Opposition from allies, and from peace movements, effectively strengthened the hands of moderates within the Bush administration, most notably Secretary of State Colin Powell, and the administration began some outreach to allies and the United Nations to build a new coalition to support a military initiative against Iraq.

The Democratic minority in Congress used this issue to criticize Bush and question his leadership, which had soared to record levels of popularity in the aftermath of the September 11, 2001, terrorist attacks in the US and the rapid retaliation against the Afghan Taliban regime and terrorist networks. The remnants of the peace movement – which for the past several years had worked in coalitions with antiglobalization efforts, and had worked on a smattering of issues including opposition to continued antiballistic missile defense development and continued sanctions against Iraq – have begun to coalesce in opposition to the anticipated military intervention in Iraq. The prospects for effective mobilization seem limited, however, should the President construct at least a symbolic international coalition, thereby preventing political elite opposition from effective dissidence, and articulate a limited set of military objectives based on limited risk to US forces, a readily achievable goal, and a clear exit strategy. The peace movement critiques based in pacifism (nonviolence), multilateralism, and humanitarianism can each be neutralized to some extent by the Bush administration's claims of self-defense, having allied support, and ousting Saddam Hussein for the good of his own people and the surrounding region. This suggests that a new symbolic frame will have to be developed to effectively mobilize peace movement opposition to future military interventions. The peace movement's continued collaboration with the antiglobalization movement seems to be the most promising incubator from which such a new frame may emerge.

The end of the Cold War, marked by the collapse of the Soviet Union, in conjunction with the popular, and internationally endorsed, short-term use of force in the Gulf War, dramatically changed the opportunities available to the peace movement. First and foremost, there is a reduced sense of urgency for action on nuclear arms control because past agreements (Strategic Arms Limitations Talks (SALT) and Strategic Arms Reductions Talks (START) Treaties) have been implemented, and followed by both unilateral and negotiated nuclear forces cuts, reducing the overall size of nuclear arsenals in the US and Russia. At the same time, the post–Cold War period provides a real open moment on policy, as political elites and policy experts are divided on appropriate foreign and military policies for the US in a dramatically changed international system. At a time when public mobilization and education might be most likely to affect policy, political activism on peace is largely absent. Longtime peace activists have organized through other issues, focusing on pursuing their visions of peace through a focus on environmental issues, human rights, or economic development. At the same time, a small segment of the movement has continued to focus on organizing against armaments and militarism, employing dramatic civil disobedience actions against military facilities and weapons producers (Marullo et al. 1996), although these actions get less attention when there is not more widespread political mobilization on issues of war and peace. And activists who might in other circumstances be engaged in peace issues have turned to domestic issues and antiglobalization protests, as in other down periods for the peace movement.

Peace Movements, Politics, and Collective Action

The brief overview of the history of peace and antiwar movements in American history underscores some fundamental points about their emergence, development, and influence, that have relevance for our understanding of social movements more generally. In this extended conclusion, we review findings and patterns from this history, with reference to significant issues in social movement theory.

It is first worth reviewing the general pattern of peace and antiwar mobilization. While some small and relatively marginal political groups, mostly internationalists and/or pacifists, are always concerned with peace and nuclear issues, they generally find it hard to reach a broad public. An apparent change in policy and the composition of people making policy affords those stalwarts to find common cause with political figures and policy experts who are normally oriented to institutional efforts. This allows both to reach a broader audience, if at a cost of a diluted message. Once the movement has begun to mobilize effectively, a synergistic interplay of factors helps it to grow, mobilizing new resources, and enlisting a range of groups and individuals not normally concerned with issues of national security. Movement opponents work to reinstitutionalize the policy debate, with a combination of conciliatory rhetoric, political openness, and explicit denigration of the expertise or loyalties of some of their critics. The possibility for meaningful influence, and sometimes a new policy reform, split the movement coalition, such that institutionally oriented actors become more connected with mainstream politics than the movement, and more comprehensive critics lose the prospect of a large audience.

As the movement recedes, however, the policies it challenged also change. And successful mobilizations leave in their wake new organizations, strategies, and activists who can invigorate subsequent mobilizations on peace (Edwards and Marullo 1995) and on other issues (Meyer and Whittier 1994). Likewise, countermovement efforts to neutralize the peace movement gains acquire experience in how to split coalitions, undermine rhetorical frameworks, and minimize the extrinsic costs of military interventions.

In the interest of clarity, we summarize our findings in regard to social movement theory.

1   Despite the best efforts of committed organizers, broad peace movement mobilization is contingent upon the constellation of institutional politics and public policy, creating a space for mobilization. Political opportunities are critical for successful

mobilization, and successful mobilization alters those political opportunities. For the peace movement, it is not institutional openings (cf. McAdam 1982), but institutional closings that matter most. Because the peace movement attempts to influence US foreign and security policy, which tends to be removed from most people's everyday concerns, it faces a formidable challenge to mobilizing under routine circumstances. The distant nature of foreign policy issues makes them difficult to use for mobilization (Rucht 2000). For each of the successful mobilizations, the peace movement was confronted with technological or policy development that directly impacted people, putting large numbers of lives at risk, making abstract issues real and powerful.

Although policy shifts can provide political space and incentives for protest movements to emerge, governments may alter their policies and/or rhetoric in order to reclaim that political space. We have seen the important role of elite actors, particularly scientists and strategic experts, who mediate between the state and protest movements, identifying which aspects of policy are most vulnerable to assault, legitimating and sometimes aiding insurgent movements, and framing solutions to the political problems that movements cause. Peace movements emerge when institutionally oriented actors lose faith in the efficacy of institutional politics, at least when not bolstered by some extra-institutional leverage. At such times, they may forge alliances with activists making broader claims and engaging in extra-institutional action. The resultant movements lodge broad claims against the state, but generally disperse after an administration reintegrates dissident elite into institutional politics, often by restoring to some extent previous policies. The cyclic nature of movement challenges reflects the shifting attention of elite actors from institutional venues to extra-institutional ones.

The concentration of power about national security in the Executive means that the extent of those shut out, in one way or another, is very large. People normally accustomed to being involved in the process of making policy, even if they frequently lose, have no interest in expanding the scope of the security policy domain generally (see Burstein 1991 on "policy domains"; also Meyer 1993; Pagnucco and Smith 1993), but have great incentive to go public when they lose access.

2   The overwhelming destructive capability of nuclear weapons limits the strategic alternative visions that can be proposed by the peace movement. The consistency of the nuclear threat, visible with the first use of nuclear weapons, and reasonably present since the development of Soviet nuclear weapons in the 1950s, presents a challenge to peace activists because it is so much taken-for-granted and so little affected by policy option offered (Marullo 1993). The risk of global destruction no longer new, activists are dependent upon changes in military strategy – such as new weapons development and deployment, or alterations in war-fighting strategies – to provide an opportunity for activists to direct new attention to the nuclear threat, and put forward an alternative vision. Yet these alternative policies offered through the political arena make no difference in changing the capability of nuclear powers to render incomprehensible global destruction in a matter of minutes.

The easiest way for the peace movement to reach and mobilize a broad public is inherently problematic: playing on public fears. While newly recognized fears of global destruction can be a motivator for action against government and current policies, they are virtually always short-lived. At once, it is hard to sustain this kind of panic without a broader analytical or ideological perspective on the arms race. More pointedly, authorities can use the same fears to legitimate and justify their own policies. "Deterrence works" is an easy example. Peace activists could illustrate convincingly the devastation of a nuclear war and lodge arguments against maintenance of the weapons that would fight such a war. At the same time, supporters of the same policies have regularly been able to respond to fear by arguing that the maintenance of a nuclear threat is the only way to avoid nuclear war and requires modernizing weapons.

3   For peace movements to mobilize sufficient support to affect policy, organizers must link very diverse constituencies, growing beyond the traditional left and pacifist core. Each of the successful mobilization surges during the last half century, built around a fairly simple and straightforward message and organizing strategy, was characterized by a "master frame" (Snow and Benford 1992; Benford 1993) that could be read differently by different audiences. As long as the difference between adherents and government policy is most salient, both moderates and fundamentalists within a peace movement coalition have more incentive to cooperate with each other. When, however, the government offers the prospect of influence, potentially transforming movement slogans to policy proposals, movement coalitions unravel.

4   Successful movement coalitions are far broader than established thinking about "challengers" versus "authorities" would have us believe (e.g., Tilly 1978). In fact, mainstream political elites, particularly scientists and strategic experts, play a critical role to peace movements, providing resources, including legitimacy, to the movement, when they "cross over" to support the movement's claims and strategies.

On occasion, experts and political elites who lose a particular debate about technical assessments or political objectives of strategy, choose to take their dispute public and direct public attention to issues normally neglected by the broader public. They play an intermediary role between the state and protest movements, identifying the elements of policy most vulnerable to challenge, providing critical information, analysis, and legitimation, thereby aiding insurgent movements. Government concessions, however, generally include formal consultation with some element of dissident elites, who are quickly reintegrated into institutional politics. Movement activists are left without ready access to media or the public, much less policy making, often feeling betrayed and sold out. The political and policy outcomes most resemble the status quo ante, much to the frustration of movement leaders who had hoped and organized for more.

5   Successful mobilization takes place when peace movement activists co-opt the resources, legitimacy, and efforts of established institutions usually inattentive to issues of national security. Whereas peace activism does mobilize new volunteers and financial support, the lion's share of effort comes from other organizations, including civic organizations, churches, and mainstream media organs. During times of peace movement quiescence, these organizations operate primarily on other terrain, sometimes not even making political claims. During periods of extensive mobilization, interorganizational cooperation (see Rochon and Meyer 1998) multiplies the effect of organizing efforts, mobilizing new groups en bloc.

6   Radical tactics, such as civil disobedience and direct action, enliven the broader movement during peaks, legitimizing and underscoring more moderate activity. While much peace protest is "polite" by the standards of the second half of the

twentieth century (Lofland 1993), all of it is not. Partisans against war have used not only dramatic civil disobedience, but also direct attacks on manufacturers and government institutions. Always a small fraction of movement activity, government can easily ignore or repress such efforts during normal political times. During periods of extensive mobilization, however, these efforts serve as punctuation marks to the larger movement, providing access to media coverage and additional attention to movement issues.

7   Activist efforts to remake world politics take place in dynamic political circumstances, such that their attempts to open the process of making security policy to new actors are countered by efforts by those in power to reinstitutionalize the debate.

The initial response is usually to ignore protest and oppositional initiatives, which in normal times almost always works. When no longer possible, during times of heightened mobilization, authorities employ a range of responses, usually in concert, including choreographing elite and expert support of current policies in mass media; discrediting the expertise or loyalties of movement leaders and critics of policy; reframing existing policies to appear more conciliatory; and/or reforming current policies to regain the support of some portion of dissident elites.

8   Even when the peace movement disappears from the news and broad mobilization ends, the infrastructure of a core remains in a sort of abeyance structure (Rupp and Taylor 1987), in which more radical and multipurpose critiques of American foreign and military policy are supported. This infrastructure proves critical during opportunities for remobilization (Marullo et al. 1996).

Each resurgence of the US peace movement throughout the Cold War and beyond was not entirely new, but instead built on the infrastructure left by its predecessors. Long enduring core peace constituencies (Wittner 1984; Boulding 1990) and key organizations, such as the historic peace churches, SANE, and the World Federalists, were instrumental in initiating resurgent protest. They sifted and filtered possible new protest strategies and policy options and designed actions around what they knew. These in turn were influenced and shaped by newer organizations, new strategies and tactics that would emerge during the surging phase. The organizational and tactical innovations of newly formed peace groups were often framed in contrast, even opposition, to those considered typical of the core constituencies and persistent peace groups who survived previous periods of decline and abeyance (Freeman 1975; Evans 1980; Carson 1981; McAdam 1982; D'Emilio 1983; Adam 1985; Isserman 1987; Brienes 1989).

One way the movement transforms during times of abeyance is the selective mortality that occurs among groups that do not survive the movement's doldrums. Such selective mortality sets the stage for the movements next resurgence by altering the domain into which new strategies are introduced. In an analysis of peace movement mortality during the decline of the nuclear freeze campaign, Edwards and Marullo (1995) found that the local peace groups more likely to survive were: older and larger in size; had broad agendas; worked in coalitions with other groups; and worked with mainstream political officials. For large and national peace groups, having more legitimacy, working across movement sectors and with mainstream political officials, and having more routinized financing increased the chances of survival. What turned out to be critical to survival was the ability to connect with other organizations on a range of issues.

For the successful test ban campaign, anti-Vietnam War movement, and nuclear freeze campaign, longstanding organizations in the peace movement industry played an important role in launching and shaping the resurgence of the movement around a new catalyst. Enlarged, sometimes overrun, by new members, they experienced leadership turnover, they refocused their own energies and resources, and they took on new developmental trajectories. Nevertheless, our point here is to stress the importance of movement's infrastructure during times of dormancy and its role as an incubator for new ideas and organizing strategies.

9   Reforms in policy and political alignments, in response to the disruption that movements create, are generally very limited in scope, far narrower than what activists demand. At the same time, they may have long-term consequences beyond what is apparent in the immediate wake of a movement. Regardless, rather small responses are usually enough to dissipate a broad movement and fragment a challenging coalition.

The successes of the peace movement during the second half of the twentieth century have been limited and mixed. Even significant victories have been incomplete and very difficult for activists to claim as the results of their efforts (Meyer 2001). Negotiated arms control agreements, a response to peace movements, have had a greater effect in pacifying public opposition than intaming the technological arms race. The movement against the Vietnam War did more to affect the disposition of presidents to commit troops to combat abroad than their capacity to do so.

At the same time, the long term consequences of apparently small concessions, can be far-reaching. While moving tests underground in 1963, for example, allowed the technological arms race to proceed unimpeded, the creation of the Arms Control and Disarmament Agency (ACDA) at the same time provided a permanent institutional place for advocates of some degree of international cooperation. Similarly, President Reagan's apparently cynical response to the peace movement, offering arms proposals calling for massive and disproportionate cuts in strategic weaponry, provided a new Soviet regime with a lever to reestablish an arms control regime, one that ultimately led to the unraveling of the Cold War and, ultimately, the Soviet Union itself.

In looking at the peace and antiwar movements in the US during the past half-century, we are struck by both great disappointments and defeats to activists, and unexpected achievements. That activists sometimes mobilize broad constituencies, and that their efforts sometimes affect policy – and subsequent rounds of mobilization, albeit less than advocates would like – must always be seen as a major accomplishment for activists. Peace activists mobilize on behalf of collective goods, and to influence the policy domain most insulated from democratic pressures and processes of all kinds. Their successes, limited as they may be, mirror the accomplishments and disappointments of real democracy.

References

Adam, Barry (1985) *The Rise of a Gay and Lesbian Movement.* 2nd ed. Boston: Twayne.
Benford, Robert (1993) Frame Disputes within the Nuclear Disarmament Movement. *Social Forces*, 71 (March), 677–701.

Boulding, Elise (1990) *Building a Global Civic Culture: Education for an Interdependent World*. Syracuse, NY: Syracuse University Press.

Boyer, Paul (1986) *By the Bomb's Early Light: American Thought and Culture at the Dawn of the Nuclear Age*. New York: Pantheon.

Brienes, Wini (1989) *Community and Organization in the New Left, 1962–1968*. New Brunswick, NJ: Rutgers University Press.

Burstein, Paul (1991) Policy Domains: Organization, Culture and Policy Outcomes. *Annual Review of Sociology*, 17, 327–50.

Carson, Clayborne (1981) *In Struggle: SNCC and the Black Awakening of the 1960s*. Cambridge, MA: Harvard University Press.

Chatfield, Charles, with Robert Kleidman (1992) *The American Peace Movement*. Boston: Twayne.

Cooper, Alice H. (1996) *Paradoxes of Peace: German Peace Movements since 1945*. Ann Arbor: University of Michigan Press.

Cortright, David (1993) *Peace Works: The Citizen's Role in Ending the Cold War*. Boulder, CO: Westview.

D'Emilio, John (1983) *Sexual Politics, Sexual Communities*. Chicago: University of Chicago Press.

DeBenedetti, Charles (1980) *The Peace Reform in American History*. Bloomington: Indiana University Press.

DeBenedetti, Charles, and Charles Chatfield (1990) *An American Ordeal: The Antiwar Movement of the Vietnam Era*. Syracuse, NY: Syracuse University Press.

Divine, Robert (1978) *Blowing on the Wind: The Nuclear Test Ban Debate, 1954–1960*. New York: Oxford University Press.

Edwards, Bob, and Sam Marullo (1995) Organizational Mortality in a Declining Movement: The Demise of Peace Movement Organizations in the End of the Cold War Era. *American Sociological Review*, 60 (December), 908–27.

Evans, Sara (1980) *Personal Politics*. New York: Vintage.

Fallows, James (2002) The Fifty-first State? *Atlantic Monthly*, 290, November, 53 ff.

Forsberg, Randall (1984) The Freeze and Beyond: Confining the Military to Defense as a Route to Disarmament. *World Policy Journal*, 1, 287–318.

Freeman, Jo (1975) *The Politics of Women's Liberation*. New York: David McKay.

Gaddis, John L. (1987) *The Long Peace: Inquiries into the History of the Cold War*. New York: Oxford University Press.

Galtung, Johan (1969) Violence, Peace and Peace Research. *Journal of Peace Research*, 6, 167–91.

Gitlin, Todd (1980) *The Whole World Is Watching*. Berkeley: University of California Press.

Herken, Gregg (1987) *Counsels of War*. Expanded ed. New York: Oxford University Press.

Inglis, Fred (1991) *The Cruel Peace: Everyday Life and the Cold War*. New York: Basic.

Isserman, Maurice (1987) *If I Had a Hammer: The Death of the Old Left and the Birth of the New Left*. New York: Basic.

Johnstone, Diana (1984) *The Politics of the Euromissiles*. London: Verso.

Joseph, Paul (1993) *Peace Politics: The United States between the Old and New World Orders*. Philadelphia, PA: Temple University Press.

Kaldor, Mary (1990) *The Imaginary War: Understanding the East West Conflict*. Cambridge, MA: Basil Blackwell.

Kleidman, Robert (1993) *Organizing for Peace: Neutrality, the Test Ban, and the Freeze*. Syracuse, NY: Syracuse University Press.

Knopf, Jeffrey (1997) The Nuclear Freeze Movement's Effect on Policy. In Thomas Rochon and David S. Meyer (eds.), *Coalitions and Political Movements: The Lessons of the Nuclear Freeze*. Boulder, CO: Lynne Rienner, 127–61.

Lebow, Richard N., and Janice G. Stein (1994) *We All Lost the Cold War*. Princeton, NJ: Princeton University Press.

Lemann, Nicholas (2002) The War on What? *The New Yorker*, 78, September 16.

Lifton, Robert J., and Richard Falk (1982) *Indefensible Weapons: The Political and Psychological Case against Nuclearism*. New York: Basic.

Lofland, John (1993) *Polite Protesters: The American Peace Movement of the 1980s*. Syracuse, NY: Syracuse University Press.

Lofland, John, and Sam Marullo (1993) Surge Soaring: Peace Activism, 1981–1983. In J. Lofland, *Polite Protesters: The American Peace Movement of the 1980s*. Syracuse, NY: Syracuse University Press, 233–72.

McAdam, Doug (1982) *Political Process and the Development of Black Insurgency, 1890–1970*. Chicago: University of Chicago Press.

McAdam, Doug, and Yang Su (2002) The War at Home: Antiwar Protests and Congressional Voting, 1965–1973. *American Sociological Review*, 67, 696–721.

Marullo, Sam (1993) *Ending the Cold War at Home: From Militarism to a More Peaceful World Order*. Lexington, MA: Lexington.

Marullo, Sam, Ron Pagnucco, and Jackie Smith (1996) Frame Changes and Social Movement Contraction: U.S. Peace Movement Framing after the Cold War. *Sociological Inquiry*, 36 (January), 1–28.

Meyer, David S. (1990) *A Winter of Discontent: The Nuclear Freeze and American Politics*. New York: Praeger.

——(1993) Peace Protest and Policy: Explaining the Rise and Decline of Antinuclear Movements in Postwar America. *Policy Studies Journal*, 21, 1–21.

——(2001) Claiming Credit: The Social Construction of Social Movement Success. Center for the Study of Democracy Occasional Paper, University of California, Irvine.

Meyer, David S., and Doug Imig (1993) Political Opportunity and the Rise and Decline of Interest Group Sectors. *Social Science Quarterly*, 74, 750–70.

Meyer, David S., and Sam Marullo (1992) Grassroots Mobilization and International Politics: Peace Protest and the End of the Cold War. *Research in Social Movements, Conflicts and Change*, 14, 99–140.

Meyer, David S., and Nancy Whittier (1994) Social Movement Spillover. *Social Problems*, 41, 277–98.

Miller, James (1987) *Democracy is in the Streets*. New York: Simon & Schuster.

Mills, C. Wright (1956) *The Power Elite*. New York: Oxford University Press.

Nixon, Richard (1978) *RN: Memoirs of a President*. New York: Grossett & Dunlap.

Page, Benjamin I., and Robert Y. Shapiro (1992) *The Rational Public*. Chicago: University of Chicago Press.

Pagnucco, Ron, and Jackie Smith (1993) The Peace Movement and the Formulation of U.S. Foreign Policy. *Peace and Change*, 18, 157–81.

Peace, Roger III (1991) *A Just and Lasting Peace: The U.S. Peace Movement from the Cold War to Desert Storm*. Chicago, IL: Noble.

Powaski, Ronald (1987) *March to Armageddon: The United States and the Nuclear Arms Race, 1939 to the Present*. New York: Oxford University Press.

Primack, Joel, and Frannk von Hippel (1974) *Advice and Dissent*. New York: Basic.

Rhodes, Richard (1986) *The Making of the Atomic Bomb*. New York: Simon & Schuster.

Rochon, Thomas R., and David S. Meyer (1998) *Coalitions and Political Movements: Lessons of the Nuclear Freeze*. Boulder, CO: Lynne Rienner.

Rojecki, Andrew (1997) Freeze Frame: News Coverage of the Freeze Movement. In Thomas Rochon and David S. Meyer (eds.), *Coalitions and Political Movements: The Lessons of the Nuclear Freeze*. Boulder, CO: Lynne Rienner, 97–126.

Rucht, Dieter (2000) Distant Issue Movements in Germany: Empirical Description and Theoretical Reflections. In John A. Guidry, Michael D. Kennedy, and Mayer N. Zald (eds.), *Globalizations and Social Movements: Culture, Power, and the Transnational Public Sphere*. Ann Arbor: University of Michigan Press, 76–105.

Rupp, Leila, and Verta Taylor (1987) *Survival in the Doldrums: The American Women's Rights Movement*. New York: Oxford University Press.

Scheer, Robert (1982) *With Enough Shovels: Reagan, Bush, and Nuclear War*. New York: Random House.

Schuman, Howard (1972) Two Sources of Anti-war Sentiment in America. *American Journal of Sociology*, 78, 513–36.

Smith, Alice Kimball (1965) *A Peril and a Hope: The Scientists' Movement in America, 1945–1947*. Chicago: University of Chicago Press, 1965.

Snow, David, and Robert Benford (1992) Master Frames and Cycles of Protest. In A. Morris and C. M. Mueller (eds.), *Frontiers in Social Movement Theory*. New Haven: Yale University Press, 133–56.

Solo, Pam (1988) *From Protest to Policy: Beyond the Freeze to Common Security*. Cambridge, MA: Ballinger.

Thompson, E. P., and Dan Smith (eds.) (1981) *Protest and Survive*. New York: Monthly Review.

Tilly, Charles (1978) *From Mobilization to Revolution*. Reading, MA: Addison-Wesley.

Weinberger, Caspar W. (1990) *Fighting for Peace: Seven Critical Years in the Pentagon*. New York: Warner.

Wittner, Lawrence (1984) *Rebels against War: The American Peace Movement, 1933–1983*. Philadelphia, PA: Temple University Press.

——(1997)*The Struggle against the Bomb*. Vol. 2, *Resisting the Bomb: A History of the World Nuclear Disarmament Movement, 1954–1970*. Stanford: Stanford University Press.

28

Ethnic and Nationalist Social Movements

Susan Olzak

Introduction and Definitions

The study of ethnic and nationalist social movements lies at the intersection of three fields: social movements, race and ethnic collective action, and nationalism. Ethnic, racial, and nationalist social movements often share overlapping themes, claims, tactics, personnel, and goals. More importantly, such movements commonly rest on founding myths organized around a specific ethnic and/or racial identity. Despite these parallels, these movements have rarely been analyzed together. Until recently, perspectives on nationalist and ethnic movements were organized separately by regional location or outcome (e.g., nationalism in Western Europe, ethnic violence in sub-Saharan Africa, etc.). As a result, the study of nationalism and ethnic conflict has become highly fragmented, which has thwarted most attempts at theoretical progress.

Recent treatments now offer a fresh approach that emphasizes the shared characteristics and causal mechanisms among movements (ethnic or otherwise) that challenge authority structures in states, institutions, and organizations (Hechter 2000; McAdam et al. 2001). For analytic purposes here, I will begin by defining the boundaries around several key forms of ethnic and racial (hereafter, E/R) and nationalist movements that vary with respect to demands, goals, and organizational forms. Once these definitions are established, I will outline a number of useful approaches that link the underlying causes of these social movements.

Social movements involve purposive collective actions that voice demands for fundamental changes in political or economic arrangements in a society. Social movements typically involve *sustained* collective action by groups favoring some form of social change (whereas collective action may be fleeting). Most scholars also assume that sporadic collective action or clashes differ from social movements in that adherents of movements tend to support a sustained set of values that define a movement's core identity (Zald and McCarthy 1977; Tilly 1978; McAdam et al. 2001).

Ethnic and Racial social movements are goal-directed collective actions that range broadly across a number of different forms of mobilization. A key identifying feature of E/R movements is that claims are made based upon particular identity or boundary, defined by the presence of racial or ethnic markers. These markers typically include skin pigmentation, ancestry, language, and history of discrimination, conquest, or other shared experience. For simplicity (and to avoid invoking unscientific assumptions about the genetic basis of racial characteristics), many researchers prefer the more generic label of *ethnic mobilization* (Olzak 1983). Mobilization efforts in E/R movements range broadly from small-scale sporadic protests that may be relatively peaceful events (such as civil rights demonstrations, marches, etc), to sustained campaigns, such as armed ethnic terrorism and ethnic civil war (Gurr 1993; Fearon and Laitin 1996). Proactive movements commonly express demands for expanded civil rights based upon past discrimination and systematic exclusion from political and/or economic participation. Other forms of ethnic movements are reactive in nature and express specific grievances directed against a particular race, ethnic target, or state authorities. The white backlash movement following Reconstruction in the United States is a prototypical example of a reactive ethnic movement.

Nationalist movements are social movements that make claims for territorial sovereignty (Hechter 2000). Most nationalist movements make claims over the legitimate right to govern a specific geographical area. Claims of nationalist movements vary from demands for regional autonomy, special status within a federation (often involving linguistic rights), to full-scale separation from multinational states, regimes, or empires. They may or may not be based on ethnic or racial distinctiveness, however, movements often voice territorial claims based upon real or presumed histories of ethnic, regional, or racial discrimination or victimization. Thus many nationalist movements invoke themes common to ethnic movements. Alternatively, nationalist movements may claim sovereign rights by invoking other types of identities, based upon religious identities, as in the case of nationalistic Islamic movements (see Snow and Marshall 1984). Alternatively, other forms of nationalist movements may make claims that they had been forcefully removed and dispersed from their ancestral homeland, as in the case of some diaspora movements. Members of nationalist movements may share a territory that lies under another jurisdiction (e.g., Quebecois nationalism), or they may be spread across multiple regions (e.g., pan-Islamic nationalism). A final type of nationalist movement might be termed nation-strengthening, or nation-building movements, in which a single identity (often ethnic in character) is being forged from many different, smaller identities. The formation of Yugoslavian identity after World War II under President Tito is one example, while efforts to establish a legitimate government authority in post-Taliban era in Afghanistan is another. A key distinction for nationalist movements is that they reflect claims to authority over territory and self-determination that are not currently being met.

The fate of nations and their challengers are inextricably linked. Because many nations also claim to be ethnically distinct, this means that ethnic social movements and nation-states depend on each other in a delicate balance of self-definition, political claims making, and contests over power, authority, and legitimacy. Thus states and social movements engage in continuous negotiations and debates over civil liberties, citizenship, and political authority.

Nationalist movements are social movements that also seek to establish new sovereignty rights (Rokkan 1970; Tilly 1975; Anderson 1991; Smith 2000). This last characteristic often brings nationalist and E/R social movements into conflict with existing regimes. Such conflict can remain quiescent for long periods of time, or they may erupt suddenly into full-blown ethnic civil wars, depending on a number of factors including regime stability, outside support, internal mobilization of resources, and reaction by state authorities to nationalist movements. Many E/R and nationalist movements voice strikingly similar claims across a wide variety of settings. Thus it seems reasonable to begin to untangle the relationships among forms of E/R and nationalist social movements by considering their common characteristics.

CHARACTERISTICS OF ETHNIC AND NATIONALIST SOCIAL MOVEMENTS

Several conceptual distinctions have facilitated the understanding of the emergence, growth, and decay of nationalist and ethnic social movements. Some (but not all) scholars distinguish *ethnic mobilization* from *ethnic solidarity*. Solidarity is characterized as the conscious identification (and loyalty) with a particular race or ethnic population, measured by attitudes or organizational involvement, and monitoring capacity. Mobilization is the capacity to harness resources (including loyalty, organizations, and material resources) in an effort to reach some collective goal. Social movement theories also distinguish various forms of movements by *their duration, target, tactics, violence*, and *audience*. These distinctions yield four broad categories of ethnic and nationalist movements: (1) regional movements that demand sovereignty over a particular territory (Laitin 1995); (2) civil rights protests that demand expansion of a group's civil and economic rights or demand an end to discrimination (Morris 1984); (3) antagonist movements directed against specific ethnic targets, including collective attacks ranging from genocide, ethnic cleansing, and mob violence, to symbolic threats (Horowitz 2001); (4) state-strengthening nationalism, which attempts to unify diverse cultures (state-building nationalism) or merge politically divided territories into one state (unification nationalism) (Hechter 2000). While studies of E/R and nationalist movements traditionally analyze these forms separately (Banton 1983; Horowitz 1985), these forms often combine in complicated ways. It bears repeating that the same ethnic event can be alternatively described as genocide or a liberation movement, depending on the actors defining the situation.

The dynamics of ethnic collective action depend on the political context, including reactions to ethnic claims by competing ethnic groups, state authorities, or other institutional leaders and elites. To the extent that E/R and nationalist social movements seek to eradicate and replace existing geographical and administrative state boundaries, they provoke reactions by state authorities that escalate into violence. This escalation into ethnic violence or rebellion is particularly true for *separatist or secession movements*, claiming rights of withdrawal from formal state authority.

Violence is also more likely to erupt when irredentist/diaspora movements claim territorial sovereignty for formerly dispersed or resettled populations (Hechter 1992; Carment and James 1995). Thus adherents justify violence in such movements as necessary aspects in the struggles for liberation, while outsiders (including state authorities) may seek to repress such movements as terrorist or genocidal in character.

An extreme form of violent social movements against a target population is *genocide* or *ethnic cleansing*. Historical examples often include claims of ethnic or racial purity that required exclusion or extermination of some other group. Most recently, this form of violence has arisen as former states (or modern empires) fragment or dissolve entirely and attempt to forge new and ethnically homogeneous identities (Jalali and Lipset 1992–3). The consequence is often a combination of pogroms, terrorist movements, disenfranchisement and other methods of physical attack such as lynchings, rape, or civil war.

Orienting Research Questions

Several key questions about the emergence and persistence of E/R and nationalist social movements drive research efforts in this area. *First, how does ethnic, racial, or national identity become transformed into social movements?* As noted earlier, most studies investigating this question have focused on a single E/R or nationalist social movement within one country. Such research tends to have limited goals, because findings are difficult to apply to other settings. Other researchers have used comparative research designs that include populations of regions or states "at risk" of experiencing ethnic conflict or nationalist movements. In this way, researchers can test theories about the emergence of various forms in different settings (Gurr 1993). There are obvious trade-offs between the amount of detail and/or statistical power that can be brought to bear in each of these designs. Comparative designs have the advantage of allowing researchers to pursue questions about the diffusion of E/R and nationalist social movements across national boundaries, while case studies can explore various historical changes in depth, holding a number of country-specific measures constant.

Scholars have analyzed the transformation of identity into collective action in terms of the dynamics of waves of protest (Beissinger 2002), rates of ethnic conflict among groups (Olzak 1992), and ethnic nationalism using a comparative/historical perspective (Brubaker 1996). Such studies generate interesting questions about the nature of internal mobilization of resources and support. Moreover, they have shown how changes in economic, legal, and political forces facilitate ethnic movements. Yet such studies have failed to draw parallels with other social movements and they have not yet connected their findings with policy in international relations or specific regional studies. Nevertheless, social movement theories have provided a rich set of hypotheses for testing arguments about the transformation of ethnic identity into social movement activity.

Second, what factors explain the emergence and persistence of E/R and nationalist movements? Answers to the question vary with disciplinary traditions, theoretical perspectives, and methodological strategies. For example, researchers using collective action perspectives tend to treat ethnic and nationalist movements as constituting a series of historically contingent events, rather than as series of predetermined stages (see also chapter 2 in this volume). This strategy has the advantage of allowing researcher to examine transitions across different forms of nationalist movements that have varying characteristics over time. For instance, Brubaker (1996: 6–12) finds that nationalism tends to reflect three major categories of collective action mobilized by national minorities, nationalizing states, and external national homelands. The most familiar of these forms include claims by national minorities (within or against existing state structures), nationalizing states (sometimes emerging from fragmented federations, as occurred after the dissolution of the Soviet Union), and claims by external national homelands for a new state (Beissinger 1996). All of these forms are variants of nationalism that share the desire for increased cultural or political rights. The three forms of nationalism diverge with respect to the degree to which they claim full sovereignty rights as a state and the rationale for making the nationalist claims to sovereignty based upon group identities. This perspective illustrates the advantage of treating sovereignty claims as a varying dimension, rather than as a defining feature of a social movement.

A third question asks, are ethnic movements truly novel, or are they are simply instrumental creatures of political movements that once, earlier in history, took other forms? Without undertaking a long historical analysis, answering this question is not easy, and it seems plausible that religious or class-based social movements are now more likely to be couched in distinctly ethnic terms and/or demand regional self-government. That we can define and analyze religious movements of awakenings, or holy wars apart from ethnic conflict means that the demands and claims can be distinguished (although this is not always easy – see Brubaker and Laitin 1998 for a critique).

Some scholars claim that ethnic and nationalist movements are distinct from other bases of political contests (such as regional or religious social movements) because they employ distinctly *modern* claims (Gellner 1983; Hechter 2000; but see Smith 2000). Yet the modern character of nationalist movements does not limit E/R and nationalist movements to a specific set of modern values or contemporary themes. Indeed, many nationalist movements (e.g., Islamic nationalist movements) have invoked themes demanding return to the past (Snow 2000). The modern character of these movements rests on the idea that there is a shared identity of a "people" with boundaries beyond a parochial village or town (Anderson 1991). Furthermore, nationalist movements stake territorial claims based upon a group's unique history, set of ethnic markers, language, phenotypes, or other characteristics that bind group members together, despite the absence of direct face-to-face interaction. That is, scholars claim that ethnic and nationalist movements differ from other types of social movements in that they make demands and moral claims of group identity and/or self-determination. Additionally, the claims of nationalist and E/R often require some authority (usually at the national or international level) to redress an existing injustice. The injustice may be a mild one, such as the fact that the group has been ignored and unrecognized, or they may involve more serious claims of victimization of terrorism or genocide. And the claims may shift from one to the other end of the continuum over time.

A fourth orienting question concerns the shift in the scope of activity: *What are the mechanisms that cause social movements to expand their scope from local concerns to encompass national goals?* Brubaker (1996) describes "nationness" as an institutional process that begins to crystallize with state-building and state-expansion. Similarly, Anderson (1991) posits a causal relationship between the rise of ethnic movements that coincided with nation-building, spread of literacy, and increasing organizational interdependence among associations, groups, and state authorities (see also Tarrow 1994). The theoretical point made here is that large-scale ethnic nationalism are more likely to be encouraged over small-scale identities as state economies and politics become more integrated. This is because the scale of social organization and political power shifts from local, parochial, and personal relations to international, associational, and impersonal multistate bureaucracies. Smaller scale identities such as kinship, family, and neighborhoods remain relevant in local settings. Yet, larger scale ethnic identities have become increasingly more important as policies regarding language, education, discrimination, affirmative action, regional taxation, and redistribution are contested at the national (or at the international) level. So ethnic groups must reorganize nationally to compete effectively for state resources. According to ecological theories of ethnic and race relations, modernization causes ethnic boundaries to continue to expand to include the largest possible subunits. In this way, modernization and national political contests create and recreate the potential for large-scale ethnic groups, political parties, and organizations (Hannan 1979; Nagel and Olzak 1982; Nielsen 1985). Larger-scale ethnic movements are also favored over smaller splinter-movements in national contests. In other words, ethnic-bloc voting only makes sense if it is substantial enough to affect outcomes. Moreover, ethnic organizations and social movements are mutually reinforcing. The existence of enlarged ethnic organizations enhances ethnic collective action on a large scale insofar as they provide organizational infrastructures, leaders, and network links.

Another set of issues raise questions about the nature of the relationship between ethnic conflict and internal civil war. For instance, they ask, *under what conditions does ethnic conflict promote civil war?* Alternatively, others are concerned with the pace of conflict, asking *does the presence of ethnic conflict prolong the duration of civil wars?* Several innovative lines of research have suggested that there is a strong link between ethnic cleavages and violence, in which group differences mobilize and sustain the capacity for groups to incite civil wars. For instance, Sambanis (2001) has analyzed whether or not ethnic and nonethnic civil wars have the same causes. This line of research is tricky, because it is difficult to demarcate when civil wars have a more or less "ethnic" character (since movements might shift their bases of mobilization over time). Nevertheless, Sambanis (2001) finds that civil wars based upon ethnic and/or religious identities are more likely to erupt in countries with high levels of ethnic heterogeneity and low levels of political democracy. In contrast, in nonethnic (or revolutionary) civil wars, economic and development indicators (especially energy consumption) have more influence than do measures of ethnic heterogeneity and indicators of democracy. Moreover, Elbadawi and Sambanis (2000) found that, contrary to expectations, civil wars in Africa over the 1960–90 period were not due to its ethnic or religious diversity, but rather their onset was due to high levels of poverty, fragile political institutions, and other economic indicators of dependence on natural resources and the absence of indigenous businesses.

Conventional wisdom (and prior research) has long supported claims that economic instability seems to generate a wide variety of rebellions, civil wars, and internal civil strife (e.g., Muller 1985; Weede 1986; Muller and Seligson 1987;

Lichbach 1989). However, as many critics have indicated, it is equally likely that economic instability *results from* prior conflict, or that economic declines follows the public's anticipation of civil unrest. In an attempt to sort out the causal ordering of economic effects on ethnic wars, Blomberg and Hess (2002) analyze the likelihood of ethnic war, genocide, revolution, and regime change (or "state failure") using newly available data on 152 countries from 1950 to 1992. They find that while the onset of ethnic war is significantly more likely following recessions, the reverse causal relationship is much weaker empirically. Such evidence largely supports the notion that economic decline raises rates of internal civil war, rather than the reverse.

Ethnic diversity also prolongs the duration of civil wars. Recently, Collier (2000), Fearon (2001), Collier et al. (2001), and Fearon and Laitin (2003) have all examined the impact of ethnic cleavages on the duration of civil wars. Collier et al. (2001) and Fearon (2001) find that the duration of violent civil conflict increases when there are a small number of large ethnic groups, when there are conflicts over land use, and when rebels have access to external (or contraband) resources. Yet, somewhat paradoxically, the capacity of either side (government or ethnic insurgents) to obtain a decisive military victory lowers the probability of a negotiated settlement among combatants, and eventually lowers the duration of the war. Not surprisingly, the evidence shows that ethnic wars and civil wars are causally and temporally related.

A sixth and final orientating question asks, when do we speak of E/R movements and when do we speak of nationalist movements? Confusion between nationalism and E/R arises because concepts of ethnicity and nation are often used interchangeably. This means that an ethnic group expressing a desire to administratively control a specific territory becomes indistinguishable from nationalism. Thus Hechter (2000: 7) defines nationalism as a process of "collective action designed to render the boundaries of a nation congruent with those of its governance unit." This definition has the advantage of treating the outcomes of movements as contingent upon various relationships of the nationalizing group *vis-à-vis* an existing set of state collectivities, empires, or host nations. Nationalism, in other words, is a variable (Hechter 2000).

This discussion prompts us to consider a continuum for nationalist movements that can be classified by the extent to which a movement's expresses goals of self-determination and sovereignty apart from an existing state. Movements can then be analyzed chronologically with respect to movement along this dimension. Such a perspective would be flexible because it allows movements to shift their scope over time, as in the case of a separatist movement emerging from a civil rights movement or cultural identity movement. This conceptualization is consistent with findings that suggest that most E/R movements tend to express relatively modest goals or reforms within an existing political structure. These are likely to include demands for increasing use of a minority language, expanded citizenship rights, or legitimation of a group's cultural practices. In contrast, nationalist movements focus on obtaining legitimate rights over territory (Hechter 2000; Smith 1991). E/R movements nearly always demand improvement in civil or economic rights of a self-conscious group and they often direct these demands to institutional authorities or state officials. In contrast, most nationalist movements aspire to *become* state authorities in their own right.

Combinations of the degree of overlap of nations and states (or their absence) can be used empirically to categorize nationalist and E/R movements aimed at making national and state boundaries coterminous with administrative units as state actors. Thus we can list irredendist, separatist, autonomy, diaspora, and civil rights movements based upon the relationship of nations to some host state or group of states. In some fundamental way, as Anderson (1991) taught us, the ideology of nationalism and self-determination creates the possibility of fission within states that consist of one or more "imagined communities." Consider, for example, the negotiations that ended World War I in Europe and carved new nations from the various existing empires and their fragments. The arbitrary nature of the resulting national boundaries cut through a variety of ethnic, linguistic, and cultural boundaries leaving a legacy that continues to affect nationalist social movements in Central and Eastern Europe. Moreover, we can trace the histories of many nationalist movements that arose in the mid-twentieth century as they generated a variety of ethnic and racial, subnationalist, and nationalist movements in the twenty-first century. Many of these movements seek to reunite those imagined communities dispersed by so-called nation-building processes. Thus Anderson's (1991) seminal work prompts us to explore how nation-building processes can identify some mechanisms underlying these social movements.

THE ROLE OF NATION-BUILDING IN PRODUCING ETHNIC MOVEMENTS

Ethnic movements are fundamentally embedded in (often contradictory) legends and myths about various group identities and actions that have shaped their histories. Language, religion, immigration, and migration histories all play a role in building the defining characteristics of a region. However, periods of nation-building apparently play a central role in determining the nature of identity of an imagined "nation." Thus one explanation for the fact that ethnic movements take on different forms is related to the events surrounding a country's national origin. The literature on state-building has suggested that ethnic movements are most likely to turn violent early in (more or less legitimate) administrative units stages of nation-building, when contested claims of power and legitimacy remain unresolved (Rokkan 1970; Eisenstadt and Rokkan 1973). In this view, nations were "birth marked" by the nature of conflicts – religious, territorial, ethnic, or otherwise – that prevailed during a particular historical period.

During periods of state-building, the content of ethnic claims (especially territorial rights) often brings them into confrontation with a nation-state that has not completely won the hearts and minds of the inhabitants of the contested territory. Outcomes depend upon complicated negotiations between opponents, nation-builders, and often-external participants, who may favor one or the other side. Although some theorists once assumed that the process of nation-building could be analyzed as an evolutionary set of stages, such assumptions seem naive today. Evidently the process of creating a legitimate nation with an accepted system of authority and leaders is better conceptualized as a dynamic set of negotiated meanings (Brubaker 1996). The problem is that multiple ethnic communities are constantly being reconstructed in any one nation-state. Social construction theories of

Coterminous—having the same boundaries

race/ethnic social movements (e.g., Nagel 1995; Cornell and Hartmann 1998) have helped clarify Anderson's (1991) claim that nations are "imagined communities," whose organizational form serves obvious political purposes and ends, but may have little factual basis.

Anderson's work also provides a useful starting place for understanding why nationalist and ethnic movements aim to remedy the lack of correspondence between state boundaries and national identity. Anderson (1991), Smith (1991), Hechter (2000), and many others have emphasized the fact that few (if any) nation-states are homogeneous entities – not only do states sometimes encompass many nations (as in the notion of multiculturalism) but many nations exist without a state. If a "nation" is demarcated by a self-identified boundary, then one nation may be dispersed across multiple state boundaries (as in the concept of a Kurdish nation), which may ultimately acquire its own state (Brass 1985).

Even if they are only temporarily successful, ethnic movements can undermine the legitimacy of the concept of a single nation existing within one administrative unit. As Anderson (1991) reminds us, ethnic/national identification as a "Nigerian," or "Indian" is easily contradicted by reality, since the vast majority of countries include population speaking multiple languages, with different ethnicities, cultures, and religions within its borders. These contradictions can render state-building efforts problematic, especially when state-builders are disproportionately drawn from a single national ethnic identity.

In this view, ethnic and nationalist movements have ideological roots in the process of nation-building. Historical evidence suggests that nation-building activities have often provoked enduring E/R social movements. For example, Smith (1979: 34) identifies a sequence of events that encourage separatism, beginning with initial state-building processes including creation of a centralized bureaucracy and diffusion of national educational institutions. A related line of research has emphasized the role of elite mobility into leading institutions also shape E/R movements. If ethnic elites find their mobility blocked, ethnic mobilization around claims of minority discrimination will arise (Williams 1994).

THEORIES OF THE DEVELOPMENT OF E/R AND NATIONALIST MOVEMENTS

Several prominent theoretical traditions have been offered to explain the emergence, growth, and decay of E/R nationalist social movements. Each is distinguished by an emphasis on one or more processes of changing economic, political and/or ideological environments as key features shaping the trajectory of these movements. Each theoretical framework has generated a number of important empirical studies, which are linked together by common theoretical concepts and mechanisms that seek to link the dynamics of changing conditions to levels of activity.

Internal Colonialism Theory

Internal colonialism theory suggests that a combination of uneven industrialization and cultural differences among regions in core nations cause ethnic grievances to become the basis of enduring political contention. In this view, the sources of ethnic solidarity include uneven regional development that reinforces or creates inequality, dependence on external or international investment and an occupational structure that is highly segregated along ethnic lines. Furthermore, according to this argument, a high level of ethnic solidarity and a division of labor segmented along ethnic lines provokes ethnic conflict in developed regions, rather than in impoverished areas (Hechter 1975).

Within internal colonies, a *cultural division of labor* often emerges, in which dominant ethnic populations monopolize administrative and supervisory occupations (and rewards), while subordinate ethnic populations are relegated to lower status occupations (often in extractive industries). These theories offer testable arguments that suggest that ethnic solidarity and political mobilization based upon ethnic and labor market cleavages triumph over other types of possible loyalties. While the arguments are predictive and highly convincing (see Hechter 1975; Hechter 2000), the empirical tests of this theory have yielded inclusive results (Ragin 1979; Nielsen 1980; Olzak 1982; Olzak and Nagel 1986; Medrano 1994).

Competition Theories

Competition theories provide an alternative explanation for understanding how changes in economic and political conditions within and among states can provoke ethnic mobilization. This perspective suggests that states, regions, or groups experiencing a decline in economic disadvantage are more likely to express claims for autonomy and political rights for minorities. According to competition theory declining inequality among regions (or groups) promotes competitive conflict among race and ethnic groups (Olzak and Nagel 1986). This is because declining inequality and intergroup contact release forces of competitive exclusion and conflict (Barth 1969). In this view, E/R social movements result from conditions of *niche overlap* (rather than from niche segregation, as in internal colonialism theory). For example, competition theorists argue that ethnic conflict rises when ethnic groups within nations come to compete in the *same* labor markets and increase their access to similar sets of political, economic, and social resources (Nielsen 1985; Olzak 1992).

A key variant of competition theory is offered by *split labor market theory*. This perspective holds that ethnic antagonism peaks when two or more ethnically or racially differentiated groups command different wage prices within the same labor market niche (Bonacich 1972). Three way-competition dynamics emerge because dominant-group employers maintain wage differences between at least two sets of workers split along ethnic lines. Mobilization based upon race or ethnic identity occurs as dominant groups attempt to reassert their dominance over newly competing groups and as formerly disadvantaged ethnic groups challenge the existing power structure and majority groups resist. Evidence on Chinese contract laborers in labor camps in Colorado (Boswell 1986) and from African-American and European immigrants in a variety of urban settings in late nineteenth-century America tend to support arguments from split labor market theories (Boswell 1986; Olzak 1992). Furthermore, this theory suggests that as the dynamics of split labor markets change over time, as the wage gap between racially differentiated groups erodes, conflict can be expected to decline proportionally. Supporting evidence on this notion has been suggested by analyses of racial conflict in contemporary South Africa (Olzak and Olivier 1998, by analyses of postindustrial conflict among white and black workers in the United States (Wilson 1978), and in analyses of race and ethnic conflict in cities around the turn of the century in the United States (Olzak 1992; Olzak and Shanahan 2002).

Economic competition perspectives have implications for political competition, suggesting that a wide variety of changes in state policies will intensify competition and mobilize ethnic populations. For instance, some Soviet and Eastern bloc observers claim that during the late 1980s, as glasnost and perestroika undercut the absolute authority of ethnic Russians within the state apparatus of many Soviet Socialist Republics, nationalist sentiment became easier to mobilize, particularly in the former republics of the Ukraine, Latvia, Estonia, and Lithuania (Ulfelder 1997). This development created the potential for new national leaders and quasi-party structures.

International relations perspectives on ethnic conflict address another impact of the role of competition in multiparty systems on ethnic conflict. Whether the potential for ethnic conflict is greater in countries with pluralist party systems or autocratic party systems has been hotly debated in this literature. However, the empirical findings suggest that strategies for containing ethnic conflict are more tractable in more democratic regimes when compared to less democratic regimes (e.g., Brown 1996). Strategies for containing violent ethnic conflict include implementation of proportional representation, direct rule, and/or granting gradualist reforms and concessions. However, Horowitz (1985, 2001), Hechter (2000), and others have documented the relative failures of proportional representation, federalism, and other structural measures designed to eradicate or diminish ethnic conflict within states. Others suggest that peaceful outcomes may depend on the future organizational strength of international human rights organizations, associations, and other nongovernmental organizations that provide external infrastructures and monitoring agencies.

Political shifts in regimes or power arrangements that offer new opportunities for formerly disadvantaged ethnic minorities within the newly democratizing states can encourage further fragmentation of ethnic movements. Some of these movements have become institutionalized in party politics. This is particularly true for the period prior to transition to democracy in former Soviet Union countries, where Community party leadership and mobility chances channeled ethnic tensions within the contests for party leadership (see Roeder 1991; Beissinger 2002). Following the breakup of Communist control, a number of Eastern European countries have witnessed a resurgence of ethnic movements, as party politics has reemerged along a number of new boundaries and identities. Competition theories would predict that mobilization rises as dominance over a single political identity declines. For example, following the decline in Communist control, gypsies in Hungary began to mobilize for civil rights in significant numbers, and Russians in Estonia and Latvia protested for expanded citizenship rights in those countries (Beissinger 2002).

The political refugees from civil wars in Bosnia and other ethnic regions provide another example of how regime changes create the potential for new ethnic movements (including ethnic wars), although resettlement programs undoubtedly undercut a group's ability to mobilize in any one country. At the same time, resettlement programs (and their opposition) often concentrate ethnic populations and create new networks that provide new recruits for mobilizing ethnic violence, as examples from the West Bank in Israel, or the Kurds in Germany, suggest. Thus transitions to democracy may mobilize ethnic movements by offering new political advantages to ethnic groups that were more easily submerged in repressive regimes.

● Rational Choice Theory

This perspective emphasizes causal factors producing E/R and nationalist social movements that shift the calculus of the costs and benefits attached to ethnic mobilization (Hechter 1987a, 2000). According to this view, modern ethnic movements occur with regularity because they have unique properties that allow them to overcome the free-rider problem that hampers recruitment and mobilization efforts. According to this view, because ethnic groups are able to form dense social networks more easily than other groups, solidarity is high, minimizing costs of mobilization. Simultaneously, ethnic groups can efficiently apply systems of monitoring behavior, insuring loyalty, and sanctioning members (Hechter 1987a). Building on rational choice models, Fearon and Laitin (1996) and Weingast (1998) have linked the strategic aspects of ethnic identity to violence, as elites build on existing ethnic loyalties. Such loyalties can prove fatal to group members. As Bhavnani and Backer (2000) argue, the presence of genocidal norms (defined as a threat of sanctions to in-group members who decline participation in ethnic mayhem) increases the scale of ethnic violence. Moreover, under conditions of strict group monitoring (under the threat of sanctions) often provokes explosive ethnic violence. However, in this view, the scale and scope of ethnic violence can be reduced when group monitoring is weak and genocidal norms lose force. Bhavnani and Backer (2000) offer an explanation for one persistent and counterintuitive finding in the literature: Despite a history of intergroup cooperation, tolerance, intermarriage, and trust among different groups interacting within a region, the intensity of ethnic killing and violence may remain high.

Similarly, theorists have extended Prisoner's Dilemma models to consider the implications of game theory for ethnic mobilization, including outbreak of ethnic war (Fearon 2001; Fearon and Laitin 2003). They find that while armed ethnic rebellions tend to last longer than nonethnic ones (Fearon 2001), a variety of ethnic and cultural characteristics have few systematic effects on the onset or duration of civil wars in general (Fearon and Laitin 2003).

Applying game theoretical models applied to four specific ethnic movements, Laitin (1995) compares violence in Basque and Catalonia in Spain and post-Soviet Georgia to ethnic mobilization in the Ukraine. Laitin (1995) finds that three factors predict the outbreak of violence, (holding a number of cultural and historical factors constant): (1) rural social structure which facilitates group monitoring and expedites militant commando operations, (2) tipping game mechanisms that explain the conditions under which costs to joining nationalist campaigns (and recruitment of soldiers to nationalist armies) are reduced, and (3) sustaining mechanisms, which rely on several random shocks which trigger a culture of violence that becomes culturally embedded in regional and collective memories (see also Gould 1999). While other scholars have not explored these processes systematically, they suggest an important way to link the structural determinants of political systems to individual-level arguments about the motivation to support E/R social movements.

Dependency Theory

Another recent perspective uses world-systems theory to consider how global processes of integration of the world's states cause ethnic movements (Olzak 1998; Olzak and Tsutsui 1999; Olzak forthcoming). Some scholars claim that the process of ethnic mobilization in periphery countries (defined by stratified systems of dominance sustained by economic, military, and diplomatic networks) has intensified ethnic conflict in recent decades, when compared to the pace in older, mostly Western European states (Young 1986). Certainly ethnic violence that has accompanied state-building during decolonization in Southeast and Central Asia, and African continents has been dramatic in recent decades. However, few studies have actually investigated whether peripheral countries are more or less at risk of ethnic conflict (but see Strang 1990; Jenkins and Schock 1992; Kposowa and Jenkins 1993). Another economic perspective considers how global processes of integration of the world's states cause ethnic movements (Olzak 1998; Olzak and Tsutsui 1999; Olzak forthcoming). Some scholars claim that the process of ethnic mobilization in periphery countries undergoing state-building has intensified ethnic conflict in recent decades, when compared to the pace in older, mostly Western European states (Young 1986). Certainly ethnic violence has accompanied state-building during decolonization in Southeast and Central Asia, and African continents (Strang 1990; Jenkins and Schock 1992; Kposowa and Jenkins 1993). The ideology of national self-determination validates moral claims of a distinct "people," to sovereignty, yet this same ideology has been an effective strategy undermining existing nation-states and their attempts at nation-building.

Some scholars find that world systems theory provides a useful explanation for the rapid diffusion of ethnic conflict in nearly every region of the world. In this view, the ideology of sovereignty validates moral claims of a distinct "people," to sovereignty, which undermines existing nation-states and their attempts at nation-building. Dependency theory explains the widespread attraction to this ideology of sovereignty and nationalism by suggesting that the world system has increasingly linked various regions, polities, and markets together into a dense, interdependent, and unitary system. It has become commonplace to notice that economic recessions, bank failures, or labor shortages now have repercussions in vastly different and formerly unconnected regions and states. Similar forms of political turbulence, including ethnic social movements, can produce serious reactions across national borders within minutes or even seconds. The implication of this political and economic integration is that integrative processes have specific, centrifugal consequences for ethnic politics. In other words, integration of the world political and economic system has encouraged local ethnic fragmentation and mobilization.

Political and Institutional Perspectives

Political perspectives emphasize the role of shifts in political constraints and opportunity structures that influence the trajectory of E/R social movements (e.g., McAdam 1982; Morris 1984; Andrews 2001). Some of these studies have focused on the civil rights' movement in the United States, as the benchmark movement for civil rights, which created a number of important "spin-off" movements in other settings. While this political opportunity structure (hereafter POS) has been influential in the study of social movements generally, a number of scholars question its ability to predict a movement given the ubiquitous nature of political change (Koopmans 2001).

In examining the international context of politics, Horowitz (1985) emphasizes the centrifugal force of ethnic political parties, which maintain ethnic loyalties through institutional arrangements and patronage based on ethnic loyalties. Such forces are particularly strong when language, religion or some other marker can distinguish a population that is geographically concentrated in a region. Other scholars have argued that while ethnic regional concentrations are important preconditions, they do not necessarily lead to ethnic violence (e.g., Brown 1996). Instead, these scholars emphasize proximate causes or triggering mechanisms, such as political changes in authority, collapse of colonial authorities or empires, or transition to market economies or democracies (Levine 1996: 322–35)

Some social scientists argue that the decline of authoritarian regimes coincides with the resurgence of ethnic or nationalist movements because the retreat of strong repressive authorities leaves a power vacuum (Gurr 1993). As the former military and administrative structures recede, local level elites mobilize ethnic loyalties and take advantage of this vacuum (Brown 1996). Along similar lines, McAdam (1982) provides evidence from the US that suggests that shifts in political opportunities (either positive or negative) drove the rates of protest activity during peak periods of civil rights insurgency. State repression may subdue such movements, but this effect is often temporary.

States use repression and concessions as substitutable and rational strategies for controlling or containing nationalism (Hechter 2000). For example, Moore (2000) suggests that accommodation and repression states shift from one strategy to the other, depending on both the virulence of dissident protest behavior and state capacity to repress these challenges. However, others have suggested the intriguing hypothesis that it is the vacillation of states itself that incites nationalist violence (Rasler 1996), signaling a weakness in the state's internal capacity to act.

The potential for ethnic separatism also influences the intensity of collective violence in a country and this effect is stronger in states with weaker political institutions. In his empirical analysis of political conflict (measured by total deaths from nonroutine political participation events), Schock (1996) finds that political opportunity measures perform better than do measures of economic inequality or economic development. In his analysis of approximately 60 countries over 1973–7, Schock (1996) finds that the potential for ethnic separatism (calculated from Taylor and Jodice 1983) increases political violence overall, but that this relationship holds only in countries with relatively low levels of political institutionalization (defined by the presence of binding rules on political participation). He concludes that his results suggest that weak states are more likely to transform ethnic grievances into political conflict and that further attempts to expand their control over minorities are especially likely to meet with ethnic resistance (Schock 1996: 127–8).

Similarly, Moaddel's (1994) analysis also showed that ethnic separatism affected both regime repression and political conflict. Contrary to dependency theories of ethnic conflict, Moaddel (1994) also found little evidence that peripheral countries experienced more political violence, once income equality and regime repression was taken into account. However, in this study political violence (measured by political deaths, civil unrest, riots, and other armed attacks, and sanctions by the state) included insurgency actions as well as state responses, it is difficult to untangle the causal priorities.

Macropolitical Structure Theories: Indirect versus Direct Rule

Hechter (2000) has argued that the seeds of nationalist movements are embedded in specific political structural arrangements in which colonialist or federated authority cedes formal authority to local leaders. Under such conditions, local elites are delegated political power and authority by centralized authorities, yet the power of local elites is fundamentally based upon regional identities and loyalties. When central authority is weakened or challenged (by external events such as war, famine, or economic crises), or when central authority is withdrawn (as in the case of the Soviet Union), local elites can mobilize on the basis of regional/ethnic identity. According to this argument, direct rule encourages both state-building nationaliza-tion (due to its centralizing authority and integration processes) and peripheral nationalism, or regional subnational movements within states.

Alternatively, when the imposition of direct rule penetrates local-level authority, peripheries and their modernizing leaders react, often with strong social movements aimed at resisting state-building efforts based in a (ethnically different) core. Hechter's (2000) analysis also suggests that some of the characteristics of direct rule, including cultural homogeneity, are endogenous. Thus it becomes difficult to test whether ethnic homogeneity is a cause or an effect of direct rule.

Brubaker (1996) has taken this theme to its logical implications in his analysis of the "new nationalisms" in Western Europe. Instead of arguing that the erosion of Soviet power and authority removed the lid on ethnic tensions, which then spilled over and diffused across former Soviet territories, Brubaker (1996) and Roeder (1991) argue that the federated system of regional and ethnically defined republics in the Soviet Union created the structural basis for ultimate disintegration of the republic. The federated system of Soviet territories also set in motion a variety of subnationalist movements that were organized around the republic's ethnic/linguis-tic/political identities.

Organizational Approaches

Organizational approaches trace the emergence of nationalist movements to changes in the scale of organizational components of authority, mobility, and social control within states. A principle of isomorphism underlies this process (Hannan 1979). To the extent that political and economic sectors expand the power of the nation-state, this expansion produces a corresponding increase in the scale of organization on the part of any potential political group. This is because modern political systems favor large-scale organization. Only those political parties, interest groups, occupational associations, and ethnic groups able to compete on a national scale survive and/or are likely to become successful. Small-scale dialects, cultural groups, and traditions may recede in importance, as larger, territorial identities become more salient to a national system of political competition.

In the study of social movements, organizational demography offers us some new insights about the founding and failure rates of ethnic organizations, their identities, and boundaries (see chapter 7 in this volume). Organizational demography has suggested several ways that social movements compete for attention, resources, and support (Minkoff 1995; Olzak and Uhrig 2001). It seems reasonable to apply some of these demographic principles of organization to the nation-state as an organizational form, especially in analyzing the emergence, persistence, and decay of this as an institutional form. Taking this process one step further, we might apply these ideas to study the impact of large ethnic organizations on nationalist movements, as they seek to forge coalitions among various irredentist and diaspora groups into broad pan-ethnic or pan-nationalist movements.

Cultural/Ideological Perspectives

Recent theoretical analysis in social movement theory suggests that group identity is both an important mobilizing strategy and a consequence of mobilization. In particular, movements articulate demands and pursue social movement "frames" (Snow et al. 1986; Snow 2000) that invoke one or more cultural themes of nationalism, rights of self-determination, expansion of human rights, and basic rights of sovereignty (see also Smith 1979, 1984; Hechter 1987b; Nagel 1994; Brubaker and Laitin 1998). Sovereignty claims usually refer to shared experiences of "a people," which need not be based in objective fact (Anderson 1991). In this view, ethnic identity is a key outcome of collective action that is socially constructed, maintained, and dissolved.

In contrast to static and primordial views of group identity, constructionist perspectives views categorical ethnic identities as the result, rather than the cause, of ethnic political mobilization (Cornell and Hartmann 1998). This perspective allows researchers to study how social mechanisms of contact, conflict, borrowing, and other forms of interaction might influence the emergence of new ethnic or racial categories. Over time, as ethnic conflicts recur along increasingly recognizable cleavages, more fluid identities become hardened into institutionalized race and ethnic categories (McAdam et al. 2001: 157). Thus, as Roy (1994) reports, beginning in 1954, relatively minor village disputes over "some trouble with cows," in Pakistan became gradually transformed and understood as part of the age-old Hindu–Muslim conflict (see also Brass 1997). As violence and revenge escalates on either side to a conflict, small-scale skirmishes became redefined as collective events requiring a response. Eventually (but not inevitably), the escalating violence led the Bangladesh–Pakistan civil war (McAdam et al. 2001: 128). Similarly, Gould's (1999) analysis of collective action in Sicily suggests that, under some conditions, repetition of disputes escalates into collective conflict. In this way, sporadic ethnic conflict becomes gradually transformed into sustained E/R social movements, as ethnic organizations, leaders, and supporters come to frame ongoing events as ethnically motivated. In analyzing forces escalating group conflict, these scholars underscore the emergent properties of both identities and conflict (McAdam et al. 2001).

Although useful for understanding particular cases of ethnic conflict, one drawback of the constructionist perspective is that it becomes difficult for researchers to determine the causal ordering of emergent group identity and ethnic mobilization. Furthermore, Smith (2000: 70) argues that the constructionist perspective overemphasizes the modern aspects of ethnicity while ignoring the symbolic aspects of identities (including cultural values and traditions) that have been carried over from premodern periods (see also Mosse 1995). Ultimately, solutions and answers to these questions are likely to be found in empirical (rather than theoretical) analysis, which can untangle the sequence of events as they unfold over time (see chapter 2 in this volume for a discussion of co-evolutionary processes).

In studying the impact of ethnic identity on ethnic social movements, Smith (1984) has provided a framework that might begin to unravel the causal steps implied by this process. In particular, he lists several "functions" of identity, which serve to designate basic cultural markers that bind them to past and present histories within time and space. Furthermore, precisely because ethnic identity is at least partially voluntary, members can enter and exit an ethnic status, creating the potential for mobilizing new recruits, supporters, and fellow travelers. Smith (1984: 119) also lists the set of conditions under which ethnic identity is likely to become activated. These include intervals (1) during prolonged periods of conflict and warfare, when group identities are under siege or are threatened by others (including third parties to the conflict, as in the Cold War), (2) during periods of secularization or cultural change, in which a technologically superior or economically dominant culture threatens a more traditional culture, and (3) during periods of intense commercialization, which integrate a society into a broader system of economic exchange which is dominated by more advanced technologies or more powerful adversaries.

Globalization Diffusion Perspectives

A number of diffusion processes encourage the spread of cross-national ideologies, resources, organizations, and leaders of ethnic and nationalism movements across regions and countries (see chapter 13 in this volume). As discussed above, the ideology of nationalism diffused across regions, legitimated by the rhetoric of national self-determination, sovereignty, and group discrimination. Similarly, social movement tactics, organizations, and claims have established a variety of international networks that share common themes, resources, and personnel. Studies of ethnic movements find that identity movements based on racial markers, linguistic, or historic patterns of subordination justify and legitimate these claims in virtually all of the world's states. For instance, Olzak and Tsutsui (1999) find that although integration into a world system of power and domination facilitates E/R movements, these effects vary considerably across countries. In addition, processes of diffusion have intensified the international scope of these movements, transforming them into highly contentious international issues.

Diffusion processes affecting the human rights movement also may have facilitated the spread and acceptance of an ideology supporting ethnic rights. In particular, as the worldwide human rights movement gained momentum, claims for national sovereignty, group rights, and individual freedom became intertwined. Recent analyses of the diffusion of world culture and ideology have shifted the emphasis of world systems theory to consider the ideological implications of the integration of the world system (Smith 1981; Meyer et al. 1997). In recent research, these scholars have considered the diffusion of human rights as key motivator of modern social movements, including ethnic ones. In this view, the fact that the diffusion of human rights organizations and intergovernmental associations (including social movement organizations) has led to the expansion of group rights in states that declared independence since 1945 (Ramirez, Soysal, and Shanahan 1997). The extension of human rights guarantees in constitutions of all newly independent states since 1960 reflects an emerging international culture. In core countries, this has the consequence of encouraging multiple movements that use conventional political avenues for protest, lobbying, and voicing grievances. In peripheral countries, however, where authoritarian regimes are less likely to embrace human rights policies, ethnic movements are more likely to be repressed.

Another globalization/diffusion approach suggests that as nation-states became linked together in networks of military and economic associations, national political boundaries weaken and political regime become vulnerable to challenges to international and external challenges. The same forces that encouraged the diffusion of nationalism as an ideology also affect ethnic movements within and between state boundaries. These processes of ethnic resurgence are not new, but they might be intensifying as political associations (such as the European Union, NATO, the UN) replace activities once controlled only by state politics. For example, ethnic movements that span borders, once called irredentist movements, are now more likely to be seen as nationalist diaspora movements (Brass 1985; Horowitz 1985). As military, economic, trade, and other international associations grew in number, the actions of individual nation-states became less salient (relative to regions, city-states, or other powerful actors within states). As states become more enmeshed in a world system of diplomats, economics, financial and military obligations, and state actions become more constrained.

As states become more integrated, influences from international associations and events occurring outside state boundaries will become increasingly salient. It seems likely that as integration of the world's states (politically, diplomatically, and economically) proceeds, ethnic groups within states will become less constrained by their own state authorities. The growing predominance of an integrated set of states ironically decreases the ability of any one state to dominate its internal borders. This happens, in part, because highly integrated nation-states cannot simply repress, jail, or torture the ethnic challengers, without risking international condemnation, sanctions, and boycotts. Furthermore, neighboring countries may directly or indirectly finance campaigns of instability, using political refugees or exiles as mercenary soldiers. There is scattered evidence in support of these claims. Indeed, a number of scholars have found that a decline in the political authority of a state coincides with an increasing number of movements based on ethnic regionalism (e.g., Brown 1996; Hechter 2000).

Another international level process suggests that social movements (such as ethnic cleansing or Islamic nationalism) that occur in neighboring countries have powerful diffusion properties. The presence of contentious neighbors also destabilizes nearby regimes (Sambanis 2001). Brown (1996) and Levine (1996) argue that elite factions (or warlords) offering military and financial support from neighboring countries have played crucial roles in prolonging ethnic wars in Africa and Central Asia in recent years. Although it is difficult to study (because many of the transactions are illegal), it also seems increasingly important to scrutinize flows of arms, mercenaries, supporting organizations, and finances that have fueled ethnic wars (without state or international sanctions) in neighboring countries (e.g., Brown 1996).

Building on this perspective Olzak and Tsutsui (1999) argue that integration of the economic and political world system has reinvigorated ethnic politics. As the world's

states have become more directly linked through communication and media channels, information about inequality and claims for redress of this inequality has
increased sharply. This leads Olzak (1998) to claim that ethnic mobilization varies
systematically among types of countries, especially between core and peripheral
nations that vary with respect to ethnic incorporation policies, economic inequality,
and economic dependency. Together, the dual trends of increasing political access
and decreasing ethnic economic disparity shape ethnic protest.

INTERNATIONAL COMPONENTS OF ETHNIC AND NATIONALIST SOCIAL MOVEMENTS

Although there is growing recognition that international forces shape the trajectories
of human rights movements, educational institutions, and environmental movements (e.g., see research by Meyer et al. (1997) and Ramirez et al. (1997)),
this perspective has not been applied to ethnic movement activity. Thus much of
what is covered in this section is speculative. It is probable that most forms of
international conflict (which, up until recently, included activities associated with
the Cold War) provide a structure for building new alliances, coalitions, and sets of
interdependent relations between countries. Each new alignment opens up the
possibility for redrawing rules of citizenship, political asylum, and deportation. As
scholars in the international relations field argue, the recent demise of the Cold War
demonstrates that new and different sets of network alliances can emerge among
former enemy camps (Roeder 1991). The reverse is equally probable, as new
enemies (with new ethnic subgroups) become salient to the world-system of political
diplomacy.

Recently, investigations of the international origins of conflicts have taken precedence over studies that focused on internal causes of ethnic conflicts within states.
For instance, it appears that changes in a state's internal capacities for dealing with
(armed) challenges to their authority affects the success of many ethnic movements.
Yet many of the shifts in a state's internal strength may be rooted in international
tensions and interactions. Many of these changes fuel the recruitment of soldiers into
nationalist armies that aim at displacing current authorities or regimes. For example,
it is well known that international wars as well as internal conflicts provide a steady
stream of political refugees seeking asylum and refugee status (Schmeidl 1997). The
Arab refugee problem in the Middle East is an especially well-known example of
ethnic strife that is both a cause and consequence of future ethnic instability. The
Bosnian tragedy provides another kind of example, as the conflict there has produced enormous numbers of refugees in Italy, Germany, Hungary, and Austria.

Taking an international perspective helps clarify how economic interdependence
among states may also foster rising ethnic subnational movements. Organizations
such as the European Union, OPEC, NATO, and other supranational organizations
promote interstate migration and decrease reliance of regions within states on the
military and economic power of the nation-state. Multistate organizations also
provide forums for subnational organizations (Koopmans and Statham 2000). In
this view, the growing network of international economic relations, exemplified by
multinational corporations, growing trade and foreign investment, and supranational economic associations, will continue to produce more large scale ethnic

What about anti-global nationalist movements?
Seems to focus on movements of the oppressed.

movements. Examples such as proposals for membership of Northern Ireland and Scotland in the European Parliament suggest that increasing economic and political interdependence has encouraged regional subnationalism in recent years.

One (perhaps unanticipated) consequence of the integration of the European monetary system is that ethnic tensions have risen rather dramatically (see Betz 1994, Betz and Immerfall 1998; Koopmans and Statham 2000). Furthermore, as labor (and capital) flows move more freely across member states as restrictions against labor mobility recede and new right-wing parties across Western Europe have mobilized sentiment against foreign workers (Kriesi 2002). To the extent that the integration of the European Union has restructured local politics within European countries, the opportunity has arisen for ethnic politics on both sides of the immigration question (Fennema 2000).

One possible outcome is that one type of ethnic identity (that of non-Europeans) will become more salient at the same time that distinct national identities within the community (French versus German) become less salient. Antiforeigner sentiment, nationalist political parties, and attacks on foreigners also appear to be rising in most Western European countries, especially in Germany, France, and England (e.g., see Tillie and Fennema 1998; van der Brug et al. 2000; Koopmans and Statham 2000; Lubbers et al. 2000; Lubbers and Scheepers 2002; Scheepers et al. 2002).

It seems reasonable to expect that if a new European/non-European boundary becomes more salient, the political and economic lines around immigration rights, unemployment and health benefits to workers, and citizenship rules will be redrawn as a consequence. The point is not just that a new amalgamated identity emerges, but rather that the social and political movements will become increasingly organized around a new boundary line (not one which reflects existing nationalities) (e.g., the phrase "foreign-born" in Western European press accounts tends to refer to immigrants from non-European countries). Because supranational organizations subsume national boundaries, they create options for drawing new lines of confrontation based on the new ingroup and outgroup boundary.

Does the increasing connectedness of international networks among nations inevitably led to rising ethnic tensions within nations? It is perhaps too early to answer this question with certainty, and there is evidence that international organizations have alternatively promoted and diffused tensions in different settings (Brown 1996; Olzak and Tsutsui 1999). Analysis suggests that at least in the short run, initial decline of state barriers and rising flows of immigrant workers (temporary or permanent) will increase the salience of some ethnic boundaries. To the extent that European workers experience competition from transnational migrants, more ethnic violence will result (Koopmans and Olzak 2002). Competition theories hold that ethnic violence would depend on the rate of in-migration, size, and wage stability in these core countries. On the other hand, if the integration of the European economy stimulates widespread economic expansion, the movement of immigrant workers from regions of low labor demand to high demand may occur more smoothly.

Military interdependence constitutes an obvious way that international relations affect conflicts within countries. Although such techniques are not new, as Enloe (1980) pointed out in *Ethnic Soldiers* (and as Tilly (1993) reminds us in *European Revolutions*), superpowers arm and train ethnic and subnational groups in order to stabilize or in some cases destabilize regimes. The cases of recent rebellions financed and supported by transnational forces (on both sides of the struggles) in civil wars in Afghanistan, Nicaragua, Vietnam, and many other settings illustrate this point. Because of the political sensitivity of national security policies, information on such alliances and funding of insurgency is difficult, if not impossible, to obtain. However, it is now clear that covert and overt military aid may have increased the mobilization potential of subnational movements considerably. Military interdependence among states fosters ethnic conflict in a less obvious way. Multistate defense organizations diminish the significance of any one-member state. Questions about whether Quebec or Scotland can and should join NATO, and on what basis, provoke just such debates and discussions. If Tilly (1993) is correct in his predictions, such processes will decrease the viability of the nation-state as an organizational form in future decades. Whether we will witness more ethnic civil wars like the one in the former state of Yugoslavia or whether ethnic tensions lead to increasing founding of ethnically homogeneous quasi-states, remains to be seen. However, it has become clear that ethnic conflict does not invariably diminish with the dissolution or splintering of a multi-ethnic state. In fact, recent events suggest just the opposite, that ethnic conflict sometimes increases as the repressive power of a state declines (Horowitz 1985). When outside nations withdraw their military presence, as happened in the case of Soviet presence in Eastern European countries such as East Germany, nationalist movements of all kinds gain momentum (Beissinger 2002).

EVALUATION OF VARIOUS PERSPECTIVES ON E/R AND NATIONALIST MOVEMENTS

For a variety of reasons, it is difficult to compare the empirical standing of various theoretical perspectives on E/R and nationalist movements. This is because the key research strategies from each tradition often vary substantially with respect to the units of analysis, selection of cases "at risk" of such movements, and the types of empirical evidence used to evaluate the theoretical arguments. Moreover, many perspectives are based in specific disciplinary traditions, for example international relations, sociology, economics, and political science, which tend to have nonoverlapping research traditions and literatures. Up until very recently, the literature on E/R and nationalist movements has not engendered much dialogue across discipline boundaries. For example, organizational theories of ethnic mobilization focus on traces of identifiable organizations, structures and leaders, while mainstream protest analysts tend to focus on events, and comparative historical approaches use rich detail to flush out specific historical contingencies. Each perspective has a set of embedded assumptions, traditions, and goals that do not lend themselves easily to direct comparison.

Despite the centrifugal force of academic disciplines, an emerging tradition in political sociology suggests that it might be useful to begin to analyze these forms together (e.g., Brubaker 1996; Hechter 2000; McAdam et al. 2001). In this view, there are similar mechanisms that can illuminate key factors responsible for the emergence, persistence, and decay of these forms of social movements. Rather than develop a variety of theories for each subtype of movement, it seems fruitful to begin with shared causal features of these movements. With more attention to the commonalities among forms of ethnic and nationalist movements, we stand to gain more understanding about how violence escalates and diffuses, or how spontaneous protests become transformed into sustained social movements that challenge existing authority structures.

Moreover, theoretical advances in sociology, political science, and psychology have suggested that analysis of particular E/R and nationalist movements might benefit directly from applications of arguments in social movement literature, rather than applying findings from specific regional studies or historical accounts of a single ethnic or nationalist movement. By this I mean an approach that seeks to emphasize the continuities (and discontinuities) among social movements and their forms, across a number of historical periods and regional settings, in an attempt to build cumulative theories of ethnic and nationalist change. I would argue that theories that seek to isolate specific instances of E/R movements and nationalism, and do not reach beyond those specific instances, tend to be self-limiting and descriptive rather than explanatory. Although it has become commonplace for scholars to assume that most if not all macrolevel processes are historically contingent and unique, such strategies hamper our ability to push theory forward and test general arguments against a variety of forms of ethnic mobilization. If each type of ethnic mobilization – from civil rights movements to ethnic civil wars – are analyzed separately by country, time period, and movement goals, it becomes impossible to know when to stop creating new and unique explanations to fit each new occurrence of a nationalist event or ethnic campaign. For this reason, I contend that comparative work that seeks to build cumulative theories that can be falsified empirically holds far more promise than do studies of movements as unique and separate events.

CONCLUSIONS

This necessarily brief review of the vast literature on ethnic and nationalist movements suggests some of the reasons why ethnic and nationalist movements seem to be erupting in virtually every society, threatening (but sometimes also strengthening) the fabric of institutions and political regimes. Instead of providing new solutions to ethnic conflict, the processes accompanying modernization, political development, economic well being, and increasingly international linkages among nations and organizations exacerbate E/R and nationalist social movements. Further, the diffusion of nationalist ideology spread by legitimating forces of international organizations seems to fuel an epidemic of proliferating ethnic identities, rather than preventing the outbreak of movements that challenge state authority.

What lessons have we learned from the study of ethnic and nationalist movements? First, we have gained many insights by considering the similar ideological and structural origins of ethnic conflicts and challenges to state authorities as social movements that are sustained by ethnic leadership, networks of organizations, flows of resources, and contentious interaction with weak states. Second, we have learned that determination of the causal ordering of ethnic heterogeneity, ethnic categories, economic inequality and mobilization is complicated by the social construction of ethnic and racial boundaries that change over time. Third, we have learned that the answers to questions about the nature and trajectory of ethnic movements lie in conducting careful empirical analyses and comparisons of different kinds of events –

ethnic, civil rights, national, religious, civil wars, and autonomy social movements of various kinds that share some (but not all) root causes.

Finally, it seems reasonable to end on a theme that underscores the benefits attached to paying attention to the international context of collective actions. Clearly the internationalization of a world economy and political integration of organizational, diplomatic, and trade linkages have prompted us to reconsider the claim that social movements are fundamentally caused by internal conditions within states. Recent sociological analyses reviewed here show that claims of sovereignty have produced strikingly similar social movements that share similar forms, goals, tactics, and ideologies. Thus, theories that focus solely on the internal bases of discontent now seem short sighted.

Applying this lesson to the next wave of E/R and nationalist movements may be instructive. Recently, new forms of nationalism have arisen in the form of fundamentalist nationalism, terrorist networks, and international networks of social movement recruitment and training. Such movements are fundamentally international in scope and are able to challenge multiple regimes simultaneously, often without warning. Such challenges defy explanations that rely on internal characteristics of existing states or leaders. By turning to explanations firmly based on theories of international connections and processes, we may be able to understand the emergence of this new form of nationalism.

Note

The author would like to thank the editors of this volume and Colin Beck for helpful comments and suggestions on earlier drafts.

References and further reading

Anderson Benedict (1991) *Imagined Communities*. 2nd ed. London: Verso.

Andrews, Kenneth (2001) Social Movements and Policy Implementation: The Mississippi Civil Rights Movement and the War on Poverty, 1965–1971. *American Sociological Review*, 66, 71–95.

Banton, Michael (1983) *Racial and Ethnic Competition*. Cambridge: Cambridge University Press.

Barth Fredrick (1969) *Ethnic Groups and Boundaries*. Sage: Los Angeles.

——(2000) Are Islamists Nationalists or Internationalists? In Kjell Goldmann, Ulf Hannerz, and Charles Westin (eds.), *Nationalism and Internationalism in the Post-Cold War Era*. New York: Routledge, 51–64.

Beissinger, Mark (1996) How Nationalism Spread: Eastern Europe Adrift the Tides and Cycles of Nationalist Contention. *Social Research*, 63, 97–146.

——(2002) *Nationalist Mobilization and the Collapse of the Soviet State*. Cambridge: Cambridge University Press.

Betz, Hans-Georg (1994) *Radical Right-Wing Populism in Western Europe*. Basingstoke: Macmillan.

Betz, Hans-Georg, and Stephan Immerfall (eds.) (1998) *The New Politics of the Right: Neo-Populist Parties and Movements in Established Democracies*. Basingstoke: Macmillan.

Bhavnani, Ravi, and David Backer (2000) Localized Ethnic Conflict and Genocide. *Journal of Conflict Resolution*, 44 (3), 283–306.

Blomberg, S. Brock, and Gregory D. Hess (2002) The Temporal Links between Conflict and Economic Activity. *Journal of Conflict Resolution*, 46, 74–90.

Bonacich, Edna (1972) A Theory of Ethnic Antagonism. *American Sociological Review*, 37, 547–59.

Boswell, Terry (1986) A Split Labor Market Analysis of Discrimination against Chinese Immigrants, 1850–1882. *American Sociological Review*, 51, 352–71.

Brass, Paul R. (1985) *Ethnicity and Nationalism: Theory and Comparison*. Newbury Park, CA: Sage.

——(1997) *Theft of an Idol: Text and Context in the Representation of Collective Violence*. Princeton, NJ: Princeton University Press.

Brown, Michael (1996) The Causes and Regional Dimensions of Internal Conflict. In Michael Brown (ed.), *The International Dimensions of Internal Conflict*. Cambridge, MA: MIT Press, 571–601.

Brubaker, Rogers (1996) *Nationalism Reframed: Nationhood and the National Question in the New Europe*. Cambridge: Cambridge University Press.

Brubaker, Rogers, and David Laitin (1998) Ethnic and Nationalist Violence. *Annual Review of Sociology*, 24, 423–52.

Brug, Wouter van der, Meindert Fennema, and Jean Tillie (2000) Anti-immigrant parties in Europe: Ideological or Protest Vote? *European Journal of Political Research*, 37, 77–102.

Carment, David, and Patrick James (1995) Internal Constraints and Interstate Ethnic Conflict. *Journal of Conflict Resolution*, 39, 82–109.

Collier, Paul (2000) *Economic Causes of Civil Conflict and their Implications for Policy*. Washington, DC: World Bank, Development Research Group.

Collier, Paul, Anke Hoeffler, and Måns Söderbom (2001) *On the Duration of Civil War*. Washington, DC: World Bank, Development Research Group.

Cornell, Stephen, and Douglas Hartmann (1998) *Ethnicity and Race*. Thousand Oaks, CA: Pine Forge.

Eisenstadt, Shulmith, and Stein Rokkan (eds.) (1973) *Building States and Nations*. Vol. 2. Beverly Hills, CA: Sage.

Elbadawi, Ibrahim, and Nicholas Sambanis (2000) Why Are there So Many Civil Wars in Africa? Understanding and Preventing Violent Conflict. *Journal of African Economics*, 9, 244–69.

Enloe, Cynthia (1980) *Ethnic Solidiers*. Athens, GA: University of Georgia Press.

Fearon, James (2001) Why Do Some Civil Wars Last So Much Longer than Others? Presented at the World Bank DECRG Conference on Civil War, University of California, Irvine.

Fearon, James, and David Laitin (1996) Explaining Interethnic Cooperation. *American Political Science Review*, 90, 715–35.

——(1999) Weak States, Rough Terrain, and Large-Scale Ethnic Violence since 1945. Unpublished manuscript, Stanford University.

——(2003) Ethnicity, Insurgency, and War. *American Political Science Review*, 97, 75–90.

Fennema, Meindert (2000) Legal Repression of Extreme-Right Parties and Racial Discrimination. In Ruud Koopmans and Paul Statham (eds.), *Challenging Immigration and Ethnic Relations Politics*. Oxford: Oxford University Press, 119–44.

Gellner, Ernest (1983) Nations and Nationalism. Ithaca NY: Cornell University Press.

Gould, Roger (1999) Collective Violence and Group Solidarity: Evidence from a Feuding Society. *American Sociological Review*, 64, 356–80.

Gurr, Ted R. (1993) *Minorities at Risk*. Washington, DC: Institute of Peace.

Gurr, Ted R., and Will H. Moore (1997) Ethnopolitical Rebellion. *American Journal of Political Science*, 41, 1079–1103.

Hannan, Michael T. (1979) The Dynamics of Ethnic Boundaries in Modern States. In John Meyer and Michael T. Hannan (eds.), *National Development and the World System*. Chicago: University of Chicago Press, 253–75.

Hechter, Michael (1975) *Internal Colonialism*. Berkeley: University of California Press.

——(1987a) *Principles of Group Solidarity*. Berkeley: University of California Press.

——(1987b) Nationalism as Group Solidarity. *Ethnic and Racial Studies*, 10, 415–26.

——(1992) The Dynamics of Secession. *Acta Sociologica*, 35, 267–83.

——(2000) *Containing Nationalism*. New York: Oxford University Press.

Horowitz, Donald L. (1985) *Ethnic Groups in Conflict*. Berkeley: University of California Press.

——(2001) *The Deadly Ethnic Riot*. Berkeley: University of California Press.

Ignatiev, Michael (1993) *Blood and Belonging: Journeys into the New Nationalisms*. New York: Noonday.

Isaacs, Harold (1975) *Idols of the Tribe*. New York: Harper & Row.

Jalali, Rita, and Seymour M. Lipset (1992–3) Racial and Ethnic Conflicts: A Global Perspective. *Political Science Quarterly*, 107 (4), 585–606.

Jenkins, J. Craig, and Kurt Schock (1992) Global Structures and Political Processes in the Study of Domestic Political Conflict. *Annual Review of Sociology*, 18, 161–85.

Koopmans, Ruud (2001) Ethnic Mobilization and Conflict in Germany. Paper presented at the Annual Meeting of the American Sociological Association, in Anaheim, CA.

Koopmans, Ruud, and Susan Olzak (2002) Right-Wing Violence and the Public Sphere in Germany: The Dynamics of Discursive Opportunities. Unpublished manuscript. Wissenschaftszentrum Berlin für Sozialforschung and Department of Sociology, Stanford University.

Koopmans, Ruud, and Paul Statham (2000) *Challenging Immigration and Ethnic Relations Politics*. Oxford: Oxford University Press.

Kpowosa, Augustine, and J. Craig Jenkins (1993) The Structural Sources of Military Coups in Postcolonial Africa, 1957–1984. *American Journal of Sociology*, 99, 126–63.

Kriesi, Hanspeter (2002) The Transformation of the National Political Space in a Globalizing World. Unpublished manuscript, University of Geneva.

Laitin, David D. (1995) National Revivals and Violence. *Archives European Sociologie*, 36, 3–43.

Levine, Alicia (1996) Political Accommodation and the Prevention of Secessionist Violence. In Michael Brown (ed.), *The International Dimensions of Internal Conflict*. Cambridge, MA: MIT Press, 311–40.

Lichbach, Mark Irving (1989) An Evaluation of "Does Economic Inequality Breed Political Conflict?" Studies. *World Politics*, 4, 431–70.

Lubbers, Marcel, and Peer Scheepers (2002) French *Font National* Voting: A Micro and Macro Perspective. *Ethnic and Racial Studies*, 25, 120–40.

Lubbers, Marcel, Peer Scheepers, and Jan Billiet (2000) Individual and Contextual Characteristics of the Vlaams Blok Vote. *Acta Politica*, 35, 363–98.

McAdam, Doug (1982) *Political Process and the Development of Black Insurgency*. Chicago: University of Chicago Press.

McAdam, Doug, Sidney Tarrow, and Charles Tilly (2001) *Dynamics of Contention*. Cambridge: Cambridge University Press.

Mazrui, Ali R. (2000) Transnational Ethnicity and Subnational Religion in Africa's Political Experience. In Kjell Goldmann, Ulf Hannerz, and Charles Westin (eds.), *Nationalism and Internationalism in the Post-Cold War Era*. New York: Routledge, 37–50.

Medrano, Juan Diez (1994) The Effects of Ethnic Segregation and Ethnic Competition on Political Mobilization in the Basque Country, *American Sociological Review*, 59, 873–89.

Meyer, John W., John Boli, George Thomas, and Francisco Ramirez (1997) World Society and the Nation State. *American Journal of Sociology*, 103, 144–81.

Minkoff, Debra (1995) *Organizing for Equality*. New Brunswick, NJ: Rutgers University Press.

Moaddel, Mansoor (1994) Political Conflict in the World Economy: A Cross-national Analysis of Modernization and World-System Theories. *American Sociological Review*, 59, 276–303.

Moore, Will H. (2000) The Repression of Dissent: A Substitution Model of Government Coercion. *Journal of Conflict Resolution*, 44, 107–27.

Morris, Aldon (1984) *The Origins of The Civil Rights Movement: Black Communities Organizing for Change*. New York: Free Press.

Mosse, George (1995) Racism and Nationalism. *Nations and Nationalism*, 1, 163–73.

Muller, Edward N. (1985) Income Inequality, Regime Repressiveness and Political Violence. *American Sociological Review*, 50, 47–61.

Muller, Edward N., and Michell A. Seligson (1987) Inequality and Insurgency. *American Political Science Review*, 81, 425–49.

Myers, Daniel (1997) Racial Rioting in the 1960s. *American Sociological Review*, 62, 94–111.

Nagel, Joane (1994) Constructing Ethnicity: Creating and Recreating Ethnic Identity and Culture. *Social Problems*, 41, 1001–26.

——(1995) American Indian Ethnic Renewal: Politics and the Resurgence of Identity. *American Sociological Review*, 60, 947–65.

——(1996) *American Indian Ethnic Renewal: Red Power and the Resurgence of Identity*. New York: Oxford University Press.

Nagel, Joane, and Susan Olzak (1982) Ethnic Mobilization in New and Old States. *Ethnic and Racial Studies*, 5, 253–75.

Nielsen, François (1980) The Flemish Movement in Belgium after World War II. *American Sociological Review*, 45, 76–94.

——(1985) Ethnic Solidarity in Modern Societies. *American Sociological Review*, 50, 133–45.

Olzak, Susan (1982) Ethnic Mobilization in Quebec. *Ethnic and Racial Studies*, 5, 253–75.

——(1983) Contemporary Ethnic Mobilization. *Annual Review of Sociology*, 9, 355–74.

——(1989) Analysis of Events in the Study of Collective Action. *Annual Review of Sociology*, 15, 119–41.

——(1992) *The Dynamics of Ethnic Competition and Conflict*. Stanford: Stanford University Press.

——(1998) Ethnic Protest in Core and Periphery States. *Ethnic and Racial Studies*, 21, 187–217.

——(forthcoming) *The Global Dynamics of Race and Ethnic Mobilization*. Stanford: Stanford University Press.

Olzak Susan, and Joane Nagel (eds.) (1986) *Competitive Ethnic Relations*. Orlando, FL: Academic.

Olzak, Susan, and Johan L. Olivier (1998) Racial Conflict and Protest in South Africa and the United States. *European Sociological Review*, 14, 255–78.

Olzak, Susan, and Suzanne Shanahan (2002) Racial Conflict in the United States, 1869–1924. Unpublished manuscript, Department of Sociology, Stanford University (forthcoming in *Social Forces*).

Olzak Susan, and Kyoteru Tsutsui (1999) Status in the World System and Ethnic Mobilization. *Journal of Conflict Resolution*, 42, 691–720.

Olzak, Susan, and S. C. Noah Uhrig (2001) The Ecology of Tactical Overlap in New Social Movements in West Germany. *American Sociological Review*, 66, 694–718.

Ragin, Charles (1979) Ethnic Political Mobilization: The Welsh Case. *American Sociological Review*, 44, 619–35.

Rasler, Karen (1996) Concessions, Repression, and Political Protest in the Iranian Revolution. *American Sociological Review*, 61, 132–52.

Ramirez, Francisco, Yasemin Soysal, and Suzanne Shanahan (1997) The Changing Logic of Political Citizenship: The Cross-national Acquisition of Female Suffrage, 1850–1990. *American Sociological Review*, 62, 735–45.

Roeder, Philip (1991) Soviet Federalism and Ethnic Mobilization. *World Politics*, 43, 196–232.

Rokkan, Stein (1970) *Citizens, Elections, and Parties*. Chicago: Rand McNally.

Roy, Beth (1994) *Some Trouble with Cows: Making Sense of Social Conflict*. Berkeley: University of California Press.

Sambanis, Nicholas (2001) Do Ethnic and Nonethnic Civil Wars Have the Same Causes? *Journal of Conflict Resolution*, 45, 259–82.

Scheepers, Peer, Merove Gijsberts, and Marcel Colnders (2002) Ethnic Exclusionism in European Countries: Public Opposition to Civil Liberties for Legal Migrants as a Response to Perceived Ethnic Threat. *European Sociological Review*, 18, 17–34.

Schmeidl, Susanne (1997) Exploring the Causes of Forced Migration: A Pooled Time-Series Analysis, 1971–1990. *Social Science Quarterly*, 78, 284–308.

Schock, Kurt (1996) A Conjuctural Model of Political Conflict. *Journal of Conflict Resolution*, 40, 98–133.

Smith, Anthony (1979) Toward a Theory of Ethnic Separatism. *Ethnic and Racial Studies*, 21, 21–37.

——(1981) *The Ethnic Revival*. Cambridge: Cambridge University Press.

——(1984) National Identity and Myths of Ethnic Descent. *Research in Social Movements, Conflict and Change*, 7, 95–130.

——(1991) *The Ethnic Origin of Nations*. Oxford: Basil Blackwell.

——(2000) *The Nation in History*. Hanover, NH: University Press of New England.

Snow, David A. (2000) Ideology, Framing Processes, and Islamic Movements. Paper presented at the Conference on Islam and Social Movements, at New York University, February.

Snow, David A., and Susan E. Marshall (1984) Cultural Imperialism, Social Movements, and the Islamic Revival. *Research in Social Movements, Conflict and Change*, 7, 131–52.

Snow, David A., R. Burke Rochford Jr., Steven K. Worden, and Robert D. Benford (1986) Frame Alignment Processes, Micromobilization, and Movement Participation. *American Sociological Review*, 51, 464–81.

Spilerman, Seymour (1970) The Causes of Racial Disturbances. *American Sociological Review*, 35, 627–49.

Strang, David (1990) From Dependency to Sovereignty: An Event History Analysis of Decolonization 1870–1987. *American Sociological Review*, 55, 846–60.

Tarrow, Sidney (1994) *Power in Movement*. Cambridge: Cambridge University Press.

Taylor, Charles Lewis, and Michael Lewis Hudson (1972) *World Handbook of Political and Social Indicators*. 2nd ed. New Haven: Yale University Press.

Taylor, Charles Lewis, and David A. Jodice (1983) *World Handbook of Social Indicators*. New Haven: Yale University Press.

Tillie, Jean, and Meindert Fennema (1998) A Rational Choice for the Extreme Right. *Acta Politica*, 33, 223–49.

Tilly, Charles (1975) *The Formation of National States in Western Europe*. Princeton, NJ: Princeton University Press.

——(1978) *From Mobilization to Revolution*. Boston: Addison-Wesley.

——(1993) *European Revolutions, 1492–1992*. Oxford: Basil Blackwell.

Ulfelder, John J. (1997) Immigration, Democratization, and Ethnic Exclusion in the Post-Soviet Baltic States. PhD dissertation, Stanford University.

Weede, Eric (1981) Income Inequality and Political Violence Reconsidered. *American Sociological Review*, 51, 438–41.

——(1986) Income Inequality, Average Income, and Domestic Violence. *Journal of Conflict Resolution*, 25, 639–54.

Weingast Barry R. (1998) Constructing Trust: The Politics and Economics of Ethnic and Regional Conflict. In V. Haufler, K. S. Uslaner, and E. Uslaner (eds.), *Institutions and Social Order*. Ann Arbor: University of Michigan Press, 163–200.

Williams, Robin (1994) The Sociology of Ethnic Conflicts. *Annual Review of Sociology*, 20, 49–79.

Wilson, William Julius (1978) *The Declining Significance of Race*. Chicago: University of Chicago Press.

Young, Crawford M. (1986) Cultural Pluralism in the Third World. In Susan Olzak and Joane Nagel (eds.), *Competitive Ethnic Relations*. Orlando, FL: Academic, 113–22.

Zald, Mayer, and John C. McCarthy (1977) *Resource Mobilization and Social Movements: Partial Theory Relations*. Orlando, FL: Academic.

29

Religious Movements

FRED KNISS AND GENE BURNS

INTRODUCTION

In 1981, in his H. Paul Douglas Lecture to the Religious Research Association, Mayer Zald laid out an agenda for the study of religion and social movements (Zald 1982). He suggested that, in the contemporary world, religion was increasingly rather than decreasingly influential. Religion, he said, was one of the chief facilitating institutions for broader social movements, and, conversely, social movement dynamics within religious organizations were an important source of religious change and vitality. In a later revision of that address, he concluded that "it is clear that the study of social movements from a resource mobilization perspective and the study of the transformation of and within religion have much to offer each other.... Both the sociology of religion and the sociology of social movements can be invigorated by continuing this interchange" (Zald and McCarthy 1987: 95). Since then, others have made this argument as well. (See, e.g., Hannigan 1991; Kniss and Chaves 1995.)

World events since 1981 have done little to cast doubt on Zald's assertion that religion has an important impact on contemporary movements, but apparently his call to scholarly arms fell on deaf ears. A quick scan of several state-of-the-art collections on social movements published since 1982 (Zald and McCarthy 1987; Klandermans et al. 1988; Morris and Mueller 1992; Johnston and Klandermans 1995; McAdam et al. 1996; McAdam and Snow 1997) shows that, out of 105 essays, only eight dealt with religion in any explicit way. Of the eight, three were authored or co-authored by Zald, one of which was a reprint of his 1981 lecture.

That is not to say that scholars have not continued to explore important questions on religion and social movements. Since 1981, much progress has been made in the social movements literature on questions relating to culture and ideology in social movements. And, in the sociology of religion, numerous lively debates have developed and continued on the relation between religion and broad social change processes such as urbanization, international migration, new religious movements, the desecularization of politics, and so on. For the most part, however, these two literatures have been parallel discourses rather than enriching dialogues. In this chapter, we update the argument that there are many fertile areas of inquiry at the intersection of religion and social movements. We do so by looking at three general empirical questions that have motivated previous research and that promise to advance our understanding of the relationship between religion and social movements.

Three Kinds of Empirical Questions

We see three general nexuses of empirical questions that might conceivably fall under the rubric of a chapter entitled "Religious Movements." The first concerns religious movements themselves, and focuses on both their causes and consequences. Most of what we now recognize as major "world religions" began as religious movements, and throughout history, religious movements have played a major role as instigators of important social change. The Protestant Reformation's impact on the Enlightenment is perhaps the most obvious example in modern Western history, but the list of examples could stretch on endlessly.

In the US, and increasingly around the world, the decades since the 1960s have seen a flowering of new religious movements. The study of new religious movements is a well-developed subfield within both the social movements literature and the sociology of religion. It is one empirical field where both groups can point to significant cross-disciplinary conversations, particularly around questions related to conversion and recruitment. But recent changes in international migration patterns suggest some new questions that are worth exploring. New religious movements are no longer primarily homegrown "cults" like Scientology, but increasingly are imports from other parts of the world. Sufism is a good recent example of an imported movement that is gaining a following outside its traditional Islamic constituency.

A second set of questions concerns social movements within religious organizations. Going back at least as far as Weber and Troeltsch, scholars have noted the importance of sectarian movements within religion for fomenting religious and cultural change. Sectarian movements are often assumed to be conservative returns to tradition. But progressive intra-religious movements have also been important sources of change and religious innovation. In the contemporary world, internal conflicts over gender, sexuality, peace and justice issues, and globalization have produced significant changes within religious institutions and communities. A third set of questions has to do with religion as a resource for or facilitator of other movements. One important way that religious movements bring about change is by building alliances with other contemporaneous movements, or, sometimes, by contesting change being fomented by other movements. Within the past two decades, resurgent "fundamentalism" and faith-based violence around the world have once again pressed these questions upon scholars. But older, perhaps more prosaic, questions remain regarding the continuing reciprocal influence between religion and movements based on gender and sexuality, the environmental movement, the peace movement, and even, more recently and once again, the labor movement.

Three Levels of Analysis

These three sets of questions regarding religious movements can be addressed at several different levels of analysis. Three seem particularly important to us and will frequently appear in the discussion to follow.

The first is the cultural/ideological level of analysis, particularly how religious ideas and values may shape collective action. We will be arguing against a too simple (and too frequent) equation of belief and action. For example, "fundamentalism" does not automatically equate to certain easily predictable political and social behaviors. On the other hand, if there is to be a fruitful interchange between social movement theory and the sociology of religion, we need to know more about how the relationship between religion and collective action operates. Religion influences social movements at the cultural level by constructing and maintaining identities, providing definitions of social problems, and supplying symbolic repertoires that justify collective action and make it meaningful.

Second, there are important questions at the organizational level of analysis. Social movements researchers and sociologists of religion have both had much to say about how organizations operate in their fields of inquiry. Religious organizations vary in their types of internal polity, as well as in the complexity and explicitness of their internal rules and regulations. This has an important influence on the "mobilizability" of religion, and on religion's ability to influence social issues that affect its interests. Further, at various times and places in history, religion has provided an alternative home for movements being confronted by an antagonistic state. Internal organizational characteristics affect the extent to which religion can be such a safe haven.

Finally, there is the macropolitical level of analysis. National and global political economies have an impact on what kinds of religious movements are possible or likely. The institutionalized relations between religion and the state, in particular, are important for what sorts of channels of influence are available to religious movements, how many and what kinds of movements can flourish, what religion's role might be in revolutionary movements, and so on. "American exceptionalism" in this regard has been of particular interest in the sociology of religion. Within the social movements literature, attention to these questions should have much to offer the dialogue between US and European theories of social movements.

In the discussion to follow, we will address the three sets of empirical questions in turn. We will highlight what we think have been the most important issues during the past several decades, what key insights have emerged from research into them, and where we think the most fruitful conversations are likely to be as we move forward.

RELIGIOUS MOVEMENTS

Although much attention has been paid in recent decades to "new religious movements" (a nonpejorative term for what are commonly called "cults"), it is important to remember that religious movements have been omnipresent through history. They occur in waves (à la Tarrow's [1994] cycles of protest), and are regularly rediscovered by sociologists. Thus "new" religious movements are an old and more or less continuous phenomenon. Particularly in the US, they have been a significant source of cultural and ideological innovation – not only in the contemporary period when various new religious movements embodied and consolidated cultural experiments from the sixties (Tipton 1982; Wallis 1984), but historically as well. Kanter (1972) made this point in her comparison of nineteenth-century utopian experiments with those of the 1960s.

Classical Studies of Religious Movements

Sociological studies of religious movements go at least as far back as Weber. He viewed charismatic/prophetic movements and sects as one of the important sources of social change in human history. In *Economy and Society*, for example, he argued that charisma arose during times of crisis or extraordinary need within a group. In transcending everyday concerns and opposing the economic and political status quo, it could have revolutionary potential. Although Weber (e.g., 1978: 1111 ff.) usually spoke of charisma as an individual characteristic, he also recognized that it only achieved social significance when it attracted a set of followers – that is, when it became a movement. Often, especially when writing about the routinization of charisma, he seemed pessimistic about its long-term survival. But elsewhere (the famous "iron cage" passage in *The Protestant Ethic* [Weber 1958: 182] is a good example), he also seemed to view it as an ever-present potential for change.

Marx, who had little to say about religious movements, was not so optimistic about their revolutionary potential. Later neo-Marxists, however, offered a more nuanced analysis of the conditions under which religious movements might promote social change and when, on the other hand, religion might be an essentially conservative force. Gramsci's work on the counterhegemonic potential of culture was a foundation for this sort of Marxist revisionism, and it has inspired studies of religiopolitical movements that draw heavily on Marxian ideas and logic. Billings (1990), for example, provides an insightful comparative study explaining why and how religion was a powerful ally of the labor movement among Appalachian coal miners, but supported the factory owners in the Piedmont textile industries. Worsley's (1957) study of cargo cults in Melanesia is another example in this tradition.

Other "classic" studies of religious movements draw heavily on the Durkheimian tradition. I speak here particularly of a number of seminal studies from the middle decades of the 1900s that offered functionalist analyses of revivalism, millenarian/messianic movements, cargo cults, and so on. Wallace's (1956) work on "revitalization movements" was especially influential. Most of the studies in this period, even if they drew on Marx as much or more than on Durkheim, were essentially functionalist in that they treated religious movements as adaptive reactions to cultural breakdown, socioeconomic decline or threat, rapid social change, or natural disaster. Religious movements offered an alternative order in the face of chaos, a promise of power and status in the face of status threats. This view of religious movements shared an outlook with dominant theories of social movements at the time. Cohn (1959), Lanternari (1963), Tuveson (1964), and Barkun (1974) are exemplars of this tradition. The old-school functionalism at the heart of these mid-century works has consigned them to the limbo of infrequent citation in the more recent social movement literature; but their prominent place in the "received tradition" in both the sociology of religion and social movement theory is evidence of the fact that the social-scientific interest in religious movements is anything but new. Having said that, we turn now to the studies of "new" religious movements that have dominated the literature on religious movements in recent decades.

New Religious Movements

The US seems to be an especially fertile ground for religious innovation. Explanations of this American exceptionalism note that ethnoreligious pluralism, a product of historical immigration patterns, has combined with the constitutional disestablishment of religion in the US to produce a vibrant "free market" of religious movements that are free to set up shop when and where they like and compete for adherents. The economic metaphor suggests that such free competition will result in high levels of religious participation on the part of "consumers" and high levels of religious innovation as "producers" attempt to appeal successfully to "market niches." (See Warner [1993] for a comprehensive review of the market metaphor applied to the sociology of religion.) This helps to explain the surprising *quantity* of religious movements in the US, but the constitutional freedom from state regulation that religious movements enjoy also has an impact on their *qualitative* characteristics. Religious movements can become a home for political and economic activities (e.g., communism) that might not receive a friendly reception in the secular public arena. This "safe haven" quality of new religious movements is one reason why religious movements have often had a complementary or symbiotic relationship to other broader social movements. We will say more about this later.

The events and social movements of the 1960s sparked a renaissance in sociological thinking about social movements. The emergence and quick rise to dominance of resource mobilization theory made the study of social movements a legitimate subfield in sociology, distinct from other forms of collective behavior with which it had been lumped theretofore. Resource mobilization theory suggested that social movements were essentially a special form of political action in which participants mobilized resources in rational pursuit of their political goals.

A parallel process occurred within the sociology of religion. As many of the countercultural and utopian experiments of the sixties took a more explicitly spiritual or religious turn, the study of new religious movements became a recognized literature in its own right, with its own widely recognized acronym for its subject matter (NRMs). Here, too, NRMs were seen as a particular form of religious action in which participants rationally pursued their goals. Stark and Bainbridge offered a rational-action based theory of NRMs that shaped much of the ensuing work (Stark and Bainbridge 1979, 1985, 1987).

Analysts of NRMs busied themselves with questions that paralleled questions being asked of other social movements by resource mobilization theorists. How did NRMs organize themselves? How did they mobilize material and symbolic resources? How did they recruit participants and maintain their commitment? It was this latter question where the most fruitful interchange occurred between sociologists of religion and social movement researchers. Lofland's (1966) work on recruitment and conversion to the Unification Church (the so-called Moonies), based on earlier work he had done with Stark (Lofland and Stark 1965) was particularly influential. Lofland proposed a seven-stage theory of conversion that began with several predisposing conditions, continued with personal contact and growing affective bonds with NRM members, and ended with an intensive inter-action within and commitment to the NRM. The Lofland–Stark model generated a multitude of empirical tests and critiques by a variety of scholars. The evidence in support of the Lofland–Stark model was mixed at best. Perhaps the most important critical response, at least with regard to the influence of NRM research on general social movement theory, was Snow's research with Machalek and Phillips, drawing heavily on his study of the Nichiren Shoshu Buddhist movement (Snow and Phillips 1980; Snow and Machalek 1984). Snow and colleagues focused particularly on the importance of friendship networks for recruitment, conversion and commitment-building. This work was an important influence on a later subliterature on friend-ship networks within social movement theory.

The importance of friendship networks for recruitment and conversion to NRMs is related to another characteristic of religious movements – the fact that they are a particularly fecund setting for identity construction and experimentation. Beckford, in particular, has argued that NRMs are responding to the decline of old national, ethnic, or religious identities under late capitalism and globalization (Beckford 1984, 1985, 1990). NRMs offer participants a chance to construct new contextual-ized identities that address contemporary social problems. These identities may be syncretic, but they also are new constructions, often combining a holistic view of spirituality and ethics with a focus on individual empowerment and freedom. Thus they may be inherently political, exercising power to address social problems in public (though noninstitutional) ways.

Here is yet another potential area of fruitful conversation between the sociology of religion and social movement research. Much of the recent work on new social movements has focused on the importance of identity politics and identity construc-tion and maintenance within the context of social movements. For example, Kriesi (1988) highlights the new social movements' dependence on informal networks of people who share common countercultural values in opposition to previously dom-inant forms of identity (such as nation or race). "They are made up of people living, working, communicating, and making politics together in pursuit of a countercul-tural design for an alternative way of life" (Kriesi 1988: 43). The sociology of new religious movements and the study of new social movements emerged and advanced relatively independent of each other. But the two communities of scholars were observing phenomena that had much in common, and they came separately to understandings that were similar in important ways.

Resurgence of Fundamentalist Movements

At about the same time as the 1970s–1980s wave of new religious movements in the US was gaining steam, there was also a resurgence of "old time religion." In fact, it may well be that the so-called "new religious right" and other fundamentalist move-ments around the world were responding to the same globalization processes and socioeconomic strains of late capitalism that were engendering the various new religious movements. Wuthnow (1983) suggests that the political activists of the religious right walked through a door that had been opened by the countercultural left and its new religious movements. That is, the new left and the counterculture had re-legitimized the role of moral discourse in the public arena. Many of the criticisms of racial inequality and the Vietnam War during the 1960s (and, later, the Watergate scandals) were expressed in religious or moral language. And the Democrats, after all, were the first to elect a "born again" president, Jimmy Carter.

Once moral discourse had become a legitimate form of political debate, the religious right was much more advantageously positioned than the left to mobilize religiomoral symbolic resources. From the 1930s through the 1960s, they had been largely out of the public eye and silent in the public square. During that time, however, they had been busy building cultural institutions such as colleges, universities, publishing houses, radio and television outlets, and so on – to say nothing of huge "megachurches" (Miller 1997). When reentering the political arena, then, they brought with them a much larger and more powerful institutional foundation than the cultural movements of the left enjoyed.

While the religious right was expanding its political influence in the US during the 1970s and 1980s, similar movements were occurring elsewhere in the world and within other religions. Most notable, of course, was the rise of a politically ambitious Islamic fundamentalism in Iran, Afghanistan, and across the Arab world. But "fundamentalist" movements also emerged within Eastern religions such as Hinduism and Sikhism, and various scholars noted a significant return to orthodoxy within Judaism, as well (e.g., Davidman 1991; Kaufman 1991).

"Fundamentalism" needs to be placed in quotes in this context, because it is a contested concept. Analysts of the phenomenon do not agree either on a definition of fundamentalism itself, nor do they agree on which religious groups belong to the category. (For a good overview of the debates, see Marty and Appleby 1994.) For our purposes here, we are referring to conservative or traditional (these terms are problematic as well, of course) religious movements that are politically active in contesting at least some aspects of modernity and the dominance of Western culture in the emerging global order. Many, but not all, combine nationalist aspirations with a traditional religious agenda.

There are two points we wish to emphasize with regard to contemporary fundamentalist movements. First, they are responding to the same social change processes as the new religious movements discussed above – especially the blurring of the boundaries between "public" and "private," and the decline of traditional identities and "metanarratives." Snow and Marshall (1984) convincingly argue this point with regard to Islamic fundamentalism, in particular. Fundamentalist movements do, however, appeal in general to a different class stratum. Many of those attracted to new religious movements are from middle- and upper-class backgrounds, and are often well-educated members of the "new class" of information and service professionals characteristic of late capitalism (Snow and Machalek 1984). Fundamentalist movements are more likely to appeal to classes that are underprivileged in the new global political economy. This may be less true of US Protestant fundamentalists, who as a group have been upwardly mobile economically since their beginning in the early twentieth century. But, in general, they continue to come from less educated backgrounds (Wuthnow 1988), and thus are less likely to benefit from the growing dominance of the "new class." Members of the working class in the US, even though they may be better off than their international counterparts, have seen their prospects decline in the global economy as more and more good jobs leave the US national borders.

Second, fundamentalist movements are organizing around issues similar to those that engage the so-called new social movements – especially gender and sexuality identity concerns. Some scholars (e.g., Riesebrodt 1993) argue that gender is the defining characteristic of fundamentalism; that, at heart, all fundamentalisms are about the defense of patriarchy. While not everyone will agree with such a strong form of the argument, it is clear that political and moral issues related to gender and sexuality occupy much of the time and energy expended by fundamentalists in the public arena. Thus it may be helpful for scholars interested in new social movements more broadly to consider fundamentalist movements, not as countermovements, but as a special subset of the new social movement phenomenon. They are products of the same global changes and are concerned with the same issues.

Incorporating fundamentalist movements into the work on new social movements is likely to generate some helpful new insights. Take the issue of informal social networks, for example. Fundamentalist movements make extensive use of such informal networks, but they have also been quite successful at mobilizing those networks into larger organizational forms – even capturing the state in several instances (e.g., Iran, Afghanistan). No other new social movement can make such a claim. Fundamentalist movements may offer important research sites for examining how informal networks transmogrify into larger political formations.

Another important set of ongoing questions in the work on new social movements concerns the role of ideological processes and the mobilization of symbolic resources. Attention to religious movements, whose *raison d'être* is the manipulation and mobilization of ideological and symbolic resources, may shed additional light on these questions. Munson (2001), for example, uses a study of the Muslim Brotherhood in Egypt to engage social movement theory's concept of "framing."

New Immigrant Religious Movements

An even more recent interest in the sociology of US religion is the growing size and significance of immigrant religions. Changes in post-1965 immigration laws have dramatically increased the quantity and quality of religious and ethnic diversity especially in urban areas, but increasingly in small-town and rural areas, as well. Of course, increased religious diversity does not equate to an increase in religious "movements" per se. However, it is not unusual for religions that were part of the mainstream establishment in their countries of origin to take on movement-like qualities upon arrival in North America. Religious ideas and organizations can easily become the basis for mobilization in defense of cultural identities or in promoting religious/cultural/ethnic revitalization. Various case studies of immigrant religion have documented this movement-like quality of transplanted religion (see especially Warner and Wittner 1998; Ebaugh 2000).

In a study of the ISKCON (Hare Krishna) temple in Chicago, Vande Berg and Kniss (2002) show how the influx of South Asian immigrants has revitalized the temple. Immigrants brought an influx of material resources as well as a new market of potential converts for ISKCON. Consequently, despite some years of institutionalization and "domestication," ISKCON in Chicago is returning to its status as a conversionist movement. This time, however, the movement is occurring primarily within Hinduism and is attracting Indian converts – as opposed to its original incarnation as a new religious movement appealing to a predominantly Euro-American constituency.

Thus it appears that we should expand the concept of "new religious movements" to extend beyond wholly "new" religious groups or "cults." We must also consider the impact of globalization and transnational migration on the importation of religious movements that may be old traditions, but are new and innovative in a particular social and historical context. The religious innovation and revitalization that results from the transplantation of old traditions will have consequences for religious movements within the "receiving" societies as well as consequences for international or transnational movements.

It is still too soon to tell what the impact of the new religious diversity will be within the North American context. But the aftermath of September 11, which energized religious actors of all sorts, gives us some indications. Interfaith responses to September 11 (and the attempt of most North American Muslims to distance themselves from radical Islamic fundamentalism) produced what seems to be an emergent coalition of the "Abrahamic" faiths that may eventually usurp Judeo-Christianity as the dominant religious category in the US. The famous Herbergian formula of "Protestant-Catholic-Jew" may be turning into "Christian-Jew-Muslim." If this should occur in North America, it could well have significant consequences for international religiopolitical movements, especially those in the Middle East. It may also produce some important realignments with regard to domestic ethnic politics. For example, Hindus and Buddhists were conspicuously absent from many of the interfaith rallies following September 11 (at least in the Chicago events that we observed). This may indicate a potential divide within the US South Asian community that previously had been much more united here than on the Asian subcontinent.

SOCIAL MOVEMENTS WITHIN RELIGION

The Place of Ideas and Issues in Intrareligious Movements

Sociologists of religion who treat denominations as important units of analysis have tended to emphasize ideological uniformity within particular religious denominations. There is also, however, a great deal of sociological literature focusing not only on religious pluralism in society as a whole but also within a given religious tradition. These studies often emphasize the different social location of various groups within the same religious tradition. They do not assume that all co-religionists hold the identical interpretation of the core of the religion or apply the religious beliefs to political matters in the same way. It is precisely in the struggles internal to a church where we find a key to understanding religion's role in social movements. Such internal struggles often involve, in particular, the social and political implications of the faith. The internal ideological divisions centered on a religion's ideas about social justice and social change can produce internal social movements that, potentially, can produce significant change within established religions as well as becoming allied with external movements.

Different political applications of a given religious tradition can develop across different contemporaneous social groups or across time. Thus it is interesting to note that white evangelicalism, a religious tradition currently associated with conservative politics, has at times been associated with egalitarian and class-based politics. Various studies of white populism in the late nineteenth and early twentieth centuries have argued that such movements have included a purist insurgency against established evangelical denominations, perhaps combined with a perception that religious leaders are too identified with the status quo and not enough with the oppressed. Thus the Puritan critique, far from being a withdrawal from the world, in that context emphasized populist activism for social and political equality (Corbin 1981; Goode 1993; Stephens 2000). Even today there is a significant social/political leftist movement within US evangelicalism, represented by publications such as *Sojourners* magazine and organizations like Evangelicals for Social Action.

Given that religious groups' internal cleavages often parallel external controversies, it is not surprising that contemporary analyses of intrareligious movements find issues of identity politics central to debates within religious traditions (e.g., Dillon 1999). For example, the place of women in the public realm was, a couple decades ago, argued to a great extent within the churches. While the question of ordination of women still remains a particular fault line within the Anglican Communion and the Roman Catholic Church, it is easy to forget that it was only a few decades ago that the presence of female ministers (or preachers) in many Christian denominations, now an unremarkable reality, was a central focus of Protestant debate, closely followed by the secular media.

Today, similarly, the ordination of gay ministers, or the legitimacy of religiously sanctioned gay marriage (or analogous unions), is a central axis of debate in numerous denominations. Religious debate about gay rights, to some extent, leads rather than follows the secular debate. The Catholic debate over homosexuality, for instance, has strongly paralleled the secular debate. Public awareness of the existence of the AIDS Coalition to Unleash Power (ACT UP) was intertwined with the group's December 1989 disruption of a mass led by Cardinal John O'Connor of New York, perceived as a prime opponent of gay rights and of effective efforts to fight AIDS. Just as explicitly antigay political organizations have become more prominent while the American population seems to move (though slowly) towards increasing tolerance, the Catholic hierarchy (though more at the Roman than American level) has largely moved to the right on gay issues, including abandoning its tolerance of the gay Catholic organization Dignity, even while American Catholics as a whole have become more tolerant of homosexuality (Burns 1999; Weaver 1999).

To take a further example of identity politics within religion not only paralleling but even somewhat defining the secular version of identity politics, it is of course impossible to comprehend American abortion politics without considering the role of religion. There is considerable evidence that the pro-life movement began as an almost entirely Catholic movement (e.g., Luker 1984), even though it is not the case that the average Catholic is reliably pro-life. The pro-life movement took on a new dimension with the rise of right-wing movements such as the Moral Majority, later followed by the Christian Coalition, which have drawn particular strength from white Southern conservative evangelicals (Guth et al. 1994).

Whether abortion is consistent with Christian belief has, then, been a particular center of debate not only within Roman Catholicism (Weaver 1999) but also within many Protestant denominations, such as the Southern Baptists. Struggles over the legitimacy of tolerance of homosexuality and abortion within Baptist theology, for instance, have remade the Southern Baptists in the wake of an intense organizational struggle over such issues (Ammerman 1990). It is clearly an overstatement to equate the rise of the religious right in the late 1970s and 1980s with theological conflicts within denominations, as many theological debates have no obvious political implications, or sometimes are applied to social causes in both left and right directions. Nevertheless, it is interesting to note that the plausibility of organizations like the Moral Majority and the Christian Coalition depend on an ability to claim allegiance within theologically conservative traditions that opposed abortion and gay rights. Some of those antigay and anti-abortion "traditions" were born (as an explicit, organized religious force) only in the last quarter century; still, what is interesting in this context is that struggles over denominational religious identity have been intertwined with conflicts over the same issues (especially abortion and homosexuality) in American society as a whole.

Again, one must remember that, while most American social movements have had a strong religious component, most religious adherents in the US typically do not connect their religion with political causes and, even when they do, they may find that the right-wing version of religion they favor is opposed by a leftist sitting in the next pew. Thus, for instance, R. Stephen Warner (1995) has noted that a pro-gay rights church originally based itself theologically within Pentecostal Protestantism and indeed was founded by a charismatic minister raised within Southern Pentecostalism, a religious tradition that has usually been antigay. But the Metropolitan Community Church that he founded, while now more theologically diverse, is a denomination that has, in recent years, arguably attained quite mainstream status. Similar studies of gender politics have argued that even apparently very traditional, patriarchal religious ideology can be used by some women in incipiently feminist directions (Rose 1987).

When sociologists attempt to take religious ideas seriously as having their own causal force, they can take at least two directions. One way is to emphasize unity of belief within a religious tradition and assume that social action on the part of believers will reflect that unity. Another approach, the one we advocate, focuses on intrareligious movements and conflict as an intracommunity argument about the meaning and application of particular religious ideas within a particular social and political context. This approach is amenable to Ann Swidler's (1986) view of culture as a "tool kit" rather than an overarching and internally consistent system of meaning. Indeed, Swidler made her original argument partly by reinterpreting Weber's Protestant ethic thesis in terms of her tool kit approach. Thus a given religious tradition includes various ideas that can be used, like tools, to build and adjust multiple social projects.

Organizational Dynamics in Intrareligious Movements

Discussions of cultural or ideological conflict within a religious tradition frequently imply a particular theory of organizational dynamics of religion as well. For instance, Finke and Stark's (1992) rational choice approach emphasizes the advantage of religious organizations that act like sects rather than churches, that is, keeping bureaucracy relatively low while ideological vitality and ideological exclusivity remains high.

Ammerman's (1990) account of the fundamentalist takeover of the Southern Baptist Convention is not just a study of the triumph of insurgent Baptist conservatism but is also a study of the battle over organizational resources. It was through a well-planned, strategically effective takeover of the denominational organization that the conservative wing was able to enforce new ideological boundaries. The story is especially interesting in the Baptist context. Since the autonomy of congregations is so central to Baptist theology, a top-down enforcement of Baptist "orthodoxy" appears inconsistent with its own tradition. Harrison (1959), however, had earlier pointed out that democratic debate and decision-making is most difficult precisely in those polity structures that emphasize local autonomy and have few institutionalized bureaucratic structures or channels of influence between the local bodies and the national agencies. Thus, internal revolutionary movements or "coups" are the only effective means of overturning authority at the top of the organization.

Indeed, there are multiple studies of religious organizations that emphasize the strong relationship between organizational structure and ideological dynamics. Chaves (1994), for example, analyzes the relationship between evolving denominational bureaucratic structures and secularization processes. There is not space here to review the vast literature on religious polity structures. But it is important to note that the form that intrareligious movements take will depend upon the polity structure within which they must operate. Internal movements within organizations with hierarchical bureaucratic structures are likely to generate movements that resemble the mobilization of "ordinary" political lobbying. Flatter structures that are decentralized are more likely to produce internal movements that resemble revolutions.

Intrareligious Movements and the State

Social movements within religious organizations are also greatly affected by the relationship between religion and the state. Religious autonomy from the state, as is the case in the US, makes religious groups an advantageous home for various kinds of movements. This is particularly true of human rights and identity movements that may face suppression by the state or the broader culture. Religious groups are free to extend sanctuary and services to people or groups who might otherwise run afoul of the law. During the Reagan administration for example, a widespread "sanctuary movement" was organized by a broad network of religious congregations. They offered sanctuary to Central American political refugees who were on the "wrong" side according to official US government policy, and who would have otherwise been classified as illegal aliens. Religious organizations thus became an important center for the US movement for peace in Central America in the 1970s and 1980s (Smith 1996).

Throughout the twentieth century, religious denominational agencies and seminaries were important "abeyance structures" (Rupp and Taylor 1987), providing a home for women's public engagement and leadership between waves of the feminist movement (Chaves 1997). Further, ordination of women clergy became an important battleground for the feminist movement. The internal women's movement was conflictual in virtually all religious organizations, and there was, of course, significant variation in the movement's success across denominations. But Chaves (1997) shows that, in those denominations where external allies supported women's equality and where the religious ideology did not pose a major block to full equality, the movement was quite successful – arguably more successful within religion than within most other social institutions.

More recently, movements for gay and lesbian rights have been particularly active within religious organizations. Again, religion's autonomy from the state plays an important role. Even though states may not be willing to recognize gay or lesbian marriage, for example, religious organizations are free to do so. This ability of religion to provide autonomous space for movements, along with the presumptive legitimacy of religious organizations' actions, makes religion a fertile ground for movement activism. It is not coincidental that virtually all religious denominations, even those who officially and publicly oppose homosexuality, are currently dealing, in one way or another, with an internal movement for gay and lesbian rights.

The "parallel" nature of religious and external movements discussed above may be a consequence of the way in which religion has been a "safe haven" for social movements in the US context. This may also have something to do with why new social movements such as the peace movement, environmental movement, gay/lesbian movement, and so on, have been more public and confrontational in Europe. In most countries in Europe, particularly Western Europe, religious organizations are much more implicated in the state apparatus, and often are subsidized by the state. There is thus no easily accessible, presumptively legitimate, institutional home for social movements outside the formal polity structure.

RELIGION AND OTHER SOCIAL MOVEMENTS

Religious Ideas and Other Social Movements

As we pointed out above, a typical "common-sense" view of religion expects that a given religion has a certain set of beliefs that all its members share, and that it has an effect on the public sphere to the extent that members try to shape the world in the direction that their beliefs mandate. Such a view regularly informs news media accounts of the role of religion in politics, when, for instance, journalists assume that Catholics are particularly opposed to abortion. It also informs many academic analyses, especially outside sociology, such as in Samuel Huntington's (1993, 1996) "clash of civilizations" argument. While such presentations often include perfunctory qualifications that internally religions can be diverse, usually such idealist analyses assume, for the most part, uniformity, in which a culture is defined by its degree of ideological consensus. Thus cultures collide because the unifying beliefs that organize those cultures contradict those of an opposing culture. Indeed, for instance, Huntington's analysis makes no sense unless one assumes that cultures are internally unified by a core of beliefs, usually of religious origin, and that such cultures are ideologically fairly autonomous of each other. Yes, there are geopolitical and other factors that are also quite relevant, but ultimately *cultures* do not clash unless cultures are built around a consensus of core beliefs.

Simplistic versions of this cultural consensus approach quickly run into trouble explaining religion and religious change. For instance, it is fairly clear that, in the United States, at least, it would be strategically unwise for a presidential candidate to attempt to woo the Catholic vote by taking a strongly pro-life stance: the hierarchy takes a strongly pro-life stand, but the laity, who comprise most of the voters, do not. Catholics are no more likely to be pro-life than the population at large, and there is some evidence that they are moderately more pro-choice (McAneny and Saad 1993; Hoge et al. 2001). Or, in Huntington's case, it is a bit difficult to understand why such monolithic cultures disappear or change. Why, for instance, were there (according to Huntington) about 22 such autonomous and internally unified cultures a century or so ago, and now there are about 6?

An approach to the role of religion in social movements, and public affairs more generally, that starts with the premise that religion can dramatically change, at least in the case of American religion, is Hunter's *Culture Wars* (1991). And yet Hunter still emphasizes conflict between two internally consistent sets of beliefs and so in some ways resembles Huntington's approach theoretically. Unlike Huntington, Hunter emphasizes cultural conflict within societies but he still sees two large, internally consistent cultures driving debate. Drawing from Wuthnow's (1988) argument that, in recent decades, American denominational divisions have become less significant than the orientations of particular congregations, Hunter argues that many of our contemporary social debates are variations of a conflict between an orthodox worldview based on traditional religious perspectives and a progressive worldview that is more secular and relativist but also includes liberal religious voices. This cultural divide cuts across denominations.

Hunter's thesis has been the basis of extended debate and critique (see especially Williams 1997). Ultimately, maintaining that such unified cultures define social debates is almost impossible to support empirically given the reality of cross-cutting cleavages (Kniss 2003). Also undermining that approach is the considerable socio-logical research that indicates that religion can provide a great deal of motivation, energy, and solidarity in social movements, but that the same religious tradition can have left-wing and right-wing manifestations (e.g., Dillon 1999). Further, while in contemporary America, levels of religious participation do predict levels of sexual conservatism reasonably well, for the most part religious behavior and religious affiliation do not predict political ideology well (Davis and Robinson 1997; Olson 1997).

Another approach treats religion as an idealist political force, but one that helps create cultural pluralism rather than cultural uniformity, and has informed a great deal of interesting scholarship. A recent, intriguing example of an argument about the power of a particular cultural or theological orientation to help shape how believers face a social problem is Emerson and Smith's (2000) discussion of how white evangelicals face race relations in the United States. Emerson and Smith argue that there have been genuine attempts by white evangelicals to reach across the racial divide and address racial injustice; but the theological emphasis on one's individual relationship to Jesus has channeled the white evangelical antiracist mobilization away from consideration of systemic or structural racism. The emphasis on individual conversion makes it difficult for white evangelicals to overcome what Lawrence Bobo (1997) would call "laissez-faire racism," that is the assumption that once direct, individual racial prejudice and hate have been addressed, no further social or policy initiatives need deal with race matters.

One could, however, ask whether Emerson and Smith can attribute the limitations of the white evangelical approach in dealing with racism so clearly to evangelical religious beliefs. Black denominations often rely ultimately on very similar religious traditions and theologies – the largest black denomination, after all, is the Black

Baptists – and yet black churches were central in the civil rights movement. (There is further discussion of black churches below.)

Yet another approach to the relationship between religious ideology and broader social movements is the view that religions *need* to be in tension with the cultural mainstream in order to differentiate themselves and offer unique spiritual and social rewards for membership (thus providing selective incentives that solve the free rider problem). This view, based on a rational-choice theory of religion, is often associated with the recent work of Finke and Stark (e.g., 1992). They expect that successful religions will maintain a strict, otherworldly perspective that will keep them internally unified and, often, uninvolved in secular public affairs. This approach implies that a religious group often becomes involved in social movements by becoming less of a vibrant sect that serves its members' religious needs and more like an established church that loses its distinctive religious quality. Becoming political means becoming less "religious" and instead becoming part of the secular world, losing the religious tension of a sect.

Numerous criticisms of Finke and Stark's assumptions (e.g., Burns 1996b) exist and there is no need to review them extensively here. One, however, is particularly relevant here: the critique of the assumption that being in religious tension with the society means being in tension with the status quo overall. For instance, Finke and Stark cite the Southern Baptists as the denomination that has most retained its sectlike character through its strict beliefs and refusal to adopt a liberal secular morality. Thus, they argue, it has retained high membership long after most of its competing sects have transformed into churches. But the Southern Baptists, through most of their history, have thrived as a white denomination in a segregated society; at best one can say that the Southern Baptist churches have acquiesced to the political and social reality of racism. From that perspective, this sect that supposedly concentrates on being in tension within the larger society, avoiding secularizing politics, has been a mainstay of the social, political, and racial status quo, especially in the South.

Thus, it is questionable whether religions really thrive by being "in tension" with the larger society. It may be more appropriate in studies of the relationship between religion and social movements to focus on how religious beliefs interact with a sense of group identity as people frame and define social problems. That is, religious believers have one foot in the church but one foot in the larger society.

Religious Organizations and Other Social Movements

One common approach to the relationship between religious organizational dynamics and broader social movements assumes that there is not much distinctive about religious versus other motivations for social movement participation. That is, religion is seen as a source of organizational resources in the same way that professional or political organizations, or social networks, can provide organizational resources. Such studies fall within the range of explanations ultimately influenced, in part, by resource mobilization theory. A now-classic work in this tradition is Aldon Morris's (1984) study of the civil rights movement. For the most part, Morris is interested in understanding how religious organizations provided organizational resources to the movement. So, also, religious civil leaders are mostly of interest in their ability to mobilize social movement resources, not in their ability to inspire the flock with biblical preaching. Still, Morris cannot easily ignore the distinctively religious identity of the Southern Christian Leadership Conference: an undertheorized discussion of the role of religious charisma in the growth of the civil rights movement is also an important part of the book's analysis.

Another example of this approach, Christian Smith's (1991) account of liberation theology, includes some consideration of particularly Catholic ideological sources of the left-wing populism that came to be known as liberation theology. But for the most part the argument is that liberation theology built its strength around organizational possibilities within the Catholic Church, so that a minority of left-wing activist bishops managed to build the Latin American Episcopal Conference (known by its Portuguese acronym, CELAM). In the first few years of the conference's existence, its organizational strength was essential to the survival and growth of liberation theology, sometimes in a context of quite violent suppression of both the leadership and grass-roots manifestations. And then ultimately it was the loss of control of the organizational structure, that is, of CELAM, that sapped the energy of liberation theology. In a more recent study of the US Central American peace movement, Smith (1996) makes the impact of religion a central theme in his analysis. As in his earlier work on liberation theology, however, he emphasizes the organizational resources provided by religion and its usefulness for framing tasks and maintaining commitment in the course of the movement.

Smith, of course, is not alone in how he incorporates religion into his analysis. It is difficult to find examples in the literature where religion *qua* religion is an important variable in the analysis. There is a gap in our knowledge of how variations in religious ideas and practices across different religious groups may affect their participation in broader social movements. It is reasonable to assume that how religious folk define moral problems or understand salvation from such problems will have an impact on how they define and act on social problems. But we know very little about this, nor about the mechanisms by which particular kinds of religious ideas may be organized into collective action.

Religion, the State, and Other Social Movements

Although often not made explicit, the question of church–state relationships is central to understanding religion's impact on other social movements. The importance of church–state relationships becomes especially clear in a comparative context. There are numerous examples of social revolutions, for instance, that have involved attacking, in part, a Catholic Church identified with an old regime. That struggle helps explain not only a good deal of the nature of the revolution but also the nature of postrevolutionary society. The anticlericalism associated with revolution and liberalism in France and Mexico, for instance, was a postrevolutionary legacy (with prerevolutionary origins) that long served as a central context for secular politics. Within the Islamic world, one of the more striking analogous cases is Turkey, an Islamic country whose political regime, following Ataturk, is so committed to secularism that religious politics is persistently the elephant in the room that the state needs to work so hard to ignore.

No matter what the particular faith under examination, the nature of the relationship that religious authorities and congregations have with states is a central variable that helps explain the nature (or absence) of religious involvement in social movements. One must consider not only the nature of the religion or whether a liberal regime exists. The same religious tradition can support diverse types of social movements. And there is not just one type of liberal church–state relationship. Indeed, there are at least two kinds, namely the liberal regime that *controls* religion and the liberal regime in which religion has a high degree of social autonomy. The French state, and the Mexican State for most of the twentieth century, fell into the former category (as does the Turkish state, to the extent that one judges it to be liberal, and at a more severe level). The American state has been the prime example of the latter.

Numerous studies of religion in America, then, emphasize or at least assume the significance of churches having a great deal of autonomy from the state. Indeed, the particular nature of the US church–state relationship may help explain the apparent paradox that religious affiliation does not predict political affiliations well, while at the same time American social movements typically have large religious components. Religion in the United States is a zone of autonomy allowing for social and ideological experimentation. Finke and Stark (1992) and Warner (1993) are particularly effective at noting this characteristic of US religion (see also Evans and Boyte 1986). The US can thus have a bit of a Wild West aspect to its religious practices, as new religious movements appear in multiple forms. But religion also is a zone of autonomy for just about any social group that wants or needs to have some autonomy from the state or from other social groups. That autonomy takes numerous forms, including the racial segregation that has been a central feature of American religious congregations. But it also accounts for why initially unpopular causes, whether temperance, racial tolerance, or gay rights often find churches to be a particularly useful vehicle, even when larger religious bodies are as hostile to the new cause as is secular society.

That type of autonomy is particularly strong in the American context, but it exists in any context in which the state recognizes the legitimacy of religious authority. Thus in the Islamic context today it is likely that religion serves as a vehicle of popular unrest precisely because the state is hesitant to crack down on anything with an Islamic identity. Far from representing a cultural consensus, in many cases anti-Western Islamic radicalism can distinguish itself from what it considers a corrupt or co-opted state and elites, because the state does not want a reputation as an enemy of religious authority or religious expression.

Jan Kubik's (1994) study of the role of Catholicism in the Solidarity movement noted that Catholicism had largely avoided conflict with the Polish Communist regime; indeed, some opponents of the regime felt that the church had been co-opted. And yet the fact that the church had an established, recognized place in the society meant that it became, both organizationally and symbolically, a central component of Solidarity's identity. The ability of churches to serve as centers of human rights advocacy under oppressive regimes, in Chile and elsewhere, is a similar phenomenon. Chile is an interesting case because, while it had the organizational autonomy that religious institutions often have, the Chilean Catholic population was particularly lax in religious observance (Brian Smith 1982, 1986). Again, the church's autonomy from the state, and its ability to support or even organize political opposition, does not necessarily depend on a strong core of shared religious beliefs in the society as a whole. Christian Smith's (1996) study of the role of US churches in opposing Reagan's Central America policy demonstrated that quite well.

Thus, even when in some ways hostile to religious practice, a state that faces a religious tradition with some degree of autonomy always faces a potential opponent. While the Shah of Iran typically made peace with religious authorities during those times that his power was threatened, the fact that Islam was an autonomous ideological and social center allowed Islam to become central to revolutionary identity. This is despite the fact that Iranian Islam had previously shown almost no history of advocacy of theocracy. Indeed, many of those who opposed the Shah saw themselves as Islamic revolutionaries and yet did not desire or expect a theocracy (Burns 1996a); again, a given religious tradition can become an ally of multiple political and ideological options.

Arguably, the French and Mexican models are most effective at restricting religion's zone of autonomy. That is, in both postrevolutionary France and Mexico, religious popular expression was not particularly difficult to pursue, but the states prevented clerics from having enough legal, or in some cases, financial autonomy to help organize opposition to the regime. Religion at the popular level could be primarily apolitical – as it typically is in the United States – but religion as a whole was apolitical as well.

CONCLUSION

Much of the foregoing discussion turns on the question of the relationship between religion and politics, an issue about which we know too little, especially with regard to social movements. The social movement literature has tended to treat the *origins* or *causes* of religious involvement in movements as an exogenous variable. Even though researchers may take religion's political *effects* quite seriously, they do not expend much energy on understanding religion itself. Sociologists of religion, on the other hand, often treat politicization as exogenous to the nature of religion. Some (as in some versions of secularization theory) even see it as a sign of religion's decline.

There are exceptions to this generalization (e.g., Kurtz 1986; Burns 1992; Demerath and Williams 1992; Kubik 1994; Kniss 1997). These studies take the internal dynamics of both religion and social movements seriously, without attempting to reduce one to the other. This nearly always requires a nuanced, historically sensitive analysis of particular cases of religiopolitical movements. In order to adequately understand instances in which religion is present in social movements (or social movements are present in religion), it is necessary to understand the history and legacy brought by each.

The advantage of these "hybrid" approaches is that they generate new research questions and insights and avoid some of the old tired debates about religion and politics (e.g., "does political involvement lead to a decline in religious vitality?"). But there are also problems with historical case-based "hybrid" studies of religion and social movements. For example, do they adequately reconcile the theoretical approaches from the two different literatures? Do they clarify systematically why classic mobilization and political process factors explain some aspects of a religious social movement while the particular religious tradition explains other aspects? Is there theoretical integration and synthesis, or is there a more ad hoc construction of theoretical claims that may even be mutually contradictory? Do they help us understand both religion and social movements in a new way that is helpful and generalizes beyond particular case studies?

Given the complexity of nuanced historical analyses, few studies of religious social movements attempt to move across different traditions or sociohistorical contexts. Usually a given study looks at one variant of Protestantism, Catholicism, or some other religious tradition, making it difficult to establish what that particular tradition brings to a social movement that another could not. We still do not know enough about how religion qua religion affects the emergence of movements within the religious field, or how it affects other social movements to which it connects in various ways. To avoid ad hoc explanations and theories, we must develop a more systematic and comprehensive understanding of the different movement possibilities within different religious traditions, and across different places and times.

References

Ammerman, Nancy (1990) *Baptist Battles: Social Change and Religious Conflict in the Southern Baptist Convention*. New Brunswick, NJ: Rutgers University Press.

Barkun, Michael (1974) *Disaster and the Millennium*. New Haven: Yale University Press.

Beckford, James A. (1984) Holistic Imagery and Ethics in New Religious and Healing Movements. *Social Compass*, 31, 259–72.

——(1985) *Cult Controversies: The Societal Response to the New Religious Movements*. London: Tavistock.

——(1990) The Sociology of Religion and Social Problems. *Sociological Analysis*, 51, 1–14.

Billings, Dwight (1990) Religion as Opposition: A Gramscian Analysis. *American Journal of Sociology*, 96, 1–31.

Bobo, Lawrence (1997) The Color Line, the Dilemma, and the Dream: Race Relations in America at the Close of the Twentieth Century. In John Higham (ed.), *Civil Rights and Social Wrongs*. University Park, PA: Pennsylvania State University Press, 31–55.

Burns, Gene (1992) *The Frontiers of Catholicism: The Politics of Ideology in a Liberal World*. Berkeley: University of California Press.

——(1996a) Ideology, Culture, and Ambiguity: The Revolutionary Process in Iran. *Theory and Society*, 25, 349–88.

——(1996b) Studying the Political Culture of Catholicism. *Sociology of Religion*, 57, 37–53.

——(1999) Abandoning Suspicion: The Catholic Left and Sexuality. In Mary Jo Weaver (ed.), *What's Left? Liberal American Catholics*. Bloomington: Indiana University Press, 67–87.

Chaves, Mark (1994) Secularization as Declining Religious Authority. *Social Forces*, 72, 749–74.

——(1997) *Ordaining Women: Culture and Conflict in Religious Organizations*. Cambridge, MA: Harvard University Press.

Cohn, Norman (1959) *The Pursuit of the Millennium: Revolutionary Messianism in Medieval and Reformation Europe and its Bearing on Modern Totalitarian Movements*. London: Harper & Row.

Corbin, David Alan (1981) *Life, Work, and Rebellion in the Coal Fields: The Southern West Virginia Miners, 1880–1922*. Urbana: University of Illinois Press.

Davidman, Lynn (1991) *Tradition in a Rootless World: Women Turn to Orthodox Judaism*. Berkeley: University of California Press.

Davis, Nancy J., and Robert V. Robinson (1997) A War for America's Soul? The American Religious Landscape. In Rhys H. Williams (ed.), *Cultural Wars in American Politics*. New York: Aldine de Gruyter, 39–61.

Demerath, N. J. III, and Rhys H. Williams (1992) *A Bridging of Faiths: Religion and Politics in a New England City*. Princeton, NJ: Princeton University Press.

Dillon, Michele (1999) *Catholic Identity: Balancing Reason, Faith and Power*. New York: Cambridge University Press.

Ebaugh, Helen Rose (2000) *Religion and the New Immigrants: Continuities and Adaptations in Immigrant Congregations*. Walnut Creek, CA: AltaMira.

Emerson, Michael O., and Christian Smith (2000) *Divided by Faith: Evangelical Religion and the Problem of Race in America*. New York: Oxford University Press.

Evans, Sara M., and Harry C. Boyte (1986) *Free Spaces: The Sources of Democratic Change in America*. New York: Harper & Row.

Finke, Roger, and Rodney Stark (1992) *The Churching of America, 1776–1990: Winners and Losers in our Religious Economy*. New Brunswick, NJ: Rutgers University Press.

Goode, Richard C. (1993) The Godly Insurrection in Limestone County: Social Gospel, Populism, and Southern Culture in the Late Nineteenth Century. *Religion and American Culture*, 3, 155–69.

Guth, James L., Lyman A. Kellstedt, Corwin E. Smidt, and John C. Green (1994) Cut from the Whole Cloth: Religion and Pro-life Mobilization among Pro-life Activists. In Ted E. Jelen and Marthe A. Chandler (eds.), *Abortion Politics in the United States and Canada: Studies in Public Opinion*. Westport, CT: Praeger, 107–29.

Hannigan, John A. (1991) Social Movement Theory and the Sociology of Religion: Toward a New Synthesis. *Sociological Analysis*, 52, 311–31.

Harrison, Paul (1959) *Authority and Power in the Free Church Tradition: A Social Case Study of the American Baptist Convention*. Princeton, NJ: Princeton University Press.

Hoge, Dear R., William D. Dinges, Mary Johnson, and Juan L. Gonzalez Jr. (2001) *Young Adult Catholics*. Notre Dame, IN: University of Notre Dame Press.

Hunter, James Davison (1991) *Culture Wars: The Struggle to Define America*. New York: Basic.

Huntington, Samuel P. (1993) The Clash of Civilizations? *Foreign Affairs*, 72 (3), 22–49.

—— (1996) *The Clash of Civilizations and the Remaking of World Order*. New York: Simon & Schuster.

Johnston, Hank, and Bert Klandermans (eds.) (1995) *Social Movements and Culture*. Minneapolis: University of Minnesota Press.

Kanter, Rosabeth Moss (1972) *Commitment and Community: Communes and Utopias in Sociological Perspective*. Cambridge, MA: Harvard University Press.

Kaufman, Debra Renee (1991) *Rachel's Daughters: Newly Orthodox Jewish Women*. New Brunswick, NJ: Rutgers University Press.

Klandermans, Bert, Hanspeter Kriesi, and Sidney Tarrow (eds.) (1988) *From Structure to Action: Comparing Social Movement Research across Cultures*. Vol. 1, *International Social Movement Research*. Greenwich, CT: JAI.

Kniss, Fred (1997) *Disquiet in the Land: Cultural Conflict in American Mennonite Communities*. New Brunswick, NJ: Rutgers University Press.

—— (2003) Mapping the Moral Order: Depicting the Terrain of Religious Conflict and Change. In Michele Dillon (ed.), *Handbook of the Sociology of Religion*. New York: Cambridge University Press, 331–47.

Kniss, Fred, and Mark Chaves (1995) Analyzing Intradenominational Conflict: New Directions. *Journal for the Scientific Study of Religion*, 34, 172–85.

Kriesi, Hanspeter (1988) Local Mobilization for the People's Petition of the Dutch Peace Movement. In Bert Klandermans, Hanspeter Kriesi, and Sidney Tarrow (eds.), *From Structure to Action: Comparing Social Movement Research across Cultures*. Vol. 1, *International Social Movement Research*. Greenwich, CT: JAI, 41–81.

Kubik, Jan (1994) *The Power of Symbols against the Symbols of Power: The Rise of Solidarity and the Fall of State Socialism in Poland*. University Park: Pennsylvania State University Press.

Kurtz, Lester R. (1986) *The Politics of Heresy: The Modernist Crisis in Roman Catholicism.* Berkeley: University of California Press.

Lanternari, Vittorio (1963) *The Religions of the Oppressed: A Study of Modern Messianic Cults.* New York: Knopf.

Lofland, John F. (1966) *Doomsday Cult: A Study of Conversion, Proselytization and Maintenance of Faith.* Englewood Cliffs, NJ: Prentice-Hall.

Lofland, John, and Rodney Stark (1965) Becoming a World-Saver: A Theory of Conversion to a Deviant Perspective. *American Sociological Review,* 30, 863–74.

Luker, Kristin (1984) *Abortion and the Politics of Motherhood.* Berkeley: University of California Press.

McAdam, Doug, and David A. Snow (1997) *Social Movements: Readings on their Emergence, Mobilization, and Dynamics.* Los Angeles: Roxbury.

McAdam, Doug, John D. McCarthy, and Mayer N. Zald (eds.) (1996) *Comparative Perspectives on Social Movements.* New York: Cambridge University Press.

McAneny, Leslie, and Lydia Saad (1993) Strong Ties between Religious Commitment and Abortion Views. *Gallup Poll Monthly,* 331 (April), 38.

Marty, Martin E., and R. Scott Appleby (1994) *The Fundamentalism Project.* Vol. 1, *Fundamentalisms Observed.* Chicago: University of Chicago Press.

Miller, Donald E. (1997) *Reinventing American Protestantism: Christianity in the New Millennium.* Berkeley: University of California Press.

Morris, Aldon D. (1984) *The Origins of the Civil Rights Movement: Black Communities Organizing for Change.* New York: Macmillan.

Morris, Aldon D., and Carol McClurg Mueller (eds.) (1992) *Frontiers in Social Movement Theory.* New Haven, CT: Yale University Press.

Munson, Ziad (2001) Islamic Mobilization: Social Movement Theory and the Egyptian Muslim Brotherhood. *Sociological Quarterly,* 42, 487–510.

Olson, Daniel V. A. (1997) Dimensions of Cultural Tension among the American Public. In Rhys H. Williams (ed.), *Cultural Wars in American Politics.* New York: Aldine de Gruyter, 237–58.

Riesebrodt, Martin (1993) *Pious Passion: The Emergence of Modern Fundamentalism in the United States and Iran.* Berkeley: University of California Press.

Rose, Susan D. (1987) Women Warriors: The Negotiation of Gender in a Charismatic Community. *Sociological Analysis,* 48, 245–58.

Rupp, Leila J., and Verta Taylor (1987) *Survival in the Doldrums: The American Women's Rights Movement, 1945 to the 1960s.* New York: Oxford University Press.

Smith, Brian H. (1982) *The Church and Politics in Chile: Challenges to Modern Catholicism.* Princeton, NJ: Princeton University Press.

——(1986) Chile: Deepening the Alliance of Working-Class Sectors to the Church in the 1970s. In Daniel H. Levine (ed.), *Religion and Political Conflict in Latin America.* Chapel Hill: University of North Carolina Press, 156–86.

Smith, Christian (1991) *The Emergence of Liberation Theology: Radical Religion and Social Movement Theory.* Chicago: University of Chicago Press.

——(1996) *Resisting Reagan: The U.S. Central America Peace Movement.* Chicago: University of Chicago Press.

Snow, David, and Richard Machalek (1984) The Sociology of Conversion. *Annual Review of Sociology,* 10, 167–90.

Snow, David, and Susan E. Marshall (1984) Cultural Imperialism, Social Movements, and the Islamic Revival. *Research in Social Movements, Conflict and Change,* 7, 131–52.

Snow, David, and Cynthia L. Phillips (1980) The Lofland-Stark Conversion Model: A Critical Reassessment. *Social Problems,* 27, 430–47.

Stark, Rodney, and William Sims Bainbridge (1979) Of Churches, Sects, and Cults: Preliminary Concepts for a Theory of Religious Movements. *Journal for the Scientific Study of Religion*, 18, 117–33.

——(1985) *The Future of Religion: Secularization, Revival and Cult Formation*. Berkeley: University of California Press.

——(1987) *A Theory of Religion*. New York: Peter Lang.

Stephens, Randall J. (2000) The Convergence of Populism, Religion, and the Holiness-Pentecostal Movements: A Review of the Historical Literature. *Fides et Historia*, 32 (1), 51–64.

Swidler, Ann (1986) Culture in Action: Symbols and Strategies. *American Sociological Review*, 51, 273–86.

Tarrow, Sidney (1994) *Power in Movement: Social Movements, Collective Action and Politics*. New York: Cambridge University Press.

Tipton, Steven M. (1982) *Getting Saved from the Sixties*. Berkeley: University of California Press.

Tuveson, Ernest (1964) *Millennium and Utopia: A Study in the Background of the Idea of Progress*. New York: Harper Torch.

Vande Berg, Travis, and Fred Kniss (2002) ISKCON and Immigrants: From Movement to Institution and Back Again. Paper presented at American Sociological Association annual meeting, Chicago.

Wallace, Anthony F. C. (1956) Revitalization Movements. *American Anthropologist*, 58, 264–81.

Wallis, Roy (1984) *The Elementary Forms of New Religious Life*. London: Routledge & Kegan Paul.

Warner, R. Stephen (1993) Work in Progress toward a New Paradigm for the Sociological Study of Religion in the United States. *American Journal of Sociology*, 98, 1044–93.

——(1995) The Metropolitan Community Churches and the Gay Agenda: The Power of Pentecostalism and Essentialism. In Mary Jo Neitz and Marion S. Goldman (eds.), *Religion and the Social Order*. Vol. 5. Greenwich, CT: JAI, 81–108.

Warner, R. Stephen, and Judith G. Wittner (eds.) (1998) *Gatherings in Diaspora: Religious Communities and the New Immigration*. Philadelphia, PA: Temple University Press.

Weaver, Mary Jo (1999) Resisting Traditional Catholic Sexual Teaching: Pro-Choice Advocacy and Homosexual Support Groups. In Mary Jo Weaver (ed.), *What's Left? Liberal American Catholics*. Bloomington: Indiana University Press, 88–108.

Weber, Max (1958) *The Protestant Ethic and the Spirit of Capitalism*. Tr. Talcott Parsons. New York: Charles Scribner's Sons.

——(1978) *Economy and Society*. Berkeley: University of California Press.

Williams, Rhys (ed.) (1997) *Cultural Wars in American Politics: Critical Reviews of a Popular Myth*. Hawthorne, NY: Aldine de Gruyter.

Worsley, Peter (1957) *The Trumpet Shall Sound: A Study of Cargo Cults in Melanesia*. London: MacGibbon & Kee.

Wuthnow, Robert (1983) The Political Rebirth of American Evangelicals. In Robert C. Liebman and Robert Wuthnow (eds.), *The New Christian Right: Mobilization and Legitimation*. Hawthorne, NY: Aldine de Gruyter, 167–85.

——(1988) *The Restructuring of American Religion*. Princeton, NJ: Princeton University Press.

Zald, Mayer N. (1982) Theological Crucibles: Social Movements in and of Religion. *Review of Religious Research*, 23, 317–36.

Zald, Mayer N., and John D. McCarthy (1987) Religious Groups as Crucibles of Social Movements. In *Social Movements in an Organizational Society: Collected Essays*. New Brunswick, NJ: Transaction, 67–95.

Index

Key reference volumes ▪ in Sociology